SELECTIONS FROM THREE WORKS

NATURAL LAW AND
ENLIGHTENMENT CLASSICS

Knud Haakonssen
General Editor

Francisco Suárez

NATURAL LAW AND
ENLIGHTENMENT CLASSICS

Selections from Three Works

A Treatise on Laws and God the Lawgiver

A Defence of the Catholic and Apostolic Faith

A Work on the Three Theological Virtues: Faith, Hope, and Charity

Francisco Suárez

Edited and with an Introduction by Thomas Pink

Translated by Gwladys L. Williams, Ammi Brown,
and John Waldron with Certain Revisions
by Henry Davis, S.J.

LIBERTY FUND

Introduction, new editorial additions, index © copyright 2015 by Liberty Fund, Inc.

The text of this edition is a reprint of the translation of *Selections from Three Works* by Gwladys L. Williams, Ammi Brown, and John Waldron, with certain revisions by Henry Davis, S.J., first published in 1944 by the Carnegie Endowment for International Peace.

Frontispiece reproduced from Raoul de Scorraille, *Francois Suárez, de la Compagnie de Jésus, d'après ses lettres, ses autres écrits inédits et un grand nombre de documents nouveaux* (Paris: P. Lethielleux, 1912), frontispiece to vol 1. © 1912 by Raoul de Scorraille.

22 23 24 25 26 C 6 5 4 3 2
22 23 24 25 26 P 6 5 4 3 2

Library of Congress Cataloging-in-Publication Data
Suárez, Francisco, 1548–1617, author. [Works. Selections. English. 2014]
Selections from three works / Francisco Suárez; edited and with an introduction by Thomas Pink; translated by Gwladys L. Williams, Ammi Brown, and John Waldron with certain revisions by Henry Davis, S.J.
pages cm.—(Natural law and enlightenment classics)
"Introduction, new editorial additions, index © copyright 2014 by Liberty Fund, Inc."
"First published in 1944 by the Carnegie Endowment for International Peace."
Includes bibliographical references and index.
ISBN 978-0-86597-516-3 (hardcover: alk. paper) ISBN 978-0-86597-517-0 (pbk.: alk. paper)
1. Canon law. 2. Natural law. 3. International law. I. Pink, Thomas, editor writer of introduction. II. Williams, Gwladys L., translator. III. Davis, Henry, 1866–1952, editor. IV. Suárez, Francisco, 1548–1617. De legibus, ac Deo legislatore. English. V. Suárez, Francisco, 1548–1617. Defensio fidei catholicae. English. VI. Suárez, Francisco, 1548–1617. De triplici virtute theologica. English. VII. Title.
262.9—dc23   KBR2074 .S84A2 2014   2014016405

LIBERTY FUND, INC.
11301 North Meridian Street
Carmel, Indiana 46032
libertyfund.org

CONTENTS

INTRODUCTION

Born in 1548 to a prominent noble family of Granada, Francisco Suárez was one of the most important thinkers of the second scholastic, that revival of Catholic school theology that centered on the study of Thomas Aquinas, and, following the early sixteenth-century example of Cajetan and Vitoria, replaced the long-established medieval practice of commentary on the *Sentences* of Peter Lombard with commentary on Aquinas's *Summa theologiae*. Suárez entered the recently founded Society of Jesus in 1564, and after undistinguished academic beginnings progressed in the study of theology and philosophy to gain a chair in philosophy at Segovia in 1571. He held a chair in theology at the Roman College, the Jesuits' college in Rome, from 1580 to 1585, but then had to return to Spain for reasons of health. There followed an unhappy period at Alcalá marked by tensions with supporters of the previous occupant of his post there, Gabriel Vásquez, who was both a more popular university teacher than Suárez and one of Suárez's main intellectual rivals in the Jesuit order. These tensions were not lessened by Vásquez's return from Rome in 1591. After teaching for more than three years at the Jesuit college at Salamanca, in 1597 Suárez moved to a chair in theology at Coimbra, where he spent the remainder of his career. He died in 1617.

Besides composing one of the last intellectually formidable exercises in Aristotelian metaphysics, the *Disputationes metaphysicae* (1597), Suárez also wrote one of the major works of scholastic moral and legal theory, *De legibus ac deo legislatore* (1612), based on his course on law at Coimbra. This work, given in selections here, also served as the basis for his political thought, outlined in that treatise and developed in two further works, excerpts from which are also presented here: his treatise on the errors of Anglicanism and in particular on the errors of King James I in relation to papal spiritual and temporal authority, *Defensio fidei catholicae et apostolicae adversus anglicanae sectae errores* (1613); and his treatise on the supernatural virtues, in part material taught by him in Rome but much expanded by him subsequently and posthumously published in 1621. The excerpts from the last treatise were taken from Suárez's accounts of faith and love, *De fide* and *De caritate*. Together these selections, originally published in the Carnegie series The Classics of International Law and now republished as a Liberty Fund edition, will give a general view of Suárez's political thought and of its basis in his moral theory.

Suárez was a natural law thinker, a tradition that stretched from the Stoicism of pagan antiquity, and which continued through medieval and early modern Catholic scholasticism to remain the basis of the Catholic moral theory of the present day; but the tradition also included Protestant thinkers of the seventeenth and eighteenth centuries such as Hugo Grotius, Samuel Pufendorf, Gottfried Wilhelm Leibniz, and Christian Wolff. Central is the idea that morality comes to us in the shape of a universal law governing the actions of all humans by virtue of their shared rational nature, hence forming a natural law. The specific systems of positive (posited) law embodied in the customs or statutes of human communities have a moral authority—that of obligation—that is derived from the moral obligations imposed by universal natural law. We have then an account of political authority, in the form of the authority of state or civil law morally to oblige us, developed out of a general theory of moral obligation. The interest of this tradition in law, therefore, goes far beyond the humanly constructed systems of positive law, of humanly made custom and statute, that are the concern of modern jurisprudence. Law is first and foremost a moral standard before it is ever to be found in humanly created regulation. Human systems of positive law are of concern to the theory of law proper insofar as they serve a central function: that of defending, through human coercive authority, existing moral obligations and of adding to those existing moral directives new ones, general adherence to which will further the good of the community. As Catholic natural lawyers were all agreed, following St. Augustine, statutes or customs which fail to do this, which because of their injustice leave us under no moral obligation to conform to them, while they may be termed 'laws' and are presented as laws by human authorities, do not constitute law of the kind with which Suárez and other natural lawyers were concerned. For they do not carry the force of moral obligation, which genuine law must do: an unjust law is not a true law (*nam lex mihi esse non videtur, quae iusta non fuerit*).[1]

How similar was the moral theory of Suárez and his Catholic contemporaries to those of subsequent Protestant natural law theorists? We can best compare Suárez with Pufendorf, who more than Grotius was to develop a serious theory of obligation and its moral psychology, and who shared with Suárez a similar conception of moral obligation's nature. In both thinkers natural law is imposed by a divine will and command communicated to us through our natural capacity for reason. Moreover, for both thinkers the moral obligation attaching to actions that comes with natural law, though imposed by divine commands, is not taken simply to be the property of being divinely commanded. Rather, moral obligatoriness is taken to be a distinctive mode of justificatory support or force, a *vis directiva,* as Suárez terms it, which divine commands generate. The force of obligation, communicated through what Suárez terms *praecepta,* or preceptive commands, parallels and operates alongside the force of advice that is communicated through *consilia,* or counsels. Where the force of *consilia* recommends, or leaves what they support advisable or a good idea, the force of *praecepta* binds and leaves what they support obligatory. Both forces or modes of support are the voice of our reason, and both directly address the will, our capacity for choice and decision, which is viewed as a capacity for free action. The natural law binds and obliges us freely to choose or decide on action that is morally good and against action that is morally bad.

This conception of moral obligation as a justificatory force binding a free will is very distinctive and is clearly absent from Locke's treatment of duty or obligation in *An Essay Concerning Human Understanding.* There Locke may appeal to natural law, but this law comes to no more than a series of punishment- or sanction-backed commands applying to the various actions we might decide on or will. There is no distinctive *vis directiva* of obligatoriness generated by those commands that applies to and binds the will itself.

---

1. St. Augustine, *De libero arbitrio,* book 1, chapter 5.

Despite this shared theory of obligation, Suárez and Pufendorf differ fundamentally in the remaining moral theory to which this theory of obligation is attached. We come to know of the content of the natural moral law, Suárez thinks, on the basis of a pre-legal grasp of what actions are morally good or bad. This grasp of a pre-legal morality of virtue, Suárez thinks, is possessed both by Christians and by rational pagans such as Aristotle, on whose theory of virtue Suárez, like other schoolmen, generally relies. Knowing what is morally good and bad, and knowing too through reason that God exists and that in freely creating us with a rational nature he wills an obligation on us to act morally, we can form rational conclusions as to both the existence of the natural law and the nature of its content. Whereas for Pufendorf, there is no pre-legal theory of virtue and vice, of moral good and bad, available to us. The notion of action that is morally good or bad simply is the notion of action that, under natural law, is permitted or prohibited. Aristotle is accorded no special authority, and moral theory has to be constructed from a general theory of advantage or disadvantage that is pre-moral and that applies to human and animal alike. This theory of pre-moral or natural good and bad has advisory force for us as rational beings and is then used by Pufendorf to generate the theory of moral law that is to bind our exercise, as rational beings, of our free will. We use reason to conclude from what is naturally good and advisable to what is obligatory, on the basis of God's will that we should do what is naturally or pre-morally good or advantageous.

Suárez's theory of moral obligation as a *vis directiva* governing free choices of the will is linked, then, to a traditionally Aristotelian-scholastic theory of virtue and of the moral good (*honestum*) and bad (*turpe*). In this he is like other Catholic thinkers of the second scholastic. Where he differs from many early modern Catholic thinkers is in his understanding of all law as legislated and as the exercise of some power of jurisdiction. For his fellow Jesuit Gabriel Vásquez or a Franciscan thinker such as John Punch, moral obligation was indeed a *vis directiva*. But it no more needed a legislator than did the recommendatory force of *consilia*. Just as some actions could be sensible or a good idea without some act of divine advice making them so, so too some actions could be obligatory and others prohibited or wrong without some act of divine command making them so. A major part of the theory of moral obligation that is developed in *De legibus* is, then, a defense of the idea that all obligation, including that of the natural law, depends for its generation on the legislative command of a superior. Suárez is accordingly committed to embedding all law and obligation within a general theory of legislation and legislative authority that extends to an ultimate and supreme legislative authority—that of God himself. The universe involves a cosmic legislative hierarchy in which its creator is also the ultimate creator of every law. Any man-made authority or law with the power to bind us owes its obligatory force to divine authority and to its legislation.

Suárez's political thought concerns both the nature of political authority in its own right and its relation to the mission and authority of the Catholic church. In this respect it goes beyond the strict concerns of the natural law on which the temporal authority of the state is based. For besides the natural law that directs us to a lower or imperfect natural happiness as conceived by rational pagan and Christian alike, there is also a supernatural or divine law, given through revelation in the Old and New Testaments, that directs us to a higher and perfect supernatural happiness that we can know of only through divinely granted faith, and attain only with the help of divinely granted grace. The divine law of the New Testament does not abrogate but goes beyond the natural law, and the authority of the church is based on that divine law. It is within this generally accepted framework that Suárez and his fellow Jesuits developed a theory of the state and its relation to the church.

Like fellow Jesuits such as Robert, Cardinal Bellarmine, and Luis de Molina, Suárez teaches that the temporal authority of the state is based independently of that of the church and is not directly subordinate to or derived from church authority. Political authority is originally given by God, not to any individual or individuals—individuals are naturally free, lacking any original authority or dominion one over another—but to human communities considered as *societates perfectae,* united by consent and capable as a unity of directing their affairs without external help. This authority could then be transferred by a community's consent to individual rulers or princes, as it mostly had been. This transfer was viewed as a form of alienation. That is, the authority could not be recovered by the community unless the conditions attaching to its original transfer had been broken, as would definitely happen if the ruler embarked on a form of tyranny that amounted to a war on his own community, which Suárez terms a war on his own state.

Jesuit writers were then agreed that the church had no direct temporal authority over earthly rulers. Since Christ's kingdom was not of this world, the pope was no *princeps mundi,* exercising earthly sovereignty over the whole world. This consensus within the order was contrary to the views of a number of previous canonists, and even of some popes including, most recently, Pope Sixtus V, who had died in 1590 when just about to proscribe Bellarmine's denial of direct papal temporal authority by placing his works on the index of prohibited books. Nevertheless the church and its earthly head the pope still had a spiritual authority over all baptized Christians, rulers and princes included. And, like his Jesuit brothers, Suárez taught that since spiritual ends were higher than temporal ones, with this authority came an indirect temporal authority to be exercised over, and for the spiritual benefit of, Christians. So the pope had the authority if necessary to absolve Christian subjects from their allegiance to spiritually abusive rulers and to punish rulers who themselves were Christian, such as heretical rulers, with sanctions ranging from the imposition of spiritual penalties, such as interdict and excommunication, to outright deposition should spiritual ends require this. Belief in at least this extensive though indirect papal authority over temporal rulers was regarded by Suárez as *de fide,* a matter of dogmatic and infallible teaching, a view shared within the Roman Curia, but not by Catholics everywhere. For Suárez's views were denied not only in Protestant lands, but also in Catholic states such as France and Venice.

Conflict had already occurred between Pope Paul V and the Republic of Venice in 1605 over a claimed immunity of Catholic clergy from the coercive power of the state, a conflict that led to a sentence of papal interdict on Venice. Further controversy over papal authority was caused by James I's imposition in 1606 of an oath on English Catholics affirming that the attribution of any authority to the pope to depose temporal sovereigns was not only false but a heresy:

I, ——, do truly and sincerely acknowledge etc., . . . that the Pope, neither of himself nor by any authority of the church or See of Rome or by
any other means with any other hath any power or authority to depose
the King . . . and I do further swear that I do from my heart abhor, detest
and abjure, as impious and heretical, this damnable doctrine and position, that princes which be excommunicated or deprived by the Pope
may be deposed or murdered by their subjects or any other whatsoever.[2]

As intended, this oath served to divide the English Catholic community,
being taken by George Blackwell, the archpriest in charge of its administration, and most of the prominent laity, but refused by the majority of the
secular clergy and by the English Benedictines and Jesuits. Following on
a series of works by Bellarmine, Suárez's *Defensio fidei* was an exercise in
controversial apologetics in reply to this oath that was commissioned by the
Roman Curia through Decio Caraffa, the papal nuncio to Madrid. With
papal approval the book gave a systematic account of state authority, of the
subordination of temporal ends to spiritual, and of the Pope's consequent
indirect temporal authority over Christians. Given Suárez's reputation, the
significance of the work was not lost on James I's government. Copies of
each of the six books of the *Defensio* were supplied to London by Sir John
Digby, James I's ambassador to Madrid, as they were printed. The complete
work was burned by the hangman at St. Paul's Cross, subversive as it was of
James I's pretensions to derive his authority to rule immediately from God
and to exercise that authority quite immune from any papal interference.

Suárez's strong view of papal authority both over the church as a whole
and indirectly over Christian rulers was always going to be unpalatable to
French Gallicans, who denied any papal temporal authority and viewed
the exercise of the pope's spiritual authority as subject to the consent of the
church. But there was a further matter that, after the assassination of two
successive French kings, guaranteed the *Defensio fidei* a hostile reception
in France. James's oath raised the issue of tyrannicide; and so, with typical
thoroughness, Suárez addressed this issue in the *Defensio* too, defending
the legitimacy of tyrannicide under certain conditions.

2. *An Act for the better discovering and repressing Popish Recusants. To be administered
to any recusant under penalty of praemunire.* 1st Parliament, Second Session: Jan 21st–
May 27th, 1606. 3 & 4 Jac. I, cap. iv. section ix.

The Council of Constance had issued a decree in 1415 condemning as heretical the following proposition:

> Any tyrant can and ought to be killed, licitly and meritoriously, by any of his vassals or subjects, even by means of plots and blandishments or flattery, notwithstanding any oath taken, or treaty made with the tyrant, and without waiting for a sentence or a command from any judge.[3]

This condemnation was seen as binding on subsequent Catholic discussion of the permissibility of killing tyrants. But few Jesuits besides Juan Azor understood this decree to be a blanket condemnation of tyrannicide. Suárez insisted on a distinction between two sorts of tyrant that had been made by Aquinas.[4] There are *tyranni a regimine,* or lawful tyrants, that is, princes with a legal title to rule, but who abuse their authority; and *tyranni a titulo,* or unlawful or usurping tyrants without even the right to rule. The latter may include previously lawful tyrants who have lost their title to rule through lawful deposition. In Suárez's view, the difference between lawful and unlawful tyrants is that an unlawful tyrant is using violence on the state by his very retention of royal power, so that the state is by that very fact involved in defensive war against him. In contrast, a lawful tyrant has just title, but is abusive in his method of rule, which aims at his private advantage against the public good. In the latter case, it need not follow that the abuses amount to an actual attack on his community, though if an attack is being made then, again, the community is involved in a defensive war against its own prince. The Council of Constance was understood by Suárez to ban the indiscriminate killing of lawful tyrants, but to leave open the possibility of killing a usurping tyrant as part of a defensive war against him by the community. Even a lawful tyrant might similarly be killed if engaged in an outright attack on his own community.

The conditions set by Suárez for permissible tyrannicide were very circumscribed; but his discussion came only three years after the assassination

---

3. Council of Constance, Session 15, 6 July 1415: *Sententia condemnationis illius propositionis Ioannis Parvi: 'Quilibet tyrannus,'* in *Decrees of the Ecumenical Councils,* ed. Tanner and Alberigo, vol. 1, p. 432.

4. Aquinas, *In quatuor libros sententiarum,* II, XLIV, 2, 2.

of Henri IV, and the apparently sympathetic treatment of the earlier murder of Henri III by his fellow Jesuit Mariana in *De rege et regis institutione* (1599) was also fresh in mind. In even discussing the topic the *Defensio fidei* contradicted earlier assurances given by the papal nuncio to France that it would not address the question of tyrannicide. As a result, Suárez's work was initially condemned, with the writings of other Jesuits, by the Paris Parlement, though the French crown was brought to retract the condemnation of Suárez along with an earlier parliamentary condemnation of Bellarmine.

Suárez writes of individuals as possessing an original and natural liberty. But the distance between his thought and any subsequent contractarianism, let alone any form of liberalism, is considerable. The consent of the community may be a condition of political subordination. But this consent is, as we have noted, an alienation and, except under limited conditions, cannot be retracted. It involves no transfer of rights or powers from individuals to their rulers, but only from the community as a whole. Moreover, the community's consent comes to no more than a shared custom of obedience under conditions that leave this custom to further the common good. And even this shared custom is not, as it would be for Hume, the ultimate source of political authority, but merely a condition under which God, the true ultimate source, grants that authority. It should also be noted that the metaphysical freedom of the individual's will guarantees no special freedom in questions of religion. As *De fide* makes clear, coercion of belief may be perfectly legitimate. The limits on such coercion are almost wholly jurisdictional and do not arise directly from the moral status of the individual. The state has jurisdiction in its own right only in relation to the ends of natural law, which is why the state cannot coerce specifically Christian belief. But the state can perfectly well coerce religious belief and practice otherwise. The state can and should force individuals out of idolatrous or polytheistic religion and into the practice of the rational monotheism that natural law requires. The church, by contrast, does have jurisdiction in relation to spiritual and supernatural ends, though this spiritual jurisdiction is limited to the baptized. But within this jurisdictional boundary coercion is again fully permitted. With the assistance of Christian rulers, the church can certainly use force and sanction on the previously baptized, in particular on heretics and apostates, to impose properly Catholic belief and practice.

We have seen that Suárez's belief in a necessary dependence of all law on legislative origin and authority was controversial at the time, although the doctrine came to be increasingly widely shared among Catholic moralists thereafter.[5] Much of the success of Suárez's views lay in his considerable synthetic ability. His writings were informed by what seemed to many of his contemporaries an exemplary mastery not only of metaphysics and moral theology and psychology, but also, more than usual for his order, of canon and civil law and commentary thereon. This synthetic ability enabled Suárez to absorb and integrate much in the positions of opponents into his own work. In particular, those of his Catholic opponents who saw the natural law as unlegislated took its origin to lie not in the decrees of God, but in our own rational nature, and to be knowable simply through consideration of that nature. But Suárez too claimed to safeguard the link between natural law and rational human nature. Though in his view natural law was the product of divine legislation, Suárez sought to agree with his opponents that the natural law is not simply posited by authority but has a content determined by that rational nature which it governs and that the law can be known and obeyed just on the basis of understanding that nature. The reconciliation of rationalism regarding the content of the natural law with a voluntarist theory of its origin in the divine will was the central distinctive feature of Suárez's *De legibus*.

Thomas Pink

---

5. By the nineteenth century we find the divinely legislated origin of natural law and obligation taught officially in Pius IX's *Syllabus errorum* (1864) and Leo XIII's *Libertas praestantissimum* (1888).

NOTE ON TRANSLATION
(from the Carnegie edition)

The translation of these *Selections* from the works of Francisco Suárez has been made from the following editions:

> *De legibus ac Deo legislatore,* first edition, Coimbra, 1612.
> *Defensio fidei catholicae et apostolicae adversus Anglicanae sectae errores cum responsione ad apologiam pro iuramento fidelitatis & praefationem monitoriam Serenissimi Iacobi Angliae Regis,* first edition, Coimbra, 1613.
> *De triplici virtute theologica, fide, spe & charitate,* first edition, Coimbra, 1621.

In the preparation of the translation, however, various other editions have been consulted, notably the Paris edition of the *Opera Omnia* published in 1856–61.[1] Several of the separate early editions of the treatises mentioned above were also referred to from time to time,[2] as was the Spanish translation of the *De legibus* prepared by Don Jaime Torrubiano Ripoll.[3]

Some mention must be made here of the numerous problems encountered in translating the *Selections.* First of all there is the fact that as both a theologian and a philosophical jurist Suárez dealt with abstract and technical ideas, with fine distinctions and precise definitions. Again, his aim throughout his work was obviously fullness of presentation rather than conciseness

---

1. For the privilege of using copies of this edition the translators and the Endowment are much indebted to the Library of Congress, the Riggs Library of Georgetown University, and the Library of the Catholic University of America.

2. For the use of these editions thanks are due especially to the Libraries of Harvard University and the Harvard Law School, and to the Woodstock College Library at Woodstock, Maryland.

3. *Tratado de las leyes y de Dios legislador,* 11 volumes, Madrid, 1918–21.

or a terse and sententious style. Then, too, steeped in the learning of the
Schoolmen as he was, he naturally employed the scholastic method of exposition, presenting in detail the arguments opposed to his own views. In spite
of its formalism there is much to be said in favour of the thoroughness of
this method, but it demands of the translator that he accustom himself to
the scholastic form of argument and that he keep constantly on the alert lest
he find himself mistaking the elaborate statement of an opponent's theories
for the author's own doctrines. For much the same reason it is hazardous for
the reader to attempt a casual survey of Suárez by dipping at random into his
pages. Finally, while Suárez was an excellent Latinist, his Latin is characterized by a marked tendency toward elliptical expressions and the habit, not
uncommon among scholars of his day in Spain, of endowing Latin words
with the meaning of their Spanish derivatives.

In coping with these problems it was necessary to obtain the services of
exceptionally competent translators who were qualified to deal not only
with Suárez's subject-matter but with scholastic argument and logic, and
who could render his profound and sometimes rather elusive thought into
clear English. At the same time it was felt that his language should not be
too much modernized in the English version. Suárez was one of the great
Schoolmen, and it seemed appropriate that the translation of the *Selections* should retain a scholastic flavour. The English text therefore repro-
duces in some measure his formal style of argument and the terms of logic
employed by him.

There are, however, certain theological and scholastic terms in the text
which are unfamiliar to laymen. To minimize the reader's perplexity over
these terms the translators, and especially the reviser, have added numerous footnotes. Other footnotes have been added with reference to citations, or as guides where Suárez has referred rather loosely to his preceding
arguments or propositions.

The treatment of citations, quotations, and certain legal terms calls for
a few words of comment. In general the aim has been to give citations in
rather full form. This would not have been possible had they been relegated
to the margins, as has been done in other volumes in this series. Suárez
himself, moreover, had made these citations an integral part of his text. In
order, therefore, to avoid confusion and undue abbreviation, which would

have tended to make such citations unintelligible to the reader, they have been retained in the text of the translation, but are set off from it by parentheses. Within the parentheses, extensions and corrections have been added in square brackets. Where Suárez has, for example, an incorrect reference to Aristotle's *Ethics,* the corrected and extended reference is thus added in brackets in the text: (*Ethics,* Bk. I, chap. ix [Bk. X, chap. ix, § 12]).

Great care has been given to the verification of references and quotations. Biblical citations have been checked against the Latin Vulgate (Paris edition of 1887), and in quotations the language of the Douay version has been employed. In dealing with the many references to St. Thomas Aquinas much use was made of the careful translation of his *Summa theologica* (2nd ed.) by the Fathers of the English Dominican Province. Canon law references were for the most part checked against the Friedberg edition (Leipzig, 1879–81) of the *Corpus juris canonici,* while in verifying and translating Roman law texts recourse was had to the several editions of the *Corpus juris civilis* by Mommsen, Kreuger, Schoell, and Kroll, published in Berlin, and to S. P. Scott's translation.[4] The texts and translations of the *Loeb Classical Library* were extensively used in dealing with Suárez's numerous references to classical authors.

The translators have felt it advisable in certain instances to employ Latin terms in the English text. Thus, in passages where Suárez distinguishes between *ius* and *lex* it has seemed best to retain those words in the translation lest the distinction be obscured by the use of the single English equivalent, 'law'. For a similar reason the words *usus, mos,* and *consuetudo* have been retained in certain passages. As regards the term *ius gentium,* Suárez employs it in both its older and its more modern signification, i.e. as embracing the laws common to various peoples, or as meaning the law applicable to the relations of independent states. Since the Latin term is familiar to readers with any knowledge of law it has not been translated except where Suárez specifically distinguishes the two meanings,[5] in which cases *ius gentium* in the sense of international law has at times been rendered as 'the law of nations.'

4. *The Civil Law,* 17 volumes in 7 (Cincinnati, 1932).
5. As in chapters xix and xx of Book II of the *De legibus infra,* pp. 401 *et seq.,* 411.

Various circumstances made it necessary to divide the work of translating among several scholars. Mr. Ammi Brown, whose suggestions regarding the choice of chapters to be included in the *Selections* were accepted in many instances, also contributed to the project by the preparation of preliminary translations of many chapters. For additional translations, and for the present form of the English version of all of the chapters except those from Book VII of the *De legibus*, Miss Gwladys L. Williams is responsible. Miss Williams also listed many of the errata in the Latin text. The twenty chapters from the seventh Book were translated independently by Mr. John Waldron. Subsequently the entire translation was carefully read by a noted English Jesuit scholar, Father Henry Davis, who gave special attention to revision and elucidation in connexion with theological terms, and who aided greatly in the verification of references as well as in compiling the Index of Authors and the List of Errata. In addition to assisting in these latter operations and in the editing of the *Selections* for publication, Mr. Walter H. Zeydel prepared the Subject Index and the Analytical Table of Contents.

NOTE ON THIS EDITION

Since the original translation of these works for the Carnegie series Classics of International Law new editions of parts of the original Latin texts of *De legibus* and of *Defensio fidei* have appeared in the *Corpus Hispanorum de Pace*. In addition there is an edition by Karl Deuringer of Suárez's Roman College lectures *De fide,* which provides an early version of the material that, subsequently greatly expanded by the author, was published posthumously in 1621 in the treatise on the supernatural virtues. The translations have been checked against these Latin texts, and where necessary some silent corrections have been made. Some explanatory notes have been revised and some further notes have been supplied. The original notes are otherwise retained in square brackets, my additional notes being without brackets.

The bibliography of works cited by Suárez refers to postclassical works, generally in the earliest printed editions. Classical works cited by him can generally be found in Loeb editions. A full list of ancient authors cited can be found in the index to the original Carnegie translation. The further reading includes Scorraille's life of Suárez and various books and papers that further explain Suárez's own psychological, moral, and political theory, or the intellectual environment within which he developed his ideas.

I should like to thank Laura Goetz of Liberty Fund for her essential editorial assistance, Professor Knud Haakonssen for his invaluable comments and advice, and Dr. Annabel Brett for her preliminary work on this edition and for very helpful advice.

CONTENTS

(from the Carnegie Edition)

A TREATISE ON LAWS AND GOD THE LAWGIVER

BOOK II: ON THE ETERNAL LAW,
THE NATURAL LAW, AND THE *IUS GENTIUM*

BOOK III: ON POSITIVE HUMAN LAW AS SUCH, AND AS IT MAY BE VIEWED IN PURE HUMAN NATURE, A PHASE OF LAW WHICH IS ALSO CALLED CIVIL

BOOK VI: ON THE INTERPRETATION, CESSATION, AND CHANGE OF HUMAN LAWS

[Chapters X–XXVII omitted from these *Selections*.]

BOOK VII: OF UNWRITTEN LAW WHICH IS CALLED CUSTOM

A DEFENCE OF THE CATHOLIC
AND APOSTOLIC FAITH

—In Refutation of the Errors of the Anglican Sect with a Reply to
the Apologie for the Oath of Allegiance and to the Admonitory
Preface of His Most Serene Majesty James, King of England

[Of this treatise, only the following Chapters are included in these
Selections: Book III, chaps. v and xxiii; Book VI, chap. IV.]

BOOK III: CONCERNING THE SUPREMACY AND
POWER OF THE POPE OVER TEMPORAL KINGS

BOOK VI: CONCERNING THE OATH OF ALLEGIANCE
EXACTED BY THE KING OF ENGLAND

A WORK ON THE THREE THEOLOGICAL VIRTUES: FAITH, HOPE, AND CHARITY

—Divided into Three Treatises to Correspond with the Number of the Virtues Themselves

DISPUTATION XVIII: ON THE MEANS WHICH MAY BE USED FOR THE CONVERSION AND COERCION OF UNBELIEVERS WHO ARE NOT APOSTATES

A TREATISE ON LAWS
AND GOD THE LAWGIVER

A Treatise in Ten Books

ON LAWS AND GOD THE LAWGIVER

By the Reverend Father FRANCISCO SUÁREZ

of Granada, Member of the Society of Jesus

Primary Professor of Sacred Theology at the celebrated Academy of Coimbra

Dedicated to the Most Illustrious and Most Reverend

D. AFONSO FURTADO À MENDOÇA

Bishop of Ejea de los Cavaleiros

With Several Indexes

COIMBRA

By Privilege of His Catholic Majesty for Castile and Portugal

From the Press of DIOGO GOMEZ DE LOUREYRO

In the Year of our Lord 1612

Dedication

When I was about to publish my book *On Laws,* most illustrious Protector, I did not deem it necessary to consider at any great length the question of what person I should select before all others as its patron, that I might commend it to his care, to be defended by his authority, or embellished by his nobility. For under no patronage could my work more happily or more safely see the light, than under that of one who caused the drafting of its first outlines, its growth into a volume, and its dissemination in printed form for the common use; since this book, the first and foremost of all the books which I have thus far published, had its origin in this kingdom [of Portugal], and is the native product of this most noble Academy. All the rest of my works were already printed, or taken from my dictation, or composed by night, in other places; and this one only, through your exhortations and at your instigation, was first composed and dictated at this distinguished seat of learning. For while you were at the helm of the University as its most equitable director, to the immense benefit of that institution, and with the overwhelming applause of the whole realm, you believed that it would be beneficial to the world of letters if I should set forth from the professorial chair, a common doctrine of laws, in such a way as to adapt it—in so far as my diligence [under these conditions] might make this possible, or usage so demanded—to the various individual branches; and therefore, you suggested that I should bend all my energies to that task, and persuaded me to obey the suggestion. Accordingly, I carried out the undertaking so gladly begun at your bidding, devoting to it—under the happy auspices of your good will—an unbroken period of two years' dictated exposition; but I did not so perfect that first draft as to fit it for the light of publication. Accordingly, I have at last polished the rough copy with such care as lay within my power, having become, according to the advice of St. Paul and at your bidding, 'all things to all men', that I might profit them all; and, having constant regard to the bidding of your will, I have fashioned the treatise with such care, that those whose words and leadership I follow are of the opinion that it should be published. Thus it was that simple justice seemed not only to ask and to urge, but also to require and to command, that you who were the instigator and originator of this work, should also be its patron; that the book conceived at your command, composed under your protection, and produced for your pleasure, should also be published under your name; a circumstance so remarkable and so glorious that my work cannot fail to derive from it great splendour and charm.[1] However, even if I were not sufficiently persuaded by the reason just set forth to dedicate these commentaries to you, how many other arguments present themselves which would in any case force me to adopt such a course, even though I were reluctant! For whether I turn my attention to the gifts with which heaven has endowed you, or to those which you have derived from your ancestors, or to those which are the products of your own labour or the acquisitions of your industry, all these attributes stand out in such dazzling splendour and shine in you with such majesty, that he who should demand greater adornments in a patron, or a stronger bulwark for his labour, might well be considered senseless. Who, indeed, can fail to see how bounteously the immortal will has imparted to your spirit those virtues which befit such a pontiff as even God Himself has painted in living colours and drawn in shining likeness. In the Hebrew High Priest and in his rich adornments, God portrayed the virtues and instilled the gifts of mind which He required also of Christian priestly dignitaries. Indeed, among all the ornaments adorning the priestly attire, that ornament held the chief

---

1. [This phrase is a somewhat arbitrary translation, as a result of the strained construction of the Latin: *sub tuo nomine lucem videat, à qua, cùm tam conspicua sit, ac praeclara,* . . . Various possible corrections of the Latin text might be offered, but, taking it as it stands, the feminine forms *qua, conspicua, praeclara,* would seem to refer to *lucem,* not to *nomine.*—Tr.]

place which was seen to be suspended upon the breast by golden chains, and on which were inscribed in large letters these two names: 'Truth,' and 'Judgment'; as if the Eternal Will preferred before all the other virtues which should adorn a pontiff, as being the chief and most noteworthy, this: that the soul of a prelate should shine with a sincere love of truth and with justice uncorrupted and equitable. These two virtues dwell in you, most illustrious Bishop; not to mention, for the present, that quality of yours which I know not how to name, whether to call it beneficence or extravagance, liberality or prodigality—the quality which moves you to lavish your resources upon the poor, to spend them for the needy, to exert yourself in behalf of those who suffer, so that you are called 'Father of those in need,' a tribute that is in truth divine. As I have said, I choose to pass over such qualities as this, and many other bright adornments of your spirit. But there is no one who fails to see—no one, indeed, who does not marvel upon seeing—how the two virtues which in their singular beauty decorated the breast of the High Priest, shine out from you with rays still brighter. For it is even as St. John Chrysostom has well said (on *Matthew*, Homily XIII): 'As a lamp that is lit cannot be hid; so it is impossible that a word of justice should be concealed.' Wherefore, indeed—however desirable it might seem to you, or to other persons, that it should be possible to conceal the ornaments of justice and integrity of which you gave such illustrious proof at Coimbra as Rector of the University, at Madrid as Counsellor to the King, at Lisbon while presiding over the Supreme Tribunal,[2] and finally, now, in the diocese of Ejea,[3] which you rule so uprightly and govern so justly that you seem to bear that laudatory inscription 'Truth and Judgment' not lightly pendant from your breast but engraved deep within—however desirable, I repeat, this concealment may seem to you—it was fitting in the very name of judgment that my book *On Laws*

2. [The Summus Conscientiae Senatus (Mêsa da Consciencia e Ordens) was a tribunal instituted by King John III in 1532 to direct the royal conscience in all matters of state. It developed later into an instrument of royal power over ecclesiastical matters.—REVISER.]

3. [Latin form 'Egitaniensis' was used for Idanha-a-Velha, a town in Portugal. Egitania was a Roman city, erected into a diocese in the sixth century and the See was transferred in the sixteenth century to Guarda where it now exists.—REVISER.]

should be dedicated to you. For Law is the sister of Justice, and both are included under one name, according to that passage from *Isaias* (Chap. xlv [, v. 19]): '[. . .] I am the Lord that speak justice, that declare truth',[4] with regard to which Cyril of Alexandria says [on *Isaias, ibid.*]: 'He calls Law, Justice.' So distinguished a devotee of Justice and the Laws cannot but welcome in a kindly spirit a treatise on the laws and on justice. And how can one whose reflections concerning the laws are so keen, one who observes them with such accuracy, fail to defend, in case of attack, a book which contains and expounds legal doctrine; how, if that book suffer from disparagement, can he fail to adorn it with praise? For you will be the more richly equipped to render this service, in that you are not only illustrious for the qualities bestowed upon you by high heaven and celestial power, but also exceedingly distinguished for these other gifts which by reason of the long-established prerogatives of noble blood have descended to you from your forebears, by so many illustrious titles. If any person desires to contemplate the glory of your lineage and the ancient[5] line of your ancestral images, let him look upon all Portugal[6]—nay, more, let him survey the whole of Spain, which so radiates the lustre of your race, that the man who fails to perceive such splendour must be deemed blind. For who is a stranger to the name and the fame of the Furtados à Mendoça? Gladly would I linger over the exposition of this point (for what man can speak adequately, when on a theme so lofty?) did I not believe that to cast verbal lustre upon a family so glorious would be to enrich[7] the sun with light, the seas with water; especially in view of the fact that you, most illustrious Bishop, nobly descended as you are, transcend your nobility of lineage in the nobility of your spirit. For to those gifts which God has lavishly bestowed upon you, and to those which you have inherited from the illustrious and venerable line of your forebears, you have by your industry and

4. [Suárez has *Loquens iustitiam, & annuntians veritatem,* whereas the Vulgate reads: *loquens justitiam annuntians recta,* translated in the Douay version as follows: 'that speak justice, that declare right things.'—TR.]

5. [Reading *antiquam* (cf. 1856 edition) for *antequam.*—TR.]

6. [Reading *Lusitaniam* for *Lusitanum,* as the context would seem to call for the former reading and the text is faulty in other respects, at this point.—TR.]

7. [*Faenerari,* evidently formed upon *faenus* ('interest upon capital,' 'gain,' 'profit,' &c.).—TR.]

labour, while diligently serving in the cause of letters, added this further qualification: the fact that our University looked up to you, as you trod its paths, not merely with congratulatory esteem, but also in just amaze and admiration. All those qualities, then, which men commonly desire in a patron, I behold in you, and possess through you in lavish quantity. But what would it avail me, that you should have conspicuous claims to renown, and should possess abundantly all that is wont to commend a patron, if in spite of your magnanimity to others the door of your benevolence were closed against me? However, while to all those who have earnestly devoted themselves to the pursuit of learning, that door has ever opened with a facility such that all men of letters acknowledge you as their outstanding protector, to me, indeed, it has always been opened so wide, in accord with your unique kindliness, that from the very day when first I took up my residence in Portugal, I have enjoyed your exceedingly generous benevolence and beneficence toward me, a generosity so great, and of so many years' duration, a generosity expressed in your speech and made public in your deeds, that there is no need for me to make it known by my own proclamation. For in truth, you have always given—and still give, most lovingly—such signal proofs of your good will toward me, that no one in all Portugal, so it would seem, can have failed to witness, directly or by hearsay, your beneficent friendliness in my behalf. Therefore, reason demands and even insists that I should strive to emulate this kindness which you lavish upon me, although in truth, its magnitude is such that I am unable to make an equal return.

Accept, then, most illustrious Bishop, the gift of this little book. Although it is unworthy of the love and benevolence bestowed by you upon me and upon our Society; although indeed, it cannot worthily repay you the many debts and favours by which we, who were already your debtors, are so bound that we are unable to render you full payment for them, in spite of the fact that we truly desire to do so; nevertheless, this gift can certainly be the evidence of a most grateful heart, and a memorial of my entire good will toward you and all yours. This is your book because it was brought to light at your bidding and under your leadership. Since, then, it came from you, let it return to you. And even as it first saw the light under so happy a star, may it thus dwell for ever under that same star, a token of my affection for you. It is yours, being your due for many reasons, although it is an insufficient and unequal repayment. May you, then, defend the work as your own, with that potent authority which you possess; may you accord it that patronage for which you are so rarely distinguished; and may you shed lustre upon it with your own bright renown. For so your courteousness demands, your kindness promises, and my reverence for you deserves.

A Treatise on Laws and God the Lawgiver

PREFACE

Setting Forth the Subject and Plan of the Whole Work

It need not surprise anyone that it should occur to a professional theologian to take up the discussion of laws. For the eminence of theology, derived as it is from its most eminent subject-matter, precludes all reason for wonder. Surely, if the question is rightly examined, it will be evident that a treatise on laws is so included within the range of theology, that the theologian cannot exhaust his subject unless he tarries for a time in the study of laws. For just as theologians should contemplate God on many other grounds, so also should they contemplate Him on this ground: that He is the last end toward Whom rational creatures tend and in Whom their sole felicity consists. It follows, then, that the sacred science has this last end in view, and that it also sets forth the way to attain that end; since God is not only the end, and (as it were) the goal, towards which all intellectual creatures tend, but also the cause of that goal's attainment. For He directs His creatures, and, having shown the way, leads them to Himself. Moreover, He checks them with admonitions, that they may not stray from the path of righteousness, and when they do stray from it, by His ineffable providence He recalls them and shepherds them back, enlightening them by His teaching, admonishing them with His counsels, impelling them by His laws and, above all, succouring them with the aid of His grace; so that Isaias most justly exclaims [*Isaias,* Chap. xxxiii, v. 22]: 'the Lord is our lawgiver, the Lord is our king: he will save us'.[1]

---

1. [This passage, though following the words of Isaias, is not given as a quotation in the 1612 ed.—Tr.]

Since, then, the way of this salvation lies in free actions and in moral rectitude—which rectitude in turn depends to a great extent upon law as the rule of human actions[2]—it follows thence that the study of laws becomes a large division of theology; and when the sacred science treats of law, that science surely regards no other object than God Himself as Lawgiver.

All this is very well (someone may argue), if the theologian, keeping within the bounds of divine laws, does not invade the domain of human laws, which both the moral philosophers, and the professors of canon and civil law, may very justly claim as their own province. For if the theologian treats of laws only in so far as they are derived from God as Lawgiver, then surely he will be discharging an alien function, if he turns aside to discuss other legislators. Moreover, since theology is a supernatural science, it should be forbidden to descend to those matters which have their source in nature and in no way rise above her. If this be not true, then the natural philosopher may also study divine laws, in addition to natural laws; and the professors of Roman, or even of Pontifical law, may usurp for themselves the lessons of the divine laws; a supposition which is clearly opposed to an harmonious division of the sciences.

These considerations, however, are not of great moment and may be disposed of almost by a single word, if one reflects that, even as all paternity comes from God, so, too, does [the power of] every legislator, and that the authority of all laws must ultimately be ascribed to Him. For truly, if a law be divine, it flows directly from Him; if, on the other hand, it be human, that law is surely ordained by man, acting as God's minister and vicar, in accordance with the testimony of the Apostle in his *Epistle to the Romans* [Chap. xiii].[3] Hence, it is not without cause that, from this

2. 'Human actions': for Suárez, properly *human* actions are the actions of normal adults. To count as properly human, and so unlike the actions of children or the mad, they must be *perfectly voluntary,* or involve a capacity to respond to and apply practical reason through the exercise of the *voluntas* or will. Given perfect voluntariness, they can also be *free,* or subject to our power of control over which actions we perform. As human in this sense they are subject to regulation by law.

3. Romans 13:1: 'Let every person be subject to the governing authorities; for there is no authority except from God, and those authorities that exist have been instituted by God.'

standpoint, at least, a discussion of all laws should fall within the scope of the faculty of theology. For, in view of the fact that it pertains to theology to look upon God as Lawgiver, and since God is the Universal Lawgiver, either through the mediation of a deputy, or by the immediate action of His own virtue (to use the terminology of the philosophers), this same sacred science must of necessity deal with all laws.

Moreover, it is a theological function to take thought for the consciences of men in this life, and rectitude of conscience rests upon the observance of laws, just as perversion of conscience rests upon their violation; for any law whatsoever is a rule which leads to eternal salvation if it is obeyed as it should be, and to the loss of that salvation if it is violated. Hence, the study of law as binding upon the conscience will also pertain to the province of the theologian.

Finally, the Catholic faith teaches not only how far we must obey God when He commands in the supernatural order; it teaches also what nature forbids, commands, or permits; furthermore, it clearly reveals to us the extent to which we must submit to the higher powers (in the words of Paul) and, indeed, the extent to which we must observe both ecclesiastical and secular laws. From these foundations of the faith, then, it is for the theologian to deduce what should be held, with respect to this or that system of laws.

One may understand, in this connexion, how theology fulfils the function in question without any imperfection or confusion; that is to say, it treats of law by the light of a higher inspiration. For, in the first place, the moral philosophers discuss many points relating to law. Thus, Plato wrote twelve books on the subject, compressed approximately into three, by Cicero.[4] Aristotle, indeed, while he did not leave any work dealing strictly with laws, did write a great deal on that subject, here and there, throughout his works on morals;[5] as did Seneca, Plutarch and others.[6]

---

4. Suárez here refers to Plato's *Laws* and Cicero's *On Laws* (*De legibus*).

5. See especially Book X of Aristotle's *Nicomachean Ethics*, which contains discussion of the necessity and effect of laws.

6. As in Seneca's *On Benefits* (*De beneficiis*) and *On Clemency* (*De clementia*), and Plutarch's *To an Untutored Ruler* (*Ad principem ineruditum*) and *Precepts on Government* (*Praecepta gerendae reipublicae*).

It would seem, however, that these philosophers recorded only the principles of jurisprudence. For their treatment was almost entirely limited to those human laws which help to keep a commonwealth or state in justice and in peace; and, at most, they touched somewhat upon natural law in so far as it can be made known by human reason and serves as guide for the moral rectitude of acquired virtues. The [Roman] emperors, too, adopted very nearly the same principle in establishing their laws; as did the other framers of civil laws; for, using philosophy as a foundation, they deduced therefrom civil laws which were in accord with reason. Wherefore, Cicero (*On Laws,* Bk. I [, chap. xxii, § 58]) makes a particular effort to confirm the statement that jurisprudence should be derived from the very springs of philosophy. Ulpian agrees with this (*Digest,* I. i. 1, § 1), when he says: 'We strive [. . .] for a true and not a simulated philosophy'. It follows thence that civil jurisprudence is nothing other than an application, or extension, of moral philosophy to the rule and government of the political conduct of the commonwealth; and therefore, in order that [this jurisprudence] may partake somewhat of the essence of true science, it must be joined or subordinated to philosophy. All this treatment of the laws, then, fails to transcend their natural end; nor does it even touch upon that end in all its phases, but only upon such phases as are necessary to preserve the external peace and justice of the commonwealth.

The canon laws, however, relate to the supernatural order, both because they are derived from the power given to Peter for the feeding of Christ's flock [*St. John,* Chap. xxi, vv. 15, 16], and also because they trace their origin to the principles of divine law, and imitate that law in so far as is possible and expedient. Wherefore, Innocent III said (*Decretals,* Bk. V, tit. 1, chap. xxiv) that the canonical sanctions were derived from the authorities of the Old and New Testaments. In the canon laws themselves, however, we may distinguish two separate ends. The one consists in the establishment in the whole ecclesiastical state of a due political order, the preservation in that state of peace and justice, and the regulation by right reason of all that relates to the external forum of the Church. The other end consists in the right and prudent ordering of all things relating to divine worship, the salvation of souls and the purity of faith and moral conduct. Hence the interpreters of canon law, by the very nature of their labours and of their own purpose, study and interpret the sacred canons from the standpoint of a superior end and aspect.

But theology embraces all these functions on a loftier plane. For it takes into consideration the natural law itself in so far as the latter is subordinated to the supernatural order, and derives greater firmness therefrom; whereas it considers the civil laws only by way of determining, according to a higher order of rules, their goodness and rectitude, or by way of declaring, in accordance with the principles of the faith, the obligations of conscience which are derived from the said civil laws. Furthermore, theology recognizes and claims as proper to itself, the sacred canons and the pontifical decrees in so far as they are binding upon the conscience and point the way to eternal salvation. Accordingly, with respect to all of these systems of law, theology conducts a divinely illuminated inquiry into the primary origins and the final ends; that is, it asks in what way the said systems derive their origin from God Himself, in the sense that the power to establish them exists primarily in God, flowing forth to men from Him either by a natural or by a supernatural course, and ever influencing and co-operating with them. Finally, theology clearly reveals the way in which all laws are standards of human action relatively to the conscience, and thus reveals also the extent to which they conduce to merit or demerit for eternal life.

Nor, indeed, are we the first among the theologians to undertake this treatment of laws. For we have as predecessors, writers of the gravest authority, in every age. In the first place, St. Thomas, in his *Summa* (I.–II, from qu. 90 to qu. 109) follows this mode of procedure when laying down a doctrine of laws; and he has been imitated by the commentators on these passages; especially, by Soto (*De Iustitia et Iure,* the first two Books) and by St. Antoninus (*Summa Theologica,* Pt. I, titles xi–xviii). Alexander of Hales ([*Summa Universae Theologiae,*] Pt. III, qq. xxvi–lx) and Vincent of Beauvais (*Speculum Morale,* Bk. I, pt. ii, first nine disputations[7]) have observed the same method. Gerson, too (*De Vita Spirituali,* Pt. III, lects. ii *et seq.; De Potestate Ecclesiastica,* Pt. I, especially *consideratio* 13), dealt with

---

7. [Suárez probably intended to say 'distinctions'.—REVISER.]

certain points relating to individual laws. [Peter Lombard,] the Master of the *Sentences,* also touched lightly (*Sentences,* Bk. III, dists. xxxvii, to end) upon the subject of divine laws; and he was imitated therein by others who undertook simply the task of commentators. Moreover, special works on certain laws have been published by other theologians, such as William of Paris[8] in his *Summa* (Pt. I, bk. ii [Pt. V, chap. i]), which book he entitled *De Legibus,* although it treats almost entirely of the precepts of the Old Law. Castro also wrote on penal laws; and Driedo, in his work *De Libertate Christiana,* treated learnedly of every kind of law; not to mention other writers in these fields.

It is, then, the common consensus of the theologians that [the study of] law has regard to the consideration of the sacred science, in so far as concerns both the essential nature of law in general, and its division under all the various species.

Therefore, the foregoing makes clear the subject-matter of this treatise and the principle on the basis of which we shall treat of that subject-matter. With this end in view, then, we shall not find it difficult to set forth a summary of all the points to be treated, a plan of discussion, and the method to be followed. For we shall speak first of law in general, then we shall pass to each of its species, and in connexion with each of these, we shall treat only of those points which are adapted to our purpose; in order that, in so far as we find it possible, we shall neither omit anything that pertains to the purpose of theology, nor appear to go beyond the bounds of the sacred science.

---

8. Now known as William of Auvergne (d. 1249), Bishop of Paris, who in his theological and philosophical writings was an early assimilator of Aristotle.

A Treatise on Laws and
God the Lawgiver

Concerning Law in General; and Concerning
Its Nature, Causes and Effects

Following the usual order of this science of law, we shall in this First Book treat only of the general nature of law; offering, however, a preliminary outline of law as it is divided into its various parts, so that some knowledge of them, even though it be a general knowledge, may be obtained. For in spite of the fact that this book is to deal with the matters that are common to all law, devoting as little attention as possible to those points which properly pertain to the individual species of law, nevertheless, it will frequently be necessary for us to make mention of those species, in order that the points which are common [to both aspects of law] may be better understood. Accordingly, it is necessary to furnish some conception of the said individual species.

However, in order to proceed more clearly, we should first dwell to some extent upon the name and the essential nature of law (*lex*).

CHAPTER I

The Meaning of the Term 'Law' (*Lex*)

1. *The definition of* lex, *according to St. Thomas.* St. Thomas (I.–II, qu. 90, art. 1) defines the term 'law' (*lex*) as follows: 'Law is a certain rule and measure in accordance with which one is induced to act or is restrained

from acting.'[1] This definition would appear to be too broad and general. For law would in that case be applicable not only to men, or rational creatures, but also to other creatures, since everything has its own rule and measure, in accordance with which it operates and is induced to act or is restrained therefrom. Moreover, law [if so defined] would relate not only to moral matters, but also to artificial matters; not only to what is good and upright,[2] but also to what is evil; since the arts, too, whether licit or illicit, have their own rules and measures, according to which their operation is promoted or restrained. Finally (and this would seem to be a graver objection), it would follow from the definition above set forth that counsels are to be included under law; for counsel is also a species of rule and measure of virtuous action inclining one towards that which is better, and restraining one from that which is less good; yet, according to the faith, counsels are clearly distinct from precepts, and therefore are not included under law, strictly speaking.[3]

2. *The divisions of* lex, *according to Plato.* With respect to the foregoing, we may note, in the first place, the division which is to be drawn from Plato's *Minos,* or *On Law* [313 B *et seq.*],[4] a dialogue in which he distinguishes between two [suggested] divisions of law: that of art, and that of custom. To these we may add a third group from the *Timaeus* [24 *et seq.*] and the *Gorgias* of this same Plato—the law of order or of natural propensity. Here, distinguishing a fourfold division of law, he gives to one part the name of natural law. We shall make some comments as to this division below (Chapter Three).[5]

For the present, we refer the expression 'natural law' not to that law which dwells in mankind, a division which we shall also discuss later, but rather to that which befits all things, in accordance with the inclination imparted to them by the Author of nature; for such appears to be Plato's

---

1. [This quotation, as given by Suárez, varies slightly from St. Thomas's text.—Tr.]

2. Suárez's term is *honestum,* meaning what is honorable or morally good.

3. 'Counsels' or *consilia* communicate advice and merely recommend; 'precepts' or *praecepta* communicate requirements and oblige.

4. *Minos:* this dialogue, though Platonic in doctrine, is now thought not to be by Plato himself.

5. [*Infra,* p. 39.—Tr.]

explanation of the term, although he admits that the law in question exists among men also, after a nobler fashion.

This third acceptation of law is therefore metaphorical, since things which lack reason are not, strictly speaking, susceptible to law, just as they are not capable of obedience. Accordingly, the efficacy of divine power, and the natural necessity resulting therefrom in this connexion, are metaphorically given the name of law. With this, indeed, the Scriptural phrase accords (*Proverbs,* Chap. viii [, v. 27]): 'When with a certain law and compass he enclosed the depths'; as do, further on, the words [*ibid.,* v. 29]: '[. . .] and set a law to the waters, that they should not pass their limits'. This sort of law is also referred to, in the term 'measure' in *Job* (Chap. xxxviii [, v. 5]): 'Who hath laid the measure[s] thereof, if thou knowest?' And we find below, the words: 'Who shut up the sea with doors' [*ibid.,* v. 8]; 'And I said: Hitherto thou shalt come', &c. [*ibid.,* v. 11].

Furthermore, it is in accordance with this acceptation that the term 'law' is wont to be applied to natural inclination; either because that inclination is the measure of the action toward which it impels one, or because it rises out of the law of the Creator. For this term 'law' is frequently applied both to the rule itself, and to the work or effect thereof, in so far as the latter conforms to the rule; just as the actual product of art is often called 'art'. It is in this sense that one may interpret the following passages, from the *Epistle to the Romans* (Chap. ii [, v. 13]): 'For not only[6] the hearers [of the law are just before God,] but the doers of the law shall be justified'; (that is to say, [doers] of the work prescribed by the law;) and from *John* (Chap. vii [, v. 19]): 'Did not Moses give you the law, and yet none of you keepeth[7] the law'. However, in these passages, the word *faciendum* (doing *or* keeping) may also be taken in another sense as equivalent to the word *observandum* (observing).

3. Paul, too, may be interpreted according to this first acceptation, when, in the *Epistle to the Romans* (Chap. vii [, v. 23]), he speaks of the

6. [I.e. not those who merely hear the law. The passage in the Bible does not contain the word 'only'.—Tr.]

7. [The Latin verb *facit* (doeth) perhaps brings out Suárez's point more forcefully than the English 'keepeth'.—Tr.]

inclination of the sensitive appetite[8] as 'the law of the members' and 'a law of sin', an inclination which St. Thomas (I.–II, qu. 90, art. 1, ad 1, and qu. 90 [qu. 91], art. 6) has called the *lex fomitis*[9] (law of concupiscence).[10] Furthermore, he there declares that this inordinate inclination of the *fomes* is called law, yet not formally, in the sense of law as a measure, but in a participatory sense, as one is wont to speak of that which is measured by law. Accordingly, St. Thomas holds, not that this inclination of the appetite comes of its very nature under the name of law, but that it does come under that name in so far as it is deprived of the rectitude of [its] original justice, owing to original sin, by operation of the punitive law of God. For in this sense, the inordinate nature of the *fomes* is not simply natural, but is a penalty of sin; and therefore, it is called 'law' in its capacity as an effect of divine law. Augustine (*De Diversis Quaestionibus ad Simplicianum*, Bk. I, qu. 1 [, no. 13]) seems to have held the same opinion, for he says: 'This oppressive and weighty burden he calls law (*lex*), for the reason that it has been decreed and imposed by divine judgment through the law (*ius*) of punishment.' Assuredly, this is to say that it was imposed by setting aside the [original] justice which endowed [the inclination] with the contrary quality of rectitude.

4. However, while the foregoing may be true, it would nevertheless seem that the inclination itself of the appetite, in so far as that inclination is purely natural, might be termed 'law' in the sense in which the natural inclination of water is so termed. For, in like manner, there would exist in man, in his purely natural state,[11] this very law of the *fomes,* although

8. The 'sensitive appetite' is the capacity for passion or nonintellectual motivation that humans share with the lower animals; it contrasts with the 'rational appetite' or will, which is the human capacity for motivation in a form that is fully responsive to reason, and which is the locus of decision-making and intention-formation.

9. The *lex fomitis,* literally 'law of kindling or incitement.' By this Suárez means the inclination of our passions toward sin, called concupiscence—concupiscence being an inclination, not itself sinful, that exists in us as a punitive consequence of original sin.

10. [In the first of these passages, St. Thomas speaks of the *lex membrorum.*—REVISER.]

11. *In puris naturalibus:* the state of pure nature refers to a hypothetical state in which humans are considered apart from their relation to any supernatural end, that is, apart from any destiny or end beyond this life. So in this state humans are being considered neither as fallen from the destiny of heaven nor as saved for it.

it would not exist as a punishment for sin. Moreover, even to-day, this inclination of the *fomes* is apparently called law not only because it is an effect thereof, but also because it is (so to speak) a measure and rule of movements pertaining to the senses and has therefore been called by Paul 'the law of the members', as having dominion, in particular, over the members of the body. Thus it is that Augustine has said (*De Genesi ad Litteram*, Bk. V [Bk. IX], chap. x): 'They have merited the operation in their members of that law which is opposed to the law of the mind.'[12] So also is it that this law has been called the law of sin, not only because it is a result of sin, but also because it inclines thereto. In this sense, indeed, the law in question did not exist in Adam before the fall. For even though his sensitive appetite lacked not its natural propensity, it did not operate of itself, nor did it dominate in any way; neither was it a rule or measure of certain movements, but was, on the contrary, entirely subject to the law of the mind. However, for the matter of metaphorical locutions, the foregoing remarks will suffice.

5. The second[13] acceptation of the word *lex* is a stricter one; for art is a work of the reason, and hence the rules that measure art may more properly be designated by the term *lex*. Accordingly, we are wont to distinguish among the military, and mercantile, and other laws; as St. Thomas has noted (I.–II, qu. 91, art. 6). The rules of correct speech, too, are customarily called the laws of grammar. And the same practice prevails in regard to other arts. Nevertheless, just as the rectitude of any art with respect to rational creatures is a relative rectitude, as St. Thomas remarks (*ibid.*, qu. 56 [, art. 3]), even so the law of an art can be termed a law only in a relative sense.

Therefore, the name 'law' is properly applied, in an absolute sense, to that which pertains to moral conduct. And accordingly, we should narrow the description given by St. Thomas, so that it runs as follows: law is a certain measure of moral acts,[14] in the sense that such acts are characterized

---

12. [This quotation, as given by Suárez, varies slightly from the text of Augustine.—Tʀ.]

13. [I.e. the second in Plato's *Minos,* although Suárez mentions it first in Section 2, *supra.*—Tʀ.]

14. *Actuum moralium:* by 'moral acts' Suárez means the free acts of adult humans that are properly subject to law.

by moral rectitude through their conformity to law, and by perversity, if
they are out of harmony with law.

6. *The true meaning of law.* Hence, although unrighteous precepts or
rules are frequently designated by the term 'law', as the saying in *Isaias* (Chap. xx [Chap. x, v. 1]) implies: 'Woe to them that make wicked
laws', and as the words of Aristotle also imply (*Nicomachean Ethics,* Bk. IV,
chap. i [Bk. V, chap. i, 1129 B]): 'A law which is made at random is evil'[15]
(take, for example, the one which in popular speech is commonly called
'the law of the world', or 'the law of the duel', or some similar laws)—
although, I repeat, this may be true—nevertheless, strictly and absolutely
speaking, only that which is a measure of rectitude, viewed absolutely, and
consequently only that which is a right and virtuous rule, can be called
law. It is on this account that St. Thomas has said (I.–II, qu. 90, art. 1
[art. 2] and qu. 96, art. 4) that an evil precept is not law but iniquity;
and St. Augustine has made the declaration, in the tractate *On Free Will*
(Bk. I, chap. v): 'That which is not just, does not seem to me to be [true]
law (*lex*).' Moreover, in his work *On the City of God* (Bk. XIX, chap. xxi),
he lays down the same assertion, with regard to *ius*. Indeed, Cicero also
has said (*On Laws,* Bk. II [, chap. v, § 11]) that law ought to be established
to the end of promoting a just, quiet, and happy life; and that, therefore,
those who are authors of unjust laws[16] [so-called], have produced anything
but [true] laws.

Plato amply confirms this assertion, in the Dialogue already cited.[17]
The reason supporting the view is also manifest in the light of what we
have said above. For law is a measure of rectitude. But an unjust law is not
a measure of the rectitude of human conduct. On the contrary, an action
which conforms to it is unjust. Therefore, [such an unjust enactment] is

---

15. [Suárez evidently is referring to the passage in Bk. V, chap. i, 1129 B of Aristotle's
Nicomachean Ethics, which reads: 'But the law also prescribes certain conduct . . . and
so with actions exemplifying the rest of the virtues and vices, commanding these and
forbidding those—rightly if the law has been rightly enacted, not so well if it has been
made at random.'—Tr.]

16. [Suárez has used the term *leges* both here and at the end of this statement. Cicero,
more logically, has *iussa* in the former position, *leges,* in the latter.—Tr.]

17. [*Minos.* See *supra,* p. 18, Section 2.—Tr.]

not law, but partakes of the name of law by analogy (so to speak) in so far as it prescribes a certain mode of action in relation to a given end. We shall discuss this point later at some length.

[7]. The foregoing satisfies the reasons for doubt, with regard to the first two heads.[18] For in the sense in which the term is here used, law is the measure, not of all acts whatsoever, but of moral acts, with respect to their absolute goodness and rectitude, by reason of which rectitude, law impels one to perform these actions. It is in this sense that Clement of Alexandria has said (*Stromata,* Bk. I [, chap. xxvi]): 'Law is the rule of the just and the unjust.'

The last objection,[19] however, postulates a distinction between counsel and law, a matter which is a cause of prolonged dispute with the heretics, although that dispute is not pertinent to the present context. Some persons hold, then, that 'law' is to be taken in two senses: in one sense, as a binding precept, and thus distinct from counsels; and in another sense, as any dictate of reason with regard to the righteousness of an act; according to which latter interpretation (so they maintain), the term 'law' includes counsels. For St. Thomas says (I.–II, qu. 19, art. 4) that every good act depends, in its goodness, upon the eternal law; and the acts enjoined by counsels are good in the highest degree; hence, such acts are included under the eternal law. However, if one is speaking (as we now are) of law in the strict sense of the term, only that is law which imposes an obligation of some sort; a point that we shall discuss more fully below.

8. Nevertheless, one should take into consideration the fact that sometimes there is laid down a law which relates to the performance of an act, so that it renders the act itself obligatory, as is the case, for instance, with the law of almsgiving; whereas at other times a law is made which deals only with the special quality of the action, or its mode of performance, a law which, although it does not require the performance of the act, does nevertheless require that, if the said act is performed, a particular mode of execution shall be observed. Of this nature, for example, is the law of attentive prayer. This precept, although it does not render obligatory the

18. [As mentioned in Section 1.—REVISER.]
19. [Cf. Section 1, discussion of counsel.—REVISER.]

act of praying, nevertheless does impose the obligation to pray with attention if one prays at all. With respect to laws of this second class, then, it
is, in a universal sense, true that (as St. Thomas has stated in the passage
cited immediately above) every act, to the extent that it is a good act, must
be in conformity with the eternal law; that is to say, with the eternal law
as it prescribes a due method of performance. This conclusion applies also
to the acts performed under counsel. Nevertheless, these acts, viewed as
such, are not said to come under 'acts of counsel'; rather, they are thus
classified to the extent that their practice or performance is counselled,
not prescribed.[20] And, speaking in this sense, we must absolutely deny that
counsel is included within the field of law.

The difference between law and counsel. Moreover, counsel is excluded
from the description of law given above, either because counsel is not,
properly speaking, a rule or measure of the goodness of an action, since
[such rules] consist rather in the laws which prescribe a given mode of
action; or else because, morally speaking, counsel does not induce to
action effectually, that is to say, by imposing a moral necessity of action,
whereas, when it is said that law induces to action, the statement must be
understood in this sense [namely, as involving moral necessity].

9. *The etymology of the term 'law'.* From these considerations, St. Thomas,
in the article cited (I.–II, qu. 90, art. 1) drew his conclusion as to the
etymology of law. For he held that the term was derived from *ligandum*
(binding), since the true effect of law is to bind, or place under a binding
obligation. This view was adopted by Gabriel (on the *Sentences of Peter
Lombard,* Bk. III, dist. xxxvii, art. 1). Clichtove (on Joannes Damascenus',
De Fide Orthodoxa, Bk. IV, chap. xxiii) quoted the same explanation of
the etymology of law, from Cassiodorus, and approved it. Moreover, the
opinion in question is in agreement with Scripture, which speaks of laws
as bands, in a passage from *Jeremias* (Chap. ii [, v. 20]): 'Thou hast broken
my yoke, thou hast burst my bands. . . .'

But Isidore (*Etymologies,* Bk. II, chap. x and Bk. V, chap. iii) believes
that law (*lex*) is so called from *legendum* (that which is to be read), a

---

20. [I.e. from the standpoint of the *method* of performance, the acts in question
come, not under counsel, but under actual law.—Tr.]

conclusion which he deduces from the fact that law ought to be written, and therefore is something to be read. However, since we are now dealing with law in a rather broad sense, the word *legendum* should be extended to include internal reading or reflection, as Alexander of Hales has noted ([*Summa Universae Theologiae,*] Pt. III, qu. xxvi, memb. 1), in order that this etymology may be suited to every law. For, just as the natural law is said by Paul (*Romans,* Chap. ii [, v. 15]) to be written in the heart, so it can and should also be read there by the mind; that is, it can and should be meditated and reflected upon, so that one's conduct may be guided in conformity therewith, according to the passage in the *Psalms,* cxviii [, v. 105]: 'Thy word is a lamp to my feet.' Moreover, in harmony with this same etymology is the Hebrew name for law (*Tora*), which signifies 'instruction'.

Finally, others hold that law is so called from *eligendum* (that which is to be selected), either because it ought to be enacted after an extensive and prudent process of choosing, or else because it points out to each individual the course which he should choose. Thus St. Augustine says, in his *Questions on the Old and New Testament* ([Pt. II,] qu. 15), if that is, indeed, his work: 'Law (*lex*) is derived from *lectio* (a collection), that is, from *electio* (a choosing); [for it is made] in order that you may know what course to select from among many.'[21]

Cicero, indeed, declares (*On Laws,* Bk. I [, chap. vi, § 19]) that the name is derived from *legendum* (in the [primary] sense of 'selecting'). 'For' (so Cicero says) 'we give to the term "law" the force of "selection", just as the Greeks call law νόμος, that is to say, [drawing the term] from the idea of granting' to each man that which is his own,[22] since law ought to be just. Accordingly, still other authorities derive the word *lex* from the fact that law legitimately moderates human actions, a derivation cited by Torquemada (on *Decretum,* Pt. I, dist. 1, can. iii).

All these derivations, then, involve some explanation truly pertinent to law. The source from which the word is derived, however, is doubtful, and a matter of slight importance.

21. [*Sic,* in Suárez's text, which reads as follows: *Lex a lectione, id est, electione dicta est, ut de multis quid eligas scias.* The passage from Augustine, however, is somewhat shorter: *Lex a lectione dicta est, ut de multis quid eligas scias.*—Tr.]

22. [This is substantially what Cicero says; but it is not an exact quotation.—Tr.]

CHAPTER II

What *Ius* Means and How It Is to Be Compared with *Lex*

1. This word [i.e. *ius*] is frequently used in connexion with the subject under discussion and is sometimes taken as a synonym for *lex,* a fact that is made evident by the *Institutes* (II. i, § 11) and the *Digest* (I. iii. 16), although at other times *ius* is taken in other senses also. Accordingly, it is necessary to explain the word *ius,* and to compare it with *lex.*

Various derivations for the term ius. First, however, we should note that three etymologies are wont to be ascribed to the former term.

The first. The first explanation is that *ius* is so called because it is close (*iuxta*). As to this explanation Connan (*Commentary on the Civil Law,* Bk. I [, chap. ii]) may be consulted. For I am passing it over, since it is not convincing to me; because, if we are considering the external form of the respective terms, there is no relation between them, *iuxta* being written not with an 's' as is *ius* but with an 'x', and if, on the other hand, it is the meaning that claims our attention, *iuxta esse* does not mean 'to be equal', but simply, 'to be close at hand'. Moreover, though the phrase does at times imply similitude or equality in some function or action, nevertheless, such an implication is made in a sense far removed from that of equity, which *ius* suggests. Consequently, this first derivation seems to me unlikely and far-fetched.

The second derivation. The second explanation, and one more widely accepted among Latin peoples, is that which derives the name *ius* from *iubere* (to command). For *iussum* is a participle of the verb *iubeo;* and if we take the second syllable from the participle *iussum, ius* is left; or, indeed, if one divides these two syllables, a sentence will be constructed in which *iussum* itself, or [the personification of] authority, will assert that it is *ius,* saying, *ius sum* (I am *ius*).

2. *The third derivation.* The third etymological explanation derives the term *ius* from *iustitia.* For Ulpian has said (in *Digest,* I. i. 1), in accordance with this explanation: '*ius,* indeed, is so called from *iustitia.*' Some persons assail this derivation on the ground that *iustitia* is derived from *ius,* rather than conversely; for that is called *iustum* (just) which is in accordance with

ius. However, that argument lacks force, since it is one thing to speak of relationship (*ordine*), or derivation, with respect to causality, and quite another, to speak of such relationship with respect to the act of denomination, or assignment of a name. For in the former sense, it is true that *iustitia* (justice) is derived from *ius;* derived, that is, from that which is in reality just and fair with regard to its object and, accordingly, with regard to its final, or formal and extrinsic cause. In this sense, indeed, *iustitia* is defined by *ius,* since, according to the *Digest* (I. i. 10), '*Ius* renders to each one that which is his due'. However, in so far as concerns the denomination and appellation of *ius* (the point of which Ulpian is speaking), *ius* could have derived its name from *iustitia;* just as 'vision' (*visus*) is such because it tends toward an object that is 'visible' (*visibile*), while the object nevertheless receives the appellation 'visible' from the very term of 'vision'. In like manner, then, *iustitia* is such, because it tends to the establishment of equity, which we say is the just mean (*medium iustum*) itself; and at the same time, this mean has been enabled rightly to take the title of *iustum* from *iustitia,* since such equity is fitted to be established through justice and is therefore called 'just' (*iusta*). And thus the term *ius* may easily have been derived through the dropping of the last syllable of *iustum;* even as we said in the case of the word *iussum.* Isidore (*Etymologies,* Bk. V, chap. iii) also has spoken to this effect, saying: '*Ius* is so called because it is just.' Augustine, too (*On Psalm cxlv,* near the end [§ 15]), remarks: '*Ius* and *iniuria* (injustice) are opposites; for *ius* is that which is just.' Therefore, even as *iustum* is clearly so called from *iustitia,* so *ius* may have derived its name from *iustum* and *iustitia,* in so far as relates to the etymology of the term.

3. Consequently, Augustine (*On the City of God,* Bk. XIX, chap. xxi) likewise deduces the following as a principle of the philosophers: 'Because they call that *ius,* which has flowed from the fount of justice (*iustitia*).'[1] For though *ius* may be, with respect to its object, the cause of *iustitia,* nevertheless, in the realm of efficient causality it is the effect of *iustitia,* since it is the latter which creates and sets up its own object, just as the other moral virtues do. Accordingly, if one were to consider this object in its potential aspect, it might be termed *iustificabile* (justifiable)—so

---

1. [This quotation, as given by Suárez, varies slightly from Augustine's text.—Tr.]

to speak—from the word *iustitia,* even as we were saying with respect to *visus* and *visibile;* but the term *iustificabile* is not in use, it is barbarous, and in its place the word *ius* (in so far as it denotes the object of justice) seems to have been introduced. And if, on the other hand, the object in question is conceived of in its active character, then it is said to be *iustum* (just), and may be called *ius.* For it is in this sense that Augustine's statement has a proper application—that is, his statement that *ius* and *iniuria* are opposites—since *iniuria* is nothing more nor less than an unjust act. So it is, too, that he has said, in the second passage cited: 'That which is done by *ius* (*iure*),[2] is surely done justly (*iuste*).'[3] And thus Bartolus (on the said law of the *Digest* [I. i. 10]) declared that *ius* in its active character is execution, and interpreted accordingly the law on which he was commenting. However, the same conception may very well be accepted with regard to *ius* in its potential aspect, also, that is to say, in its [potential] nature (*in habitu*); because, as I have said, the question is not one of causal emanation, but simply one of the assignment of a name, just as *scibile* (that which may be known) derives its name from *scientia* (knowledge), even in a potential sense (*in habitu*).

Therefore, this third derivation is in no way unsuitable; and although it is uncertain which of these two conclusions comes nearer the truth, either one will serve for our present purposes.

4. *The meaning of the term* ius. In accordance, then, with those two derivations of the term, the word *ius* has two principal meanings. These have been noted by Driedo (*De Libertate Christiana,* Bk. I, chap. x). For, according to the last-cited derivation, *ius* has the same meaning as *iustum* (that which is just), and *aequum* (that which is equitable), these being the objects of *iustitia.* Yet one must take into consideration the fact that the word *iustitia* has [also] two acceptations. In the first place, this word may stand for every virtue, since every virtue in some wise is directed toward and brings about equity. In the second place, it may signify a special virtue which renders to another that which is his due. Accordingly, the word *ius* conforms, in due proportion, to each of these two meanings [of *iustitia*].

2. [I.e. *iure fit.*—Tr.]
3. [I.e. *iuste fit.*—Tr.]

For, in the first sense, *ius* may refer to whatever is fair and in harmony with reason, this being, as it were, the general objective of virtue in the abstract. In the second sense, *ius* may refer to the equity which is due to each individual as a matter of justice. This latter acceptation is more common, since *ius* so taken is most particularly wont to be related to justice in the strict sense. Thus, St. Thomas (II.–II, qu. 57, art. 1) has said that such justice constitutes the primary basis and significance of *ius*. And in consequence, he well concludes (*ibid.,* ad 2) that *ius* is not *lex,* but is rather that which is prescribed or measured by *lex.* This view should, I think, be understood in a relative sense. For the laws which pertain to justice in the special sense [likewise] involve a special form of *ius,* that referred to in the above-mentioned strict acceptation of the term. Whereas *lex* understood in the general sense, and in so far as it may have a place in all the virtues, will look to *ius* in the broad and general acceptation of the latter term; in accordance with Cicero's statement (*On Laws,* Bk. II [, chap. v, §§ 11–12]), that in the very name of *lex* there is inherent the essential force of that which is *iustum* and of that which promotes *ius,* inasmuch as true law ought to prescribe what is just and fair, as I also have declared.

5. *The true meaning of the word* ius. According to the latter and strict acceptation of *ius,* this name is properly wont to be bestowed upon a certain moral power which every man has, either over his own property or with respect to that which is due to him. For it is thus that the owner of a thing is said to have a right (*ius*) in that thing, and the labourer is said to have that right to his wages by reason of which he is declared worthy of his hire. Indeed, this acceptation of the term is frequent, not only in law, but also in Scripture; for the law distinguishes in this wise between a right (*ius*) [already established] *in* a thing and a right *to* a thing; as it also distinguishes among rights of servitude or rights of rural or urban estates, rights of use or enjoyment, and similar rights, concerning which one may consult Brisson (*De Verborum Significatione,* Bk. IX, word *ius,* at great length). And in Scripture, we read that Abraham said (*Genesis,* Chap. xxiii [, v. 4]) to the sons of Heth: 'Give me the right of a burying-place' (*ius sepulchri*), that is, the power of burying (*facultas sepeliendi*); in another chapter (*Genesis,* Chap. xxxi [, v. 21]) it is said of Jacob that, when he departed from his father-in-law, he carried away with him 'all

that belonged to him' (*Omnia quae iuris sui erant*); and similar passages
are frequent. Again, it would seem that *ius* is so understood in the *Digest*
in the passage (I. i. 10), where justice is said to be the virtue that renders to
every man his own right (*ius suum*), that is to say, the virtue that renders
to every man that which belongs to him. Accordingly, this right to claim
(*actio*), or moral power, which every man possesses with respect to his own
property or with respect to a thing which in some way pertains to him, is
called *ius,* and appears to be the true object of justice. Hence, *ius* is also
wont to be given the connotation of relationship, as is stated in another
passage of the *Digest* (I. i. 12); for, in such a context, the word seems to
refer to a certain bond or connexion born of relationship itself. In this
sense, one person is said to succeed by right (*ius*) of kinship; another, by
right of adoption; yet another, by right of appointment or testament. So it
is, also, that the *Digest* (II. xiv. 34) makes the statement: 'The right of kinship cannot be repudiated;' while another passage (*ibid.,* XLVIII. xxiii. 4)
declares that the right of kinship is restored to the son. It is consequently
inferred that [the term *ius*] is applied not to the blood-relationship itself,
but to the moral claim (*actio*), or faculty, born of that relationship. The
same explanation holds in the case of other passages.

6. *Another meaning of the term* ius. However, according to the other
etymology, which derives *ius* from *iubendum* (ordering), the true meaning of *ius* would seem to be *lex.* For *lex* is based upon ordering (*iussio*), or
command. The jurisconsults, indeed, often give the word this signification; as when they say, 'We are following this or that law (*ius*)', or, 'This is
a point on which the law (*ius*) is certain and firmly established', or when
they make similar statements. Again, [*ius*] seems to be given this meaning
whenever it is distinguished from fact; as when a discrimination is made
between ignorance of law (*ius*), and ignorance of fact, a distinction which
is frequent in law (*ius*), and among the Doctors. There is in the *Digest,*
a title [i.e. XXII. vi], 'On ignorance of law, and of fact'. Hence it is, that
what is in harmony with reason is said to be lawfully done (*iure fieri*), as
if to say, 'done in conformity with law' (*legi conforme*). It is thus, too, that
Sallust (in *The Conspiracy of Catiline*) would seem to have defined *ius,* saying: '*Ius* is civil equity, either sanctioned by written laws or institutions,
or else drawn from custom.' This description has apparently been given

primarily with a view to the civil laws only, but if the word 'civil' is suppressed, [the definition] will be easily adaptable for the canon laws as well, and the positive divine laws. It does not seem applicable to natural law, however, unless we say that the latter law is written in the minds of men; whereas the term *ius* is indeed applied to natural law, as is evident from the title of *Institutes,* I. ii: *De Iure Naturali & Gentium & Civili* (Concerning natural law, the law of nations and the civil law), a title which we shall discuss later. Finally, the description in question appears to have been given rather with respect to the effect of law (*lex*) than with respect to the true rational basis thereof. Or, at least, it would seem to be rather a description of the object set up by the law, than a description of the law itself; since law constitutes equity, or is the measure and rule thereof, but is not properly speaking equity itself.

7. Isidore (*Etymologies,* Bk. V, chap. iii, cited above) adds that *ius* and *lex* are comparable as are genus and species; for he holds that *ius* is the genus while *lex* is the species. He appears to offer as his reason the argument that *ius* consists of laws (*leges*) and customs. Whereas *lex* denotes a written constitution, as the *Decretum* (Pt. I, dist. 1, cans. ii, iii, and iv)[4] indicates. St. Thomas, too (II.–II, qu. 57, art. 1, ad 2), apparently follows Isidore when he declares that the rational basis of that which is equitable and just, if it is drawn up in written form, is law (*lex*). These writers, indeed, would seem to have taken their opinion from Augustine (*De Diversis Quaestionibus LXXXIII,* Qu. xxxi), who says: 'In the law (*lex*), *ius* is that which is embodied in the writing set before the people that they may obey it.'

Cicero (*On Laws,* Bk. I [, chap. vi] and Bk. II [, chap. v]), on the other hand, believes that only that is true law (*lex*), which dwells in the reason; while that which appears written externally, he calls law (*lex*) in the popular sense. Accordingly, he speaks of the divine mind as the supreme law (*lex*); he then gives the name [of *lex*] to reason as it exists in the mind of the wise man; whereas he declares that written law is designated as *lex* in name rather than in fact.

However, it has now come about through usage that the term *lex* is properly applied both to written and to non-written law, so that *ius,* in so

4. [Can. iv merely gives a definition of *mos.*—REVISER.]

far as it refers to *lex,* is used interchangeably with that term, and the two words are considered as synonyms.

8. *The act of a judge is sometimes equivalent to* ius. In consequence, to be sure, the word *ius* has come to possess certain other connotations which have not been transferred to the term *lex.* For the act of a judge is thus wont to be designated by the term *ius,* either because it ought to be performed in accordance with the laws (*leges*), or because it sometimes seems to establish a law (*lex*), as it were; so that the judge, when he exercises his office, is said to declare the law (*ius dicere*). This is the source of the title of *Digest,* II. iii: 'If anyone fails to obey him who declares the law.' Moreover, in the canon law (*Sext,* Bk. I, tit. II, chap. ii), we find the words: 'He who pronounces judgment outside the territory [of his jurisdiction] may be disobeyed with impunity.' This statement may be interpreted as referring both to [judicial] sentences, and to law (*lex*) in the sense of a statute. And the *Digest* (I. i. II) even speaks of a judge as administering law (*ius reddere*) when he makes an unjust decision, the reference being not to what he [actually] does but to that which he ought in duty to do. Furthermore, the judge is in this sense said to summon a subject to law (*in ius vocare*), with the meaning, in any case, that he does so for the purpose of testing the law, a point that is brought out in another passage (*ibid.,* II. iv. I). However, these words could be interpreted as referring to a summons to the place of judgment. For there has also been transferred to the term in question the signification of 'a locality where judgment is rendered', as the above-mentioned passage of *Digest,* I. i. II, notes. Accordingly, among Roman[5] peoples, 'to go to law' (*ire in ius*) is the same as to go before the Praetor or to the seat of the Praetor, as Brisson above cited, notes (*De Verborum Significatione,* Bk. IX, word *ius*), basing his comment upon Donatus [on Terence's *Eunuch,* Act IV, sc. vii], Victorinus [*Comment. on Cicero's De Inventione,* Bk. II, tit. 4] and a number of laws. Furthermore, this is also the interpretation given above by St. Thomas (II.–II, qu. 57, art. I, ad I), of the phrase in which one is said 'to appear before the law' (*comparere in iure*). In this passage, he adds still another meaning to the word in question, for he says that even the art itself by which one

---

5. [*Latinos,* evidently referring to peoples living under the Roman law.—Tr.]

determines what is just, is sometimes called *ius*. Thus he appears to give a tacit explanation of the above-cited law of the *Digest* (I. i. 1, § 1), in which Ulpian quotes with approval the definition of Celsus, namely: '*Ius* is the art of the good and the equitable.' For this definition would seem to be suited, not so much to law (*lex*) itself, as to jurisprudence (*iuris pruden-tiae*), unless 'art' is taken in a broad sense, as referring to any method or measure of operation.

9. *How* ius *is to be distinguished from* aequum et bonum. Lastly, two points remain to be explained. One consists in the following question: How may *ius* be distinguished at times from *aequum et bonum* (the equi-table and the good), if *ius* is precisely the same as that which is just, while the latter is in turn precisely the equitable and the good, or if [*ius*], being taken as equivalent to *lex,* is the essential principle of the just and good itself, as we have declared?

Nevertheless, this distinction between *ius,* on the one hand, and that which is equitable and good, on the other, is clearly evident from the many references cited by Luis Vives (in the *Scholion* on Augustine, *On the City of God,* Bk. II, chap. xvii). Accordingly, Quintilian (*Institutes of Oratory,* Book IV [, chap. iii, § 11]), has said: 'the nature of the judge should [. . .] be ascertained: that is, whether he is more inclined[6] to [a strict interpretation of] the law (*ius*), or to an exercise of equity.' Again (Bk. VI [, chap. v, § 5]), he asks: 'Should the plea be based on law (*ius*), or on equity?' Cicero, too (in *Brutus* [Chap. xxxix, no. 145]) has written: 'Crassus spoke at great length, in opposition to the written law, in support of the good and equitable.'

Aristotle accordingly propounds this [very] doubt in the *Ethics* (Bk. V, chap. x [, § 8]); and, in this same chapter x [, § 3], he replies in effect that equity is the rectification of that which is [legally] just (*iustum*).

In order that this statement may be understood, one should distinguish respectively between the words 'just' (*iustum*) and 'equitable' (*aequum*), 'justice' (*iustitia*), and 'equity' (*aequitas*).

---

6. [*Appositus* in Quintilian; in the Latin text, *opposita,* evidently an error in quota-tion or a misprint.—Tr.]

For the just is twofold; first, what is naturally just, this being equivalent to what is right according to natural reason, [a phase of the just] that is never defective, provided that the reason itself does not err; secondly, what is legally just, that is to say, what is constituted by human law, [a phase] that is often defective in specific cases, though just in a general sense. Neither is a given law (*lex*) unjust for this reason, since it must necessarily be enacted in general terms. Rather (so Aristotle says), the fault arises neither from the law nor from the lawgiver, but from the subject-matter itself.

Moreover, in accordance with this twofold division of *iustum,* a twofold form of *iustitia* may in due proportion be distinguished.

In similar fashion, the term *aequitas* is customarily interpreted as having a twofold sense. In one sense, it stands for natural equity, which is identical with natural justice, and to which the term *aequum* corresponds, in so far as the latter is equivalent to that which is naturally just. It is with this meaning, indeed, that the civil laws frequently mention natural equity. For example, the *Digest* (XXXVIII. xvi. 1, § 4) declares: 'Grandsons[7] succeed to the position of sons, by natural equity'; and again (*ibid.,* XLVIII. xvii. 1): 'The very nature of equity suffers no one to be condemned unheard.'[8] To this kind of equity, 'the equitable', in the general sense of the term, corresponds. Thus it is that the *Digest* (XII. vi. 14) says: 'This is naturally equitable: that no person be enriched to the hurt of another.'[9] Moreover, equity so interpreted, is not an emendation of [legal] justice (*ius*), but rather the source or rule thereof, as the *Digest* (L. xvii. 91 [90]) indicates in the statement: 'In all matters, but especially in law (*ius*), equity must be considered.'

10. *Aequitas* may be taken in another sense, however, as being a prudent moderation of the written law (*lex scripta*), transcending the exact literal interpretation of the latter; and, in this sense, *aequitas* is spoken of in the *Digest* (XXXIX. iii. 2, § 5) as being opposed to *ius* in its strict meaning.

---

7. [This section of the *Digest* concerns certain situations in which the son ceases to be the father's heir.—Tr.]

8. [This quotation, as given by Suárez, varies somewhat from the text of the *Digest.*—Tr.]

9. [This quotation, as given by Suárez, varies somewhat from the text of the *Digest.*—Tr.]

So, also, Terentius Clemens has said: 'Between *ius* and *aequitas,* there is this distinction: *ius* is that which exacts that all things be strict and inflexible; whereas *aequitas* to a great extent abates the rigour of *ius.*' Furthermore, in view of this interpretation of 'equity', the terms 'equitable' (*aequum*) and 'good' (*bonum*) are applied—by antonomasia so to speak—to that which does indeed of itself possess these qualities, even though it may appear to be at variance with the letter of the law (*lex*). Aristotle, too, understood 'equity' in this sense, when he spoke of it as the emendation of that which is just, that is to say, legal, and gave to the virtue from which it springs the name of *epieikeia* (equitable interpretation).[10] St. Thomas also (II.–II, qu. 120) enters into a discussion of this virtue. For to this [form of equity] does it pertain to act, in particular cases, in opposition to the words of human law (*lex*), when the observance of that law would be contrary to natural equity. Under such circumstances, indeed, the judge is said to act, not according to law (*iure*)—not at least, according to the letter of the law as it stands—but in accordance with what is equitable and good; and this, in turn, is to observe the law (*ius*) itself, with respect to its intention, while the contrary mode of action would be to violate the law. Such is the view expressed in the Code of Justinian (*Code,* I. xiv. 5): 'There is no doubt but that he attacks the law (*lex*) who, while accepting its words, labours against its spirit.' And therefore, it is possible that jurisprudence has been called the art of the good and the equitable because, in the interpretation of the laws, the good and the equitable should always be regarded; even if it be needful at times to temper the rigour of the words, in order not to depart from what is naturally equitable and good. For a further discussion of this matter, see Covarruvias (on *Sext, De Regulis Iuris,* rule *possessor* Pt. II, § 6, no. 3).

11. *Concerning the distinction between* ius *and* fas. Another point should be made clear, namely, the question of what *fas* is and how it may be

---

10. *Epieikeia:* in Greek, fairness or equity. Aristotle in *Nicomachean Ethics,* Book V, Chapter 10, 1137a30, discusses how in the interests of justice general laws may be recti- fied or reinterpreted better to fit particular cases unforeseen by the legislator; *epieikeia* is the kind of justice involved in so rectifying or reinterpreting a law. Suárez later distin- guishes *epieikeia* understood as such rectification from the more general phenomenon of simply interpreting what a law says (see Book 2, chapter 16).

compared with *ius* and *lex*. For Isidore (*Etymologies,* Bk. V; chap. ii) says: '*Fas* is divine law; *ius* is human law.' The same distinction is brought out in the *Decretum* (Pt. I, dist. i, can. i), where it is expounded with the aid of this example: '[The right] to pass through another's field is *fas;* it is not *ius.*' But it would seem that all this should be interpreted in accordance with the passage immediately following; for, in that passage, *ius* is understood strictly in the sense of 'written law' (*lex*), and *fas,* in the sense of 'equity' and as a just exception—so to speak—[from the letter of the law]. Thus, in the example above-mentioned, passing through another's field is spoken of as not being *ius,* for the reason that it is in general prohibited rather [than permitted] by human law (*lex*); and nevertheless, if this act of transit is performed for reasonable cause and without consequent damage, it is *fas,* that is to say, it is permissible. Moreover, this is the explanation contained in the Gloss with respect to the passage in question; as it is also the explanation given by Henry of Ghent (*Quodlibeta,* IX, qu. 2 [qu. 26]).

St. Thomas (II.–II, qu. 57, art. 1, ad ult.), however, offers a different explanation of the words above quoted. For he maintains that the term *ius,* in accordance with a certain exclusive signification, befits the laws (*legibus*) which are ordained for men in their mutual relationships rather than those laws which govern men in their relation to God; because we cannot render our account to God on a basis of equality, and therefore (according to St. Thomas) *fas* rather than *ius* is the term for law (*lex*) in so far as the latter has regard to [man's relationship with] God.

But, whatever the fact may be with respect to this exclusive significance of the word *ius*—a significance that is not alien to Latin usage—*fas* is called divine law by Isidore, not because it regulates the rendering of [man's] debt to God, but because it is based upon natural equity and consequently upon natural reason, which is divine law.

However, leaving aside the metaphorical connotations and the distinctions which are not pertinent to our present purpose, we shall deal here, in a general sense, with *ius* in its second and proper connotation; and accordingly, the term will become synonymous with *lex,* in so far as we shall now be speaking of *lex,* too, in its general aspect.

CHAPTER III

The Extent of the Necessity for Laws, and of Their Variety

1. Having treated of the terms *ius* and *lex,* we must first demonstrate, before we inquire into the nature of *lex,* that it actually exists.

This demonstration will best be effected by explaining the necessity for *lex;* since, in these matters which relate to the moulding of moral conduct (*mores*), nothing superfluous should be allowed, nor may anything necessary be lacking. Necessity, however, is usually divided into two kinds. One is the absolute necessity in accordance with which a given thing is said to be necessary of itself and for itself, in an absolute sense. Thus, there is attributed to God a necessity for His existence in accordance with His actual existence; and it is of this necessity that we are now speaking. The second kind is a relative necessity, having respect to some particular end or effect. This kind is subdivided into two phases: one phase is that of simple necessity; the other, that of necessity for the attainment of the better state, this latter phase being, in stricter parlance, utility.

2. *Law, in an absolute sense, was not necessary.* Accordingly, two points seem, generally speaking, to be certain. The first point is this: absolute necessity does not pertain to law as such. The proof of this assertion is as follows: such necessity is an attribute proper to God, Who alone is a Being existent *per se* and necessary in an absolute sense; whereas every law is either a created thing or at least one which presupposes the existence of some creature on whose account it is established; for God cannot be subjected to law; and therefore, inasmuch as a created thing is not absolutely necessary, law in like manner lacks the attribute of absolute necessity. In addition, I shall state that, if one is speaking of law in the strict sense of the term (as we are now doing), it can [be considered to] exist only in view of some rational creature; for law is imposed only upon a nature that is free, and has for its subject-matter free acts alone, a point which we shall note below; accordingly, law cannot be more necessary than a rational or intellectual creature; and rational creatures are not characterized by an absolute necessity for their existence; therefore, neither is law itself characterized by this sort of necessity.

The sole doubt that could occur in this connexion would be one relating to the eternal law, which we shall for the present assume to exist. For that law is God Himself; therefore, it is as immutable and eternal as He, and consequently, as necessary. However, I shall reply briefly that what constitutes eternal law is indeed absolutely necessary, as the argument proves, but that it does not possess this attribute in its character as law, since it embraces a connotation of freedom, a point that I shall demonstrate below.[1]

3. *If the creation of a rational creature is assumed to have taken place, law has become useful, and absolutely necessary in the necessity of its purpose.* Secondly, I make the following assertion: if the creation of rational creatures is assumed to have taken place, law, both absolutely and with a view to attaining the better state, has become necessary in the necessity of its purpose. This truth is (so to speak), in connexion with the subject under discussion, a self-evident principle.

Moreover, in so far as concerns the first part [of the assertion]—the part relating to absolute necessity—one may adduce the argument that an intellectual creature, by virtue of the very fact that he is a created being, has a superior to whose providence and control he is subject; while, for the very reason that he is intellectual, he is capable of being subjected to moral government, which is effected through command (*imperium*); and therefore, it is connatural to such a creature, and necessary to him, that he be made subject to some superior who will govern him through command, that is, through law.

Furthermore, this creature, because of the very fact that he has been made out of nothing, may be bent to good or to evil. This I assume, for the present, on the basis of the common opinion of the Fathers. Consequently, not only is he capable of being subjected to law, whereby he may be directed towards the good and held back from the evil, but furthermore, some such law is absolutely necessary for him, that he may live as becomes his nature. Or, we may argue also from the converse. For he who is subject to no law cannot sin; but a rational creature does possess the power to sin; and therefore, he is of necessity subject to law.

1. [*Infra,* p. 161, *De Legibus,* Bk. II, chap. ii.—Tr.]

Nor is it pertinent to argue that the said creature may, through grace or glory, become impeccable. For, in the first place, we are speaking here of natural necessity, asserting that from this standpoint, if one assumes the creation of rational nature, law is necessary. Moreover, the gift [of grace] through which such a nature becomes impeccable does not involve a removal of that nature's subjection to law, in so far as concerns the acts which it is free to exercise, but on the contrary causes it to obey the law without fail.

The second part of our assertion—that which relates to utility—is clearly proved on the basis of the first part. For necessity pertaining to an end must include utility; and furthermore, these words (*Psalms,* xviii [, v. 8]) have been written with regard to laws: 'The law of the Lord is unspotted, converting souls', &c., as has also this passage from *Proverbs* (Chap. vi [, v. 23]): 'The commandment is a lamp, and the law a light.' And there are similar passages which we shall examine later, and which point out a great utility in law.

4. However, since this utility or necessity is not one and the same in the case of all laws, it will be worth while, for the purpose of presenting the attribute in question with clearness and accuracy, to distinguish among the various kinds of laws, and to explain the particular necessity or utility characteristic of each kind. For thus we shall clearly perceive, not only that law in general does exist, but also the number of particular species of which that whole is composed. This latter point must also be ascertained in order that we may fully define the question involved in the entire subject-matter of this treatise, namely, the question of whether or not law exists. For we have already pointed out that the said subject-matter embraces every species of law. Moreover, this procedure will be opportune for our understanding of the terms to be used throughout the entire treatise.

5. *The division of law into its various categories.* In the first place, then, we may assume that law is divided into four different categories, a division which was laid down by Plato, in the *Timaeus* [24 *et seq.*] and in the *Phaedrus,* as follows: divine law; celestial law; natural law, and human law. The second of these terms is rejected by the theologians, because it is either superfluous or else involves erroneous doctrine. For by 'celestial

law' Plato meant fate, and a certain necessity of action proceeding from
the ordered movement and influence of the heavenly bodies; and therefore, if he understood that celestial law was of such a nature that it was
not subject to divine providence, or that it imposed a necessity upon all
things, even upon men, with respect to operations proper to the soul,
[his interpretation] involves a false and heretical conception, opposed to
the divine government and to the freedom of the will. If, on the other
hand, he referred in the expression 'celestial law', merely to Aristotle's
statement that this lower world is so conjoined with the heavenly spheres
that it is governed thence, that is to say, governed through natural influ-
ences and vicissitudes dependent always upon God, affecting bodies, not
souls—if this was what Plato had in mind—it was not necessary to set
up this separate category of law; because, to the extent that it may be
called law, it is comprised under the head of the natural law, as we shall
prove. This second term therefore being omitted, the other three are in
use even among the theologians, though in a slightly different sense from
that understood by Plato.

6. *The conception of 'divine law', in Plato; and the [two] ways in which
the term is used.* Thus divine law, according to Plato, is a rational principle
existing in the mind of God, and governing the universe. This law is also
recognized by the theologians, who, however, call it the eternal law. For
the term 'divine law' may be used in two senses: in one sense, as dwelling within God Himself; in the other, as being decreed directly by God
Himself, though existing outside of His Being. Plato gave to the term the
first connotation, while the theologians, agreeing with Augustine, and for
the purpose of distinguishing that form of law from the other, which God
promulgates outside of His own Being, call the former 'the eternal law';
and we, too, shall call it by this name. With respect to this thing which
is called eternal law, it as certainly exists in God, as does His providence
over the universe; for the term refers simply to the essential principle of
this providence, a principle dwelling in God, or to some element of that
providence.[2] As to the question of whence it derives the name and nature

---

2. [The antecedent of *eius* might be *ratio, providentiae* or *Deo.* The second alternative
is perhaps the one best suited to the context.—Tr.]

of 'eternal law', however, that is a point which we shall explain in the first part of the next Book.

From the foregoing, one may easily understand what necessity and utility characterize the law in question, since it is identical with the law of divine providence. For just as it would be impossible for the universe to continue in existence apart from divine providence, so would it be impossible apart from this divine and eternal law; and furthermore, all utility and benefit flowing forth to this universe from divine providence should also be ascribed to this same divine law.

St. Thomas (I.–II, qu. 91, art. 1, ad 3) observes, however, that the utility of the said law consists, not in the fact that it is itself ordained to the end, but rather in the fact that it directs all other things to their own ends, by appropriate means. For the law itself cannot be ordained to an end, since it is God Himself, Who is the ultimate end of all things.

A first division of law: into temporal and eternal. Finally, from this first divine or eternal form of law, one may infer a first division of law into the eternal and the temporal. For we assume that there is nothing eternal outside of God; yet, it is evident that there are many laws in existence outside of Him; and therefore, there must be established, in addition to the eternal law, other and temporal laws, which consequently differ [from the former] as the created differs from the increate, since whatever is eternal is increate, and what is temporal is created. Thus it becomes evident that there is established a divine law, that is, one which exists in God Himself. The manner, however, in which divine law is established by promulgation directly from Him, will be made clear in the discussion that follows.[3] In fine, there is a law that exists in God Himself; for all the foregoing arguments point to such a conclusion.

7. *A second division of law: into natural and positive.* Accordingly, from the other two classes of law laid down by Plato, a second division of law may be deduced, consisting in a subdivision of created law into natural and positive. This division is recognized by all the theologians, too, and repeatedly by the Fathers, whether under the name of *lex,* or under that of *ius*—positive and natural.

---

3. [*Infra,* p. 152, *De Legibus,* Bk. II, chap. i, *passim.*—Tr.]

Take, for example, the *Etymologies* (Bk. II [, chap. x] and Bk. III [Bk. V, chaps. ii *et seq.*]) of Isidore. The point is also brought out in the *Decretum* (Pt. I, dists. 1 *et seq.*). It may be inferred, too, from Augustine (*On the Gospel of John,* Treatise VI [, chap. i, no. 25]). Paul (*Romans,* Chap. ii [, v. 14]) indicates the same division, as the ordinary Gloss on the passage notes, when he says: 'The Gentiles who have not the law, do by nature those things that are of the law.'[4] The said division is also to be found in the civil law, in both the *Institutes* (I. ii) and the *Digest* (I. i [. 3]). Cicero, too, in his work *On Laws* (Bk. I [, chap. vi, §§ 18–19]), specifically demonstrates that natural law was established prior to all human law. He discusses this point quite fully (*ibid.,* Bk. II), also. Reference may also be had, in this connexion, to the *Nicomachean Ethics* of Aristotle (Bk. V, chap. vii), where he in like manner divides law into natural and conventional.

In what senses the term 'natural law' is employed by the different writers. However, with respect to 'natural law', it should be noted that this term is variously understood by the philosophers, the jurisconsults and the theologians. For Plato, in the works above cited, apparently understands 'natural law' as referring to every natural inclination implanted in things by their Creator, whereby they severally tend towards the acts and ends proper to them. For just as he has said that the divine law is the eternal rational principle dwelling in God, whereby all things are governed, even so has he given the name of natural law to the participation in this rational principle that has been instilled into all creatures in order that they may tend toward their appointed ends. St. Thomas (I.–II, qu. 91, art. 2) has even said that all things ruled by divine providence partake in some fashion of the eternal law, to the degree that they derive from its efficacy, propensities toward their proper acts and ends. But the jurisconsults, while they hold that the natural law is common to other living beings as well as to men, apparently exclude inanimate things from participation in this law, a fact which is evidenced by the *Institutes* (I. ii, § 1) and by the *Digest* (I. i. 1).

8. *'Law', in its strict meaning, is not to be attributed to insensate things.* However, as I stated in the First Chapter, 'law' is to be attributed to

---

4. [The better version is: 'The Gentiles who, by nature, have not the Law, fulfil the requirements of the Law.' This version fits St. Paul's use of the word φύσει better. The Gloss, however, states what Suárez gives in the text.—REVISER.]

insensate things, not in its strict sense, but metaphorically. Accordingly, of natural law in that first and most general acceptation, we need say nothing more at present than what we have already remarked in Chapter One, and what we shall remark below,[5] in connexion with the eternal law. Not even brute animals are capable of [participating in] law in a strict sense, since they have the use neither of reason nor of liberty; so that it is only by a like metaphor that natural law may be ascribed to them. For, even though they differ from insensate things in this respect, namely, that they are guided not merely by the force of nature, but also by knowledge and natural instinct, an instinct which is for them a form of law; and although the second interpretation of the jurisconsults can therefore be sustained, after a fashion; nevertheless, absolutely speaking, that interpretation is metaphorical and to a great extent dependent upon analogy. Accordingly, we shall pass over it also, for the present; for later (in Bk. II, chap. viii [chap. xvii]), in our exposition of *ius gentium*,[6] we shall attempt to explore the true meaning of the [divisions of law] above mentioned.

9. *What constitutes natural law, strictly speaking.* Natural law, then, in the proper sense of the term—the natural law which pertains to moral doctrine and to theology—is that form of law which dwells within the human mind, in order that the righteous may be distinguished from the evil, in accordance with the passage in the *Psalms* (iv[, vv. 6, 7]): 'Who sheweth us good things? The light of Thy countenance, O Lord, is signed upon us.' Such is the explanation of St. Thomas in the passage (I.–II, qu. 91, art. 2) wherein he concludes that the natural law is, 'a participation in the eternal law on the part of the rational creature.'

Moreover, in another passage (on the *Sentences,* Bk. IV, dist. xxxiii, art. 1), St. Thomas says: 'Because man [alone] among living beings is cognizant of the essential nature of his end and of the comparative relationship between the work and the end, the natural power of comprehension implanted in

5. [*Infra,* pp. 152 *et seq., De Legibus,* Bk. II, chaps. i–iv.—Tr.]

6. *Ius gentium:* the law of nations, which Suárez will take to consist in (a) obligatory customs governing relations between political communities, such as those governing treatment of prisoners and of ambassadors, and international trade; and (b) civil laws found within the generality of states, such as those governing currency or religious sacrifice. Suárez will argue that the *ius gentium* is part of positive law.

him, which is directed toward befitting action, is therefore spoken of as the *lex naturalis,* or *ius naturale* (natural law), while in the case of the other animals, it is called *naturalis aestimatio* (instinct). This is plainly Cicero's opinion, also (*On Laws,* Bk. II [, chap. iv, no. 8]). For, after writing the words above quoted, on the eternal law, he adds: 'Wherefore that law which the gods have given to the human race has been justly praised; since it is the reason and mind of a wise being, suited to commanding and to restraining.'

So it is, then, that the law in question is called natural, not only in so far as the natural is distinguished from the supernatural, but also in that [what is natural] is distinguished from what is a matter of free choice.[7] This is the case, not because the execution of that law is natural, or the result of necessity, as is the execution of the natural inclination of the brutes or of inanimate objects; but because the law in question is (so to speak) a kind of characteristic of nature, and because God Himself has annexed that law to nature. Moreover, in this respect the natural law is also divine, being decreed, as it were, directly by God Himself. Such was the opinion of St. Thomas, as expressed in the above-mentioned passage (Qu. 91 and qu. 94, art. 6), where he cites the words of St. Augustine (*Confessions,* Bk. II, chap. iv), spoken to God, 'Thy law is written in the hearts of men', words which had reference to natural law; wherefore Augustine has said, in another work (*On the Sermon of Our Lord on the Mount,* Bk. II, chap. ix), that there is no soul, 'in whose conscience God does not speak. For who save God writes the natural law in the hearts of men?' Isidore (*Etymologies,* Bk. V, chap. ii) more explicitly calls this law divine. And finally, it is evident from the foregoing how necessary and useful the said law is; since on it rests the capacity of discriminating between the righteous and the evil[8] in the rational nature. All this, however, requires a lengthy explanation; but let us reserve that explanation for the following Book, lest we invert the proper order and cause complete confusion.

10. A certain subdivision of natural law remains for discussion. But first, we must say a word concerning Plato's fourth division of law, called by him the human, and relating to the law designated by Aristotle [*Nicomachean*

---

7. [Simply *a libero,* in the Latin.—Tr.]
8. *Honestum et turpe:* the morally good and the morally bad.

Ethics, Bk. V, chap. vii] as 'conventional law', which he describes thus: 'It is that form of law which is a matter of indifference, originally, but of great moment, once it has been established [as a law].'[9] This comment is to be understood as referring to the subject-matter of the said law, since the latter relates to actions which apart from that law would not be a matter of obligation, but which are rendered obligatory by it. Finally, to this same division belong those laws which Cicero (*On Laws,* Bk. II [, chap. v, no. 11]) distinguishes from eternal and natural law, calling them popular. We, however, divide created or temporal law into natural and positive, after the manner of the theologians; since the term 'positive' covers a wider field than does 'human'. For it is to be noted that the philosophers have not recognized man's supernatural end but have dealt only with a certain felicity in this life, or rather, with a certain state conducive to passing it in peace and in justice, and have considered the subject of laws, from the standpoint of this temporal end; so that they have merely distinguished natural law from human law, which we may call 'civil', and to which we shall presently devote some words.[10] However, since it is a doctrine of the faith that men are ordained to the supernatural end of the future life by fitting means which are to be sought after in this life, sacred theology rightly infers that this natural law is necessary for a reason vastly different [from the reason recognized by the philosophers], and that men need more laws of a positive nature than were discerned by those same philosophers.

11. *In what ways human nature may be considered, with respect to the laws which it needs.* With respect to the natural law, then, it is the teaching of theology that man may be considered from the standpoints of a twofold nature and dual light of reason. The first standpoint deals with pure nature, or the substance of the rational soul, and consequently with the light of reason that is connatural to man. The second deals with the nature of grace infused into man from above, and with the divine and supernatural light of faith which rules and guides him in this life. Moreover, in accordance with these two principles, [theology] distinguishes two aspects of natural

9. [More exactly, Aristotle wrote: 'The conventional kind is that which might originally have been determined either way with equal justice, but which, when once determined, is then no longer indifferent.'—REVISER.]

10. [*Infra,* p. 53, Section 20, this Chapter.—TR.]

law. The one is absolutely natural, [even] with respect to man. The other, although it is supernatural in its relation to man (since the whole order of grace is supernatural in that respect), may nevertheless be called natural in relation to grace. For grace also has an essence and a nature of its own, to which the infused light is connatural, and to which it is connatural not only to direct men toward righteous, good, and fitting behaviour in supernatural matters, but also to dispel darkness and errors relating to the purely natural law itself and to enjoin on the basis of a higher reason the observance of that same natural law. Two aspects of natural law, then, may be distinguished: the one purely natural; the other, supernatural in an absolute sense, but natural in a relative sense, as compared with grace. Wherefore, since the natural law even in its purely natural form is divine, its source being God, far more truly is the natural law of the divine order, a divine law. For the former [phase of natural law] is from God through the medium of nature, whence it flows as a property of nature; whereas the latter phase is [directly] from God, Who by His own action infuses grace and actual supernatural enlightenment, and Himself guides men to fulfil the commands of that law through aid supplied by a stimulating and assisting grace.

12. Finally, both phases of this law may be termed connatural to humanity, in so far as that which is concreate with nature and has always persisted in nature may in a certain sense be called natural. For in this sense, the law of connatural grace, also, has always existed among men; since the light of faith has never been lacking in mankind as a whole, nor in the whole Church, nor have men ever been without a supernatural divine law, in the absence of which they could not have striven toward eternal beatitude. Wherefore, when the conditions of men are, as is customary, distinguished through laws—that is to say, distinguished as being [respectively] the conditions under natural law, under written law, and under grace—then, in the case of the first state, one should understand by natural law, both the law of nature alone, and that which is connatural to grace, or the law of faith. For the world could never have been entirely without this law, in accordance with the ordinary course of providence, since it has always been possible for the doers of the law to be justified by divine aid; as may be inferred from the *Epistle of Paul to the Romans* (Chaps. ii and iii). So,

also, the necessity and the utility of natural law, as explained in this latter sense, become evident; that is to say, it is necessary and useful because grace and faith have always been necessary, and the law in question is connatural to them. [Natural law served] this purpose, too, namely: that man might have a law through the observance of which he could, by divine aid, obtain remission of sins and eternal life.

13. *What is positive law?* With respect to the third division of law, the positive, it should be noted that the term 'positive' is applied to that law which is not inherent in nature nor in grace, but has been laid down in addition to them by an extrinsic principle endowed with power, wherefore it is called 'positive', having been added, as it were, to the natural law, not flowing therefrom of necessity. Thus, by some persons, it has been called 'the posited law' (*ius positum*), a point that is brought out in Connan's *Commentary on the Civil Law* (Bk. I, chap. viii). Again, a remark made by Aristotle (*Ethics,* Bk. I, chap. ix [Bk. X, chap. ix, § 12]) is suitable to the positive law thus interpreted. He says: 'law [. . .] is a rule, emanating from a certain wisdom and intelligence, that has compulsory force.' For though Aristotle was referring only to human law, nevertheless, his words are in themselves comparatively general; and so also the term 'positive law' has a wider application than has 'human law'.

14. *A division of positive law into divine and human.* Thus the theologians deduce a third division, that of positive law into divine and human. That positive law is called divine which has been established directly by God Himself, and added to the whole body of natural law. Of human positive law, we shall speak presently. Apart from these two phases, however, there can be no other positive law relating to mankind, since there are no other legislators. For the angels have not such power over men, since it is not a part of their nature, nor has it been granted by God to them, inasmuch as[11] their possession of that power has not, to our knowledge, been revealed to anyone, so that, consequently, we cannot divine [its existence].[12] Accordingly, the term 'divine law' is here used to refer, not to

11. [Interpreting the single word *id* as referring to the angels' possession of the power.—Tr.]

12. [Simply *divinare illud,* in the Latin.—Tr.]

the law which exists within God, but to that which emanates in a special manner from Him; for it denotes, not law that has been conceived, but law that has been made known, and in this among other respects it differs from the divine law as the latter was described by Plato.

Again, this [positive] law differs from the natural, interpreted in all its perfection as above set forth, in the fact that the natural law is not specifically added by God to nature itself, or to grace; whereas this [positive] law is specifically established and added thereto. Thus the natural law is not conferred, in itself and primarily, as a specific gift of law; rather it is conceived of as being that gift attached either to nature itself, or to faith and grace. For he who gives the form, gives also those things that are consequent upon the form. This [positive] law, on the other hand, is essentially and primarily bestowed, as a gift added to nature and to grace. Whence there has followed the custom of calling this branch simply 'the law' (*lex*), as is evident from the entire *Epistle to the Romans,* and from other passages of Scripture of which we shall speak presently. And therefore, the expression 'divine law', as such, is usually understood as referring to this [part of positive law]; and we, too, shall use the term in that sense, for the most part.

15. From the foregoing, it is also easy to discern the necessity of that divine law.

With respect to this point, it should be noted (lest one chance to be deceived by a verbal ambiguity) that St. Thomas (qu. 1, art. 4 [I.–II, qu. 91, art. 4]) adduces four reasons on account of which the divine law is necessary; reasons which, when attentively considered, will be found to contain proof only with respect to the divine law—whether natural or supernatural—in so far as it is connatural with grace, but not with respect to the positive supernatural law [i.e. positive divine law],[13] according to the sense in which we are now speaking.

The first of the four reasons is this: that such divine law may direct man to a supernatural end. The second, that it may aid man in natural matters

---

13. [The reader will remember that Suárez is here speaking only of divine positive enactments that are superadded to the natural and the supernatural law, as, for example, the divine positive laws in the matter of the Sacraments and the Ecclesiastical hierarchy referred to below.—REVISER.]

also, lest he err therein. The third, that it may furthermore be able to govern and order his interior acts. The fourth, that it may forbid all evil; for it is impossible that human law should do so. There is a passage in *Psalms,* xviii [, v. 8], too, which St. Thomas applies to these four properties: 'The law of the Lord is unspotted, converting souls: the testimony of the Lord is faithful, giving wisdom to little ones.' For this last phrase contains the first reason, since it is through wisdom that man is ordered to his supernatural end. The last reason, indeed, is comprehended in the third or penultimate property; for the law in question depends upon God's truth; it cannot be subject to error; more than that, it is able to correct and repress the errors of nature. Again, the third reason enters into the second property; for the divine law is justly said to convert the soul, in that it directs interior acts.[14] Lastly, this law is called unspotted, because it permits no evil.

All of these reasons furnish proof chiefly with respect to the divine law as it is connatural to grace. This is especially true of the first and second reasons, a point which I have also touched upon above. For the third and the fourth have application even to the purely natural law, since that law also prescribes internal acts that are good, and forbids those which are evil, while it does not actually permit of any act that is wrong. The divine positive law, as we are now speaking of it, is on the contrary concerned ordinarily with external acts.[15] This fact is evident in the case of the Old Law, and also in that of the New, in so far as the latter deals with the Sacraments and the Ecclesiastical hierarchy. Furthermore, God does not forbid all evils through positive law; rather does this prohibition pertain to the divine natural law of both orders, as has been explained above.[16]

16. *The divine [positive] law is necessary not in an absolute sense but on the basis of a presupposition.* From the foregoing, we conclude that the divine positive law was necessary, not in an absolute sense, relatively to

---

14. 'Interior' or 'internal acts' here are principally acts of the will or our capacity for deciding and intending what to do, these acts of the will being what law immediately governs.

15. 'External' or 'exterior acts' are not acts of the will itself, but of further capacities subject to the will, as when someone moves his hand (external act) on the basis of a prior decision to move it (internal act).

16. [*Supra,* this Section.—Tr.]

[man's] supernatural end but on the presupposition of the institution of
the Synagogue or of the Church. Relatively to such institution, the said
law may be considered as an absolute necessity; although, with respect to
the end itself, it serves rather for the better state and the greater instruction of mankind, either that men may be restrained in their excessive
blindness and depraved morals, or for the sake of [their] greater perfection
and enlightenment, that perfect virtue and holiness may be attained [by
them]. The rational basis of the foregoing statements is as follows: even
though some supernatural law, as well as some supernatural knowledge,
may have been necessary, that law which was connatural to grace itself
would have been able to suffice; therefore, the need to add another and
positive law sprang from the particular institution of the mystical spiritual
body, so to speak. The existence of this institution being granted, the reasons adduced by St. Thomas may very well be applied, in due proportion,
to this positive divine law.

The said law is wont to be further subdivided into the Old and the
New Laws, a division which we shall explain more fully in Books Nine
and Ten.[17]

17. It remains to discuss positive human law, which is so named because
of the proximate source from which it flows.

For this law is called human, not because it was imposed by men,
nor because it exists in them as in those persons who are to be governed
by it; since these facts, although they do apply to the law in question,
are not characteristics peculiar to it, but are shared in common with
all [the divisions of] law of which we treat, whether divine or natural.
Thus, according to such a derivation, human law would be distinguished
rather from angelic law, that is, from the law imposed on the angels, with
which we are not dealing. Again, the said law is not called human from
its subject-matter; that is to say, it is not so called on the ground that it is
established with regard to human, and not to divine affairs. For although
this derivation may perhaps be suitable with reference to the law which
the philosophers have called 'human', nevertheless, it does not actually

---

17. [Not included in these *Selections*.—Tr.]

represent their meaning nor is it adequate, since human law covers a wider field, as we shall see.

What is human law; and why is it so called? This law, then, is called human for the reason that it was devised and established proximately by men. But I say 'proximately', because the original derivation of every human law is in a certain sense traced back to the eternal law, according to the Scriptural passage (*Proverbs,* Chap. viii [, v. 16]): 'By me princes rule, and the mighty decree justice'; and furthermore, as to the binding force[18] [of such law], that flows from the power given by God, since, 'There is no power but from God' (*Romans,* Chap. xiii [, v. 1]). However, that law itself which is called human is an act of man, and accordingly, it is proximately established by him; for which reason it is given this epithet of 'human'. Thus Plutarch (*Comment.* [*Ad Principem Ineruditum*]) said that learning was a requisite in the prince. For, 'justice is the end of law; law is the work of the prince; and the prince is the image of God governing the universe.' Augustine, too (*On the True Religion,* Chap. xxxi), says: 'The founder of temporal laws, if he is a good and wise man, consults the eternal law in order to discern [. . .] in accordance with its immutable rules, what temporal commands and prohibitions should be laid down.' Elsewhere (*On the Gospel of John,* Treatise VI [, chap. i, no. 25]), Augustine says that God has apportioned human laws to mankind through its rulers.

Human law is therefore the work of man, derived proximately from his power and wisdom, and ordained for its subjects as a rule and measure of their actions.

18. *What is the necessity for human law?* From the preceding statements, the necessity, or the utility, of this human law is also readily to be seen. For as St. Thomas ([I.–II,] qu. 91, art. 3) has noted, its necessity springs from the fact that the natural, or the divine law, is of a general nature, and includes only certain self-evident principles of conduct, extending, at most, to those points which follow necessarily and by a process of obvious inference from the said principles; whereas, in addition to such points, many others are necessarily involved in the case of a human commonwealth in

---

18. *Vim obligandi:* power or force to oblige or impose obligation. Suárez often refers to obligation as a *vis directiva* or directive force.

order that it may be preserved and rightly governed, so that it was necessary for human reason to determine more particularly certain points relating to those matters which cannot be defined through the natural reason alone, a determination that is effected by means of human law; and therefore, such law was most necessary. Accordingly, Plato (*Laws,* Bk. IX, not far from the end [875]) says: 'It is necessary for men to lay down laws in order that they may live accordingly; for if they lived without laws, they would in nowise differ from the most savage beasts.' Similarly, Aristotle (*Politics,* Bk. I, chap. ii [chap. i, no. 12, 1253 A]) has declared: 'Even as man, when perfected, is the best of all animals, so, when separated from law and justice, he is the worst of all.'[19]

19. Moreover, relying upon both authors, it is possible to explain more fully the necessity involved. For that necessity is founded on the fact that man is a social animal, requiring by his very nature a civil life and intercourse with other men; therefore, it is necessary that he should live rightly, not only as a private person, but also as a part of a community; and this is a matter which depends to a large extent upon the laws of the individual community. It is furthermore necessary that each person should take counsel not only for himself, but also for others, preserving peace and justice, a condition that could not be brought about in the absence of appropriate laws. Again, it is necessary that those points which relate to the common good of men, or of the state, should be accorded particular care and observance; yet, men as individuals have difficulty in ascertaining what is expedient for the common good, and moreover, rarely strive for that good as a primary object; so that, in consequence, there was a necessity for human laws that would have regard for the common good by pointing out what should be done for its sake and by compelling the performance of such acts. Accordingly, Aristotle ([*Ethics,*] Bk. X, chap. ix [, no. 14]) says: 'Public regulations and provisions must clearly be established by law, and the good ones are established by laws zealous[20] of good.' Wherefore Cyril (*Against Julian,* Bk. III, not far from the beginning [Migne, *Patrologia Graeca, loc. cit.,* no. 81]) remarks: 'Nor is there

---

19. [This passage in Latin, as given by Suárez, varies slightly from the Greek text of Aristotle.—Tr.]

20. [*Studiosos* evidently for *studiosas,* the feminine form, referring to *leges.* The Greek, of which the Latin is a paraphrase, would seem to confirm this suggestion.—Tr.]

any doubt but that laws direct one toward what is good and compel one to recede from baser things; and consequently, no person in his senses will contradict the laws or the lawmakers.' Positive laws, then, were both useful and necessary. Accordingly, in former times, when inanimate laws had not been established, the princes were (so to speak) animate laws, by whose will the peoples were ruled; as St. Augustine records (*On the City of God,* Bk. IV, chap. vi), citing Justin Martyr.

20. *The last division of law: into civil and ecclesiastical. What is the civil law?* And lastly, this positive law is divided into civil and ecclesiastical; a division which was not recognized by the philosophers, since they knew nothing of the supernatural end, or of the special power [relating thereto]. For this reason, the human law, in their writings, is the same as the civil law, which Augustine is accustomed to call the temporal; for it is that law which is devoted to the political government of the state, the guarding of temporal rights, and the preservation of the commonwealth in peace and justice. Accordingly, civil laws are concerned with these temporal or bodily goods.

Again, what are the ecclesiastical laws? In addition to such laws, however, the Christian religion recognizes certain ecclesiastical or canon laws which are contained in the sacred canons and in the pontifical decrees. Some persons call these not human but divine, for the reason that they are derived from a special power, especially conferred by God, and relate chiefly to a supernatural end, to divine worship and to the salvation of souls. Nevertheless, in point of fact, they are human laws; as has been well taught by Giovanni d'Andrea, whom Panormitanus (on *Decretals,* Bk. II, tit. VII, chap. i, no. 7) cites and follows, and as one may clearly infer from the *Decretals* (Bk. IV, tit. XIV, chap. viii). The reason for this is that the said laws are proximately established by the human will, although they differ from civil laws with regard to the power that is their immediate source, and with regard to their end and to their subject-matter, as we shall see below. However, the reason or necessity for such laws was, in due proportion, the same. For (so we assume) God founded a special congregation of the faithful, which should be one body, and which we now call the Church; and He did not make specific provision, through the law which He Himself had established, for everything that might be fitting in the spiritual direction of the Church, but simply laid down certain essential bases for this spiritual commonwealth. The other matters, however, He left to be provided for, through His ministers and ecclesiastical pastors, partly with the purpose that all points might be ordered agreeably and in a manner adapted to mankind, and partly because it was not possible to determine every point specifically in such a way that it would be immutable. Therefore, this process of determining took place through canonical laws, so that such laws were as necessary in the spiritual commonwealth of the Church as civil laws, in the temporal commonwealth.

21. From the foregoing divisions, then, the variety, necessity, and manifold constitution of law become sufficiently evident.

To these divisions, there are frequently added others, which are either doubtful or of [only] apparent importance, and over which, therefore, we need not for the present linger, since they will be better touched upon in their proper places. Of such sort is the division of law into instructive (*ostendens*) and mandatory (*praecipiens*), of which we shall speak in a subsequent Book, and one which may perhaps be an unnecessary classification. Again, there is another general division of law, into affirmative and negative, the former prescribing what should be done, the latter opposing or prohibiting what should be avoided. These two forms of law are manifested in all those which we have enumerated; for they differ only in the subject-matter of what is prescribed, which is to do or not to do, so that there is consequently a certain difference in their modes of binding. Of this difference, we shall treat more properly in Chapter Thirteen.[21] Next, one may add the divisions of human law into penal and non-penal, and into the merely prohibitory, and that which annuls; terms which are familiar enough. Concerning the actual concepts involved, however, special discussions will be undertaken in the later pages of the work. Finally, it may seem that the *ius gentium* has been omitted from the number of the divisions mentioned; but in Chapter Eight of the next Book,[22] we shall explain how that body of law is included within the forms above-mentioned.

---

21. [Suárez discusses this point, not in Chapter xiii, but in Chapter xv of Book I. Chapter xv is not included in these *Selections.*—Tr.]

22. [Suárez's real discussion of this point is found in Chap. xvii of Book II of *De Legibus, infra* pp. 374 *et seq.*—Tr.]

CHAPTER IV

What Acts in the Mind of the Lawmaker Are Necessary for the Making of a Law?

1. The points with which we have so far dealt relate only to the determination of the question of whether or not law exists. Moreover, we have demonstrated the necessity as well as the existence, not of one law only, but of various kinds or species of laws. We have explained the names of these species, and their rational bases, in order that our discussion of the subject may be clear and expeditious.

We should examine next the question, 'What is law?' Of this question, we shall treat in an abstract and general manner, postponing for the appropriate places, the difficulties arising in the case of particular laws. Moreover, we shall speak always from a human standpoint and in accordance with our own [human] mode of conception; yet we shall have to apply certain expressions to the divine law, or mind, excluding imperfections.

In this Chapter, then, and in the Chapter that follows, we shall discuss the genus under which law is comprehended; and later we shall inquire into the specific differences within that genus.

2. *Law pertains to the intellectual nature.* Thus we assume, first, that law is a thing which pertains to the intellectual nature as such, and accordingly, to the mind thereof; both intellect and will being included under the term 'mind', for it is with that understanding that I am now speaking. The truth of this assumption is sufficiently evident in itself, since law implies a moral relation to the performance of a given action, and since no aspect of nature save the intellectual is capable of such a relation. Moreover, properly speaking, only those who have the use of intellect and reason are governed by law, or are capable of being so governed; and therefore, it is still far more necessary that there be a mind in one who is to govern by means of laws. Law, then, is a thing that pertains to the mind. Furthermore, if it is said, by an extension of terms, that God conceives a given law for natural or irrational things, that is the case only in so far as things lacking intellect are in need of a superior governing mind, in order that the work of nature may be a work of intelligence; and thus from every standpoint, law must be related to mind. Such has been the concept of law entertained by all

the wise, even by the philosophers, as is evident from the passages cited in our preceding Chapters from the works of Plato, Aristotle, and Cicero.

3. *Law is based, not upon a habit, but upon an act.* Secondly, I assume that law—properly speaking, and especially in so far as it exists in the lawgiver—is based upon a concrete act, and not upon a habit or power. This is clearly true, because that which is called law has the virtue of proximately moving its subjects and imposing an obligation upon them; but this virtue does not exist in potency or habit, save basically and remotely; therefore, it must exist in some act. Moreover, commanding, ordering and similar functions imply an act; and such functions are discharged through law, either formally, or (as it were) through a moral activity; hence, law consists in an act.

However, in order that we may explain what this act is, it will first be necessary to enumerate all the acts which may concur to make laws, and to describe the sequence or order of these acts. For they may be either interior, and elicited by the intellect or the will; or exterior, and prescribed; and all of them are necessary for the ultimate effectiveness of the law.[1]

4. *Concerning the subject [or state] with respect to which the law may exist.* For the clarification of this point, I shall note, thirdly, that law may be considered from a threefold standpoint, with respect to its state or subject. First, it may be considered as it is in the lawmaker himself; in which sense, as we were saying above,[2] law is conceived in the mind of God from eternity. Secondly, law may be considered as it exists in the subjects on whom the law is imposed; from which standpoint, it is customarily said that the law of nature has been instilled into the minds of men. Thirdly, it may be considered as it is in some different symbolic manifestation (*signum*), or some other external materialization (*materia exterior*); for example, in writing or even in a spoken word that declares the will of a superior.

As to law when considered with respect to the two latter states, no difficulty can arise. For law, taken in the third sense, consists formally in some external act, by means of which the lawgiver makes known his thought;

---

1. [An elicited act issues from, and is actualized in the faculty; a prescribed act is one that is actualized in the will or other faculty and is so elicited by command of the will.—REVISER.]

2. [See *supra*, p. 37, Chap. iii, §§ 2 *et seq.*—TR.]

such an act as speech is among men, or writing. Thus Aristotle (*Ethics*, Bk. X, chap. ix [, no. 12]) has said that, 'law [. . .] is a rule, emanating from a certain wisdom and intelligence'. Gabriel, too (on the *Sentences*, Bk. III, dist. xxxvii), defines law as a sign making sufficiently manifest the will or the thought of the prince. I have said, indeed, that this sign is an activity or act, including the term of duration of the said act, when the latter is permanent and embodies perfectly the character of a sign. For written law is accordingly called law, not only when it is at the time put into writing, but in so far as the term of that writing is permanent and indicates always the thought of the prince. Similarly, if a law is handed down merely by [the spoken] word, and even though the audible word passes away, then, in so far as this word endures in human memory, the law is said to be sufficiently enduring. For it is thus that unwritten law is sometimes preserved through tradition. In like manner, custom, too, may at times attain the force of law, as we shall see below.[3]

No other difficulty arises with regard to this category of law, except in connexion with the promulgation of law, a point of which we shall treat later.[4]

5. *Law in the subject resides solely in an act of the mind.* Furthermore, with respect to law as it may exist in its human subject, such law unquestionably consists in an act of the mind, and of itself requires only a judgment by the intellect and not an act of the will, since an act of the will is necessary to the observance or execution of the law but not to its existence. For law precedes the will of the subject and is binding upon that will; whereas an act of the intellect is necessary in order that the law itself may thereby be brought before and into direct contact with the will; and consequently, a judgment by the reason is required. It is in this sense, indeed, that the natural law is commonly spoken of as the natural judgment of the human reason; in so far, that is, as the said law exists in man as in one who is subject to it. Joannes Damascenus, too, speaks in this same manner, saying (*De Fide Orthodoxa,* Bk. IV, chap. iii [chap. xxii]): 'The law of God, as it

3. [*Infra*, p. 527, *De Legibus,* Bk. VII, chap. iii, no. 10.—TR.]
4. [Suárez's discussion of promulgation, found in Book I, chapter xi, of his *De Legibus,* is not included in these *Selections.*—TR.]

draws near to us, enkindling our minds, attracts them to itself and arouses our consciences, which are themselves said to be the law of our minds.' The same is true, in due proportion, with respect to positive laws. For after they have been enacted, they are applied to each individual through a judgment of the reason, to the extent that what was not necessary *per se* is judged necessary by virtue of the law, so that this act of judgment is now the law (so to speak) as it exists in the subject himself.

In this connexion, to be sure, there has occurred a question as to whether in the case of these positive laws, there is sometimes required on the part of the subjects an act of the will that accepts the law. However, this point should be discussed in relation to human laws, to which it is pertinent. For the present, let us consider it a certainty that such an act is not a requisite for the essential principle of the law as such, and possibly not for any law, unless it be on account of some defect of power in the lawmaker. Accordingly, with regard to this aspect of law, nothing further of a general nature need be said. For the special difficulty which may arise from it, in connexion with natural law, will be better dealt with, in the following Book.

6. *Acts of the intellect and of the will are necessary for the making of law.* There remains, then, the matter of the law as it exists in the lawmaker himself. With respect to this phase of the question, it is certain, to begin with, that both the intellect and the will intervene in the making of law. But it is necessary to explain what acts are involved in connexion with that process.

In the first place, law, in so far as it is externally imposed upon the subjects, is a species of means for securing their welfare and peace or happiness. And therefore, one may assume first of all that the will of the lawmaker includes the purpose of promoting the common welfare, or the good government of the subjects. From this purpose there follows forthwith in the intellect a consideration of this or that [possible] law, as to which of them is just, or suitable for the commonwealth. These two acts are seen to occur successively and with ratiocination, in men; but in God, without imperfection, as a simple act in the order of reason.

How many acts are proximately necessary in the intellect and the will for the making of law? However, the said acts intervene only remotely in the making of law, and therefore it would seem clear that the essence of the law is not found in them.

It appears, then, that after these acts are performed, there is direct intervention, on the part of the intellect, by an act of judgment through which
the lawmaker decides and decrees that a given provision is advisable for
the commonwealth, and that it is expedient that this provision should be
observed by all. This fact is manifest since, without such an act of judgment, the law could not be prudently and rationally enacted; and it is part
of the character of law that it shall be just and, consequently, prudent. For
prudence[5] commands, as St. Thomas (II.–II, qu. 47, art. 8) teaches, citing
Aristotle (*Ethics,* Bk. VI, chaps. x *et seq.* [chaps. v *et seq.*]). Wherefore, just
as in the case of each private person there is required a prudence that serves
for the right direction of individual acts, whether with respect to himself
or with respect to another private person, so, in the case of a prince, there
is required a prudence that is political; that is to say, one that is construc-
tive in relation to the building of laws, in accordance with the passage in
Proverbs (Chap. viii [, v. 15]) where Wisdom says: 'By me kings reign, and
lawgivers decree just things.' The teaching of St. Thomas (II.–II, qu. 50,
art. 1), together with that of Aristotle (*Politics,* Bk. III, chap. iii [chap. vii]),
on this point, is also excellent.

7. Secondly, it is certain that there is required, in addition to this act
of judgment, an act on the part of the will, by which the prince agrees,
chooses, and wills that his subjects shall be obedient to that which his
intellect has judged expedient. On this point all the Doctors, too, are in
agreement, at least with regard to positive laws; a fact which we shall demonstrate in the next Chapter. Moreover, the reason in support of the point
is, briefly, this: law does not merely enlighten, but also provides motive
force and impels; and, in intellectual processes, the primary faculty for
moving to action is the will.

Some one, to be sure, may ask: 'And what is this act of will?' There is,
indeed, cause for doubt since simple or inefficacious willing[6] is insufficient. For God possesses such a will with regard even to those things which
He counsels but does not prescribe; and among men, although a superior

---

5. *Prudentia:* prudence in the wide sense of general practical wisdom, a virtue of the
intellect as it responds to reason and directs the will.

6. *Voluntas simplex aut inefficax:* a preference or wish that falls short of an actual
decision that something occur.

might in this sense desire that something should be done by a subject, and might inform the latter of this desire, that would not suffice to constitute a command. On the other hand, an efficacious will would not seem to be necessary; for God does not possess this sort of will with respect to all things prescribed by Him. If He did, all these precepts would be executed, since His efficacious will would infallibly be fulfilled.

8. *What efficacy of act is requisite in willing, in order to set up a law.* The reply [to the doubt above set forth] is that there is a necessity for some act of an efficacious will, a will which in God is that of His good pleasure,[7] as is proved by the argument first set forth; but it is not necessary that this willing should relate to the observance or execution of a law, since execution is a thing which follows later, as is also proved by the last argument adduced. Accordingly, it is inherently necessary that [the said act of will] should relate to an obligation imposed on the subjects; in other words, that it should be a will to bind the subjects; for without such a will, [the act] cannot be binding upon them. And this will to bind suffices, in so far as willing is concerned.

The truth of the first assertion is evident, because the obligation is a moral effect, and voluntary on the part of the prince; also, because the acts of agents do not transcend their own intentions; and furthermore because, in accordance with the same reasoning, there can be no vow without the will to bind oneself; wherein [a vow] is like a law, a fact which we have mentioned in another work (Vol. II, *De Religione,* Treatise VI, bk. I, chap. ii).[8] The second assertion is also clearly true, since we assume that there exists in the lawmaker, the power to bind; and therefore, if he furthermore possesses the will to bind, nothing else can be required, in so far as relates to the will. It may be objected that the will to command is necessary, and that this will suffices even in the absence of the will to bind. I reply that these are not two separate forms of willing, but one and the same form described in different terms, a point which I shall explain below.

9. The will in question may be described in yet another way, as being the will to bring about a given action because that action is necessary to

7. [Termed by theologians *voluntas beneplaciti,* which simply means the will of God in reference to what we know is pleasing to Him.—Reviser.]
8. [Not included in these *Selections.*—Tr.]

the preservation of equity or the mean in a particular matter of virtue. For the will of a superior has this moral efficacy, namely, that it can lay a binding obligation upon his subjects, and make that a requisite matter for virtue, which was not in itself essential; as, for example, when it makes fasting on a certain day necessary for the mean of temperance. For though this fast is not always necessary to the observance of the law, nevertheless, when it shall be necessary, [the imposition of such a restriction] does not exceed the power of the lawmaker.

This, then, is the correct explanation of the object with which the efficacious will of the legislator is concerned. For, even though that object may be moral rather than physical, the efficacious will may be exercised with respect to it; and not only the human will, but also the divine, as I have elsewhere expressly said[9] and as I shall later repeat in the treatise on grace.[10]

In this connexion, indeed, there was a special difficulty in regard to the natural law; but this point will be treated to better advantage in the following Book.

10. *The act of the intellect which some persons call intimation is not a requisite for the making of law.* The sole remaining question is whether or not, subsequently to the acts of the intellect and of the will already mentioned, some other act on the part of the legislator himself is a requisite for the making of law. For many persons believe that an additional act of the intellect is indeed necessary, one to which they give the name of intimation, explanation or notification of the will of the superior with respect to the inferior; because this act, such persons say, involves the real essence of command and may be expressed in the phrase, 'Do this', so that, as I shall point out below, they find the real essence of law in the said act. The basis of their opinion, moreover, is their belief that in every moral operation the act in question is necessary, after the election [by the will] in respect to execution. Aristotle, too, touched upon this view, in declaring (*Ethics,* Bk. VI [, chap. v]) that to command was the most perfect act of prudence. St. Thomas did likewise (I.–II, qu. 17, art. 1) when he taught that the act of commanding is an act of the intellect.

9. [*Supra,* pp. 59–60, Sections 7–8, this Chapter.—Tr.]
10. [Not included in these *Selections.*—Tr.]

11. I hold, indeed, speaking generally of command over the personal acts and powers of the person himself who exercises the command, that there is no necessity for an act of the intellect directed immediately toward the executory power, subsequently to the choice, or act of willing, by which one definitely and effectively wills to perform some external act, with all the special accompanying conditions required for action in view of the circumstances and the executive power. I go further, and hold that such an act [of the intellect] is not even possible. For the executory power is not aware of the force of the command; and solely the placing of the object before the will, not the application of the power to the act, pertains to the intellect. To the will pertains the subsequent application of the other powers in actual use. This is the more common opinion, one which I derive from St. Thomas (I.–II, qu. 17) and from the authors to whom I shall refer in the following Chapter. I have touched upon the same matter more frequently, and at sufficient length, elsewhere (Tract. *De Praedestinatione,* Bk. I, chaps. xvi and xvii and *De Religione,* Tr. IV, bk. i, chap. i and Tr. VI, bk. i, chap. xii).[11]

12. This doctrine having been laid down with respect to each person's command over himself, it is still needful to state that, with respect to the command of one person over another, the only necessary requisite, following the act of will on the part of the lawmaker which I have explained above,[12] is that the lawmaker should manifest, indicate or intimate this decree and judgment of his, to the subjects to whom the law itself relates. For this is essential, since if he did not do so, the will of the prince could not be binding upon his subject, inasmuch as it would not be made known to that subject, a point which we shall discuss more fully when we treat of promulgation.[13] It is clear, moreover, that this [act on the part of the lawgiver] suffices, since the will of the prince is of itself efficacious. For that will is derived from a sufficient authority and is, so we assume, accompanied by an absolute and binding decree; consequently, if the said will is adequately revealed to the subject, it effects that which is willed;

---

11. [Neither treatise included in these *Selections.*—Tr.]

12. [*Supra,* p. 56, Section 4, this Chapter.—Tr.]

13. [Suárez discusses promulgation in Book I, chapter xi of the *De Legibus,* a chapter not included in these *Selections.*—Tr.]

hence, it establishes an obligation; the law is accordingly consummated; and therefore, nothing further is necessary. This argument will stand out more clearly in the light of the statements to be made in the following Chapter.

13. It is clear, however, that such instruction as to [the lawgiver's] intention[14] consists of some utterance, the term 'utterance' being understood to include any indication or manifestation whatsoever, given to another person, of an internal act. That utterance, indeed, properly considered with special reference to its relation to a creature, is effected by means of an act which passes on and is finally received in some way into the person to whom the utterance is addressed; a fact which is manifestly true in the case of human interrelations, and which I believe to be true, among the angels, also, in a sense appropriate to them. For if the one who speaks, causes no impression on the one to whom he speaks, the former will not be making his thought manifest to the latter.

Moreover, the same is true with respect to God in relation to His creatures. For God gave no intimation to Adam of His will concerning abstention from eating of the tree of life, save through some revelation made to Adam himself; and if God makes manifest in the Word, to one of the blessed, that which He wishes to be done, the very vision of the Word in the blessed has the force of an utterance and intimation from God, concerning the precept in question.

The utterance directed by the creature to God, however, involves another principle, of which I have spoken elsewhere ([*De Religione, ubi*] *de Oratione, loc. cit.*),[15] but which is not pertinent here, since the creature cannot give commands to God.

14. *In addition to the acts enumerated, an act of the intellect for communicating with the subject is required.* Thus, from the foregoing, I conclude that, subsequently to the above-mentioned[16] act of the will, there is required of the lawmaker only an act of the intellect which will be needed in order to communicate a given matter or decree to the subject.

---

14. [The Latin has simply, *illa . . . intentione.*—Tr.]

15. [Not included in these *Selections.*—Tr.]

16. [Reading *praedictum* for *praeditum,* in accordance with the 1856 edition.—Tr.]

And, in consequence, there may be a necessity for a new act of the will to produce some sign which will make manifest the previous act of the will. Just as we are required to have an understanding of the words which we are about to utter, and a will to move our tongues, so also in due proportion it is required that the prince shall conceive, through his intellect, a way to effect an intimation of the law, and that he shall, through his will, choose to execute this intimation. The foregoing statement may in due proportion be applied with respect to God; for it is thus that He executes this intimation, even as He executes His other effects.

Finally, one may also infer that there takes place within the legislator, and subsequently to the aforesaid act of the will, a new act of the intellect, by which the legislator perceives his own will; just as we understand that there is in God, subsequently to His act of willing, that knowledge which is called the knowledge of vision.[17] Thus it also results that the lawgiver, after having knowledge of his law, exercises judgment as to its subject-matter in yet another manner than that which he formerly employed; for at first, he judged[18] it only as being suitable matter for his command, whereas afterwards he judged it as being necessary to moral rectitude, by virtue of his decree. All of which is so manifest that it requires no new proof. We shall speak in the following Chapter, however, of the way in which these elements concur to make law and, accordingly, of the act on which law is founded.

CHAPTER V

Is Law an Act of the Intellect or of the Will? And What Is the Nature of This Act?

1. *The first opinion: law is held to be an act of the intellect.* In the light of the assumptions which I have made in the previous Chapter, the question will turn almost entirely upon a manner of speaking. Nevertheless, it

---

17. [The *Scientia visionis,* or knowledge of vision in God has for its object Himself, and all things and events outside God which are, were, or will be.—REVISER.]

18. [Reading *iudicabat* for *indicabat* in accordance with the 1856 edition.—TR.]

should be briefly discussed, because of the variety of opinions on this subject.

According to the first opinion, then, law is an act of the intellect. This is the view held by St. Thomas (I.–II, qu. 90, art. 1); and Vincent de Beauvais (*Speculum Morale,* Bk. V, pt. II, dist. 1), often speaks thus in his discussion of the matter. The same opinion is adopted by the Thomists, Cajetan, Conrad Koellin, and others (thereon and on I.–II, qu. 17; qu. 58, art. 4; qu. 60, art. 1). Mention should also be made of Soto (*De Iustitia et Iure,* Bk. I, qu. i, art. 1), Torquemada (on *Decretum,* Pt. I, dist. III, can. iii), Alexander of Hales ([*Summa,*] Pt. III, qu. xxvi, *ad primum*), Richard Middleton (on the *Sentences,* Bk. III, dist. xxxiii, art. 2, qu. 6, ad 3), Antoninus ([*Summa,*] Pt. II, tit. IV, chap. x [Pt. I, tit. xi, chap. ii]), William of Paris (Tr. *De Legibus*), and Corduba (Bk. II, *Quaestionarium Theologicum,* qu. 10). Moreover, the opinion in question is wont to be proved, first, by the argument that the Scriptures, as well as the Fathers, philosophers and jurisconsults, assign law to the reason, or to wisdom. For example, in *Proverbs* (Chap. viii [, v. 15]), Wisdom declares: 'By me [. . .] lawgivers decree just things.' So, also, Clement of Alexandria (*Stromata,* Bk. I [, chap. xxv], not far from the end), declares that law is good opinion and that good opinion is that which is true. Moreover, he adds: 'Consequently, certain persons have said law is right reason, which prescribes those things that should be done, and prohibits those that should not be done.' Again, Basil (*On Isaias,* Chap. viii, in vv. 19–22) says: 'Law is a teacher and instructress' (*doctrix & magistra*).[1] Joannes Damascenus (*De Fide Orthodoxa,* Bk. IV, chap. xxiii [chap. xxii]) has also attributed to law the function of teaching.

2. Furthermore, Plato (Dialogue, *Minos,* or *On Law,* at the beginning [314 C D]) calls law, 'the upright opinion of the state', that is to say, the true opinion. And later, he asserts that law is 'the operation of truth'. Aristotle (*De Sophisticis Elenchis,* Bk. I, chap. xii, at the end) has likewise said that law is 'the opinion of the multitude'. Again, in the *Letter to Alexander,* preceding the *Rhetoric to Alexander,*[2] he defines law as the 'utterance of a command, with the common consent of the state, etc.' And in a closely

---

1. [Basil has: *lex est veritatis magistra.*—REVISER.]

2. [In Preface to *Rhetoric to Alex.* = 1420 A.—TR.] The *Rhetoric to Alexander* and the *Letter to Alexander* are now thought not to be by Aristotle.

following passage (*Rhetoric,* Chap. i), he says: 'Law is the common consent of the state, a consent which prescribes in writing the way in which each act is to be performed.' In this passage, Aristotle also embodies law as bidding and precept; although frequently, in other passages, he nevertheless attributes the function of commanding to reason and to prudence (*Ethics,* Bk. VI, chaps. ix *et seq.; Politics,* Bk. I, chap. iii [Bk. III, chap. xi]).

Thus he has said (*Ethics,* Bk. X, chap. ix) that law is 'a rule, emanating from a certain wisdom and intelligence'. We have also cited above many of the words of Cicero, in which he indicates that law is in the reason: that first, indeed, it is in the Mind of God; and that, through participation in this [Mind, by the human reason], the said reason contains the natural law and prudence, from which source the laws of states should be derived. This point is fully dealt with, in the *Laws* (Bks. I and II, shortly after the beginning [Bk. I, chap. vii and Bk. II, chap. iv]) where, among other remarks, Cicero lays down the conclusion that, 'Law is right reason in commanding and forbidding'. And in fine, it is in like vein that Papinian (in *Digest,* I. iii. 1) calls law 'a common precept', declaring it to be 'the decree of prudent men'. Marcianus, too (*ibid.,* 2), says, quoting Chrysippus: 'Law is the queen, princess and leader of human and divine affairs.' These, indeed, are the functions of reason, to which the rule and direction of actions pertain.

3. *The first opinion is confirmed by reasoning.* Various arguments are advanced for the confirmation of this first opinion.

The first argument is as follows: it is the function of law to regulate, wherefore it is customary to define law as a 'regulation by the reason'; yet regulation pertains not to the will, but to the intellect, since it involves a certain ratiocination, so that those things which lack reason cannot regulate; therefore, law is an act of the intellect.

Secondly, it is the function of law to enlighten and instruct in accordance with the words [of the *Psalms,* cxviii, v. 105], 'Thy word is a lamp to my feet, [. . .]' and of this passage, also [*ibid.,* xviii, v. 8]: 'The law of the Lord is unspotted, converting souls: [the testimony of the Lord is faithful,] giving wisdom to little ones'; and the act of enlightenment pertains to the intellect.

Thirdly, law is a rule, as we said at the beginning, in accordance with a passage of Basil (on *Isaias,* Chap. i, in v. 9)[3] where he calls it 'a rule of the just and the unjust'. This view is also supported by the *Digest* (I. iii. 2). Thus it is that the laws of the Church are called canons—that is to say, rules—as Isidore (*Etymologies,* Bk. II [, chap. x]) remarks. But the will is not a rule; rather should it be regulated by the reason itself. Therefore, law dwells in the reason.

4. Fourthly, we have the argument that no act of the will can be designated as law. For [such an act would fall into one of two classes.]

First, it might be the will of a prince or of a superior that a particular act shall be performed by the subject; which is not the case, since such a will is neither necessary nor sufficient; for God imposed upon Abraham a true precept concerning the sacrifice of Abraham's son, yet God did not will that this sacrifice should be executed; and conversely, however much a superior may will and desire that a given act be performed by a subject, he imposes no obligation if he issues no precept. Thus the theologians say that we are not bound to conform to the divine will, even the efficacious divine will, unless there is added to it a precept concerning the execution of the will in question. Therefore, law does not consist in such an act of the will.

Secondly, [the act] might consist in the will to bind the subject; a will which is also insufficient, unless it is made known. Indeed, some persons add that a will of this sort in the prince is not necessary to his establishment of the law, for if the prince wills to command, by the very act of commanding, he makes law, even though he reflects not at all upon the binding obligation involved. Bartholomew Medina goes further and says (on I.–II, qu. 90, art. 1) that, even though [the prince] may be [definitely] unwilling to impose the obligation, nevertheless, if he wills to command, he does impose it, and makes law. Just as one who makes a vow without willing to bind himself, nevertheless vows truly (says Medina) and becomes bound; and just as he who makes a deceitful promise under oath, without intent to lay himself under a binding obligation, is bound by the sanctity of the oath, to fulfil the promise; even so, he who wills to

---

3. [Evidently a reference to the end of Section I of this Chapter, although the reference to Basil (on *Isaias,* Chap. viii) given at that point is not precisely that which is given here.—Tr.]

command, imposes a binding obligation, by the efficacy of the command, even though he be unwilling to do so.

Accordingly, no other act of the will than the will to command, is necessary to law; and the will to command does not constitute law, unless it is followed by the command itself, which pertains to the intellect; therefore, law dwells in the intellect.

5. *In what act of the intellect does law dwell?* However, there exists among those persons who have advanced this opinion, a controversy as to what act of the intellect contains the essential principle of law; that is to say, a controversy as to whether this act is the judgment of the reason which precedes the willing, or the command which is said to follow after. For certain of these authorities declare that the act in question is the judgment of the reason. William of Paris held this view; and he was followed by Conrad Koellin (on I.–II, qu. 91, art. 1). St. Thomas, also (I.–II, qu. 91, art. 2 [art. 1]), clearly says that law is a dictate [of practical reason] in the prince. Moreover, if we take into consideration the testimony cited, especially that of the philosophers, it would appear to have reference to this judgment of the reason. Again, the properties which consist in enlightening, and in serving as a rule and a measure, are appropriate to such a judgment of the reason, and not to the command in question, for the latter is said to be of a quality that merely impels and does not make manifest any truth.

Nevertheless, in opposition to this opinion, we have the fact that this judgment does not possess any efficacious force for binding, or for moving in a moral sense; yet such a force is essential in law. Moreover, in so far as concerns the judgment involved, a precept would seem to be in nowise different from a counsel; since even one who gives counsel passes similar judgment in regard to the action whose performance he counsels. Accordingly, if God should make manifest to us nothing more than this judgment, He would be giving us not a law, but a counsel, in connexion with those acts, to be sure, the contraries of which are not intrinsically wicked.

6. *Some say that law is the act of the intellect which is called 'command'* *(imperium).*[4] Other authors therefore, assert that law resides in the act of the intellect subsequent to willing, an act to which they give the name

---

4. [The editions of 1612 and 1619 place this subheading beside the following paragraph (under Section 7). The correct position, however, is evidently beside Section 6, as indicated by the Paris edition of 1856.—Tr.]

of 'command' (*imperium*). However, this act, if it is not in the form of a locution, is certainly a fiction, as we have remarked above.[5] And if it is in that form, then it will have the nature of a sign, so that it will be not so much law, as the sign of law; or, at the most, it will be called law, even as written law or that promulgated orally is so called. But this external or written law has the force of law only in that it stands for something else, something in which there dwells the virtue of law; therefore, it necessarily presupposes the existence of another thing which is law in its essence;[6] and this is the very object of our inquiries. Nor may it even be said that the internal locution, as we conceive it in the mind of the prince, constitutes law; for this locution, too, has force and efficacy only in that it is a sign, so that it necessarily presupposes the existence of that which is law in its essence.[7]

7. Furthermore, with respect to God, there is a special reason on account of which it would seem that the said act [of the intellect] is not to be attributed to Him as necessary for the establishment of law. For either this act is in the form of an externally active impulse, as some persons hold it to be, distinct even in God from His proper judgment and cognition; or else it is in the form of a mental locution; yet neither of these alternative assertions is acceptable; therefore, . . .

The minor premiss can be proved, in so far as concerns its first part, by demonstrating that no such act exists, since its existence is vainly posited, and the act is inconceivable; but we have treated of this point, elsewhere (*De Religione*, Pt. I, tr. II, bk. I, chap. x).[8] Here, however, we shall provide a brief demonstration, as follows: on the part of God, such an impulse cannot be necessary for the establishment of law; for God, in establishing law, does not impel one physically toward the act prescribed by the law, but merely imposes an obligation which is of a moral nature and cannot be thus physically brought about, a fact which would seem to be self-evident.

5. [*Supra*, p. 56, *De Legibus*, Chap. iv, § 4.—Tr.]

6. [*Principaliter.* Cf. *Mos. et Rom. Leg. Coll.*, 12, 7, 5 as cited in Harper's Dictionary. Some of the examples cited by Du Cange also suggest this interpretation. On the other hand, some readers may prefer the translation: '. . . another thing which is primarily law.'—Tr.]

7. See note 6.

8. [Not included in these *Selections*.—Tr.]

The other part of the minor premiss, indeed, the part relating to a locution, is easily demonstrated. For a locution on the part of God, externally
actualized, can be nothing more nor less than an infusion of enlightenment or of intelligible forms, or the production of some sign making
manifest Himself or His will; but all this, God does through His will, nor
is any impulse or act of the intellect subsequent to the act of the will, more
necessary for this effect than for other effects.

In nowise, then, may law, as it exists in God, be assigned to an act
consequent upon [an act of] will. The same is therefore true with respect
to any lawmaker whatsoever; since all lawmakers participate in the basic
characteristics of law, which dwell in God by His essence, so that in due
proportion [all] imitate those characteristics.

8. *The second opinion: law is held to be an act of the will.* There is, then,
a second general opinion, according to which law is an act of the lawmaker's will. In support of this opinion, one may cite all those who assign
command to the will, as do Henry of Ghent (*Quodlibeta,* IX, qu. 6),
Gabriel (on the *Sentences,* Bk. II, dist. xxxvii, qu. 1, art. 1, not. 3), Major
(on the *Sentences,* Bk. III, dist. xxxiii, qu. 7), Occam (on the *Sentences,*
Bk. III, qu. xxii [qu. xii], art. 4), Almain (*Moralia,* Tract. III, chap. ii),
and Angest (on the *Moralia,* Tract. I, pt. III, corol. iii).⁹ Bonaventure also
supports this view, when he says (on the *Sentences,* Bk. III, dist. xvii, art. 1,
qu. 1, *ad penult.*): 'The will is that within which resides the rule and command of what is in the person who wills.'¹⁰ Joannes Medina (*Codex de
Oratione,* Qu. 2) expresses himself in like manner. The opinion in question is furthermore attributed to Durandus and to Gregory of Rimini (on
the *Sentences,* Bk. I, dist. xlvii) in so far as they assert that the divine will
is a rule to which we are all bound to conform. Scotus,¹¹ too, is cited in
behalf of this opinion, in that he says, in certain passages (on the *Sentences,*

---

9. [The opinion is found in *Bipartitum in Morali philosophia opusculum per
magistrum Guillelmum Manderston Scotum,* Paris, 1517. The work should be ascribed to
Jerome Angest, as Raynauld states.—REVISER.]

10. [It is in replying to this that St. Bonaventure states that the will commands.—
REVISER.]

11. Scotus: John Duns Scotus (1265?–1308), a leading Franciscan theologian and
philosopher. Associated with the Franciscan order, Scotism was an important school of
thought in early modern Catholicism and had considerable influence on Suárez,

Bk. II, dist. vi, qu. 1 and dist. xxxviii, qu. 1, *ad ult.* and *quodlib.* 17), that
the ordering of another to the performance of any action is a function that
pertains to the will. And in yet another passage (*ibid.*, Bk. III, dist. xxxvi,
qu. 1, art. 2), he assigns the function of command to the will. This same
view is defended at length by Castro (*De Potestate Legis Poenalis,* Bk. II,
chap. i).

9. Moreover, [this second opinion] can be upheld by argument. First,
it may be argued that Scripture and the civil laws (*iura*) give the name of
law (*lex*) to the will of God, and to the will of the prince. 'He hath made
his ways known to Moses: his wills to the children of Israel' (*Psalms,* xxxii
[cii, v. 7]), that is to say, He hath made known His precepts. Again, we have
the words: 'Teach me to do thy will' (*ibid.,* cxlii [, v. 10]). In the second book
of *Machabees* (Chap. i [, v. 3]), we read: 'And [may he] give you all a heart to
worship him, and to do his will [. . .]', that is, to obey His law. Thus Christ
our Lord has said, in the Lord's Prayer: 'Thy will be done', which was to
say, Thy law be obeyed. Again, in the prayer in the garden He said: 'Not my
will, but thine be done', that is, thy command be done. For so it had been
written of Him, according to the *Psalms* (xxix [xxxix, vv. 8, 9]): 'In the head
of the book it is written of me that I should do thy will.'

The customary reply [to the argument based on these passages], an
answer drawn from the Master of the *Sentences* [Peter Lombard] (in the
Sentences, Bk. I, dist. xlvii) and from St. Thomas (*Summa,* Pt. I, qu. 19,
art. 9 [art. 11]), is that the passages in question refer to the will as expressed
by some sign,[12] which is will not strictly but metaphorically speaking.

10. However, even though the will when expressed by a sign may be so
called [only] in a metaphorical sense, it must be indicative of some true
will. For, why should it be called will metaphorically, unless because it has
a relation to true will? And it has no such relation save as a sign, wherefore
it is called 'the will, as expressed in a sign'. Hence, the will which it has
indicated is that which is fulfilled in the strict sense, and which has been
designated in the passages above-cited by the term 'law'. Accordingly, in

---

12. [St. Thomas, *loc. cit.,* explains that in God the *voluntas beneplaciti* is the divine
will strictly so called, but when God manifests His will by some sign this is called
voluntas signi and is His will understood metaphorically, i.e. by the sign.—REVISER.]

the civil law (*ius*) also (*Digest,* I. iii. 19), law (*lex*) is said to have its own will; for written or external law undoubtedly indicates the will of the prince, and this is declared to be the will of the law itself; therefore, will of that sort is law existing in the prince himself.

Thus we read (*Digest,* I. iv. 1 and *Institutes,* I. ii, § 6) that, 'What the prince has decreed, has the force of law', words which certainly indicate an act of the will.

One may also cite the philosophers who say that law 'is the decree and resolution of the state', as Plato puts it in the Dialogue already cited (*Minos* [314 B]); or that it is the consent of the state, in the words of Aristotle (*Rhetoric to Alexander,* Chaps. i and ii). For a decree indicates an intention of the will and—a clearer example—consent is an act of the will.

Anselm, also, in his *De Voluntate Dei,* has attributed [the function of giving] precepts to the divine will; and again, in the *De Conceptu Virginali et Originali Peccato* (Chap. iv), he has assigned to the will the function of commanding.

11. *The second opinion is confirmed on the basis of the characteristic properties of law.* Secondly, the opinion in question may be proved primarily on the basis of the characteristic properties of law. For all those properties which were attributed to an act of the intellect, are more appropriate to the will, and there are certain properties which are appropriate to the will and cannot be attributed to the intellect; therefore, . . .

The major premiss is clearly true, because, in the first place, there is assigned to law the attribute of being a rule and a measure; and this characteristic is particularly appropriate to the divine will, as may be inferred from various statements made by St. Thomas (I.–II, qu. 4, art. 4; qu. 19, art. 9; II.–II, qu. 26, last art.; and, more expressly, II.–II, qu. 105, art. 1). He says that the divine will is the first rule by which human actions should be measured; but that the wills of human superiors constitute a secondary rule, imparted by the first. The reason supporting this view is the fact that we ought to do or will that which God wills that we should, as Anselm declares in the work, *De Voluntate Dei.*

12. Another characteristic property of law is that it enlightens and directs the subject. In connexion with this property, indeed, we should note that it may be attributed to law, in so far as the latter dwells within

the subject himself; in which sense there is no doubt but that law is an act of the reason and, formally speaking, enlightening reason, as we have remarked in the preceding Chapter. Consequently, in reading the various authorities, one should take care lest he be led astray through ambiguity. For these authorities, inasmuch as they define law in terms of reason, are often speaking of it as it exists in the subject himself, in which sense the natural law is said to be right reason, imparted by nature; and thus it is that law enlightens, since it reveals the will of the lawmaker. Therefore, it would seem that there dwells within the lawmaker himself that will which objectively (so to speak), or even effectively, enlightens the subject; in accordance with the words of Anselm (*De Voluntate Dei* [Chap. iv]): 'The will of God is the master of the human will.'

13. The third characteristic property which we were to discuss, is that law orders. But this property is one which most properly pertains to the will; as Scotus (in the passage cited above) rightly declares, and as I have demonstrated in my Treatise on Predestination.[13] Moreover, the point can be well confirmed by the statement of St. Thomas (*Summa*, Pt. I, qu. 107, art. 1) that one angel through his will orders his concept [to be made known] to another angel, and in this way speaks to him; hence, the function of ordering pertains to the will. This explanation applies to the matter in hand. For such ordering by law takes the form either of a relation of the means to the end, or of a locution which indicates the will of the prince. And in either form, the ordering is most properly attributed to the will. For it is the will that orders the means to correspond to the end, since it is the will itself which strives towards the end, chooses the means for the sake of the end, and so decrees that these means be put into execution; and it is also the will that gives the command for the locution, while in God, or in an immaterial inferior being, the ordering of the locution is likewise accomplished through the will. Therefore, ordering by law, in so far as this property exists in the superior who orders or employs the locution, is always a matter pertaining to the will.

14. Hence, there is yet another way in which to meet the customary objection that a superior issues no command if he does not make his will

13. [This treatise is not included in these *Selections*.—TR.]

known, even though he may wish that a given act be performed by the subject. For it is replied that this intimation may be external and that such an intimation is not pertinent to the discussion, since it does not reside within the lawmaker but is simply a transient act, affecting either the subject or some other external matter, in accordance with the statements made in the preceding Chapter;[14] whereas intimation as it exists in the lawmaker would seem to consist pre-eminently in a will to intimate externally, which in its turn is an intimate part or else a consequence of the will to bind, so that, for this reason also, law pertains principally to the will.

15. *Some characteristic conditions requisite for law, which are appropriate only to an act of the will.* It remains for us to prove the second part of the first antecedent: namely, that some characteristic conditions requisite for law are to be found in an act of the will and not, strictly speaking, in an act of the intellect.

The first condition. The first of these conditions consists in the moving and bringing of the subject to the performance of an action, omission being always included under the term, 'action'. For the principle that moves and brings one to the performance of an action is the will, since the intellect is a motive force with regard more to the special mode of action (*specificationem*), and is therefore said to direct rather than to move.

The second condition. The second condition is the possession of a binding force; and this condition, properly speaking, dwells in the will, not in the intellect. For the intellect is able merely to point out a necessity existing in the object itself, and if such a necessity does not exist therein, the intellect cannot impart it [to the object]; whereas the will endows [the object] with a necessity which did not formerly characterize it; and, in the matter of justice, for example, it causes a thing to be of a given importance; and again, in connexion with other virtues, it creates a necessity for acting here and now, which would not exist under other circumstances and *per se*.

The third. The third condition consists in the fact that lawmaking is an act of jurisdiction and of superior power, a matter upon which I shall

14. [*Supra*, pp. 61 *et seq.*—Tr.]

comment below.[15] Consequently, it is (so to speak) the use of a form of dominion; and use is an act of the will, particularly the use of dominion, which is a free act.

The fourth. The fourth condition consists in the fact that law is an act of legal justice. For the prince, when he makes law, should have regard above all for the common good, which is a matter pertaining to legal justice. And such justice is a virtue of the will, although it may require the direction of prudence, a requirement which is common to all the virtues of the will. From this it follows simply that prudence is in the highest degree necessary to lawmaking, as is rightly demonstrated by the grounds supporting the first opinion; but it does not follow that this must be a formal act of prudence; even as just distribution and right choice depend upon prudence, while nevertheless they constitute formally an act of the will operating through the medium of distributive justice or of some other moral virtue.

16. One may adduce as a final argument the fact that it is possible, in the light of the remarks I made when setting forth the first opinion, to understand how difficult it is to designate the act of the intellect that constitutes law; whereas it is easy to make such a designation in the case of the will. For the will of a superior to bind a subject to a given act, or—what is equivalent—to set a given matter within the sphere of obligatory virtue, is well denoted by the term 'law'. This is true, both because of all the facts that we pointed out in connexion with the characteristic properties of law; and also because nothing antecedent to this will can have the force of law (a matter on which we have also touched), since it cannot induce necessity, while all that is subsequent [to the said will] is rather the sign of law that has already been conceived and established in the mind of the prince, since even the mental locution itself is only a mental sign.

To these fundamental statements, Bartholomew Medina could have made no answer other than a denial that a will to bind on the part of the prince is necessary for lawmaking, and for binding through law.

17. *The doctrine of B. Medina concerning the will to bind, is assailed.* This answer, however, is apparently a denial of what the other authors of the two opinions consider as a certainty; unless perhaps, there is some ambiguity in the wording. For it is a certainty that, in the case of these moral

15. [*Infra*, p. 81; Section 24.—Tr.]

effects which depend upon the will, the agents do not act without intention or in excess thereof; but binding by means of law is a moral effect
and one which depends upon the free will of the lawmaker; therefore, in
order that this binding effect may be accomplished, intention and will on
the part of the legislator are necessary, for otherwise, the said effect would
take place without intention, an inacceptable conclusion.

The truth of the minor premiss is self-evident, and the same author
(B. Medina) accordingly admits that law requires the concurrence of the
will; while the major premiss is commonly accepted by the theologians,
and, what is more, by the jurists. It is in this sense that they make the statement (*Decretals,* Bk. III, tit. v, chap. xxxviii) that the acts of agents do not
operate in excess of their intentions.

This conclusion, moreover, is made manifest by a process of induction,
since it is for this reason that excommunication imposed without intent to
bind is not binding, and absolution given without intent to absolve does
not take effect, the same being true with respect to the other Sacraments;
and in like manner, a vow or a marriage or a similar act, engaged in without intent, is not valid. The reason for this invalidity is the fact that all the
virtue of such actions flows from or through the medium of the will. And
again, it is the will that confers being as though it were the form. For an
external act performed without intent is not, from that standpoint, a true
moral act, but rather one that is feigned.

18. *To will to command, and to will not to bind, are incompatible
intentions, repugnant [to reason], unless ignorance is involved. Similarly, in
the case of vows, the intent to vow, and the intent not to bind [oneself], are
incompatible.* Wherefore, with respect to the example of the vow, it is
in my opinion certain that the said vow is not binding if it was made
without intent to bind; a point which I have brought out elsewhere
(*De Religione,* Tr. VI, chap. iii).[16] However, just as in the case of vows,
a situation is frequently conceived of, in which some one vows with the
intention of vowing and has at the same time the intention not to bind
himself, even so B. Medina conceives of a similar situation in the case
of a legislator who has the will to command and not to bind. Under

16. [Not included in these *Selections.*—Tr.]

those circumstances, says Medina, the legislator nevertheless does bind. However, unless ignorance is involved, such intentions are incompatible and involve a [mutual] contradiction, when the first intention is to vow, or to command, in very truth and not fictitiously. For willing to command is nothing more nor less than willing to bind, or at least, willing to indicate a will to bind; and the same is true in due proportion with respect to vows. If, on the other hand, the intention is not of the sort described, but is simply an intention to command or to vow outwardly, then doubtless the result is nil, and no true law is decreed, nor is any true vow made. For it is certain that a fictitious promise that does not bind can be made; but this sort of promise can occur in no other [than a fictitious] way. In due proportion, the same holds true of precepts; and therefore, if it were known to a subject that his superior had not the intention of binding, although he might give utterance to words of command, that subject would certainly not be bound; a point on which [the authorities] agree, with respect to the case of excommunication above mentioned. Again, and conversely, we have the words of St. Thomas, who says (II.–II, qu. 104, art. 2) that the will of a superior, in whatsoever fashion it may become known to his subject, is a kind of precept; a statement which cannot be understood save with reference to this will to bind.

19. *In the case of an oath there may exist, together with an intent to take the oath, the intent not to bind oneself.* In the case of oaths, however, the principle is not altogether the same. For it is possible that one may have the intention of taking an oath, that is, of calling God to witness, and may nevertheless intend not to bind himself; so that if, under such circumstances, an obligation does arise (and this is a debatable point), it results not from the personal will, but from the natural precept whereby every individual is bound to render true that statement which he has called upon God to witness. This fact I have elsewhere (*De Religione,* Tract. V, bk. II, chap. vii)[17] discussed at length.

On the other hand, the obligation imposed by the law cannot arise save from the will of the lawmaker; and therefore, an act of that will is necessary. Thus Gabriel has rightly said (on the *Sentences,* Bk. III, dist. xxxvii)

17. [Not included in these *Selections.*—Tr.]

that, howsoever well the will of a superior may be made known, no obligation results unless he wills that his inferior shall be bound by that will. But my assertion[18] contained this reservation: 'unless . . . there is some ambiguity in the wording.' For it may not be necessary that the lawmaker should conceive directly and expressly of the obligation of the subject and should be directed toward it by his will, since it may suffice if he intends, for example, to command that a given thing shall be of a given degree of importance, or that a particular act shall be part of the necessary subject-matter of temperance, or if he vaguely intends to command in so far as he is able. But these [modes of willing] involve only slight differences; since every one of them includes the intention to impose a binding obligation, and since [actually] intending not to bind is wholly repugnant to them all, unless the agent is absolutely ignorant of what he wills. And in that case, this ignorance itself would prevent the existence of an entirely true will to bind, or—consequently—of a true law; a point which I made in connexion with the similar matter of vows. In so far as concerns the necessity for such willing, then, this second opinion is undoubtedly the true one.

20. *The third opinion: affirming that law is composed of both acts.* The arguments which we have advanced in favour of [each of] these opinions, thus seem to indicate that the act of the intellect and that of the will are both necessary for law; so that a third opinion may be held, according to which law is composed and compacted of the acts of both faculties. For in these moral matters, one need not seek a perfect and simple unity; on the contrary, that which is morally a unity, may be composed of many elements that are physically distinct and that are of mutual aid. So it is, then, that for law there are two requisites: impulse and direction, or (so to speak), goodness and truth; that is to say, right judgment concerning the things that should be done and an efficacious will impelling to the performance of those things; and therefore, law may consist of both an act of the will and an act of the intellect.

This opinion, indeed, is usually attributed to Gregory of Rimini (on the *Sentences,* Bk. I, dist. xlviii [Bk. II, dist. xxxv,] only qu.). Nevertheless, he does not there discuss this matter, nor does he make any other statement

---

18. [*Vide* the first sentence of Section 17.—Tr.]

than that he who acts out of harmony with God's will and good pleasure, acts in opposition to the eternal law. In this connexion, Gregory cites Augustine's assertion (*Against Faustus,* Bk. XXII, chap. xxvii) that the eternal law is the reason or the will of God, an assertion in which Augustine lays down no definite decision [regarding the two faculties]. Gabriel (*ibid.,* Bk. III, dist. xxxvii, only qu., at beginning), more definitely upholds the opinion in question, when, after saying with regard to the external law (that is, with regard to law as it exists in the subject) that it is 'a true sign making known to the rational creature that right reason which dictates that he is bound, etc.', he declares that [the said law] 'is the dictum of him who dictates or binds, etc., for the purpose of indicating that the right reason of the one who commands, together with his will, is the basis of the binding obligation incumbent upon the inferior; that is to say, the force by which the inferior is bound'.[19] But the law is the true basis of the obligation; and therefore, Gabriel holds that in the prince himself the law is the reason of the prince combined with his will, and furthermore declares that this will is a will to bind the subject, as he has stated above.

Wherefore, just as free will is wont to be defined as a faculty of the will and of the reason, so law, which is customarily called the free will of the prince, may not improperly be considered an act of each of the two faculties.

21. It may also be added that, although the term law (*lex*) in its complete and adequate sense embraces both acts, nevertheless, from another standpoint, the act of the will and that of the intellect may each be spoken of as law, under diverse aspects. The words of Augustine in the passage above-cited (*Against Faustus*) are not out of harmony with this manner of speaking, and the passage is interpreted accordingly. For if one has in mind the moving force in law, so that law is said to be the power in the prince which moves and makes action obligatory, then, in that sense, it is an act of the will. If, on the other hand, we are referring to and considering that force in law which directs us toward what is good and necessary, then law pertains to the intellect. Moreover, it appears to consist in an

---

19. [This passage is a conflation of two passages in Gabriel Biel, *loc. cit.* The first passage is found in the paragraph, *Lex obligatoria.* The second is found in the paragraph, *Dicitur dictantis,* the two being in the same column, one at the beginning, the other near the end, of the edition referred to in the Index of Authors Cited.—REVISER.]

active judgment and—in so far as it exists within the prince—to follow upon, not to precede the will. To be sure, it appears to do so, not after the fashion of an impelling act that is not a judgment (a view which has been sufficiently disproved), but after the fashion of an active judgment in which the prince, having issued his decree, decides that a given act absolutely must be performed by the subjects, to whom the said decree should therefore be made known. For I have in the preceding Chapter expounded the fact that, in the mind of the prince, this judgment follows upon the willing; so that, in this sense, it may be said that the law is written in his mind, which is the source of every external law. The similar judgment which takes place within the subject will be (so to speak) a law derived from that law which exists within the prince.

22. *A definite judgment is laid down with regard to the whole controversy.* The opinions above set forth are credible, and the one last stated seems sufficiently acceptable, as well as reasonable. However, in order to pass some judgment on the question as a whole, we shall set aside the natural law, and therefore the eternal law, also, [for separate consideration,] since they involve a special difficulty with regard to this very point, namely: whether and in what way they have the true and proper nature of law; a matter of which we shall treat in the following Book.

The present controversy, then, simply concerns law as it is constituted through the will of some superior. With respect to this form of law, it is certain either, that it consists of an act of the reason and an act of the will or, at least, that it assuredly does not exist apart from both of them; in such wise that, if it consists of one of the two only, it is nevertheless intrinsically dependent upon the other. For this fact is proved by all the arguments adduced in support of the first two opinions.

23. From this, indeed, we draw a second inference, namely, that it is not possible to give efficacious proof with regard to the manner of speaking adopted for either of those opinions. For the evidence adduced in support of the first opinion proves merely that law is not made without the guidance of prudence. Therefore, when the philosophers cited in that connexion attribute law to the reason, they refer, not to an act of the intellect resulting in the prince from the will whereby he chooses to bind his subjects, but to a judgment which precedes, directs, and (as it were) regulates that will. For

the assertion made by them is simply that the will of the prince does not suffice to make law, unless it be a just and upright will; so that it must have its source in an upright and prudent judgment. As to this judgment, it is clearly not law, if it is considered in itself and as prior to the [act of] will. Accordingly, these philosophers call law right reason, having regard to its root; just as Cicero, *On Laws* (Bk. II, chap. iv), has said that virtue is the right reason of life.[20] However, the arguments advanced in defence of this opinion, have been answered in the process of confirming the second opinion. But the evidence adduced in support of the latter merely proves, strictly speaking, that the binding obligation imposed by law is derived from the will of the legislator. For this suffices in order that it may be said that he who observes God's law is doing God's will, or acting in accordance with that will; and it suffices also to allow of the converse assertions. However, the arguments set forth in behalf of this opinion are, to my mind, more convincing if we assume that law is that act of the prince which of itself and by its own force creates an obligation and binds the subject. It may, indeed, be objected that the term 'law' (*lex*) refers, not to a binding act, but to the sign of such an act, or to the act of the intellect from which the said sign is proximately derived.

24.[21] *The assertion that law is an act of the will, is better understood and upheld.* Wherefore, and thirdly, I add that, with regard to the essence of the matter, a more intelligible and more easily defensible assertion is this: law in its mental aspect (so to speak), as it exists in the lawmaker himself, is the act of a just and upright will, the act whereby a superior wills to bind an inferior to the performance of a particular deed. I find a proof of this assertion in the arguments advanced in support of the second opinion. For though such an act of the will cannot take effect in the subject unless it be sufficiently propounded to him, nevertheless this act of propounding is an application of the cause that creates obligation, rather than the true cause and basis of obligation.

25. *With respect to the application of the term,* 'law' (lex) *signifies primarily the external rule, and the sign [thereof], of the person commanding.* Lastly,

20. [The exact words of Cicero are: *Ratio profecta a natura, et ad recte faciendum impellens et a delicto avocans* (Reason derived from nature, urging men to right conduct and diverting them from wrongdoing).—REVISER.]

21. [Latin text incorrectly has '34'.—TR.]

however, I assert, with respect to the application of the term 'law' (*lex*), that it seems to have been used primarily to denote the external rule of the person commanding, and the sign making manifest his will. For it was in this sense that Aristotle (*Ethics,* Bk. X [, chap. ix, § 12]) declared law to be a rule emanating from a certain wisdom [etc.]; and that he elsewhere (*Rhetoric to Alexander*) speaks of it as the common wish of the people, set down in writing. Isidore, too, assumes this to be the case, when he says that *lex* is derived from *legendum* (that which is to be read, &c.), and should be in written form.

According to this acceptation of the term, then, one may well defend the view that law, as it exists within the prince, is that act of the intellect whereby he proximately dictates the external law, or that act which is by its very nature suitable for the dictation and manifestation of this [external law].

For, just as the external law is in a sense a proximate rule for the will of the subjects, even so, in due proportion, the law which is written (as it were) in the intellect of the prince, is a rule for this same will of the sub-ject, one from which the rule of external law is proximately derived when it is set forth to the subject. However, it is derived, as the saying goes, in the form of another intimation or impelling force; yet this intimation is nothing more nor less than the external locution that is directed and (so to speak) dictated by the intellect of the prince, through that judgment which his will has already approved, or in so far as that locution is derived from the said [intellectual] act as already defined and decreed through the volitional act of the same prince; a point which is made sufficiently clear by what we have said above.

CHAPTER VI

Is It Inherent in the Nature of Law That It Should Be Instituted for Some Community?

1. Having discussed the question of the general class in which law is to be placed, we should inquire into the distinguishing marks by virtue of which it acquires the [particular] nature of law. What these distinguishing marks are, we shall ascertain while explaining certain characteristic conditions

which are necessary to the true nature of law. And at the same time, we shall explain the causes of law, since the true and intrinsic conditions characterizing law can have no better source than those causes; neither can the said distinguishing marks be understood or explained, without reference to the subject-matter, object and end of law.

It is inherent in the nature of law that it should be instituted for certain beings. In the first place, then, as to the essential nature of law, it is clear that law is instituted for a certain being or certain beings; for, in the words of Paul (*Romans,* Chap. iii [, v. 19]): 'Now we know, that what things soever the law speaketh, it speaketh to them that are in the law.' Thus, law essentially implies a certain habitual relation (*habitudo*) to those upon whom it is imposed; and consequently, in order to explain the essential nature of law, it is necessary to make clear the terms of this relationship.

Human beings alone are capable of [subjection to] these laws. We assume, moreover, that law should be instituted for human beings, since inferior creatures are not capable of [subjection to] true law (which is the topic under consideration), as has often been remarked; for they are not capable of moral acts. And the angels, although they are capable of [subjection to] the divine law, are nevertheless not included within the range of our present discussion, as I said in the Preface. However, the statements which we shall make with respect to natural and divine law may easily be applied, in due proportion, to the angels.

Law as we are treating of it must, then, be imposed upon human beings; and accordingly, every law may in this sense be called human, as I have remarked above,[1] even though, to avoid ambiguity, it is not so called.

2. *Is it inherent in the nature of law that it should be instituted for some community?* These statements having been assumed to be true, there arises a doubt as to whether law can be instituted for one individual only, or whether it is inherent in the nature of law that it should be instituted for a multitude of men, or a community.

For we presume it to be a manifest fact that a human community is capable of [subjection to] laws and even stands in special need of them,

---

1. [*Supra,* pp. 50–52; *De Legibus,* Chap. iii, §§ 17–18.—Tr.]

since the arguments advanced in the preceding Chapter offer convincing proof of this assertion. Accordingly, it is also clear that, as a matter of regular and ordinary procedure, law is indeed instituted for some community, or multitude of men; a fact which is sufficiently evident through usage itself, and which will become still more manifest from what we have yet to say. The difficulty, then, consists in the question of whether or not the said fact is inherent in the nature of law.

The first and affirmative opinion. The first opinion as to this question is affirmative, namely, that only that precept is law which is instituted in general for all the persons included within a given community; whereas that precept which is imposed upon a single individual is not law. The foundation customarily adduced for this opinion is a passage in the *Decretum* (Pt. I, dist. IV, can. ii), taken from the *Etymologies* (Bk. I, chap. xxi [Bk. II, chap. x and Bk. V, chap. xxi]) of Isidore. In this passage, Isidore lays down various conditions for law and the last condition is, 'that it shall have been written for no private benefit, but for the common advantage of the citizens'. This text, however, does not provide a compelling argument, since it is one thing that a law should be imposed upon a community, and quite another, that it should be imposed for the good or the advantage of that community. For it may be that a precept is imposed upon a particular individual and is nevertheless imposed with a view to the common good. Thus, Isidore, in the passage cited, is laying down a necessary condition, not with respect to the person on whom the law is to be imposed, but with respect to the end on account of which it is to be imposed, namely, the common good. This condition I shall explain in the next Chapter.

3. It may be objected that the condition in question, if so interpreted, had already been included under another, laid down by Isidore in the same Chapter, the condition 'that law be just and righteous'; for law will not have these qualities, unless it is ordered for the common good.

But that objection is not valid; first of all, because many of the conditions that Isidore lays down in this Chapter are so related that one is included within another or inferred therefrom, and nevertheless all are added to the list for the sake of a more complete explanation. Thus, in the mere condition that law should be just, there are included the conditions that law should be [such that obedience] is possible and that it should be useful. For how will law be just, if [obedience thereto] is impossible, or useless? And nevertheless, these three conditions are separately enumerated.

Accordingly, with still more reason could this last condition have been added, in order to explain clearly the particular justice and rectitude which are required of law. For an act may be just and righteous, even if it be not directed to the common good; and it will suffice if such an act is not [positively] opposed to that good. But with respect to law, the additional requirement is made that, in order to be just, law must be ordered for the common good.

4. Neither, apparently, can there be any doubt as to the fact that this was Isidore's meaning [*Etymologies,* Bk. V, chap. xxi], as is evident from that adversative expression, 'written for no private benefit but for the common advantage of all'.[2] For it is not impossible that a law should be imposed upon the community, yet imposed for private benefit, since tyrannical laws are possessed of both characteristics simultaneously. But Isidore speaks of the two qualities above mentioned as if they were mutually opposed. Therefore, he is not speaking of the community upon which the law is to be imposed, but simply maintains that, on whomsoever it may be laid, the law must be imposed for the common advantage.

It is in this sense, too, that St. Thomas (I.–II, qu. 90, art. 2) has interpreted the statement of Isidore. For, in the body of the article cited the whole argument of St. Thomas tends towards a declaration that the intention of a lawgiver in making a law ought to be directed towards the common good, since the common happiness should be a measure, and as it were, a first principle, by means of which the justice, utility and fitness of a law are measured. Wherefore, he concludes: 'any other precept in regard to some individual work, must needs be devoid of the nature of a law, save in so far as it regards the common good. Therefore, every law is ordained to the common good.' In these words St. Thomas would seem to indicate that law may contain precepts of an individual nature, provided that these precepts be related to the final end of law. Moreover, this passage in the

---

2. [Suárez has *communi omnium utilitate* as translated above; but the text of Isidore, *Etymologies,* Bk. V, chap. xxi, has *communi civium utilitate* (the common advantage of the citizens).—Tr.]

text under discussion [*Decretum,* Pt. I, dist. IV, can. ii] was similarly understood by Archidiaconus, Dominicus de Sancto Geminiano, Torquemada and many persons to whom I shall refer in the next Chapter.

5. Secondly, this [first and affirmative] opinion is wont to be proved on the basis of a passage in the *Digest* (I. iii. 1) in which the statement is made that a law ought to be 'a common precept'. Nevertheless, the word 'common' is also ambiguous; for, as Jason (on that passage, in the beginning [*Digest, ibid.*]) notes, together with Fulgosius, law may be termed a common precept for three [distinct] reasons: first, because it has been instituted by the common consent or authority; secondly, because it should be common to all; thirdly, on the ground that it serves the common good. However, in the above-cited law of the *Digest,* it is not stated that the second mode of being common is necessary in an absolute sense to the nature of law, or of a common precept. Wherefore, the Gloss on that passage [*Digest, ibid.*] refers to these alternative interpretations: '[the precept] is common, that is to say, decreed for the common advantage, or given in common to the whole body.' Thus the first condition will suffice for the essence of law, even without the second.

Thirdly, the opinion in question may be proved from a passage in the *Decretals* (Bk. I, tit. II, chap. i) which says: 'Let the statutes of the canons be observed by all'; assuming, consequently, that they should be imposed upon all. This text, however, is greatly weakened by the Gloss on the passage [*Decretals, ibid.*]; for, to the word 'canons', it attaches the comment: 'general; for some canons are personal, and some are local.' Consequently, there would seem to be no doubt that the statement in question is to be interpreted with suitable discrimination, that is, interpreted as meaning that the canons are to be observed by all to whom they are addressed, or upon whom they are imposed. But as to whether there are always a number of such persons in the case of each canon, or whether it is possible that there should be a canon constituted for the purpose of binding one person only, that is a point not dealt with in this Gloss.

6. *The second opinion, which denies that it is inherent in the nature of law that it should be instituted for some community.* Therefore, there may be a second opinion according to which, it is not inherent in the nature of law that it be imposed upon a community or multitude of men, although it

may for the most part happen that law is thus instituted, since rules of conduct are ordinarily applicable to many persons in common. However, they may at times be constituted for this or that individual.

In behalf of this opinion, we may cite St. Thomas (I.–II, qu. 90, art. 2), in so far as he declares that an individual precept, when related to the common good, assumes the nature of law. Moreover, in the answer to the first objection, he brings out the same idea. And in answering the third objection, he lays down the general rule that a precept which is directed to the common good has the nature of law.

The Gloss (on *Digest,* I. iii. 1) upholds this view more expressly when it states that the law in question[3] does not provide a definition of the term 'law', since there is some law that is not common. The same opinion is evident in another Gloss (on *Decretals,* Bk. I, tit. ii, chap. i), wherein a distinction is made between general, and personal canons. Furthermore, this distinction occurs very frequently among the canonists as is clear from the words of Archidiaconus, Dominicus de Sancto Geminiano, and Torquemada (as cited above). The Gloss (on *Digest,* I. iii. 3) makes this same distinction, when it discriminates between law in general and special law (*ius*), declaring that the former is imposed upon the multitude, while the latter may be private. Other Glosses (on *Code,* X. xxxii (xxxi). 61 and 63) contain similar statements. Arguments [in defence of this negative opinion] may be based, first, on the two laws cited above [*Code, ibid.*]. For they are true laws, and nevertheless, they are decreed for certain special individuals. Secondly, the said opinion would seem to be expressly laid down in a law of the *Digest* (I. iv. 1, § 2), as follows: 'Of these (namely, these laws), some are personal.' Moreover, the same view is set forth in the *Institutes* (I. ii, § 6, word *Plane*). A third argument is the fact that the canons also distinguish private from public law, maintaining that the former should be imposed upon private persons, and the latter, upon the community. This we infer from two chapters of the canon law (*Decretals,* Bk. III, tit. xxxi, chap. xviii; and more extensively, *Decretum,* Pt. II, causa xix, qu. ii, can. ii).

3. [I.e. *Digest,* Book I, tit. iii, law 1, referring to the statement that law is a common precept. Cf. the first sentence of Section 5.—Tr.]

7. This [negative] opinion is confirmed by reasoning. Finally, this [negative] opinion may be confirmed by reasoning. In the first place, it is reasoned that a just precept may be imposed upon a single subject, for the sake of the common good, and by virtue of the power to rule the commonwealth and its individual members; hence, such a precept will be of the same essential nature as a precept imposed upon many or upon all the members of that community; and therefore, it will be a true law. The proof of the first consequent is the fact that, with respect to the essence of a precept, it would seem to be an extraneous circumstance that this precept should be imposed upon one person only, or upon many; just as it is an extraneous circumstance in the case of heat that it should exist in one subject or in many, and extraneous in the case of speech that it should be addressed to one, or to many. The second consequent is proved as follows: the precept in question, if it were imposed upon many, would be law; therefore, it is also [law, when imposed] upon one individual, since it has indeed been proved to be of the same nature [in both instances]. And it can happen that this precept is imposed upon one individual and not upon many persons, owing simply to the fact that the necessity for it is found to exist in only one individual.

Secondly, one may reason thus: law is the rule of the moral actions of man, as has often been said; and not only the human community, but also individual men have need of this rule; therefore, law *per se* implies a relationship not with the human community, exclusively, but also with individual human beings.

Thirdly, law is made with reference to a person, and consequently with reference to a true person, not less than to a fictitious one; but on the contrary much more so, for a fiction always presupposes the truth which it imitates; and a community is a fictitious person, whereas an individual human being is a true person; therefore, an individual person is not less capable [of being the subject] of law than is a community.

Fourthly, when a law is established for a community, either it binds only the community, as such, or else it binds also the individual members of that community. The first alternative is not necessarily the true one; nor is such ordinarily the situation, as is self-evident. Furthermore, even if it were, then the community would be as an individual person, whence one would again conclude that a law may be made with respect to one person only. If, on the other hand, the second alternative is held to be true, from this fact, also, one would infer that it is possible for a law to be made for a single individual, if it is appropriate in regard to him and necessary only for him.

8. *Preference is given to the opinion according to which it is inherent in the nature of law that it be made for a community.* This controversy may depend, to a large extent, on the use of the term ['common']. However, the absolute statement should be made that it is inherent in the nature of law, as signified by this name, that it be a common precept; that is to say, a precept imposed upon the community, or upon a multitude of men.

This is the assumption made by Isidore and St. Thomas (as cited above, and in other places to be mentioned later). It is the teaching, too, of Panormitanus (on *Decretals,* rubric of Bk. I, tit. II), of Felinus (on *Decretals,* Bk. I, tit. II, chap. vi, no. 5), and of Jason and Fulgosius (on *Digest,* I. iii. I). For though they say that law may be termed a common precept in its habitual relationship (*habitudo*) to him who makes it, to the end for which it is made, and to those upon whom it is imposed, they nevertheless give sufficient indication[4] that law, in the proper sense of the term, requires these three elements in conjunction, rather than separately. Antonio Gómez has expressed the same opinion in a passage (on *Tauri.,* Law I, no. 5) where he lays down as a requisite for the nature of law the stipulation that it must be common, rather than particular, with reference to a given person. Other authorities, to whom we shall refer below, and in the following Chapter, have expressed themselves similarly.

9. This contention may be proved, first, by a certain process of induction. For the eternal and natural law are sufficiently common in character, as is clearly evident; the divine law, also (both Old and New) was laid down for communities: the Old Law for the Jewish people; the New for the Catholic Church and the entire world. And not only the law as a whole, but also its individual precepts, have been laid down generally. This is not to say that such individual precepts are laid down for each and every member of the community, since that is not necessary, nor is it

---

4. [Reading *indicant* for *indicat.*—Tr.]

pertinent to the nature of law; rather, it is to say that, even though there have been imposed, among the common precepts, laws which are binding upon such and such particular members, according to their [respective] functions and capacity, these laws are nevertheless always laid down in a general and common form. Furthermore, even the divine precept imposed upon Adam in the state of innocence was imposed not upon him solely and personally, but upon him as the head of all nature; and it would have endured always in that state, binding all persons, so that, to this extent, it had the true nature of law. A proof of this contention is the fact that, although God imposed the precept upon Adam alone, before He formed Eve (as related in *Genesis,* Chap. ii), nevertheless, Eve also was bound thereby (as is evident from Chapter iii of that same Book).

The precept that God imposed upon Abraham concerning the sacrifice of his son cannot, however, be said to be law, in the proper sense of the term, but must be termed [simply] a command in accordance with the usual manner of speaking.

10. With regard to the civil law, indeed, this point would seem to be made sufficiently manifest in a passage of the *Digest* (I. iii. 8). For there we find the statement: 'Laws are made, not for individual persons, but in general terms.' Proof of the same view, in connexion with canon law also, may be derived from a chapter of the *Decretum* already cited (Pt. II, causa XIX, qu. ii, can. ii), in that this chapter contains the assertion that the canons and decrees laid down by the Fathers are public laws. Moreover, the private law which is also mentioned in that passage is not canonical law, but one of a very different nature, as we shall observe. So it is, too, that Gregory IX, in the Preface to his *Decretals,* makes the following statement: '[. . .] law (*lex*) is promulgated for this reason, that the evil appetite may be restrained under the rule of *ius,* through which rule, humankind is instructed that it may live [. . .] righteously.' Aristotle, also, has said, in the *Ethics* (Bk. VI [, chap. viii]), that the faculty or prudence required for lawmaking is architectonic, or regal, since the principal act of this prudence is the making of laws, as St. Thomas (II.–II, qu. 50, art. 1, ad 3) has declared. Moreover, the said prudence looks to the community and is concerned therewith, so that law (according to the opinion of Aristotle) also looks to the community. Thus Aristotle has asserted (*Art of Rhetoric,*

Bk. I, chap. iv [, § 12]) that, 'it is on the laws that the safety of the State is based'. Again (*Rhetoric to Alexander,* Preface), he has said that law is, 'reason as defined by the common consent of the State', &c., assuming that it is established for the direction of that same community. Plato (*Laws*) often repeats this assertion; and all the philosophers express themselves similarly. Accordingly, Biesius (*De Republica,* Bk. IV [, section *Leges*]) says that, 'Laws are public precepts of life which it behoves all persons to obey at all times', &c. Therefore, according to the common usage of the laws (*iura*), the jurists and the sages, there is no doubt that the word 'law' (*lex*) refers to a public precept, imposed upon some community and not simply upon one or another single individual.

11. *The same opinion is more fully confirmed in the light of the [other] properties of law.* The foregoing may be further demonstrated in the light of the other properties of law. One of these is that law should be perpetual, as we shall show below;[5] yet a precept for one person only cannot possess this attribute, since such a person is not perpetual; whereas the community is perpetual, at least through a process of succession so that, in relation to the community, law in the true sense is possible. Neither is it of any consequence that even a precept imposed upon the community may be temporary. For this fact gives rise, at most, to the conclusion that not every precept imposed upon a community is law; a point which we shall consider later, but which does not interfere with the necessity that every law should be imposed upon the community, if it is to be perpetual. The same truth may be established by assuming that this perpetuity exists with respect [also] to the lawmaker. For it is inherent in the nature of law that it shall not depend upon the life of the lawmaker, as we shall demonstrate below;[6] and this condition can exist only in the case of laws that are common, since an individual precept, imposed solely upon a single individual, lapses with the death of the person who lays down the precept, or it lapses when that person has been removed from his office, as common opinion and custom testify. The reason for this is a matter of which we shall treat

5. [Suárez has reference to chap. x of Bk. I of *De Legibus,* which is not included in these *Selections.*—Tr.]

6. [Suárez discusses this point in *De Legibus,* Bk. I, chap. x, §§ 9 *et seq.,* which chapter is not included in these *Selections.*—Tr.]

below.[7] Neither has it any bearing upon the point under discussion, if a precept decreed for the community is annulled by the death of him who lays down the precept, provided (as I shall point out, later[8]) that this precept is not laid down in the form of a law. For from this annulment, it would follow merely that not every precept imposed upon a community is law; and this is in agreement with the assumption that a law ought to have that perpetuity and that independence of the person imposing it, which it does not have unless it is a precept imposed upon a community.

It will be objected that such an assumption is applicable only in the case of human laws; since in the case of divine laws, whether natural or positive, the Lawmaker cannot pass away or suffer change, and since such laws depend always upon Him in regard to their institution and persistence, [so that their perpetuity is not dependent upon the perpetuity of those subject to them]. I reply that this objection is without force. For it is in view of this fact—namely, that divine laws have clearly been laid down for the community—that we have accordingly made the additional observation above set forth,[9] regarding human laws, in order to make it clear that every precept, whether human or divine, possessed of the stability which law by its very nature requires, is to be considered as relating to some community.

Thus the precept imposed by the paterfamilias upon his slaves, or even his children, or indeed, his whole household, is not law, as St. Thomas declares (I.–II, qu. 90, art. 3, ad 3); either because it has not been instituted for a sufficient community, again as St. Thomas asserts in that same passage, or else because it has not been instituted by means of a true compulsory authority, this being necessary for [the constitution of] law, a fact that is pointed out by Aristotle (*Ethics,* Bk. X, last chapter [, § 12]).

12. Finally, proof of the opinion in question may be drawn from another attribute of law, namely, the fact that law is the rule and measure of an action from the standpoint (so to speak) of its subject-matter and of the mean of virtue. For in this sense, law is said to be the rule of the just and of the unjust, as I have noted above,[10] referring to Basil and to other authorities. And in like manner, that which is laid down by means of law

7. See note 6.
8. See note 6.
9. [I.e. in the immediately preceding paragraph.—Tr.]
10. [*Supra,* p. 66; *De Legibus,* Bk. I, chap. v, § 3.—Tr.]

is called by Aristotle (*Ethics,* Bk. V, chap. i), legitimate or legal justice, as St. Thomas has observed (I.–II, qu. 90, art. 2). Law, then, is a kind of rule establishing or pointing out, in regard to its own subject-matter or the operation with which it is concerned, that mean which is to be preserved for the sake of right and fitting action; and this rule is in itself universal, having relation to all persons, in due proportion; therefore, law is in itself general, and consequently, in order that any law may be law in a true and perfect sense, it must possess this characteristic.

If, on the other hand, there are certain precepts which do not possess it, either they are not laws at all, or else—assuming that they are considered as being laws—they are thus considered to the extent that they do in some wise partake of the said characteristic. We may also add that it pertains to this general or common character of law that the latter shall be instituted universally, without regard for persons and without unjust exceptions, as is indicated in the *Decretals* (Bk. I, tit. ii, chap. vi). Many expressions, too, in the laws there cited would seem to point to the same conclusion, presupposing the existence of the first conditions, or universality of law, and adding this last condition as necessary to the justice of law, a matter concerning which we shall speak a little later.[11]

13. *The contrary opinion is refuted by means of arguments.* However, the foregoing explanation may be expanded by answering the arguments which have been advanced [to the contrary].

Of these, the arguments first set forth are easily disposed of. For we admit, with respect to the first, that Isidore and St. Thomas, in the passages cited, did not seek to treat directly of the condition in question; rather, they assumed its existence. Accordingly, the same St. Thomas, when expounding a passage in Aristotle (*Commentary on Ethics,* Bk. V, chap. i, lect. 2) which he also cites in the article above mentioned [I.–II, qu. 90, art. 2] says, more clearly, that those things are called legally just, which are productive of happiness in relation to the political community for which the law was established. In this passage, he is speaking of human law, but the same reasoning applies, in due proportion, to the remaining forms of law. With respect to the other laws, and the objections brought

---

11. [*Infra,* p. 116; *De Legibus,* Bk. I, chap. ix.—Tr.]

against them, our reply is that, though the words are not in themselves so convincing but that they may be weakened through some interpretation or evasion, nevertheless, when taken in conjunction with different laws and with the interpretations of wise authorities, they possess considerable force for the confirmation of the truth above set forth.

14. We turn, then, to the reply to the later arguments.

First, with respect to St. Thomas, we assert that in the passages cited from his works, he never excludes the condition which we are discussing, and that he speaks of the individual precept not in relation to the person upon whom it is imposed but in relation to the particular deed with regard to which it is established. As to this deed, he declares that it must contribute to the common good, and that, if the precept laid down for the deed does possess this quality, it will have the nature of law—provided, at least, that it possesses the other characteristics required for law.

With respect to the Gloss, however, and the remarks of other Doctors therein cited, our reply is that these should be interpreted or admitted in accordance with the laws to which those Doctors allude, and that if they intended to convey some other meaning, their opinion is not to be approved. Thus, in regard to the two laws of the *Code* (X. xxxii. 61 and 63), it is true that in a certain sense they deal with the welfare of private individuals named in them; but nevertheless, in so far as they involve any command, they are instituted not for those individual persons but for the community and for all persons who are subject to the lawmaker, persons whom they bind to the observance of a particular immunity enjoyed by the aforesaid individuals. And in like manner, we shall explain in Book VIII[12] that a privilege, although it may seem to be of an individual nature, can have the character of law. I add, furthermore, that in the case of the laws under discussion a favour is granted not only to the individual persons therein named but also to their successors in perpetuity, so that these laws partake of a perpetual and common quality; for the families involved might have constituted a large portion of the community and possibly a portion of the most important group. Accordingly, the laws in question, in spite of the fact that they may appear to be special when viewed in one

---

12. [Not included in these *Selections.*—Tr.]

aspect, are in their own way general, even though they are never established save by way of constituting a privilege, as is evident from usage.

15. To the second argument, drawn from law 1 and section 1,[13] I reply that laws of privilege are there called personal, being so designated by reason of the proximate advantage toward which they are directed; while they nevertheless do relate to the community in a certain sense, that is, with respect to the persons for whom they lay down a command; a point which we have just explained, and shall discuss more at length when treating of privileges.[14]

What private law is; and why it is so called.[15] The reply to the third argument is this: the term 'private law' is to be taken, in those canons, in a very different sense. For the name 'private law' is therein given, either to a vow made by the special inspiration of the Holy Ghost, or to the divine inspiration itself through which man is specifically called to some higher good. This appellation is metaphorical; for such 'law' is not law, in the proper sense and of the kind which we are now discussing. Rather, it is so called because it is written in the heart and partakes of some of the effects of law, as we have said elsewhere in treating of vows.[16]

16. As for [the argument drawn from] reasoning, the reply is easily made on the basis of the foregoing remarks.

Law and precept are not interchangeable. What is in law that is not in precept; and how the two differ. For, with respect to the first reason adduced, it is evident from those remarks, that precept and law are not interchangeable; since, though every law is a precept, not every precept is a law. On the contrary, a law must satisfy certain special conditions, among which is the requirement that it shall be a common precept, in the sense expounded above.[17] Furthermore, in so far as the moral aspect is concerned, it is not necessary to inquire minutely as to whether precept and law are essentially

---

13. [I.e. *Digest,* I. iv. 1, § 2.—TR.]

14. [Suárez also discusses privilege in Bk. I, chap. viii of the *De Legibus,* which chapter is not included in these *Selections.* He touches on this subject in chapter vii, *infra,* pp. 111 *et seq.*—TR.]

15. [In the Latin, this subheading appears opposite the end of Section 14.—TR.]

16. [Suárez's treatise on vows is not included in these *Selections.*—TR.]

17. [*Supra,* p. 86; § 5 of this Chapter.—TR.]

distinct; since, [from the moral standpoint,] granting that they may not be physically distinct with respect to the natural species of acts involved, it is sufficient that they should be distinct morally, or (as it were) in their artificial being. For law is (so to speak) a certain artificial product resulting from a given act with the accompaniment of given circumstances, conditions or habitual relations, without which it is not true law, even though it may be of the same nature with respect to the act of commanding. It may also be added that legislation, with reference to the act of prudence from which it proceeds and the righteousness which characterizes it as it issues from the legislator, possesses a special kind of virtue distinct from that of an individual and private precept, so that, in this sense, it may be called law, being thus rendered essentially distinct from a private mandate.

17. *In what sense law is said to be common, and instituted for the community.* To the first confirmation, we reply that it is true that law implies a relationship with individual persons, in so far as they are parts of the community upon which the law is imposed as a rule of action, so to speak.

The reply to the second confirmation is this: law is called general, not because it is necessarily imposed upon the community as a community and as a mystical body; but because it should be propounded in general terms, such that it may apply to each and every person, in accordance with the exigencies of the subject-matter, in which sense it is true that law is instituted as a rule for persons who are real, not simply fictitious. It should be added, indeed, with regard to the third confirmation, that ordinarily law is framed for the community not collectively, but distributively, that is to say, framed to the end that it may be observed by each and every member of the community, in the proper distribution, according to the nature of the law; for this provision is always implied.

However, a law may sometimes be established for the community itself, viewed as such; that is to say, it may be established by forbidding or prescribing an act which can be performed only by the community acting as a community; a fact which is made evident by the statutes of various societies, universities, [cathedral] chapters, colleges, &c., providing for certain points in connexion with the public and common acts of that mystical body. For such laws are true laws, provided that they satisfy the other requisite conditions, even though their commands be laid upon one individual community only, if that community is a perfect one; as I shall presently explain.[18] This is true because, in the first place, although it may be called a fictitious person, it is a community in an absolute sense, has the perpetuity required of law, and relates directly to the common good. Secondly, moreover, the individual members of that community are always bound through such a law to refrain from operating or co-operating in opposition to it.

18. *Of what nature a community must be, in order that it may be capable of [subjection to] law in the strict sense.* But some one will inquire, and not without reason, what must be the nature of a community that is capable of [subjection to] law in the strict sense.

I reply briefly that different kinds of community suffice or are required in accordance with different kinds of law.

How many different kinds of community there are. In the first place, then, a distinction may be made with respect to communities. For there is a certain natural form of community, brought about solely through the conformity [of its members] in rational nature. Of this sort is the community of humankind, which is found among all men. Another form, however, may be termed the political or mystical community, constituted through a special conjunction in the case of a group that is morally a unit. The natural law relates to the former type of community, this law being revealed to every man by the light of reason; since it is established, not for any one individual as such (not because he is Peter, for example), but for each person as a human being. This observation may be made in regard both to the purely natural law, and to the supernatural law, in so far as the latter is connatural to grace.

The latter form of community may be subdivided.

For certain [examples of it] may be thought of as additions to nature, yet brought about not by human but by divine law, in that they have been established by God Himself, under some head designated by Him, and with a unity directed toward some supernatural end. In former times, the Jewish synagogue was a community of this kind; and now, a much more perfect example is the Catholic Church, which was founded not for

18. [*Infra*, p. 99; § 21 of this Chapter.—TR.]

one or another people but for the whole world, by Christ Himself, under one and the same faith, which was to be professed through certain signs established by Christ and under obligation of obedience to one [visible] head to whom He Himself entrusted His representation upon earth. For this sort of community, then, positive divine laws are by their very nature primarily made. For example, the Old Law was given to the Jewish people, and the law of grace, for the Universal Church. Canon laws, too, are made for this same body, though not all of them are established for the Universal Church at large; rather, they are established in accordance with the intent or the power of the person who decrees them, as we shall see later.[19]

19. In addition to these forms of the community, there is that which has been humanly assembled or devised, and which is spoken of as a gathering of men who are united under the bond of some law. Examples may be drawn from the *Digest* (XII. i. 27) and from the *Decretals* (Bk. V, tit. xxxi, chap. xiv), and the Gloss thereon. These passages make it clear that a multitude of men does not suffice to constitute a community, unless those men are bound together by a particular agreement, looking toward a particular end, and existing under a particular head.

So, also, Aristotle has said (*Politics,* Bk. III, chap. x [chap. ix]) that a state is a multitude of citizens who have, indeed, a mutual bond of a moral nature. This kind of community, moreover, is wont to be divided by the moral philosophers and the jurists into perfect and imperfect. A perfect community is in general defined as one which is capable of possessing a political government; and this [type of community], in so far as it is such, is said to be self-sufficient within that [political] order. Thus Aristotle (*ibid.,* Bk. I, chap. i) and St. Thomas (I.–II, qu. 90, art. 2) have asserted that the city state is a perfect community, and that, *a fortiori,* a kingdom or any other higher body or community of which the city state is a part will be a perfect community. For there may be a certain latitude in [the definition of] these communities, and even though individual ones, viewed in themselves, may be perfect, nevertheless that community which is part of another is in this respect imperfect; not in an absolute sense, but comparatively or relatively speaking. Again, among the communities in question,

---

19. [*Infra,* p. 124; *De Legibus,* Bk. I, chap. ix, § 9.—Tr.]

some are called real or local, because they are enclosed within certain real or local boundaries, as in the case of a city state or of a kingdom; while others are called personal, because they are considered in connexion with persons rather than with localities; as in the case of any religious community, for example, or confraternity, or similar group, which may also be perfect communities if they have perfect government and a moral unity. On this [personal kind of community], one may consult the jurists (*Digest,* III. iv. 1 *et seq.*[20] and XLVII. xxii).

20. *What is an imperfect community?* The term 'imperfect community' may, indeed, be applied not simply in a relative but in an absolute sense to a private household over which there presides the paterfamilias. This possibility has been noted by St. Thomas (I.–II, qu. 90, art. 3, ad 3) and by Soto (thereon; and *De Iustitia,* Bk. V [Bk. I], qu. i, art. 2) and it may be inferred from Aristotle, in the passage quoted above.

One reason, to be sure, is that such a community is not self-sufficient, as we shall presently explain. A further reason is that in such a household the individuals are not united as the principal members for the composition of one political body, but merely exist therein as inferiors destined for the uses of the master, and to the extent that they are, in some sense, under his dominion. Therefore, a community of this sort, *per se* and within its proper limits, is governed not by a true power of jurisdiction but by the power of dominion, so that it partakes, according to the diversity of dominions, of diverse kinds of command with regard to diverse [persons]. For there is one right, or dominion, so to speak, held by the paterfamilias over his wife; another, over his children; and another, over his servants or slaves. Consequently, neither [a private household] possesses a perfect unity or uniform power, nor indeed, does it enjoy a truly political government; and therefore, such a community is called imperfect, without qualification.

21. *Human laws ought to be framed only for perfect communities.* Accordingly, this distinction having been assumed to exist, it should be stated that human laws may properly be laid down for any perfect community, but not for one that is imperfect.

---

20. [Suárez cites this title of the *Digest* as: *Quid cuiusque universalitatis,* &c., while Krueger's edition of the *Digest* gives the title as: *Quod cuiuscumque universitatis.*—Tr.]

The first part of this statement is proved by the fact that every perfect community is a true political body, governed by means of its own jurisdiction, which has a coercive force that is legislative. Furthermore, the precepts and rules of living propounded for such a community, if they fulfil the other conditions required for law, may constitute legal justice and the mean to be observed in every matter of virtue befitting the said community; and therefore, these rules or precepts will have the true nature of law. Finally, even as that community is perfect, just so a precept imposed upon it may in an absolute sense be called a common precept, and therefore, a law.

22. The second part [of the same statement] is suggested with sufficient force in Aristotle's *Ethics* (Bk. X, last chapter) and by a passage in St. Thomas (I.–II, qu. 90, art. 3, ad 3), in that these authorities maintain that a community consisting of one household is not sufficient [as a source] for law, in the proper sense of the term. The reason supporting this doctrine may be drawn from Aristotle's argument that there is not found, in such a community, the true jurisdiction, nor the coercive force, required in the case of a true lawgiver. The reason, in turn, on which this contention is based, is the quasi-natural imperfection of that community, inasmuch as the latter is not in itself sufficient to attain human happiness in the mode in which such happiness is humanly attainable. Or, to put the matter more clearly, the parts of the said community do not furnish one another sufficient support or mutual aid, such as human society requires for its own ends or its own preservation; consequently, this kind of community is subordinated—naturally, as it were—to a perfect community, as the part is subordinated to the whole; and therefore, legislative power dwells, not in such a community, but only in one that is perfect. This reasoning properly refers to civil laws, but may be applied in due proportion to those which are ecclesiastical; since ecclesiastical legislative power, although it is derived not from the community but from Christ, is nevertheless communicated and distributed to the human community, in a fitting and properly proportioned manner.

23. *Objection.* An objection to the foregoing remarks will, however, be raised. For it follows from what has been said that law in the true sense of the term cannot be established [even] in a perfect community,

if it is established solely for a particular part of that community; but this would seem to be a false deduction; therefore, . . . The inference is clearly true, because a decree relating to a single household or an imperfect community is not law, since that imperfect community forms part of one that is perfect; and therefore, the same will be true of any part of a city state, for it, too, is an imperfect community and part of a perfect community. The minor premiss, indeed, is proved by the fact that it is not proper to the nature of law to be binding upon all the members of a state; therefore, it may be binding [only] upon a part of them, and nevertheless be true law.

With respect to this point, some jurists assert that law made by the prince in order to bind one part of the state—for example, a fourth part only—is not a true law and has no binding force. So Angelus de Ubaldis has declared; and he has been quoted and followed by Jason (on *Digest* I. iii. 1, no. 2), who bases his opinion solely on the principle that a law should be a common precept.

24. *Solution.* Nevertheless, I reply that it is one thing to speak of such a law from the standpoint of its justice or injustice, that is, its regard for persons, and another thing, to speak of it from the standpoint of the lack of an adequate community on which it may be imposed.

For we are not treating, at present, of the former question; though even in that respect we cannot say that the said law is intrinsically bad, or unjust; since there may exist at times a sufficient cause and reason for imposing a burden upon one part [of the community], and not upon another part, either on account of the site and location, because the state has need of the service in question in that particular part, or on account of the condition of the particular persons involved, as is clear from the laws of taxation.

The second question, however, is pertinent at this point. With regard to that question, we assert that it is not inherent in the nature of law that it should necessarily be made for the entire community taken as a whole, so to speak. For there may reside in a portion of that whole, a community that is in itself sufficient, and a basis that is sufficient, for the perpetuity of a law and for the derivation of the latter from a political jurisdiction pertaining directly to the common government.

Moreover, this may occur in various ways. In the first place, it may occur if a law is made with respect to a particular function or employment, with the result that it applies to particular workmen, and to no other persons. Secondly, it may occur if the law is made for persons of a certain kind or condition—for example, plebeians or nobles, descendants of the Hebrews, converts from among the Saracens, or any group of a similar nature. Thirdly, the law may be made in behalf of the inhabitants of a given part or quarter of the city state and not for any other persons, in such a way that it is enacted, not only with reference to those who are at the time residing in the said regions, but in perpetuity, to the end that it may endure for all their descendants without distinction.

For any one of these modes of generality will suffice to satisfy the essential requirements of law, provided that the requirements of justice are observed: since the first mode is absolutely general, within its proper field of distribution; the second partakes of the same general nature, if we assume that its range of application is just; while the third is also impartial by its very nature with respect to all persons, since it is not impossible for any one to dwell in the region specified. And similar arguments may be applied to any other law of this kind.

CHAPTER VII

Is It Inherent in the Nature of Law That It Be Enacted for the Sake of the Common Good?

1. The other characteristic conditions of law depend largely upon this characteristic.[1] We have therefore given it the second place [in our discussion of the said conditions], in spite of the fact that Isidore placed it last. Moreover, we shall at the same time explain the intrinsic end of law.

It is inherent in the nature of law that it be enacted for the common good. With respect, then, to the question above set forth, there is no dispute among the various authorities; on the contrary, this axiom is common to them all: it is inherent in the nature and essence of law, that it shall

---

1. [I.e. upon the characteristic, suggested in the chapter title, that law must be enacted for the sake of the common good.—Tr.]

be enacted for the sake of the common good; that is to say, that it shall be formulated particularly with reference to that good. So St. Thomas maintains, in a passage (I.–II, qu. 90 [, art. 2]) commented upon by Cajetan, Conrad Koellin, and other modern authorities; and also, by Soto (*De Iustitia*, Bk. I, qu. i, art. 2), Castro (*De Potestate Legis Poenalis*, Bk. I, chap. i), Antoninus (*Summa Theologica*, Pt. I, tit. XI, chap. ii, § I and tit. XVII, § 3), as well as all the Summists on the word *lex*. Navarrus, too (in his commentary *On Ends*, No. 28), brings out this point well; as does Gregory López (on *Las Siete Partidas*, Pt. I, tit. i, law 9), in which latter passage Alfonso, King of Spain, requires that his own laws shall fulfil this very condition. The same view is held, moreover, by all the commentators on civil law (*Digest*, I. iii. 1), who assert that law should be 'a common precept', that is to say, one 'established for the common advantage', as the Gloss on the above-cited law of the *Digest* explains. Bartolus, Jason, and others follow the Gloss on this point. Isidore (as cited in *Decretum*, Pt. I, dist. IV, can. ii) has set forth the doctrine more clearly, as I have explained in the preceding Chapter; and he is followed by the other canonists thereon.

2. Furthermore, the same truth may be inferred from the words of Aristotle, who says (*Ethics*, Bk. III, chap. vi [*Politics*, Bk. III, chap. ix, 1280 A]) that the end of the state is to live well and happily. Accordingly, he adds [*ibid.*, 1280 B]: 'Those who have a care for the good government of the state, engage in public deliberation on virtue and vice';[2] of course, by means of laws. Thus Aristotle subsequently (*ibid.*, Bk. IV, chap. i, 1289 A) declares that, 'The laws should be adapted to the commonwealth, and not the commonwealth to the laws'. Similarly, Marsilio Ficino, in connexion with the argument of Plato's dialogue, *Minos*, draws from the latter's opinion (as it is expressed both there, and in the works on *Laws* and on the *Republic*) the following description of law: 'It is the true essence of government, and guides that which is governed to the best end, through fitting means.' Furthermore, Plato, in this same dialogue [*Minos*, 314 D], calls that law noble, which establishes that which is right, in matters (*ordine*) of state and

---

2. [A translation of the original Greek of Aristotle reads: 'Those who care for good government take into consideration the question of virtue and vice in states.'—TR.]

in the plan of government.[3] Again in the dialogue, *Hippias,* or *The Beautiful* (shortly after the beginning [284 D]), he says: 'In my opinion, indeed,
law is established for the sake of its utility, and legislators give law as the
greatest good to the state; for, if law is removed, we are unable to live legitimately in a state.' In the work *Laws,* too (Bk. I [631]), Plato demonstrates
at length that, 'laws are established for the sake of virtue' and in order to
promote the common peace and happiness. Cicero (*Laws,* Bk. III) makes
the same point in a very full discussion. And Plutarch (*Problemata* in 40)
declares that, of all the things within a state, goodness of laws is to be
deemed the most excellent for this reason, namely, that such laws work
most to the common good.

3. This truth is indeed self-evident in the case of divine laws; so that it
does not call for demonstration. For though the said laws are necessarily
directed to the honouring of God (since He cannot will anything apart
from Himself, or act save for His own sake), nevertheless in those laws
He seeks not His own profit, but the good and happiness of humanity. Wherefore, since the divine works are superlatively perfect, and of a
finely proportioned suitability, divine laws, in so far as they are given to a
particular community, are accordingly given with a view to the common
good and felicity of that community; a fact which becomes easily evident
through a process of induction, with respect both to natural law and to
the positive divine laws. Neither is there any force in the objection that
through these laws God frequently provides for the private welfare of this
or that individual; as when through the law of penance He provides for
the salvation of the sinner himself, and as in other cases. This objection, I
repeat, has no force. For, in the first place, the good of private individuals
(as I shall shortly point out in greater detail) forms a part of the common
good, when the former is not of a nature to exclude the latter good; being
rather such that it is a necessary requisite in individuals—by virtue of the
law in question as it is applied to individuals—in order that the common
good may result from this good enjoyed by private persons. Moreover,
and in the second place, the divine laws relate principally to eternal bliss,
which is in itself a common good, and which is striven after, essentially

3. [This is a rather loose paraphrase of Plato's words.—Tr.]

and for its own sake, by every individual without regard to any community other [than the eternal]. Wherefore, St. Thomas has said (*Summa,* Pt. I, qu. 23, art. 7 and qu. 98, art. 1) that the multiplication of human souls, even though it results only in a difference in their number, is not simply an incidental effect, but one that is sought for its own sake in view of the immortality of those souls and their capacity for happiness.

4. With respect to human laws, indeed, of whatsoever order, the reason [supporting the conclusion set forth in Section 2] may be inferred from the essential condition of law discussed in the preceding [chapter]. For just as laws are imposed upon a community, so should they be made principally for the good of that community, since otherwise, they would be inordinate. This is true because it would be contrary to every consideration of rectitude that the common good should be subordinated to the private good, or the whole accommodated to a part for the sake of the latter; and therefore, since law is made for a community, it should of its very nature be directed primarily to the good of the community.

Again, an excellent argument may be deduced in connexion with the ends [of law]. For ends should be in due proportion to acts, and to the original principles of and faculties pertaining to those acts; but law is the common rule of moral operations; consequently, the first principle of moral operations should also be the first principle of law; but their final end—that is to say, happiness—is the first principle of moral actions, since in moral matters the end to be attained is the principle of action, so that the final end is [also] the first principle of such acts; and the common good, or happiness of the state, is the final end of that state, in its own sphere; hence, this common good should be the first principle of [human] law; and therefore, law should exist for the sake of the common good. This reasoning is very nearly the same as the reasoning of St. Thomas (I.–II, qu. 90, art. 2); and it finds excellent illustration through the teachings of St. Augustine, where (*On the City of God,* Bk. XIX, chap. xvi) he infers from the due relationship of the part to the whole, and of one household to the state (of which, as he says, [the household] is the beginning or minute element), that domestic peace is related to civil peace. And he adds: 'Thus it is that the paterfamilias ought to derive from the law of the state, those precepts by means of which he so governs his household that it accords with the civil peace.' And therefore—so Augustine holds—it is far more obligatory that the laws of the state should serve the common peace and the good of the state.

5. Another reason is clearly to be derived from the origin of human law. For the governing power that resides in men flows either immediately from God, as in the case of spiritual power, or immediately from men themselves, as in the case of purely temporal power; but, in both instances, this power has been primarily given for the general good of the community; and therefore, that good should be held in view, in the process of lawmaking.

The truth of the minor premiss in so far as relates to the first statement, on spiritual power, is evident from the Scriptures: since it is for this very reason that Prelates are called shepherds (who should lay down their lives for their sheep), stewards (not masters), and ministers of God (not primary causes); consequently, they are bound to conform to the divine purpose, in the exercise of such power; but the principal purpose toward which God works, is the common good of men themselves; therefore His ministers also are bound to serve this end; and accordingly, the Scriptures rebuke with the utmost severity those persons who abuse that power for their private advantage. When, on the other hand, the power has been granted directly by men themselves, it is most evident that it has been granted not for the advantage of the prince but for the common good of those who have conferred it; and for this reason, kings are called the ministers of the state. It is to be noted that they are also the ministers of God, according to a passage in *Romans* (Chap. xiii [, vv. 4, 6]), and these words from the *Book of Wisdom* (Chap. vi [, v. 5]): 'Because being ministers of his kingdom', &c. . . . Therefore, they should use that power for the good of the state, from which and for the sake of which they have received it. Thus it is that Basil (Homily XII: *On Proverbs,* at the beginning [No. 2, near end]) has rightly said that a tyrant differs from a king in this respect, namely, that the former in his rule seeks after his own advantage, the latter, after the common advantage. Aristotle (*Ethics,* Bk. VIII, chap. x and *Politics,* Bk. III, chap. v [chap. vii, 1279 A B]) writes to the same effect; and St. Thomas (II.–II, qu. 42, art. 2, ad 3 and *De Regimine Principum,* Bk. III, chap. xi) agrees with this view.

Now the first consequent is proved by the fact that one of the principal acts of the power in question is law. For law is (so to speak) an instrument by means of which the prince exercises a moral influence upon the state, in order that he may govern it; and therefore, law should serve the common good of that same state.

6. *Objection.* It may be objected, however, in opposition to the condition in question, that there are many laws which are ordered to the good of private individuals; as, for example, the laws made in behalf of wards, those in behalf of soldiers, and similar laws. Wherefore, in the *Digest* (I. i. 1 [, § 2]) and in the *Institutes* (I. i, § 4), a distinction is made between two kinds of laws: those which are ordered to the general good, or the welfare of the state; and, on the other hand, those which relate to the private good of individuals. Moreover, the *Digest* (I. iv. 1 [, § 2]) also contains the statement that certain laws are of a personal nature, with an effect that is limited to the individual for this reason, namely, that they are made solely for his benefit. This is especially evident in the case of privileges, to which the *Decretum* (Pt. I, dist. III, can. iii) refers as private laws since, assuredly, they are granted for the private advantage of the persons on whom they are conferred; therefore, not all laws are ordered to the common good.

From yet another standpoint, it would seem insufficient that laws should be directed to the common good. For frequently they redound to the harm and detriment of many persons; yet evil should not be done that good may result, nor should certain persons be enriched at the expense of other persons, according to a rule of the *Sext* (Bk. V, tit. XII, rule xlviii). The major premiss is clearly true when, as a first example, many kingdoms are subject to one and the same king; for a law which is useful to one kingdom often is harmful to another, and the same situation may occur within a single kingdom, among its different cities. Again, the law of prescription, in order that it may endow one person with ownership of a given possession, deprives the true owner of his possession. Frequently, too, that which seems advantageous to the community is onerous and troublesome to a great number of private persons; and indeed, the laws at times inflict evil directly upon certain individuals, as is the case with punitive laws.

7. *The objection is answered.* To the first part of this objection, the various authors make varying replies, as does Navarrus, above (*On Ends,*

Nos. 28 and 29). In my opinion, however, the matter is clear and may easily be explained by the application of a double distinction.

The first [member of this distinction] relates to a twofold common good enjoyed by the state. One phase of this good is that which is of itself and primarily common, being subject not to the dominion of any private person but to that of the whole community, for whose use or enjoyment it is directly ordered. Examples of this form of good are temples or sacred things, magistracies, common pastures or meadows, and the like, mentioned in the laws above cited, and in other laws under the title *De Rerum Divisione.* But the other form is a common good only in a secondary sense and because it redounds [to the general welfare], so to speak. In a direct sense, however, it is a private good, since it is immediately subordinated to the dominion and advantage of a private individual. Yet it is also said to be a common good; either because the state has a certain higher right over the private goods of individuals, so that it may make use of these goods when it needs them, or also because the good of each individual, when that good does not redound to the injury of others, is to the advantage of the entire community, for the very reason that the individual is a part of the community. Thus the civil laws (*Institutes,* I. viii, § 2; *Authentica,* Coll. II [, tit. ii, Pref., § 1 = *Novels,* VIII, Pref., § 1]; and other, similar laws) declare it to be expedient for the state that the citizens should be rich and that no one should abuse his possessions.

8. *A twofold subject-matter of the common good, with which law may be concerned.* The other member of our twofold distinction is that which is generally made with respect to human acts. In these, we distinguish the proximate subject-matter with which they are concerned, from the motive or reason because of which [they are executed]. For, in view of the fact that law is a moral act, these two factors should be distinguished in the case of law, also. Therefore, the subject-matter with which law is concerned, may sometimes be the common good for its own sake and primarily; while at other times it is a private good for its own sake and primarily, but a private good which redounds to the common welfare.[4] Accordingly, a distinction of this kind, also, was laid down with respect to laws, in those above cited,

----

4. [*Commune . . . per redundantiam.*—Tr.]

as I have, moreover, explained at greater length in my work, *De Religione* (Treatise V; that is, in Bk. II, chap. xxii[5] of the part on oaths). For certain laws deal directly with subject-matter that is common; others, with the good of individuals; but the reason why law deals with either kind of subject-matter is the common good, which therefore should always be the primary aim of law.

9. *Objection.* In regard to this point, however, it may be asked whether this good should be deliberately aimed at, in the intention of the person acting, or whether it should [simply] be the [natural] end of the actual work imposed, to use the terminology of St. Thomas (II.–II, qu. 141, art. 6, ad 1). For it would seem that the intention of the agent is extrinsic, that it may vary as the result of external accident, and that the essence of a law is not dependent upon this intention; yet the work imposed does not always and by its own virtue tend to the common good, unless it is made to do so by another, so that, in like manner, the aim of the work would seem to be neither essential nor sufficient.

The subject-matter of law should be advantageous for and adapted to the common good, not through the intention of the law-maker, but of itself. I reply briefly that for the validity and essence of a law, it is necessary only that its subject-matter be advantageous to and suitable for the common good, at the time and place involved, and with respect to the people and community in question. For this utility and fitness are not bestowed by the lawgiver, but are assumed to exist; and therefore, in so far as relates to their existence (so to speak) they are not dependent upon his intention. Wherefore it also follows that such subject-matter ought of itself to be referable to the common good, since every useful good as such is fit to be directed to the end for which it is useful, and in this sense, the aim of the work imposed and not that of the agent, is the necessary factor in the matter under discussion.

The reason for the foregoing statements is clear; since even if a legislator makes a law from hatred, for example, or from some other perverse motive, if the law itself nevertheless works to the common good, that fact suffices to give the said law validity. For the perverse intention is strictly

5. [Not included in these *Selections.*—Tr.]

a personal factor, and its effect does not extend to the work imposed, in so far as the latter relates to the common advantage. Thus, the perverse intention of a judge does not affect the validity of his sentence, unless that intention is in [actual] opposition to the equity of the sentence; and similarly, the perverse intention of him who administers [a sacrament] is in no way detrimental to that sacrament, unless such an intention is in opposition to the essence thereof. Just so, then, in the matter under discussion, the common good must be sought in the law itself, and not in the extrinsic intention of the lawgiver. Augustine gives an excellent portrayal of this view when he says (*On Free Will,* Bk. I, chap. v): 'A law which has been made for the protection of the people, cannot be censured on the ground of any evil desire, since he who made it, if he did so at God's bidding (that is to say, in accordance with the precepts of eternal justice), may have performed this [legislative act] apart from any experience of such desire; if, on the other hand, evil desire was associated with his making of the decree, it does not follow [merely] from that fact, that it is necessary to obey the said law in such a spirit; for[6] a good law may be made, even by one who is not himself good.' Moreover, just below this passage, Augustine calls attention to an excellent argument, namely, that one may without evil desire conform to a law, even though he who made the law may have done so in a spirit of evil desire.

10. *Reply to an objection.* Accordingly, in the light of the foregoing remarks the first part of the objection is easily answered; since that part involves simply the conclusion that the proximate subject-matter of law is not always that common good which, *per se* and primarily, dwells within the community as such; and it is thus that the distinction laid down in connexion with the laws above cited, is understood. For it was laid down with regard to subject-matter; and the laws in question are said to turn about private benefits having as their subject-matter the personal welfare of the [individual] citizens themselves, welfare which, viewed from another standpoint, includes the common welfare, as we have remarked. With respect to these legal precepts it should also be noted that they never

---

6. [The '&' before *quia* has not been taken into account in the translation, since it does not appear in the text of the Migne edition of St. Augustine's works.—Tr.]

fall under the head of law when they relate merely to this or that individual, but do come under that head in so far as they deal with [all] persons of a certain condition (such as wards, soldiers, &c.), or with [all] persons of a certain origin (for example, nobles), or with [all] the successors of a given family; and in this sense, they look to the common good, because of a common participation (so to speak) in their universal effects, that is to say, because such good affects a large number of persons, as was pointed out at the end of the preceding Chapter.

However, when the *Digest* (I. iv. 1) states that a regulation issued by a prince, does not at times extend its application beyond the particular person involved, the term '[princely] regulation' is apparently not used in the sense of strict law, but rather in that of any edict or decree whatsoever, issued[7] by the prince in favour of or adversely to some specific person; since such a regulation, unless it has [also] a wider scope and a more enduring force, is not law in the strict sense. This point, too, was brought out in an earlier Chapter.[8]

11. In the light of the foregoing remarks, it is evident what should be said in regard to privileges, a matter apparently touched upon by the *Digest* (*ibid.*), also. Thus the Gloss (on *Decretum,* Pt. I, dist. iv, can. ii) answers that it is through the condition in question that law is distinguished from privilege.[9] This reply is sharply attacked by Castro (cited above), on the ground that it leads to the conclusion that a law decreed by a prince, concerning payment of a perpetual tribute to himself and for his own advantage, would have to be called a privilege. However, this objection to the words of the Gloss has little force. For the tribute in question would be either just, or unjust. If it were just, then the law itself would be just, and would serve the common good, even though it would [also] be to the advantage of the prince; because, in the first place, the welfare of the prince, viewed as such, is considered as the common welfare, inasmuch

7. [This word may be understood from the genitive form of *principis,* or it may be a translation of *constitutum* read as *constituto.* The accusative form is possibly the result of an error, here.—Tr.]

8. [*Supra,* p. 83; *De Legibus,* chap. vi, §§ 2 *et seq.*—Tr.]

9. [The Gloss simply comments that if law was made for private advantage it would be privilege.—Reviser.]

as he is a public personage, pertaining to the whole community;[10] and furthermore, because a just subsidy bestowed upon the prince by the state constitutes a common good, benefiting the state as a whole. If, on the other hand, the tribute should be unjust and tyrannical, then it would not be law, but would on the contrary have the character of an inequitable and unjust privilege. Moreover, this reply which is contained in the Gloss would seem to be in accord with Cicero's statement (*Laws*, Bk. III [, chap. xix, no. 44]) that, 'Our forefathers [. . .] desired no laws to be made which penalized private individuals; for to do so would be to make a law of personal privilege'.

12. *Privileges are true laws.*[11] Nevertheless, I am of the opinion that the said condition was not laid down by Isidore, to the exclusion of privilege from the essential realm of law. For in the first place, this same Gloss (on *Decretum*, Pt. I, dist. III, can. iii) declares that a privilege is law, and requires of it a compliance with certain other conditions which are laid down by Isidore as he is quoted in a different passage (*Decretum*, Pt. I, dist. IV, can. ii). Another reason for my opinion is the fact that the clause in question was framed for the immediate purpose of excluding tyrannical laws, or those which do not tend toward the common good, even though it may be that they do not look to any private good, either; so that evil laws are necessarily excluded through the said condition, even if they are not privileges. Finally, my opinion is supported by the fact that it was perhaps not needful to exclude privileges. This is a point which I shall discuss in the proper context. For the present, I shall merely assert that, in so far as relates to the common good, it is not unreasonable that a privilege should have the character of law. For even though its proximate subject-matter may be the private good of a particular family or household, or that of particular individuals—this being, perhaps, the reason that Isidore gave privileges the name of 'private law', in the Chapter[12] of the *Decretum* above cited (Pt. I, dist. III,

10. [Simply, *persona publica, & communis.*—Tr.]

11. [In the Latin text of the 1612 Coimbra edition on which this translation is based, the subheading appears a little below the marginal references, 'Gloss' and 'Decretum'. However, the edition of Paris, 1856, places the subheading at the beginning of Section 12, which would seem to be the correct order.—Tr.]

12. [For *chapter* read *canon.*—Tr.]

can. iii)—nevertheless, from a formal standpoint, [a privilege] should look also to the common good. In this connexion, one may consult the *Decretum* (Pt. II, causa I, qu. vii, can. v, argument, and Section *Nisi rigor* [same canon]; also Pt. II, causa I, qu. vii, can. xvi) and the remarks of St. Thomas (I.–II, qu. 97, art. 4, ad I). For the good conceded by the privilege should be a private good [only] in such a way as to redound to the common welfare, in the fashion explained above. Moreover, the particular grant of privilege should be of so rational a nature, that it will work to the common advantage if [other, and] similar privileges are granted for similar causes. Privileges, then, are not excluded from the strict and essential character of law, under this head. And as to the question of whether they are excluded on the ground that they relate to private individuals, or whether they may [in spite of this fact] be laws in the true sense of the term—especially if they are of a perpetual nature—that is a matter which we shall discuss in Book Ten.[13]

13. The question is less difficult in regard to laws of taxation. For these laws are imposed upon a community (a fact which is self-evident) and relate directly to the common good; since, as I have said, though they may seem to be directed to the advantage of the prince, nevertheless, if they are to be true laws, they must have in view the common welfare; because such taxes are granted to the king only to the extent that he is a public personage pertaining to the whole community,[14] and on condition that he shall use them for the good of the community. Thus a canon of the Council of Toledo (Eighth Council, Chap. x, *De Regibus*)[15] contains the qualification: 'Not having respect to those rights which concern private advantage, but taking counsel for the country and the people.'

14. As to the other part of the objections, we may make the general reply that it is a natural characteristic of human affairs that they are not uniform in every way. And thus it frequently happens that what is expedient for the whole community, will be harmful to this

---

13. [This discussion is in Book VIII of the *De Legibus,* which is not included in these *Selections.*—Tr.]

14. [*Persona communis & publica.*—Tr.]

15. [This Chapter of the Council of Toledo deals in one of its sections with the obligations of kings and all civil rulers.—Reviser.]

or that individual; but, since the common good is preferred to private good whenever the two cannot exist simultaneously, therefore, laws are made in absolute form, for the sake of the common good, and take no account of individual cases. This point is brought out in a number of laws (*Digest,* I. iii and *ibid.,* i; *Decretals,* Bk. III, tit. xxxi, chap. xviii and *Decretum,* Pt. II, causa vii, qu. i, can. xxxv). However, it is sometimes the case that several kingdoms, or several communities, are gathered together under one king; externally (so to speak) since, in actual fact, they do not form among themselves a single political body, but have come under the power of that king through various titles, and as the result of external accidents. In such cases, it would be unjust to bind the different kingdoms by the same laws, if those laws were advantageous to one kingdom, and not advantageous to another. For under these circumstances, the comparison would be made, not as between the common and the private good, but as between one common good and another, also common, each of which requires, *per se* and separately, that provision be made for it through its own laws just as if it were still under a separate king; even after the manner adopted by the Pope, when he lays down [separate] rules for different religious orders, in so far as they are distinct communities, each in need of its own laws. On the other hand, when the various communities are [in reality] parts of one and the same kingdom, or political body, then the welfare of each individual part is to be regarded as private in relation to the welfare of the whole, for which the laws are essentially and primarily made.

Two precautions, however, should be taken. For one thing, the harm to private individuals should not be so multiplied as to outweigh the advantages accruing to other persons. Again, dispensations or exceptions should when needed be annexed [to laws]; for in such cases of necessity, this is in the highest degree permissible, and sometimes even a matter of obligation.

15. From the foregoing we readily perceive what statements should be made regarding harm to private persons. For harm of this sort is accorded less consideration and consequently is sometimes permitted, as in the case of prescription, which regards the common good; that is to say, it regards peace, the avoidance of litigation, &c. At times, such harm is actually [one

of the ends] sought [by legislation]; for example, by punitive laws, which are at the same time necessary to the common good.

Thus we have the explanation of the two other conditions of law laid down by Isidore, in the same passage [cited in *Decretum*, Pt. I, dist. IV, can. ii], namely, that law must be necessary, and that it must be useful. These conditions are explained by St. Thomas (I.–II, qu. 95, art. 3) in such a way that he connects necessity with the removal of evil (as when a law is made in order to avert some evil from the state) and utility, with the promotion of good; a distinction which is well made, in that it prevents either of the two conditions from seeming to be redundant. Nevertheless, in both cases, the promotion of the common welfare should be borne in mind. For a given evil must be removed in such a way that no other greater evil will afflict the state in consequence; since otherwise, the law in question would be, not necessary, but pernicious. And again, a given useful result must be attained in such fashion as not to impede thereby the attainment of a result still more useful, nor to afflict the community in consequence with evils greater [than those from which it would otherwise have suffered]. All these terms, then, serve to explain one and the same property in law, although they explain it in diverse aspects, for the purpose of a fuller exposition, a fact which suffices to prevent the said terms from being superfluous.

16. *Is a general law, established with the intention of injuring a particular individual, unjust and invalid?* At this point, it is customary to inquire whether a law established in general terms, but with the intention or fraudulent design of having it work harm to a single individual, is unjust, or invalid.

For the jurists are wont to say that such a law is so unjust that it is permissible to appeal therefrom, or to take exception to it on the ground of fraud. Statements to this effect may be found in the comments of Bartolus on the *Digest*, (I. i. 9, qu. 5, no. 53), Panormitanus (on *Rubric* of *Decretals*, Bk. I, tit. II, no. 2), Felinus (on *Decretals*, Bk. I, tit. II, chap. vi, no. 5), Jason [on *Digest*, I. iii. 1, no. 4] and Gregory López, as cited above [on *Las Siete Partidas*, Pt. I, tit. i, law 9].

Nevertheless, these authors do not hold that laws of this kind are always invalid, or unjust. For doubtless they may sometimes be enacted for a reasonable cause, permitting harm to a private individual for the sake of the common good, rather than [deliberately] seeking to inflict such harm, or even seeking to do so as a just penalty. Again, if it so chances that the lawmaker was moved by an unjust intention owing to private hatred, that fact (as has been said above) will not be detrimental to the law itself, nor to the justice thereof, if in other respects this law is necessary to the common good. So Felinus has declared at length, in the passage already cited [on *Decretals,* Bk. I, tit. II, chap. vi, concl. I]. Moreover, he adds (*ibid.,* concl. 3) that the same conclusion holds true of a law made in favour of a private individual or of a family, if the said law redounds to the common advantage; a fact which is sufficiently clear in the light of what we have already said.[16] Thus the authorities above cited[17] are referring—when they speak of injustice and fraud—to cases involving an attempt, without just cause, to inflict harm upon a third party under the guise of a general law. For in these cases the injustice is manifest, and consequently a suitable method of self-defence is likewise permissible, and befitting; and it is of such self-defence that these authors treat, since the subject falls properly within their field.

CHAPTER IX

Is It Inherent in the Nature of Law That It Be Just, and Established in a Just Manner? In This Connexion the Other Conditions of Law Laid Down by Isidore Are Discussed

1. Now that we have expounded the conditions required of law with respect to the persons or causes that may be considered as extrinsic, the intrinsic conditions (so to speak) present themselves for discussion, whether intrinsic in the act to which a legal precept may apply, or intrinsic in the very process of making the law. We reduce these conditions to a question of justice; and under justice, we include all the conditions laid down by

---

16. [*Supra,* p. 109; § 9, this Chapter.—Tr.]
17. [*Vide* the second paragraph of this Section.—Tr.]

Isidore in a passage (*Etymologies,* Bk. V, chap. ii [chap. iii]) where he speaks thus: 'Law will be all that which is established by reason, provided that it is in harmony with religion, agreeable to [moral] discipline and conducive to welfare.'[1] However, Isidore would seem to be speaking here of human custom, rather than of law in general, although the words might be made applicable to all phases of law. In other chapters, indeed (*ibid.* chap. xxi and Bk. II, chap. x), he enumerates other conditions—or the same ones, with greater clarity—for he says: 'Law will be righteous, just, practicable, and in harmony with nature and with the custom of the country, and suitable to the time and place.' St. Thomas, also (I.–II, qu. 95, art. 3), interprets these conditions as referring to human law.

Nevertheless, owing to the fact that either all or at least the chief of the said conditions, are applicable to every kind of law, and because it is necessary to have a knowledge of them in order to draw up a definition of law, an explanation of the conditions is fitting at this point.

However, we shall reduce them all to the two conditions suggested in the title of this Chapter, namely, law shall be just, and law shall be established in a just manner. These conditions, we expressly undertake to expound; and, in connexion with them, we shall discuss certain others, viewing them as corollaries.

2. *The first assertion: It is inherent in the nature of law that it shall prescribe just things.* My first assertion, then, is as follows: it is inherent in the nature and essence of law that it shall prescribe just things.[2]

This assertion is not only indubitably true by the light of faith, but is also manifest by the light of natural reason. Accordingly, it is made not only by the theologians and Fathers whom I shall cite below, but also, in various passages, by the philosophers named in the preceding Chapter.[3]

A twofold sense in which law may be regarded as just. Moreover, it may be expounded in the following manner. The statement that law ought to

1. [*Quod saluti proficiat.* The word *saluti* may refer either to physical welfare or to spiritual salvation; for the interpretation of the term in this particular context, cf. the penultimate paragraph of Section 10, *infra,* p. 126, and note 16, p. 126.—TR.]

2. [*Ut praecipiat iusta.* A strictly literal translation is necessitated by the argument in a later part of this same Section. Cf. last words of first paragraph on p. 118.—TR.]

3. [Not included in these *Selections.*—TR.]

be just, is susceptible of two interpretations. First, the question of justice may be viewed from the standpoint of the very act which the subject is, by virtue of the said law, obliged to perform; that is to say, the act must be such that it may be justly executed by him. Secondly, the question may be considered in regard to the law itself; that is, the law must be imposed upon men without the infliction of injury. For sometimes an act may be such that it is possible for the subject to perform it justly—as in the case of a fast on bread and water—while the superior [nevertheless] does this subject an injury by prescribing such an act. This distinction has been pointed out by St. Thomas (I.–II, qu. 96, art. 4). Our assertion, then, should be interpreted according to the first standpoint, or first kind of just law; for in order to set it apart from the second standpoint, we have said that a law ought to prescribe just things.[4]

Again, 'justice' sometimes signifies a special virtue; while at other times it refers to all the virtues. But in the present case, our assertion that law should be just must be taken in a general sense, as meaning that whatever the law prescribes should be such that it may be executed justly and virtuously, that is, righteously.[5] Even this condition, however, is susceptible of a twofold interpretation; that is, it may be interpreted negatively, meaning that what is prescribed shall not be unjust or base; or it may be interpreted positively, meaning that what is prescribed shall be just and righteous.

3. The said condition, then, is to be understood principally in the first sense; and accordingly its truth is self-evident.

Nevertheless, it exists for one reason in the case of divine laws, and for another reason in the case of human laws.

For in the former case the reason is the essential rectitude of the divine will, since God is superlatively good and therefore incapable of commanding anything evil.

There is the further reason that God cannot be a contradiction to Himself, and therefore cannot lay down mutually contradictory precepts at

---

4. [Cf. note 2, p. 117, *supra*.—Tr.]

5. [*Iustè, & honestè, seu studiosè*. The adjective, *studiosus* (*vide* Du Cange on this word), has sometimes been used in the sense of *bonus, probus;* and in this context it seems advisable to give the adverb a corresponding interpretation, rather than the usual one of 'zealously'.—Tr.]

one and the same time, while they continue to be thus contradictory. The prescribed deed, then,—a deed which, for the purposes of argument, we have assumed to be unjust or base—will be of such sort that it is in nowise separable from its iniquity (as in the case of lying, or entertaining hatred against God, or failing to believe when He speaks with sufficient evidence, or similar conduct); or else, the said deed will be such that its wickedness can be removed by a change in the subject-matter, or by the adoption of a [special] mode of action (as in the slaying of a human being, or other act of this kind). When the deed [prescribed] is intrinsically evil in the former sense, it is for that very reason prohibited by natural law, and consequently by God, as the Author of natural law; therefore, it is impossible that positive divine law should contain anything contrary to this natural justice, although it may contain many precepts in addition to those of natural justice, precepts which are most righteous in their own order. If, on the other hand, the deed in question is of the latter sort, it will be righteous for the very reason that it is prescribed by God; a point which may be illustrated by the deed of Abraham and also by similar cases which we shall discuss later, when we treat of dispensations from natural law. For this latter form of command occurs (a point which should be noted), not in divine laws of a general nature but, at most, in certain rare personal precepts. Accordingly, it is quite clear, with respect to divine laws, that they are always characterized by the kind of justice in question.

4. In the case of human laws, however, this [condition which we have been discussing in the two preceding sections] is founded upon another principle. For a human legislator does not have a perfect will, as God has; and therefore, of himself and with respect to the deed [prescribed], such a legislator may sometimes prescribe unjust things, a fact which is manifestly true; but he has not the power to bind through unjust laws, and consequently, even though he may indeed prescribe that which is unjust, such a precept is not law, inasmuch as it lacks the force or valid-ity necessary to impose a binding obligation.[6] To be sure, I am speaking

6. Suárez understands as law that form of directive which, *inter alia,* possesses the force of moral obligation. If we cannot be under a moral obligation to act unjustly—and we cannot—precepts which require unjust actions of us cannot be laws properly speaking.

of unjust deeds which are opposed to natural or divine law. For if a deed is wicked solely because it is prohibited by a human law, and if the latter can be withdrawn by means of a subsequent law, then this second precept will not relate to an evil deed, since—through the revocation of the earlier law—the evil of the [prescribed] deed is removed. The reason for our assertion thus becomes clear. For, in the first place, the [legislative] power in question is derived from God; and those things which are from God, are well ordered; therefore, the said power has been given for good and for edification, not for evil or destruction. And secondly, no inferior can impose an obligation that is contrary to the law and the will of his superior; but a law prescribing a wrongful act, is contrary to the law of God, Who prohibits that act; therefore, [the former law] cannot be binding, for it is not possible that men should be bound, at one and the same time, to do and to abstain from doing a given thing. Moreover, if a wrongful deed is prohibited by divine law, no law made by an inferior can annul the obligation imposed by the superior; consequently, [such an inferior] cannot impose an obligation, for his own part; and therefore, his law on the deed in question cannot be valid.

It was to this justice of law, indeed, that St. Augustine referred, when he wrote (*On Free Will,* Bk. I, chap. v): 'In my opinion, that is not law which is not just.' Moreover, one may interpret as a reference to the same justice, the words of St. Augustine in another passage (*On the True Religion,* Chap. xxxi): 'A founder of temporal laws, if he is a good and wise man, will consult the eternal law in order to discern, [. . .] in accordance with its immutable rules, what from a temporal standpoint should be avoided or prescribed.' Wherefore, just as the eternal law prescribes only that which is just, since this law is essential justice itself, even so, true human law ought to be a participation therein, and consequently cannot validly prescribe anything save that which is just and righteous; a condition which accords with the verse in *Proverbs* (Chap. viii [, v. 15]): 'By me kings reign, and lawgivers decree just things.'

5. *In what way an act prescribed by law is characterized by positive righteousness.* From the foregoing, we draw the further conclusion that the condition in question, even when positively interpreted, pertains to the essential nature of law; although it is not to be applied in one and the same manner to each individual [legal precept].

The first part of this statement may be demonstrated to be true on the basis of our preceding remarks; for if the act prescribed is not of itself evil and if it is prescribed by a superior, then, for this very reason, it may righteously be executed, since by virtue of the precept of the superior it acquires a certain righteousness, even though it may not always possess that quality inherently. For, even as an act not of itself evil becomes evil through the just[7] prohibition of a superior, so an act not of itself either good or evil, will become good through a law which justly prescribes it; and accordingly, law always relates to a good act, since it either presupposes that the act is good, or causes it to be so.[8]

Thus the second part of the same statement is also manifestly true. For, in some cases, it is presupposed that [certain] acts prescribed by law are of themselves good and righteous. Such acts acquire through law merely a necessary and obligatory character; since they were formerly optional and the failure to perform them was not evil, whereas such failure does become evil after the making of the law, and the act in question becomes essential to righteousness, manifest examples of this sort being found in the acts of hearing mass and of fasting, or in similar acts. Sometimes, on the other hand, a law is made with regard to a deed which is in itself indifferent; as in the case of laws concerning the carrying of arms, or abstaining therefrom, at a certain time or in a certain place, and similar matters. In such a situation, the act [prescribed] becomes good both by the efficacy [of the law] and by virtue of the end to which that law is directed. This righteousness ordinarily relates to some special virtue, in accordance with the capacity of the subject-matter with which the law is concerned, inasmuch as the said law establishes a certain moderation in regard to that [subject-matter]. Examples of this kind are found in the law of fasting, or the law prohibiting the use, at a stated time, of stated foods that are in themselves

7. [Reading *iustam,* with the Paris edition, 1856; not *iniustam,* with our own Latin text from the Coimbra edition, 1612.—Tr.]

8. Law as natural law gives obligatory force to features of an action that already made the action good and so already justified its performance. By contrast, law in positive form itself contributes a further reason for the action and so itself causes the action to be good. When some new enactment of positive law makes an action legally obligatory, that feature of being now legally obligatory itself justifies the action's performance and makes it good.

a matter of indifference; and in other laws of a like nature. Sometimes, however, the righteousness may be a matter solely of obedience, or legal justice. Examples of this sort are the law which prohibits carrying arms, and other, similar laws.

Thus law must be just from the standpoint of its subject-matter, in one of the ways above described.

6. *In what way a law concerned with the permission of evil is just.* Nevertheless, an objection may be raised at this point, with respect to human laws which permit some evil and which apparently do not relate to what is just. Augustine (*On Free Will,* Bk. I, chaps. v and vi) discusses this objection at considerable length; and we shall return to the point later.

For the present, I shall answer briefly that the subject-matter of such a law is not the evil deed involved, but the permission of that deed; and permission of an evil deed may in itself be good, inasmuch as God wills that it shall be granted; accordingly, a law of this sort deals with subject-matter that is just. And if it is urged that the permission is not the subject-matter but the effect of the law, I answer, first of all, that the permission does not result from the law, save in so far as [the latter] prescribes that the act in question shall be permitted, and not punished or checked; for otherwise, the true and essential principle of the law could not subsist, as is evident from its general nature, and as I shall explain more fully below.[9] Secondly, if any one should venture to speak of the said act as being the subject-matter of the law, I would reply as follows: the act itself may be considered in either of two aspects; that is to say, as capable of being performed (in which sense it is evil), or [simply] as permissible, so to speak (an aspect in which it is not wrongful subject-matter, nor subject-matter contrary to reason). In other words, this act is not fit subject-matter from the standpoint of its capacity to be legally obligatory, but it is capable of being permitted, since with respect to the purpose of such [legal] power, it does not necessarily call for prohibition or punishment and is, therefore, in itself just subject-matter in relation to the law in question.

7. From this [first] assertion, thus expounded, we are able to draw two inferences.

9. [The discussion of permission of evil deeds is found in *De Legibus,* Bk. I, chap. xv, §§ 5 *et seq.,* a chapter not included in these *Selections.*—Tr.]

The first corollary: Righteousness is inherent in the nature of law; and the remaining conditions laid down by Isidore are reduced to this one [condition of righteousness]. One inference is as follows: to the said assertion, there pertains, most of all, the first condition laid down by Isidore (*Etymologies,* Bk. V, chap. xxi), namely, the condition that law shall be righteous, a requirement which is sufficiently clear from the very nature of the term. I shall add, moreover, that to this quality of justice in law, we may very well reduce all the conditions laid down by Isidore in the passage cited above, and also in the *Decretum* (Pt. I, dist. i, can. v), in which passage he first says: 'Law will be all that which is established by reason'; that is to say, law ought to be in accord with reason; and this [in turn] is equivalent to requiring that law shall be just, in the sense explained above. Furthermore, this condition includes virtually all the justice of law, in its entirety. For law cannot be in absolute conformity with reason, unless it is just in every respect. Accordingly, St. Thomas (I.–II, qu. 95, art. 3) accepted this requirement, not as a special condition of law, but as a general one virtually including all other conditions, so that he does not discuss the others.

8. Secondly, then, Isidore [*Etymologies,* Bk. V, chap. iii] requires of law, 'that it shall be in harmony with religion'; a requirement which St. Thomas expounds in the place cited in connexion with human law, saying that law should be in harmony with religion, in so far as it ought to correspond to divine law. However, this correspondence consists simply in not prescribing what divine law prohibits, and in not prohibiting what divine law prescribes; so that, in like manner, it may be said that to be in harmony with religion is the same as to be righteous.

Nevertheless, it is possible to extend the condition to apply to all law, and it is also possible to understand religion more exactly, as the true mode of worshipping the true God. For, in this way, it becomes clear that the eternal law, viewed as externally preceptive for its proper occasions, is in the highest degree harmonious with divine worship; since God ordains all things to His own honour and glory through this law. Consequently, He especially prohibits all sin, since sin is opposed to His law and His goodness.

Furthermore, the natural law, being the first participant in this [eternal law], prescribes as a principal requirement, the worship of God. For it was in view of this precept that Paul wrote (*Romans,* Chap. i [, vv. 20, 21]) that the heathens were inexcusable. Because that, when they knew God, they have not glorified Him as God. Accordingly, the natural law does not merely refrain from prescribing anything incongruous with the religion of the true God; rather, it does not even permit such a thing. For though the individual precepts of that natural law do not all prescribe the worship of God, yet that law does not prescribe anything that cannot be done to the glory of God, and this is equivalent to being in harmony with religion.[10]

9.[11] Furthermore, it is a self-evident fact that the condition in question applies to positive divine laws; since the latter have always been laid down in a manner eminently in harmony with divine worship and religion, for given times and given peoples, as we shall see later when we treat of such laws, and as one may well infer from the words of the Apostle to the *Hebrews* (Chap. vii [, v. 12]): 'the priesthood being translated, it is necessary that a translation also be made of the law.' For even though that statement was made with special reference to the Old Law, it may rightly be based upon this condition of law, namely, that law should be in harmony with religion, so that a change in the former is consequently necessary when religious rites have undergone change. Thus Augustine is wont to explain on this basis the consonance and character of the two kinds of law; a matter on which he touches in the *Confessions* (Bk. III, chap. xxxvii [chap. vii]), and which he pursues at length in his work *Against Faustus,* and in numerous other passages.

Again, human laws, if they are canonical, are by their very nature directed primarily to the ends of divine worship and religion; and accordingly, almost every one of them deals with this subject-matter. A few [individual precepts], indeed, may be concerned with other subjects; but even in these cases, there is always the greatest regard for that which befits and harmonizes with religion.

Finally, with respect to civil laws, while these do not *per se* serve such an end, they are nevertheless subordinate to it, and consequently should not

---

10. [The argument seems loose here, but the Latin does not warrant a more pointed rendering.—Tr.]

11. [Latin text incorrectly has '8'.—Tr.]

be incompatible therewith; if they are incompatible, they cannot be just; and in this sense, civil laws should be in harmony with religion.

For the condition in question may be expounded from either a positive or a negative standpoint; and even though the former standpoint is applicable in the case of certain laws, in regard to other laws the latter suffices, that is to say, it suffices that such laws shall be not incompatible with the true religion; all of which is a matter pertaining to their righteousness.

10.[12] Thirdly, Isidore [*Etymologies,* Bk. V, chap. iii] requires of law 'that it shall be agreeable to [moral] discipline'; a condition which is explained by St. Thomas [I.–II, qu. 95, art. 3, with the comment,] 'because it should be in due proportion to the law of nature'.[13] This proportion must consist in nothing more nor less than the quality of not deviating from the precepts and rules of the law of nature; since a human lawgiver ought to conduct himself in his legislative acts as a disciple of natural law (so to speak), and ought to prescribe those things which are in harmony with its teaching.

These assertions are, to be sure, correct. Nevertheless, if we interpret this condition as referring to discipline in relation to the subjects [upon whom laws are imposed], we may well say that every law lays down suitable doctrines for its subjects, and is thus agreeable to discipline;[14] since every law is a species of instruction for the subjects, in accordance with the words [of the Psalmist (*Psalms,* xviii, v. 8)]: 'The law of the Lord is unspotted, . . . giving wisdom to little ones.'[15] For every just law is, in a sense, a law of the Lord, and gives wisdom to little ones; accordingly, it is, with respect to those little ones, a species of doctrine; and therefore, it is rightly asserted of all law, that it should be agreeable to discipline. But the instruction in habits of conduct (for it is of such instruction that

12. [Latin text incorrectly has '9'.—Tr.]

13. [The exact reading of this passage in Question 95, art. 3 of I.–II which Suárez is here quoting is: *inquantum est proportionata legi naturae* (inasmuch as it is proportionate to the natural law).—Tr.]

14. *Disciplina* or 'discipline' here means the inculcation of moral and intellectual virtue.

15. [This is the incomplete form in which Suárez quotes the verse. The complete verse is as follows: 'The law of the Lord is unspotted, converting souls: the testimony of the Lord is faithful, giving wisdom to little ones.'—Tr.]

we are speaking) which is said to be in consonance with discipline, is that which promotes virtue, or that which promotes other ends in such a way as to do no injury to righteous habits, being, rather—to the extent of its influence—advantageous to such habits. For this [third] condition, also, may be interpreted either positively or negatively; and both modes of interpretation are adequate, each in due proportion. To be sure, it is hardly possible that there should exist any law not repugnant to righteous habits of conduct, which would not be in some way agreeable to righteous discipline, assuming—as is indicated in the last of the [three] conditions mentioned—that with respect to its remaining qualifications, the said law is beneficial to the state.

For Isidore [*Etymologies,* Bk. V, ch. iii] adds [another requirement for law], namely, 'that it shall be conducive to welfare'.[16] St. Thomas I.–II, qu. 95, art. 3, interprets this condition, saying, 'in so far as it is adapted to the advantage of mankind', whereby he relates this requirement to the one mentioned above, the utility of law in promoting the common good. And in this sense, the said condition may be applied to every law, as we have already explained. However, it is possible to interpret the phrase in question theologically, as referring to the salvation of the soul, in preference [to the interpretation first suggested]. This spiritual welfare may have been what Isidore had in mind. For the Holy Fathers are wont to refer to such welfare by the term *salus.* If a law is just, it will indeed conform to such a condition,[17] since observance of a just law is essentially conducive to salvation.[18]

Thus all these [qualifying] remarks constitute [simply] an exposition of the righteousness of law, in so far as relates to the required observance thereof on the part of the subject. Nor are the said remarks superfluous for that reason. For the consideration of these diverse aspects [of law's righteousness] leads to a clearer understanding of that quality of law, and of its relation to higher goods that pertain both to God and to the soul.

16. [*Saluti.* For the twofold connotation of this term, cf. the remainder of this paragraph, and note 1, beginning of this Chapter, *supra,* p. 117.—Tr.]

17. [Simply *erit talis.*—Tr.]

18. [I.e. *salus.*—Tr.]

11.[19] *The second corollary: A law devoid of righteousness not only has not the nature of [true] law, but furthermore is neither binding nor capable of being obeyed.* Our second inference [from the first assertion], above set forth, is: a law not characterized by this justice or righteousness is not a law, nor does it possess any binding force; indeed, on the contrary, it cannot be obeyed.

This is clearly true, because justice that is opposed to this quality of righteousness in law, is in opposition to God Himself, since it involves guilt, and offence against Him; and therefore, it cannot licitly be obeyed, because it is not possible licitly to offend God. Furthermore, injustice of this sort is to be found only in laws laid down by men; but one must obey God rather than men; and therefore, such laws cannot be observed in opposition to the obedience due to God, just as one does not obey the praetor in defiance of a command issued by the king. So Augustine argues, *a fortiori* (*De Verbis Domini*, Bk. I, serm. vi, c. 8 [*Sermons,* lxii, no. 8, Migne ed.]).

In cases of doubt as to the righteousness of a law, it must be assumed to be righteous, and accordingly, must be obeyed. However, all the Doctors indicate that the evidence of injustice in the law must be such as to constitute a moral certainty. For if the matter is doubtful, a presumption must be made in favour of the lawgiver; partly because he has and is in permanent possession of a superior right; partly, also, because he is directed by superior counsel and may be moved by general reasons hidden from his subjects; and partly because the subjects, if this presumption in his favour did not exist,[20] would assume an excessive licence to disregard the laws, since the latter can hardly be so just that it is impossible for them to be treated as doubtful, by some individuals, apparently for plausible reasons. Such, indeed, was the opinion upheld by Augustine (*Against Faustus,* Bk. XXII, chaps. [lxxiv and] lxxv), and quoted in the *Decretum* (Pt. II, causa XXIII, qu. i, can. iv).

The question, indeed, of the degree of certitude—regarding this injustice in a law—that is necessary in order to oblige men not to obey that law, is repeatedly dealt with in comments on I.–II [, qu. 96, art. 4],

19. [The Latin text incorrectly has 'io'.—Tr.]
20. [Simply *alias,* in the Latin.—Tr.]

on conscience. Furthermore, we shall make some comments on this same point below,[21] when we discuss the binding force of law, and especially that of human law. For doubts of the kind in question are particularly wont to occur with respect to law of this sort [i.e. human law], and they may take many diverse forms; so that this subject will be disposed of more fittingly and more fully in that [later] context. On the other hand, the question of how in a doubtful case a presumption is made in favour of the prince, is treated at length by Panormitanus (on *Decretals,* Bk. I, tit. II, chap. vii, no. 14), Felinus (*ibid.,* nos. 60 *et seq.*) and Torquemada (on *Decretum,* Pt. II, causa XI, qu. iii, can. i, concls. 6 and 7, nos. 8 and 9, and *ibid.,* can. xciii, at end).

12.[22] *The second assertion: it is inherent in the nature of law that it be justly established.* My second assertion is as follows: it is inherent in the nature of law, that it be justly established; and if it is established in any other way, it will not be true law. The first part of this assertion is commonly accepted as true. Moreover, since in the case of divine laws it is a quite self-evident fact that they are justly established, it is in regard to human laws that we shall explain this assertion; which St. Thomas [also] has set forth in the question above cited (I.–II, qu. 96, art. 4). All the commentators on this passage, and others, to be cited presently, [agree on this point].

The said assertion, however, finds a first and general proof in the fact that conformity with reason is inherent in the nature of law, a fact proved by all the arguments adduced just above and acknowledged, moreover, by all the philosophers there cited; but in order that law may be in conformity with reason, it is not enough that the subject-matter of law should be righteous; on the contrary, its form must also be just and reasonable, which is to say that law must be established in a just manner; therefore, this latter requirement is likewise essential to the nature of law.

A second and specific argument is based upon the supposition that, when we declare establishment in a just manner to be inherent in the nature of law, we refer to a just mode of operation, not as regards the [legislative] agent, but as regards the product of his efforts. For, with respect to the mode

---

21. [*Infra,* pp. 142 *et seq.*—Tr.]
22. [The Latin text incorrectly has '10'.—Tr.]

of operation in its relation to the agent, it is necessary, not only that there be no defect in the law itself, but also that the agent be moved by a virtuous impulse, not by hatred or cupidity, and that for his part he conduct himself prudently in regard to the mode and circumstances of his action. But this good or virtuous behaviour on the part of the legislator who makes a given law, is not necessary to the validity of the law. For a prince may conduct himself wickedly and unjustly when he makes a law, while the law which he makes may nevertheless be just and good, and also valid. With respect to the law itself, however, the requisite mode involves not only righteousness in the subject-matter of the law, but also righteousness in its form. A law, then, is said to be just when the form of justice is preserved in it, a point which St. Thomas (*ibid.,* art. 4 and qu. 95, art. 3) neatly expounds.

13.[23] *Three phases of justice must be observed in order that a law may be made justly.* A fuller explanation may be offered, as set forth below. For in order that a law may be made justly, three phases of justice must be perceptible in its form.

The first phase is legal justice. It is the function of this form of justice to seek the common good and, consequently, to guard the due rights of the community; but law ought to be directed chiefly to this purpose, as we have shown; and therefore, law should be made in a just manner from the standpoint of legal justice. Thus it is that St. Thomas (*ibid.*) declares that law should be just in having as its goal the common good.

The second phase is commutative justice. It is the care of this phase of justice that the legislator shall not exceed his own power in laying down his commands. Such justice is in the highest degree essential for the validity of a law. Consequently, if a prince legislates for persons who are not subject to him, he sins against commutative justice in so far as those persons are concerned, even though he may be requiring an act that is in itself righteous and advantageous. And accordingly, St. Thomas has said that in a law justice on the part of the legislator is a requisite.

The third phase of justice is distributive. This also is a requisite of law. For in the process of laying down commands for the multitude, [law] distributes the burden, as it were, among the various parts of the state,

---

23. [The Latin text incorrectly has 'II'.—Tr.]

for the good of the latter, and must therefore preserve in that distribution a proportionate equality, which is a matter pertaining to distributive justice. Accordingly, a law which apportions burdens unequally will be unjust, even if the thing which it prescribes is not inequitable. It is in this sense that St. Thomas (*ibid.*) has asserted that a proportionate equality is required in the form of a just law.

From the foregoing, moreover, he correctly concludes that, in addition to its inequity from the standpoint of subject-matter, a law can be unjust in three ways, namely: because the end in view is private advantage, not the public good; or, because of a defect in power on the part of the [legislative] agent; or, because of a defect in the form [of the law], that is, a defect of just distribution.

It is clear, then, that just enactment from all the standpoints above mentioned is essential to law.

14.[24] *Proof that justice is necessary to the validity of a law.* Moreover, the second part of our assertion[25]—namely, that this justice [in enactment] is so necessary to law that without it law is invalid and ceases to bind—is expressly upheld by St. Thomas in the same place [I.–II, qu. 96, art. 4]; by Soto [*De Iustitia et Iure,* Bk. I, qu. v, art. iii], B. Medina and others (on that passage of St. Thomas); by Castro (*De Potestate Legis Poenalis,* Bk. I, chap. v), Victoria (*Relectio: De Potestate Papae et Concil.,* no. 18), Panormitanus (on *Decretals,* Bk. I, tit. ii, chap. vii, no. 9), Felinus (*ibid.,* nos. 40 and 41) and others. This view is also favoured by the *Digest* (I. i. 1); and the interpreters of that passage may be consulted. St. Thomas, too, interprets as referring to this phase of justice, the words of Augustine above cited (*On Free Will,* Bk. I, chap. v): 'That is not law which is not just.' Still more pertinent to this point is the remark which he makes in the *City of God* (Bk. XIX, chap. xxi): 'What is done according to law (*iure*) is done justly (*iuste*), and what is unjustly done, cannot be done according to law. For the unjust decrees of men should not be thought of or spoken of as laws, since even they themselves define law as that which has flowed from the fount of justice.'[26]

---

24. [The Latin text incorrectly has '12'.—Tr.]

25. [*Vide* Section 12.—Tr.]

26. [This quotation, as given by Suárez, varies somewhat from the text of Augustine.—Tr.]

15.[27] Finally, it is in this sense that we shall rightly interpret the second condition of law laid down by Isidore in the last of the passages above cited. For he says that 'law should be righteous and just'; and the first of these attributes relates to the subject-matter of law, as I have pointed out in a preceding statement; so that the second relates to the form of the law, as it were—that is to say, [it implies] that [law] must be justly enacted.

Moreover, this part of our discussion may be demonstrated by reasoning, if we shape our argument in accordance with the three standpoints regarding justice which were indicated by St. Thomas as follows: the end, the [legislative] agent, and the form.

For with respect to the first standpoint, all those statements are applicable which we made in Chapter Seven,[28] where we proved that there is no law that is not enacted for the common good. Consequently, under this division of justice, which we call legal, are included certain[29] conditions of law laid down by Isidore in the aforementioned passage [*Etymologies,* Bk. V, chap. xxi and *Decretum,* Pt. I, dist. IV, can. ii], namely: law must be necessary, it must be useful, and it must serve the common welfare. Accordingly, we shall omit the discussion of those conditions in the present context, inasmuch as we have expounded them above.

Again, as to justice on the part of the [legislative] agent, or commutative justice, everything set forth in Chapter Eight[30] is pertinent; and consequently, it is also sufficiently clear that a law enacted [by an agent] without jurisdiction is null.

16.[31] *Concerning the necessity of distributive justice for the validity of a law.* Thus there remains to be proved only the assertion regarding the other and third part of justice, which relates to the form, that is, to distributive equity.

27. [The Latin text incorrectly has '13'.—Tr.]
28. [*Supra,* p. 102.—Tr.]
29. [*Illae.* Isidore specifies various other conditions in Chapter xxi of the *Etymologies.*—Tr.]
30. [Omitted from these *Selections*—Tr.]
31. [The Latin text incorrectly has '14'.—Tr.]

As to this factor, it is manifestly essential to the justice of law; since, if a law is imposed upon certain subjects, and not upon others to whom its subject-matter is equally applicable, then it is unjust, unless the exception is the result of some reasonable cause; a point which we have demonstrated above.

Again, the imposition of equal burdens upon all persons, without regard to the strength or capacity of each, is also contrary to reason and to justice, as is self-evident. And as to the fact that such injustice suffices to nullify a law, this is expressly affirmed by St. Thomas [I.–II, qu. 96, art. 4], when he says: '[Precepts] of this sort are manifestations of violence, rather than laws, and therefore they are not binding in conscience.' In my opinion, this statement should be interpreted as referring to cases in which the disproportion and inequality of a law are so great that the latter redounds to the common detriment, and results in a grave and unjust burdening of many members of the community.[32] If it so happens, however, that a law is in itself useful, while some exceptional instance to which it applies involves injustice, the law would not on that account be entirely null, nor would it cease to bind the other subjects. For, strictly speaking, no positive injustice (as it were) is done these subjects in the imposition of such a burden upon them, since the burden would not in itself be wrongful and since there results simply a measure of disproportion as between certain individuals and the community as a whole, a disproportion which would seem insufficient to nullify the law. But if, by an exception in favour of certain persons, others are burdened to a degree that exceeds the bounds of equity, then, to the extent of that excess, the law will fail to bind; while it will nevertheless be able to bind in other ways wherein it is not unjust. An example of this sort may be noted in the case of the laws on taxes, to which we shall later devote some remarks.

This part of our argument, moreover, may be further clarified by an explanation of the third principal condition for law, as laid down by Isidore [*Etymologies,* Bk. V, chap. xxi]—namely, that law must be practicable[33]

---

32. [Simply *eius,* the grammatical antecedent evidently to be understood from the preceding adjective *commune.*—Tr.]

33. [Literally, of course, 'possible', i.e. possible to observe.—Tr.]

(*possibilis*)—as well as by an explanation of other points which he also mentions in that context, as follows: '[law must be] in harmony with nature and with the custom of the country, and suitable to the time and place.' For all these latter factors evidently serve to define that practicability, as we shall [presently] explain.

17.[34] *The third assertion: it is inherent in the nature of law that it shall relate to a practicable object.* My third assertion, then, is this: it is inherent in the nature of law that it shall be practicable. This assertion, interpreted in a general sense, is applicable to every law.

However, in order that it may be proved and expounded, we should note that the term *possibilis* admits of two distinct interpretations: first, as opposed, absolutely, to *impossibilis;* secondly, as opposed to what is difficult, oppressive, and burdensome.

Taken in the first sense, this property of practicability is[35] a self-evident [requirement of law], whatever the evasive arguments heretics may employ. For that which does not fall within the realm of freedom does not fall within that of law; but what is absolutely impossible does not come within the realm of freedom, since the latter of its very nature demands power to choose either of two alternatives; and therefore, [what is impossible] cannot be the subject-matter of law. Similarly, in cases of transgression or omission which cannot be reckoned as involving guilt or calling for punishment, it is impossible for law to intervene. For it is a part of the intrinsic nature of law that it shall contain some intrinsic element of obligation; but the omission to perform impossible deeds cannot be accounted guilt (any more than the performance of what is absolutely necessary is accounted deserving of a reward); and therefore, laws cannot be concerned with matters of this sort.

18.[36] *The assertion laid down by the Council of Trent is confirmed.* Moreover, in this [first and absolute] sense, at all events, the Council of Trent (Sixth Session, and Chap. xi, canon 18) laid down the same assertion with

---

34. [The Latin text incorrectly has '15'.—Tr.]
35. [The Latin text at this point has *non* (not), evidently an error. It has been corrected in the 1856 Edition of Paris, which omits the *non*.—Tr.]
36. [The Latin text incorrectly has '16'.—Tr.]

regard to divine laws, also.[37] Bellarmine, too (*De Iustificatione,* Bk. IV, chap. xi), and Andreas de Vega (*Tridentini Decreti de Justificatione Expositio et Defensio,* Bk. XI, chap. ix), opposing the heretics[38] of that time, furnish extensive proofs to the same effect, based upon the Scriptures, upon the writings of the Fathers, and upon reason. Consequently, it is clear, *a fortiori,* that it is still more necessary for human laws to be practicable [in the absolute sense], because they are derived from a lesser power and are a participation (so to speak) in the divine law, and because the arguments adduced with respect to divine law, apply *a fortiori* with respect to these [human precepts].

There is the further argument that Augustine (*De Natura et Gratia,* Chap. xcvi [Chap. lxix]) says, not merely that God does not command that which is impossible, but also that, 'It is a matter of firmest belief that a just and good God cannot have commanded impossibilities'. How, then, shall man have been able to command impossibilities? In this connexion, there is a vast difference between God and man. For God can command certain things impossible to nature, being able to render them possible through grace, which He for His part does not withhold in so far as it is necessary to the observance of His commandments; and consequently, the commandments of God relate always to something which is possible [of achievement], since that which we are able to achieve through those who befriend us, we are in an absolute sense able to achieve, provided that this friendly assistance is surely to be had and ready to hand. Human beings, however, cannot supply the power necessary for the fulfilment of precepts, and therefore they must necessarily assume that this power exists either by the force of nature

37. The canon of Trent is from the decree of 1547 on justification, and it reads: 'If anyone says that the commands of God are impossible to keep even for a human who is justified and established in a state of grace, let them be anathema.'

38. The heretics here are the Protestants who are seen as detaching law from freedom. The sense in which, according to Suárez, it must be possible for us to obey the law is that we must be free to do so, where freedom is understood, not just as a power to do right, which might be consistent with a necessity of doing right, but as a power over alternatives. Law addresses the exercise of freedom because it is concerned with actions deserving of punishment and reward, and only actions involving the exercise of freedom are deserving of punishment and reward.

or through grace, according to the character of the precept in question. At this point, to be sure, difficulties might be raised as to the possibility of loving God, of overcoming concupiscence, and of obeying the commandments; but we shall take up these matters in the treatise On Grace.[39]

19.[40] The words of Isidore [*Etymologies,* Bk. V, chap. xxi], when he requires of law that it shall be practicable, should, then, be interpreted in accordance with this last part of our discussion. For Isidore is speaking principally of human law, and therefore, in order to explain the kind of practicability [to which he refers], he adds the phrase, 'in harmony with nature'; that is to say, regard being had for the frailty and the constitution of nature. This condition, God Himself, in His own way, observes. For He refrains from prescribing that virginity be preserved by all persons, since this would be impossible, according to nature. So, also, the canon law refrains from prescribing that communion be received on all feast days, because such a practice could not be worthily observed, in view of the conditions inherent in nature. The same argument applies to other instances. Under this head comes the contention (upheld by St. Thomas) that law should be adapted to the subjects, in accordance with their [varying] capacities, so that the same fasts are not imposed upon children as upon their elders.

Isidore makes a further addition [*ibid.*], in the words, '[in harmony] with the custom of the country'. For custom is a second nature; and therefore, that which is repugnant to custom is held to be decidedly repugnant to nature and, consequently, almost morally impossible. This condition, however, should be understood as referring to custom that is righteous and advantageous to the state. For evil custom should be amended by law; and even though [a given custom] may have been at one time

---

39. [Not included in these *Selections.*—Tr.] According to Suárez, the Law of the New Testament, insofar as it directs us to a supernatural end that is impossible for our unaided nature and imposes commands on us that we are not free to keep without assistance, is by its very nature as obligatory law accompanied by the assistance of divine grace that gives us freedom to keep the law and attain the end to which the law directs us.

40. [The Latin text incorrectly has '17'.—Tr.]

advantageous, nevertheless, if the state of affairs has undergone so great a change that [the same custom] ceases to be of advantage and the opposite course becomes expedient for the common good, then, in that case also, it will be possible for law to override custom; a point which we shall discuss later, in the proper context.

Finally, Isidore adds [*Etymologies,* Bk. V, chap. xxi], 'suitable to the time and place' [as qualifying words], since regard should be had for these circumstances, in every prudent act. In this connexion, however, they are to be considered, not from the standpoint of the act of command, but from that of the subject-matter or act which is prescribed, since not in every place, nor at every time, are the same actions suitable; wherefore, in the process of legislation, the said circumstances should be accorded the most careful consideration, as Augustine, too (*Confessions,* Bk. III, chap. xxxvii [chap. vii]), has rightly declared.

If, however, we give this matter proper attention, we shall see that the circumstances in question are also determining elements of the practicability of any law whatsoever, since a given thing may be regarded as morally impossible at one time and as easily [accomplished] at another time; the same argument being applicable in due proportion to matters of locality. Sometimes, moreover, these circumstances may affect the righteousness [of a law], owing to similar reasons.

20.[41] Finally, the explanation of the conditions discussed above enables us to understand that, in so far as these conditions may be pertinent to the substance and validity of law, they are correspondingly necessary either to the justice or to the requisite practicability of human law; since legislative power has been granted to men in conjunction with such just limitations.

The determination, however, of the cases which involve a substantial defect in regard to such conditions, must be left to prudent judgment; and this judgment must be based upon a high degree of certainty, if a law is to be adjudged invalid on such grounds. For the statement which I made above,[42] namely, that the injustice [of a law] must be clear and beyond

41. [The Latin text incorrectly has '18'.—Tr.]
42. [Referring evidently to Section 11.—Tr.]

doubt [if the law is to be declared invalid], is a statement which applies in the present[43] connexion with much greater force. This is true, partly because of the reasons set forth in that earlier passage, since they hold good also for the matter now under discussion; and partly because less danger exists in connexion with this matter, since the doubt [in this case] turns solely upon a temporal objection.

The difference between injustice from the standpoint of subject-matter, and injustice from the standpoint of mode. For we must note the difference between injustice in a law from the standpoint of subject-matter, and injustice therein from the standpoint of mode.

In the former case, if the injustice clearly exists, it is on no account permissible to obey the law—not even for the sake of avoiding any damage or scandal whatsoever—since it is never permissible to do wrong for the sake of any end.

But in the second case, though the law may not of itself be binding, a subject may obey it if he so chooses, provided he does not co-operate in [any resulting] injustice; for he has the power to cede his own right. Accordingly, it is much more credible, that he can be bound to obey in a doubtful case. And, indeed, even in cases of indubitable injustice [i.e. from the standpoint of mode], the subject may sometimes be bound to obedience in order to avoid scandal; since the latter must be avoided, though some temporal damage be suffered in consequence. This view is supported by the *Decretals* (Bk. II, tit. xxvi, chap. ii); it also finds a basis in Augustine (*De Verbis Domini,* Serm. vi [*Sermons,* lxii, Migne ed.] and *On Psalm cxxiv*); and it has been noted by St. Thomas (I.–II, qu. 96, art. 4). Adrian (*Quaestiones Quodlibeticae,* No. 6, ad 1), too, may be consulted in the same connexion; as may Gabriel (on the *Sentences,* Bk. IV, dist. xvi, qu. 3 [*Dicitur autem lex*]), the jurists (on *Decretals,* Bk. II, tit. xxvi, chap. ii), Panormitanus (on *Decretals,* Bk. I, tit. ii, chap. vii, no. 9), the Cardinal (on *Decretum,* Pt. I, dist. l, can. xxxvi), and Bellarmine (*De Romano Pontifice,* Bk. IV, chap. xv).

---

43. [I.e. with respect to the just *establishment* of a law, rather than with respect to the justice of the *act* thereby imposed.—Tr.]

CHAPTER XII

What Definition of Law (*Lex*) Is Derived from the Conditions of Law Above Set Forth?

1. The method above indicated[1] was employed by St. Thomas (I.–II, qu. 90, art. 4), when, from the characteristic properties of *lex* as he had recorded them, he drew a definition of the term, a definition which I shall presently quote. For other definitions of *lex* have been laid down, and these have been cited and rejected by Soto on St. Thomas (*De Iustitia et Iure,* Bk. I, qu. i), by Castro (*De Potestate Legis Poenalis,* Bk. I, chap. ii) and by other modern authors. It is unnecessary, however, to dwell upon this point, since the descriptions in question are not true definitions, but eulogies of law, or else refer not to law in general, but to some particular law. Thus Cicero (*Laws,* Bk. I [Bk. II, chap. iv]) has said that: 'Law is something eternal existing in the mind of God', and (Book II [, chap. iv]), that it is: 'The right reason of supreme Jove', descriptions which are suitable for the eternal law. In another passage [*Laws,* Bk. I, chap. vi], indeed, he declares that law is 'Right reason,[2] implanted in nature'. Similarly, Clement of Alexandria has also said that law is 'right reason'. And these statements are applicable to natural law. Aristotle, however, in the *Rhetoric to Alexander,* has asserted that, 'Law is the common consent of the state,' &c., and again (*Ethics,* Bk. X, last chapter [, § 12]), that it is, 'a rule emanating from a certain wisdom', &c. These assertions may fittingly be applied to human or civil law. Similar declarations are found in several passages of Isidore (*Etymologies,* Bk. II, chap. x and Bk. V, *passim*), whom we have frequently cited, and to these passages Gratian refers in the *Decretum* (Pt. I, dists. i and iv). Moreover, definitions of a like nature may be inferred from various laws of the *Digest* (I. i and iii).

2. *Various definitions of law.* A more general definition may be drawn from the statement made by St. Thomas (I.–II, qu. 91, art. 2 [art. 1])

---

1. [*Hanc methodum,* evidently referring to the method of definition implied in the chapter heading.—Tr.]

2. [Suárez has *Rectam rationem,* although Cicero's phrase is *ratio summa* (the supreme reason).—Tr.]

that: 'Law is a dictate of practical reason emanating from the prince who rules some perfect community.' Castro, however, defines law differently (*De Potestate Legis Poenalis,* Bk. I, chap. i), as 'The righteous will of one who represents the people, when that will is promulgated either orally or in writing, with the intention of binding the subjects to obey it'. These definitions express the personal opinions of the individuals who framed them, a practice which should be avoided, in so far as is possible; for a definition ought to consist of a primary principle (as it were), on a universally applicable basis. Furthermore, the definition last quoted contains certain elements which are not strictly necessary, or which require fuller explanation. Take, for example, the statement that [law] is a righteous will; for, strictly speaking, it could fail to be righteous in an absolute sense. Again, [we may question] the phrase, 'one who represents the people', since [the legislator] may be either the people themselves, or some one who does not represent the people but is nevertheless charged with caring for them. And as for the first of the two definitions, it is applicable to law only in so far as law dwells within the mind of the prince; whereas, in the present discussion, we are treating also of external law.

Thus Gabriel (on the *Sentences,* Bk. III, dist. xxxvii, art. 1 [, par. *Lex obligatoria*]) has defined law as: 'The explicit sign made by right reason when the latter dictates that some one shall perform or shall refrain from performing a given action.' It would seem that this definition is approved by Aristotle, when he says [*Nicomachean Ethics,* Bk. X, chap. ix, § 12] that, 'law [. . .] is a rule emanating from a certain wisdom,[3] [etc.]'. One ought not, however, to limit the definition to the external sign alone. Moreover, the entire definition above quoted may be applied to numerous precepts or signs which are not, properly speaking, laws.

Finally, the same is true of other, similar definitions which can be found in the works of Gerson (Pt. III, tract. *De Vita Spirituali,* Lect. 10 and Pt. I, tract. *De Potestate Ecclesiastica et Origine Iuris et Legum*).

---

3. [Reading *prudentia* for *providentia,* which is evidently an error. This definition, in the fuller form already quoted, is as follows: 'law . . . is a rule, emanating from a certain wisdom and intelligence, that has compulsory force.' The leaders and the bracketed 'etc.' have been added by the translator.—Tr.]

3. Consequently, that deduced by St. Thomas (I.–II, qu. 90, art. 4) has more frequently been adopted, namely: 'Law is an ordinance of reason for the common good, promulgated by one who is charged with the care of the community.' Alexander of Hales, too (*Summa Universae Theologiae,* Pt. III, qu. xxvi, memb. 4 [memb. 3]), offers almost the same definition.

In the first place, the definition in question[4] contains as its generic term, the expression, 'ordinance of the reason', an expression which is to be interpreted in an active and not a passive sense. For the ordinance is laid upon the subjects through the law, but the act of ordering issues from the lawgiver; this act whereby he orders, is given the name of an active ordinance; and that active ordinance must emanate from the reason; therefore, it is called an ordinance of the reason. But this term (whatever may be the particular sense in which it is employed by the authors [of the definition]) is not of itself restricted to an act of the intellect, nor to one of the will. For, in the case of both faculties, there may be an ordinance, and that ordinance which pertains to the will may be said to pertain to the reason, either because the will itself is a rational faculty, or, in any case, because it ought to be directed by right reason, especially in the law-making process. The term in question may even be applied to an external as well as to an internal act; for an external precept is also an ordinance of the reason, that is to say, an ordinance dictated by the reason.

The remainder [of this definition], however, is added by way of differentiation, and includes virtually all the conditions of law, as is sufficiently evident from what we have already said.

4. *Objection.* A question may indeed arise owing to the fact that the said definition contains no limitation whereby counsel is excluded from the nature of law. Accordingly, some persons grant that counsel is comprehended within law, a supposition which—as I indicated above,[5] and as I shall repeat in the following Chapter[6]—is, strictly speaking, not true.

---

4. [I.e. the one just quoted from St. Thomas's work, and found, in similar form, in the work of Alexander of Hales.—Tr.]

5. [*Supra,* p. 23; *De Legibus,* chap. i, § 7.—Tr.]

6. [Not included in these *Selections.*—Tr.]

Solution; and the difference between law and counsel. I therefore reply that counsel is excluded in a twofold manner by the definition in question.[7] For counsel, as such, is not of its very nature derived from a superior in so far as he possesses power over and charge of his subjects; whereas law should be an ordinance of the reason such that it emanates thus from one having charge of the community, even as this very definition provides, for the definition must be understood in its essential terms and formally.

Similarly, prayer, or petition, should be excluded from this ordinance of the reason. For these three things—precept, counsel and petition—agree in this respect: that, through each of them, one person is ordered or directed to action by means of another's reason, so that each of the three may be said to be an ordinance of the reason. And nevertheless, they differ one from another. For a petition is normally addressed by an inferior to a superior; although it may occur between equals and may sometimes proceed from a superior with respect to an inferior, which, however, does not apply in so far as regards the true nature of petition. Indeed, even in such an [abnormal] situation, the one submits himself, in a sense, to the other; as I have remarked above. Counsel, on the other hand, passes essentially between equals; and if it implies a certain pre-eminence on the part of the counsellor, that pre-eminence is one of wisdom only, not of power. But law essentially proceeds from a superior with respect to an inferior; and this is indicated by the definition under discussion. Accordingly, counsel is in this way sufficiently excluded from partaking of the nature of law. Furthermore, the kind of ordinance in question should be interpreted as being an efficacious ordinance that has compulsory force, as Aristotle declared; and this specification would seem to be laid down in the word 'promulgated', since true promulgation apparently does not pertain to counsel. For the word promulgation implies an order for the purpose of creating an obligation, and it is in this respect most of all that counsel differs from law.

5. *Another objection.* Finally, there would seem to be [another] objection to this same definition of law, namely: the fact that it is possible that a

---

7. Counsel neither obliges nor by its nature derives from a superior with the authority to oblige.

prelate may, in accordance with right reason, and by making his will sufficiently clear to the community, order those subject to him to execute a
given act; and that [in so doing] he will nevertheless not be making a law,
since [his order] does not involve a perpetual and stable precept, such as is
requisite, according to what we have said, to the nature of law; so that the
entire definition given above is applicable [, it would seem,] to precepts
promulgated for a community, even when they have been enjoined only
for a day.

Solution. To this objection, I reply briefly that either St. Thomas understood 'law' in the broader sense, including thereunder every precept of
this sort; or else, the first part of the definition should, indeed, be so interpreted that the phrase 'an ordinance of the reason' is made to refer solely
to ordinances that are stable and enduring.

The definition laid down by the author. Therefore, law may perhaps be
more briefly defined as follows: law 'is a common, just and stable precept,
which has been sufficiently promulgated'. For this generic definition has
also been laid down by St. Thomas (qu. 96, art. 1, ad 2 [I.–II, qu. 96, art. 4])
and by the jurist [Papinian] (*Digest,* I. iii. 1); and by means of that definition, particular precepts are excluded, while by means of the remaining
terms, all those elements are provided for which can be desired in the
case of law, as is easily apparent to any one who reflects upon the remarks
made above.

CHAPTER XVIII

Are All Men in This Life Subject to Law and Bound by It?

1. We have said that the chief effect of law consists in its binding power,[1]
and that all its other effects have their roots in that one alone. Binding power, however, must of necessity relate to some one on whom it is
imposed; and therefore, in order to provide a perfectly clear understanding

---

1. The chief effect of law, through the exercise of its power to bind, is to impose
obligation.

of this effect, it is necessary to explain what persons fall under the binding power of law, or are capable of so doing. For although we have already demonstrated that law is established for men, and for men considered in common—that is to say, established for some community—still, we have not explained whether all men are capable of being subject to this obligation, or whether some are (so to speak) exempt.

This question has been discussed by St. Thomas (I.–II, qu. 96, art. 5), in special relation to human law; for he may have thought the discussion unnecessary with respect to law in general, in view of the fact that absolutely all adult human beings in this life (for of such are we speaking) are most clearly subject to some law.

However, the heretics of the present age force us to deal generally, at this point, with the said question. In the course of this investigation, we are not asking what men are bound by positive laws—divine or human; nor even what men are bound by the natural law. For these are points to which we shall later[2] give special consideration. Much less, then, do we inquire whether all men are bound by all laws, since it is clear that every individual is not bound by each and every law. For such a state of affairs, in so far as concerns positive laws, is neither necessary nor possible; as is self-evident. Therefore, we inquire solely whether the binding force of law, as such, or of some particular law, considered abstractly or in itself alone, extends to all men in such a way that there is no one of them not subject to the yoke of some law.

2. *The heretics exempt all just men from [the yoke of] law.* For the heretics of the present age hold that just[3] men are exempt from the yoke of law; nor are they speaking simply of human law, as some persons believe, but rather of law in the absolute sense, a fact which may clearly be inferred from the fundamental principles that they uphold.[4]

---

2. [*Infra,* this Chapter.—Tr.]

3. [Just; that is, those who are in God's grace and favour.—Reviser.]

4. By 'heretics of the present age' Suárez means Luther and his followers. These he sees as committed to denying that the just are subject to law. For in Luther's view, as Suárez supposes, the just are justified or accounted just by their faith alone; their actions bring no desert of reward or punishment. But the possibility of bringing such desert is, in Suárez's view, essential to actions' being subject to obligation or law.

These principles have been carefully and accurately explained by Peter Canisius (*De Verbi Dei Corruptelis,* Bk. I, chap. xi), by Salmerón (on the *Epistle to the Galatians,* Disp. xiv) and by Cardinal Bellarmine (*De Iustificatione,* Bk. IV, chap. i) where the latter cites, among other blasphemies pronounced by Luther, the following, from one of Luther's sermons: 'Let us beware of sins, but far more of laws, and good works; and let us give heed only to the promise of God and to faith.' [Bellarmine] furthermore relates that [these heretics] interpret Christian liberty as consisting in the just man's freedom from the duty of fulfilling the law before God, so that all works are indifferent to him, that is to say, neither prescribed nor forbidden.

They base their view partly upon their own errors, partly upon certain misinterpreted Scriptural passages.

The principal basis of that view is their denial of true justice[5] and of the necessity of works for the attainment of justice. For they say that men are justified solely through their acceptance by God, and through the lack of any extrinsic imputation [of sin] by Him; a state attained by every person who firmly believes that his sins have been forgiven him, or rather, are not imputed to him, because of Christ's merits. Furthermore, they say that this faith suffices for salvation, whatever works a man may do. From this basic argument, it necessarily follows that a just man, as conceived by them, is not bound by any law, provided he remains steadfast in the faith; since, whatever works he may perform while believing that they are not imputed to him, he does not incur any punishment, nor are his acts imputed to him as sin. Thus, these heretics would not seem to deny that men are bound by law, in such a way as to imply in their denial that works opposed to law are not sins; on the contrary, they teach that, from other standpoints, all the works of the just are sinful, that it is impossible even for the just to fulfil the law of God, and similar doctrines which presuppose that law has binding force and is a rule for such works. They assert, then, that this obligation is morally removed (so to speak) or rendered ineffective, by that faith of theirs; since [such faith] renders one not liable to punishment,[6]

5. [Justice; that is, justification. The heretics held that justification was imputed through the merits of Christ.—REVISER.]

6. [A necessarily free interpretation of the Latin word order, *non facit hominem reum poenae* (does not render one liable to punishment).—TR.]

and since, by reason of it, one's deed does not appear as evil in the sight of God, even though it may in itself be evil.

Another basis for their view is derived from a certain false distinction made between the law and the Gospel, which we shall consider below, when we treat of the law of grace.[7] And as for the Scriptural testimony on which they make a show of reliance, that will be discussed in the following Chapter.[8]

3. *The Faith teaches that all men in this life are subject to law.* But the true Catholic belief is that all men in this life are subject to law to such an extent, that they are bound to obey it, and become legal culprits in the sight of God, if they do not voluntarily observe the law. This is a certain conclusion, and one of faith, defined in the Council of Trent ([Sixth Session,] Chap. xi and canons 18, 19 and 20), where the Council particularly mentions the just and the perfect, since it lays down a doctrine specifically in opposition to heretics. But it does not omit the general doctrine, for it makes this statement: 'Moreover, no one, howsoever truly he may have been justified, should consider himself free from the obligation to observe the commandments.' If, then, no one is exempted from that obligation, all men in this world are certainly subject to laws.

The truth of this conclusion may be proved inductively, as follows: from the beginning of their creation men were subject to natural law and, furthermore, Adam and Eve were subject to a prohibition against eating of the tree of knowledge, even though they were just and in a state of innocence. Moreover, it is manifest that, after the fall, and before the advent of Christ, the Jews were under the written law and the rest of mankind, under natural law (to omit human laws for the time being from our discussion). Such is the explicit teaching of Paul (*Romans,* Chaps. i and ii), who shows that the Jews as well as the Gentiles were transgressors of the law; the former, of the written law, and the latter, of the natural law, which they manifested as being written in their hearts whenever they observed any part of it. And these laws were not less binding upon the just than upon the unjust, since they were laid down for all without distinction.

---

7. [Not included in these *Selections.*—Tr.]
8. [Not included in these *Selections.*—Tr.]

Moreover, the natural law is binding essentially and intrinsically, both before and after the states of justice or injustice; but the written law had its inception among the just, inasmuch as it was given to the whole of that faithful people, which included Moses, Aaron, and many other just persons, while the law of circumcision had even before that time been given to Abraham, who was just.

4. Subsequently to the advent of Christ, however, there have been no just persons outside of the Church; and therefore, with regard to the men who are entirely outside of it, we can only say that the unbelieving Gentiles are bound by that same natural law, since no dispensation [therefrom] has been granted to them, nor has any grace been imparted to them. Furthermore, it is certain that they are bound to accept the faith and the law of Christ, as He Himself testifies, when He says (*Matthew,* Chap. xxviii [, vv. 19, 20]): 'Going [therefore], teach ye all nations; baptizing them in the name of the Father, and of the Son and of the Holy Ghost. Teaching them to observe all things whatsoever I have commanded you.'

As to the Jews, it is also manifest that they are bound by natural law, and subject to the same precept as the Gentiles with respect to receiving baptism and accepting the faith and the law of Christ; a fact which Mark made sufficiently clear, saying (*Mark,* Chap. xvi [, vv. 15, 16]): 'preach the Gospel to every creature. . . . he that believeth not' (that is to say, believeth not with a living faith that works through charity)[9] 'shall be condemned.' Furthermore, those Jews, although they are no longer bound in actual fact by the written law, since it has been abrogated, nevertheless sin through a faulty conscience when they fail to observe it; for Paul (*Galatians,* Chap. v [, v. 3]) testifies,[10] 'to every man circumcising himself, that he is a debtor to do the whole law'.

5. *Wicked Christians are bound by the law of the Gospel.* I come now to the Church of Christ, to which the words of the heretics especially refer, and in that body, I distinguish the wicked from the good, or just.

---

9. [The parenthetical phrase was inserted by Suárez.—Tr.]

10. [The word *Testificatur* is also quoted in the Latin text, but the actual Scriptural sentence begins: 'And I testify again' (*Testificor autem rursus*).—Tr.]

As to the wicked, it is manifest that they are bound by the law, seeing that they are wicked for this very reason, namely, that they fail to observe the law. The heretics will perhaps assert that these persons are sinners, not for the simple reason that they fail to observe the commandments, but because they thus fail while they are without faith; that is to say, because they have not a firm faith, while acting contrary to the law, that such evil works are not imputed to them and do not cause them to lose the goodwill and favour of God in which they consider that their justness rests. But this error may easily be refuted by means of the words of Christ, Who, in the sentence of condemnation of the bad Christians (*Matthew,* Chap. xxv [, vv. 41 *et seq.*]), condemns them, not because they have not believed, nor because while disobeying the precepts, they have lacked faith in the non-imputation [of sin against them], but simply because they have not performed the works of mercy and because, accordingly, they have failed to observe the law of mercy and charity. This point has been discussed by Augustine, in the works (*De Fide et Operibus,* Chap. xv and *De Octo Dulcitii Quaestionibus,* Chap. [Qu.] i) in which he amasses a number of other Scriptural passages as testimony confirming the position in question. At present, however, it is not necessary to dwell at length upon this phase of the subject, either; for with respect to these baptized evildoers, also, the heretics do not deny that such persons are subject to the law, but [merely] err in their mode of explanation, a matter of which we shall treat presently, and more fully, in the treatises on Grace and Faith.[11]

6. It remains, then, to speak of the just among the faithful. Some of these persons may be baptized only in desire and may be said to be of the Church in this sense, that is, by merit, though they are not so numbered; whereas others are baptized persons in actual fact and are numbered among the living members of the Church.

With regard to the first group, it is clear that they are bound at least by the law of baptism, over and above the obligations imposed by natural law and by faith, hope, charity, and penitence. However, we shall demonstrate later,[12] and in the proper contexts, that even just persons who have been

---

11. [Not included in these *Selections.*—Tr.]
12. [*Vide infra,* p. 796.—Tr.]

baptized are bound by human laws, both civil and ecclesiastical, and also by the positive divine law laid down by Christ.

Accordingly, we undertake at this point to prove [the existence of a similar obligation] in regard to divine, moral, or natural law.

The first proof is as follows: the law is so essential, so necessary in its very nature, that it cannot be abolished, as we shall demonstrate in the following book.

7. Secondly, Christ did not abolish the law, but on the contrary confirmed it, at the very beginning of His preaching (*Matthew*, Chap. v), where He clarified it and purged it of the corruptions of the Pharisees and the imperfections of the Mosaic law, and, having added counsels and means for the observance of the law, perfected and in a certain sense enriched it. Moreover, it is certain that all these teachings were laid down by Our Lord for His future Church, for the just as well as for the unjust, since He says [*ibid.*, vv. 20 *et seq.*] to all: '[. . .] Unless your justice abound more than that of the scribes and Pharisees, you shall not enter into the kingdom of heaven', and so forth. Especially should one reflect upon the words [*ibid.*, Chap. vii, v. 13], 'Enter ye in at the narrow gate [. . .]'. For He most clearly speaks of the observance of His commandments as 'the narrow gate', commandments which He declares to be included in the principle, '[. . .] whatsoever you would that men should do to you, do you also to them' [*ibid.*, v. 12]; and He teaches that this principle pertains to the Gospel and relates to all who profess the Gospel.

8. Thirdly, all that Christ taught on the night of His Supper, with regard to the observance of precepts and particularly of charity, has a special pertinence in relation to just persons who have been baptized. For the Apostles were just and had been baptized, and to them He said (*John*, Chap. xiv [, v. 15]): 'If you love me, keep my commandments'; again [v. 21], 'He that hath my commandments, and keepeth them; he it is that loveth me'; yet again [v. 23], 'If any one love me, he will keep my word' and [v. 24], 'He that loveth me not, keepeth not my words'; and also, in Chapter xv [, v. 9], 'Abide in my love', and in a subsequent verse [14:] 'You are my friends, if you do the things that I command you.' These conditions have the force of a threat, and indicate the necessity for observing the commandments in order that charity may be preserved; and therefore, the just are bound to

such observance, and without it they will not preserve [their] justness. An infinite number of similar passages from the Scriptures might be adduced, but there is no need to dwell upon a matter that is clear and evident by the light of natural reason—in so far, at least, as moral precepts are concerned.

9. *The fundamental arguments of the heretics are refuted.* The basic position of the heretics involves a number of errors, of which we cannot treat at this point, but which are to be discussed in various parts of this work. For in the first place, their assertion that the divine commandments are impossible of fulfilment has been rejected above,[13] and [the validity of this rejection] will be made more evident in the treatise on Grace.[14] Secondly, in that same treatise we shall refute their declaration that all the works of the just are sins, and particularly the declaration that these works are mortal sins. Thirdly, we shall lay down the distinction between the Old and the New Laws at the end of this treatise [*De Legibus,* Bks. IX and X][15] and shall assail the false distinction devised by the heretics. Fourthly, in the treatise on Grace,[16] we shall pluck out the root of all the heresies, which is imputed justness, and we shall demonstrate in that treatise that men are truly, actually and intrinsically justified through an inherent justness given by Christ, and that, through this same justness, their sins are truly and completely remitted, not merely covered over or left free from imputation of punishment. Accordingly, it will become clear and indisputable that the works of the just are weighed, estimated and imputed by God, according to their character in point of fact. Consequently, if they are good works, they are imputed for reward; if slightly evil, for temporal punishment, unless they are blotted out by penance and satisfaction; if they are grave sins, they are so imputed as actually to destroy the just character [of the doer] until that character is restored through penance.

10. Thus, the basic position of the heretics is contrary also to natural reason, and most decidedly inconsistent with divine goodness. For sin, as such, cannot fail to be displeasing to God, since '[. . .] to God the wicked and his wickedness are hateful alike' [*Wisdom,* Chap. xiv, v. 9]. It is

13. [*Vide* Section 2 of this Chapter.—Tr.]
14. [Not included in these *Selections.*—Tr.]
15. [Not included in these *Selections.*—Tr.]
16. [Not included in these *Selections.*—Tr.]

furthermore inconsistent with divine justice that sins should be more easily forgiven, or should not be imputed, to those who commit them while
possessed of more faith in God Himself; which would be as if He Himself granted licence to sin, by promising that sins would not be imputed
against those who believe that they are not.[17] This is true especially in
view of the fact that such a promise is vain and fictitious, since it appears
nowhere in the New Testament, any more than it does in the Old. On
the contrary, Paul says (*Romans,* Chap. ii [, v. 16]) that God shall judge the
secrets of men by Jesus Christ according to the Gospel—which will be,
assuredly, according to the law and the truth, not according to the false
opinions of men.

Finally, I ask of these heretics whether or not men were justified in
the faith of Christ before His advent. If they answer in the negative, they
gravely offend against the universal redemption of Christ and contradict
explicit passages in the Holy Scriptures. 'For there is no other name under
heaven given to men, whereby we must be saved' (*Acts,* Chap. iv [, v. 12]);
since, as Paul testifies (*Romans,* Chap. iii [, v. 25]), God hath proposed
Him alone to be a propitiator through faith in His blood. If, on the other
hand, [the heretics] affirm that justification has always been effected
through faith, then, in order to be consistent, they must say that it has
always been effected without law or works, and through non-imputation
[of sins] combined simply with faith on the part of men. Therefore, these
same heretics will be forced to assert also that the just, under the natural
or the Old Law, were not subject to the law, nor did they sin against it
even in transgressing it, provided that they transgressed with faith in the
non-imputation [of their act]. What, then, remains for them to attribute
especially to the Gospel? Consequently,[18] this basic position is impious
and vain.

17. [Simply *illam,* in the Latin.—Tr.]
18. [I.e. since no such special function remains.—Tr.]

On the Eternal Law, the Natural Law, and the *Ius Gentium*

[INTRODUCTION]

After treating of law in general, it is logical that we should pass on to the individual kinds thereof, among which the eternal law has first place, on account of its dignity and excellence, and also for the reason that it is the source and origin of all laws.

But we shall discuss this kind more briefly than the others because, with respect to human affairs it is less applicable in itself to the uses or function of law; and because the eternal law is in great measure wont to be confused with divine providence, which is dealt with according to our plan in the first part of this treatise.

However, we shall combine the treatment of the natural law with that of the eternal law, partly for the sake of completeness in our work; partly because the natural law is the first system whereby the eternal law is applied or made known to us; and partly because these two laws differ as law by essence, and law by participation, or (so to speak) as symbol and symbolized, a point which we shall later explain.[1] But at this point we are interpreting natural law strictly, in so far as it is contained in natural reason alone; for that law which is connatural with grace or faith is purely supernatural, and will in consequence be expounded later when we treat of the law of grace,[2] although what we shall say about the natural law may, in due proportion, be applied also to the law of grace.

---

1. [*Infra*, p. 173 *et seq.*; *De Legibus*, Bk. II, chaps. iii and iv.—TR.]
2. [Not included in these *Selections.*—TR.]

With respect to the former, we must note that the natural law is made known to men in a twofold way; first, through the natural light of reason, and secondly, through the law of the Decalogue written on the Mosaic tablets. Thus it was that, in one passage, St. Thomas (I.–II, qu. 94) treated of the natural law under the former aspect, and later (qu. 100), he treated of it under the latter aspect.

But, since this law which was inscribed upon tables of stone is indeed the same as natural law in its substantial binding force, the wider knowledge of the latter being brought about solely by that written law, we shall consequently include in this work a consideration of all points relating to the Decalogue. But we shall consider later, in our discussion of the Old Law [*De Legibus,* Bk. IX],[3] whatever has been added to the Decalogue from the law of the Old Testament, with regard either to penalties or to certain special circumstances, or to the increase of some particular obligation. In this later context, we shall duly see whether the law of the Decalogue has in any respect ceased to operate, or whether it still endures.

Finally, because the *ius gentium* is of all systems the most closely related to the natural law, we shall discuss that, also, at the end of this Book.

CHAPTER I

Is There Any Eternal Law; and, What Necessity Is There for the Same?

1. *The first argument.* The reason for doubt lies in the fact that a law necessarily requires some one upon whom it may be imposed; and from eternity[1] there was no one upon whom law could be imposed; therefore, no system of eternal law could [actually] have existed. The truth of the major premiss is clear: for law is an act of sovereignty; and a contradiction is involved in the existence of sovereignty, unless there is some one over whom it may be exercised. The minor premiss may also be proved, because from eternity there was only God, and neither law nor sovereignty can be imposed upon Him.

3. [Not included in these *Selections.*—Tr.]
1. [I.e., before time and creation.—Tr.]

The second argument. A second argument is as follows: by a similar process of reasoning there existed from eternity no dominion, nor any jurisdiction, nor any government, because there was no being upon whom God might exercise dominion, or whom He might govern; but law is an act of government and of dominion, or jurisdiction, and therefore, for the same reason, law cannot have been eternal.

The third argument. Thirdly: promulgation is essential to law, as we have said;[2] but from eternity promulgation was impossible, since there was no one to whom law might be promulgated, nor could it be promulgated within God alone; therefore, . . .

The fourth argument. Fourthly: if there were any eternal law, it would be intrinsically and absolutely necessary, as well as unchangeable; for nothing is eternal save what is intrinsically necessary; and no law is of itself and absolutely necessary, as we said above;[3] therefore, there is no eternal law.

2. *It is the common opinion of the theologians that eternal law does exist.* Nevertheless, it is the common opinion of the theologians, that in God some kind of eternal law does exist. Thus St. Thomas (I.–II, qu. 91, art. 1, and qu. 93, throughout) teaches; as do Cajetan, Soto, and other commentators on that passage from St. Thomas, as well as Vincent de Beauvais (*Speculum Morale,* [Bk. I,] pt. II, dist. 1), Alexander of Hales (*Summa Universae Theologiae,* Part III, qu. xxvi, membrum 1), Antoninus (*Summa Theologica,* Pt. I, tit. XI, chap. i, § 4, and tit. XII, at the beginning) and Torquemada (on *Decretum,* Pt. I, dist. 1, can. i). The same conclusion is to be deduced from Augustine (*On the True Religion,* Chap. xxx [Chap. xxxi]; *On Free Will,* Book I, chaps. v and vi; and *Against Faustus,* Bk. XXII, chap. xxvii). And Cicero, also (*Laws,* Bk. I, and Bk. II [, chap. iv, § 8]), proclaims this law most of all, and asserts in the following words that it was recognized by the wisest philosophers: 'I find that it has been the opinion of the wisest men that Law is not a product of human thought, nor is it any enactment of peoples, but something eternal which rules the whole universe by its wisdom in command and prohibition. Thus they

2. [Suárez discusses promulgation in Book I, chapter xi of the *De Legibus,* a chapter not included in these *Selections.*—Tr.]
3. [*Supra,* p. 37; *De Legibus,* Bk. I, chap. iii, § 2.—Tr.]

have been accustomed to say that Law is the primal and ultimate mind of God, whose reason directs all things either by compulsion or restraint.' Plato, too, distinguished four kinds of laws in *Timaeus,*[4] calling the first divine law, whereby he clearly refers to this eternal law through which God governs the universe. The same conception is expounded in the *Dialogues: On Laws* (Bk. X, *passim*).

3. St. Thomas also demonstrates this truth, arguing that there must be in God Himself some kind of law, and that this law cannot be other than eternal in its nature, so that, consequently, there must exist in the universe some kind of eternal law. The minor premiss is assumed on the ground that God is unchangeable, and that nothing new can be added to Him [i.e. to His nature]. The major premiss is also clearly true, since God exercises providence and since it is therefore necessary to assume the existence in Him of some eternal and active reason controlling all the order and government of the universe, in accordance with the words of Boethius (*The Consolation of Philosophy,* Bk. III [, metrum ix]): 'O Thou, who governest the universe by Thy eternal reason'; therefore, this eternal reason of God has the true nature of law; because as Isidore (*Etymologies,* Bk. II, chap. x [, § 3]) said: 'If law consists in reason, then everything which is made known through reason will be law.'[5]

This argument is confirmed by Augustine on the ground that every human law is mutable and exposed to defects and errors; so that he necessarily assumes the existence of some unchangeable law, which stabilizes and serves as a measure for [these human laws], in order that right may be done through conformity with [this immutable] standard, which can be none other than the eternal law.

Finally, every specific[6] law presupposes the existence of something which is law in essence; and this essential law is eternal; therefore, . . .

---

4. [See *supra*, p. 39; *De Legibus*, Bk. I, chap. iii, § 5.—Tr.]

5. [The translation of this quotation from Isidore is based upon the text of the Oxford edition: . . . *si ratione lex consistat, lex erit omne iam quod ratione constiterit,* and not upon the apparently inaccurate wording used by Suárez: *Si ratione lex constat, lex erit omne, quod ratione constiterit.*—Tr.]

6. [Suárez has simply *participata.*—Tr.]

4. *Objection.* Some persons may object, however, that these arguments prove only that there exists in God the eternal reason determining the acts that are to be performed, a rational principle which we call Providence, while they do not prove that this principle existed as strict law from eternity. For Providence connotes an eternal relation, and law, a temporal one, as the arguments set forth at the beginning of the Chapter indicate. Wherefore, this eternal reason may at the most be called law in a material sense (as it were) and in reference to that act of the divine will or intellect which is law, but it may not be given that name in the formal sense, in so far as relates to the strict connotation of the term 'law' and all the conditions required therefor; just as active creation may be said to be eternal in a material sense, when regarded as the act of God, but not formally and absolutely, in so far as it is [essentially] creation. The same must be said of the power to exercise dominion and the like.

St. Thomas (I.–II, qu. 91, art. i, ad 1), however, maintains that the law in question is eternal, even in a formal sense and viewed as law, strictly speaking, because, 'The eternal concept of divine law has the nature of an eternal law, in that it is ordained by God for the government of things foreknown by Him.'

But, although St. Thomas may rightly say that the rational principle governing that which is destined to be performed, exists eternally within God and has the nature of an idea; nevertheless, he does not explain how that principle possesses from eternity the nature of law, nor in what way it differs therefrom, when regarded as an idea; nor does he seem to answer satisfactorily the difficulties advanced.

5. Therefore, lest we dwell exclusively on a matter of terminology, it remains for us to determine what is clear as a matter of actual fact, to what extent the question turns upon the use of terms, and what reason of an absolute nature may be adduced in favour of the phraseology adopted.

Two phases of law. A solution to the objection. Therefore let us distinguish in law, two phases. One is that which exists in the inner disposition of the lawmaker, in so far as the law in question has already been defined in his mind, and established by his absolute decree and fixed will. The other is that phase in which a law is externally established and promulgated for the subjects.

It is evident that in the former mode the eternal law does exist in the mind of God: a fact proved by the reasons advanced in favour of the true opinion. But as for the latter mode, it is equally certain that this law of God did not exist in that second phase from eternity; and this conclusion is proved by the reasons for doubt set forth at the beginning of the Chapter, as will more clearly appear from the answers which we shall give to each of the said reasons. Furthermore, law regarded in the former aspect is an immanent act, wherefore it may exist eternally in God, even though it connotes relation to a temporal effect, as in the case of predestination or providence; whereas law in the latter aspect connotes a transient action in relation to God. For although this eternal law of God, in so far as it is properly law, may be laid down for those who are subject thereto, through acts immanent in those subjects, nevertheless, these same acts are external in relation to God, and necessarily temporal; so that the law in question cannot be eternal as regards this second phase.

But if any one quibbles over words, saying that this law in its first phase is not law, because it has not been, but is yet to be established, I shall reply, in the first place, that there should be no such controversy over terms, for the usage of the Fathers and of philosophers in this matter is sufficient to warrant this application of the name 'law', in an absolute sense; and secondly, I shall argue that an excellent reason may be advanced in favour of this nomenclature, a reason by which it may even be demonstrated that the law under discussion is, in this [first] phase, not merely a law which is yet to be established, but one which has been established from eternity after its own manner, as the replies to the arguments set forth above[7] will show.

6. *Solution of the first difficulty.* Therefore, the reply to the first difficulty is that, just as the divine will is eternal, so also is [the divine] sovereignty, for this sovereignty, as regards its essence, consists in that very will alone, as I have already said.[8] And if this sovereignty be given the name of reason or judgment as to activities to come, such reason or judgment also has existed eternally in the mind of God. A question is also brought up in connexion with that [first] argument, as to whether this eternal law is in

7. [*Vide* Section 1 of this Chapter.—Tr.]
8. [*Supra,* p. 72; *De Legibus,* Bk. I, Chap. v, § 11.—Tr.]

any way applicable to God Himself; that is, whether it serves in any way as a measure and rule for the acts of the divine will, a point which we shall take up in the following Chapter.

Solution of the second difficulty. The reply to the second argument is that the exercise of dominion and of government is a transient act, and that true dominion connotes a certain relationship to a thing existing at the actual moment, so that the terms which are derived from these acts are temporal; whereas law as such, especially in its relation to God, does not necessarily connote a transient act; for in that first phase, which is of an essential nature, [the idea of law] is sufficiently verified in the immanent act, as we have explained.

7. *Answer of certain writers to the third argument.* The third argument is disposed of in various ways. Some authorities hold that the eternal law is not termed a law in relation to created beings, that is, in relation to men, because it is not a rule imposed upon them, but relates rather to the external works of God, since it is a rule and measure of all His acts. According to this explanation, the law in question is not a law regulating conduct (so to speak) but one governing the creations of the Artificer; for all things made by God are related to Him who made them. Wherefore, just as the idea of the artificer may be called a law, which he prescribes for himself, that he may produce works in accordance with it, even so is this eternal law the archetype in accordance with which God as the Supreme Artificer has willed from eternity to fashion all things. Consequently, the argument based on promulgation[9] loses all force. For promulgation is necessary in the case of a law regulating conduct, but not in the case of one governing the production of works.

Furthermore, the other arguments [adduced above] also lose their force. For this is not a law which is imposed upon subjects, nor does it relate to government.

However, such an explanation is not satisfactory.

This answer is rejected. In the first place, it is contrary to the opinion of Augustine and the theologians, and to that of Cicero and of the philosophers as well. For all of these writers speak clearly of a law which is the rule

9. [*Vide* Section 1 of this Chapter.—Tr.]

of human acts and the pattern of all other laws existing in the minds of men, or capable of emanating therefrom, whether or not the eternal law contains within itself many [kinds of law], a point which we shall discuss later.[10]

Then, in the second place, the explanation in question is unsatisfactory, because the terminology involved in it is highly figurative and would be unfitted to the subject-matter of law, by reason of its mere metaphorical significance; for the fact itself which lies beneath the metaphor consists in nothing more nor less than the ideas which we have already discussed in the first part of this treatise,[11] and connotes relation to nothing but [ideas].

In the third place, just as providence connotes relation to that which is cared for by it, and nevertheless can be eternal, although the things cared for are temporal; so also law can connote a relation to [temporal] subjects, and still be eternal.

8. *The reply made to the [third] argument, by Alexander of Hales.* Hence, Alexander of Hales [*Summa Universae Theologiae,* Pt. III, qu. xxvi, membrum 1], gives a different reply, derived from Isidore (*Etymologies,* Bk. II [, chap. x]); for Alexander holds that the term *lex* (law) is derived on the one hand from *legendum* (reading), and on the other hand from *ligandum* (binding), and that, with respect to the former derivation, the law of God is eternal, since it was read in His mind, while, with respect to the other derivation, it is not eternal, and under that sole aspect requires promulgation. If one objects that a law which does not bind does not deserve the name of law, he is met with the reply [of Alexander] in the *Summa* to the effect that it is sufficient for the nature of law that it should of itself have binding force, although in point of fact it may not yet be binding inasmuch as it has not yet been applied.

While this doctrine is perhaps true, it would not seem to solve the difficulty raised in the argument about promulgation; for [according to the said doctrine] either it must be asserted that promulgation is not necessary for the essence of law, but only for the effect thereof, which is to bind—a statement that seems contrary to the common definition of law; or, at least, an explanation is not given as to how the law in question may

10. [*Infra,* p. 173; Chap. iii.—Tr.]
11. [I.e. Book I of *De Legibus.*—Tr.]

be a true law without promulgation. Indeed, with regard to the twofold etymology for the word 'law', which Alexander of Hales assumes, in the passage cited, I find in Isidore not both derivations, but only that based upon *legendum;* neither is the latter etymology [expounded by Isidore] in any metaphorical sense; on the contrary, it is understood in a sense that is strictly literal. However, the derivation of the term is not of any great importance; for in order that anything may be termed law in an absolute sense, it is not enough that it should be possible to apply the etymology of the word *lex* correctly to that thing.

9. *The third reply based upon St. Thomas.* In the third place, then, St. Thomas (I.–II, qu. 91, art. 1, ad 2), attempts to explain how an eternal promulgation has not been lacking to the law in question: for he says that promulgation may be made orally or in writing, and that law has received promulgation in both ways from God its promulgator, because both the word of God and the writing of the Book of Life[12] are eternal.

Objection. However, some persons object, with respect to the first method of promulgation, that the utterance of the Word is not in itself required for the law of God, since the Word is personal and not essential, and because if it were essential, the Father alone would have promulgated this law and would have been the Legislator.

Against the second method of promulgation it is furthermore objected that writing has little to do with promulgation if we regard the divine knowledge, when that writing does not and cannot become known to those who are subject thereto. For promulgation should be made to those upon whom the law is imposed; whereas such writing could not have been read by any one from all eternity, nor was there any one in existence from eternity, for whom the law in question could have been promulgated.

Neither is the explanation of St. Thomas (*ibid.,* ad 1) satisfactory, when he says that created beings existed at that time in the foreknowledge of God; for promulgation is made not to creatures foreknown as the objects of knowledge, but to those actually existing in themselves. Otherwise, the

---

12. *Liber vitae* refers to God's choice and foreknowledge of those whom from all eternity he has predestined to the eternal life of heaven. See Thomas Aquinas, *Summa Theologiae,* Part I q24, articles 1 and 3.

law of Moses and the law of grace would also have been promulgated from eternity, and would consequently be eternal law.

10. But the first objection is of little weight, because, in the first place, what St. Thomas says concerning promulgation in the Word may be understood in an applied[13] sense and not in a literal one, just as ideas are said to be contained potentially in a word; and thus St. Thomas himself explains, for he duly maintains that, in so far as the essential concept of a term is concerned, it should be strictly interpreted. Then, in the second place, it is no part of the essence of law that it should be promulgated both orally and in writing; on the contrary, it is enough that what is written should be publicly made known. For the sake of the completeness and nicety of his doctrine, however, St. Thomas wishes to explain that both modes exist in God. Hence, it is not unfitting that one mode should be personal and the other, essential. Neither does it follow from this, that the Father alone is the Legislator or Promulgator, since the essential mode suffices in both cases.

To the other objection, St. Thomas replies implicitly [I.–II, qu. 91, art. 1, ad 2] by adding the limiting phrase that the law in question 'has received promulgation, in so far as relates to God . . . but in so far as relates to the creature who hearkens or regards, promulgation of law cannot be eternal.' Hence, his statement (*ibid.,* ad 1) as to creatures foreknown from eternity does not indicate that, in his opinion, the existence of creatures as objects of [divine] knowledge from eternity suffices to constitute an eternal promulgation in so far as they are concerned; rather is it an assertion that, in so far as concerns God, a law could have been established from eternity by which future creatures were to be governed.

11. *Actual promulgation is not of the essence of the eternal law.* And from this exposition of the doctrine of St. Thomas, it is clearly inferred that, according to his belief, promulgation actually made to subjects is not of the essence of this eternal law, but that, on the contrary, it suffices that the law should already have been made on the part of the Legislator, to become effective at its own proper time. Alexander of Hales was, indeed, of the same opinion. And I also regard it as true. I may add that this

---

13. [*Appropriatio* is a term used by theologians to signify our human way of applying certain divine attributes to one Person of the Trinity rather than to another.—REVISER.]

circumstance is peculiar to the law under discussion, for that law may be regarded as consummate and perfected, for the very reason that it has been established in the mind of the Lawgiver; whereas other laws are not complete until they are actually promulgated. This argument may also be added, that the eternal decree of God is immutable and is, without any change on its part, of binding force at its own proper time; while the decree of man is changeable, wherefore, as long as it is not promulgated in the form of law, it has more the character of a proposal to enact a law than that of a law firmly established and enacted.

Hence, with respect to this eternal law, absolutely speaking, no other public promulgation is necessary to make it actually binding, beyond the requirement that it shall come to the notice of the subject. And therefore if, through an interior revelation, a decree of the divine will should be made known to us, this fact would suffice to give such a decree binding authority, which would not be true in the case of a human law. For although a [temporal] subject may know that a law has already been written out by the king, he is not bound thereby until it is promulgated.

Ordinarily, however, God does not bind men by the eternal law, save through the medium of a law which is external and which constitutes a participation in and manifestation of the eternal law. So it is that, when other laws are promulgated to men, the eternal law itself is at the same time externally promulgated. Accordingly, in the case of this law, in so far as it is eternal, its promulgation, properly speaking, has no place.

In the fourth argument, this question arises: whether the eternal law is to be ranked among the free, or among the necessary acts of God. But this matter will be more properly treated in Chapter Three.

CHAPTER II

What Is the Immediate Subject-Matter of the Eternal Law? Or, What Actions Are Commanded or Governed by That Law?

1. We have said that the eternal law exists; consequently, we must explain what that law is.

However, since every law is the standard of certain acts that it regards as the material and object of which it properly treats, this point also must be taken into consideration in connexion with the eternal law. Hence, in order to make clear the nature of the eternal law, it is well that we should first set forth the subject-matter with which it deals; for this matter bears the relation of object to it, and every act is properly explained in terms of its object.

Now, there are three orders or kinds of acts in connexion with which a doubt may occur as to whether or not they are regulated by the law in question. The first and highest order comprises certain acts of God Himself which are immanent in Him, that is to say, the free acts of the divine will. The second and lowest order comprises the acts of the inferior natural agents which are devoid of reason. The third consists of the free acts of rational creatures.

We shall speak briefly of each of these classes.

2. *Whether the eternal law is the rule of the immanent acts of God. The negative solution.* In the first place, then, a doubt may be raised as to whether the eternal law is the rule of the immanent acts of God.

In order to separate what is certain from what is uncertain, we assume that the acts of the divine intellect and will—in so far as they regard God Himself and have no relation to His creatures, as these are destined to exist in the future—do not fall under the eternal law and are not regulated by it. This is the opinion of St. Thomas (I.–II, qu. 93, art. 4), as well as of Alexander of Hales [*Summa Universae Theologiae,* Pt. III, qu. xxvi, membrum 1], and all the Doctors, who postulate the existence of this law on the ground that divine providence exists, thus maintaining that providence almost coincides with the law in question. Divine providence, however, relates to the works of God, and not to God as He is in Himself. Therefore, the eternal generation of the Son of God, or the procession of the Holy Spirit,[1] does not come under that law; for they are altogether natural, and are not due to any direction or impulse proceeding from a

---

1. [In theological language, the Son proceeds by generation from the Father; the Holy Ghost proceeds from Father and Son. This is called the procession of the Holy Ghost, or, in the Latin text, *productio.*—REVISER.]

dictate of the [divine] reason or from an exercise of the [divine] will, an impulse which would pertain to the nature of the law. In accordance with the same reasoning, the love with which God loves Himself has its source not in the eternal law, but in [His own] nature. However, the reason for all this is that the law does not relate to matters which are essentially and intrinsically necessary, for these matters require no rule, since they intrinsically possess a definite mode of existence, and are, of themselves, right.

Whether the eternal law is a rule governing the free acts of God, operating externally. Therefore, the difficulty has to do only with the free acts which are in God; and which, in so far as they are free, may be called moral, although, in so far as they operate externally, they may be said to relate to art [rather than to morals].

3. It may, then, be asserted, or conceived, that the eternal law is the measure and rule of the free acts of God, in both of these aspects.

First, [those acts are so regulated] in so far as they are moral and righteous; for they are ruled by the divine reason as by a natural law of God Himself.

The proof of this statement is that God always acts according to right reason, not the reason of another, but His own; and therefore, the rectitude of the free acts of God's will is measured by the judgment of His own intellect, because, according to the logical order, the judgment is prior to the act which it is judged necessary to perform; hence, the judgment in question, in its relation to the divine will, has the nature of eternal law. This argument may be confirmed and made clear by means of certain examples. For if God speaks, He speaks truth, since lying is evil in His judgment; and if He promises, He fulfils, because He judges that fidelity is right and in harmony with His own nature; and for the same reason He takes pleasure in that which is morally right, while sinful acts are displeasing to Him, for right reason dictates that this should be so. Therefore, in His own moral acts, He is led by His eternal reason as by law. So it is that, to this extent, the eternal law has been imposed on God Himself, in so far as relates to the moral acts of His will and the righteous character of those acts.

4. With respect to the second aspect [the same relationship] may be discerned. The eternal law may be conceived of as one which God as an Artificer has imposed upon Himself, that He may perform His works in

accordance with it. For God, although He might have made and ruled the world in any one of various ways, has determined to constitute and govern it according to a certain definite law. Thus, for example, He has determined to establish the elements and the heavenly bodies after a certain order, and to confine the waters within certain places. So also He has determined to visit sins with corresponding punishments, to give rewards, on the other hand, for meritorious conduct, and to govern the world by certain specific laws. Therefore, in the light of this reasoning, it may properly be said, that the eternal law applies to God's works as they come from Him in the capacity of supreme Artificer and Governor; and that consequently it applies directly to the free acts of God's will, from which all such works directly issue. The foregoing argument is confirmed by the fact that on this account it is said that God cannot perform certain acts by the ordinary law, that is, by the law which He has imposed upon Himself, or that He cannot perform them according to His regulated power,[2] that is, according to the power reduced to a definite order through this same law, a point which Scotus has noted (on the *Sentences,* Bk. I, dist. xliv, only qu.). Therefore, if God should set free from hell any one of those who had died in mortal sin, it would be said that He was making use of His power to grant dispensations, and not that He was acting in accordance with the established law. Hence, the free works of God are ruled by a law set up by God Himself. Neither does it seem unfitting that the same will should be a law to itself with respect to acts that are distinct in their nature. For the will can issue commands to itself, and the lawgiver can be bound by his own law.

5. I assume from what has been said in the preceding Book, that law, properly understood, is the rule of moral actions, in so far as their rectitude is concerned; but that the term 'law' may also be used, at times, with reference to the rules of art or of some form of government. In either sense, then, the eternal law may be termed law; and, consequently, we may make reply to the question in hand, in either sense.

---

2. [Theologians distinguish between the absolute and the ordinary or regulated power of God. The absolute power extends to all that is not intrinsically impossible; the ordinary power is regulated by the divine decrees. Thus, God could preserve man from death, but He has decreed otherwise.—REVISER.]

The first proposition: The eternal law is not a rule of divine acts, in so far as they are moral. Therefore, I hold in the first place, that the eternal law as a rule of free and upright conduct should not be understood as being imposed upon God Himself; nor should the divine will be conceived of as good and upright because of conformity to the eternal law, as though it were subject thereto. St. Thomas (I.- II, qu. 93, art. 4, ad 1) and Alexander of Hales (*Summa Universae Theologiae,* Pt. III, qu. xxvi, memb. 8, art. 1) held this view; and Anselm (*Cur Deus Homo,* Bk. I, chap. xii) was of the same opinion, saying that God is entirely free from law, so that what He wills is just and fitting; and that, furthermore, what is unjust and unfitting does not fall within the scope of His will, not because of any law [prohibiting it from so doing], but because such matters have no relationship with His freedom.

6. This first proposition is explained by the fact that such a law must needs be understood as being either positive or natural; but it cannot be understood as existing in either way; therefore [that law cannot be in existence]. The first part of the minor premiss is proved as follows: a positive law is one which is established by the free will of some one able to command, and to lay an obligation by his precept or will upon the being on whom the law is imposed; but God has no superior, neither can He bind Himself through precept or law, for He is not superior to Himself; therefore, He can in no way be subject to positive law.

This argument is confirmed by the fact that in relation to God, nothing is evil on the ground that it is prohibited, whether as an act of commission or as one of omission; for howsoever strong a prohibition may conceivably exist with respect to a given act, if God moves in opposition to that prohibition, the act will be good, since it will proceed from the primary standard of goodness; and, therefore, positive law in relation to upright conduct has no application to the divine will. Hence, notwithstanding any law whatsoever made by Himself for the government of Creation, God may disregard that law, making use of His absolute power, as in the distribution of rewards or punishments, and so forth; because He is not bound to the observance of law. For He is Sovereign Lord and not confined within any order; so that He is not to be compared with any human legislator, the latter being a part of his own community, whatever may be the way in which the human lawgiver is bound by his own law. But if, apart from any general law, God makes a promise, He is indeed bound to keep that promise, not because of positive law, but because of the natural rectitude which, by virtue of the promise, attends its fulfilment. The matter of whether or not natural law intervenes, in this obligation, will be discussed below.

7. *Objection.* One may object that if God, after decreeing absolutely that something is not to be done, should then do the same, He would act improperly, and that it is, therefore, impossible for Him to commit an act so prohibited. Consequently, a free decree of God has the force of positive law with respect to His will, since He cannot righteously do that which in itself and apart from His decree, He might freely have done.

Solution. I reply that God is unable to act in opposition to His own decree, not on account of any prohibition which the decree carries with it, but on account of the repugnant nature of that act itself; for if He should move in opposition to an absolute decree, there would be in existence, at the same time and from eternity, contrary decrees about the same thing and with respect to the same point of time; that is to say, He would have willed absolutely two contradictories, a conception which is repugnant to reason. Moreover, He would [, under such circumstances,] be acting against the efficacy of His own will and rendering it ineffective and inconstant, which is also repugnant to reason. Hence, it must further be said that, granted that it implies not a physical contradiction (so to speak), but solely a moral one, for God to change His decree, and further, granted that once He has made a decree, it is contrary to due order that He should act in opposition thereto, nevertheless, these facts result not from any prohibition but from the intrinsic nature and essence of God; a point of which we shall presently speak in discussing [His] truthfulness, [His] fidelity, and similar matters. For just as it is unfitting that divinity should deceive, even so it is unfitting that divinity should be inconstant. Thus, His inability to will in opposition to His own decree arises, not from any prohibition, but from the nature of the case, if we suppose some object to have been placed in such a position [as to be contrary to a divine decree].

8. *Why an active dictate of God as to what must be done, has not the nature of law in relation to Himself.* The latter half of the minor premiss,[3] which

---

3. [See first sentence of Section 6, *supra*, p. 165.—Tr.]

concerned natural law, is proved thus: although it cannot be denied that in the divine intellect the first place is taken, in the logical order, by the active dictates whereby God judges what is worthy of His goodness, justice, or wisdom—as He does in the following: 'One may not lie; promises must be fulfilled'—nevertheless, in relation to the divine will these active dictates cannot have the nature of law. This is true, first, because they do not lay down any precept, or make known the will of any being, but simply reveal the fact, by indicating what the nature of the case determines, whereas law is either the will or the intimation of the will; therefore, . . . Secondly, in God reason and will are not, in point of fact, distinguished, wherefore St. Thomas (I.–II, qu. 93, art. 4, ad 1) has said, that the will of God regarded as such, cannot rightly be called rational, for it is rather reason itself; therefore, just as the eternal reason of God is not regulated by law, neither is His will so regulated, even with respect to its free acts, being, on the contrary, righteous in itself, as His reason is essentially righteous.

St. Thomas, again (in Pt. I, qu. 21, art. 1, ad 2), must be interpreted thus, when he says: 'It is impossible for God to will anything other than that which is approved by the rule of His wisdom. This rule is, as it were, the law of justice, according to which His will is right and just.' For the expression, 'as it were' (*sicut*), indicates a reference not to the *true* nature of law, but only to a certain analogy and proportion, and in order to explain this point, St. Thomas adds [*ibid.*]: 'Hence what He does according to His will He does justly, as we also do justly whatever we do according to law; but we, indeed, act in accordance with the law of some superior; whereas God is a law unto Himself.' That is, He is righteous in Himself, apart from law, as if He were a law unto Himself.

Finally, the foregoing may be explained on the ground that the judgment of reason is necessary to God, solely because nothing can be willed unless foreknown; nevertheless, [this judgment] has not the office of (as it were) binding or determining His will; on the contrary, His will is in itself right and good, and consequently the dictate of reason, which is understood to take logical precedence in the intellect, cannot, in relation to the divine will, possess the nature of true law. It may be objected that, even if [this rule of reason] cannot be called coercive law, it can be described as a directive law indicating the propriety or goodness of the end in view. My reply is that this description does not suffice for a moral law, a fact which is evident from what has been said above and which will be more fully explained in the later passages on natural law. Moreover, a metaphorical way of speaking is clearly not permissible, unless sanctioned by usage.

9. *The second proposition: The eternal law may be called a law of action in regard to the things governed but not in relation to God Himself.* I hold in the second place, that the eternal law, since it is a law of government or (so to speak) of operation by an artificer, may be said to have the nature of law in regard to the things governed, but not in relation to God Himself or His will. This is the opinion expressed by St. Thomas (I.–II, qu. 93, art. 4, ad 1), and also by Vincent de Beauvais in *Speculum Morale* (Bk. I, pt. II, dist. i). It may be expounded first by means of examples. For God, in laying down any law—as, for instance, the rule that in accordance with His judgment, a certain good work should have a certain reward, and a given sin, a given punishment—thus brings it about that the doer of good shall be worthy of that particular reward, and that the sinner shall be liable to that particular punishment; so that the things themselves which are to be governed do straightway become subject to the law in question. But God is not subject to it; on the contrary, He remains always exempt from law, so that He is able to act as He wills; and in the natural order the same situation exists.

The opinion in question may also be expounded by reasoning, as follows: when God framed the eternal law with respect to the government of His creatures, He ordained this law as applying to those creatures themselves, that they might be directed in accordance with it; but He did not impose the law upon Himself, in such a way that He should be compelled to govern thereby. Moreover, law in the proper sense of the term is the regulation of an inferior by a superior, through the direct command of the latter. But if this definition is extended and applied in a metaphorical sense, a due proportion should always be observed, in such a way that the term still refers to the action of a superior upon something under his authority. Therefore the rational principle inherent in divine providence partakes, in accordance with this proportion, of the nature and name of law, a fact which will be made more evident in the following section.

10. *Whether irrational and inanimate creatures are subject to the eternal law.* Secondly, a question may be raised as to whether all created things,

even those which are irrational or inanimate, and which perform their actions not freely, but from natural necessity, are included under the head of this eternal law.

The reason for raising such a question may be that St. Thomas (I.–II, qu. 93, arts. 4 and 5) favours the inclusion under that law of necessary actions of creatures, an opinion derived from Augustine (*On Free Will,* Bk. I, chaps. v and vi), who declares that the eternal law is reason dwelling within the mind of God, whereby all things are directed to their proper ends, through means in harmony with these ends. Furthermore, in another work (*De Diversis Quaestionibus LXXXIII,* Qu. xxvii), Augustine says: 'An immutable law governs all mutable things, in a most beautiful manner.'

Argument for the affirmative. Moreover, in defence of this view, one may argue thus: just as our will controls our bodily members and imposes upon them, by its command, the necessity of action, even so the divine will governs all created things and imposes necessity upon them, according to the varying capacity of each of these things, and in agreement with the words of the Old Testament (*Psalms,* cxlviii [, v. 6]: 'He hath made a decree, and it shall not pass away'; and again (*Proverbs,* Chap. viii [, v. 29]), 'and set a law to the waters that they should not pass their limits', this latter passage being expounded in *Job* (Chap. xxxviii [, v. 11]) as follows: 'I said, hitherto thou shalt come, and shalt go no further, and here thou shalt break thy swelling waves.' For these laws, although given in time, had their source in the eternal law.

11. *Argument for the negative.* But, on the other hand, it may be argued that no irrational nature is capable of [subjection to] law in the proper sense of that word, as Augustine has expressly declared (on *Leviticus,* Qu. 74 [*Questions on Heptateuch,* Bk. III, qu. 74], and this is stated in *Decretum,* Pt. II, causa xv, qu. i, can. iv). The same argument may be drawn from the words of Paul, in 1 *Corinthians* (Chap. ix [, v. 9]), wherein he refers to the law, 'Thou shalt not muzzle the mouth of the ox that treadeth out the corn', and adds: 'Doth God take care for oxen?' 'Care', that is, involving the imposition of a law. For divine providence, in a general sense, is concerned even with irrational creatures, a fact which is not to be doubted, but such care as is specifically provided through laws, is peculiarly directed toward intellectual beings. Consequently, Paul adds

that the law in question was written for the sake of men, since the labourer should not be deprived of his hire.

One may also resort to logical reasoning, as follows: law, of its nature, involves a bond or moral obligation; and only intellectual creatures are capable of bearing such an obligation; neither are they thus capable with respect to all their actions, but only when they act freely, since all morality depends upon liberty.

12. *Solution of the question.* I reply briefly, that the problem concerns a mode of speaking; and that, nevertheless, if we examine the phrase of Augustine, who is the foremost author treating of eternal law, it will be seen that he included under this term all things, natural as well as moral. For he wished while using the term to explain the efficacy of divine providence, in relation not only to free actions, but to natural actions as well, and to the whole order of the universe; that is, he wished to explain in what way all things are subject to divine government and obey that government, in accordance with its efficacious power. This intention is evident from various previously cited passages in the works of Augustine (*On Free Will,* Bk. I, chap. vi, and *On the City of God,* Bk. V, chap. xi; Bk. IX, chap. xxii), in which he says that there is nothing in the universe not subject to the laws of divine providence; that the holy angels foresee temporal changes in the eternal and immutable laws of God, existing in His wisdom; and later (Bk. XIX, chap. xii), that, 'Nothing is exempt from the laws of the Supreme Creator and Governor, by Whom the peace of the universe is administered.'[4]

13. However, I think that two analogous concepts (as it were) are comprehended under this general acceptation of the term 'eternal law'. One concept is derived from the idea of law, since that law whereby God is said to govern natural or irrational things, is metaphorically called a law or precept. The other connotes a relation to the creatures themselves, and complements the first concept; for the subordination and subjection of irrational creatures to God is but loosely and metaphorically called obedience, since it is more properly a kind of natural necessity; while, on the other hand, the eternal law, in so far as rational beings are thereby governed as moral beings and as members of society, has the true nature of

---

4. [This quotation, as given by Suárez, varies slightly from the Augustine text.—Tr.]

law, and obedience in the true sense is paid to it. It is in this latter acceptation, as I have remarked above,[5] that the expression, 'eternal law' should
be considered, in the present discussion; so that, using the term strictly,
we shall not extend its application to irrational objects.

14. *Whether all human actions are the proper subject-matter of eternal law.*
A further inquiry may be made, as to whether all moral or human actions
are the subject-matter of this eternal law. There can, indeed, be no doubt
in so far as evil actions are concerned, for they are all forbidden by the
law in question, as we have pointed out above.[6] With respect to actions
morally indifferent, however, there is some doubt, since they are neither
forbidden nor prescribed, and consequently do not seem to be the subject-
matter of any law in the mind of God. As great or even greater doubt exists
concerning good works which are not necessary to [the ultimate] end [of
man], but are more excellent [than their alternatives]. For this reason,
some authors say that the eternal law, strictly interpreted as a command,
does not apply to such works; but that they are included under the more
general conception of that law, inasmuch as it embraces any disposition
whatsoever made by the [divine] Ruler, including permission and counsel.
For permission is applicable to the indifferent actions and counsel to those
actions which are more excellent [than their alternatives].

15. However, it may be asserted in an absolute sense, that all moral
actions in some way come under the eternal law, even when the latter is
conceived of in its strictly preceptive character.

This assertion may be expounded by means of a certain distinction
pointed out above, the distinction between a law enjoining the performance of some action and one laying down specifications and enjoining
a given mode of performance with regard to that action. Accordingly, we
hold that the acts in question are the [proper] subject-matter of eternal
law, whether the latter commands their performance, prescribes a particular mode of acting, or prohibits some other mode.

[The foregoing] may be elucidated as follows: in the first place, in so far
as concerns the good or best actions, there is, according to St. Augustine,

5. [*Supra,* p. 169; § 11.—Tr.]
6. [*Supra,* p. 168; § 9.—Tr.]

almost no deed that is the subject-matter of counsel, which, in the preparation of the soul, might not also be the subject-matter of precept, if that
deed be necessary to the glory of God. This is especially true in relation
to the eternal law, through which God binds man so that the latter shall
be prepared to perform all such deeds, if God Himself should so will,
or if they should be necessary for some other reason. Just as marriage—
although it is not a deed enjoined by counsel, but one of the lesser goods,
neither is it, as a general rule, a deed enjoined by precept—falls nevertheless by natural law, under the head of a bounden duty when it is necessary
for the preservation of the race, in which case it comes under the eternal
law as well. In this sense, then, there is no good action which does not
come under the eternal law in its preceptive character. Moreover, when the
performance of such actions is not necessary, though they may seem to
be advised or approved, a mode of performance is nevertheless prescribed
by the eternal law, and this mode must be observed, if the actions are to be
executed aright. Accordingly, we say that they come under a preceptive
law which relates to their mode of performance, that is to say, one which
specifies that mode. The same statements are clearly true with respect to
indifferent actions. For it is commanded that, if they are performed, they
must be performed for the sake of a good end, and it is forbidden that
they be executed for their own sake; so that, if they are regarded strictly
as indifferent acts, they may be said to come under the eternal law in its
prohibitive character, according to a very credible opinion of St. Thomas
[I.–II, qu. 18, art. 9] to the effect that there is no such thing as a human
action indifferent in the concrete.[7] Thus, in relation to the actions under
discussion, the eternal law may be interpreted as containing two precepts:
one concerning their performance for the sake of a good and proper end,
if they are actually performed; another forbidding their performance for
their own sake, as, for example, idle words are prohibited.

16. *In what sense Augustine has asserted that nothing can escape the sway
of the eternal law.* Thus we may understand, at last, in what sense there is

7. [St. Thomas states that though some actions, as walking, eating, are morally
indifferent (neither good nor bad) in the abstract, there is no morally indifferent act in
the concrete, for if one deliberately walks or eats, there must be some motive for doing
so.—REVISER.]

truth in the assertion of Augustine, made in the passages cited above[8] and frequently repeated elsewhere, namely: that there is nothing which can entirely escape the sway of the eternal law, whether in heaven, on earth, or in hell, whether in sinning or in acting righteously. For although a man may in sinning act contrary to one eternal law of God, he comes [through that very deed] under another law which prescribes that one must pay by suffering, in exact proportion to the defect in his act. So St. Thomas has held (*ibid.,* qu. 93, art. 6); and Augustine (*De Catechizandis Rudibus,* Chap. xviii [, no. 30]), also, saying: 'God knoweth how to govern spirits[9] that forsake Him, and out of their just misery, to rule the lower parts of His Creation with the laws, most fitting and harmonious, of His wondrous dispensation.' Another remark of Augustine (*Confessions,* Bk. I, chap. xii) also bears upon this point: 'For it is even as Thou hast ordered, O Lord, that every sinful affection shall be its own punishment.'[10] Indeed, if the matter is duly considered, that law which is fulfilled in the wicked by punishment, and in the righteous by reward, has no reference to a preceptive law governing moral actions on the part of intellectual creation, but is a mensurative law (so to speak) relating to the rewards and punishments in question, and brought through the efficacy of divine providence to the desired end.

CHAPTER III

Is the Eternal Law an Act of the Divine Mind, Differing in Concept from Other Laws; and Is This Law One, or Manifold?

1. From our previous discussion it is evident that the eternal law dwells within the divine mind, since outside it nothing is eternal. It is likewise evident that it exists in the form of a second and ultimate actuality.[1] For

---

8. [*Supra,* p. 170; § 12.—Tr.]

9. [St. Augustine, in his *Retractationes* (II, chap. xiv) corrects *animas* of the Latin text to *spiritus,* for he was speaking of the Angels.—Reviser.]

10. [This quotation, as given by Suárez, varies slightly from the Augustine text.—Tr.]

1. [Power is a first actuality when compared with action. *Actus primus* is the faculty prepared to act; *actus secundus* is the exercise of the faculty.—Reviser.]

law, in so far as it dwells in the lawgiver, consists in an act of this kind, and not by way of a habit, or first actuality, and this is especially so in God, Who is a pure act in the highest degree.[2]

One may ask then whether this law resides in His intellect or in His will; for Augustine (*Against Faustus,* Bk. XXII, chap. xxvii) seems to have left that point undecided and ambiguous, saying: 'The eternal law is the divine reason, or the will of God, commanding the preservation of the natural order, and forbidding its violation.'

2. *Whether the eternal law is a free or necessary act of God. The opinion of some who confound ideas with the eternal law.* However, before replying to this latter question we inquire further whether the eternal law implies a free or a necessary act in God. For some say that it is solely divine ideas, whereby the external world is produced; because these persons think, not that the law in question has the function of commanding, but merely that it is a rule in accordance with which God makes all things. Upon this opinion, the conclusion would seem to follow, that just as the ideas exist in the divine intellect by natural necessity, and not freely, so does the eternal law necessarily exist.

3. *Solution: The eternal law exists in a free act of God.* It must be asserted, however, that the eternal law involves not a necessary, but a free act of God. This is the view held by St. Thomas, by Alexander of Hales, and by other authorities, in the passages cited.

The same conclusion may be deduced from the words which we have just quoted from Augustine; for the eternal law has as its subject-matter the external works of God, since He commands that the natural order be observed and forbids that it be violated, and since the natural order does not exist, save in created things; and therefore, just as these works are freely created, so does the eternal law involve a free relationship.

This argument is confirmed by the fact that no law can exist save in relation to what must be ruled thereby; and the eternal law, as has been said, is not imposed upon God or upon the Divine persons; so that it exists for the sake of created things, and therefore implies a free relation towards

---

2. [*Actus purus* of the text, as applied to God, means that there is no potentiality in God; He is the fullness of being and of perfection.—REVISER.]

them. Thus it is that St. Thomas (I.–II, qu. 91, art. 1, ad 1) says: 'The eternal concept of the divine mind has the character of eternal law, in so far as it is ordained by God for the government of things foreknown by Him.'[3]

Wherefore, as regards the above-mentioned doctrine of ideas, it may be denied, in the first place, that the eternal law, as law, partakes of the character of ideas; for an idea is set up as a principle of operation on the part of the artificer himself, rather than in the form of a command or impulse, relating to the thing which is to be produced in conformity with the idea; and so it is more probable that law and idea differ from each other in their concepts, a point which will be better established by our later discussion.

The difference between ideas and exemplars. Secondly, indeed, we must add that even if one follows the doctrine in question, it is more appropriate to say that ideas, not in themselves, but considered as exemplars, have the nature of eternal law. For ideas differ from exemplars in that ideas are wholly natural in God, so that they concern even those things the existence of which is [merely] potential; whereas exemplars involve a free relation, since they connote a causality in some sense actual, in such wise that something is or will be done in imitation of them. Thus it is that law may involve an idea in the sense described above, but not in the sense in which it is absolutely necessary.

4. *The eternal law comprehends or requires an act of the divine will.* Therefore, the conclusion with regard to the first doubt is, that the eternal law necessarily includes or postulates an act of the divine will; since freedom, even the freedom of God, is formally in the divine will, and the eternal law is a free principle residing in God, wherefore it includes [an act of His] will. For this reason, it is true, even with respect to the eternal law, that, as we said above, no law as such is absolutely necessary; for the eternal law itself, in so far as it is a freely established law, is not absolutely necessary. Nor is this fact inconsistent with its eternal character, for within God, even that which is free may be eternal. Neither is it opposed to the immutability of the eternal law, since the free decrees [thereof] are also immutable.

5. From the foregoing, another conclusion may be drawn, namely, that the eternal law does not consist in acts of the divine intellect, in the sense

3. [Not an exact quotation.—TR.]

that those acts precede, in our concept of them, the free decrees of God. The proof of this conclusion is the fact that in the said acts, as such, there is no freedom, and consequently, no law. For this reason, also, neither providence nor predestination is conceived of as existing in the divine intellect, before any free decree of God's will, for both providence and predestination connote free acts; and, therefore, the eternal law may not be thought of as existing within the divine intellect, as such.

Objection. But one may object that within the divine intellect, as so conceived, there are contained dictates of the natural law; for example: 'Lying is forbidden'; 'Promises must be kept'; 'Evil deeds must be punished'; and the like. Hence, with respect to these dictates, at least, the eternal law exists within the divine intellect prior to any act of God's will. This, then, was apparently the light in which the eternal law was viewed by Cicero (*Laws,* Bk. II [, chap. iv, § 8]) and other philosophers treating of the same.

Solution. Nevertheless, our reply is that if the dictates in question are considered in relation to the divine will itself, that is, in so far as they give expression to those things which are to be willed by God Himself, as such, then the said dictates do not possess the character of law, as we have already pointed out; and if, on the other hand, they are considered in relation to the created will, in so far as they declare what is to be done, or what is to be avoided, by that will, then again, they have not the nature of law until the divine will is superadded to them, since they are not commands, nor do they have any actual effects, being (so to speak) a speculative knowledge of the acts in question, as we shall explain below, in treating of the natural law.[4]

6. *The eternal law consists formally in a free decree of God, Who lays down the order to be observed in the [separate] parts of the universe, with respect to the common good.* Secondly, one may conclude from the above, that it is quite legitimate to assert that the eternal law is a free decree of the will of God, Who lays down the order to be observed: either generally, by the separate parts of the universe with respect to the common good (whether this decree be immediately congruous to common welfare, in relation to

---

4. [*Infra,* p. 194; Chap. v.—Tr.]

the universe as a whole, or whether it be thus congruous, at least, in relation to the individual species thereof); or else specifically, by intellectual creatures in their free actions.

This assertion may be proved, first, by what we have said in the Fifth Chapter of the preceding Book. Secondly, we may find support also in the opinion of Joannes Damascenus (*De Fide Orthodoxa,* Bk. II, chap. xii), as expressed in the passage wherein he refers to the view of Gregory Nazianzen (*Orations,* ii: *De Paschate* [*Orations,* xxxviii: *In Theophania*]), who says that after the creation of the spiritual and the physical worlds, it was necessary to create a being composed of both elements. To this he adds: 'However, by the word "necessary" (*Oportebat*) I refer simply to the will of the Creator. For no law or sanction [more] fitting than this can be imagined or devised, &c.'[5] The remark of Augustine (*On the City of God,* Bk. II, chap. xix) is also to the point: 'In the heavenly and the angelic court, the will of God is law.'[6] His will, then, is the eternal law of the entire universe, although it is especially assigned to the heavenly court, because there God's will is known as it is in itself, and because it is the first and proximate rule of action for all the blessed.

7. Furthermore, as for the manner in which God is said to command irrational creatures, He does so not through His intellect, but proximately and immediately through His will; for he rules these creatures not by words but by acts, and He works more directly through His will than through His intellect, as I assume from what has been said in the first part.[7] Therefore the eternal law, in so far as it is concerned with these lower creatures, is rightly thought of as residing in the will of God, Who ordains that to each of them shall be given its particular nature, tendency,

---

5. [The Latin translation of this passage from Joannes Damascenus (in the Migne edition, Vol. 94, col. 919) differs somewhat from Suárez's rendition. The Migne version reads: *Hoc porro verbo decebat, nihil aliud indicatur, nisi voluntas opificis. Haec quippe lex et sanctio est: congruentissima, nec quisquam fictori dicturus est.* . . . . The passage in Suárez reads: *Hoc autem vocabulo, Oportebat, nihil aliud à me indicatur, quam opificis voluntas. Hac enim nec lex, nec sanctio ulla congruenter fingi, excogitarivè potest, &c.* Note that the word *oportebat* (implying necessity), which Suárez emphasizes, appears to be a substitute for *decebat* (implying seemliness).—Tr.]

6. [Not an exact quotation.—Tr.]

7. [Cf. the early sections of this Chapter.—Tr.]

and place. Thus, for example, that law which is spoken of in *Proverbs* (Chap. viii [, v. 29]) as follows: 'And [He] set a law to the waters that they should not pass their limits', when considered as temporal and as established outside of God, is nothing other than the natural tendency imparted to the water and causing it to remain so quietly in its own place that it does not rise upward, but is confined by the bounds of its nature. Such is the meaning to be drawn from *Job* (Chap. xxxviii [, v. 8]) and from the *Psalms* (ciii [, vv. 6–9]). This law, then, as it exists in eternity in the mind of God, is none other than God's will, whereby He has decreed that the waters shall be set in a particular place and endowed with a particular tendency, so that they shall not transgress the bounds prescribed to them; and the same conclusion applies to other [precepts of this sort].

Therefore the eternal law, when metaphorically conceived (so to speak) in relation to merely natural and irrational creatures, is rightly established in the will of God.

8. Moreover, the same is true of that eternal law in so far as it has ordained that a given thing shall be done with respect to intellectual creatures without their free co-operation: as in the case either of those acts which are natural and which such creatures therefore perform by a necessity of nature; or those which God works in the said creatures without their free co-operation, as when He creates, illuminates, calls, or in some other similar way provides for them, or even when He rewards or punishes them. Again, if the eternal law be thought of as having the true nature of law, in relation to the moral obligation of intellectual creatures, then it is the eternal will of God, according to which rational wills must operate, if they are to be virtuous. For, as Augustine (*De Diversis Quaestionibus LXXXIII,* Qu. xxvii) has said, 'Only when we will virtuously, do we act according to law; and in other acts, we are acted upon according to law; for the law itself remains unchangeable', &c. Accordingly, we may apply at this point the general remarks made with respect to the same opinion, in the Fifth Chapter of the preceding Book.

9. *In what act of the intellect the eternal law must be placed, if it formally consists in acts of the intellect.* However, if any one should wish, in the light of those remarks, to consider the eternal law as existing in the divine intellect, it would not be difficult to explain that [conception of it also].

Such a person must, however, regard that law as residing within the divine intellect subsequently, in the logical order, to the aforesaid decree of God's will. For it cannot be denied that this decree constitutes (so to speak) the very soul and virtue of the law in question, and that from it is derived all the power [of the law] to bind or impart an inclination effectively. Nevertheless, assuming the existence of the decree, one may conceive that knowledge of it exists in the mind of God, a knowledge which follows upon the decree itself, and that by reason of the said decree the divine intellect thereupon passes precise judgment, as to what course must be taken in the government of created things; so that this intellect preconceives within itself the law which is to be prescribed in due season for each one of those things. It is thus that I understand the following passage from St. Thomas (I.–II, qu. 92 [qu. 91], art. 1, ad 1): 'The eternal concept of God, whereby He ordains that which relates to the government of things foreknown by Him, is the eternal law of God.'[8] For this ordination is none other than the decree of the [divine] will which we have discussed, and which, being known by the [divine] intellect, determines it in governing created things according to such a principle or law. Furthermore, perhaps because both [the divine intellect and the divine will] concur in making law, and both forces, each in its own way, are true in a proper sense, the two terms have been employed disjunctively by Augustine (*Against Faustus* [Bk. XXII, chap. xxvii]).

10. *On the distinction between the eternal law of God and His ideas.* In the third place, from the foregoing it is sufficiently manifest in what respects the eternal law is distinguished conceptually from the [divine] ideas.

For if that law consists in a decree of the [divine] will, the distinction in question is evident; since an idea certainly resides in the intellect.

If, on the other hand, we are speaking of the eternal law as it exists in God's intellect, and especially if we speak of ideas as exemplars, there is no distinction, according to some authorities. Nevertheless, St. Thomas (I.–II, qu. 93, art. 1, ad 1) expressly distinguishes between the two, and according to his teaching, the distinction may be explained in various ways, as follows. First, ideas are properly concerned with the creation or production of things;

8. [Not an exact quotation.—Tr.]

whereas law is concerned with their government, as St. Thomas declared in the passage quoted above; wherefore, just as ideas are to be distinguished from providence, so they must also be distinguished from the eternal law. Secondly, the true difference seems to have been implied above, namely, that an idea has only the character of an exemplar in relation to God Himself, so that He works in accordance with it, while it serves (so to speak) merely as a concrete pattern for the works of God; whereas the divine law as law has rather a dynamic character, giving rise to an inclination or obligation to action; and these diverse characteristics are entirely sufficient to constitute a conceptual distinction. Finally, from the foregoing it is clear that law as such is imposed upon subjects, that is to say, upon inferiors: for law ordains how things in subjection shall operate, each according to its own mode; whereas an idea is not properly imposed upon the thing represented in it, but is rather fixed formally [that is, as an idea] in the mind of the artificer, so that he may work in accordance with it; hence, the distinction is clear.

11. *On the distinction between the eternal law of God and His providence.* Fourthly, one may furthermore perceive from the foregoing remarks the respects in which the eternal law is distinguished from providence. With regard to providence, also, there is wont to be doubt as to whether it resides in the intellect or in the will, since it includes acts on the part of both. Therefore, in order that providence and law may be compared, they should be examined in relation to each other, with due regard for proportion, that is to say, in so far as each resides in will or each in intellect; so that they seem not to be mutually distinct, even conceptually. For providence is the principle of the government of all things, a principle existing from eternity in the divine mind; and this very principle is the eternal law in its general connotation, as may be inferred from the words of St. Thomas (*ibid.,* qu. 92, art. 2, ad 1 [qu. 91, art. 1, Corp.]); hence, providence and the eternal law apparently are not to be distinguished as two attributes, but are the same thing, receiving different names under different aspects. And if, on the other hand, the eternal law is to be interpreted, not in this broad sense, but in its restricted and proper sense, as concerned with intellectual creatures, and properly binding upon them, then, [even] when so interpreted, it will constitute a part (so to speak) of divine providence. For it is the work of the providence of God to lay down laws for rational

creatures; indeed, providence is rather a special and peculiar form of moral government, appropriate to those intellectual natures for whom God has a special care, as Paul has indicated (*1 Corinthians,* Chap. ix [, vv. 9–10]). And, therefore, the eternal law will always coincide with providence, if the two are compared in due proportion. So St. Thomas seems to hold [I.–II, qu. 91, art. 1, Corp. and qu. 93, arts. 1 and 4], with regard to the eternal law and providence, as does Alexander of Hales (*Summa Universae Theologiae,* Pt. III, qu. xxvi, memb. 1); and Augustine ([*Against Faustus,* Bk. XXII, chap. xxvii] and *On the True Religion,* Chap. xxx, at the end, and Chap. xxxi, at the beginning, and *De Diversis Quaestionibus LXXXIII,* Qu. xxvii) favours the same opinion.

12. *Solution.* Nevertheless, St. Thomas (*De Veritate,* Qu. 5, art. 1, ad 6) distinguishes the eternal law from providence, saying: 'Providence [. . .] signifies, not the eternal law, but something consequent upon the eternal law'; and in expounding this assertion, he adds that the eternal law is to be referred to providence, as a general principle is referred to particular conclusions or actions; even as, with us, first principles of practice are referred to prudence. Thus he explains that the acts or effects of divine providence are to be attributed to the eternal law as to a source whence they proceed, and not as to a proximate dictate concerning the specific execution of particular deeds.

A more complete explanation of this view may be given as follows: the divine reason, in so far as it has the nature of law, establishes general rules, as it were, in accordance with which all things should be actuated and should operate; whereas providence makes specific disposition of particular things and acts, and is consequently the principle (so to speak) according to which the law is executed and applied. This explanation seems to be in harmony with the literal meaning of the terms themselves; for *lex* implies *ius,* which has been established in general, as we have observed above,[9] while providence implies the care which should be taken with respect to particular acts.

13. *On the effects of the eternal law.* Fifthly, the effects of the eternal law may incidentally be deduced from the foregoing, by comparison with the

---

9. [*Supra,* p. 26; *De Legibus,* Bk. I, chap. ii.—Tr.]

effects of providence. For it is often asked whether the eternal law produces all the effects which providence produces.

In this comparison, the eternal law must be conceived of in all its
amplitude. For if it is conceived of in a narrow sense, as law that, strictly
speaking, lays down moral commands for intellectual creatures, then it is
clear that not all the effects of providence, but only the morally good acts,
are [likewise] effects of the eternal law; because the natural effects [pro-
duced by providence] do not emanate from the eternal law regarded in this
aspect. Morally good acts, however, are truly effects of this law, since the
law of itself incites to them and supplies the obligation to perform them.
On the other hand, morally evil acts, in so far as they are evil, are not the
effects of the eternal law, although they are the subject-matter of this law,
which prohibits them; just as such evil acts are not effects of providence,
because they are not effects due to God, if we regard His providence,
although they are indeed the subject-matter of His providence, both in so
far as the very prohibition [against evil acts] is a part or principle (so to
speak) of divine providence, according to St. Thomas's way of speaking,
and also, in so far as the acts in question are permitted, or punished, or
regulated to some good end, by divine providence. Thus, although sin as
such is not essentially derived from the eternal law nor in harmony with
it, but, on the contrary, opposed thereto, yet in its material aspect it is
derived from this law, whereby God has willed to co-operate with His
creatures;[10] and furthermore, punishment of sin also proceeds from the
eternal law. Thus, as Augustine (*Enchiridion,* Chap. c) says with respect
to those who sin, 'In so far as they themselves are concerned, they have
done what God willed not to be done; but in so far as relates to God's
omnipotence, they have in no wise been able to accomplish such a deed,[11]
for through the very fact that they acted in opposition to God's will, His
will concerning them was done.' Augustine (*Confessions,* Bk. IV, chap. ix)
speaks of the sinner, again, in the same strain, as follows: 'And he who

10. [Suárez means that God co-operates with the physical act of the sinner.—REVISER.]

11. [Reading *valuerunt,* in accordance with the Migne edition of Augustine, not
voluerunt (willed), which we assume to be a misprint in our own Latin text. It should
be noted, however, that the phrase as a whole differs in the two texts. The Migne edition
has *efficere valuerunt;* our own text has *facere voluerunt.*—TR.]

forsaketh Thee, whither goeth he, or whither fleeth he, save from Thee well pleased, to Thee who art angry? For where doth he not find Thy law in his punishment?'[12]

14. In speaking of the eternal law in its widest sense, however, it may be said that all the effects of providence are, in some manner, effects of the eternal law; since all the governmental force of divine providence is contained in principle (as it were) within the eternal law, and thus every effect of providence has its root (so to speak) within that law. This was the opinion of St. Thomas (*De Veritate,* Qu. 5, art. 1, ad 6); and the same conclusion may be drawn from the remarks of Augustine (*Confessions,* Bk. IV, chap. ix).

Objection. But one may object, that law is framed for universal application, whereas God through His providence at times acts outside of law; hence, the effect of such an act cannot be said to result from the eternal law, although it may well proceed from His providence. For example, the fact that the sun at one time stands still is an effect of divine providence, but not of the eternal law, since, on the contrary, it is a precept of the eternal law that the sun shall move continuously.

Solution. The reply to this objection is that the eternal law is most universal, and that what appears to be a departure from one part of it or even a dispensation (so to speak) therefrom, is, when viewed in another aspect, in harmony with that same law, being in accordance with another part of it. Thus, in the example given, although the fact that the sun stands still is not a result of the eternal law as it prescribes the order to be observed in the movements of the heavenly bodies—nay, more, although that fact is a dispensation therefrom—nevertheless it is congruous with another precept of the eternal law, whereby God wills that the prayers of those that love Him shall be heard, when they pray in due manner and for a just cause. Wherefore, Augustine (*Against Faustus,* Bk. XXVI, chap. iii) said: 'We give the name of nature to that course which is known to us and customary in nature, and whatever God does contrary to this customary course, we call a prodigy or a miracle. Nevertheless, God in no wise acts in opposition to that supreme law of nature, which is beyond the knowledge [of men . . .], even as He does not act in opposition to Himself.'

12. [Not an exact quotation.—Tr.]

15. *Whether the eternal law is one or manifold.* In the sixth and last place, from the preceding discussion we may determine this question: whether the eternal law shall be spoken of as one or manifold.

With respect to this question, St. Thomas (I.–II, qu. 93, art. 1, ad 1) holds that the law is one, so that it is not manifold even in thought; for he made this the distinguishing mark between ideas and law, namely, that ideas are multiplied, whereas the eternal law is simply one. Vincent de Beauvais cited above [*Speculum Morale,* Bk. I, pt. 11, dist. i] apparently is of the same opinion.

However, this distinction is not easy to grasp; for ideas are multiplied, not objectively, but merely according to diverse relations of reason with respect to objects; and, in the same way, precepts and laws are also multiplied in the mind of God. It is even as we said, a little above: there is one mode of law in relation to irrational things, and another in relation to rational beings, and touching the latter, we may distinguish in God's mind law which is purely natural, or law which is positive.

And if the objection is raised, that from all these considerations, there proceeds one law wholly simple and all-sufficing, which regulates all the universe, then likewise it may be maintained that there dwells in the mind of God one all-sufficing idea of the universe, of which other ideas, distinct in their nature, are (as it were) but parts. Wherefore, Augustine (*On Free Will,* Bk. I, chaps. v and vi; *On the True Religion,* Chaps. xxx and xxxi)— who in these passages and repeatedly, elsewhere, refers to the eternal law as being simply one—speaks in the plural, in his work *On the City of God* (Bk. IX, chap. xxii), of the eternal and immutable laws which reside in the divine wisdom, and furthermore remarks, in the *De Catechizandis Rudibus* (Chap. xviii), that God in His wisdom has been able to regulate the inferior parts of creation with the laws that are most appropriate.

16. *The conclusion drawn by the author.* This whole question, indeed, turns upon a manner of speaking; and the doctrine of Alexander of Hales (*Summa Universae Theologiae,* Pt. III. qu. xxvi, memb. 6), is sufficiently credible; namely, that under varying aspects, the eternal law may be spoken of as one or as manifold in nature.

For, in an absolute and essential sense, this law is one, and entirely simple, as is evident; and, nevertheless, it comprehends within itself many laws distinct in their character, as is proved by the argument set forth above. Neither is this doctrine surprising; for the natural law [also] is spoken of as one, yet it contains many precepts; although, in the case of the natural law, this is true in a very different sense, for the natural law has the unity characteristic of a collection, whereas the unity of the eternal law is derived from absolute simplicity.

However, we may add, in view of the opinion of St. Thomas, that there is a certain reason for the existence of unity in law, greater than the reason for unity in idea. For an idea connotes only a relation to an exemplar, that is, to something modelled on the idea, and therefore it is diverse in nature according to the diversity of the exemplars; whereas law has the general good in view as its end, just as providence has; and accordingly all the precepts of law which are ordained to the same kind of end, are held to constitute one law in general and in the concrete.[13] Therefore, since God has in view the most universal end of all, the law in His mind is said to be one, even as His providence is said to be one.

CHAPTER IV

Is the Eternal Law the Cause of All Laws?
Is It Manifested and Does It Exercise Binding
Force through Them?

1. We have discussed the essential reason, the universality, and the necessary character of eternal law; and there is no need to discuss the causes of that law, for it is God Himself and therefore has no cause. Indeed, at most, it may have an essential reason, either in the sense in which the divine will is the primary reason of the divine law, as constituted in God from eternity, or else in the sense in which the divine wisdom may be called the reason of His most just will, wherein the efficacy of the eternal law is founded, as we have explained.[1] I repeat, then, that nothing remains to be said concerning the causes of that law.

---

13. [*Vnum ius, & vnam legem,* in the Latin.—Tr.]
1. [*Supra,* p. 175; Chap. iii, § 4.—Tr.]

As to its effects, moreover, in so far as concerns the acts prescribed by it or resulting from the impulse given by it, we have also mentioned in passing those points which the scope of our discussion seemed to render essential. Therefore, it remains merely to speak of the way in which the proximate and (as it were) intrinsic effect of law—which is to lay a binding obligation on the subjects—befits the eternal law.

In order that this point, which is a moral one, may be treated without ambiguity of language, I assume that the discussion turns upon the truly binding aspect of the eternal law, in its relation to men, and likewise—in due proportion—to the angels. For in so far as that law relates to the lower creatures, it is clear that it creates not true obligation, but rather an instinct, or inclination, or impulse, naturally determining those creatures to pursue one definite course; and this effect neither pertains to law, strictly speaking, nor requires [for its elucidation] any doctrine other than the philosophical.

2. *The eternal law in its preceptive aspect, and when sufficiently promulgated, has binding force.* With regard to this aspect of the eternal law, then, we hold that the said law contains in itself a binding force, if it is sufficiently promulgated and applied.

The proof [of this assertion] is that otherwise it would not be law in the true and proper sense, since it is of the essence of law to have binding force, as has been demonstrated above.[2] Furthermore, God has supreme power to give commands, and hence to create binding obligations, for the precept of a superior gives rise to the obligation of obedience; and it is through His eternal law that He does command, for God's conception of His dominion does not originate in time; and therefore His binding power is exercised by means of this same law.

One may object that, according to the above argument, He imposes binding obligations from eternity, since the law itself is eternal: an inference which is clearly false, so that [the premiss from which it follows is likewise false]. We reply by denying that this inference follows. For providence is eternal, and yet it does not govern from eternity, inasmuch as government implies transitory action with respect to creatures in existence

---

2. [*Supra*, p. 24; *De Legibus*, Bk. I, chap. i, § 9.—Tr.]

at the time; so that the eternal law in like manner is enacted from eternity, and nevertheless it has binding force, not from eternity, but in time, since binding implies a relation to creatures actually existing.

This point having been established, it remains for us to explain in what way the law in question exerts binding force: that is, whether it binds directly, by its own virtue, or mediately, through other laws which have their source in it.

3. *Whether other laws derive their binding force from the eternal law.* In order to explain this point, however, we must discuss the principal question involved, that is, whether or not the origin of all laws is in the eternal law, or in other words, and in the usual phrasing, whether or not all laws are the effects of the eternal law, and so participate in it that they derive a binding force therefrom.

A reason for doubt. There may be a reason for doubt as to this matter; for we are speaking either of divine or of human law, and neither of these could properly be said to be an effect of the eternal law; therefore, . . .

The first half of the minor premiss may be proved as follows: the divine law is a mandate of God Himself; accordingly it dwells in Him, and hence it does so from eternity, so that it is that same eternal law; therefore, it is not an effect of the eternal law. The [attempted] proof of the latter half of the minor premiss is this: if the human law were an effect of the eternal, it would share in the binding force of the latter; hence, it would bind, not by a human, but by a divine obligation; and this conclusion is clearly false. The last inference, in its turn, is proved thus: the natural law is binding by a divine obligation, only because it participates in the eternal law; and therefore, if the human law similarly participates therein, it will also be binding by that same obligation.

4. *The affirmative solution.* Nevertheless, it must be stated in the first place that, in some way, every law is derived from the eternal law, and receives binding force from the same. This is the opinion of St. Thomas (I.–II, qu. 93, art. 3), Alexander of Hales (*ibid.,* qu. xxvi, memb. 7), and other theologians. The same conclusion may be inferred from the words of Augustine (*On the True Religion,* Chap. xxxi) when he says that this [eternal law] is 'the law of all the arts', and when he adds a little farther on, that 'He who makes temporal laws consults, if he is good and wise,

the eternal law on which no soul may pass judgment, so that he may discern, in accordance with its unchangeable rules, what should in time be prescribed or forbidden.' To the same effect, Augustine remarks elsewhere (on the *Gospel of John,* Tract. VI [, no. 25]): 'God imparts human laws themselves to mankind, through the medium of emperors and kings.' And again (*On Free Will,* Bk. I, chap. vi): 'There is nothing just in temporal law, save that which is derived from the eternal.' And the same author (on *Exodus,* Qu. 67 [*Questions on Heptateuch,* II, qu. 67]) declares that: 'The eternal law is God's law,[3] a law which all pious minds consult in order that they may act or issue commands or lay down prohibitions, according to whatever they may find therein.' In this connexion, it should be noted incidentally that not all men who act righteously consult the eternal law as it is in itself, that is, as it exists in God; for perchance some who lack faith may not know that law, as it is in itself; and furthermore, there are many who do not have this law in mind at the very time when they act virtuously or command aright. Hence it is said that [persons who do act righteously] are consulting the eternal law either as it is in itself or else through something which partakes of its nature, such as natural reason or the light of faith, a matter explained by St. Thomas in the passage cited *supra (ibid.,* art. 2), and by Alexander of Hales (*ibid.,* memb. 2).

Many of the philosophers, however, have attained, through the effects of the eternal law, a conception of that law as existing in God Himself, and consequently they have perceived that every righteous and true law established among men emanates from the eternal, either immediately as the natural law does, or through the medium of the latter, as is the case with human laws. Therefore Cicero (*Laws,* Bk. II [, chap. iv, § 8]), after he has praised 'that chief law', namely, the eternal, adds, 'Because of it, that law which the gods have given to the human race is rightly praised', and so forth. In another work (*Philippics,* II [XI, chap. xii, no. 28]), Cicero has said: 'Law is nothing other than right reason, derived from the will of the gods, enjoining that which is righteous, prohibiting that which is wrongful.' Wherefore, Demosthenes [*Against Aristogeiton,* p. 774], also,

---

3. [Augustine reads: *lex Dei sempiterna est,* while Suárez varied not only the wording, but also the order of the phrase by writing, *Lex . . . aeterna Dei est.*—Tr.]

according to Marcianus, Jurisconsult (*Digest,* I. iii. 2), has declared that, 'Law is that which all men should obey, [. . .] since every law is (so to speak) the invention and the gift of God.'

5. A general argument may also be adduced, in that the eternal law is essentially law, while every other law exists by participation therein; hence, necessarily, every other law must be an effect of the eternal. It may also be noted that there are two requisites for law: one is that it be just and congruous with reason; the other, that it possess efficacious binding force; and all created right reason is a partaker of that divine light which has been shed upon us, while all human power is bestowed from above and comes from the Lord God; therefore, all law existing among men is derived from the eternal law. Both of the requisites in question have been named by divine wisdom, which has said (*Proverbs,* Chap. viii [, v. 15]): 'By me kings reign', referring, that is, to power; and also, 'and lawgivers decree just things', that is to say, with reference to right reason.

6. We shall explain our argument more fully, however, by discussing the two divisions of the reason for doubt above set forth.[4]

Cajetan [on I.–II, qu. 93, art. 3, ad 2] touches upon the first part of this doubt, the part which has to do with divine law; and he replies that the supernatural reason is divine law, and that it is a participation in and an effect of the eternal law, even as St. Thomas (Qu. 91, art. 4, ad 3 [I.–II, qu. 93, art. 3, ad 2]) holds. Wherefore, Cajetan adds, the divine law is not reason as it exists in God, but reason as it exists in man, for the supernatural government of himself or of others. This statement may be understood as applying, in due proportion, to divine natural law. In order, however, to understand this matter more fully, we must remember, as I have said at the beginning of the preceding Book,[5] that law may be thought of as existing either in the lawgiver or in his subjects: strictly and formally speaking, in the former; but in the latter to the extent that it is applied through certain signs issuing from the lawgiver. The divine law, then, in so far as it resides in the lawgiver, dwells in God Himself, since He alone is the real Author thereof; but it dwells in men also, in their capacity as subjects, even in the

4. [See Section 3 of this Chapter, *supra,* p. 187 of this Translation.—Tr.]
5. [Book I of the *De Legibus.*—Tr.]

case of those men who govern; for they, too, are subject to the divine law, and are, in their relation to others, merely promulgators and declarers of the law which is in God. Thus, in one passage of the New Testament, the old [Hebraic] law is said to have been given through Moses (*John,* Chap. i [, v. 17]), and in another passage (*Acts,* Chap. vii [, v. 53]), it is said to have been given to Moses himself through the angels. Nevertheless, the binding force did not come from the will of Moses, or from the will of the angels, but immediately from God's will; and accordingly it dwelt in Him alone as in the Lawgiver. Moreover, the same is true, in due proportion, of the law of grace and of the natural law.

7. Therefore, it follows that the divine law, in so far as it resides in the lawgiver, is not an effect of the eternal law, but is rather that eternal law itself, the latter being conceived of in a particular and incomplete sense.

We may, indeed, distinguish two aspects of the eternal law. In one aspect, it is eternal, and being so, is independent of external promulgation, neither has it relation to creatures existing for the moment. In the other aspect, this law is promulgated and binding at the present time, and consequently has a temporal relation to creatures existing at the time. In this sense, it may be called divine. Accordingly, this latter term connotes the condition of adequate external communication and promulgation. That same law, indeed, may more properly be called divine law, when it has external existence in the subjects and servants of God, that is to say, in any knowledge or sign whereby it is adequately promulgated to them. In this sense, we may assert that the divine law is a partaker in the nature of the eternal law, more excellent than any other: partly because the eternal law is more perfectly embodied in it; partly, also, because the divine law emanates more directly from the eternal; and finally, because the binding force of the divine law proceeds immediately from the same divine authority.

Thus we dispose of the first part of the difficulty stated.[6]

8. And in regard to the other part of the doubt set forth above, we must deny the inference there made, namely, that the binding force of human law is divine. For there is a great difference between the nature of divine law and that of human law; since human law, not only as it

---

6. [See Sections 3 and 6, *supra,* pp. 187 and 189 of this Translation.—Tr.]

exists in relation to its subjects but also as it exists in its own legislator, is something created and temporal, inasmuch as this law is formed and perfected in the mind and will of man, being, in the direct sense, a law of man and not a law of God Himself. Accordingly, under both aspects, human law is an effect of eternal law, as is proved by the argument set forth above; for this human law, as existing in its author, is law by reason of its participation [in the eternal]. Moreover, it emanates from a power given by God Himself, of which we read in the New Testament (*Romans,* Chap. xiii [, v. 1]). It has also a binding force, in so far as it is dependent upon principles of the eternal law, such as the precept that obedience is due to superiors. And finally, in order that [human law] may be righteous, it should conform to the eternal. Hence, in all these ways, the former is an effect of the latter. Accordingly, it was to this human law that Augustine particularly referred in the passages cited above.[7] Whence it results that the law in question, in so far as it exists in the subjects, is not so directly an effect of the eternal, as is the divine law itself. For human law is made known to its subject through the mediation of men, the latter being not only an incidental cause (so to speak) that is, not merely the cause that proposes and applies this law; but also the essential cause, or that which creates the law. For this law receives its force and efficacy directly from the will of a human legislator.

The difference between the eternal divine law, and human laws. From the foregoing, there follows also the difference which was assumed in the difficulty already set forth; for in the case of the divine law, the obligation is derived immediately from God Himself, since in so far as that law exists in man, it has no binding force save as it manifests the divine reason, or will. In human law, however, the obligation is not derived immediately from God; for in so far as human law exists in those who are subject thereto, it has an immediate relation to the will of the prince who[8] has the power to establish a new law, distinct from divine law, and from his will the obligation directly emanates, although fundamentally this obligation proceeds in its entirety from the eternal law.

7. [*Supra,* pp. 187–88.—Tr.]
8. [For *quem,* read *qui.*—Tr.]

9. *The eternal law is not known in itself to man in this life, but becomes known through other laws.* Furthermore, from what has been said above, one may conclude that the eternal law is known to men in this life, not through itself, but either in other laws or through them. For men in this life cannot know the divine will, as it is in itself, but know it only in so far as it is revealed to them through certain signs or effects. Hence it is a peculiar characteristic of the blessed that, contemplating the divine will by intuition, they are governed thereby as by their own laws; a point which I have already mentioned,[9] when citing Augustine. Human wayfarers, then, know the eternal law through participation therein, and, in an immediate sense, through just laws which are temporal and created; for even as secondary causes reveal the primary cause, and creatures, the Creator, so do temporal laws, which constitute a participation in the eternal, reveal the source from which they flow. Nevertheless, as I have said, not all men attain to this knowledge; since not all are able to discern the cause in the effect.

In what sense it is true that all have a knowledge of the eternal law. Thus, indeed, all men necessarily behold within themselves some sort of participation in the eternal law, since there is no rational person who does not in some manner judge that the virtuous course of action must be followed and the evil avoided; and in this sense, it is said that men have some knowledge of the eternal law, as St. Thomas, Alexander of Hales, and other theologians, including Augustine (*On Free Will,* Bk. I, chap. vi and *On the True Religion,* Chap. xviii), have said.

Nevertheless, not all men have knowledge of that law formally, from the standpoint of their participation therein; so that the eternal law is not known to all by such direct knowledge as to be the formal object thereof. Yet some men attain to this knowledge either through natural reasoning, or more perfectly through the revelation of faith; and accordingly, I have said that the eternal law is known to some men only in laws that are secondary to it, whereas to others, it is known not only *in* those laws but also *through* them.

10. *On the manner in which the eternal law binds its subjects.* Finally, the foregoing discussion makes manifest the way in which the eternal law exercises binding force.

---

9. [*Supra,* pp. 187–89; § 4 this Chapter.—Tr.]

For regarded strictly, as being eternal, it cannot be said actually to bind; but it may be said to have a potentially binding character[10] (if we may explain the matter thus), or to suffice of itself for the imposition of a binding obligation. The reason for this statement is that a law cannot actually bind, unless it is externally promulgated; and the eternal law, as such, is not externally promulgated; therefore, . . . Furthermore, the eternal law as such does not connote a temporal effect already accomplished, because this would be inconsistent with its eternal character; but actually to bind is a temporal effect; therefore, . . . Thus it also follows that the eternal law never binds through itself and apart from every other law, and that, on the contrary, it must necessarily be united with some other law in order actually to bind. For it never binds thus, unless it is actually and externally promulgated; and it is not promulgated, save through the promulgation of some divine or human law. So that we may also say that the eternal law never binds directly, but on the contrary, does so through the medium of some other law. [In the different cases,] however, [this act of binding indirectly is executed] in different ways.

For when the binding force is applied through a divine law, the chief and proximate cause of the obligation is the eternal law itself, and the external divine law which intervenes under such circumstances is only a sign that indicates the law which has primary binding force. This fact is manifest in the case of positive divine laws; but in the case of the natural law, the matter presents some difficulty, which we shall explain in the following Chapters.

However, when the application of the eternal law is made through a law that is human, then, although the eternal contributes to the binding obligation, in the character of a universal cause, the proximate cause of the obligation is nevertheless this same human law; for it binds not only as a sign of the divine will, but proximately, as the sign of a human will. Accordingly, in the case of human laws the eternal law binds less proximately, so to speak.

Concerning this law, it would seem that the foregoing remarks suffice.

10. [The Latin has simply *dici poterit obligativa.*—Tr.]

CHAPTER V

Is the Natural Law Natural Right Reason Itself?

1. *Various opinions on the formal basis of the natural law.* We have assumed and demonstrated in Bk. I, chap. iii, that there is some form of natural law, and as we inquire into the nature of this law, the fact of its existence will become more certain.

Some persons have asserted, then, that the law in question is none other than rational nature itself, as such.

However, this assertion may be advanced with more than one meaning, so that we should take into account the fact that rational nature may be considered in two different aspects: from one point of view, it may be regarded as it is in itself, that is to say, on the basis of the fact that, by reason of the essential characteristics which it possesses, certain things are in accord with it, and other things, in disaccord; from another point of view, it may be regarded on the basis of its power to judge, by the light of natural reason, concerning these very things which accord or disaccord with it. This twofold method of consideration has been suggested by St. Thomas (I.–II, qu. 94, art. 2), in the passage wherein he first discriminates among the various inclinations inherent in human nature, in accordance with which inclinations, reason dictates concerning those things which are good or evil for human nature; and he effects this discrimination in order that he may deduce therefrom the precepts of natural law.

The sense of the questions under discussion is expounded. Accordingly, a twofold interpretation may be applied to the assertion that the law of nature is rational nature itself. In the first place, this assertion may be understood to refer to nature itself, strictly speaking, and in so far as, by reason of its essential character, certain actions are naturally appropriate to it, and contrary actions, inappropriate. According to the other interpretation, the statement in question is to be understood as referring to nature on the basis of the [power of] rational judgment which is inherent in it, and with respect to which it has the character of law.

2. *The first opinion: affirming that the natural law consists formally in rational nature itself, in the sense that it involves no inconsistency, and is the basis of moral goodness in actions.* There is, then, the first opinion, asserting

that rational nature, strictly speaking, is natural law itself, in the sense that rational nature involves no inconsistency and is the basis in human actions, either of all their righteousness (through their accord with the said rational nature), or else, on the contrary, of their turpitude (through their disaccord with that nature).

So Vázquez[1] (on I.–II, disp. 150, chap. iii), has pointed out in a particular passage, a doctrine which he frequently repeats throughout his entire discussion of the subject, although he does not cite any authority for such an opinion.

The basis of this belief is, that certain actions are so intrinsically bad of their very nature, that their wickedness in no way depends upon external prohibition, nor upon the exercise of judgment, nor upon the divine will; and similarly, other actions are so essentially good and upright that their possession of these qualities is in no sense dependent upon any external cause. So I assume, at least, from the common opinion of the theologians (on the *Sentences,* Bk. II, dist. xxxvii); from the words of St. Thomas (I.–II, qu. 100, art. 8 [, ad 3]), and from the Relectio X (*De Homicidio,* nos. 1 et seq.) of Victoria. Moreover, in the following sections, we ourselves confirm this point.

Briefly, the underlying reason for such a view is that moral actions have their own intrinsic character and immutable essence, which in no way depend upon any external cause or will, any more than does the essence of other things which in themselves involve no contradiction, as I at present assume from the science of metaphysics.

3. From the foregoing, then, the first argument is formulated, as follows: the upright character or the turpitude of such actions is to be found in their conformity [or lack of conformity] with some law, and not with a judgment pronounced by reason; therefore, the character of the said actions is determined by their conformity with the rational nature itself,

---

1. Gabriel Vázquez or Vásquez (1549–1604), an eminent Jesuit contemporary of Suárez, who in his commentary on the Prima Secundae of Aquinas's *Summa Theologiae* provides a rationalist or intellectualist theory of natural law as existing, with its power to oblige, independently of any legislative act, whether of intellect or will, of God. For Vázquez the source of natural law lies in our rational nature and in the consistency or inconsistency of actions with that rational nature, not in the legislation of any lawgiver.

and consequently, that rational nature in itself is the natural law, with respect to all those things which are prescribed or forbidden, approved or permitted by the natural law.

The truth of the major premiss may be assumed either from the passage in *Romans* (Chap. iv [, v. 15]): 'For where there is no law, neither is there transgression'; or from the definition of sin given by Augustine (*Against Faustus,* Bk. XXII, chap. xxxvii [chap. xxvii]): 'It is a word, an act or a desire opposed to God's law'; or from the words of Ambrose (*On Paradise,* Chap. viii): 'Sin would not exist if no prohibition existed'; or, finally, from the fact that all the goodness of virtue is measured by some standard which is of the nature of law.

The proof of the minor premiss runs as follows: lying, for example, is not evil because it is adjudged by reason to be evil; rather, the converse is true, that lying is adjudged evil because it is essentially evil; therefore, it is not judgment that measures the evil of this action, and consequently, it is not a prohibitory law on the subject. Wherefore, other conclusions may be proved by the converse reasoning, as follows: the action in question is evil for this reason, namely, that in its very essence it is out of harmony with rational nature; hence, [that] nature itself is the standard by which this action is measured, and, consequently, that nature is the natural law.

4. A second argument may also be advanced, as follows: the precepts of this [natural] law are either principles self-evident from their very terms, or manifest conclusions necessarily derived therefrom and prior to every judgment framed by reason, not only to judgments of the created intellect, but also to those of the divine intellect itself. For just as the essence of things, in so far as it does not involve a contradiction, is in each case of a given nature, by virtue of the fact that it is such inherently and prior to any causality on the part of God and (as it were) independently of Him; even so, the righteousness of truth and the evil of falsehood, are such of themselves and by virtue of eternal truth. Hence, with respect to such actions and precepts, a judgment cannot have the nature of law, seeing that prior to every [possible] judgment they possess their good or evil character, and are prescribed or forbidden accordingly; and therefore, with regard to these same actions and precepts, there can be nothing endowed with the character of natural law, save rational nature itself.

In the third place, with respect to the nature of other, inferior things, the standard according to which they are good or evil, appropriate or inappropriate, is the very nature of the particular thing in question. For example, heat is inappropriate to water, and cold is appropriate; since water, by virtue of its very form and nature implies cold and not heat, being, indeed, opposed to the latter. Consequently, if one wishes to fix a standard and (as it were) a law, of movements appropriate or inappropriate to a given object, he will find no such standard and law outside the bounds of that object's nature. Accordingly, then, [the standard in question] dwells in like manner, in rational nature; and in this harmony or discord between a free act and rational nature itself, as such, consists the goodness or turpitude of that act; so that, more properly speaking, that nature falls into the category of law.

5. I believe that the opinion expounded above contains the true doctrine in its fundamental assumption regarding the intrinsic goodness or turpitude of actions, whereby they fall under the sway of the natural law commanding or forbidding them: a matter which I shall elucidate in the course of this Chapter's argument.

Nevertheless, this opinion, in so far as it relates to the exposition of the natural law, and this mode of speaking of the said law, are not, in my opinion, acceptable.

The first opinion as to the basis of the natural law is rejected. The first reason for my objection is that the mode of speaking in question, as we shall presently see, is foreign to the teaching of all theologians and philosophers.

Secondly, the rational nature itself, strictly viewed in its essential aspect, neither gives commands, nor makes evident the rectitude or turpitude of anything; neither does it direct or illuminate, or produce any of the other proper effects of law. Therefore, it cannot be spoken of as law, unless we choose to use that term in an entirely equivocal and metaphorical sense, a use which would render the entire discussion futile. For, we assume, in accordance with the common opinion found not only in the words of the Doctors, but also in the canon and the civil law, that the body of natural law (*ius*) is a true body of law, and that particular natural law (*lex*) is true law.

[6.] Thirdly, the reason for our statements is the fact that not everything which forms the basis of the goodness or rectitude of an act prescribed by law, and not everything which is the ground for the turpitude of an act forbidden by law, may [in themselves] be called law; and, consequently, although the rational nature is the foundation of the objective goodness of the moral actions of human beings, it may not for that reason be termed law; and, by the same token, that nature may be spoken of as a standard, yet it is not correct to conclude on that ground that it is law, for 'standard' is a term of wider application than is 'law'. Wherefore, the entire argument[2] would proceed from the general to the particular by means of affirmative deduction, a faulty method of procedure.[3]

The foregoing assumption may be illustrated in many ways.

In the first place, the practice of almsgiving is an example. The indigence of the poor man and the capacity of the giver are the basis of the goodness or obligation involved in almsgiving; and, nevertheless, no one holds that the need of the poor man is the law that imposes almsgiving.

The words of St. Thomas (II.–II, qu. 141, art. 6), concerning temperance, furnish a similar example, when he says that the need of the body is the rule of temperance; yet no one will say that this need is the law [of temperance]; on the contrary, it is the foundation of the law. In that same passage (ad 1), indeed, St. Thomas says that happiness is the rule of human actions in so far as they are morally good; and yet that happiness is not law.

It is evident, then, that the basic principle of a rule and standard, has wider connotations [than that of a law]. Moreover, the end is the rule and measure of the means, but it is not law; and the object is the rule and measure of actions, and similarly, it is not law. Otherwise, [if we do not accept this view,] our abuse of terms will leave us floundering in ambiguity.

7. *The opinion above set forth is assailed on the ground of the absurd conclusions consequent upon it.* Furthermore, we may construct a [contrary] argument, based upon the absurd conclusions to be inferred from the opinion above set forth.

One example is the conclusion that it would be no less fitting that God should have His own natural law, binding and obligatory on Him, than

---

2. [In support of the opinion rejected by Suárez.—Tr.]

3. [I.e., Suárez argues that we should not suppose that because rational nature is the measure and basis of right conduct it is a law.—Reviser.]

that men should be subject to such a law; a deduction which is manifestly absurd. [Yet] such an inference is clearly to be drawn; for to God also, falsehood, for example, is repugnant, being incongruous with the perfection of His nature; therefore, the very nature of God is a rule of rectitude with regard to the speaking of truth, and a rule of evil with regard to falsehood; and, consequently, the nature of God would be law with respect to Him, no less than human nature is law with respect to mankind. For the fact that the will of God is so righteous that it could not fail to conform with His nature, when [the latter] makes any demand as being necessary to rectitude, has no relation to the essence of law, which is attributed only to the essential characteristics of a standard of measurement found in the divine nature. Accordingly, St. Thomas (Pt. I, qu. 21, art. 1, ad 3) says that God's justice looks to that which befits Himself, in that He renders to Himself that which is due to Himself; therefore, God's nature itself is the measure of His actions, in that He acts in a manner congruous with and fitting to that nature, and, consequently, His nature will be law.

In like manner, and in accordance with the same reasoning, divine goodness, as it is made manifest to the blessed, will be the law of beatifying love, since that goodness is the measure of rectitude for such love and the standard regulating the mode which the blessed should observe in loving. And it is of slight importance that this love is or is not necessary, inasmuch as this law is wholly natural, and requires as its essential principle a standard existing in nature itself.

8. It would follow, therefore, that natural law is not divine law, nor does it come from God.

The proof of this conclusion is as follows: according to the opinion expounded above, the precepts of the natural law are not from God, inasmuch as they are characterized by a necessary goodness, and inasmuch as that condition [of necessary goodness], which is in rational nature and by reason of which that nature is the standard of such goodness does not depend upon God for its rational basis, although its actual existence does depend upon Him. For the fact that falsehood, for example, is discordant with the rational nature, is not a fact derived from God, nor is it dependent upon His will. Indeed, in the order of thought, it is prior to the judgment of God. Hence, natural law is prior to the divine judgment and the divine will of God; and, therefore, natural law does not have God for its author, but necessarily dwells within rational nature in that manner, in such fashion that it is inherently endowed with this essence, and no other. However, we shall demonstrate in the following discussion, that this conclusion cannot be admitted as true.

And, finally, with respect to human laws themselves, since they should be just and righteous, one would necessarily assume that there exists in them some basis of justice and rectitude; for everything that is just and right is just in accordance with some rule and to the extent of its conformity with that rule. Hence, for example, the common welfare, or the community itself, in so far as a particular thing or act prescribed by human law is the due of the community, or advantageous to it, would be a law (so to speak) prior to human law itself, and (as it were) a law regulating human law, since it would be the standard with which the latter should accord. Yet no one will make such an assertion.

We conclude, then, that the essential principle of a standard or foundation for rectitude does not suffice as the equivalent of the essential principle of law; and, consequently, that rational nature merely as such, may not fittingly be called natural law.

9. *The second opinion: asserting that the law of nature is a certain natural force, which we call natural reason.* There is, then, a second opinion [regarding the formal basis of natural law].

According to this opinion, two aspects of rational nature are distinguishable: one being that nature itself, in so far as it is (so to speak) the basis of the conformity or non-conformity of human acts with itself; the other consisting in a certain power which this nature possesses, to discriminate between the actions in harmony with it and those discordant with it, a power to which we give the name of natural reason.

With regard to the first aspect, rational nature is said to be the basis of natural rectitude; but with regard to the second, it is said to be the very precept [*lex*] of nature which lays commands or prohibitions upon the human will regarding what must be done [or left undone], as a matter of natural law [*ius*]. This appears to be the opinion of the theologians, as one gathers from St. Thomas (I.–II, qu. 94, arts. 1 and 2 and on the *Sentences,* Bk. IV, dist. xxxiii, qu. 1, art. 1), and from Alexander of Hales (*Summa*

Universae Theologiae, Pt. III, qu. xxvii, memb. 2, art. 1). Moreover, the same view is held by Abulensis [Tostado] (on *Matthew,* xix, qu. 30), Soto (*De Iustitia et Iure,* Bk. I, qu. iv, art. 1), Viguerius (*Institutiones Theologicae,* Chap. xv, § 1), in many instances by other theologians; by the jurists on *Digest,* I. i; and by Albert of Bologna (Tract. *De Lege, Iure et Aequitate,* Nos. [Chaps.] xxv and xxvi), who especially may be consulted, in a passage wherein he refers to other authorities. The philosophers, too, frequently speak in this vein, as we have previously noted (Bk. I, chap. iii).[4]

10. *Confirmation [of the foregoing opinion] from Scripture.* The opinion in question may also find a basis in the words of Paul (*Romans,* Chap. ii [, vv. 14–15]), who, after saying: 'For when the Gentiles who have not the law, do by nature those things that are of the law, these having not the law, are a law to themselves', adds, as if to indicate the way in which the Gentiles are a law unto themselves and the nature of that law: 'Who show the work of the law written in their hearts, their conscience bearing witness to them.' For conscience is an exercise of the reason, as is evident; and conscience bears witness to and reveals the work of the law written in the hearts of men, since it testifies that a man does ill or well, when he resists or obeys the natural dictates of right reason, revealing also, in consequence, the fact that such dictates have the force of law over man, even though they may not be externally clothed in the form of written law. Therefore, these dictates constitute natural law; and, accordingly, the man who is guided by them, is said to be a law unto himself, since he bears law written within himself through the medium of the dictates of natural reason. St. Thomas confirms this view (I.–II, qu. 91, art. 2) in his comment on the passage from Psalm iv [, vv. 6–7]: '[Many say,] Who sheweth us good things? The light of thy countenance O Lord, is signed upon us'; for these words, [according to St. Thomas], mean that man participates by the light of reason in the eternal law, which dictates what must be done or left undone. This [rational illumination], then, is the natural law; for the latter is nothing other than a natural participation (so to speak) in the eternal law.

4. [Of the *De Legibus.*—Tr.]

11. *Confirmation [of the same] from the Fathers.* The opinion under discussion may also be confirmed by the authority of the Fathers. For Basil, according to St. Thomas (I.–II, qu. 94, art. 1, obj. 2), has said that synteresis,[5] or conscience, is the law of our intellect; and this statement is unintelligible, unless it refers to the natural law, as St. Thomas remarked in the passage cited, a passage apparently derived from Basil (Homily XII: *On Proverbs,* at the beginning). Joannes Damascenus (*De Fide Orthodoxa,* Bk. IV, chap. xxiii), also, would seem to have been speaking of this same law, when he said: 'The law of God, enkindling our minds, draws them to itself, and rouses our consciences, which, in themselves, are spoken of as the law of our minds.' These words are explained by Clichtove [on Joannes Damascenus' *De Fide Orthodoxa,* Bk. IV, chap. xxiii, near the beginning], as follows: 'The law of our minds is natural reason itself, in which there is fixed, stamped and inborn the law of God, by which through the medium of an inner light, we are able to distinguish between good and evil', &c. St. Jerome (Letter cli, qu. viii [Letter cxxi, *Ad Algasiam,* Chap. viii, Migne ed., Vol. XXII, col. 1022]) expresses the same opinion when he calls this law, 'the law of intelligence, which is disregarded by the very young, and unknown to infants, but which, when intelligence begins to assert itself, comes to the fore and lays down commands regarding those things which cannot be made to accord with pure rational nature.' He adds, moreover, that Pharaoh, when he was roused by the law of nature to a recognition of his own guilt (*Exodus,* Chap. ix), was urged by nothing other than right reason. Maximus of Turin (Tom. V, *Biblio. Centur.* V, chap. xiii),[6] too, says that, 'The law of nature is natural reason, which holds captive the mind in order to destroy irrational impulse.' And Augustine (*On the Sermon of Our Lord on the Mount,* Bk. II [, chap. ix, § 32]) declares that, 'There is

5. *Synteresis* or *synderesis* is the shared understanding of the fundamental and general principles of natural law given us by our rational nature. *Synteresis* is commonly seen as a *habitus* or disposition to make particular judgments.
   Conscientia, by contrast, is the individual's application of the fundamental principles of natural law, known through *synteresis,* to arrive at judgments of how to act in particular cases. *Conscientia* consists of the exercise and application of the *habitus* (cf. note 2, p. 233) that is synteresis.
   6. [*Centuriae Magdeburgenses,* V, chap. x, gives a brief account of Maximus of Turin.—REVISER.]

no soul [. . .] capable of reasoning, in whose conscience God does not speak. For who save God writes the natural law in the heart of man?'[7] It is in this same vein that Augustine [*ibid.*] treats of the above cited passage from Paul (*Romans,* Chap. ii [, vv. 14–16]). Ambrose discusses this point similarly and at great length, in the passage (*Letters,* Bk. V, epistle xli [*Letter* lxxiii, Migne ed.]) in which he says, among other things, that, 'The law in question', namely, the natural law, 'is not written but innate; neither is it perceived through any reading, but rather is it made manifest within the individual as by a flowing natural spring.' Isidore (*Etymologies,* Bk. V, chap. ii [chap. iv]) wrote to the same effect. And, finally, Lactantius (*Divine Institutes,* Bk. VI: *De Vero Cultu,* chap. viii) describes the natural law in the words of Cicero (*The Republic* [Bk. III, chap. xxii, § 33]), saying: 'Right reason is, indeed, true law, in harmony with nature, diffused among all men, constant, eternal, calling them to the observance of their duty in its commands and prohibitions', &c.

12. *The opinion, above set forth, is confirmed by reasoning.* The opinion above set forth may be briefly supported by reasoning, in accordance with what has been said.

First, [we may argue] by means of an adequate discrimination: for natural law resides in man, since it does not reside in God, being temporal and created, nor is it external to man, since it is written not upon tablets but in the heart; neither does it dwell immediately within human nature itself, since we have proved that it does not do so; nor is it in the will, since it does not depend upon the will of man, but, on the contrary, binds and (as it were) coerces his will; hence, this natural law must necessarily reside in the reason.

Secondly, one may adduce the argument that the legal effects which may be thought of in the case of natural law, proceed immediately from a dictate of the reason, for that dictate directs and binds and is a rule of conscience which censures or approves what is done, so that law of the kind in question consists in the said dictate.

Thirdly, the exercise of dominion and the function of ruling are characteristic of law; and in man, these functions are to be attributed to right

7. [Not an exact quotation.—TR.]

reason, that he may be rightly governed in accordance with nature; therefore, the natural law must be constituted in the reason, as in the immediate and intrinsic rule of human actions.

13. *Whether the natural law consists in a [second] act or in a habit of mind.* It is furthermore usual to ask, at this point, whether the natural law consists in a [second] act, or in a [mental] habit—that is to say, in the light of natural reason itself, or, in other words, some first act.[8] For theologians disagree on this question also; and many prefer to answer that the law under discussion consists in the second act,[9] since law is an exercise of authority, which consists in action, and since such action is, strictly speaking, a directive rule. This is the common opinion of the Thomists (I.–II, qu. 94, art. 1), for it is thus that they interpret St. Thomas's meaning, as is evident from Cajetan, Conrad Koellin, and others. On this point, we may also refer to Antoninus ([*Summa Theologica,*] Pt. I, tit. XIII, chap. i, at the beginning), and Soto (*De Iustitia et Iure,* Bk. I, qu. iv, art. 1). Alexander of Hales, on the other hand ([*Summa Universae Theologiae,*] Pt. III, qu. xxvii, memb. 2, throughout three articles), judges natural law to be a [mental] habit. One may argue, on behalf of this latter opinion, that the natural law is said to be congenital with nature, and is permanent; characteristics which befit not a [second] act, but a habit. For, by the term 'habit', we understand, not a quality superadded to a faculty, but the light of the intellect itself, as it is regarded in its first act.[10] Bonaventure (on the *Sentences,* Bk. II, dist. xxxix, art. 2, qu. 1, ad ult.), expressing yet another view, asserts that the term 'natural law' signifies in one sense a habit, and, in another sense, natural precepts themselves, in so far as these exist objectively in the mind, or synteresis. St. Thomas, however, says that the term properly refers to an act, or a judgment, on the part of the reason; although, in another [, less strict] sense, it denotes a habit, in so far as the natural precepts remain permanently in the mind.

---

8. [Cf. Chapter iii, sect. 1, note 1 (p. 173), where *actus primus* is explained as the faculty. One might employ the crude comparison of an engine that is just ready to start working (*actus primus*); the pulling of a lever will set it free for its *actus secundus.*—REVISER.]

9. See note 8.

10. [*Vide* the preceding note for an explanation of 'first act'.—REVISER.]

14. *The opinion of the author, and the solution of the question.* The question seems to me, indeed, to turn upon the use of terms; and I have no doubt but that, it is in the actual judgment of the mind that natural law, in the strictest sense, exists. I must add, however, that the natural light of the intellect—which is inherently to prescribe what must be done—may be called the natural law, since men retain that law in their hearts, although they may be engaged in no [specific] act of reflection or judgment. It must be taken into consideration, then, that natural law, as we are now using the term, is looked upon as existing not in the Lawgiver, but in men, in whose hearts that Lawgiver Himself has written it, as Paul says, and that, by means of the illumination of the mind, as is intimated in Psalm iv. Therefore, just as human law, in so far as it is external to the legislator, implies on the part of the subject not only active knowledge thereof, or an act of judgment, but also a permanent sign of its existence, contained in some written form which is always able to awaken knowledge of that law; even so, in the case of natural law, which exists in the lawgiver as none other than the eternal law, there is, in the subjects, not only an active judgment, or command, but also the [mental] illumination itself in which that law is (as it were) permanently written, and which the law is always capable of incorporating in action.

15. *In what way the natural law may be distinguished from the rule of conscience.* Thus, it is easy to understand a comparison between the natural law and conscience. For sometimes these two forces are thought of as identical (a fact which we have already gathered from Basil and Joannes Damascenus), on the ground that conscience is nothing more or less than a dictate regarding what ought to be done.

Nevertheless, strictly speaking, the two are different. For the term 'law' signifies a rule in general terms regarding those things which should be done; whereas 'conscience' signifies a practical dictate in a particular case, wherefore it is the application of the law to a particular act (so to speak) rather than [the law itself].

From these facts, it also follows that 'conscience' is a broader term than 'natural law', since it puts into application, not only the law of nature, but also every other law, whether divine or human. Indeed, conscience is wont to apply not merely true law, but even reputed law, in which sense it sometimes occurs that conscience is in error. [True] law, on the other hand, can never be in error, for, by the very fact that it was erroneous, it would fail to be law, an assertion which is especially true with respect to the natural law, of which God is the Author.

Finally, law is properly concerned with acts which are to be performed; while conscience deals also with things which have already been done, and consequently is endowed not only with the attribute of imposing obligations, but also with those of accusing, bearing witness, and defending, as may be gathered from St. Thomas (Pt. I, qu. 79 [, art. 13], and I.–II, qu. 19, art. 6), in certain passages, wherein he treats of conscience. Alexander of Hales, too, is especially to be consulted on this point (*ibid.,* Qu. xxvii, memb. 2, art. 3); as is also Bonaventure (on the *Sentences,* Bk. II, dist. xxxix, art. 2, qu. 1).

CHAPTER VI

Is the Natural Law in Truth Preceptive Divine Law?

1. *The reason for doubt is explained.* The reason for doubt on this question originates in the fundamental grounds of a previously cited opinion, referred to in the preceding Chapter, which was there propounded and which has not yet been explained. For in its true sense, a preceptive law never exists without an act of willing on the part of him who issues the command, as has been shown in the First Book; but, [so runs the doubt,] the natural law is not dependent upon the will of any giver of commands; hence, it is not law in the true sense.

The truth of the minor premiss is established by the points adduced in the preceding Chapter, namely: that the dictates of natural reason, wherein natural law consists, are intrinsically necessary and independent of every will, even of the divine will, and prior, in concept, to the free act by which something is willed; examples of such dictates being the precepts that God must be worshipped, parents must be honoured, lying is evil and must be shunned, and the like; all of which has been sufficiently proved above. Therefore, the natural law cannot be called true law. This statement is further confirmed by the fact that [this so-called law] is not a true command; and hence, it is not true law.

The truth of the antecedent is evident. For the natural law is one of two things. First, it may be a command laid upon man by himself; which is not actually the case since a command of this kind either does not exist save as an act of judgment manifesting the truth of the matter in hand, or else, if it be an expression of the will or of a choice already made, is not in itself necessary to action, nor does it impose an obligation, but [merely] leads to the actual execution of the act in question, so that it neither suffices for, nor contributes anything to, the true or proper character of law. Or, secondly, natural law may be the command of a given superior; but this assertion is also untenable, in view of the argument above stated, namely, that the natural law dictates concerning what is good or evil, without reference to the will of any superior.

2. From the foregoing it would also seem to follow that the natural law may not properly be termed divine, not with the implication, that is, that it has been given by God as by a lawmaker.

But I repeat, *as by a lawmaker,* since it is clear that natural reason and its dictates are a divine gift, descending from the Father of Light. It is one thing, however, to say that this natural law is from God, as from an efficient primary cause; and it is quite another thing to say that the same law is derived from Him as from a lawgiver who commands and imposes obligations. For the former statement is most certain, and a matter of faith, both because God is the primary cause of all good things in the natural order, among which the use of right reason and the illumination which it affords constitute a great good; and also because, in this sense, every manifestation of truth is from God, according to the saying in the *Epistle to the Romans* (Chap. i [, v. 18]): 'For the wrath of God is revealed from heaven against all ungodliness and injustice of [those] men that detain the truth of God in injustice.' Paul, in explaining why he uses the expression, 'the truth of God', adds (*ibid.* [, v. 19]): 'Because that which is known of God is manifest in them. For God hath manifested it unto them'; by means, surely, of the natural light of reason, and by means of visible creatures whereby the invisible things of God may come to be known. It is in this sense, then— that is, as referring to an efficient cause and to the function of instructing, so to speak—that the words of Paul above-cited, are interpreted by Chrysostom (Homily III, *On Romans* and more at length, Homilies XII and XIII, *To The People*); by Theophylact also, on the same passage from Paul; by Ambrose, on the same; by Cyril (*Against Julian*, Bk. III, near the end, § *Nam quod summa, et seq.* [Vol. LXXVI, col. 666, Migne ed.]), and, most excellently, by Augustine (*Sermons*, lv, *De Verbis Domini* [Letter cxli, Vol. XXXVIII, col. 776, Migne ed.] and *On the Sermon of our Lord on the Mount*, Bk. II, chap. ix [, § 32]), who says in the latter work: 'Who save God writes the natural law in the hearts of men?'

Therefore, without doubt, God is the efficient cause and the teacher (as it were) of the natural law; but it does not follow from this, that He is its legislator, for the natural law does not reveal God issuing commands, but [simply] indicates what is in itself good or evil, just as the sight of a certain object reveals it as being white or black, and just as an effect produced by God, reveals Him as its Author, but not as Lawgiver. It is in this way, then, that we must think of [God in relation to] the natural law.

3. *The first opinion: holding that the natural law is a law not truly preceptive, but rather demonstrative.* On this point, the first opinion which we shall discuss is, that the natural law is not a preceptive law, properly so-called, since it is not the indication of the will of some superior; but that, on the contrary, it is a law indicating what should be done, and what should be avoided, what of its own nature is intrinsically good and necessary, and what is intrinsically evil.

So it is that many writers distinguish between two aspects of law, the one indicative, the other preceptive, and hold that the natural law is law in the first sense, not in the second. This is the view expressed by Gregory of Rimini[1] (on the *Sentences*, Bk. II, dist. xxxiv, qu. 1, art. 2, shortly after the beginning, § *Secundum corollarium*), who refers to Hugh of St. Victor (*De Sacramentis Christianae Fidei*, Bk. I, pt. vi, chaps. vi and vii) and who is followed by Gabriel (on the *Sentences*, Bk. II, dist. xxxv, qu. i, art. i); Almain (*Moralia*, Bk. III, chap. xvi) and Corduba (*De Conscientia*, Bk. III, qu. x, ad 2).

---

1. Gregory of Rimini (ca. 1300–1358), an Augustinian friar whose commentary on Lombard's *Sentences* Suárez treats as proposing a purely intellectualist or rationalist theory of natural law and the obligation to obey it. Suárez's interpretation of Gregory is controversial.

Accordingly, it seems that these authors would grant that the natural law is not derived from God as a Lawgiver, since it does not depend upon His will, and since, in consequence, God does not, by virtue of that law, act as a superior who lays down commands or prohibitions. Indeed, on the contrary, Gregory, whom the others follow, says that even if God did not exist, or if He did not make use of reason, or if He did not judge of things correctly, nevertheless, if the same dictates of right reason dwelt within man, constantly assuring him, for example, that lying is evil, those dictates would still have the same legal character which they actually possess, because they would constitute a law pointing out the evil that exists intrinsically in the object [condemned].

4. *The second opinion: affirming that the natural law is truly divine and preceptive.* The second opinion, at the opposite extreme to the first, is that the natural law consists entirely in a divine command or prohibition proceeding from the will of God as the Author and Ruler of nature; that, consequently, this law as it exists in God is none other than the eternal law in its capacity of commanding or prohibiting with respect to a given matter; and that, on the other hand, this same natural law, as it dwells within ourselves, is the judgment of reason, in that it reveals to us God's will as to what must be done or avoided in relation to those things which are conformable to natural reason.

This is the view one ascribes to William of Occam[2] (on the *Sentences,* Bk. II, qu. 19, ad 3 and 4), inasmuch as he says that no act is wicked save in so far as it is forbidden by God, and that there is no act incapable of becoming a good act if commanded by God; and conversely, . . . ; whence he assumes that the whole natural law consists of divine precepts laid down by God, and susceptible of abrogation or alteration by Him. And if any one insists that such a law would be not natural but positive, the reply is, that it is called natural because of its congruity with the nature of things, and not with the implication that it was not externally enacted by

2. William of Occam or Ockham (ca. 1285–1347), an English Franciscan theologian and philosopher who is taken by Suárez as a leading proponent of a purely voluntarist theory of natural law and the obligation to obey it as resting on no more than contingent and revocable acts of the divine will. It is controversial how accurate Suárez is as an interpreter of Ockham.

the command of God. Gerson also inclines to this opinion (Pt. III, tract. *De Vita Spirituali Animae,* Lect. I, corols. 10 and 11; *Alphabetum Divini Amoris,* 61, littera E and F);[3] and says accordingly (*De Vita Spirituali Animae,* Lects. II and III), that the natural law which exists within us is an expression of the upright dictates, not only of the divine intellect, but also of the divine will. Peter d'Ailly (on the *Sentences,* Bk. I, qu. xiv, art. 3), too, defends this view at length, saying that the divine will is the primary law and therefore able to create men endowed with the use of reason but totally destitute of law. The same opinion is supported at length by Andreas a Novocastro (on the *Sentences,* Bk. I, dist. xlviii, qu. 1, art. 1).

These authorities also add that the whole basis of good and evil in matters pertaining to the law of nature is in God's will, and not in a judgment of reason, even on the part of God Himself, nor in the very things which are prescribed or forbidden by that law. Their opinion would assuredly seem to be founded upon the fact that actions are not good or evil, save as they are ordered or prohibited by God; since God Himself does not will to command or forbid a given action to any created being, on the ground that such an action is good or evil, but rather on the ground that it is just or unjust, [simply] because He has willed that it shall or shall not be done, as Anselm (*Proslogion,* Chap. xi), indicates, saying: 'That is just which Thou dost will; and that is not just which Thou dost not will.' Such is the view held also by Hugh of St. Victor (*De Sacramentis,* Bk. I, pt. iv, chap. i); and by Cyprian, in a work (*De Singularitate Clericorum*) attributed to him.

5. *The first proposition: Not only does the natural law indicate what is good or evil, but it also contains precepts and prohibitions regarding both good and evil.* However, neither of the opinions above set forth appears to me to be satisfactory; and consequently I hold that a middle course should be taken, this middle course being, in my judgment, the opinion held by St. Thomas and common to the theologians.

My first proposition, then, is as follows: Not only does the natural law indicate what is good or evil, but furthermore, it contains its own prohibition of evil and command of good. This is the inference which I draw from the words of St. Thomas, in the passage (I.–II, qu. 71, art. 6, ad 4)

---

3. [Gerson does not deal with this point very clearly in his *Alphabetum.*—Reviser.]

where he says that, in so far as human law[4] is concerned, not all sins are evil simply because they are prohibited; but that, with respect to the natural law, which is contained primarily in the eternal law and secondarily in the judicial faculty[5] of natural reason, every sin is wrongful simply for the reason that it is forbidden. In a subsequent passage (*ibid.,* qu. 100, art. 8, ad 2), he says that God cannot deny Himself and therefore cannot abolish the order of His own justice; by which St. Thomas means that God cannot fail to prohibit those things which are evil and contrary to natural reason. Bonaventure (on the *Sentences,* Bk. II, dist. xxxv, *dub.* 4, *circa literam*) is of the same opinion; and Gerson (Tr. *De Vita Spirituali,* Lect. II, in entirety, especially coroll. 5) also writes clearly to this effect, when he defines the natural reason as follows: 'The natural law in its preceptive character is a sign impressed upon every man who is not deficient in the due use of reason, a sign making known the divine will that rational human creatures shall be bound to perform certain actions or to refrain from other actions, in the attainment of their natural end.' This definition is perhaps more comprehensive than necessary, and at present we avail ourselves of it only in so far as it serves our purpose. The assertion in question is also assumed to be true, by some of the authorities who hold the second of the two opinions discussed above; and it is furthermore defended at length by Victoria (Relectio XIII: *De Pervenientibus ad Usum Rationis,*[6] Nos. 8 *et seq.*).

6. *The foregoing proposition is confirmed by reasoning.* This proposition may be proved, first, on the basis of the peculiar nature of law. For the natural law is truly law, inasmuch as all the Fathers, theologians, and philosophers so speak and think of it; but the mere knowledge or conception of anything existing in the mind cannot be called law, a fact which is self-evident and which follows also from the definition of law given above; therefore, ...

A second argument may be drawn from those actions which are evil, in that they are prohibited by human law. For in the case of such acts, also, if

---

4. [St. Thomas, in the passage cited, uses the term 'positive law'.—Tr.]

5. [Suárez has *indicatorio,* apparently a misprint, as St. Thomas, in the passage cited, employs the term *indicatorium.*—Tr.]

6. [In the Lyons Edition of 1586 and in Simon's edition, 1696, the title of this Relectio reads: *De eo, ad quod tenetur homo cum primum venit ad usum rationis.*—Tr.]

a man is to be guilty of sin, it is necessary that there be a preceding mental judgment indicating that the thing in question is evil; yet that judgment has not the nature of a law or prohibition, since it merely indicates [a quality] existing within that thing, whatever the source of the quality may be; hence, by the same reasoning, although in those matters which fall within the province of the natural law as it relates to good or evil actions, a judgment pointing out the good or evil involved in a particular thing or act must necessarily precede [that act]; nevertheless, such a judgment has not the character of a law or of a prohibition, but is merely a recognition of some fact already assumed to be true. Accordingly, the act which is recognized as evil by the said judgment, is not evil for the reason that it is thus considered, but because it actually is evil, and is, in consequence, truly adjudged to be so; therefore, that judgment is not a rule of evil or of good; and consequently, neither is it a law nor a prohibition.

Thirdly, if the assertion in question were not true, God Himself would be subject to a natural law relating to His will; since even in God, an intellectual act of judgment logically precedes an act of His will, a judgment indicating that lying is wicked, that to keep one's promises is wholly right and necessary [, and so forth]; and therefore, if such an act of the intellect is sufficient to constitute the essence of law, then there will be a true natural law, even with respect to God Himself. For in such a case, the fact that God has no superior, will not serve as an objection, since the natural law is not imposed by any superior. Neither is any objection to the argument in question involved in the identity [of the action of God's will with that of His intellect], since a distinction in thought is sufficient, in order that God's will may truly be said to be directed to that which is manifested by His intellect, and since by that manifestation [the object of the law] is proposed [to the will]; so that [such a distinction] suffices to make [these intellectual manifestations] law; for that process is said to suffice for the essence of law.

Finally, a judgment showing the nature of a given action is not the act of a superior, but may, on the contrary, be that of an equal or of an inferior who has no binding power; and consequently, it is impossible for that judgment to have the nature of a law or of a prohibition. Otherwise, a teacher when he points out what is good and what is evil, would be imposing a law, an assertion which cannot [truthfully] be made. Law, then, is that sort of authority which can impose a binding obligation; whereas the judgment in question does not impose an obligation, but [simply] points out what obligation should be assumed to exist. Therefore, if this judgment is to have the nature of law, it must indicate some sort of authority as the source of such obligation.

7. However, some one may object that these arguments have weight only with respect to 'law' [in the strict sense of] the term, and may therefore easily be rendered inefficacious by the declaration that the natural law is not termed law in the rigorous sense in which law is said to be a universal precept imposed by a superior, but is so termed for the more general reason that it is a measure of moral good and evil, such as law is wont to be.

But in answer to this objection, I shall argue further that what is opposed to the natural law is necessarily opposed to true law and to the prohibition of some superior; so that the natural law, as existing in man, points out a given thing not only as it is in itself, but also as being forbidden or prescribed by some superior. The consequent is clearly true; for if the natural law consists intrinsically in its simple object as the latter is in itself, or in the manifestation of the same, then the violation of the natural law will not be of itself and intrinsically opposed to the law of any superior inasmuch as a man would violate the natural law, even independently of all laws imposed by a superior, if he acted in opposition to those natural dictates.

The antecedent, then, may be proved, first, from the words of Augustine (*Against Faustus,* Bk. XXII, chap. xxvii), when he defines sin thus: 'It is a word, deed, or desire opposed to the eternal law', and adds that 'The eternal law is the reason and will of God'; indicating that he believes it to be the nature of sin that it should be contrary to the strict law of some superior. Wherefore, in another passage, Augustine (*De Peccatorum Meritis et Remissione,* Bk. II, chap. xvi [, § 23]) says: 'Nor can that be sin, whatever it may be, concerning which God has not enjoined that it shall not be.' And, farther on, he adds: 'How can [. . .] forgiveness be bestowed by God's mercy if there is no sin; or how can a prohibition by God's justice not exist, if there is sin?' his meaning being that it is no less repugnant to reason that sin should exist and not be forbidden by God, than that there should be need of forgiveness without the fact of sin. This opinion is confirmed by the definition of Ambrose (*On Paradise,* Chap. viii): 'Sin is violation of the divine law and disobedience to the heavenly mandates.' But an offence against the natural law is sin in the true sense; therefore, such an offence is a violation of a divine and heavenly mandate; and consequently, the natural law, as it exists in man, has the force of a divine mandate, indicating such a mandate (so to speak) and not merely the nature of its own subject-matter. Finally, the words of Paul are in agreement with the truth which we are discussing, for he says (*Romans,* Chap. iv [, v. 15]): 'Where there is no law, neither is there transgression.' For clearly, he is speaking of the whole law, not merely with reference to ceremonial and judicial precepts, but also with reference to the moral precepts which are part of the law of nature; because the teaching of Paul is valid for all law (natural law also being so classified), that is to say, the teaching that of itself and without the spirit of grace, the law worketh wrath. And thus it is that the passage in question is commonly interpreted, since otherwise the doctrine of the Apostle would not be complete, a fact which will be brought out more fully in our treatise on Grace.[7] He holds, then, that every sin is contrary to some law. This conclusion, moreover, should be understood as applying to true preceptive law; both because that sort of law is referred to throughout the chapter cited, and also because words ought not to be given a strained interpretation without authority or unless there exists an urgent necessity.

8. Furthermore, the proposition in question[8] may be supported by *a priori* reasoning; since all things which are declared evil by the natural law, are forbidden by God, by a special command and by that will whose decree binds and obliges us, through the force of His authority, to obey those [natural precepts]; and, therefore, the natural law is truly a preceptive law, that is to say, one which contains true precepts.

The truth of the consequent is evident.

The first proof of the antecedent premiss is as follows: God has complete providence over men; therefore, it becomes Him, as the supreme

7. [Not included in these *Selections.*—Tr.]

8. [I.e., the assertion made at the beginning of Section 5 of this Chapter; *supra,* p. 210.—Tr.]

Governor of nature, to prohibit evil and prescribe that which is good; hence, although the natural reason reveals what is good and what is bad to rational nature, nevertheless God, as the Author and Governor of that nature, commands that certain actions shall be performed or avoided, in accordance with the dictates of reason.

Secondly, whatever is contrary to right reason is displeasing to God, and the opposite is pleasing to Him; for the will of God is supremely just, and therefore, that which is evil cannot fail to displease Him, nor can that which is righteous fail to please Him, inasmuch as God's will cannot be irrational, as Anselm (*Cur Deus Homo,* Bk. I, chap. viii) says; consequently, the natural reason which indicates what is in itself evil or good for mankind, indicates accordingly that it is in conformity with the divine will that the good should be chosen, and the evil avoided.

9. *Objection.* One may object that the existence in God of a will which approves or disapproves, does not imply as a necessary corollary that this will is compelling in a preceptive sense. For in the first place, we are not for that reason bound to conform to every expression of the divine will that is a matter of simple volition; nor even to every approving and efficacious volition; but only to those volitions whereby God wills to bind us, as I gather from St. Thomas (I.–II, qu. 19 [, art. 11]). Wherefore, by this same reasoning, although the works of counsel[9] may be pleasing to God, it is not to be inferred on that account that His will commands that they be performed. And [similarly]—to take a second example—whatever I do contrary to reason is displeasing to a just man or to one of the blessed, and nevertheless their will in the matter is not a command.

Solution. My reply to this objection is, in the first place, that the question concerns not simply any complaisant will, but that will which is so pleased by something, in so far as it is good, that the contrary—or that which is opposed thereto by the lack [of some quality], through omission—is displeasing as being evil; and the works of counsel are pleasing not in this fashion, but in such a way that their opposites, that is, omission to

---

9. *Opera consiliorum* or actions by which Christians follow the evangelical counsels or recommendations of Christ to pursue in various ways poverty, chastity, and obedience. The evangelical counsels are held in Catholic theology to be just that—advisory counsels, not obligatory commands.

perform them, involves no displeasing evil, so that the complaisance with which these works are regarded, is called simple will; whereas the former sort of will, according to which one thing is pleasing in such fashion that another thing is unrestrictedly displeasing, is held to be will in a more absolute sense.

Secondly, I reply that such a will must be regarded as existing in God as the supreme Governor, and not as it may be found in a just individual, whether in this life or in the state of glory. For God, in that absolute disapproval or complaisance, wills absolutely that the deed in question shall be done or left undone, in so far as relates to His office as a just governor; and therefore, this volition is of such a nature that through it He wishes to oblige His subjects to perform a given action or to leave it unperformed. For the volition under discussion cannot be an efficacious volition, willing that a certain action absolutely must or must not be performed; since in that case, no action could ever be done [or left undone], save in accordance with God's will, which nevertheless is clearly not the fact. Neither is such [a mode of willing] proper to the office of Governor, to whom it pertains, to will the good in such fashion that evil is [nevertheless] permitted, and secondary free causes are [nevertheless] allowed to use their free wills, without let or hindrance. Therefore, the volition in question must be binding volition, for it is thus that [God] provides for His subjects in this matter, as befits a righteous and prudent providence.

10. Wherefore the [first] proposition[10] is confirmed; for offences against the natural law are said in Scripture to be opposed to the divine will. Thus Anselm declared (*De Voluntate Dei* [, Chap. ii]): 'Whoever resists the natural law, fails to fulfil the will of God.' The proof of this declaration is manifest, since a transgressor of the natural law is, in the divine judgment, deserving of punishment; hence, he is a transgressor against the divine will—for that slave shall be beaten with many stripes who does not the will of his lord, as is said in (*Luke,* Chap. xii [, v. 47]); and therefore it follows that the natural law includes the will of God [among its various elements]. Conversely, to him who does the will of God, is promised the

---

10. [See Section 5 of this Chapter; *supra,* p. 210.—Tr.]

kingdom of heaven (*Matthew,* Chap. vi [, v. 33]; *1 John,* Chap. ii [, v. 17]), a promise which must be interpreted as referring particularly to the preceptive will [of God], for it is written: 'If thou wilt enter into life, keep the commandments'; hence, whosoever obeys the natural law does God's will; and therefore, the natural law includes the preceptive will of God.

The same assertion may be further confirmed, as follows: the divine will indicated by an external sign,[11] and as such ascribed by the theologians to God, extends even to those matters that pertain to the natural law, a fact which one infers from St. Thomas (Pt. I, qu. 19, last art.), as well as from Peter Lombard (*Sentences,* Bk. I, dist. xlv) and others, and which is, moreover, self-evident; for whosoever violates the natural law draws away from the will of God, and when, in the Lord's Prayer [*Matthew,* Chap. vi, v. 10] we pray, 'Thy will be done', we are asking also that it be done in the observance of the natural law; therefore, the natural law, as it exists in us, is an indication of some divine volition; hence, it is pre-eminently an indication of that volition whereby He wills to oblige us to the keeping of that law; and thus it follows that the natural law includes the will of God.

A third confirmation is the fact that a sin against the natural law is offensive to God, being characterized, therefore, by a certain infinite quality; consequently, it betokens opposition to God, as the Maker of that law, for it connotes a virtual contempt of Him; hence, the natural law includes God's will, since without an act of will, no legislation exists.

The final confirmation is this: the binding force of the natural law constitutes a true obligation; and that obligation is a good in its own way, existing in point of fact; therefore, this same obligation must proceed from the divine will, which decrees that men shall be bound to obey that which right reason dictates.

11. *The second proposition. The prohibition or [affirmative] command is not the whole reason for the good or evil involved in the transgression, or the observance of the law of nature; on the contrary, it presupposes the existence of*

---

11. [According to our way of thinking, the divine will properly so called, that is, the absolute volition itself, in respect of what God wills, is the *voluntas beneplaciti;* an external indication of the divine will is the *voluntas signi,* and this term is applied by a process of metonomy to the divine will itself.—REVISER.]

some [such inherent quality]. My second assertion is as follows: this divine volition, in the form of a prohibition or in that of an [affirmative] command, is not the whole reason for the good or evil involved in the observance or transgression of the natural law; on the contrary, it necessarily presupposes the existence of a certain righteousness or turpitude in these actions, and attaches to them a special obligation derived from divine law. This second assertion is drawn from the words of St. Thomas, in the passages above cited.

The first part of the proposition may be deduced from an axiom common to the theologians, that certain evils are prohibited, because they are evil. For if they are forbidden on that very ground, they cannot derive the primary reason for their evil quality from the fact that they are prohibited, since an effect is not the reason for its cause.

This axiom, indeed, has a basis in the words of Augustine (*On the Sermon of our Lord on the Mount*, Bk. II, chap. xviii [, § 59]), in the passage where he says that there are certain acts which cannot be committed with a righteous intention, for example, debaucheries, adulteries, &c.; or more clearly (*On Free Will*, Bk. I, chap. iii) when he quotes Evodius as saying that adultery is not an evil because prohibited by law, but rather that the converse is true, [i.e., adultery is so prohibited, because it is evil], a statement of which Augustine tacitly approves. Moreover, the same opinion is held by the Scholastics, Durandus (on the *Sentences*, Bk. II [Bk. I], dist. xlvii, qu. 4, nos. 7 and 8), Scotus, Gabriel, and others (on the *Sentences*, Bk. III, dist. xxxvii), as well as by Cajetan (on I.–II, qu. 100, art. 1), Soto (*De Iustitia*, Bk. II, qu. iii, art. 2), and other theologians, cited above. We have also the clearly expressed opinion of Aristotle (*Nicomachean Ethics*, Bk. II, chap. vi [, § 18]), who says: 'There are some passions which essentially have their evil nature implied in their very names, for example, malevolence, shamelessness,[12] and envy; and a number of actions, such as adultery, theft, or murder. For all these and others like them are censured because they are intrinsically wicked.'

This doctrine also finds support in the metaphysical principle that the nature of things is immutable in so far as their essence is concerned, and

---

12. [For *imprudentia* read *impudentia*.—Tr.]

hence also, in so far as concerns the consistency or inconsistency of natural properties. For although it is possible that a given thing may be deprived of a natural property, or that it may take on that of an opposite character, nevertheless it is not possible that such a [changed] condition should be connatural to that thing; a fact which Victoria has brought out at length (Relectio X: *De Homicidio,* Nos. 4 *et seq.*), which Soto has touched upon in the passage last cited, and which we mention elsewhere (*Metaphysicarum Disputationum,*[13] Disp. XXXI, at the beginning, and *De Deo Uno et Trino,*[14] Tract. III, bk. IX, chap. vi), in treating of created essences.

There is [also] an *a posteriori* confirmation of these statements; for if hatred of God, for example, involved no essential and intrinsic evil existing prior to its prohibition, then it would be possible for this hatred to be unprohibited. For why shall it not be allowed, if it is not in itself evil? Hence, it could be permitted, and it could be righteous. But this conclusion is clearly repugnant [to reason. Therefore, such an act must be essentially evil.]

Finally, the truth of this first part of our second assertion is sufficiently proven by the cause for doubt postulated at the outset [of this Book][15] together with the basic reasons which are stated in the preceding Chapter in support of the first opinion.[16] And we shall have more to say upon this point when we treat of the indispensable character of the law in question.

12. As for the latter half of this second proposition, its truth may be inferred from what we have already said in connexion with the former conclusion. For the natural law prohibits those things which are bad in themselves; and this law is true divine law and a true prohibition; hence it must necessarily result in some sort of obligation to avoid an evil which is already evil of itself and by its very nature. Neither is it irrational to suppose that one may add to an act which is of itself righteous, the obligation to perform it; or that one may add to an act of itself evil, the obligation to avoid it. In fact, even when one obligation already exists, another may be added thereto, especially if it be of a different character, as is clearly true

13. [Not included in these *Selections.*—Tr.]

14. [Not included in these *Selections.*—Tr.]

15. [In Section 1, Chapter i. See p. 152.—Tr.]

16. [I.e., the opinion set forth at the beginning of Section 2 of Chapter v. See p. 194.—Tr.]

of a vow, a human law, and similar matters. Therefore, the law of nature, as it is true divine law, may also superimpose its own moral obligation, derived from a precept, over and above what may be called the natural evil or virtue inherent in the subject-matter in regard to which such a precept is imposed. This point will presently be more fully expounded, when we reply to the contrary argument.

13. *The third proposition. The natural law is truly and properly [divine] law; and God is its Author.* From the foregoing, then, I conclude and state as my third proposition that the natural law is truly and properly divine law, of which God is the Author.

This conclusion follows clearly from the discussion set forth above, and is taken from the works of the Fathers already cited, as well as from passages in Epiphanius and Tertullian, which are to be cited below, and from a work of Plutarch (*Comment. In Principe Requiri Doctrinam,* near the beginning [*Ad Principem Ineruditum,* 3, p. 780]).

Moreover, its truth may be demonstrated as follows: the natural law may be considered as existing either in God or in man; and as existing in God, it implies, to be sure, according to the order of thought, an exercise of judgment on the part of God Himself, with respect to the fitness or unfitness of the actions concerned, and annexes [to that judgment] the will to bind men to observe the dictates of right reason. This entire matter has already been sufficiently explained. Moreover, it may have been this doctrine that Augustine intended to suggest in the passage (*Against Faustus,* Bk. XXII, chap. xxvii) wherein he said: 'The eternal law is the divine reason and will commanding the preservation of the natural order, and forbidding its disturbance.'[17] For the particle *vel* is frequently understood in the sense of a connective, especially when the words between which it is placed are so related to each other that they are not to be separated [in meaning]; and this is true of the terms 'divine reason' and 'divine will', with respect to the eternal law; so that Augustine has included both.

Consequently, we may not approve the assertion of the Doctors cited in a later passage,[18] namely, the assertion that [the action of] the divine will,

---

17. [Not an exact quotation.—TR.]
18. [I.e., at the end of Section 18, *infra,* pp. 225–26.—REVISER.]

whereby the natural law is sanctioned, does not presuppose the existence of a dictate of the divine reason declaring that a given act is righteous, or that it is evil; nor the further assertion that the will of God does not presuppose in the object, the existence of an intrinsic harmony or an intrinsic discord with the rational nature, by reason of which it wills that one thing be done and another avoided. For it is evident from our discussion of the second conclusion that such suppositions are false and opposed to the essence of the natural law.

Therefore, although the obligation imposed by the natural law is derived from the divine will, in so far as it is properly a preceptive obligation, nevertheless [such action on the part of] that will presupposes a judgment as to the evil of falsehood, for example, or similar judgments. However, in view of the fact that no real prohibition or preceptive obligation is created solely by virtue of such a judgment, since such an effect cannot be conceived of apart from volition, it is consequently evident that there exists, in addition, the will to prohibit the act in question, for the reason that it is evil.

Wherefore one concludes, finally, that the natural law, as it exists in man, does not merely indicate what is evil, but actually obliges us to avoid the same; and that it consequently does not merely point out the natural disharmony of a particular act or object, with rational nature, but is also a manifestation of the divine will prohibiting that act or object.

14.[19] *A satisfactory answer is given to the argument at the root of the two contrary opinions.* It remains for us to reply to the argument at the root of the two [contrary] opinions. For the whole matter turns upon the following hypothesis: 'Even if God does not issue the prohibition or commands which are part of the natural law, it will still be wicked to lie, and to honour one's parents will still be a good and dutiful act.'

Two points must be considered, in connexion with this hypothesis: one is the question of what conclusion is to be drawn from it, once it has been posited; the other is the question of whether the hypothesis is admissible.

The reply of Medina to this fundamental opposing argument. To the latter of these queries Bartholomew Medina (on I.–II, qu. 18, art. 1) makes the reply that the hypothesis is inadmissible, because if it is assumed to be

19. [The Latin text incorrectly has '4'.—Tr.]

true, a contradiction is implied, as follows: lying, for example, is not a sin, because it is not forbidden by any law; and it is a sin, because it is contrary to reason and essentially incongruous with rational nature.

But, in opposition to this reply, one may urge that in the order of thought, such an act is evil, prior to the existence of any prohibition against it, by any law, in the strict sense of the term; that, therefore, even though one accepts the hypothesis in question, and so assumes that the action is not forbidden by God, it still does not follow that such an action is not evil, since by its very nature it does possess this quality, apart from any prohibition; and [finally] that for these reasons the self-contradictory conclusion mentioned above does not follow.

15.[20] To this in turn one may reply that, although the negative proposition in the said conclusion does not follow on intrinsic grounds (as they say), or *a priori*, it does follow *a posteriori* and by extrinsic principles; for if the actions in question were not forbidden by God, then they would not be displeasing to Him, and consequently they would not be evil; yet, from another point of view, they are assumed to be evil; and thus the self-contradictory conclusion would indeed follow [upon the hypothesis which we are discussing]. Similarly, we may argue that, [according to this hypothesis,] if God willed that I should hate Him, then surely hatred of God would not be evil; yet, if my emotion *is* one of hatred, it is necessarily evil; and, therefore, that same contradictory conclusion would follow. Again, if God willed that fire should be cold by nature, that condition would surely result; but, since such a condition would be self-contradictory, it is impossible that God should will its existence. According to the reply [of Medina], then, one assumes that there is an inconsistency involved in the supposition that an act may in itself be evil and yet not be forbidden by God.

The reply of Medina is excluded. However, I do not see that his opinion can properly be supported by drawing [, from the hypothesis in question,] this inconsistent conclusion that a given action would [consequently] be evil and not evil at one and the same time. For, in arguing thus, one is guilty of a *petitio principii*[21] and of reasoning in a vicious circle. Hence,

---

20. [The Latin text incorrectly has '5'.—Tr.]
21. [That is, assuming in a proof that which has to be proved.—Reviser.]

another mode of proof must be adopted. *A more fitting reply.* Accordingly, as a result of that hypothesis, whether it be admissible or inadmissible, the sole inference is that a certain evil quality residing in a human act, or in the failure to perform that act, does not formally consist in a lack of conformity with a true precept or law, whether prohibitive or preceptive. Wherefore, if this hypothesis is posited, there follows, properly enough, the conclusion that such and such an action is evil, and not forbidden; but it cannot therefore be inferred that the two conditions are in reality separable, which is the only point pertinent to the matter under discussion.

16.[22] Nevertheless, one may urge that the foregoing remarks lead to the conclusion that, if we assume the truth of the hypothesis that an act may be evil independently of the existence of any prohibitory law, or prescinding from and putting aside the law, then it will follow also that this act is morally evil, since it is assumed to be a free act; but the evil quality of a free act, because of disaccord with rational nature as such, is itself a moral evil; so that, consequently, the act in question is morally wrong, and not by reason of any prohibitory law; hence, it is also a sin, apart from all question of disaccord with a prohibitive law. Thus the entire foundation of the opinion which we have been discussing, falls to the ground.

To this argument, however, some writers, as B. Medina notes in the passage cited above, reply by distinguishing between an evil act and a sin, on the ground that the former term is more comprehensive and does not necessarily imply opposition to any law, which is not true with respect to a sin. Wherefore, these authors admit that in the case supposed the act in question would be evil; but they deny that it would be a sin. However, this is a difficult distinction; and it appears to be somewhat discordant with the doctrine of St. Thomas, for according to that doctrine, sin is nothing other than an action that is evil because it deviates from its proper end, that is, evil because, when it is or ought to be performed in view of some particular end, it does not work duly to that end, that is to say, it deviates therefrom. Consequently, if such an action is in the moral order and is human, the very fact that it is an evil act because of its deviation from right reason makes it a sin, as St. Thomas (I.–II, qu. 21, art. 1) declares; for that

22. [The Latin text incorrectly has '6'.—Tr.]

action deviates from the proper end toward which it should be directed, is therefore evil, and is consequently a sin.

Accordingly, other authorities reply that the action in question is indeed a sin, but that it does not involve guilt, if it is not contrary to law. But this statement, also, would seem to be opposed to the opinion of St. Thomas, as expressed in the same question (art. 2), in the course of which he says that in the case of free actions, sin and guilt are interchangeable terms and differ merely relatively, and as a matter of terminology. For a given act is termed a sin with reference to the fact that it deviates from its end; whereas it is called guilt with reference to the agent to whom it is imputed. But a free act, by virtue of the very fact that it is free, is imputed to an agent; hence, if it is both free and evil, it is in consequence a sin and involves guilt; and, therefore, even in the case supposed, and apart from the law of God, such an act would involve guilt. And thus, all the arguments set forth above [as a solution to the difficulty] in question, are bereft of force.

17.[23] *The true reply to the difficulty.* Therefore, my own reply [with regard to that difficulty] is that in any human act there dwells some goodness or evil, in view of its object, considered separately in so far as that object is in harmony or disharmony with right reason; and that, in its relation to right reason, such an act may be termed an evil, and a sin, and a source of guilt, in view of the considerations above mentioned, and apart from its relation to law, strictly speaking. In addition to this [objective goodness or wickedness], human actions possess a special good or wicked character in their relation to God, in cases which furthermore involve a divine law, whether prohibitory or preceptive; and in accordance with such laws, these acts may in a special sense be said to be sins or to involve guilt in the sight of God, by reason of the fact that they transgress a true law of God Himself. It was to this special form of wickedness that Paul [*Romans,* Chap. iv, v. 15] apparently referred in the term 'transgression', when he said: 'For where there is no law, neither is there transgression.'

A human action, then, opposed to rational nature, will not be characterized by this latter type of depravity, if one grants the supposition that God does not [positively] forbid this particular action; for, under such

23. [The Latin text incorrectly has '7'.—Tr.]

circumstances, it does not involve that virtual contempt of God which is involved in the violation of a law with respect to the legislator, as Basil declares (on *Psalms,* xxviii) in commenting upon the text: 'Bring to the Lord glory and honour.' The words of Paul (*Romans,* Chap. ii [, v. 23]) are in accord with this belief, when he says: 'By transgression of the law, thou dishonourest God.' Wherefore, Augustine has said (*On True Religion,* Chap. xxvi): 'A prohibitory law redoubles [the guilt incurred through] all sins committed.' And in connexion with this statement, he adds: 'For it is not a simple sin to be guilty, not merely of that which is evil, but also of that which is forbidden.'

18.[24] It is in this sense that St. Thomas (I.–II, qu. 71, art. 6, ad 5), too, seems to distinguish between a sin as contrary to reason and a sin as an offence against God, holding that in the former aspect it is treated by the moral philosophers, and in the latter aspect by the theologians. In the first case, then, the evil act would be a sin and would involve guilt in the moral order, but not in a theological sense, that is to say, not in relation to God. A similar interpretation should be given, so it seems, to the words of St. Thomas when, in the passage above cited, he answers the fourth objection, saying that the sins in question, in relation to the eternal law, are evil because forbidden; evil, surely, with that theological wickedness (so to speak) which such an act would not possess, unless it had been forbidden. Thus it is, apparently, that we must understand the argument which he appends, and which otherwise would be obscure. For, after saying that every sin is evil because forbidden relatively to the eternal law, St. Thomas adds [*ibid.,* ad 4]: 'For by the very fact that [such an act] is inordinate, it is repugnant to the natural law.' This argument seems to prove that the sin is prohibited because evil, rather than the converse proposition. That is true, in speaking of the evil of irregularity in the moral order; and nevertheless, by reason of such irregularity, the eternal law is imposed, together with a divine prohibition in relation to which such a sin has a particular repugnance; and consequently that sin is also characterized by a special depravity which it would not possess if the divine prohibition had not intervened, and it is in view of this depravity that the character

24. [The Latin text incorrectly has '8'.—Tr.]

of sin considered theologically becomes complete, as well as that of absolute culpability in the sight of God. Victoria and some other theologians
have apparently spoken to the same effect. And accordingly, the replies
[of opponents] set forth above are without force save that which consists
solely in words.

19.[25] Therefore, from the hypothesis in question, if it is thus explained
and its truth conceded, there can be drawn no conclusion opposed to
our opinion, nor to the arguments by which we have proved that opinion. For, admitting the soundness of such a supposition, in the sense
explained, nevertheless the natural law, thus viewed, truly and properly
forbids anything in human actions which is in itself evil or inordinate;
and if no such prohibition existed, that action would not possess the
consummate and perfect character (so to speak) of guilt and of an offence
against God, which undeniably exists in actions that are contrary to the
natural law as such.

[20.] *Whether God can have abstained from prohibiting by His own law
those things which are opposed to natural reason.* Moreover, in order that
it may be entirely clear wherein this divine prohibition can intrinsically
and essentially be a characteristic of the natural law, we should turn to
the exposition of a second point, namely whether the hypothesis under
discussion is admissible, i.e., whether it is admissible that God by an act of
His own will has abstained from imposing, in addition, His own law that
prescribes or forbids those things which in any case fall under the dictates
of natural reason.

Two possible ways of speaking may be considered in connexion with
this hypothesis.

The first and affirmative opinion. In the first place, we may say, indeed, if
we have in mind the absolute power of God, that He can abstain from laying down such a prohibition, since no implied contradiction is evident in
this statement, as would seem to be proved by the arguments accumulated
by William of Occam, Gerson, and others in defence of their opinion.
Nevertheless, such cannot possibly be the case, if we have in mind the
ordinary law of divine providence, that is, the law which is in harmony

25. [The Latin text incorrectly has '9'.—Tr.]

with the nature of things; for this assertion at least is proved by the arguments opposed [to the assumption in question] and adduced in favour of our own opinion; and it is also strongly supported by Scripture and by the Fathers. Indeed, that same assertion would seem to provide an argument sufficiently strong, in favour of asserting that the natural law includes a true command of God, because the natural law is that law which harmonizes with the nature of things.

21.[26] *A second opinion, denying that the hypothesis is admissible.* Another way of arguing may be as follows: the hypothesis is absolutely inadmissible, because God cannot fail to prohibit that which is intrinsically evil and inordinate in rational nature; neither can He fail to prescribe the contrary. Such is clearly the opinion of St. Thomas (I.–II, qu. 72, art. 6, and more clearly *ibid.,* qu. 100, art. 8, ad 2), inasmuch as he says that the decree of divine justice with regard to this [natural] law is immutable, a statement which cannot be taken as referring to an immutability existing solely on the assumption of a [divine] decree; for in that sense every decree of God in connexion with any positive law whatsoever, is immutable. Therefore, St. Thomas must be speaking of immutability in an absolute sense. Hence, he holds that God cannot abandon the order of His justice in this matter, just as He cannot deny Himself or be unfaithful to His promises. The same opinion is clearly supported by B. Medina [on I.–II, qu. 18, art. 1]; and, more fully, in the aforecited Relectio XIII: *De Pervenientibus ad usum rationis,*[27] nos. 9 and 10, part ii, by Victoria, in the passage where the latter holds that it is neither probable nor intelligible that any one could sin and not be under some superior and some precept, or law, of that superior. Accordingly, just as it is impossible that a man possessing the use of reason should be unable to sin, or that he should be under no superior, even so, [Victoria] believes it is equally impossible that God should be able to abstain from prohibiting those things which are evil in themselves, or from prescribing those which are necessary to natural rectitude. Finally, the reasoning whereby we have proved that God is in fact the Author of this law [of nature], proves also that such a law is necessary, in an absolute sense,

26. [The Latin text incorrectly has 'II'.—Tr.]
27. [See note 6 *supra,* p. 211.—Tr.]

inasmuch as God cannot fail to be displeased with actions of the sort in question, as befits His goodness, justice, and providence.

22.[28] *Objection.* However, in order that the above argument may be elucidated, the following objection is raised: a divine command is an act of the will or at least presupposes the existence of volition and derives its origin therefrom; and the divine will is free in all of its external actions; hence, it is free even with respect to the act of volition in question; consequently, it is able to refrain from performing that act; and, therefore, it is able to refrain from imposing the precept under discussion.

The solution offered by some. To this objection, some persons reply that it suffices for the existence of the natural law, that there should be a natural dictate of the divine intellect whereby it judges that these evil actions should be avoided, and the good actions performed. For, in regard to those things which of themselves and intrinsically possess such qualities, that dictate is not a free act, but a necessary one; from the said dictate of divine and eternal law, in this matter, there necessarily issues a certain participation therein by the rational creature, assuming that he has indeed been created; and from this participation and derivation, without any further act of the divine will, there flows forth to the rational creature, as a natural consequence (so to speak), a special obligation, because of which he is bound to follow right reason as an indicator of the eternal rule that dwells in God. Accordingly, whatever may be true of the free actions of the divine will, this obligation and these prohibitions are necessary effects of the divine reason.

This reply is rejected. However, this reply is unintelligible, since the mere dictate of intelligence apart from will, cannot have the nature of a precept with respect to another being, nor can it impose upon that being, a particular obligation. For an obligation is a certain moral impulse to action; and to impel another to act is a work of the will. Moreover, the entire obligation in question does not transcend the force of the object, which is in itself good or evil, and from which the action involved derives its own essential goodness or evil; and the judgment of the reason[29] merely has

---

28. [The Latin text incorrectly has '12'.—Tr.]

29. [I.e., the judgment of the reason by which the obligation was assumed to be created.—Tr.]

the office of applying and pointing out this object.[30] Finally, the natural reason, by pointing out good and evil, has no more extensive nor stronger binding force because it is a participation of the divine reason, than it would possess in itself and viewed as being non-derivative.

23.[31] *The true reply to the objection: it is shown how, in spite of the existence of divine freedom, God cannot fail to prohibit, by some law, those things which are intrinsically evil.* Therefore, I hold with Cajetan (on I.–II, qu. 100, art. 8), that although the divine will is absolutely free in its external actions, nevertheless, if it be assumed that this will elicits one free act, then, it may be necessarily bound, in consequence, to the performance of another action. For example, if through the divine will an unconditional promise is made, that will is obliged to fulfil the promise; and if it be the divine will to speak, or to make a revelation, that will must of necessity reveal what is true. In like manner, if it is the divine will to create the world, and to preserve the same in such a way as to fulfil a certain end, then there cannot fail to exist a providential care over that world; and assuming the existence of the will to exercise such providential care, there cannot but be a perfect providence, in harmony with the goodness and wisdom of the divine will. Accordingly, assuming the existence of the will to create rational nature [in such fashion that it shall be endowed] with sufficient knowledge for the doing of good and evil, and with sufficient divine co-operation for the performance of both,[32] God could not have refrained from willing to forbid that a creature so endowed should commit acts intrinsically evil, nor could He have willed not to prescribe [, for performance by that creature,] the necessary righteous acts. For just as God cannot lie, neither can He govern unwisely or unjustly; and it would be a form of providence in the highest degree foreign to the divine wisdom and goodness, to refrain from forbidding or prescribing to those who were subject to that providence, such things as are [, respectively,] intrinsically evil, or necessary and righteous.

30. [I.e., it has not the office of endowing such objects with an essentially good or evil character.—Tr.]

31. [The Latin text incorrectly has '13'.—Tr.]

32. [The thought of Suárez should not be misunderstood. He does not mean that God co-operates in evil as such, but that He co-operates in the physical act of the sinner.—Reviser.]

Therefore, in the [alleged] argument, we must make a distinction as to the minor premiss. For, absolutely speaking, God could have refrained from laying down any command or prohibition; yet, assuming that He has willed to have subjects endowed with the use of reason, He could not have failed to be their lawgiver—in those matters, at least, which are necessary to natural moral rectitude. In like manner, the arguments suggested above are sufficiently cogent, since God cannot fail to hate that evil which is opposed to right reason, and since, moreover, He entertains this hatred, not merely as a private individual, but also as Supreme Governor; therefore, because of this hatred, He wills to bind His subjects lest they commit such evil.

24.[33] *Another objection. The solution of this objection, in the course of which it is shown what declaration of divine natural law God is obliged to give, in order that men may be bound by that law.* Secondly, however, the objection is raised, that the will of the lawgiver does not suffice for the completeness of law, unless a publication, or declaration, of that will also takes place; and there is no reason which makes it obligatory that God should declare His will; hence, it is possible that He may refrain from making such a declaration, since He is free to refrain; and, therefore, it is possible that He may not establish the law in question, nor create any binding obligation through it, inasmuch as no obligation exists, independently of the declaration.

To this second objection I shall reply, in the first place, that if that volition on the part of God is essential to a fitting and prudent providence and government over mankind, it is in consequence necessary that, by virtue of this same providence, that divine volition shall be capable of being made known to men; and this process is sufficient for the nature of a precept and of law, nor is any other form of declaration necessary. Wherefore, it may further be stated that this very faculty of judgment which is contained in right reason and bestowed by nature upon men, is of itself a sufficient sign of such divine volition, no other notification being necessary. The proof of the foregoing is as follows: the faculty of judgment contained in reason, of itself indicates the existence of a divine providence befitting God, and morally necessary for His complete dominion and for the due subjection

---

33. [The Latin text incorrectly has '14'.—Tr.]

of mankind to Him, within which providence the legislation in question is comprehended. Moreover, for this same cause, it is revealed by the light of natural understanding, that God is offended by sins committed in contravention of the natural law, and that the judgment[34] and the punishment of those sins pertain to Him. Hence, this natural light is of itself a sufficient promulgation of the natural law, not only because it makes clearly manifest the intrinsic conformity or non-conformity of actions [with respect to that law,] a conformity and non-conformity which are indicated by the increate light of God; but also because it makes known to man the fact that actions contrary [to the law so revealed] are displeasing to the Author of nature, as Supreme Lord, Guardian and Governor of that same nature. This, then, suffices for the promulgation of the law under discussion, as St. Thomas has held (I.–II, qu. 90, art. 4, ad 1). On this account, moreover, the natural law is called the law of the mind, as has been noted by Epiphanius ([*Panarium Adversus LXXX*] *Haereses,* Bk. LXIV, in words quoted from Methodius, at end of that section [*Haeres.* liv, no. lxi]), and as Tertullian suggests (*Contra* [*Adversus*] *Judaeos,* Chap. ii).

However, certain difficulties and certain rather obscure questions still remain in connexion with this matter. One question is this: does a transgression of the natural law, as we have explained such a transgression, involve any special kind of evil, distinct from that which the act would involve (according to the hypothesis discussed above) solely by reason of its non-conformity with rational nature as such? Furthermore, if that evil is of a special kind, what is its quality, and to what extent is its existence due to the force of the natural law? Again, one may ask whether it is possible to be invincibly ignorant of this special aspect of the natural law; and whether, assuming the existence of such ignorance, the commission of an act contrary to reason would be an offence against God; and whether it would involve infinite wickedness, that is to say, whether it would be a mortal sin. But these questions pertain rather to the subject-matter of sins,[35] and, accordingly, I shall pass over them for the present, so that we

34. [The text has *indicium,* evidently a misprint for *iudicium.*—Tr.]
35. [Suárez has reference here to his Disp. xv, *De Peccatis* of Tract. *De Fide,* not included in these *Selections.*—Tr.]

may not digress too widely from our [immediate] purpose. Meanwhile, Victoria (aforesaid Relectio, *De Pervenientibus ad Usum Rationis*), Gerson (*De Vita Spirituali,* said Lectio II, a little before the First Corollary) and other authors already cited may be consulted.

CHAPTER VII

What Is the Subject-Matter Dealt with by Natural Law; or, What Are the Precepts of That Law?

1. We assume from the foregoing discussion that the subject-matter of natural law consists in the good which is essentially righteous, or necessary to righteousness, and the evil which is opposed to that good; in the one, as something to be prescribed, in the other, as something to be forbidden.

The proof of this assumption is as follows: since the law in question is true law and God is its Author, it cannot be other than righteous; and, therefore, it cannot prescribe anything save that which is righteous, neither can it prohibit anything which is not opposed to righteousness. Moreover, this law prescribes that which is in harmony with rational nature as such, and prohibits the contrary; and it is evident that the former[1] is not otherwise than righteous.

The difference between the natural and other laws. Indeed, the natural law differs from other laws in this very respect, namely, that the latter render evil what they prohibit, while they render necessary, or righteous, what they prescribe; whereas the natural law assumes the existence in a given act or object, of the rectitude which it prescribes, or the depravity which it prohibits. Accordingly, it is usual to say that this law forbids a thing because that thing is evil, or prescribes a thing because it is good. We have already touched on this point, in the preceding Chapter.

2. *Whether or not everything that is righteous and every opposing evil fall within the range of the natural law.* The difficulty then turns upon the question of whether or not every moral good, and every contrary evil fall within the range of the natural law.

---

1. [I.e. that which is in harmony with rational nature, as such.—Tr.]

The opinion of those who assert that only commonly applicable, general principles fall within the range of the natural law. For certain authorities have declared that the subject-matter of this law includes only general and self-evident principles concerned with goodness or evil in the moral sense, such principles as: 'one must do good, and shun evil'; 'do not to another that which you would not wish done to yourself', and that it does not include the conclusions drawn from these principles, as for example: 'a deposit must be returned'; 'usury must be shunned.' St. Thomas (I.–II, qu. 94, art. 2), is frequently cited in defence of this opinion, as is also Durandus (Tract. *De Legibus*). I have not been able to secure the work of the latter, but Torquemada (on *Decretum,* Pt. I, dist. 1, can. vii, no. 3) refers to him. Other jurists, too, support the same view to such a degree that, in their opinion, [even] the Commandments of the Decalogue embody principles, not of the natural law, but of the *ius gentium,* which these authorities regard as possessing a different character. Soto (*De Iustitia,* Bk. I, qu. v, art. 4) apparently inclines to this same opinion, as I shall point out more fully in the following Chapter. Moreover, the authors cited appear to base their stand upon a manner of speaking employed by the Roman jurisconsults, who do not attribute to the natural law those actions which are dictated by reason and solely through a process of rational reflection, as may be gathered from various passages of the *Digest* (I. i. 1, 2, 3 and 9, and others, also XVI. iii. 31).

3. The basis of the opinion above set forth may, in the first place, be the fact that the natural law is one to which nature itself gives an immediate inclination; and only first principles are of this kind, since those which are arrived at through reasoning have rather their origin in man himself. Hence, even with respect to habits[2] themselves, a distinction must be drawn between a habit of applying principles and one of applying conclusions. In the second place, the law which deals with first principles is absolutely immutable, both in its essence, and also from the standpoint of mankind, since ignorance of it is impossible; but that law which is

---

2. *Habitus* or dispositions that enable one more easily and readily to perform the actions or mental operations to which they dispose one. Virtues and vices are *habitus,* disposing one to virtuous or vicious action.

concerned with conclusions, is mutable, and ignorance thereof is possible. Thirdly, if the opinion in question were not correct, even the virtuous acts prescribed by men would pertain to the natural law, since they are drawn from that law by a process of reasoning. Fourthly, if the said opinion were incorrect, the *ius gentium* would not be distinguishable from the natural law; but would on the contrary be a part or a subdivision of the latter.

4. *The question is answered; and it is shown that the natural law embraces all moral precepts which are plainly characterized by the righteousness neces-sary to virtuous conduct.* Nevertheless, we must assert that the natural law embraces all precepts or moral principles which are plainly characterized by the goodness necessary to rectitude of conduct, just as the opposite precepts clearly involve moral irregularity or wickedness.

This is the opinion of St. Thomas (I.–II, qu. 91, art. 2; qu. 94, arts. 2 and 4 [art. 3]; qu. 95, art. 2; qu. 100, arts. 1, 2, and 3), as set forth in several passages, in connexion with which Cajetan, Conrad Koellin and other commentators express a like view; as does Soto, also (*De Iustitia,* Bk. I, qu. iv, art. 2; qu. v, arts. 1 and 2; Bk. III, qu. i, arts. 2 and 3). One gath-ers that the theologians cited in the preceding Chapter are of the same mind. And this is also true of Torquemada (on *Decretum,* Pt. I, dist. 1, can. vi, in many articles, especially the first and last) and Covarruvias (on *Sext,* rule *peccatum,* Pt. II, § 11, no. 4); as it is of Aristotle (*Nicomachean Ethics,* Bk. V, chap. vii), in the passage where he divides all law into two kinds, natural and legal, including under the former head all that which involves necessary and immutable truth. Cicero expresses this same view, in his work (*On Invention,* Bk. II [, chap. xxii]), defining the natural law as, 'That which is imparted to us, not by mere opinion, but by a certain innate force, as is the case with religion, piety,' &c. Isidore (*Etymologies,* Bk. V, chap. iii [chap. iv]), too, is of a similar mind, when he expounds the natural law by means of still other illustrations. Augustine (*On Free Will,* Bk. I, chap. iii) expresses himself in like manner, in that he classifies adultery as being contrary to natural law,[3] for the same principle would apply to every offence of a similar sort. Finally, the conclusion in question may be deduced from the *Psalms* (iv [, vv. 6–7]): 'Who sheweth us good

---

3. [This is a rather loose paraphrase of Augustine's reasoning.—TR.]

things? The light of thy countenance, O Lord, is signed upon us.' For we rightly conclude from this passage that all those things which natural enlightenment makes evident, pertain to the natural law. This conclusion may be confirmed from the words of Paul, in his *Epistle to the Romans,* Chap. ii [, v. 14]: 'The Gentiles who have not the law do by nature those things that are of the law'; whence he infers that the Gentiles are a law to themselves; yet those things which are clearly recognized by means of natural enlightenment, whether they be recognized with or without reflection, are rightly said to be produced by nature; therefore, . . .

5. *The assertion in question is confirmed by reasoning.* The assertion in question[4] may also be demonstrated by reasoning. For those things which are recognized by means of natural reason, may be divided into three classes. First, some of them are primary and general principles of morality, such principles as: 'one must do good, and shun evil', 'do not to another that which you would not wish done to yourself', and the like. There is no doubt but that these principles pertain to the natural law. Again, there are certain others, more definite and specific, which, nevertheless, are also self-evident truths by their very terminology. Examples [of the second group] are these principles: 'justice must be observed'; 'God must be worshipped'; 'one must live temperately'; and so forth. Neither is there any doubt concerning [the fact that] this group [comes under the natural law], a point which will become evident, *a fortiori,* as a result of the discussion that is to follow. In the third class, we place those conclusions which are deduced from natural principles by an evident inference, and which cannot become known save through rational reflection. Of these conclusions, some are recognized more easily than others, and by a greater number of persons; as, for example, the inferences that adultery, theft, and similar acts are wrong. Other conclusions require more reflection, of a sort not easily within the capacity of all, as is the case with the inferences that fornication is intrinsically evil, that usury is unjust, that lying can never be justified, and the like.

The assertion set forth above may, then, be understood as applicable to all these [principles and conclusions]; for all of them pertain to the natural

4. [*Vide* the first sentence of Section 4 of this Chapter; *supra,* p. 234.—Tr.]

law. And if this truth is established with regard even to the conclusions of any one of these classes, then, the same truth will, *a fortiori,* be established with regard to the other conclusions mentioned, provided only that a degree of evidence involving certainty is reached.

6. Therefore, the proof follows; first, by a process of induction. For the precepts of the Decalogue are precepts of natural law, a fact accepted by all. Yet they do not all embody self-evident principles. On the contrary, some of them require reflection, as is also evident. This point is still more clear with regard to many natural precepts which are included within those of the Decalogue; as, for example, the prohibitions against simple fornication, against usury and against vengeance inflicted upon an enemy by one's own authority, all of which according to Catholic doctrine, indubitably pertain to natural law. In like manner, the affirmative commands to keep vows and promises, to give alms out of one's superfluous possessions, to honour one's parents, are natural precepts, not only according to the faith, but also according to the philosophers and all right-thinking persons. Yet the conclusions [leading to these precepts] are not reached without reflection and, in some cases, a great deal of elaborate reasoning.

Secondly, we may advance the argument that all the [acts] dealt with by these principles and conclusions,[5] are prescribed because they are righteous, or forbidden because they are evil, while the converse [i.e., that they are righteous because prescribed, or evil because forbidden] is not true; therefore, the said [acts] do not fall under positive law; and, consequently, they do come under natural law. For, as I have noted above, there is no branch of law outside [of these two]. The truth of the first consequent is evident from the fact that a positive law is properly one which involves additional obligation, beyond what is demanded by the intrinsic character of the subject-matter; for, as Aristotle has said [*Nicomachean Ethics,* Bk. V, chap. vii], positive law concerns those things which were of no import, before the enactment of the law. The truth of the antecedent is also clear. For the truth of a principle cannot stand, apart from the truth of the conclusion that is necessarily drawn [therefrom]; accordingly,

---

5. [A rather free rendering of *illis membris* (those members [of the threefold classification]).—TR.]

if a conclusion relating to righteousness necessarily follows, from natural principles, then, even apart from any external law, that conclusion is righteous *per se* and by its intrinsic force; and therefore, when a law is [justly] applied [to such matter], it is applied because its object is necessarily righteous; the converse is also true, in the case of prohibitions and that which is [necessarily] evil.

7. Thirdly, no one is doubtful as to the primary and general principles; hence, neither can there be doubt as to the specific principles, since these, also, in themselves and by virtue of their very terminology, harmonize with rational nature as such; and, therefore, there should be no doubt with respect to the conclusions clearly derived from these principles, inasmuch as the truth of the principle is contained in the conclusion, and he who prescribes or forbids the one, necessarily prescribes or forbids that which is bound up in it, or without which it could not exist. Indeed, strictly speaking, the natural law works more through these proximate principles or conclusions than through universal principles; for a law is a proximate rule of operation, and the general principles mentioned above are not rules save in so far as they are definitely applied by specific rules to the individual sorts of acts or virtues.

Finally, all these precepts proceed, by a certain necessity, from nature, and from God as the Author of nature, and all tend to the same end, which is undoubtedly the due preservation and natural perfection or felicity of human nature; therefore, they all pertain to the natural law.

8. Gratian (*Decretum,* Pt. I, dist. 1, at beginning), indeed, adds that the natural law is that which is contained in the law and the Gospel. If this is true, not only the precepts which we have mentioned, but also the precepts which God transmitted through Moses, or which Christ laid down in the New Law, will come under the natural law; for these precepts are embodied in the Gospel and the [Old] Law. The Gloss, tacitly replying to this remark of Gratian, contains in connexion with that passage a comment that the natural law is therein called by Gratian the divine law, a comment which indicates that [the natural law, as interpreted by Gratian] includes not only the natural divine law, but the positive divine law as well. This view is adopted by several of the jurists, also. Moreover, St. Thomas says (on the *Sentences,* Bk. IV, dist. xxxiii, qu. 1, art. 1, ad 4)

that 'The term "natural" is sometimes applied, not only to that which is derived from an intrinsic principle, but also to that which is infused and impressed by a Superior Agent, namely, God; and it is so interpreted by Isidore, when he says that what is contained in the Law and the Gospel is natural law.' For the words in question, although they are taken not from Isidore, but from Gratian [*Decretum,* Pt. I, dist. 1], are apparently based upon a passage of Isidore (*Etymologies,* Bk. V, chap. ii), which Gratian cites just below in Chapter One of the same distinction of the *Decretum,* and which reads: 'All laws are either divine or human; divine laws are founded upon nature, human laws upon custom.'

Nevertheless, the interpretation in question is apparently not the one supported by the Fathers cited above. For, in the first place, they explain with sufficient clarity the kind of natural law to which they have reference, namely, that which is common to all nations and which has been established by natural instinct, not by any decree; a distinction by means of which they differentiate it from the civil law. Wherefore, these same authorities are clearly speaking of the law (*ius*), or rather, of the legal rules (*legibus*), whereby men have from the beginning been governed, whether by virtue of the strictly natural establishment of these rules, or else by their establishment on the basis of natural [principles]. The said authorities, then, do not include [under the natural law] supernatural or positive divine law. Neither is it probable that they include, under the term, 'natural law', all the ceremonies of the Old Law, or the ordinances relating to the Sacraments.

9. *The words of Gratian are explained.* Accordingly, I maintain that Gratian does not say that the natural law includes all those things which are contained in the Law and the Gospel; neither does he so describe or define the natural law. He merely asserts that it is comprehended within the [Old] Law, at least in so far as relates to its moral precepts and the precepts of the two Tables; and also within the Gospel, both in so far as the Gospel (*Matthew,* Chap. v) expressly confirms and expounds the precepts of the Decalogue, and in so far as the whole of the natural law is virtually contained in that principle which is laid down in the first of the Gospels (*Matthew,* Chap. vii [, v. 12]): 'Whatsoever you would that men should do to you, do you also to them.' This last text especially, seems to have

been in Gratian's mind; so that his words should be assembled as follows [*Decretum,* Pt. I, dist. 1]: The natural law is the rule whereby each of us is commanded to do to another, what he would wish done to himself, a rule which is contained in the Law and the Gospel.[6] Hence, Christ, according to the Gospel, has said: ['All things therefore whatsoever you would that men should do to you, do you also to them. For this is the law and the prophets.']

The explanation given by St. Thomas (I.–II, qu. 94, art. 4, ad 1) is very similar; as is also that of Torquemada (on *Decretum,* Pt. I, dist. 1, art. 3, ad 4), although he does not speak consistently, for he favours now one interpretation, now another, and first rejects the opinion expressed in the Gloss, later approving the interpretation of St. Thomas, in Article 4, an interpretation which, subsequently, he has undoubtedly repudiated.

However, it remains to be explained at this point, whether all the conclusions which are clearly drawn from the principles of the natural law are, in an absolute sense, an integral portion thereof; and what, or how necessary,—that is to say, how evident,—a connexion between the two must exist in order to bring about their inclusion therein. This point, indeed, will in part be more easily disposed of, [than if we were to discuss it here independently,] when we reply to the foregoing arguments, and in part when we demonstrate in subsequent chapters the immutability of the natural law.

10. In regard to the bases of the contrary opinion, I deny, in the first place, that St. Thomas was of this opinion. The fact that he did not take such a view, has been made sufficiently clear by the foregoing discussion. Nor was Soto's opinion different [from that of St. Thomas], as Soto himself has quite fully explained (*De Justitia,* Bk. III, qu. i, art. 3). As to that held by the jurists, this is a point which I shall discuss in the following Chapter.

Moreover, my reply to the first argument[7] [in defence of the contrary opinion] is as follows: whatever is the result of a necessary dictate of the

6. [This sentence is a paraphrase of, rather than a quotation from Gratian. Likewise from Gratian is the succeeding sentence, including the bracketed verse 12 from *St. Matthew* Chap. viii, for which Suárez wrote simply 'etc.'—Tr.]

7. [*Vide* Section 3 of this Chapter; *supra,* p. 233.—Tr.]

natural reason, is, as a matter of necessity, consequent upon nature, and is derived from a natural inclination, whether the said dictate be formulated directly, or indirectly through reflection. For not only the inclination which is a direct product [of the natural reason], but also that which is indirectly consequent thereon, flows from nature; and not only the internal principle of the impulse, but also the impulse itself, and the end that it seeks, are natural. Furthermore, the moral question, that is, the obligation, is little affected by the fact that reflection is or is not involved, provided that the obligation itself has an intrinsic connexion with the object [of the impulse], and with nature as well.

As to the second argument,[8] I shall demonstrate below that the natural law is not, strictly speaking, mutable, although certain precepts of that law may involve subject-matter that is more or less mutable, a fact which does not alter the formal character of the law.

11. *Whether all virtuous actions come under the natural law.* In connexion with the third argument,[9] a special difficulty is raised, namely, the question of whether or not all virtuous actions fall under the natural law. This question is discussed in two passages by St. Thomas (*ibid.,* qu. 94, art. 3 and qu. 100, art. 2), who answers it affirmatively, explaining, however, that under natural law, he includes not only precepts, but counsels [of perfection] as well. Our inquiry, on the other hand, properly concerns the precepts [alone]. Therefore, it would be easy for us to dispose of the difficulty in question by the same method as that which we applied to our discussion of the eternal law: namely, by stating that all virtuous acts, in so far as relates to the specifications—that is, the manner—according to which they should be carried out, fall under the natural law; although they are not all prescribed [by that law] in an absolute sense, that is, in so far as actual performance is concerned.

However, St. Thomas, in the former of the two passages cited above, also propounds a different answer, involving the distinction that the term 'virtuous acts' may be considered to have a twofold sense, one of which has reference to the principle of virtue residing within those acts—reference,

---

8. [*Vide* Section 3 of this Chapter; *supra,* p. 233.—Tr.]
9. [*Vide* Section 3 of this Chapter; *supra,* p. 233.—Tr.]

that is, to the fact that they are [in one way or another] virtuous;[10] while the other sense is absolute, referring to the acts as they are in themselves. St. Thomas affirms that, in the first sense, all virtuous acts come under the natural law, but he denies that this is true in the second sense.

This distinction may be expounded in two ways. First, it may be explained as meaning that every virtuous act, when viewed in the light of its specific nature as virtue, comes under a natural precept prescribing not only the mode of performance, but also [the obligation] to perform it; for it is thus, in a strict sense, that we speak of precepts. If, on the other hand, we are to consider individually all virtuous acts of whatsoever kind, then, in this sense, not every such act comes under a natural precept.

This latter part [of our explanation] is plainly true; both with respect to acts falling under the counsels of perfection; and also with respect to many good acts which (although they are not characterized by the highest degree of moral excellence, and therefore are not matters of counsel, nor even matters of a necessary nature, so that they are consequently not [made obligatory] by any precept) are nevertheless righteous and may licitly be performed, as is the case with the act of marriage, &c.

12. *Whether there is attached to every virtue, a natural precept requiring the exercise of that virtue, at one time or another.* A difficulty arises, however, with regard to the first part of the explanation, a difficulty as to whether there exists in connexion with every virtue, a natural precept requiring the exercise of that virtue at one time or another. For, as a general rule, it is a sufficiently self-evident fact that this is the case; but the rule does not seem to hold with regard to certain virtues, such as liberality, which by its very nature would seem to exclude any attendant obligation, or *eutrapelia* (urbanity), which also appears to be in large measure a matter of choice.

An exact treatment of this difficulty, indeed, would necessitate an examination of all the virtues. Consequently, I shall state briefly that if the term 'precept' is taken in its rigorous meaning, as involving obligation under pain of mortal guilt, then precepts are to be applied not to every sort of virtue, but only to the more important ones, a fact which is proved

10. [An unusual but attested meaning of *studiosi. Vide* Du Cange, *Glossarium Mediae et Infimae Latinitatis,* Vol. vii; under *studiosus.* St. Thomas, in the passage cited, used the term *virtuosus,* in the corresponding context.—Tr.]

by the argument set forth above. With regard to truth, [for example,]
many persons hold that this virtue is never in itself obligatory under pain
of mortal guilt, unless there is attached to it an obligation of justice or
of some other similar virtue which is involved in it; [otherwise, truth] is
not prescribed under penalty of mortal guilt. If, however, we are speaking
more broadly, so as to include obligations under pain of venial guilt, there
is probably, in that sense, no virtue the practice of which is not at one time
or another obligatory. For, in view of the fact that the perfect rectitude of
an individual man, his proper behaviour, both relatively to himself and
in his relations with others, results from the possession of all the virtues
collectively, it is probable that there are for each of the virtues respectively
occasions on which it ought to be practised, owing to a special obligation
attaching to each, with respect to which neither liberality nor any other
virtue is an exception.

13. [Secondly,] the distinction in question may be interpreted in another
sense. A virtuous act may be considered as such either in its objective
aspect (as, for example, the act of eating or of abstaining therefrom); or
in its formal aspect, as when the action is considered with reference to the
fact that it involves the mean [between two extremes]. St. Thomas [I.–II,
qu. 94, art. 3 and qu. 100, art. 2], then, is speaking of virtuous actions
regarded in the latter aspect, when he says that they fall under the natural
law, in that this law has regard to what is righteous.

With respect to this point, we must bear in mind the fact that there
are two ways in which a given act may be found to contain the mean of
virtue. In the first place, this may be discerned from the very nature of
the case, in that—given the subject-matter of a particular act, a particular
individual performing the same, and particular circumstances surround-
ing its performance—it is found, solely by means of reason and natural
reflection, that the conduct in question involves the mean of a virtue, so
that, in such a situation, the natural law clearly imposes an obligation [to
perform the said act]. Secondly, however, it may happen that the mean
of a virtue is placed in some particular subject-matter by the sole force of
positive law, as in the case of fasting, or in that of the just price of a certain
article. Under such circumstances, doubt exists as to whether the natural
law has application. For St. Thomas appears to speak indifferently and in

general terms on this point, and evidently it is thus that he is understood by Cajetan and other commentators. On the other hand, one may argue that in this second situation, either the obligation of the positive law is abolished,[11] or else the obligations concerning the act in question are multiplied. But I shall deal with this matter more properly in explaining the effects of the natural law. For the present, I merely assert, that the natural law does indeed play a part in this situation, not so much as creating an obligation of itself, but as giving efficacy to positive law.

14. The fourth[12] argument raised a grave question as to the distinction between the natural law and the *ius gentium,* a distinction which cannot be clarified without a clear exposition of both of the systems to be contrasted. Consequently, we shall postpone the treatment of that point to the last part of this Book,[13] where, after a complete discussion of the natural law as it is in itself, we shall say something regarding the *ius gentium;* for in this context we may more fittingly explain the difference between these two forms of law.

CHAPTER VIII

Is the Natural Law One Unified Whole?

1. Three questions may be asked at this point. First, with respect to a single individual, is the natural law one unified whole? Secondly, with respect to all men and in all places, is it one unified whole? Thirdly, is it also such a unified whole with respect to all times and every condition of human nature?

Before replying separately to these questions, however, I must again call attention to a fact which I have noted above, that this natural law may be conceived of either in its relationship to pure nature,[1] or in its relationship

---

11. [I.e., in the sense that it is absorbed within the natural obligation to which it gives rise.—Tr.]

12. [*Vide* Section 3 of this Chapter; *supra,* p. 233.—Tr.]

13. [Chap. xvii; *infra,* p. 374.—Tr.]

1. [Pure nature, that is, human nature conceived of as not yet elevated by supernatural grace. We may speak of human nature under three aspects: namely, pure, fallen, and redeemed.—Reviser.]

to [divine] grace, in so far as the latter has also a nature of its own. In this sense, then, it is manifest that there is a twofold natural law; the one phase that of humanity, so to speak; the other, that of grace. For these two phases are of different orders, and are directed to widely different ends. Accordingly, one of the two is wholly connatural with human nature; the other, wholly supernatural. Cajetan (on I.–II, qu. 100, art. 1), clearly teaches that this distinction exists, and the same conclusion is to be drawn from St. Thomas himself (I.–II, qu. 100, art. 1, and more clearly in art. 3). Therefore, the three questions enumerated above may be discussed from the standpoint of each of these two divisions; and indeed, everything that we say concerning the natural law may, in due proportion, be applied to both divisions. However, we almost always speak, by way of example, of the law that is wholly natural, partly because that law is better known, and partly because authorities usually adopt this manner of speaking.

2. *With respect to any one, there are many natural precepts; yet all of these form one unified body of law.* Turning to the first question, then, we must state that with respect to any one individual, there are many natural precepts; but that from all of these there is formed one unified body of natural law. It is thus that St. Thomas [I.–II, qu. 94, art. 2], Soto, and others explain this matter. Moreover, the same conclusion is drawn from the *Digest* (I. i. 1, § 2), in the following passage: 'This law is made up of natural precepts.'[2] The basis of this unity, apart from the common manner of speaking, consists, according to St. Thomas, in the fact that all natural precepts may be reduced to one first principle in which these precepts are (as it were) united; for where there is union, there is also a certain unity. Basil (*Regulae Fusius Tractatae,* Interrogatio 1), too, upholds this opinion when he says that a [relative] order exists between the divine commands, one of them—that enjoining the love of God—being the first, the other—that enjoining the love of one's neighbour—being the second, as stated in *Matthew* (Chap. xxii [, v. 39]); and that the remaining natural precepts are reduced to these two, as to primary principles, a fact which Paul also has indicated (*Romans,* Chap. xiii [, v. 8]). Finally, it may be added that all natural precepts are united in one end; in one author or lawgiver, also; and in the one characteristic of avoiding evil

2. [Not an exact quotation.—Tr.]

because it is evil, and of prescribing good because it is right and necessary; so that these facts suffice to constitute a moral unity.

3. However, in order that the multitude of precepts may be reduced to some kind of order, they may be distinguished from one another under various heads. For example, they may be distinguished with reference to the persons for whom they are—objectively, so to speak—ordained. Thus, certain precepts relate to God; certain others to one's neighbour; and still others, to the individual himself. Or, the precepts in question may be distinguished according to the virtues [which they prescribe]. For some relate to justice; others to charity or natural love; and so on. Or, again, they may be distinguished according to their respective relations to the intellect. It is thus that natural precepts are classified by St. Thomas, Cajetan, and others, even as propositions necessarily true are classified by the philosophers. For certain of these precepts are manifest in and of themselves, and with respect to all men, as is the case with the most universal precepts. Others are manifest in and of themselves, and in an immediate sense, but not in so far as relates to our apprehension, although they may have this character in so far as relates to the wise. As examples of this group, we have certain precepts regarding individual virtues, and the Commandments of the Decalogue. However, there are still other precepts, which call for reflection [in order that they may be known], and this group, in turn, admits of gradations; for certain of these precepts are recognized easily, others with difficulty. The distinctions above set forth will be useful in examining the matter of ignorance in regard to natural law, a point which we shall presently discuss.

4. Lastly, St. Thomas (*ibid.*, qu. 94, art. 2), followed by Cajetan and others, traces this variety in the natural precepts to the varied natural inclinations of mankind. For man is (as it were) an individual entity and as such has an inclination to preserve his own being, and to safeguard his own welfare; he is also a being corruptible—that is to say, mortal—and as such is inclined towards the preservation of the species, and towards the actions necessary to that end; and finally, he is a rational being and as such is suited for immortality, for spiritual perfection, and for communication with God and social intercourse with rational creatures. Hence, the natural law brings man to perfection, with regard to every one of his tendencies and, in this capacity, it contains various precepts—for example, precepts

of temperance and of fortitude, relating to the first tendency mentioned above; those of chastity and prudence, relating to the second tendency; and those of religion, justice and so forth, relating to the third tendency. For all these propensities in man, must be viewed as being in some way determined and elevated by a process of rational gradation. For, if these propensities are considered merely in their natural aspect, or as animal propensities, they must be bridled, that virtue may be attained, as Aristotle (*Nicomachean Ethics,* Bk. II, chap. ix) and Chrysostom, in an excellent passage (Homily XIII, *To the People,* near the end), have said; and on the other hand, if the same propensities are considered with respect to their capacity for being regulated by right reason, then proper and suitable precepts apply to each of them.

5. *The natural law is a single unit with respect to all men.* In answer to the second question,[3] the statement must be made that this natural law is a unified whole with respect to all men and in all places. This is the opinion of Aristotle (*ibid.,* Bk. V, chap. vii) and likewise of Cicero, whose remarkable words have been quoted above [Chap. v, p. 185] and cited by Lactantius (*Divine Institutes,* Bk. II, chap. vii and Bk. V, chap. viii). St. Thomas ([I.–II,] qu. 94, art. 4), and all the commentators on that passage may also be consulted in this connexion.

The rational basis of this position is that the law in question is (so to speak) a peculiar quality accompanying not the particular rational faculty of any given individual, but rather that characteristic nature which is the same in all men. Furthermore, synteresis is one and the same in all men; and, absolutely speaking, the recognition of the truth of conclusions might be one and the same; therefore, the law of nature is also one and the same [in all men].

Objection. At this point, one encounters the objection that various nations have followed laws contrary to natural precepts; and that consequently, the natural law is not the same in all nations. The truth of the antecedent is clear from the words of Jerome (*Against Jovinianus,* Bk. II [, no. 7]), of Theodoret (*Curatio,* Bk. IX) and of St. Thomas (*ibid.*), where the latter declares, on the authority of Julius Caesar (*Gallic War,* Bk. VI

---

3. [I.e. the second of the three questions enumerated in Section 1 of this Chapter.—Tr.]

[, chap. xxiii]), that formerly, among the Germans, theft[4] was not considered iniquitous. Castro also (*De Potestate Legis Poenalis,* Bk. II, chap. xiv), following Plutarch, says the same thing of the Lacedaemonians. Moreover, Plutarch, in his account of the life of Lycurgus [*Lycurgus,* Chap. xv, no. 6] relates that adultery was approved by the latter.

Solution. To this objection, following St. Thomas (*ibid.*), I shall reply briefly that the natural law in so far as relates to its substance is one and the same among all men, but that, in so far as concerns the knowledge of it, that law is not complete (so to speak) among all.

6. I shall expound this statement briefly. For, as I have previously remarked, the natural law may be considered in its first act,[5] and as such, it may be regarded as the intellectual understanding itself; so that it is therefore evident that in this sense, the natural law is one and the same in all men. Furthermore, it may be the same with respect to the second act,[6] that is, in actual cognition and judgment, or again, in a proximate habit induced by such act; and in this sense, the natural law is in part [the same] in all who have the use of reason. For in so far, at least, as regards the primary and most universal principles—no one can be ignorant of this law, inasmuch as those principles are by the very terms defining them completely known and to such a degree in harmony with and (as it were) fitted to the natural bent of the reason and will, that it is not possible to evade them. Thus it is that St. Thomas (*ibid.,* art. 6), has said that the natural law, at least in so far as such principles are concerned, cannot be eradicated from the hearts of men. And it is in the same sense, that some writers interpret Aristotle (*Nicomachean Ethics,* Bk. III, chap. i [, § 15]), when the latter says that any person may well be censured if he is ignorant of universal [principles]. On the other hand, one may [less reprehensibly] be ignorant of particular precepts; and, assuming the existence of such ignorance, some nations may have introduced rules contrary to the natural law, although these rules were never regarded by them as natural, but were considered as positive human rules.

4. [Caesar employs the word *latrocinia* (acts of brigandage).—Tr.]

5. [*Actus primus* is the faculty prepared to act; *actus secundus* is the activity realized. Cf. *supra,* p. 173, note 1, and p. 204, note 8.—Reviser.]

6. [The meaning of this expression is explained in the preceding note.—Reviser.]

7. Whether ignorance of natural precepts can be invincible. The negative opinion on this point. In this connexion, however, a question arises as to whether such ignorance of natural precepts can be invincible.[7] Castro [*De Potestate Legis Poenalis,* Bk. II, chap. xiv] indicates that this is not possible; and the same opinion has been held by some other theologians, as may be seen in the works of Alexander of Hales (Pt. II, qu. 153, membrum 3), and of Durandus (on the *Sentences,* Bk. III, dist. xxv, qu. 1). Moreover, certain jurists also favour this view, as is evident from the words of Gratian (*Decretum,* Pt. II, causa 1, qu. iv, can. xii); and from the Gloss (on *Decretals,* Bk. I, tit. iv, chap. ii).

The opinion of Suárez. But since it is customary to treat of this point more at length in dealing with the subject of sin ([Disp. XV, *De Peccatis* of Tract. *De Fide,*[8] in which is cited] St. Thomas, I.–II, qu. 76), my opinion shall be briefly stated here, as follows: it is not possible that one should in any way be ignorant of the primary principles of the natural law, much less invincibly ignorant of them; one may, however, be ignorant of the particular precepts, whether of those which are self-evident, or of those which are deduced with great ease from the self-evident precepts.

Yet such ignorance cannot exist without guilt; not, at least, for any great length of time; for knowledge of these precepts may be acquired by very little diligence; and nature itself, and conscience, are so insistent in the case of the acts relating to those [precepts] as to permit no inculpable ignorance of them. The precepts of the Decalogue, indeed, and similar precepts, are of this character. The truth of the foregoing has been sufficiently indicated by Paul (*Romans,* Chap. ii [, vv. 12 *et seq.*]), for he was speaking of the transgression of the precepts in question, when he said of the Gentiles that they were given over [by God] to reprobation, on account of their sins. The same may be inferred from the *Decretum* (Pt. II, causa xxxii, qu. vii, can. xiii). However, with respect to other precepts, which require greater reflection, invincible ignorance is possible, especially on the part of the multitude, a fact which is also to be inferred from the *Decretum* (*ibid.,* qu. iv, can. vii).

---

7. Ignorance if invincible is outside the power of the individual to avoid, and so is not the individual's fault.

8. [This disputation of Suárez is not included in these *Selections.*—Tr.]

The reason for this, is self-evident. See Corduba (*Quaestionarium Theologicum*, Bk. IV, qu. iv), and Soto (*De Iustitia*, Bk. I, qu. iv, art. 4).

8. *The natural law is a single law, with respect to all times, and every condition of human nature.* The last statement to be advanced is that the natural law is a single law with respect to all times and every condition of human nature.[9] So Aristotle teaches (*Nicomachean Ethics*, Bk. V, chap. vii) using the phrase 'everywhere and always'; and Cicero (*The Republic*, Bk. III [, chap. xxii]) supports the same view; as does Lactantius ([*Divine Institutes*,] Bk. VI, chap. viii), who says: 'all nations in every time,' &c. The reason for these statements, indeed, is the same; namely, that the law in question is the product, not of any [particular] state in which human nature is found, but of human nature itself in its essence. However, there are some who may say that, although this is true with respect to the universal principles of the natural law, it does not hold with respect to the conclusions drawn therefrom; but that, on the contrary, one must distinguish between two states of human nature, namely, the incorrupt and the corrupted states, a diverse form of the natural law being applied to each. For in the former, the natural law demanded, for example, the liberty of all men, common ownership, and the like; whereas, in the corrupted state, it demands servitude, division of property, &c., a conclusion which may be gathered from the *Digest* (I. i. 4), and also from the *Institutes* (I. ii, § 1).

9. This distinction, however, is not a necessary one. For, in the first place, the examples cited and any similar examples which may exist, pertain not to the natural law, in its proper and positive sense, but to the *ius gentium* (a point which I shall later explain more fully).[10] Wherefore, true natural precepts—generally speaking, at least—are commonly applicable to both the incorrupted and the corrupted states.

In the second place, it is one thing to speak of the existence of such precepts (as it were) and another thing to speak of their actual binding force or application. Therefore, although a given condition may demand the application of one precept and not of another, the natural law is

---

9. [This introduces Suárez's answer to the third of the questions propounded in the opening paragraph of this Chapter, *supra*, p. 243.—Tr.]

10. [*Infra*, p. 374; Chapter xvii of this Book.—Tr.]

nevertheless always the same, and comprises the same precepts; since the latter are either principles, or else conclusions derived therefrom by a necessary inference, and consequently possess a necessary quality of which they are not devoid with respect to any condition whatsoever.

Finally, it may be asserted that in connexion even with the natural law one may consider either its negative or its affirmative precepts. The negative precepts must necessarily be and have always been the same for all conditions [of human nature]; for they prohibit actions intrinsically evil, which are therefore evil for every such condition. Furthermore, they are binding without intermission,[11] and consequently, binding also for every [human] condition, whenever their proper subject-matter shall be involved.

The affirmative precepts, on the other hand, in like manner prescribe actions which are righteous of themselves, and consequently possess always this same righteous nature; and, nevertheless, since they are not binding without intermission, it may be that in connexion with one particular [human] state there will arise occasions to observe certain of these precepts, and in connexion with another [human state], occasions for the observance of other precepts. Yet this fact does not suffice to justify the assertion that the law itself is diversified in character. For even in the corrupted state of [human] nature, a time of peace is one thing, a time of war is quite another thing, and during these times respectively, diverse precepts must be observed. Furthermore, the art of medicine is one and the same art, even though it prescribes that certain things shall be done in time of health, and other things in time of illness. It is in such a sense, then, that the natural law is always one and the same.

CHAPTER IX

Is the Natural Law Binding in Conscience?

1. Thus far, we have expounded the nature and causes, that is to say, the subject-matter, of the natural law. Next in order we must treat of the

---

11. [*Pro semper.* A precept binds *semper,* if it may never be violated; it binds *semper et pro semper* if it must be continuously fulfilled. An example of the first kind of precept is: 'Honour thy father and thy mother'; an example of the second: 'Thou shalt not steal'.—REVISER.]

effects of that law, of which the chief, or very nearly the sole effect, is its binding force, for if the natural law does have other effects, they too may be reduced to this one. Its binding obligation, then, and the mode in which it so binds, must be discussed.

2. *An assertion: The natural law is binding in conscience.* In the first place, we must establish the fact that the natural law is binding in conscience.

This conclusion is unquestionably true, being a matter of faith, according to the theologians. It may be deduced, moreover, from the words of Paul (*Romans,* Chap. ii [, v. 12]): 'For whosoever have sinned without the law,'—the written law, undoubtedly—'shall perish without the law'; that is, [they shall perish] because they have violated the natural law. With regard to the latter, Paul adds [*ibid.,* vv. 14, 15]: 'The Gentiles, who have not the law, do by nature those things that are of the law [. . .], their conscience bearing witness to them.'

As for the reasons in favour of the above proposition, however, the first is that the natural law is the law of God, as has been shown. Secondly, this law is the proximate rule of moral goodness; and therefore, moral evil is wont to result from defiance of this law, so that sin is defined as an act contrary to God's law. Although Augustine and St. Thomas offer this explanation in connexion with the eternal law, yet, touching the subject-matter of the natural law also, whatever is to any extent contrary to reason, is to the same extent contrary to the eternal law, a view which is held by St. Thomas himself (I.–II, qu. 71, art. 6, ad 4 and 5). For the eternal law, as I have said above, is not the proximate rule for man, save in so far as it is explained by the natural law; and it may consequently happen that the latter, considered in all its latitude, shall be binding both under pain of mortal, and under pain of venial guilt; a fact which is clearly to be gathered from the above-cited passage in the Epistle of Paul, and which may easily be proved by induction. The reason for this assertion, indeed, is that the subject-matter of the law in question is often extremely weighty, and necessary to the observance of divine or neighbourly charity—and, consequently, necessary to the attainment of human felicity. However, the question of the occasions on which the precepts of this law are in one way or another binding, is not pertinent at this point, but will be explained when we deal with the subject of sin [Disp. XV, *De Peccatis* of Tract. *De*

Fide[1]], and the essential distinction between venial and mortal sin; and
the same matter will also be touched upon later [in this work[2]], in our
discussion of human law.

3. As against this truthful assertion, however, it may in the first place be
urged that the natural law is a dictate of natural reason; but natural reason
knows nothing of eternal punishment; hence, this law cannot be binding
under pain of eternal punishment; and consequently, it cannot bind under
pain of mortal guilt. The truth of the latter consequent is evident, because
that sin is mortal which leads to eternal punishment. And the truth of
the former consequent is proved, since a law cannot be binding with the
sanction of a punishment which it can neither indicate nor inflict. It is on
this ground that Gerson (Tr. *De Vita Spirituali,* Pt. III, lect. iv, [corol. 1,]
alphab. 62, lit. G)[3] apparently denies the possibility that the natural law,
as such, may bind under pain of guilt, and particularly, mortal guilt. However, we shall speak more fully, in the next Book, chapter xviii [chap. xxi][4]
of this author's expression of opinion, and his meaning.

For the present, we simply assert that, according to the faith, it cannot
be denied that a transgression of the natural law suffices for the incurring
of eternal punishment, even if the transgressor be ignorant of every supernatural law. For this fact is convincingly established by the testimony of
Paul, and by the arguments already adduced. Neither is it to be contro-
verted by the objection set forth above, for even though, in us, the natural
law is reason itself, nevertheless in God, it is the Divine reason or will,
and therefore it suffices that God Himself should know the penalty due to
transgressors of that law. For in order that the subject and transgressor of
the law may incur a given penalty, it is not necessary that he himself shall
be aware of the penalty attaching to his transgression; on the contrary, it
suffices if he commits an act that deserves such punishment; a truth which
Gerson himself admits (*ibid.,* Lect. ii).

---

1. [Not included in these *Selections.*—Tr.]

2. [*De Legibus,* Bk. III, chaps. xxv and xxvii. These Chapters are not included in the
Selections.—Tr.]

3. [Gerson does not deal with the subject very clearly in *Alphabetum Divini
Amoris.*—Reviser.]

4. [Not included in these *Selections.*—Tr.]

4. A second possible objection [to the assertion that the natural law is binding upon the conscience], is that this law does not create obligation, but merely assumes its existence; hence, such obligation is not the effect of the natural law. The truth of the antecedent is evident; for this law prohibits a given thing because that thing is evil; and therefore, prior to the existence of the said law, there exists the obligation of avoiding such an evil. The same is true, in due proportion, with respect to the command and precept to do good [simply] because it is good. However, we have already given a partial reply to this objection, and the question will, moreover, recur below; so that, for the present, we shall content ourselves with stating briefly that the objection in question proves our very proposition. For if the natural law does forbid a thing because that thing is then evil, it also draws in its train its own especially imposed obligation of avoiding the thing in question; for this is an intrinsic characteristic of any prohibition. Furthermore, [the objection mentioned above] proves at the same time that this law assumes the existence of something which pertains to an intrinsic debt of nature, since everything owes it to itself, in a sense, to do nothing inconsistent with its own nature; but, in addition to this, the law imposes a special moral obligation, which we speak of as an effect of that law. It is customarily called by the jurists a natural obligation; not because it is not moral, but in order to distinguish it from civil obligations. Wherefore, these same persons also admit that it is an obligation binding in conscience, and so term it, as is evident from the Gloss (on *Digest,* I. i. 5, word *obligationem*); from Panormitanus, and from other canonists (on *Decretals,* Bk. III, tit. XLIX, chap. viii).

5. *Whether every obligation induced by the natural law is binding in conscience.* Thirdly, with respect to the obligation in question, and in order that it may be more fully explained, a question may be raised as to whether it is universally true that an obligation imposed by the natural law is one that is binding in conscience. A reason for this doubt may be that every obligation springing from a moral virtue pertains to the natural law; since, as we have said above, this law lays men under an obligation to practise all the virtues, and nevertheless, not every sort of obligation springing from a moral virtue is binding upon the conscience; therefore, . . .

The minor premiss is clearly true, since obligations of gratitude, for example, are not binding in conscience, the same being true with respect to obligations of this or that friendship. A confirmation of this argument lies in the fact that the obligation to undergo punishment which results from guilt, is a part of the natural law; and nevertheless, that obligation is not binding in conscience; therefore, . . .

6. *The distinction made by some authorities, between legal and moral right, as an aid to solving the difficulty.* With regard to this point, some authorities distinguish a twofold duty—that is, legal and moral—each aspect of which springs from the natural law. The first, they say, is not binding in conscience; only the second is thus binding. Covarruvias supports their opinion (on *Decretals,* Bk. III, tit. xxvi, chap. vii, no. 10; *ibid.,* no. 9; on *Sext,* Chap. *quamvis pactum,* pt. II, § 4, no. 5 [no. 6]), and cites St. Thomas (II.–II, qu. 106, art. 1, ad 2, and art. 5), naming debts of gratitude as an example. But it is in an entirely different sense that St. Thomas himself, in the passage cited [by Covarruvias], draws a distinction between legal debts and debts of virtue as he calls the latter, from which [second group], he surely does not exclude obligations binding in conscience; inasmuch as he uses the expression 'virtue', for the very reason that [the obligations in question] must necessarily [be observed], as a requirement of virtuous conduct, although they are not so rigorous that human laws bind men to observe them—for in this case, [St. Thomas] would use the term 'legal debt.'

A natural obligation, strictly speaking, always carries with it an obligation in conscience. Wherefore, if we are speaking in a strict sense of a natural obligation, it certainly cannot be separated from an obligation in conscience, since, if that natural obligation consists in [a duty] to avoid something, it must spring from the intrinsic evil of the action [prohibited], which, for that reason, is to be avoided, as a matter of conscience; and if, on the other hand, the natural obligation consists in [a duty] to do something, then it springs from the intrinsic connexion between the required action and that which is good from the standpoint of moral virtue, which we are bound in conscience also to observe in our actions, so that the omission of a required action is in itself wicked. A confirmation of the foregoing lies in the fact that to break the natural law without sinning involves an inconsistency, as is evident from the definition of sin given above; and therefore the existence of an obligation which is imposed by the natural law, but which is not a matter of conscience, also involves an inconsistency.

7. *In what sense a moral obligation does not carry with it an obligation in conscience.* However, lest there should be some ambiguity in our use of terms we must note that, according to the common mode of speech, the expression, 'a moral obligation', is occasionally applied to something which ought to be done, not as a matter of necessity, but rather because it is preferable, pertaining (as it were) to a counsel of perfection included under some virtue in its broad [optional] aspect; and in this sense, it is true that not every moral obligation is one of conscience, that is to say, binding under pain of guilt. But [such a duty] does not constitute a true obligation under the natural law. Yet it may have been with reference to these duties that Covarruvias made his assertion. Thus, the reply to the reason for the doubt set forth above,[5] becomes evident. By way of confirmation, moreover, we may add that Bartolus ([*Tractatus Super Constitutionem*] *Ad Reprimendum,* [fol. 77 of his *Consilia, Tractatus, Quaestiones*] on the word, *denunciationem,* § *sed dico,* no. 10) makes to the proposed rule an exception of the obligation to suffer punishment. But it is not a necessary exception, since this obligation is not an obligation to perform any act, but rather a duty to submit to the punishment which is to be inflicted by another; and the exception is unnecessary for this reason especially, that within the bounds of natural law one does not incur the burden of any punishment, save that which is to be inflicted by God and which has no relation to the strict obligation now under discussion.

8. *Whether or not every obligation in conscience is an effect of the natural law.* Lastly, we may inquire whether the converse proposition is true, namely, that every obligation binding in conscience is an effect of the natural law, and that consequently every such obligation may be called natural.

The reason for doubting this proposition is that human laws also, as we shall see, are binding in conscience; so that the obligation in question is an

---

5. [*Vide* Section 5 of this Chapter, *supra,* p. 253.—Tr.]

effect not of the natural, but of the positive law. Furthermore, there exist obligations in conscience which are derived immediately from the positive supernatural law, as, for example, the obligation to make confession, or to keep the seal of confession; wherefore, such an obligation may be called supernatural, and is therefore in no wise an effect of the natural law. Finally, if the said proposition were not [open to question], there would exist one and the same adequate effect of natural law, and of law in general; and consequently, all laws other [than the natural] would be superfluous.

9. But, on the other hand, it would seem that an obligation in conscience arising from human law, is indeed an effect of the natural law. For any objection to this view would be drawn chiefly from the fact that the will of the prince plays a part [in such a law]; yet this contention would not constitute a [real] obstacle, since even in the obligation resulting from a vow, the personal will of the one making the vow plays a part, yet the obligation in question is nevertheless an effect of the natural law. And just as the natural law commands the fulfilment of what has been promised of one's own will, so also does it command the performance of that which has been enjoined by the will of a superior.

Likewise, in the case of prescription, a part is played by that human law which transfers the ownership of a thing from one person to another; and yet the resulting obligation not to deprive another of the property which he has obtained by prescription, is a natural obligation, the violation of which would be theft.

The same appears to be true of the obligation which arises upon the establishment of a law determining the price of a given thing, for there springs up immediately a resultant obligation of justice, the violation of which would be theft and therefore contrary to the natural law.

10. Secondly, not only the obligation resulting from human law, but also that resulting from divine and supernatural law, would seem to be an effect of the law of nature. For it is the opinion of the theologians, that the failure to assent to matters of faith which have been sufficiently made known, is opposed to the very light of nature, which, under such circumstances, clearly indicates that these matters are worthy of belief and should therefore, according to right reason, be believed. Wherefore, the theologians also say, more commonly, that no one is turned away through sin

from his supernatural end, without being diverted from his natural end, as well; and the reason for the truth of this statement must be that one always violates the natural law [in violating the supernatural law]; hence, conversely, the obligation to observe supernatural precepts is always an effect of the natural law. Moreover, the additional reason may be adduced, that nature is the foundation for grace, as well as for every human law.[6] Again, the natural principles in accordance with which a man ought to be governed in moral matters, are so general in character, as virtually to include every obligation; and consequently, no obligation can be made applicable to man save through the mediation of those principles; therefore, just as all human knowledge is an effect of first principles, even so, every obligation in conscience is an effect of the natural law, in so far, at least, as it comprehends those first principles.

11. *The doubt propounded above, is resolved; and the assertion is made that not every obligation in conscience is immediately and essentially an effect of the natural law.* This question may be briefly resolved, in accordance with a certain distinction which was suggested above and of which the authorities make no mention. We may speak, then, either of an immediate and essential effect, or of a remote effect which may sometimes be essential and sometimes, incidental.

Accordingly, I assert first of all that not every obligation in conscience is immediately and essentially an effect of the natural law. The reasons first[7] set forth prove this assertion. For no one will say that the obligation to observe a fast day ordered by the Church is a precept of the natural law, nor even that it is an obligation of faith, properly speaking. Accordingly, with respect to the third precept of the Decalogue,[8] as it has been handed down in the written law, the theologians distinguish between two [obligations], namely, the worship of God, and the keeping of the Sabbath day. The first, they say, is an effect of the natural law; but this is not true of the second, since it would not fall under the head of an obligation if it were

6. [I.e., nature is the foundation for the bestowal of grace and for the very existence of human law.—Reviser.]

7. [*Rationes priori loco factae,* i.e. the reasons set forth in the second paragraph of Section 8 of this Chapter, pp. 255–56.—Tr.]

8. [I.e. keep holy the Sabbath day.—Reviser.]

not for the fact that a positive law of God has intervened. Finally, there is the *a priori* argument, that the natural law is not the proximate rule of all human actions.

12. *In what sense it may be said that every obligation in conscience is an effect of the natural law.* I must, however, make this second assertion: there is no obligation in conscience which is not in some way an effect of the natural law—mediately and remotely, at least. The second group of arguments proves this fact.[9]

We must, indeed, note the difference between an obligation which arises from civil law, that is, from merely human law (as I term it in order to exclude the canon law, which for the present I include preferably under the supernatural), and one which arises from the divine law supernaturally given by God.

For, with respect to a human law and the obligation proceeding therefrom, the natural law may be spoken of as a cause *per se,* since, in truth, every such obligation is *per se* founded upon principles of the natural law, known through the natural light [of reason]. For, although the civil law is not deduced speculatively (as it were) through an absolute inference drawn from the principles of the natural law, being, on the contrary, established by some act of determination, through the will of the prince; nevertheless, granting this assumption as to an act of determination, [the conclusion] that such a human law must—in actual practice, at least—be obeyed, is deduced from natural principles. And, in this sense, the obligation imposed by that civil law is said to be an effect of the natural law considered as a cause *per se,* not proximate but universal (so to speak) and modified by a specific [agency], which is human law. In this connexion (because of certain arguments set forth above) one must also take into consideration the fact that human law sometimes has the effect of imposing a simple obligation to perform, or to refrain from performing, a given act. In such a case, the obligation in question is derived from human law, strictly speaking and in an immediate sense, but remotely, it is derived from the natural law. Sometimes, however, human law has other effects,

---

9. [*Argumenta posteriori loco facta,* i.e. the arguments adduced in Sections 9 and 10 of this Chapter, pp. 256–57.—Tr.]

relating to the subject-matter itself with which virtuous actions are concerned. And in that case, it may frequently happen that, though a change may be effected in this subject-matter through human law, or through the *ius gentium,* or even through the will of a private individual, nevertheless, later, the obligation to observe this or some other [special] manner of acting may arise directly from the natural law. Such is indeed the case with respect to the above-cited examples relating to prescription, division of property, and vows. But the reason is that, under these circumstances, the change is made merely in the subject-matter; and it is of no importance whether that change be made owing to one cause or owing to another; for once it has taken place, the natural law forthwith imposes a binding obligation to the same effect, as is illustrated in the examples already set forth, and as we shall explain more fully in the following Chapters.

13. However, with respect to the supernatural obligation proceeding from the divine law, a further distinction must be made, touching the natural law.

For if we are speaking of that natural law which is connatural with grace, it may be compared with any positive law whatsoever, belonging to the supernatural order, just as a comparison is made between a purely natural law and one that is civil; since the same proportionate relationship exists [in both cases]. Indeed, a similar statement may be made with respect to the canon law in its human aspect; for in so far as that law proceeds from a supernatural power, it is *per se* founded upon supernatural principles connatural with grace itself, and therefore derives its origin from grace, as from a universal cause, indirectly, to be sure, but *per se* and connaturally.

If, however, we are speaking of the natural law in its stricter sense, as law proceeding from the light of nature alone, there is also, indeed, a supernatural obligation existing in a sense as an effect of that law, not, however, *per se,* but merely incidentally. The arguments above set forth prove the former portion of this proposition. The proof of the latter portion is as follows: natural knowledge cannot be the cause *per se* of supernatural knowledge, since the former pertains to an inferior order; but natural knowledge can be a necessary condition in order that a given object may be duly referred to supernatural knowledge, as is evident from the treatise

De Fide.[10] In this sense, then, a natural dictate may be assumed to exist, and may be necessary to the binding force of a supernatural precept.

CHAPTER X

Is the Natural Law Binding Not Only with Respect to the Virtuous Act but Also with Respect to the Manner of Its Performance, in Such a Way That This Law Cannot Be Fulfilled, Save by an Act That Is Good in Every Particular?

1. The consideration of this question is essential to a perfect understanding of the strength and efficacy of the natural law, and of its exact binding force.

St. Thomas has discussed this matter when treating of the commandments of the Decalogue, in a passage which we shall expound here almost in its entirety (I.–II, qu. 100 [, art. 9]), together with an earlier one (qu. 95); for the precepts of the Decalogue are natural precepts, although they were laid down in the Old Law in a special manner. In the first of these two passages, then, St. Thomas (*ibid.*) inquires whether or not the mode [of performing an act] of virtue falls within the scope of precepts. He asks the same question (*ibid.,* art. 10) regarding the mode [of performing an act] of charity, and distinguishes many conditions which are required for a virtuous action, holding that some of these conditions come under the natural law, while the rest do not.

The difference between the affirmative and the negative precepts. Before we set down his doctrine, however, let us make a distinction between the negative and the affirmative precepts, which do agree to a certain extent in that, just as the affirmative precepts prescribe nothing save that which is righteous, so the negative precepts forbid nothing save that which is evil; since (as we have often said) those things which are forbidden by the natural law are not evil because they are prohibited, but are prohibited because they are evil. The two kinds of precepts differ, however, in that

10. [Of this Tractate, only Disp. XVIII (*De Mediis*) is included in these *Selections.*—Tr.]

the negative may be fulfilled without action, in so far as the form of the precept is concerned; for men conform to them, simply by abstaining from the forbidden act. Thus, the question propounded above has scarcely any application to the negative precepts, save perchance to the extent that the latter may be fulfilled through a will to refrain from doing what is prohibited, a point which we shall touch upon presently. But that question does have strict application to the affirmative precepts, which—as is evident—must be fulfilled by a positive act.

2. *The difference between fulfilling a precept, and refraining from the transgression thereof.* Furthermore, we should note that, properly speaking, it is one thing, to refrain from transgressing a precept, and another thing to fulfil that precept. For he who does not offend against a commandment, does not transgress the same; and nevertheless it is not always true that he who does not offend against a commandment, fulfils it. For one who is invincibly ignorant of a given precept, who is drunk, or asleep, who is incapable of action, or who has any other, similar excuse, does not offend against that precept; yet he does not fulfil it—especially not, if it be affirmative—since he does not do what the law prescribes, which would be, properly, the fulfilment of the law. Indeed, if we use the word ['fulfil'] in a moral sense, it is not enough to do what the law commands; we must do it freely, and in human fashion, as I shall presently show.[1] Wherefore, the question under discussion does not relate to the non-transgression of a precept, since such non-transgression may exist apart not only from virtuous action but even from any action at all, a fact which is evident from what has already been said. For it may happen that one abstains from offending against the precept, because one is asleep.

The question, then, relates to the situation in which no excuse exists [for the omission of a given act], but rather, the law has to be positively[2] (so to speak) fulfilled, if offence against it is to be avoided. Under such circumstances, it is clear that [this] necessary act is righteous by its very nature, since—as I have said previously (Chap. vii)—the natural law does not prescribe acts of any other sort, and cannot be fulfilled save through

---

1. [*Infra*, p. 263; § 4 this Chapter.—Tr.]
2. [I.e. by a positive act.—Reviser.]

the act which it prescribes; but, in view of the fact that the demands of virtue are not satisfied by the doing of a righteous act unless that act be performed in a righteous manner, according to the saying in *Deuteronomy,* Chap. xvi [, v. 20]: 'Thou shalt follow justly after that which is just'—in view of this fact—we are moved to inquire whether this entire procedure must necessarily be followed in order to fulfil the natural law.

3. *On the conditions requisite to a good moral action.* Finally, we should distinguish three conditions which are required in the case of a moral action in order that it may be good. These were included by Aristotle under two heads. For the sake of clearness, however, we have made the triple distinction as indicated, a point which we shall explain more fully in the discussion that follows. The first condition is that the act shall be performed with sufficient knowledge; the second, that it shall be freely and deliberately performed; and the third, that it shall not only concern a righteous object, but shall also be attended by all the circumstances requisite to the righteousness of an act.

Aristotle adds another condition, which he puts in the third place, and which we could regard as the fourth, namely, that the act in question shall be performed firmly, readily, and with pleasure, that is to say, as an act that proceeds from habit. We may, however, omit this last condition, since it is universally considered to be certain and indubitable that neither the natural law nor any other law makes such a mode of action obligatory.

This fact is manifest, in so far as relates to laws other [than the natural]; since these laws do not prescribe the said mode, directly and formally (as is readily apparent from a consideration of all legal systems, both positive divine laws, and human); and since, moreover, the prescription of that mode does not follow from the precepts contained in the laws in question, inasmuch as all these precepts may be fulfilled without adopting the mode. The same reasoning will afford [similar] proof in so far as relates to the natural law, especially since the natural law prescribes nothing save that which is inherently necessary to righteousness, whereas the mode under discussion is not necessary to a righteous performance, although it may be desirable and appropriate. Furthermore, the natural law is binding from the beginning [of one's life], before—if we take into consideration the nature of the case—it has been possible to acquire habits [of fulfilling that law]; for one must acquire those habits through his own acts. Again, to have or not to have a habit is not in itself subject-matter for a precept, since precepts are imposed with respect to human actions; and as to the fact that certain habits may or may not follow upon such actions, this depends either upon the nature of the latter, as is the case with acquired habits, or upon the grace of God, as is the case with [habits] divinely infused; so that such a result is not a matter of precept. Hence, although it may happen that, from a continuous observance of precepts, the habit and the above-mentioned facility of execution may be acquired; nevertheless, this acquisition is an incidental matter so far as the precept itself is concerned; for the precept is observed before the habit is acquired, and it may very well happen that a precept—for example, that of fasting—is observed for a long time without the acquisition of the habit of fasting or of facility in the same, if outside of the season of fasting, one eats sumptuously, even though he does not exceed the bounds of natural temperance.

Accordingly, waiving this [fourth] condition, with respect to which no difficulty arises, we shall speak of the other conditions; for they require some explanation.

4. *The first proposition. The mode of voluntary action falls under a precept of the natural law, and is a requisite for the observance of that law.* I hold in the first place, then, that the mode of voluntary action is a matter which falls under a precept of the natural law; and that, consequently, this mode is a requisite for the observance of the natural law.

So St. Thomas teaches (I.–II, qu. 100, art. 9), as do all the commentators on that passage of his works.

Moreover, the proof of this proposition is as follows: the natural law is founded in reason, and immediately directs and governs the will; consequently, the binding force of the natural law is imposed *per se* (so to speak) and primarily upon the will; therefore, this law is observed only by the mediation of the will; hence, the mode of voluntary action is *per se* a matter of precept, and a requisite for the observance of the law in question.

A second proof is this: human action comes directly under the natural law, and an act is not human unless it be perfectly voluntary and, consequently, free—in relation, at least, to the circumstances of this life; therefore, the mode of acting which we are discussing [likewise] falls directly under the natural law; hence, whoever involuntarily performs an act in accordance with the law, although he may seem to observe it, is a transgressor of the law; as one may infer from a passage in the works of Augustine (*Contra Duas Epistolas Pelagianorum,* Bk. II, chap. ix), and from numerous other statements which he makes, to the effect that where a good action is done not from a love of justice but from a fear of punishment, it is not well done; especially not, when the fear is so servile as to be coupled with a disposition to abstain from performing the act prescribed, save for the fact that a penalty attaches to its non-performance. To the same effect, St. Thomas (*ibid.,* art. 9, ad 3) has held that performance [of prescribed acts] without sadness is included under the precepts of the divine law, since he who acts sadly, acts unwillingly. For this assertion is true of the sadness originating from an entirely contrary disposition, in accordance with which one intends not to obey a precept if he is not forced to do so. Such an unwilling disposition, then, is especially contrary to the natural law, which applies directly even to internal acts; and therefore, conversely, the mode of voluntary action is necessarily included in that which is prescribed by this law.

5. *Objection.*[3] One may object that, although this reasoning duly proves the necessity, at least, for not coupling with the execution of the law an [actual] disposition to refrain from acting in the absence of any penalty or other similar compulsion, the same reasoning nevertheless does not prove the necessity of a positive mode of voluntary observance of the law. For a middle course may perhaps be taken; that is to say, the deed may be performed neither willingly nor unwillingly, and such [a performance] will suffice, since the law prescribes only that the deed be done.

Solution. My reply to this objection is that, in the argument last adduced,[4] it is assumed that the act whereby the command is observed should be a human act, as is made sufficiently evident in the arguments previously set forth; and it cannot be human unless it is voluntary and

---

3. [The text has *Solutio* (Solution), evidently printed here by confusion with the immediately following catch phrase. The context indicates that *Obiectio* was the term intended. Cf. note 11, p. 269.—Tr.]

4. [I.e. the second argument of Section 4 of this Chapter; *supra,* p. 263.—Tr.]

proceeds from the will, for otherwise it should be designated as passivity rather than as human activity. However, since not everything which proceeds from the will is voluntary, absolutely and properly speaking, the argument in question[5] shows that the voluntary disposition should be such as not to admit, in conjunction with itself, any contrary will inherently opposed to the precept, and that, accordingly, will in the absolute sense is necessary for the observance of the natural law.

In order to explain the matter more fully, we may distinguish at this point between two different situations. One is that the act prescribed should, simply in itself, be voluntarily performed; the other is that this act should be voluntarily performed, while regarded, moreover, as being prescribed, so that the willingness extends also to the actual observance of the precept. These two situations may indeed be distinguished. For one who is ignorant of the precept of almsgiving cannot will to observe that precept; and nevertheless, he might voluntarily perform an act of almsgiving. The conclusion in question, then, may be understood as applying to both kinds of will. For the former is necessary as the basis of the prescribed act, in order that this act may be human and correspond to the subject-matter of the precept; while the latter form of willing would also appear to be necessary in order that the observance of the precept may be moral, that it may be the effect of the law or precept, and that this fact may be attributed to the man himself, for otherwise it would be merely an accidental occurrence that the external act was in conformity with the precept.

6. *Some objections to the proposition stated above.* A difficulty arises, however, in relation to each of these two phases of our proposition.[6] As to the first, the difficulty is that, apparently, a precept is sometimes fulfilled through an action performed without the use of reason and therefore not voluntary in a human fashion. But we shall discuss this problem [more fully] in connexion with the next proposition. The second hypothesis leaves room for doubt because it leads to the conclusion that a formal act of obedience—that is, of willingness to obey the precept—is necessary for

5. [I.e. the second argument of Section 4 of this Chapter; *supra*, p. 263.—Tr.]
6. [I.e. the proposition stated at the beginning of Section 4 of this Chapter; *supra*, p. 263.—Tr.]

the observance thereof; a conclusion which is absurd, and contrary to all the authorities. Another conclusion which would follow [from the same hypothesis]—the conclusion that to act with displeasure regarding a precept is always a sin, so that [under such circumstances] the precept is not fulfilled—is also inacceptable. For he who gives an alms, even if he does so with displeasure, nevertheless obeys the precept.

The objections are answered. I shall reply to the first [of the objections in connexion with the second hypothesis[7]] by denying the validity of the consequent. For it is one thing to will to do that which is prescribed, and another thing, to will to do the same because it is prescribed and with that fact as the motive for one's action. I hold that the first form of willing is a requisite, and that this requisite is satisfied by the simple fact that the precept is not unknown and the will desires that which has been prescribed. Yet such a disposition does not suffice for a formal act of obedience. On the contrary, the second form of willing is also necessary for that act, that is to say, it is also necessary to act formally from the particular motive mentioned. But this requisite is certainly not essential to the [actual] fulfilment of the precept, since it is not a requisite prescribed in the law itself, neither is there any reason which makes it obligatory. Accordingly, there are few persons who execute in this [formal] fashion, the works enjoined by natural precepts; for, on the contrary, [the majority execute them] with attention fixed upon the righteous character pertaining to the individual precepts themselves.

7. *What sort of displeasure as to the prescribed deed is inconsistent with a fulfilment of that [precept].* Again, as to the second part [of the objections to the hypothesis in question[8]], I shall reply [once more] by absolutely denying the validity of the consequent.

---

7. [I.e. the objection that it would be necessary to conclude that a formal act of obedience is required for the observance of the precept. The context calls for this interpretation of *priorem partem.* Moreover, Suárez has already said that he postpones the discussion of the objection to the first *hypothesis* until he takes up the next proposition.—Tr.]

8. [I.e. the objection that it would be necessary to conclude that to act with displeasure regarding a precept is always a sin, so that such an act does not constitute a fulfilment of the precept; cf. the preceding footnote.—Tr.]

For, in the first place, there may be a certain kind of displeasure which is merely natural, and which arises from some [involuntary] repugnance on the part of the subject, or from some human inconvenience consequent upon [the observance of the precept involved]; a form of displeasure which is not in itself wicked, and which does not necessarily render the act in question evil.

Furthermore, a distinction should be made even with respect to the displeasure which is voluntary and entertained through deliberate consent; for a twofold displeasure [of this voluntary sort] may be conceived, in the present connexion. One phase is a displeasure in the very observance of the precept, but displeasure in a composite sense (so to speak) when, notwithstanding the obligation imposed by the natural law, a man would will not to observe that law, if he did not fear the penalty attaching to nonobservance, or some other evil, a point which we have already discussed in connexion with that fear which is servilely submissive. This phase, moreover, includes an intrinsic contradiction to the precept involved, and therefore is intrinsically evil, and contrary to the natural law. For such displeasure, although it does not exclude the possible existence of an absolute will to perform the deed [prescribed], which a servile fear commands more efficaciously [than the precept], does nevertheless exclude the existence of a will to observe the law; and it implies the existence of a contrary disposition, which in itself, and with respect to the will, is absolute, although it may be modified by fear.

However, there may exist another kind of [voluntary] displeasure, relating to the occasion (so to speak) of a particular precept and to the fact that the obligation involved in that precept falls upon one at a particular moment. This displeasure, indeed, is not intrinsically evil, and may coexist with an absolute disposition to obey the precept; so that, even when there is such an attitude of displeasure, the said precept may be observed, since, as is evident, that attitude is not incompatible with a sufficient willingness to obey.

8. *The second proposition: to act wittingly is, in a certain sense necessary for the fulfilment of a natural precept.* My second proposition is this: to act wittingly—that is, with knowledge—is in a certain sense necessary for the fulfilment of a natural precept.

The argument in support of the proposition is as follows: a precept is not obeyed, save by a human action; and an action is not human, unless it proceeds from knowledge; therefore, . . . The truth of the major premiss is sufficiently well established in the discussion of the first proposition, upon which this second assertion necessarily follows. Furthermore, a confirmation of the same truth consists in the fact that knowledge would seem to be no less necessary for the observance of a precept than for its transgression; and some knowledge is indeed necessary for the latter act; therefore, . . .

It may be objected that, on the contrary, sometimes the transgression of a precept occurs apart from any knowledge of that precept and through ignorance. The reply to this objection is that, in such a case, the essential knowledge, at least, was required and within reach, and was unattained, through negligence; and that this negligence suffices to constitute a transgression, since evil arises in the case of any defect, while the fulfilment of a precept is a good act and accordingly involves of necessity a faultlessness in all respects (*integram causam*) of which knowledge is one [essential] element.[9]

9. *What knowledge and how many kinds thereof should exist concerning the prescribed action, in order that the latter may be carried out.* It should also be noticed that this knowledge may be twofold.

For example, it may relate to the prescribed action as it is inherently;[10] and it is with respect to this [sort of knowledge], particularly, that the arguments set forth above have application. For it is evident that the knowledge of an action is necessary in order that this action may be performed voluntarily, since knowledge is the root of that same voluntary quality.

Objection. One may object to the foregoing, however, on the ground that he who has ignorantly or unwillingly performed a [prescribed] action is not bound to repeat that action later; which is an indication that he has already fulfilled the precept. The antecedent is clearly true; for if restitution has been made against the debtor's will, the latter is free from the obligation to make restitution; in like manner, if tithes have thus been

---

9. [Suárez is here referring to the maxim: *Bonum ex integra causa, malum ex quocumque defectu.* That is, in every good act, the object, the motive, and the circumstances are all relevant to the morality of the act. If any of the three is evil, the act is evil.—Reviser.]

10. [I.e. the prescribed *action* itself as opposed to the fact that it is prescribed. *Vide infra*, p. 269, the first sentence of Section 10 of this Chapter.—Tr.]

paid, or rather, extracted from an unwilling individual, he is not bound to pay them a second time; again, if an alms has been given by a drunken person, his obligation [to bestow that alms] no longer persists; and finally, the same is true with respect to positive precepts, as in the case of one who hears Mass under compulsion or fasts against his will because he is deprived of food, and as in similar cases.

Solution.[11] My reply is that, in all these instances, the natural precepts are not observed; for serious offences are committed against them. Therefore, I deny the validity of the consequent in the argument set forth, since, in each of the cases mentioned, the precept involved ceases to bind, not because it has been fulfilled, but because the object which the law enforced has been withdrawn. Thus, the obligation to make restitution ceases because the debt has been extinguished by the restitution of the thing itself, even though it was extorted from an unwilling agent; for willingness on the part of the debtor, as is evident, is not always necessary to the discharge of a debt. The same argument holds true in due proportion with respect to the payment of tithes; we shall presently apply it also to the giving of alms. Concerning the positive precepts, indeed, we shall speak in the following Book. For the present, I shall observe [simply] that, in the sight of God, a precept is not fulfilled in the fashion described above; although, in the external forum, it is fulfilled to the extent of evading punishment, provided the prescribed act is substantially executed. For if one should under compulsion attend Mass in such a way as not to give heed to it, he will not even externally fulfil the command involved. In accordance with the same reasoning, if any one while drunk reads the whole of his divine office,[12] he fulfils no precept; for he does not *recite*[13] the office, and therefore, he is still under an obligation to do so later.

10. *Whether knowledge of the prescribed action,* as being prescribed,[14] *is necessary for the fulfilment of a precept.* One might express oneself differently,

---

11. [The text has *Obiectio* (Objection), evidently for *Solutio,* by confusion with the preceding catch-phrase, *Obiectio.* Cf. note 3, p. 264.—Tr.]

12. [*Breviarium,* which is frequently used for the divine office which a priest is bound to recite daily.—Reviser.]

13. [The italics are supplied by the Translator.—Tr.]

14. [The italics are supplied by the Translator.—Tr.]

however, with respect to knowledge of the actual precept; knowledge, that is, of the fact that the act in question is prescribed. Thus there might be some doubt as to whether such knowledge is necessary to the fulfilment of the precept. For the human and moral action which is prescribed may be performed, without that knowledge. As to this contention, however, there is probably some difficulty in the case of a positive law, a point which we shall discuss later.[15]

Reply. But, for the present, I shall say briefly that, without the knowledge in question, a precept may be observed in a material sense (so to speak) which will suffice to exclude sinning directly against that precept, as is proved by the reasons already set forth; yet, even so, it would not be observed in a formal sense, nor in human fashion; accordingly, the knowledge of which we are speaking is necessary in order that this act may be human with respect to the observance of the precept, in accordance with our discussion of the preceding[16] proposition. Wherefore, if any one happens knowingly to have given alms at a time when a natural precept bound him to do so, and if he acted while ignorant of that obligation, then, although he has not transgressed the precept, he cannot properly be said to have fulfilled it; for, in so far as that precept is concerned, he has performed the act casually and (as it were) incidentally. To go a step further, it may happen that, if the ignorance was vincible, he has thus sinned against that very precept, since by reason of his disposition—that is, his knowledge at the time—he may have exposed himself to the peril of transgressing the precept in the very fact that he was ignorant of the obligation imposed thereby.

It may be objected that, if any one while ignorant of a precept—for example, the precept of almsgiving—has performed the act [prescribed thereby], he is not bound to give the alms again, at a later time, even though he comes to know of the precept; therefore, this is an indication that it has been fulfilled by him. One may reply to the objection on the basis of what has been said above, denying the consequent on the ground that affirmative precepts do not bind one to uninterrupted fulfilment of

---

15. [*Infra,* p. 417; *De Legibus,* Bk. III, chap. i.—Tr.]
16. [*Vide* the first sentence of Section 4 of this Chapter, p. 263.—Tr.]

them, but impose their obligation only when the particular occasion so demands; whereas this act of almsgiving caused the need of [the alms-giver's] neighbour to cease, so that the obligation imposed by the precept also ceased to exist, not because the precept was fulfilled, but because the subject-matter and the occasion for the prescribed act were wanting; whence one may infer that, if this same occasion or necessity persists, then, the obligation of fulfilling the precept will also persist.

Lastly, it may be inferred incidentally from the foregoing that there arises from the very existence of every precept the obligation to have knowl-edge of it, since, in a moral sense, it could not otherwise be observed. So St. Thomas has rightly maintained ([I.–II, qu. 100,] art. 9), asserting that he who ignorantly performs an act which is prescribed by law, performs the prescribed deed by chance, and incidentally; whereas the precept imposes the obligation of observance for the precept's sake and intentionally, as has already been shown; therefore, it imposes the obligation of knowing, and furthermore, of reflecting upon it.

11. *The third proposition: the natural law imposes an obligation as to the mode of practising virtue.* In the third place, I hold that the natural law also imposes an obligation as to the mode of practising virtue.

In order that this proposition may be understood, we must explain what we mean by the phrase, 'the mode of practising virtue'. For under that phrase we include everything required in order that an act may be righteous and good in an absolute and moral sense; and for this it is nec-essary that the act in question shall be directed to a good object, not only materially, but also formally—that is to say, it shall be inspired by a righteous motive. This was the meaning of Aristotle (*Nicomachean Ethics,* Bk. II, chap. iv), when he said that, in order that a virtuous work may be performed with [all due] care, it is not sufficient that the acts involved shall themselves be just or temperate; for it is furthermore required 'that the agent shall perform them while he is in the following state of mind: first, he shall act knowingly; secondly, he shall act by deliberate choice and for the sake of those acts themselves; thirdly, he shall act with a firm and unchangeable spirit'.

Of these three conditions, the second is that which is pertinent to the matter in hand; for within it, Aristotle would seem to have included our first proposition, as well as the third, which we have just laid down. Accordingly, some authors subdivide that [second] condition into two parts, as follows: first, one must act voluntarily, for this is acting from choice; secondly, one must act for righteousness' sake. Although Soto (*De Iustitia,* Bk. II, qu. iii, art. 9) rejects this subdivision, for the reason that Aristotle treats of the condition in question as a single unit, nevertheless, the doctrine itself is true; and it will be profitable to distinguish between those [two] parts, in this discussion, for the purpose of explaining the binding force of the natural law.

Thus, to act by deliberate choice pertains to our first proposition; to perform acts 'for the sake of those acts themselves',[17] that is, for righteousness' sake, pertains to the third proposition. Under the head of righteousness, moreover, I would include all that is necessary in order that an act may be characterized by every condition required for righteousness in an absolute sense; since no one acts with intent toward righteousness unless he does so under the proper attendant circumstances.

The phrase 'mode of practising virtue' thus includes all the points mentioned above; so that we hold it to be included under natural law.

12. The conclusion just set forth, then, is taken from the above-cited passage of St. Thomas [I.–II, qu. 100, art. 9], who has thus distinguished between the natural and the positive law, a distinction which cannot be understood in any other way. Accordingly, he holds, not only that the natural law binds one to act voluntarily, but also that it binds one to act thus voluntarily for the reason already set forth, that is, for righteousness' sake, in which [form of action] the mode of practising virtue is comprehended. Soto, on that passage (*ibid.,* answer to third objection), clearly upholds the same doctrine, expounding in this wise the teaching of St. Thomas.

Nevertheless, there are certain authorities who do not accept that distinction, but rather maintain, in an absolute sense, that the mode of practising virtue is not included within the obligation imposed by the natural law. This would seem to be the opinion held by Joannes Medina (*Codex*

---

17. [Reading *ipsa* for *ipsam* to correspond with the preceding quotation from Aristotle, although Suárez may have intended here, not a quotation, but a paraphrase influenced by the following *honestatem.*—Tr.]

de Oratione, Qu. 16; *De Horis Canonicis Iterandis*); and Navarrus (Tr. *De Horis Canonicis et Oratione,* Chap. xx, no. 29), and on *Decretum* II. xi. iii. 55 [, conclusio v, no. 72] and in *Summa,* Chap. xxi, no. 7). For one who pays a debt obeys the natural precept regarding payment, even if he performs this act in an improper way; and one who gives an alms obeys the natural precept of compassion, even if he is actuated by vainglory.

13. *A reconciliation of the two opinions.* However, these [conflicting views] may be reconciled in a few words, as follows. Although a particular precept of the natural law may be observed by means of an act which is good in itself but which is, as a matter of fact, performed in an evil way, the natural law as a whole may not be thus observed; and in this respect, it differs from human law. For human law may be observed by means of an evil act, in such a way that no part of it is violated, since the evil attaching to the act in question is often opposed, not to any human precept, but to a natural precept. This is clearly the case, when, for example, a person receives communion unworthily at the Easter season, an act which is in no way contrary to ecclesiastical law since the precept which it violates, namely, that of receiving communion worthily when one does receive it, is not a human but a natural precept, and the latter [form of law] alone is violated under these circumstances.[18] But the same natural law which prescribes the doing of a righteous act, prescribes also that this act shall be done with [all due] care, for such a specification is itself a dictate of the natural reason and consequently a part of the natural law; therefore, whenever a particular natural precept is fulfilled by means of an evil act, the law of nature itself is violated.

14. *Doubt.* It may be asked, however, whether this twofold, or virtually twofold, obligation springs from one and the same natural precept, or from different precepts. In connexion with this question, we may avail ourselves of a distinction which we may assume to be valid.

For sometimes the circumstance of evil annexed to [a given act] is opposed to a virtue of a different sort [from that involved in the act]; as in the example cited, regarding a vainglorious intent attached to an act of compassion, that

---

18. [In the present law of the Church, canon 861 of the *Codex Iuris Canonici* rules that a sacrilegious communion does not fulfil the paschal precept.—REVISER.]

is, of almsgiving, the evil in this case being opposed to humility, and not to compassion itself. Under these circumstances, then, there is a twofold obligation springing from diverse precepts; accordingly, in such a case, it must be affirmed that one natural precept is completely observed by means of an act which is good in itself, but which is performed in an evil way; and nevertheless, the natural law [itself] is not completely and absolutely observed, since [in this observance of one natural precept] another is violated.

Sometimes, on the other hand, it may happen that the evil involved in a given act is contrary to the very virtue enjoined by the precept apparently observed in the substance of that act; as when a person prays with recollection, but in an unsuitable place, or under other circumstances opposed to the reverence due to God in prayer. In such cases, it may be truly said that one and the same precept is obeyed with respect to its substance, and violated with respect to the attendant circumstances. For, even though a virtuous act necessarily involves both an [external] object and intrinsic circumstances, nevertheless, it must not be thought, in consequence, that this act is regulated by a number of distinct precepts, referring [respectively] to its object and to the individual circumstances connected with it. On the contrary, a single natural precept is laid down, prescribing an act of a specific righteous character, such as to require specific accompanying circumstances; and accordingly, this same precept can be observed in so far as relates to the substance of the external act while it is violated with respect to the other circumstances involved.

CHAPTER XI

Does the Natural Law Impose as an Obligatory Mode of Action That Mode Which Springs from the [Natural] Love of God, or from Charity?

1. St. Thomas treats (I.–II, qu. 100, art. 10), in this connexion, of the question above set forth. However, that question involves many points which relate to other matters, especially matters of faith, charity, and grace; and [in the passage cited] it is dependent upon St. Thomas's previous remarks (*ibid.* qu. 18) concerning the requisites for moral goodness in a human

action. Consequently, that question might well be disregarded, at this point; and yet, in view of the fact that it is complementary to our subject-matter, and inasmuch as it includes some remarks necessary for the explanation of the force of the natural law, we shall deal with it briefly here, postponing for treatment in the proper passages, in so far as is possible, those points which are foreign to the matter in hand.

It is necessary to assume, indeed, that one may speak either of the natural love of God or of an infused charity;[1] for in our title we have suggested that by the term 'charity' infused charity is to be understood, but that the term 'love' refers to the natural love of God, viewed as the end of nature. Accordingly, it is also possible to speak relatively of the natural law; to speak, that is, either of the purely natural law that accompanies pure nature in so far as the latter is illuminated solely by natural reason, or else of the law that is connatural with grace and with the light of faith, which we may call divine by antonomasia.

2. Therefore, when we speak of the love of God as the Author of nature, we assume, in the first place, that there may exist in human nature such love, even above all things, and essentially distinct from a love that is infused, although it may be impossible that [this natural love] should be perfectly possessed without the aid of grace. In our treatise *De Gratia*[2] we shall touch upon this point, showing by what powers this love can be elicited; and, in our discussion on charity,[3] the distinction in question will be more fully expounded.

We assume, secondly, that the natural law contains a special precept enjoining the love of God, as the Author of nature, an assumption which will also be proved in our discussion of charity.

The assertion is made that the natural law obliges man, viewed simply with respect to his nature, to order himself and all his [works] towards God

---

1. 'Infused charity': love of God considered as a supernatural virtue that has to be given to us by God, being infused by divine grace. The supernatural virtues of faith, hope, and charity all have to be infused by God because they are beyond our own unaided ability to acquire. Charity contrasts with a natural love of God, as enjoined by natural law and acquired by us through the exercise of our own powers of reason.

2. [Not included in these *Selections*.—Tr.]

3. [Only Disp. XIII of Suárez's *De Charitate* is included in these *Selections*.—Tr.]

[as his final end]. Thirdly, it follows upon this assertion, that the natural law, taken as a whole, obliges man, viewed in the light of pure nature, to refer himself and all his [works] to God as his final end; for thus to refer oneself and one's [works] is involved in a love of God above all things. However, since this precept is in affirmative form, it is binding not continuously, but only at suitable times; and therefore, that love is not necessary in order that other precepts may be fulfilled completely and without the transgression of some natural precept. For at times there may occur a fit occasion for the honouring of one's parents which is not an occasion calling for the love of God; and under such circumstances, I may fulfil the precept of filial piety, even though—in so far as concerns the part of the active agent—such fulfilment may be in no wise motivated by the love of God.

Every work whereby a natural precept is fulfilled tends of its own nature to God as its final end. Fourthly, however, we must add that every work whereby a natural precept is fulfilled tends of its own nature towards God as its final end, and in itself contributes to His glory. For every such work issues from God as its chief and primary source; moreover, through it the will of God is in actual fact fulfilled, even if the agent does not formally work to this end; and again, it is a righteous work, and one suited to the final natural end of man, which is, primarily, God.

3. *A solution of the question: in what sense one should understand the assertion that the love of God is an obligation of the natural law.* The foregoing, then, provides a sufficiently clear solution for the question of the extent to which this obligation may be derived from the pure law of nature and from the pure love of God as the Author of nature, a love which is in harmony with natural reason. For, in this order, the mode of acting from the love of God consists simply in the activity of that love itself, or of something else, under the command of that love.

The former kind of action will be required only on occasions when the precept [enjoining it] is in active force; and consequently, by reason of that same precept, this mode of love is essential in order that the natural law as a whole and collectively may be fulfilled, although it is not essential to the fulfilment of individual moral precepts, since the latter do not all impose, as an obligation, the love of God.

The second kind of action, if the command in question is assumed to be formal, is manifestly not required; for no particular precept is laid down regarding this point, nor do the other individual precepts impose this obligation. The truth of the foregoing is self-evident, since, if it were not true, right action would always be joined of necessity to an actual love of God, and to assert that such is the case would be absurd. If, on the other hand, we refer [merely] to a virtual command [of love], that is, to a relationship with some previous action of the agent himself, even this mode of action is not required for the observance of other precepts. For, in the first place, this act of love may not have taken place previously, yet an occasion may be offered for some good act in accordance with another natural precept; and, in the second place, even if such an act of love did occur previously, it may exercise no influence here and now, inasmuch as there is no recollection thereof nor any virtue from it that persists.[4]

I shall add, moreover, that not even the habitual disposition of such love is required, for he who is in a state of mortal sin is not considered to possess that habitual disposition, and nevertheless he may observe some natural precept. Therefore, it is sufficient that there should exist the natural relation or tendency which is included in the righteous action itself, by its very nature, as has been explained.

4. *The opinion of Gregory that nothing created is rightfully lovable for its own sake, and that God alone is thus lovable.* In this connexion there is wont to arise a dispute regarding the view of Gregory of Rimini, who has said (on the *Sentences,* Bk. II, dist. xxxix, qu. i, art. 1, concl. 2) that nothing created is rightfully lovable for its own sake, and that God alone is thus lovable; whence he infers (in art. 2, corols. 1 and 2) that it is not possible for men to act righteously unless they act for the love of God, to Whom they refer their deed, either actually or virtually—that is, by the force of some previous act of love. He finds proof for his statement in various passages of Augustine (*On Christian Doctrine,* Bk. I, chaps. xxvii and xxxvii; *De Trinitate,* Bk. IX, chap. viii and *De Diversis Quaestionibus, LXXXIII,* Qu. xxx) wherein he says that it is perverse to enjoy any created thing

---

4. [In this passage Suárez states that a morally good act need not be based on either the actual or the virtual love of God.—REVISER.]

beyond[5] God. Wherefore, he asserts, in another work (*On the Customs of the Catholic Church,* Bk. I, chap. xiv), that all good things must be referred to the highest good, a fact from which he infers (*ibid.,* chap. xv) that virtue is nothing other than the highest love of God; so that he defines all of the virtues (*On the City of God,* Bk. XIX, chap. xxv) in accordance with this love, asserting in consequence that it is pride to love even these virtues themselves for their own sake. The reason for this view, indeed, is that God alone is supremely good, and that therefore He alone is to be desired for His Own sake. And furthermore, if the view in question were not correct, any good created thing could be loved for its own sake.

5. However, this discussion is not appropriate to the present context; for it pertains to a matter dealt with by St. Thomas in a passage (I.–II, qu. 18) where he treats of the requisites for moral rectitude in a human action. In discussing the subject of faith, too, it is also customary to deal with this question owing to the case of unbelievers who have no knowledge of God.

The opinion of Gregory is rejected. Briefly, I hold that the opinion of Gregory, above set forth (p. 277), is probably not sound nor based upon any sound foundation. For a thing that is morally good is lovable for its own sake, and suffices to render this act [of love] moral, even if one's thought is not of God [on the occasion in question] and was not previously directed to Him in such a way that a past act of loving God has a certain present influence upon the [present] act [of love for the created thing]. Moreover, it is one thing to love something as being the supreme good; but it is different to love a thing as being a good which is in itself lovable. The first kind of love pertains strictly to God; but the second is imparted by God Himself to every morally good thing; and therefore, in so loving that which is morally good, one commits no offence against God. Neither does the foregoing lead to the conclusion that all good created things are lovable for their own sake, because there are no goods of this inferior [created] order, either useful or enjoyable, which are to be desired

---

5. [Reading *praeter* for the *praepter* found in our Latin text. The 1619 and 1856 editions have *propter,* but *praeter* would seem to make Augustine's argument clearer. St. Augustine's words are: *Neque enim ad aliquid aliud Deus referendus est. Quoniam omne quod ad aliud referendum est, inferius est quam id ad quod referendum est* (*De Diversis Quaestionibus,* Migne ed., Vol. xl, col. 20).—REVISER.]

only for their goodness. Finally, although a created thing which is morally good may be loved for itself, it is not loved as an ultimate end. On the contrary, the love in question tends of its own nature, towards God; and this fact suffices to prevent the assertion that man enjoys rather than uses such good.[6] He might, indeed, be said to enjoy such [a lesser good], if he should set it up as his ultimate end; and it was to this latter action that Augustine referred, calling it pride. Therefore, the authority of Augustine does not stand in our way, nor does the argument of Gregory have weight; and consequently, the opinion of Gregory is commonly rejected by the theologians in their treatises on faith, as we shall see—God willing—in the proper place. One may also consult Soto (*De Iustitia*, Bk. II, qu. iii, art. 10) and [Joannes] Medina (*Codex de Oratione*, Qu. 16, and [Bartholmaeus Medina] on I.–II, qu. 18, art. 9).

6. *The mode of action that springs from infused charity is not required for the observance of the natural law.* Secondly, there remains for discussion the mode of action that springs from infused charity.[7] With respect to this point, it is certain that such a mode is not necessarily required for the fulfilment of the purely natural law, since it is [a virtue] of a much higher order. But there may be a doubt as to whether or not, assuming the elevation of man to a supernatural end, this circumstance is required even for the fulfilment without sin of the natural law. For such seems to have been the meaning of those writers who have said that man is not, at any given time, fulfilling any divine precept whatsoever, unless he is in some sense acting from charity. *The opinion of Denys, the Carthusian, and a criticism of that opinion.* This opinion was held by Denys, the Carthusian (on the *Sentences,* Bk. I, dist. xvii, qu. 1, art. 3), and the same view was supported, a few years ago, by Michael Baius,[8] who declared [cf. *De Charitate, Iustitia, et Iustificatione,* Bk. I, chap. vi] that every action which does not spring from charity comes from a corrupt concupiscence and is therefore evil.

---

6. 'To enjoy' or *frui* is contrasted with 'to use' or *uti.* The first is to love and possess something as an ultimate end, and God is the only proper object of such *fruitio;* the second is to love and possess something by reference to some further end. For the distinction see book one of Augustine's *De Doctrina Christiana.*

7. [*Vide* the second paragraph of the first section of this Chapter, *supra,* p. 275.—Tr.]

8. [*For* Caius *read* Baius.—Tr.]

7. Nevertheless, such an opinion is entirely false and erroneous, or, at least, it affords great occasion for error. In order to demonstrate this proposition, however, we must take it up point by point.

For the opinion in question may first be interpreted as referring to a habit of charity or, what is the same thing, to a state of grace; and in this sense it is erroneous, and was virtually condemned in the case of the Lutherans, at the Council of Trent (Session VI, canon vii).[9] For, according to this opinion, all works done outside the state of grace would be contrary to the divine precept, and therefore would be sins; a conclusion from which it would follow that all works by which a sinner remotely disposes himself for grace are sinful. This consequent has been condemned in the Council above mentioned, and justly so, since the sacred Scriptures very frequently counsel works of this kind, such as holy fear, almsgiving, prayer and the like.

However, Baius would perhaps reply that habitual charity is required for the avoidance of sinning, but that it is not sufficient to one's attainment of remission of sin; for habitual justness may be attained without [consequent] remission of sin. This reply, however, involves another error, namely, that it is possible for true justness and charity to exist *de facto* in a man while he is in a state of sin; a proposition which is contrary to that same Council in the same Session VI (canon vii). Nor does such a reply dispose of the definition cited above, since in that definition the Council referred to works preceding justification, which involves not merely the remission of sin, but chiefly the infusion of justness, as is evident from the teaching of the same Council. And furthermore, remote dispositions[10] are directed not only to the remission of sin, but also to an infusion of justness, and therefore, it is impossible that such works should be evil or against the law of God.

8. Finally, there is this clear argument: that the necessity of habitual grace or charity in order that individual precepts may be observed without

---

9. The canon reads: 'If anyone says that all works done prior to justification, for whatever reason they are done, are in truth sins or deserving of the hatred of God; or that the more fervently one strives to dispose oneself for grace, the more gravely one sins, let him be anathema.'

10. [I.e. preliminary acts by which one prepares for justification.—Tr.]

fresh transgression, springs neither from the purely natural law, as has been shown,[11] nor from that law which is connatural with habitual grace itself or charity; for there is no necessary connexion between such habits and the particular obligation [to observe those individual precepts], nor can it be proved that there is such connexion, on the basis of any principle of probable validity. Neither does [the necessity in question] spring from any special positive law of God, since it is nowhere found that such a law has been established, a point which we shall presently demonstrate, in replying to the objections.

Accordingly, all theologians require for certain acts which are especially holy an habitual sanctity in the person performing them, that they may be performed worthily and without sin; as, for example, in the administering of the sacraments of the living. The same state of habitual sanctity may be required on the occasion of a deed involving imminent danger of death, or because of some similar occasion; although this requirement is a special one, emanating from the law of charity or of religion. But a general requirement of habitual sanctity applying to all acts cannot be founded upon any law, nor conceived by any plausible reasoning.

9. *Another interpretation of the question.* Secondly, the opinion under discussion[12] may be understood as referring to an actual love of charity; so that, for the observance of any precept whatsoever of the natural law, it may be necessary that one shall order himself toward God, through a supernatural love that is the personal act of the agent, or an act coexistent with the deed through which the [natural] precept is observed, or one which shall have preceded that observance and shall virtually influence it.

However, this interpretation also may easily be refuted, on the basis of the principles already laid down. For it must be taken as referring, either to a love of God above all things, or else to another, imperfect and merely affective love, which is supernatural and through which the observance of any precept may be directed toward God.

If the former of these alternatives be maintained, one is led into the difficulty already mentioned, and a new one is added. For the act of loving

---

11. [*Supra,* this Chapter.—Tr.]

12. [I.e. the opinion of Denys, the Carthusian, and Michael Baius; *vide* Section 6, *supra,* pp. 279–80, and the opening sentences of Section 7.—Tr.]

God above all things is not separate from the habit of thus loving Him (whether the act proceeds from the habit or proximately prepares [the soul] for it, alternatives which have no bearing upon the point under discussion); and therefore, if this love is necessary, either as existent in the act or as having preceded it and not having been withdrawn (for the latter condition is required in order that [the love] may exert a virtual influence), then the state [of the agent] will necessarily consist also in a state of grace and of charity; but [the suggestion of such a requirement] has been rejected. Furthermore, there would also be demanded an act of perfect charity, influencing the prescribed action; and this supposition is a new absurdity. For, just as we are prepared for the attainment of a state of habitual justness by means of good works which precede that state of justness, in so far as these works may be brought about by the Holy Spirit disposing us thereto, but not indwelling within us, according to the Council of Trent (Session XIV, chap. iv), even so are we made ready to obtain the aid and receive the impulse [of grace], through which, proximately, we are prepared for that state of justness and for the love of God above all things. Therefore, it is no less absurd to lay down as a prerequisite to individual acts observing moral precepts, the infused act of the love of God above all things, than it is to lay down as a prerequisite the habitual state of such love. Moreover, the arguments which we have adduced in opposition to the opinion of Gregory apply in due proportion when opposed to the opinion now under discussion; a point which I shall now expound in connexion with the other part of our discussion.

10. If there is demanded, accordingly, not a love above all things, but another and lesser love, which will be sufficient in order to refer a given act to God as its supernatural end; then, in the first place, it is difficult to distinguish such an affection—one which partakes of a supernatural complacency in, or good will towards God, and which is apt to be elicited by infused charity—[it is difficult, I say, to distinguish such an affection] from the love [of God] above all things and the love that justifies. For the present, however, I shall postpone this question to another and more fitting place, and shall demonstrate, following the appropriate line of argument, that the opinion under discussion is false and arbitrary, even in the sense just set forth. For such an obligation does not proceed by the very

nature of the case from the principles and light of faith; nor, on the other hand, can it be shown that God has laid down for men as ordained for a supernatural end, any special command always to discharge or to observe the precepts of the natural law, out of this sort of love or this reference of one's acts [towards Him]. In opposition to the assumption [that this obligation exists], one may apply, in due proportion, all the arguments that we have used in opposing the opinion of Gregory.

And furthermore, such reference [of one's acts to God], or such love, is not necessary in a general sense and *per se* even to the observance of other supernatural precepts. For the precept of faith is fulfilled by the act of believing, prior to any act of true love of God; one may make a similar statement regarding the precept of hope, as is to be inferred from the teaching of the Council of Trent (Session VI, chap. vii); and the precept enjoined by religion concerning divine worship or that concerning prayer may be observed in the same fashion.

One may go farther and say that, although a state of grace is required in the case of some external acts, as I have just pointed out, on account of their special sanctity, nevertheless, even for such acts, this special love, whether actual or virtual, is not necessary, provided the agent is assumed to be in a state of grace; on the contrary, a religious intention, one that regards the virtue of religion, is sufficient. And similarly, if an occasion should arise either for professing the faith or for witnessing to the honour of God, this may be done from an impulse towards the faith and the confession of it, or from an impulse towards divine worship and the honouring [of God], involved in religion, even if it is not done by a formal act of charity. In no wise, then, is the mode of acting out of charity a requirement for the observance of other precepts, apart from the special precept of charity, which is binding not uninterruptedly but only at certain times and on certain occasions, as will be pointed out when we deal with that special matter.

11. *Objection.* But an objection may be raised, first, on the basis of several passages from Paul (*1 Corinthians,* Chap. x [, v. 31]): 'Do all to the glory of God'; (*Colossians,* Chap. iii [, v. 17]): 'All whatsoever you do in word or in work do all in the name of the Lord Jesus Christ, giving thanks to God and the Father by Him'; and (*1 Corinthians,* Chap. xvi [, v. 14]): 'Let all your things be done in charity.'

Secondly, various passages from the works of Augustine are cited by way of objection, passages in which he declares that any act performed not from charity is performed from a corrupt concupiscence, and is therefore evil. Accordingly, he says (*Retractationes,* Bk. I, chap. xv): 'Will without charity is wholly a corrupt concupiscence.'[13] And again (*De Gratia et Libero Arbitrio,* Chap. xviii): 'What is done without love is not well done.'[14] He also has numerous similar passages (*De Gratia Christi et de Peccato Originali,* Bk. I, Chap. xxvi).

Thirdly, Dionysius argues that God, in His precepts, seeks to make us lovers of Himself; hence, if those precepts are not observed from a love of God, His will is not done; and therefore, the precepts are not fulfilled.

12. *Solution of the objection.* My reply to the passages from Holy Scripture, cited as testimony, is, first, that they contain the best of counsels; secondly, they may contain a precept which is to be interpreted in one of two ways.

One interpretation is that all our works, in so far as their essential character is concerned, should be such that they tend to the glory of God, even if they are not actually related to this end. [Such an interpretation] accords with the words of Christ (*Matthew,* Chap. v [, v. 16]): 'So let your light shine before men, that they may see your good works and glorify your Father who is in heaven.' For the meaning of these words is not that it is necessary to perform the works with the [specific] purpose of having them seen by others who will glorify God, since such a purpose, even if it is good in itself, is nevertheless not required, nor is it ordinarily advisable, because of the peril [of vainglory which it involves]. The meaning, then, is that these works should be of such nature that, if they are seen, the glory of God may result from them.

According to the other mode [of interpreting the testimony of the Scriptures], that testimony may be understood to contain an affirmative precept that is always binding, but not uninterruptedly save with respect to the preparation of the soul; that is, with respect to our state of readiness to do all things for the glory of God, whether from charity or as a confession of the name of Christ, when such acts are necessary or becoming.

---

13. [Suárez quotes Augustine in substance.—Tʀ.]

14. [The words of St. Augustine are: *Si fiat sine charitate nullo modo fiat bene,* Migne ed., Vol. xliv, col. 903.—Rᴇᴠɪsᴇʀ.]

13. *Explanation of the passages from Augustine.* To the passages containing the testimony of Augustine we shall reply specifically and in the proper places, in *De Fide* and *De Charitate;*[15] for the works of Augustine contain difficult passages on both these virtues.

For the present, I will say that the words of Augustine may be expounded in the same way as those of Scripture; so that the expression to act from charity does not signify 'to be evoked or commanded by charity', but rather, 'to act in accord with it', so that the act in question is such that by charity it may be directed and performed, charity thus being always and inherently a rule (so to speak) of a good deed, although not necessarily a [moving] principle as well, nor an end [specifically] sought by the agent. Accordingly, when [Augustine, *De Gratia et Libero Arbitrio,* Chap. xviii] says that, 'An act is not well done that is done without love', it is just as if he said, 'not done in accord with love', or 'done [in a spirit] alien to love'. When, indeed, he says [*Retractationes,* Bk. I, Chap. xv][16] that will without charity is wholly a corrupt concupiscence, this statement also may be explained as referring to the will in itself, and not to its individual acts; and the whole will may be termed a corrupt concupiscence in a moral, but not in a rigorously physical sense, for a will destitute of charity is regularly overcome by corrupt concupiscence, although at times it may act from a love of righteousness, without any relation to charity, as we shall show at greater length in the treatise *De Gratia.*[17]

Some persons, to be sure, also explain that, in the passages cited (*De Gratia et Libero Arbitrio,* Chap. xviii, *De Gratia Christi et de Peccato Originali,* Chap. xxvi), Augustine means by the word 'charity', not the infused theological virtue, but a general love of moral good, that is, of right conduct for the sake of justness itself. Nevertheless, in the Chapters cited, he clearly

---

15. [Only Disp. XVIII of the Tractate *De Fide* (*infra,* p. 837) and Disp. XIII of *De Charitate* (*infra,* p. 910) are included in these *Selections.*—Tr.]

16. [St. Augustine there says: *Quod si quisquam dicit, etiam ipsam cupiditatem nihil aliud esse quam voluntatem, sed vitiosam peccatoque servientem; non resistendum est, nec de verbis, cum res constet, controversia facienda.* (And if any one should say that even concupiscence itself is nothing more nor less than will—a will, however, that is vicious and the servant of sin—that statement should not be combated; nor should a controversy be raised as to terms, when the facts of the matter are clear.)—Reviser.]

17. [Not included in these *Selections.*—Tr.]

speaks of the charity which is referred to in the precept of Christ (*John,* Chap. xiii [, v. 34]): 'A new Commandment I give unto you; that you love one another'; and in that other precept (*Deuteronomy,* Chap. vi [, v. 5], *Mark,* Chap. xii [, vv. 30–1]): 'Thou shalt love the Lord thy God with all thy heart [. . .] and thy neighbour as thyself.' [Augustine] is also speaking of the charity concerning which Peter said (*1 Peter,* Chap. iv [, v. 8]), that it 'covereth a multitude of sins'; and to which John referred [*1 John,* Chap. iv, v. 7] in the words: '[Dearly beloved,] let us love one another: for charity is of God.' For Augustine cites these passages in the context under discussion, in order to explain what sort of charity it is to which he refers. As yet, I have not found the other passage from the *Retractationes.* But let this suffice us, as far as the discussion of Augustine is concerned.

14. To the argument from reason one may reply, in agreement with St. Thomas, whom Soto and others follow, that the purpose sought in a precept is not itself enjoined by the precept. Accordingly, although God purposes pre-eminently, that we shall act from charity, He nevertheless does not impose this command with respect to all actions, neither does He impose it by virtue of [every] individual precept, but only by the special precept of charity, which is to be observed on the proper occasions. Save for this special necessity, then, not only the natural law, but also the supernatural law, may be observed without following the mode in question. For thus the Christian sinner by the act of belief fulfils the law of faith, even though he does not believe from the motive of charity, and attains the end proximately sought by God in that precept; for this proximate end is contained within the precept [of faith] itself; although the extrinsic and remote end may not be attained. The same is true of the other precepts also.

CHAPTER XII

Does the Natural Law Not Only Forbid Certain Acts, but Also Invalidate Contrary Acts?

1. In discussing the binding force of natural law, we have in consequence dealt with almost all the effects which are usually assigned to law in general. For it is evident from what has already been said, that this law prescribes certain good actions and prohibits evil ones, but that permission

and punishment, properly speaking, have no place therein. The reason for this is that a violation of the natural law results in a desert of punishment, in relation to divine providence and justice, to which pertains the assignment of that penalty; nevertheless, natural reason cannot define this punishment, and therefore, such and so great a penalty does not, strictly speaking, result from the authority of some merely natural law; but rather, the said desert of punishment follows from a natural and intrinsic condition of guilt, so that, even if the penalty were not fixed by any specific law, the guilt could be punished by the decision of the competent judge.

Permission has no place in the natural law. Whence it follows that true permission has no place in this law, since it permits nothing which is evil in itself to be done licitly, a self-evident fact, inasmuch as the law in question is opposed to actions that are intrinsically and *per se* evil. It also follows that this natural law does not permit intrinsically evil actions to be done with impunity, in so far as punishment can result from the said law, that is to say, in so far as relates to a state of liability to punishment; since it never impedes, nor can of itself impede, such a state. For if it is said that this law permits either those indifferent actions which it does not prohibit, or those good actions of which it approves, although without prescribing them, it may be answered that neither attitude is equivalent to true legal permission, so to speak. For the former is simple negation, inasmuch as an action is spoken of as indifferent which is neither prescribed nor forbidden, nor yet approved; while the latter attitude is more than a permission, since it is a kind of positive concession, a matter which has been touched upon above and which will be more fully discussed later,[1] when we treat of the *ius gentium*. And with respect to these points, if the natural law is considered in so far as it establishes the manner in which [a given action] must be executed in order that it may be done righteously and blamelessly, then the question is one which pertains to law as prescribing a given manner and forbidding another, a matter also touched upon above; so that, with regard to these effects [of the law], nothing more need be said.

2. The only question remaining for discussion, then, is this: When and in what way may the natural law have not only obligatory or prohibitory force, but also the force which invalidates an act done in contravention of

1. [*Infra*, p. 374; chapter xvii.—Tr.]

such obligation? This doubt is especially pertinent with respect to negative precepts, but it may be extended to apply to affirmative precepts, in so far as the latter logically prohibit acts contrary to those which they prescribe.

The reason for this difficulty. The reason for the doubt, indeed, is that to invalidate is not to prescribe, but [actually] to do something [beyond that]; whereas the natural law, as such, apparently has power solely to give commands, and not to abolish the power of ownership, for example, or to do anything similar. This point may be confirmed by induction. For the natural law forbids the contracting of marriage after the taking of a vow of chastity, or after betrothment to another person; and nevertheless, such a marriage is valid. The natural law also forbids the selling of anything for more than a just price; and yet such a sale is not rendered void by the law of nature. Therefore, the same will hold true of all similar cases. For the efficacy of the natural law is the same in all cases; nor does it employ any special language for prohibiting, such that, on account of this diversity in wording, we might say that it does invalidate at times, but not always, a statement which may be made with regard to positive law.

3. *Actions opposed to the natural law are not only perverse, but sometimes invalid.* Nevertheless, it is certain that, at times, acts committed in opposition to the natural law are not only evil, but also invalid. The writers on the subject assume this to be certain in many of the questions which they discuss specifically; such questions as whether or not these acts—for example, a contract effected under the influence of fear, violence, fraud, or some similar condition—are nullified by the natural law or only by the positive law. They assume, then, that such contracts may be null under both heads. Furthermore, this position is confirmed by the following examples. A second marriage made during the lifetime of a former spouse is null by the natural law. The same is true of a marriage, let us say, between brother and sister; and still more certainly true in the case of a marriage between father and daughter. So also a usurious contract is invalid by the natural law, that is, it is null in so far as any obligation to pay usurious interest is concerned. The same conclusion holds with respect to a contract made by means of a grave fraud. And there are many similar examples.

In order, however, that we may establish a rational basis [for all of them] and may satisfy the foregoing objections, it is necessary to assign some rule for determining when an action prohibited by the natural law is valid, and when it is invalid. For the fact that either situation may occur is demonstrated by the examples already adduced; but the distinction cannot be based upon the words of the natural law itself, as has rightly been objected. Whence, then, shall we derive that distinction?

4. *The rules for ascertaining when acts are invalid by the natural law.* Two rules especially present themselves.

The first rule. The first is as follows: when an act is forbidden by the natural law because of some defect of power, or because of the incapacity of the subject-matter, then, the act is null and void, by its very nature. The example cited in connexion with a second marriage demonstrates this point; as do, in general, the cases in which a gift has been made of a thing which has previously been validly and permanently donated; for such a [second donation] is null, since he who is giving or transferring the thing for the second time has already ceased to have power over it. This consideration will make clear the difference between a transfer effected subsequently to a prior transfer, and one effected simply after a prior promise. For both of these transactions are opposed to the natural law, and nevertheless, one is valid and the other is invalid; since the earlier transfer has extinguished the ownership of the thing transferred, and thus has also extinguished the power over that thing; whereas the promise does not do away with the ownership, and therefore does not do away with the power [of the promisor], although it may place him under an obligation to use the property in the manner agreed upon. According to the same reasoning, a contract or a consent extorted through substantial fraud (as it were) is null by the natural law; since the fraud impedes true consent, and causes it to be involuntary, and since a human contract cannot be perfected without an exercise of the will. The same reasoning applies to other [similar] acts. Thus the rational basis of the [first] rule is easily evident; for, in these and like cases, the substantial principle (so to speak) of the validity of the action is destroyed, this principle being a moral power, that is, a power that has attached to it, a sufficient exercise of the will; and there is no valid act without power and volition.

5. *The second rule.* The second rule is this: when an act is forbidden on account of some unseemliness or turpitude discerned in its subject-matter, then it is also invalid when that same turpitude persists in the effect itself

of the act, or, as the jurists say, when the turpitude has a continuous cause. This rule I take from a similar statement in the Gloss (on the *Constitutions of Clement,* Bk. III, tit. XII, chap. i, word *inhibentes,* at end), from yet another passage in the Gloss (on *Decretum,* Pt. I, dist. X, can. x), from Decio (on *Decretals,* Bk. II, tit. XX, chap. ii), and from other authorities to whom Covarruvias refers (on *Decretum,* Bk. IV, pt. II, can. vi, no. 6, at the beginning); it may also be inferred from the following words of the civil law (*Digest,* XLV. i. 35, § 1): 'That agreement which the laws prohibit ceases to have a binding effect, if the cause of its prohibition is to be perpetual; as, for example, when any person enters into an agreement of marriage with his own sister'. On this passage, the Gloss notes that such a promise is invalid, by the natural law itself. Thus the [second] rule is confirmed by the above-cited example of a marriage between blood relations of the first degree. For in that case there is no lack of power, that is, no lack of dominion over oneself for the purpose of giving oneself in matrimony; nor is there a lack of volition, in so far as the parties to the contract are concerned; but that unseemliness from the standpoint of nature which causes such a marriage to be forbidden, endures perpetually, if the marriage in question endures; therefore, even the duration itself is forbidden, and is thus invalid. The same condition is seen to exist with respect to the example of usury. For usury is forbidden because it is unjust, and this injustice consists in the retention of the profit received, as well as in the act of receiving it, so that the prohibition against usury has an invalidating effect [upon such retention]. From the foregoing, the rational basis [of the second rule] is also evident. For if it is contrary to the natural law to invest a given act with validity, that act may not be performed by any one, since the law of a superior authority stands in the way; and, in the case in question, the very validity of the act is contrary to the natural law, since it is characterized by the same cause of turpitude [as that which characterizes the subject-matter of the act] and, consequently, cannot endure; therefore, the act involved is without valid effect. One may consider accordingly the difference between this [second] rule and the preceding rule. For in the case of the first rule, the act is prohibited, on the ground that it is wrongful and null because of a defect of power; whereas, according to the second rule, the act is null by reason of an intrinsic and perpetual wickedness, and consequently by reason of the very fact that a [natural] prohibition exists, since, apart from these considerations, an absolute power over the subject-matter involved in the act was not lacking.

6. *When an act forbidden by the natural law is nevertheless not rendered null.* Aside from the cases just discussed, however, the natural law, although it may prohibit an act, will not render null the effect of that act; for if one assumes the existence of a power sufficient to produce such an effect, and if, besides, the effect may endure without turpitude and with a righteous use, there is no reason for it to be invalid.

This point is best brought out in the case of a marriage entered into, in contravention of a simple vow of chastity. For that vow has not destroyed, but has enchained the power which a man has over his own body; and, in other respects, a marriage contracted contrary to that vow has, in so far as an actual surrender [of the body] is involved, a greater efficacy (so to speak) than a promise has, and may also have a righteous use, at least in discharging, [though] not in seeking the [conjugal] debt; therefore, such a marriage may rightfully be valid.

In like manner, an unjust sale leaves behind it, to be sure, a perpetual obligation of making restitution for the excess price; yet, if this restitution is made, all turpitude in the validity and perpetuity of that contract disappears; and consequently, there is no reason for the contract to be invalid in an absolute sense. Thus the reply to the objections set forth above is evident. In connexion with these examples, we may also take into consideration the fact that the prohibition is not (as it were) direct or absolute, with respect to the substance of the act in question, but either proceeds from some general law, such as that which enjoins the observance of a vow, or refers solely to a particular mode or excess involved; so that it is not strange that this prohibition does not make the act itself invalid.

CHAPTER XIII

Are the Precepts of the Natural Law Immutable of Themselves and Intrinsically?

1. In the foregoing discussion we have treated of the substance and binding force of the natural law. It remains to speak of the stability, or immutability, of that law.

Change, with respect to any law, indeed, may be conceived of in two ways: namely, as change through addition; or else as change through subtraction, or diminution.

Here, however, we are not speaking of the process of addition; since addition does not constitute a change when the earlier law is left in its entirety, but rather, there takes place a perfecting and extension which contribute to human utility, as St. Thomas has said ([I.–II,] qu. 94, art. 5). And, in like manner, Ulpian (in *Digest,* I. i. 6) says that the civil law is built up by the addition of various [precepts] to the natural law. Furthermore, the divine law, too, has added many [precepts] to the law of nature, as has the canon law to both of these. For, as we shall see below,[1] human laws determine many points which have not been determined by the natural or the divine law, and which were not capable of being suitably determined by them.

The meaning of the question [set forth in the Chapter heading] is weighed; and an explanation is given as to what sort of immutability is under discussion. We are treating, then, of a change in the strict sense, a change brought about by subtraction from a law or from the obligation imposed by it. And this change in things is wont to occur in one of two ways; that is, either as a change in a thing that becomes intrinsically defective, or as one occurring externally through some agent having the necessary power. Either mode is applicable to law, for sometimes a matter[2] becomes itself deficient, for it changes from a useful thing to one that is harmful, or from a rational thing to one that is irrational; whereas, at other times, it is abolished by a superior, as we shall see later, in connexion with positive laws.[3] Both changes, moreover, may occur either absolutely and entirely, with respect to the whole law, such a change being spoken of as the abrogation of a law; or with respect to a particular point, in which case the change is called a dispensation, or special relaxation. Thus, an inquiry might be made into all these

---

1. [*Infra,* p. 374; Chapter xvii.—Tr.]

2. [The Latin text has *res* (a thing) where *lex* (a law) might well be expected. Very possibly *res* is used by confusion with the immediately preceding *rebus* and *rei.* However, even though the rather vague *res* be accepted as the correct reading, the argument will be materially the same as if the emendation were made.—Tr.]

3. [*Infra,* p. 374; Chapter xvii.—Tr.]

modes of change, in connexion with the natural law; but in this Chapter we shall speak only of intrinsic changes, while in the following Chapters we shall investigate the question of those effected by external agents.

2. *Solution. The natural law cannot of itself lapse or suffer change, whether in its entirety, or in its individual precepts.* I maintain, then, that properly speaking the natural law cannot of itself lapse or suffer change, whether in its entirety, or in its individual precepts, so long as rational nature endures together with the use of reason and freedom [of will]. For this latter hypothesis is always presupposed and assumed to be true; since, if this [rational] nature were wholly abolished, then the natural law—because it is a property (so to speak) of this nature—would also be abolished in so far as its [actual] existence is concerned, and would endure only objectively as an essence, or potentially, in the mind of God, just as would rational nature itself. Indeed, in such a situation, even the eternal law would not have the character of true law, for there would be no creature for whom God might lay down commands. It is necessary, then, to assume the existence of rational nature; accordingly, we shall assert that the natural law cannot lapse or suffer change of itself, whether completely or in part.

This is the inference to be drawn from the works of St. Thomas (I.–II, qu. 94, arts. 4 and 5, and qu. 100, art. 8; II.–II, qu. 66, art. 2, ad 1, and qu. 104, art. 4, ad 2), of Vincent de Beauvais (*Speculum Morale,* Bk. I, pt. ii, dist. 3 [dist. 2]), and of other authorities to whom I shall refer in Chapters xiv and xv. The same inference may be drawn from the works of Augustine (*De Diversis Quaestionibus LXXXIII,* Qu. liii; *On the True Religion,* Chap. xxxi, and *On Free Will,* Bk. I, chap. vi); Lactantius ([*Divine Institutes,*] Bk. VI: *De Vero Cultu,* chap. viii); Aristotle (*Nicomachean Ethics,* Bk. V, chap. vii); Cicero (*Laws,* Bks. I and II; *The Republic,* Bk. III), as well as from the *Institutes* (I. ii, § 6 [§ 11]).

The first proof of this view, indeed, is the fact that the natural law may be considered as existing either in God or in man. And as it exists in man, it cannot suffer change, since it is an intrinsic property which flows of necessity from that [human] nature as such or (as some persons maintain) this natural law is the rational nature itself; and, therefore, a contradiction would be involved, if that nature should remain fitted for the use of reason while the natural law itself was abolished. If, on the other hand, the law in question is considered as it exists in God, then, as has been demon-strated above,[4] it is impossible not only for the said law to be abolished by a judgment of the divine intellect, but also for it to be abolished by that will, whereby He wills either to prescribe certain good things, or to avert[5] certain evil things.

3. Secondly, I argue as follows: no law can lapse of itself save through revocation by the lawgiver; unless it does so either because it was not of a permanent nature, being constituted rather for a definite period of time with the expiration of which the law itself also expires and wholly ceases to be, or else because some change occurs in the subject-matter, by reason of which change the law is now unreasonable and unjust although formerly it was just and wise. For if the law was set up for an indefinite period, without any limit, and if no change has been made with regard to its subject-matter, one cannot conceive how it should cease to have force while its object and subject persist, inasmuch as it is not abolished by the legislator, according to the assumption which we have made. Yet, neither of those modes [of abrogation][6] apply to the natural law.

This statement is clearly true with respect to the first mode. For the pre-cepts of the natural law are necessary and characterized by eternal truth, since (as I have said above)[7] that law comprises self-evident moral prin-ciples together with all the conclusions—and only those conclusions—which are drawn therefrom by a process of necessary inference, whether proximately or through a series of such inferences. But all of these ele-ments are eternally true, [since] this truth in the principles does not subsist apart from the truth of the conclusions in question, the principles them-selves being necessarily true by their very definition. Therefore, all of the precepts in question are of a perpetual character. And, consequently, they cannot cease to be, solely through lapse of time.

With regard to the second mode [of abrogation], indeed, the truth of our conclusion may easily be demonstrated, by means of the same principle.

---

4. [*Supra*, p. 211, Chapter vi, §§ 6 *et seq.*—Tr.]

5. [Or 'forbid', reading *vetare* for *vitare.*—Reviser.]

6. [I.e. abrogation through change in the object of a law, or abrogation through change in its subject-matter.—Tr.]

7. [*Supra*, p. 232, Chapter vii of this Book, *passim.*—Tr.]

For a judgment which is necessarily inferred from self-evident principles can never be false; and, therefore, it cannot be irrational or unwise. But every judgment derived from the natural law is of such a character that it rests either upon self-evident principles or upon deductions necessarily drawn therefrom; and, therefore, however much things themselves may vary, there can never be a variation in such judgment.

4. Thirdly, another inference may be drawn by distinguishing in this law between affirmative and negative precepts and by showing that neither sort of precept can of itself lapse or cease to be of binding force.

For, in the first place, the negative precepts prohibit things which are in themselves and intrinsically wrong; and, therefore, they are binding for all time, and continuously, both by reason of their form, since negation destroys everything, and by reason of the fact that what is in itself evil should always and everywhere be avoided; hence, according to the same reasoning, these precepts cannot of themselves cease to exist, inasmuch as a thing which is in itself evil cannot cease to be evil.

The affirmative precepts, on the other hand, although they are binding for all time, are not continuously binding. Therefore, this kind of precept, although it is natural, may be binding at one time and not at another, or upon one occasion and not upon another. Yet it does not for this reason suffer change, since such is its nature, and since (so to speak) it was made from the beginning for given occasions or conditions, and not for others; and nevertheless, it retains its proper force for all time, and is binding for all time, though not continuously. Thus, for example, the precept which imposes confession, although it may not be binding for this particular month and is binding for the Lenten season, does not therefore suffer change, but always in its nature remains the same. This proposition may also be stated in broader terms, as follows: the affirmative precepts of the natural law are of binding force only for those occasions upon which the failure to perform the act prescribed would be of itself and intrinsically evil; accordingly, just as that omission cannot fail to be evil, so, in like manner, the obligation imposed by an affirmative precept, and compelling the performance of the action opposed to the omission, cannot of itself lapse or undergo change; and, therefore, such a precept is necessarily always binding with respect to the time to which it refers, and consequently always imposes also a binding obligation not to entertain the contrary purpose, or an obligation to obedience, at least, in the preparation of the spirit.

5. Fourthly, this truth is to be expounded and confirmed by answering the objection which may be urged against it at this point. For Aristotle says (*Ethics,* Bk. V, chap. vii) that natural justice, that is to say, justice which exists by nature, is not as a whole changeable, but that [human rules of such justice] may at times be liable to change.[8] St. Thomas also makes this statement (I.–II, qu. 94, art. 5), saying that the natural law, in so far as relates to its primary principles, is entirely immutable; while with respect to its conclusions for the most part, it is unchanging, yet it does change in certain cases, which are in the minority, owing to particular causes which then occur. St. Thomas [*ibid.,* art. 4] confirms the above view, by means of the example afforded by the natural precept which commands that a deposit shall be returned to the owner when the latter asks for it, a precept which is not binding in cases where the deposit is sought for the purpose of harming the commonwealth. The same argument may be applied in connexion with the natural precept on the keeping of secrets, which is negative and which may nevertheless be violated, if such violation is necessary for the defence of the state or of an innocent person. Likewise, the precept, 'Thou shalt not kill', is a natural one, and nevertheless, it is permissible to kill in self-defence. A more complex example may be noted in the case of the precept which prohibits the contracting of marriage with one's sister or with one's mother; a natural precept which nevertheless, in the event of necessity relating to the propagation of the human species, is not binding. Thus it was not binding, in point of fact, at the beginning of creation, as will become evident from our discussion of matrimony.[9] Finally, St. Thomas confirms this view by reasoning, arguing that speculative and natural science is characterized by more certitude than moral and practical science, while, nevertheless, in physical and natural science, although the universal principles do not fail, the conclusions—even those

8. [Aristotle says: 'Amongst the gods, perhaps, that which is just may be absolutely immutable. Amongst men there is a kind of natural justice, although all human justice is conceivably liable to change.'—REVISER.]

9. [Not included in these *Selections.*—TR.]

that are necessary—at times do fail; therefore, the same may happen in moral matters, and accordingly, the natural law may undergo change. The truth of the consequent is proved by a parity of reasoning; for, just as physical matter is changeable, so also human affairs, which are the matter of the natural law, are much more changeable; and, therefore, that law itself is likewise subject to change since, even as it derives its specific form from its subject-matter, so does it imitate and participate in the very nature of that matter.

6. *In what way the natural law is immutable; and in what way it undergoes change.* However, all these statements, rightly explained, confirm rather than weaken our assertion. We should consider, then, that those things which stand in a certain equivalence and relationship, as it were, [to other things], are in two ways liable to actual change, or to virtual change (that is to say, a cessation of being), as follows: these things may change either intrinsically, in themselves—as when a father ceases to be a father, if he himself dies—or extrinsically, simply through change in another—as when a father ceases to be such, owing to the death of the son. For this cessation on the part of the father is not [actually] change, but is [merely] conceived or spoken of, by us, as being a manner of change. In the positive law, then, change may occur in the former of the two modes, for this law may be abrogated; whereas, with regard to the natural law, that is by no means the case, since, on the contrary, it is liable to change only in the second manner, that is, to change through changing subject-matter; so that a given action is withdrawn from the obligation imposed by the natural law [with respect to it], not because the law is abolished or diminished, since it always is and has been binding in this sense, but because the matter dealt with by the law is changed, as will presently be made clear through the examples adduced.

Wherefore, we should go farther and take into consideration the fact that the natural law, since in its own set terms it has been written not upon tablets or upon parchments but in the minds [of men], is not always formulated in the mind according to those general or indefinite terms in which we quote it when speaking or writing. For example, the law concerning the return of a deposit, in so far as it is natural, is mentally conceived, not in such simple and absolute terms, but with limitations and circumspection; for reason dictates that a deposit shall be returned to one who seeks it rightfully and reasonably, or in cases involving no objection based upon just defence, whether of the state, of oneself, or of an innocent person; yet this law is usually quoted simply in the following terms: 'A deposit must be returned'; because the rest is implied, nor is it possible to make in the shape of a law humanly drawn up a complete statement of all points involved.

7. *An explanation of the admissions made by St. Thomas and by Aristotle, that change may take place in natural precepts.* Therefore, when St. Thomas asserts [I.–II, qu. 94, art. 5] with Aristotle [*Nicomachean Ethics,* Bk. V, chap. vii] that certain precepts of the natural law suffer change or lapse or admit of an exception in a few cases—that is to say, occasionally—he is speaking of change in the loose sense of the term, simply by metonymy and extrinsically, by reason of a change which occurs in the matter [dealt with by that law], as is evident from a passage already cited (I.–II, qu. 100, art. 8); and with respect to this point, he makes a distinction between certain precepts which are natural in relation to other precepts, and those which are natural in relation to universal principles. For some precepts deal with matter that does not admit of change or limitation, as is the case with the general principle, 'One may not do evil', or, sometimes, with the special precept, that 'One may not lie'; while there are other precepts which can undergo change in the matter involved and therefore do admit of limitation and exceptions of a sort. Consequently, we often speak of these latter precepts as if they were framed in absolute terms under which they suffered an exception, the reason for this apparent exception being that those general terms do not adequately set forth the natural precepts themselves, as they are inherently. For these precepts, thus viewed as they are inherently, do not suffer any exception; since natural reason itself dictates that a given act shall be performed in such and such a way, and not otherwise, or under specific concurrent circumstances, and not unless those circumstances exist. Indeed, upon occasion, when the circumstances are changed, the natural law not only refrains from imposing the obligation to perform a certain act—such, for example, as the return of a deposit—but even imposes the [contrary] obligation to leave the act undone.

8. Thus, the example of the deposit, cited above, is easily explained. For even if in a particular case it ought not to be returned, the precept

of the natural law does not for that reason suffer change; because, from the outset, it was established with reference not to this situation, but to certain others, indicated by right reason; just as he who fails to fulfil a promise, because of a notable change in the circumstances involved, does not himself change; neither does the law requiring the observance of good faith; the subject-matter, however, has undergone a change, but from the very beginning a virtual exception was made with regard to this change, by means of a condition implied in the promise itself, so that it is not a true or intrinsic, but [merely] an apparent change, and one so termed through an extrinsic process of metonymy. The same is true, then, in the case of a deposit, even if a promise to return that deposit is annexed to [the act of making] it. This assertion is supported by Augustine (*On Psalms,* v [, § 7]), and is also set forth in the *Decretum* (Pt. II, causa xxii, qu. ii, can. xiv).

The same view applies, in due proportion, to the natural precept enjoining the keeping of secrets; since a secret is a kind of deposit which is given that it may be guarded, and which is accepted under promise of preserving it, [in so far as is possible,] without causing harm or injury to a third person. For this condition is necessarily implied, in order that the promise may be licit. We are speaking, however, of natural secrets; for the seal of confession involves an obligation of a higher nature.

Finally, the view in question also holds true with respect to the fifth precept of the Decalogue, 'Thou shalt not kill', which includes, in so far as it is a natural precept, many conditions, [so that it means,] for example, 'Thou shalt not kill upon thine own authority, and as an aggressor'; points which are to be discussed in their proper context, and to which we shall give some attention in Chapter xv. Of the last example, which is, indeed, more obscure, I shall speak in the following Chapter.

9. *A reply is made to the contrary position.* To the above argument, I reply by admitting, with due regard for proportion, the truth of the analogy drawn from physical conclusions. For physical propositions, although they are said to be defective at times, are nevertheless not defective as scientific conclusions; since as such they are deduced not inevitably, but with this limitation, namely, that certain conclusions result *per se* from certain causes, unless these causes are checked. Thus, with respect to the case under discussion, a natural precept—as I have pointed out—does not lay

down an absolute command in regard to some particular subject-matter, [the command,] for example, that a deposit must be returned; rather does it command that [the act in question] must be performed, assuming that the proper circumstances exist, a point which has been sufficiently explained. For it is only in this way that such conclusions are necessarily inferred from natural principles; and they are not natural precepts, save as they are necessarily deduced from those principles. Therefore, neither is any objection to our view involved in the fact that the subject-matter is changeable. For the natural law discerns the mutability in the subject-matter itself, and adapts its own precepts to this mutability, prescribing in regard to such subject-matter a certain sort of conduct for one condition, and another sort of conduct for another condition; so that the law in itself remains at all times unchanged, although, according to our manner of speaking and by an extrinsic attribution, it would seem, after a fashion, to undergo change.

10. *Can the natural law be eradicated from the minds of men, and so undergo change? The reply.* Another difficulty is wont to occur in this connexion. For it seems that the natural law may be effaced from the minds of men; and accordingly, that it is subject to change through separation from its subject (as it were); just as knowledge, which with respect to its object is immutably true, may in the subject become corrupted through error. But this difficulty, in so far as it is relevant to our discussion, has been dealt with sufficiently above (Bk. II, Chap. viii, *supra,* p. 243), where we spoke of the ignorance that may exist under this law. Therefore we shall assert, briefly, that this law cannot be entirely effaced from the minds of men, but that there may be ignorance with respect to some of its precepts, an ignorance which, moreover, is perhaps not shared by all men; for, although certain nations are in error in regard to one precept and others in regard to another precept, there nevertheless seems to be no one precept that is not made manifest to some men, at least, through the light of nature. This fact suffices to enable one to make the absolute assertion that no precept of the natural law can be totally eradicated, even through ignorance. I shall add, moreover, that, through error or ignorance, the law does not change in itself, but is obscured or not known, which is a very different matter.

For, although all the precepts of the natural law may be immutable, yet not all are equally manifest; so that it is not incongruous that some of them should fail to be known.

Another difficulty arises here, as to *epieikeia;* a difficulty that is more serious and that requires special treatment, which we shall devote to it in a later chapter (Chap. xvi).

CHAPTER XIV

Does the Natural Law Admit of Change or Dispensation through Any Human Power?

1. Although this question may seem to have been settled by the preceding discussion, nevertheless there are certain Doctors of great authority who lay down an absolute statement to the effect that sometimes a dispensation from the natural law may be made through human agency, or this law may be changed by means of human law, whether the latter be the *ius gentium* or the civil law. This statement does not apply, indeed, to all the precepts of the natural law, for [the said Doctors] admit that such change can have no place in the primary principles of that law, or in the conclusions immediately derived therefrom, with respect to which, in their opinion, all that was said in the preceding Chapter holds good.

The opinion of those who assert that a dispensation from the natural law may be made through human power with respect to a specific point. They maintain, then, that only with regard to certain things, or certain precepts more remote [from the primary principles], can that change be effected; a change which is not universal, by a process of abrogation, but specific, by a process of dispensation or diminution. This opinion is expressly set forth in several passages of the Gloss (on *Decretals,* Bk. III, tit. xxx, chap. xxiv, word *exemptus*). The same opinion is observed in the Gloss (on *Digest,* I. i. 4, word *nascerentur,* and on *Digest,* I. i. 6, § 1). It is also followed by Abbas [i.e. Panormitanus] (on *Decretals,* Bk. III, tit. xxx, chap. xxiv, no. 4, Bk. I, tit. IV, chap. xi, no. 3, and Bk. I, tit. II, chap. vii, no. 11). On which (viz. *Decretals,* Bk. I. tit. II, chap. vii) one may also consult Felinus (No. 26), Innocent, and others, all of whom are commonly agreed upon this position. However, the opinion in question has been more fully and clearly expounded by Angelus de Clavasio ([*Summa,*] on word *Papa,* No. 1), where he speaks especially of papal dispensations. Navarrus (*Consilia seu Responsa,* Bk. II, *Qui filii sint legit.,* no. 8 [*Consilia,* Bk. III, *De Sponsalibus,* Consil. III, no. 8]) also says that the Pope can limit a natural or a divine law, and that he can grant dispensations therefrom. The same doctrine is laid down concerning the Pope by Thomas Sánchez (*De Sancto Matrimonii Sacramento,* Bk. VIII, disp. vi [, no. 4]), who also refers to many of the jurists, and to Cano (*Relectio: De Poenitentia,* Pt. V), from among the theologians. However, we have already, in another passage (*De Voto,* Bk. VI, chap. ix)[1] sufficiently refuted the opinion of the latter [i.e. Cano] on this point. Henríquez (*De Eucharistia,* Bk. VIII, chap. xiii), too, may be cited in defence of the view in question. But in the case of these writers and of others who discuss the same point, it should be noted that at times they are speaking generally of divine law and of the power of the Pope to grant dispensations therefrom, [so that] they confuse under the heading of divine law, both the natural and the positive divine law. But we are speaking definitely and specifically, and at present are dealing solely with natural law in its relation to any human power and to the action of that power, whether such action be a dispensation, a precept, or a legal institution constituted either by a legal precept, or by custom, whether particular or world-wide; [the latter sort] being customarily called the *ius gentium,* a matter which I shall discuss below.[2] With positive divine law, however, we shall deal in the last Book of this treatise.[3]

2. The opinion which we are discussing, then, may be confirmed, first, by various examples [of change].[4] The first example, and a common one, relates to a division of ownership rights; for by the natural law all things were [originally] held in common, and nevertheless a division of property was introduced by mankind. On this point, see the *Decretum* (Pt. I, dist. i, can. vii; Pt. I, dist. viii, can. i).

---

1. [This passage is to be found in Tom. II, bk. vi, chap. ix of Suárez's *De Religione,* a tractate not included in these *Selections.*—Tr.]

2. [*Infra,* p. 374, Chapter xvii.—Tr.]

3. [Book X of the *De Legibus,* not included in these *Selections.*—Tr.]

4. [As distinguished from human dispensations from the natural law, discussed in the next paragraph.—Tr.]

Indeed, it is even said in one Chapter of the *Decretum* (Pt. II, causa XII, qu. i, can. ii), that the division of property was introduced as a result of [human] iniquity; not because the introduction itself was evil, but because it was occasioned by sin, according to the interpretation of all the writers cited below. The second example is similar [to the first], and concerns liberty, which is proper to mankind by the law of nature, and is nevertheless taken from men by human laws. On this point, one may consult the *Digest* (I. i. 4; I. v. 4) and the *Institutes* (I. ii, § 1 [§ 2]). The third example relates to that precept of natural law which prohibits taking away the property of another, a precept which would seem to be changed through the introduction among men of [the institutions of] usucaption and prescription. The Gloss cites this example in connexion with the above-mentioned law (*Digest,* I. i. 4). The fourth example is drawn from the natural precept which rules that a marriage is effected through the mutual consent of the man and the woman; a precept which is changed by men, so that a marriage may not be effected thus, unless there are also witnesses present. A similar example is that of the law regarding the execution of a will, or the donation of one's own property; for, according to the natural law, these acts might be performed according to the owner's will, and nevertheless this natural precept is changed or limited by men; so that, for example, a will may not be made, save as a formal testament, &c.

3. Secondly, and as the principal [argument], there are adduced various examples of human dispensations from the natural law. The first of these examples relates to dispensation from vows and oaths, which derive their binding force from the natural law. The second concerns dispensation from marriage that is [merely] ratified,[5] which we assume to be dissoluble through a papal dispensation, although it is indissoluble by the natural law. The third example is that of a dispensation as to the residence of bishops, which, according to the Council of Trent (Session XXIII, chap. i: *De Reformatione*), is a matter of divine natural law, and which nevertheless is subjected to daily dispensation, as is well known. Nor will the common

---

5. [A Christian marriage contracted with all canonical requirements is called *ratum* or ratified. When consummated, it is called *ratum et consummatum*. The papal power extends only to the dissolution of a ratified, not consummated marriage, and is called the power of dispensation.—REVISER.]

explanation apply to this example, namely, the explanation that [the exceptions in question] are not dispensations, but interpretations of the natural law. For, in the first place, it is evident from obvious examples that this faculty [of residence outside the diocese], has been granted in many cases in which the obligation of [episcopal] residence had not ceased to exist, and in which there can be no convincing reason for supposing that this was done solely through interpretation, the obligation having rather been removed by the authority of the Pope, through a relaxation of the said obligation, which constitutes a dispensation. And in the second place, [the act] is often so named in the indults themselves, and even by the Council of Trent (Session VI, chap. ii: *De Reformatione*). The fourth example is that of dispensation from impediments which make a marriage invalid by natural law; for Angelus, in the passage above cited [*Summa,* on word *Papa,* No. 1], relates that a dispensation was given by human[6] law, in the case of a marriage between brother and sister; and nevertheless that relationship is a diriment[7] impediment imposed by the law of nature.[8] Further examples are then adduced by the jurists relating to dispensation from the duty of paying tithes, which they declare to be derived from divine natural law. Moreover, an example is found in the exemption of clerics from secular jurisdiction; an exemption which [the jurists] also judge to be derived from divine natural law, and with respect to which the Pope nevertheless grants dispensations, permitting a cleric to be punished by a temporal judge, even in a criminal case. Other examples of a similar kind may be found in the works of Felinus (on *Decretals,* Bk. I, tit. xxxiii, chap. xvii, nos. 7 *et seq.*).

6. [Reading *humano* for *naturali,* because of the context. *Vide,* especially, the opening sentence of this paragraph.—Tr.]

7. [The impediments to a marriage by canon law are of two kinds, diriment and impedient. The diriment impediments make the marriage invalid *ab initio,* while the impedient make it merely illicit.—Tr.]

8. [Suárez here relies on Angelus de Clavasio, who states (*loc. cit.*) that St. Antoninus informs us that Pope Martin V gave a dispensation, making valid a marriage between brother and sister. The same statement is found in the *Summa Sylvestrina* and in Parisio's *Consilia.* In point of fact, St. Antoninus relates that the dispensation was for the man to marry, not his sister, but the sister of a woman with whom he had had illicit relations (*Summa Theologica,* Pt. III, tit. i, chap. xi).—Reviser.]

4. Thirdly, it is argued that this dispensation with respect to certain natural laws is often necessary for the welfare of souls, as is evidenced by the examples adduced; and, therefore, it is not probable that God has left men without this remedy, since it pertains to God's providence to grant to men the power practically necessary for the proper government of the state. From this principle, then, we infer that there resides in men the power to punish malefactors, even with the death penalty; to deprive them of their property when the welfare of the state so requires; and to do similar things. Hence Angelus, in the passage cited above, has said that God would not have been a good Father to His family, had He not left a shepherd set over His flock who could provide for all cases that arose, and that were, of necessity, expedient [for the common good]. He [i.e. Angelus] cites Richard Middleton (on the *Sentences,* Bk. IV, dist. xxxviii, art. 9, qu. 1) on this point, saying merely that right reason dictates that there should be in the Church some representative of God who may reasonably take measures against the dangers to individuals after weighing their infirmities and advantages. The foregoing may be demonstrated by means of analogy: for unless the Pope so framed his own laws as to grant the bishops power to dispense therefrom in cases of necessity when he himself could not be approached or consulted, he would not be making proper provision for the Church; and therefore, on the basis of this principle, authorities generally conclude that in such cases [of emergency] inferior officials may grant dispensations from the laws of the superior; hence, a similar conclusion with due modifications would hold true in the case under discussion. In fine, all admit that by this reasoning it is possible for the natural law to be subjected to interpretation; but the principle that applies to interpretation applies likewise to dispensation, for both require the same power, since authentic interpretation of a law can be made only by its author; hence, on the same ground, the [possibility of] dispensation must be allowed, since frequently one cannot provide through interpretation alone for all the cases which arise.

5. *The second and more common opinion, that the natural law cannot, in any of its precepts, be abrogated or dispensed from, by human authority.* According to the contrary opinion, however, the natural law cannot be subjected, in any of its true precepts, to abrogation, diminution, dispensation, or any

other change of a similar sort, by means of any human law or power. This is, without doubt, the common opinion of the theologians, to whom we shall refer more at length, in the following Chapter. Particularly, indeed, is it the view of St. Thomas (I.–II, qu. 100, art. 8), as expressed in several passages cited in the preceding Chapter [*ibid.*, qu. 94, art. 5] and, especially, concerning the Pope in the *Quaestiones Quodlibetales* (Quodl. IV, qu. viii, art. 13). The same opinion may be noted in a passage from Alexander of Hales (Pt. III, qu. xxvii, memb. 4, in its entirety), although in a preceding section (memb. 2, § 2 [memb. 3, art. 2]), he speaks obscurely of the mutability of the natural law, as we shall observe in the following Chapter. The view in question is held also by the theologians who absolutely deny that the Pope can grant dispensations from divine law; for if he cannot do this with respect to positive divine law, much less is it possible for him with respect to the natural law, which is also divine and, besides, less subject to change. However, we shall refer again to these authorities, when we treat below of the law of grace.[9] This view of the natural law, indeed, is expressly maintained by Almain in his *De Potestate Ecclesiae* (Chap. xiii, concl. i [, propositio 1]); and he holds to the same opinion in another work (on the *Sentences,* Bk. IV, dist. xv, qu. 2, art. 1). Sylvester (word *Papa,* Qu. 16) and Abulensis (on *Exodus,* Chap. xx, qu. 35, at the middle) also support this opinion. And Victoria (in *Relectio* II [IV]: *De Potestate Papae et Concilii*) frequently makes the same assumption; as do Driedo (*De Libertate Christiana,* Bk. II, chap. iv, at end) and Soto (*De Iustitia,* Bk. I, qu. vii, art. 3 [, ad 3]; Bk. IV, qu. iii, art. 1, ad 1, and Bk. X, qu. iii, art. 4), the latter extending his statement even to the special example of the residence of bishops. The modern theologians, too, are commonly agreed upon this view. And as for the jurists, several of the Glosses on *Decretum* (Pt. II, causa xxv, qu. ii [qu. i], can. vi), throughout this and the following text, as well as the Gloss on *Decretals* (Bk. III, tit. VIII, chap. iv), suggest this opinion, although they couch it in obscure terms. The doctrine is stated more clearly by Torquemada (*Summa,* Bk. III, chaps. liv and lvii) and Navarrus (*Consilia,* Bk. IV, *De Desponsat. Impuberum,* no. 16 [*De Sponsalibus,* Consil. xxxix]); it may be inferred from the comments of the

---

9. [The treatise *On Grace* is not included in these *Selections.*—Tr.]

latter on the *Decretals* (Bk. V, tit. vi, chap. vi [*Consilia,* Bk. V, *De Judaeis,* Consil. iii], next to last Gloss in its entirety); [and it is also stated thus clearly] by Covarruvias (on *Sext,* rule *peccatum,* Pt. II, § II, nos. 3 *et seq.* and rule *quamvis pactum,* Pt. II, § 4, no. 6, and *Epitome* on *Decretals,* IV [*De Matrimonio,*] Pt. II, chap. vi, § 9, no. 3); Barbosa (on *Digest,* rubric XXIV. iii, pt. ii, no. 104) and Albert of Bologna (tract. *De Lege, Iure, et Aequitate,* Chap. xxvi, nos. 3 *et seq.*). Furthermore, the said opinion is in my own judgment entirely true, although, regarding certain points thereof, there may be some disagreement as to terminology.

6. *In what ways a thing may fall under the natural law.* Therefore, in order that we may briefly set forth the truth, it should be noted that there are many ways in which a thing may be spoken of as pertaining to the natural law.

In the first and most fitting sense, it may be spoken of thus when some natural precept prescribes the thing in question; and this is the sense proper to the natural law, with which we are dealing. For such a situation, it is necessary that natural reason, viewed in its essential character, shall dictate that something is necessary to right conduct; whether it so dictates without reflection or as the result of a single act of reflection, or of several such acts; for as long as the inference is always inevitable, this latter consideration[10] is of slight importance, as I have frequently remarked.

According to another manner of speaking, however, a thing is said to pertain to the natural law merely in a permissive, negative, or concessive sense, to put the matter thus. Under this classification many things fall which, from the standpoint simply of natural law, are permissible, or conceded, to men—such things as the holding of goods in common, human liberty, and the like. With respect to these things, the natural law lays down no precept enjoining that they shall remain in that state; rather does it leave the matter to the management of men, such management to be in accord with the demands of reason. Thus it can be said that nakedness is natural to man, and that this nakedness would not require covering in the state of innocence; whereas, in the condition of fallen [human] nature,

---

10. [I.e. the question of whether reflection is involved; and if so, what degree of reflection.—Tr.]

natural reason imposes a different requirement. So also liberty is natural to man, since he possesses it by virtue of natural law; yet the law of nature does not forbid the loss of his liberty.

In yet another sense, a thing may be spoken of as pertaining to the natural law, for the reason that it has its foundation in a natural disposition, although it is not absolutely prescribed by natural law; for example, the fact that, as the *Digest* records (XXXVIII. vi. 7, at end), the son inherits from a father who dies intestate; for the natural law, although it does not absolutely prescribe that this shall be so, does incline toward this arrangement, which follows from it naturally (so to speak) unless an impediment arises from some other source. So, too, the practice of giving credence to two witnesses, or the fact that they are sufficient for human requirements of proof, may be said to pertain to the natural law—not in its prescriptive, but in its approving and permissive character—unless for special causes some other requirement is added, or imposed [in substitution].

In the present discussion, then, we are speaking (as I have pointed out) of the natural law in the first sense; but in connexion with certain arguments, we shall say something concerning that law in the latter sense.

7. *A point to be noted.* With respect to the first mode, however, it should be further noted that, among the precepts of natural law, there are certain precepts—dealing with pacts, agreements, obligations—which are introduced through the will of men: for example, the laws relating to the observance of vows and of human promises, whether these be made in simple form or confirmed by oath; and the same is true of other contracts, according to the particular characteristics of each; and true, also, of rights, natural and legal,[11] arising therefrom.

There are other natural laws, however, which are directly binding, in their very subject-matter and independently of any prior consent by human will: for example, the positive precepts of religion in relation to God, of filial piety, of mercy, and of almsgiving to one's neighbour; and the negative precepts against killing, those against slander, and similar

---

11. [Giving to *actio,* in the rather doubtful phrase *iuribus, vel actionibus,* the quite common connotation, 'right to sue', or 'right to take legal action.'—REVISER.]

prohibitions. In both kinds of precepts[12] there is involved the same necessity in so far as concerns the formal character of law, and, consequently, there are the same uniformity and immutability; but with respect to the subject-matter, the second group of precepts possesses a greater degree of immutability, since they have not for their subject-matter (so to speak) human free will, which is exceedingly changeable and frequently requires correction and alteration.

8. I hold, first: that no human power, even though it be the papal power, can abrogate any proper precept of natural law, nor truly and essentially restrict such a precept, nor grant a dispensation from it.

The first assertion: no human power can abrogate any natural precept. The first proof of this assertion is drawn from the statements made in the preceding Chapter; for it has been shown in that Chapter that the natural law, in so far as its precepts are concerned, is by its very nature unchangeable; and men cannot change that which is unchangeable; therefore, . . . This argument is confirmed and made clear by the fact that the natural law, in all its precepts, relates to the natural qualities of mankind; and man cannot change the nature of things; therefore, . . . Secondly, the assertion in question is proved by the fact that, in the case of every precept of natural law, God is the Lawgiver; and man cannot change a law that God has established, since an inferior cannot prevail as against his superior, a point which is brought out in the *Decretum* (Pt. I, dist. xxi, can. iv) and the *Constitutions* of Clement (Bk. I, tit. iii, chap. ii), therefore, . . . Thirdly, there is the argument that the natural law is the foundation of human law, and that therefore, human law cannot derogate from natural law; since if it did so, it would destroy its own foundation and consequently itself. Fourthly, if human law could derogate from natural law, it would be possible for the former to make an enactment in opposition to the latter, since one can conceive of no other way of changing natural law; but [human law] cannot make such an enactment; therefore, . . . The minor premiss is proved thus: what is contrary to natural law is intrinsically evil; therefore,

---

12. [I.e. those introduced by human will, and those which are binding independently of the human will. This classification should not be confused with Suárez's subdivision of the latter group into affirmative and negative precepts.—Tr.]

the human law in question would relate to an intrinsically evil matter, and in consequence would not [truly] constitute law either in general or in particular. A confirmation of this argument is the fact that, for this same reason, a custom opposed to natural law cannot inaugurate a legal rule. On this fact, see the *Decretals* (Pt. I, tit. IV, can. xi) and the Gloss thereon. The latter passage notes that the natural law is immutable in so far as concerns its commands and prohibitions. There is another, similar passage in the Gloss (on *Decretum,* Pt. I, dist. V, pars I, § I), where Gratian says that the natural law is unchangeable; a statement which he repeats in the following distinction (*Decretals,* Pt. I, dist. VI, § I [following can. iii, citing the words of Gratian]).

9. *Objection.* It may be objected that all these remarks apply rightly to the abrogation or absolute change of any natural precept, but not to dispensations upon the occurrence of a legitimate cause; for it is not probable that God has granted to mankind authority to abrogate or restrict [the natural law] without cause; nor do men of themselves possess such authority, as is proved by the arguments already presented. But the case is otherwise with respect to just dispensations. For, although a man may not grant such a dispensation on his own authority—a fact which is also proved by the arguments in question—nevertheless, he may do so with authority from God, since an inferior is in this sense able to grant dispensations from the law of a superior, and since it seems probable that man, acting as vicegerent on earth of God, is likewise able to grant dispensations for a just cause and by divine concession from the laws in question, inasmuch as this [ability on the part of man] is pertinent to the good government of the universe, as we were reasoning above.

10. *Solution.* However, in answer to this objection, it may be urged, first, that God Himself is not able—at least, not by ordinary law—to grant dispensations with respect to any precept of natural law. For if, at times, He does work some change in these precepts, He is making use of His absolute power, and indeed, of His supreme dominion, as we shall explain in the following Chapter; and therefore, it is improbable that He has given to men, ordinary power for granting dispensations with respect to any natural precept. This is especially evident, in view of the conclusion which will follow clearly upon the solutions to the arguments, and the

content of Chapter xvi—namely, that this power is not necessary to men for the proper conduct of government.

Secondly, it may be answered that, if such power did reside in men, it would be found not only in the Pope, but also in the Emperor, or temporal king, in so far as those natural precepts are concerned which have to do with temporal affairs, as is the case with nearly all the precepts which relate to one's neighbour; and both [of these conclusions] are false; therefore, . . . The consequent is explained as follows: although the Pope has supreme power in the Church, nevertheless, the Emperor also holds power from God and acts, in his own realm, as the minister of God, according to the statement made by Paul in his *Epistle to the Romans* (Chap. xiii); moreover, from the standpoint of the natural law, one can think of no person other [than the Emperor], prior to the institution of the Papal dignity, who was the minister of God within the state in so far as such an act was concerned; and even now, the Emperor will have the same power, provided that the Pope places no impediment in his way. The minor proposition, moreover, in so far as it concerns the Emperor, is stated in the *Constitutions* of Clement (Bk. II, tit. xi, chap. ii, at end): 'Neither could the aforesaid remedy of the defect [of jurisdiction] with respect to a subject, reasonably have been applied to those things through which it would have been possible to do away with the right of self-defence—springing from the law of nature—against a criminal charge, especially a charge that was so grave; for it would not be permissible that the Emperor should abolish those things which proceed from the natural law.' The same general conclusion is to be drawn from the *Decretals* (Bk. V, tit. xix, chap. iv), where these words appear: 'Since the crime of usury is held in abhorrence in the pages of both Testaments, we do not see that any dispensation can be granted with regard to that crime.' For the Pope tacitly infers from the fact that the said crime is execrated in both Testaments, that it is contrary to the natural law, and consequently beyond the bounds of possible dispensation in an absolute sense, wherefore it lies beyond them in so far as every human power is concerned.

Thirdly, one may answer that with respect to the precepts in question, the same principle is applicable to the parts and to the whole. For in the case of the necessary proposition applied by logicians to a matter which is natural, falsity in a single instance is no less inconceivable than the falsity of the whole universal proposition; but every natural precept deals with such a natural matter, and is characterized by the absolute truth which is necessary from the very nature of the case; therefore, just as a natural precept cannot be abrogated, so it cannot be changed in any particular instance, and consequently cannot be subjected to dispensation. The force of this argument, however, depends upon the statements to be made in the following Chapter and in the answers to the arguments.[13]

11. *The second assertion: those precepts of the natural law which depend upon the consent of the human will for their binding force, may at times be subjected to human dispensation.* My second assertion is this: the precepts of the natural law which depend for their preceptive binding force upon a prior consent of the human will, and upon the efficacy of that will to issue in some action, may sometimes be subjected to human dispensation, involving not a direct and absolute abolition of the obligation of natural law but a certain remission that affects the subject-matter [of the precept in question].

The truth of the first and negative member of this assertion is readily apparent in the light of the preceding assertion, since the said precepts, when viewed in themselves, possess an intrinsic rectitude that can never be abolished or violated if they are applied to their [proper] subject-matter; as is evident in the case of precepts such as the rule that good faith must be observed towards God and man, and the like. Moreover, the other and affirmative member [of the assertion] is most effectually proved by the example of a vow, that of an oath, and similar examples. It has been fully explained in our tractate *De Voto* (Bk. VI, chap. ix)[14] and will be clarified below in the replies to the various arguments. The reason, indeed, [in support of this affirmative statement], is none other than the fact that to change or to vary the subject-matter in question is not contrary to natural law, since such a variation depends upon a change of [human] volition. By the same reasoning, moreover, this [kind of dispensation] is not beyond

---

13. [I.e. the arguments set forth in the latter part of this Chapter.—Tr.]

14. [This is found in Suárez, *De Religione,* Tom. II, bk. vi, chap. ix, which is not included in these *Selections.*—Tr.]

the power of a human superior, either in so far as the will of the subject depends upon that superior, or in so far as the latter is the vicar of God. Furthermore, once this change has been effected, not only is there no obstacle necessarily opposed to the abolition of [that particular] obligation of the natural law, but the obligation lapses even of itself, and ceases to exert a binding force. Nay, more; a private individual can sometimes do away with the natural obligation arising from a promise (for instance, by remitting it) or with the obligation arising from a loan (by making it completely a gift). Accordingly, it is thus that one should conceive of the above-mentioned relaxation of natural law—the relaxation involved in this kind of dispensation, which, indeed, strictly speaking, is not from natural law, but may be called a dispensation from a vow or from an oath, since it is effected through an act of remission (so to speak) by a superior power, of [its own] jurisdiction; although [such relaxation] is (strictly speaking) a dispensation in fact, rather than in law, as Albert of Bologna has rightly remarked (*De Lege, Iure, et Aequitate,* Chap. xxvi, nos. 3 *et seq.*).

12. *The third assertion: through human law the subject-matter of the natural law may be so changed, that in consequence of this change in the matter, the obligation imposed by natural law will also change.* My third assertion is this: through human law, whether it be the *ius gentium* or the civil law, there may be effected in the subject-matter of the natural law a change of such sort that, by reason thereof, the obligation imposed by natural law will also change. It would seem that a number of civil laws should be understood in the light of this conclusion; or that the jurists should be thus understood when they say that some part of the natural law is withdrawn, through the *ius gentium* or the civil law. This point is clearly brought out in the *Digest* (I. i. 4 and 6) and in the *Institutes* (I. ii, § 1). The third assertion is furthermore confirmed by many of the examples adduced to illustrate the first basis of the contrary opinion, as we shall see when we expound those examples. And finally, the rational basis of the said assertion is the fact that such a mode of change is not inconsistent with the necessary and unchangeable character of the natural law; and that, for the rest, it is convenient and frequently necessary for men, in accordance with the various changes of estate which befall them. In this connexion, too, one may fittingly apply the familiar illustration drawn from Augustine, namely,

that just as the science of medicine lays down certain precepts for the sick, others for the well, certain precepts for the strong and others for the weak, although the rules of medicine do not therefore undergo essential change but merely become manifold, so that some serve on one occasion, and others, on another occasion; even so, the natural law, while it remains [in itself] the same, lays down one precept for one occasion and another, for another occasion; and is binding [in one of its rules] at one time, though not binding previously or subsequently, and this without undergoing any change in itself but merely because of a change in the subject-matter.

13. *The arguments are answered.* A reply must be made, then, to the arguments supporting the first opinion,[15] in so far as those arguments may be opposed to the foregoing assertion.

Reply to the first argument. Thus, with respect to the first example laid down in connexion with the first argument and relating to ownership in common and division of property, Scotus (on the *Sentences,* Bk. IV, dist. xv, qu. 2, art. 1) and Gabriel (on the *Sentences, ibid.,* qu. 2, at the beginning), say that, before the commission of sin, a precept was laid on mankind ruling that all property should be owned in common: whereas, after the commission of sin, this law was annulled, so that the division of property was not then contrary to the law of nature. This opinion, however, with regard to that first precept, is not acceptable to me, since I do not see the necessity for such a rule. For if it is conceived of as being a positive precept, the assertion is gratuitous, since it cannot be proved; and if the precept is conceived of as natural, proof must be offered of the necessary connexion between community of property and the state of innocence, proof which would seem not to exist, since, without prejudice to the rectitude of their conduct, men could in that state of innocence take possession of, and divide among themselves, certain pieces of property, especially those which are movables and necessary for ordinary use. This fact has been noted by Almain (on the *Sentences,* Bk. IV, dist. xv, qu. 2, art. 1, *secunda propositio*). Moreover, the conjectures that Scotus employs to prove this precept—that is to say, the conjecture that community of property in such a state would be better adapted to promote

15. [*Vide* p. 301; Section 1 of this Chapter.—Tr.]

the sustenance and peace of mankind, and similar suppositions—prove merely that at that time a division of property was not necessary; or, at most, they prove that ownership in common would have been more useful in that state, but not that it would have been necessary. Just as, conversely, the advantages which show that a division of property is better adapted to [human] nature in the fallen state are proof, not that this division of ownership is a matter prescribed by natural law, but merely that it is adapted to the existing state and condition of mankind. Yet we must note that, according to the opinion of Scotus, the admission is, not that there has been any intrinsic and true change in natural law, but simply that there has been a cessation in its binding force, owing to a change made by men and therefore made in the subject-matter itself.

14. *A division in the natural law, into the negative and the positive aspects.* The common reply, then, with respect both to the example in question and to many other examples, is that there are two senses in which a matter may fall under the natural law; namely, a negative, and a positive sense. It is said that [a given action] falls negatively under the natural law because that law does not prohibit, but on the contrary permits [the said action], while not positively prescribing its performance. When, however, something is prescribed by natural law, that prescription is said to be positively a part of natural law; and when any thing is prohibited thereby, the thing thus prohibited is said to be positively opposed to natural law.

A division of property is not contrary to positive natural law. Hence, a division of property is not contrary to positive natural law; for there was[16] no natural precept to forbid the making of such a division. Therefore, when certain legal precepts are said to be opposed to the law of nature, they are to be thought of, in their negative relationship to natural law; for ownership in common was a part of natural law in the sense that, by virtue of that law, all property would be held in common if men had not introduced any different provision. Such is the deduction to be drawn from St. Thomas (II.–II, qu. 66, art. 2, ad 1 and I.–II, qu. 94, art. 5, ad 3), Conrad Koellin

16. [I.e. at the time when the division was made. Some such phrase was evidently in Suárez's mind when he changed at this point from the present to the imperfect tense.—TR.]

(*De Contractibus,* Qu. 10), Covarruvias (on *Sext,* rule *peccatum,* Pt. II, § 11, no. 3), and Navarrus (on *Decretals,* Bk. V, tit. VI, chap. vi, notab. II [*Consilia,* Bk. V, *De Iudaeis,* Consil. iii], next to last gloss).

15. *The objections raised by Fortunius in opposition to the doctrine above set forth.* This response, however, has been impugned among the jurists by Fortunius Garcia (on *Digest,* I. i. 4, no. 8). For, according to the distinction above set forth, liberty would not be more a part of natural law than would slavery; nor ownership in common, more than division of property; a proposition which is opposed to the laws already laid down and to the general opinion. The truth of the consequent is evident, [first,] in that division of property also comes under natural law, negatively speaking, since it is not prohibited. Secondly, this truth is evident because, if the case were otherwise, it would follow that, relying upon natural law, one man could licitly deprive another of his liberty and reduce him to slavery, since in so doing the former would not in any way be acting contrary to a precept of natural law; a conclusion which is evident, inasmuch as liberty is only negatively said to be a part of the law of nature, that is, it is said to be a part simply because it is not forbidden [by the said law], not because it is prescribed by some positive precept; hence, an action opposed to liberty is not forbidden by natural law. In the third place, it would also follow, if the case were otherwise, that men could licitly, of their own will and through force, usurp all the property of others as well as jurisdiction and also dominion over other men; for in so doing they would be acting, not in opposition to any precept of natural law, but merely in opposition to that which was permitted by virtue of natural law, a line of conduct which is not essentially evil. Accordingly, it would seem that certain jurists have found in this argument the source for their opinion when they say that temporal kings may, of their own absolute power and arbitrarily, transfer rights of ownership over property or usurp those rights for themselves. Almost to the same effect is a statement in the Gloss (on *Decretum,* Pt. II, causa IX, qu. iii, can. xxi, words *ad nos*), although the Gloss does not declare that the prince may so conduct himself without just cause. Angelus de Clavasio (on *Digest,* VI. i. 15, § 1 [*Summa Angelica,* word *Dominium*] upholds the same opinion. Nevertheless, these statements are most absurd, a fact which is self-evident, since they are opposed

to peace and justice among mankind and to every law imposed by nature upon every man.

16. *The objections are answered, and the doctrine in question is more fully expounded.* But the objections above set forth proceed from a faulty understanding of the distinction in question; and in order that this distinction may be better grasped, we must assume the existence of another distinction in law, one which we have marked out above. For we have said[17] that *ius* sometimes signifies *lex;* while at times it means dominion or quasi-dominion over a thing, that is, a claim to its use. At present, then, we make the same statement with respect to the natural law.

Accordingly, the distinction laid down by St. Thomas and commonly agreed upon should be understood as relating to the preceptive natural law, and with reference to the subject-matter under discussion. From this point of view, it is manifest that a division of property is not opposed to natural law in the sense that the latter absolutely and without qualification forbids such division. The same is true with respect to slavery and other, similar matters.

If, however, we are speaking of the natural law of dominion,[18] it is then true that liberty is a matter of natural law, in a positive, not merely a negative sense, since nature itself confers upon man the true dominion of his liberty. Common ownership of property would also pertain in a certain sense to the dominion held by men by virtue of natural law, if no division of property had been made, since [in that case] men would have a positive law [on this matter] and a claim[19] to the use of common property, a fact which is self-evident and rightly demonstrated by the objection first laid down.

For liberty rather than slavery is of natural right, for this reason, namely, that nature has made men free in a positive sense (so to speak) with an intrinsic right to liberty, whereas it has not made them slaves in this positive sense, strictly speaking. Similarly, nature has conferred upon men in common dominion over all things, and consequently has given to every

---

17. [*Supra,* p. 30; Bk. I, chap. ii, § 6.—Tr.]
18. [The Latin has *iure naturali dominativo.*—Tr.]
19. [The Latin has *actione* for *actionem;* or, possibly, for the plural, *actiones.*—Tr.]

man a power to use these things; but nature has not so conferred private property rights in connexion with that dominion, a point well brought out by Augustine (on the *Gospel of John,* Tract. VI, at end: chap. i, dist. viii). On such common dominion, Soto (*De Iustitia,* Bk. IV, qu. iv, art. 1) and Molina (*De Iustitia et Iure,* Tract II, disp. iii) may be consulted.

17. From the foregoing discussion, the reply to the other inferences also becomes clear; for none of those examples is conclusive, since they are incompatible with this positive law of dominion which nature has given either to all collectively, or to individuals separately. Therefore, although nature may not have prescribed that things should always be owned in common (in which sense it is said that community of property comes negatively under natural law), nevertheless, while that condition of common ownership did exist, there was a positive precept of natural law to the effect that no one should be prohibited or prevented from making the necessary use of the common property. This positive precept in its own fashion is even now in existence with regard to those things which are common, and for so long as they are not in any way divided; for no one may be prohibited from the common use of such things, generally speaking—apart, that is, from cases involving special necessity or a just cause. Moreover, in the same way, and arguing conversely, although division of property may not be prescribed by natural law, nevertheless, after this division has been made and spheres of dominion have been distributed, the natural law forbids theft, or the undue taking of another's property. It is, indeed, for this reason that all the things involved by inference in the objection under discussion are impermissible; a point which is clearly evident. Furthermore, Covarruvias (*Variarum Resolutionum,* Bk. III, chap. vi [, no. 6]) and du Pineau (on rubric of *Code,* IV. xliv, pt. I, chap. i, nos. 14 *et seq.*) may be consulted in this connexion.

18. But the second example still presents a difficulty; for a division of dominion, in so far as liberty is concerned, has been made by nature; how, then, can it licitly be abolished?

Why the natural law of dominion may be changed by human agency, while this is not true of the preceptive natural law. Another and general difficulty also arises, as to why the natural law of dominion, even if positively given by nature itself, may be changed, and may at times be licitly and validly abolished by human agency, whereas the preceptive natural law may not be thus changed.

My first response with respect to the second example is that nature, although it has granted liberty and dominion over that liberty, has nevertheless not absolutely forbidden that it should be taken away. For, in the first place, for the very reason that man is lord of his own liberty, it is possible for him to sell or alienate the same. A commonwealth, too, acting through the higher power which it possesses for the government of men, may deprive a man of his liberty for a just cause (as when it does so by way of punishment). For nature also gave to man the use and possession of his own life; yet he may sometimes justly be deprived of it through human agency.

19.[20] *A solution of the difficulty; and the reason for the difference in question.* The general reason, however, for the difference between the preceptive law and the law concerning dominion is that the former kind comprehends rules and principles for right conduct which involve necessary truth, and are therefore immutable, since they are based upon the intrinsic rectitude or perversity of their objects; whereas the law concerning dominion is merely the subject-matter of the other preceptive law, and consists (so to speak) of a certain fact, that is, a certain condition or habitual relation of things. And it is evident that all created things, and especially those which are corruptible, are characterized through nature by many conditions that are changeable and capable of being abolished by many causes. Accordingly, we say of liberty and of any similar lawful right, that even if such a right has been positively granted by nature, it may be changed by human agency, since it is dependent, in the individual persons, either upon their own wills, or upon the state, in so far as the latter has lawful power over all private individuals and over their property, to the extent necessary for right government.

The remaining examples of this group, indeed, are easily disposed of, in the light of the foregoing discussion.

For the third example, dealing with prescription, proves merely that civil laws may for a just cause change or transfer rights of dominion; and

---

20. [The context seems to indicate that section number 19 should be placed here and not with the following paragraph, as in the Latin text. The 1856 edition has designated both this, and the following paragraph, as Section 19.—Tr.]

that, when this change has been made, it may be said that the natural law is changed in an extrinsic sense, inasmuch as the prior law lapses when the subject-matter has changed and another law becomes binding; all of which is not incompatible with what we have said above but, on the contrary, confirms our remarks.

The fourth example, to be sure—the example respecting testaments and contracts—proves simply that human law is able to add something to natural law; a statement which is also true. Neither does there follow from that fourth example any conclusion incompatible with a positive precept of natural law; since that law does not prescribe, for example, that a marriage ceremony celebrated without the presence of a certain number of witnesses shall be valid, but has a negative force in this respect, in that it does not [specifically] require witnesses. From this fact, it results that, as long as positive law does not demand those witnesses, a marriage celebrated without them is valid by virtue of natural law; but after positive law has laid down such a condition for the validity of a contract, natural law does not conflict with this positive rule, but rather, in its own fashion, binds one to the observance of the latter, and the same statement applies to other forms devised by human law.

20. *Answer to the second argument.* As to the second argument, which involves examples of dispensations granted by men from the natural law, the reply is that this argument conforms to the second assertion,[21] and affords proof of it.

In what way the natural law lapses through dispensations granted by prelates with respect to vows and other matters. For the first example, relating to vows and oaths, clearly deals with subject-matter that depends upon human will and consent; and therefore, in the case of dispensations from such vows and oaths, there is no essential relaxation of a precept of natural law, but [merely] the remission of a debt which came into existence by human consent, so that the obligation imposed by natural law lapses in consequence, a fact which I have elsewhere expressly discussed (Tracts. *De Iuramento* and *De Voto* in the work *De Religione*).[22]

---

21. [*Vide supra*, p. 312.—Tr.]
22. [Not included in these *Selections*.—Tr.]

The second example, concerning a marriage that has [simply] been rati-fied,[23] is of the same kind; for in that case also, a human contract underlies the natural obligation, and by reason of this contract a dispensation may be granted from the said obligation. However, it may be objected that the natural law prescribes that this bond shall be indissoluble; to which I reply that the natural law does not lay down this prescription in such a way that it is intrinsically evil, in an absolute sense, for the contract in ques-tion to be dissolved. For the truth of such an assertion is not sufficiently proved on the basis of natural principles. On the contrary, it is proved merely that the contract cannot be dissolved by private authority and the will of the contracting parties. For such a dissolution cannot be accom-plished without some prejudice to the community, or to the conservation of nature itself, which, through the bond in question, has in a certain fash-ion acquired a right, such that this bond cannot be dissolved by private authority. No contradiction to this aspect of natural law is involved when a dispensation is granted by public authority, and accordingly no dispensa-tion from preceptive natural law, strictly speaking, takes place in the cases in question. The fact that such a dispensation may be granted, however, by public authority is not contrary to but rather in harmony with nature itself; since nature itself is able (so to speak) to cede its right, for the sake of some greater good which will also redound to its own advantage. For, indeed, the administration of the rights that pertain to the common good of nature has been committed to the power having in charge the welfare of the commonwealth; and therefore, it is not contrary to natural law that the said act should be dissolved by public authority. The questions, how-ever, of whether that power is supernatural or may exist in pure nature,[24] whether matrimony is a simple contract and not a sacrament, and why [a dispensation[25]] may take place in the case of a marriage which is merely ratified but not in the case of a consummated marriage, must be treated in our discussion of matrimony.[26]

---

23. [*Vide* note 5, *supra*, p. 303.—REVISER.]

24. [Pure nature, that is, nature regarded as nature, without reference to its present elevated state.—REVISER.]

25. [That is, dissolution.—REVISER.]

26. [Not included in these *Selections*.—TR.]

21. *Whether the Pope can grant dispensations from the obligation of epis-copal residence when this is a matter of natural law.* With respect to the third example, dealing with dispensations from the obligation of epis-copal residence [in the diocese], a question may be raised as to whether this obligation of residence is derived from natural law, or from positive divine law; however, since that question is not pertinent to the present context, I [simply] assume that it is derived from natural law. According to this assumption, Soto (as I have already remarked, *supra*[27]) denies that the dispensation whereby this obligation is relaxed is a true dispensation, and regards it, on the contrary, as a mere interpretation that the natural law is not binding in the case in question. For the precept involved, since it is affirmative, is not binding continuously; and therefore, occasions may eas-ily arise upon which, or with respect to which, that precept is not binding, so that, on those occasions, there will be an opportunity for interpretation. Such a reply, however, is effectually disproved by the reasons set forth in the course of this argument. For, wherever a simple interpretation takes place, the obligation is not thereby abolished, but is assumed and declared to have been removed already; whereas, with respect to the sort of situation under discussion, it is evident and is widely known from experience that licences and dispensations have often been granted in cases wherein the obligation had not lapsed of itself and could not with a secure conscience be passed over, upon private authority, through any doctrinal interpre-tation (so to speak) simply because of the existence of such and such a cause—cases in which, nevertheless, permission having once been granted through the Pope on the basis solely of this same cause, it is indubitable that [the bishop in question] might with an undisturbed conscience fail to meet the requirements of [episcopal] residence; which therefore indicates that in such instances there is a true relaxation [of obligation] through the power of jurisdiction. Furthermore, it may not be asserted that such an interpretation concerns a doubtful case and consequently calls for jurisdic-tion, since no doubt is assumed to exist. On the contrary, it is assumed to be certain that the cause in question is not such that of itself it avails to extinguish the obligation. This point is also made evident by the fact that

27. [Sect. 5; p. 305.—Tr.]

the cause is often extrinsic with respect to the said obligation; as when a public advantage is involved in relation to the government of the whole realm, or in the assisting of a Catholic prince for the common welfare of the Church or the State, or in other and similar cases which of themselves do not avail as excuses and which depend in large measure upon human decisions, so that they may suffice to justify a dispensation, but not to extinguish *per se* the obligation in question.

22. *The opinion of the author, that human power may grant a dispensation from the requirement of episcopal residence. The reason [for this belief] is also set forth.* I grant, then, that this act is a [true] act of dispensation. I maintain, however, that such dispensations do not fall under the preceptive natural law regarded in its essential aspect, but that they occur in its subject-matter, changing this matter in so far as it depends also upon human consent or human will; so that, once this change has been made, the natural precept itself ceases, of itself, to be binding.

This assertion may be explained by the fact that the said obligation of residence arises only through a pact and a bond between the bishop and the Church; but such a pact and bond are contracted by the exercise of human will, and consequently, in this respect, are subject to change—at least, through the public authority (a point on which the *Decretals* (Bk. I, tit. VII, chap. ii) should be consulted); accordingly, they may be relaxed through this same power, and therefore, the natural obligation which arises from them may also be changed or abolished.

The same point is further demonstrated as follows: this pact between an individual bishop and his church is, from the very nature of the case, subject to the supreme pastor; so that in the said pact there is included the condition that he shall offer himself to the service of that church with accompanying subordination to the supreme pastor, who possesses a superior power over the church in question and is also charged with the immediate care thereof. When the Pope, however, grants a dispensation from [the obligation of episcopal] residence, he himself decrees how provision shall be made for the particular church involved, throughout a particular period of time, and takes upon himself (as it were) the burden of this church; so that it therefore follows that the bishop himself is freed from his personal obligation not through a dispensation from a natural precept, but because the pact which he made with his church, and from which the obligation involved in that precept arose, is thus in point of fact fulfilled. Or rather, this obligation is fulfilled in a different way, also comprehended in the pact itself, provision being made for the church in the manner prescribed by the supreme pastor for a reasonable cause. For such is the assumption to be made; namely, that this condition which is comprehended within the bond itself is a just one.

23. *Dispensations from diriment impediments to matrimony, which arise from natural law, cannot be granted by the Pope.* In regard to the fourth example, concerning impediments which invalidate by the force of natural law, we now assume that it is more probable that dispensations from such impediments cannot be granted through human power. For example, when a man has contracted and consummated a marriage with one woman, human power cannot grant a dispensation allowing him to marry another woman during the lifetime of the former spouse, in such a way that both bonds remain valid, or the prior bond is dissolved; for neither of these alternative effects can be brought about through human power. And the same is true of similar cases. Therefore, such examples rather tend to confirm the first assertion. For impediments of the kind in question, if they are natural, depend upon pure reason and not upon human volition. Accordingly, we do not believe that a dispensation has ever been granted in the Church with respect to the marriage of brother and sister, and yet if that has been done, we must believe that it was done in adherence to the opinion that such a relationship is not a diriment impediment by natural law. On this point, we shall add a number of remarks in the proper context, and also some further comment in our next Chapter.

24. The other examples, indeed, are in no way pertinent to the question. For in the case of privileges regarding tithes there is derogation[28] not from natural law, but from a provision laid down by man, since the support of the ministers of the Church falls under natural law, but the form and the distribution of that burden among the faithful are matters of human law and human decision, and since it is in these matters only that

---

28. 'Derogation': the removal of part of a law, by contrast to its abrogation or complete removal. See also Book 7, chapter 19, section 3.

change is wrought, as I have elsewhere explained at length (in Tract. II, *De Virtute et Statu Religionis,* Bk. I, chap. xiv).[29]

Again, ecclesiastical immunity of persons [from secular jurisdiction]—granting that this comes under divine natural law, a question with which we are not at present dealing—is not violated or diminished, in itself, nor in so far as it may be enjoined by a natural precept, by the fact that sometimes a given cleric is by Papal authority deprived of that immunity and subjected to lay power; the reason for this fact being either that the lay[30] power on that occasion serves as the minister of the Pope, or, at least, that natural reason prescribes the existence of this immunity only with accompanying dependence upon and subordination to the supreme pastor of the Church. Accordingly, the case under discussion involves no dispensation from preceptive natural law. For natural law does not prescribe that clerics should be immune in such fashion that, even for a just cause, a prelate of the Church, and especially the supreme prelate, would not be able to hand them over to the authority of the secular arm, it being self-evident [that such ability does exist]. Therefore, when clerics are thus handed over, not only is it not a relaxation of natural law, but, indeed, it is rather a proper execution of the justice dictated by divine and by natural law.

Other examples, to be sure, adduced by Felinus—whom we have cited[31] in the same connexion—I shall omit from motives of prudence. For many of the said examples are excluded as a result of the foregoing remarks; others are improbable; while others, again, are not pertinent to the case in question, but bear rather upon the subject of dispensations from divine positive law, a subject which must be treated below,[32] in its proper place.

25. To the reasoning set forth above, I reply that it confirms the second assertion and does not militate against the first. For in the case of those obligations which depend upon human consent or upon a pact made by men, such a need for dispensations may frequently arise; and consequently, it is in harmony with the nature of divine providence that it should have left this power in the Church. We have availed ourselves of

29. [Not included in these *Selections.*—Tr.]
30. [Reading *laica* for *Ecclesiastica.*—Reviser.]
31. [*Supra,* Sect. 1; p. 301.—Tr.]
32. [*Vide* next Chapter.—Tr.]

this argument in our treatises, *De Iuramento* and *De Voto* in the work *De Religione.*[33] Moreover, the subject-matter of such obligations is essentially mutable and variable, and human volition frequently consents imprudently to some obligation; so that this subject-matter was well suited for the power of dispensation. But when the natural law is binding by virtue of reason alone in a matter which is independent of prior human consent, not only can there be no necessity for dispensation, but dispensation is even repugnant to reason.[34] For if a given thing is forbidden by natural reason, it is intrinsically evil; and therefore what necessity can there be for dispensation from such a law? If, on the other hand, that thing is prescribed by natural law, then, there may arise a necessity [for such an exception], and the law in question will not be binding, nor will dispensation be necessary; or else, if in spite of the said necessity the law is binding by virtue of reason, failure to observe that law in such a situation is essentially evil, so that, consequently, there can be no necessity for permitting this non-observance.

Thus, the other examples adduced in the passage mentioned above lose their force: examples which might be more or less pertinent with respect to positive divine law, and which will be dealt with in the proper place, for they are not well adapted to this discussion of natural law. But the observations concerning interpretation, added at the conclusion of our argument, will be dealt with in the Sixteenth Chapter.

CHAPTER XV

Whether God Is Able to Grant Dispensations from the Natural Law, Even by His Absolute Power

1. *The reason for the difficulty.* The reason for this doubt is that every lawgiver can grant dispensations with respect to his own law; for this is true so generally and in a degree so free from exception, in the case of human legislators, that even if they grant dispensations without cause those dispensations are valid. Hence the same is true to a far greater degree when

---

33. [Not included in these *Selections.*—Tr.]
34. [Taking *ratio* as the antecedent of *illi.*—Tr.]

God is the Legislator; and therefore, since He is the Author of the natural law, He must be able to grant dispensations from it.

This argument is confirmed by the fact that He would seem to have acted thus when He granted to Abraham a dispensation from the Fifth Commandment of the Decalogue (*Genesis,* Chap. xxii), to Osee, a dispensation from the Sixth Commandment, bidding Osee take to himself a wife of fornications (*Osee,* Chap. ii [Chap. i]); and to the children of Israel, a dispensation from the Seventh Commandment (*Exodus,* Chap. xii [, vv. 35–6]) on the occasion when they despoiled the Egyptians, by His authorization.

2. *A threefold classification of natural precepts is pointed out.* Let us distinguish among three classes of natural precepts: some are principles of the most universal sort, for example, that one should not do evil, and that one should follow after the good; others, indeed, are immediate conclusions, intrinsically united in an absolute sense with the said principles, examples of this group being the Commandments of the Decalogue; in the third class, are still other precepts, much more remote from the first group of principles, and remote even from the commands of the Decalogue, as well. We shall give examples of this third class later.

As to the first class, there is no controversy among those who write on the subject. For it is certain that no dispensation can apply to this group, with respect to any man acting freely and as a moral being. For if God should ordain that man be deprived of the capacity for every moral action, by impeding his free use of reason and will, man would be excused from obligation to any natural law, since he would not be able to act well or ill, morally; yet this would be not a dispensation from natural law but an impeding of the subject's capacity to bear the obligation in question, just as, under present conditions, an infant is not, strictly speaking, bound by the natural law. But if, on the other hand, man is left capable of free action, he cannot be absolved from obligation with respect to all the aforementioned principles of the natural law. For, whatever dispensation we may assume to have been granted, it is necessary that those principles should be the rule of righteous conduct; since the dispensation either does make the action—or its omission—licit, or else it does not do so, and since, if the latter supposition is true, there is no dispensation, whereas, in the former case, it is necessary that reason should judge that the said action is here and now permissible, so that the dispensation consequently cannot apply to the principle in question—namely, that one must strive after the good—a point which will become more clear from what follows.

Therefore, the controversy concerns the two other classes of precepts. And the Doctors treat especially of the second class, for they say little concerning the third, with which we shall therefore deal briefly at the end of the Chapter.

3. *The first opinion: asserting that God is able to grant dispensations with respect to all natural precepts.* There is, then, the first opinion, involving the general assertion that God is able to grant dispensations with respect to all the precepts of the Decalogue. This consequently amounts to saying that God is able not only to grant such dispensations, but also to abrogate the whole of that law, doing away entirely with its binding or prohibitory force. If this were done, then—according to the opinion in question—all the things forbidden by the law of nature would be permissible, however evil they may now seem to be; whence one finally arrives at the conclusion that God is able not only to refrain from forbidding these actions, but even to command that they be done; for if they are not evil but, on the contrary, permissible, why should He not be able to prescribe them?

This was the opinion supported by Occam (on the *Sentences,* Bk. II, qu. xix, reply to third doubt), whom Peter d'Ailly followed (on the *Sentences,* Bk. I, dist. xiv [qu. xiv, ad 2]), and Andreas a Novocastro (on the *Sentences,* Bk. I, dist. xlviii, qu. i, art. i). Gerson (*Alphabetum Divini Amoris,* lxi, *lit.* E and F)[1] also inclines to this view; and Almain (*Moralia,* Bk. III, chap. xv), too, treats of it as probable, although later, indeed, he rejects it. These authors rest their case chiefly on the position that all actions which come within the range of the law of nature are evil only in so far as they are prohibited by God; and He acts freely in prohibiting them, since He is Supreme Lord and Governor. There is also the argument that the opposite position[2] does not involve any contradiction of this reasoning; for, once the prohibition is abolished, all the remaining points easily follow.

---

1. [Gerson does not deal very clearly with the subject.—Reviser.]

2. [I.e. the view that those things which are prohibited by the natural law are evil *per se,* and not because they are prohibited.—Tr.]

4. *This opinion is rejected.* This opinion, however, is rejected by the rest of the theologians as false and absurd; and it is to be condemned *a priori* on the basis of what was said above (Chap. vi; p. 206), where we have shown that, although the natural law, as properly a divine law, includes the commands and prohibitions[3] of God, it nevertheless assumes that there dwells in its subject-matter an intrinsic righteousness or wickedness, wholly inseparable from that matter. Furthermore, we showed in the same passage that, even though one assumes the existence of divine providence, it is not possible that God should refrain from forbidding those evils which are indicated by natural reason to be evils. And though we may suppose, indeed, that an additional prohibition imposed through the will of God may be withdrawn, nevertheless, it is wholly repugnant to that which is essentially and intrinsically evil that it should cease from being evil, since the nature of the thing cannot undergo change. Consequently, no act of the sort in question can be freely performed, without being evil and discordant with rational nature, as we have pointed out in the passage mentioned [*supra*, p. 217; Chap. vi, § 11], citing Aristotle [*Nicomachean Ethics*, Bk. II, chap. vi, § 18] and others. This fact, indeed, would appear to be self-evident. For how could it ever happen that a voluntary act of hatred of God, or of lying, should not be wrong? Therefore, the foundation of this opinion is entirely false; that foundation being the belief that all evil in human actions springs from an external prohibition. Therefore, lest we labour over an equivocation, we must consider separately the question of whether an external prohibition established by God might fail to be established by Him, either in the case of all such prohibitions, or in the case of one in particular. For, with respect to this sort of prohibition, there is more room for doubt, as I have remarked in that same Chapter vi; nevertheless, I showed it to be more probable that these prohibitions are inseparable from divine providence. Passing over this question, however, we now make a general inquiry as to whether God could bring it about that those actions which are forbidden by the law of the Decalogue should in no way be evil, so that they would not be forbidden as evil through any demonstrable law of the natural reason. It is in this sense, indeed, that we shall declare the opinion of Occam and of others to be false.

3. [*Prohibitionem*, possibly for *prohibitiones*.—Tr.]

5. An absurdity following upon the rejected opinion, namely: it would be possible for God to command that He Himself be held in hatred. Wherefore, *a fortiori,* it is evident that it is much more absurd to say that God could command man to hold Him in hatred, a conclusion which would plainly follow from that [rejected] opinion. For if He is able to refrain from forbidding that act, and if, with the prohibition abolished, the act is not evil, then He is able to command that it be done. Yet this consequent is clearly absurd, because God cannot bring it about that He Himself should be worthy of hatred; for that would be incompatible with His goodness. Nor can He even bring it about that it should be right and proper to hate an object that is worthy of love. Furthermore, a certain contradiction would be involved in such a situation; for obedience to God is a virtual love of Him, and the obligation to obey springs, above all, from love; therefore, it would be contrary to reason that one should be bound by a precept to hold God Himself in hatred.

The same argument may be presented in connexion with lying. For if God were able to command that lies be told, then He Himself would also be able to lie; a conclusion that is false, for if it were true, all certitude of faith would perish.[4] This reasoning, indeed, also affords proof with respect to dispensations; for if God is able to grant dispensations in all matters, then He is able to grant them in the case of lying—not only profitable,[5] but also injurious lying—and in any matter whatsoever; so that far more truly will He be able to grant dispensations for Himself (so to speak), or rather, able to lie without receiving a dispensation, since there would exist no prohibition with respect to Him, and since it is asserted [according to this first opinion] that the action in itself, apart from such a prohibition, is not evil.

6.[6] *The second opinion: asserting that the precepts of the Decalogue which are called those of the Second Table can be subjected to dispensation by God; whereas those of the First Table cannot.* The second opinion is that of Scotus

---

4. [Suárez here refers to the certitude of faith, which is based on the truthfulness of God in revelation.—REVISER.]

5. [A profitable (*officiosum*) lie is one from which the liar secures a benefit for himself or others.—REVISER.]

6. [This Section is incorrectly numbered '7' in the Latin text.—TR.]

(on the *Sentences,* Bk. III, dist. xxxvii, sole qu. [, concl. 4]), who is followed by Gabriel in the latter's comments on that passage (*ibid.,* qu. 1,
art. 2). Almain, too, is cited on the same passage. This opinion distinguishes between the precepts of the First Table, and those of the Second.
Three precepts of the Decalogue are said to belong to the First Table,
precepts which have regard to God. Concerning these, it is held that the
first two, which are negative, cannot be subjected to dispensation; but
that the third, in so far as it involves the circumstance of the Sabbath, was
liable both to dispensation and to abrogation; a fact that is manifest to
all persons, since with respect to that particular circumstance it was not a
natural precept but a positive one, although, in so far as this Third Commandment comprises in an absolute sense an affirmative precept enjoining divine worship, [Almain] doubts whether it is liable to dispensation.
All this part of the second opinion, indeed, I shall discuss below. The
remaining seven commandments are said to be commandments of the
Second Table; as, in general, all those are called which deal with one's
neighbour or with created things; and every one of these, in the opinion
of Scotus, is subject to dispensation.

7. Scotus adduces two special grounds for his view. One of them is as
follows: if the said commandments were not subject to dispensation, the
divine intellect, anticipating its act of will, would necessarily judge that
certain actions are to be regarded with love, and certain others with hatred;
so that, consequently, it would impose upon that divine will the necessity
of loving the acts which [the intellect] prescribes and hating those which
it prohibits; but, this Scotus deems to be absurd, saying, moreover, that he
has elsewhere demonstrated [its absurdity].

His second ground is that human blessedness does not depend upon
any act relating to created things; for only by love of God Himself can
God make man blessed. Accordingly, no act of the human will respecting
a creature is a necessary means to the blessedness of man, in so far as the
absolute power of God is concerned; neither is [an act of this kind] necessarily an obstacle excluding that happiness; hence, no such act relating to
a creature is necessarily prescribed or forbidden by God; and therefore, He
is able to grant dispensations from any of the said acts. Wherefore, Scotus
draws the inference that those seven precepts of the Decalogue are not

conclusions deduced by an absolute necessity from self-evident principles, but are simply characterized by the highest degree of harmony with the nature of man, with the result that they are [respectively] prescribed, or prohibited; so that, accordingly, they are subject to dispensation. Moreover, Scotus adduces, as an example, the slaying of a man; the prohibition against this act not being inferred of necessity from natural principles; a point that was brought out (he says) in the case of Abraham. Bonaventure (on the *Sentences,* Bk. I, dist. xlvii [, qu. 4, conclusio, scholion]) seems to have held almost the same opinion, the only difference being that, with respect to the commandments of the First Table, he denies without exception that dispensations are possible. As for the commandments of the Second Table, however, he makes absolutely the contrary assertion, and believes that this is the opinion of Bernard (*De Praecepto et Dispensatione,* Chap. v). But concerning the latter's meaning, I shall speak later.[7] It is possible, indeed, that Bonaventure's meaning was the same.

8. In connexion with this opinion of Scotus, one must take into consideration, first of all, the fact that he does not so much admit that dispensations are possible in the case of natural law—formally speaking, as it were (that is, speaking properly and rigorously of the commands of the natural law)—but rather excludes from this law, the precepts of the Second Table, consequently conceding that they are subject to dispensation. Whence it seems to follow that he admits of no strict precept of the natural law save those which have regard to God. Both these points are clearly evident, since the law of nature is that law which imposes an obligation by the force of reason alone; whereas the excluded precepts have not this quality, according to Scotus, since (so he says) they are not of necessity inferred from the principles of nature, so that [the acts which they prohibit] are not intrinsically evil save by virtue of the fact that they are forbidden; therefore, . . .

9. *The opinion above set forth is rejected.* In both respects, then, this opinion is entirely unacceptable to me. For, in the first place, if the precepts of the Second Table were not part of the natural law, then, before the time of the law which was given through Moses, they would not have

7. [*Infra,* p. 346; § 24.—Tr.]

been binding upon men by the force of natural reason alone; and a special divine prohibition could not have been made known through that Mosaic law, if reason did not reveal an intrinsic wickedness in the [prohibited] acts. Hence, even after the giving of the law, these moral precepts would not have been binding upon the peoples for whom the Mosaic law had not been given. And furthermore, not even for us, at the present time, would they retain their force, since all the commandments, in so far as they were [merely] positive commandments embodied in that law, have lapsed; unless it be said that they were renewed by Christ in the Gospel. This latter assertion is, indeed, true; but it results in a reversal of the argument, for Christ laid down, not moral precepts of a positive character, but natural precepts which He [merely] amplified, so that, if they still endure, it is for this very reason, namely, that they are natural precepts. Again, the whole of the consequent under discussion would seem to be opposed to the words of Paul, when he said, in his *Epistle to the Romans* (Chap. ii [, vv. 14 and 12]: '. . . the Gentiles who have not the law, do by nature those things that are of the law,' and, '. . . whosoever have sinned without the law, shall perish without the law'; that is, without positive law and on account of natural law alone. And in that *Epistle to the Romans* [Chap. i, v. 28], Paul is speaking of sins against the commandments of the Second Table, when he says: '. . . God delivered them up to a reprobate sense, to do those things which are not convenient,' &c.

10. It may be answered that, even if the precepts in question are not absolutely necessary by the natural law, they are nevertheless in such harmony with nature that they were introduced and accepted by all nations; a fact which suffices for the conclusion that, apart from any positive prohibition laid down by God, men would sin by transgressing these precepts.

But the contrary is true; for it would follow from the foregoing argument that these commandments would be, at most, a part of the *ius gentium,* as Scotus plainly seems to believe when he compares them with the precepts concerning division of property; and the *ius gentium,* indeed, can be changed, not only by God, but even by man, a point which I shall make below.[8] This fact, moreover, is clear because, if a given country

8. [*Cf.* Chapter xx, especially Sec. 6; pp. 379 *et seq.*—Tr.]

were practising not individual, but community ownership of property, we should not be able to condemn that custom as evil; and therefore it would follow that the same should be said regarding the commandments of the Second Table, a statement which would be absurd in the highest degree. If it were not thus absurd, then the custom of a barbarous people who practised not individual but community ownership of wives would not call for condemnation as being intrinsically evil; an assertion that no one will make. Accordingly, as we have noted above, certain peoples have approved of adultery and others have failed to condemn theft, errors which are most severely condemned in them; whereas, if the said errors were opposed simply to the *ius gentium* they would not be altogether worthy of condemnation, since not all kingdoms and countries are bound to accept in their own practice the whole of the *ius gentium,* which is, strictly speaking, a human body of laws. Finally, Paul also, *loc. cit.* [*Romans,* Chap. ii, v. 15], would seem to exclude the possibility of such an answer,[9] in the words: 'Who shew the work of the law written in their hearts'—written, assuredly, by the Author of nature, as all the commentators explain, declaring therefore that the Author of this law is God Himself, [promulgating it] through the light of nature. I shall offer as a confirmation of this point, another passage from Paul (*ibid.,* Chap. xiii [, v. 9]): 'Thou shalt not kill; thou shalt not commit adultery[10]. . . . [and if there be any other commandment,] it is comprised in this word, Thou shalt love thy neighbour as thyself.' In these words Paul teaches that the commandments in question are intrinsically, and from the very nature of the case, bound up with love of one's neighbour; and that they are part of the Decalogue only as they are necessary to the love of one's neighbour; yet it would seem to be self-evident that such love pertains most especially to the natural law, since without that love it is impossible to preserve nature itself, not only in so far as relates to proper order and to development, but also with respect to its very existence; and therefore, the same should be said with regard to all the commandments under discussion.

9. [I.e. the answer suggested at the beginning of this Section (10).—Tr.]

10. [The Vulgate version of this passage reads: *Non adulterabis; Non occides.* Suárez has: *Non occides, non maechaberis.* The order used by Suárez is that of *Exodus,* Chap. xx, vv. 13, 14.—Reviser.]

11. *Not only the precepts relating to God are necessary by virtue of the natural law, but the same is also true of many which relate to one's neighbour.* Hence, indeed, it necessarily follows that not only the precepts relating to God are absolutely necessary by the force of natural law, for the same is also true of many precepts which relate to one's neighbour. Moreover, the philosophers have apparently recognized this fact, as is clear from Aristotle (*Nicomachean Ethics,* Bk. II, chap. vi and Bk. V, chap. vii), Cicero (*The Republic* [Bk. I, chap. iv]), and Plato (*The Republic* [Bk. I, chap. viii and chaps. xix–xx]), as well as from St. Thomas [I.–II, qu. 94, art. 5] and the other theologians. The rational argument, too, which may be inferred from what has already been said, affords convincing proof of this point. And furthermore, its truth is made manifest by a process of induction; for the Eighth Commandment, at least, 'Thou shalt not bear false witness', is entirely a necessary commandment, as is clear, *a fortiori,* from the remarks made above,[11] with respect to the evil[12] of lying. Likewise, stealing in the formal sense, and if we restrict our meaning to the very nature of theft, can never be permissible. For if the taking is permissible, the other person (from whom I am taking the thing in question) is not reasonably unwilling that I should do so; if such unwillingness is not reasonable, there is no theft; therefore, conversely, when the other party is reasonably unwilling, the taking is not permissible; hence the act of theft and the fact of permissibility are mutually repugnant; and therefore, this precept [prohibiting theft,] is also necessary in an absolute sense. Moreover, the same argument holds in connexion with homicide, as I shall explain in dealing with the third opinion.

12. The arguments of Scotus, indeed, are not convincing.

The arguments of Scotus are answered. For the first argument, as Bassolis, Cajetan, and others have observed, tells equally against the first part of Scotus's own opinion; since, if any commandment of the First Table is incapable of being subjected to dispensation, then the divine intellect also, in so far as it acts before the will,[13] necessarily determines that this commandment shall be observed; and consequently, the will—even the

---

11. [*Supra,* p. 330; § 5.—ED.]

12. [Read *pravitate* for *parvitate.* The 1856 Paris edition has the correct reading.—TR.]

13. [There is no actual priority of intellect and will in God. It is we who conceive a priority.—REVISER.]

divine will—conforms of necessity to this judgment, in spite of the fact
that the latter deals with a created thing, that is, with human conduct
or actions. Therefore the consequent in question, in so far as it relates
to the divine intellect, involves no contradiction. For God passes necessary judgment concerning every necessary truth, whether it has to do
with increate or with created subject-matter, and whether that subject-
matter be speculative or practical—that is, capable of being acted upon
by man. In so far, indeed, as relates to God's will, if one is referring to
a simple disposition of approval or disapproval, then it is possible that
God should even entertain such a disposition as a matter of necessity,
with respect to that which He judges to be essentially good or essentially
evil; especially if one assumes the action of free will on His part in the
creation of man. If, however, the reference is to some act of absolute
will,[14] that imposes a precept or binds men by a positive and superadded
obligation, then, from this standpoint,[15] the consequent may, with some
force, be contested as to both its parts. However, we have already demonstrated the more probable opinion to be that, even in this sense, there
is no obstacle to prevent the divine will from being bound of necessity
to the prohibition in question, on the basis of the assumption that He
determined to create human nature and to govern it—that is, exercise a
fitting providential care over it.

The second argument of Scotus, however, is derived from an extrinsic
relation; for the intrinsic evil or good of a given act is to be estimated in
accordance with its object and not on the basis of its habitual relation to
the ultimate end, or of its necessity for the attainment of that end. Accordingly, a jocose or profitable lie[16] does not, strictly speaking, deprive a man
of his ultimate end, since it is a venial sin; yet it does not admit of dispensation. And if it is urged that an impediment exists in the fact that as long
as that sin persists,[17] beatitude cannot be attained[18] until the obligation

---

14. [The *voluntas beneplaciti* in God is the act itself by which God wills something,
since God wills that which He wills because it is well pleasing to Him.—REVISER.]

15. [Simply *sic* in the Latin.—TR.]

16. 'Profitable lie': *mendacium officiosum,* a lie aimed at providing a benefit.

17. [I.e. as long as it has not been forgiven.—REVISER.]

18. [*Obtinere,* evidently for *obtineri.* The 1856 Paris edition has the correct form.—TR.]

to pay the penalty is discharged,[19] then it is evident that the assumption is false. For there are many acts in relation to creatures, and omissions of such acts, which may be necessary to the attainment of beatitude, or which may impede its attainment. It was for this reason, indeed, that Paul said that they who commit such acts shall perish without the law. Therefore, although the substance of beatitude consists in God alone and in acts relating to Him, nevertheless, those acts which relate to creatures may be an impediment to beatitude, or a necessary means to its attainment, in so far as they result in offence to God, or involve obedience to Him.

13. *The third opinion: affirming that the negative Commandments of the Decalogue do not admit of dispensation; except in the case of the Fifth Commandment, from which dispensations may be granted, as they may in the case of the affirmative commandments.* The third opinion is that of Durandus (on the *Sentences,* Bk. I, dist. xlvii, qu. 4 [, no. 18]) and of Major (on the *Sentences,* Bk. II, dist. xxxvii, qu. 10 [Bk. III, dist. xxxvii, qu. 11, art. 8]), who distinguish between the negative and the affirmative commandments, although they do not entirely agree with each other. For Major declares that the negative commandments do not admit of dispensation, save in the case of the Fifth Commandment, 'Thou shalt not kill.' Durandus, however, while laying down the same rule in regard to an exception, has said that if the words 'Thou shalt not kill' are taken in a general sense, as relating to every homicide, then, in that sense, they admit of dispensation; whereas, if they are taken as referring to the slaying of a human being in so far as that slaying is prohibited by natural reason, then, according to such an interpretation, not even the Fifth Commandment is liable to dispensation.

But surely it was not necessary to make this distinction. For slaying, in that first sense, does not come under the prohibition laid down by the law of nature, since the prohibition implies [only] a certain general concept, treating of this concept of slaughter as apart from the qualities of justice and injustice, and since it is evident that slaughter simply as such is not prohibited by the natural law. With respect to the Fifth Commandment, then, strictly speaking, the exception is made without cause, as will become clear. Moreover, the two authors in question might, in the

---

19. [In every sin theologians see a *reatus culpae* and a *reatus poenae.*—REVISER.]

same manner, have made an exception with respect to the Seventh Commandment, or proposed distinctions within its range, since the taking of another's property may sometimes occur justly.

14. As to the affirmative precepts, however, Major makes the absolute assertion that all of them admit of dispensation.

He proves this statement, first, by the argument that God is able to refrain from co-operating with man in the performance of any prescribed act whatsoever. But this argument is irrelevant because such a withholding of co-operation is equivalent not to the granting of a dispensation but to a withdrawal of the power to act. For who would say that one man grants to another man a dispensation from the obligation to hear Mass, by forcibly detaining that other person or by wounding him so severely that he is unable to hear Mass?

Major's next proof is that God is able to give for any designated period of time whatsoever the privilege of refraining from the performance of the prescribed act, or is able even to prescribe the performance of some different act, so that He is therefore able to grant in this way a dispensation extending over the whole of a lifetime. Neither is this argument convincing, however, if we take into consideration the fact that an affirmative precept is not binding continuously, and that, in the case of purely natural law, it is specifically binding at no other time than that which is determined by the occurrence of a necessary occasion or opportunity. Accordingly, although it may happen that a whole lifetime passes without the occurrence of such an occasion or opportunity, and therefore without any exercise of binding force on the part of the precept, no dispensation is involved [simply] for that reason. For such a situation may arise even naturally, and without the intervention of a miracle. At best, then, this argument proves that God is able to bring it about that, on each of the occasions [otherwise] coming under the precept, the necessity for obeying it shall not occur, either because some other precept more urgently demands obedience, or because the circumstances involved undergo change. But if Major means to say that, while those circumstances remain unchanged under which a natural precept is binding, God is able to grant licence to refrain from fulfilling that precept, then this author does not prove his point, but, on the contrary, merely assumes it to be true.

15. *Durandus declares that the Commandments of the First Table do not admit of dispensation; but that this is not the case with the Commandments of the Second Table.* Durandus, indeed, distinguishes between the Commandments of the First Table and those of the Second Table, asserting that the former do not admit of dispensation, whereas the latter do admit of it. He defends this assertion with the following argument: every matter from which there may be withdrawn the essential reason for the obligation involved, admits of dispensation; but those matters which have annexed to them an inseparable[20] obligation, do not admit of dispensation; and the matters to which the precepts in question relate, come under these two classifications respectively; therefore, . . .

Durandus proves his minor proposition by analogy, thus: dependence upon God is a condition inseparable from man; but the dependence of one man upon another is a condition separable from any given individual; so that, accordingly, the worship of God is inseparable from the obligation to worship Him; but the honouring of parents may be separated [from the corresponding obligation]. Therefore, it is impossible for God to do away with the obligation to believe in Him and show Him reverence; whereas it is possible for Him to bring it about that parents should not be honoured.

In my opinion, however, the argument is in both its parts ineffective, and the distinction lacking in consistency.

The first proof of my assertion is as follows: [The dependence in question] is a very different matter from dependence upon God for one's existence, inasmuch as the latter kind of dependence is absolutely necessary, since without it man could not continue to exist, whereas he may exist without performing any practical action in relation to God, and may even perform good acts with respect to other objects. Again, although God might have brought it about that Peter, for example, should not derive his [physical] being from [those persons who do happen to be] his parents, nevertheless, that would not be equivalent to granting Peter a dispensation from the precept enjoining that one shall honour his parents; and if, on the other hand, we assume that he has received his [physical] being from those persons, there is involved forthwith a dependence inseparably

20. [The Latin has *separabile*, evidently for *inseparabile*.—Tr.]

connected with the obligation to honour the said parents, even as the obligation to worship God is inseparable from dependence upon Him.

From the foregoing, [my objection to] the second part [of Durandus's contention] becomes clear. For if we are referring to the obligation itself, that is equally inseparable [from both kinds of precepts], if we regard the matter with due proportion—that is to say, if we assume the derivation of the obligation from the appropriate cause; and if, on the other hand, we are referring to the acts by which the said obligation is discharged, then, just as God is able to bring it about that a man may never in the whole course of his life perform an act of honour toward his parents, and may be without sin despite this omission, even so is He able to bring it about that a man may never perform an act of divine worship, [and nevertheless not sin in so abstaining]; so that neither case permits of dispensation, or else it is possible for dispensations to be granted with respect to both of the precepts in question.

16. *The fourth opinion: asserting that none of the Commandments of the Decalogue admits of dispensation, even by the absolute power of God.* There is, then, a fourth opinion, according to which, simply and absolutely, none of the Commandments of the Decalogue admits of dispensation, even by the absolute power of God. St. Thomas (I.–II, qu. 100, art. 8) holds this opinion, as do also Cajetan and others who comment upon that passage in the works of Thomas, such as Soto (*De Iustitia,* Bk. II, qu. iii, art. 8), Victoria (Relectio: *De Homicidio*), Viguerius (*Institutiones Theologicae,* Chap. xv, § 1, versu. 7), and Vincent de Beauvais (*Speculum Morale,* Bk. I, pt. ii, dist. 6). Altisiodorensis on Peter Lombard (*Summa Aurea in IV ll. Sententiarum,* Bk. III, tract. vii, chap. i, qu. 5); Richard Middleton (on the *Sentences,* Bk. III, dist. xxxvii, art. 1, qu. 5); de la Palu and Bassolis, expounding the same passage of Peter Lombard also support this view. Others, such as Abulensis (on *Exodus,* Chap. xx, qu. 35) and Molina (*De Iustitia et Iure,* Vol. VI, tract. v, disp. 57, no. 6) hold the same opinion.

The basic argument supporting the view of St. Thomas is as follows: those commandments which involve an intrinsic principle of justice and obligation are not liable to dispensation; and the Commandments of the Decalogue are of this nature; therefore, . . . The major premiss is clearly true, according to the following reasoning: a contradiction is involved in conceiving of [one and the same] thing as being obligatory and as not being obligatory; and that which is subjected to dispensation by that very fact ceases to be obligatory; yet, if it is inseparable from obligation, it necessarily retains that obligatory quality; and therefore, a contradiction is involved in conceiving that anything of this sort[21] is subjected to dispensation. Accordingly, St. Thomas further declares that not even God is able to grant [such] a dispensation; for He cannot act contrary to His own justness; and nevertheless He would so act, if He granted licence to do that which is *per se* and intrinsically unjust.[22]

17. This argument is assailed, however, by the authors who advance other opinions, on the ground that the said argument either follows a vicious circle, or applies equally to every precept and to the dispensation therefrom. The proof of this statement is as follows: if St. Thomas means to say that, as long as the obligation stands and endures, there can be no room for dispensation, this would be true of every law, since it is inconceivable that a dispensation should be granted, making it permissible to act against a law, while the obligation imposed by that law endures, for the nature of a dispensation consists in the very fact that it does away with the obligation resulting from the law, so that a contradiction of terms is involved in speaking of such a dispensation; but the alternative interpretation [of the argument] is that the obligation in question cannot be removed in the case of natural precepts, and this is the point to be proved, so that, since this very point is assumed to be true, the argument moves in a vicious circle.

18. *The fourth opinion is approved and expounded.* The reply is that the obligation in question is twofold. One phase of it proceeds from the law itself, as an effect of that law, and as to this phase, the objection clearly holds good; but in the above argument St. Thomas is not speaking of this form of obligation. The other phase is one arising from an intrinsically fit proportion between the object and the act in relation to right reason, or rational nature; and with respect to this obligation, the argument of St. Thomas holds.

---

21. [I.e. anything inseparable from obligation.—Tr.]
22. [*Iniustum;* unjust, that is, in the Scriptural sense of unrighteous.—Tr.]

For (as has often been said) the natural law forbids those things which are in themselves evil, in so far as they are evil in this sense; and therefore, it assumes that such objects or acts themselves involve an intrinsic obligation, requiring that they shall not be loved, or that they shall not be performed. Conversely, this same law prescribes that which is good, in so far as the latter involves an intrinsic and necessary connexion with rational nature. Such obligation, however, is inseparable, not for the reason that it does not admit of dispensation (for we should then be arguing in a vicious circle), but because it is assumed to exist intrinsically in the things themselves, prior to the existence of any extrinsic law, so that, as long as these things themselves remain, the said obligation cannot be abolished. For it is not dependent upon any extrinsic act of willing; neither is it something distinct, but rather an entirely intrinsic mode of action (so to speak) or—as it were—a relation which cannot be prevented from arising, once the foundation and term of the relation have been established. This reasoning is confirmed, moreover, by what has been said with respect to the other opinions, and by our statements in Chapter vi.

19. The fourth opinion, then, formally and properly speaking, is true. For, assuredly, we cannot deny that God sometimes brings it to pass that those material acts shall be permissible which otherwise—if God Himself and God's power did not intervene—could not licitly be performed. Accordingly, in order to understand how this may be and why [such intervention] is not a dispensation and is not so termed, we must distinguish in God various characteristics.

For He is supreme Lawgiver, wherefore he has the power to impose new and various commandments. He is also supreme Lord, and is able to change and to grant rights of ownership. Furthermore, He is supreme Judge, and has the power to punish or to render to every man his due.

Properly speaking, then, [the power of] dispensation pertains to God under that first aspect, since it is one and the same power that abrogates laws and makes laws. Accordingly, in order that God may be understood to grant a dispensation, it is needful that, while exercising this [legislative] form of jurisdiction only, without adjoining to it the power of dominion by means of which He changes the objects themselves, He shall render permissible that which previously was not permissible. For if through His own power of dominion He brings about a change in human dominion, that is not the granting of a dispensation, but an abolition of the subject-matter, of a law, as is evident from what we have said above. Now at no time when God renders permissible an act which has seemed to be prohibited by the natural law, does He do so purely in the capacity of Legislator; on the contrary, He makes use of another power; and therefore, He is not granting a dispensation.

20. This fact may be perceived in considering the examples already set forth.

For when God bade Abraham slay his son, God issued this command as Lord of life and death; since, if He Himself had willed to slay Isaac by His own hand, He would have had no need of any dispensation, but could have performed the deed by His own power of dominion; and therefore, in like manner, He was able to use Abraham as His instrument; nor does the Fifth Commandment forbid one to be God's instrument in slaying, if God Himself shall so command.

St. Thomas holds the same opinion in regard to the taking to himself, by Osee, of a wife of fornications. This is evident from the passage cited (I.–II, qu. 100, art. 8, ad 3, and II.–II, qu. 154 [, art. 2, ad 2]). For God has power to transfer to a man *dominium* over a woman without her consent, and to effect such a bond between them that, by virtue of this bond, the union is no longer one of fornication.

According to the opinion which is more probably correct, Osee received the harlot as his wife. However, though this is true with respect to God's absolute power, the passage in *Osee* [Chap. i] does not make such an interpretation compulsory; for God commanded Osee to take to himself this woman who had previously lived in fornication, not merely to use her, but also in matrimony and as his spouse. Such is the interpretation of Jerome, Theodoret, and others, as well as Irenaeus (*Against Heresies,* Bk. IV, chap. xxxvii [chap. xx]) and Augustine (*Against Faustus,* Bk. XXII, chaps. lxxx and lxxxv, and *Against Secundinus the Manichean,* Chap. xxi).

According to the same line of reasoning, God did not grant a dispensation to the Hebrews when He conceded to them the spoils of the Egyptians; but rather, He either made a gift of these spoils, acting as supreme Lord, or else, at least, paid them the wages of their labours, acting as supreme Judge, according to the words of the *Book of Wisdom* (Chap. x [, v. 19]).

All similar cases, then, are to be interpreted in like manner; nor could one interpret them otherwise, owing to the reason above set forth.

Moreover, the same conclusion may be applied to affirmative commandments, in connexion with which the argument is simple. For these commandments are binding, not continuously, but upon the occurrence of an occasion which involves necessity with respect to the object in question; and God has power either to change the object, by ceding His right or changing the rights of men, or else to remove the necessity by adding new circumstances which will impede its existence; yet the commandment remains intact in such a way that, of itself, it is always binding for the proper occasions; and this is an indication that no dispensation has been granted.

21. Accordingly, St. Thomas, in the passage above cited (I.–II, qu. 100, art. 8), concludes, in his reply to the third objection, that this kind of change is possible not only to God but, at times, to men as well. [This is true,] indeed, in the case of the negative commandments, when their subject-matter falls under human dominion and can be changed by human beings, in the way which we have described above in connexion with the law of prescription. In the case of the affirmative commandments, however, [the conclusion of St. Thomas holds true] when men are able to change the circumstances that brought about the necessity for acting, or they are able to impose a more weighty precept: as, for example, when the king commands a son not to succour his parent when the latter is in extreme need, in order that this son may rather succour the imperilled state.

But God, because of His unique excellence, is able, when He so wills, to make use of His absolute power and dominion. From this fact, one deduces the reason that such changes cannot be made by men with respect to the subject-matter of all negative commandments which can be so changed by God. Take, for example, the commandment against adultery; for, in truth, a man has not, as God has, that power over the person of a woman that enables him to give her into the possession of another at will; and consequently, even human laws have availed through prescription to change rights of ownership over property, whereas they have not availed in the same way to change rights of ownership over wives. Accordingly, even while human law remains the same, that which was formerly a theft could cease to be theft; but that which is essentially an act of adultery, cannot cease to be adultery.

22. *Which natural precepts are entirely immutable.* Furthermore, from the above remarks, it may incidentally be deduced that whenever the subject-matter of a precept is such that the rectitude or evil involved does not depend upon the divine power of dominion, the said precept is not only one which does not admit of dispensation, but it is also immutable in such a way that what is prohibited by it cannot for any reason be made licit. For, properly speaking, this situation is found to occur solely in the case of negative precepts.

The First Commandment of the Decalogue is of this character, in so far as it is a negative commandment and prohibits men from having or worshipping more than one God. For this precept can in nowise undergo change, since [that which it prohibits] is opposed to the very essence of the ultimate end and to the excellence of God, as well as to His unity, which He Himself cannot change; for He is unable either to set up any other God, or to create anything worthy of honour equal [to that due to Him]; and therefore, the power to change this commandment or its subject-matter does not fall under divine dominion.

The same is true of the Second Commandment: partly because it involves a prohibition against lying, which cannot for any reason be made righteous, so long as it continues to be lying; but chiefly because it prohibits men from making God the Author of lying, a prohibition which extends also to irreverence toward God, a thing so incompatible with the divine authority, that He cannot cede His right (so to speak), in that respect.

In this sense, indeed, Scotus's assertion that these [two] commandments are more strictly immutable than the others, is a true assertion.

23. *Whether God is able to concede, or permit, in the case of any person, that through all eternity that person may refrain from executing any good impulse toward God Himself.* As to the Third Commandment, however, it is certain, since this precept is affirmative, that God can bring it about that the said precept shall often not be binding when otherwise, according to the common course of things, it would be binding. Whether He is able to

give a man permission to refrain throughout all the days of his life and—a more difficult supposition—throughout all eternity, from executing any good impulse toward God Himself, or tendering any direct and proximate act of worship, is a point on which Scotus has not unreasonably felt doubt. Some of the Thomists, indeed, are of the opinion that this is not possible, whether through dispensation, properly speaking, or even through a change in the subject-matter [of the precept]. If, however, we are considering pure and absolute power, no implication of a contradiction is involved in this assertion, since there does not follow from it the inference that the person in question is unable to perform good acts in practical relation to created objects. For the quality of goodness in these acts does not depend upon a previous formal act in relation to the ultimate end; and moreover, they tend by their very nature toward that end, so that, both mediately and remotely (or, as it were, substantially), they may be said to include the worship of God. If, on the other hand, we are considering the divine power as it is joined with the infinite wisdom and goodness of God, and if we speak in this sense, then, practically (as it were), it is more credible that God is unable to cede His own right in this respect; for that would seem to be an act of irrational prodigality, especially [if executed] with respect to a rational created being and for all eternity.

In the other commandments, however, I do not find this sort of immutability on the part of the subject-matter; an exception being made solely in the case of lying, as I have already remarked.[23] In the case of lying, there is perhaps a special reason for the immutability, either in the fact that lying is also an evil with respect to God Himself; or, again, in the fact that lying, of itself, is not limited to created matter, nor does it depend upon God's dominion over that matter or over the person involved, since, on the contrary, a lie can be told in any matter whatsoever and concerning any person; or, finally, in the fact that the perverseness of lying does not depend upon any dominion, or divine law, but arises directly from the disaccord between the words and the mind.

24. *The sense of Bernard's assertion that the commandments of the Second Table can be changed by God.* In fine, from the remarks above made,

---

23. [*Supra*, p. 330; this Chapter, § 5.—Tr.]

one may interpret the sense of St. Bernard's assertion (in *De Praecepto et Dispensatione,* Chap. v) that those things which pertain to the Commandments of the Second Table can be changed by the authority of God, if He so commands. For St. Bernard is speaking, not of the commandments themselves, formally considered, as it were; but of the actions with which those commandments are concerned. With regard to the latter, he says that even though they are never permissible *per se,* they can be made permissible by the authority of God if He commands it. This assertion is true, in the sense expounded above; yet such an exception amounts, not to a dispensation from a commandment of the Second Table, but to a change in the subject-matter of the commandment, as we have already remarked. However, in view of the fact that this change, when it is wrought through the peculiar dominion and power of God, is (so to speak) outside the natural course of things, and beyond the realm of the laws of ordinary providence—in view of that fact, I say—such a change is sometimes spoken of as a dispensation; not, indeed, a dispensation from any strict natural precept (nor has St. Bernard so stated, as will be evident, if we read his words with care), but a dispensation from the ordinary course of things and the ordinary law of providence, a law dependent upon the divine will. The words of Bonaventure, too, appear to have the same sense; for he follows the opinion of St. Bernard.

It may be objected that, in consequence, the distinction drawn by Bonaventure between the commandments of the First Table and those of the Second will no longer exist; a distinction also favoured by St. Bernard, for immediately afterward (*ibid.,* Chap. vi), he says that certain precepts are of so immutable a nature that not even by God Himself can they be changed. One may easily reply, on the basis of what we have already said, that the difference consists in the following fact: the commandments of the First Table are such that it is impossible not only that a formal dispensation should be granted from them, but even that such a change should be brought about in the actions which they forbid as to make these actions permissible or righteous; so that it is accordingly impossible that the said acts should, even in their substance, be made righteous by the authority of God Who would so command. For in no way can hatred of God, or adoration of an idol, or the worship of any god other than the true God, be made righteous since the quality of perverseness is inseparable from these acts considered in themselves, if they are freely performed; a statement that does not always apply to the acts that come under the commandments of the Second Table. This assertion should be taken, not in a universal, but in an indefinite sense; for some commandments of the Second Table may also be immutable in this manner, a point which Bernard openly admits (*ibid.*, Chapter vi, above cited) and which we have sufficiently explained in the foregoing pages.

25. *Whether, apart from the Decalogue, there are certain natural precepts from which dispensations can be granted, by divine power.* There remains for discussion the question of whether, apart from the Decalogue, there are some natural precepts which, strictly and formally speaking, can be relaxed by a divine dispensation. For Soto [*De Iustitia*, Bk. II, qu. iii, art. 8], affirms this, and he is followed by B. Medina (on I.–II, qu. 100, art. 8), who ascribes this opinion to St. Thomas. It may be so ascribed because the latter says (I.–II, qu. 94, art. 5) that with respect to some conclusions, at least, the natural law may be changed in certain special cases; as in the case of the precept concerning the return of a deposit (an example used by the authors in question in order to prove that the natural law admits of dispensation). Or, the said opinion may be ascribed to St. Thomas, because he asserts (in the aforesaid [I.–II,] qu. 100, art. 8) that dispensations can occur from the precepts which are laid down for the purpose of determining the special modes of complying with the Commandments of the Decalogue; so that, for example, if the law should distribute sentry duty among the citizens in order that the city might be guarded, dispensations from this duty could be granted to certain persons. (For that is the example given by St. Thomas, and also applied by Soto to the question under discussion.) Altisiodorensis [*Summa*, Bk. III, tract. vii, chap. i, qu. 5], seems likewise to have been of this opinion; inasmuch as he distinguishes in laws, four degrees of necessity. Of these, the fourth is not pertinent to our question, since it is that degree of necessity which proceeds from a human law. In the third grade, Altisiodorensis places those precepts that are dependent upon a human act, the existence of which[24] they presuppose; such, for example,

----

24. [Reading *quem* for *quam,* in accordance with the Paris edition of 1856.—Tr.]

as the precepts relating to the observance of vows, oaths, contracts, &c. And with respect to these there is little doubt, as is clear from the preceding Chapter. As regards the first grade of necessity, then, Altisiodorensis declares that the precepts falling under this head do not admit of dispensation, whereas the laws of the second grade do admit of dispensation. He cites by way of example the law against taking several women in marriage [at one time]. Moreover, he sets forth the rational basis of his view: that those precepts are characterized by a secondary degree of necessity which are in a certain sense necessary to the preservation of charity, but not in an absolute sense necessary to charity itself; inasmuch as those which are necessary in the latter sense, constitute the precepts of the first degree of necessity. St. Thomas strongly favours this view (on the *Sentences,* Bk. IV, dist. xxxiii, qu. 1). For he maintains (art. 1) that the rule of the natural law which forbids a plurality of wives belongs not to the precepts of the primary degree, but to those of the secondary degree; and accordingly, he adds (art. 2) that God could have granted a dispensation in the case of that precept [against polygamy].

Moreover, the same reasoning will apply to the natural precept prohibiting marriage between brother and sister. Thus it is that we read that Abraham had Sarah, his sister, to wife. A similar conclusion applies to the precept prohibiting dissolution of the bond of a marriage that has been consummated. For these and the like are natural precepts, and nevertheless, God has power to grant dispensations from them.

Soto's position would appear to be based upon the fact that the said precepts are neither proximately nor remotely contained, strictly speaking, in the laws of the Decalogue, in the sense in which conclusions are contained in the principles [from which they are derived]. Accordingly, it is his opinion that [these rules] are not inferred as necessary consequents, and are therefore not characterized by such a high grade of necessity that it is impossible to grant dispensation from them.

26. *The solution: it is not possible that God should, properly speaking, grant dispensations from any natural precept.* Notwithstanding the foregoing, we must assert that God does not, properly speaking, grant dispensations with respect to any natural precept; but that He does change the subject-matter of such precepts or their circumstances, apart from which they themselves

do not possess binding force, of themselves and without dispensation. I believe that this is the meaning that St. Thomas has in mind (aforesaid I.–II, qu. 100, art. 8), as well as Cajetan, Richard Middleton and others.

I shall prove the validity of that opinion, first, by excluding the examples adduced in opposition to it.

The first example had to do with the failure to return a deposit in a case of necessity. But that clearly does not involve a dispensation. For, if it did, [the inference would be that] any individual might grant himself a dispensation with respect to the natural law involved; since on his own authority he is able—nay, more—he is bound, to refrain from returning the deposit in such a case. There occurs, then, a change in subject-matter, through which change it is brought about that this subject-matter does not fall under the precept in question; a fact which I have already pointed out (Chapter Three).[25] Therefore, it is not pertinent to adduce in this connexion the remarks made by St. Thomas in Article 5, qu. 94 [of I.–II], since he is speaking, in that passage, not of a dispensation but of a change in subject-matter.

The second example related to the defence of a city, through sentry duty assigned by law; which is much more beside the point. For such assignments are made only by human law, so that it is not strange that they should admit of dispensation, not only by God but even by man. Consequently it is also a mistake to cite the above-mentioned article of St. Thomas (I.–II, qu. 100, art. 8), since he is speaking there of the specific determination[26] of natural law through human law; a fact which is clearly brought out by the example adduced.

27. The third example mentioned by Altisiodorensis is that of the precept concerning the observance of vows, a precept from which dispensations may be granted. As to this point, it is also clear from our remarks in the preceding Chapter that when a vow is cancelled this fact does not constitute a dispensation from natural law; but rather, certain subject-matter pertaining to that law is removed. In this same way, and in no other, is

25. [This is found in Chap. xiii, *supra;* p. 296, *et seq.*—Tr.]
26. [Determination; that is, where natural law is vague, human positive law sometimes prescribes a more exact determination of it. This is clear in the matter of contracts.—Reviser.]

God able to abolish the obligation imposed by a vow; for He is not able to bring it about that a vow shall remain intact, and that the natural law shall [, in such a case,] not bind the person under that vow to a fulfilment of the same. God has the power, then, to abolish the vow, and to withdraw the corresponding obligation imposed by natural law, without granting any dispensation. Furthermore, I shall add in this connexion (although it may be that my point turns simply upon a manner of speaking) that, even if the Pope, when he cancels a vow, is said to be granting a dispensation in the strict sense with respect to that vow, nevertheless, if God, acting in Himself, remits the vow, it cannot so well be said that He is granting a dispensation therefrom as that He is annulling it. The reason in support of this view is that God remits the debt due to Him, in the capacity of the true master of that debt, so that He bestows a gift or annuls a debt, but does not grant a dispensation; just as, when one man remits to another man a promise made to himself, he does not grant a dispensation, but rather annuls that promise; whereas, with respect to the Pope, the case is otherwise, for he acts by the power entrusted to him and as the steward (so to speak) of the Lord. A sign of this distinction, moreover, is the fact that God may do away with a vow for no cause but His own will alone, a circumstance which is characteristic of annulment, whereas the Pope cannot grant dispensations without cause.

28. The fourth example had to do with the precept that prohibited the taking of several wives [at one time]. And the other precepts regarding this same subject of marriage are of the same grade and order. With respect to this group, I consider that all such precepts are of the sort that found their binding force upon human consent and contract. This I assume from my treatise on marriage;[27] and it is, furthermore, evident by induction in the case of the precepts mentioned. For all of these are founded upon the character of the contract involved, as a character in harmony with rational nature. From this, then, it follows that all such precepts are mutable in so far as their subject-matter is concerned. For the said contract consists in a mutual surrender of bodies; and therefore God, Who is the supreme Lord of those bodies, may change or regulate the transfer of dominion

---

27. [Not included in these *Selections*.—Tr.]

over the body of another that is effected by such a contract, so that, when this change has been made, the law founded upon this contract will lapse, not through a dispensation from the law, but through an annulment— whether in whole or in part—of the contract itself.

The foregoing may be confirmed and made clear by analogy; since the precepts in question may be compared with the natural precept against fornication, from which there can be no dispensation, inasmuch as access to a woman not one's own cannot be rendered righteous. Nevertheless, in view of the fact that it has been possible for a woman who did not [previously] belong to a man (for example, to Osee) and who could not have belonged to him without her consent, to be made his through the power of God, whether absolutely or [solely] for the purpose in question—in view of this fact, I say—one may assert that it was possible for access to such a woman to be made righteous, not through a dispensation from the precept against fornication, but by making the act no longer an act of fornication, as it would have been formerly.

Arguing in like manner, then, but conversely, withdrawal from one's own wife, in so far as the marriage bond is concerned, is an act opposed to a natural precept. For there does not exist in man the power to deprive another man of ownership which the latter has acquired, even though he be willing.[28] But God does possess this power; so that He is able to change the subject-matter of the law in question, and, consequently, to bring it about, without any dispensation, that the obligation imposed by that law shall lapse.

In fine, the following argument may be adduced in explanation: as I have said in the preceding Chapter, there are, among the laws relating to matrimony, some which look to the final purpose of matrimony and the conservation of nature; and accordingly, since this conservation pertains to the Author of nature, the objective of the said precepts therefore includes an intrinsic relation (so to speak) to the Author of nature, or a dependence upon Him, so that they are not quite absolute, but (as it

---

28. [Since this statement is not universally true it appears that Suárez must be referring to the dominion acquired by the marriage contract, which is certainly inalienable.—REVISER.]

were) conditioned. So, for example, the dissolution of a marriage upon the authority of the persons involved is not permissible, because private individuals may not, on their own authority, do anything that works to nature's harm; wherefore it is understood that, in the case of the precept in question, an exception is made with respect to the authority of God, as the Author of nature; and therefore, when God prescribes that the situation be otherwise, this constitutes, not a dispensation, but an observance of the precept in accordance with the condition included therein; even as we shall point out below, with respect to human precepts, noting that when it is ordered in the precept or rule itself, that a given act may not be performed without permission, the granting of permission under these circumstances is not the granting of a dispensation, but an execution of the law according to the order and mode prescribed by it.

Not by any [alleged] example, then, can it be proved that true dispensation by God may take place with respect to the precepts of natural law.

29. Finally, this [additional] argument may be used in explanation, namely: if a precept is natural, then, in so far as it possesses this characteristic, it follows as a necessary consequence from natural principles; and therefore, dispensations are no more possible in the case of these precepts than in the case of the principles themselves. This inference is clearly true, because every falsity or defect in a conclusion goes back to a falsity or defect in the principle, or to a change therein; while the truth of the antecedent is evident for the reason that, if [the precept in question] does not follow of necessity, it is, in consequence, not binding by virtue solely of reason or of reflection, so that it does not involve a purely natural obligation.

The same explanation applies to both the affirmative and the negative precepts.

For if an affirmative precept does not follow necessarily from natural principles, the act which it prescribes is therefore not absolutely requisite to righteous conduct by the force of reason alone; so that this act is not prescribed, nor does it fall under a natural obligation, unless there is involved, in addition, some will which imposes the necessity [of action]. Wherefore, conversely, the omission of the act on certain occasions or under certain circumstances will not of itself and intrinsically be evil. For if this omission is intrinsically evil at a certain time or upon a certain occasion, and is not thus evil at other times and upon other occasions, then, to be sure, there will be for that [first occasion] a natural precept which makes the act in question obligatory, while there will not be a precept of this sort with respect to those other occasions. Accordingly, as long as that occasion of intrinsic evil and all its circumstances continue to exist, the precept cannot fail to be binding; whereas, if the occasion and the circumstances change, then it will be possible for the obligation to cease; not, however, through dispensation, but for the reason that it is the nature of an affirmative precept to be binding for all time, but not on all occasions.

In the case of a negative precept, however, if the precept is to be a natural one, it must forbid the act in question because that act is bad, and so much so as to be characterized by an essential and intrinsic badness; otherwise the precept would not be natural, since a natural precept does not cause, but [merely] points out the wickedness of the action prohibited. For if an act is not in itself of this essentially evil nature, then, [if it is to become evil,] there must be some will that makes it so.

30. It may be objected that one and the same act can be essentially evil at times, and nevertheless, at other times, not essentially evil. However, it may be argued to the contrary, that the said act cannot possess both of these qualities with respect to its subject-matter when the same circumstances or conditions prevail. For, since[29] the goodness or wickedness of an act arises from its harmony or disharmony with rational nature, it is not possible that one and the same act, accompanied by identical conditions, should be *per se* both disharmonious and harmonious with that nature, inasmuch as mutually contradictory relations do not spring from the same basis; and therefore, in order that these diverse relations may arise, even at diverse times, it is necessary that changes to accord with them should be made in the conditions qualifying the subject-matter. Thus, to take another's property, for example, is sometimes evil and sometimes good; but it is not both evil and good under identical circumstances; rather, it will be an evil act when extreme necessity does not exist, and a good act

---

29. [*Cum.* The construction of the Latin sentence is hardly logical; one would expect not a causal conjunction here, but, rather some connective with the sense of 'and' before the subsequent phrase, 'it is not possible'.—Tr.]

when the situation is indeed one of extreme necessity; for the right to use such property varies, according to these considerations of appropriateness. This being the case, then, a negative precept of the natural law prohibiting such an act does so not in the abstract, but simply in so far as that act is evil and, accordingly, in so far as it relates to subject-matter affected by circumstances of the sort mentioned; therefore, the said precept, considered in relation to its own proper subject-matter, cannot lapse; and, consequently, no dispensation from it can be granted with respect to that subject-matter.

Moreover, this principle applies universally to all the precepts of natural law, and points to the intrinsic difference in this respect between such precepts and those of positive law. No exception or limitation, then, is possible in the case of natural law, if we are speaking of that law in the strict sense, and of true dispensation. And if St. Thomas or some other weighty authority has at times expressed a different opinion, he is taking the term 'dispensation' in a broad sense, as denoting a change of obligation springing from a change in the subject-matter, on occasions when the latter change is wrought by God through a certain supreme power, in a manner removed from the ordinary course of things; a point which we have expounded at sufficient length in our reply to the opinion of St. Bernard.

CHAPTER XVI

Does the Natural Law Afford Any Opportunity for
Epieikeia (Equity) or Interpretation, Whether Made
by God or by Man?

1. *It is the common opinion of the authorities that the natural law can be subjected to interpretation.* Two questions are brought up in this Chapter heading. One question is as follows: Does the natural law afford any opportunity for *epieikeia?* The other is this: If the natural law does afford such an opportunity, may the interpretation be made only by God, or by men also?

As to the first question, almost all the authorities seem agreed that the natural law may receive interpretation through *epieikeia;* a point which will become evident from the remarks we shall presently make.

But they disagree [as to the second]; for certain authorities say that this *epieikeia* with respect to the natural law may be made by God alone. This opinion is attributed to St. Thomas (on the *Sentences,* Bk. IV, dist. xxxiii, qu. 1, art. 2), where he speaks in particular of the natural law as prohibiting the possession of a plurality of wives. Nevertheless, he uses the term 'dispensation', in this passage. Moreover, in like manner, Richard Middleton thereon [on the *Sentences,* Bk. IV, dist. xxxiii, art. 1, qu. 1], Peter de la Palu (*Supplement to Gabriel*), as well as others mentioned in the same context, use in the same connexion this term, 'dispensation'. So, also (as we have remarked in the treatise, *De Voto,* Bk. VI[1]), many theologians give the name of dispensation to the interpretation of the law in obscure cases. From what has already been said, indeed, this kind of explanation would seem to be necessary. For, as has been demonstrated, strict dispensation has no place in the natural law; and therefore, if any dispensation seems to occur, it must be in the nature of an interpretation. This form of dispensation, moreover, would appear to be necessary; because the natural law, in so far as concerns certain precepts which are rather far removed from first principles, deals with subject-matter which is changeable and which in many cases may cease to exist, as Aristotle has said (*Nicomachean Ethics,* Bk. V, chaps. vii and xii [chap. x]); so that *epieikeia* is also necessary in connexion with that law, since otherwise the latter would often be unjust.

That this function pertains to God alone is proven, indeed, by the fact that he whose part it is to establish the law is the one to interpret the law.

2. *The opinion of those who say that* epieikeia *may take place in connexion with the natural law, and that it may at times be effected through a human being.* Other authorities hold, however, both that *epieikeia* may take place in connexion with the natural law, and also that it may at times be effected through a human being; for example, through the Pope, or some like person endowed with power. Cajetan (on II.–II, qu. 120, art. 1) upholds both of these assertions, although he does so more expressly in the case of the first one; Soto (*De Iustitia,* Bk. I, qu. vii, art. 3, ad 3, and Bk. X, qu. iii, art. 4) maintains the same view; Navarrus does likewise, at length

---

1. [This tractate is found in Suárez's *De Religione,* which is not included in these *Selections.*—Tr.]

(*Consilia*, Bk. IV, *De Desponsatione Impuberum*, Consil. IV, nos. 16, 17), adducing various examples, where he also cites Covarruvias (on *Decretals*, Bk. IV, pt. II, chap. vi, § 9); and Felinus writes in the same vein (on *Decretals*, Bk. I, tit. ii, chap. vii, no. 26); while mentioning other authors. Moreover, all the authorities whom we mentioned in Chapter xiv as saying that men may grant dispensations with respect to the natural law, can, *a fortiori*, be cited in defence of the opinion in question.

Furthermore, the rational basis of the said opinion is the fact that this interpretation or *epieikeia* is often morally necessary, as we have proved just above; so that it would seem probable, not that God has reserved the function to Himself, but that, on the contrary, He has committed it to the men whom He has constituted as His ministers. The consequent is proved by the fact that, otherwise, God would have failed to provide for men in [certain] necessary matters; and that would not be consistent with His providence. This latter conclusion is clearly true, because direct recourse to God Himself is not possible for man, nor is it consonant with the natural order; and therefore if, when the occasion arose, there did not exist in men the power to interpret the law of nature even while exceeding the letter of that law, and if there [nevertheless] existed exigent cause for such interpretation, men would be perplexed and a miracle, or some special divine revelation, would be necessary for the direction of their actions; a condition which would be repugnant to any wise providence. Just so would it be repugnant among men for a prince to reserve to himself the interpretation of his laws in such a way that his ministers might not interpret any of them under any circumstances, even when it should be impossible for them to have recourse to the prince himself.

3. *Another opinion, which maintains that the natural law is not susceptible of* epieikeia. However, there may be a third opinion, which denies, with respect to the first point under discussion, that the natural law is susceptible of *epieikeia*, and which consequently does away with the very basis of the second doubt. For it follows from that assertion, that not even God Himself is able to except any case from the natural law by a process of true and strict *epieikeia*; since, if the natural law itself is not susceptible of such interpretation, it is not strange that this act cannot be performed, even by God.

That first basic point, then, would seem to be proven by what we have already said with regard to dispensations;[2] since, for the same reason that a law is incapable of dispensation, it is furthermore incapable of such interpretation. This assertion is proved by the fact that the precepts in question are incapable of dispensation for the very reason that they are characterized by an intrinsic principle of justice, or due rectitude, or (which amounts to exactly the same thing) for the reason that the precepts of the natural law[3] are certain necessary propositions that follow, by an inevitable process of deduction, from natural principles; and propositions of this kind cannot fail or be false in any individual case; therefore, it cannot, through any act of interpretation, become permissible to do that which is forbidden by the said precepts (since what they forbid is intrinsically wicked), or to leave undone what is prescribed by them (since what they prescribe is *per se* essential to rectitude). There is the additional argument that, if [the conclusion in question][4] were not true, the dictates laid down by natural law would be found to be false with respect to cases in which there should occur any interpretation of the sort mentioned; and that is an impossible supposition, as we have already remarked.

4. *Judgment is passed upon the opinions in question, and the last opinion is preferred and expounded.* This last opinion, indeed, in so far as regards true *epieikeia* seems to me to be, strictly speaking, a true opinion. *The distinction between* epieikeia *and 'interpretation'.* However, in order that the views expressed by other authors may be understood and the whole subject better explained, it behoves us to distinguish between the interpretation of a law and true *epieikeia,* or equity. For 'interpretation of law' is a term much broader than *epieikeia;* inasmuch as the relationship between the two is that of a superior to an inferior, since every instance of *epieikeia* is an interpretation of law, whereas not every interpretation of law is, conversely, an instance of *epieikeia.* Cajetan (on II.–II, qu. 120, art. 1) has noted this distinction, saying that often—or rather, always—laws require interpretation because of the obscurity or ambiguity of their terms or for other,

---

2. [*Supra,* p. 326 *et seq.;* Chapter xv.—Tr.]
3. [Simply, *huius legis.*—Tr.]
4. [I.e. the conclusion that the natural law is not susceptible of *epieikeia.*—Tr.]

similar causes; yet, not every interpretation of this kind is an instance of *epieikeia,* but only those interpretations in which we consider a law as failing in some particular instance, owing to its universal character—that is, owing to the fact that it was established for all cases and so fails to meet the requirements of some given instance that it cannot justly be observed with respect thereto.

The same opinion may be derived from the *Nicomachean Ethics* (Bk. V, chap. x) of Aristotle, for it is in this sense that Aristotle calls *epieikeia* a rectification of legal justice, since it interprets a law as not calling for observance in cases in which such observance would be a practical error and opposed to justice or natural equity, wherefore it is said to be a rectification of the law. However, there may be other interpretations of law which do relate, not to its rectification, but only to the explanation of its sense in regard to those points in which given laws are ambiguous. Thus, for example, when we interpret the question of whether a law prohibits a contract, or invalidates it, we are not in any way rectifying the law, but are simply inquiring into its true meaning. So it is, then, that interpretation in general differs from interpretation as it takes place through *epieikeia.*

5. Next, it should be noted that the natural law may be regarded from either of two standpoints: from the one standpoint, as it is in itself; from the other, as it may happen to be laid down through some positive law. For one form of positive or written law, as Cajetan also observes (*loc. cit.*), is constitutive of new law, and this form is positive in the strict sense, whether it be divine or human; whereas another form is merely declarative or (so to speak) a reminiscence of the natural law, as were the moral precepts of the Decalogue in the Old Law and as those human laws are which involve natural justice—for example, those which rule that a deposit must be returned, that a promise must be fulfilled, that a wife must not be separated from her husband; and others of a similar nature. There are indeed some natural precepts, such as the rule that simple fornication should be avoided, which are not prescribed by any positive law, since human law does not declare or prescribe everything. Thus, the natural law may be considered either as it is in itself, just as it is conceived or dictated by right reason or else as it is expressed in a certain number of set words, through some written law.

6. *The first assertion: many natural precepts require frequent interpreta-tion and exposition.* Accordingly, I hold, first: that many natural precepts require a great deal of exposition and interpretation in order that their true sense may be established. This assertion may be understood to refer both to the natural law as it is in itself and to the same law as it is written in one that is positive; and from both standpoints, the truth of the assertion is manifest.

It may be proved, first, by a process of induction, as follows: in the case, for example, of the precept bidding that homicide be shunned, interpre-tation is especially necessary, in order that one may understand what is meant here by the term 'homicide'; for not every slaying of a human being is homicide as forbidden by natural law, but [only] that slaying which takes place on private authority and for its own sake (that is, intention-ally), or else by way of attack; whereas that slaying which takes place on lawful authority, or by way of prudent self-defence, is not thus forbidden. Similarly, as to the precept which enjoins the fulfilment of a vow made to God, our interpretation is that this precept should be understood as apply-ing to the vow in accordance with the intention of the one who vows and, consequently, as not binding in cases not falling within his consciousness nor included in his intention. The same interpretation will apply to the other examples which we shall presently mention.

The basic reason underlying this line of argument is as follows: not all natural precepts are equally well known or equally easy to understand, and they require interpretation in order that their true sense may be under-stood without any diminution or addition.

Furthermore, it may be stated by way of elucidation that human actions, in so far as concerns their rectitude or wickedness, depend to a great extent upon the circumstances and opportunities for their execution, and that in this respect there is great variety among them; for some are of a more unmixed character (so to speak) than others, and require fewer conditions in order to bring out their good or bad character. The natural law, more-over, does not in itself prescribe any act save in so far as it assumes that act to be good, nor does it prohibit any save in so far as it assumes that the act is intrinsically evil. Therefore, in order to understand the true sense of a natural precept, we must inquire into the conditions and circumstances under which the act concerned is essentially good or evil; and this inquiry is spoken of as the interpretation of a natural precept with respect to the true sense of that precept.

Accordingly, it is evident that such interpretation is necessary to mankind; necessary, that is, for the sake of mankind. For God and the angels do not, of themselves, have need of this interpretation. On the contrary, they are directly cognizant of the nature of a given precept, and of the mode and the conditions of its operation with respect to its subject-matter.

It is also evident that the interpretation in question can and should be made, not only by God, but also by men. For it is man himself who ought to inquire into and understand the true sense of the natural law; and if he is unable to grasp this sense by himself, he ought to learn from others, as one may frequently do simply through instruction [from teachers] not endowed with the power of jurisdiction.

However, I shall discuss presently the sense in which such interpretation does upon occasion pertain to the authority of a superior.

7. *The second assertion: true* epieikeia *has no place in natural law, in so far as the latter is natural.* Nevertheless I hold, secondly: that true *epieikeia* has no place in any natural precept, in so far as the latter is natural; that is to say in so far as it is viewed in the light of its inherent nature. Consequently, such *epieikeia* cannot be applied by man, nor by God Himself.

This doctrine is confirmed and explained by examples, through a varied process of induction. This latter statement follows from the first. And the first is proved by induction from the very examples that other authors adduce in favour of the contrary position.

One example is drawn from the law concerning the return of a deposit, an example of which Cajetan makes use; for in the case of this precept, our interpretation is that the said precept is not binding when the return of the deposit would be contrary to justice or to charity. But this interpretation is not *epieikeia* relating to the natural precept itself, viewed according to its inherent nature; for the precept in question, as such, is embodied in right reason, and right reason lays down, not an absolute dictate that deposits must be returned, but a dictate that they shall be returned only under certain implied conditions required by the principles of justice and charity. Accordingly, the interpretation in this case is not made with respect to the universal character [of the precept] (as Cajetan asserts), but is rather a declaration of the true universality of the law itself, in so far as its inherent nature is concerned, that is to say, in so far as the said law is contained in right reason. Such interpretation, then, is not *epieikeia.*

Another example is adduced by Navarrus (on the *Constitutions of Clement,* Bk. V, tit. iv [*Consilia,* Bk. V, *De Homicidio*]), in connexion with the precept, 'Thou shalt not kill,' on the ground that the said precept does not extend to killing that is necessary for self-defence. This limitation, however, is an instance, not of *epieikeia,* but of simple interpretation as to the true sense of the precept in question. For who would say that the statement to the effect that it is permissible to slay malefactors, on public authority, notwithstanding the Fifth Commandment of the Decalogue, constitutes *epieikeia,* or emendation, of the Commandment? Surely no one will make such an assertion; for that statement is merely a declaration of the true sense of the precept. Therefore, the same may be said of the statement regarding self-defence, since [the two declarations] have an identical rational basis.

Another example is also given by Navarrus in a passage (on *Sext,* Bk. II, tit. i, chap. i [*Commentarius de Iudiciis,* n. 71]) which explains that the natural law concerning the observance of an oath does not bind one to observe an unlawful statute. As to this limitation, it is clear that no *epieikeia* is involved, but simply an explanation of the nature of an oath, for it is not in accord with that nature to render obligatory anything that is unlawful. Accordingly, Navarrus himself confesses that interpretation by *epieikeia* is not involved in these two instances.

However, he adds a third example and holds that it does involve true *epieikeia.* For, as Navarrus remarks, the law of nature prescribes that an inferior should obey a superior; yet an exception from this rule is made in the case of exemptions, since the existence of exemptions indicates that the inferior is not bound to obey the superior. Still less, however, is this an instance of *epieikeia.* For, in the first place, an exception from law through privilege is not *epieikeia,* as Cajetan has rightly observed (*supra*); and the exemption in question is nothing more nor less than a species of privilege. In the second place, the law on this point ceases to be binding as the result of a change in subject-matter (namely, the fact that he who was an inferior ceases, through exemption, to be such, as Navarrus himself admits); but this cessation is not *epieikeia.* If it were, prescription would involve *epieikeia* with respect to the natural law forbidding retention of another's property; and similar situations would arise in connexion with other laws impossible to enumerate. The reason for this is that law is not amended through a change in subject-matter; and furthermore, in the case of the law under discussion, there occurs not even any true interpretation, or any change, but merely a cessation through an extrinsic process of metonymy, as has been pointed out in Chapter Thirteen.[5]

8. Lastly, Navarrus cites vows as an example, for interpretation frequently occurs with regard to them. But what I have said about oaths[6] is likewise to be applied to vows. For at times they are interpreted solely in order to explain their nature. An example of this is the fact that they are not binding if their subject-matter is illicit or requires impossibilities; and so on. In such instances, indeed, there is no trace of *epieikeia.* To be sure, an interpretation is made, at times, of the intention of the person who vows, limitations being set to that intention even though the words of the vow may seem to be general. This, indeed, involves a form of *epieikeia,* since it is an emendation of the vow with respect to the general character thereof. Nevertheless, such *epieikeia* affects, not the natural law regarding the fulfilment of a vow, but the vow itself, which is (so to speak) a private precept of positive law; and accordingly, this *epieikeia* of the vow results merely in an explanation of the form of the promise that is the subject-matter of the vow which, in this case, falls under the natural law; so that with respect to that law no *epieikeia* is involved, but rather a simple explanation of the subject-matter in question. We have said that dispensation from a vow is dispensation, not from the natural law itself, but from its subject-matter, so that when this subject-matter has been withdrawn the obligation imposed by natural law also lapses; and a similar assertion is true, in due proportion, of the situation under discussion.

Similarly, the example adduced by Soto also ceases to have force—the example of the natural precept which binds bishops with respect to their

5. [*Supra,* pp. 298 *et seq.*—Tr.]
6. [Suárez's discussion of oaths is not included in these *Selections.*—Tr.]

place of residence and which, Soto says, is at times revoked through interpretation by *epieikeia*. For although I pass over the fact that such an exception is not interpretation unless there be some change in the obligation,
which was truly involved therein and which is thus removed; still, even if
it were interpretation, it would be *epieikeia* not with respect to the natural
law, but with respect to the pact—that is, the promise—or the obligation
by which a bishop is bound to his church and upon which is founded
this precept of natural justice. For if such an obligation is able at any time
to cease through interpretation, the whole interpretation turns upon the
pact and upon the intention to bind oneself, an exception being made for
a situation that was understood [to be exceptional] though not expressly
mentioned. For example, we might make the interpretation that a bishop
may absent himself on account of grave illness or some other similar and
urgent necessity; and so on.

9. *The same solution is confirmed by reasoning.* Finally, an exposition [of
the view above taken] may be made on the basis of reasoning.

For, in the first place, *epieikeia* is an emendation of a law, or of that
which is legally just. But the natural law cannot be amended, inasmuch
as it is founded upon right reason, which is unable to be deficient in
truth, since in so doing it would no longer be right reason. Therefore, in
accordance with the same argument, the justice which corresponds to this
natural law is incapable of lapsing, since it is legal in such a sense as to be
natural also. Moreover, that which is naturally just cannot lapse, since it
arises (so to speak) from an extrinsic conformity and harmony of extremes,
unless there be some change in the extremes; in which case, indeed, there
is a change in the subject-matter of the law and the mean of virtue is not
the same, so that, in consequence, the just course is no longer the same.
Wherefore, although the obligation imposed by the law ceases to bind,
this is the result not of *epieikeia* but of a change in subject-matter.

In the second place, the matter may be more fully expounded by means
of the following argument. In so far as the natural law is concerned, there
never occurs through interpretation any exemption from the said universal
law for the reason that it is universally imposed; and only such an exemption, as has already been remarked, is *epieikeia*. This assumption is manifestly true; for a dictate of right reason, considered in itself and as being

practically true, is universally imposed, not with respect to the cases in which it may lapse, but simply with respect to those circumstances under which it never lapses; otherwise, it would not be a true dictate and, consequently, it would not be necessary or right, nor would it embody a natural precept. Thus, philosophical science does not declare in an absolute sense that every man has only five fingers, but does so in a limited sense, with the provision that natural causes shall be properly adapted and not impeded; in consequence, this declaration is never at fault; and if it were, it would not be a scientific conclusion.

10. In the third place, a certain process of induction may be applied to our explanation. For the precepts of the natural law are either positive or negative. The former are of such a nature as to be always binding [in the abstract,] though not [specifically] binding with respect to all occasions; but in the cases for which they are always binding, there is no opportunity for interpretation, since there is none for variation; for it is necessary that, with respect to the occasions to which they refer, these precepts should be always and infallibly binding. In so far, however, as these same precepts are viewed as not binding for all occasions, the times when they do impose a binding obligation may be determined in either of two ways. One way is determination through positive law; and in such cases that determination will permit not only of interpretation and *epieikeia*, but also of dispensation; all of which considerations, since they relate not to the natural, but to positive law, have no bearing on the question in hand. The determination may be made, then, in another way, through natural reason itself; and in these cases, although reason may determine that a precept is binding at one time but not at another, *epieikeia* plays no part, since there is involved no exception from the law, nor any emendation of the precept, but rather a simple understanding of the same. Therefore, *epieikeia* has no place in such precepts; for it is not possible to perceive in connexion with them any other mode of determining obligation or lack of obligation, with respect to a particular case. For if reason determines that a given precept is not binding at a certain time, it is to be understood by virtue of this fact itself that the said precept, in its very nature, has not been established with reference to the occasion and the circumstances occurring at such a time. Thus, for example, in the case of the precept enjoining fraternal

correction, reason itself determines, in so far as this is a natural precept, that it is not binding when there is no hope of any fruitful result from such correction; a determination arrived at, not through *epieikeia* but because the precept in question by its very nature is not binding for all occasions and because the circumstance in question is one of those under which it is not binding. It is so, too, that I would understand the precept concerning the return of a deposit, if this precept is to be conceived of as affirmative; since it is binding, not continuously, but for the time when the deposit can be returned suitably, that is to say, without prejudice or injury to another person. Accordingly, with respect to these precepts *epieikeia* does not occur.

11. I come now to the negative precepts, the nature of which is such that they always and upon all occasions impose a binding obligation to shun evil for the reason that it is evil; for that obligation is of the very nature of a negative precept of the natural law, and in the light of this fact it is not subject to *epieikeia;* since it is impossible that a thing which is of itself and intrinsically evil, should become good, or not evil, while the object and the circumstances remain the same; accordingly, we assert that such a result cannot be brought about through dispensation; and therefore, still less can it be brought about through *epieikeia.* The proof of the consequent is as follows: that which cannot be otherwise than evil, never fails to be evil; hence, it never fails to be prohibited; and therefore it cannot truly be declared to be not forbidden by the natural law with respect to some particular time or occasion, the declaration which would be proper to *epieikeia.*

Moreover, if a change occurs in the object, or in the intrinsic circumstances, and if by reason of this change the act in question ceases to be evil, then that is not *epieikeia,* because it does not turn upon subject-matter comprehended under the aforesaid natural law; it is, rather, a comprehension, or interpretation, of the subject-matter of the law and of its purposes. Thus when we interpret the law against stealing as not forbidding that one person shall, in cases of extreme necessity, take from another person those things which are necessary for life, that is not *epieikeia* but rather a strict interpretation of the law in question. For it prohibits only theft, that is, the taking of another's property when the owner is reasonably unwilling, or the taking of that which is another's property in so far as relates to owner-ship and to use; whereas the taking of another person's property in cases of extreme necessity is not a matter having to do with what is absolutely another's possession, since with respect to such a time all things are common property, nor is it a case in which the owner is reasonably unwilling.

So also, with regard to the example of the deposit, if the precept on that point is considered as negative—let us say, as a precept enjoining restitution, which is equivalent to non-retention, of another person's deposit—then the precept in question is not so unlimited [as it would seem, when viewed affirmatively], but merely forbids the retention of the deposit unreasonably or without compelling cause.

Accordingly, then, true *epieikeia* cannot be considered as taking place in connexion with the negative precepts of the natural law.

12. *Objection.* It may be objected that, in consequence of this same reasoning, *epieikeia* can never be considered as taking place in connexion even with the positive precepts. This [, it will be argued,] is clearly true, because an act either remains always attended by the same circumstances, in which case, it is impossible that a negative precept forbidding the act should be binding at one time and not binding at a later time; or else it does undergo change in its attendant circumstances, in which case, again, *epieikeia* will play no part; and this same reasoning is applicable, in due proportion, to affirmative precepts.

A twofold distinction between the positive and the natural law, which disposes of the objection. The objection may be answered by a denial of the consequent. For there we should make note of two differences between positive and natural law, differences which to a great degree clarify the matter under discussion.

First. The first is that, in positive law, while the whole subject-matter of an act, together with all its intrinsic circumstances, remains the same, it is nevertheless possible for the binding obligation [imposed by that law] to lapse through a process of equitable interpretation (although it may be necessary for some extrinsic circumstance to arise which will force one to make such an interpretation); and that process will be *epieikeia,* in the strictest sense of the term. This fact is clearly brought out by the common example of the prohibition against carrying arms at night. For in the case

of a necessity which is evident, and so urgent that permission from a superior cannot be obtained [in time], we justly supply the interpretation that,
under the existing circumstances, the precept is not binding—not because
the subject-matter involved fails to be that of the precept in question, but
because, even though the subject-matter is the same, the evil [of the act]
is separable from that subject-matter, if the prohibition is removed, and
because under the conditions stated it is improbable that the intention of
the lawgiver extended to the case in question.

In regard to the natural law, however, so long as the subject-matter
remains unchanged and the same intrinsic circumstances persist, we cannot, solely on the basis of extrinsic occasions, interpret a prohibitory law as
not binding. For it is not possible to eliminate the evil from such subject-
matter while its intrinsic conditions persist, and consequently not possible that the natural prohibition should be eliminated, even though some
extrinsic end, or the circumstances, may vary.

*It is proved that lying is intrinsically evil, and can therefore on no ground
be made essentially righteous.* This is made particularly clear by the example of lying, which I assume to be so intrinsically evil that it cannot be
permissible because of any occasion or extrinsic necessity, so long as it
continues to be lying. This view accords with the teaching of St. Augustine (*On Lying* and *Against Lying to Consentius;* also, *Letters,* viii [xxviii
in Migne ed.] *To Jerome;* and following letters). The same doctrine was
upheld by St. Basil (*Regulae Brevius Tractatae,* Regula 76), and by Jerome
(*Apology against Rufinus* and *Letters,* lxv [cii]), and it has also been accepted
by all the theologians, including Peter Lombard (*Sentences,* Bk. III,
dist. xxxviii) and St. Thomas (II.–II, qu. 110, art. 3). The said doctrine
has a strong basis, too, in the words of Christ (*John,* Chap. viii [, v. 44]),
when he says of the devil: 'He is a liar and the father of lies'; for lying
cannot be from God, but must be from the devil, wherefore he is called
its father, that is, its inventor. Accordingly, the contrary has been written
of God (*Psalms,* v [, v. 7]): 'Thou shalt destroy all who speak lies.' And
therefore, in the *Decretals* (Bk. V, tit. xix, chap. iv), it is said that Holy
Scripture prohibits lying to save another person's life; while the opposite
view is consequently condemned in Cassian (*Collationes,* No. xvii) as an
error; a matter that is discussed more fully in another context. Castro

(*Contra Haeres. [Adversus Omnes Haereses,]* the word *Mendacium*) may also be consulted on this point. No other reason can be given for this most truthful doctrine than the fact that the extrinsic end, or extrinsic necessity, does not change the object [of lying] or the intrinsic conditions requisite thereto; while it is precisely from this object that lying derives its intrinsic evil. Accordingly, no opportunity is afforded in the matter of lying for either dispensation or *epieikeia,* such as to make lying permissible because of any extrinsic occasion, necessity, or end. Therefore, whenever any natural precept seems not to be binding upon some particular occasion, it must be that there is some change in the subject-matter of the act involved, the subject-matter whence the act derived that evil character which causes it to be prohibited by the natural law. Accordingly, such a change differs greatly from the change taking place in the case of positive law when *epieikeia* occurs; for in the latter case, it is only the prohibition that lapses, while its subject-matter remains unchanged; whereas in the former case that is by no means true; for, on the contrary, the subject-matter is removed, and as a result of this change in the subject-matter, the evil [attending the act] is dispelled.

13. *The second difference.* The other difference[7] is as follows: in the case of positive law, when there occurs an interpretation by *epieikeia,* it does not refer to the act forbidden by the law, nor to any obscurity in the words of that law; on the contrary, it is assumed that this act is one forbidden in its specific nature, and that it is described by the terms of the law, taken in their proper sense; while the whole interpretation and conjecture turns upon the intention of the lawmaker, on the ground that he did not intend to include the case, or act in question, as corresponding to these specifications. This, then, is true *epieikeia,* which may be termed an emendation of the law—emendation that accords with the verbal form of the law, justifying the words (so to speak) in the light of the lawgiver's intention and presumed equity. This procedure, however, has no place in the natural law, because [a prohibition contained in the latter] is primarily based, not upon the will that prohibits, but upon the nature of the inherently evil act

---

7. [I.e. the other of the two differences between the positive and the natural law referred to in Section 12, second paragraph.—Tr.]

itself; and therefore interpretation of such prohibitions has place only in relation to subject-matter when an act, considered in the abstract, is evil not intrinsically but only in so far as it is concerned with a given subject-matter, in a given way (as we have explained in connexion with homicide, the taking of another person's property, the retention of a deposit, and other, similar acts). Accordingly, in so far as concerns this kind of law, interpretation by emendation of the law does not occur, since the latter is always adapted to its subject-matter; on the contrary, interpretation of this sort occurs only by way of an explanation of the matter involved and of the evil by which that matter is inherently characterized. For it is solely on the basis of this evil that the prohibition exists, or the law is enacted, whether they be regarded as indicative of evil, or as prohibitive thereof. Under such circumstances no interpretation through *epieikeia* can occur to the effect that the act in question, in so far as it turns in a particular manner upon particular subject-matter, may be permissible in consequence solely of the legislator's intention, as this intention is conjecturally deduced from an extrinsic occasion, necessity, or purpose.

Therefore, the comparison between the natural and the positive law is not correctly drawn.

14. *Objection.* Nevertheless, it may yet be urged that there are some natural precepts which admit of interpretation through *epieikeia,* in the strictest sense of that term. For, with respect to the very same acts, accompanied by all the intrinsic circumstances which ordinarily suffice for a prohibition of natural law against those acts, we offer the interpretation that the said natural precepts are not binding in certain cases, owing to some extrinsic necessity, or some extrinsic purpose. Of this sort is the precept forbidding marriage with one's own sister, a prohibition which, in a case of extreme necessity and for the sake of the preservation of the race, does not have binding force. The same is true of the precept prohibiting marriage to a second wife during the lifetime of the first wife, especially when the first marriage has been consummated. For, in cases involving the same necessity as regards the human race, and provided that the first wife was sterile, it would be permissible to take a second wife. Again, among the precepts concerning those impediments which by the natural law invalidate marriage, many similar cases will be found.

15. *Solution.* It may be replied, however, that the general rule already laid down is true, namely, the rule that it is impossible—so long as the subject-matter of a negative, natural precept remains the same—for the forbidden act to be considered licit, through *epieikeia,* and solely on account of an extrinsic cause or purpose, or an extrinsic necessity. For the reasons and examples adduced above are convincing proofs of this fact. If, indeed, such [an interpretation] should seem to occur in connexion with a particular precept, and with respect to a particular case, one of two explanations will apply. Either the precept in question is not in an absolute sense a natural precept, but is [merely] related very closely to natural law, and accepted and approved by human custom, so that it is, absolutely speaking, a precept of the *ius gentium* only, and therefore susceptible of change or alteration in a given case; or else, if the precept is natural in an absolute sense, its subject-matter will be, not the act in question, absolutely and abstractly considered, but that same act taken in conjunction with some intrinsic circumstance the removal of which will make it possible for the obligation to lapse, not, indeed, through *epieikeia,* but through a defect in the subject-matter itself.

However, the application of the said general rule to the individual precepts is not a part of our present purpose, but pertains rather to a variety of matters. Thus the Doctors argue as to the nature of the above-mentioned precepts concerning marriage, and differ in their conclusions. Assuming, however, that those precepts are truly natural, we may here reply that they do not absolutely prohibit marriages between brother and sister, for example, or with a second wife, but rather prohibit them only in so far as they are harmful to human nature, and therefore opposed to natural rectitude, according to right reason; while, on the other hand, in the cases of necessity mentioned above,[8] this argument ceases to have force and the marriages in question attain to the highest degree of suitability to nature and are consequently righteous, since they are entered into solely for the sake of the necessary conservation [of the race], which is the intrinsic and not the extrinsic end of the act in question. Accordingly, on such occasions, the subject-matter of the negative precept is changed.

8. [*Illius necessitatis.*—Tr.]

The foregoing may be clarified by an analogous argument: for the mutilation of one's own body, save in case of necessity and for the preservation of life, is intrinsically evil; and nevertheless, when the case is one of necessity in order that the body may be preserved, such mutilation is permissible; for the mutilation is neither prohibited nor essentially evil save in so far as it is injurious to life; and in the situation described it is not injurious but necessary. In like manner, a word uttered when no good end is in view, nor any end in harmony with nature, is evil and prohibited by the natural law; but the same word, uttered for a fitting purpose, is not prohibited, since it would be evil not as viewed in itself but as being idle and useless, a defect which disappears when the word is directed to that [righteous] end.

Careful consideration, then, should be given to the quality and nature of the subject-matter. For, according to its capacity, the condition of this subject-matter is morally changed in relation to the end or the necessity that may be involved; since the act is such that by its very nature it seeks to be ordered toward a particular end, in some particular manner; and, such being the case, the necessity that arises has a resulting effect upon the subject-matter of the precept and changes it, so that, in consequence, the obligation imposed by the natural precept ceases to exist, not because the precept, in its own subject-matter, fails to be binding always and for all occasions without exception, but because, once the subject-matter has been changed, the precept in question, considered as a natural precept, no longer has application to that subject-matter.

16. *The third assertion: the natural law, as established through positive law, may admit of* epieikeia. Therefore, I hold, thirdly, that if the natural precepts are considered in so far as they have been established through positive law, then they admit of exception by *epieikeia,* especially in relation to the intention of the human legislator; although, considered in themselves and [purely] as natural precepts, they do not, strictly speaking, admit of such *epieikeia.* The remarks frequently met with in the works of other authors may be explained in the light of this assertion. Cajetan, especially, speaks expressly of these precepts as they are constituted through human laws. Others also speak of them as being framed in general terms without the moderation that is later added by *epieikeia;* a conception which does

not apply to these precepts when they are viewed as natural, since in that capacity they are not formulated through any general statement, save in the sense that [their definition] includes everything necessary to indicate the presence of intrinsic evil and is in consequence unable to admit of exceptions. So it was, for example, that we referred to the prohibition against stealing, as such, or the prohibition against homicide in so far as homicide is essentially evil. In the light of this consideration, indeed, the reason supporting [our third] assertion becomes clear. For human laws often overlook the said consideration, and prescribe a given act in absolute terms. This point is illustrated by [the precepts enjoining] the return of a deposit or the fulfilment of a promise; laws which, propounded in this absolute form, may admit of *epieikeia*. I maintain, indeed, that this process of *epieikeia* should be understood as relating to the intention of a human lawgiver. For frequently it may happen that such a lawgiver has had no thought for an exception of this kind; neither has he expressly intended to allow it, but has, on the contrary, set up the law in absolute form and without limitations, in terms which of themselves extend their application to the [exceptional] case in question; while we nevertheless interpret them as not extending to that case. With respect to the will of the human legislator, this interpretation is *epieikeia,* since it is (so to speak) an emendation of that will; but in itself, and with respect to the natural law, it is merely an explanation of a change that has occurred in the subject-matter, by reason of which change the act referred to—since it is accompanied by particular circumstances—does not *per se* involve any evil, nor does it fall under the natural law. Thus the entire assertion which we have laid down is easily proved.

Furthermore, it would be my opinion that many of the authors cited speak loosely and improperly, at times, of interpretation of the natural law, bestowing the name of *epieikeia,* or exception to the law, upon that which is merely an explanation of the law's subject-matter and its true sense. We should not dispute concerning terms, however, when the facts themselves are clear; although, in order to explain the force of the law and to speak consistently of its interpretation, the doctrine above set forth would seem to be needful.

Is the Natural Law Distinguished from the *Ius Gentium* in That the Latter Pertains to Mankind Only, While the Former Is Shared in Common with Dumb Animals?

1. Having given an exposition of the natural law, and before we pass to a discussion of positive law, we shall find it worth while to treat, at the close of this book, of the *ius gentium,* in so far as the latter partakes of the true character of law. For it has a close affinity with the natural law, so that many persons confuse it therewith, or hold that the *ius gentium* is a part of the natural law; and, furthermore, even in those aspects wherein the two are distinguished, the kinship is very close and the *ius gentium* constitutes an intermediate form (so to speak) between natural and human law, a form more closely allied to the first of these extremes, so that we shall find it easy to make a transition to true positive law through a discussion of the *ius gentium.*

The existence of the *ius gentium,* then, is assumed by all authorities to be an established fact, or so we gather from their very frequent use of the term. For the *ius gentium* is often mentioned in the civil law (*Digest,* I. i. 1, § 2 and *Institutes,* I. ii), and in the *Decretum* (Pt. I, dist. 1, which is based on Isidore, *Etymologies,* Bk. V, chap. ii [chap. vi]); by the Doctors of both canon and civil law, in their comments on the above-mentioned passages and *passim;* and by St. Thomas (II.–II, qu. 57, art. 3) and the theologians.

2. *Various meanings of the word* ius *are explained.* However, since the word [*ius*] is an ambiguous term, we must distinguish between its different meanings, that we may employ it only in that acceptation which is pertinent to our purposes. For *ius* sometimes refers to the moral right to acquire or retain something, whether that right involve true dominion or merely a partial dominion; and the said right is, as we learn from St. Thomas (II.–II, qu. 57, art. 1), the true subject-matter of justice. On the other hand, *ius* sometimes means law, which is the rule of righteous conduct; and in this sense it is that which establishes a certain equity in

things, so that, as St. Thomas holds (*ibid.,* art. 1, ad 2),[1] it is the expression [of right,] that very acceptation of *ius* which we first noted; but this expression of right is law itself (again according to St. Thomas, *ibid.*), and accordingly *ius* is synonymous with law, as we have observed in the Second Chapter of the preceding Book.[2] Therefore, in order that there may be concise terms at our disposal, we may speak of the first sort of *ius* as 'equitable' (*ius utile*), and of the second as *ius* in relation to [legal] propriety (*ius honestum*); or we may speak of the former as 'real' (*ius reale*), and of the second as 'legal' (*ius legale*).

Both kinds of *ius,* then, may be divided into the natural law, the *ius gentium,* and the civil law. For the *ius utile* is called natural when it is granted by or originates within nature, as liberty may be said to spring from the natural law. That *ius* is called civil which has been introduced by civil law—as is the case, for example, with the right of prescription; that which is founded upon the common usage of mankind—as, for example, the right of passage over public highways, or the right to enslave introduced by war—is termed *ius gentium.* In this sense, the [threefold] division in question relates to the subject-matter of justice. And this standpoint accords, perhaps, with the teaching of St. Thomas in the passage above cited (*ibid.,* art. 3).

At present, however, we are speaking of the *ius gentium,* not in this acceptation, but rather as a species of law. For the *ius legale* is also wont to be divided into the three groups aforementioned; since, in *Digest,* I. i. 1, § 2, it is explicitly stated that law has been made up from natural precepts,

1. [*Ratio.* This word, as used by St. Thomas Aquinas and by Suárez, is susceptible of various interpretations. Since an English version of St. Thomas has been prepared and published by English members of the Dominican Order, their rendering of *ratio* is here accepted by the present translator.

The passage in St. Thomas which Suárez cites (II.–II, qu. 57, art. 1, ad 2), is Englished in the Dominican translation as follows: 'Just as there pre-exists in the mind of the craftsman an expression of the things to be made externally by his craft, which expression is called the rule of his craft, so too there pre-exists in the mind an expression of the particular just work which the reason determines, and which is a kind of rule of prudence. If this rule be expressed in writing, it is called a *law,* which according to Isidore (*Etymologies,* Bk. V, chap. i) is a *written decree:* and so law is not the same as right, but an expression of right.'—Tr.]

2. [*Supra,* pp. 26 *et seq.*—Tr.]

or from the precepts of the nations, or from those of civil law. This division is indicated in the same manner in *Institutes,* I. ii. We assume that the division is a good one, in view of general usage and opinion. And since we have sufficiently examined the two extremes of the group [i.e. natural law and civil law,] in the last Chapter of Book One, it remains for us to treat now of the second sort of law [i.e. the *ius gentium*]; the discussion of which we have postponed to this place, because an understanding of the *ius gentium* depends upon its comparison with the natural law. Such a comparison will also clarify the rational basis and true significance of the entire division mentioned above.

3. *The first opinion of the jurists, distinguishing natural law from the* ius gentium, *in that the former relates also to brutes while the latter pertains only to mankind.* In explaining this *ius gentium,* then, one is confronted with various opinions. We shall deal with the first of these in the present Chapter; and the others, we shall discuss later.

Jurists usually distinguish the natural law from the *ius gentium,* in that the natural law is shared in common with brute creation, while the *ius gentium* is peculiar to man. Thus, in *Digest,* I. i. 1, § 2 [§ 3] and in *Institutes,* I. ii, it is written: 'The natural law is that which nature teaches to all animate creatures; for it does not pertain exclusively to the human race, but is shared in common with all animate creatures born on land or sea, and with all birds as well.'[3] Moreover, various examples are given, such as the union of male and female, and the generation and education of children. And with regard to the *ius gentium,* the following words are added [*Digest,* I. i. 1, § 4]: '[The law] of nations is that used by the nations of mankind.' Furthermore, it is said to differ from the natural law, because it is common only to men in their mutual relations; although, subsequently, the *Digest* (I. i. 9) further states that the name *ius gentium* is given to 'that [law] which natural reason has established for all mankind and which is uniformly observed by all men'. Thus it is clear that the *ius gentium* is held to be natural as well, but in a special sense peculiar to mankind; a fact that is also brought out by certain examples mentioned in *Digest,*

---

3. [This quotation is not identical with the *Digest* and *Institutes.* It follows the *Digest* more closely.—Tr.]

I. i. 2, 3, namely: 'reverence toward God; obedience to one's parents and to one's country; the repelling of violence and injury.' Therefore, in the same context (*ibid.*, 3), a rule is laid down to the effect that it is contrary to the *ius gentium* 'for man to plot against man'. Furthermore, mention is also made (*ibid.*, 4 [and 5]) of 'manumissions' and 'slavery'; and likewise of 'wars of kingdoms; division of property and of ownership rights; commercial intercourse and other contracts of sale', and of like matters. Similarly, use is made, in *Institutes,* I. ii, § 4 [§ 2], of these very examples, with the exception of the examples concerning religion and filial piety towards one's parents and one's fatherland.

4. Wherefore, according to the opinion above set forth, the division of *ius,* or *lex,* into natural law, *ius gentium,* and civil law, should be reduced to consist of two bipartite groups in such a way that law will first be divided into natural and civil, and natural law will then be subdivided into two kinds; that is, into the natural law which is common to all animate creatures and which has without qualification retained the name of natural law, according to one acceptation of the term; and the natural law which is peculiar to mankind and has been given the name of *ius gentium.*

The reason for this subdivision, indeed, may be that the two rational bases thereof are in point of fact truly distinct and may involve different aspects and moral effects, so that it has proved fitting to distinguish between them and to provide each with its own suitable appellation; nor does it seem possible to give a better explanation of these appellations.

Furthermore, the difficulty touched upon[4] is easily resolved; for we now see clearly how the division in question may be adequate, while the term 'natural law' may still be used in its more general meaning. Nor does St. Thomas appear to dissent from this opinion (I.–II, qu. 95, art. 4, ad 1, more at length, II.–II, qu. 7 [qu. 57], art. 3) when he acknowledges that there are two modes of natural law, and adapts the terms in question to them. For it is so that Conrad Koellin (on I.–II, qu. 95, arts. 2 and 4) interprets him, in the passage in which he thus expounds the opinion of the jurists and declares that St. Thomas expressed himself in similar fashion, although the philosophers speak in a different vein.

---

4. [Cf. the beginning of this Chapter.—Tr.]

5. *Authorities who disagree with this opinion of the jurists.* However, this interpretation, assigned by the jurists, is condemned by Lorenzo Valla (*Elegantiarum Latinae Linguae,* Bk. IV, chap. xlviii). Connan (*Commentary on the Civil Law,* Bk. I, chap. vi), too, rejects such a subdivision of the natural law and maintains, accordingly, that the *ius gentium* is not distinguishable from the natural law, so that neither Aristotle nor the other ancient philosophers made the distinction in question or recognized the existence of the *ius gentium.* Soto (*De Iustitia,* Bk. III, qu. i, art. 3) also rejects the explanation offered by the jurists. These authorities base their opposition primarily upon the fact that there is no natural law common to men and to other animate creatures, since brutes are not capable of rendering true obedience or justice or of suffering true injury.

The reply to this contention, and in defence of [the opinion of] the jurists. To this contention, on the other hand, Albertus Magnus ([Tract. III, chap. iii,] on Aristotle's *Ethics,* Bk. V, chap. vii), Torquemada and Covarruvias (cited below), reply that the natural law is said to be shared in common with the brutes, not formally, so far as concerns the basic character of right (*ius*) and law (*lex*), but materially, with respect to acts falling under the law in question; for the performance of such acts is common to men and to brutes, as is evident from the examples adduced in the law and relating to the union of the male and the female, the generation of children, &c.

But opposed to this consideration is the fact that this material sharing of acts in common with the brutes has no bearing on any distinction between *ius* and *lex;* so that, in this sense, and for this reason alone, the proposed classification is unsuitable and crude.

[The jurists] may reply, however, that this very fact of material agreement serves to explain the varied character of the naturalness (so to speak) of law in man. For natural law, taken in its general sense, consists in dictates of natural reason, dictates which at times owe their origin to an inclination of the *genus* [*animal*], that is, of the sensitive nature, as such, whereas at other times they result from the characteristic inclination of rational nature, as such; and in accordance with these basic inclinations the natural law is distinguished as being common [, or not common,] to both brutes [and mankind], from the standpoint, that is to say, of the type of inclination upon which it is founded.

6. Nevertheless, even this last explanation does not dispose of the difficulty. For, in the first place, according to these statements [the right] to repel force with force would have to be constituted not under the *ius gentium,* but under the natural law, since that right is not laid down in the precepts of the former system. The consequent is proved by the fact that such an act is common to men and to brute animals, and springs from the general inclination toward self-preservation. For just as reproduction arises from the natural inclination to preserve the species, so self-defence is the result of the innate tendency to preserve one's own life and one's own being; and both inclinations are common to men and to other animals, so that the act in question is wrongly classified under those sanctioned by the *ius gentium.*

In the second place, it would seem erroneous to assert that the natural law, in so far as it has the true nature of law, is founded upon the basis of a sensitive nature, in the sense in which that nature is shared in common with the brutes. For the natural law should always be considered as elevated to a superior plane by reason of a rational difference; since this system of law is regulated through its conformity not to sensitive but to rational nature, and since, moreover, it relates to sensitive nature only in so far as the latter is restricted and especially perfected by the said rational difference; and therefore the above-mentioned generic resemblance [between man and brute] is not pertinent to a discrimination of natural law [from other forms of law].

The truth of the consequent seems evident. And the truth of the antecedent is proved, first, by the fact that whenever the natural law enjoins anything for the sake of the preservation of the sensitive nature, the injunction always includes a rational mode [of performance]. Thus the dictates of the natural law with respect to the union of male and female differ greatly from the dictates of natural brute instinct, as is clearly evident in the matter of matrimony. The same distinction may also be noted, in due proportion, in connexion with the education of children, the preservation of one's own life, and similar matters.

Secondly, the antecedent is confirmed by the fact that, with respect to those very actions which are common materially to man and the brutes, the natural law forbids in man many things from which the brutes are not restrained by natural instinct. For example, it forbids promiscuous intercourse; that is to say, simple fornication and sexual intercourse with a mother or a sister, restrictions which are not laid also upon the brutes.

Hence there arises another or third argument; for it would follow from the opinion under discussion that such negative precepts are part of the *ius gentium,* and not natural precepts; a supposition which would be entirely absurd. The truth of the consequent is evident from the fact that the said precepts are so entirely peculiar to man that they cannot possibly be said to be shared by brute creation; for, although a given act may after its own fashion be common to men and to the brutes, nevertheless, the omission of that act is not common to both, and it is this omission which is the proper subject-matter of the laws in question. This last argument, indeed, has more evident force in connexion with the precepts enjoining the worship of God and the honouring of one's parents and one's neighbour. For it is absurd to deny that these precepts are absolutely a part of natural law, and to affirm that they are, on the contrary, merely subject-matter of the *ius gentium.* The same is true, moreover, of the commands relating to the restitution of the property of another, the return of a deposit, the observance of good faith, speaking the truth, and similar matters; all of these being peculiar to mankind and not common even in a material fashion to the brutes, while they nevertheless pertain most decidedly to the province of the natural law.

7. To these arguments, however, one may reply, in accordance with the civil law, that the *ius gentium* is in reality natural law,[5] and is often so referred to in civil law, as is evident from the *Digest* (XVI. iii. 31) and the *Institutes* (II. i, §§ 1, 11; I. ii, § 11). Therefore, it would not be absurd, speaking with this fact in mind, to call the precepts just enumerated, and even all the precepts of the Decalogue, a part of the *ius gentium.* For no denial is thereby made of the fact that they are [also] a part of the natural law, properly and strictly so called; on the contrary, there is indicated a peculiar aspect—and characteristic property (as it were)—of that law in relation to human nature. Thus the entire discussion would revolve simply

---

5. [This statement can only be inferred from the citations to the *Digest* and *Institutes.*—Tr.]

about the use of a word, or at least about the necessity or utility of making the distinction in question in a particular sense.

However, although this reply may be valid from one standpoint, the second argument adduced above nevertheless retains its force and proves the extreme impropriety of saying that the natural law has been laid down for the brutes in common with men. Furthermore, and in order that there may be no contention as to mere words, it will be necessary to make an absolute declaration in accordance with the opinion above set forth, stating that the *ius gentium* is intrinsically and essentially natural law, that is to say, a part thereof. But such a statement cannot be made to apply to all [the precepts] adduced as being part of the *ius gentium*. For some of these involve matter not only [intrinsically] necessary, but also shared in common with brute creation, as is proved by the arguments given above; while others of those precepts are not only concerned with matter peculiar to mankind but also unrelated to any intrinsic necessity, as will become clear from what follows.

8. *The refutation of a second [false] opinion, which distinguishes the* ius gentium *from the natural law on the ground that the natural law reveals itself without reflection, or at least with the simplest kind of reflection, while the reverse is true of the* ius gentium. Therefore, we shall furthermore repudiate the opinion of certain theologians who hold that the precepts of the *ius gentium* are characterized by an intrinsic necessity, and that this system differs from the natural law [only] in that the latter is revealed without reflection—or at least with the simplest kind of reflection—while the precepts of the *ius gentium* are deduced by means of many and comparatively intricate inferences. This conclusion may be inferred from Soto (Bk. I, qu. v, art. 4); and certain modern Thomists also appear to adhere to it, since they so interpret St. Thomas, whose opinion we ourselves shall subsequently attempt to interpret.

We reject the view in question, then, because, in the first place, many matters are said to fall under the *ius gentium* which nevertheless are not characterized by the intrinsic necessity that has been mentioned: take, for example, division of property, slavery, and other points, which we shall consider below.

Secondly, and principally, we base our objection on the fact that the *ius gentium* cannot possibly be concerned with primary moral principles nor with conclusions necessarily drawn therefrom, since all these principles and conclusions are included under the natural law strictly so called, as we have already proved (Bk. II, Chap. vii, *supra*, p. 233). This argument is confirmed by the fact that all the precepts written by God upon the hearts of men pertain to the natural law, as is indicated by the words of Paul (*Romans*, Chap. ii [, vv. 14–15]); and all precepts which may clearly be inferred by reason from natural principles are written in [human] hearts; therefore all such precepts pertain to the natural law.

On the other hand, the precepts of the *ius gentium* were introduced by the free will and consent of mankind, whether we refer to the whole human community or to the major portion thereof; consequently, they cannot be said to be written upon the hearts of men by the Author of Nature; and therefore they are a part of the human, and not of the natural law.

Now if the truth of this latter statement must of necessity be admitted—and we show that it must—with regard to certain precepts of the *ius gentium,* we should not confuse the *ius gentium* with the natural law; neither is it necessary solely on account of inferences, although they may be many, to give such a name[6] to that law which is simply natural. For the [fact that a precept calls for] reasoning does not exclude the true and natural necessity of that precept, recognized as such; and the further fact that this reasoning proceeds through many or few inferences, more or less clear, is entirely incidental.

9. *A third [false] opinion, which distinguishes the natural law in that it is binding independently of human authority, while this is not true of the* ius gentium. Some authorities maintain, indeed, that the natural law embraces conclusions so essential that, independently of the assumption of the existence of human society, or a society dependent upon human volition, these conclusions would obviously follow upon natural principles; and the said conclusions do not come under the *ius gentium;* whereas there are others which also follow upon natural principles, necessarily, yet not absolutely but rather in conjunction with the assumption of the existence of human society and in view of certain circumstances essential for the preservation of that society; so that precepts relating to such conclusions

---

6. [I.e. the name of *ius gentium.*—Tr.]

constitute the *ius gentium.* It would seem that this view may be derived from St. Thomas (II.–II, qu. 57, art. 3).

However, such a view does not explain the true and proper character of the *ius gentium,* or the difference between that system of law and the natural law.

The opinion above set forth is rejected. For there are many precepts of the natural law which are not binding, and which have no application save in conjunction with an assumption of some kind. For example, the prohibition against stealing has no application unless there has been a division of property and of property rights. Likewise, the precept of obedience to one's master is inapplicable, save on the assumption of the existence of slavery; as is also the precept requiring justice in contracts, unless one assumes the existence of commercial intercourse among men. The same is true of many other matters which clearly pertain to the natural law; for these matters are so righteous in themselves that the contrary is forbidden because it is evil, and not conversely.

The following argument may also be adduced: the mere fact that a conclusion follows from the principles of nature [only] upon the assumption that particular subject-matter exists, or a particular human status, does not involve a variation in the kind of law derived from the intrinsic nature of the case, and not from the human will; on the contrary, [the necessity for such an assumption] implies merely a distinction in the actual subject-matter of the law. For example, the law relative to observing a promise and keeping faith with God and men is a natural precept; and nevertheless, it can have no application, save upon the assumption that a promise has been made. So, also, in the discussion of simony [*De Religione,* Tract I, Bk. IV: *De Simonia*],[7] it is said that the selling of an object consecrated by men is opposed to the natural law, although this prohibition involves the supposition that consecration has been introduced by human law. Therefore, although it is from the assumption that the conclusion follows, an assumption that regards only the subject-matter of the precept, still, if the inference involved is clear from self-evident [natural] principles, the conclusion in question pertains to the natural law and not to the *ius gentium.*

7. [Not included in these *Selections.*—Tr.]

Consequently, in order that the *ius gentium* may be distinguished from the natural law, it is necessary—after making the assumption with regard to a particular subject-matter [for the precepts in question]—that, in addition, these precepts should follow not as a manifest conclusion [from natural principles] but rather by an inference less certain, so that they are dependent upon the intervention of human free will and of moral expediency rather than that of necessity.

In my opinion, then, our conclusion should be as follows: the *ius gentium* does not prescribe anything as being of itself necessary for righteous conduct, nor does it forbid anything as being of itself and intrinsically evil, whether [such commands and prohibitions] are absolute or whether they involve an assumption of the existence of a particular state and set of circumstances; on the contrary, all such matters pertain to the natural law; accordingly, it is from this standpoint that the *ius gentium* is outside the realm of natural law; neither does it differ from the latter in that the *ius gentium* is peculiar to mankind, for that characteristic pertains also to natural law, either in large part, or even entirely, if one is speaking of right (*ius*) and law (*lex*) in the strict sense.

CHAPTER XVIII

Does the *Ius Gentium* Command or Forbid a Given Act; or Does It Merely Concede or Permit?

1. *The opinion of some—who hold that the* ius gentium *is not imperative, but merely permissive in character—conceding that certain actions may be performed, or, on the contrary, left undone.* Because of certain points which were dealt with in the previous chapter, Connan (*Commentary on the Civil Law,* Bk. I, chap. vi, no. 5), who is referred to and followed by Vázquez ([on I.–II,] Disp. 157, chap. iii), has held that the *ius gentium,* as distinguished from the natural law, includes within its scope, not precepts or permissions,[1] but merely certain concessions, that is to say, certain

---

1. [The Latin has *promissiones* (promises); although this word may be a slip for *permissiones* (permissions), which would seem better adapted to the discussion here.—Tr.]

authorizations or permissions to perform or not to perform a given act, not merely with impunity but even justly and with rectitude; and yet these concessions are of such sort that the contrary behaviour is not evil or unjust. Those who advance this opinion add further that it is an essential characteristic of the *ius gentium* that it be adapted to human nature, viewed not in an absolute manner but as it is already constituted in civil society; for there are many rules useful to men living in a community which do not affect, in an absolute sense, the well-being of [human] nature considered in itself.

Therefore, those concessions which, because of a common utility, are made to men living in society, as concessions authorizing behaviour that is virtuous, but not essential to virtue nor yet prescribed, are said [by the authorities in question] to pertain to the *ius gentium*. And if any act be prescribed, it will fall either under the natural law, if the command depend upon the force of reason, or under the civil law, if the command shall issue from human will possessing authority; as was proved by the arguments set forth in the preceding Chapter. Therefore, in order that the *ius gentium* may be distinct [from natural law], it must have a concessive and not a preceptive character.

This statement is confirmed by the negative authority, at least, of St. Isidore and St. Thomas. For Isidore (*Etymologies*, Bk. V, chaps. iv and vi) confirms it when he says that the natural law is that which is common to all nations; although he does not define the *ius gentium*, but merely explains it by means of certain examples having simply the nature of concessions and not that of precepts, as we shall see below. St. Thomas also said [II.–II, qu. 57, art. 3] merely that the *ius gentium* was founded by men in the social state, living in society, in order to further their own welfare; a fact which may be deduced by rational reflection. But he did not say that the *ius gentium* was established in preceptive form.

2. *The opinion above set forth is rejected.* Frankly speaking, however, I do not clearly understand the foregoing opinion. For I must ask whether *ius* is taken as consisting merely in a moral right of use or abstention; or whether it is taken as being equivalent to law, that is, to a rule of reason, either preceptive in the strict sense of the term, or indicating approbation of certain things as righteous. The former interpretation is not to the point, as is evident from what has already been said; unless perhaps the

authorities who advance the opinion in question wish to deny that there is any *ius gentium* in the form of true law, a denial which they do not make. Neither are they able to offer any reason for their admittance of such a branch of the *ius gentium,* namely, the right of use, into the field of *ius* and not into the field of *lex.* Furthermore, it will become apparent from what we shall say below, that there is the same reason for its admittance into both fields. If, on the other hand, those same authorities are speaking of that *ius* which is also true *lex,* or a rule of virtuous conduct, then their doctrine may easily be refuted.

For I shall prove, in the first place, that there is no greater reason to distinguish from the natural law a *ius gentium* of a concessive, than to distinguish therefrom one of a preceptive character; since, in the case of the law [*ius*] of nature, there are many acts which may be performed with rectitude by virtue of natural precepts [*lex*], and which [nevertheless] are not prescribed, nor are their contraries prohibited; accordingly, there may also be a concessive form of natural law, exemplified by the natural law concerning the taking of a wife, or concerning the retention and preservation of one's own liberty, for such behaviour is righteous and is permitted but not prescribed by natural law.

In this sense, moreover, a twofold natural law is wont to be distinguished; the one phase being positive—that is, preceptive—and the other, negative—that is, non-prohibitory—as may be learned from the words of Covarruvias (on *Sext,* rule *peccatum,* Pt. II, § 11, no. 3). In a preceding passage, too, when discussing the immutable character of the natural law, we explained this same distinction. It is based upon the fact that natural reason dictates not only what is required, but also what is permissible.

Therefore, when it is said that the *ius gentium* confers the faculty to perform a given act righteously, I ask whether that faculty has its source— in so far as it is just and righteous—in natural reason, regarded absolutely, or in some human agreement. If it be answered that the source is in natural reason, then the law in question will be natural law, even though it be merely permissive in character. If, on the other hand, the source is said to be in some human agreement, then, either the arguments already advanced, to the effect that the said law is not *ius gentium,* as distinct from civil law, are valid arguments; or else—if notwithstanding this consideration it is possible for a concessive *ius gentium* of such a variety to exist, distinct from the civil law and constituting (as it were) an intermediate form between the natural and the civil law—then, in accordance with the very same reasoning, the existence of a similar but preceptive form of law will be possible.

3. To this it may be replied that the law in question does spring from the force of natural reason alone; yet it is fitted, not for men in an absolute sense, but for men as congregated in some human society; and, consequently, it is distinguished from the primary natural law as a secondary phase (so to speak) and is called the *ius gentium.*

This statement may be clarified by means of the customary examples relating to the topic under discussion. Thus war, for instance, is said to fall under the *ius gentium,* not because there is any precept rendering war obligatory, even if one assumes that a just ground therefor exists, but because war is permitted as being righteous. But this kind of law clearly assumes the existence of human society. Likewise, the division of fields or lands and of dwelling places, and the settlement of common boundaries, are said to come under the *ius gentium.* But these acts manifestly presuppose the establishment of human communities; and, with this assumption made, all the said acts are permissible by the force of natural reason alone, although they may not be necessary, in an absolute sense.

On the other hand, it is to be noted, first, that this very separation into nations and division into kingdoms, pertain to the *ius gentium,* as is indicated in the *Digest* (I. i. 5); but prior to this division, nothing save the existence of men in their natural state is to be assumed; and, therefore, the *ius gentium* does not always originate from the assumption [of some form of human community], but may on the contrary be based upon the purely natural characteristic which makes of man a social animal, together with the natural principle that a division into states is best adapted to the preservation of human beings.

Secondly, I argue that, even though the existence of human communities is assumed in the acts or laws under discussion, that fact does not prevent the concessive law in question from being natural. For that assumption is made merely in order that subject-matter for such a law may result; but the rule of reason itself existed before the existence of that subject-matter, and is always a natural rule. A proof of this argument is the fact that a preceptive law often has not any subject-matter through which its binding force may become active, unless one assumes the existence of community and social life among men; and, nevertheless, such precepts are always part of the natural law, as has been proved above and as the very authorities in question concede; therefore, the same will be proportionately true in the case of a concessive law, for it would seem that no convincing argument for differentiating between the two cases can be adduced.

4. Next, I shall prove that concessive law is not to be separated from all preceptive or prohibitory law; and that, in so far as concerns the matter in hand, if the one form of law pertains to the *ius gentium,* the other does also; or if the one is natural law, then the other is likewise natural law, so that the distinction made between them is not valid.

The former point may be explained, first, by the example of privilege. For by the very fact that a privilege is conceded to one person, all others are commanded not to impede that person's exercise of it. Indeed, it is on the basis of this argument that we have already explained the basic characteristic of law in the case of privilege; and the basis is the same in the case of all concessive law.

Secondly, the same point is made clear by running through the examples of the *ius gentium* which were laid down by Isidore [*Etymologies,* Bk. V, chap. vi].

The first example is 'the occupation of places for settlement'. For permission to occupy such places is so conferred upon any individual by the *ius gentium,* or rather by the natural law, that no person may justly interfere with another person who occupies in any manner whatsoever a place not previously occupied by another; so that the concession in question has annexed to it this [prohibitory] precept.

The second example is 'the right of building'; and the third, 'the right of fortification'. To these examples the same reasoning applies; for it is inconsistent that one should have a free right to build upon or fortify land or possessions occupied by himself, and that at the same time it should be possible for others justly to hinder or disturb him in the exercise of that right. Hence, [in these two instances also,] there is a necessary connexion between concessive and [prohibitive] preceptive law.

The fourth example relates to 'wars', and through it, the connexion above mentioned is made more clearly evident. For, in the first place, [the existence of a right to make war] presupposes the existence of a precept forbidding that warfare to the aggressor; since defence is permissible to one party, for this very reason, namely, that another party unjustly initiates a war. And, in the second place, with respect to the party who is defending himself, it frequently happens that the right in question carries with it not only the permission to make war, but also a command to make use of that permission, this being especially true in the case of a prince, for he is bound to defend the state. The same statement holds good with regard to other persons who are bound to act in defence of the common welfare or even, at times, in simple defence of their own lives. If, on the other hand, the war be aggressive, then, by the very fact that this aggression is permitted to one party as against another, the latter is forbidden to defend himself; for he is bound to render obedience and to give up to that other party that which is the latter's right, or else to accept a just punishment.

5. The fifth and sixth examples relate to 'captivity and slavery'; for in these matters also it is evident that if one party is permitted to reduce another to captivity or to slavery, even though the process may involve coercion of the second party, then, by that very fact, the latter must be obedient and must make no resistance, since it is impossible that there should be a war that is just on both sides.

The seventh example is the right of 'postliminium', in connexion with which the same reasoning holds, in due proportion. For 'postliminium' is the right either of recovering one's lost liberty or of returning to one's former [civil] status after release from the chains of captivity;[2] and within this right is necessarily comprehended a command to restore such and such a person to his former rights, or a prohibition against depriving him of such rights after they have been recovered.

The eighth example has to do with 'treaties of peace' and the ninth, with 'truces'. Under these heads we may consider first the power to make peace or grant truces, acts which are indubitably righteous in themselves,

---

2. [*Post exitum a liminibus captivitatis* (literally, 'after egress from the portals of captivity'), a phrase which points to the etymological connotations of *postliminia*.—Tr.]

and often useful or necessary; yet joined to this power is the obligation not
to violate treaties of peace or harm the enemy during a period of truce.

The tenth example is 'the obligation to respect inviolability of ambassadors', an obligation which is clearly expressed in the form of a command.
Yet two elements of this obligation may be distinguished: one, the right to
send ambassadors to other princes or provinces; the other, a command and
an obligation to preserve the immunity of those ambassadors.

Finally, the last example is 'the prohibition against marriage with the
foreign born', a matter in which not only the [negatively] permissive, but
also the preceptive element is openly set forth. Indeed, since this rule is
negative in form, one can scarcely discern in it anything in the form of a
concession. However, I shall explain a little later[3] the way in which this
example relates to the *ius gentium.*

6. It may be contended that, although it is true that something in the
nature of a precept is always joined to a concessive law, nevertheless [these
two elements] may frequently fall under different categories. For often,
when a concessive civil law has been laid down, there follows in consequence a rule of natural law: for example, when a law granting title of
ownership by means of prescription has been enacted, and a prescriptive
right acquired, there results a rule of natural law forbidding any one to
take, against the owner's will, the property which has been acquired by
prescription; and, again, in the case of a privilege which has been granted
by an individual or by a rule of human law and which exempts a given
person from the payment of a tribute, there is a resultant rule of natural
law prescribing that this tribute shall not be demanded of the grantee.

Accordingly, with respect to the examples above cited, one might say
that the permission or concession involved in each falls under the *ius gentium;* while, on the other hand, the precepts attendant upon these examples are a part of preceptive natural law.

7. In view of this objection, I have proposed a second part for our
[general] assertion, namely, that [the distinction in question] is inapplicable to the present subject-matter.

---

3. [*Infra*, p. 393.—Tr.]

For by a similar process of induction, one may demonstrate that the concession, as well as the prohibition laid in consequence upon other parties, pertains to natural law; or, if either one of them is absolutely a part of human law, it will be the concession rather than [the prohibition], and [yet], once the concession has been granted, the obligation resulting therefrom will be natural.

In the first place, this is, in my opinion, clearly proved through the first four examples of Isidore, namely: the occupation of places for settlement; building; fortification, and defence through just warfare. For the law applying to all of these acts is the natural law, that is to say, they are all permitted by the natural law; and, in like manner, the obligation incumbent upon one person to refrain from violating such rights when they are possessed by another person pertains to a natural precept. It is only the actual exercise of these rights which may be said to fall within the field of the *ius gentium* by reason of the custom of all nations. And this exercise of rights is a matter pertaining to fact, and not to law.

The same holds true, in due proportion, with regard to the eighth, ninth and tenth examples, which relate respectively to peace, truces, and ambassadors. For all the rules on these points have their foundation in some human agreement, in which both the power to contract a treaty or convention, and the obligation arising from that treaty or convention and demanding good faith and justice, have regard to the law of nature. Only the exercise of these powers may be termed a part of the *ius gentium,* owing to the accord of all nations with respect to the principle of the exercise of such faculties, in general. And this actual use of the powers in question is the effect of law, and not law itself; for the law under discussion does not spring from such use; on the contrary, the use has its source in the law.

8. In the fifth and sixth examples, however, relating to captivity and slavery, human usage appears to have introduced an element that is not derived immediately from the dictate of natural reason, namely: the fact that a title of capture in a just war is sufficient ground for holding another person prisoner even against his will and by force, or indeed, for the acquisition of ownership rights by one man over another; and, consequently, for the introduction of slavery in the case of one person in his relation to another. For the natural law does not of itself prescribe such a procedure,

although it does not forbid the same, provided the war in question be just. Therefore, the specification of that right [to impose captivity or slavery], is a form of penal law[4] (so to speak) introduced by human usage and adverse to those who wage an unjust war. For there is imposed upon such persons, by way of punishment, the condition that they shall become captives or slaves if they are conquered. So understood, indeed, this law is not concessive, but directly punitive; and exercises over the guilty a binding punitive force proportionate to that exerted by other penal laws of a civil character, which we shall discuss below in Book Five.[5] But whatever may be the nature of the law in question, in so far as it actually confers the power to reduce men to captivity or to slavery, it is a rule of positive law and does not depend upon the force and exercise of natural reason, even if one assumes the existence of human communities; and therefore, it does not pertain to the *ius gentium* as defined by the opinion[6] [which we are now combating.]

9. Again, the same conclusion is still more evident in the case of the eighth[7] example, relating to the right of postliminium, wherein there would seem to be more of civil than of natural law or of the *ius gentium*. For this rule apparently softens the punishments of captivity and slavery, or in general of property losses or of depredations committed by enemies, which are especially apt to occur in wars; a procedure which is not so universally recognized by all nations [as is the right to make captives or slaves], but which is accorded particular notice by civil laws. Moreover, in accordance with the fact that the said procedure is recognized by established law, the rule of postliminium consists not merely in a grant of permission but in a law the observance of which is truly obligatory. For a rule of law that softens some penalty is no less binding than one that has fixed a penalty.

---

4. 'Penal law': a law with punishment for its breach attached. Laws that are *purely penal* involve no obligation to keep the law and so no consequent guilt for their breach, but still impose an obligation to suffer a punishment or penalty for that breach. In effect, the lawgiver imposes a charge on certain actions without condemning them as wrong.

5. [Not included in these *Selections*.—Tr.]

6. [I.e. the false opinion stated at the beginning of this Chapter.—Tr.]

7. [*Octavo*, evidently an error for *septimo* (seventh).—Tr.]

Finally, with respect to the last example,[8] there clearly exists a prohibition, and not merely a permission, in the rule that marriages should not be contracted with the foreign born. Furthermore, it is evident that this law or usage was in neither sense common to all nations, for, on the contrary, it appears to be chiefly the peculiar custom of believers both formerly, under the Old Law, and now, under the New; so that the rule in question is divine or canon law, rather than [a precept of the *ius gentium*], and if it has been observed by certain nations, it has apparently come not so much under the said *ius gentium* as under civil law.

We conclude, then, that the *ius gentium* is not properly distinguished from natural law on the ground that the former is concessive only; and the latter preceptive. For one of two alternatives will apply: either the two characteristics are found in both systems of law; or else, if a [legal] precept does pertain to natural law, then the concession duly corresponding to that precept also has its source in that same natural law.

CHAPTER XIX

Can the *Ius Gentium* Be Distinguished from Natural Law as Simply as Positive Human Law?

1. *The* ius gentium *properly so called is not included under natural law.* From what has thus far been said, the conclusion seems to follow that the *ius gentium,* properly so called, is not contained within the bounds of natural law, but that on the contrary it differs essentially therefrom; for although it agrees with natural law in many respects, nevertheless, the two are distinct from each other owing to practical differences in their respective characters.

Wherein the ius gentium *agrees with natural law.* The *ius gentium* and natural law agree, first, in that both are in a sense common to all mankind. And on this ground each may be called a law of nations (*gentium*), if we are to confine our attention to terms alone. The characteristic of being

8. [I.e. the tenth (the prohibition against marriage with the foreign born). Suárez has already returned briefly to the eighth, ninth, and tenth examples, in the last paragraph of section 7.—Tr.]

common to all nations is clearly evident in the case of natural law, and for that reason the law of nature itself is called, in the *Digest* (I. i. 9), the law of nations (*ius gentium*); as may be noted in the wording of many laws. However, this name is more properly bestowed upon the kind introduced by the custom of nations, and on this point the *Institutes* (I. ii, § 4 [§ 2]) may be consulted.

Secondly, these two kinds of law agree in the fact that, just as the subject-matter of the *ius gentium* has application to men alone, so also the subject-matter of the natural law is peculiar to mankind, either in its entirety, or in great part; as is perhaps sufficiently evident from what we have said in Chapter Seventeen. Consequently, many examples which the jurists classify under the head of the *ius gentium* because of this characteristic alone, fall only nominally under the *ius gentium,* strictly viewed. For in reality such examples pertain to the natural law; as in the case, for instance, of reverence towards God, the honouring of one's parents, and dutiful patriotism, all of which are mentioned in the *Digest* (I. i. 2 and 3), although they were rightfully omitted from the *Institutes* by the Emperor [Justinian]. Of like character, if they are strictly interpreted, are other examples which Isidore enumerates [*Etymologies,* Bk. V, chap. vi]; such as the observance of treaties of peace, of truces, of the immunity of ambassadors, and similar matters. But as for the sense in which such instances were interpreted by Isidore, that is a point of which we shall speak below.[1]

Thirdly, the *ius gentium* and natural law agree in that both systems include precepts, prohibitions, and also concessions or permissions; as has been made sufficiently clear in Chapter Eighteen.

2. *In what way, chiefly, the* ius gentium *differs from the natural law.* On the other hand, the *ius gentium* differs from the natural law, primarily and chiefly, because it does not, in so far as it contains affirmative precepts, derive the necessity for these precepts solely from the nature of the case, by means of a manifest inference drawn from natural principles; for everything of this character is [strictly] natural, as we have already demonstrated, [and therefore pertains to natural law]. Hence, such necessity [as may characterize the precepts of the *ius gentium*] must be derived

---

1. [*Infra,* p. 398, § 6.—Tr.]

from some other source. Similarly, the negative precepts of the *ius gentium* forbid nothing on the ground that the thing forbidden is evil in itself; for such prohibitions are [properly within the province of] the natural law. From the standpoint of human reason, then, the *ius gentium* is not so much indicative of what is [inherently] evil, as it is constitutive of evil. Thus it does not forbid evil acts on the ground that they are evil, but renders [certain] acts evil by prohibiting them.

These differences are, indeed, real and (as it were) essential differences in law; and therefore, from this standpoint, a distinction exists between natural law and the *ius gentium*.

Secondly, and consequently, the two systems under discussion differ in that the *ius gentium* cannot be immutable to the same degree as the natural law. For immutability springs from necessity; and therefore, that which is not equally necessary cannot be equally immutable. This point will be expounded more fully in the following Chapter.

Thirdly, it follows from the above that even in those respects in which they seem to agree, these two systems of law are not entirely alike. For, in its universality and its general acceptance by all peoples, the natural law is common to all, and only through error can it fail of observance in any place; whereas the *ius gentium* is not observed always, and by all nations, but [only] as a general rule, and by almost all, as Isidore states [*ibid.*]. Hence, that which is held among some peoples to be *ius gentium,* may elsewhere and without fault fail to be observed. Furthermore, although the *ius gentium* is regularly concerned with subject-matter peculiar to mankind, it may upon occasion make some disposition regarding matters that pertain to brutes also; for example, in the permitting of promiscuous sexual intercourse or fornication and in connexion with the repelling of violence, in so far as such acts may in some manner be encouraged or restricted through the *ius gentium*.

The latter, then, differs in an absolute sense from natural law, and particularly by reason of the first difference [mentioned above].

3. *The* ius gentium *should be termed positive and human, in an absolute sense.* Therefore, the conclusion would seem to be, in fine, that the *ius gentium* is in an absolute sense human and positive.

This proposition may be inferred from the words of St. Thomas ([I.–II,] qu. 95, art. 4), who divides positive law absolutely into *ius gentium* and civil law, saying that both are human law, derived from natural law. However, since these terms are potentially ambiguous, it is necessary to do away with that ambiguity and to expound the true meaning of St. Thomas's remarks.

For law may sometimes be called human, not with respect to its author but with respect to its subject-matter and because it is concerned with human affairs; and in this sense the natural law itself is human, since it governs the human race and directs the actions of mankind. It is thus that Aristotle (*Nicomachean Ethics,* Bk. V, chap. vii) seems to have understood the term 'human law', which he himself, in the terminology of his translator,[2] calls *ius politicum* (political law) or *civile* (civil). Accordingly, he divides civil law into natural and conventional, referring by the latter term to what we call positive civil law. St. Thomas (*ibid.,* art. 2) also seems to have interpreted human law in this sense, for he divides it into that which derives its force from natural reasoning and that which derives it from the free will of men; two divisions which seem to be equivalent simply to natural and positive law. Moreover, St. Thomas (*ibid.,* art. 4) calls positive law human, and he holds every law established by men to be of this character. He also makes a subdivision of laws; for there is in his classification one branch in the form of [general] conclusions, which derives its force from the natural law, and which we speak of as declaring rather than making law; whereas the other branch exists in the form of specifications which introduce a new law, and this form we call positive law, in an absolute sense. Therefore, St. Thomas, in the passage cited above, is apparently speaking of the *ius gentium* as human and positive law in the first of these two senses. For he clearly says that the *ius gentium* exists in the form of a [general] conclusion and derives its force from the natural law. He appears, moreover, to maintain this same opinion in another passage (II.–II, qu. 57, art. 3, *in corpore*). Nevertheless, the term in question may be understood properly as referring to positive and human law, that is, to law constituted by men; but that law is said to be constituted in the form of a [general] conclusion, and not a specification, since [St. Thomas]

---

2. [I.e. the translator of the Greek into the Latin.—Tr.]

does not interpret the force of the *ius gentium* as leading to complete and concrete specification; on the contrary, he holds that the *ius gentium* is established with general force in the form of a conclusion not absolutely necessary, but so in harmony with nature that it is inferred (as it were) at the instigation of nature. This is the interpretation given to the words of St. Thomas, and followed by Soto (*De Iustitia,* Bk. I, qu. v, art. 4; more at length in Bk. III, qu. i, art. 3). Cardinal Bellarmine (*De Clericis,* Bk. I, chap. xxix, last edition) likewise follows St. Thomas, and Covarruvias (on *Sext,* rule *peccatum,* Pt. II, § 11, no. 4) holds the same opinion.

4. Nor is this opinion denied by the jurists who divide the *ius gentium* into two branches, primary and secondary, and who hold that the former is included within the natural law whereas the latter is positive human law; a classification which may be found in Albert of Bologna (*De Lege, Iure et Aequitate,* Chap. xxvii), and in du Pineau (on *Code,* IV. xliv). For such a method of division differs merely in the choice of terms, while it agrees in point of fact with the doctrine above set forth, since the so-called 'primary'[3] *ius gentium* is intrinsically natural law and is called *ius gentium* only because the nations have it in common.

But here we are employing the term in a precise sense, in so far as it is derived from considerations of origin and authority, so that we are referring to that secondary *ius gentium* which the above-mentioned jurists declare to be positive human law.

The assertion in question may also be proved by reasoning, in view of what has already been said. For it suffices that law should be divided into natural and positive, properly so called, or into divine and human law, each of these being named according to its author, since the two branches are mutually exclusive, as is evident; but it has been shown that the laws of the *ius gentium* are not natural law, properly and strictly speaking, and consequently not divine; and therefore, they must be positive and human.

This argument is confirmed by the fact that natural law is that law which springs not from [human] opinion, but from the evidence afforded by nature, as Cicero has pointed out. Hence, every law that does not

---

3. [A free translation of *primaevum,* which may have been written inadvertently for *primarium,* the term used in the first sentence of the present Section.—Tr.]

arise in this way is positive and human. And the *ius gentium* is of this latter variety, because it came into existence not through [natural] evidence but through probable inferences and the common judgment of mankind. Therefore, . . .

5. *In what way the* ius gentium *and civil law differ.* It now remains for us to explain in what manner the *ius gentium* differs from civil law. For all positive law laid down by mankind for the governance of the purely political order is called by Aristotle (*Nicomachean Ethics,* Bk. V, chap. vii), 'conventional';[4] and the same sort of law may, it seems, be called civil, according to Isidore (Bk. I, dist. i [*Etymologies,* Bk. V, chap. v]), and the opinion held by St. Thomas in the places cited [I.–II, qu. 95, art. 4; II.–II, qu. 57, art. 3].

You may say that the *ius gentium* and civil law differ in that the latter is the law of one state or kingdom, while the former is common to all peoples. One objection to this reply is that the difference pointed out is merely a difference between the greater and the less,[5] and far from essential. A second and more formidable objection is based upon the fact that it seems impossible that the *ius gentium* should be common to all peoples and should nevertheless have its origin in human will and opinion. For it is not customary that all peoples[6] should agree with respect to matters that are dependent upon human opinion and free will, since it is characteristic of mankind that there should be almost as many sentiments and opinions as there are individuals; and therefore, it would seem either that the *ius gentium* is not human law, or else that it cannot differ in the manner described from civil law.

6. *Solution.* For the solution of this difficulty, then, I offer the following explanation.

The precepts of the *ius gentium* differ from those of the civil law in that they are not established in written form; they are established through

---

4. ['Conventional', that is, the kind which might originally have been determined either way with equal justice (Aristotle, *ibid.*).—REVISER.]

5. [According to the principle that greater and lesser do not constitute a specific difference.—REVISER.]

6. [Reading *nationes* in the place of *rationes. Vide* footnotes 8 on p. 403, and 2 on p. 410.—TR.]

the customs not of one or two states or provinces, but of all or nearly all nations. For human law is twofold, that is to say, written and unwritten, as the legal systems above cited maintain and as we shall later perceive. It is manifest, moreover, that the *ius gentium* is unwritten, and that it consequently differs in this respect from all written civil law, even from that imperial law which is applicable to all. Furthermore, unwritten law is made up of customs, and if it has been introduced by the custom of one particular nation and is binding upon the conduct of that nation only, it is also called civil; if, on the other hand, it has been introduced by the customs of all nations and thus is binding upon all, we believe it to be the *ius gentium* properly so called. The latter system, then, differs from the natural law because it is based upon custom rather than upon nature; and it is to be distinguished likewise from civil law, in its origin, basis, and universal application, in the manner explained above.

It seems to me that this is the opinion expressed by Justinian in the passage (*Institutes,* I. ii, § 1 [§ 2]) where he says: 'The *ius gentium,* indeed, is common to all the human race, for because of imperative usage and human needs the nations of the earth have established certain laws for themselves.' In this passage, the phrases 'imperative usage' and 'have established' are to be carefully weighed; for the latter implies that the law in question was established not by nature but by men, and the phrase 'imperative usage' indicates that it was introduced not by a written instrument but through use.

Isidore (*Etymologies,* Bk. V, chap. iv) evidently holds the same view, for he first distinguishes the three kinds of law aforementioned and then defines the natural law as 'that which is common to all nations, in that it exists everywhere[7] through natural instinct and not through any formal enactment.' Herein he supports our own statement and virtually holds that the *ius gentium* is not based upon natural instinct alone. Later on (Chap. v [Chap. vi]), after giving examples of the *ius gentium,* he accordingly concludes: 'Therefore, this system of law is called the *ius gentium* because almost all nations make use of it.' In making this assertion Isidore

---

7. [For *utrobique,* read *ubique,* the term actually used by Isidore. *Vide* W. M. Lindsay's edition of the *Etymologies,* Oxford, 1911.—Tr.]

by implication defines the *ius gentium,* indicating that it is a system of law common to all nations, and constituted not through natural instinct alone but through the usage of those nations. Neither should the particle 'almost' be lightly passed over; for it shows that there is no altogether intrinsic and natural necessity inherent in this law, and that it need not be absolutely common to all peoples, even apart from cases of ignorance or error, but that, on the contrary, it suffices if nearly all well-ordered nations shall adopt the said law. St. Thomas appears to me to be of the same opinion, as I shall presently explain; and the other authorities cited above undoubtedly hold the same view.

7. The validity of this view may be proved, first, by an adequate enumeration of the various parts involved; for such an explanation of the *ius gentium* involves no inconsistency whatever, but is, on the contrary, manifestly credible, as I shall demonstrate at greater length immediately below; and, furthermore, one could not distinguish the *ius gentium,* by any mode more satisfactory, from the other two extremes, [that is, from natural and civil law], a fact that is sufficiently proved by all we have said above; therefore, . . .

Secondly, the same view is upheld by several examples already adduced. For the custom of receiving ambassadors under a law of immunity and security, if considered in an absolute aspect, does not spring from any necessity of the natural law, since any community of men might have failed to have within its territory any ambassador of a foreign community, or it might have been unwilling to receive such ambassadors; yet this reception is an obligation imposed by the *ius gentium,* and to repudiate those ambassadors would be a sign of enmity and a violation of the *ius gentium,* although it would not be an injury committed in contravention of natural reason. Accordingly, even though it would be contrary to the natural law not to respect their immunity, for the reason that such an act would be contrary to justice and due good faith, if we assume that they have been received on the basis of some implied agreement, nevertheless that assumption and that implied agreement would have been introduced by the *ius gentium* under the conditions stated. The same argument may be applied in the case of any contract or commercial agreement; for three separate factors may be distinguished in connexion with such an agreement. The first is the specific method of making the contract, a matter which ordinarily pertains to civil law, and which is frequently decided in accordance with the will of the contracting parties, if their will conflicts with no existing legal rule. The second factor is the observance of the contract after it has been made; and this matter, as is evident, pertains to the natural law. The third factor is the freedom to contract commercial agreements with persons not actively hostile or unfriendly in sentiment. This freedom is derived from the *ius gentium;* for it is not an obligation imposed by natural law considered in itself, inasmuch as a state might conceivably exist in isolation and refuse to enter into commercial relations with another state even if there were no unfriendly feeling involved; but it has been established by the *ius gentium* that commercial intercourse shall be free, and it would be a violation of that system of law if such intercourse were prohibited without reasonable cause. It is in this light, I believe, that one should interpret the following passage from the *Institutes* (I. ii, § 1 [§ 2]): 'By this *ius gentium* almost all contracts—those of purchase, those of sale, &c.—have been introduced.' Moreover we might make similar comments with regard to other examples.

8. *Twofold form of the* ius gentium. For the clearer presentation of this point, I shall add that a particular matter (as I infer from Isidore and other jurists and authorities) can be subject to the *ius gentium* in either one of two ways: first, on the ground that this is the law which all the various peoples and nations ought to observe in their relations with each other; secondly, on the ground that it is a body of laws which individual states or kingdoms observe within their own borders, but which is called *ius gentium* [i.e. civil law] because the said laws are similar [in each instance] and are commonly accepted.

The first interpretation seems, in my opinion, to correspond most properly to the actual *ius gentium* (law of nations) as distinct from the civil law, in accordance with our exposition of the former.

The examples mentioned above concerning ambassadors and commercial usage also pertain to this first aspect.

Similarly, in my judgment, the law of war—in so far as that law rests upon the power possessed by a given state or a supreme monarchy, for the punishment, avenging, or reparation of any injury inflicted upon it by another state—would seem to pertain properly to the law of nations. For it was not indispensable by virtue of natural reason alone that the power in question should exist within an injured state, since men could have established some other mode of inflicting vengeance, or entrusted that power to some third prince and quasi-arbitrator with coercive power. Nevertheless, since the mode in question, which is at present in practice, is easier and more in conformity with nature, it has been adopted by custom and is just to the extent that it may not be rightfully resisted.

In the same class, I place slavery. For peoples and nations, in their relations with one another, put into practice the law regarding slavery, although that institution was not necessary from the standpoint of natural reason; for, as I have said, another mode of punishment could have been introduced. Under present conditions, however, the law in question exists in such form that the guilty are bound to submit to the punishment of slavery in accordance with the manner in which that custom has been introduced, while the victors, on their side, may not justly punish their conquered enemies more severely at the close of the war unless there exists some other special ground for punishment which would justify such a course of action.

Likewise, treaties of peace and truces may be placed under this head [that is, under the law of nations, or *ius gentium* in the strict sense of the term]; not in so far as relates to the obligation to observe such treaties after they are made, since this obligation pertains rather to the natural law, but in so far as [offers of] such treaties should be heeded and not refused, when presented in due manner and for a reasonable cause. For while such compliance is to a great degree in harmony with natural reason, it appears to be still more firmly established by usage itself and by the law of nations, [thus] falling under a more binding obligation.

There are other examples of the same sort which could be pointed out and expounded.

9. The rational basis, moreover, of this phase of law consists in the fact that the human race, into howsoever many different peoples and kingdoms it may be divided, always preserves a certain unity, not only as a species, but also a moral and political unity (as it were) enjoined by the

natural precept of mutual love and mercy; a precept which applies to all, even to strangers of every nation.[8]

Therefore, although a given sovereign state, commonwealth, or kingdom may constitute a perfect community in itself, consisting of its own members, nevertheless, each one of these states is also, in a certain sense, and viewed in relation to the human race, a member of that universal society; for these states when standing alone are never so self-sufficient that they do not require some mutual assistance, association, and intercourse, at times for their own greater welfare and advantage, but at other times because also of some moral necessity or need. This fact is made manifest by actual usage.

Consequently, such communities have need of some system of law whereby they may be directed and properly ordered with regard to this kind of intercourse and association; and although that guidance is in large measure provided by natural reason, it is not provided in sufficient measure and in a direct manner with respect to all matters; therefore, it was possible for certain special rules of law to be introduced through the practice of these same nations. For just as in one state or province law is introduced by custom, so among the human race as a whole it was possible for laws to be introduced by the habitual conduct of nations. This was the more feasible because the matters comprised within the law in question are few, very closely related to natural law and most easily deduced therefrom in a manner so advantageous and so in harmony with nature itself that, while this derivation [of the law of nations from the natural law] may not be self-evident—that is, not essentially and absolutely required for moral rectitude—it is nevertheless quite in accord with nature, and universally acceptable for its own sake.

---

8. [Reading *nationis* in place of *rationis*. This word has elsewhere been read as *nationis* and so translated. See for example Ernest Nys: *Le Droit de la Guerre et les Précurseurs de Grotius* (Brussels and Leipzig, 1882), p. 11; and *The Collected Papers of John Westlake on International Law,* edited by L. Oppenheim (Cambridge, 1914), p. 26. In all of the available editions of Suárez, however, the term in question is *rationis.* Cf. footnote 6, p. 398, and 2, p. 410.—Tr.]

10. The second kind of *ius gentium*[9] embodies certain precepts, usages, or modes of living, which do not, in themselves and directly, relate to all mankind; neither do they have for their immediate end (so to speak) the harmonious fellowship and intercourse of all nations with respect to one another. On the contrary, these usages are established in each state by a process of government that is suited to the respective courts of each.[10] Nevertheless, they are of such a nature that, in the possession of similar usages or laws, almost all nations agree with one another; or at least they resemble one another, at times in a generic manner, and at times specifically, so to speak.

This fact may be illustrated, moreover, by means of examples.

In the first place, the example of religion, mentioned by the jurisconsult [, i.e. Justinian],[11] may be adapted to our purpose. For the worship of God pertains, in an absolute sense, to the natural law, but the purely particular and specific determination [of the details] thereof is a matter for positive divine law; while in the natural order such specific determination would pertain to civil or private law. Nevertheless, in a certain intermediate fashion, the worship of God seems to have been determined by the *ius gentium*. For example, the custom of conducting this worship through sacrifice is not, absolutely speaking, a matter of natural law; yet almost all nations seem to have agreed on that custom, as we have already remarked in treating of that particular subject; and therefore, the said custom may properly be described under the head of the *ius gentium*. Similarly, the fact that there may exist within the state a class of men especially set aside for the worship of God does not seem to be a matter of the natural law in the absolute sense; yet it is so in harmony with that law that almost all nations and states have agreed upon such an institution, at least in a general manner, however widely they differ as to individual details; so that, in this respect also, religion may be said to pertain to the *ius gentium*.

It is in the same manner, apparently, that many of the examples given by Isidore [*Etymologies*, Bk. V, chap. vi] come under the *ius gentium;* that

---

9. [I.e. civil law.—TR.]
10. [I.e. suitable to the legal system already established.—REVISER.]
11. [*Digest*, I. i. 2.—TR.]

is to say, such examples as the occupation of places by settlement, matters relating to buildings, those relating to fortifications, and the use of money; even many private contracts may in this [secondary] sense be said to pertain to the *ius gentium;* as, for instance, contracts of purchase and sale, and of like nature, engaged in by the individual nations internally. Under this same head I should place the matter of postliminium, if indeed there is a real agreement among the nations on that subject; for, as I have said, it seems rather to relate very closely to civil law.

With even greater reason I shall classify in the same manner the prohibition against marriage with persons of an alien religion; for, in reality, wherever such a restriction exists, it concerns not the general intercourse and fellowship of the human race, but rather the individual interest of the nation within which the prohibition is found. And if there be a great similarity among the various nations in this matter (an assumption which is, in my opinion, quite doubtful) the said prohibition may reasonably be considered as pertaining to the *ius gentium.*

In the foregoing, then, our opinion on the subject under discussion has been sufficiently set forth and defended.

CHAPTER XX

Corollaries from the Doctrines Set Forth Above; and in What Way the *Ius Gentium* Is Both Just and Subject to Change

1. *How the* ius gentium *may be common to all nations, and yet not be the natural law.* From what has been said above, it is easy to explain the remaining points that we may wish to discuss in connexion with the *ius gentium.*

In the first place, one readily understands how this law may be common to all nations, although it is not the natural law; so that a certain difficulty, left unanswered in the Chapter immediately preceding, is solved.

For if we are speaking of the *ius gentium* properly so called, that is, in the first of the two senses expounded above,[1] it is easily apparent that

---

1. [See *supra,* p. 401, Chapter xix, § 8.—Tr.]

this system of law, simply as the result of usage and tradition, could have been gradually introduced throughout the whole world, through a successive process, by means of propagation and mutual imitation among the nations, and without any special and simultaneous compact or consent on the part of all peoples. For the body of law in question has such a close relationship to nature and so befits all nations, individually and collectively, that it has grown, almost by a natural process, with the growth of the human race; and therefore it does not exist in written form, since it was not dictated by a legislator, but has, on the contrary, waxed strong through usage.

On the other hand, as to the *ius gentium* when interpreted in the second sense, it is easy to explain the source of the great similarity of forms in which that law exists among the various nations; although, in other respects and essentially, this phase of the *ius gentium* is [simply] civil law. The explanation regarding that similarity is, partly, that the resemblance is not always perfect, but lies only in a certain general and common character, as I have explained above; partly, that such a common character, although it is not in an absolute sense derived from natural law, is nevertheless so closely related to, and so thoroughly in accord or harmony with nature, that through it the individual nations could easily have been led to adopt the rules in question; and partly, that tradition and a mutual imitation, dating from the beginning of the human race and growing with the growth and dissemination of that race, may have added their influence in this matter.

2. *In what sense St. Thomas is to be understood when he asserts that the precepts of the* ius gentium *are conclusions drawn from principles of the natural law.* In the second place, we [now] understand in what sense the words of St. Thomas ([I.–II,] qu. 95, art. 4) are to be taken, when he says that the precepts of the *ius gentium* are conclusions drawn from principles of the natural law; and that these precepts differ from the civil law in that the rules of the latter are not general conclusions, but specific determinations of the natural law.

This doctrine refers especially to the *ius gentium* strictly speaking and interpreted in a common and general sense, that is to say, regarded in the first of the two aspects described. Moreover, although Conrad Koellin interprets the doctrine in question as being couched in the customary

language of the jurists, we prefer to agree with Soto and others in considering that [St. Thomas] speaks of the precepts of the *ius gentium* as [general]
conclusions of the natural law, not in an absolute sense and by necessary
inference, but in comparison with the specific determinations of civil and
private law. For in this latter system of law [one of two events must occur]:
either a merely arbitrary specific determination is made, of the sort concerning which it is said that 'What the prince decrees has the force of law',
not because his will alone suffices as a rational basis, but because that particular determination might reasonably have taken one of various forms,
and because there is frequently no ground on which one form should be
preferred to another, so that it is said that the determination is made by the
will [of the prince] rather than in accordance with reason; or else, where
there exists some special reason for a preference, that reason is weighed in
relation to the particular and (as it were) material circumstances, so that
the determination has reference rather to the circumstances of a situation
than to the substance thereof. In the *ius gentium,* on the other hand, the
precepts are of a more general character, for they take into consideration
the welfare of all nature, as well as conformity to her primary and universal principles. Consequently, such precepts are said to be conclusions
drawn from natural principles, since their appropriate character and moral
value are immediately made manifest by the force of natural reflection;
an appropriateness and value which have induced men to introduce the
customs in question, more because of the pressure of necessity—as the
Emperor Justinian has said—than because of [deliberate] will.

3. *True equity and justice must be observed in the* ius gentium. Thirdly,
from the foregoing we conclude that equity and justice must be observed
in the precepts of the *ius gentium.* For such observance is included in the
essential character of every true law, as has been shown above; and the
rules pertaining to the *ius gentium* are indeed true law, as we have already
declared, and are more closely related to the natural law than are those of
the civil law; therefore, as Covarruvias (*Variarum Resolutionum,* Bk. II,
chap. iii, no. 2) has well noted, it is impossible that these precepts of the
ius gentium should be contrary to natural equity.

A difference between the ius gentium *and the natural law.* I must add,
indeed, that there is a difference between the *ius gentium,* and the natural

law in its strict interpretation. For the latter not only prescribes the performance of good acts, but also prohibits all evil acts in such a way as to be tolerant of none; whereas the *ius gentium* may permit some evils, as Matienzo (*Recopilación,* Bk. V, tit. XI, law I, gloss I, no. 3 [no. 5]) has remarked. This statement would seem to apply especially to that form of the *ius gentium* which is in point of fact civil law, but which is called *ius gentium* by analogy and owing to mutual agreement thereon among the nations. For just as certain evils are tolerated by civil law, so also they may be tolerated by the *ius gentium;* since this very toleration may be so necessary, in view of the frailty and general character of mankind or of business affairs, that almost all nations agree in manifesting it. Of this nature, apparently, are the toleration of prostitutes, the toleration of deception that is not excessive in the matter of contracts, and similar instances.

4. *Objection.* However, an objection may be advanced on the basis of a law in the *Digest* (IV. iv. 16, § 4), and the Gloss on that law. For the text in question contains the following words: 'It is naturally permissible for the contracting parties to circumvent each other in regard to the purchase and selling prices'; and the Gloss on this passage explains the term 'naturally' (*naturaliter*) as being equivalent to 'by the *ius gentium*'. The same statement is found in yet another law of the *Digest* (XIX. ii. 22, § 3).

Matienzo (as cited above) replies to this objection, while upholding the interpretation of the Gloss in regard to the word 'naturally', that the expression 'is permissible' (*licere*) ought not to be understood in its strict sense, as when one speaks of something permissible and righteous; since it would be a contradiction in terms to assert in this sense that the practice of mutual deception is ever permissible, whether in regard to prices of purchase and sale or in any other transactions whatsoever. For among the precepts laid down by Paul are these words (2 [1] *Thessalonians,* Chap. iv [, v. 6]): 'That no man [. . .] circumvent his brother,' to which the following is added: 'because the Lord is the avenger of all these things.'

The expression 'is permissible', then, ought to be taken in a broad sense and as relating to human judgments, in accordance with the fact that a thing is said to be permissible when it is done with impunity and tolerated by usage, which is the same as to say that it is permitted. Or else one may offer the following explanation, which amounts to very nearly the same thing: the act in question is 'naturally permissible'—that is, 'permissible by the *ius gentium*'—which is to say that it is 'not forbidden' thereby; this permissibility being based, not on the fact that natural law in its strict sense does not prohibit the said act, but rather on the fact that the *ius gentium,* inasmuch as it is a human system of law, does not include a special prohibition as to the point in question, decreeing on the contrary that the act is not punishable and is not to be considered as a crime in a human state or court of justice. In this sense, indeed, the laws cited tend to confirm the doctrine set forth.

5. Covarruvias [*Variarum Resolutionum,* Bk. II, chap. iii, no. 2], however, does not approve of the interpretation of the Gloss with respect to the word 'naturally'; and he furthermore disapproves of such a loose interpretation of the word 'permissible', especially in view of the fact that the passage from the *Digest* (XIX. ii. 22, § 3) cited in this connexion reads: 'it has been naturally conceded' (*concessum est*), &c. Accordingly, he explains the word 'circumvent' (*circumvenire*) by saying that it is to be taken not in its strict sense, as referring to deception through trickery and fraud, but in the sense in which it refers to human ingenuity and skill in that the buyer tries to lessen as much as possible the estimated value of a given article, while the seller attempts to increase that valuation, not by fraud and trickery but within the limits of a just price and of right reason.

This sort of circumvention seems to have been described by Solomon in the *Proverbs* (Chap. xx [, v. 14]): 'It is nought, it is nought, saith every buyer: and when he is gone away, then he will boast.' Hence, in the *Digest* (*ibid.*) under discussion, the words 'Wherefore [. . .] it is naturally conceded that one may buy for less, what is worth more, and may sell for more that which is worth less,' are to be understood according to the opinion just set forth as applying within the limits of a just price, inasmuch as the buyer attempts to purchase at the minimum just price, and the vendor attempts to sell at the maximum just price. When interpreted thus the laws cited present no difficulty; although this interpretation has no bearing on the present question, so that I shall not linger over a discussion of it.

6. *The* ius gentium *may be changed by the consent of men.* Fourthly, from the above discussion one may infer [the corollary] that the *ius gentium* is subject to change, in so far as it is dependent upon the consent of men;

and in this respect, also, the *ius gentium* differs from the natural law, as is evident from what we have already said.

Some, indeed, say that the former may be changed by private authority, in that an individual may surrender his own right, even if that right is derived from the *ius gentium*. For it is thus that a religious renounces the ownership of temporal goods, and even the capacity for such ownership. However, this [sort of mutability] is not peculiar to the *ius gentium*, nor does the latter system of law differ therein from the natural law, if one interprets precisely, as being concessive, that which some persons call negative. For, in the same manner, a religious renounces his *natural* right to take a wife; and again, a given person may make himself a slave by renouncing his natural liberty; just as one may likewise renounce his right to privileges individually granted by the civil or canon law.

Therefore, the corollary must be understood as referring to the *ius gentium* as a system of law that contains prohibitions or precepts. For these are of themselves subject to change; and the reason [for their mutability] is that the things prohibited by the *ius gentium* are not, absolutely speaking, evil (in themselves and intrinsically) in view of two facts: first, because the precepts in question are not deduced from natural principles by a necessary and evident inference; secondly, because the obligation imposed by the *ius gentium* does not spring from reason alone, apart from human obligation of every sort, even from that which has its source in general custom. Hence, in so far as pertains to the subject-matter of that system of law, it is not absolutely inconsistent with reason that the said law should be subjected to change, provided that the change be made on sufficient authority.

7. *By whom and in what manner the* ius gentium *may be changed.* In this connexion, I must furthermore note that such changes may be effected in the *ius gentium* in different ways. They may occur in connexion with that phase of the said law which is common merely in that several nations[2] agree upon the suitability of certain precepts; on the other hand, they may occur in that phase of the *ius gentium* which is common, owing to the usage and customs of all nations, in so far as there exists among them any fellowship or intercourse.

2. [Reading *nationum* for *rationum*. Cf. footnotes 6 on p. 398 and 8 on p. 403.—Tr.]

For [the *ius gentium*] in the former phase may be changed by an individual kingdom or state to an extent affecting that state alone; since the law in question, as it exists within the said state, is intrinsically (so to speak) nothing more or less than civil law, and is called *ius gentium* only because of its kinship and harmony [with the laws] of other [states], or because it is so closely related to the natural law that it is in consequence applied universally to all or almost all nations. Considered in itself, however, as it exists in each separate state, this form of law is dependent upon the particular determination [of general law], the power and the custom of that state in itself, without respect to any other. Therefore, such law may be changed in any one country, by that country, even though the others do not consent; for individual nations are not bound to conform to others. For example, a certain state might decree that prostitutes are not to be tolerated within its territory; or that all unjust sales, made at any excessive price whatsoever, shall be rescinded; or that [its citizens] shall not use money; or similar decrees might be made with regard to other kinds of exchange.[3] For although these alterations may not actually be made, since there is no cause for them and no advantage attached to them, nevertheless, they are not inconceivable from the standpoint of righteousness and the power [of the individual state].

8. In connexion with the other phase of the *ius gentium* (law of nations), however, changes are far more difficult, for this phase involves law common to all nations and appears to have been introduced by the authority of all, so that it may not be annulled [even in part] without universal consent. Nevertheless, there would be no inherent obstacle to change, in so far as the subject-matter of such law is concerned, if all nations should agree to the alteration, or if a custom contrary to [some established rule of this law of nations] should gradually come into practice and prevail. That event, however, although it might be conceived of as not contrary to reason, yet seems impossible, practically speaking.

But in another sense a given community may ordain that, within its own territory and among its own subjects, the law in question shall not

---

3. [Reading *pecunia; sic de aliis generibus commutationum,* in accordance with the Paris edition of 1856, instead of *pecunia, sed de aliis generibus commutationum,* as in our own Latin text.—Tr.]

be observed. This mode [of change] is both conceivable and practicable. For it was thus that the rule of the *ius gentium* as to the enslavement of prisoners taken in a just war was changed in the Church; so that to-day this rule is not observed among Christians, in accordance with the early custom of the Church, which is (so to speak) a special form of 'the law of Christian nations' (*ius gentis fidelis*) and one to be observed strictly, as has been noted by Bartolus of Sassoferrato (on *Digest,* XLIX. xv. 24, no. 16) and also Covarruvias (on *Sext,* rule *peccatum,* Pt. II, § 11, no. 6), who refers to many others.

9. *A difference between the* ius gentium *and the civil law.* From the foregoing, another distinction may be inferred; a distinction which is wont to be drawn between the *ius gentium* and the civil law, with respect to this same point. For the civil law is said to be subject to change in its entirety, while the *ius gentium* is said to be so subject not entirely but partially; since this distinction should not be understood as relating to an absolute power of change (so to speak), that is, to the mutable nature of these two bodies of law themselves; because, speaking in this sense, both are inherently mutable, as is proved by the arguments stated above. On the contrary, we must conceive of the distinction in question in accordance with the moral power and usage of men. Similarly, this difference must not be understood to relate to the entire body, taken as a whole, of each system; for neither the *ius gentium,* nor the civil law is, practically speaking, mutable in its entirety, seeing that neither may be entirely abrogated by the human race as a whole; a fact which is sufficiently evident from what has already been said. The rules of the civil law, then, in so far as relates to the individual precepts, are considered as being readily subject to complete repeal or alteration; whereas those of the *ius gentium* are said to be subject to abrogation only in part.

10. Finally, the constitution and nature of the *ius gentium* would seem to be sufficiently clear from the foregoing discussion, in so far as relates to that law in itself and viewing it with respect to its own peculiar character. Furthermore, solutions have been found for all the difficulties touched on in the foregoing Chapters; difficulties which seemed for the most part to depend either upon modes of verbal expression in the laws and in weighty authorities, or else upon various examples adduced by those laws and authorities.

But emphasis should not be laid upon such points, because the verbal expressions in question could have been used in different senses; and because, moreover, the *ius gentium* is a form of law, intermediate (as it were) between the natural and the civil law. For, in a certain sense, the *ius gentium* is in harmony with the natural law, because of the common acceptance and universal character of the former, and the ease with which its rules may be inferred from natural principles; although this process of inference is not one of absolute necessity and manifest evidence, in which latter respect the law in question agrees with human law. Accordingly, certain natural precepts, which have been established simply by deduction and the formulation of which requires that process, have occasionally been called precepts of the *ius gentium;* and, in like manner, examples of the *ius gentium* are sometimes confused with examples of the natural law. Nevertheless, strictly speaking, and making a proper distinction among the respective characters [of the different sorts] of law, the examples relating thereto and the various precepts involved must also be mutually distinguished.

On Positive Human Law as Such, and as It May Be Viewed in Pure Human Nature, a Phase of Law Which Is Also Called Civil

[INTRODUCTION]

1. In the First Book we divided temporal law into the natural and the positive, and consequently, since the eternal law and natural temporal law have been discussed, the discussion of the positive [temporal] law should follow.

However, in that very passage, [Bk. i, chap. iii, § 14,] we subdivided this phase into the divine and the human. Of these, the divine is in truth the more noble and the worthier, but the human is better known to us, and closer to [human] nature, since it pertains to the same order. Accordingly, as the existence of nature is presupposed for the existence of grace, so human law by its very nature is prior in the order of its generation to divine law, since the latter is supernatural and relates to the order of grace. Therefore, we shall treat of human law before treating of divine law.

And as to positive law in its general aspect, apart from any division into divine and human, this is a matter which we need not discuss. For, aside from its mode of origin, which is explained in the negative statement that the precepts of positive law, whether divine or human, are characterized not by an intrinsic necessity, existing in themselves, but by a necessity resulting from an extrinsic will—aside from this fact, I say, and aside from the statements relating to law in general which were made in the First Book— practically nothing remains to be said, of a general nature, that would be useful as practical doctrine or even possessed of any speculative significance.

Moreover, when both the human and the divine branches of positive law have been explained, all the questions pertaining to their mutual accord or distinction that might call for discussion, will have been explained.

2. *Human law* (lex) *is divided into that which is common law* (ius) *and that which pertains to the particular law* (ius) *[of a single community].* However, in the opinion of Justinian (*Institutes,* I. ii. 1), human law (*lex*) may be divided into that which pertains to common law (*ius*) and that which pertains to the particular law (*ius*) [of a single community].

The former relates to the *ius gentium* and is comprehended within that term. We have already discussed that phase of law sufficiently.

At present, therefore, we are dealing with particular human law [of individual communities] to which the name of positive human law has been applied, and which is said to be peculiar to any given state, commonwealth or similar perfect community.

Human law is divided into civil and canon. Accordingly, human law of this kind is in turn divided into civil and canon. For though canon law is of itself capable of being common to the whole world, even as the Catholic Church is universal, nevertheless, in point of fact, it is a law peculiar to the community of the Church of Christ, and not common to all nations, since they are not all a part of the Church. Furthermore, in the manner of its enactment, it is positive human law in the strict sense, and of a very different character from that of the *ius gentium,* while in many respects it bears a likeness to the civil law. For these two branches of law agree in the fact that both in common possess the character of positive human law. One may note, however, that there exists between them a difference, consisting in the fact that civil law pertains entirely to the natural order in so far as regards its origin and authority, for though it is not enacted directly by nature, it is nevertheless enacted through the authority connatural to man. Canon law, on the other hand, is properly speaking, that law which is enacted by man through a supernatural authority.

Therefore, following the order of doctrine, and beginning with those points which are easier to comprehend, we deem it advisable to speak of civil law before speaking of canon law. We shall, however, discuss the common basis of positive human law, in connexion with civil law. For the doctrine will thus be grasped more readily and will easily be adapted to the canon law by the addition of those elements which befit the latter because of its supernatural authority, a matter which we shall take up in the following Book.[1]

From the foregoing, it also follows that, within the civil law itself, two states may be distinguished: one, the civil law in itself, simply as it existed among the Gentiles and exists now among unbelievers; the other, civil law as it exists when joined with faith and as it may be practised among believers in the Christian Church. These two states differ only in non-essentials, and therefore, we shall speak of civil law in a general sense. However, when any special point arises, calling for explanation, we shall not pass it by, but shall adapt the general doctrine to the present state of the Church.

CHAPTER I

Does Man Possess the Power to Make Laws?

1. We are speaking (as I have said) of man's nature and of his legislative power viewed in itself; for we are not considering, at present, the question of whether anything has been added to or taken from that power through divine law, a matter which will be taken up later.

The question under consideration, then, is as follows: is it possible— speaking solely with reference to the nature of the case[2]—for men to command other men, binding the latter by [man's] own laws?

A reason for doubting that they can do so, may lie in the fact that man is by his nature free and subject to no one, save only to the Creator, so that human sovereignty is contrary to the order of nature and involves tyranny.

This doubt is confirmed by history; for [such sovereignty] was in point of fact thus introduced, and it is written (*Genesis,* Chap. x [, vv. 8, 10]) of Nemrod: 'he began to be mighty on the earth. [. . .] And the beginning of his kingdom was Babylon'—that is to say, his kingdom began through force and might. Similarly, Lucan [*The Civil War,* Bk. X, line 21] said of Alexander that he was, 'A fortunate freebooter'. This was the meaning of Augustine, also, in his work *On the City of God* (Bk. IV, chap. iv). Thus it

1. [Not included in these *Selections.*—Tr.]
2. [With reference to a power inherent in human nature.—Tr.]

is that we read in *Osee* (Chap. viii [, v. 4]): 'They have reigned, but not by me: they have been princes, and I knew not [. . .].'

Secondly, the same doubt is confirmed by the words of Augustine, who discusses (*On the City of God,* Bk. XIX, chap. xv) the fact that God said (*Genesis,* Chap. i [, v. 26]): 'Let us make man', &c., 'and let him have dominion over the fishes of the sea, and the fowls of the air, and the beasts [and the whole] earth';[3] whereas He did not say: 'Let him have dominion over men', a distinction which indicates that such domination is not natural to man. 'Therefore,' says [Augustine, *ibid.*], 'the first just men were not kings, but shepherds of flocks, and they were so called.' Thus Gregory the Great, too, indicates (*Moralia,* Bk. XXI, chap. x, or xi [*Libri sive Expositio in Lib. B. Job,* Bk. XXI, chap. xv] and in the *Regulae Pastoralis,* Pt. II, chap. vi) that authority of this kind was introduced through sin and acquired through usurpation.

Thirdly, the doubt may be confirmed by the testimony of a number of passages which show that God alone is the king, the lawgiver and the lord of men.[4] 'For the Lord is our judge, the Lord is our king, the Lord is our lawgiver' (*Isaias,* Chap. xxxiii, v. 22). And again, 'There is one lawgiver, and judge', &c. (*James,* Chap. iv [, v. 12]).

Finally, we have this confirmation, namely: there is no true law save that which is binding in conscience; but one man cannot bind another in conscience, since this power would seem to be exclusively a property of God, Who alone can save and destroy; therefore, . . .

2. At this point, mention might be made of various errors among the heretics; but it will be better to touch upon those errors later.

The affirmative conclusion, which is a matter of faith. Accordingly, leaving them aside, we shall make first the following statement: a civil magistracy accompanied by temporal power for human government is just and in complete harmony with human nature. This conclusion is certainly true, and a matter of faith. It may be sufficiently proved by the example set by God Himself, when He established a government of this kind over

---

3. [Suárez has simply *bestiis terrae* (the beasts of the earth) in the place of the Vulgate reading, *bestiis, universaeque terrae.*—TR.]

4. [Reading *dominum* for *dominium.*—TR.]

the Jewish people, first by means of judges, and later by means of kings, endowed doubtless with the princely office and temporal power, and held in such veneration that they were even called gods, according to the passage in *Psalms* (lxxxi [, v. 1]): 'God hath stood in the congregation of gods: and being in the midst of them he judgeth gods.' Nor is there any validity in the objection which may be made that those judges and kings had their power from God Himself; for that power nevertheless did not in itself exceed the limits set by nature, even though the mode through which it was held was extraordinary and the result of a special providence; and therefore, this [divine derivation of the power in question] does not render it impossible for the power to be held justly in some other way. Furthermore, from that same contention there follows this argument, namely, that power of that kind is in harmony with nature itself, in so far as it is necessary to the proper government of a human community.

Again, this contention derives a fuller confirmation from human custom, since kings existed long before the times of which we were speaking, even kings who were holy and praised in the Scriptures, as was Melchisedech (*Genesis,* Chap. xiv and *Hebrews,* Chap. vii). Abraham, too, is thought to have been a king or sovereign prince. Moreover, a like example is to be found in *Job,* &c.

And finally, we read in *Proverbs* (Chap. viii [, v. 15]) the general statement: 'By me kings reign.'

The point is clearly set forth in the writings of the Holy Fathers, to whom I shall refer in the course of our discussion.

3. *The basic reason for the assertion.* The basic reason for this assertion is to be sought in Aristotle's *Politics* (Bk. I [, chap. v, 1254 B]). This reason is expounded by St. Thomas (*Opuscula,* XX: *De Regimine Principum,* Bk. I, chap. i), and also, very neatly, by St. Chrysostom (*On First Corinthians,* Homily XXXIV [, no. 5]). It is founded, moreover, upon two principles.

The first principle is as follows: man is a social animal, and cherishes a natural and right desire to live in a community. In this connexion, we should recollect the principle already laid down, that human society is twofold: imperfect, or domestic; and perfect, or political. Of these divisions, the former is in the highest degree natural and (so to speak) fundamental, because it arises from the fellowship of man and wife, without which the human race could not be propagated nor preserved; wherefore it has been written, 'It is not good for man to be alone'. From this union there follows as a direct consequence the fellowship of children and parents; for the earlier form of union is ordained for the rearing of the children, and they require union and fellowship with their parents (in early life, at least, and throughout a long period of time) since otherwise they could not live, nor be fittingly reared, nor receive the proper instruction. Furthermore, to these forms of domestic society there is presently added a connexion based on slavery or servitude and lordship, since, practically speaking, men require the aid and service of other men.

Now, from these three forms of connexion there arises the first human community, which is said to be imperfect from a political standpoint. The family is perfect in itself, however, for purposes of domestic or economic government.

But this community—as I have already indicated, above—is not self-sufficing; and therefore, from the very nature of the case, there is a further necessity among human beings for a political community, consisting at least of a city state (*ciuitas*), and formed by the coalition of a number of families. For no family can contain within itself all the offices and arts necessary for human life, and much less can it suffice for attaining knowledge of all things needing [to be known].

Furthermore, if the individual families were divided one from another, peace could scarcely be preserved among men, nor could wrongs be duly averted or avenged; so that Cicero has said (*De Amicitia*):[5] 'Nothing in human affairs is more pleasing to God our Sovereign, than that men should have among themselves an ordered and perfect society, which (continues Cicero) is called a city state (*ciuitas*).' Moreover, this community may be still further augmented, becoming a kingdom or principality by means of the association of many city states; a form of community which is also very appropriate for mankind—appropriate, at least, for its greater

---

5. [This passage is not found in *De Amicitia*. A very similar passage is found in Cicero's *De Republica*, Bk. VI, chap. xiii, which reads: *nihil est enim illi principi deo, qui omnem hunc mundum regit, quod quidem in terris fiat, acceptius quam concilia coetusque hominum iure sociati, quae civitates appellantur* (For nothing of all that is done on earth is more pleasing to that supreme God who rules all this world than the assemblies and gatherings of men associated in justice, which are called States).—TR.]

welfare—owing to the above-stated reasons, applied in due proportion, although the element of necessity is not entirely equal in the two cases.

4. *In a perfect community, there must necessarily exist a power governing that community.* The second principle is as follows: in a perfect community, there must necessarily exist a power to which the government of that community pertains. This principle, indeed, would seem by its very terms to be a self-evident truth. For as the Wise Man says (*Proverbs*, Chap. xi [, v. 14]): 'Where there is no governor, the people shall fall'; but nature is never wanting in essentials; and therefore, just as a perfect community is agreeable to reason and natural law, so also is the power to govern such a community, without which power there would be the greatest confusion therein.

This argument is confirmed by analogy with every other form of human society. For the union of man and woman, since it is natural, consequently involves a head, the man, according to this passage from *Genesis* (Chap. iii [, v. 16]): '[. . .] thou shalt be under thy husband's power.' Thus it is that Paul says (*Titus*, Chap. ii [, v. 5]): 'Let women be subject to their husbands.'[6] To this, Jerome [on *Titus*, Chap. ii, v. 5] adds the words: 'in accordance with the common law of nature.' Similarly, in that second relationship of parents and children, the father has over his child a power derived from nature. And in the third, the relationship of servants and master, it is also clear that a governing power resides in the master, as Paul teaches [*ibid.*, v. 9], also in *Ephesians*, Chap. vi [, v. 5] and *To the Colossians*, Chap. iii [, v. 22]), saying that servants ought to be obedient to their lords, as to God. For though the relationship of servitude is one derived not entirely from nature, but rather through human volition, nevertheless, given the existence of this relationship, subordination and subjection are obligatory by natural law, on the ground of justice. Filial subjection, too, is supported by this same natural bond and basis, that is to say, natural origin, from which it derives a higher degree of perfection

6. [Suárez probably had reference to *Ephesians*, Chap. V, v. 22, of which this passage is a direct quotation. The passage in the *Epistle to Titus* reads: *Ut . . . doceant adolescentulas . . . subditas viris suis* (That they may teach the young women . . . to be obedient to their husbands).—Tr.]

by the title of [filial] piety. This point, moreover, is emphatically brought out in the Fourth Commandment of the Decalogue.

Finally, it follows from all this, that in a domestic community, or family, there exists by the very nature of the case, a suitable power for the government of that community, a power residing principally in the head of the family. Furthermore, the same situation is necessarily found to exist in the case of any community whatsoever that consists of one sole household, even though that community be founded, not upon the bond of matrimony, but upon some other kind of human society; and therefore, it is likewise necessary, in the case of a perfect society, that there shall exist some governing power suitable thereto.

5. *The reason* a priori. There is, in fine, an *a priori* reason in support of this view, a reason touched upon by St. Thomas in the *Opuscula* [XX: *De Regimine Principum,* Bk. I, chap. i] above cited, namely: that no body can be preserved unless there exists some principle whose function it is to provide for and seek after the common good thereof, such a principle as clearly exists in the natural body, and likewise (so experience teaches) in the political. The reason for this fact, in turn is also clear. For each individual member has a care for its individual advantages, and these are often opposed to the common good, while furthermore, it occasionally happens that many things are needful to the common good, which are not thus pertinent in the case of individuals and which, even though they may at times be pertinent, are provided for, not as common, but as private needs; and therefore, in a perfect community, there necessarily exists some public power whose official duty it is to seek after and provide for the common good.

The righteousness of and necessity for civil magistracy are clearly to be deduced from the foregoing, since the term 'civil magistracy' signifies nothing more nor less than a man or number of men in whom resides the above-mentioned power of governing a perfect community. For it is manifest that such power must dwell in men, inasmuch as they are not naturally governed in a polity by the angels, nor directly by God Himself, Who acts, by the ordinary law, through appropriate secondary causes; so that, consequently, it is necessary and natural that they should be governed by men.

6. *The second conclusion.* I hold, secondly, that a human magistracy, if it is supreme in its own order, has the power to make laws proper to its

sphere; that is to say, civil or human laws which, by the force of natural law, it may validly and justly establish, provided that the other conditions essential to law be observed.

This conclusion is certainly true; and it has, moreover, been laid down by the philosophers—by Aristotle (*Politics*, Bk. I throughout and *Ethics*, Bk. X, last chapter), by Plato (*Laws* [Bk. III, 684 c] and *The Republic* [Bk. I, chap. xii, 339]) and by Cicero (*On Invention*, Bk. I [, chap. i] and *Laws* [Bk. I, chap. vi]). The theologians, too, and other Doctors whom I have cited above (Bk. I, chap. viii)[7] agree with the conclusion in question. A great deal of support may also be drawn from Covarruvias (*Practicae Quaestiones*, Chap. i; and on *Sext*, rule *peccatum*, Pt. II, § 9, no. 6).

The proof of the [second] conclusion. Moreover, the reason [on which the said conclusion is based,] is as follows: a civil magistracy is a necessity in the state for its government and regulation, a fact which has already been pointed out; but one of the most necessary acts is the establishment of law, as is evident from what we have said above (Book One); therefore, this legislative power does exist in a political magistracy. For he who is invested with a given office, is invested with all the power necessary for the fitting exercise of that office. This is a self-evident principle of law.

[7.] *A corollary.* Whence it follows that such power to make human laws is identified with the human magistracy endowed with supreme jurisdiction in the state.

This fact is evident from what has already been said (in Bk. I, chap. viii),[8] where we showed that the power in question pertains to a perfect jurisdiction. That entire discussion should be applied here. Moreover, it holds true in a universal sense. For solely in the prince, or [supreme] magistrate, does that public power reside which is ordained for public action, concerns the community as a whole, and includes an efficacious binding and compelling force; yet this twofold force is essential to law, according to Aristotle (*Ethics*, Bk. X, last chapter), the *Digest* (I. iii. 7), and, also, the proof adduced above; and therefore, only that magistrate who has supreme power in the commonwealth, has also the power to make human, or civil

---

7. [Not included in these *Selections*.—Tr.]
8. [Not included in these *Selections*.—Tr.]

law. Finally, this supreme power is a certain form of dominion, but a form of dominion that calls, not for strict servitude to a despot, but rather for civil obedience; therefore, it is the dominion of jurisdiction, of the sort that resides in the prince, or king.

8. *Objections to the corollary.* Certain jurists, however, qualify these statements, declaring that it is true of the precepts of the law which is commonly applicable or relative to a [whole] kingdom, but that it is not true of municipal precepts, or statutes relating to particular communities;[9] a qualification which may be encountered in referring to Felinus and to the authorities whom he cites in his commentary (on *Decretals,* Bk. I, title II, chap. vi, nos. 9 and 10). These jurists base their opinion upon the contention that many communities not possessing jurisdiction do possess the power to make statutes. Their argument may be confirmed by the fact that the civil laws often distinguish jurisdiction from sovereignty, that is to say, from the power of sovereign command, as one may gather from the *Digest* (L. i. 26 and II. i. 3); but law, properly speaking, is related to the power of sovereign command, as may easily be seen from what we have already said regarding the essence of law; and therefore, the power which is *per se* necessary to law, is not the power of jurisdiction.

9. Nevertheless, the reply is that this qualification is unnecessary, unless, perchance, there is some ambiguity in the use of terms. For the arguments above set forth furnish universal and unqualified proof. St. Thomas makes this clear in the passage (II.–II, qu. 67, art. 1) where he proves that jurisdiction is necessary in order to pass a sentence for the reason that jurisdiction is necessary to law, because a sentence is a particular law and also has coercive force; and thus, *a fortiori,* any law howsoever particular its character may seem, requires jurisdiction; for no [other] law is ever so particular in character as a sentence, and the latter always has or always should have annexed to it some means of coercion—as is evident from the *Ethics* of Aristotle (as cited above) and from the laws already mentioned—since directive without coercive force is of no value. Indeed, no one has

---

9. [*Statutis particularium populorum.* The translation, 'communities', would seem to be justified here by the necessity for a contrast with *regni* (kingdom), above, as well as by the appearance of *Communitates* (communities) in the next sentence.—Tr.]

ever doubted that jurisdiction is required for the passing of a sentence. And thus our contention is confirmed; for if jurisdiction is necessary for the declaration of law, it is much more necessary for the making of law.

10. *The objections to the corollary are answered.* As to the fundamental position of the authors in question, the [basic] assumption which they make may be denied. For statutes are either not true laws or else not made without jurisdiction; points which will be accorded more attention in later pages.

As for the confirmation, in so far as concerns the laws cited in that [confirmatory argument], I shall point out that the term 'jurisdiction', in the full and proper sense, refers to political—that is, governmental—power of dominion, the sense in which we are here using the word. And jurisdiction, thus interpreted, is included as intrinsically a part of political sovereignty, in order to differentiate the latter from tyranny. Such is the argument set forth in the *Decretum* (Pt. II, causa XXIII, qu. i, can. iv), in the passage where supreme governmental power over the state is called 'legitimate sovereignty' (*legitimum imperium*); and the degree and mode of sovereignty will be in accordance with the degree and mode of jurisdiction. Sometimes, to be sure, 'jurisdiction' is understood strictly according to the etymology of the term, as signifying the simple power of passing judgment. For law is properly declared, or interpreted, by means of a sentence; and, if one is speaking in this sense, it is not incongruous that the power to judge should reside in a given person apart from the legislative, although such a person is never without some coercive power, such as would seem at times to be denoted by the word 'sovereignty', when the latter, also, is strictly interpreted. Thus it is that, on the other hand, the power given to the magistrate for the punishment of crimes and extending even to the death penalty, is ordinarily spoken of in the civil law simply as sovereignty, and is apparently so treated in the laws above mentioned, as well as in another law of the *Digest* (L. xvi. 215). In such cases, moreover, it is customary to give this power the name of 'unmixed sovereignty' (*merum imperium*), as may be seen by consulting the *Digest* (II. iv. 2) and the Gloss (thereon;[10] and on similar passages); although, in point of fact, it is impossible that such sovereignty should exist apart from

10. [The words of the Gloss are: *Imperium, s. merum quod est gladii potestas.*— REVISER.]

the power of jurisdiction, just as, conversely, it is impossible for jurisdiction to exist apart from every element of sovereignty. This point is brought out in that passage of the *Digest* (I. xxi. 5)[11] which declares that when jurisdiction has been given, a certain element of sovereignty is also given, 'For there is no jurisdiction without a measure of coercive power.'

Relatively speaking, then, these two attributes are separated, not in actual fact, but only in a certain usage of the terms; so that the legislative power, being—as it is—a power of sovereign command, is accordingly one of jurisdiction.

11. *The objections to the first conclusion are answered.* So it is that, in so far as concerns the reason for doubt,[12] the deduction [involved in that reason] is denied. For though man was not created or born subject to the power of a human prince, he has been born potentially subject (as it were) to such power; and therefore, it is not in opposition to preceptive natural law that one should be thus subjected in fact, even though this subjection is not derived directly from nature. On the contrary, it is consonant with natural reason that a human commonwealth should be subjected to some one, although (as we shall see) natural law has not in and of itself, and without the intervention of human will, created political subjection.

It is [merely] an accidental quality of human principates that empires have been established tyrannically. With regard to the first confirmation of the doubt, we admit that empires and kingdoms have often been established or usurped through tyranny and force; but we deny that this fact is due to the essential character, or nature, of such principates, tracing it rather to the abuse of man. Consequently, we furthermore deny that kingdoms were established in this fashion from the very beginning, a denial which has already been supported by means of examples. Moreover, the words of Osee, quoted above,[13] referred specifically to the kings of Israel, who were set up without the sanction of God's Will, as Ribera explains at

---

11. [The title of this Chapter in the *Digest* reads: *De officio eius, cui mandata est iurisdictio,* not *De eo, cui mandat. est iurisd.,* as it is given in the text of Suárez.—Tr.]

12. [I.e. the reason (set forth in the third paragraph of Section 1 of this Chapter) for doubting the general proposition that man possesses the power to make laws.—Tr.]

13. [In Section 1 of this Chapter. The passage quoted is from *Osee,* Chap. viii, v. 4: 'They have reigned, but not by me: they have been princes, and I knew not: [. . .]'.—Tr.]

length, when expounding this passage [in his *Commentarii in 12 Prophetas Minores*]. These words may, however, be applied to all tyrants, or to all persons who rule unjustly even though they be true kings, or to those who are ambitious to govern though they are unworthy and unfitted to do so. Such persons, indeed, are frequently spoken of as reigning not by God, and not because they are false kings but because they rule in a way that fails to accord with God's will, or else for the reason that God permits rather than ordains their elevation to such office, a point which is made by Origen (*Homilies*, IV, *On Judges*).

12. *Human principates did not originate with nature, but neither are they contrary to nature.* As to the second confirmation, that drawn from Augustine [*supra*, Section 1 of this Chapter], I reply that the passage cited indicates simply that human principates did not originate with nature, but does not indicate that they are contrary to nature. To be sure, Augustine here gives expression to the opinion that the dominion of one man over another is derived from the occasion created by sin, rather than from the primary design of nature; but he is speaking of that form of dominion whose concomitants are slavery and a condition of servitude. And Gregory the Great[14] expresses himself more clearly with regard to the governing power; but he should be interpreted as referring to coercive power and the exercise thereof; since, in so far as directive power is concerned, it would seem probable that this existed among men even in the state of innocence. For a hierarchy and a principate exist among the angels, too, as is evident from the language of the Scriptures, from the words of Dionysius [the Areopagite] (*Concerning Ecclesiastical Hierarchy*, Chap. ix), and from those of Gregory (*Homilies*, XXXIV, *In Evangelia*). Moreover, our own preceding arguments may be considered as applicable to the state of innocence, since they are based, not upon sin nor upon any defection from order, but upon the natural disposition of man, the disposition to be a social animal and to demand by nature a mode of living in which he dwells in a community, the latter necessarily requiring to be ruled by means of public power. Coercion, on the other hand, presupposes the existence of

---

14. [Gregory the Great (*Moralium Libri* and *Liber Regulae Pastoralis*) was also cited in connexion with the second confirmation. *Vide* Section 1 of this Chapter.—Tr.]

a certain amount of defection from order, and therefore, with reference to coercion, it may be said that this power was introduced in consequence of sin. Similarly, a wife's subjection to her husband is also natural, and such subjection would exist in the state of innocence; yet it was after the commission of sin that these words were spoken to Eve: 'Thou shalt be under thy husband's power' (*Genesis*, Chap. iii [, v. 16]), the reference being to a proportionate coercive force, as Augustine has indicated (*De Genesi ad Litteram*, Bk. XI, chap. xxxvii).

13. Turning to the third confirmation [*supra*, Section 1, at end], based upon certain Scriptural passages, we reply that, in these passages, that is attributed to God which is His, but that is not denied to men which may be shared by them. Accordingly, Isaias[15] [*Isaias*, Chap. xxxiii, v. 22] exhorts his people to trust in God and in His protection, because he holds that God is the true lord, king and lawgiver, that is to say, lord, king and lawgiver in a superlative and unique sense; but, [in making such an exhortation,] he does not exclude that people's right to have its own human king, a king who in his own proper degree might also have been lord, &c. Again, it is possible to give a similar interpretation to the passage in *James* [Chap. iv, v. 12], concerning the supreme lawgiver and judge, as is indicated by the words, '[There is one lawgiver, and judge,] that is able to destroy and to deliver'. For these attributes would seem to be proper to God. A satisfactory exposition of this passage may, indeed, be supplied by interpreting the word 'one' as denoting identity rather than singularity, so that the sense would be: he who is lawgiver is also judge; nor should the function of judgment be usurped by one who is not the lawgiver and has not the lawgiver's power. Thus it is that Saint James adds [*ibid.* v. 13]: 'But who art thou that judgest thy brother?'[16] He does not deny, then, that men can be legislators and can pass judgment, but he does reprove those who judge rashly and thus usurp the office of judges and legislators.

To the fourth confirmation [*supra*, this Chapter, Section 1], we shall reply later, in treating of the obligation imposed by human law.

15. [*Isaias* and *Saint James* are quoted in Section 1 of this Chapter, in the course of the third confirmation of the doubt.—TR.]

16. [The Vulgate has 'neighbour'.—TR.]

CHAPTER II

In What Men Does This Power to Make Human Laws Reside Directly, by the Very Nature of Things?

1. *Reasons for doubt.* The reason for doubt on this point is the fact that the power in question dwells either in individual men; or in all men, that is to say, in the whole body of mankind collectively regarded.

The first alternative cannot be upheld. For it is not true that every individual man is the superior of the rest;[1] nor do certain persons, [simply] by the nature of things, possess the said power in a greater degree than other persons [, on some ground apart from general superiority], since there is no reason for thus favouring some persons as compared with others.

The second alternative would also seem[2] to be untenable. For in the first place, if it were correct, all the laws derived from such power would be common to all men. And secondly, [so the argument runs] no source can be found, from which the whole multitude of mankind could have derived this power; since men themselves cannot be that source—inasmuch as they are unable to give that which they do not possess—and since the power cannot be derived from God, because if it were so derived, it could not change but would necessarily remain in the whole community in a process of perpetual succession, like the spiritual power which God conferred upon Peter and which for that reason necessarily endures in him or in his successors, and cannot be altered by men.

2. *The first opinion.* It is customary to refer, in connexion with this question, to the opinion of certain canonists who assert that by the very nature of the case this [legislative] power resides in some supreme prince upon whom it has been divinely conferred, and that it must always, through a process of succession, continue to reside in a specific

---

1. [This would seem, in the light of the context, to be the most acceptable interpretation of Suárez's argument at this point, although the Latin text is ambiguous: *quia neque omnes sunt aliorum superiores.*—Tr.]

2. [Suárez is apparently presenting here the arguments opposed to the very alternative which he nevertheless accepts. (*Vide* the first sentence of Section 3 of this Chapter.) Thus the word *videtur* (would . . . seem) should not be overlooked by the reader.—Tr.]

individual. The Gloss (on *Decretum,* Pt. II, causa VII, qu. i, can. ix) is cited [by way of confirmation]; but the passage cited contains simply the statement that the son of a king is lawfully king, which is a very different matter, nor does it assert that this mode of succession was perpetual among men. Another Gloss (on *Decretum,* Pt. I, dist. x, can. viii) is also cited, because it declares that the Emperor receives his power from God alone. But that Gloss, in its use of the exclusive word 'alone', is intended to indicate simply that the Emperor does not receive his power from the Pope; it is not intended to deny that he receives it from men. For, in this very passage, it is said that the Emperor is set up by the army in accordance with the ancient custom mentioned in the *Decretum* (Pt. I, dist. XCIII, can. xxiv). The said opinion, then, is supported neither by authority nor by a [rational] basis, as will become more evident from what follows.

3. *The opinion of the author.* Therefore, we must say that this power, viewed solely according to the nature of things, resides not in any individual man but rather in the whole body of mankind. This conclusion is commonly accepted and certainly true. It is to be deduced from the words of St. Thomas ([I.–II,] qu. 90, art. 3, ad 2 and qu. 97, art. 3, ad 3) in so far as he holds that the prince has the power to make laws, and that this power was transferred to him by the community. The civil laws (*Digest,* I. iv. 1 and I. ii. 2, § 11) set forth and accept the same conclusion. And it is upheld at length by Castro (*De Potestate Legis Poenalis,* Bk. I, chap. i, § *Postquam*), as well as by Soto (*De Iustitia et Iure,* Bk. I, qu. i, art. 3). One may also consult Soto (*ibid.,* Bk. IV, qu. ii, arts. 1 and 2), Ledesma ([*Theologiae Moralis,*] II, Pt. IV, qu. xviii, art. 3, doubt 10), Covarruvias (*Practicae Quaestiones,* Chap. i, [no. 2,] first concl.), and Navarrus (on *Decretals,* Bk. II, tit. 1, chap. xiii, notab. 3, no. 119).

The basic reason in support of the first part of the conclusion is evident, and was touched upon at the beginning of our discussion, namely, the fact that in the nature of things all men are born free; so that, consequently, no person has political jurisdiction over another person, even as no person has dominion over another; nor is there any reason why such power should, [simply] in the nature of things, be attributed to certain persons over certain other persons, rather than *vice versa. The power held by Adam over*[3] *his descendants.* One might make this assertion only: that at the beginning of creation Adam possessed, in the very nature of things, a primacy and consequently a sovereignty over all men, so that [the power in question] might have been derived from him, whether through the natural origin of primogeniture, or in accordance with the will of Adam himself. For it is so that Chrysostom (on *First Corinthians,* Homily XXXIV [, no. 5]) has declared all men to be formed and procreated from Adam alone, a subordination to one sole prince being thus indicated. However, by virtue of his creation only and his natural origin, one may infer simply that Adam possessed domestic—not political—power. For he had power over his wife, and later he possessed the *patria potestas* over his children until they were emancipated. In the course of time, he may also have had servants and a complete household with full power over the same, the power called 'domestic'. But after families began to multiply, and the individual heads of individual families began to separate, those heads possessed the same power over their respective households. Political power, however, did not make its appearance until many families began to congregate into one perfect community. Accordingly, since this community had its beginning, not in the creation of Adam nor solely by his will, but rather by the will of all who were assembled therein, we are unable to make any well-founded statement to the effect that Adam, in the [very] nature of things, held a political primacy in the said community. For such an inference cannot be drawn from natural principles, since it is not the progenitor's due, by the sole force of natural law, that he shall also be king over his posterity.

But, granted that this inference does not follow upon natural principles, neither have we sufficient foundation for the assertion that God has bestowed such power upon that [progenitor], through a special donation or act of providence, since we have had no revelation to this effect, nor does Holy Scripture so testify to us. To this argument may be added the point made by Augustine and noted in our preceding Chapter [Chap. i,

---

3. [The marginal subheading, *Quam potestatem habuit Adamus posteros,* should read: *Quam potestatem habuit Adamus in posteros,* the reading found in the editions of Mayence, 1619 and Paris, 1856.—Tr.]

sect. 1], namely, that God did not say: 'Let us make man that he may have
dominion over men', but rather did He say: [Let us make man that he may
have dominion] over other living creatures.[4]

Therefore, the power of political dominion or rule over men has not
been granted, directly by God, to any particular human individual.

4. *Two standpoints from which the whole multitude of mankind may be
regarded.* From the foregoing, it is easy to deduce the second part of the
assertion [at beginning of Section 3], namely, that the power in question
resides, by the sole force of natural law, in the whole body of mankind
[collectively regarded].

The proof is as follows: this power does exist in men, and it does not
exist in each individual, nor in any specific individual, as has also been
shown; therefore, it exists in mankind viewed collectively, for our foregoing division [into the two alternatives] sufficiently covers the case.

However, in order that our argument may be better understood, it must
be noted that the multitude of mankind is regarded in two different ways.

First, it may be regarded simply as a kind of aggregation, without any
order, or any physical or moral union. So viewed, [men] do not constitute
a unified whole, whether physical or moral, so that they are not strictly
speaking one political body, and therefore do not need one prince, or
head. Consequently, if one regards them from this standpoint, one does
not as yet conceive of the power in question as existing properly and formally; on the contrary, it is understood to dwell in them at most as a
fundamental potentiality,[5] so to speak.

The multitude of mankind should, then, be viewed from another standpoint, that is, with regard to the special volition, or common consent, by
which they are gathered together into one political body through one
bond of fellowship and for the purpose of aiding one another in the attainment of a single political end. Thus viewed, they form a single mystical
body which, morally speaking, may be termed essentially a unity; and that
body accordingly needs a single head. Therefore, in a community of this
kind, viewed as such, there exists in the very nature of things the power of

---

4. [Suárez merely paraphrases Augustine's statement in these two passages.—Tr.]
5. [The Latin has simply *radicaliter.*—Tr.]

which we are speaking, so that men may not, when forming such a group, set up obstacles to that power; and consequently, if we conceive of men as desiring both alternatives—that is to say, as desirous of so congregating, but on the condition (as it were) that they shall not be subject to the said power—the situation would be self-contradictory, and such men would accordingly fail to achieve any [valid end]. For it is impossible to conceive of a unified political body without political government or disposition thereto; since, in the first place, this unity arises, in a large measure, from subjection to one and the same rule and to some common superior power; while furthermore, if there were no such government, this body could not be directed towards one [common] end and the general welfare. It is, then, repugnant to natural reason to assume the existence of a group of human beings united in the form of a single political body, without postulating the existence of some common power which the individual members of the community are bound to obey; and therefore, if this power does not reside in any specific individual, it must necessarily exist in the community as a whole.

5. To what has been said above, we should add the statement that the power in question does not reside in the multitude of mankind by the very nature of things in such wise that it is necessarily one sole power with respect to the entire species, or entire aggregate, of men existing throughout the whole world; inasmuch as it is not necessary to the preservation or welfare of nature, that all men should thus congregate in a single political community. On the contrary, that would hardly be possible, and much less would it be expedient. For Aristotle (*Politics,* Bk. VII, chap. iv [, § 7]) has rightly said that it is difficult to govern aright a city whose inhabitants are too numerous; accordingly, this difficulty would be still greater in the case of a kingdom excessively large, and therefore, it would be greater by far (we are referring to civil government) if the whole world were concerned.

Consequently, it seems to me probable that the power of which we speak never existed in this fashion in the whole assemblage of mankind, or that it so existed for an exceedingly brief period; and that, on the contrary, soon after the creation of the world, mankind began to be divided into various states in each one of which this power existed in a distinct form. Thus it is that Augustine (*On the City of God,* Bk. XV, chap. viii) concludes from the Fourth Chapter of *Genesis,* that Cain, before the Flood, was the first to establish an individual kingdom and commonwealth. Moreover, in another passage of the same work (Bk. XVI, chap. iv), Augustine adds that, according to the Tenth Chapter of *Genesis,* after the Flood, Nemrod was [the first to do so]. For Cain first brought about a division of the perfect community, separating himself from his father's family; and Nemrod did likewise, at a later period, with respect to Noe.

6. Finally, it may be concluded from the foregoing that this power to make human laws of an individual and special nature, laws which we call civil, as if to indicate that they are ordained for one perfect community— it may be concluded, I say—that this power never existed in one and the same form throughout the whole world of men, being rather divided among various communities, according to the establishment and division of these communities themselves. Thus we also conclude that—before the coming of Christ, at least—this civil power did not reside in any one specific man with respect to the whole world. For at no time did all men agree to confer that power upon a particular ruler of the entire world, neither have we any knowledge of its bestowal upon some particular individual by God; inasmuch as such an idea might most easily be entertained with regard to Adam, and we have already shown it to be inapplicable to him [*supra,* Section 3 of this Chapter]. Finally, as is evident in the light of history, no one has ever acquired such power through war or any other similar means.

As to what should be said, however, with respect to the situation after the advent of Christ, that is a matter which I shall take up in the following Book.[6]

The manner in which the precepts of the ius gentium *were introduced.* But these statements are not incompatible with what we have already said regarding the *ius gentium.* On the contrary, they serve to confirm those earlier assertions. For even though the whole of mankind may not have been gathered into a single political body, but may rather have been divided into various communities, nevertheless, in order that these communities might be able to aid one another and to remain in a state of

---

6. [Not included in these *Selections.*—Tr.]

mutual justice and peace (which is essential to the universal welfare), it was fitting that they should observe certain common laws, as if in accordance with a common pact and mutual agreement. These are the laws called *iura gentium;* and they were introduced by tradition and custom, as we have remarked, rather than by any written constitution. Moreover, they comprise that twofold body of law—special and common[7]—which Gaius distinguished in the *Digest* (I. i. 9).

CHAPTER III

Has the Power of Making Human Laws Been Given to Men Immediately by God as the Author of Nature?

1. *A reason for doubt.* A reason for doubt on this question may lie in the fact that it apparently follows upon what has been said above that this power over an entire community of men assembled together is derived from them as individuals, and through their own consent. For such power springs from the same source as does the very community in which it resides; and that community is welded together by means of the consent and volition of its individual members; therefore, the power in question also flows from those same wills.

The major premiss is manifestly true, because, once the community is assumed to exist, it follows that this power likewise exists; for he who gives the form, gives, too, those things which are consequent upon the form; and therefore, whoever is the proximate author of the said community, would seem also to be the author and bestower of its power. But, on the other hand, it may be contended that before men congregate into one political body this power does not reside in the individuals, whether wholly or in part, and that, furthermore, it does not exist even in the rough mass (so to speak), or aggregate, of mankind, a point which was made in the preceding Chapter; and therefore, the power can never flow immediately from men.

---

7. [That is to say, the law of each state and the law common to all men.—Tr.]

2. *The common and true opinion.* On this question, the common opinion appears to be that the said power is given immediately by God, as the Author of nature, in such a way that men in a sense dispose the matter involved and render the recipient capable of wielding the power, yet the form is imparted, as it were, by God, Who is the Giver of the power. Such is the view suggested by Cajetan (*Opuscula,* Vol. I, tract. ii: *De Potestate Papae,* Pt. II, chap. x, reply to 2d confirmation [chap. ix, *ad id vero*]), by Covarruvias (*Practicae Quaestiones,* Chap. i [, no. 6]), by Victoria, more at length, in the *Relectio* that treats of this power [*De Potestate Civili*], and by Soto (*De Iustitia et Iure,* Bk. IV, qu. ii, art. 1).

Moreover, one might adduce as an argument the fact that, as I remarked above,[1] if we assume that men have willed to gather together into one political community, it is not in their power to set up obstacles to this jurisdiction; and this is an indication that the jurisdiction does not flow proximately from their wills as from a true efficient cause. Thus, in regard to matrimony, we rightly infer that the husband is the head of the wife by grant of the Author of nature Himself, and not by the will of the wife; for though they may contract the marriage by their own will, nevertheless, if they do contract it, they cannot prevent the establishment of this superiority.

This view is confirmed by Saint Paul, who says (*To the Romans,* Chap. iii [Chap. xiii, vv. 1, 2]): '[. . .] there is no power but from God [. . .] and therefore he that resisteth the power, resisteth the ordinance of God'; therefore, the power in question is also of God; and consequently, it is derived immediately from Him, since it has no other prior, or more immediate, source.

3. *The acts of legislative power.* Secondly, it is held that this power embraces several acts which appear to transcend human authority as it exists in individual men; and this is an indication that such power is not from them, but from God. The first of these acts is the punishment of malefactors, extending even to the death penalty. For, since God alone is the Lord of life, it would seem that He alone could have granted the power

---

1. [*Supra,* p. 419, § 3, chapter i, of this Book.—TR.]

[to impose this penalty]. Thus it is that Augustine has said (*De Natura Boni, Contra Manichaeos,* Chap. xxxii): 'There is no power to hurt unless it comes from God.' The second act is the establishment, in a certain matter, of the mean of virtue necessary to its rectitude.[2] Thirdly, to this [righteous] state has been added the effect of binding the conscience, as we shall see below, and this effect would seem to pertain most especially to divine power. The fourth act is the infliction of punishment for injuries done to individuals; for it has moreover been written (*Romans,* Chap. xii [, v. 19]): '*Revenge* is mine; I will repay, saith the Lord.'[3] This, then, is an indication that the power in question is divine; for otherwise, men would have been able to seize for themselves some other means for the avenging of injuries, and that would be opposed to natural justice.

4. One part of this opinion[4] is clear and beyond dispute; but another requires explanation.

The first part is the contention that the power under discussion comes from God as its primary and principal Author. For this appears to correspond with the clearly expressed opinion of Paul and to be sufficiently well proved by the arguments already set forth. Moreover, since this power is a part of the nature of things, and since—whether it be physical or moral—it is in an absolute sense a good thing, extremely valuable and necessary for the good estate of human nature, it therefore must flow from the Author of that nature. Finally, since the persons who wield this power within a human community are the ministers of God, they accordingly administer a power received from God; and therefore, God is not only the chief Author of this power but its exclusive Author.

The other part of this opinion, however, calls for an explanation, as to how God may be said to confer the power in question immediately.

5. *In what way the afore-mentioned power is given by God.* With respect to this point, I shall say briefly that, in the first place, this power is given

2. [For example, the legislator may order certain acts to be performed as acts of the virtues of temperance, justice, and so on.—REVISER.]

3. [The words *dicit Dominus* (saith the Lord) are not a part of the quotation in the Latin text.—TR.]

4. [I.e. the opinion in Sect. 2, *supra,* p. 436.—TR.]

by God as a characteristic property resulting from nature, just as the bestowal of the form involves the bestowal of that which is consequent upon the form.

The first proof of this assertion is the fact that God does not give this power by a special act or grant distinct from creation; for if He did so, that grant would necessarily be made manifest through revelation, and this is clearly not the case, since if it were, such power would not be natural. Therefore, the power is given as a characteristic property resulting from nature, that is to say, resulting through a dictate of natural reason, since the latter shows that God has sufficiently provided for mankind, and has therefore given it the power necessary to its preservation and proper government.

6. *When the afore-mentioned power manifests itself.* In the second place, I declare that this power does not manifest itself in human nature until men gather together into one perfect community and are politically united. My assertion is proved as follows: the said power resides not in individual men separately considered, nor in the mass or multitude of them collected, as it were, confusedly, in a disorderly manner, and without union of the members into one body; therefore, such a political body must be constituted, before power of this sort is to be found in men, since—in the order of nature,[5] at least—the agent of the power must exist prior to the existence of the power itself. Once this body has been constituted, however, the power in question exists in it, without delay and by the force of natural reason; and consequently, it is correctly supposed that it exists as a characteristic property resulting from such a mystical body, already constituted with just the mode of being [that it has] and not otherwise. Wherefore, even as man—by virtue of the very fact that he is created[6] and has the use of reason—possesses power over himself and over his faculties and members for their use, and is for that reason naturally free (that is to say, he is not the slave but the master of his own actions), just so the political

---

5. [The order of nature, that is, the order of reality, as distinguished from the order of thought.—Reviser.]

6. [Reading *creatur,* with the Paris edition of 1856; not *creditur,* the reading of our own Latin text.—Tr.]

body of mankind, by virtue of the very fact that it is created in its own fashion, possesses power over itself and the faculty of self-government, in consequence whereof it also possesses power and a peculiar dominion over its own members. Moreover, by a similar process of reasoning, just as freedom [of will] has been given to every man by the Author of nature, yet not without the intervention of a proximate cause—that is to say, the parent by whom [each man] is procreated—even so the power of which we are treating, is given to the community of mankind by the Author of nature, but not without the intervention of will and consent on the part of the human beings who have assembled into this perfect community.

Nevertheless, just as, in the former case, the will of the parent with respect to generation only is necessary, but no act of will endowing the child with freedom, or with the other natural faculties which are not essentially dependent upon a special act of will on the part of the parent, being on the contrary a natural consequence; even so, with respect to the matter under discussion, human will is necessary in order that men may unite in a single perfect community, but no special act of volition on their part is required to the end that this community shall possess the said power, which arises rather from the very nature of things, and from the providence of the Author of nature, so that in this sense it is rightly said to have been conferred immediately by Him.

7. *The afore-mentioned power is not immutable.* I shall add that, thirdly, although this power is (so to speak) a natural attribute of a perfect human community, viewed as such, nevertheless, it does not reside immutably therein, but may be taken from that community—by its own consent or through some other just means—and transferred to another [seat of authority].

This fact is sufficiently evidenced by usage, and it will, moreover, be explained more fully by the inferences to be drawn below. First, its truth may be demonstrated by means of the example already adduced, that is to say, by applying this example in due proportion. For freedom from servitude is a natural property of man, and is therefore wont to be described as an effect of natural law; yet man can by his own volition deprive himself of this property, or can even for a just cause be deprived thereof and reduced to slavery; and therefore, in like manner, a perfect human community, though by nature it may be free and may possess within itself the power to which we refer, nevertheless can be deprived of that power in one or another of the ways already mentioned. Thus it may be considered that, even though the physical properties emanating from nature are wont to be immutable from the standpoint of nature, nevertheless, these quasi-moral properties—which are like titles of ownership, or rights—can be changed by means of a contrary will, in spite of their derivation from nature; just as [, to be sure,] even those physical properties which have the contrary quality, or are derived from some contrary disposition, are sometimes liable to change, as is evident.

8. A second proof of the same contention is based upon a certain similarity and, from another point of view, upon a dissimilarity, between the power in question, and that which is derived from a special divine disposition—such a power, for example, as that of the Pope.

For though this power has been bestowed by Christ upon a specific individual duly chosen, it may be renounced by the Pope himself, who may deprive himself thereof, if he so wishes; at least, he may do so if the Church accepts the resignation, as I here assume. In this respect, then, there exists a certain similarity, since the human community, too, though it has received this power from God, may, if it wishes, deprive itself thereof.

A dissimilarity exists, however, as to mode. For in the first place, the Pope, once he has been elected, cannot for any cause whatsoever be deprived of his power or dignity, by the whole body of mankind, if he himself is unwilling. By Christ alone, Who gave that power, can he be so deprived. The commonwealth, on the other hand, can on some occasions, and for just cause, be divested of its liberty through some coercive measure, such as a just war. Again, a dissimilarity exists because the papal power cannot be so changed as to be transferred by one person to a community, since it is not within the power of man to alter the monarchical government of the Church; whereas the human community, on the other hand, may transfer its own jurisdiction to a single individual or to some other community, as will be made clear. Thus the power under discussion is not only mutable, but even more mutable [than that derived from a divine disposition], and more dependent upon human will.

In the third place, a reason for this difference may be found in the fact that those things which are the result of a special disposition are dependent upon the will of him who orders the disposition, a will which cannot be changed by his inferiors; whereas the power in question results, not from such a disposition, but from nature, and is therefore bestowed in such form as befits the rational nature and accords with right reason and prudence. And natural reason declares that it is not necessary to rational nature—nor even conformable to it—that the said power should reside in an immutable form within the community as a whole, since the latter, so viewed, and without the addition of any specific qualification or the making of any change, would scarcely be able to put this power to use; and therefore, the power is so given by nature and by the Author of nature, as to be capable of undergoing such change as may be expedient for the common good.

CHAPTER IV

Corollaries from the Doctrine Set Forth Above

1. From our discussion in the preceding Chapter, we may draw certain inferences which will throw a great deal of light on all that we have to say.

The first inference is this: although the power in question is in an absolute sense an effect of the natural law, its specific application as a certain form of power and government is dependent upon human choice. This inference may be explained as follows: political government, according to the doctrine set forth by Plato in the Dialogue on *The Statesman,* or *On Kingship*[1] [Chap. xxxi, 291 D], and in the *Republic* [Bk. I, chap. xii; Bk. IV, *passim,* especially at end, 445 D E], as well as by Aristotle in the *Politics* (Bk. III, chap. v), and in the *Ethics* (Bk. VIII, chap. x), takes three simple forms. These forms are: monarchy, or government by one head; aristocracy, or government by the few and the best; and democracy, or government by the many and the common people. From these, it is possible to

---

1. [This is the usual English translation of the Greek title for this Dialogue, referred to in our Latin text as *Dialogo Civili, seu de Regno.*—Tr.]

make up various mixed forms of government, that is to say, forms compounded of these simple ones by drawing either from all three or from two of them. Bellarmine (*De Potestate Summi Pontificis,* Bk. I, from the beginning and through several Chapters) may be consulted, for he has treated of the matter at length and very satisfactorily. Thus men are not obliged, [simply] from the standpoint of natural law, to choose any given one of these forms of government.

Monarchy is the best form of government. We grant, indeed, that monarchy is the best among the three; as Aristotle demonstrates very fully and as one may infer from the government and providential plan of the universe in its entirety, the government and plan which ought to be the most excellent, so that Aristotle concludes (*Metaphysics,* Bk. XII, at end [1076 A]): 'Therefore, let there be one prince.' This conclusion is also supported by the example of Christ the Lord in the institution and government of His Church. And, finally, the prevailing usage among all nations is an argument in favour of the same view. Although—as I was saying—we grant this to be true, nevertheless, other forms of government are not [necessarily] evil, but may, on the contrary, be good and useful; so that, consequently, men are not compelled by the sheer force of the natural law to place this power either in one individual, or in several, or in the entire number of mankind; and therefore, this determination [as to the seat of the power] must of necessity be made by human choice.

Moreover, experience similarly reveals a great deal of variety in connexion with this [most excellent type of government]. For monarchies may be found in this place or in that, and rarely in their simple form; since—given the frailty, ignorance and wickedness of mankind—it is as a rule expedient to add some element of common government which is executed by a number of persons, this common element being greater or smaller according to the varying customs and judgment of men. Accordingly, this whole matter turns upon human counsel and human choice.

We infer, then, that by the nature of things, men as individuals possess to a partial extent (so to speak) the faculty for establishing, or creating, a perfect community; and, by virtue of the very fact that they establish it, the power in question does come to exist in this community as a whole. Nevertheless, natural law does not require either that the power should be exercised directly by the agency of the whole community, or that it should always continue to reside therein. On the contrary, it would be most difficult, from a practical point of view, to satisfy such requirements, for infinite confusion and trouble would result if laws were established by the vote of every person; and therefore, men straightway determine the said power by vesting it in one of the above-mentioned forms of government, since no other form can be conceived, as is easily evident to one who gives the matter consideration.

2. *When the civil power flows from the community.* The second inference [to be drawn from the preceding Chapter] is as follows: civil power, whenever it resides—in the right and ordinary course of law—in the person of one individual, or prince, has flowed from the people as a community, either directly or indirectly; nor could it otherwise be justly held.

This is the common opinion of the jurists, as indicated by their comments on certain laws of the *Digest* (I. iv. 1 and I. ii. 2). Moreover, the same conclusion is upheld in these laws themselves; by Panormitanus and other canonists (on *Decretals,* Bk. IV, tit. xvii, chap. xiii); by St. Thomas (I.–II, qu. 90, art. 3 and qu. 97 [, art. 3]); by Cajetan (in the above-cited work, *De Potestate Papae,* Pt. II, chaps. ii and x [chap. ix]); by Victoria (in his *Relectio* on this very subject [*De Potestate Civili*]); and by other authorities to whom reference has been made.

[This] power, in the very nature of things, is lodged immediately in the community. A reason for this view, supplied by what we have said above, is the fact that such power, in the nature of things, resides immediately in the community; and therefore, in order that it may justly come to reside in a given individual, as in a sovereign prince, it must necessarily be bestowed upon him by the consent of the community.

Again, the same view may be explained by means of a comprehensive enumeration of the various aspects of the matter.[2]

The first title of royal power is derived immediately from God. For [in the first place,] the power in question may be considered as having been

2. [I.e., the various titles to monarchical power. This enumeration extends throughout the remainder of Section 2, and through the whole of Sections 3 and 4.—Tr.]

bestowed upon kings immediately by God Himself. Yet such a bestowal, although it has sometimes occurred—as it did in the case of Saul and in that of David—has nevertheless been extraordinary and supernatural in so far as concerned the mode [of imparting power]. In the common and ordinary course of providence, however, such cases do not come to pass, since—in the natural order—men are governed in civil affairs not by revelations, but by natural reason. Neither may a valid objection be based upon the assertions in certain Scriptural passages, as in the Fourth Chapter of *Daniel,* that God gives kingdoms and changes them at His will; or as in the Forty-fifth Chapter of *Isaias,* which declares that God made Cyrus a king; wherefore Christ said [to Pilate] (*John,* Chap. xix [, v. 11]): 'Thou shouldst not have any power against me, unless it were given thee from above.' For the meaning of these passages is simply that all of the events mentioned come to pass only through the special providence of God, Who either ordains or permits them, as Augustine has said (*On the Gospel of John,* Tract. VI [, chap. i, § 25] and *Against Faustus,* Bk. XXII, chap. lxxiv); but this fact does not prevent such [bestowals and transferences of power] from being executed by human agency; just as all the other effects wrought through secondary causes are attributed primarily to the providence of God.

3. *A second title of royal power: hereditary succession.* A second possibility is that this power may reside in a king through hereditary succession. Some jurists, indeed, are of the opinion that such was the case from the very beginning; but others rightly point out that succession necessarily presupposes the existence of dominion or power in the person succeeded, so that we must of necessity trace it to some one who was not the successor of another, since the succession cannot reach back *ad infinitum.* Therefore, with respect to that first[3] possessor, we ask whence he has derived the kingdom and power, since he does not possess it inherently and by natural law. Title by succession, then, cannot be the primary source of this power as it resides in the sovereign. Therefore, the first possessor must have derived the supreme power directly from the commonwealth, while his successors must derive it from that same source indirectly, [yet] fundamentally.

---

3. [Reading *primo* (the unaccented adjective) in accordance with the 1619 and 1856 editions, instead of *primò* (the accented adverb).—TR.]

Moreover, since any possession passes into the hands of a successor with its accompanying obligations, the conditions attaching to the kingly power when it was transmitted by the commonwealth to the first king, pass to his successors, so that they possess that power together with the original obligations.

4. *A third title of royal power: a just war.* A third title of royal power is wont to arise on the basis of war, which must be just war in order to confer a valid title and dominion. Consequently, many persons believe that kingdoms were originally introduced through tyranny rather than true power. This belief is attested by Alvaro Paez (*De Planctu Ecclesiae,* Bk. I, chap. xli), by Driedo (*De Libertate Christiana,* Bk. I, chap. xv), and by Petrus Bertrandi (in his treatise *De Origine et Usu Iurisdictionis,* Qu. 1). Accordingly, when the kingly power is held solely through unjust force, there is no true legislative power vested in the king; yet it is possible that, in the course of time, the people may give their consent to and acquiesce in such sovereignty, in which case the power in question is [once more] traced back to an act of transmission and donation on the part of the people. It may sometimes happen, however, that a state not previously subject to a king is subjected through a just war. But such an event is always an incidental circumstance (as it were) of the punishment of some wrongdoing; so that the state in question is bound to obedience and to acquiescence in such subjection; and therefore, this mode [of acquiring kingly power] also includes, in a sense, the consent—whether expressed or [implicitly] due—of the state.

However, we are now treating of this power chiefly in so far as it is inherently capable of being introduced and bestowed upon one man. And finally, if we give the matter sufficient consideration, we shall find that when such subjection to one king is imposed by means of a just war, it is presupposed that he possesses the royal power by virtue of which he is able to declare that war; and this power is simply a just extension (so to speak) of the power of his kingdom; so that such kingly power is always to be traced back to some individual who attained it, not through war, but through just election or the consent of the people.

We rightly conclude, then, after this comprehensive enumeration [of the various titles to royal power], that the said power has been derived [in every case] by the prince from the state.

5. *The royal power viewed formally as such pertains to human law.* It may, indeed, be objected that from our conclusion it follows that this royal power pertains exclusively to human law, a deduction which would seem to be contrary to the language of the Scriptures: 'By me, kings reign [. . .]' (*Proverbs,* Chap. viii [, v. 15]); and again, 'For he is God's minister,' &c. (*Romans,* Chap. xiii [, v. 4]).

Another deduction from the same conclusion is that the kingdom must be superior to the king, since it has given the king his power; whence a further inference is drawn, namely, that the kingdom may, if it shall so choose, depose or change its king, a deduction which is altogether false.

Consequently, Victoria (above cited [*De Potestate Civili*]) held that the royal power should be described absolutely as derived from divine law and as having been given by God, with the intervention of human choice. On the other hand, Bertrandi, Driedo (above cited) and Castro (*De Potestate Legis Poenalis* [Bk. I, chap. i]) uphold the opposite doctrine, which is doubtless the true doctrine, if one is speaking in a formal sense of the royal power as such and in so far as it exists in one man. For this governing power, regarded from a political viewpoint and in its essence, is undoubtedly derived from God, as I have said; yet the fact that it resides in a particular individual results—as has been demonstrated—from a grant on the part of the state itself; and therefore, in this sense, the said power pertains to human law. Moreover, the monarchical nature of the government of such a state or province is brought about by human disposition, as has already been shown; therefore, the principate itself is derived from men. Another proof of this derivation is the fact that the power of the king is greater or less, according to the pact or agreement between him and the kingdom; therefore, absolutely speaking, that power is drawn from men.

6. The passages cited from Holy Scripture, however, are to be interpreted as having two meanings. One is as follows: the power in question, viewed in itself, is derived from God; and it is just and in conformity with the divine will. The other meaning is this: assuming that the said power has been transferred to the king, he is now the vicar of God, and natural law makes it obligatory that he be obeyed. The case is similar to that of a private individual who surrenders himself by sale to be the slave of another; so that the resulting power of *dominium* has, in an absolute

sense, a human derivation, yet the slave is [also] bound by divine and natural law—once we assume that the contract has been made—to render obedience to his master.

Thus the reply to the confirmation [of the opposing view] consists clearly in a general denial of the [second] deduction [and its corollary].[4] For, once the power has been transferred to the king, he is through that power rendered superior even to the kingdom which bestowed it; since by this bestowal the kingdom has subjected itself and has deprived itself of its former liberty, just as is, in due proportion, clearly true in the case of the slave, which we have mentioned by way of illustration. Moreover, in accordance with the same reasoning, the king cannot be deprived of this power, since he has acquired a true ownership of it; unless perchance he lapses into tyranny, on which ground the kingdom may wage a just war against him, a point which we consider elsewhere.[5]

7. *There are no laws established universally for the whole world, which are binding upon all.* A third inference to be drawn from our preceding Chapter[6] is as follows: in view of the nature of things—that is to say, according to the natural and ordinary course of human events—there are no civil laws established universally for the whole world and binding upon all men.

This fact is evident, indeed, from the term itself, since we are speaking of human laws as strictly distinguished from the *ius gentium,* and therefore called civil, for the reason that they are peculiar to one city state or one nation, as the *Digest* (I. i. 9) declares. We are furthermore speaking of laws which can be established by natural power, omitting for the present the consideration of supernatural power. Accordingly, such laws demand, as by an intrinsic condition, that they should not be of a universal nature.

The reason [in support of our third inference] is the fact that *a priori* there is in existence no legislative power with jurisdiction over the whole

---

4. [I.e. the deduction 'that the kingdom must be superior to the king', and the consequent inference 'that the kingdom may, if it shall so choose, depose or change its kings'. *Vide* the second paragraph of Section 5 of this Chapter, p. 446.—Tr.]

5. [*Defensio Fidei Catholicae,* Bk. VI, chap. iv, *infra,* p. 803, and in Disp. XIII of *De Bello,* Sec. viii, *infra,* pp. 975–77.—Tr.]

6. [*Vide* the first sentence of this Chapter, *supra,* p. 441.—Tr.]

world, that is, over all mankind; and therefore, no civil law can be thus universal. The consequent is clearly true, since no law extends its force beyond the limits of the legislator's jurisdiction. 'For we know', says Paulus [*Digest,* II. i. 20], 'that every law is addressed to those who are under the jurisdiction of that law'; since 'he who pronounces judgment outside the territory [of his jurisdiction] may be disobeyed with impunity,' as the laws declare; and therefore, much less are we bound to obey, outside his own territory, the person who decrees law, or legal precepts [for that territory]. The antecedent, moreover, is manifestly true in the light of what has already been said. For the power in question does not reside in the whole community of mankind, since the whole of mankind does not constitute one single commonwealth or kingdom. Nor does that power reside in any one individual, since such an individual would have to receive it from the hands of men, and this is inconceivable, inasmuch as men have never agreed to confer it [thus], nor to establish one sole head over themselves. Furthermore, not even by title of war, whether justly or unjustly, has there at any time been a prince who made himself temporal sovereign over the whole world. This assertion is clearly borne out by history. And therefore, the ordinary course of human nature points to the conclusion that a human legislative power of universal character and world-wide extent does not exist and has never existed, nor is it morally possible that it should have done so.

However, an objection with respect to the emperor would straightway present itself [to those who support the view above set forth]. I shall deal with this objection in the following Book.[7]

Thus the whole world—even though it be governed and bound by civil laws, as is morally certain in the case of all nations enjoying any form of civil government and not entirely barbarous—is nevertheless not ruled throughout by the same laws; on the contrary, each commonwealth or kingdom is governed, in accordance with an appropriate distribution, by means of its own particular laws.

And as to how the power in question finds a place within the Church of Christ, or whether it has been specifically instituted therein, these are questions which we shall discuss later.

---

7. [Bk. IV, chap. iii, which is not included in these *Selections.*—Tr.]

8. By way of a fourth inference, we may briefly deduce from the discussion [in the preceding Chapter], the ways in which this power to make human laws may be imparted.

In what ways this power of making [human] laws may be imparted. For it should be pointed out that, originally, the said power can be received directly from God; since there is no other possible origin for it—as we have shown in that previous Chapter—and since God, as the Author of all good things, is therefore the Author of all powers and especially of this power. For the latter most particularly rests upon divine providence, being necessary to good moral conduct, and to the proper preservation and government of mankind. Consequently, the said power must have been transferred to some possessor immediately by God; for if it resides mediately in any being, it necessarily resides immediately in some other being, since it cannot be traced back *ad infinitum.*

There are two ways, however, in which this power may be derived from God; that is to say, it may be derived naturally, as from the Author of nature, or supernaturally, as from the Author of grace. We shall treat of the latter mode in Book Five,[8] but the first has been sufficiently expounded in our previous discussion.

Accordingly, it is furthermore clear that the power in question may [also] be received immediately from men, and mediately from God. Indeed, such is usually the case with regard to natural power. For though it resides immediately in the community, it is conferred through the latter upon kings or princes or senators, since it is rarely or never retained in the community as a whole in such a way as to be administered immediately thereby. Nevertheless, after that power has been transferred to a given individual, and even though it may pass as the result of various successions and elections into the possession of a number of individuals, the community is always regarded as its immediate possessor, because, by virtue of the original act of investiture, it is the community that transfers the power to the other possessors. The case is similar to that of the papal power which, in spite of the fact that it is transferred to various persons in turn, as the

8. [Not included in these *Selections.*—Tr.]

result of various elections, comes always to every one of these persons from God, its immediate source.

9. But we must distinguish at this point between two customary modes in which any power may be held; that is to say, it may be held as ordinary, or as delegated power.

For what we have said above holds true with respect to ordinary power; since such power is indeed derived immediately from God, in the case of the community, and transferred by the community to the prince in exactly the same way, so that he wields this power as its proper owner and as one entitled to it by virtue of his peculiar office.

With respect to the second mode, however, a question may be raised as to whether such power can be delegated. That question is suggested by Bartolus (on *Digest,* I. i. 9, qu. 2 at beginning, subques. 5, no. 20) and by Panormitanus (on *Decretals,* Bk. V, tit. xxxix, chap. liii). Moreover, this doubt may have reference to all human legislative power, both supernatural and natural and with respect to every status. Such would indeed seem to be the scope of the question as it is raised by the authors above-mentioned. These authorities lay down without qualification the doctrine that the said power is capable of being delegated; a conclusion drawn by Panormitanus from the following phrase in the afore-cited Chapter of the *Decretals* [*ibid.*]: 'Certain citizens of Pisa, deputed by popular power to promulgate the statutes of the city', &c. The same inference is customarily derived also from the first law of the *Code* [I. i. 8, § 33].

10. But we must note that there are two ways in which this commission or delegation may take place.

What power is capable of being delegated. First, there may be a delegation of power to frame a law, decreeing whether or not it is just, useful or necessary, and in what terms it shall be incorporated; but the power of the delegate does not extend to the ability to endow the law with binding force nor, consequently, to the ability to promulgate it as law. In this sense, it is manifest that the power in question can be delegated; although, in point of fact, this constitutes a delegation, not of jurisdiction, but simply of a form of ministry that requires knowledge and skill. This kind of delegation, then, would seem to be effected by way of consultation, as it were.

And speaking from this standpoint, the said delegation takes place daily. Indeed, it would hardly be possible, otherwise, for laws to be made by princes, since the latter could not accomplish unaided all that is necessary to the process of legislation. Moreover, the laws cited above, if duly examined, prove this point and no more.

From the other standpoint, then, we have true delegation when the promulgation of a law is entrusted to any person in such a way that he is able to give it authority and validity, by his own will and independently of the confirmation or approval of the delegating party. This mode of delegation is neither so frequently nor so easily employed [as the first mode]. Accordingly, Bartolus (in the passage cited above) makes a distinction between the community and the prince, saying that the community may delegate this power when holding it in its ordinary phase and when able to wield it in accordance with the community's own choice and will; whereas the princes and judges to whom this jurisdiction has been entrusted—continues Bartolus—may not delegate it; because, in the first place, their [personal] activities are required when this charge is committed to them, so that they may not transfer the said charge to another (as is argued in *Digest*, I. xxi. 1), and furthermore because the power in question would seem to exist in those [princes and judges] solely in a delegated form and therefore may not be subdelegated by them.

11. However, passing over the first member [of Bartolus's distinction], which is clearly valid, we find that the second requires explanation.

For if it is understood as referring to the emperor, to kings, and to other princes, into whose hands this power of the state has been absolutely transferred, a false doctrine is involved; since in the case of such princes the power in question is not delegated but ordinary, inasmuch as it is perpetual and pertains to them by virtue of their office. Moreover, these princes may grant that power in its ordinary form to certain inferior states or rulers; why, then, may they not transfer also the function of delegating the same power? For in truth, there is no obstacle, in so far as concerns the power itself, which renders it incapable of being delegated. Bartolus himself upholds this supposition; and its truth is rendered still more clear by the fact that any power of a purely jurisdictional nature—such as the power under discussion—is capable of being delegated. Accordingly, the transfer of the said power from the state to the prince is not a delegation but a transfer (as it were), that is to say, an unlimited bestowal of the whole power which [formerly] resided in the community; and therefore, just as it was possible for the community to delegate that power, so also is it possible for the prince to make a similar delegation. Neither is the said power committed to him in such a way as to require his [personal] activities any more truly than this requirement is made in the case of the community. On the contrary, the power is granted to him absolutely, to be used by him personally or through agents, in that way which seems most expedient to him. Moreover, in the light of this same reasoning, the Pope, too—and not only the Pope but bishops, also—may delegate their legislative power whenever they are legislators with ordinary power; so that the arguments adduced above are [likewise] valid with respect to them.

12. *What power is incapable of being delegated.* Thus the opinion set forth by Bartolus applies solely in the case of those magistrates and judges to whom the power in question has been delegated by the supreme sources of power. For the arguments advanced by Bartolus are valid only in those cases. To be sure, since he refers particularly to communities, a verification of his opinion may be found in those commonwealths which are free in fact and which retain in themselves the supreme power, though they commit the task of legislation to a senate, or to a leader, [and in the latter case,] either to the leader alone or to him in association with the senate. For such legislators are perhaps simple delegates; and they will consequently be unable to delegate [, in turn,] their own power, unless this very ability is expressly provided for in the delegation [of power to themselves], or unless it is rendered clear by the light of custom that the power in question has been committed to them with that provision, a supposition which relates to fact rather than to law, so that we cannot make a more definite assertion as to this point. Furthermore, we are for the same reason unable to make any statement with regard to the actual delegation of this power, that is to say, any statement as to the persons in whom such delegated power may reside; for this is a matter which depends upon the free exercise of the will, and concerning which nothing is decreed by the common law.

CHAPTER XXXII

Are the Laws Peculiar to Some Kingdom or Domain Binding on the Men of That Domain, When They Are Dwelling outside Its Territorial Limits?

1. There are four ways in which any person may be related to a given domain or diocese: first, as a permanent inhabitant[1] thereof, actually living and residing therein; secondly, at the opposite extreme, as one who has neither of these relations with the domain in question; thirdly, as a permanent inhabitant of this domain, having his domicile therein, but dwelling abroad at the time; fourthly, as being present in the said domain, but having neither domicile nor origin therein.

There is no occasion for dispute with regard to the first and second situations. For, as to the first, what was said in the preceding Chapter[2] has special application, since all the elements necessary for the actual status of a subject and consequently for the binding obligation of law are present in this first case. In the second situation, on the other hand, it is clear that there is no possibility of legal obligation, because there is no title existing under which the status of a subject may be imposed. But in connexion with the third and fourth, there are two doubtful questions which must be discussed.

2. *The reason for the doubt.* The first question is stated in the title of this Chapter. There is indeed cause for the doubt indicated therein, since the subject, although he is actually living or travelling outside the boundaries of his own state, always remains a subject, as long as he does not change his domicile, and since we have already said[3] that the law binds all subjects and all parts of the community, wherefore the law is binding, even in the case in question. The confirmation of this view is drawn, first, from an argument based on [the absurdity of] the converse supposition: for an inhabitant of another kingdom, while dwelling in this one, is not bound to observe the laws of the latter kingdom, a fact which seems to

1. [*Incola.*—Tr.]
2. [Not included in these *Selections.*—Tr.]
3. [Bk. III, chap. xxxi of *De Legibus,* which is not included in these *Selections.*—Tr.]

be expressly defined in the *Decretals* (Bk. V, tit. xxxix, chap. xxi); and therefore, he must be under the obligation of observing the laws of his own domain, since if he were not so bound he would be freed, solely on account of his absence, from the obligation of obeying the laws of either country, an assumption which is evidently absurd.

The second confirmation of the same view is that if a bishop makes a rule for the diocese in question, ordering for example that all persons subject to him, who enjoy a benefice within that diocese, must reside therein during a given period of time under pain of a given punishment or censure, then he so binds the holders of such benefices, wherever they may be, that if they do not return to the diocese within the prescribed time, they incur the said penalty or censure, as a general rule, apart from ignorance of the order on their part, or inability to comply therewith. Hence, a provincial statute is binding upon those belonging to a diocese, even while they are travelling elsewhere; and therefore, the same is true of any similar law.

3. *The negative conclusion: this is the opinion commonly held.* Nevertheless, it must be stated, that no law is binding outside the limits of the territory of the superior or prince by whom it is decreed; so that the inhabitants of that country, generally speaking, do not sin if they violate the law in question while they are outside this territory. Such is the common opinion of the Doctors on the *Sext* (Bk. I, tit. ii, chap. ii) and on the *Decretals* (Bk. V, tit. xxxix, chap. xxi); of Sylvester (on word *excommunicatio,* Pt. II, no. 7); as also of Angelus de Clavasio and the other summists (on word *lex*); and of Covarruvias (on *Sext,* Pt. I, § 10, no. 3). This conclusion is derived from the passage in the *Sext* already cited (Bk. I, tit. ii, chap. ii), in which it is stated that one who is living outside a particular diocese and disobeys a law made by the bishop thereof, does not therefore incur the sentence imposed by that law. However, the reply may be made that in the passage under discussion, the reference is not to the binding authority of the law, but rather to the censure, and that in the latter case the principle involved is different; for the imposition of a censure pertains not to the directive, but to the coercive power of the law, and therefore is not a practice to be extended outside of the territorial limits, since the superior or judge may not punish outside of the territory, although he may issue orders and

impose obligations. This would appear to be the meaning of the Pope when he adds, in explanation of the above-mentioned passage (*Sext, ibid.*), these words: 'since he who pronounces judgment outside the territory [of his jurisdiction] may be disobeyed with impunity'; for pronouncing judgment is the same as passing a sentence. Nevertheless, the intention of the Pope was doubtless to assert that the statute involved was not [actually] violated by the subject in such a situation; that it is for this reason that the subject does not incur a censure; and that, therefore, even the directive force [of the law] would not be binding in the said situation. Moreover, the person who does not obey the statute, under the circumstances supposed, is not contumaciously disobedient to the Church; and this in turn is an indication that the person in question is not bound by that statute, even with respect to its directive force. The truth of the antecedent is evident, since if the said subject were contumacious he might accordingly be excommunicated, and consequently would incur a legal censure. For excommunication, to follow the more probable opinion, may be inflicted upon an absent subject, even though he be dwelling in foreign territory, provided a sufficient cause for censure is assumed to exist; and contumacy is a sufficient cause, according to the passage (*Matthew*, Chap. xviii [, v. 17]): 'If he will not hear the church, let him be to thee as the heathen and publican'. Therefore, just as [liability to] a censure does not bind an absent person, neither does a law. It clearly follows that, although the statute in question may have been published without any provision as to censure or penalty, but simply with the force of a directive law binding in conscience, nevertheless, it will not be binding upon absent subjects, since its power to lay an obligation upon the conscience is not enlarged by reason of the censure [of the court]. For the imposition of a censure rather assumes the existence of jurisdiction and the power to bind; and when a censure is attached, the jurisdiction [of the law] is not for that reason extended[4] or restricted. Thus, from the text cited, the best argument may be drawn as to any law proceeding from a power limited to a definite territory; and whether this law be ecclesiastical or civil, the same conclusion in due proportion holds true.

4. [Reading *extendatur* for *extenuatur.*—Tr.]

4. But all the authorities do not agree as to the rational basis for the assertion in question.[5] For some explain the fact stated, by referring it to the intention of the legislator, on the ground that he intended merely to bind the subjects living within his own territory; wherefore these persons say that the conclusion which we have laid down is true only if the law is couched in general terms, since in that case, no other—that is to say, no more extensive—intent on the part of the lawmaker, is expressed; and, therefore, if the legislator declares in explicit terms that he wishes to bind [all] subjects, wherever they may be, then—according to those [who favour the opinion above set forth]—the law is binding even upon subjects outside the territory. Thus the persons who hold to the said opinion limit the aforementioned statement in the *Sext,* (Bk. I, tit. II, chap. ii). In favour of the view in question, Bartolus (on *Code,* I. i. 1, nos. 44 *et seq.*) is usually cited. However, this stand, as ascribed to Bartolus, is criticized by Panormitanus (on *Decretals,* Bk. V, tit. xxxIx, chap. xxi); Navarrus (*Enchiridion,* Chap. xxvii, no. 272); Sylvester, *ibid.,* [Sect. 3]; Covarrubias, *ibid.,* [Sect. 3] and all the other authorities. And the matter is made entirely clear in that passage of the *Sext, ibid.,* where the Pope states the reason for his proposition, as follows: 'since he who pronounces judgment outside the territory [of his jurisdiction] may be disobeyed with impunity.' These words indicate a defect not merely of will, but also of power, a fact which is self-evident and which is, moreover, corroborated by the *Digest* (II. i. 20), whence the assertion in question has been taken, the commentators being commonly agreed upon this point in connexion with the latter passage, also.

Therefore, the true reason for the statement under discussion is that the jurisdiction of any one state or particular prince does not include the power of making laws which shall be valid outside the state or kingdom; a fact which I have elsewhere expounded more fully, in a passage where I have treated of other phases of this matter (Vol. V, *De Censuris Ecclesiasticis,* Disp. V, sect. IV[6]), which pertain more especially to censures. Neither

---

5. [I.e. 'no law is binding outside the limits of the country of the lord or prince by whom it is decreed'; &c. Cf. *supra,* § 3, p. 454.—TR.]

6. [Not included in these *Selections.*—TR.]

is this reason entirely alien to the mind of Bartolus; for he touches upon it in the place cited, [on *Code*, I. i. 1, nos. 44 *et seq.*] and draws this very conclusion from the *Digest* (I. i. 9), in which [civil] law (*lex*) is defined as the particular law (*ius*) of any given state.[7] Therefore, just as in philosophy we are accustomed to say that an action does not continue outside its sphere of activity, owing surely to a defect of power and not of will; even so the activity of jurisdiction in the making of any law is limited to a specific territory, and hence that law is not binding outside those territorial limits. Therefore, it is clearly to be inferred that the lawgiver cannot bind a subject outside the existing boundaries of the state, even if he has a decided intention of doing so, and expressly states that intention in the words of his [law].

5. *When a prince may punish a delinquent subject outside of his own territory.* But we must interpret the foregoing as referring to the peculiar directive obligation imposed by law upon the conscience, for this is the proper and immediate effect of law.

If, however, one is discussing coercion by means of a penalty, it is the opinion of the jurists that when a subject has committed a crime outside of the state, the prince may inflict upon him the punishment imposed by his own law for his own territory, provided that the penalty is not imposed *ipso iure,* but is still to be imposed, and provided that the crime thus committed outside the realm is later punished within that same realm. Thus Abbas [i.e. Panormitanus] (on *Decretals,* Bk. V, tit. xvii, chap. i, no. 8) teaches; and indeed it will be found that this is all that Bartolus meant in the passage cited, if that passage is carefully read.

The reason for the opinion above set forth is that under the conditions specified the penalty is imposed not outside the territory in question, but within it; for it is assumed that this punishment must be imposed by human agency, and judges do not inflict punishment upon or exercise power over those who are dwelling outside the territory, but do so only

---

7. [Suárez wrote: . . . *Lex dicitur ius proprium civitatis.* The *Digest* (*loc. cit.*), has: *Quod quisque populus ipse sibi ius constituit, id ipsius proprium civitatis est vocaturque ius civile, quasi ius proprium ipsius civitatis.* The point of the reference is that the *Digest* recognizes particular law.—REVISER.]

when the latter return to the country. This view, then, is not in conflict with the *Sext* (Bk. I, tit. ii, chap. ii): for, in the first place, it has reference [only] to statutes accompanied by a sentence of censure, through which sentence the censure is inflicted *ipso iure;* and, furthermore, that kind of a statute necessarily supposes and requires a peculiar power to lay a binding obligation upon the conscience, rendering the transgressor contumacious and worthy of censure. By the same token, the reason set forth in the *Sext* (*ibid.*) does not conflict with the limitation in question, since a legal precept designating the penalty to be imposed even for a crime committed outside the limits of the state, and the execution of that precept, are not equivalent to 'pronouncing judgment' outside the territory [of the lawmaker].

6. Hence, also, we clearly see the rational basis for this difference between a law imposing punishment *ipso facto,* and a law merely declaring a punishment that is to be imposed. For the first kind of law of itself inflicts a penalty and thus necessarily extends its binding character and power of execution outside its own territory; and this it cannot do otherwise than by obliging the guilty person to execute the penalty upon himself, which is impossible, as has been proved. For if the law in question cannot compel one to, or restrain one from an action, much less will it be able to compel one to the execution of the penalty. Whereas a law which imposes a penalty that is to be inflicted by a judge, is by the very nature of the case, a statute binding the judge to act in accordance with it, rather than a statute binding upon the criminal; and the judge dwells within the territorial limits of the state. The objection may be raised that the [guilty] subject is also bound in conscience to submit to the punishment in question. Our reply is that the said subject, strictly speaking, is not bound by this law until after sentence has been passed, when he is assumed to be already within the limits of the state.

Hence Panormitanus has rightly noted that it is necessary not merely that any crime punishable by such a law should be evil because it is forbidden by the law in question, but also that the supposition should exist that the deed is essentially evil, or in some other way sufficiently forbidden. For that law, as has been proved, can not itself prohibit the deed, outside of the limits of the state; and therefore it can not designate any penalty for the same, unless the deed is for some other reason assumed to be evil or sufficiently prohibited.

7. *A reply to the arguments to the contrary.* As to the reason for the doubt which was mentioned at the beginning [of this Chapter][8] we may reply, in accordance with what has been said above, that a subject living outside the territorial limits of the state, although he does not lose his status as a subject in the essential sense—or basically, so to speak—does nevertheless lose that status, in a temporary sense; that is to say, he ceases to exercise it in relation to the laws of his country, since he is living beyond the range of their [normal] operation.

However, in the first confirmation of [the view set forth in Section 2 of this Chapter], it is pointed out that a certain difficulty exists in connexion with the interpretation of a statement in the aforesaid Chapter xxi [*Decretals,* Bk. V, tit. xxxix, chap. xxi], which pertains rather to the following point. Briefly, then, I answer that the statement in question refers, not to a statute or law, but to a general sentence, or a personal and temporary precept. As to the difference arising from this fact, and the reason therefore, I shall speak presently of these points.

8. In regard to the second confirmation [of the above-mentioned view], the Doctors add certain limitations to the proposition stated [in connexion with the said confirmation]. This may be deduced from Sylvester, [on word *excommunicatio,* Pt. II, no. 7] and from Angelus de Clavasio (on word *excommunicatio,* Pt. I, no. 10), who reduce the limitations to this principle: that, outside of the territory in question, no one is bound when the agent, and the object of the operation, and the action itself, are entirely without the limits of the state. Whence it is to be inferred that if the agent is outside, while the object with respect to which he offends is inside, then the obligatory force of the law may be applicable. Covarruvias, however, explains this limitation in different words, although their ultimate significance may be the same; for he says that a law is not binding outside the limits of the state, unless the subject-matter of the law has in view the welfare of that same state, that is to say, the avoidance of injury or harm to it, or some similar purpose.

8. [*Vide* Section 2, p. 453.—Tr.]

In my opinion, this is the true doctrine. I have explained it more fully in a passage already cited [Vol. V, *De Censuris,* Disp. V, sec. iv];[9] and from the statements made there, I infer that, strictly speaking, the proposition in question is not limited by the said doctrine, since offences contrary to a law of the sort under discussion should be considered as having been committed, not without, but within the territory [of the lawmaker]. For if the law is, for example, affirmative, directing that some act be performed within the state, the failure to observe this law is considered to have occurred where the prescribed act should have been performed, since one would seem to perpetrate an offence in that place in which he fails to do what he ought, just as, on the other hand, he would seem to sin wherever he does what he should not have done. This analogy is borne out by a statement in the *Digest* (L. xvii. 121). But if the law be negative, and if its transgression shall result in an injury to the state, then the offence is clearly consummated in that state: even as a person corporally outside the limits of the state or kingdom would, if he shot an arrow and thus killed a man within those boundaries, be clearly held to have sinned in the territory of the said state, thus transgressing the law and incurring, in consequence, a liability to the censure, if the latter should be provided for by the law in question: all of which I have said in the passage cited above. These remarks, then, are applicable to the second confirmation, and constitute a sufficient comment upon it.

9. *The same assertion, due proportion being observed, may be made with respect to exempt localities when they are enclosed within a state.* There may be some doubt as to whether the same assertion may be made with respect to exempt localities when they are otherwise enclosed within a state. But this doubt occurs more frequently in connexion with the canon, than with the civil laws; and, besides, I have treated of the question sufficiently in the place above-mentioned [*De Censuris,* Disp. V, sect. iv].[10] Therefore, I shall simply state that the same assertion does indeed hold true with respect to localities of this kind; a reply which is, as I have said in the aforesaid passage, the common solution of the question. This opinion is held also by de la Palu (on the *Sentences,* Bk. IV, dist. xviii, 2d part of quest. 2, art. 2)

---

9. [Not included in these *Selections.*—Tr.]
10. [Not included in these *Selections.*—Tr.]

and by Gabriel thereon (on the *Sentences, ibid.,* concl. 6), by Antoninus (*Summa,* Pt. III, tit. xxiv, chap. lxxv, § 1) and is supported by the *Summa Rosella*[11] (word *excommunicatio,* Pt. VII, § 3), the *Armilla*[12] ([word *excommunicatio,*] No. 30) and by the canonists (on *Sext,* Bk. I, tit. XVI, chap. vii and on the *Constitutions* of Clement, Bk. V, tit. VII, chap. ii). The same view is supported by the laws above cited, in so far as it may be inferred from them that a prelate cannot exercise his jurisdiction within the exempt territory, a limitation which applies to every superior. From this fact, we draw the conclusion that the exempt locality, in so far as jurisdiction is concerned, is considered as outside the [enclosing] state; since, except in cases expressly mentioned in the law, an ordinary superior of the said state may not execute therein any act of jurisdiction; and the act of binding by a statute or law, in the place exempted, is an exercise of jurisdiction in that place; as is evident from the *Sext* (Bk. I, tit. II, chap. ii), already cited. Therefore, the same argument exists in regard to the exempt locality; and to that locality one may well apply the principle under discussion, namely, that 'he who pronounces judgment outside the territory [of his jurisdiction] may be disobeyed with impunity.'

CHAPTER XXXIII

Are the Laws Peculiar to Some Domain Strictly Binding upon Aliens While They Are Living within That Domain?

1. I have treated of this question at length in Vol. I, *De Religione,* Tract. II, bk. II, *De Festis,* Chap. xiv,[1] in connexion with the precept for the observance of festivals; and therefore, avoiding repetition in the present context, I shall note briefly the points which I there set forth and shall add certain observations more suited to this passage.

Three elements are to be distinguished in law. Three elements, then, must be distinguished in every law: first, its binding force with respect to the

---

11. [*Summa Rosella, liber qui Rosella casuum appellatur.*—REVISER.]
12. [*Aurea Armilla* by Bartholomeo Fumo, O. P.—REVISER.]
1. [Not included in these *Selections.*—TR.]

conscience, which I call its directive force; secondly, its coercive force, by means of which one may be punished according to law; and lastly, the force by which a definite form is laid down for contracts and similar legal acts, so that it sometimes happens that an act otherwise performed is not valid. The question placed at the head of this Chapter will be considered in relation to these three points, since they present their own difficulties.

2. Regarding the first element there are various opinions, which I have set forth in the place cited [*De Religione, ibid.*].[2]

The basis of the negative opinion. Those who hold to the first opinion absolutely deny that a person may be bound by the laws of any place, unless he has a fixed and perfect domicile therein. In favour of this view, I have cited as authorities, in the passage already referred to, de la Palu, Medina, Archidiaconus, Hostiensis and others; but I myself have rejected the view as improbable.

The second opinion. According to the second opinion, the laws of a locality are binding upon those aliens who are permanent residents of that locality to the extent, at least, of establishing a quasi-domicile therein; but this binding force does not hold with respect to other persons living in the said locality for a brief season, or passing through it. I have cited Felinus, Antoninus and others, in support of this opinion.

However, the basis of both views is very nearly the same, namely, that non-resident foreigners are not subjects; for the status of subject, in so far as concerns the direction of conduct, and binding obligation, is acquired only through domicile, or, at least, through quasi-domicile. *Proof by means of examples.* In addition to this argument based on reason, [certain supporters of the theory stated above] cite the example of unbelievers who are not bound by the laws of Christians, although they live among the latter; the example of members of religious orders in relation to secular persons; and that of novices in relation to professed religious. But I shall pass over these instances, since they are not pertinent; for they have to do not only with those who pass through a territory, but also with those possessing a fixed domicile in it. Of these cases I shall speak later (Bk. IV, last chapter).[3]

2. [Not included in these *Selections.*—Tr.]
3. [Not included in these *Selections.*—Tr.]

The confirmation [of the theory in question] may be derived from the disadvantages [which would result if the opposite were true]; for, in that case, unbelievers when passing through Christian territories would be bound to observe the laws or rites of Christians, abstaining from meat on the days when it is prohibited, and so forth, which would be absurd. Moreover, the monks residing in the territory in question would be obliged to observe the synodal fasts, and such an obligation would be a grave burden, since they have many other fasts of their own, which the laity are not bound to observe, according to the decrees of the regulars. It would also follow that a religious of a given province is bound to observe the fasts, festivals, and laws on similar matters, peculiar to another country, when he is a guest therein, even if these regulations are not common to his whole organization. And in like manner, a novice would be bound to observe the rules of a religious order as long as he dwelt in the house of that order. But these suppositions are not acceptable.

3. *The law of a territory is binding in conscience upon aliens while they live therein, and in the same way as upon permanent inhabitants.* Nevertheless, it must be asserted that the law of a locality is binding in conscience upon aliens and guests as long as they dwell therein, and in the same way as upon the permanent inhabitants. This is the common opinion of those who have interpreted *Code,* I. i. 1 and *Decretals,* Bk. V, tit. xxxix, chap. xxi, especially Innocent [IV], Hostiensis, and Panormitanus; it is brought out also in a passage of the *Sext* (Bk. I, tit. ii, chap. ii), on which Geminiano and Sylvester (word *excommunicatio,* Pt. II, no. 4) have commented fully; and I have likewise referred to many others in the place cited. I have verified this same opinion by citing the authority of Augustine and the custom of the Church, as well as by various arguments.

The true reason, however, is that a law is made for general application within a given territory, as we assume, and is therefore binding, for the period of their residence, on all persons actually living therein.

It is necessary to peace and good conduct in any locality that aliens, while they are living in that locality, shall conform to the customs of conduct of its people, lest scandals result. The deduction is proved, first, because from the standpoint of the final cause it is morally necessary for the good government of a province, locality or territory that the laws made for the same should have this [universally binding] effect; for it is necessary to peace and good conduct in that locality that aliens should conform to the customs of conduct of its people, as long as those aliens live with the people in question; a fact which is frequently indicated in the *Decretum* (Pt. I, dist. xii, can. iv; Pt. I, dist. viii, can. ii; Pt. II, causa xvi, qu. vii, can. xxii), and which experience makes sufficiently clear. For otherwise, disputes and scandals would result. Therefore, since laws are established with a view to the common welfare, peace and good conduct of the country, it is necessary that they should possess the [universal] force in question.

Secondly, the same conclusion may be proved from the standpoint of the efficient cause, that is to say, from the standpoint of the legislator's power. For every civil governor has the power necessary to preserve his state and to safeguard its morals; therefore, he has also the power to make laws which are binding upon all living within his domains; since it is on this ground that he is empowered to punish aliens who commit crimes therein; hence, by reason of these faculties he possesses [likewise] the power to bind by his laws all persons engaged in activities within his realm, in so far as such an act of compulsion is necessary to the welfare of his realm.

4. *Proof of the above proposition, from the standpoint of the aliens.* Thirdly, the same truth is evident from the standpoint of the aliens, since there are grounds sufficient to justify their subjection to such an extent that they may be bound by the laws of the territory; and this degree of subjection is all that is required. Therefore, the truth of the major premiss is evident partly because power in the sovereign and subjection in the governed are correlative, and we have proved the existence of the power in the prince, so that there is a corresponding subordination in the other extreme; and partly in view of the fact that, just as this obligation is (as it were) transient and relative, even so a temporary subjection (so to speak) is sufficient therefor, the sole requirement for that subjection being actual sojourn and presence, even though the sojourn may be of short duration. For just as a man in changing his domicile from one place to another by this very act manifests his will to be bound permanently by the laws of that new territory, or else becomes bound in consequence of his act and despite his will to the contrary; even so any person who wills to sojourn in a given

locality for a brief time, by that very act manifests or should manifest a will to subject himself temporarily to the government of that territory, in everything relating to general habits of conduct and laws. This statement is confirmed by the converse argument. For an inhabitant of any territory, withdrawing from it for a brief period, at once and throughout that period ceases to be bound by the laws thereof, according to the argument of the preceding Chapter; and consequently, during that time, he is not actually a subject. Hence the converse will also hold true; for the principle is the same, and equity demands that in both cases equality—that is to say, due proportion—shall be observed.

5. *The reply to the basic argument of the contrary opinion.* The basic argument of the contrary opinion has been refuted by the foregoing remarks. For we have already proved that in the case posited neither jurisdiction nor subjection is lacking, and we have elsewhere demonstrated (*De Censuris,* Disp. V, sec. IV)[4] one by one the following points: first, that a quasi-domicile is sufficient to establish the obligation in question; secondly, that a sojourn of a few days will suffice; and finally, that the said obligation should be extended in a proportionate degree to travellers remaining for a brief period in a guesthouse. Moreover, what we said in that same passage, with respect to the law on the observance of festivals may well be extended to all laws, including those of a civil nature, with which, also, we dealt there in passing, but at some length.

In what fashion this doctrine may be applied to persons of religious calling. It may furthermore be added incidentally that this doctrine is applicable to religious persons who are pilgrims or guests in alien provinces or religious houses, in so far as relates to the peculiar regulations of those provinces or houses. I mention this fact, because some writers hold that persons of a religious calling, when travelling, are exempt from such regulations on the ground that they have no territory of their own, since the spirit of religion may be [considered as being] diffused throughout the whole Church. But this fact does not prevent the religious from having their own domiciles, according to the argument in the *Sext* (Bk. V, tit. VII, chap. i); and as to the point in question, the separate monasteries and provinces may have

---

4. [Not included in these *Selections.*—TR.]

their own observances. We hold, then, that aliens are bound by these, for the time that they remain in such surroundings, due proportion being observed; for the principle involved is the same [as that in the case of the permanent residents], unless religious custom itself concedes to the aliens some particular exemption.

6. *Not merely on account of scandal are aliens bound by the laws of the locality, but also because of the laws themselves and because those aliens are in a sufficient state of subjection.* Finally, it is evident from the foregoing that certain persons have been mistaken in saying that aliens are bound to observe these laws, merely to avoid scandal. For this is not true. If it were, they would not, in the absence of [possible] scandal, be bound in an absolute sense and in secret, to obey these laws. Therefore, it must be stated that, although the occurrence of actual scandal accidentally increases the obligation, nevertheless, scandal is not therefore the true basis of the obligation; on the contrary, it is at most an occasion or motive which impels the legislator to make the law. But the obligation to obey this law does not lapse even if the particular motive does lapse; just as the carrying of arms in a given place or at a given time is forbidden in order that quarrels may be prevented, and women are forbidden to adorn themselves in this or that specified way, that scandal may be avoided, while nevertheless, after the laws have once been established, the obligation to abstain from these acts exists not merely on account of the scandal, but *per se,* by reason of the laws themselves. So it is in the case under discussion; for the necessity of avoiding scandal and of maintaining morality within a state may cause the making of laws for all who are living in that locality; and, accordingly, after the law has been made, aliens are bound to conform thereto, not only for the sake of avoiding scandal, but also because of the law itself and because they are in a sufficient state of subjection, as has been explained.

7. *A doubt.* But one may ask whether a law for any state or territory may be made which is binding only upon the aliens dwelling therein. For Innocent [IV] says (on *Decretals,* Bk. V, tit. xxxix, chap. xxi) that such a law cannot bind non-resident foreigners unless it is formulated in general terms, and is binding *per se* upon the inhabitants and concomitantly (as it were) upon the non-residents. It may be that Innocent was influenced

by the fact that the principle of uniformity, and of the accessory which follows upon the primary factor[5] would apply in the latter case; whereas this principle could not be applied if the law related only to non-resident foreigners, who, essentially and directly, are not subjects of the commonwealth or prince in question.

The true answer. A law may be enacted for any country, binding upon such aliens as reside therein when such a law could promote the common welfare. Nevertheless, I think that the contrary opinion is true—a view which Hostiensis supports, on this same passage [*Decretals,* Bk. V, tit. xxxix, chap. xxi, no. 7], also; Panormitanus, more decidedly; and Sylvester, too. The principle, however, is the same, applied in due proportion; for it concerns the general welfare of the state or commonwealth to regulate the manner in which non-residents shall conduct themselves while there, and to determine the means necessary for this end. Otherwise, the state would not be sufficiently protected. Nor can such power reside in any source other than the state itself or its governor, since the guardianship and care of the locality have been entrusted to him. Therefore, just as the said non-residents have a peculiar mode of living, that is to say, of being located in a given place, so in many matters they may require special statutes. Hence, they may be bound by such statutes; since they are constituted subjects to this extent by the mere fact of their sojourn, as we have already pointed out. But we assume that these laws must be just, and suitable, not only to the locality in question but also to the non-residents themselves, observing a due proportion between the two; for thus the said laws will satisfy every qualification for placing those non-residents under a valid obligation.

8. *On coercive force: the reason for the doubt.* On the second point, regarding coercive force, that is, the question of whether by that force also a law is binding upon foreigners—in other words, upon non-resident aliens—a special reason for doubt is derived from the *Decretals* (*ibid.*), in which the following question is raised: when a bishop issues in his diocese this general decree, 'If any one shall be guilty of stealing, let him

---

5. [An example of this maxim would be a promise confirmed by oath. The oath is accessory; the promise is the primary factor or principal. If the promise lapses, the oath lapses also.—Reviser.]

be excommunicated,'[6] will the decree be binding upon aliens? To this the Pope replies that it is binding only upon the subjects of that bishop, a reply for which there can be no other reason than the fact that the bishop does not have coercive power over aliens, but has it only over subjects.

The reply contained in the Gloss is rejected. The Gloss thereon [on *Decretals, ibid.*] replies, as to this point, that such a decree of excommunication applies to foreigners, not as such, but in so far as they have become subject by reason of their offence; and accordingly holds that the text [of the Pope's answer] must be interpreted as referring to those who are subjects by whatsoever title. However, this explanation in reality inverts the force of the Pontiff's response, and renders it frivolous and absurd. For that is the very point at issue, namely, whether the said aliens are subject by reason of their offence; hence [the Pope] is speaking of subjects, not in the sense employed [by the Gloss], but in that in which inhabitants are designated simply as subjects. Furthermore, a certain inconsistency is involved in the reply quoted from the Gloss. For in a case of punishment by excommunication, the proximate reason for the subjection of the offender cannot be the fact that an offence has been committed in a given place; on the contrary, one must necessarily assume the existence of an obligation to obey the prelate of that locality, since for excommunication there must have been contumacy in regard to the Church, and since an offence against the natural law, as such, is not a sufficient ground. This being the case, as I presume from the very nature of the question, a condition of subjection existing before the commission of the offence must consequently be assumed, from which subjection arises the obligation of obeying a law embodying a given prohibition under pain of excommunication. Hence, since the discussion in the text concerns this censure, aliens may not be classed as subjects by reason of an offence, but are termed thus, because they were inherently subjects, before the law or offence in question existed. So also Panormitanus and others interpret this same text [on *Decretals, ibid.*], admitting, in consequence, that aliens are not included under the censure when it is imposed in a general decree.

---

6. [This quotation, as given by Suárez, varies slightly from the text of the *Decretals.*—Tr.]

9. *The opinion of the author.* Nevertheless, it must be admitted that a law made for a given territory does apply, even as to its coercive force, to non-resident foreigners who linger therein; that is to say, such foreigners may be punished in that territory for the transgression of the said law, either through a judge, or through the force of the law itself, if the latter carries with it a penalty, *ipso facto.* This is the opinion of the authors cited above, as well as of the commentators on the *Decretals* (Bk. V, tit. xxxix, chap. xxi). The reason is evident, since the same title of subjection, or power, is operative in regard to this coercive force, as that which was shown to be valid in regard to directive force. Indeed, directive power would not be efficacious unless coercive power were annexed thereto. Besides, if an alien is bound, essentially and in conscience, to obey the law of a particular state, then, by transgressing that law he commits an offence in that territory and against that state; and therefore, by reason of this offence also, he remains subject to the coercive power of the commonwealth in question, according to an *Authentica* on the *Code,* III. xv [*Novels,* LXIX, chap. i].

10. However, the following limitation is usually added: that the non-resident foreigner shall not be superior in rank to the author of the law in question, since no superior can be subjected to an inferior by coercive authority. For instance, if a bishop should impose a prohibition upon his clerics under pain of excommunication to be incurred *ipso facto,* and if his metropolitan should act contrary thereto, even in the bishopric of the former, that metropolitan could not [by this act of disobedience] incur the penalty of excommunication. This fact is noted by Sylvester (on word *excommunicatio,* Pt. I, no. 9) and by Panormitanus, on the *Decretals* (Bk. V, tit. xvii, chap. i, no. 11 [no . 12]), the latter touching upon the same point elsewhere (on *Decretals,* Bk. II, tit. ii, chap. xx).

Soto also expresses this opinion in a passage (on the *Sentences,* Bk. IV, dist. xxii, qu. 2), wherein he extends the rule to apply to prelates of equal rank, saying that neither the archbishop, nor another bishop, offending within the diocese of a suffragan or bishop, can be bound by the censure of the latter. Panormitanus, however, rightly asserts that this principle applies to a superior in jurisdiction; for although one prelate may be the equal or even the superior of another in dignity, while he remains within the diocese of the latter, he can be bound by its laws, wherefore he can also be bound by its censures or punished on account of an offence committed within that diocese.

This holds true with respect both to ecclesiastical laws and to civil laws, according to an opinion also expressed by Innocent, on the *Decretals* (Bk. I, tit. xxxIII, chap. xvi), and supported by the *Digest* (I. xviii. 3). The reason for this view is that a dignity without jurisdiction does not exempt the person enjoying that dignity from subjection because of an offence, just as it does not exempt him from the obligation of obeying the law violated; and therefore, such dignity is incidental (so to speak) in relation to jurisdiction.

One bishop cannot be punished by another of equal rank. The foregoing holds true [only] from the standpoint of ordinary law, and on condition that a given person is not [specifically] exempted by reason of the said dignity; for in that case, one bishop cannot be punished by another bishop of equal rank.

On the other hand, when any person is superior in jurisdiction, it is clear that he may not be bound by an inferior (*Decretals, ibid.*). Moreover, just as such a superior is not subject with respect to coercive power or punishment, neither is he subject with respect to directive force or obligation in so far as this obligation exists by virtue of a law; for the principle is the same in regard to both sorts of subjection, the law itself being dependent upon jurisdiction. Whether or not the person in question may be bound for some other reason, however, is a point which we shall discuss later, when treating of the lawgiver himself;[7] for as to this question almost the same principle holds.

11. *The passage cited from the* Decretals *refers not to a law or to a statute, but to a precept or sentence passed by an individual.* Therefore, in answer to the objection made on the basis of the *Decretals* (Bk. V, tit. xxxIx, chap. xxi), it must be said that in that passage the reference is not to a law or to a statute, but rather to a precept or sentence passed by an individual, although it may be made in general terms; a fact which is clear from the text, and which is agreed upon by all the interpreters thereof.

---

7. [Bk. III, chap. xxxv of *De Legibus,* which is not included in these *Selections.*—Tr.]

The difference between these. But it is necessary to explain the difference between a statute and a precept, that is, a general sentence passed by an individual.

Panormitanus thereon (*Decretals, ibid.*), gives the following answer: such a sentence operates [only] at the time when it is passed, so that it binds only those whom it finds at that time suited to be so bound; whereas a law is always operative and therefore always binding [even] upon persons who have newly become subjects.

The explanation given by Panormitanus is rejected. However, this answer is not acceptable, first, because according to the *Decretals* (*ibid.*), a general sentence of the sort described does not include foreigners, even if they are actually present within the territory affected thereby when the sentence is promulgated; but if a precept or sentence is framed in terms of a statute it will apply to foreigners; and therefore a distinction must be drawn [between the sentence passed by an individual and the statute], and not merely in relation to persons subject at some future time, even if we assume that equal subjection—that is, equal presence in the territory affected—exists [in both cases]. Secondly, the explanation given by Panormitanus is unsatisfactory, because even in relation to the future, the distinction in question does not hold good. For if, through a precept issued by an individual, sentence is declared in regard to some offence that may be committed in the future, such a sentence likewise holds good for that future time; it has reference always to that time; and it extends its application to persons newly born in the region affected, as well as to those who newly transfer their domicile thither, even if the said persons were not subjects at the time when the precept was imposed.

Another point to be considered is that a statute not only prescribes or forbids, but also punishes of its own force and *ipso facto,* and contains within itself a sentence legally framed; but the obligation imposed by the precept [of an individual] extends, no less than does the binding force of a legal sentence, to those who, after the first publication of such a statute [or precept], come into the territory in question and there commit the offence. Consequently, as far as this point is concerned, there is the same principle applicable [to a statute, and] to a general precept issued by an individual and including a general sentence which imposes a penalty, *ipso facto,* upon future transgressors. For if in the case of a statute one takes into consideration that permanence whereby it is always applicable and therefore always binding, why shall not the same quality of permanence be considered in the case of a precept issued by an individual, which also endures, according to his intention, so long as he lives or while he remains in office? And if, on the other hand, in the case of a [violated] statute it is understood by a fiction of the law that judgment is handed down at the time when the offence takes place in a given territory, even if that offence is committed by a foreigner who recently has come thither, then why will not the same legal fiction hold good of a judgment declared in the precept of an individual?

12. *The difference between a law, and a simple precept issued by an individual.* Therefore, I maintain that the distinction to be drawn is due to the differing characters of a law, and a simple precept issued by an individual. For a law, as I have said previously[8] is perpetual; while the precept of an individual is transitory, and easily subject to change. Hence it follows that a law by reason of its perpetuity is likened to custom, and is held to be well known to all, and laid down for observance by all. On the other hand, the precept of an individual has not this equivalence to custom, nor is custom introduced thereby, since a precept is easily changed, nor is it wont to be so widely known; so that a precept of itself binds only the inhabitants of a territory, its true and permanent subjects; whereas a statute is binding upon all who reside in that territory.

Therefore, another distinction should be taken into consideration, namely, that a law (*lex*) is made for a given territory, since it is the 'law of the state' (*ius civitatis*) as Bartolus said, or 'law of the territory', (*lex territorii*), according to Panormitanus, and consequently is binding by means (so to speak) of the territory itself; that is to say, in so far as the persons bound dwell within that territory, just as a local interdict binds those living in a given locality. On this account a statute, outside the territory for which it is decreed, has no binding force over persons who are in other respects subject to it, a fact which we have noted above.[9] On the other hand, the precept of an individual—that is, a personal precept—is

---

8. [*Supra*, p. 138; *De Legibus*, Bk. I, chap. xii.—Tr.]
9. [*Supra*, p. 453; chap. xxxii.—Tr.]

directly applicable to the persons of all subjects, so that it presupposes subjection and is therefore not binding upon aliens even when they are living in the territory affected. On the contrary, it may bind subjects even though they are living outside of that territory, as I have said elsewhere (Vol. V, *De Censuris,* Disp. V, sect. v),[10] in a passage wherein I made many observations on this difficulty. Here, however, I have merely attempted to indicate wherein the doctrine in question is applicable to all human laws, including civil laws.

13. *The third [element, or source of] doubt.* A third point proposed above [Section 1, this Chapter] is whether or not a law prescribing a given form for legal trials, contracts, or other similar acts, and invalidating those carried out in any other form, is efficacious within its territory, even over non-subjects.

An alien making a will or contract ought to observe therein the form prescribed in the locality where he is. Upon this point, it must be briefly said that, in this respect, also, the law must be obeyed in its own territory, and that the act in question must be adjudged in accordance with that law. Such is the opinion held by Bartolus, Jason and others, on the *Code* (I. i. 1); by Felinus, on the *Decretals* (Bk. IV, tit. 1, chap. i, nos. 2 and 23 *et seq.*); and, with excellent comments, by Panormitanus (*Consilia,* Pt. II, no. 52), and Tiraqueau (*De Iure Primogenitorum,* Qq. 46 and 48). The meaning of this statement, indeed, is that an alien who makes a will or contract in a given territory, ought to observe in so doing the form prescribed by the laws of that realm. Therefore, when the said form is not observed, the contract in question is invalidated by the force of the disregarded law, and will be void even though made by an alien; a rule which holds also with regard to the other acts mentioned.

The reason for this fact is that the said law is a rule governing the act itself, in so far as relates to the power of binding by virtue of locality, as I have already pointed out.[11] Therefore, this law obliges all persons in that locality to observe also the form of procedure which it prescribes; and, just as it includes the power to punish, so also it includes the power to

10. [Not included in these *Selections.*—Tr.]
11. [*Supra,* p. 463; § 3, this Chapter.—Tr.]

invalidate. [The truth of] the consequent is made evident by the same reasoning [as that applicable to the antecedent], and also by the fact that the act in question is subject to the law without qualification; and, therefore, that same act is subject in relation to its entire validity. *The confirmation.* The confirmation of this statement is that acts which require a certain customary form and solemnity are not valid without the support of law (*Digest,* II. xiv. 6); and in the situation described above, the law does not support the act, but rather is opposed to the same; therefore, that act will have no validity. Finally, in matters and acts of this kind, the local custom should be observed; and consequently, the local laws should also be observed. This doctrine is supported by those same civil laws to which the authors above cited refer at length; and since these laws fall properly within the field of those authors, I will not tarry longer over a discussion of this point.

14. *Hence it is inferred that a positive law nullifying the validity of the act, consequently nullifies its binding character.* However, from the foregoing remarks, we may infer that the validity of the acts in question, and their binding force in the court of conscience, must be viewed in accordance with laws of this character; since a positive law nullifying such actions has the same effect upon their binding force. The same statement must be made with regard to legal trials; for they should be carried on in accordance with the form and mode prescribed by the laws of the place in which they are conducted; and to these laws, therefore, the alien litigant must conform. Otherwise, that is to say, if his actions are rendered null by the local laws, he will achieve no valid result. And the same holds true with regard to other [acts of a legal nature, on his part]. We assume in all cases, however, that the laws are just and have regard to the property located in that place, and to the acts performed therein; since the said property and acts must be subject, on the ground of locality to the jurisdiction of the territory in question, even if [the person involved] is not subject thereto inherently and in a personal sense, that is to say, not subject in matters apart from the locality; all of which the above-cited authors set forth at greater length.

In what sense an alien is bound to pay taxes. At this point there arises the question of taxes, and whether a foreigner is bound to pay them. This point, also, must be settled according to the principles stated above. For if a tax is owed by reason of property located in a certain place, or an act performed in that place, then there will be an obligation to pay that tax, even on the part of an alien, generally speaking, and assuming that the tax is a just one. But such an obligation does not exist with respect to other taxes, which are of a personal nature. On this entire question, I shall have much to say in Book V.[12]

12. [Not included in these *Selections*.—Tr.]

On the Interpretation, Cessation and Change of Human Laws

CHAPTER IX

Are There Occasions When a Law, as a Whole, Automatically Ceases to Exist, with the Cessation of Its Cause?

1. *A law is of itself perpetual, and it is enacted for the sake of the community.* Since a law is essentially perpetual, and is enacted for the sake of the community, it is manifestly incapable of lapsing through the disappearance of its efficient cause.

For a law does not cease to exist because of the legislator's death, nor because his successor dies, a point that is clearly demonstrated by our earlier discussion;[1] and therefore, it is not abolished by the mere passage of time, since it should [as a general rule] be established as valid for an indefinite period. If, indeed, it is occasionally possible for a law to be enacted with reference to a specified period, that is nevertheless an exceptional occurrence and such a law carries with it—subjoined, as it were—its own abrogation, which is to become effective at the time so specified and which comes under another class of annulment, discussed below [in Chapter xxv].[2]

Again, laws do not lapse from any defect on the part of those for whom they are enacted. For a state or a people, viewed as a community,

---

1. [*De Legibus,* Bk. I, chap. xx, which is not included in these *Selections.*—Tr.]
2. [This Chapter is not included in these *Selections.*—Tr.]

is essentially perpetual, persisting through a continuous process of succession; and though a given state, or people, may suffer complete annihilation, such an event is rare and, practically speaking, does not call for consideration.

Therefore, the only way in which a law can cease to exist is as the result of a change in the object to which it relates. This change, in a physical sense, may occur in any one of various ways; but for present purposes we need to consider only such changes in the subject-matter of laws as concern the essential reason for the imposition of the legal obligation upon that subject-matter. For, assuming that the said reason persists, the [corresponding] law will not cease to exist on the ground [of a change in its object]; and accordingly, it will not in any sense cease to exist, unless it is repealed, since it is derived from no other mutable cause as a factor in its preservation, a point which we have made [above, in Book I, chapter x].[3]

If, however, a change does take place in the object of the law, that object being regarded from the standpoint above specified, then, whatever may be the source of this change, we are confronted by the same question, namely: whether or not, by virtue of the said change in its subject-matter, the law itself ceases to exist; for this is equivalent to inquiring whether, upon the complete disappearance of its entire reason or end, the law also disappears, being altogether extinguished and abolished. But I have employed the phrase, 'upon the complete disappearance of its entire reason'. For we are not at this point concerned with cessation in regard to some particular act, nor with any similar change of a partial character, transpiring only on one occasion, or with respect to a given part of the law's subject-matter and for a given period of time; inasmuch as our discussion of this partial change, contained in the preceding Chapter [Chapter viii],[4] will suffice. It would indeed be possible to consider in this context a different aspect, of partial change, either perpetual change affecting some notable part of the subject-matter of the law, or temporary change affecting the whole of that subject-matter; but I shall deal with these aspects in closing.

3. [This Chapter is not included in these *Selections*.—Tr.]
4. [This Chapter is not included in these *Selections*.—Tr.]

2. *The cessation may be either contrary or negative.* The other distinction, however, which was also laid down in the preceding Chapter[5] (a distinction turning upon the two ways in which the [essential] reason or end of a law may cease to exist, namely, contrary and negative), most emphatically demands consideration at this point: partly in order that we may see whether or not both [modes] may relate to the law as a whole, and partly in order that we may explain which of these [modes] leads to the disappearance of the law itself.

The object of a law, then, is said to alter by contrariety,[6] whenever—as the result of a change in subject-matter or in [external] considerations or circumstances—the observance of the law becomes unjust, or somehow evil; or if its observance is rendered impossible, or at least so difficult and laborious as to be considered impossible for practical purposes and with respect to the community as a whole; or, finally, if such observance comes to be wholly useless and vain from the standpoint of the common good. On the other hand, a negative change will take place when the reason for the enactment of a law has departed entirely from the subject-matter thereof, although, despite the disappearance of that reason, the subject-matter in itself is neither evil, nor impracticable, nor useless, nor unjust.

3. *A change with contrary effect destroys the validity of a law.* Whenever there occurs, then, in the entire subject-matter of a law, a change resulting in a contrary effect,[7] no occasion for doubt or argument arises. For all authorities acknowledge that under such circumstances the law *ipso facto* ceases to exist; inasmuch as these very circumstances divest it of its just character, wherefore it is divested of its character as law, since (as we have often said, quoting Augustine [*On Free Will,* Bk. I, chap. v]) an unjust law is not law.

The antecedent is clearly true. For a law enjoining anything wrong, impossible of fulfilment, or devoid of usefulness for the common good,

---

5. [Not included in these *Selections.*—TR.]

6. [The terminology is technical and impossible to translate without circumlocution. Cessation of law is said to be *contraria,* when its observance would be harmful. It is said to be *negativa,* when the reason for the law has ceased to exist.—REVISER.]

7. [I.e. an effect through which the observance of the law becomes harmful or impossible.—TR.]

is unjust and null, a point which is made manifest by our discussion in Book I;[8] and as the result of a change with contrary effect occurring in the object [of a prescription], the thing prescribed becomes wrong, impossible of fulfilment, or useless, as we have already explained; therefore, if a law should continue to exist [after such a change had transpired], it would then be enjoining something wrong and would thus itself be wrong, or else impossible or useless, wherefore it would be unjust.

Consequently, in the event of such [a change], it is not necessary for the prince to revoke the law before the latter can licitly be disobeyed; nor is it necessary even that the said law be abolished by custom, since its non-observance becomes just prior to the introduction of that custom; and for these reasons I have declared that the law ceases, *ipso facto*, to exist. This truth is, indeed, self-evident whenever the very observance of the law becomes wrong, since the continued existence of an obligation to do wrong is inconceivable.

Moreover, the same assertion applies when [this observance] becomes impossible; for no one is bound to attempt the impossible. Furthermore, in so far as relates to the community, a virtual impossibility suffices [to dissolve the obligation]. Accordingly, when such an impossibility presents itself,[9] the law in question ceases *ipso facto* to exist for the community. Therefore it also ceases to exist for individuals.

The same reasoning is once more applicable when the subject-matter of a law becomes useless and vain from the standpoint of the common good. For, by virtue of that fact, such subject-matter is rendered incapable of imposing a legal obligation upon the community, and consequently, incapable also of imposing it upon individuals.

There must be evidence of such change before the law can lose its force. It is necessary, however, that such a change, effected universally in the entire subject-matter of the law, shall be a clear and evident fact; for, in doubtful cases, a law always retains its rightful force and foothold (so to speak) and the presumption is always in favour of the justice of the law. The chief

---

8. [Chapter ix of the *De Legibus; supra*, p. 116 *et seq.*—Tr.]

9. [This English clause is an interpretation of a single word, *tunc,* in the Latin text.—Tr.]

argument in support of this contention is the fact that, when the change is not evident and clearly apparent to all, a lack of significance and universality in that change is indicated. Therefore, in so far as concerns this point, there seems to be no need of additional distinctions as to greater or lesser doubt. On the contrary, certain knowledge should be absolutely required, although it will suffice if this knowledge is based upon the public and undeviating opinion of the people.

4. Accordingly, we are now confronted solely with a certain difficulty in regard to those occasions on which the essential reason for the law ceases generally to exist, but in a negative sense only. For it would seem that such a cessation does not suffice to destroy the force of the law as a whole.

The first argument in support of this view is as follows: the same proportion and relationship apparently exist between the whole [reason] and the whole [law], as those which exist between the respective parts; but, when a negative[10] cessation takes place in a particular case, in the reason for a law, the obligation imposed by the law does not [on that account] cease to exist; and therefore, when there is a general cessation of the reason, the law as a whole is not thereby destroyed.

Secondly, it is argued that the negative cessation of the reason for a law is not manifestly attended by an immediate cessation of the will of the prince; therefore, the law does not necessarily pass immediately from existence. The consequent is clearly true, because it is from the will of the prince that the law derives its binding force. The antecedent, moreover, has been proved above:[11] for it is possible either that the will of the prince may be motivated at the outset by several reasons, of which the principal one or the one best known—not the whole number—is declared by him; or, at least, his will may be motivated by one reason at the outset, while the motivation is continued later by a different reason, as we remarked previously in our discussion of tributes.[12]

A third argument is this: when the reason or object of a law ceases in a purely negative sense, the law can still be observed without sin;

---

10. [The Latin at this point has *illo modo*, evidently referring to *negatiuè*, above.—Tr.]
11. [*Supra*, pp. 55 *et seq.*; *De Legibus*, Bk. I, chaps. iv and v.—Tr.]
12. [*De Legibus*, Bk. V, chap. xiii, which is not included in these *Selections*.—Tr.]

consequently, by virtue of the same binding force, it should be observed as long as it has not [positively] been revoked. The antecedent is an assumption based on the very meaning of the terms involved. The truth of the consequent is proved, indeed, by the fact that under the circumstances described no peril is involved in the observance of the law, whereas great peril may attend its transgression, partly because the cessation of the prince's will cannot immediately become a certainty, and partly because grave moral evils might ensue if so extensive a licence were granted to the people.

Finally, one could cite, in support of the same view, those writers who declare that a law does not cease to exist although the reason for the law may disappear. To these authors I have alluded at the beginning of the preceding Chapter [Bk. VI, chap. viii].[13]

5. *On what occasions a law ceases to exist upon the disappearance of the reason for the law.* Nevertheless, the commonly accepted opinion is that a law ceases to exist, when the reason for the law disappears in a general way, that is to say, more frequently than not in regard to the community as a whole.

This opinion is, first of all, the view of those persons who assert that, when the reason for a law disappears in a particular case (even though this cessation be purely negative), the obligation imposed by the law also disappears, in so far as concerns that particular case. For these same authorities are compelled, *a fortiori,* to make a similar assertion with respect to total cessation. Accordingly, we may cite Panormitanus, on the *Decretals* (Bk. III, tit. XLIX, chap. viii [, no. 38]) in support of the said opinion. Innocent, Antoninus and other writers mentioned in the preceding Chapter[14] clearly indicate, in their comments on this passage, that they support the same view. The point is more clearly made, to be sure, by Peter Ledesma ([*Theologiae Moralis,*] Pt. II, chap. iv, qu. xvii, art. 2, 3d doubt, ad 4 and qu. xviii to 12th doubt after the second conclusion, and 14th doubt after the third conclusion), and by Covarruvias (on *Decretals,* Bk. IV, pt. II, § 9, no. 8 and *ibid.,* Bk. III, tit. XXVI, chap. x, no. 9) where he cites Fortunius (*De Ultimo*

---

13. [Not included in these *Selections.*—TR.]
14. [Not included in these *Selections.*—TR.]

Fine Utriusque Iuris Canonici et Civilis, Illat. xv and xvi). Castro (*De Potestate Legis Poenalis,* Bk. I, chap. v, docum. 3) upholds a like opinion, as do Cajetan (on II.–II, qu. 147, art. 5, and in other passages above cited) and, in general, the commentators on St. Thomas (I.–II, qu. 96, art. 6). Soto expresses himself in a similar manner, but he appends a limiting condition which it will be necessary for us to consider before recording his true argument and solution.

6. A question may be raised, then, as to whether, when the reason for a law ceases in a general way to exist, we should conceive of the law as also ceasing to exist, *ipso facto,* in such a way that its non-observance on the part of the subjects would be licit, nor would it be necessary for them to await a proclamation or revocation by the prince; or whether [, on the other hand,] we should say that the law becomes void for the reason that with the disappearance of its cause, the prince is bound to abolish that law.

For the remaining authorities (with the exception of Soto), even though they may not expressly bring up this point, are clearly referring to cessation *ipso facto.* Confirmation of their view[15] may be found in the fact that if that view were not correct,[16] the disappearance of the law in this special mode would not differ from a revocation thereof; rather, at most, a legitimate cause for abrogating the law would be assigned in consequence of the said [mode of disappearance], even as many other causes may be assigned. A further confirmation is the fundamental assumption that an effect ceases with the cessation of its cause; an assumption which is understood to refer to cessation *ipso facto,* as we deduce from a chapter of the *Decretals* (Bk. II, tit. xxiv, chap. xxvi). Thus the explanation of this cessation is customarily concerned with the true and adequate cause on which the effect depends for its continued existence, in accordance with the purport of the Gloss on that passage, and more clearly with other parts of the Gloss (on *Decretals,* Bk. I, tit. ix, chap. xi, word *cessante;* on *Decretum,* Pt. I, dist. lxi, can. viii, § 2 (*Sed sciendum*), word *causa;* on *ibid.,* Pt. II, causa i, qu. vii, can. vii, and the text itself). But when we speak in the present discussion of the cessation of the cause, or reason, or end of a law, we are speaking [precisely] of

15. [Simply *hoc,* in the Latin.—Tr.]
16. [Simply *alias,* in the Latin.—Tr.]

the adequate cause; otherwise, it would not be said, that the cause ceases in an absolute sense. Therefore, when this adequate cause ceases, the law also should cease, *ipso facto,* for both the will of the prince and the utility of the law are dependent upon the said cause. Accordingly, if such a reason had not existed from the beginning, the law could not have been set up justly; and therefore, it cannot justly be kept in existence independently of that reason.

7. Nevertheless, Soto clearly supports the contrary view. For he says (*De Iustitia et Iure,* Bk. I, qu. vi, art. viii): 'If the cause has totally ceased to exist, then the law also should cease to exist; nevertheless, it does not lose its force until it is abrogated by the prince or by custom.'[17] It is evident that Soto is speaking here of the negative cessation of the cause, since he denies that its occurrence with regard to a particular instance would suffice to deprive the law of its binding force in that instance. In another passage (*ibid.,* Bk. III, qu. iv, art. v, ad 1) he practically repeats this assertion, saying: 'For though it may be incumbent upon the prince to change this [law], it is not permissible for his subjects to act in opposition thereto, so long as the natural law concedes permission (that is to say, permits the thing legally prescribed), unless [the precept in question] has become contrary to natural law.'[18] Soto, then, does not believe that a law ceases to exist *ipso facto,* before abrogation, so long as the reason therefor does not cease in such a way that the thing prescribed becomes contrary to the law of nature.

To be sure, he does not state the basis of his opinion, but he does indicate that, as long as the subject-matter of a law is capable of involving a binding obligation, so long will the law endure, provided it is not repealed. Yet the subject-matter of the law does not become in general incapable of involving such an obligation simply because the reason for the law ceases to exist. For this subject-matter may [still] be not evil, and [even] useful to the state, though it may not be such as it was formerly nor [absolutely] necessary, as it was before; because this [change in the reason] does not sufficiently justify the immediate and necessary conclusion that the said law is abrogated.

---

17. [This quotation, as given by Suárez, varies slightly from Soto's text.—Tr.]
18. [This quotation, as given by Suárez, varies slightly from Soto's text.—Tr.]

A confirmation of the foregoing argument may be derived from the objections [to the opposing view]. For it is contrary to a due regard for order that the law laid down by a superior should be disobeyed without his consent, as long as it is licitly and easily possible to obey that law, inasmuch as such disobedience may give rise also to scandal and disturbances or to fraud within the state. A middle course, then, may be pursued in our deductions, as follows: when the cause or reason of the law ceases in a general sense, the law also ceases, in itself and *ipso facto;* but, in spite of this cessation, the subjects cannot licitly begin to act in opposition to the said law before the prince has proclaimed its cessation, because this limitation is expedient for the common good. We arrive at that conclusion in the same way as we arrived at the assertion made by us in the preceding Book,[19] namely, that a penalty is often incurred *ipso facto,* but has no binding force before a declaratory decree is issued.

8. *The subject-matter of human law is twofold.* In order to expound my opinion, I assume from what has been said above that the subject-matter of human law is twofold.[20] For one phase of that subject-matter is of such a character that, viewed in itself, it is righteous and involves an act of virtue. Examples of this sort are the precept on fasting, that on praying, and so forth. The other phase is in itself of a neutral character. Examples of such subject-matter are the bearing or not bearing of arms; the taking of this or that object from a given place, and similar instances.

In consequence of this dual subject-matter, there arises another difference, relating to the laws themselves. For, inasmuch as all human laws establish some deed of commission or of omission as coming under the head of a given virtue or vice (a fact which we have already pointed out), consequently, when the subject-matter of a law is essentially and of itself endowed with a righteous character, it is established proximately through the said law under the head of that virtue to which of itself and intrinsically it pertains. For example, fasting is put into the category of temperance, while omitting to fast is intemperance; and other examples could be pointed out, in like manner. Moreover, the same holds true in all cases in

---

19. [Not included in these *Selections.*—Tr.]
20. [*Supra,* pp. 50 *et seq.; De Legibus,* Bk. I, chap. iii, §§ 17 *et seq.*—Tr.]

which a standard of virtue may, through the efficacy of a law, be founded
upon such subject-matter. A case in point is that of the law fixing a given
price. For, prior to the establishment of the law, this price did not represent a standard of justice; but after it has been determined by the law, it
does embody such a standard; and, therefore, the act prescribed by the
said law is put into the category of justice, while the violation of the law
becomes an act of injustice.

On the other hand, when an act is itself of a neutral character and is
not prescribed by any law that makes of it an intrinsic standard of virtue,
but is legally prescribed or prohibited simply because of its utility in the
attainment of some extrinsic end—when such is the case, all the righteousness of the act must be ascribed to the said end, on the basis of which
righteousness[21] the act becomes in its turn obligatory and necessary, by the
force of the law.

Thus we come at length to the conclusion that, in so far as concerns the
laws of the first group,[22] the extrinsic end of the subject-matter involved
in a precept is never adequate for the law; since intrinsic righteousness and
the characteristic of virtue are directed always to a proximate and intrinsic
end, and to an end, moreover, which is in itself sufficient, though every
extrinsic end cease to exist. As for the laws of the second group,[23] however,
the extrinsic end is [necessarily] adequate [to justify the various precepts],
inasmuch as their subject-matter is not essentially and for its own sake an
adequate [justification] of these precepts, being adequate only because of
its utility in regard to some extrinsic end.

9. *A law prescribing an [essentially] virtuous act does not cease to exist, upon
the disappearance of an extrinsic end.* Accordingly, I hold, first: that a law
prescribing an essentially good act, establishing it as falling intrinsically
within the subject-matter of virtue, does not cease to exist because some
extrinsic end of the law wholly disappears; even though [this end] may be
all that is required in so far as the legislator's intention is concerned, and

---

21. [Assuming that the Latin word *illa* is not a misprint for *illo*. If we read *illo,* the
translation will perhaps be smoother: 'on the basis of which', referring to the extrinsic
end.—Tr.]

22. [I.e. those laws whose subject-matter is in itself a standard of right conduct.—Tr.]

23. [I.e. those laws whose subject-matter is in itself of a neutral character.—Tr.]

may perhaps have been so regarded [by him] that he would not have made the law independently thereof.

A proof of this assertion is supplied by the argument set forth in defence of Soto's opinion. For, despite the disappearance of every extrinsic end, the subject-matter of such a law remains in itself righteous, and suitable for law by the sole force of the intrinsic end involved, that is to say, because of the righteousness of the act in question; furthermore, this intrinsic end is always sought by the legislator, since he based the necessity and means for the said act upon this kind of virtue; consequently, despite the disappearance of every extrinsic[24] end, the law possesses a sufficient justification for its continued existence; and, therefore, it will not be rendered void.

A confirmation of the foregoing argument will be found (if the matter is carefully examined) in the fact that, under the circumstances described, the adequate cause of the law does not cease. For the most potent cause, end and proximate reason (so to speak) of the said law, consist in the righteousness of the act which it prescribes. Therefore, there is no reason why the law should cease to exist.

Finally, as long as the prescribed subject-matter together with the formal reason therefor shall endure, the obligation imposed by the precept remains. For, as St. Thomas has declared (I.–II, qu. 100, art. 9, ad 2), what the legislator purposes to prescribe, is one thing, while the end for which he purposes to prescribe it is another; and accordingly, just as the precept is of itself binding with respect to the former, and not with respect to the latter, even so, conversely, as long as the former endures—and provided that it shall continue to include a reason sufficient to justify the precept, this precept, too, will endure, though its extrinsic end may cease to exist.

The point may be clarified by means of examples. For though a law on fasting be established for the purpose of mortifying the flesh, and though a community be conceived of which does not need such a means for the attainment of that end inasmuch as it possesses many other means [for the same] or a similar purpose, this law—I repeat—will nevertheless be binding, a fact not open to dispute; but if the act prescribed by it should

---

24. [Reading *extrinseco* with the 1856 edition, not *intrinseco*, which is the term here used. The context clearly indicates that the former reading is correct.—Tr.]

cease to be an act of temperance, as might occur in a case of extreme necessity, then, indeed, the law would lapse. Similarly, if some law should fix the price of wheat, the binding force of that law would endure, even if all the extrinsic reasons or other advantages thereof should disappear, as long as that price continued to be equitably just in the sense that it did not become manifestly inequitable; but if, on the other hand, the situation should alter to such a degree that the sum fixed would be manifestly unjust, the law would cease to exist. Similar illustrations could be drawn from other situations.

10. *When the adequate end of a law, both extrinsic and intrinsic, ceases to exist, the law itself ceases.* Accordingly, one infers that if the adequate end, both intrinsic and extrinsic, of the law in question should cease to exist, then the law itself would cease. However, careful reflection will show that in such a case the end does not simply disappear in a negative sense, but is transformed with contrary effect, since the subject-matter does not retain its virtuous character, but rather becomes vicious, so that it is incapable of serving as subject-matter for a binding law. Evidence confirming this assertion is found in the fact that, under the circumstances described, the binding force of the law will lapse not only in general but also in particular cases, with respect to the act or the subject-matter involved. Accordingly, it also happens, that in such a case the law ceases *ipso facto,* without any other revocation[25] or declaration [of its cessation]. For it lacks a foundation, nor can its binding force be applied to unsuitable subject-matter.

A common example is offered by laws imposing tributes for certain works or ends. When such a work or end has been accomplished, the law of itself ceases to exist, because the reason for the law then ceases, not merely in a negative sense, but even with contrary effect, inasmuch as the tribute becomes from that moment unjust. When, on the other hand, the intrinsic end does not cease to exist, although the extrinsic ends disappear, then just as the law itself does not *ipso facto* come to an end, even so it is not necessary that this law be abrogated by the prince. For the righteousness of the subject-matter may suffice to sustain the law; unless the latter

---

25. [Reading *revocatione,* in accordance with the Paris edition of 1856, not *recordatione,* the reading of our own Latin text.—REVISER.]

becomes from some other cause harmful to the state, or intolerable; since in that case there might be another reason creating an obligation to repeal the law, or that law might even come to an end of itself, provided that its harmfulness and oppressiveness are of a general character and excessive in their degree. For such a cessation, as is clearly evident, would be not of a negative, but of a contrary nature.

The difference between a law and a precept. Furthermore, and lastly, I must note with respect to this [first] assertion[26] that it refers to law in the strict sense of the term. For in so far as concerns precepts laid down by an individual, solely by virtue of the obedience due to him, these may frequently be such that, when their end or cause ceases to exist, the obligation imposed by them also ceases, even though the act prescribed is in some other respect intrinsically righteous, as in the case of fasting or praying. For example, if a superior should prescribe that a fast be observed once a week during a particular month; if it is evident that the precept is imposed because of some special need or occasion; and if this need or occasion comes to an end before the month expires, then we consider that the precept, too, has ceased to exist. For, in the case of such precepts, the whole reason for prescribing, consists in the extrinsic end involved, not in the intrinsic[27] righteousness, although the latter is presupposed. Evidence of this truth is afforded by the fact that the transgression of such a precept is not an act of intemperance, for example, but one of disobedience; whereas we find a different situation in the case of a true law. Such a law aims primarily at the rectitude of virtue under which the prescribed act is classified as if by its very essence.

11. *A law prescribing an act of a neutral character, for the sake of an extrinsic end, itself ceases to exist when its adequate end ceases.*[28] I hold, secondly: that when an act of a neutral character in itself is prescribed by a law for the sake of an extrinsic end, then, if the adequate end of the said law ceases, in a general sense, to exist, the law itself ceases *per se* and *ipso facto,* as does the obligation which it imposes.

---

26. [*Vide supra,* p. 486; the first sentence of Section 9 of this Chapter.—Tr.]

27. [Reading *intrinseca* for *extrinseca.*—Reviser.]

28. [Reading *cessat,* with the Paris edition of 1856, not *cesset,* with our own Latin text; and omitting again, in accordance with the 1856 edition, the final and redundant *lex* of our text.—Tr.]

The reason for this fact is that, in the situation described, the negative cessation of the end is transformed into a contrary effect, inasmuch as it unfits the subject-matter in question for law. This assertion is proved as follows: an act which is in itself of a neutral character can never be prescribed of itself or for its own sake; for an act of that sort, considered as such, is not of itself desirable from the standpoint of righteousness; on the contrary, if it is thus prescribed [for its own sake], it will not be rightly prescribed; moreover, it is still more certain that such an act does not afford subject-matter for law, unless it is prescribed for the sake of some common advantage which it may promote or because of which it may be necessary; but when the end of the law ceases in a general sense to exist, the act in question necessarily becomes useless with respect to the common good; therefore, it becomes for this very reason incapable of being rendered obligatory by human law, and the law itself consequently ceases *ipso facto*. The consequents and the major premiss are quite clearly true in the light of our previous remarks. The truth of the minor premiss, moreover, becomes evident through our hypothesis. For we have assumed that the adequate end for the sake of which the act was prescribed, ceases to exist. Yet it is impossible that this should occur save [for one of two reasons]: either because the good which was the proximate aim of the act in question is no longer advantageous for the common good of the state; or else because the act itself is no longer useful with respect to such advantage. But in either case the act becomes useless and vain from the standpoint of the common good, and consequently ceases to be fit subject-matter for law.

It may be objected that, even though the act be useless with respect to the end sought by the law, it may possibly be useful for the attainment of other ends. My reply is that this [objection] is of an incidental and individual nature, since, in so far as concerned the aforesaid act, the law has had regard only to the aforesaid justification of advantageousness and public benefit, so that consequently, when the justification has been removed, the subject-matter of the law ceases to exist and therefore the law, too, ceases. For even though the act in question may be useful from some other standpoint, the law concerning the act was not established with a view to that [other] end; and accordingly, such utility is not regarded as necessary to the state until a law has been established with respect to the said act and in consideration of the said end.

12. *A decree of the prince is not required in order that such a law shall cease to be binding.* From the foregoing, it follows, first, that a situation of this kind does not require a decree of the prince, in order that the law may permissibly be disobeyed after having ceased in the manner described, since that law fails, *ipso facto.* The sole requirement, then, is that this cessation shall be a matter of clear and public knowledge owing to evidence of a fact generally established throughout the state or community. For, by virtue of the very fact that the law ceases to exist in the aforesaid manner, it is no longer law; consequently, it is not of itself binding; and therefore, in order that its cessation may be effective with respect to the community, it suffices if that cessation is publicly known to the said community.

Nor does any sufficient reason arise, which would make it necessary to await a decree of the prince. For [such a decree, if] it [were required at all,] would be required either as an instrument of repeal, which is not the case, since the law has passed away of itself; or else it would be required as an authentic proclamation, an alternative which it is also impossible to support satisfactorily, inasmuch as this act of proclamation is not necessary in the nature of things, nor do we find it specifically prescribed by positive law. Moreover, one should not, in this connexion, compare the cessation of a law with the incurring of a penalty. For a penalty by its very nature is violent and is imposed from without, wherefore it inherently requires the action or concurrence of a judge, unless the contrary has been expressly provided by law. Consequently, a penalty is not incurred *ipso facto,* independently of any legal declaration thereof; and even if it were incurred *ipso facto,* that would not prevent the passing of a declaratory sentence regarding the crime, save in cases in which the law does [specifically] preclude such a sentence or in which there is some other manifest [cause precluding it], since there always exists a presumption in favour of the accused to the effect that he is not liable to a penalty until he has been condemned. In such a case, however, the cessation of the law is not a violent occurrence; on the contrary, by means of that cessation the state is restored (so to speak) to its pristine status and liberty, while [the law] gives place to that [free status]; and therefore, there is no necessity for a decree of the sort described, to serve as a declaratory sentence.

It will be objected that [a declaration] is required by way of promulgation, for promulgation is necessary in the annulment of a law that is being revoked by the prince. I reply that the principle involved in this case is different; for revocation depends upon the will of the prince, which must be revealed to all, whereas the cessation of a law when the cause of the law ceases to exist, depends not upon the prince's will but upon the very fact [that the cause disappears], so that it suffices [in this latter situation] if the bare fact is known to all. For example, if a tax for the purpose of building a bridge has been imposed by law, and if it is a matter of public knowledge that the bridge is completed and no more is being expended upon it, such a situation constitutes a sufficient promulgation of the fact that the tax has ceased to be imposed; and other, similar examples might be adduced. Public and sufficiently certain knowledge, then, of a general cessation on the part of the cause is all that is required [as a promulgation of the law's cessation]. And [, at the same time,] this is a minimum requirement. For I do not think it would suffice [as a promulgation] if [the cessation of the cause] were known to this or that particular individual, since the law does not cease to exist with respect to such individuals until it ceases with respect to the whole community, and since, in order that the law may cease for the community, it is necessary that the cessation of its cause shall have taken place in such a way that the fact can be made manifest to the community and becomes accordingly a matter of public knowledge.

The foregoing, moreover, has reference especially to cases in which the observance of a law is becoming unjust, for in such cases the fact of the law's cessation is more clearly evident. Furthermore, a law may be described as unjust, not only when it causes specific harm, but also when it is wholly useless and unjustified by reason.

13. *A distinction made by the jurists is examined.* Secondly, the remarks made above may serve to show how acceptable that distinction is, which some jurists have drawn, between a law made for the purpose of doing away with the ills that frequently follow upon a given fact, and [, on the other hand,] a law made essentially for the sake of some [positive] good and utility. For these jurists hold that laws of the former kind cease to exist, with the cessation of the [possibility of such] ills; whereas laws of the latter kind by no means cease, even though the reason for their utility may do so.

This is the view suggested by the Gloss (on *Decretals,* Bk. II, tit. xxiv, chap. xxvi, word *cessante,* near the beginning [word *causa,* near the end]). Proof with regard to the first class [of laws] is afforded by that text and by the example of an oath, which is prohibited solely because of the danger of perjury and is therefore permissible when that danger ceases to exist. Proof as to the second class, on the other hand, is based upon laws in two chapters of the *Decretum* (Pt. II, causa xxxii, qu. i, can. ii; *ibid.,* qu. vii, can. xxvii), which are in no wise pertinent, since they deal with matrimony, an indissoluble bond to which a different process of reasoning applies. The same distinction is suggested by Navarrus (in *Summa,* Chap. xvi, nos. 36 and 37) in a passage where he agrees with Cajetan that clandestine marriage may have been permissible (at least, before the Council of Trent)[29] upon the cessation of the possibility of consequent ills that caused its prohibition; while he nevertheless declares that the obligation imposed by a law does not cease to exist [merely] because its end ceases with respect to a particular case, if that end was a good to be acquired through a means prescribed by the law. Navarrus, then, speaks in this passage not only of the general cessation of a law, but also of cessation in a particular case, as I have noted above.

14.[30] But, as a matter of fact, and formally speaking, there would seem to be no difference [between the two classes of laws in question]. For if a law is laid down for the purpose of avoiding certain ills, the object of that law is the warding off of the ills. Accordingly, the same reasoning applies to the cessation of that object, and to other cases, whether in general or in particular. And therefore, the only possible difference is a material one, so to speak. For a law established solely for the purpose of avoiding certain ills, does not as a rule prescribe any act for its own sake and because of its [essential] goodness, nor does such a law prohibit any act because of its [essential] evil; rather [is it established] in order to avert an occasion for evil; and under these circumstances, when the object [of the law] lapses in a general and negative sense, it lapses with contrary effect, also, since the act in question becomes vain and unfitted to be the subject-matter of law.

29. [A decree of the Council of Trent, usually referred to as *Tametsi* (Session XXIV, chap. i), invalidated clandestine marriages.—Tr.]

30. [This Section is incorrectly numbered '41' in the Latin text.—Tr.]

Thus we have elsewhere remarked [*De Voto,* Bk. IV, chap. xviii, sect. 4],[31] in connexion with a vow to abstain from entering a certain house (a vow taken in order to avoid an occasion [of evil]), that when this occasion ceases to threaten, the vow is no longer binding. For in such a case, abstention from entrance into the house is a matter of indifference and has no religious significance. The same reasoning, then, will apply in due proportion with regard to a law.

To be sure, a law which prescribes a given act both for its own sake and also in order to promote some good end does not immediately lapse when that end ceases to exist, since in the act itself there may persist the intrinsic righteousness which is the [partial] cause of its prescription. If, on the other hand, [this intrinsic virtue] is not found to exist in the act—which is, on the contrary, of an essentially indifferent nature—then, certainly, we must come to the same conclusion regarding the law which prescribes such an act in order to achieve some good, and the law prohibiting an act in order to avoid some evil. This is sufficiently clear from the foregoing discussion. Conversely, when a law which prescribes or prohibits anything for the purpose of avoiding an evil, does involve subject-matter that is good and advantageous in itself apart from the avoidance of the evil—in that case—the said law would not lapse, even if the necessity for avoiding the ill should cease to exist. For all our remarks in connexion with the first assertion would be applicable in such a situation.

A distinction which should be carefully considered.[32] With reference to this point, careful consideration should also be given to the following distinction: whether a thing is prohibited because of the peril [inherent in it], or solely because of its [possible] future effect. For ordinarily a prohibition is laid down on account of a danger which is inherent in the prohibited action itself, so that, even though it is clear and certain that there will be no future effect—that is to say, none of an injurious nature— nevertheless, the obligation and effect attendant upon the obligation will not cease to exist, since the act remains always inherently capable

---

31. [Not included in these *Selections.*—Tr.]

32. [The Latin subheading, partially illegible in our own Latin text, should read: *Distinctio diligenter notanda.*—Tr.]

of causing the harm in question, a fact which I have discussed at greater length in the preceding Book.[33]

Consequently, the example of clandestine marriage, adduced by Cajetan and Navarrus, is not in my opinion acceptable. For peril is so bound up with that act as to be inseparable therefrom both in general and in particular, and therefore, the obligation imposed by that prohibition never lapses, since it is an unquestionable fact that one ought to guard against all evils. Accordingly, in the sense that marriages made in these days in the presence of the parish priest and of witnesses may be clandestine because of failure to publish the banns in accordance with the prescription laid down in the *Decretals* (Bk. IV, tit. III, chap. iii, § 1), such marriages are illicit, even when the object of the precept prohibiting them ceases, in a negative sense, to exist; unless other legitimate causes present themselves, giving rise to a judgment by *epieikeia*,[34] to the effect that the precept regarding that incidental rite is not binding on a given occasion and at a given time. It is thus, indeed, that Navarrus [*Summa*, Chap. xvi, nos. 36 and 37], finally seems to explain the example in question.

15. *A statement as to when the obligation of fraternal correction lapses.* Thirdly, the foregoing incidentally does away with a difficulty, the solution of which was postponed in the preceding Chapter for this context, a difficulty relating to the precept of fraternal correction. The obligation imposed by this precept ceases, even in a particular case, upon the cessation of the hope that correction will be beneficial and, accordingly, through a negative cessation of the reason for the law; so that, in view of the fact that this hope does ordinarily cease in general, we are [apparently] obliged to say, that the precept in its entirety ceases to exist.

To this statement, B. Medina [on I.–II, qu. xcvi, art. 6], Ledesma [*Theologiae Moralis*, Pt. II, chap. iv] and Covarruvias [on *Decretals*, Bk. IV, *De Sponsalibus et Matrimoniis*, Pt. II, § 9, no. 8 and *ibid.*, Bk. III, tit. xxvi, chap. x, no. 9] reply that the law of fraternal correction was laid down for the private good of individuals, and therefore may lapse with respect to individuals whenever the end thereof ceases in a particular instance, even

33. [Bk. VI, chap. xxiii, which is not included in these *Selections.*—Tr.]
34. [I.e. equitable interpretation.—Tr.]

though it be merely a negative cessation; whereas this is not the case with respect to laws whose end is general and universal, such laws, for example, as the precept on fasting and others of a similar nature.

To tell the truth, however, I do not sufficiently grasp the meaning of this distinction, nor its rational basis, since all laws exist for the sake of the common good, though this good may be sought and attained, not directly in connexion with the community, but in connexion with individual cases. For the law of fasting is of this nature, being directed to the good of the Church, yet its utility applies to individuals. And so it is that the precept of fraternal correction, too, is a common precept, while its fruit is nevertheless sought among individuals and in particular cases. Accordingly, there is no difference [in this respect] between the two precepts.

Wherefore, it is easier to reply—as Ledesma also (*ibid.*) briefly indicates—that, in fraternal correction, no part is played by *epieikeia,* nor by a cessation of the obligation involved, resulting from the cessation of the object [of the precept]; for this is an affirmative precept, not continuously binding, nor is there a specified occasion on which it binds, and without this specification, *epieikeia* (as I have above remarked) can play no part. Thus, the obligation imposed by the affirmative precept of fraternal correction does not cease to exist, when there is no hope of fruitful results; rather, this obligation—which is in itself indefinite—is simply not definitely laid down for that occasion, since right reason dictates that it is not binding then, inasmuch as the time is not advantageous, nor is the subject properly adapted. Even so, the precept of almsgiving binds one to succour the needy; and nevertheless, if that succour should be harmful, or if it should be clear and certain that the person in need would not profit by the alms, the precept would fail to be binding, not through a process of cessation nor through *epieikeia,* but because such an occasion would not be one for which the precept in question—being a natural precept, not merely one of positive law—is binding. And I must add that in so far as the reason for the precept can be said to cease in such a case, it ceases not merely negatively, but also by contrariety; for under these circumstances correction would not be an act of virtue, but would be idle, useless, and possibly harmful, rather than beneficial, to one's neighbour.

16. Finally, from the foregoing remarks, it will be easy to dispose of the reasons for doubt laid down at the outset [Sect. 4, *supra,* p. 481].

The first of these turned upon the objection that the preceding discussion apparently led one to conclude that no difference exists between the general, and the particular cessation of a law, when such a cessation is due to the fact that the object [sought by the law] has ceased in a purely negative sense and proportionately, that is to say, in general and in particular; a conclusion which would nevertheless seem to be opposed to the commonly accepted opinion already set forth. The inference is clearly true, because a law never ceases to exist generally as a result of a purely negative cessation of its object; rather must this object cease in a contrary sense, at least, in the sense of becoming a useless act and consequently unfit to be the subject-matter of a law; and if the object does cease thus in a particular case, the obligation imposed by the law will also cease in that particular case; therefore, [. . .]

The difference between the cessation of a law in general, and its cessation in particular. [To this objection,] I reply that the difference consists in the following facts: when the adequate object of a law ceases in the manner already described, the absolute reason for establishing the law will cease in consequence, since this cessation of the object is necessarily attended by the loss of all utility for the purposes of law, on the part of the subject-matter; whereas, on the other hand, if the general object of the law persists, even though it may cease with respect to a particular act, the reason for a general law will endure unimpaired, that reason which has regard, not for individual occasions, but for what occurs most frequently; so that, even if the said object ceases negatively in a particular case, the act prescribed does not become useless, nor does the reason for establishing the law cease by contrariety in that case, since this general reason may impel one to the act, for the sake of the general good and of conformity to the said law and to the whole body [under that law], as has been explained in the preceding chapter.

17. As to the second reason [for doubt—Sect. 4, *supra*], relating to the will of the prince, a reply is easily drawn from our previous remarks. For when the reason for a law ceases in general, the law is rendered useless by that very cessation, and its subject-matter becomes incapable of causing a

just obligation; so that the will of the legislator must necessarily cease in consequence, partly because he has willed to impose a binding obligation justly and to such an extent as is licitly possible (no other presumption being acceptable), and partly because, once the subject-matter of the law has changed, he would not be able to impose such an obligation [through that law], even if he did so will. And if it is assumed (an additional point which was brought up in connexion with this same argument) that when the first reason ceases to exist another reason takes its place, as is ordinarily held to occur in the case of taxes, the reply to this is that the first law has ceased to exist, and no other law has been made. Consequently, if the prince wishes to make the act in question obligatory on the basis of a new reason that arises, it will be necessary for him to legislate anew, or promulgate his wish to this effect; otherwise, and merely by the force of that earlier law alone, his subjects cannot be bound.

As to the third reason [for doubt—Sect. 4, *supra*, p. 481], either this constitutes a proof of the first assertion [Sect. 2, *supra*, p. 479], if, when the extrinsic end of the law ceases to exist, its subject-matter still retains a righteous character and is of itself advantageous for the common good; or else, if this same reason is applied to the occasions when the object of the law ceases absolutely, we deny that it is possible for the law to be obeyed licitly under such circumstances, since such obedience would be a vain and idle action; and even if the act itself could be performed with rectitude, owing to some other and specific benefit sought by the agent, that is too extrinsic and incidental a consideration to result in the perseverance of the original law, which did not impose any obligation to act in that manner or for the sake of that end. Neither can such a non-observance of the law—which has now manifestly and publicly ceased to exist—be attended by moral ills; just as such ills need not be feared in consequence of the non-observance of a law that is manifestly and publicly unjust, from which greater ills would result if, on the contrary, the observance thereof were obligatory.

18. *A law may be rendered useless in regard to one of its parts, and not in regard to another part.* Finally, it is possible to form in accordance with what we have said as to the total cessation of a law, a judgment regarding the cessation of a given part of a law, in so far as that part relates not to a particular person or case but to a whole community.

For a law may prescribe many things or comprise various members, and may become useless in regard to one of these factors while it does not become useless in regard to the others. And in such a case, the same judgment applies to this part, whose reason has ceased to exist (provided that it is separable from the remainder of the law), as that which applies to a law in its entirety [when the reason therefor disappears]. For the same argument holds [in the two cases]. In fact, that law, which seems to be a single unit, is actually multiple, and thus it is that one of these various laws ceases to exist without a corresponding cessation of the others. If, on the other hand, a law should embrace many factors in such a way that they were mutually inseparable and that there existed a practically indivisible obligation, since the good involved [depends on] the whole cause, and evil would result from defect [in the observance of any member[35]—if, I say, the law were of this sort]—it would be necessary to consider carefully the question of whether or not a whole law becomes unjust or useless, or more harmful than beneficial, on account of a defect in one of its parts. If this is the case,[36] the law as a whole will cease to exist. But if, despite that defect, the law remains just, and more beneficial than harmful, it will not cease *ipso facto* before being repealed.

When is a law said to be suspended, but not abolished? We must also take into consideration the fact that if a law is to cease in an absolute sense, it is necessary that the reason for the law cease in a general sense, permanently. For if that reason seems to lapse thus for a limited time only, then the result will be a suspension of the obligation imposed by the law, rather than the extinction of the law itself; because the latter becomes useless or unjust, not absolutely, but merely for that temporary period. Accordingly, a limited cause [of cessation] produces a limited effect, so that the law is suspended, but not extinguished.

---

35. [Suárez is here applying rather loosely the principle that regulates human actions. The morality of an act depends on object, motive, and circumstances. That an act may be good, all three determinants must be not opposed to rectitude. If any one of the three is evil, the act is evil. The principle is enunciated, *Bonum ex integra causa, malum ex quocumque defectu.*—Reviser.]

36. [A free translation of *& tunc.*—Tr.]

Of Unwritten Law Which Is Called Custom

[INTRODUCTION]

Thus far we have confined our discussion principally to written law. At this point, however, we must turn to a particular study of custom in so far as it embodies law or brings it into being. This order Gregory IX followed in the First Book of the *Decretals;* treating first of constitutions, then of rescripts, and finally of custom. For even if we grant a priority in time to custom over written law, nevertheless it is the more reasonable procedure to take up the written law first, since its matter is more definitely fixed and its field more thoroughly explored.

It is to be added that among human laws those in a written form are earlier than those in an unwritten one, even though many jurists, whose doctrine Rochus Curtius follows in his treatise *De Consuetudine* (at the beginning),[1] assume it as a certainty that consuetudinary law arose first.

For even though men took up a life in common without laws before such were written—as is clear from the *Digest* (I. ii. 2)—it is to be inferred that they held in the place of law, not custom, but rather the personal rule of the king, which is neither law nor custom. This, in fact, is suggested by the language of the *Digest* (*ibid.*), but from the *Institutes* (I. ii, §§ 9–10) it may be inferred that the consuetudinary law was of earlier date among the

---

1. [In the Preface.—REVISER.]

Lacedemonians than the written law among the Athenians, from whom the civil law took its origin. Whatever may be the truth on this point, it is now clear that custom is often of earlier origin than written law and that frequently it is also more recent.

It is certain, in any case, that the written is the principal form of law, and that from it custom derives in great measure its force and meaning, as is clear from the *Decretals* (Bk. I, tit. iv, chap. xi) and what is there noted. This Book, then, finds its proper place here after what has preceded. In it we have followed the usual arrangement: we shall begin with a definition of custom in the light of its necessary conditions and its causes; we shall then discuss its effects; we shall conclude by treating of its abrogation or alteration.

CHAPTER I

The Definition of Custom, Usage or General Conduct, Forum, and Stylus,[2] and How Each Differs from Written Law

1. Custom, according to Isidore (*Etymologies,* Bk. II, chap. x and Bk. V, chap. iii), is a kind of law instituted by general conduct, which is accepted as law when law is lacking. He seems to have derived his definition from the passage in Tertullian (*On the Soldier's Chaplet* [Chap. iv]): 'In civil matters custom is accepted as law when the latter is lacking.'

A threefold difficulty with respect to this definition immediately presents itself. First of all, as to the generic classification: for custom would appear to belong rather to the domain of fact than to that of law; it is, then, not a law, but a fact or action frequently repeated. For this reason, Isidore immediately adds [*Etymologies,* Bk. II, chap. x] that custom is called such 'because it is in common usage'. But usage clearly implies not law but fact. And so in controversies as to whether in a certain matter there is or is not a custom, we are wont to say that the question is one of fact, not of law.

---

2. *Forum* or *forus* covers customs of judicial procedure; *stylus* covers customs of writing or speaking, especially in legal contexts. Suárez discusses these at length in Book 7, chapter 5, below, 'Of the Various Divisions of Custom on the Basis of Subject-Matter.'

The second difficulty arises out of the use of the term *mores* (general conduct): for it would seem to include the thing to be defined in the definition, since *mos* (general conduct) and *consuetudo* (custom), appear to be the same thing, differing only in name. In defining the term *mos* (general conduct) in the same passage (*Etymologies, ibid.;* also cited in *Decretum,* Pt. I, dist. I, cans. iv and v), Isidore says that, '*mos* is *consuetudo,*'[3] and what is astonishing, in the same place, he seems to repeat his error more unmistakably: '*mos* (general conduct)', he says, 'is custom which arises only[4] from general conduct.' Here he includes in his definition not only the thing but the very term to be defined. Again, his statement that '*mos* is custom that arises out of the general conduct of the people only' increases the confusion with the implication that it is possible for custom to be introduced in some other way.

The words 'which is accepted as law', in the second part of his definition, give rise to a third difficulty. They refer, as we shall point out later, not to an essential characteristic of custom itself but to its effect. They seem, also, to convey the opinion that consuetudinary law is not true law, but is reputed as law, and this, too, is false. Other difficulties on this point we shall deal with more conveniently as they arise in the course of the discussion.

2. *Second opinion.* The foregoing difficulties have their origin chiefly in the ambiguity of Isidore's terms. Their exact meaning must, therefore, be fixed as a first step to an understanding of the matter of this discussion. We must, then, notice first of all the three terms: *usus, mos, consuetudo.* All three, it must be noted, are closely kindred in meaning, inasmuch as they are strictly predicated only of free actions. There is, however, some distinction among them.

Definition of usus. In its strict theological meaning, *usus* (usage) signifies an act by which the will freely carries out that which it elects. This is in accordance with the teaching of St. Thomas through the whole of qu. 16 of I.–II; and with that of Augustine (*De Trinitate,* Bk. X, chap. xi, and *De*

---

3. [This passage in Isidore reads: *Mos est vetustate probata consuetudo* (*Mos* is custom approved by time).—TR.]

4. [The Roman edition of Isidore's *Etymologies* by Faustinus Arevolo in a note, Tom. III, p. 192, states that Isidore often uses *tantumdem* for *tantum.*—REVISER.]

Diversis Quaestionibus LXXXIII, Qu. xxx). In these passages, Augustine contends that only a rational animal can properly be said to exercise usage, since only such a being freely applies itself or other beings to action: such application he defines as usage. Consequently, usage is, in strict philosophical terminology, predicated of any act of usage whatever, viewed absolutely, since it is any free exercise of a faculty in the adaptation of means to an end, just as any act of joy in regard to the achievement of the end is called fruition. In the speech of every day, however, usage signifies a repetition of like actions. In this way, as Gregory López notes ([on *Las Siete Partidas,*] Pt. I, tit. ii, law 1 [*glossa* b]), usage is said to grow out of actions repeated without change over a long and uninterrupted course of time. It is for this reason that he contends in his note that usage is a matter of fact, that is, of repeated, free, similar actions with respect to one thing. In the law referred to, on the other hand, usage is said to be that which results or springs from the repeated action. This would imply the possibility of a third meaning of the term, a point we shall take up in a moment.

3. *Definition of* mos. The term *mos* (general conduct), according to St. Thomas, (I.–II, qu. 58, art. 1), is predicated not only of rational but of irrational beings also. For even in Scripture (2 *Machabees,* Chap. xi [, v. 11]) men are spoken of as acting *after* the *manner* of brutes; sometimes in a good sense, as: 'Rushing violently upon the enemy, like lions' (*leonum more*); at times, in a bad one, as in *4 Esdras* (Chap. viii [, v. 29]):[5] 'Those who have lived after the manner of cattle' (*mores pecudum*); at still other times, with an indifferent meaning, as (2 *Machabees,* Chap. x [, v. 6]), '[They had kept the feast of the tabernacles when] they were in the mountains, and in dens like wild beasts' (*more bestiarum*).

Mos, *properly so-called is found in free actions only.* Nevertheless, as St. Thomas rightly observes (on the *Sentences of Peter Lombard,* Bk. III, dist. xxiii, qu. 1, art. 4), this term *mos* (general conduct) is predicated of brutes only by similitude, or analogy, in so far as they always follow the same manner of acting by instinct; for *mos* in its proper meaning is found in free actions only. For the characteristic of morality (*genus moris*) begins

---

5. [*4 Esdras* in the Vulgate, *2 Esdras* in Anglican versions; an apocryphal book, frequently quoted.—Tr.]

only where the dominion of the will is found, as the same St. Thomas has said (*ibid.*, Bk. II, dist. xxiv, qu. 3, art. 2). Only the free act, therefore, is properly called moral. The reason is that the free act alone merits praise or blame, but a 'moral' act is similarly capable of praise or blame.

Consequently, it is stated by Aristotle (*Nicomachean Ethics,* Bk. I, chap. xiii [, § 20]): 'When we speak of a person's moral character (*mores*), we do not say that he is a philosopher or a man of quick appreciation, but that he is gentle or temperate.' *Mos,* therefore, properly so called, is nothing *else* than a frequent repetition of, or continuance in, similar, human moral actions over some length of time. Thus, we say that this or that was done in accordance with general conduct. So, in *St. John* (Chap. xix [, v. 40]) we read, 'as the manner of the Jews is to bury', and in *Genesis* (Chap. 1 [, v. 3]), 'for this was the manner with bodies that were embalmed'. In the same way those who mutually conform in moral conduct are said to be of one manner (*Psalms,* lxvii [, v. 7]): 'who maketh men of one manner to dwell in a house.'

Whence we may say that the distinction between *mos* (general conduct) and *usus* (usage) is this: the term *usus* may be applied equally to a general habit of action and to single actions; the term *mos,* on the other hand, may not be properly applied to a single action as *usus* may be, but only to a repetition of like actions. Wherefore, if the term *usus* is taken to mean a repetition of acts, it would seem not to differ in sense from the term *mos.*

St. Thomas adds in the passage referred to above [on the *Sentences,* Bk. III, dist. xxiii, qu. 1, art. 4] that the term *mos* is used in another sense to signify a tendency to similar actions, that is due to their frequency; this tendency is nothing *else* than a certain *habit.* We might speak of *usus* in the same way, according to the opinion of Alfonso [X] in the law we have cited [*Las Siete Partidas,* Pt. I, tit. ii, law 1]. That law, since it includes several elements, I shall discuss presently.

4. Of custom regarded as factual (as it is stated in *Sext,* Bk. I, tit. iv, chap. i) the same observations may be made. *Consuetudo* (custom) and *mos* (general conduct)—as St. Thomas remarks in the same passage [on the *Sentences, ibid.*]—are practically the same, since both words have the same meaning, namely, frequency of moral actions. For custom, strictly so-called, is found only in free actions, since in necessary actions it is more

correct to say that there never is any force of custom, and therefore, it does not exist in brutes, though by analogy it is sometimes attributed to them (*Institutes,* II. i, § 15).

Again, custom resides not in single acts, but in the frequency of them. This Isidore suggests [*Etymologies,* Bk. II, chap. x] and St. Thomas [on the *Sentences, ibid.*] very clearly states: 'Custom imports a certain frequency with respect to actions which it is in our power to do or not to do.'

I have noted, however, that this remark applies only to custom factually considered, because we must distinguish two elements in custom. The one is the frequency of actions, as such, which we may call formal custom. This, as we have said, is matter of fact—as usage is. The other is an after-effect of the repeated acts. This after-effect may be physical, as habit, which is not infrequently called custom but somewhat improperly by jurists, since it has reference to custom as fact. We shall, therefore, include it under the first head. A second after-effect may be one of the moral order, after the manner of a power or a law binding to such action, or nullifying another obligation. This may be called consuetudinary law or a legal rule introduced by custom.

For, just as custom induces a tendency to similar actions and a consequent ease and pleasure in their performance—and this is not only a moral but also a physical effect—which we call habit; so, in like manner, the customary action establishes a moral power or obligation, or, as we shall see later, changes established obligations, by creating not a physical but a moral power or bond which we call law. Thus, just as the word *mos* from meaning a repetition of free actions, has come to signify the habit or inclination itself, so custom, even though its primary reference is to actions as such, has been capable of being transferred to mean a juridical element (which is the result of the repetition of actions) by which it brings into being [now as law, not as physical habit] the repetition of like actions. The term for the cause is wont to be applied to the effect, and vice versa: thus we may apply the word custom either to the frequency of action or to the legal rule created by it.

Here we have the principle of distinction between the words *mos* and *consuetudo* used by Isidore in the passage just quoted [*Etymologies, ibid.*]: *mos* refers only to the physical acts; *consuetudo,* however, implies also the element of law. The term *usus* may be employed in the latter sense, according to the third meaning given it in the law referred to above—although it has other meanings. Isidore, however, as may be seen from his comments on this passage, applies the term *usus* only to facts.

5. *Definition of custom of law and custom of fact.* It is now clear that in discussing the nature of custom, it is necessary to make clear under what aspect we are considering it: regarded as matter of fact it must be defined in one way; as matter of law, in another. St. Thomas's definition of custom is, as matter of fact, excellent [on the *Sentences, ibid.*]: 'Custom is the frequency of free actions all performed in the same way', that is, the frequency of the free use of anything that lies in our power.

It is to be noted, however, that not every sort of factual custom has the power of creating a legal rule. An evil custom, for instance, creates no legal force; nor does one that grows out of the observance of a law—although it is spoken of as custom. An example of the latter use of the term is found in the Second Chapter of the Gospel according to *St. Luke* (Chap. ii [, v. 27]): '[And when his parents brought in the child Jesus] to do for him according to the custom of the law.' This kind of custom is often called *mos,* as in the Fifteenth Chapter [, v. 1] of the *Acts,* circumcision is described as being done 'after the manner of Moses'. There are numerous other like customs which we may pass over as irrelevant to our present discussion.

And therefore, to limit our definition to such custom of fact as is capable of introducing law, we must include in the definition, this term or something equivalent, namely, that custom is a legitimate repetition of actions in consonance with some law; or, that it is one in which all the conditions required by the law are fulfilled, or something to that effect. The definition of Isidore can be said to hold of custom understood in this sense; that is, the word *ius* must be taken, not in its formal, but in its causal[6] sense. If, however, we take into account the intent of Isidore, the context of his definition, and the strict meaning of its words, it is probable that he was not speaking in this sense.

6. Wherefore, even though it is probable that Isidore, in the passages cited [*Etymologies,* Bk. II, chap. x; Bk. V, chap. iii], was considering custom

---

6. ['Causal,' warranting the introduction of new law through custom.—Tr.]

under both its aspects and was speaking in the passage quoted in the *Decretum* (Pt. I, dist. i, chap. iv), of custom as fact—for speaking thus, *consuetudo* and *mos* are the same; and that it was in this same sense that he said: 'custom is so called because it is in common use'; nevertheless, in the passage cited in the *Decretum* (*ibid.,* chap. v), where he gives the definition we have quoted, he seems to have been considering custom as a juridical element, that is to say, as law itself, which grows out of the factual custom or the repetition of the acts. Thus the way is made clear for solving the difficulties presented at the beginning of this Chapter.

7. To the first of these, indeed, we reply that in custom, two elements are to be found: the factual and the juridical, and therefore, we speak of it at times in one sense, at other times in the other sense. And since in relation to the laws which Isidore is discussing in that last passage, the juridical rather than the factual aspect of custom is more pertinent, he defined it under that aspect and under the category of law. His definition is adapted from the *Digest* (I. iii. 32), in the first part of which we read: 'In matters concerning which we do not use written laws, it is necessary that we preserve what has been introduced by conduct and custom'; and farther on [*ibid.,* § 1]: 'Long continued custom may not unwarrantably be cherished as law, and this kind of law is said to be constituted by general conduct (*mores*).' So also in the law of Spain ([*Las Siete Partidas,*] Pt. I, tit. ii, law i [law 4]), custom is defined as: 'Unwritten law which has grown out of long and continuous usage.' In the same manner, the jurists define custom under the same category (on rubric of *Digest,* I. iii), and Bartolus (on *Digest,* I. iii. 32, in his *Lecture* and in *Repetition,* Qu. i), rightly distinguishes the two meanings of the word in almost the same manner in which we have. The phrase *non scriptum* (unwritten) added to the definition by the Spanish law and by many Doctors is virtually included in the statement that this law is established by general conduct (*mores*), which sufficiently distinguishes it from written law. In Chapter Three, I will give this phrase fuller discussion.

8. Hence, the second difficulty is easily resolved: for, juridically considered, custom may correctly be defined as law founded by 'general conduct', since 'general conduct' regards fact and not law: thus, the thing to be defined is not in this case included in the definition; for the

consuetudinary law is brought in by the repetition of free acts, and this repetition is called general conduct. So, also, there would be no fault in the logic, if the definition of custom as law were to include the term custom as fact, provided the distinction of meanings with respect to custom is kept clear.

Isidore's sentence that '*mos* is custom which arises from "general conduct" (*mores*) only'[7] has an excellent sense and is faultless, if we remember that the term *mores* is often predicated of single moral acts considered separately [that is, without reference to their being or not being actions done in observance of a custom]. *Mos,* however, as signifying custom is used as a kind of collective term, including the whole number or the repetition of acts. Thus *mos* (a customary mode of conduct), may be said to grow out of *mores* (general conduct), that is, out of free, 'moral' actions.

We may also consider that not any conduct (*mos*) but only the general and public conduct of the community is sufficient for bringing in consuetudinary law—the subject of our discussion—in the sense that it is able to introduce the strict obligation of law. For the private conduct of one person, or of a family, does not found a legal rule—as we shall see later. It is said, therefore, that the custom which suffices to introduce law must be drawn from the general conduct of the people: it must, that is, be so general as to arise out of the conduct of the community as a whole—of all, or the greater part of its members.

Lastly, Isidore adds to his definition the qualifying term 'only' to denote that only that conduct suffices for custom constitutive (if I may use that term) of law, which has come into being by usage alone and general conduct, without the assistance of statute and written law to introduce it. For a general line of conduct that has come into being through law, cannot, as such, bring in law, much as it may help to strengthen law already existing, as we shall point out later.

9. As for the third difficulty: we have already stated that although consuetudinary law is an effect of custom as fact, we must keep the two distinct and remember that our present concern is a definition of custom

---

7. [This appears to be a paraphrase of the same passage in Isidore, *Etymologies* (Bk. II, chap. x, and Bk. V, chap. iii), found near the beginning of this Chapter.—Tr.]

not as fact but as law, and that when the phrase 'which is accepted as law' is added to our definition, the effect of custom is not stated definitely, but its essential quality is explained.

It is said to be 'accepted as law', not because it is not true law, but because Isidore restricts the term *lex* to law in written form only. It is for this reason that he says that consuetudinary law is accepted as written law where the latter is absent.

Bartolus (on *Digest,* I. iii. 32, in *Repetition,* no. 6), states that by this phrase the distinction is drawn between custom and a right (*ius*) which arises from the usage of a single person, or which is not accepted in the place of law, nor is it a regulative right, but rather something that is itself regulated by some law. In order to grasp this point we must recall what has been said at the beginning of this treatise,[8] namely, that the term *ius* has two meanings. According to the one, it signifies a moral power of use: and this is ownership or quasi-ownership; for it may include an established right in holding a thing or a right to have a thing and can be called generally a right of ownership or quasi-ownership. In this sense, *ius* refers rather to fact [than to law]. In the second sense, *ius* is a right that carries the power to bind and command: this we may call the right of law, or legal right. The private usage, then, of a single person can confer a legal right to hold a thing, that is, ownership of a thing, or the right to a servitude (*ius servitutis*) and the like, as is the case in prescription.[9] This kind of right has not the force of law, and so it is correctly held to be not a regulative right, since it neither prescribes nor ordains anything, but rather a regulated right, since it has been acquired by the operation of some law. Custom, however, in the sense of our present discussion, is not of this latter kind, but is a legal right: it is so called because it is accepted as law and because for that law such custom is required as is established by the general conduct of those who employ the custom, that is, the community itself.

8. [*Vide supra,* p. 28.—Tr.]

9. [The right to a servitude, as the right of way, or of retaining ancient lights, is the right which a dominant tenement has established over a servient tenement by prescription or law. This right is the second meaning of *ius,* for it connotes forbearance on the part of others, against whom a prescriptive right has been set up.—Reviser.]

10. *The difference between custom and prescription is noted.* Therefore, we have briefly indicated the distinction between custom, with which we are concerned, and prescription.[10] The two words are often used as completely synonymous because of their likeness in some details. They are, however, in their proper connotations, radically different.

Bartolus (*Repetition,* no. 10 to the said question 1, at end), as well as other earlier commentators whom he cites, makes this point, as do other later writers, such as Panormitanus (*De Consuetudine,*[11] Chap. xi [no. 20]) and Rochus Curtius (*De Consuetudine* [Sect. iii]), with Gloss thereon (on word *legitime*), and Aimone Cravetta (*De Antiquitatibus Temporum,* Pt. IV, at beginning), Balbus (*De Praescriptionibus,* Pt. I, qu. 10), Rochus Curtius (*ibid.,* Sect. v, no. 3) and Covarruvias (on *Sext,* rule *possessor,* Tom. I, pt. II, § 3, no. 2), Matienzo (*Recopilación,* Bk. V, *De Matrimonio,* Tit. VII, law I, gloss 6, no. 3) and Luis de Molina Baetico[12] (*De Hispanorum Primogenitorum Origine et Natura,* Chap. vi, no. 10). The latter, Molina, sets down numerous distinctions on this point; but disregarding them (in detail), the root of the distinction [between custom and prescription] is more clearly perceived from what he says.

Because in prescription as well as in unwritten law, there enters an element both of fact and of law, which is introduced by fact; therefore, prescription requires a certain custom, and unwritten law, again, sometimes requires a custom which is in a certain sense prescriptive, that is, one that is indubitable and in accordance with law.

11. *The first difference.* They differ, first of all, and chiefly, in the kind of right which each establishes. Prescription, in its strict sense, does not

---

10. 'Prescription' in a wide sense can be used to mean custom. In a narrow sense it involves something importantly different: the acquisition of a right or of a title to something through use over a period of time fixed by law. For further discussion of the nature of prescription by Suárez see section 11 below and also Book 7, chapter 8, 'Concerning another division of custom into that which is valid by prescription and that which is not.'

11. [The Latin text incorrectly has: *de Constitutionibus.* It should read: *de Consuetudine* (of custom). This refers to Title IV of Book I of the *Decretals.* Henceforth in Book VII, the commentaries of Panormitanus, Rochus, and other canonists on this Title of the *Decretals* will be referred to as: *De Consuetudine.*—TR.]

12. [Not to be confused with Luis Molina (1535–1600), Spanish theologian.—TR.]

introduce a legal or regulative right, as does law. It confers rather a right of ownership or one of a similar kind to the use or enjoyment of some corporeal thing, as a house, an article of clothing, or an incorporeal right, as the exercise of jurisdiction or the right of suffrage. Therefore, they differ also in the custom of fact by which the one and the other kind of right is introduced; for, the custom which establishes prescription demands conditions different from those which establish law. A custom of the people is essential for legal right; the usage of a private person is sufficient for prescription, unless the object that is to be the matter of prescription is to be acquired by a corporate body. Some of the jurists cited employ the term 'custom' whensoever it is a corporate body that establishes prescriptive right, or whensoever prescription is established against a corporate body. This use of the term is improper. The acquired right is not law but ownership or some right of use. In these cases the community acts as a single private possessor and owner: whether the person establishing prescription or against whom a prescription is established is an actual person or only a fictitious one is an entirely material [—not a formal—] distinction.[13] But we must not quarrel over terms.

12. *The second difference.* Another difference is that for the validity of a true, legal custom—the subject of this discussion—the consent of the community, or of the prince against whom (as it were) the custom is set up, is necessary; but it is unnecessary in prescription to secure the consent of him against whom the prescriptive right is established, as I have noted elsewhere (Tract. II, *De Religione,* Bk. I, chap. v, no. 19).[14] It is for this reason,[namely,] that for setting up a custom, no legal title is necessary, since consent is sufficient; whereas to establish prescription, a legal title is necessary. This is the doctrine of the Gloss, Abbas [i.e. Panormitanus] (*De Consuetudine,* Chap. xi [, no. 30]) and of others (*De Consuetudine,* Chap. xi). This test is, however, a negative one, that is, it does not give final certainty in this matter: for legal title is often

---

13. [A material distinction, in the terminology of Suárez, is one that does not affect the main issue. Thus, the distinction between paying a debt with paper money or with coin is only a material or objective distinction. The debt is paid, whatever the medium.—REVISER.]

14. [Not included in these *Selections.*—TR.]

demanded for a prescription, but not always; while for custom, title is never demanded. For this reason, also, in prescription evidence of good faith is necessary; in custom, however, it is not always necessary, at least, not in the beginning.

Finally, although in the case of each, some period of time is a requisite element, yet it is not the same in each case. In prescription, its length is that which is fixed by law; in custom, on the other hand, either the law does not fix the time necessary for the custom to be set up, or such a fixed period is not *per se* necessary; rather, that period suffices which gives time for the prince or the people to manifest consent—as I shall explain further on. Other differences are set forth by the authorities we have cited, but they lack foundation in reason or are such that their examination need not detain us.

CHAPTER II

Does Custom Always Introduce Unwritten Law, and Is the Definition Given Complete?

1. This question is raised by the presence in Isidore's definition of the phrase [in *Etymologies,* Bk. II, chap. x], 'when law is lacking'. He inserted it, evidently, either to make it clear that custom must be unwritten law; or, to point out that we are to assume that there is no written law [against which custom is set up]. Each of these interpretations would seem to be open to doubt. In the first place, because consuetudinary law is often found in written form: the feudal laws and our own Spanish rules of judicial procedure are considered as such. It is not, therefore, of the essence of consuetudinary law that it be unwritten. As to the second interpretation, there is also a doubt for we must notice that custom often derogates from existing law, as will be made clear later: it cannot, then, be true that custom may not suppose the existence of written law. From this observation, we see that a third difficulty may be brought forward here, one respecting that other phrase [in Isidore's definition (*ibid.*)], 'which is accepted in the place of law'. For, as a matter of fact, the custom is not accepted in the place of law, but rather abolishes it, so that the custom imposes no obligation to a course of action, but at most does no

more than permit it. A fourth objection may be added, namely, that this definition nowhere touches on the element that is of the substance and essence of custom, that is to say, its acceptance by the common consent of the people.

2. *The true interpretation of the phrase 'when law is lacking'.* I answer, first of all, that the proper meaning and basis of the phrase 'when law is lacking' is that consuetudinary law is commonly introduced in default of law: for where there is already written law, custom calculated to introduce law is not needed; the written law suffices. Indeed, such custom does not seem to be morally possible, since it is of the essence of custom that it be established not by explicit but by tacit consent, as Bartolus notes (on *Digest,* I. iii. 32, in *Repetition,* no. 7) and as is clearly to be seen from the *Institutes* (I. ii, § 9). Thus, if a custom has arisen through the influence of a written law, it lacks for that reason power to introduce law; for it was begun and continued, not that men should be bound by it, but that they should obey some law already in existence. Nor is there any difficulty against our position in the fact that sometimes a custom is said to be introduced subsequently to a law. For this has reference, either to custom of fact only, which does no more than confirm the law; or, to a custom limiting or interpreting the law, and in this respect—as I shall show later—able to create new law. It is thus, it will be noted, not based upon the law, but is an addition to the law.

Thus, custom is most properly pronounced to be unwritten law, and is held to be such in the *Digest* (I. iii. 36 and I. i. 6, and in *Institutes,* I. ii, §§ 3 and 9). The reason is that it does not of its nature demand a written instrument, nor does it flow from written law; nor even from the personal or express precept of the superior: it is introduced by usage, for this is embodied not in writing nor in words, but in facts. This is the doctrine of the theologians on certain church laws which have come down by tradition. Of these, we shall have something to say in the two following Chapters.

3. The jurists, however, dispute whether a written instrument is so incompatible with custom that if consuetudinary law be reduced to writing it ceases by that very fact to be such and becomes law of another order. Some have asserted that it does, as Bartolus notes (*ibid.* [, no. 8]), and

as Gratian indicates in the *Decretum* (Pt. I, dist. I, can. v, § *cum itaque*). In that passage, Gratian says that a custom not expressed in writing is properly called a custom, but that one reduced to writing becomes a constitution. Rochus Curtius (*De Consuetudine,* in Pref., nos. 5 and 6) and Baldus (on *Digest,* I. iii. 32) concur in this opinion. And Jason says (on *Digest,* XXVIII. vi. 2) that custom reduced to written form by one who lacks the power of making laws persists as custom, despite such written form. The truth of this is clear: this written form is not written law; but it may serve for remembrance and as a source of proof, just as we refer to the Fathers to prove traditions that are unwritten. If, however, custom be reduced to writing by one who has authority to establish law, it ceases to be custom by the very fact that it is so written: it is now written and not unwritten law, and is law not by tacit but by express consent. It may be added that even though the law is written in legal form by one possessing authority to establish laws, nevertheless, if he does not intend, in giving it written form, to add any new force to that of custom, nor to publish or declare it authoritatively as a sufficient custom, it has no more than the force of custom, just as, in the opinion of many, is the case with the laws of judicial procedure. If, on the other hand, the authority fixes the custom in the strict form of written law, and in words that pronounce it binding, it is by that act no longer custom but written law.

4. It appears to me, however, that even in this last situation the custom retains its own force and the essential character of custom unless it be abolished by a special written statute. Bartolus (on *Digest,* I. iii. 32, in *Repetition,* no. 8) was of this opinion, and other jurists frequently speak to the same effect (thereon and on *Digest,* XXVIII. vi. 2), including Antonio de Butrio (on rubric *De Consuetudine,* Chap. xi), and others cited by Rochus (*ibid.,* nos. 5 and 6). This can be proved also from the canon law (*Sext,* Bk. III, tit. IV, chap. ii), where it is said that: 'A custom of this kind is approved by Apostolic authority and demand is made that it be inviolably observed.'

Such a written law, then, does not abolish the custom which it orders to be observed, rather it adds new force to it; and, as the Gloss on that law observes, from being a particular custom it thus becomes a common law. There is no contradiction in the fact that there should be two founts of obligation—that is, of custom and of written law—for the same thing, any more than that there should be two statutes relating to the same thing. Thus, written laws themselves often cite both customs and statutes as at the same time giving proof of the rectitude of a provision and of the obligation which exists in respect of it. An example of this is the canon law (*Decretals,* Bk. IV, tit. xviii, chap. iii) which says: '[this doctrine] is approved both by ancient custom and by the laws.'

Nor is the continuance of the custom and of its obligation useless, notwithstanding the existence of a written law on the matter. The reason is that if the custom is a particular one and the supervening written law is general law—as in the *Decretals* (Bk. IV, tit. iii, chap. iii), and if there is effected a derogation from that law by privilege, nevertheless, where the earlier custom existed in that matter, it is not held to have been derogated from by that privilege, unless there is an express derogation from the custom also.

There is here no question of a mere manner of speaking, but it is one of fact, for it may be of the utmost importance as regards moral effect, that a custom which had its beginning without benefit of law should stand as concurrent authority with the statute, and remain in full force as unwritten law; for the mere coexistence of a written law does not make impossible an unwritten law existing with its own peculiar force and in its own terms. The custom should, however, be complete and established with sufficient firmness before the written law comes into being; for if it exists only in inchoate form and the binding force is (as it were) anticipated and introduced by the statute, it will, clearly, be no more than simple written law.

5. *In what manner custom ought to assume the existence of law.* To the second objection, that concerning a custom contrary to law—which seems to assume the existence of law—a reply is ready at hand, namely, that it is not against the nature of custom that there be in existence law of some sort on the subject, but only that there be a written law ordaining the very course of action which the custom is to bring in. But a custom which derogates from a law does not suppose a law that regards the same object as the custom, but rather the contrary, namely, that what the law forbade the custom permits—or conversely.

Bartolus (on *Digest*, I. iii. 32, in *Repetition*, no. 6) explains the phrase 'where law is lacking' in a different manner. He holds, that this phrase denotes that the custom is not to be condemned by the law: for, if the custom is not against the law, the law is clearly defective in respect of the rule which the custom is bringing in; if, on the other hand, the custom is contrary to the law, it should prevail over the law, and thus the latter should cease to exist in order that the custom may prevail. For if a custom of fact is counter to written law and does not remove it, then custom will under no circumstance be able to introduce law. This doctrine is true and ingeniously conceived, but it does not, I believe, express Isidore's thought, which was much simpler, as I have explained in a previous passage. Nor was it necessary to explain this point in detail in a definition, since, in the nature of things, it is clear that a custom could not introduce one legal rule contrary to another already existing, without cancelling it; for the simultaneous existence of two laws in mutual opposition involves a contradiction.

6. There remains the third objection: a custom derogating from a law already in existence is strictly custom, and is not law. My first reply to this objection is to remark that in the realm of moral actions, under the term 'habit', absence [of action] is understood to be included: thus, Augustine's definition of sin includes not only a word, or act, and the like, [contrary to the law of God,] but also the omission of words or actions in contravention to law. Thus, then, when custom is called law, one is to understand even its power to abrogate law.

For one law voiding another is true law, even though it may not prescribe a course of action opposed to that prescribed by the law it has annulled. In the same way, then, a custom abrogating a written law is called unwritten law, since it is accepted as an abrogating law. Whence, it is said that just as permission[1] is included among the effects of law, and as a permissive law is held to be true law—since, even though it does not enjoin the commission of permitted action, it enjoins permission to do it—so custom, introducing law that derogates from statute, does so, indeed, not as imposing an act contrary to the previous law, but only as

1. [For *promissio* read *permissio*.—Tr.]

permitting that act. It thus enjoins permission for the act; that is to say, it forbids that any one be forced to obey the derogated law, or that he be punished for not obeying it.

7. The definition of Isidore set forth at the beginning of the treatise is approved. I have recorded a fourth objection, because some have found fault with Isidore's definition as incomplete. Owing to the lack of some such words as 'by consent of the people', or 'by common consent', or, even, 'of the people', they say that the phrase should not be, as it is in Isidore's words, 'established by general conduct' (*mores*), but rather 'established by the general conduct of the people'. This is the opinion of Bartolus (on *Digest,* I. iii. 32, in *Repetition,* no. 6). In fact, he approves in this passage another definition, setting forth, by the addition of several terms, the conditions requisite for custom. Other canonists also object to Isidore's definition as too brief. Not a few offer other definitions. These we need not rehearse, both because they are of no use to us here, and because they are to be found in Hostiensis (*Summa, De Consuetudine*), in Rochus (*De Consuetudine,* Pref. nos. 13, 14), and in the passage of Bartolus (*ibid.,* no. 1 [no. 6]), in which he rejects his earlier opinion and takes his stand on Isidore's definition, just as it is.

It is my opinion, then, that none of those additional terms is necessary: they do not clarify the definition; rather, they obscure it. For, if we add to the definition the words 'the consent of the people', the question arises immediately: 'Of what people?' Is the consent of the council sufficient? The like question arises on each of the other terms.

The words 'established by general conduct' (*mores*) sufficiently includes the element of consent; since, as I stated before, the general conduct is voluntary. It must be understood, of course, that the general conduct must be such as to suffice for establishing law. What conditions should obtain for this sufficiency, or, upon whose consent those conditions ought to depend, it is neither proper nor necessary to include in the definition. It is enough that the essential and formal character of the thing defined be given in the definition: an enumeration of all its causes is not called for. Such matters are more properly taken up in the course of the discussion.

CHAPTER III

Of the Varieties of Custom, and
Whether It Includes Forum and Stylus[1]

1. Since custom may be of many sorts, and since our discussion deals not with custom in general but only with that which pertains to human law, and has the force of introducing or of annulling it in some way, a review of the different kinds of custom is called for to clear the way for a discussion of that custom which is our proper concern. Such a review will assist us to a clearer and more precise concept of the nature of custom.

We will give special attention to custom as fact [rather than as law]. From this study we shall see to what extent law can arise from custom; for in this matter it must be noted that the clear understanding of the consuetudinary law depends upon the clear understanding of the fact as the prime cause and root of the law.

2. *The first division of custom: that which has to do with things and persons taken separately or together, and that which has to do with the actions of men.* We may begin by distinguishing two kinds of custom: that which, as its subject-matter, has things or persons, considered separately or together; and that which is concerned with human acts. This distinction is touched upon and illustrated with examples, in [*Las Siete Partidas,*] Pt. III [Pt. I], tit. ii, law 4. Thus, the custom of paying or not paying tithes of the fruits of the field or of the vineyard pertains to things and (as it were) imposes a burden upon them, and the custom of paying or not paying personal tithes or personal taxes pertains to persons; the custom of fasting or praying, however, clearly pertains only to human acts.

Some writers maintain, therefore, that the first two kinds of custom— those, namely, relating to things alone, or to persons alone—or both together, pertain rather to prescription than to law, since directly and of themselves they give only an [established] right to hold a thing (*ius in re*), or a right to claim a thing (*ius ad rem*), or a right against a person

---

1. [There appears to be an error in this title. No mention of 'forum' or 'stylus' is included in this Chapter. A discussion of these terms is found, *infra,* pp. 544 *et seq.,* Chapter v, sections 3 *et seq.*—TR.]

(*ius in personam*), and that this is a kind of moral power, and not law.[2] They argue that even though out of this moral right there arises an obligation in conscience to pay the tithes and the like, that obligation does not arise directly from the custom, but from the law of natural justice, which obliges men to render to others their due. Thus, as a result of prescription, there follows the obligation not to take away the thing obtained by prescription, an obligation which is derived immediately from the natural precept against stealing. And thus, also, from a servitude acquired by prescription allowing passage over a field, there follows, from the same principle, the right that one should not be obstructed in the exercise of the right. The same principle applies to any custom whatever relating to a thing or to a person.

But a custom concerned with human acts is said to pertain not to prescription but to law. The reason is that no one, as we said in the preceding Book,[3] establishes a prescriptive right concerning his own action, but he can be bound by custom, and by that custom there is established a consuetudinary law with respect to his personal acts.

3. But this doctrine calls for further explanation, chiefly, because there would seem to be *no* custom that is not concerned with human acts, since every custom consists of a frequency of human acts. If you say that all customs consist of acts, but that they are not all concerned with human acts, then the reply would be that if such were the case, there would hardly be any custom which is concerned with human contingencies. For though a custom of fasting be observed by human acts, nevertheless, those actions are concerned both with matters that are the object of temperance, and with that person who does them, whose passions it moderates. This is true of all customs. And if those customs which have to do with the goods of others or with persons distinct from the person observing the custom, are said to be concerned chiefly with things and

---

2. [*Ius in re*, as the right which a worker has to keep the wages he has received. *Ius ad rem,* as the right which a worker has to get his wages. *Ius in personam,* as the right a man has that other people should not impede his free actions. This is a right to claim a forbearance. The right to life is an example, under different aspects, of all three.—Reviser.]

3. [Not included in these *Selections.*—Tr.]

persons, then it is true, of course, that a prescriptive custom is in a sense concerned with the things of another, since no one establishes a prescriptive right against his own property; and it is also concerned with a person distinct from him who establishes the right. This statement is true for two reasons: because prescriptive custom pertains to the matter of justice, and therefore ought to consist of acts which have regard to another; and because prescriptive right is always established against some person who must necessarily be a person distinct from him who has exercised prescription.

4. *The aforesaid explanation is rejected.* Nevertheless, the division so stated is not satisfactory. First of all, since in prescription properly so called a distinction must be made between the person against whom the prescriptive right is established, and the subject-matter of the prescription. For, in the first aspect, every prescriptive custom is engaged, as is obvious, with a person; in the second, however, it is engaged not only with a thing and a person, but with human facts. Thus, a prince can establish prescription against his vassals that they should render this or that person service, either in war or at his place of residence, or on his lands. A custom of such service or ministry creates a prescriptive right with respect to similar acts, just as the custom of fasting is said to create the obligation of fasting.

And so, in the same way also, a custom which affects another person, and actions and property which are put at the service or use of another, may, without the support of prescription, create law. Thus the pious custom in the Church of making voluntary offerings, of which the *Decretals* (Bk. V, tit. III, chap. xlii) speaks, is concerned with the objects offered as its proximate matter, with God as the person to Whom they are offered, and with the Church or the priests as the persons for whose use they are offered: nevertheless, out of such a custom, concerning such matter and such persons, an obligation in law can arise. In fact the commoner opinion is that it does arise, as may be seen from the text just quoted. And although it is probable that the obligation can be sufficiently explained as a form of prescription, it is nevertheless certain that it can bring in the obligation of a human law, if other conditions are fulfilled. For in the case of a mere custom of private devotion, such as attending a procession on a certain day, or assisting at the divine office without a real obligation[4] so to do, that custom could establish a law enjoining that act. Why, then, cannot the custom of making an offering have the same effect? Finally, on the contrary, not every custom which affects personal action not done in the service of others suffices for establishing a legal rule: the customs of writing, painting, and the like are concerned with facts but they do not suffice to make law.

5. *How the aforesaid division of custom should be interpreted.* That division of custom, to serve the purpose of our present discussion, should be understood not in a material sense (so to speak) but in a formal one, that is, it should be determined rather by the purpose or scope—as I may call it—of the custom.[5] For one kind of custom would seem to be directed toward establishing right relating to things or between persons: such may properly be said to be concerned with things and with persons. It is true that this sort of custom should be regarded as pertaining to prescription and not to unwritten law, which, by a substitution of terms, we are here calling custom. Nor is there any difficulty in the fact that such a custom may at times be engaged with human acts as its proximate matter. And this, either for the reason that in such a case these acts are regarded not as human acts in the sense that freely willed acts are, but as things of such or such worth and value; or, at least, because such a custom is rightly included in that custom which is concerned with persons, since through it the person remains liable and bound—not, however, by custom as law, but by a right affecting the person acquired by another in virtue of the custom, and this right is a prescriptive one. So also, contrariwise, a custom, or rather usage, through which a prescriptive right to an action is wont to be obtained, although it may seem to affect as its proximate matter the action to which a right is obtained by prescription, nevertheless falls directly upon the person who was formerly responsible for the action, and by this quasi-custom he is freed of obligation.

4. A real obligation is that of a cleric (laity are free of any actual obligation to say the office).

5. [That is, we should distinguish custom from custom, not on the ground that they differ in regard to material and objective actions, but because their purposes are distinct.—REVISER.]

6. The second kind of custom is of its nature classified solely with respect to the usage or non-usage of like acts, as they are exclusively the acts of the agent himself. These acts may be immanent (as it were) as fasting and praying, &c.; or, they may be acts that terminate in an external object, as writing, plowing, and so on, whether they have relation to another person or are free of such a relation. The reason is that all these acts are capable of developing custom because of their very nature, or because of their uprightness without regard to any right acquired through them in respect of another person or thing.

To this sort of custom belongs that which is capable of bringing in a preceptive rule; and in that respect it may be said to be concerned with acts, since it intends by its nature their use or exercise. Customs that concern extrinsic objects and persons must not, however, be excluded from this class. The reason is that through them also a particular obligation of human law may come into being, if they are performed only under that aspect [—that is, as being prescribed—] as the argument concerning the custom that creates obligation proves. Similar examples could be easily adduced.

For the custom of almsgiving can be such as to introduce law, because even though almsgiving is concerned with an extrinsic object and a person distinct from the donor, it can be performed on the ground of pity, and as a good practice of the agent himself, without any relation to any right which another [the recipient] has. The general ground, therefore, would seem to be that such acts, although they have a relation to another, and involve matter extrinsic to the agent, may become obligatory by the mere force of custom—although by them no right is yielded to another—just as they can be commanded by human law, or, as a man may bind himself to such an act by a vow or by a mere promise. We must add, however, that not every such custom, even though it deals with mere facts, is sufficient to establish unwritten law. Only that custom which is concerned with free actions in so far as they are good or bad relatively to the common good, can do that. For as it is the nature of law either to command or prohibit actions of this sort, so the same nature is necessary for legal custom, if I may so speak. Thus, we exclude such customs as that of writing and the like, which are morally indifferent, private, and of their nature produce only facility or skilful usage in actions of that kind, but impose no obligation of exercise; as custom—of the sort that we are discussing—of its nature does.

7. *The second division of custom: universal and particular.* Secondly, this moral custom [, that is, custom founded on human acts,] can, in its main division, be differentiated into most common, that is, universal; common, that is, public; particular, that is, private. This division is derived in part from the *Digest* (XXX. l. 3), and is more fully set forth by Hostiensis (*Summa, De Consuetudine,* Chap. xi, no. 11), by Baldus, and others cited by Rochus (*De Consuetudine,* in Pref., nos. 20, 21). But they explain the division differently, as may be seen by reference to their works.

For my part, however, under the first category [, universal custom], I include, most of all, those customs of the whole world which constitute the *ius gentium,* as I have stated in Book Two.[6] For that *ius gentium* is true law, and in its own order it binds as true [particular] law, as I have there proved. Furthermore, that *ius gentium* is unwritten, a fact that is also obvious. Therefore, it was introduced by the usage and general conduct, not of one or another people, but of the whole world. Hostiensis, therefore, calls it universal, that is, most common custom. Consequently, in passing, we can understand that the definition of custom, given above on the authority of Isidore, is strictly applicable to the *ius gentium.* Nor is this attribution [of being due to custom] contrary to the rectitude of the *ius gentium,* viewed in itself, because the *ius gentium* is truly a kind of custom; and so it has its force not solely in virtue of natural law, as I have proved, nor by virtue of the will of some human prince, as is evident.

The principle of custom should be restricted for the present purpose so that it excludes the law of nations. Nevertheless, if we restrict the name and character of custom to what we at present are dealing with, namely, civil, that is, human law,[7] as contradistinguished from the *ius gentium,* then, by the

---

6. [*Supra,* p. 405.—Tr.]

7. [The difficulty in adequately rendering Suárez's argument here has prompted the following elucidation.]

Suárez is proving that custom gives rise to law. However, he restricts custom to that particular kind of custom which is common custom (i.e. civil), not wishing to include universal custom, for he is considering particular laws of particular places. He

name of custom is to be understood only the custom that is common [not universal], which we can call civil custom; and with due proportion, the definition of custom is to be restricted so that by the term law [in the definition of custom] is to be understood human, that is, civil [positive] law, including also canon law. Or else, at all events, this restriction is to be understood as indicated by the phrase *moribus utentium institutum* (instituted by the general conduct of those who employ the custom). The reason is that the said phrase signifies that this kind of law [, due to custom,] should be introduced as new law, either in a particular place or province, that is, introduced as law over and above the common laws of nations, which are considered virtually natural laws. The point can be further explained when we say that the law [introduced by custom] is reputed as law, when written law is wanting, whereas the *ius gentium* is introduced not as though in default of written law, but as being in itself necessary, and whereas also, because of its nature, it postulates that character of necessity, since on no other basis than that of necessity could it be introduced by mankind.

In what manner ecclesiastical traditions embody law. So we shall set aside for the present the first member of our division. Under the head of this sort of custom may be included ecclesiastical traditions whose beginnings and whose author we do not know, but which are observed by the Universal Church, for these embody unwritten law and are strengthened by the practice of the whole Church. For since the Church is essentially universal, for the whole world, these customs may properly be said to be universal, and most generally adopted. On these traditions we shall add in the following sections a few remarks from which it will be seen whether they

---

wishes it understood that he is speaking of human (civil) law, not of the *ius gentium*, and that it is human law to which he is referring in the phrase *moribus utentium institutum*. His restriction is the more reasonable, because, as he says, a law that is introduced by a general manner of conduct is a new law and is introduced in particular localities, not in all places, as is the *ius gentium*, the latter being a kind of natural law, introduced by and for all mankind in all places. He makes his point still clearer by saying that consuetudinary law arises only in default of positive written statute. This is not true of natural law, because it does not arise and come into being in default of written statutes, but develops because it is essentially necessary. So, too, there is no other way, humanly speaking, for the *ius gentium* to be introduced than by way of necessity, for it applies to and is necessary for all mankind. It could not, therefore, have ever arisen if it merely supplemented particular local laws.—REVISER.]

are to be counted amongst those traditions which are capable of establishing unwritten human law.

8. *By private custom is to be understood*[8] *that of one person or that of an imperfect community which cannot enact laws.* Particular, private custom is that which is followed by one person only, or by an imperfect community, a community whose consent is not sufficient to institute law, such as a private household or family, which is unable itself, or through its head, the father of the family, as I have shown in Book One,[9] to make laws. Such private custom we shall not, therefore, count for the present as custom, for the same reason, namely that it cannot establish law.

This is the common teaching of the jurists such as Bartolus (on *Digest,* I. iii. 32, in *Repetition,* no. 6) and Antonio de Butrio (*De Consuetudine,* Chap. xi [, no. 45]) and others. The reason is that if a custom is that of a private person, such a one cannot impose a law upon himself, nor establish an obligation by the mere force of repeated acts, even though the person have a fixed will of acting always in that way. If a promise be added, an obligation arises, not by reason of the custom but by virtue of the promise; and this not by reason of law, but by reason of the fact, that is, of the vow or pact, for on that basis, natural law creates an obligation, as I explained in the treatise on vows.[10] So true is this, that even though the agent may have, in another capacity, the power of making law, he cannot establish it by personal custom, a point which Rochus has noted (*De Consuetudine,* Pref., nos. 16 and 22). The same principle with respect to himself applies to the prince as to a private person, for in his personal actions or in their repetition he acts as a private person, not as prince, nor can he command himself by placing a legal obligation directly on himself as we saw above. So, furthermore, from the private or personal custom of the prince, no consuetudinary law falls upon his subjects. And this, both for the reason that, first, one of the conditions requisite for consuetudinary law is that it be introduced by the tacit consent of the people, and such consent does not intervene, except by the usage and conduct of the people themselves.

8. [The 1612 edition here used has 'not to be understood'.—Tr.]
9. [Chap. vi, § 22; *supra*, p. 100.—Tr.]
10. [Not included in these *Selections.*—Tr.]

Without that condition, therefore, the private custom of the prince is insufficient. Again, the subjects are not bound to imitate the prince in their actions, even his most praiseworthy and repeated acts, unless he enjoin it. He does not, however, sufficiently enjoin an action by simply observing a private custom, since thereby there is no express or tacit sign of his will to command it—as is clear. Bartolus has well said (on *Code,* VIII. lii. 2, at the beginning): 'The power of establishing consuetudinary law is given to the prince only when it is yielded by the consent of the people.' Thus, it is clear that personal custom never establishes law.

9. The same principle holds with respect to the custom of an imperfect community—one family, for instance—since one family is incapable of imposing upon itself an express law, as I demonstrated in Book One, and is, then, much less capable of establishing a tacit law, such as custom is.

Furthermore, although such a community can establish certain private ordinances, which, even though they do not bind as law, do so at least as pacts or mutual agreements; still, the persons of such a community cannot be even thus bound, it seems clear, on the ground of custom alone, because the pact or the promise is not created by custom alone, unless prescription intervenes, or some law or institution is assumed upon which such consent to the binding power of the pact is founded. For the same reason, although the father of a family can impose a precept within his family, he cannot bind them by his own custom, since personal custom is not a tacit sign of a precept.

10. *What custom establishes law.* We are left with the conclusion, therefore, that custom of the second sort only, that which we have called the common, or public custom, is capable of introducing positive human law properly[11] so called. The word custom, in this discussion, has reference to this sort alone. This is the meaning of the term as used by Bartolus (on *Digest,* I. iii. 32, in *Lecture,* no. 4 [in *Repetition,* no. 6]) and Baldus (on *Code,* rubric VIII. lii), Panormitanus, Rochus and all the commentators (*De Consuetudine,* Chap. xi). This is clear both from a sufficient enumeration of its parts, and from our discussion on the definition of custom, the second part of which we shall explain more fully in the following Chapter.

11. [For *propriis* read *proprii.*—Tr.]

It should, however, be noted that it is one thing for a community to be capable of possessing the power of making laws, another that it should actually possess such power. For only those sovereign commonwealths which have not transferred their jurisdiction to some prince have this power *per se* in respect to their civil laws. The capacity, however, for making laws resides in all perfect communities, that is, cities or peoples, which have the power to be bound by their own laws, whether common or municipal, even though they have a prince over them, since, with his consent at least, they can make laws.

The public custom, therefore, of any community that has the capacity of being bound by its own laws, may establish law, in so far as it rests with the community so to do, even though it may not actually have the power of making laws. It is true that such a custom calls for the fulfilment of more conditions in order to establish law in a community *de facto* lacking that power, than in one that has it, because, for that effect, at least the tacit consent of the prince is necessary, as we shall explain later.

11. We conclude then, at length, that according as the communities are more or less extensive or general, we can distinguish a number of kinds of public custom which are included in the second group of our division. Out of this variety of custom arise a variety and multiplicity in consuetudinary law. For if the community is ecclesiastical, its custom will introduce ecclesiastical law; if lay, it will introduce civil law. Likewise, if the custom be that of the whole Church—to refer to our first division—it will introduce common canon law, concerning which there are many decrees (in *Decretum*, Pt. I, dist. xi); if that of a whole province, the consuetudinary law will be (as it were) national; if one of a particular bishopric, the law will be (as it were) synodal or diocesan;[12] if that of a private chapter or community, the law will be (as it were) municipal. The same sort of relation will hold true of the civil customs. For if the custom be that of one kingdom, it will be (so to speak) that of the realm, that of a province, or national; if it is the custom of a city, it will be municipal. But common civil law of this order cannot be found apart from the *ius gentium*, since

12. [Synodal, because passed in Synod; diocesan, because extended to the diocese, but not to the province.—REVISER.]

the various realms are not able to be at one in the general conduct of the citizens. And even though the realms are sometimes alike in respect of a certain custom, it is by way not of one entity but of several similar entities, just as in various kingdoms they will have many laws that are alike, but the law of one is not binding on the subjects of any other, nor conversely.

I do not think that praetorian law should be placed in this class, whatever certain jurists may hold—see Rochus (*De Consuetudine,* no. 22)—since the two, consuetudinary law, that is, and praetorian, involve conditions repugnant to each other, as will be clear to any one considering the matter. I shall, therefore, pass it over as scarcely relevant to our subject.

CHAPTER IV

Of a Third Division of Custom: That Which Is in Accordance with Law; That Which Is outside Law; and That Which Is Contrary to Law: and of Certain Points of Ecclesiastical Traditions

1. A third principal division of custom is made under the following heads: that which is according to law; that which is outside the law; that which is contrary to law. This division is that made by Abbas [i.e. Panormitanus] (*De Consuetudine,* Chap. xi, near end), Antonio de Butrio (*ibid.* [Chap. x]), Rochus (*ibid.,* Sect. V, no. 5) and Cardinal[1] (*ibid.,* Qu. 45 [quoted by Rochus, *loc. cit.*]), and is that implied by Hostiensis (*Summa, De Consuetudine,* no. 11). This triple comparison may be made in respect of the natural law, of positive divine law, and of human law: thus, in respect of these three kinds of law, there arises a threefold division, each consisting of three members.[2] Of each of these, we shall speak briefly. We shall touch upon them all, in order that, having set aside those matters that are irrelevant to our discussion, and having briefly treated of those points which are of less difficulty, we may pass on to matters that are germane to the subject and present greater difficulty.

1. [Gratian, Italian canonist, later Cardinal.—REVISER.]
2. [The complete division is: *Consuetudo iuxta, praeter, contra legem naturalem, legem divinam positivam, legem humanam.*—REVISER.]

2. With respect, then, to the natural law, it would seem that no moral act can be outside it, at least, in the concrete; for every concrete moral act is—according to the more probable opinion—either good or bad. Such an act must, then, be either in conformity or at variance with the natural law since the natural law is a rule for all human acts. But custom is constituted by concrete human acts. Therefore, every such act must be either in conformity or at variance with the natural law. No custom, then, can be outside that law.

3. *What acts are in accordance with the natural law, and what contrary to it.* Nevertheless, since we speak of the natural law as forbidding certain acts, or as rigorously enjoining the performance of other acts, so we may say that a particular custom is in accord with the natural law, since it proceeds from it, and through it the natural law itself is observed. A custom of an entirely opposite character will be contrary to law, since by it the law is violated—if no more than slightly.

A third kind of custom will be outside the natural law when it consists of actions that are, according to a probable opinion, indifferent in the concrete;[3] or of good actions, which, although they are approved by the natural law or enjoined by it as to mode or precise character—that is, if they are done, they should be done in this or that way—are not absolutely enjoined as to performance: they are performed without the command of the natural law.

4. The first sort of custom, then, namely, that according to the natural law, although it may, as is obvious, be excellent, has not that moral effect which is the subject of our present treatment. For it does not introduce new positive law in respect of the same acts, since those acts are done not with such intention or will [of introducing custom]; but rather with the intention of fulfilling the natural law, as we noted above.

Such custom is, of course, useful for adding strength (so to speak) as far as we are concerned, to the natural law, by keeping fresh its memory, and by facilitating its observance on the part of the whole community. Such

---

3. [According to St. Thomas Aquinas there are no human acts which, in the concrete, are neither good nor bad. But the Scotist school maintained that there could be such, as, for example, the picking of a straw from the ground.—REVISER.]

a custom may at times—if it be approved by prudent, wise, and virtuous men—serve to interpret the law of nature.

A custom contrary to the law of nature has no effect. A custom contrary to the law of nature is not worthy of the name of custom; it rather merits that given it in the language of the laws—a corruption. It can, therefore, have no effect as law, either by abrogating or introducing law, as St. Thomas teaches (I.–II, qu. 97, art. 3, ad 1) and as is made clear in *Decretals* (Bk. I, tit. IV, chap. xi) and *Decretum* (Pt. I, dist. VIII, can. v and Pt. I, dist. VIII, can. ii), together with similar chapters in Distinction viii of the *Decretum*. Moreover, a custom of this kind is said (in *Authentica*, CXXVII, Coll. IX, tit. IX, chap. i = *Novels*, CXXXIV, Chap. i) to derive no cogency from any period of observance, however long. The reason is evident, since the law of nature is, as we have seen, immutable and so cannot be abrogated. Furthermore, such acts contrary to the law of nature have an essentially evil character, and it is inconceivable that they should have obligatory force. These arguments prove not only that no binding law can be introduced through such acts, but also that they cannot abrogate the obligation of the natural law or extinguish any of its precepts, either in whole or in part, since in respect of these, the natural law is, as we saw in Book Two, immutable.

The third kind of custom, that which we spoke of as outside the natural law, may be thought of as composed of actions essentially good or of indifferent actions.

The first kind is true custom, fit by its nature to introduce law, if other elements concur. It is with this custom that we shall principally have to do. But a custom constituted by indifferent actions, regarded in itself and its object, can have no effect on the introduction of law, since indifferent acts, as such, cannot be strictly enjoined. Still, if in them there is found some usefulness essentially good, some law might be introduced through them as custom, or at least, human law abrogated. This point we will explain later when we speak of the effects of custom.

5. *A question.* The question here arises whether this doctrine holds true of custom with respect to the *ius gentium*. We are not here dealing with a custom in conformity with the *ius gentium*, since it is clear that such a custom is a continuation of universal custom, and is consequently the same

law and not a new one. Nor does any difficulty present itself in regard to custom outside that *ius gentium*, for such a custom can be essentially good, and can be capable of establishing law, if no obstacle exists.

The difficulty arises then with respect to custom contrary to the *ius gentium:* some jurists, among them Panormitanus (*De Consuetudine*, Chap. xi, no. 23) and Rochus (*De Consuetudine*, Sect. V, no. 16), unreservedly deny that it can introduce law. Their denial is grounded on the opinion that the *ius gentium* is truly and strictly the natural law. We, however, have in a previous passage[4] drawn a distinction between the two; and so, when the term *ius gentium* is [, in the light of that distinction,] used in its proper sense, the reason urged [by those authors] is of no value.

6. *Parts of the* ius gentium *can be abrogated by custom.* I believe, therefore, that it must be stated that it is not absolutely inconceivable that a part of the *ius gentium* should be abrogated by custom. The reason is that that [act] which is contrary merely to the *ius gentium* as such, is not intrinsically evil, since what is opposed [to such action] is not essentially a matter of obligation of the natural law. The example usually adduced is from the Gloss (on *Digest,* VIII. vi. 14), for it is a rule of the *ius gentium* that no one be deprived of his possessions, even for the public service, without compensation, and still, through custom, a rule might be introduced that possessions may be taken without compensation. Some deny the force of this example, but they do so without good reason; for since custom can establish the mode and conditions of ownership, it can establish the principle that private possessions be held on the condition we have mentioned, and as a kind of servitude to the public welfare. Nevertheless, if the matter be carefully considered, there is here no formal derogation of any law through such custom, but rather a change in the subject-matter of law, just as the same sort of change may be made in the natural law, as I said above, and as appears from the example we gave concerning prescription and the like. Thus, the objections usually brought against our assertion are solved by this one argument.

An example more to our point is that respecting the slavery of prisoners captured in war, a practice that was introduced by the *ius gentium,* and

4. [*Supra,* pp. 394, 405, 406 *et seq.*—Tr.]

which can be abolished by custom in such a way that in a given province it is no longer permissible, and the same holds true, in my opinion, as to the division of ownership rights. An example may also be offered from the case of the Church; for the Lenten fast of forty days is (as it were) a part of the *ius gentium,* and yet it has been changed in some places by custom, at least partially, with respect to some of the early days of Lent.[5]

7. *Morally speaking, the* ius gentium *cannot be abolished as a whole.* It should be added that while admitting the possible abrogation through custom of some portion of the *ius gentium,* nevertheless, it is morally impossible that the whole of this law could be abolished, since in that case all nations would have to concur in a custom contrary to the *ius gentium:* which is morally impossible. And this, both for the reason that such uniformity in any matter is hardly found, and especially for the reason that the *ius gentium* is in close harmony with nature. Whatever, then, is contrary thereto is of rare occurrence. It follows from this (a consideration that should be noticed in this matter) that a custom contrary to the *ius gentium* can be approved and tolerated in the case of one people, in such fashion that it does not result in serious harm or prejudice to another people. Thus, if in some territory, passage over highways were permitted only under irksome conditions, such a custom could not extend to foreigners who in their territory allow such passage without such conditions, save in the case of a toll levied for a just cause, and one applying equally to strangers. Under those circumstances, such a custom would no longer be contrary to the *ius gentium.* But it would be otherwise, if the just cause for this condition should cease to exist. For then it would be contrary to the natural law to extend such a custom to foreigners, because it would be opposed to that law to deprive of their rights by the law of that custom the persons who were obliged to obey it, since they do not come within the jurisdiction of those who could rightfully introduce such a custom.

8.[6] But from the foregoing may be drawn an objection to the solution just given. Thus, a prince may not enact anything contrary to the *ius*

---

5. The custom of Lenten fasting varies within the Latin part of the Catholic church: in the Roman rite, it begins on Ash Wednesday; but in the Ambrosian rite of Milan which lacks Ash Wednesday, it begins only later, after the first Sunday in Lent.

6. [Section number missing in Latin text.—Tr.]

gentium, because his power and jurisdiction are inferior thereto—as Baldus states (*Libros Feudorum:* Tit. *De Nat. Feud.,* Chap. i and Tit. *Qui Feudum Dare Possunt,* Chap. i, last section), in which he is followed by Jason (on *Digest,* XLIII. xii. 2, in *Repetition,* no. 3); therefore, neither can the custom of one nation derogate from the *ius gentium,* because the custom is not more powerful than the law of a prince.

A reply to this may be made, first, by a denial of the inference for the reason that the joint consent of the people and of their prince to the custom can be of more weight than the consent of the prince by which he enacts law. For it is probable that the prince might not be able to compel his subjects to accept a rule contrary to the *ius gentium,* and still that rule could be established by common consent and custom.

Secondly, I maintain that a prince may, perhaps, enact a law contrary to the *ius gentium* by derogating from it in some matter which it is expedient not to observe in his realm and relatively to his subjects, as, for example, he might enact a law that in his realm there should be no slaves, but that all men should be free, or something similar. For this exercise of power is not opposed to [natural] reason, nor to the proper government of the state. Hence, just as a prince might enact law against another custom, so also he might make a rule contrary to that portion of the *ius gentium* which affects his government; and the reason is that, because of its universality alone, the *ius gentium* is not there the stronger or more immutable with respect to his subjects: it is so only with respect to other nations.

9. In the second place, the third division set forth above is to be applied also to the positive divine law: for some customs are in accordance with it, others are outside it, and still others, contrary to it.

With respect to the first group, that custom is said to be in accordance with the divine law which includes the observance of a certain body of divine positive law, that is strictly preceptive. For, if the term law in this case be given a broader interpretation so as to include the counsels [of perfection], then we may say that a custom in accordance with the counsels may be held to be according to the divine law. Nay more, every morally good custom to which Christ gave specific approval can be said to be in accordance with the divine law; and in this sense, no such custom can be outside that law. For the present, however, we shall call every custom made up of acts in accordance with the divine law, yet not prescribed thereby, a custom outside that law; therefore, a custom by which a divine precept is fulfilled, we shall call a custom in accordance with that law.

Under this latter heading, then, certain unwritten traditions of the Church would seem most properly to belong. For when the divine law as to baptism, or the Eucharist and the like, has been put into written form, any custom in accordance therewith is not part of the unwritten law, as is evident from the foregoing, since such a custom has the written law for its source, and it initiates nothing new in law. Hence, though this may sometimes be called a custom or *mos* (general way of acting), as is evident from *St. Luke* (Chap. ii [, v. 27]) and *Acts* (Chap. vi [, v. 14] and Chap. xv [, v. 1]), it is to be understood as custom of fact, and an observance of some written law, and not as a distinct law in itself. The unwritten traditions of the Church can belong to this class.

10. *Tradition and custom are not the same.* Nevertheless, at the outset we must note that, strictly speaking, tradition and custom are different things. Tradition relating to general conduct—and it is of this tradition that we are here speaking—is evidently the first institution of some action or of a mode of acting; or it may be understood as meaning a body of doctrine through which such an institution is given or made known to men. Custom, on the other hand, which embodies the tradition, is the fulfilment, and (as it were) the preservation of the original tradition. Hence, tradition may be written or unwritten, but custom exists as usage, and so is unwritten. Thus, St. Paul said (*2 Thessalonians,* Chap. ii [, v. 14]): 'hold the traditions which you have learned, whether by word or by our epistle'; that is, whether orally only or in writing; and thus he assumes that both kinds of tradition exist. When he says 'hold', he commands the usage and the execution, wherein consists the custom. The same is to be gathered from the passage in the *First Epistle to the Corinthians* (Chap. xi [, v. 23]): 'For I have received of the Lord that which also I delivered unto you'; that is, by word first, and later, in writing, by his epistle. He indicates usage and custom when he adds [*ibid.,* v. 33], 'Wherefore [. . .] when you come together to eat' &c. Thus, Tertullian also, in Chapter iii of his work *On the Soldier's Chaplet:* 'If no Scripture has determined this [tradition], certainly custom has corroborated it, and the custom, without doubt, originated in

tradition'; and he adds in the next Chapter: 'There is offered you tradition
to authorize it, custom to confirm it, and faith to live it.' Therefore, he
distinguishes custom from tradition, so much so, indeed, as to say: 'How
can a practice be observed which has not been handed down by tradition?'

11. But on this point it is further to be noted that just as custom sometimes emanates from the written divine law, so it could have emanated
from and have taken its rise from the same law in unwritten form. For as
written form is not, as we said above, of the essence of law as such, it is
much less of the essence of divine law. Indeed, New Law, of its nature, as
we shall show in Book Ten,[7] demands no more than an oral form, and was
thus handed down in the beginning, as is evident from various passages
in Paul. It is most certain that there are now many unwritten traditions of
the Church which emanated from a divine command, and which embody
such commands, as may be gathered from the Council of Trent (Session IV).
The same will appear in the treatise relating to the Sacraments and to
Faith, on which we shall have to speak at length,[8] and is also clear from the
learned chapters of Bellarmine in *De Verbo Dei* (Bk. IV [, chaps. v *et seq.*]).

However, such are not truly customs of law, but customs of fact; since,
although they contain unwritten law, they are not laws established by
custom; rather, the custom emanated from divine law. Hence, such law
is not human, but divine; and the traditions themselves are called divine,
even though they have been preserved by custom. Such custom added no
new element to their binding power as law, although it has the highest
value for the interpretation of the law: for as custom manifests the divine
precept, so, too, it sets forth (so to speak) the mode of observance, that is,
the conditions of its fulfilment.

What customs emanate from Apostolic precepts. I note, in passing, that
besides these traditions, there are other unwritten traditions, which are
believed to have originated not from divine, but from Apostolic precepts
and laws: the law, for instance, of the Lenten fast, and of the observance
of the Lord's Day, and the like—which are called Apostolic traditions. The
custom of observing these traditions can be styled Apostolic law. This is

---

7. [Not included in these *Selections.*—Tr.]
8. [Not included in these *Selections.*—Tr.]

not consuetudinary law, since the custom did not initiate the law, but the reverse; and so these are customs—in the sense that we are using the word here—not of law, but of fact.

Sometimes an ecclesiastical custom may originate apart from any precept. But at times, a custom of the Church, although observed universally, could have originated without the aid of any express precept, written or oral, whether of divine or of Apostolic origin, as seems likely in the case of certain sacramental[9] ceremonies. Here we find custom existing without any binding tradition, but not altogether without tradition. For the very initiation of a custom by the Apostles, and approval by the first pastors of the Church, gave to a practice the force of tradition. Thus, Augustine said (*On Baptism,* Bk. IV, chap. xxiv): 'What the Universal Church holds, and has always held, even though it be not defined by the Councils, is most properly believed to have been handed down by Apostolic authority.' The reason is that these immemorial customs, if they are observed by the Universal Church, are believed to have had their beginning in the days of the Apostles, and that, not independently of their teaching and their authority, at least by way of approval.

12. *What ecclesiastical custom is there outside divine law?* The second kind of ecclesiastical custom, namely, that which is outside divine law, may now be easily explained. For such in general is every custom which, on the one hand, has not proceeded from, nor is, on the other, contrary to a divine precept. But this is not enough to warrant the inclusion of such custom with that which embodies unwritten law, unless it be added that it came from no express law, Apostolic or human, as I have said a little above,[10] as is clear from our discussion on the definition of custom; and as we shall soon repeat in dealing with human law. But if a custom is outside divine law, and took its rise from no express law, then it is of itself sufficient for establishing unwritten consuetudinary law by the tacit consent of the people, and of prelates, or princes.

Such are those traditions which the Universal Church observes, yet which are not expressly commanded by Christ our Lord or by the Apostles;

---

9. [Suárez means that certain ceremonies came into existence by custom, and the Church sanctioned them, so that they became what are called 'Sacramentals', such as blessing with holy water, blessing the fire, ringing the church bells.—REVISER.]

10. [*Supra,* this Chapter, § 9.—TR.]

as, for example, lay communion under one kind, infant baptism, etc. But it must be noted that universal ecclesiastical customs of this kind do not always establish unwritten law that obliges their adoption, or observance as [legal] custom: as, for instance, making the sign of the cross on the forehead, or prayer towards the East—which Tertullian (*On the Soldier's Chaplet*, Chap. iv) and Basil (*De Spiritu Sancto*, Chap. xxvii, which is cited in *Decretum*, Pt. I, dist. xi, can. v), and others whom I cited in another passage include under such traditions. They also put forward as examples of this sort of tradition, customs which do not bind under precept. Such traditions, for all that, do establish a sort of law, or rather, indicate one that approves (as it were) of such acts. For such a custom of the Universal Church, although it is not a matter of special obligation, in respect of some particular usage, still does impose the obligation of believing that such a usage is licit and holy. It does so, both because the usage is always regarded as having Apostolic approval, and because the authority of the whole Church guarantees it [to be licit and holy], since the Universal Church cannot err in morals by following a sinful practice or by approving it.

13. *A custom contrary to divine law is of no effect.* There can, finally, exist a custom contrary to the divine law, a custom which the Scripture calls, in a disapproving sense, the 'tradition of men' (*Matthew*, Chap. xv [, v. 3]): 'Why do you also transgress the commandment of God for your tradition?'; and, that which is referred to in *Mark*, Chap. vi [Chap. vii, v. 8]: '[leaving the commandment of God, you hold] the tradition of men.' Hence, Paul said (*Colossians*, Chap. ii [, v. 8]): 'Beware lest any man cheat you [by philosophy, and vain deceit;] according to the tradition of men [. . . and not according to Christ]'. These traditions, too, St. Peter (*1 St. Peter*, Chap. i [, v. 18]) called vain. Custom of this kind cannot, therefore, have the moral effect of law, and so it in no way concerns us. For it is impossible that such custom should abrogate a divine law. This is the doctrine of St. Thomas, as we saw (I.–II, qu. 97, art. 3, ad 1), and that of Panormitanus, with the Gloss, and others (*De Consuetudine*, chap. xi).

And the reason is that even though the matter of such a law be not intrinsically evil, but evil only because it is prohibited, and as such not essentially impossible of initiation by custom; still, because the prohibition is a divine one, men cannot prevail against it, since men cannot change the divine law or the divine will. Nor can God be thought of as conniving at such custom and abolishing the law because of it, as we shall see later that men may do [in the case of human law]. There is no principle or ground for imputing such a possibility to the divine will; nor would it be expedient, or befitting the divine authority; His law must be immutable, as we shall see later when we come to deal with the law of grace.[11]

A custom in respect of divine law can be its interpreter. Some, however, of the jurists to whom we have referred, assert that custom can have the effect of limiting and relaxing (as it were) the divine law if a reasonable cause exists. This must not be taken as meaning a limitation or dispensation properly so called, which has for its effect a partial abrogation of the obligation of a previously existing law. In this sense, the assertion is clearly false. The reason that holds good in respect of the entire law, holds equally good for any part thereof, in due proportion, as we shall state at greater length (Book Ten).[12] Therefore, this [apparent limitation and relaxation of the law] should be looked upon rather as a kind of interpretation of the law; for custom may thus interpret even the divine law, which in such a case, and because of such an intervening cause, is not binding, because it was not framed for such a situation.

14. *On custom which is in accord with, outside, and contrary to human law.* It remains for us to apply the same third division[13] to human law, for it is with that law we have chiefly to deal, and because in such law it happens more commonly that a custom may be in harmony with, outside of, or contrary to law. Indeed, there is no dispute concerning these two latter groups, nor need we add any special remarks about them here, since the main discussion regarding them will be found in the following Chapters. But concerning the first group, some jurists contend that no custom can exist which is in accordance with human law. This was held by Felinus (on *Decretals,* Bk. I, tit. III, chap. i, no. 17), by Antonio de Butrio thereon, as well as Giovanni da Legnano and Dominicus de Sancto

11. [Not included in these *Selections.*—TR.]
12. [Not included in these *Selections.*—TR.]
13. [I.e. of custom, *vide supra*, p. 528.—TR.]

Geminiano (on *Sext,* Bk. I, tit. II). Others, however, to whom I have previously referred, who propound this third division, hold the opposite opinion, for they advance it particularly with respect to human law. *Custom in observance of human law is one of fact.* The difference of opinion is not actual, since the latter group are speaking of custom of fact, while the former are speaking of custom of law. It is clear that there are customs of fact in accordance with human laws, as the custom of hearing mass on feast days, or of going to confession during Lent, and the like. Thus, human law is like the divine or the natural law, in that there may exist a repetition of actions in conformity with it—in short, a custom of fact.

15. Nevertheless, it is certain that no new unwritten or consuetudinary law is introduced by means of such a custom, and the aforesaid authors are speaking in this sense when they say that even though a people obey a law for a thousand years, they do not thereby introduce custom [, i.e. consuetudinary law]. The reason is touched upon above: such custom of fact is merely a form of observance of a pre-existing law; and so it does not tend to the introduction of any new law, since the custom was formed or continued not for that purpose, but only to fulfil a law already in existence.

Nor does the prince [, in tacitly accepting such a custom of fact,] form a new purpose of introducing another legal rule relating to that matter, since he is merely continuing (as it were) the intent that was always in his mind, that his law should be observed. Wherefore, Baldus truly says (on *Code,* VIII. lii. 3 [in commentary, Sect. 3, *Leges*]) that a custom in harmony with law is not regulative in character but is imitative of the law, or executory as it were. From which the Gloss (on *Sext,* Bk. I, tit. IV, chap. i) and Panormitanus (*De Consuetudine,* Chap. xi, no. 21) correctly infer that if that law be abrogated by a later one, the custom [that grew out of its observance] is abolished also, even if no mention is made of it. The reason is that it does not add any new obligation, and it is held to be established, not on its own merits, but as something annexed to and founded upon the law; and so it has no binding force when the law which forms its basis is abolished. Whether, when it existed as a custom first, and later a written law was established, the custom can persist after the revocation of the written law, is a point we have touched upon in a previous Chapter. The reader may consult Felinus (on *Decretals,* Bk. I, tit. III, chap. i, last rule to no. 15, particularly limit. 7) and Rochus (*De Consuetudine*, Sect. 5, no. 7), for further study of this question.

16. *What effects the aforesaid custom has.* But even though this custom does not introduce law, it may have some influence on pre-existing law as regards its preservation and future effects. In this sense, it is said first of all, to confirm the law. Thus, Gratian (in *Decretum*, Pt. I, dist. IV, can. iii) held that: 'Laws are established when they are promulgated; confirmed when they are approved by the general conduct of those who use them.' The same is made clear in the *Code* (VIII. lii. 3). And Bartolus (on *Digest*, I. iii. 32, in *Repetition*, no. 4) explains the matter well when he says that 'such custom confirms the law not directly, but by removing that which would prevent[14] the law from exerting its efficacy, namely, the contrary custom and the abrogation of the law'. So, in almost the same way, this sort of custom may be said to render aid to the law, as may be gathered from the *Decretals* (Bk. II, tit. xxxix, chap. xiv), since the custom makes easier the observance of the law, and in a certain sense, makes the law itself less liable to change, as we have just explained.

Another effect of this custom is to interpret the law; indeed, it is called in the canon law (*Decretals*, Bk. I, tit. iv, chap. viii) and in the civil law (*Digest*, I. iii. 37): 'an excellent interpreter of the law'. Bartolus (on *Digest*, I. iii. 32, in *Repetition*, nos. 4 and 5) and Panormitanus (*De Consuetudine*, Chap. viii, no. 28 [no. 7]) speak of it in the same way. The reason is that it indicates in what sense the law was originally made and received. But if at any time this custom induces such an interpretation as to introduce some change from the first form of the law, the custom will then be something more than a mere interpretation, and will, in that respect, be a custom not in accordance with the law, but one that is superadded to it. On this point, the same principle applies as in custom contrary to the law, since the custom introducing change is in some respect in opposition to the law as it was at first, for it is said to derogate from that law in some particular.

---

14. [The term *removens prohibens* means, literally, removing an obstacle. For example, if I cut a string which is holding up a weight, the weight will fall. The string prevented it from falling. My action removed the obstacle to the fall of the weight. My act was *removens prohibens*, or a cause *per accidens* of the fall of the weight.—REVISER.]

We shall, then, treat of it with regard to this effect at the same time that we deal with custom that abrogates law.

17. Finally, it is usual to speak of another effect of this kind of custom, which is called the extension of law. Thus if, for example, a law is made originally for laymen only, and then through custom comes to be observed by clerics, it may happen that by reason of custom it will bind clerics also, who would otherwise not be bound by the force of the law itself. This may be gathered from Panormitanus through his comment (on *Decretals,* Bk. II, tit. xxvii, chap. viii, no. 4), Felinus (on *Decretals,* Bk. I, tit. ii, chap. x, no. 62 [no. 65]), Covarruvias (on *Decretals,* Bk. IV, *De Matrimoniis,* Pt. II, chap. vi, § 10, no. 18 [no. 35]), and Tiraqueau (*De Iure Primogenitorum,* Qu. 44), who hold that a just custom, one common to clergy and laity, binds clerics; and that, therefore, *a fortiori* a custom of the clergy will bind the clergy, even if that custom is established in accordance with a law for laymen.

But on this point it must be remembered that a custom according to law in the sense that it exists by force of law and by its command, is one thing; and that a custom according to law in the sense that it is modelled on the law, and is like to and imitates it, is another matter. Here we understand the term 'custom according to law' in the first sense. Such custom does not really extend law except, possibly, by way of the interpretation that it may give to the words of the law. Nor, in the above example, does custom accord with law in that [, i.e. the first] sense, since it proceeds not from the civil law, but from the free will of those who have wished to perform what the civil law prescribed, even if they were not bound thereby—which was the case of the clerics in our example. Hence it may be said that that custom—of the clerics—was according to the civil law only by imitation; it is not, therefore, strange that it should introduce new law. For custom has this force *per se* according to the *Code* (VIII. lii. 3); and the fact that it is an imitation of another and extrinsic law is of no importance, nor does it take from the custom its force. Hence it is that this custom is not properly an extension of the prior law, but the establishment of new law of another order or jurisdiction. For the obligation which arises concerning such persons comes really not from the force of the prior civil law, but from a new ecclesiastical law introduced by custom of the clergy. That kind of custom, as such, is thus shown to be of the type which is outside the law.

CHAPTER V

Of the Various Divisions of Custom on the Basis of Subject-Matter

1. *Custom is either canonical or civil.* Customs may, in a fourth way, be grouped on the basis of the things or subject-matter with which they are concerned, and on this principle a number of subdivisions, or easier classifications, can be included in custom. Thus, custom may be distinguished as canonical or civil, just as written law is divided into similar branches. For if a custom relate to spiritual matters, it will be canonical, as the custom of fasting, or that of the observance of a feast-day. And in general, every custom, proper to the clerical order as such, is canonical, even when it might sometimes seem to be concerned with secular matter; for it always touches upon such matter as affecting the property of churches, or the property or persons of clerics, and under this aspect it is sacred or spiritual. But a civil custom is one that is proper to laymen, and is rightly concerned with subject-matter that is temporal. For it resembles civil law, as may be seen from the reasoning of the *Code* (VIII. lii. 3).

2. One may object that this division is not an adequate one, because there are customs observed in common by the clerics and the laity and binding upon both orders—as we saw from Panormitanus and other writers in the preceding Chapter—and such a custom must be called not canonical or civil, but mixed. To this I reply first, that such a custom includes clerics merely in their character as citizens, as its subject-matter pertains to temporal government and to the common welfare of the state. As such it is a civil custom: partly, since it tends wholly towards a temporal end and falls within secular authority; partly also, because it emanates from the state as a human organization; whence the law or custom will be termed a civil one. Nor is there any unfitness in the fact that such a custom should bind clerics as citizens, because they are included in the term state (*cives*), as Bartolus (on *Digest,* L. i) and Panormitanus (on *Decretals,* Bk. II, tit. xxvii, chap. viii) note. And, again, they may be bound by the written civil law, in respect of its directive force, as has been previously explained. Custom may, on the other hand, relate to clerics as such or simply as Christians, in which case the custom is essentially a canonical one. The

reason is, that only a canonical custom can bind clerics as such, and only such a custom is of that higher order of custom which can include laymen also; for custom always follows the principle of written law and [therefore] depends upon a power and jurisdiction of the same order [as law].

Customs may be canonical in two ways. In the first place, the subject-matter and object of a spiritual custom may relate to clerics and to laymen as Christians, and such a custom makes no distinction between the two orders and is canonical: as the custom of observing a feast-day is common to both. A custom may be canonical, in the second place, solely on account of some propriety or likeness; as, for example, for the reason that in a certain locality both civil and ecclesiastical judges observe the same custom in their decisions. Thus, strictly speaking, we have here not a single custom, but two, one canonical and the other civil, which are regarded as one merely by a combination of the two. Thus, our division is an adequate one; and, in passing, we have said all that is necessary in exposition of it. It will also be of service in our use of terms in the following discussion.

3. Custom may, again, on the basis of its subject-matter be divided into general conduct (*mos*), strictly so called; and style (*stylus*), rite (*ritus*), and forum (*forus*). This division will become clear from our explanation of the last three terms, for we include under these words every other custom not comprehended under general conduct (*mos*), strictly so called.

The meaning of style. In the first place, then, style means some special usage of writing or speaking, as may be inferred from the *Decretals* (Bk. V, tit. xx, chap. vi), where, for determining what are genuine Papal rescripts, it is said that, among other matters, style must be taken into consideration. Some hold, from that passage, that the term in question means [in law] only a customary manner of writing, for this is the meaning given the term in the *Decretals* (Bk. II, tit. xxx, chap. viii). This is the opinion of Rochus Curtius, also (*De Consuetudine*, Preface, no. 28 [no. 27]), and of others whom he cites. The translation of the word, too, favours this definition; for its primary meaning apparently is a bronze instrument for writing; the word was then applied to the writing itself (*Code*, I. ii. 1); and thence to the fashion or arrangement of the writing. But even though the term is so used in the above-cited laws, that fact does not exclude other meanings, for it also signifies a 'usage' or manner of speaking. Thence also the word would seem to have served to signify a certain usual mode to be followed in judicial procedure. Thus Cynus (on *Code,* VIII. lii (liii). 1 [2, no. 7]) said that style is the practice of some court, and Baldus holds the same (on *Code, ibid.,* 3). By a substitution of terms the practice of the Roman curia is thus usually called its style. And what Bartolus says (on *Digest,* I. i. iii. 32, in *Repetition,* no. 10, at end of qu. 1), on this matter is almost of the same import, namely, that style is a custom which relates to a method of speaking or proceeding—that is, in court. On this account, Bartolus says (on *Code,* VIII. lii (liii). 2, no. 9) that style may be established only by the judicial acts of those whose business lies in the courts. Angelus de Ubaldis (on *Institutes,* I. ii, § 9), however, insists that style has the same meaning with reference to legal decisions as it has in other matters. This is certainly true in the general meaning of the word, but when we consider its use in connexion with the explanation or the introduction of law, it seems to mean properly a certain order in the drawing up of judicial decisions; including thereunder all [legal] documents, bulls, and rescripts. For even if in executing them, judicial procedure does not intervene, yet their style is considered in judicial decisions. Many points relating to this word have been collected with erudition by Cristóbal de Paz in his writings on the laws of Spain (on *Las Siete Partidas,* Pt. I [, nos. 34–40]) which are called styles.

4. *What is style of fact?* So, not to linger upon the mere meaning of the word, and to come to the matter as it pertains to law, we can distinguish— as we have done in the case of custom—two kinds, style of fact and style of law. To my mind, style of fact is not so much the frequency of the actions of writing, speaking, or proceeding, in a certain way, as that quasi-conventional form which is wont to be kept in the order of speaking, writing, or procedure, so that in the different parts, there will be used such and such words, or that the parts will be arranged according to a certain method or order. This meaning is evident from general usage, and from the laws cited; and may also be inferred from the *Code* (I. ii. 1), where it says: 'The style of the last will must be free';[1] that is, the form of making testamentary disposition of property. The reference here is clearly to style as matter of

---

1. [This quotation, as given by Suárez, varies slightly from the text of the *Code.*—Tr.]

fact and means not frequency of actions, but the form followed in drawing up such a document. The term is also more clearly used in the same sense in the *Code* (X. x. 3). So, too, Terence in *The Lady of Andros* [Prologue, line 12] said: 'But there is a difference in the sentiment and the style.' But since it is especially in speaking or writing that such a form is customarily employed, the usage itself, or the custom of speaking and writing in this manner, is termed style. And so style signifies a custom as fact, and in this meaning it was used by Baldus (on *Code,* I. ii. 1 and IX. xlix. 7). But this view must be understood to apply not absolutely to every custom, but only to custom in matters of the kind to which I referred above.

5. If, then, there arises from such a style of fact an obligation to observe such a method or order in passing judgment or in procedure, then in this respect style will be a special and unwritten law. Whence, since it does not seem ordinarily possible that this obligation can be introduced through style as fact in such wise as to have the force of law, except in those things which concern judicial matters, style would seem specifically as an element of law to be restricted to a customary order in court proceedings, as we said in citing Bartolus. For in other matters, utterances, or writings, a usage of speaking or writing according to such and such a mode, would seem to have too little relation to the common good to make it possible for the said usage to establish law. But in judicial matters it may be of great importance, so much so, as Ancharano remarked (*Consilia,* 53), that the style of the court makes law in cases where there has been no legal decision.

Various effects of style are touched upon. Accordingly style, as a thing properly termed judicial, relates to judicial procedure. Hence, style is a certain kind of unwritten law, which sometimes creates a positive obligation, allowing no departure therefrom, according to the *Code* (IX. xxxv. 11); at other times, it abolishes an obligation in such a way that, although by the general law a decision should be handed down by the court, yet because of the style of the court, this is held to be unnecessary. Upon still other occasions, style establishes an interpretation of the law, even an authentic one, such as must be followed. In what manner style may be introduced, so as to have those effects, must be explained in its due relation to custom, and wherever it possesses any special peculiarity, that will be pointed out in the course of our discussion.

6. *What are the laws of style and what is their nature?* Thus, at length, we can understand what the laws of style are, and what is their nature. When a law is said to be a law of style, the term may be understood in two ways. One way is that this denomination be derived from the object of the law, that is, the subject-matter with which the law is concerned. Such a law of itself does not, properly, pertain to custom, but rather to written law, which arranges for the style to be observed in judicial procedure, just as the rhetorical rules that are given, for the orderly arrangement of the matter, for the dignity, clarity, and grace of written or spoken compositions, may be called the laws of style. Of such sort are the laws of style of the Spanish Kingdom, in which the style of conduct or custom is frequently cited. So, I am of the opinion that this denomination was derived from the subject-matter itself, although Cristóbal de Paz (on *Las Siete Partidas,* Pt. I, no. 53 [no. 73]), explains this rubric [on style] otherwise. A law of style may, in a second way, take its name from the intrinsic mode whereby it has been introduced through usage alone in such forensic or judicial subject-matter, and so is properly unwritten law, and a form of custom, as has been explained.

7. *The meaning of rite.* The second member of our division is rite (*ritus*). For Rochus Curtius places it among those matters which relate to custom, when he says (*De Consuetudine,* Pref., no. 28) cited from Panormitanus (on *Decretals,* Bk. I, tit. xi, chap. ix): 'Rite is a custom that gives solemnity in the performance of some action; so that when usage provides for the solemnity of an action, it may be called rite or observance.' His only reference in support of his definition is to a passage (*De Consuetudine,* Chap. xi) in which no particular mention of rite is made. According to this description, even style may be a form of rite, although not every rite may be called a style. Panormitanus (on *Decretals,* Bk. III, tit. xxx, chap. xxxii) gives it a more restricted meaning: 'Rite signifies general conduct in spiritual matters.' According to this definition, not every solemnity of action may be called a rite, but only that expressed in sacred matters, as in sacrifice, the Sacraments, and the sacramentals; or in prayers, or in the divine offices. This seems to be the general ecclesiastical usage of the word. Indeed, Panormitanus never proved that the word signified a species of custom; for, on the contrary, he said (on *Decretals,* Bk. I, tit. xv [tit. xvi, chap. iii]):

'Rite is a certain form and solemnity in an action relating chiefly to the sacramental act.'

8. *Rite of fact and of law.* Accordingly, the doctrine that we have set forth concerning style should, it would seem, be applied also to rite. For a rite may be factual, or legal. Likewise, rite of fact, primarily and of itself, consists in a certain solemnity or ceremony in some action. In the three Chapters of the *Decretals* cited, it is used with this meaning. Whence neither custom nor frequency of actions are of themselves necessary for rite of this sort: for more commonly it is introduced prior to any kind of usage, either by word, as when Christ our Lord instituted the essential rite of the Sacraments; or, again, by writing, as is clear in many of the accessory solemnities and sacred observances instituted by the Church. But it is not intrinsically impossible, and in fact it often happens, that a rite of this sort should be introduced by usage and custom. Such a custom may be, therefore, spoken of as a certain rite, and this is the meaning of the authors quoted above. But it will be necessary to distinguish between the rite as fact, and the rite as law. For in the first aspect, it is a repetition of actions in a certain manner and in a certain matter; in the latter, it may be an unwritten law with respect to that matter, which has been initiated by that repetition. Thus, almost all canonical customs in actions concerning the divine worship, in so far as they give to those actions a form, or special mode, may be called rites. What, however, is the nature of that law, and how it is introduced, must be determined from the general rules concerning custom. For there is no peculiarity in this kind of observance, such that it cannot be treated of, under the principles that apply to custom.

9. *What is forum?* A third branch of custom in this general classification is 'forum'. This term is not commonly used in this sense in the general law, and so Bartolus, Panormitanus, and Rochus, and other writers on custom make no mention of it. But in the laws of our kingdom, Spain, forum is reckoned among the customs (*Las Siete Partidas,* Pt. I, tit. ii, law 7), as Gregory López notes [*glosea* n], in commenting on that law.

When the derivation of this word is considered, it would seem to mean the same, or almost the same, as style in the sense in which we have explained that term. For in popular usage, forum usually means a public place set apart for trafficking and the business of selling, and is so used by Isidore (*Etymologies,* Bk. XV, chap. vi). And, it is because courts are usually held in such public places that Isidore believes that the name has been transferred to mean the place of judgment. The term 'forum', he says (*Etymologies,* Bk. XV, chap. ii and Bk. XVIII, chap. xv) signifies a place for conducting litigations; and the word is said to have been derived from the verb *fari* (to speak). This derivation is contained in the *Decretals* (Bk. V, tit. XL, chap. x). Hence, the word also means the special domain of each judge or prelate, in which sense it seems to be used in the *Decretals* (Bk. II, tit. II), as Hostiensis, Panormitanus, and others have noted in commenting on that title. Hence, also, by an extension of meaning, judicial actions are wont to be called 'forensic actions'—as they are in the *Digest* (II. xii. 9). So also, public documents are termed 'forensic instruments' and these are accepted as proof in the court, as may be seen in the *Code* (IV. xxi. 20, § 2). So, then, customs relating to the order of judicial procedure are called forensic customs.

10. In Spain, then, these customs are held to be included under the name of forum; for the laws which are spoken of as those of the forum, take their origin from usage, as is said in the preface to the collection of those laws. There is also no doubt that in such matters usage may initiate law; there is no reason for doubting that custom can establish law in that matter, any more than in other matters. Hence it is said in the *Digest* (XL. vii. 21): 'We ought to follow the custom of those who are handling the matter.' Elsewhere the *Digest* (L. xiii. 1, § 10), expressly states: 'High regard is to be cherished for a custom of the Court.' Bartolus makes a note of the same tenor (on *Digest,* I. iii. 32).

In what manner forum and style differ. In this sense, then, it is evident that forum differs only slightly from style, and thus, although in the laws of Spain those of forum and style are distinct, still the latter are held to be quasi-interpretative of those of the forum, as is stated in the rubric on the laws of the forum. Nevertheless, forum and style are distinct. My ground for this statement is that forum does not, as is the case with style, signify an order or mode in the use of words, or in procedure, but apparently designates all the laws that are competent by reason of judicial authority, or have a relation to it and its usage. Therefore, the whole body of laws relating to the use of judicial authority can, apparently, be designated by the name of forum, the name being taken in a collective sense, although even individual laws of this sort are usually called *fora*—in Spanish, *fueros*.

11. *Whether forum includes written and unwritten laws without distinction.* For these reasons, some writers maintain that in this acceptation, forum signifies not custom alone but both written and unwritten laws indifferently—the latter being those introduced by custom in relation to matters of jurisdiction and judicial procedure.

This opinion was held by Burgos de Paz (Law 1, *Tauri.*,[2] No. 385): 'for the laws of the forum are written, yet they are properly comprehended under the name of forum'. But the more common opinion of Spanish jurists is that these rules are not of legal validity, save by force of custom, so that a written law of forum has no legal force, nor sufficiency as proof, unless its usage has been proved. This is the teaching of Gregory López (on *Las Siete Partidas*, Pt. I, tit. ii, law 7 and Pt. VII, tit. xv, law 28), of Suárez[3] (*Prooemium Fori*, Nos. 1, 2, and 3), of Diego Valdés in *Additions*;[4] of Cristóbal de Paz (in rubric to law on style, Pt. I, no. 36), and others on *Tauri.*, Law 1 (which is law 3 of tit. i, Bk. II of *Compilación*), from which the same conclusion is drawn.

But if this is true, then certainly the laws of the forum, as written laws, are not legal prescriptions. For a written law does not derive its essence and force from usage, but from enactment and promulgation. These laws, however, were not instituted or proposed as in themselves binding, but only in so far as their usage was manifest. They are, then, mere registers of custom, and frequently their rules—despite their written form—are to be classified as unwritten and consuetudinary. That they exist in written form is not incompatible with this character, as we pointed out before.

12. But whatever may be true of these special laws of forum, there is no doubt that there could have been written laws relating to the whole body of forensic business, and again, that others could have been introduced by

---

2. [Marcus Salon de Pace, *Ad Leges Taurinas insignes Commentarii* (Pinciae, 1567).—Reviser.]

3. [This is Rodrigo Suárez; sometimes spelled Juárez or Xuárez, a Spanish jurist of the 15th century.—Tr.]

4. [D. Jacobus Valdés, *In Comment. ad prooemium fori Roderici Xuárez, Additiones.*—Reviser.]

custom; and so, all that we have said as to factual style, or about written or unwritten law, may, in due proportion, be applied to forum. We may also add that, even though in the Kingdom of Castile the forensic laws were limited to the subject-matter of judicial procedure, it is possible that in the other kingdoms, as in Aragon, &c., they were interpreted in another manner and with a wider meaning.

13. For, in those places, the forum would seem to be the name given to the ancient laws of those kingdoms, which are peculiar to them and which had been confirmed by (as it were) inviolable usage, especially those which pertained to the mode of government and of the exercise of jurisdiction of the prince, and of [the manner of] subjection of people and nobles. It is possible that they included other matters also; and it is not clear to me whether they owed their origin to express institution, or were introduced by custom. For they might have had their origin in either manner, if, as we assume, they are just and reasonable. With the exception, therefore, of these special terms or customs, all other laws introduced by usage, in whatever moral matter, retain the general name of custom. Thus, it becomes clear that this classification multiplies consuetudinary law not formally (as it were) but only materially; that is, with respect to the things or the subject-matter with which law is concerned. The same is true of other like groupings which could easily be thought out.

14. *Division of custom into positive and negative.* Lastly, we must note another division of custom: into positive, and privative or negative custom, a division which may be useful in our later discussion. The former takes its origin from positive usage and consists, in so far as it is a custom of fact, in a certain repetition of actions, and therefore, as law, it sets up a disposition or an obligation to act. The latter sort, on the other hand, is passive in character and originates from non-usage, and so it is sometimes named [negative custom]. To the extent that this non-usage is frequent and continuous, it possesses the character of a custom, which consists (as it were) of fact; and where it establishes some legal rule, it merely fosters a disposition or obligation to refrain from action. But, at this point, we must mark the distinction between negative and privative non-usage, a distinction which we shall more fully explain in our discussion of privilege.

Negative non-usage does not establish custom—as Paul de Castro rightly noted (on *Digest,* I. iii. 32)—because it is not an action, nor a moral omission, and so does not possess the character of a moral and voluntary usage, without which the introduction of custom is not possible.

But privative non-usage which is continuous, or repeated upon due occasions, does establish moral custom for quite the opposite reason. The chief reason here is that such non-usage cannot practically exist without a positive act in the sense that theologians use the term in discussing acts of omission. This [quasi-positive act in non-usage] may happen in two ways. In the first, because non-usage consists in the absence of some proper circumstance, or of some formality in a positive action; for example, the contracting of an incestuous marriage without a dispensation. For on account of its frequent occurrence, many conclude with Navarrus that this is a true custom which might have abolished that impediment [to marriage]. This sort of custom must be called not merely negative, but positive, since it consists not in a simple omission but in the performance of an action implying a negation [of the law]; nor would the mere negation suffice to establish custom without the action. It may, again, happen that the non-usage consists in the mere absence of action at a due time; as the omission to hear mass, despite the law, on a certain day. For such a custom to establish law, this omission must be voluntary, and at least in that respect it involves an action [of the will]; but formally, it consists in the absence of due action, and thus the custom is called privative.

Such a custom can also be called desuetude, although this term may be ambiguous, as is observed by Rochus Curtius (*De Consuetudine,* Pref., nos. 30 and 31), since desuetude in its proper meaning seems to assume the [previous] existence of custom: for it is because it recedes from custom that it is termed desuetude, whether the recession be by means of contrary actions, and so through a custom positively contrary in character, or whether the recession occurs solely through the omission of an ancient usage. It may, it is clear, occur in either way.

Thus, desuetude may occur through contrary custom. A negative custom may also exist, but it is not desuetude, if it does not assume the existence of a contrary custom. Desuetude can, indeed, be said to exist even without any regard to actual previous custom, but only to one that might or should have come into being. This apparently is the meaning in which the jurisconsult Julianus uses the term in the passage cited in the *Digest* (I. iii. 32 [, § 1], at end). In this sense, desuetude consists formally in the absence of due actions and thus, properly, it signifies a negative or privative custom. So for the sake of clearness we shall use the term in this sense. As to how it may possess the moral force and effect of custom, we shall see in the discussion that follows.

CHAPTER VI

What Is a Good and Reasonable Custom and What Is an Evil and Unreasonable One

1. This is another possible division of custom and one which we must make in order to explain the moral nature and the effects of custom. I have thought, then, that a discussion of it should be taken up at this point. A twofold division, however, is suggested by the title: one into the good and bad, the other into reasonable and unreasonable. These divisions are not synonymous; the second implies an element not included in the first. We must, then, take up each division separately.

2. *Good and bad customs.* When, then, custom is divided into good and bad, we must take the words in the sense of moral goodness and rectitude, and of the evil contrary thereto. The reason is that other sorts of goodness, regarded in themselves, or of evil contrary only to them, do not render men or their customs either good or bad. We are here considering custom solely in its moral aspect, and as it is able to constitute or annul some rule of human conduct. Accordingly, no third group, such as indifferent custom, is added here. Such a custom, according to the more probable opinion, is either not possible in usage and practice, as is more likely, or, even if such be admitted, it is, viewed as indifferent custom, irrelevant for setting up law, unless it is converted to some kind of rectitude, in a way presently to be explained.

A bad custom can be only one in fact, never in law. Hence, we see that this division of custom is concerned with custom of fact; for legal custom cannot be of an evil character, or opposed to rectitude, since this very evil would be in contradiction with the nature of law. For, just as a statute if it is evil is no true statute, so also, an evil law is no law; and therefore, an evil custom can exist only in fact and can never establish a legal rule, unless the element of evil is taken away.

Our present division is, then, based upon custom as a fact common and public in some community. Thus, this division is of itself sufficiently clear, first with respect to the existence of both members, since just as individual persons may follow good or evil customs, so may a whole people or community; secondly, with respect to its sufficiency as we have already explained; and, finally, with respect to the distinction between the members, a distinction which is evident from the terms themselves.

3. *A good custom is of a twofold character.* In order, however, that we may explain more fully the meaning of this distinction and difference in its parts, I note, further, that a custom can be good in two ways: in one, it can be good in so far as its object is alone concerned; in the other, it can also be good from the character of the agent and from the circumstances of the morally good actions by which the custom is introduced. In this latter meaning custom is called good in the absolute sense; in the former it is so only under one aspect—that is, objectively—if the other requisite conditions are lacking.[1] The reason is that absolute good arises only when all elements [in an act] are good, and therefore a custom to be absolutely good must be brought into being through acts good in every respect; for a custom to be good only objectively, however, it is sufficient that it be concerned with an object good of its nature, that is, either with acts which are in their object good or with those which could be performed with moral rectitude, and done from a just motive.

In a similar—even if not exactly the same—way a subdivision of bad custom may be made. For, since evil is the result of a defect of any kind at all,[2] so through whatsoever element a custom is bad, it can be called

---

1. [That is, an act is morally good absolutely if object, motive and circumstances are good; it is good only under one aspect, if the object alone is good, but motive and circumstances not so.—REVISER.]

2. [A reference to the teaching on the moral act: *Bonum ex integra causa; malum ex quocumque defectu.* An act is good, if all its determinants are good. It is bad, if any one determinant is bad. The determinants are: object, motive, circumstances.—REVISER.]

so absolutely. Nevertheless, one custom may be evil in view of the object of the actions which by their frequency constitute the custom, that is, because they are evil in virtue of their object.

Another custom, on the other hand, may be concerned with subject-matter not evil in itself, and nevertheless be, in another aspect, evil in respect of the agent, or of some other circumstance, or condition which precludes goodness. When, then, custom is intrinsically and from its object evil, it deserves not the name of custom, but of abuse or corruption, as is said in the case of laws. For such a custom is not capable of establishing true law, nor is it possible that through it a customary act can become good or not evil. But if the custom be at least objectively good, or not evil, although it may have been introduced not in a praiseworthy way, but through evil actions on the part of the agent, it nevertheless retains something of the character of a good custom, and from that aspect it is not inconsistent that it may preserve or establish some rule of unwritten law.

4. *A custom intrinsically evil establishes no law.* For a clear exposition of the foregoing, I add the further observation that it is possible for a certain custom to be bad of its nature, because the actions constituting it are either intrinsically evil, or because they are, as prohibited actions, so evil that they cannot be made good actions by any human power. Such a custom is properly called an evil custom by reason of its object. It is certain that this sort of custom cannot introduce law, since it is opposed to either the natural or the divine law, of which we have treated before.

In another way, however, an action or the subject-matter of a custom can be evil merely because it has been forbidden by human law. It cannot be said of such a custom that it is simply no custom, and of no moment, as will be evident from what will be said immediately, and from the discussions in the subsequent Chapters. The following rule is applicable to this sort of custom, namely: 'Many actions are forbidden to be done, but once done, they are valid.' The reason is that this kind of custom is not essentially evil, nor does it contain evil from which it cannot be separated by human power and will; and so, while in its inception the custom is bad, it can lack evil in fact, if the evil at last ceases, or if human prohibition is withdrawn. Thus, such a custom is absolutely and without qualification evil not by reason of its subject-matter when viewed in itself, but only by reason of the presence of a human prohibition, and in virtue thereof. There is, therefore, no radical impossibility of its introducing law.

The same will be all the more true, if the actions through which a custom is established are neither evil in themselves, nor even forbidden by human law, but are done with some evil circumstance on the part of the agents. But since such a circumstance may be separable from the action, the custom may be valid as to the substance of the action, but not as to its circumstances; just as we have said elsewhere concerning a vow. Thus, if there be a custom of celebrating some feast by means of unfitting sports, or by bull-fighting, such a custom is not truly binding in respect of the manner of the celebration, but can be so regarding the observance of the feast. This is the principle we must go on, unless it is in some way made clearly certain that it was not the will and consent of the people to bind themselves otherwise [than as to the manner of celebration]—for, as we shall state below, a custom cannot be introduced without consent. In this case, that circumstance [, unfitting sports, &c.,] may be said to be of the substance of the custom, and in consequence, the custom is bad intrinsically, owing both to its object on account of the said disorderly nature thereof and to its essential connexion with the action [of celebrating the feast in such a way]—at least from the main intention of the agents.

5. *Reasonable and unreasonable custom.* Now we must give our attention to a difficulty raised with respect to the other member of our division, the one which distinguishes customs as reasonable or unreasonable. For it is not quite clear whether these two sorts of custom are the same as the other two which we have enumerated; nor is it clear by what rule they are to be distinguished both from one another and from those others.

The Doctors experience difficulty on this point and express various opinions. First, Navarrus (*De Alienatione Rerum Ecclesiasticarum ac De Spoliis Clericorum,* Sect. 14) defines that as a reasonable custom, 'which is not directly or indirectly contrary to natural or divine law'; and conversely, 'every custom which is directly or indirectly opposed to natural or divine law and such custom only' is unreasonable. To say that a custom is contrary to the natural or the divine law is to say that it is evil by reason of its object or subject-matter, as is evident from what we have set down in a previous paragraph. Moreover, Navarrus proves his proposition. He cites, first, the authority of Augustine (*Letters,* cxviii, Chap. ii [*Letters,* liv, Chap. ii, in Migne ed.]) to the effect that: 'what is proved to be neither contrary to Catholic faith, nor opposed to good morals, is to be treated as indifferent'. In the second place, he says that that which is in conflict with natural or divine law cannot be established by custom; and conversely, that whatever is not so opposed, may be established thereby; and therefore Navarrus concludes that the first of these is unreasonable custom, and the latter, reasonable.

The inference is clear, since evidently no custom can prevail unless it is reasonable, and no custom can be denied introduction save an unreasonable one. The proof of his antecedent is that whatever may be established through human law can be established by a custom; and, conversely, that what may not be introduced by custom cannot be introduced through human law. Human law, however, can establish whatever is not in conflict with natural or divine law, but not what is repugnant to them—according to the reasoning of the *Decretum* (Pt. II, causa xxvii, qu. i [qu. ii, can. xix]), the *Constitutions* of Clement (Bk. II, tit. xi, chap. ii). Therefore, Navarrus repeats this same opinion elsewhere (*Consilia,* Bk. III, *De Censibus* [, cons. vii]), saying that a custom is not unreasonable, unless it is opposed to natural or divine law. This is also the opinion of Gerson (*Alphabetum Divini Amoris,* Pt. III, lxii, letter P),[3] and *Supplement* to Gabriel (*on the Sentences,* Bk. IV, dist. xlii, qu. i, art. 3, doubt 6 [sole qu. conclus. 9, doubt 6]).

6. Other writers, however, state the matter otherwise, and say that every bad custom, because it is contrary to law—whether natural, divine, or human—is unreasonable. Whence, they hold, on the contrary, that that custom is reasonable, which is good at least in respect of the action itself, and is of a subject-matter not prohibited, whatever may be the extrinsic and accidental evil it may take on from the agent. In support of this position the Gloss (on *Decretals,* Bk. I, tit. iv, chap. xi, word *rationabilis*) is cited, to this effect: 'I call that reasonable which is not disapproved by the laws.' This is more clearly stated in another Gloss (*ibid.,* chap. iii, word

---

3. [The reference is to Gerson, *Sermo coram Rege Franciae,* 7ª *consideratio,* and *Tractatus de Potestate Ecclesiastica et de Origine Juris et Legum, consideratio 10,* may be found in Vol. IV *Gersonii Opera Omnia* (Antwerp, 1706).—REVISER.]

canonicis): 'A custom opposed to a canonical ordinance is not valid'; and this seems to take its force from the text of the *Decretals* itself (Bk. I, tit. IV, chap. iii), wherein it is stated that a certain custom is said to be not reasonable, since it is 'in conflict with canonical ordinances'. The conclusion is that it is sufficient that a custom be bad for the reason that it is forbidden by the ecclesiastical law, for it to be held unreasonable. This is the tenor of the *Decretals* (Bk. II, tit. XXVI, chap. xii), inasmuch as that Chapter decrees that 'nothing can be obtained by prescription which is contrary to obedience'.

Many other similar laws are cited by the aforesaid Glosses. This position can be confirmed by reason, on the ground that a just law is reasonable; and that, therefore, a custom opposed thereto is unreasonable; therefore, every custom which is evil, either from the nature of the object, or from the fact that it is forbidden by divine or human law, will be unreasonable: conversely, every custom not so forbidden will be reasonable.

7. *First reply in refutation of the preceding opinion.* Nevertheless, my first reply in refutation of the opinion thus set forth is as follows: that the distinction between reasonable and unreasonable customs is not to be found in the fact that they are or are not forbidden by natural or divine law; nor to be found in goodness or evil which they possess by virtue of their object, or subject-matter. The proof is that, although every usage contrary to divine or natural law is unreasonable, yet it is not such custom only that is unreasonable—as I shall make clear by two proofs.

The first is that, if we speak of usage regarded in its relation to the initiation of consuetudinary law, then a certain usage or custom might be wholly good in fact, and still be unreasonable in its relation to the initiation of law; and this, not because it is deficient in goodness, but rather because (so to speak) it is excessive. But such a custom is not contrary to natural or divine law, either directly or indirectly. Therefore, . . .

The major premise is evident from the example of a custom observed by a whole people of hearing Mass daily, an act of the greatest rectitude; but if this custom were observed with the intention of establishing law, it would be in that respect imprudent, and on that account the custom could be termed unreasonable. The same is true of like customs. This reason, however, is not convincing, because it is not the custom that is unreasonable, but the intention of initiating obligation through it, or in regard to it rather is unreasonable, and as such may be said to be contrary to natural law. Similarly, a positive law enjoining that practice would not be unreasonable in respect of its subject-matter considered in itself; but the law itself would be so, and as such would be opposed to natural reason and prudence.

Now if, on this ground, this subject-matter may be termed unreasonable—not because it is evil, but because it is lacking in fitness for a general law—so, on the same ground, it is contrary to natural reason, which dictates that not all good actions are to be the matter of human law. The same principle applies, in due proportion, to the obligation induced tacitly by custom and explicitly by law.

On this ground alone, then, it is proved that a consuetudinary law can be unreasonable, and therefore void, even though the custom in itself is not unreasonable, a very true statement; just as it is possible for a law to be bad, although the action directed by the law may not be bad. Nevertheless, the argument would seem to be a sufficient refutation of Navarrus' thesis [in *Consilia,* Bk. III, *De Censibus,* Consil. vii], both because it demolishes the basis of his argument, as I shall presently show, and again because he[4] seems to think that a custom is not unreasonable in relation to the initiation of law, save in so far as it is directly or indirectly opposed to divine or natural law in the actions that constitute it, or in the fact itself of the custom, as Navarrus pointed out in the basis of his argument.

8. *Second refutation.* Secondly, however, that opinion of Navarrus is more clearly refuted by the fact that many customs, not contrary to divine or natural law, are held to be unreasonable in the field of law. And they are unreasonable not only in relation to the establishment of law on account of an excess of goodness, but absolutely and in themselves, on account of some defect or irregular quality which, although it does not attain to that quality of evil [which would make it intrinsically unreasonable], is sufficient to constitute the custom a truly unreasonable one: therefore, in order that a custom be accounted reasonable it is not sufficient that there

---

4. [Reading *ille* for *illa,* though *illa* might stand in spite of its being strange to say that an opinion can think; *illa . . . videtur sentire.*—REVISER.]

be that twofold negation, nor that it be good, or [at least] not evil, so far as its object is concerned.

A proof of the antecedent of my argument is derived from the custom of not obeying in all its details a general interdict laid upon a place, a custom that is discussed in the *Decretals* (Bk. I, tit. IV, chap. v), and which is there called unreasonable, although it contains nothing opposed to natural or divine law. Abbas [, i.e. Panormitanus] (*De Consuetudine*, Chap. v, no. 3 [no. 2]) makes the observation that every custom that is contrary to what is good is unreasonable, and this is in accord with the *Decretals* (Bk. III, tit. I, chap. xii). He understands, however, by the contrary of what is good—that is, what is fitting—those actions which do not always include something opposed to divine or natural law; as, for example, that laymen should be seated in choir with the clergy. This is not contrary to divine or natural law, yet it is not fitting, and it is, therefore, impossible for this practice to be introduced by a custom. The canonists hold the same thing with regard to the custom of clerics engaging in hunting for the sake of pleasure, as does Giovanni d'Andrea (on *Decretals,* Bk. V, tit. XXIV, chap. ii). Rochus (*De Consuetudine,* Chap. xi, no. 30) refers to a number of such instances.

Yet Navarrus would say that these and similar acts are indirectly opposed to law, either natural or divine. But this solution is not satisfactory. First, because it is impossible to define adequately in what that indirect contrariety consists, since the act can exist in its totality without any violation of law, natural or divine; again, because a deed forbidden by human law appears to be all the more indirectly contrary to the natural law, since the natural law enjoins obedience to superiors, and yet Navarrus admits that the custom in question is not either directly or indirectly against divine or natural law; and, finally, because there is the fact that the custom is not evil from its matter or its object but is, for all that, held to be unreasonable.

9. *Navarrus's argument turned against him.* And now, the first principle of Navarrus's argument can be turned against him, for it is not true to say that human law can command whatever is not opposed to divine or natural law. For although it cannot enjoin the performance of anything in conflict with these laws, it does not follow that it is able to prescribe everything not in opposition to them—as has been stated above. This is

clear from a consideration of the works of the counsels [of perfection]; or, of those good actions which are not compatible with the counsels, such as marriage; and (which is more to the point) of those actions which are less proper or less decorous—though they are not contrary to the said law—as in the case of a law prescribing the playing of games which are somewhat unseemly or not expedient, even if they are not bad; or a law granting to clerics some way of acting or some habit not sufficiently upright, and the like. Therefore, human laws can be unreasonable, even if they are not evil in virtue of matter forbidden by divine or natural law. So, too, the same can be true in the case of customs.

10. *For a custom to be unreasonable it is not necessary that it be contrary to the canon law.* Then, in reply to those who hold the second opinion,[5] I observe that for a custom to be unreasonable, it is not sufficient that it should be opposed to the canon law, nor is this opposition always necessary [for the custom to be so]. Panormitanus and almost all the other commentators (*De Consuetudine,* Chap. xi, no. 5) are of this opinion, including Bartolus (on *Digest,* I. iii. 32 and on *Code,* VIII. lii. 2). I shall refer in a moment to the opinion of certain other writers also.

The first part of this assertion is proved from the fact that an unreasonable custom cannot prevail in opposition to human law, as is clear from the *Decretals* (Bk. I, tit. IV, chap. xi); and yet, as I shall prove below, it is possible that a custom contrary to human law can prevail against that law. Therefore, not every custom which is in conflict with human law can be held to be unreasonable.

The second part of our assertion is evident in respect of those matters which are contrary to divine or natural law, even if they are not especially forbidden by human law. In addition to these, however, there are some things which, while not especially prohibited by any law, possess an impropriety, or some condition, on account of which they are thought of as unsuitable, or unworthy of being established by custom. Hence, a custom relating to such matters will be unreasonable even if it is not contrary to the canon, or to the civil law.

5. [Cf. Section 6, this Chapter.—TR.]

The antecedent of this argumentation is founded on the words of Paul in *1 Corinthians* (Chap. xi [, v. 4]): 'Every man praying or prophesying, with his head covered, disgraceth his head'; and later [*ibid.,* v. 6]: '[But if] it be a shame to a woman to be shorn or made bald, [let her cover her head].' Now, these and similar things are not absolutely forbidden by natural law as morally bad, but nevertheless, while they are forbidden by no positive law, divine or human, yet they involve a certain lack of decorum, as is signified by St. Paul, when he adds [*ibid.,* vv. 14–15]: 'Doth not even nature itself teach you, that a man indeed, if he nourish his hair, it is a shame unto him? But if a woman nourish her hair, it is a glory to her.' On this passage Ambrose comments [on *1 Corinthians,* Chap. xi, vv. 14–15]: 'He wishes that this practice be regarded as naturally good, and that it be almost a positive command.' Ambrose here properly uses the words 'naturally' and 'almost', because, the positive law apart, this propriety is natural, in the sense that the natural law prohibits the contrary not strictly but only 'almost'. That limited prohibition is sufficient, however, to render a custom unreasonable, if opposed to what is becoming. This is also made evident in those activities which—while not forbidden by positive law, nor possessing within them an intrinsic evil—theologians speak of as 'suggestive of' evil, since they involve some danger of moral harm, especially if they are frequently done or generally permitted: such as the sale of judicial offices, or the reception of gifts by ministers of justice; or similarly the practice of bestowing a spiritual favour upon the offering of a temporal gift, even though the latter is not given as the price of the former; or the failure of prelates to visit and correct their flocks—and the like. Therefore, customs in matters of this sort, apart from any law prohibiting them, are deservedly held to be unreasonable.

Finally, this matter can be explained from what we have already said on the subject of oaths and vows: that there are some things which, although they are not evil as actions, are evil as promises: as that a husband should promise not to accuse a wife of adultery; or a promise not to revoke a will, and the like. Thus a promise can be unreasonable, even if its subject-matter is forbidden by no law.

The same, therefore, is true of custom. Such in general is any custom which affords a licence to sin: as would be a custom which gave illegitimate children an equal status with lawful heirs, or, one which punished homicide with a light pecuniary fine. These and other illustrations are more discursively treated by Rochus (*De Consuetudine,* Chap. xi, no. 26).

11. *The author's conclusion that a custom can be evil, although its subject-matter is not evil.* Whence I conclude that a custom can be unreasonable, even if its subject-matter is not evil, as is evident where its subject-matter happens to be unbecoming, or where it brings with it an element of danger, or possibilities for harm if it should be introduced into common public observance; and this, despite the fact that it is neither evil in itself, nor forbidden by any positive law, such as may be the case in many of the examples cited.

And, on the other hand, it is possible that a custom may be bad at least in its inauguration[6] and in the actions by which it is introduced—since they are prohibited at least by human law—and nevertheless may not be unreasonable, because, apart from human law, its subject-matter is not entirely unsuitable for the introduction of a custom respecting it. This quite clearly is the opinion of Panormitanus (*De Consuetudine,* Chap. xi, no. 4), where he says that the principle of that law, that 'the authority of custom of long standing is of no little moment', can be applied to a bad custom also. For such a custom can, if it is reasonable, prevail against a law; hence, Panormitanus assumes that a bad custom can be reasonable. But this statement is to be understood of that sort of custom which, though bad in its inception, can cease to be bad when established—a matter which we shall explain later.

12. Our conclusion, then, is that the division of custom into good and bad is not the same as that into reasonable and unreasonable. The justification for this statement is found in the fact that the goodness and the evil [in customs] are derived from their objects, or from some law not forbidding the actions or forbidding them; their reasonableness or unreasonableness, however, should—it seems—be judged from their fitness for general usage and for consuetudinary law, as I shall explain in the following

---

6. [*In fieri* strictly means 'in its becoming'; *in facto esse* means 'in its actual existence'. Thus, we speak of marriage *in fieri,* which is the making of the contract, and of marriage *in facto esse,* which is the married state.—REVISER.]

Chapter. Nor do the observations made by those who maintain the second opinion opposed to ours, refute this assertion, since the laws and glosses they cite in their support speak in a different sense, as will be presently explained in another section regarding this division. The question there to be answered is: in what manner can a custom contrary to law be a reasonable one? This we shall deal with later on, where we consider in what manner a custom may prevail in opposition to human law.

13. It remains, however, to ask in what consists the unreasonableness of a custom; or, what, beyond and apart from prohibition, is required to make it unreasonable; and conversely, what, apart from goodness, is necessary in order that a custom may be held to be reasonable; and, finally, by what test this can be discerned. Panormitanus treats of this subject at length (*ibid.,* Nos. 5 and 6), where he rehearses many opinions on this point. This is also fully discussed by Rochus (*De Consuetudine,* Sect. 2, no. 20), Bartolus (on *Digest,* I. iii. 32 and on *Code,* VIII. lii. 2), on which Jason and others comment and Menochio adduces many examples (*De Arbitrariis Iudicum Quaestionibus et Causis,* Bk. II, centuria 1, case 82). They all, however, set forth this division in one of two ways, as well as the distinction existing between the members of it.

14. *What is an unreasonable custom?* They do so, first, on the basis of the effects of the customs, namely, that that custom is considered unreasonable which will be opposed to the liberty of the Church; or which will afford in some way licence or occasion to sin; or which will be harmful to the general welfare; or which will have some such condition annexed to it—even if the custom is not contrary to divine law. For if a custom should have such a condition, it is always judged as being in the highest degree unreasonable.

On the contrary, however, that custom will be judged reasonable which will not be contrary either to divine or to natural law, or which will not possess any of the aforesaid conditions. It is possible that Navarrus, as quoted above [*Consilia,* Bk. III, *De Censibus,* Consil. vii], meant nothing more than this; and he seems to have thought that all these conditions could be summed up directly and indirectly by the phrase [opposed to natural or divine law]. To me, however, this seems to make the matter much more obscure, because one cannot understand his exposition without reference to similar examples. For the indirect opposition of which he speaks is never necessarily such that, by reason of it, the matter of the custom is truly and strictly of an intrinsic malice contrary to the natural law, since in fact, as I have shown earlier, this is not necessary to unreasonable custom.

15. Another mode of making answer to this, is to say that no absolutely general criterion can be laid down in this matter: decision must be left to the judgment of a prudent mind. This rule is stated by the Gloss (on *Sext,* Bk. I, tit. ii, chap. i, word *rationabile*), and is followed by Francus de Franchis, and other writers on that law. This was also the opinion of Hostiensis (*Summa:* on *Decretals,* Bk. I, tit. iv, chap. xi, § *Quid sit consuetudo*), and his doctrine is accepted by Giovanni d'Andrea, Panormitanus, and others in their comments (*De Consuetudine,* Chap. xi). Bartolus and other authorities take the same view.

Those writers who do not reject the first mode of answering the question, but accept it as useful for forming the mind of the judge in a particular case, do leave the final decision to the judgment of a prudent man. These writers are here speaking of the judge who is to decide in the external forum on the character of a custom: with due proportion this mode may also be applied to the case of a confessor in his judgment in the internal forum, and to a divine in giving an opinion. The aforesaid writers understand that this principle has application in the absence of a declaration by positive law as to whether or not a custom is unreasonable; if such a declaration has been made by law, generally speaking, this is the criterion to be applied, as I shall presently explain. Finally, Baldus (on *Digest,* I. iii. 32), and Jacobus Fontanus (in his scholium on *Sext,* Bk. I, tit. ii, chap. i) add that in a case of doubt the custom is to be presumed reasonable, and that judgment must be given in its favour. I interpret this statement to apply when a custom is ancient, and has been observed by good men, or by all men in common. When explained in this way, this solution seems to me entirely sound.

16. Yet for the fuller exposition of the above point, we must add the rule inserted in the *Decretals* (Bk. III, tit. xi, chap. i), where those customs are held to be unreasonable 'which are neither favoured by reason, nor in harmony with the sacred ordinances'. This phrase is derived from the Lateran Council under Alexander III (Pt. I, chap. xvi [Pt. III, chap. xvi,

ann. 1179]), where it was positively enjoined that those customs are to be observed, 'which are favoured by reason, and are in harmony with the sacred ordinances'. From the words of either passage the inference is to be drawn that a custom is unreasonable if it is without rational basis, even though it be not clearly contrary to reason.

But in order to judge whether a custom is wholly lacking in rational basis it will be necessary to recall that for our present discussion, the reasonableness or unreasonableness of a custom is to be judged chiefly by the criterion of its moral effect, and that this can be manifold. For at one time the custom has the effect of creating an obligation with respect to its observance; at another, of permitting such and such a usage by revoking a law prohibiting it; occasionally, too, it has no more than the effect of approving such an action, or at most, of reasonably urging and inclining men to use it. The effect, then, in respect of which the custom is said to be reasonable or unreasonable, must be carefully weighed that the custom may be so judged. For it may call for the fulfilment of more conditions to achieve one purpose or effect, than to achieve another. Thus, the fulfilment of more conditions is required for a custom to have the power of introducing law, for instance, than is required for a custom to be merely good: and so, in order that it be reasonable, in relation to this end [of establishing law], it is necessary to consider whether the custom possesses, in addition to its character of goodness, the other conditions required for a just law; as, that the burden of its observance be tolerable, and also that it be useful for the public welfare. If, however, a custom is regarded in its relation to the revocation of a human law, in order that it be reasonable, it is not necessary that it be not a bad one—at least not bad because it is prohibited; but it will suffice that, of itself and apart from any prohibiting law, it is not evil. It must, however, have some reasonable cause, on account of which it may be established against the existing law; because otherwise it would be established against the law in an unreasonable way. For, in general, the revocation of a just law without cause is unreasonable. This we shall show later.

17. *Two principal effects in this subject-matter of a custom. The best rule for discerning whether a custom is reasonable or unreasonable.* Wherefore, in

considering a custom in relation to those two effects which are of chief importance in this subject-matter—namely, that of enforcing the performance of similar actions, and that of giving release from the obligation to such actions, despite the law—the best rule, it seems to me (assuming the moral rectitude of the subject-matter, at least in respect to its not being repugnant to divine and natural law), is to test the custom by the conditions necessary for a just law, or for the just revocation of a law. For if these conditions shall have been found to be present in due proportion in the custom, the custom will be judged reasonable in the same proportion; if, however, these conditions are lacking, the custom will be unreasonable, by comparison with such and such an effect.

I find this rule laid down by Geminiano (on *Sext*, Bk. I, tit. II, chap. i), and Antonio de Butrio (*De Consuetudine*, Chap. xi), who are followed by Sylvester (on word *consuetudo*, Qu. 1), Soto (*De Iustitia et Iure*, Bk. I, qu. VII, art. 2), and Sánchez (*De Sancto Matrimonii Sacramento Disputationum*, Bk. VII, disp. iv, no. 41 [no. 14]). I have used here the words 'by comparison', &c. because, if the custom is to be judged apart from these conditions, and merely in the sense of usage, or voluntary repetition, it will be judged to be a reasonable one, if its matter is not bad. According to this rule, it will be easy to pass judgment upon a custom, in relation to whatever other effect it may have, as we shall make clear in subsequent Chapters dealing with these effects.

In the next section,[7] another subdivision of unreasonable custom will be explained.

CHAPTER VII

What Sort of Custom Is or Is Not Condemned in Law

1. Another division of custom now requires explanation, that, namely, of custom condemned in law and that permitted by the law. This division, although it is related to the preceding group, is yet distinct from

---

7. [I.e. of the following Chapter.—Tr.]

it, as we shall see. The title of the question is understood as concerned with positive human law; for what concerns the natural law in the matter has been sufficiently discussed in a former Chapter.[1] For a custom which has been found by a prudent judgment applying right reason to be unreasonable will also be condemned in natural law; and a custom which has not been found unreasonable by right reason will not be condemned by the law. Divine law, however, has no rule on this matter, as is evident.

A custom to be condemned by law ought to be declared unreasonable or specifically prohibited upon that ground. It will, then, be necessary first of all to learn what kind of custom is to be held as condemned by positive law. Some writers hold that every custom expressly and specifically abrogated by law is condemned in law. Others add that this abrogation is not enough, but that it is necessary that the custom be forbidden by law. Others, again, hold that even such prohibition is not sufficient, but rather that it is necessary for the custom to be declared unreasonable through law or else that it be prohibited specifically on this very ground, that is to say on the ground that the custom is unreasonable. This last assertion is the true one, and the one more commonly accepted. It is clearly held by Navarrus (*Consilia,* Bk. III, *De Censibus,* consil. vii), Covarruvias, and other writers presently to be cited. We must, then, explain and demonstrate it.

2. *First conclusion.* Therefore, I assert that human law at times abrogates custom; and that at times also it prohibits custom; and that at other times it condemns custom. I say, also, that these three effective dispositions of law are distinct. I do not find the foregoing statement set forth very explicitly by the authorities; in fact, I find even that they frequently confound the meaning of these three. Yet the three are really distinct, as can be gathered from the common teaching on these matters. Indeed, even a fourth member might be added, namely, 'an unqualified opposition to a custom'. But this last, although it is in some respects distinct, seems rather to coincide with the third. I shall, therefore, prove the truth of each of the three separately.

---

1. [*Supra,* p. 529; Chap. iv.—Tr.]

As to the first point of our first conclusion, in respect to the question of abrogation, or revocation of a custom, I say that it does no more than annul an existing custom. For the phrase derogating from or revoking or (what is the same thing) a revocatory clause proposed in law in absolute terms, can, in the strict meaning of the words, apply only to a past fact: therefore, a law abrogating a custom can affect only a custom already in existence. Just so a written law revoking a contrary law relates to one already in existence: for if there were no law that pre-existed, the revocation would be unnecessary, and even useless. Nor could such a law have been made, except in a case of error, or on the condition that if there is such a law, it be revoked. Therefore, such a law always has reference to a previously existing one. The same is true, then, of a law revoking a custom.

In what way one must understand the clause 'notwithstanding any custom whatever'. It follows from this that when there is attached to a law the clause, 'notwithstanding any custom whatever', as in the *Constitutions* of Clement (Bk. I, tit. iii, chap. vii), and in similar laws, that phrase revokes only a custom already existing: it does not prohibit future custom, since such a clause regards not the future, but merely the past. A custom which can have existence only in a future time, and does not yet exist, cannot be in opposition to a law in the present. Such a clause can annul only a custom which can operate against the law, and hence this law relates solely to an existing custom, and does not extend to future custom. The same is true of every revoking clause, however phrased, unless a qualifying note is added to it.

This position is supported by the consideration that such an effect is of a burdensome character; the meaning, then, of the words of such a clause should not be extended beyond their force and strict meaning. Usage also confirms this opinion; for when a lawgiver wishes to extend the effect of law beyond the usual one, he makes an explicit statement of that intention, as we shall presently explain.

3. *A simple abrogation of a custom is not equivalent to a condemnation of the same.* For almost the same reasons, a simple abrogation of a custom is not equivalent to a condemnation thereof, since a custom can be abrogated, not because it is unreasonable, but simply for the reason that it pleases the lawmaker so to do, since he judges that, under present conditions, this

course is more expedient. It is, obviously, possible for a certain custom to be, in a certain situation, in some way inexpedient, even if it is not essentially bad or unreasonable. This seems to be self-evident if we keep in mind what was said in a previous Chapter[2] about bad and unreasonable custom. When, therefore, a law revokes a custom simply or without any further declaration, there is no presumption that the law condemns it as unreasonable. Just as, when a subsequent law revokes a prior one, it is not therefore to be presumed that it condemns the earlier one as bad or unreasonable. Generally speaking, from a legal standpoint, what is not proved to be evil, nor condemned as such, is not presumed to be bad, but rather is presumed to be good, even if some other course is at the time preferred because it can produce more useful effects, or is judged to be here and now more expedient.

Finally, this opinion is clearly to be gathered from the passage in the *Sext* (Bk. I, tit. II, chap. i), which says that a law does not abrogate a reasonable custom, 'unless an express provision is made in the law'.[3] These words imply, therefore, that law does at times revoke a reasonable custom, and that, from the fact of revocation alone, no conclusion is to be drawn that the custom is unreasonable or condemned.

This doctrine is in both its members that commonly taught, a fact that can be seen from the Gloss on the *Constitutions* of Clement (Bk. I, tit. III, chap. vii, word *consuetudo*) and Alexander of Imola thereon [*Consilia,* Bk. VI, consil. 134, no. 33], Dominicus de S. Geminiano (on *Sext,* Bk. I, tit. II, chap. i), Angelus de Clavasio (*Summa,* on word *consuetudo,* no. 9) and Sylvester ([word *consuetudo,*] Qu. 6, no. 10), although the latter seems to contradict the first part of our thesis. Of this obscurity I shall, however, speak in a moment. Ancharano, Panormitanus, and others (on *Decretals,* Bk. I, tit. II, chap. xiii) hold the same opinion, as also does Felinus (on *Decretals,* Bk. II, tit. XIX, chap. ii, no. II), where he cites Bartolus, Baldus and other writers. Navarrus, (*Consilia,* Bk. III, *De Censibus,* consil. vii), and Covarruvias (*Variarum Resolutionum,* Bk. III, chap. xiii, no. 4, concl. 4)

---

2. [*Supra,* p. 553; Chap. vi.—Tr.]

3. [Suárez indicates by italics that this statement is a direct quotation from the canon law. As a matter of fact, only the clause 'unless an express provision is made' is a verbatim citation from the *Sext;* the first part of the statement being a paraphrase.—Tr.]

are also in agreement with us here, although the latter seems to hold a different doctrine on the second point, where he agrees with Antoninus, whose opinion I shall discuss immediately.

4. Antoninus ([*Summa Theologica,*] Pt. I, tit. xvi, § 6) seems to hold a doctrine opposed to that set down in the first member of our assertion, and cites in his support the authority of Archidiaconus and Giovanni d'Andrea (on *Sext,* Bk. I, tit. ii, chap. i). For Antoninus says that even though the law does not condemn the contrary custom, if it abolishes that custom simply and without qualification, nevertheless, it is to be understood as abolishing not only existing custom but future custom also. This seems to be the import of the teaching of Angelus de Clavasio (*ibid.*) and of Sylvester (*ibid.,* no. 9), in the case of laws that carry a clause derogating from a custom. In support of their opinion they cite the authority of Bartolus and Antoninus, and derive it from the arguments of Panormitanus (on *Decretals,* Bk. II, tit. xix, chap. ii, no. 8) and those of Felinus (*ibid.,* no. 11). They seem to hold [that the law *condemns* future custom] even if the law does not expressly prohibit for the future. This seems to be the trend of their argument, namely, that the law is continuously in force; therefore, if the law once and for all explicitly derogates from a custom, it does so for all time, and is continuously in opposition thereto. Covarruvias (*Variarum Resolutionum, ibid.,* concl. 2), also, can be cited as holding this opinion. In the passage in which he seems to do so, he uses the word *reprobandi* (condemning), which involves a different principle, as I shall presently show.[4]

Other authors, however, to avoid self-contradiction, speak not of a law merely revoking a custom, but only of that which stands unconditionally opposed to a custom. But this involves still another principle, as I shall immediately make clear by indicating the words by which such opposition arises out of the law, and what effect such opposition has. And so the argument advanced [against our position] may at most have some force in the case of a law that stands in unconditional opposition to a custom, but it has no weight against the doctrine we have laid down. For a law dealing

4. [*Infra,* Section 7.—Tr.]

merely with a past action always has, of course, force against that action; but it never can have force against something in the future, which was not in being when the law was enacted.

5. *A law prohibiting a custom contrary to it has reference to both past and future customs.* As to the second point of our first conclusion, that concerning law prohibiting a custom, it must be said that the law forbidding a custom contrary to it, annuls not only past custom, but also future custom: or rather, it sets up a barrier to or prevents its introduction; it does not, however, on that account, condemn such a custom.

The first part of this assertion assumes that law does sometimes prohibit a future custom. This is the common doctrine, and as an example of such prohibition there is usually offered the law of the *Digest* (XLVII. xii. 3, § 5). This law, it is true, refers to a municipal ordinance, but it is cited for purposes of comparison. Thus Tiraqueau (*De Utroque Retractu,* Pref., no. 17) infers from this law that 'when a law condemns (that is, prohibits) a future custom, it does so by specifying that custom'. Hence the authors just cited, Antoninus, Angelus de Clavasio and Sylvester accept the first part of the above conclusion. Navarrus and Soto (*De Iustitia,* Bk. I, qu. VII, art. 2), have done the same more explicitly.

The reason here is clear, since a prohibition has reference to actions in the future: for it cannot forbid those which are past; nor can it forbid present actions, not, that is, in so far as they have already taken place, but only to the extent that they may not persist in the future, for only as such are they capable of prohibition. Hence, if a law prohibits a custom, it opposes not only that which has been established, but that which is to be established, and, in so far as the law of itself can do so, it sets up an obstacle against its introduction.

Now the law is understood to prohibit a custom, first, if it expressly prohibits that any custom be permitted introduction contrary to that law; or when it forbids its introduction, as Navarrus says. Again, the law does so—as is probable—when it absolutely prohibits every contrary custom, even if that law does not expressly mention the future or the introduction of the custom, as when it says, 'It is our will that no custom have force against this law', or carries a clause to that effect. Such a law would seem to have reference to all such custom, both that which is in existence and any that can be introduced. It would seem also to oppose all such, because the words are quite absolute and universal in application, and apply without distinction of past and future, and there is no evident reason why their application should be restricted.

The writers of whom we have been speaking interpret as of the same import a clause which derogates without qualification from a contrary custom. Antoninus speaks in this sense, when he says that a custom is abolished absolutely by such a law. Such a meaning can be inferred from the example which he brings forward from the *Code* (XI. lviii [IV. xxxii. 26, § 3]), where it is said: 'Nor is it permissible for a judge to increase the said rate of interest by reason of a custom existing in the region.' These words would seem not only to revoke an existing custom, but also to oppose it absolutely, even for the future, because these words include not merely a revocation, but also a prohibition. This is evident from the words *nec licet iudici* (nor is it permissible for a judge): for the words *non liceat* (it is not permissible) express a prohibition, and are, therefore, addressed to judges exercising their office not only at that time, but at all future times. The words apply, accordingly, to future custom in the time of any judge whatsoever. The reason given above is rightly applicable here, namely, that the law is continuously in force.

But from this passage [, i.e. *Code,* IV. xxxii. 26, § 3] Bartolus infers only that the law revokes a custom of the past. Nevertheless, in the context of that law, the force of those words would seem to be stronger. I gather, however, from the opinion of Bartolus that the words [of such a law] are not to be readily extended to future customs, but are extended only when this is demanded by the strict meaning of the words.

6. *A law prohibiting a future custom does not therefore condemn it.* The second part [of our assertion in Sect. 5]—namely, that a law which prohibits absolutely a custom in the future, does not therefore condemn such a custom—has been taught more explicitly by Navarrus in the passage cited (*Consilia,* Bk. III, *De Censibus,* consil. vii) than by the other writers on this matter. He says that a custom is not unreasonable from the fact that a law is in opposition to it, annulling it or commanding that it be not established, unless the law at the same time declares that the custom is unreasonable or a corruption of law.

This doctrine may be inferred from a passage of Bartolus (on *Digest,* I. iii. 32, in *Repetition,* after opposit. 10 [opposit. 11], no. 5), in which he makes a distinction between a condemnation and a prohibition of a custom—even when the prohibition is explicit and relates to the future. And the proof which we used to establish the first conclusion concerning law which revokes custom, can be used with little change here. That consideration is especially applicable which is drawn from the argument that a written law can revoke an existing custom, not on the ground of its being unreasonable, but for other reasons. So also, a written law can forbid the future establishment of the custom, not because it is unreasonable, but because for other considerations it seems expedient to the lawmaker to forbid it: either because he presumes that the reasons moving him to revoke it will be continuously applicable, and so he is moved by them to prohibit it; or because he may wish, perhaps, through the addition of the prohibition to give greater inducement and compulsion to the observance of the law. Therefore, from the prohibition for the future alone, we cannot infer or presume that the custom[5] is unreasonable, or that it is condemned as such. But what effect such a law may have on the custom thus prohibited, we shall see in the following Chapters.

7. *A custom is condemned when it is expressly declared to be unreasonable.* I come, therefore, to the third point of our first conclusion, that which deals with custom condemned by law. For the conclusion to be drawn from the foregoing discussion is that a custom is condemned in law, when to a revocation or prohibition there is added in express terms the declaration that the custom is unreasonable.

Such a declaration is made in the laws in various ways. An example is the passage in the *Sext* (Bk. III, tit. iii, only chap.), where the words, 'disapproving entirely of that custom', are used. In the *Decretals* (Bk. II, tit. xix, chap. ii), we read: 'we condemn such a custom'. In the *Decretals* (Bk. I, tit. iv, chap. v), a certain custom is made void since 'by reason thereof the force of ecclesiastical discipline would be broken'. Again (*ibid.,* chap. iii), a custom is abolished 'because it is held to be not reasonable', and (*ibid.,* chap. vii), 'since this is rightly thought to be

---

5. [Reading *consuetudo* for *lex.*—Reviser.]

not so much a custom as a corruption'. In the *Decretals* (Bk. III, tit. VII, chap. iii), a certain custom is termed 'evil', and later another is declared to be 'contrary to what is proper, opposed to rectitude and in violation of the canonical ordinances'. Accordingly, I think that the principle stated above is valid when a custom is termed 'an abuse', and is declared as such not to be of obligation, as is stated in the *Decretals* (Bk. I, tit. IV, chap. x).

When, therefore, in some such fashion, a custom is condemned, then the law has the force, not only of prohibiting it, but also of declaring it to be bad—as Covarruvias held (*Variarum Resolutionum, ibid.*, conclusion 2). Thus, the law is said to revoke such custom specifically. For the same reason words of this kind are necessary, because without them the law does not state what the character of the custom was or is; it does no more than forbid it.

8. Whence, it follows that, even though it is a custom of the past which the law annuls, if, by way of justification, it adds that the custom is corrupt or is unreasonable, by that very fact the law also forbids and condemns a future custom of the same sort, as long as the circumstances remain the same.

This opinion is that of Panormitanus (on *Decretals*, Bk. II, tit. XIX, chap. ii, nos. 7 and 8), and Tiraqueau (*De Utroque Retractu*, Pref., nos. 18 and 19), who refers to many other authorities. Their argument in proof of this opinion is that an unreasonable custom is prohibited by every law and for all time, according to the *Decretals* (Bk. I, tit. IV, chap. xi), and other Chapters. Navarrus was also of this opinion, and the passage in the Gloss (on *Decretals*, Bk. I, tit. IV, chap. xi, word *rationabilis*) is of the same sense: 'that is a reasonable custom, which the laws do not condemn'. The word 'condemn' (*improbandi*) here is to be taken in its proper meaning, and it must be understood in the same sense where it is stated at the end of the Chapter that reasonable custom is one 'which is not opposed to the canonical ordinances'—those ordinances, namely, as Navarrus notes, which condemn unreasonable customs. Whence the same Gloss adds, an unreasonable custom is one 'which is condemned by law', and from all the laws which it cites, it is clear that the word 'condemned' is used in its proper sense.

Finally, writers must be understood in this sense when they say that a custom condemned in law can no longer be valid; and although they sometimes use the word 'derogation' in this connexion, they can be modestly interpreted as holding the doctrine here set forth. The proper definition of the term 'derogation', and the difference between a custom from which there has been a derogation and one that has been prohibited or condemned, I shall explain in Chapter xvi of this Book.

9. *Condemnation of a custom can be effected in a twofold manner.* It remains to notice that this condemnation of a custom can be understood as accomplished by the law in two ways: by a mere declaration of law, or by way of regulation as well. The former takes place only when a custom is either so clearly evil as to be contrary to natural or divine law; or when it is evidently useless, and harmful to or at variance with the general welfare. The latter way seems to be used when it is not immediately evident from natural or divine principles alone that the custom is unreasonable, and nevertheless for the sake of greater decorum, or for the good of religion, or for the rigour of discipline, the law provides that the custom in question is to be held as unreasonable. For unquestionably it is possible for human law, and especially for the canon law, to do this, since such a regulation by the law may be in the highest degree proper in the interest of good morals.

The distinction between these two modes of condemnation is to be seen in the language of the laws themselves. For sometimes a custom is condemned by the phrase *declaramus* (we declare), as in the *Decretals* (Bk. I, tit. IV, chap. x). At other times, however, the verb *irritare* (to make null and void) is used, as in the *Decretals* (*ibid.,* chap. v), where it is said: 'We have decided that such a custom is to be made null and void.' These words indicate, in their *strict* sense, that such a custom previously and of itself was not void; and consequently, that it is not essentially unreasonable, but only that it has been made void by law. This point is admirably made by Molina, in his work *De Iustitia et Iure* (Tract. II, disp. 79). Still, I hold that by such nullification, a custom of that character has remained for ever condemned by law. For that nullification (*irritatio*) was not a nullification of some particular fact, nor was it (so to speak) a transitory one; it was constitutive of law, and as such, universal and perpetual; therefore, it applies always, and always resists a custom of that kind as an unreasonable one. This is made clearer by the fact that this voiding [law] was imposed not as the punishment of a fault, but for the reason that, 'if such a custom were to stand, the force of church discipline would be broken'. [This voiding law] was, then, set up in essential opposition to the establishment of a custom in that matter, to prevent for all time the disruption of the force of church discipline that would be brought about through such a custom. For it is not alone the intrinsic character of the things to be done or not to be done that determines the nature and condition of a discipline, but rather the fact that the law rules that this or that must or must not be done. It is for this reason that we said that the condemnation of the custom of which we have been speaking was not a purely declaratory one, but rather one regulatory in its nature.

10. In this sense, also, are to be understood many laws condemning certain customs or prescriptions, which, from the nature of the case alone, do not immediately seem to be unreasonable. In the same way, some decrees condemn customs which unsettle canonical ordinances, or curtail them, as being opposed, that is, to the exactitude intended by them. Moreover, in this sense is to be understood the Gloss quoted above (on *Decretals,* Bk. I, tit. IV, chap. xi, word *rationabilis*), which says that a custom is unreasonable which the law condemns. This meaning would seem to be the only one admitted by Baldus (*Consilia,* Vol. V, cons. 401 [cons. 349]), when he said that in order that a custom may be spoken of as reasonable, it is enough that it be not condemned. Yet this statement does not seem to be strictly true; since a custom can be essentially, and of its own nature, unreasonable, although it has not been condemned in law.

It is possible, then, that these writers intended their words as applying only to the external forum; or, at all events, that opinion can be understood to refer to a condemnation by law, either on some particular ground, or, at least, upon general principles—as, for instance, that the custom weakens the force of church discipline, or that it derogates from the liberty of the Church, or for some reason of a similar character.

Finally, a distinction can be drawn between these two modes of condemnation; for that which is purely declarative seems to be the more immutable of the two, as founded in natural reason alone, or in the divine law; the other, which is positive, since it emanates from human law, can suffer change, either through new law, or sometimes by reason of change in the matter itself. This is the opinion of Panormitanus (on *Decretals,* Bk. II, tit. xix, chap. ii, no. 8, and *De Consuetudine,* Chap. xi, no. 12 [no. 21]), as we shall explain at greater length in Chapter xvi of this Book.

CHAPTER VIII

Concerning Another Division of Custom into That Which Is Valid by Prescription and That Which Is Not

1. This is the last division of custom, and I have determined to discuss it in this Chapter, because a clear notion of it is necessary both for a treatment of this matter, and for the explanation of the effects of custom. In this whole matter, the chief difficulty centres round the nature of custom valid by prescription, and we shall, therefore, give most of our attention to that; for when that has been made clear, it will be easy to explain the nature of custom not validated in that way.

Certain civil jurists, we must begin by noting, have said that there is no such thing as consuetudinary law obtained by prescription. Cynus and Pierre d'Ailly, who are referred to by Abbas [, i.e. Panormitanus,] (*De Consuetudine,* Chap. xi, no. 7) and Angelus de Ubaldis (on *Code,* VII. xxxix. 8) held this opinion. They were induced to think so, because custom is not settled law; but rather it settles law. For it is thus, as we have pointed out in Chapter One of this Book, that the custom of which we are treating is to be distinguished from prescription. The custom, accordingly, that we are here discussing, is not prescription; it cannot, therefore, be validated by prescription.

The logical validity of this argument is established as follows: when it is said that a custom is validated by prescription, the assertion is made either of a custom of law or of a custom of fact. But the first cannot be separated from the second, because whatever is established by prescription is established through prescription by a usage of some sort. Therefore, if the legal custom is validated by prescription, it must be validated by some usage, which is nothing else than the custom of fact itself. With reference to that, we must ask in turn: by what usage can it be validated by prescription? By some usage distinct from itself, or by itself? But not the first, because we observe a custom not by another usage, but by its own, because custom is itself a usage, and a usage is not exercised by a different one. Otherwise, we should be involved in an infinite series. Nor is custom established by itself, since it is not a prescription as assumed; and nothing comes under the heading of prescription except by some specific act of prescription.

Several confirmatory arguments are advanced for this position. One is based upon the fact that every prescription requires good faith, but this requirement is not necessary in this sort of custom, for it can sometimes, as we have said, be established by means of sinful actions. Likewise, a prescription demands a definite period of time, fixed by law; but in the case of this custom there is no law that requires a fixed time for the prescription. Finally, every prescription is obtained against some individual who is unwilling to have it established; but this element is not present in the custom of which we are speaking. For all these reasons, validation by prescription cannot be demanded in this sort of custom, and therefore the distinction laid down by us cannot stand.

2.[1] *The existence of a customary prescription is approved.* Nevertheless, we must assert first, that there is a custom which settles law, that is, which is legal, and which can be validated by prescription. This statement is explicitly made in the canon law (*Decretals,* Bk. I, tit. IV, chap. xi), in the words: *legitime praescripta* (legitimately established by prescription); it is sufficiently suggested by the *Sext* (Bk. I, tit. IV, chap. iii), as also in the *Decretals* (*ibid.,* chap. viii), on which the Gloss comments in the last note, as well as in the *Decretals* (Bk. II, tit. XII, chap. iii), on which the Gloss also comments (on words *De Consuetudine*), and in other passages to which writers on this matter refer.

In connexion with these references, the reader must remember that the laws use a different manner of language, when they deal with the true prescription of things, or of private rights. [This caution must be given] since we are dealing, not with prescription, but with legal custom. In respect of that, we find scarcely any law requiring that a custom be validated

---

1. [This section-number omitted in text.—Tr.]

by prescription, except[2] the aforesaid last chapter (*Decretals,* Bk. I, tit. IV, chap. xi). For the *Sext* (Bk. I, tit. IV, chap. iii) may perhaps refer to prescription, since it treats of the custom of a bishop with respect to his exercising his jurisdiction without the advice of his cathedral chapter. But the *Decretals* (Bk. I, tit. IV, chap. viii), makes no mention of a prescriptive custom by name, but merely says: 'If the custom has been such as to prejudice the common law [. . .].' *Decretals,* Bk. II, tit. XII, chap. iii, is best interpreted as relating to a true prescription concerning a right of election, and *Decretals,* Bk. I, tit. VI, chap. l, deals with prescription, also, in speaking of the subject of elections, as do other Chapters which are cited.

Nevertheless, one law is sufficient to oblige us not to depart from its terms. Upon this point, the canonists thereon (on *Decretals,* Bk. I, tit. IV, chap. xi) are agreed: Panormitanus (*De Consuetudine,* Chap. xi, no. 7), Rochus (*De Consuetudine,* Sect. 3, at the beginning) who deals with it at great length, Antonio de Butrio and others thereon (*De Consuetudine,* Chap. xi), and Cardinal[3] (on *Decretum,* Pt. I, dist. VIII, can. vii). Bartolus mentions this view explicitly, in writing against Peter, to whom he alludes (on *Digest,* I. iii. 32, in *Repetition,* Qu. 2, no. 15). Baldus, Jason and others set forth the same opinion on this matter (on *Digest,* I. iii. 32). The Gloss (on *Digest,* L. xvii. 166 [54]) provides an excellent statement of the same tenor.

Now, even though it may seem to be a mere matter of words, I think that it is necessary for a clear discussion [of prescriptive custom] that we give some attention to the manner in which the jurists just mentioned speak of it, defining it rather from the connotations of the word 'prescription', than from the nature of the custom itself. Thus, Panormitanus says that for a custom to be [prescriptive] means no more than that it has been secured through the running of a period of time required for a prescription. Rochus (*De Consuetudine,* Sect. 3, at the beginning), in like manner, says that to assert that a custom ought to be established by prescription, is equivalent to saying that it demands a certain duration of time. Baldus (on *Digest,* I. iii. 32, opposit. 7) states that a prescriptive custom is one which

2. [For *praepter* read *praeter.*—Tr.]
3. [I.e. Gratian.—Tr.]

is perfected and firmly grounded through lapse of time. Bartolus, however, explains the term 'validated by prescription' as meaning 'established by custom after the manner of a servitude'. This latter definition would seem to be different from the preceding one, yet both are true when their meaning is properly interpreted.

3.[4] *Both custom itself and the right acquired through it can be validated by prescription.* Therefore, in order to explain better the above assertion and its basis in reason, I note that, just as of a true prescription, so also of a custom, it is true to say that both the custom, and the right which has been acquired thereby, can be validated by prescription. Thus, in the case of a true prescription, a house, a servitude, or an action can be said to be the objects of prescription: consequently, the custom of making use of such a thing is the prescription itself. However, it is not such, unless it has been consummated within a required period of time, along with other circumstances. Therefore, when such is the case, it is also termed a 'prescriptive', to distinguish it from an inchoate custom, or from one imperfect in some other way.

So then, a custom of the sort that we are here discussing, can, in so far as it is a legal entity, be validated by prescription, since prescription has been acquired by means of a custom that has been consummated, that is, by a custom fulfilling the conditions required by law. This is the doctrine of Bartolus, and he bases it upon analogy with a prescription of a servitude. For although there is a difference in the rights acquired in a servitude and in those of an unwritten law, nevertheless, the manner whereby each is established, is—with due proportion—the same. Thus, also, a consuetudinary law may be said to be validated by prescription.

Whence, also, it is to be said that the custom of fact itself, through which a legal right is established, in so far as it requires the assistance of the law to attain a certain degree of perfection and consummation, may be termed a prescription: for the right itself cannot be said to have been validated by prescription, unless the approach thereto (so to speak) may be called a prescription. And, therefore, such a custom of fact may be said to be prescriptive, in order to distinguish it from a custom which is inchoate

---

4. [The section number is omitted in the Latin text.—Tr.]

or imperfect; that is, in order to show that it has fulfilled all the conditions called for by the law, and that especially which touches the time of its running. This is the meaning of the words of Baldus and Panormitanus (*supra*) and that of the Gloss (on *Digest*, L. xvii. 54) when this Gloss speaks of a firmly grounded custom.

4. *Refutation of the contrary opinion.* The basis, then, of the contrary opinion is easily destroyed. Primarily, the opinion is based upon an ambiguity in the terms. For, when, earlier in this Book,[5] we distinguished custom from prescription, we also pointed out that these words are sometimes taken in a broad meaning and used interchangeably. For even prescription is a custom brought to its culmination in a certain way; and, every custom brought in like proportion to completion is usually called a prescription; in the same way, a custom can be called a prescription, as well in law as in fact, as has been explained. When, therefore, in an earlier Chapter we distinguished custom from prescription, we were using these two terms in their strict meaning. For the present, however, we assert that it is possible for a custom, even a legal one, to be, and to be spoken of as prescriptive in the broader sense of that term.

Custom and prescription when used in the broad meaning are equivalent to each other; but in their exact meaning they are distinct. Our answer to the argument for the contrary opinion is that a custom in its character of a legal rule takes its epithet 'prescriptive' from the character of the custom by which it is acquired; but that a custom of fact takes that epithet from the conditions wherewith it was involved in order to be such: namely, because it is of long duration, is voluntary, is observed by common consent, and the like. So the custom itself can be said to be prescriptive, for the reason that it has that completeness (as it were) by its own intrinsic and essential perfection. Further, we can say almost the same thing of any prescription properly so-called.

In reply to the confirmatory argument for the contrary assertion, I say that it proves no more than that this custom is called 'prescriptive' owing to conditions different from those which are proper to a true prescription, and that consequently prescription properly so-called and prescriptive custom

---

5. [*Supra*, pp. 509 *et seq.*—Tr.]

are not identical. It does not, however, prove that this custom is not prescriptive in the broader meaning of that word [as we have defined it].

5. From this solution of the arguments opposed to ours, it is clear that this use of the adjective 'prescriptive' and this definition of its meaning, indicate that there is a kind of custom which requires, together with the fulfilment of other conditions, a certain duration of time in order that it may be true custom, and be without qualification called such by the law. This is the cardinal point of our present discussion, and that which we must now take up to establish our conclusion.

In the first place, the question may be asked, whether legal custom occasionally requires for its validity the running of a fixed length of time, that is, a period and duration such as are demanded for a true prescription. On this point, it may be noted that the opinion of some theologians denies that a definite time is required for establishing a legal custom, that is, one establishing unwritten law; they hold that this period should be defined at the discretion of a prudent man. This Soto held (*De Iustitia,* Bk. I, qu. vii, art. 2), and his opinion is followed by many of the modern commentators upon St. Thomas (I.–II, qu. 97). They are induced to think so because this period is not fixed by the nature of the matter, as is self-evident; nor, again, is it fixed by canon law, nor by civil—at least by common civil law—hence, [they say,] it is not possible for such period to be defined in any other manner than by the decision of a prudent judgment. The validity of the inference appears self-evident; no other way of fixing the period of time can be thought of. The proof of the minor premiss is that all laws, canonical as well as civil, which designate a certain time for the running of the prescription period, have reference to a private prescription, or to a legal disposition, as in the case of ownerships, servitudes, and of similar rights; hence, the argument runs, the periods fixed by these laws cannot be extended in such wise as to regulate legally the period of time requisite for a legal custom.

6. The antecedent, as far as canon law is concerned, is proved from the fact that all the laws which are cited on this point clearly refer to prescription properly so called, a fact which I have noted.[6] This can be seen in

---

6. [See *supra,* Section 2.—Tr.]

the entire title concerning custom [, i.e. *Decretals,* Bk. I, tit. iv], in which custom validated by prescription is dealt with only in the last Chapter of this title; and that Chapter makes no mention of the length of time necessary for the running of such custom.

In relation to the civil law, the truth of the statement in the antecedent[7] is a better ascertained fact. Abbas [, i.e. Panormitanus] (*De Consuetudine,* Chap. xi) expressly admits it, and because of it[8] some civilians deny that a custom can be validated by prescription, as I have said. Those who hold the opposite opinion ought to produce a text to prove it. And hence I have referred only to the common law that prevails generally; for the matter might be otherwise in the case of the special law of a particular kingdom. But of this I speak later. The validity of the inference [in proof of the subsidiary argument] is demonstrated from the fact that a true prescription is very different from a custom: so different, that what is determined in the one, cannot, with any foundation, be extended to the other. This is especially true, since with respect to each the reasoning is not the same: for in a prescription, a right is acquired by one person against another, contrary to the latter, who is deprived of his own property, or of his right; and it is for this that it has been necessary to fix definitely a certain time within which the [former] owner of a right can and ought to exercise diligence, in order to recover his own property, or to preserve his own rights, so that if he neglects to do so, he may be justly deprived of them. For this reason, then, according to the character of the property involved, and according to the presence[9] or absence of the person prescribed against, a longer[10] or shorter time[11] is usually defined for the establishment of a prescription. In the establishment of a custom, however, no prescriptive right is acquired against an unwilling person; in fact, the custom is founded upon the tacit

---

7. [That time is not of the essence of consuetudinary law.—REVISER.]

8. [The opinion of Panormitanus.—REVISER.]

9. [Suárez is referring here to the knowledge or ignorance on the owner's part of the act of the person attempting to obtain the prescriptive right.—TR.]

10. [For *mais* read *maius.*—TR.]

11. [Suárez probably intended to say: 'according to the presence or absence of the person prescribed against, a *shorter or longer* time is usually defined for the establishment of a prescription', since a shorter space of time is usually required for the prescriptive period to run against an owner who is present.—TR.]

consent of the prince, as we say below; and hence it has not been necessary to define the length of the period whenever there is sufficient ground for assuming his tacit consent: the mere continuity of the custom for a longer or a shorter period suffices.[12]

7. *A definite time is required for a custom obtained by prescription. [Suárez rebuts the argument developed in Sections five and six.]* Nevertheless, I assert that for the prescriptive custom of which the laws speak—at least those in the *Decretals* (Bk. I, tit. iv, chap. xi), previously referred to—a certain, and definite time must be fixed. The secondary question, whether that period should be of this or that number of years, we shall discuss later. This is the opinion of the doctors of both the canon and civil law. The canonists, including Giovanni d'Andrea, Panormitanus, Antoninus and Rochus (*De Consuetudine,*[13] Sect. iii, no. 1), give it as their doctrine in their comments on this chapter.

This is the doctrine, likewise, of the Gloss and of the Doctors (on *Sext,* Bk. I, tit. II [tit. iv], chap. ii, and on *Decretum,* Pt. I, dist. VIII, can. vii; *ibid.,* dist. XI, can. iv; *ibid.,* dist. XII, can. vii). It is that maintained by Abbas [, i.e. Panormitanus] and Felinus (on *Decretals,* Bk. I, tit. XXXIV, chap. i [, no. 6]). It is set forth as the common teaching by the jurists (on *Digest,* I. iii. 32), by Bartolus (*ibid.,* qu. 2, at the beginning, no. 14); by Baldus and Jason (*ibid.,* no. 41 [no. 27] and on *Institutes,* I. ii, § 9). The teaching of these writers is followed by Gregory López (on *Las Siete Partidas,* Pt. I, tit. ii, law 5, gloss 4 [*glossa* g]), by Burgos de Paz (in Bk. I in *Tauri.,* no. 205), by Alexander of Imola (*Consilia,* Vol. II, consil. 66 [consil. 68, no. 1]). It is the opinion, also, of St. Antoninus (Pt. I, tit. xvi, only chap., § 4), Angelus de Clavasio (in his *Summa,* on word *consuetudo,* no. 8), Sylvester ([word *consuetudo,*] Qu. ii [, no. 6]), and Antonius Corduba ([*Quaestiones,*] Bk. I, qu. xii, ad 4). Finally, Navarrus (in *Consilia,* Bk. I, *De Consuetudine,* consil. ii [consil. i]) and Molina (*De Iustitia,* Tract. II, disp. 77), propound the same opinion.

It does not, then, seem safe to dissent on a moral question from an opinion which is so generally received. This is especially true, since this

---

12. [Reading *sufficit* for *sufficiat*—REVISER.]
13. [For *De Constitution,* read *De Consuetudine.*—TR.]

whole question is so intimately dependent upon positive law—in which case, the opinions of those who are experts in that branch of law must have greater weight than the opinions of those who are not thus expert. Again, no convincing argument in support of the opposite assertion can be given.

8. The first proof of our assertion [*supra*, Section 7] is taken from the *Decretals* (Bk. I, tit. IV, chap. xi), where, among the conditions of the custom there mentioned it is specified that it must be the result of prescription. But it cannot be said to be the result of prescription, except in relation to a definite, legitimate time, during which it should continue in order to be established by prescription.

An evasion. Some reply to the above argument, that such custom is said to be prescriptive, not univocally—as is the case with rights of ownership and other similar rights, which are obtained by prescription—but by analogy only, and because it is modelled upon true prescription in the sense that it is firmly grounded by running for a certain length of time, which if not that fixed by law, is at least that defined as sufficient by a prudent judge.

The evasion is rejected. But this evasion is arbitrary, and is contrary to all the authorities. Furthermore, it seriously impairs the force and utility of that law [*Decretals, ibid.*]. Wherefore, although it may be true that custom is different from prescription, nevertheless, it is necessary that this kind of custom which is spoken of as prescriptive, should accord with true prescription at least in the requirement of a long period of time within which it is said to be established, that is, validated by prescription; otherwise the term has no definite meaning.

When, then, that same law [*Decretals, ibid.*] requires that the custom be established by prescription, in language of the same character as that employed in other decrees demanding that a right of election, or other similar right, shall be lawfully established by prescription, we must hold that the law speaks univocally, at least respecting the period of time requisite: otherwise, it would leave the peculiar prescriptive character of the custom unexplained. Therefore, Panormitanus and almost all the writers have made it plain that the custom must be established by prescription, that is, must be obtained by reason of a period of time of length sufficient for a prescription. Even the word prescription itself connotes a fixed length of time: what is left to the free decision [even of a prudent judge] cannot be definite, or prescribed.

9. *The expression 'a long time' legally means at least ten years; nor is the determination of this period left by the law to the judgment of a prudent individual.* In the second place, a confirmation of our assertion is to be drawn from the term 'a long continued custom' which is used in that same chapter [*Decretals, ibid.*]. This term is taken from the civil law (*Code,* VIII. lii. 1, and from *ibid.,* 2). In other passages, it is spoken of as custom 'of long standing' (*diuturna*), as it is in the *Institutes* (I. ii, § 9) and in the *Digest* (I. iii. 33).

The phrase 'a long time', however, or 'long continued', is not an indefinite one in law, nor is it left to the discretion of a prudent individual, but means a period of at least ten years. The phrase, then, 'a long time', taken absolutely, refers to a period marked off, on the one hand, from a period of less than ten years[14]—which is held to be a brief period; and on the other hand, from a period longer than twenty years—which is termed 'very long': hence, the phrase denotes a period from ten to twenty years. According, then, to the variety of the attendant subject-matter or circumstances, the law usually requires a period of ten or twenty years. All of the foregoing is clear both from Rubric in *Code,* VII. xxxiii and from laws 1 and 2 and the following title (*ibid.,* xxxiv). Hence, when a law requires a long time for the sufficient confirmation of a custom, or its validation by prescription, the phrase is not indefinite in its meaning, but definite: its meaning is fixed by law, and it definitely indicates a period of at least ten years.

10. If, then, any one of the conditions of prescriptive custom is to be left to discretion, it must not be that which relates to this requirement of a full ten-year period, for this is (as it were) an essential requisite for custom, as such. This is the sense of Gloss 1 (on *Sext,* Bk. I, tit. IV, chap. iv), where it says that in the canon law a custom validated by prescription is one of forty years' duration, but that for a custom as custom, that is, for one intended to introduce new law, a period of ten years, at least, is required: this period, at least, is understood as referring to a long-continued custom.

14. [See also *infra,* pp. 656 *et seq.*—Tr.]

Accordingly, if any discretion were to be allowed [a place in the determination of the time element in prescriptive custom], it could be only in cases where the custom has run for a period of more than ten years: and then only to determine whether that period should (as it were) be automatically sufficient; or, whether at that point the decision of a prudent judge is required to determine whether this length of time suffices, or whether a longer period should be awaited.

However, not even in such a case should discretion be admitted: partly because it would subject long-continued custom too much to restriction, and would deprive it of a proper certainty without good reason; partly, and this is the most important consideration, because in whatever way the fixing of the length of time is left to the discretion [of a judge], there will follow not only a destruction of the true character of prescriptive custom but also of every appearance of one, or even of the appellation prescriptive as it is suggestively[15] applied to any custom, as the first argument in support of our assertion sufficiently proves.

The words of *Decretals,* Bk. I, tit. IV, chap. viii, are of no slight support to our position here: 'If such a custom shall have been approved, which does prejudice to the common law.' These words assume that such a custom is not left to the discretion of any one (for if this were so, the custom could hardly or not at all be approved); but that the custom has its essence and formality as custom defined by the law, and, accordingly, a definite time within which it accomplishes its prescriptive effect—as is there noted by the Gloss.

11. Another argument in confirmation of our assertion is this: the contrary opinion assumes that a long continuance of time is not essentially, but only incidentally, required in a custom which the law calls prescriptive. The conclusion is false. Therefore, . . .

The truth of our conclusion in the foregoing proof will be clear from a consideration of the principle on which the contrary opinion rests. Those who follow that opinion hold that the custom is required for the effects

---

15. [*Coloratae:* The term '*coloratus*' means 'giving a colour to' or 'suggestive of'. The phrase '*titulus coloratus*' is frequently used to signify a title to an office that has some specious justification.—REVISER.]

attributed to it, only as a sign of the tacit consent of the prince; hence, they conclude that this kind of custom does not call for a fixed number of years, but only for such a length of time as is needed for indicating in the judgment of an upright man the [tacit] consent of the prince. Therefore, I infer that in that opinion[16] the time element is incidentally required, because it is accidental that the token of consent is completed in a longer or shorter time; for a definite length of time is not *per se* demanded as a necessary condition for that manifestation. Therefore, the inference in the opinion aforesaid is obvious.

Its falsity, however, is proved: First—and here the points we have established earlier in this Chapter must be kept in mind—for the reason that it does not leave this kind of custom even a shadow of a prescriptive character: for a prescription of its essence requires time to run in its favour, and time is definitely determined, as is clear from the language of all the laws [that touch upon it]. Again, and the point is most important, this opinion is contrary to the fact that a custom is frequently actually completed and has become prescriptive in cases where the judgment of a prudent man would not be—human law apart—that the custom sufficed as evidence of the consent of the prince. It is clear, then, that such a custom is not a prescriptive one merely because it has endured a sufficient time to indicate the existence of the prince's consent to the mind of a prudent judge; but rather, it is because it has been validated by prescription, that it indicates the consent of the prince: therefore, such a prescription cannot be said to be established in such a length of time as only the judgment of a prudent mind can determine: therefore, it can be established only in a length of time that is fixed by law. The logical soundness of these conclusions is self-evident. The truth of the antecedent of my proof will be clear from what we shall have to say in Chapter xvi, concerning a custom which is sufficient for the revocation of a law.

12. *Reply to the basis of the contrary opinion.* I deny, therefore, the minor of the argument for the contrary opinion, and I assert that this period of time has been defined by positive law, both canonical and civil, each within its own sphere.

---

16. [For *Hinc ergo in foro ex,* read *Hinc ego infero in.*—Reviser.]

The determination of the time necessary can be made in two ways. This
determination of time may, it must be understood, be effected in two ways.
In the first, explicitly and specifically: in the manner, that is, of which we
are speaking in the present discussion, and which will be explained more
in detail in Chapters xv and xvi. We admit that the laws do not explicitly
define the period necessary for this particular subject-matter of laws, that
is, of legal customs. The reason is that this mode of explicit determination
is not a necessary one; there is another that is sufficient.

In the second way, then, the length of time [necessary for the validation
of a custom by prescription] is determined implicitly, and (as it were) by
the proper application of general principles expressed in the language of
law itself to the case of custom of this kind. It is in this sense, then, that I
assert that a fixed length of time is necessary according to law for a custom
to become validated by prescription.

For the law itself has distinguished in general: customs that are immemorial, of very long standing, of long standing, and [lastly] common
customs, those, that is, existing for a brief period; and the law has determined beforehand for each of these its own manner of duration or definite
period; as we, in company with Panormitanus and others, have noted.
This determination by the law is, however, a general one, and applies
properly to a custom of fact which can establish a right (*ius*) whether of
law, or of ownership, or of any other moral power. This opinion will be
seen to be that of Baldus (*Consilia,* Bk. V, cons. 34 [cons. 349,] no. 2) and
of Petrus Philippus Corneus (*Consilia,* Bk. IV, cons. 188, no. 10).

In particular, however, respecting a custom which establishes or destroys
a legal right, the laws determine that [the period of time] ought to be very
long or protracted, or that the custom should be validated by prescription,
as we have shown. Hence, the laws make it clear that a certain definite
time is necessary for such a custom. Thus, this declaration of the law is
clearly not a mere extension of the principles applicable to a prescription
properly so called so as to cover a legal custom; it is derived from a general determination of time requisite, under this or that denomination, in
custom itself. The truth of this assertion will be the more clearly realized
when it is recalled that the distinction between custom and prescription,
as set forth in the argument of the contrary opinion, is not sufficient.

For even though in the case of a legal custom, it is not necessary that the period of time be defined, as in the case of prescription, upon the ground that the custom is initiated in opposition to some person who is passively or actively unwilling that the custom be established, nevertheless such a determination of the running time of the custom can be necessary on another ground no less urgent: in order, that is, that we may have a definite and legal token of the consent of the prince, and that a matter so grave, public, and general in character, should not be left to the uncertain decision of a prudent individual: for it is obvious that even unwritten law ought to be as definite and uniform as possible.

This determination of the period of time is further necessary, because it must sometimes take the place of the [express] consent of the prince, so that such consent will be recognized as given in law itself, even if it is evident that it was not personally granted by the prince himself—a point which we shall discuss later.[17]

13.[18] *At least ten years are required for a prescriptive custom.* It remains for us to inquire how long is this period of time which is required for prescriptive custom. This definition cannot be properly made in general terms: for a longer or shorter period may be necessary, as the effects and circumstances of the custom vary. Hence, I shall here do no more than state in a general way that a period of at least ten years is required, on the principle that a long time is necessary, a period which, in law, comprises at least ten years. This has been expressly determined by a law of Spain ([*Las Siete Partidas,*] Pt. I, tit. II, law 5), where, speaking of a legal custom, it lays down a period of 'ten or, alternatively, twenty years'. Why this law laid down this alternative requirement will be stated in Chapter xv.

I have used in my assertion the words 'at least', because in some cases, more time is required. In Chapters xv and xvi I shall explain what those cases are. Our assertion, as thus explained, is the common one with all the authorities whom I have cited, and it does not involve any new difficulty

17. [The principle of the 'legal consent' of a superior is important. Laws are framed sometimes in such a way that a custom begun and persisted in may automatically receive the consent of the superior.—REVISER.]

18. [This Section incorrectly numbered '14' in the Latin text.—TR.]

except one, and that I shall take up in Chapter xvi, because it is more relevant to the matter of that Chapter.

14.[19] *A continuity of time is required in order that the custom may be said
to be lawfully validated by prescription.* It may, again, be asked whether this
period of time must be continuous. I reply that it must be so in order that
the custom may, in the definition of the aforesaid last Chapter [*Decretals,*
Bk. I, tit. IV, chap. xi], be said to be lawfully prescribed. All the commentators on that law are agreed on this point. And they dwell upon the word
'lawfully', since it signifies that the custom must have the same continuity as that demanded by the laws for prescription: but it is clear that an
uninterrupted period is necessary for prescription; the same, therefore,
is necessary for a custom valid by prescription. This was the doctrine of
Frederick de Senis (*Consilia,* 91, no. 5), who, for the reason we have given,
has inserted in his definition of custom the condition that the custom be
observed without interruption over the usual length of time.

Antonio de Butrio holds the same view (*De Consuetudine,* Chap. xi), as
does Jason (on *Digest,* I. iii. 32 in *Repetition,* no. 41). This is the teaching,
also, of Sylvester (word *consuetudo,* Qu. 5 [, no. 8]) and of Panormitanus
(*De Consuetudine,* Chap. xi, no. 19).

This doctrine is confirmed by the fact that when in law a period of
time is put down as necessary for anything, the rule, in cases of doubt and
generally, is to suppose that the law requires continuous time—as Lapus
(*Allegationes Iuris,* xlvii) has stated. Sylvester (word *religio,* Pt. V, qu. 5
[qu. 4]) supports this opinion, and he cites the language of the Gloss on
rubric of *Digest,* XLIV. iii. This view is also that of Navarrus (*Consilia,* 87
[89], *De Regular.,* no. 1) and he cites the text of law 1 of the same title of
the *Digest.*

These passages just cited, however, prove hardly anything, and although
the next to the last Gloss on the aforesaid law 1, gives some indication, [it
is not strictly to our point,] since it is speaking of a prescription.

15.[20] But the question may be asked, in what way or when is a custom held to be interrupted. For in the case of a custom no possession is

---

19. [This Section incorrectly numbered '15' in the Latin text.—Tr.]
20. [Latin Text incorrectly has '51'.—Tr.]

necessary, nor is any other legal ground required beyond the worthiness of the custom, hence it cannot be interrupted on those grounds, as is the case with a prescription. Nor, [so this question runs, can it be interrupted] for lack of good faith, since that too is unnecessary. My reply is that in a certain sense good faith is necessary in order that a custom may establish law, as I state below. Hence, wherever good faith is necessary for a custom, the latter may be interrupted for the lack of it, as happens in the case of a true prescription. For there is a parity between custom and prescription on this point, as will become more clear from what will be said in Chapter xv.

Where, however, good faith is not necessary, custom can be interrupted only by means of actions in opposition to it. Panormitanus thinks that a single contrary action is sufficient to effect this result, because by that act the people give sufficient indication of their unwillingness that this custom be introduced. Thus, if the observance of the custom proceeds in violation of a law, then it may be interrupted by actions in observance of the law. For those actions oppose the custom in question, and they retract the prior will, either of establishing new law, or of revoking the earlier one.

What actions are necessary to interrupt a custom. Further, the mingling of contrary usages due to contrary acts makes it impossible that a certain tacit will of the prince be inferred—a point of very great importance with respect to the power of the custom to produce its effect, as we shall see. In order that an act may be sufficient to interrupt a custom, on the one hand, it will be necessary that it be done by the whole community in which the custom has been followed—for the acts of a few private individuals do not obviate the consent of the community, and so they cannot interrupt a general custom; or on the other hand, it will certainly be sufficient if an act contrary to the custom be done with the public authority of the one holding the necessary power—as that some individual should be publicly punished for observing the custom, or that a similar official act should be done, whereby it is proved that this custom was not in accord with the will of the prince.

16. *Custom is divided into customs which are and those which are not validated by prescription.* The second of the two principal assertions of this Chapter must now be made: that not every custom is established by prescription, and that, accordingly, custom may be divided into customs

which are validated by prescription, and those which are not. All the writers agree in making this assertion, but only a few explain its meaning in the sense in which we understand it. For we can speak of custom of fact only and custom of law only.

With reference to the first of these the truth of our proposition is self-evident. The aforesaid last chapter [*Decretals,* Bk. I, tit. IV, chap. xi] indicates this sufficiently, in the words, 'unless the custom has been validated by prescription according to law'; for these words clearly imply that there can be a custom that is not legally validated by prescription. Again, from the very fact that a prescriptive custom requires [for its introduction] a certain period of time, it will be clear that before the completion of this period, the custom will not have been validated by means of prescription; and yet it will still be a custom of a definite character. This does not mean that the custom in this latter case initiates law: it exists merely as a series of repeated acts.

With respect to those customs that initiate law, the meaning of our assertion is that not only custom which has been validated by prescription, but also that which is not prescriptive can sometimes establish law. This is the sense of the assertion as I make it, as it was apparently that of Panormitanus when he said, (in commenting on *De Consuetudine,* Chap. xi), that a prescriptive custom is required by the canon law only when the custom is in opposition to law, but not, however, when the custom is outside law, his meaning being that in such a case a custom can initiate law, and this, even if the custom has not been itself validated by means of prescription.

This view of Panormitanus seemed objectionable to Rochus (*De Consuetudine,* Sect. 3, no. 5), and for this reason, apparently, he did not admit the existence of a custom not validated by prescription, except inchoate and imperfect customs, which are not yet in the form in which they are able to establish law; or in the case of certain lines of conduct or customs of a few individuals, which practices are wont to be held up as examples for imitation, and are more accurately termed observances. Rochus (*ibid.,* Pref. no. 23) has a lengthy passage on this distinction.

A legal custom may exist independent of prescription, and of the determination of a definite period of time. I understand the above assertion, however, in the sense in which I first stated it: for I think that a legal custom can exist, apart from prescription and from a definite determination of a certain period of time; an example of this kind being a custom which is created with the knowledge and toleration of the prince. This sort of custom initiates law, not after the manner of prescription, but in virtue of a tacit personal consent [of the prince], which consent can be sufficiently indicated by a non-prescriptive custom—as seems to be self-evident. In such a case, the opinion of Soto [Sect. 5] could be valid, an opinion which I attacked inasmuch as he spoke in general terms; and yet even with this limitation in respect of time required for a legal custom, it does not seem that the judgment should be left to the decision of a prudent individual but that some more certain rule will be necessary.[21] This point, however, I shall explain more conveniently in chapters xv and xvi.

17. *What is the meaning of custom in the absolute sense?* Finally, however, the question may be asked whether this division [of custom][22] in legal usage is analogical, [i.e. not a strict distinction,] in such wise that under the term custom in its absolute sense only prescriptive custom falls, whilst the term is applied to other kinds of custom only when they are adequately explained. This point has been touched upon by Abbas [, i.e. Panormitanus] (on *Decretals,* Bk. I, tit. vi, chap. fifty, no. 9 [no. 4]), Giovanni d'Andrea, and Antonio de Butrio (on the same chapter of the *Decretals*). Abbas holds that a custom absolutely so called in law ought, in a doubtful case, to be understood as meaning prescriptive custom. Baldus (*Consilia,* Bk. V, cons. 349, no. 20) inclines to the same opinion, and he is followed by Petrus de Ubaldis (*Super Canonica Episcopali et Parochiali,* Chap. v, no. 2 [no. 13]), by Rochus (*De Consuetudine,* Sect. 3, no. 1) who also cites Baldus (tit. *De Feudorum Cognitione,* Chap. i). Baldus here states that a custom which is not validated by prescription is no custom at all, but a mere will to establish the same.

These authors likewise maintain that this opinion can be proved best from the aforesaid chapter fifty [*Decretals,* Bk. I, tit. vi, chap. fifty]. At the beginning of that chapter, the condition there applied is referred to in

21. [In Section 5, Soto is cited as having held that no time is determined by law for the establishment of a legal custom.—REVISER.]

22. [Into customs validated or not validated by prescription.—TR.]

these words: 'That the expression of the opinion of those who by law or custom ought not to be present should have no validity'; and later, at the end of the Chapter, we find the words, 'But it is not clear from this [, i.e. from the fact that they did elect,] that the right of election belongs to them by law or by prescriptive custom.' But I do not see how from these words it is to be inferred that the word 'custom', understood in its absolute sense, is to signify only a prescriptive custom. The conclusion seems rather to be, that the word 'custom' is of a general and indifferent character, and that it is for this reason that the words stating that the right has not been obtained by prescription were added in the response, in order to indicate that not any kind of custom, but only that which is prescriptive, could be sufficient for giving the right of election without a law [granting that right].

18. My opinion, then, is that if we keep in mind the true meaning of the word 'custom', we find that it is a general and indifferent term. This was the view held by Giovanni d'Andrea (on *Decretals*, Bk. III, tit. XXVIII, chap. ix), and that also of Petrus de Ubaldis, as he records in the passage cited. It is that, also, of the Gloss (on *Sext*, Bk. I, tit. IV, chap. iv, word *consuetudo*), above cited, which refers to the opinions of other writers.

The proposition can be proved, whether we regard custom as one of fact or as unwritten law. First, a custom of fact, does not, of its nature, imply any limits in respect of a definite period of time, either long or short; and it is, therefore, not differentiated by reason of these variations of time. Nor do I find in the law a basis for the other interpretation, even if the word 'custom' is used in the law without a qualifying word. Again, as to custom embodying unwritten law established by a custom that of its nature does not require a determined period for its running, we find that it is law in the strict sense of the term, and that it is consistent with the proper definition of custom exactly as is a custom validated by prescription.[23]

Accordingly, I do not see a basis for that general rule;[24] and this chiefly for the reason that all the laws which are cited by the aforesaid authors,

---

23. [Reading *praescriptae* for *praescripta.*—REVISER.]

24. [The rule stated in the opinion of Abbas [, i.e. Panormitanus], laid down near the beginning of Section 17, *supra*, p. 595.—TR.]

deal with true prescription and not with consuetudinary law. Hence, wherever the word *custom* is used without a qualifying epithet, we must, I think, determine the nature of the custom there spoken of by a careful consideration of the subject-matter of the custom and of the kind of effect with which we are dealing. For, if that effect is such that it can be introduced only by prescription, or through a prescriptive custom, it will be clear that the intention of the author is to refer to a prescriptive custom; if, however, the matter does not demand a prescriptive custom, there is no ground for understanding the term in that restricted sense; rather, it is to be there read either as meaning custom without reference to a distinction in kind, or to custom other than prescriptive, the nature of which is clear from its own context, or from its closer application to other laws. Finally, the above-cited authors say virtually the same thing by reason of the limitations which they attach to their own rule, and by the laws which they cite in justification of these limitations.

CHAPTER IX

Concerning the Causes of Custom and in Particular Who Can Introduce It

1. *The cause of a custom is explained.* We have explained, so far as appeared necessary, the nature and essence of custom, both in general and in particular. It remains for us to explain its causes and effects.

First, as to the causes. Almost all of these have been touched upon in explaining the definition and divisions of custom and only its efficient cause remains to be more fully explained.

For in the case of custom, there is no question of any special matter and form of which it is composed; but in so far as the custom is a juridical entity, the matter with which it deals is the same as that of written human law. The written law and unwritten law differ not in the matter with which they deal, but only in the mode of expression employed in their institution. Hence, in consuetudinary law, there is no special form, sensible and external, except the actions [constituting the custom], which must be external and sensible, and these, in so far as they are tokens of consent, may be called the unwritten words by which this kind of law is engraved upon the memory of men. Consequently, no special promulgation is required in this form of law, because custom, through the usage itself, is its own public manifestation and promulgation.

The intrinsic form,[1] however, of this branch of law, is a certain 'will'— which under another aspect is the efficient cause of the obligation created by the custom. Of this we shall speak in a moment. If, however, we consider a custom merely as fact, the matter which constitutes it is the acts themselves in the frequency of which the custom consists. And since the custom should be useful and morally good, its form (as it were) will be its moral goodness and the usefulness in the single acts that make it up, and in their repetition; or, at least, the continuity or uninterrupted repetition of the actions for a sufficient time, can be said to be (as it were) its form. All these elements of custom are in some way connected with its sufficient[2] cause, and we shall discuss them more at length when we come to deal with that.

The final cause of custom, however, is, with due proportion, the same as that of written law, namely, the public utility, or that factor of the custom which makes it morally good; this element, objectively regarded, has the character of purpose, and [as such], in part at least, will be identical with the effects of custom. I shall discuss this cause at greater length in connexion with these effects. The efficient cause, then, is the only one needing elucidation.

2. *The efficient cause of custom is twofold.* It is possible, however, at this point, to distinguish proximate and primary, among human causes, for it is of these that we are treating. The proximate cause, I term the men themselves who introduce the customs, for they inaugurate and continue a usage by their acts, thus producing the custom. I name as the primary cause, however, the sovereign power, or the prince if, by chance, his authority is necessary to give force to the custom. Whence the first of these two causes is called the proximate, especially in reference to a custom of fact, for the reason that it effects the custom directly and immediately. Of custom as

---

1. [That is, the formal element which makes custom law.—REVISER.]
2. [*Sufficientis.* Suárez probably intended to write *efficientis* (efficient).—TR.]

law, however, the prince is the principal cause. He may also be called the immediate cause by reason of the immediacy of the law-making power exercised, even though he may not be such by reason of the immediacy of his personal agency, as is evident.

Three things must be borne in mind with respect to the proximate cause: the agent, the external action or the frequency of the action, and the internal will or consent. Baldus noted this, as cited in the last Chapter [*supra,* Chap. viii] and added a fourth element—time. This latter is not, however, a cause, but at most is a requisite condition. On this point, we have said something in the preceding Chapter, and we shall discuss it more specifically in those that follow. We must, then, here offer a brief explanation of these three elements [of a proximate cause].

3. *A perfect community is necessary for the establishment of a custom.* Concerning the first of these [, i.e. the agent], the question is raised: who is capable of introducing custom? In the first place, all maintain that a private person is not adequate therefor; but that a perfect community is required. This is sufficiently evident from the considerations brought forward in the Second Chapter of this Book, on the second division of custom, in which the proof of this point is given. This doctrine is excellently stated in *Digest,* I. iii. 32.

4. An objection, however, may be made, based on the fact that sometimes a private individual or a private community may, by means of a custom, acquire a privilege—as will be pointed out in the following Book.[3] But a privilege is a kind of law and private legal rule. [Therefore, . . .]. Again, it is possible for a person, by virtue of a private custom, to be exempt from a legal obligation. Therefore, such a custom is a legal one. The antecedent of this last proof is evident from the fact that in the correction of his subjects, a bishop is bound by common law to proceed after seeking the advice of his chapter, and yet by custom he can be excused from so doing, as appears in *Sext,* Bk. I, tit. iv, chap. iii. This rule is also derived from *Sext,* Bk. II, tit. xiii, chap. i, where we find the words: 'Since the common law establishes a contrary rule [. . .]'. And this can

---

3. [Not included in these *Selections.*—Tr.]

be proved also, from the reason that the law can be thus annulled only in part, which annulment is called derogation of law (*Digest*, L. xvi. 102). Therefore, by the custom of one person a derogation may be made from the law, at least in regard to the person in question.

5. *A private custom could exempt from common law in two ways.* My reply first of all to the first portion of the argument just set forth, is that we are not here concerned with a privilege, which is a private written law, but with law that is unwritten, and which possesses a true legal character. Moreover, I maintain that a privilege is acquired rather through a prescription properly so-called than by means of a true custom of the sort we are here discussing, as we shall see in the next Book.[4] For it is evident that a prescription is introduced by a private person and by a private usage or custom.

Our reply then to the second part of the above contention is that there are only two ways in which a private custom could exempt from an obligation of a common law.[5] In one way, by the obtaining of a prescriptive right through it, the acquisition of which may change the matter of the common law, and consequently may terminate the obligation of that law. Thus, a private custom can exempt, or rather remove the obligation of the common law from a certain person; for there is here no derogation from the common law, but an abolition of its subject-matter.[6] This may occur even in the natural law through a change of circumstances, as has been frequently stated, and it is a known fact even in prescription. This is the case with the laws cited above, as is clear from the language of the laws themselves.

In the second way, private custom might be conceived *per se* and directly as derogating from the common law by withdrawal from its obligation, but this we maintain is impossible, because a private custom of violating even a positive statute never excuses the fault; on the contrary, it normally rather increases it. And this is the meaning of the laws when they say that no prescription can be established in opposition

---

4. [Not included in these *Selections*.—Tr.]
5. [Reading *excusare* for *excusari*.—Reviser.]
6. [Reading *ablatio* for *oblatio*.—Reviser.]

to rightful obedience, as is clear from the *Decretals* (Bk. II, tit. xxvi, chap. xii), on which the same doctrine is noted by the Gloss. It is held likewise by other commentators on that Chapter, on the principle that no person can be exempt from due obedience by means of his disobedience; nor may one through abuses of his own derogate from the power of a superior, or in any other way diminish that power. Thus, the Doctors also assert that a subject cannot depart from a precept or the wish of his superior, because this act of its nature is a fault of disobedience.[7] On this point, Archidiaconus (on *Sext,* Bk. III, tit. iv, chap. v) may be consulted, and also Felinus (on *Decretals,* Bk. I, tit. ii, chap. viii, no. 30, words *quarto limita*).

It is not, then, possible for an individual subject to exempt himself from a law by means of his own evil custom. Whence, the fact that a derogation from the law can be partially made by one having the legal power so to do, does not imply that an individual subject, who does not possess such power, can do so; nor is it presumed that a superior has granted the subject a dispensation (as it were) on the ground of his abuse, because a will that would have the effect of weakening discipline would be an unreasonable one, and contrary also to the force and efficacy of all law.

6. *By what community the introduction of a legal custom is possible.* Our second assertion here is that a legal custom can be introduced not by any community whatever, but only by one possessing the capacity for legislative authority over itself; or, at least, by a community of sufficient perfection to be the subject of law properly so-called.

This assertion is the commonly accepted one on the point that a perfect community is required for the introduction of a custom: a state, for instance, or a similar community. This conclusion may be drawn from the aforesaid law 32 [*Digest,* I. iii. 32, § 1], where is first stated the principle that an ancient custom has the force of law, and then is added a statement of the ground in reason for the principle, namely, that the laws themselves derive their force from the fact that they have been accepted by the judgment of the people: the same, therefore, must be said of those unwritten laws of which the people have approved. The reference here

---

7. [Reading *inobedientiae* for *obedientiae.*—Reviser.]

is clearly to a perfect community and one having from its first establishment the inherent power to make its own laws. In law 35 [*Digest, ibid.,* 35] there is added the clause that 'a custom is introduced by the tacit agreement of the citizens': but the citizens constitute the state; and a state is a perfect community. In law 37 [*ibid.,* 37] such a custom is called a law of the state. The same is laid down in the *Institutes* (I. ii, § 9, and following sections).

7. Whence the assertion is made by the Doctors generally, that only a people which possesses legislative authority can introduce a custom. This statement is made by Bartolus, Jason and others, in commenting on *Digest* (*ibid.,* 32). It is made by Panormitanus, Rochus and others (*De Consuetudine,* Chap. xi). Innocent (on *Decretals,* Bk. I, tit. ɪɪ, chap. xii), Felinus (on *Decretals, ibid.,* chap. vii, no. 25 and on *ibid.,* Bk. II, tit. xxvɪ, chap. xi) and Navarrus (Comment. *De Spoliis,* Sect. 14, no. 7)—all hold this opinion. The names of other writers who follow this doctrine are set down by Tiraqueau (*De Iure Primogenitorum,* Qu. 16).

Giovanni d'Andrea, for this reason, puts it in the definition of custom (*De Consuetudine,* Chap. xi), that it should be the law of a people which by public authority has power to enact law. Barbatia [*Repertorium, De Consuetudine,* No. 9] and others, including Angelus de Clavasio (*Summa,* word *consuetudo,* No. 7), agree with this statement. The latter says that for custom there is required a people competent to enact law. Sylvester ([word *consuetudo,*] Qu. 3) states this doctrine very clearly, but St. Thomas does so even more satisfactorily when he says (in I.–II, qu. 97, art. 3, ad 3) that a community by which a custom can be introduced, should be either a free commonwealth, that is, one possessing sovereign power; or, if it is not a sovereign community, it should have that power by virtue of the tacit consent of the prince to whom it owes allegiance. Accordingly, I chose my words advisedly when I said that there was required a community 'which has the capacity for legislative authority', because it is not necessary that it be in actual possession of this power, for this can be supplied through the permission or tacit consent of the prince. The capacity, however, for such active power is necessary, because it should be a perfect community; but every perfect community, as was stated, has an inherent capacity for such power.

8. Panormitanus (*De Consuetudine,* No. 1), develops an objection to this doctrine from the fact that a community of clerics is able to establish a custom opposed to the canons, according to the *Decretals,* (Bk. I, tit. IV, chap. xi), and yet is not able to enact a law contrary to the canons (*Decretum,* Pt. II, causa xxv, qu. ii, can. vii, and other similar canons). He therefore concludes that [legal] custom can be established by a body that does not possess the power of making laws.

We can urge a second objection to the same effect, namely, that a community of lay persons cannot make a law of the Church, as is self-evident, and yet by means of a custom of their own, they may establish a law of the Church, such as a law of fasting, or of the observance of some feast. Again, a community of merchants has not power to make law, yet a custom of theirs can establish a legal rule, as is clear from the observations of Bartolus and others (on *Code,* IV. xviii. 2). Furthermore, women are not able, in the common opinion of writers on the subject, to enact laws; yet a community of women can, through their own custom, introduce a legal rule, as in the case of an institute of nuns. This is the opinion of Bartolus (on *Digest,* I. iii. 32 and on *Code,* VIII. lii. 2). Moreover, many authorities, whom Tiraqueau refers to in *De Iure Primogenitorum* (Qu. 16), say that the custom of one family can make a law for that family, although it has no legislative power.

9. *The answer to the objection.* On account of the first objection given above, Panormitanus (tit. *De Consuetudine,* No. 8) rejects the aforesaid definition of Giovanni d'Andrea. Yet an answer to Panormitanus's objection is easily made: in the first place, a clerical community has power to make a law, at least, one not opposed to the canons, and this is enough to give them authority to introduce a custom, and hence, consuetudinary law. Nor is it a difficulty against our doctrine that a clerical community actually have more extensive power to introduce law through custom, than by means of statutes, since it could have that power by special grant of the law and of the Popes—and this for the special reason which is examined by Abbas [, i.e. Panormitanus,] (*ibid.,* Chap. xi, no. 8), by Rochus (*De Consuetudine,* Chap. xi, sect. 3, no. 9) and by other writers on that same Chapter. It is, nevertheless, always true that no custom is introduced, save by one having legislative power. This matter is better explained by the

doctrine stated above: it is not necessary that a community be in actual possession of legislative power, but it suffices that it have the capacity for such power. However, this capacity is truly possessed by a clerical community; for the power of enacting statutes contrary to the canons could be given to it, even if the grant has not actually been made.

10. *An objection.* But in that case, a second objection presents itself, namely, that which is based upon the fact that a community of laymen has no capacity to enact a written law of the Church. *The answer.* The first answer to this can be found in my statements in the treatise *De Voto,* Bk. IV, chap. ix:[8] namely, a community of the people, practically,[9] and if we regard only the nature of the case, is capable of legislative power, even in matters of religion and of divine worship; and therefore, even though this power has at present in the Church been raised to a higher order and committed to the rulers of the Church, the people are, nevertheless, permitted by the consent of these prelates to bind themselves in matters of that kind through their own customs, with the tacit assent of their prelates, in the manner which we shall explain in the following Chapter.

Another reply may be given, namely, that it is sufficient that this community constitute a perfect society, and have of itself a passive capacity for such a law, so as to possess the power of originating a law in a spiritual matter through custom which has the consent, tacit or expressed, of its spiritual superiors. It was to indicate this fact that I included in my assertion these last words: 'or at least that it be such a community as can be the subject of law properly so-called'. *A twofold [legal] capacity may reside in a community.* For, a twofold capacity may be considered to reside in a community, one to make law, another to receive law. Although at present their earlier power to make ecclesiastical laws does not exist among Christian lay people, nor perhaps, even a capacity to do so, at least according to ordinary law; nevertheless, the laity has a passive capacity—that is, the capacity for receiving such law—and this capacity, I say, is necessary and sufficient, in order that by the custom of such a community, with the

---

8. [Not included in these *Selections.*—Tr.]

9. [In other words: 'as far as the people are concerned, i.e. they are members of the Church and could be given the power'.—Reviser.]

tacit consent of its prelate, [legal] custom may be introduced. I say that this capacity is necessary: for no form can be introduced except in matter capable of receiving it; so also the law of a spiritual custom (so to speak) cannot be introduced in its own way except in a subject with a capacity to receive ecclesiastical law. I say that is sufficient, for it is enough that the community be considered as in some way complete and perfect in a particular order: for a community entirely imperfect and restricted has no capacity for law strictly so called, although it can be the subject of a precept, as I have shown in Chapter ix of Book I.[10] But in every perfect community, custom is sufficient for introducing law, if the consent of the ruler is given for the custom.

11. *The answer to the third objection.* The answer to the third objection is now clear. For a community of merchants, for instance, can introduce custom in proportion to its capacity for law. Bartolus (on *Code*, IV. xviii. 2) says, that it can enact statutes. On the interpretation that must be given to this remark, I have spoken in Book III.[11] For if that body of merchants be regarded in itself, it has the power to frame conventional statutes[12] only, but not true laws. If, however, it be regarded as united with the prince or as wielding authority granted by him, this merchant body has power to frame statutes of a quasi-municipal character. Hence, it can establish custom, which has, with the same limitations, the force of law.

This seems the evident conclusion to be drawn from the *Code* (VIII. lii. 3), where at the beginning, the Emperor [Justinian] makes the unqualified assertion that an approved custom tenaciously preserved, resembles a law: words that can have application only to a people possessed of the power of making law. He adds immediately, 'and what is known to have been observed by offices, courts, cities, or corporate bodies'—of course, with the consent of the prince, as the Gloss there states. Hence, it is sufficient that a community possess legal capacity, 'together with the tacit consent of the Prince or Prelate'.

---

10. [This is found in Chap. vi. of Book I, *supra,* pp. 82 *et seq.*—Tr.]

11. [Chap. iii, *supra,* p. 434.—Tr.]

12. [That is, statutes which regulate the convention that rule in the merchant body.—Reviser.]

Solution of the fourth objection. The fourth objection is refuted in the same way: for, a community of women can have a capacity for law, and so a custom among them, accepted by the prelate, can establish law. This is the express teaching of Bartolus (on *Code,* VIII. lii. 2, no. 13).

Answer to the last objection. The answer to the last objection is that the statement there quoted[13] is false; for a private family cannot establish a true legal custom, since of itself it is essentially without legal capacity, even of a merely passive kind. The reason is that it is a wholly imperfect community, and can never by its own customs introduce a legal rule, even with the consent of the prince. A family as such, and apart from its social relations, has no capacity for law, not even for law imposed upon it by the prince—as I have stated in Chapter ix of Book I.[14] Nor, again, can a family introduce a custom applicable to others, because the custom of one is not binding upon another; nor can it be presumed that it is the will of the prince to bind a perfect community because of the custom of an imperfect portion thereof, as we shall explain in discussing the point next to be taken up. In what manner this principle is relevant to the question of custom abrogating law, will be easily explained in view of this last consideration.

12. *In order that a custom may be established, it is necessary that it be observed by at least the greater part of the community, and this is sufficient.* The third principal assertion in this Chapter is the following: For a custom to be established by the people, it is necessary that it be observed by at least the greater part of the community; and such observance is sufficient. This proposition is accepted by all the authorities to whom I have made reference. A full treatment of it is to be found in Bartolus (on *Code, ibid.,* no. 12) and in Rochus (*De Consuetudine,* Sect. 4, from no. 2).

The proof of the first part of this assertion is that the source of a custom ought to be practically the whole community, inasmuch as its custom applies to all; that of the smaller portion of the community is not sufficient for the custom to be imputed without qualification to the community as a whole, or for it to carry with it the consent of the community. Again, for the enactment of a law through the express will of the community, the

13. [*Vide* the last sentence of Sec. 8, *supra,* p. 603.—TR.]
14. [*Supra,* p. 116.—TR.]

consent of a minority is not sufficient; nor is it sufficient in elections, and in other acts, which ordinarily are done or can be done by the community as a whole: much less, then, will it suffice for establishing legal custom.

An objection. One may object that this rule is to the point, where the consent of the whole community is the real cause of the law, but not so, where the law is established by means of a custom with the consent of the prince. *The solution.* I answer that we must determine whether it is of the express or of the tacit consent of the prince that we are here speaking. If we speak of his express will, then it is true that the prince can enact law, if he so choose, which has regard for the custom of a few persons only, if this seems to him better or more expedient: this, however, will be not consuetudinary law, but rather a written law, or one expressly enacted. If, by the consent of the prince, we here mean tacit consent, then this cannot be reasonably presumed solely on the ground of a custom observed by the smaller portion of a community, even if it has been adequately tolerated: and this, both for the reason that the presumption is not based upon any law, and because the prince is not to be considered as desiring through such an unwritten law to force the consent of a people who do not consent. Rather, the prince is held to give his tacit consent—other conditions having been fulfilled—because the people give theirs and tacitly petition his own. But[15] the consent of a minority in the community is not that of the people as a whole. Therefore, . . .

13. The second part of the third assertion, namely, that the usage of the larger portion of the community is sufficient for the establishment of custom, is based upon the converse reason: namely, that in every community the consent of a majority thereof is usually sufficient for the validity of its acts in matters where law has not made some special provision[to the contrary]. Thus, in the case of a corporate body, the consent of the major part is held to be that of the whole body. This principle is set forth in the *Digest* (L. i. 19). Felinus, too (on *Decretals,* Bk. I, tit. ii, chap. vi, no. 17), has noted this, adducing many examples. We, also, have already touched upon this point in earlier passages. Therefore, in the present case, the

---

15. [Reading *at* instead of *ut.*—REVISER.]

custom of the greater part of the community is to be held as that of the whole community, and hence, this is sufficient.

Almost all the authorities cited above are of this opinion, for they require [for the introduction of custom] no more than this [consent of the majority]. How such consent of a majority is sufficient for a custom in derogation of law, I shall discuss in Chapter xvi. Angelus de Clavasio, indeed, adds (*Summa,* on word *consuetudo,* no. 7) that in that case it is necessary for two-thirds of the community to give their consent. He cites the *Digest* (III. iv. 3 and 4); and accepts the opinion of Panormitanus (*De Consuetudine,* Chap. xi, no. 18), who treats this question at some length.

But however the matter is explained, the restriction made, is not necessary in the present case. For if it means that two-thirds of the people should give their consent, and should observe the custom, then this statement is not true, since it is based upon no law. For in the laws just cited, there is no statement to that effect, but only the statement that the presence of two-thirds of any community is necessary for its acts to be held as done in the name of that community. Indeed, the Gloss on those laws notes that the consent of the two-thirds who are present is not necessary, but that the consent of the majority of those present is sufficient. This principle is admitted by Panormitanus in respect of the matter under discussion; and in this sense he reads *Digest,* L. i. 19 and *Decretals,* Bk. III, tit. xi, chap. ii. If, however, that assertion means no more than that the presence of two-thirds of the community is necessary, the requirement would seem to be a superfluous one in the case of a popular custom, since it is obvious that when a custom is a long-continued one, almost the whole of the population is necessarily present.

14. Panormitanus has for this reason added the note that 'it is necessary that at least two-thirds of the community be aware of the custom which is introduced'. But this has rather to do with the other conditions which are requisite with respect to the consuetudinary actions, namely, that they be publicly performed. The necessary consequence of such performance is that if the custom is thus publicly observed by the greater portion of the community, not only that portion of the community, but others also, will have a knowledge of it. However, so general a knowledge of the custom is not essential; for, even though many may be ignorant of it, so long as that

custom is known to the larger part of the community, this is sufficient. The reason is that the consent of those who are thus ignorant of it is not necessary, nor is even a knowledge of the custom on their part called for: it is sufficient that this custom be of itself a public one.

It is for this reason that Rochus (*De Consuetudine,* Chap. xi, sect. 4, no. 24 [no. 2]) said that a knowledge of the custom by the people, or by a majority of them, is requisite for the validity of a custom. He discusses this point thoroughly, and strengthens it [by citing authorities]. Gregory López ([on *Las Siete Partidas,*] Pt. I, tit. ii, law 5, gloss 4 [gloss 3]) who is followed by Burgos de Paz (in Law I: *Tauri.,* no. 205), agrees with this view, saying that in a custom observed by the greater portion of the people, there is always a sufficient representation of the whole people, and that the ignorance of it, on the part of some, cannot set up a barrier to its introduction.

How the reckoning of the 'majority' is to be made. It remains that we explain in what manner the computation of this greater portion should be made, or of what persons it must be composed. There is a general agreement on this point, that there should be reckoned in this number only persons who can give consent to consuetudinary law. All infants and all persons mentally defective are therefore excluded. Some would also entirely exclude women on the ground that they can exercise no legislative authority. Among men, they exclude all below the age of twenty-five years. However, I cannot find any basis in law or any justification in reason for the exclusion of the last two groups. This question, however, will be better settled when we come to consider the separate effects of law.

CHAPTER X

By What Acts Custom Is Introduced

1. The assertion of this Chapter is, briefly, that a custom is not introduced except by a repetition of public and voluntary acts, and for the reason that the consent of the people is necessary for the establishment of a custom.

Custom is established by a repetition of public and voluntary acts. That custom is introduced by repeated actions would seem to be an assertion not requiring proof. First, as to a custom of fact: the custom is essentially nothing more than a repetition of actions; this has been made clear above; and therefore, with respect to such a custom, even though the single actions may be said to be the efficient cause of it, nevertheless, the repetition of or the sum of the acts would rather seem to be the essence of it, and (as it were) its formal element. Then, with respect to custom as law, it is to be remarked that such custom is introduced by one of fact, and hence it also must be initiated through a like repetition of acts. This part, then, of our proposition would seem to be sufficiently established by the fact that by definition, a custom should be instituted by the general conduct of those who employ it. But general conduct arises from the repetition of certain actions by the people.

This part of our proposition may also be proved from the word *consuetudo* (custom): for 'custom' is so called because, as Isidore says (*Decretum*, Pt. I, dist. I, can. v), it is usage in common. But how can it be common usage except through a repetition of actions? Likewise, a custom is termed long-continued usage (*Decretum*, Pt. I, dist. XI, can. iv, and *Digest*, I. iii. 35). Again (*ibid.*, 32) the people are spoken of as having declared their will by the language of deeds in a custom. But deeds do not exist except by repetition of acts, and this repetition we call 'frequency'. Therefore, . . .

2. *First objection.* It may be objected, indeed, that at times a mere omission of an action is sufficient to introduce a custom. I have already pointed out, however, that a moral omission is included under the heading moral acts, and that wherever such omission is sufficient, then a repetition of such omissions is also necessary. When and in what way such omission suffices for establishing custom we shall see in Chapter xvi.

Second objection. Secondly, one may object that it is asserted by Doctors of high authority that a single action is sometimes sufficient for introducing a custom, as Bartolus notes (on *Digest*, I. iii. 32 and on *Code*, VIII. lii. 2). Panormitanus (*De Consuetudine*, Chap. xi, no. 17), also accepts this doctrine, with respect to an action that is of its nature permanent in the sense that the act continues in its effect, and endures for sufficient time; thus, by the one bestowal of a benefice, a custom is established in that bestowal, if it has endured in point of fact for a sufficient time (on *Sext*, Bk. III, tit. IV, chap. v). He notes again that by the one act of building a bridge, a [legal] right is acquired, when the bridge has stood for a sufficient time.

However, these and similar examples are matters of prescription, for which indeed, a particular act consisting of a human operation is not *per se* essential; an habitual possession, if I may use the word, is sufficient, together with the fulfilment of the other conditions. The reason is that more commonly, prescription is concerned with persons or things—as has been sufficiently touched upon in the first and second Chapters of this Book—and hence, when a single action is sufficient [to establish a right of prescription], what continues is not the act itself, but its effect or term: the possession of the benefice, for instance, or [continued existence] of the bridge.

Still, the element of frequency of using the bridge or holding the benefice is morally present in these examples and the like. But in custom of the kind of which we are now treating, and generally in custom which has as its matter human acts as such, it is impossible for the custom to be introduced without a multitude and frequency of actions, for the reason that those separate actions do not by themselves endure for a long period of time, and custom should be a protracted [usage]. Whence it is impossible that the custom should be such [, i.e. protracted], except through a succession of actions.

Objection. One may object that although the individual action is transitory, it may be held to endure morally, so long as it is not revoked, even if it is not repeated.

Solution. My reply is that this holds true of guilt or continual[1] fault, but not of a custom: for no one is said to observe a custom of stealing merely because he stole upon one occasion, and did not make restitution for a long time thereafter. This principle is especially true because, in the matter of initiating or revoking a law, it is not possible that the people who have performed one act of keeping some feast-day or a fast, for example, should go on for a long time without performing either similar acts, or contrary acts. Therefore, it is true absolutely and without qualification, that

---

1. [Suárez is here using the word *habitualem* in the sense of persisting, not in that 'of frequently taking place'.—REVISER.]

for a custom, a frequency of actions is required. Bartolus, in his remarks (on *Code,* VIII. lii. 2, no. 12), sets forth this opinion at some length, as does also the Gloss (on *Decretum,* Pt. I, dist. 1, can. v, and on *Decretals,* Bk. I, tit. IV, chap. xi), on which Rochus, treating the matter at length (*De Consuetudine,* Sect. 5 [Sect. 4], no. 36), says that this doctrine is generally received with hardly any dissent.

3. *What frequency of actions is required for the establishment of custom.* Furthermore, these Doctors raise a question as to what frequency of actions is necessary or sufficient for the establishment of a custom of this character. For certain early jurists said that two actions are enough. Bartolus, in the passage cited above, notes this opinion, and he is followed in Rosella[2] (word *consuetudo*) and by Sylvester (word *consuetudo,* Qu. 4 [Qu. 3]), who accept the opinion but make certain distinctions. These writers cite the *Code* (I. iv. 3) and the *Decretum* (Pt. II, causa xxv, qu. ii, can. xxv), in which they call one repetition of the same criminal act, 'a custom'. But, as Bartolus has rightly said, the word 'custom' must there be understood as meaning a certain usual mode of action, such as is sufficient not for the introduction of a law, but only for the justification of a heavier punishment, and for the prevention of a too facile grant of pardon, and similar effects of fact, rather than of law. Hence, Bartolus and others generally reject this opinion, since no criterion can be found for fixing a definite number, nor do the laws prescribe one. Whence they assert that the matter is to be left to the decision of a prudent judge.

One should have recourse to the judgment of a prudent man. This opinion of these writers seems to me certain, when it is applied to our subject-matter of legal custom strictly so called, whatever may be the number of acts necessary to establish a true prescription or other effects of 'fact', so to speak.

4. The matter may be made clear as follows. Sometimes the custom of which we are speaking must, in order to initiate or abrogate law, be validated by prescription; at other times, that is not necessary. When, therefore, validation of the custom by prescription is called for, the first consideration must be the number of years required therefor, according to

---

2. [*Summa Rosella* of Baptista Trovamala.—Tr.]

the principles we shall lay down in the following Chapters. Attention must then be directed to the question whether, in the successive years, the custom requires one act only or many acts: for, if it requires only one, as in the observance of a certain feast, or of fasting on a particular day, then as many acts are necessary as the number of years required for the running of the prescriptive period. If, however, the custom requires many acts in a fixed number of years, then the number of actions will be proportionate with the number of years necessary for the prescription. It is possible, however, that the number of actions in the successive years may be not an absolutely definite one, but subject to some condition or occasion—as the custom of public prayer, or other like exercise, may find place only upon such and such an occasion or in response to the need of the moment. Thus, the number and frequency of the occasions will indicate the required frequency of the actions—done at the time they are called for, and with no omission of the act on those occasions.

Likewise, in respect of a community, these actions are to be taken as one act, in so far as the community acts either as one in the form of a corporate body or a college, as in electing or ordaining[3] or the like; or, as the whole body or the greater part thereof concur in the action, although each person acts upon his own account, as in observing a feast, or a fast, &c. Therefore, in cases where the whole community participates, few actions are required. For they are multiplied in virtue of the separate actions of the observance of the custom: and this, not only in proportion to the magnitude of the population—in the great numbers of actions which are done at the same time by all the members of the community—but also in proportion to the length of time during which custom is observed, that is, the repetition of those actions on successive occasions by the individuals.

But when there is no requirement of a definite continuity of time, then, just as the length of the period within which the custom must be continued is an arbitrary one, so also is the frequency of the actions, which will be fixed according to the exigencies of the subject-matter, or of the occasions for which the custom must be (as it were) sustained in observance.

---

3. [For *eligendo ordinando* read *eligendo, ordinando.*—Tr.]

Since, also, the custom in question requires the consent of the people and of the prince, such a multiplication of actions will be held sufficient as will make known the consent of the people and the tacit approval of the prince.

Hostiensis (in *Summa* [Bk. I, rubric iv, no. 5]) states the doctrine in much the same way—as do Archidiaconus (on *Sext,* Bk. I, tit. ii, chap. i), Panormitanus (*De Consuetudine,* Chap. xi, no. 17) and Bartolus (on *Code,* VIII. lii. 2, no. 12). This doctrine is followed by other writers also.

Whether the same assertion holds true of style or custom of judicial acts, I shall discuss at the close of the following Chapter.

5. *Public observance of custom is necessary.* From the above discussion, it is evident that it is necessary that the observance of a custom be public, and consequently, that the customary actions be publicly performed: partly in order that all the people or a majority of them may unite in giving their consent to such a custom; and partly also, in order that the custom in question may, in so far as such public observance can do so, be made known to the prince whose consent also is needed.

An act can be public in two ways. An action, however, can be public in two ways, namely, in fact and in law: as an act is usually said to be notorious in a twofold sense, namely, with a notoriety of fact or law.

What is publicity in fact and at law. In the former manner, an act is notorious which, although it is the action of a private person and done on private authority, is yet performed publicly in the sight of other persons, and not furtively or in secret. In the latter manner, however, an act is termed a public one which is done by public authority and in a juridical fashion; for example, as the sentence of a judge, and the like.

When, therefore, a custom itself is one observed by private acts, it is certain that in order to establish a consuetudinary law, the acts must—for the reasons just given—be performed publicly, at least after the first-named manner, and with notoriety of fact. The reason is that actions done privily and in secret, indicate, by the fact that they are so done, that they are not performed with the consent of the people nor of the prince; and therefore, unless the acts be public, at least with the notoriety of fact of which we have spoken, they cannot be suitable for the establishment of a public custom. This condition is so stated in [*Las Siete Partidas,*] Pt. I, tit. ii, law 5.

CHAPTER XI

Whether Judicial Cognizance of the Frequency of Actions Is Requisite for the Introduction of a Custom

1. *Is judicial cognizance necessary for the introduction of a custom?* Our present Chapter seeks an answer to the question whether it is essential for the introduction of a custom that the sufficiency of the number of acts constituting it be defended or proved in court by the public authority.

Some authorities assert that it is necessary that the custom be approved by legal decision in its favour.[1] This is the doctrine of the Gloss (on *Decretals*, Bk. I, tit. IV, chap. xi and on *Decretum*, Pt. I, dist. VIII, can. vii; on *Institutes*, I. ii. 9, word *diuturni*), and in the Gloss (on rubric to *Code*, VIII. lii). It is followed by St. Antoninus ([*Summa Theologica,*] Pt. I, tit. xvi, § 4).

This doctrine is founded first, upon *Decretals*, Bk. V, tit. XL, chap. xxv, where a certain custom is alleged to be insufficient, because it was not established by a decision in its favour when impugned. This is noted by the Gloss on that Chapter, which cites in confirmation, the example of a prescription for the validity of which an appeal is necessary, according to the *Digest* (VIII. vi. 18, § 2). 'Thus it would seem,' says the Gloss, 'that it [, i.e. an appeal,] is required in a custom validated by prescription.'

Secondly, the *Digest* (I. iii. 34) is cited in favour of this opinion. That law states that when a custom is cited as proof, the first point to be examined, is 'whether that custom also has been confirmed when impugned'.

Thirdly, this view is favoured by the law of Spain ([*Las Siete Partidas,*] Pt. I, tit. II, law 5), which holds that a custom of ten or twenty years'

---

1. [I.e. 'custom proved by a judicial decree after it had been disputed' (*Contradictorio judicio*). This term is explained by Panormitanus, in his Commentary *De Consuetudine*, Chap. xi (p. 124 of the Venice edition, 1569). The term means that a judicial decision is given in favour of a custom which has been challenged by a plaintiff. His words are: '*Quod parte contradicente, vel semel saltem fuerit judicatum consuetudinem esse.*'—REVISER.]

standing must be observed in the future if, during that period, judgment has been given in accordance with that same custom.

Fourthly, the proof may be added that, until the custom has thus been confirmed, it cannot become sufficiently known and of a public character suitable for its observance to become binding upon other persons, or for it to give a peaceful conscience to those observing it.

Thus, if one asks how many judicial acts are necessary to establish a custom, the answer of the Glosses is that a reaffirmed judgment in conformity with and approving the custom is necessary. The sole proof of this opinion is derived from the *Code* (I. iv. 3).

2.[2] *A judicial act is not necessary for the introduction of custom.* This opinion, however, is false, and the contrary view is the common one among the canonists and the jurists,[3] as is stated by Abbas [, i.e. Panormitanus,] (*De Consuetudine,* Chap. xi, no. 16), and also by Bartolus (on *Code,* VIII. lii. 2 and on *Digest,* I. iii. 32 in *Repetition,* qu. 2). Jason states the same opinion in his comment on the same law (on *Code,* VIII. lii. 2, and on *Digest,* I. iii. 32, no. 51, col. 12), as does Rochus (*De Consuetudine,* Sect. 4, no. 34), where he gives the names of other writers who teach the same doctrine. Gregory López sets forth this view (on *Las Siete Partidas,* Pt. I, tit. ii, law 5, *glossa* c), as does Peter de Salazar (*De Consuetudine,* Bk. I, chap. vii).

The first proof of our assertion is that custom does not require for its establishment such a judicial act, either by reason of its nature or from the obligation of positive law: there is, therefore, no ground on which such an act is necessary.

The general inference of this argumentation is clear: every condition or cause requisite for a custom ought to be based upon some law; otherwise, the assertion of such a condition or cause as an essential one is gratuitous and unfounded.

The proof of the major premiss is derived, first, from the fact that there is no reason in the nature of things why such a judicial act should be necessary. For, as Bartolus says, the general consent of the people, or a greater

---

2. [Figure 2 is omitted in Latin text.—Tr.]
3. [Reading in *legistarum* for *legislatorum.*—Reviser.]

part thereof, sufficiently manifests popular consent; and the public usage, as such, can of itself be known to the prince, so that his tacit consent may be assumed. Hence, there is no reason why a judicial act should, from the nature of the case, be necessary. As to the second member of our premiss, the positive laws which speak of custom that is reasonable, never require this condition [of a judicial act], but only that it be of a prescriptive, immemorial, or of an ancient character, and the like. This is clear from the *Decretals* (Bk. I, tit. IV, chap. xi) and the *Digest* (I. iii. 32) and other laws of a similar nature.

3. I offer as a second argument, one drawn from reason: this requirement of a judicial act for the establishment of the custom supposes that it has been impugned in the courts: what, however, if in fact the custom is never impugned? If it were not thus challenged, its establishment could never be effected. But that is contrary to all law and to all reason.

It may be said [in reply to this argument] that the custom is not confirmed in a space of ten or twenty years only, if it had not been put to the test of trial in which it was impugned, yet, if the custom lasts for a longer period, say for thirty years or more, then such lapse of time makes up for the required judicial actions. It is the opinion of Burgos de Paz (Law I, *Tauri.*, no. 247) that this holds true, at least in Spanish law. But with respect to the common law, this view is untenable, since according to that law a custom of ten years' standing is held to be ancient, and for such a custom to be complete and perfect under the rules of that law, the condition [of a judicial act] is not necessary, as has been proved. Regarding the law of Spain on this point, I shall add a note shortly.

4. I shall add another argument, an excellent one, it seems to me, suggested by Panormitanus. It is that the aforesaid condition [of a second judicial act] involves a certain contradiction. For if a second decision in a trial where custom is impugned, is required, then, either it is impossible that a first just decision favouring the custom can be given, and thus the establishment [by it] of a perfect custom is made impossible, a proposition that our opponents do, of course, deny; or the [second] decision of the court supposes the custom to have been a perfect one before its decision was given—in which case, that decision is clearly not essential to the custom and at most does no more than record it.

The proof of the first member of the foregoing proposition is that, if a [second] judicial decision in favour of the custom is necessary for the establishment of the custom, then no custom can be complete before a first decision is given, since a condition necessary to its perfection is lacking. Yet, such a first decision cannot, therefore, declare the custom be complete; or that an action done in virtue of the custom is valid and permissible; or, finally, that the custom can establish any obligation. The reason is that such a decision must contain error in defiance of the plain truth, even though from the standpoint of those who demand a second judicial declaration, the custom was not a custom before that first decision was given.

From this reasoning, the second member of our proposition also is clear: for, if the custom is truly and justly declared by the court [in a second decision] to be a perfect one, then it was perfect before the declaration. The judicial decision in question does not complete the custom, but merely declares what it is.

5. *Reply to the basis of the contrary position.* The reply to the first state-ment contrary to our thesis,[4] that drawn from the *Decretals* (Bk. V, tit. XL, chap. xxv) is, first, that this law has reference not to a legal custom, but to a prescription of a right of election, which is a very different matter. As to that, the matter can be open to dispute, but upon it no proof appli-cable to our present subject can be based. In the second place, the words in the *Decretals* (*ibid.*) here referred to are not found in the decision, but in the allegation of the party against whom the case was settled, as is evident from the context. Thirdly, those words are interpolated not in order to suggest that a decision in favour of a prescriptive custom impugned is necessary for [the validity] thereof—for this is so clearly false, that it is improbable that this allegation was even put forward—but only to dem-onstrate that such a custom was not sufficiently proved from the evidence which the contesting party had brought forward.

Whence Panormitanus (on *Decretals, ibid.,* no. 13) says that the infer-ence to be made from the text of the law is not that which our adversaries

---

4. [*Supra*, p. 615.—Tr.]

here have drawn from it, but rather its opposite. The example, however, which the Gloss brings forward (on *Digest*, VIII. vi. 18), has no bearing upon the present matter, because in that law the custom in question is not a legal custom, but one concerning a prescription of servitude; and, again, because a reference to that law in our present question is irrelevant, for it sets forth, not the manner of acquiring a servitude by prescription, but merely the manner in which the servitude is not lost. As to this latter point, it lays down the principle that the servitude is not lost through non-usage when there is no occasion for its use. The law holds that such non-user is a merely negative non-user and not privative in its effect, a point that we shall more fully explain later in treating of the loss of privileges. Since sometimes, the occasion for the use [of the servitude] does not arise unless a certain previous conditional action takes place, the law makes it clear that prior to the occurrence of such an occasion the servitude is not lost merely on the ground of non-user. The principle has special application to urban servitudes as is shown from the *Digest* (VIII. ii. 6). From that law, therefore, nothing as to the necessity of a further challenge[5] of the prescription, especially in a court of law, can be inferred.

6. *The answer to the second statement.* My reply to the [second] contrary thesis based upon the *Digest* (I. iii. 34), is that this law makes simply the following assertion: for the examination and proof of a custom it is a point of great importance to know whether the custom has ever been confirmed when impugned; and therefore, this point should be determined first [in establishing such proof]. This principle is a valid one in the sense that such judicial decision is of considerable use in the proof of a custom; it is not so in the sense that such judicial decision is demanded to establish the truth and consummation of the custom.

I shall not avail myself of the other, negative reading of the text of the law: namely, that it is of much importance 'whether or not the custom was also confirmed in a contested trial'.[6] Thus stated, the matter is very clear: for a knowledge of such a rejection of a custom can be highly pertinent in

---

5. [A further challenge, that is, in the sense of an appeal as indicated in the third paragraph of Section 1 of this Chapter; *supra*, p. 615, cf. also note 1 on that page.—Tr.]

6. [Suárez is here apparently giving a negative paraphrase of the text of the *Digest*.—Tr.]

a question of its establishment, since through a decision given against the custom, there is an interruption, or a cessation of the presumption of a tacit consent of the commonwealth, or of the prince. The former reading of the law is, however, held to be the genuine one. The Gloss and the Doctors have explained it in various ways, as can be seen by reference to them.

7. *The answer to the third statement.* We now pass to the third statement namely, that drawn from the law of Spain. As to the meaning of that law, our commentators have some difficulty, and certain of them attempt to interpret it as relating to a prescription. They do so, however, without justification: both because the law very clearly has reference to custom, as will be evident to any one who examines it; and because the interpretation they give the law does not hold even for prescription, or, at least, it involves them in the same difficulty with respect to it.

Others, however, admit that by the special law of Spain,[7] two judicial decisions rendered in favour of impugned custom are necessary in order that a custom be confirmed. This is the view of Burgos de Paz (Law I, *Tauri.*, no. 247). But even though the words of the law, literally taken, favour this opinion, the meaning is so absurd that it does not seem admissible, because, as I have said before, this condition involves a contradiction. The reason is that if this requirement of two decisions were to hold, the first decision could never be justly given in favour of the custom, or in accord with its terms.

Two parts of the law distinguished. We must, then, it seems to me, take two parts of that law separately: the first is, that the custom to which it refers must be one that has been completely established and is having its effect as law; the second is, that such a custom shall be irrevocable by virtue of the rule embodied in that law. For the first of these, therefore, a repeated judicial decision is not necessary—and this is the matter of present concern to us. For the second, such a judicial decision would seem to be necessary—and in this respect, this law would seem to be one peculiar to Spain. Therefore, the question of its present existence as a matter of usage, or that of its interpretation, does not now concern us. And this sense is easily inferred from the words of the law itself: 'If

---

7. [*Las Siete Partidas*, Pt. I, tit. ii, law 5, previously referred to, *supra*, p. 616.—Tr.]

the people shall have observed a custom for ten or twenty years with the knowledge of the sovereign and without his forbidding it, then they are free to follow that custom in the future.' This is the first part of the law; in it nothing more is required for a legal custom. Then, however, follow the words: 'Such a custom is to be observed in the future, if within this same time, a judicial decision shall have been twice given in favour of the aforesaid custom.' This is the second portion of the law, and in it the custom is no longer called one that the people 'are free to follow', but one that is strictly 'to be observed'—and it is for this effect of irrevocable obligation that that condition [of two decisions in favour of the custom] was specifically set down as requisite. This interpretation of that law will become clearer from what we shall have to say in what remains of our present discussion and from that to be taken up in Chapter xvi.

8. *The answer to the fourth statement.* Our reply to the fourth statement,[8] drawn from reason, is that, at most, it demonstrates that a decision given in favour of an impugned custom is of value in proof of the custom, and for the publication thereof—and this we readily concede. Nevertheless, before that decision was given, the custom was a true one; and, indeed, while the custom is still in the process of development, such a decision cannot be given in virtue of the custom, as I have already demonstrated. Again, before a judicial decision can be given, the custom must be sufficiently proved; therefore, before such a decision can be given, there can be a moral certitude as to the character and sufficiency of the custom which has been established; indeed, for those who cannot of themselves pass an opinion upon the character and sufficiency of the custom, a probable opinion of the Doctors is adequate proof.

What is the value of the opinion of a learned Doctor. Bartolus, in fact holds (on *Digest,* I. iii. 32, qu. 4), that the opinion of even one learned Doctor is sufficient, and on this point he is followed by many weighty authorities, whose opinions have been very carefully compiled by Mascardi (*De Probationibus,* Concl. 426), and by Sánchez (*De Sancto Matrimonii Sacramento,* Bk. VII, disp. xvii, no. 8).

8. [*Supra,* p. 615.—Tr.]

This view must be understood with the qualification that it holds only if this one Doctor's opinion is not contradicted by that of other authorities; and even in that case it is truer to say that it is necessary that several Doctors of high authority should be in agreement with his opinion concerning the custom, or that the statement of the one Doctor be supported by the weighty reasons of other authorities. This may have been the meaning intended by King Alphonso in (*Las Siete Partidas,* Pt. I, tit. ii, law 5), which states that two concordant decisions are sufficient to establish the certitude and proof of the custom in question in such wise that no decision counter to them is possible, nor fuller proof of the custom demanded. The matter could be very properly settled in this manner, although the basis of the arrangement could not be the common law. For *Code,* I. iv. 3, to which the Glosses above mentioned refer, deals not with this point, but with the need of caution in granting pardon to an individual who commits an offence a second time. This relates solely to a matter of fact, and to the beginning of a custom not strictly so called, or a habit, as I have stated above.

9. Panormitanus, however, basing his opinion upon the teaching of the Doctors of both the canon and civil law, adds that although a decision of a judge is not necessary for a custom, it can nevertheless be of assistance not only in proving, but also in establishing it. His reason is that if a judge decides against a law, with the knowledge of the people and without their opposing it, the consent of the people with respect to the custom to be introduced is made known. But surely if the judicial decision was just, it had to assume the custom to be a perfect one, and one in derogation of the law: hence, such a decision cannot serve to establish the custom; it can only indicate and strengthen it. If, however, the decision was unjust, it offers no good ground for presuming the consent of the people to the custom, since the people cannot easily resist a judge, or contradict him. From such a decision, then, it is not the consent of the people to the custom, but only their tolerance of it that is to be inferred, since they cannot oppose the decision. Accordingly, Antoninus and Rochus set down a number of conditions that must be fulfilled for such a reason to have any value. I pass over a discussion of those conditions, since, notwithstanding such a judicial decision or judgment, the same number of actions are required for

the custom, and the same period of time is necessary for its prescription. For an unjust decision cannot remit any of these requirements—nor is the contrary based on any known legal rule.

10. Sylvester, on the other hand, asserts (word *consuetudo*, Qu. 4 [, no. 7]) that in the case of judicial acts a judicial decision can assist in the establishment of a custom: 'in such wise that from two decisions, with a proper lapse of time intervening, and with the consent of the people, given either from the beginning or after the event, a valid custom is to be presumed;' and this because these decisions have an aptitude for establishing a custom (*Digest*, V. ii. 5 and XXIX. v. 3, § 1).

This assertion calls, however, for further examination and clarification. For it is certain that just as through extrajudicial acts, in reference to the making of contracts and wills, and in other observances, consuetudinary law can be established respecting actions of a like kind; so, by judicial acts there can be introduced custom respecting similar acts. These latter customs are, as I said above, known as those of 'style'. This contention is clear both from what has been said above, and by parity of reasoning, or even, *a fortiori*. For this reason I add that just as for an extrajudicial custom no decision handed down by a court is required, so neither is one necessary for a judicial custom—for one, that is, arising from judicial acts. The reason is that there are many judicial acts which are distinct from judicial decisions, and such acts can be repeated over a period of time sufficient for the establishment of a custom; and this, without any judicial decision having been given for or against the custom. In such a case, therefore, the custom is established without a judicial decision having been passed upon it; for all the reasons which hold for an extrajudicial custom, hold equally for such acts and such custom.

Indeed, even though these judicial acts are declarations of law and even though they are judicial decisions repeated many times, there will never be necessary a judicial decision which (as it were) reciprocally decides on the custom of giving such decisions. And so, formally, and properly speaking, for the establishment of a judicial custom, there is never required, in addition to the acts themselves that expressly initiate a custom, any decision given in favour of such custom, when it is impugned, nor any decision that a legal rule has been established by that custom. And this is true also if the custom is concerned with this or that way of proceeding to judgment, or with the pronouncing of judgment after one or another style; the custom is introduced, essentially, by the repetition of the acts of judgment themselves. Thus there is no proper, formal distinction between judicial and extra-judicial actions [in respect of the conditions requisite for the establishment of custom].

11. *The opinion of other writers.* Yet many writers assert that in the giving of decisions and even in judicial acts, two actions are sufficient for the establishment of a custom. This seems to be Sylvester's opinion in the passage quoted above (Section 10). It is that of the Gloss (on *Digest,* I. iii. 32, word *inveterata*), and of Giovanni d'Andrea (on *Decretals,* Bk. V, tit. XL, chap. xxv), and, that also of Bartolus (on *Digest,* I. iii. 32, in *Repetition,* Qu. 4). Many other writers in speaking of style indicate that two actions are sufficient for the establishment of a style; and a style is, as I have stated above, nothing more than a custom in matters of this special kind. This seems to be the opinion of Decio (on rubric to *Digest,* I. iv, no. 35), where he states that lapse of time is not required for style. Rebuffi (Tr. *De Consuetudine,* in *Repetition,* Art. 2, gloss 13, nos. 10 and 17) even says that usage, or a plurality of acts is not necessary for proof of style, and he cites other authorities in support of his opinion. Cristóbal de Paz (on rubric to law on style, Pt. I, nos. 76 *et seq.*) defends this latter opinion, and he cites Cynus (on *Code,* VIII. lii (liii). 2 [, no. 7]), who states that the authority of style is so great, that even if the style is brought in by a single judge, it will have the force of law, and by style he means one established by general conduct without the aid of written law. Cristóbal de Paz sets forth the same opinion at length (*ibid.,* nos. 86 *et seq.*).

Much of what Antonio de Butrio has to say on the observance [of style] in his comments (*De Consuetudine,* Chap. xi) would seem to confirm this opinion. Rochus, quoting him (*De Consuetudine,* Pref. no. 27) speaks to the same effect. They assert that a fixed period of time is not required [for the establishment of a style], but that two or three acts are sufficient to make the observance of it binding in judicial actions. And this, especially if such an observance is declarative and interpretative of law. Finally, many of the remarks made by Rochus (*De Consuetudine,* Qu. 5, no. 34) on use and custom are to the same effect, especially that in which he contends that two acts are sufficient for a custom, particularly in judicial matters.

12. *What must be said of judicial acts.* Nevertheless, having reviewed the essential elements of the question and taken into account the points of difference in the matter involved in it, I find nothing peculiar in this respect in judicial acts, setting aside those in which the person and authority of the sovereign prince vested with legislative power are involved. For his power is a special one in respect to certain matters, as I shall immediately explain. Therefore, although it is certain that law can be established by means of unwritten style, as all jurists teach in their commentaries (on *Decretals,* Bk. I, tit. II, chap. xi and on *Code,* VIII. lii. 2) and as, in particular, Baldus asserts (on *Code,* IX. xlix. 7), as well as Jason (on *Digest,* XXX. lxxi, § 2, no. 5); nevertheless, I do not find that it is defined in any law that two acts or any fixed number of them are sufficient for establishing a legal style, nor that such is proved by any plausible reason; nor that any distinction has been established in this respect between style and customs made up of other kinds of acts.

What duration of time is required in judicial act. I assert, therefore, that in judicial acts, just as in others, there are required such a frequency of the act and such a lapse of time as is sufficient either for validating the custom by prescription, or for manifesting sufficiently the common consent of the prince and of the people.

13. And, first of all, this is the meaning of the laws, which require absolutely for style or its acts frequent use and custom. This is evident from the *Code* (VIII. lii. 1), which uses the words: 'when those acts have been proved, which have been frequently used in the city in the same kind of controversy'. The same is also evident from the *Digest* (V. ii. 5)—cited by Sylvester [word *consuetudo,* Qu. 4] which says: 'when [certain practices] are constantly in use'; for the word 'constantly' signifies more than two actions. The other law, however (*Digest,* XXIX. v. 3, § 1), cited by Sylvester, is in no way applicable to the present situation. In the same way, the other laws which require a frequency of acts do so in general terms and without determination as to number.

Moreover, this is clearly the meaning of Bartolus (on *Digest,* I. iii. 32, no. 14); for, even in the case of judicial decisions, he requires for the establishment of custom a period of ten years and the tacit consent of the people. Decio (on rubric to *Digest,* I. iv, no. 35), states the same doctrine more clearly. He says that for the establishment of a style of the legislator no lapse of time is required; that in other cases, however, a lapse of time is necessary for the introduction of the style. He then proceeds to the conclusion that the frequency of actions necessary be determined by a prudent judgment, in the manner explained earlier in this Book. Saliceto (on *Code,* VIII. lii. 2, no. 23) holds the same view. He says that the repeated acts of a single judge do not establish a style, unless he is a magistrate clothed with sovereign authority. This opinion is defended by Baldus in his comment (on *Code,* VIII. lii. 3), and by Bartolus (on *Digest,* XXVII. i. 30, near the end). Many arguments in favour of this view are to be found in Burgos de Paz (in Pref. to the laws: *Tauri.,* nos. 220 *et seq.*), and in Cristóbal de Paz (on Rubric to law on style, Pt. I, nos. 86 *et seq.*).

The reason on which these laws and legal opinions are based has already been touched upon: it is that neither a judge nor his subordinates possess the power to make law, even if they should expressly wish to do so; they cannot, therefore, by two or three acts tacitly establish law: such authority has not been granted them either by reason or by the law.

14. *An objection.* It may be objected that even though this may be true of certain judicial acts which are preparatory (so to speak) to the decision itself, it is not true of that decision, for the latter has a special character in that by it law is stated and made clear: it would, therefore, seem to have the power of making law, since it is passed by public authority. This would seem to be especially true where the judicial decision has been twice handed down and accepted by popular consent, for it then seems to be law approved by common consent.

Solution. I reply that if the judge giving the decision is not a sovereign prince, and so does not possess legislative authority, his decision, even if it is given more than once, or if it is repeated by different judges of the same rank, has not, on the mere ground of the number of acts performed, the effect of making law. This is the meaning of the *Digest* (I. iii. 38), where it says: 'or of cases always decided in the same way'. The reason is that those decisions are not sufficient to establish law either after the manner of a custom, for reasons already given; or after the manner of a written law, since a judge possesses no power to make law. In this respect, such a decision is different from one which is given by a sovereign prince: for that of the prince has the force of establishing law, not through the medium of custom, but by means of written law, in the manner described in Books Three[9] and Four[10] of this treatise. In the case, then, of a decision handed down by the prince, two acts are not required: one only is sufficient.

In the case of an inferior judge, however, not even many repeated acts suffice, according to an express provision of the emperor given in the *Code* (VII. xlv. 13). On the ground of that law, the Gloss (*De Consuetudine,* Chap. xi, word *legitime*) says that two occasions do not suffice 'since,' in the words of the law, 'judgment must be given not by precedents, but by laws'. Hence, the decision of a private judge has some weight of authority; and if he is a senator of the commonwealth or of the kingdom, the authority of his decision will be much greater; and it will be further enhanced by the handing down of decisions in agreement with his own: but even so, these decisions will have the authority not of law, but rather of an opinion of a Doctor of high authority, or even of many Doctors, as is evident from the decisions of the Rota[11] and the like. And if in a kingdom it is especially provided by statute, that judges shall not dissent from a decision which has been handed down twice or oftener by the royal senate, that rule will be one peculiar to the realm in question; and that, not by virtue of a custom, but by that of written law. Such law apart, however, the tacit consent of the people, or of the prince, is not to be presumed, unless a sufficient lapse of time, and a sufficient frequency of actions make such consent clear.

15. *Two kinds of style taken into account.* In reply to the objections contrary to our thesis in respect of style, I reply that any assertion touching that kind of custom must take into account the two kinds of style: that which has the force of law, and that which is merely factual. As to the first,

9. [Only Chapters i–iv and xxxii–xxxiii of this Book are included in these *Selections. Vide supra,* pp. 415–75.—TR.]

10. [Not included in these *Selections.*—TR.]

11. [The Rota, called the Sacred Roman Rota, is a Roman ecclesiastical tribunal established early in the fourteenth century to hear cases of appeal to the Holy See. Under present discipline it decides, in the second instance, on appeal, cases tried by Ordinaries. Matrimonial cases now form a large part of its business.—REVISER.]

I assert that it does not exist until the style has either been approved by written law or established by a completed prescriptive custom; or, at least, when it is a style so clearly of the sovereign prince who has authority to make law, that he sufficiently declares through it his will that it be law. Again, the term 'style' may be used of custom based on the authority not of the sovereign prince, nor of the law, nor established through a sufficient custom; that is, it may be used of style that has become usual through a few actions—and such a style, I say, is to be followed and observed, not because it is legally binding but because it displays a prudent and fitting mode of action. It is to be observed unless the most urgent reasons are brought against it, or some grave necessity compels a contrary procedure. This, it seems to me, is the purport of the remarks of Rochus and Antonio de Butrio on observances and style of fact, as well as the remarks of many other writers referred to in Section 11 of this Chapter.

CHAPTER XII

Whether Only Voluntary Acts Avail for the Introduction of Custom

1. That the actions by which a custom is established must be voluntary is the certain and generally accepted doctrine on this point.

The acts establishing a custom must be voluntary. This assertion is proved as follows: the actions constituting a custom are of effect in the establishment of the custom only in so far as the consent of the people is manifested through them. But they cannot manifest that consent unless the acts are voluntary. The acts, therefore, by which a custom is established must be voluntary.

The inference is evident. The minor premise is an unquestioned principle of moral philosophy. The major premise is likewise generally agreed to by all the Doctors who deal with this subject. For this reason, as we also saw in the first Chapter of this Book, many writers desire that this consent be expressly included in the definition of custom; that it must be included, at least implicitly, all agree. The reason is that, even though the consent of the prince is also necessary, as we shall state presently, nevertheless, his consent assumes the consent of the people, with which, in this usage, he complies. This is manifest when the custom derogates from the law of the prince; yet the same is true when the custom establishes law, since this legal custom originates (so to speak) with the people, and thus assumes their consent. Whence, even though the expression of the people's consent is necessary in some way for the validity of all law, the mode of its expression need not be the same with respect to this unwritten law [of custom] as with respect to written law. For, primarily and directly, the law emanates from the prince, and he requires consent from the people in obliging them to accept the law, as I have stated in Books Three[1] and Four.[2] But legal custom originates with the people by their willing that the law be introduced, in so far as they have the power to do so, and by their tacitly requesting consent thereto from the prince. It is for this reason that their customary acts must be voluntary.

2. *A custom cannot be established by means of acts done in ignorance or in error.* From this principle I infer that a custom cannot be established by means of acts done in ignorance, or in error, since these are involuntary. This is the doctrine set forth in the Gloss (on *De Consuetudine,* Chap. xi), and that of the Cardinal[3] on the same passage. It will be found also in the Gloss (on the *Decretum,* Pt. I, tit. VIII, chap. vii), in Innocent (on Rubric to *Decretals,* Bk. I, tit. iv, no. 4); in the Gloss and Bartolus (on *Code,* VIII. lii. 2, qu. 17, at the end); also in Baldus (on *Digest,* I. iii. 32, in the fifth objection).

The others, to whom I shall refer, assert almost the same thing except that they add a qualification and a proof from the *Digest* (I. iii. 39), of which we shall speak presently. The stronger proof is that drawn from the *Digest* (*ibid.,* 32), inasmuch as it places the whole force of custom in the consent of the people, which is, obviously, nullified by error. This position is also supported by the *Digest* (*ibid.,* 35) which states that a custom has the force of law from the tacit agreement of the citizens; now a true agreement is lacking where an error intervenes. The law farther on in the same title of the *Digest* (*ibid.,* 36) says that consuetudinary law is of great

---

1. [Only Chapters i–iv and xxxii–xxxiii of this Book are included in these *Selections. Vide supra,* pp. 415–75.—Tr.]

2. [Not included in these *Selections.*—Tr.]

3. [I.e. Gratian.—Reviser.]

authority, 'for the reason that it has been proved so clearly that it had no need of being reduced to writing'. But a custom introduced through error cannot have such authority; nor can it be held to have been truly proved, but merely thought to be so. So also in the *Code* (VIII. lii (liii). 2 [1]), it is said: 'An anterior custom, and a reason [for acting] which has resulted in a custom must be preserved.' This law, then, assumes that a custom should emanate from reason, and not from error. For if it has been established through error, upon discovery of the error, there disappears the apparent reason which might justify such a custom; and consequently the custom itself lapses also, because it cannot persist without a reason. Wherefore, even though the custom will seem to prevail and to establish law before the error is detected, it will do so only from an erroneous persuasion; for when the truth is known, the force of the custom vanishes. It was never, therefore, true law, but was merely thought to be such; and the same is true of the custom itself.

3. *Objection.* The objection is brought against this reasoning, that the passage from the *Digest* (I. iii. 39), says: 'What has been first introduced not by reason, but through error, and was then held to be binding through custom, does not hold in similar cases.' The apparent inference from this text is that a custom established and confirmed by error is valid as to that subject-matter in respect of which it was initiated, but that it must not be extended to similar cases. This is the opinion of Bartolus (on *Digest,* I. iii. 32, no. 5, and *ibid.,* 33, and on *Code,* VIII. lii. 1 [, no. 21], with the Gloss thereon) as well as that of Baldus, and other authorities. Panormitanus holds the same view (*De Consuetudine,* Chap. xi, no. 12), as does Antonio de Butrio on the same Chapter. Rochus is in agreement with these writers (*De Consuetudine,* Sect. 4, at the beginning), and cites others whose opinion may be summarized in three points.

First, they assume that a custom founded upon certain knowledge and without error, and with other adequate conditions, is not only valid in the subject-matter with which it is concerned, but may also be extended to similar matters. They add, secondly, that a custom established through error is also valid in its own subject-matter. Thirdly, they conclude that the latter custom differs from the first, [only] because it cannot be so widely extended to similar cases.

Explanation of the law which has been brought forward as a proof. While the first of these points seems to have been most favourably received by the jurists, I find great difficulty in accepting it. But, since it cannot be properly analysed or explained in general terms, we shall deal with it when we come to the chief particular effects of custom.

The second statement, however, is directly opposed to our assertion, and these writers prove it not by any argument but by a reference to *Digest,* I. iii. 39, nor do they answer the argument advanced in support of our thesis—that error annuls consent—whereas they themselves use the same argument to prove their third point.

4. *The foregoing interpretation of the above-cited law is attacked.* Accordingly, I do not think that this [second] opinion is valid with respect to true custom, with which alone we are at present dealing. This I shall prove in detail, assuming certain points which have been conceded by the Doctors above cited. In the first place, Cynus and other ancient authorities, with whom Bartolus also agrees, qualify that assertion for the reason we have given. They hold that that assertion does not apply to a custom which is opposed to law. Their reason is that if the people act contrary to law from ignorance, or if they err in their judgment of its terms, it is clear that they have no intention of derogating from the law.

In what manner, then, is *Digest,* I. iii. 39 to be explained in its relation to a custom of this [erroneous] sort? For is not such a custom a very clear example of custom introduced without reason and through error? Indeed, many writers in touching on custom of this kind hold that the law of the *Digest* is to be read as referring especially to custom established in opposition to a positive law, inasmuch as it refers to custom 'not initiated by reason', in order that it may not seem to be referring to unreasonable custom.

Moreover, concerning even a custom that is outside the law, Bartolus and others distinguish between error of fact and error of law. Respecting a custom established by an error of fact, they admit that it is invalid owing to a defect in consent, according to *Digest,* II. i. 15. If the error be merely one in respect of the law, they say that the custom is nevertheless valid, with the aforesaid limitation, however, that it is not to be extended to similar cases.

5. Therefore, we admit that the first member of this latter assertion thus distinguished is not contrary to our contention, and we attack the second member of that assertion; for an error concerning the introduction of law removes the element of consent in introducing it. For in those customs which are outside the law there can be no error as to law, save by the misapprehension that their subject-matter is either forbidden or enjoined. For under the misapprehension that the matter is prohibited, the custom is not one intended for establishing new law, but rather one in derogation of [misapprehended] existing law. But no custom can derogate from law where there is no law in existence from which departure is made. Again, an erroneous custom of the second sort [, based on the misapprehension that the matter is enjoined by law,] cannot establish law, since it was formed not with that intention, but rather with that of obeying the law [, misapprehended as existing]. For, just as a custom that has sprung from true law does not establish any legal rule, as we said above, neither is it possible for a custom which has grown out of a falsely presumed legal obligation to establish any legal rule, for the popular consent is annulled by the false presumption— as will be more clearly evident from what we shall say in the following Chapters. Therefore, a custom derived from error never has the effect of establishing law, even in its own subject-matter. Whence it is clearly the more logical and better grounded conclusion that it is not to be extended to other cases.

Accordingly, I do not approve of the example which Rochus borrows from Baldus, to the effect that if a people are accustomed not to reap a crop of grain from a certain locality, because they believe that this is forbidden, this custom establishes law, for the reason that even though the people are in error as to the law in the matter, they do consent to the fact. But I hold that such material consent to fact is not sufficient: rather, to establish law, they must consent to the fact as establishing a legal rule. The reason is (as Rochus himself admits in the Chapter to which I have referred and as will be said in that which here follows) that law is not established by a custom apart from a purpose to establish a custom, that is, a legal custom. Now error takes away such purpose, as we have clearly demonstrated. Therefore, . . .

An excellent example is that of religious profession tacitly made which is not established as valid by any usage, so long as error concerning the validity of the previous profession persists, owing to want of consent. This is a well-known example.[4]

6. *Answer to the objection drawn from* Digest, *I. iii. 39.* But in regard to the argument drawn from *Digest,* I. iii. 39, my first reply is that this law can be explained as having application to a legal prescription, but not to a true legal custom. For in the case of prescription, it can happen that a custom may originate without a reason, that is, without a true title, and in error, when the custom begins in good faith and so continues and persists up to the point of the establishment of a valid prescription. But this can scarcely be understood of a true and legal custom; and this, both for the reasons we have already set forth as to the force of error in annulling consent; and because consuetudinary law cannot be established without a ground in reason. However, that last clause of the above-cited law, ['it] does not hold in similar [cases,] might not seem applicable to prescription, since there is never question of extending the identical prescription to subject-matter other than its own, merely because of a similarity existing in such subject-matter. Whereas, if the manner of establishing prescription is identical, in another similar situation, the same prescriptive right will arise.

Nevertheless, I think *Digest,* I. iii. 39 is correctly interpreted in regard to this point by the legal rule that 'what is a matter of special concession to any one, ought not to be used as a precedent by others' (in *Sext,* Bk. V, *De regulis iuris,* rule 74). This opinion is confirmed by another rule (*ibid.,* rule 78), which states that, 'what has at times been granted, on account of necessity, cannot be employed as an argument' [in other cases]. It is also stated in the *Digest* (I. iv. 1), that grants to particular individuals are not to be set up as a precedent. Thus, what *Digest,* I. iii. 39 may have been framed to say was, that what is permitted to one person on the ground of

---

4. [Suárez here refers to the case of a Religious who takes vows invalidly, in consequence of some unknown defect. In order to validate the vows, such a Religious must give explicit consent, and take the vows again, conscious of their previous invalidity. No amount of religious observance, as though the vows had been valid, is of any avail.—REVISER.]

a consuetudinary prescription made in good faith, but lacking in reason and founded in error, cannot be taken advantage of by others, even if in other respects their cases are identical or similar. This is the interpretation of the law that I draw from the Gloss on *Digest,* I. iii. 14, which is similar to the passage in the *Digest* which we are discussing. The one law assists us to the correct reading of the other.

7. *Objection.* A difficulty against this reading of the law may be drawn from the fact that the law of which we are speaking [law 39] is found under the title *De Legibus* [*Digest,* I. iii], whereas the laws that precede and follow it deal with legal custom.

Solution. But it is not to be wondered at, if, to avoid another absurd reading of law 39, we extend somewhat the meaning of the word 'custom' in that context. And we do so especially, since many points in those laws apply equally to both sorts of custom,[5] and the Doctors, in expounding these common points and setting forth the conditions of custom, succeed only in confusing everything, as I have frequently remarked. The common example, which the jurists use as an illustration of an established custom, that if the owner [that is, the buyer] of wine has placed his hand upon the cart,[6] from that moment the wine will be at his own risk, certainly refers to a custom of prescription. The explanation of the Gloss on the aforesaid law[7] is that such a custom is not transferred to any like cases, that is to say, as a prescription against persons against whom no prescriptive right was set up in virtue of such a custom as we have mentioned. The whole of this matter may be considered as relating to the title *De Legibus;* for although this custom does not make law, it does change the subject-matter of the

---

5. [I.e. legal custom and prescriptive custom.—Tr.]

6. [Presumably a cart belonging to another person who has agreed with the buyer of the wine to transport it to the buyer's house. Though the translation is exact, is it not rather a case of the buyer of the wine accepting responsibility of transport, and thus freeing the seller of the wine from all liability? At owner's risk, as we say. The argument of Suárez is somewhat difficult to follow here.—Reviser.]

7. [The Gloss says: 'If the owner of wine put his hand to the cart even to help, the wine is then at his own risk.' This is contrary to reason, and is a custom introduced by error; it is therefore not a valid custom in the case of other liquids, even though this custom was afterwards approved with certain knowledge and with tacit consent.—Reviser.]

law, in such wise that by reason of the custom the laws must be applied in a different way in a case of this kind.

8. *Another interpretation of the law, i.e.* Digest *I. iii. 39.* Secondly, if we wish to read the aforesaid law 39 [*Digest,* I. iii. 39] as applying to true legal custom, we shall reply that it does not say it is possible that a custom may be introduced without reason, and by error; but rather that it sets forth the contrary. This is the meaning of the Glosses cited in our assertion, and in our reasoning, which refer to this law in support of the interpretation they set forth.

Hence, the sense of the words, 'it [, i.e. the custom,] does not obtain in other cases, of a like sort' is not that the custom does obtain in that particular matter, but that it does not in similar matters. For probably this same statement could be made of every custom, even of one established with certain knowledge, as I state later on. Certainly, if other customs extend [, as our opponents hold,] to similar cases, a custom [founded upon error and lacking reason] would also extend to like cases if it were true law [; but this our opponents deny]. The ground of this conclusion is that such extension can never be made except in so far as the reason of the law permits, a principle that is verified in every true law. Therefore, that interpretation of the law is at variance with sound reason. Therefore, the meaning of the words, 'that it does not obtain in other cases, of a like sort' will be that such a custom does not persist, and that when the error is recognized, there exists no right to perform actions similar to those which were previously done in error, that is, in observance of a custom which was thought to be, but was not, legitimate. This interpretation is neither absurd, nor does it do violence to the words [of the law], and thus read, the aforesaid law 39 proves our assertion, as the Glosses imply.

9. *The kind of ignorance or error that does not establish custom.* Finally, the inquiry can be made on this point, namely: what sort of ignorance or error is to be understood here [in the assertion that custom is not established by acts arising from ignorance or error]?

For on this point also, Cynus and the other jurists distinguish, as usual, between the motive [, i.e. cause,] and the final cause,[8] and they say that

---

8. [Aristotle recognizes four causes of being (*Physics,* II. iii; Loeb ed., Vol. I, 129): (*a*) material; (*b*) formal; (*c*) moving, or efficient; and (*d*) final. In the scholastic philosophy,

the assertion [which we are here defending] must be understood of an error as to the final cause [of the custom], not as to its moving cause. But I have had much to say of this and similar distinctions in my other works (*De Iuramento,* Bk. II, chap. xi, and *De Voto,* Bk. I, chap. xi),[9] and what I have there said is applicable in due proportion to the present question.

The assertion must be understood of an ignorance which relates to the substance of a custom. I shall, therefore, here content myself with saying that the assertion of this Chapter must be understood as pertaining to an ignorance concerning those things which relate to the substance of the custom, whether in respect of the law or of the fact on which the law is founded. Ignorance of this kind precludes the necessary consent, as has been previously stated. If, however, the ignorance is one that concerns other motives which are accidental, no hindrance is created, since such ignorance does not destroy consent. Some writers, however, interpret the aforesaid law 39 [*Digest,* I. iii. 39], as applying to this sort of error regarding incidental matters. They assume that the law states that a custom in accordance with law is established despite the existence of errors of this sort. But these writers have not been able to explain satisfactorily why they should have to say that such a custom does not hold in similar cases, since an error that does not touch essential matters cannot present an obstacle to such extension, if a true custom [, as they teach,] is permitted such extension. In the light of this interpretation, their teaching is not conclusive.

---

following Aristotle, the immediate moving cause is called the efficient cause (*causa efficiens*); and the ultimate purpose of the action, the final cause (*causa finalis*). The efficient cause is that which, by its action, produces an effect substantially distinct from itself. In other words, it is the cause '*cuius virtute effectus immediate producitur*'.

Efficient causes acting towards ends are distinguished as (*a*) acting by intelligence; or (*b*) acting by nature. For example: the sculptor using the chisel (intelligent efficient cause) produces the statue which he intended (this intention, or purpose, being the final cause). The final cause, or end, therefore, is that for the sake of which the effect, or result of any action is produced. See St. Thomas Aquinas, *Summa Theologica,* I.–II, qu. 1, art. 2. But, where the efficient cause acts through nature alone, the intention of a rational creature is not involved; thus, excessive heat coming in contact with a piece of paper *of its own nature* reduces that paper to ashes.—Tr.]

9. [Not included in these *Selections.*—Tr.]

10. *A custom is not established by means of acts done by compulsion or from grave fear.* In the second place, it is to be inferred from this assertion that a custom does not prevail, nor is it established validly by acts done under compulsion or from grave or unjust fear. This is substantially the doctrine of Bartolus (on *Code,* VIII. lii (liii). 2, qu. 18 in its entirety, and in no. 19, in reply to the last objection but one [and *ibid.,* no. 23]), and of Antonio de Butrio (*De Consuetudine,* Chap. xi). But Rochus Curtius (*De Consuetudine,* Sect. 5, no. 3) seems to hold the contrary opinion, for he says that a custom is established by acts done from fear. However, he refers to the above-cited authors, and evidently intends his own assertion to be understood in the light of the assertions of these writers. Hence, Rochus does not differ from us; but by acts done from fear he means either that the fear is of slight and trifling importance, or, at least, that the acts, though inspired by fear at the time of their performance, are later freely confirmed and accepted in the course of time. For that is Bartolus's doctrine also. The ground on which our present inference is drawn is that force and fear preclude the consent required for the introduction of custom. This, however, applies to compulsion strictly so called.

11. *In what way fear may cause an involuntary action.* A difficulty may be raised as to the validity of customary acts done out of fear, because, although fear may make an act involuntary under one aspect, still of itself it leaves the act an entirely voluntary one.[10] Whence arose the occasion for the dispute as to whether from the nature of the case fear alone is sufficient to invalidate a forced consent, in such wise that the consent shall not have the effect of establishing consuetudinary law, and as to what kind of fear can have this effect. But since the question is general and one that arises in connexion with other matters, and since I have discussed it at length in

10. [The concept of a *voluntarium* and of the species into which it is divided is of the first importance in ethics and Catholic moral theology, &c. A *voluntarium* is an act that proceeds from the will with a clear [i.e. 'intellectual'] knowledge of the purpose [i.e. nature] of the act. The act of jettison [, of throwing the cargo out of the ship in order to escape shipwreck by lightening it,] is, under the circumstances, an absolutely voluntary act; but there is, in the will, as an active faculty, a *certain reluctance* in throwing cargo away, and consequently, the act, though absolutely voluntary in the will, is done with regret, and under that aspect, it is called and is an involuntary act *secundum quid,* i.e., the act would not be done under other more favourable circumstances.—REVISER.]

De Iuramento (Bk. II, chap. ix) and in *De Voto* (Bk. I, chap. vii),[11] I now refrain from discussing it.

In connexion with the present subject-matter, there is greater reason why fear precludes the establishment of custom. I shall say no more than that there is a much stronger reason why, in the case of custom, fear should be a bar to validity: and it is that, for a custom, mere actions are not sufficient; it is essential that those actions be performed with the intention of introducing custom, and this intention is commonly tacit rather than expressed. But when the actions are done solely from fear—when they would not be done except under its compulsion—they lack that intention; nor can such an intention be morally presumed, since the fear in itself, in a certain way, excludes it. Thus, a frequency of actions done solely from fear, is never sufficient evidence of the public consent of a whole people to the establishment of a custom. There is the additional consideration that the prince cannot be presumed in such a situation to give his consent, since he does not wish his subjects to be forced to adopt customs of that kind under unjust fear. And if he himself brings force and fear to bear [upon his people], he commits an injustice, because he would *morally* oblige the people to adopt the custom, as I have said in connexion with the passage cited above, in similar cases.

CHAPTER XIII

Whether the Consent of the Prince Is Necessary for the Introduction of a Custom, and What Must Be the Nature of This Consent

1. We must devote this Chapter to inquiries respecting the principal efficient cause of consuetudinary law. In this, the consent of the prince must first of all be recognized as necessary for the introduction of a custom. This assertion I have derived from the common teaching of the Doctors. The opinion of the few who teach otherwise, I shall discuss at a later time, to better advantage.

---

11. [Not included in these *Selections.*—Tr.]

We must, then, in order to distinguish what is certain from what is uncertain, mark the distinctions that exist between peoples [in respect to their power to make laws]. For, in the first place, a custom can be that of a people which is in possession of supreme legislative authority, a status enjoyed only in the domain of the civil law, and by those commonwealths which acknowledge no superior in temporal affairs.

Various classes of communities distinguished. In respect of communities of this sort, our assertion does not seem to be pertinent, but it is true in so far as it has reference to them. For in a state of this kind, the sovereign is the whole commonwealth, and so, if a custom is accepted by such a people, the consent is necessarily given by the sovereign, since in this case the two are identical. *Digest,* I. iii. 32 refers clearly to a community so organized.

A first class of community.[1] But if the sovereign power has been transferred to a senate, and some disagreement arises in that body, then it is necessary that a majority of its members hold to the custom, for otherwise the custom cannot be said to be observed by the larger portion of the community in respect of its power to establish law. And the senate could not be regarded as tacitly giving its consent, if the major part thereof does not hold to the custom. Accordingly, our assertion is found to be true with regard to peoples possessing such legislative authority, and of them nothing further need be said.

2. *A second class of community.* We may, next, have a people which recognizes a superior, but holds from him the authority to make laws or municipal statutes, even as, according to *Digest,* I. i. 9, the cities especially have by commonly accepted law. It is certain that just as such a community is empowered to enact written law, so it can introduce law by custom (*Digest,* I. iii. 32 *et seq.*). Whence, just as they can enact law without the renewed consent of the prince, so they can establish customs. Nevertheless, the consent of the prince is not entirely lacking in such a case, since he has given it through his permission to make laws, and wishes it to be continuously available. Thus, under such an arrangement, the prince need not have particular knowledge of a custom newly introduced into

---

1. [Suárez really discusses four classes of communities in this passage, though his marginal notes indicate only three.—Tr.]

this or that city; for even without this special knowledge, he could give an antecedent consent (so to speak) and has done so when he granted to the people permission to enact in one form or another a particular law for themselves, should they wish to do so.

Wherefore, if the permission were given under the limiting condition that the law must be later confirmed by the prince, it could not be strictly binding before such consent had been obtained, as seems to be the situation in Spain. Under such an arrangement, our assertion would not apply. For it would then be necessary that the custom be confirmed by the prince also, and hence a renewed consent would be required from him, since a renewed confirmation is not had without such consent. Such a community, then, is, to that extent, to be held as, in a certain sense, lacking in authority to make laws apart from the prince. Of this matter we shall speak presently: for we shall have to introduce this point again, in our discussion of the nature of that confirmation and the means of obtaining it.

3. *A third class of community.* Furthermore, there are communities which possess no power of making statutes or enacting laws, even of a municipal character, but who must accept those given to them either by a sovereign prince, or by their overlords or pastors. This is the relation which the Universal Church bears to the supreme Pontiff, and the particular churches to their respective pastors. For the people have no power to make canon laws; nor have the clergy such power apart from their superiors or without their superiors' concurrence—the peculiar differences in the various laws and communities being always taken into account.

The first opinion. Many secular communities stand in this same relation to their sovereigns, as is self-evident. Hence, some authorities have said that these communities cannot introduce a custom without the special tacit consent of the prince himself (which I term his personal will); so, for such a custom they demand both a knowledge and a toleration of the custom on the part of the prince.

This is the doctrine of the Gloss (on *De Consuetudine,* Chap. xi), and it is followed by many writers. It is stated by Panormitanus in his comments on this law, and it is expressly set down by Innocent (on rubric *De Consuetudine,* no. 4 [*Ex parte*]). It is found, again, in the Gloss (on *Code,* VIII. lii. 2), which cites the authority of Giovanni d'Andrea and Azo.

This is also the opinion of Gregory López ([on *Las Siete Partidas,*] Pt. I, tit. ii, law 3, gloss 7 [*glossa* f]) and would seem furthermore to be that of St. Thomas (I.–II, qu. 97, art. 3, ad 3). St. Thomas says that in those communities which have a superior, custom is so far able to introduce law 'as is tolerated by those whose office it is to give law to the people. From this toleration they may be considered as approving of the rule established by the custom.' With this doctrine, Soto agrees (*De Iustitia,* Bk. I, qu. vii, art. 2), as do Sylvester (word *consuetudo,* Qu. 3), Driedo (*De Libertate Christiana,* Chap. xii), and Angelus de Clavasio (word *consuetudo,* No. 9 at the beginning). But, in fact, many of these authorities can without difficulty be understood in the sense which I shall explain.

4. A proof of this opinion can be developed, first, from the *Digest* (I. iii. 32), where the whole basis of custom is founded upon the consent of a people, which can give force and efficacy to its own laws. This, then, was the primary force of the custom among the people, when they still retained the sovereign power; therefore, after the people has handed over that power to the prince, the force of custom will mainly depend upon his consent. For this reason, it is necessary that he should have previous knowledge of a custom, since without that no consent is possible.

The second proof is taken from *Las Siete Partidas* (Pt. I, tit. ii, law 3), where, among the conditions for custom, it is laid down that it be introduced with the consent of the prince.

Thirdly, it is argued from reason that legislative authority is no less necessary for the establishment of unwritten law, than of written law, as is clear from our discussion upon laws in general. But legislative power does not exist in these peoples—this is the supposition of the argument—either because they never had this power, as is the case with the canon laws, or because they have transferred that authority to the prince, as is the case with the civil laws. Therefore, it is necessary that the one in whom the sovereign power resides should give force to custom by his will and consent.

5. *Distinction between the power of making ecclesiastical laws and the power of making civil laws.* Some Doctors, however—but not many— seem to admit that this opinion is true of the canon laws, but deny that it is so of civil laws. They submit, as the ground of their distinction, the fact that the power of making the canon laws never resided in the people,

but in the prelates; on the other hand the authority to enact the civil laws was originally vested in the people. This is the view of Antoninus ([*Summa Theologica,*] Pt. I, tit. xvi, § 2). Covarruvias follows St. Thomas (I.–II, qu. 97, art. 3), and also, very clearly, Driedo (*De Libertate Christiana,* Bk. I [, chap. viii]).

The distinction is attacked. But I cannot approve of this distinction, since I feel certain that it is not valid: for, although the civil power was originally in the community, after the community has transferred it to the prince, the former no longer has that power in itself. The people, therefore, are in this case not less dependent upon the prince than if the community had never possessed the power to make laws.

Those writers might here object that when the people transferred their power to the prince, they did not give it up entirely, but only for the express uses (so to speak) of government, and for framing written laws and oral precepts; they surrendered it, that is, in such a way as always to reserve to themselves the power of introducing customs. But this view cannot be well-founded, since it is not proved from any law, nor does it appear in a perfect monarchy, either by custom or through any other evidence. Still, in a given kingdom, the royal power may be limited in that or some like fashion, at least by tacit agreement; as, for example, where the monarchy is not absolute, but partly democratic—as we made clear above in our discussion of the acceptance of law.[2] Yet this is not the usual situation, and the exception rather strengthens the rule to the contrary. Again, this opinion does not seem probable, for the reason that a temporal sovereign can revoke the private customs prevailing among his people, and can, for a [good] reason, prohibit their introduction. On the same principle, the prince may ordain that a custom shall be invalid if it lacks his express consent; which is evidence that the entire legislative authority of every sort has been transferred to him.

6. *The consent of the prince is necessary for the validity of a custom.* The third and true opinion is that which first of all lays down the general principle that the consent of the prince is necessary for the validity of a custom. For this is the common teaching of the Doctors, as I have said,

---

2. [*De Legibus,* Bk. I, chap. xi, no. 7, which is not included in these *Selections.*—REVISER.]

and is effectually demonstrated by the proof given in our discussion of the first opinion. [The third,] however, further specifies that this consent of the prince can be understood in two ways. One, I term personal, because it is given by the prince in person, either by expressly consenting, or by antecedently permitting the introduction of a custom, or by approving it subsequently or contemporaneously, and this either in express terms, or when being aware of the custom he does not check it. The second kind of consent we may term legal or juridical, because it is given not by the prince personally, but through the law itself. Thus, if the prince enacts a law to the effect that a custom which contains such and such conditions shall be valid, he thereby gives his consent, which is applied in particular to like customs which are introduced in virtue of that law.

Hence, we assert that consent of the first sort is not always necessary, the latter being sufficient. For it is self-evident that the first sort of consent is sufficient. That such express consent is not necessary, and that consent of the second sort is sufficient, I shall prove as follows. The law is never silent, and the will of the prince, speaking through the law, is no less efficacious than his immediate wish and command. What occasions are proper for the one or the other mode of consent, I shall discuss in the following corollaries [to this general principle].

7. *First inference: that the personal consent of the prince is not required.* My first inference is that, when a law is established by prescriptive custom, the personal consent of the prince is not required; nor, therefore, is any special knowledge of the custom on his part called for: but the custom is efficaciously established, even though he may have no specific knowledge of it, or may not have manifested his will with respect to it, either tacitly or expressly.

This is the common opinion of the jurists according to Panormitanus (*De Consuetudine,* Chap. xi, no. 13). The same is set forth in the Gloss (on *Decretum,* Pt. I, dist. iv, can. iii, § *leges,* after the canon, at end and also *ibid.,* dist. viii, can. vii, in the last words), if the latter Gloss is carefully weighed, and by Cardinal Alexander[3] thereon, at the end. The same position is held by Antoninus and Barbatia and others (*Repertorium, De Consuetudine*), to which Rochus Curtius (*De Consuetudine,* Sect. 4, no. 24)

3. [I.e. Giovanni de Sangiorgio.—Tr.]

refers many times. This opinion is held also by Dominicus de Sancto Geminiano (*Summa,* Dist. xi, near end), Angelus de Clavasio (*Summa,* word *consuetudo,*[4] no. 9), and Sylvester ([word *consuetudo,*] Qu. 4). The last-named two writers assume that a prescriptive custom suffices, even though the Pope has no knowledge [of the custom]. Felinus (on *Decretals,* Bk. II, tit. xxvi, chap. xvi, no. 11) teaches the same, although he qualifies his assertion with respect to certain special cases which touch upon other matters. Among the theologians who defend this opinion are: de la Palu ([*On the Sentences,*] Bk. IV, dist. xlii, qu. 3, art. 1, no. 7 [, concl. 3]), *Supplement,* Qu. 2, art. 2, concl. 3,[5] Antoninus ([*Summa Theologica,*] Pt. I, tit. xvi, § 2), and Sánchez (*De Sancto Matrimonii Sacramento,* Bk. VII, disp. iv, nos. 11 and 14, and disp. lxxxii, no. 20), who cites a number of other writers.

8. The principal basis of this opinion is taken from the *Decretals* (Bk. I, tit. iv, chap. xi), where only two conditions are required for a custom, namely, that the custom be reasonable, and '[validated] by prescription'. To demand, then, another condition, namely, one not included in these, is to demand a condition without a basis in law, in fact, one contrary to the law. But special knowledge [of the custom] on the part of the prince is such an added condition not included above. Therefore it is not necessary; and, therefore, neither is his personal consent necessary—since it is impossible without such knowledge.

This assertion is confirmed and explained as follows: the prince had the power to enact a general law approving a custom fulfilling such and such conditions laid down by him and giving validity to it without a renewed consent or knowledge of it on his part. But this he has done by means of that provision. Therefore, . . .

The major premiss is evident, for this course of action does not exceed the power of the prince, and this mode of manifesting his will is entirely sufficient, as I have shown; it is also the most convenient way, because it is practically impossible that all customs should come to the knowledge of the prince—as is noted (in *Sext,* Bk. I, tit. ii, chap. 1); and on other

---

4. [The Latin text incorrectly has *confessio.*—Tr.]

5. [This reference to *Supplement* is apparently copied from Chap. xix, sect. 26, *infra,* p. 729, where *Supplement* of Gabriel Biel is cited as parallel to the passage from de la Palu; but the reference is wrong.—Reviser.]

grounds it is expedient that reasonable customs should be observed and receive their [legal] force. Therefore, . . .

Finally, a confirmation of our assertion can be drawn from the similitude between this kind of custom, and prescription properly so called. It is because of this likeness that the custom of which we are speaking is called prescriptive: for in a prescription, knowledge on the part of the individual against whom the prescription is being established, is not necessary; so, also, a custom is said to be obtained against the prince by prescription, if it fulfils the terms of such prescription. Therefore, a custom of this sort, to be valid, does not call for a knowledge of it on the part of the prince.

9. *An objection.* An objection may be raised, namely, that the above holds true only of a custom abrogating law—which point is dealt with in the *Decretals* (Bk. I, tit. IV, chap. xi)—not, however, of a custom establishing law, because with respect to this custom there is no such rule. Again, it may be objected that the same holds true at most only for canon law, and canonical custom; for in the civil law no such rule can be found to have been laid down.

The solution. My reply to the first part of this objection is that this rule in principle includes *a fortiori* custom constitutive of unwritten law, for the reason that the same power is necessary for abrogating a law of a prince, as is required to introduce a new law not contrary to the old. From another aspect, however, the need of the consent of the prince for permitting the revocation of the prince's own law would seem more necessary than that for the establishment of new law: since the revocation would seem to derogate more from his will and authority [, than would the introduction of new law]. This point is emphasized in the above-cited text [*Decretals, ibid.*]: 'Although the authority of an ancient custom is not slight, yet it is not to prevail so far as to prejudice even a positive law unless, &c.' Therefore, since this character is granted to a custom, if it has these two conditions aforesaid (Section 8, *supra*), every consuetudinary law that fulfils the said conditions is absolutely approved.

10. In reply to the second part of the objection, however, it is to be said first of all that, granting that the civil law has not declared this principle so expressly, nevertheless, it does not deny the validity of custom which

fulfils those two conditions, whatever may be true of its effects, of which we shall speak in another place.

In fact, the civil law teaches virtually the same doctrine on this point, that the canon law sets forth in a clearer manner. For in the *Digest* (I. iii. 32) we find the words: 'It is most correctly admitted that laws are abrogated, not only by the decision of the lawgiver, but also through disuse, with the tacit consent of all.' In these words, a distinction is drawn between the people and the lawgiver, and the decision of the latter is not required. Further, in the following laws [*ibid.*, 33 and 35], nothing more is required—assuming that the custom is reasonable—in order that the custom may have legal force, than that it be protracted, 'of long standing', or 'observed for many years'. In the *Digest* (*ibid.*, 38) it is added that the Emperor has ordained that an immemorial custom 'is to have' the force of law. In the civil law, then, according to its commentators, it is provided that a prescriptive custom is sufficiently complete, without any new knowledge of it on the part of the prince.

II. *If a custom does not prevail in virtue of a prescription, then a personal consent is necessary.* My second inference is that when a custom does not prevail in virtue of prescription, then the personal consent of the prince is requisite, that is, at least a tacit consent; and that, therefore, it is also necessary that he should have knowledge of the custom. This point we concede to the writers who defend the first opinion,[6] among whom is St. Thomas, whose language concerning the consent of the prince is general, and whose words can be interpreted as referring to either of the two ways by which the prince—as we have explained—may give his consent. This would seem also to be the opinion of Sylvester [word *consuetudo*, Qu. 4] and St. Antoninus [*Summa Theologica*, Pt. I, tit. xvi, § 2], who, while quoting and following the opinion and words of St. Thomas, nevertheless admit that sometimes a custom of which the prince is ignorant, does prevail. Finally, the authors cited for the opinion we have just discussed admit this.

It is, further, proved by a sufficient exclusion of possibilities. The sovereign's consent is necessary; but in custom of this sort that consent is

6. [*Supra*, p. 639.—Tr.]

not given in virtue of any law, nor does any law definitely fix the terms under which it is given. Hence, his consent must be personal; and for this, knowledge is necessary. This reasoning is also confirmed by the arguments brought forward for the first opinion.

12. *What sort of consent of the prince is necessary.* On the question, however, whether such consent of the prince should be positive and explicit, or whether one which is inferred is sufficient—that is, it is sufficient that he knows and tolerates the custom or offers no opposition thereto—St. Antoninus indicates (*ibid.*), that an express consent is necessary, especially in the case of the supreme Pontiff. And this view might be urged in that toleration alone, even assuming that a knowledge of the custom exists, does not sufficiently indicate consent, because many things are allowed to be done which are not approved, according to the *Decretals* (Bk. III, tit. v, chap. xviii).

A tacit consent is sufficient. Nevertheless, St. Thomas (I.–II, qu. 97, art. 3, ad 3), expressly teaches that a tacit consent is sufficient. This is accepted by other writers, and usage proves that tacit consent is regarded as of equal effect with explicit consent, as, with reference to this kind of custom, the aforesaid law 32 [*Digest,* I. iii. 32] states. It is necessary only that it be morally evident that the toleration is not merely permissive but an active or approving one; whether it is such will be easily seen from the circumstances and from usage, especially either when the approval is reasonable, or when, by a permission alone, the safety and well-being of the subjects is inadequately provided for, as I shall explain in the following Chapters. Nor in this matter is any exception to be made in the case of the supreme Pontiff. There is no law or reason for making such exception necessary. In some special cases, however, his explicit consent will perhaps be necessary, when the gravity of the matter or some particular law indicates that it is called for. But this can happen in the case of other princes also, and hence the rule we have given is, strictly speaking, a general one.

13. *What consent of the prince is necessary.* To the basic principle of the contrary opinion, a ready reply is possible. For *Digest,* I. iii. 32 proves merely that there is required [, for custom,] the consent of him who is in possession of the supreme legislative authority, but it establishes no proof in favour of this or that mode of consent; nor does it obviate the possibility

of this consent being given by law; in fact, it indicates that it can be so given, as I have argued. In the same way, the Spanish law [*Las Siete Partidas,* Pt. I, tit. ii, law 5] requires no more than that the custom be established with the consent of the prince. With this principle our theory is in agreement, and the law does not say that knowledge or personal consent of the prince is always necessary. If this law [, i.e. *Las Siete Partidas,*] had decreed that the consent of the prince must be of the latter kind, the law of Spain would have been a particular kind of law, and not one demanded by the nature of things, nor of the general type of law.

The argument from reason for the contrary opinion serves only to prove the first member of our assertion, and to confirm the last. Nor does it hold against our second member, since in that part of our assertion we also say that the authority of the prince is a cause in the establishment of prescriptive custom, and that it does, through the medium of the prince's law, give validity to such custom.

CHAPTER XIV

What Sort of Custom Has the Effect of Establishing Unwritten Law?

1. We have discussed the essence and the causes of custom; now it remains for us to speak of its effects. For although we have, in passing, touched upon some of them, we must, to make our doctrine serviceable, apply these principles which have been set forth in a general way to the several effects.

Four effects of custom. Four effects are usually attributed to custom: namely, the establishment, the interpretation, the confirmation, and the abrogation of law. To these are reduced all other conceivable effects of custom. We shall, however, pass over the third one of these, because its effect is not so much one of law as one of fact; for a custom which is said to confirm law is derived from law itself, and so it does not confirm law by the introduction or the addition of new law beyond the written law, as explained above (Bk. VII, chap. ii, *supra,* p. 513). Hence, it confirms a law by the fact merely that it either brings men more readily to the observance or knowledge thereof by increasing in some way its authority and man's sense of its value; or, at least, by guarding the law against revocation and (as it were) keeping it from the influence of a contrary custom, and so preserving it from the abrogation which might be effected by such a custom. I have discussed this effect also, *supra* (Bk. I, chap. xi),[1] nor is there need for us to add here to the further remarks on this matter, given in Books Three[2] and Four,[3] in our discussion of the acceptance of human law.

The second effect, however—namely, the interpretation of law—inasmuch as it can pertain to law, is, as I shall show,[4] included under the first effect. Thus, the two remaining effects alone need to be explained; and we shall speak of the first one in the present Chapter, and of the last in a later Chapter.[5]

2. The first effect, then, of legitimate custom, is to establish unwritten law where neither written nor traditional law exists. I repeat 'where no written [. . .] law exists' because if there precedes, in point of time, a written law in conformity with custom, and if the custom grows out of this law, then the custom does not, as I have said, establish law. If, however, a law contrary to the custom exists first, then such a law must first be abolished, as I shall prove in the following Chapters. Our assertion, therefore, applies properly to custom which is outside law,[6] one, namely, that is neither forbidden nor prescribed by a legal rule.

I have added also, '[. . .] nor traditional law exists', since not every unwritten law is a law of custom: that only is such which has its origin in the general conduct and usages of a people. For sometimes, although it may not be written, the law may derive its origin from the prince himself, or from the [ruling] prelate, who enjoins, at least orally, that a precept of a general and enduring nature shall be law; and that law may be preserved

---

1. [Not included in these *Selections.*—Tr.]

2. [Only Chapters i–iv and xxxii–xxxiii of this Book are included in these *Selections.*—Tr.]

3. [Not included in these *Selections.*—Tr.]

4. [In Chapter xvii of the present Book.—Tr.]

5. [Chapter xviii of this Book.—Tr.]

6. [The reader will remember that customs are, *iuxta, contra,* or *praeter legem;* i.e. in accordance with, contrary to, and outside law. It is the last kind that is neither prevented nor forbidden by any existing law.—Reviser.]

subsequently, solely through the usage and tradition of his subjects. This will also be unwritten law, but it will be the unwritten law of tradition, not of custom. Of this character are many laws of the Church, which are in force through tradition, as I have indicated, *supra* (Chapter ii, p. 513).

It is necessary, therefore, in order that a custom of fact may introduce that form of unwritten law which is called the law of custom, that there be previously in existence no law [on the matter in question] laid down by the superior either in written or in oral form. Thus defined, our assertion on this point is certain.

This doctrine is found in both canon and civil law (*Digest,* I. iii. 32 *et seq.,* and *Code,* VIII. lii, in entirety, and the whole title of *Decretals,* I. IV, and of *Sext,* Bk. I, tit. IV). It is assumed in *Sext* (Bk. I, tit. II, chap. i), and in *Decretum* (Pt. I, dist. I, can. v, and Pt. I, dist. VIII, can. vii). Again, it appears throughout *Decretum,* Pt. I, dist. XI, where in canon vii, Augustine, *Letters,* lxxxvi is cited; again in *Decretum,* Pt. I, dist. XII, can. xi where [Augustine,] *Letters,* cxviii, chap. ii is cited; and Tertullian (*On the Soldiers' Chaplet,* Chap. iv) says that, 'custom is received as law even in the civil law when the latter is wanting'.[7]

The Doctors in theology are in accord upon this point, as well as the jurists of both canon and civil law, and it is the general teaching of the Church, respecting which doubt is not permissible.

3. *Proof of the assertion.* The ground in reason for this assertion may be given as follows: in a legitimate custom, all the elements essential for the establishment of a true precept or law can be present; therefore, it is able to establish law. The minor premiss is proved first by the fact that three or four elements are necessary and sufficient for law: namely, fitness of subject-matter, power, and will sufficiently manifested externally; and all of these can be present in this kind of custom.

The fitness of subject-matter in this case is evident, for the custom in question should be reasonable; but it will be such in relation to this effect, provided its subject-matter is not opposed to natural or divine law, and if it is useful for the general welfare, and not excessively onerous, or a deviation from the general mode of upright living; and finally, it should be such that a

---

7. [Tertullian has *cum deficit lex.*—REVISER.]

written law enacted in this matter would be just, as I have stated in a previous Chapter (Bk. VII, chap. iii *supra*, p. 519). In respect of subject-matter, therefore, a reasonable custom has a fitness for the establishment of law.

Whence, the gravity of the law will be in proportion to that of its subject-matter: for if its matter is serious, the precept will be a grave one, binding under pain of mortal sin; if, however, the matter is not thus serious, the law will be law only in a limited sense, imposing a light obligation. Again, if the subject-matter pertains to spiritual welfare, the custom will belong to the ecclesiastical jurisdiction; but if it relates to temporal good, it will pertain to the civil jurisdiction, as I pointed out above. Finally, as touching this element of subject-matter, the custom will preserve in all respects an analogy with the written law.

4. *Authority requisite for the validity of a custom.* On the second element necessary for law, it is evident from the discussion of the preceding Chapter that power is not lacking for the establishment of this kind of custom. For a legitimate custom proceeds either from a free people, and hence from one having supreme power, and, therefore, the power of enacting law; or from one having a pastor or prince by whom it is governed. In this latter case, if a legitimate custom is thought of—as it should be—as proceeding not from a people regarded apart from its sovereign, but from the people jointly with its head, and displaying in some sufficient way his influence, either by his having given the people the power to make its own municipal laws or statutes, or by his approval of the custom, an approval given either by law itself [cf. Chapter xiii, this Book], or by his proved tacit will, then in a people thus conjoined with its head there resides sufficient power to make laws, as is evident. Therefore, . . .

It is usual to inquire at this point, whether one family can establish a custom through a continuous succession, and in so far as the family is regarded as perpetual. But I have just stated above that a true custom is not established by a private family. Hence, even if a family remains always in existence, the fact is of no importance, because a custom never can originate from that source, nor, therefore, can it be continued in existence. Again in the Ninth Chapter of Book One of this treatise,[8] it was proved

---

8. [This is found in Chapter vi of Book I, *supra*, p. 82.—Tr.]

that one family has neither the authority to make law, nor the capacity to receive law, save by way of privilege. Hence, it cannot introduce law by its own custom, even though it may acquire a privilege, as I shall state below. Rochus (*De Consuetudine,* Sect. 4, nos. 6 [nos. 62] *et seq.*) has much to say on this matter, as has Antonio Gabrieli ([*Communes Conclusiones,*] Bk. VI, tit. *De Consuetudine,* concl. 5).

5. *Of the will requisite for the establishment of custom.* The same conclusion holds with regard to [the third element for the enactment of law,] the element of will. For, in free peoples, it is to be supposed that the greater number of the people and the magistracy concur voluntarily in a custom. In other communities, the consent of the prince, expressed in one or other of the modes we have spoken of, is added to the will of the people or to that of the greater number. Thus, always, there concurs [in the introduction of custom] the sufficient will of one who has the power of making law.

We need only note at this point that although the will of the prince or that of the prelate is the principal one in this matter, nevertheless, in a certain sense, more depends upon the will of the people. The reason is that it is to the will of the people that the prince (so to speak) conforms by granting that people permission (as it were) to introduce such legal custom as it may wish; or by approving of the popular intention, or confirming it.

It is of the utmost importance to note whether the custom as such was willed. Therefore, in respect of this effect, it is of the first importance to note that it is not enough that certain acts on the part of the people are frequently performed, from which results a custom of fact; but that it is essential that this very custom be intended by them; so that the acts are thus repeated to establish that custom for the common good, or for the integrity of religion, or for some like virtue which it contains. This is explicitly taught by the Glosses and the Doctors to be cited forthwith.

We have shown above that this last factor is of the essence of custom: since a custom cannot be voluntary except in so far as it is intended. This can also be shown from the nature of law; for it is of the essence of law, that its enactment be intended by the sovereign. But whatever is of the essence of law in general, or of positive law [in particular], is of the essence of legal custom also; for what is of the essence of the genus must be included in the species. It is on the ground of the truth of this principle that I advise that attentive thought be given as to whether the customs in question are intended as such, or whether they come into being in some other way; for if the customs come into existence in the latter fashion, they are not properly legal customs carrying a binding obligation of law. Thus, there is a general custom that sleep intervenes between the evening meal and holy communion: this, however,[9] was not intended in itself, but arose out of the ordinary habits of men's lives. Whence this sort of custom, as I have elsewhere remarked, does not establish any obligation.

6. *What must be the character of the will to establish a custom.* Furthermore, not only an intention to establish a custom of fact is required, but also one to make a legal custom, or (what is the same thing) to establish a custom that is binding. For these two sorts of custom are quite different in character; since a custom can be directly intended, and yet intended not as binding, but to be observed out of devotion, and as a matter of perfection. This is evidently the case with personal and private customs, but the same can be true even of the customs of a whole people. Thus, there prevails among Christian peoples the custom of paying honour to the Blessed Virgin at the sound of the evening bell,[10] which is practised out of devotion only, and not under obligation. Bellarmine (*De Romano Pontifice*, Bk. IV, chap. xviii) held that many of the customs observed among Christian peoples are of such a character; that, for instance, of receiving [on the forehead] the blest ashes on the first day of Lent, and that of receiving a palm on Palm Sunday, and of taking holy water at the door of the church. Such also is the custom among many peoples of going to church at daybreak, as is also the practice of hearing Mass for devotional reasons on days that are not holy days of obligation, and such also is the custom, on feast-days, of not taking breakfast before Mass. These customs, and others like them, even though they are practised by a majority of the people as a matter of devotion, establish no obligation in law. Indeed, Soto (*De Iustitia*, Bk. IX, qu. iii, art. i) includes in this class even the custom of presenting offerings at the church for [Masses for] the dead on All Souls' Day; and this is also

9. [Reading *at* for *ad.*—REVISER.]
10. [I.e. the Angelus. The custom was to sound the bell half an hour after sunset. This was called the Evening *Ave* or the Angelus, from the opening word of the salutation, *Angelus Domini nuntiavit Mariae.*—REVISER.]

probably true of other voluntary offerings, except when the church shall have obtained a prescriptive right to such donations, as I have stated in my treatise on religion (*De Religione,* Tr. I, bk. II, chap. v [Tr. II, bk. I, chap. v]).[11] I have noted there, with Cajetan and Soto, that an examination must be made of the intention with which the customs were introduced, for if they begin from a motive of devotion, and continue as such, they do not establish a true [legal] custom.

7. Hence, the Gloss (on *Decretum,* Pt. I, dist. VIII, can. vii), says that for a [legal] custom it is essential that it be observed with the will and intention that 'it become a law for posterity'. The same statement is repeated in another Gloss (on *De Consuetudine*), on which Abbas [, i.e. Panormitanus,] also, comments (*ibid.,* no. 17) to the same effect: 'that it [, i.e. the factual custom,] must be observed with the intention of establishing a [legal] custom.' Rochus Curtius sets forth the same view thereon at length (*De Consuetudine,* Sect. 4, no. 36), and cites the authority of other writers for his opinion.

The reason on which this opinion is founded is also clear: the acts of those observing the custom cannot have an effect not included in their intention. Again, it is of the essence of law that it is made with the intention of obligating those subject to it. Likewise, no one puts himself under a strict obligation unintentionally, as is clear in the case of a vow, or of a promise. And although a people that lives under a superior may seem to bind itself not by a custom, but rather by unwritten law, and therefore by the will of its sovereign, nevertheless, since the prince does not wish to impose a greater obligation through custom than the people are willing to bear, an intention on the part of the people to establish, in so far as they have power to do so, a true custom and its accompanying obligation is an essential condition of such a [legal] custom.

8. *The evidence of a will to establish a custom.* Finally, the evidence of this will and of this obligation is the custom of fact itself. For thus Julianus asked in his commentary (in the *Digest,* I. iii. 32, § 1): 'What difference does it make whether the people declare their will by a vote, or by facts and deeds?' Other laws are of the same tenor.

---

11. [Not included in these *Selections.*—Tr.]

Lastly, the custom [of fact], from common acceptance and as a kind of natural token, has come to be received as evidence sufficient to indicate such a will of the people, when it has been continued for an adequate time, and by a sufficient frequency of actions. A special difficulty, however, respecting this intention and its tokens, we have not touched upon here, since we shall be able to do so to better advantage in the following Chapters.

CHAPTER XV

How Long Must Custom Endure in Order to Suffice for the Establishment of Law?

1. *Of the time required for the establishment of a custom.* In the preceding Chapters, we have sufficiently discussed the number and frequency of the acts adequate for a custom, and now it remains only to speak of the length of time necessary for the same. For although we have pointed out that one sort of custom is established by prescription, and there is another that is not so established, we have not explained in what way these types of custom suffice for the establishment of law; nor how much time each requires for that effect. We must, then, take up these points in the present Chapter.

2. *A prescriptive custom is of itself sufficient to establish law.* In the first place, it is certain that a prescriptive custom is sufficient of itself for the introduction of law. This is clearly inferred from the *Decretals* (Bk. I, tit. IV, chap. xi), as I have explained in a former Chapter, in accordance with the common teaching of the Doctors cited therein.

First opinion. But as to the time that is necessary for such prescription, there are various opinions. Some ancient writers demanded an immemorial length of time; but this opinion is without adequate basis, and has been abandoned as obsolete.

Second opinion. Others require a space of forty years in the case of a canonical custom, as did Hostiensis (in *Summa,* on *Decretals,* Bk. I, rubric iv, § *Obtentum* [, no. 3]). But this rule has application to those customs which are contrary to law, not to those which are outside law.

True opinion. A period of ten years is requisite and sufficient. Whence, for
the latter sort of custom, ten years is held to be necessary and sufficient,
even where canonical subject-matter is concerned. This was the teaching of
the Glosses referred to above, and that of Bartolus, Panormitanus, Rochus,
and others in passages frequently cited. The same is held by Covarruvias
(*Variarum Resolutionum,* Bk. I, chap. xvii, no. 8, § *Quarto*), who refers to
these and other writers, and Navarrus (in *Summarium de Consuetudine,*
Consil. I, chap. xiii, no. 19).

The proof of the first part of our assertion is that the laws declare that
a custom which is ancient, or of long standing, is sufficient to establish
a legal rule; and ten years are necessary and sufficient for a custom to be
termed ancient and of long standing. Therefore, . . .

The premises of this argument call for no further proof here, since we
have dealt with them in an earlier passage.[1]

The proof of the second part of our assertion is that the custom in question is not contrary to law, but is, as we assume, outside of law. But we
know from the matter of prescriptions that for those prescriptions which
are not contrary to law, no more time is required in the canon than in the
civil law for establishing the prescription; and in respect of this condition
of the time requisite, a prescriptive custom follows the mode of a prescription, as I have said above. Therefore, . . .

3. *A note.* I note, however, that the phrase 'a long time' is not, in
the eye of the law, a single, fixed measure of years [, but one that var-
ies]: when the parties to the prescription are present, ten years, and
when they are absent, twenty years[2] (*Institutes,* II. vi, § 1 [II. vi, Pref.]).
Nevertheless, the above-cited Doctors make no distinction between a
prescriptive custom when parties are present and such a custom when
they are absent; they do not, that is, require twenty years for the latter, and ten, for the former, but lay down the absolute requirement of
ten years in all cases. Indeed, Bartolus (on *Digest,* I. iii. 32, in *Repetition,*

---

1. [*Supra,* Chap, viii.—Tr.]
2. [This was the rule of Justinian regarding real estate, which was acquired 'by possession for a long time, that is, after ten years, where the parties are present, and after
twenty, where they are absent'. It was provided that personal property, however, should
be 'acquired by use for three years' (*Institutes,* II. vi).—Tr.]

no. 14) expressly states that in the present matter, that distinction is not to be made, for the reason that "'absent parties" can have no place here, since the people (as a whole) are always present, even if some of them are absent'. In these words, he indicates that this kind of custom is not obtained by prescription against people of other countries, but is established among the citizens themselves, who must be present at least in the majority, since, as we have said above, they must have knowledge of it, if the custom is to be valid. Gregory López ([on *Las Siete Partidas,*] Pt. I, tit. ii, law 5, gloss 4 [gloss 5, *glossa* a]) and Burgos de Paz (Law i, *Tauri.,* no. 207) subscribe to this opinion.

But this reasoning does not seem to be altogether adequate; since, as I have said in an earlier passage, this custom, in its own way, is acquired by prescription against the prince, and he may be absent or present, and so in respect to him the prescription of this custom ought to require a length of time in proportion to that of a true prescription. Therefore, when the prince is absent, a period of twenty years ought to be necessary.

4. *Whether the distinction above made should apply in the present case.* For this reason, other authors think that this distinction ought to apply also in the matter of our present inquiry. This is the view of Sylvester (word *consuetudo,* Qu. 2), and it is recorded by Hostiensis (in *Summa,* on *Decretals,* Bk. I, rubric iv, no. 3). He states in this passage that some of the canonists also held this opinion, and that many jurists take the same view with regard to civil customs; and refers [in particular] to Azo (in *Summa* on rubric of *Code,* VIII. lii). And in the aforesaid *Las Siete Partidas* (Pt. I, tit. ii, law 5) this distinction is set down, together with the statement that custom is established through usage by the people during a period of ten or twenty years. On the ground of this law, certain writers hold that at least in Spain—because of this special law—such a distinction must be made. They argue that since the distinction in question is not unsuitable or useless, and does no more than require a custom of ten years in the case of present parties, and twenty years in the case of absent ones, this opinion is tenable, with regard to this part of the matter.

5. *Ten years is a sufficient time for the establishment of a custom.* Nevertheless, I hold that ten years is in all cases sufficient for a custom to be held as establishing law and as being validated by prescription.

The first proof is that drawn from the common teaching on this matter, which, not without reason, omits the use of that distinction in the case of prescriptive custom, although it is invoked in the cases of prescription properly so called. The same teaching I find in our Molina (*De Iustitia,* Tr. II, disp. 77), by comparing that disputation (77) with those that precede it and deal with the time requisite for true prescription in various matters.

A second proof is the way in which custom is [in practice] accepted so that no account need be taken of the presence or absence of the prince in order to establish a custom by prescription in opposition to a law, a principle admitted by all. I use the words 'to establish a custom by prescription', because as I say below, the absence or presence of the prince may be of great importance in regard to other effects of non-prescriptive custom, and this, not that it is important in itself, but for the reason that his knowledge of the custom may be more readily and more certainly presumed when he is present than when he is absent.

A third and excellent proof is drawn from this last note. It is not required in custom of the latter sort that it be established by prescription with any reference to the prince, save to the extent that he is ignorant of the custom, or can be supposed to be ignorant of it; therefore, the presence of the prince or his absence is of no importance in settling the question of whether this custom may be established by prescription within such and such a time. For if the prince himself is acquainted with the custom, whether he is present or absent, the prescription is not necessary, as I say below. If, however, he is ignorant thereof, it is of no consequence that he be present, since although he be present in body, he is not so in mind, and hence the prescription will be established in as short a time against an absent person, as against one who is not aware of it, since such a person in either case is absent.

6. *An objection.* One may object that, in regard to a prince who is present, the presumption is that he can more easily have knowledge of a custom, and hence a shorter time ought to be sufficient for his gaining such knowledge. Again, if that proof [set forth above, to which objection is here made,] were valid, it would be more true to say that a period of twenty years is always necessary, since this prescription is always against

a person formally absent, that is, against one who is unaware [of the custom].

The solution. My reply to the first part of the above objection, is that in this kind of prescription attention is to be paid not to the ease or difficulty in the acquisition of knowledge of the custom on the part of the prince, but to the necessity of the common good which is served by the prescription. For it is very expedient for the general welfare that the people observe customs that are reasonable and confirmed by sufficient usage, and to this end it is fitting in the highest degree that such customs have the binding power of law. Prudent men, therefore, realizing this need, hold that a period of ten years is sufficient [to establish a legal custom], irrespective of the presence or absence of the prince.

The ground in reason in this case is that a custom of this sort is of itself adequately confirmed, and the time allowed for its introduction is ample, in any case, for the prince to have knowledge of it, if he wishes to do so; a greater or lesser ease [in his obtaining such knowledge] would seem to be of no importance. And this is the more true because, in the prescription of a custom, the prince is not to be considered as having a will in opposition to the movement, especially with regard to this effect of bringing in an obligation not contrary to his law; he is not, that is, in the situation of the owner of a thing against whom a prescription is acquired. The reason is that the bringing in of this obligation is in no way prejudicial to the prince, nor is it counter to his jurisdiction, since it is an outgrowth of his law and useful for good government. Thus the character of this custom is not that of prescriptions in other subject-matters.

And so we answer the second part of the objection by denying the conclusion. For, since the laws lay down no distinction on this point, but demand only a 'long-continued' custom, the shortest period within the meaning of the phrase 'a long time', is to be understood here. And this for two reasons: because this is the more favourable interpretation and the one to be followed where there is question of the common good; and because, in respect of prescriptive custom, it is only the ignorance of the prince, whether he is absent or present, that is to be taken into account. This is not true of prescription properly so-called, for the same length of time suffices, other things being equal, whether the owner of the thing has knowledge of the usage of the person acquiring the prescriptive right or not.[3]

7. *The contrary opinion of some Doctors does not affect this reasoning.* We need not consider at length the views of the authors cited for the opposite opinion. They are, in the first place, relatively few in number; and again, even of these, some authors are probably discussing not legal custom alone but custom in general, as it includes that by which prescriptions are acquired. This, as I have remarked before, is the common practice of jurists. Certainly, it is the practice of Sylvester in his discussion on the word *consuetudo,* and of other summists and jurists—as will be clear to any reader of their works. It is for this reason that they discuss custom under this distinction, and not because they believe it should be applied to every kind of custom, even to custom in regard to moral acts.

It was in this sense, perhaps, that King Alphonso spoke in law 5 [of *Las Siete Partidas,* Pt. I, tit. ii]. But this also bears, as I shall indicate in the next Chapter, another interpretation. Or, if he wished to introduce new law and to approve the opinion of Azo—whose works are said to have been the source of the laws of *Las Siete Partidas*—then that special law was, in my opinion, brought in not by custom, even in Spain [, but by enactment of the king].

8. It remains for us to discuss custom that is not validated by prescription. For sometimes such custom can suffice to establish law; and consequently it is possible that this result may be effected in a shorter period than ten years, in cases where a knowledge of the custom on the part of the prince is present. This was the opinion of Antonio de Butrio (*De Consuetudine,* Chap. xi), St. Antoninus, Sylvester, Angelus de Clavasio and others who agree with him, as we shall see when we discuss a similar question in a following Chapter. For these writers distinguish between a prince who is aware of, and one ignorant of, a line of conduct of the people; and they hold that a shorter time is required when the prince knows of the custom than when the opposite is true. But a custom of ten years is sufficient to establish law, even when the prince has no acquaintance with the custom:

---

3. [In ordinary prescriptions, however, the consideration of presence or absence of the owner of the thing is important.—Tr.]

hence, a shorter time will suffice for that effect when he has knowledge thereof. But a prescriptive custom is not established in a period shorter than ten years. Hence, a non-prescriptive custom, which is known to the prince, can introduce a rule of law. Thus, we see the occasion when a prescription is required, namely, when the prince is ignorant of the custom; also, when a prescriptive custom is not necessary, that is, when the prince is aware of the custom. The reason for this distinction is that although the laws say that a custom of long standing is sufficient, they never state that one of a shorter period is not sufficient.

And, to take another ground, a custom of a shorter period will, in the nature of things, suffice for this effect, if the prince is aware of the custom. The reason is that under these conditions a custom of shorter duration can reveal adequately the consent of both the prince and the people, as appears evident. Therefore, a non-prescriptive custom may be sufficient, since the sole requirement is that there shall exist adequate evidence of the will of the legislator. And this is the difference that marks these two kinds of custom: that a prescriptive custom establishes a legal rule, not because it is evidence of a fresh consent of the prince, but because it includes all the elements required by law, in which a previous will of the sovereign is included. For it, therefore, no new knowledge of the custom on the part of the prince is called for, nor is the consideration of the possibility of his having such knowledge relevant here. But a non-prescriptive custom can operate only as a token of his will and as a sign of a fresh consent on his part; and this may be given to a custom of shorter duration, of which the prince has knowledge. It is self-evident that there never can be any evidence of such will and consent on the part of a sovereign ignorant of such a custom.

9. *The term of observance for the validation of a custom in less than ten years is not a fixed one.* But the question may be urged, what period of time under ten years is adequate for the establishment of a custom of this kind? My reply is that a definite term cannot be fixed by any conclusive reasoning, both because the law is silent on this point, and because this signification [of consent]—since it is expressed through facts—depends upon inferences which are not equally valid in the case of all customs. And so the evidence of the prince's consent can be adequately manifested in a shorter

period in the case of some customs, than in that of others. For some customs are made up of actions which are repeated more frequently, and are of a character more general and more public than is the case with others; and so, other things being equal, in the case of those customs, the fact of the sovereign's knowledge will be more speedily established, and thus—if he voluntarily tolerates the custom—evidence of his tacit consent is given.

Again, for establishing a presumption of the prince's consent in such cases, his presence or absence may be factors of great importance: for he is presumed to know what happens in a locality in which he is present, but not what is done in his absence, unless other proofs are available.

Evidence of proof of custom. Furthermore, for calculating the probabilities in the case of a custom of this kind, certain considerations brought forward in our discussion of judicial acts[4] may be of use. Thus, especially, a decision handed down in favour of a custom, if it be published and confirmed by the sovereign prince, would be fully sufficient evidence of his consent. Indeed, even if that opinion were known as having been given by a judge of a lower court, and were tolerated, it would be of no slight force as evidence.

Likewise, a judicial decision by any prudent judge at all may, of itself, give authority to the custom, since it is possible for the decision to be a just one, in view of a custom that is not prescriptive. The reason is that since the establishment of such a custom does not call for a fixed length of time, but depends rather upon certain probabilities in the situation, a decision in favour of the custom may be given on grounds of prudence and of the probabilities of the case, and so the custom, although it has not been validated by prescription, is held to be adequate [for the bringing in of law], on the ground that it is an adequate indication of the will of the prince and of the people. Whence, although such a decision is in itself not absolutely necessary for the validity of the custom in question—because this validity is itself assumed as the ground of the decision, and is but declared by it, as we have argued above in a similar case—nevertheless, if such a decision has at some time been delivered, it confirms in a high degree the probable validity of the custom. And if it be many times repeated, a strong moral

---

4. [See Chap. xi of this Book, *supra*, p. 615 *et seq.*—Tr.]

certitude will exist in favour of the custom, for it will have been greatly confirmed by the testimonies of prudent men.

In what sense the opinion of Soto is to be applied here. Finally, we can apply to custom of this sort the opinion of Soto and other writers [*supra*, p. 583], who say that the length of time necessary for the establishment of custom must be determined by the judgment of prudent minds, at least, when it is a question of interpreting the mind of the prince and of the people. The authority of the writers can, therefore, be cited in support of this part of our argument, for they clearly assume that a non-prescriptive custom can have the force of introducing a rule of law.

10. *A doubt.* One difficulty arises, however, from the foregoing discussion: a custom of fact can never, it would seem, be a satisfactory indication of the will of the prince and of the people. For, as has been said, a custom ought to arise out of an intention to establish consuetudinary law, and such intention can never be sufficiently inferred from a mere repetition of like actions unless that intention is expressly declared, since the same acts could be repeated in the same manner without that intention. It is to be added, as I have noted in my work, *De Religione* [Tr. II, bk. 1, chap. v],[5] that even though a custom may have its origin in a devotional practice, that intention can easily be changed later, and the very same actions may be done with a purpose of creating an obligation, even if no change is evident in the actions themselves. This difficulty is more a practical than a speculative one, and it has application as much to a prescriptive as to a non-prescriptive custom.

The acts constituting the custom must be repeated with the intention of establishing law. For a custom will never establish a rule of law by prescription, even if it lasts for a thousand years, unless the frequency of the acts arises from the intention of creating a legal obligation. Indeed, I think that it is even necessary that the custom be observed with that intention during the entire period of ten years, since otherwise, the customary actions cannot be said to concur as an expression of the popular consent essential for establishment of the custom by prescription. By what test, then, is this intention to be recognized?

5. [Not included in these *Selections*.—Tr.]

11. This question is touched upon by Angelus de Clavasio ([*Summa,*] word *consuetudo,* nos. 4 and 5), and he says in effect, that it must be decided on the basis of the frequency with which the actions are repeated and their number, or the fact that they are of a public character and widely known, and done with the consent of the people. But these tests and others like them do not solve the difficulty, since they may apply not less to a simple custom observed out of a devotional or other voluntary reason, than to one observed with the intention of establishing a binding rule of consuetudinary law.

Rochus proposes the same doubt (*De Consuetudine,* Sect. 4, no. 36), when he deals with the seventh requisite for custom, and refers the reader to question 6, after the Gloss, namely, to Sect. 5 from no. 10 onwards. In no. 27 of this Section he again proposes the question clearly, and he says merely that in the case of doubt it must be judged that each person observing the custom is to be held as acting with the intention of introducing a [legal] custom, when he does the act as by right, that is, in the belief that he has the right to act thus in future. But as to when a person acts, as though exercising a right, Rochus says this must be determined from the nature of the acts. Thus, if the acts are of the sort that are usually done out of pure friendship—as dining in the house of a friend—even if they are repeated many times, they are not regarded as done with the intention of establishing a right; the case is otherwise, however, with regard to actions which are wont to postulate a right. For this opinion, Rochus cites many Doctors.

But, in the first place, that rule, this method of interpretation, and these examples, seem to have reference rather to custom in virtue of which a prescriptive right is acquired, than to legal custom. For in the first case, the party observing the custom is presumed, when a doubt is to be settled, to be seeking or exercising his own right, because that right is useful or favourable to himself; but why, in the case of legal custom, is it to be presumed that any one in doubt would wish to establish a rule of consuetudinary law which is burdensome and inconvenient to himself? Again, in the present subject-matter, the nature of the actions cannot be used as a test of the probable intention of the agents; for the same acts are, from their very nature, such as may be performed, either out of devotion, or as a following of a counsel [of perfection], or as the fulfilment of a precept—as are evidently the making of offerings in the church, or fasting, or the observance of feasts [of the Church year], and the like.

12. Finally, the same question is propounded by Peter of Ravenna (Tr. *De Consuetudine,* Sect. 1, no. 15). His sole reply is to appeal to those points of doctrine concerning the prescription of incorporeal rights, which are treated by Innocent [IV] (on *Decretals,* Bk. I, tit. v, chap. iii, and other places), and by Bartolus and others. All these writers have in mind prescription properly so-called, in which it is easier to discern whether a usage is one of law or simply one of permission, in which, in case of doubt, the party using the prescription is presumed to intend possessing the right of ownership, or of the servitude, or the like. But this does not hold in the matter at present in question—for the reason we have already given.

A distinction to be noted. We must note also that the authors cited treat especially of the proof of a custom in the external forum; we, however, are dealing with the forum of conscience. In that forum a judgment on a prescription and on its usage is more easily arrived at. The reason is as follows: the one who establishes a prescriptive right is either a private individual, in which case he will be the witness of his own intention, or else some community, in which case the judgment of the conscience rests not upon the community as such, but upon individual members thereof; however, the individuals, in turn, can and ought, in conscience, to presume the right on behalf of the community, as is clear from the reasons we have already given. A legal custom, however, always depends upon the intention of the people as a whole, and individuals are, therefore, not bound to presume an intention of establishing a legal precept; and this because such a precept is not favourable, but burdensome to the community.

13. *When there is a doubt, a custom should be regarded as one of devotion, or of rectitude, rather than as a legally binding rule.* I say, then, that it is not easy to judge of the obligation of a precept established through a custom, and that in a case of doubt, other things being equal, it is wiser to incline to the judgment that the custom is observed rather out of devotion, or rectitude, or perfection, than for the purpose of establishing a legal obligation. It is a general rule that, in a case of doubt, no one is presumed as

willing to be bound, as I have noted in the treatise on the matter of vows.[6] Again, it is not expedient that precepts be multiplied where they are not morally certain, or at least not highly probable.

The mode and intention with which a custom has been established is to be left to the judgment of a prudent man. I note further that judgment as to the manner of introduction of a custom, and the intention with which it has been introduced, must be left to the discretion of prudent minds; and that no more definite rule can be laid down here, since the law makes no disposition in this matter, and the subject is in itself elusive and obscure, as the difficulty we have just discussed shows.

However, in any inquiry as to the intention with which a custom is established, the following criteria will be of assistance.

First criterion. First, if the custom is of long standing, and has to do with matters onerous and difficult, and if, finally, the custom is observed by the major part of the people—since the people do not commonly agree in the performance of acts of this sort save when they feel an obligation to do so—we have sound evidence that the people then are led [to act as they do] from a sense of obligation that is already established or is being established by it.

Second criterion. Secondly, if prudent and conscientious men think ill of those who do not observe the custom, or if the people generally are scandalized at non-observance of it, we have another strong indication of an intention on the part of the people to introduce consuetudinary law.

Third criterion. Thirdly, if the prelates or the governors of the realm gravely censure and punish those who do not follow the custom, that also is no slight indication.

Fourth criterion. Fourthly, if the subject-matter of the custom is evidently of itself of such advantage to the state that it may be prudently held that the binding force of the custom is highly expedient for the general welfare, the presumption is admissible, in a case of doubt, that the custom has been deliberately introduced.

---

6. [Not included in these *Selections.*—Tr.]

CHAPTER XVI

Concerning the Causes and Effects of Unwritten Law Introduced through Custom

1. Reference to the principles that we have already set forth in our discussion of written human laws makes lengthy treatment of our present question unnecessary. For it is clear from what we said there that, generally speaking, everything which has been set forth concerning the causes and effects of human law, holds, in due proportion, for law introduced through custom, with the exception of such assertions as touch upon the material or sensible form of the law, and its promulgation. The reason for this qualification is evident, since this consuetudinary law of which we are speaking is not essentially different from written law, and is so only in the kind of outward expression by which in it the will of the legislator is manifested—which expression I call the sensible form of that law. For in law, strictly so called, the will of the legislator is given outward expression in some form of writing, or, at least in an express statement made by him; in consuetudinary law, however, neither a written nor an oral expression of that sort has place, rather it is manifested in the form of external acts, as has been explained.

Custom, as a public token, is its own promulgation. It is for this reason that in the case of law [strictly so called] in addition to the enactment of the law by the legislator, its promulgation is required; for the enactment of the law is not in itself a public expression unless knowledge of it is spread abroad. A custom, on the other hand, is itself an outward expression, of its very nature public, and known to the people observing it; and hence it does not need any other promulgation. The reason is, as I shall point out more fully in a moment, that a custom binds only a people which makes use of it, and so there is no necessity for any other promulgation or publication. For in order that a custom be extended to other peoples, it is necessary that they adopt and copy it; and thus, this imitation will effect among them the introduction of a like custom and promulgation. If, however, one people adopt the custom of another people, not through a custom of its own creation, but through a statute directing the observance among them of a custom practised elsewhere, their law will then be not consuetudinary, but written law, and will, as such, require its own form and promulgation.

But in the other causes [that are essential for law], when due proportion has been observed, there is no difference between these laws [, i.e. written and consuetudinary], since, as I have said, their subject-matter should be morally good, adapted to the public weal, and finally, reasonable. And thus it is clear that reason is (as it were) the soul of both kinds of law, and that both are chiefly dependent upon the will of the prince who possesses the power of legislation; a power which is, in the case of each kind of law, the true efficient cause, as the will [of the prince] is (so to speak) the substantial form.[1]

2. *The effects of custom may be inferred from the foregoing discussion.* In the same way, we can deal with the effects [of consuetudinary law]. For custom is, of its own virtue, binding in conscience, since it is true law (*Decretum,* Pt. I, dist. xi, can. vii). This is the common teaching of the Doctors, as may be seen in Felinus (on *Decretals,* Bk. IV, tit. i, chap. i [, no. 18]) and in Rochus (*De Consuetudine,* Sect. i, nos. 12 and 13), who cites other authorities. So also the obligation of the law of custom will be serious or light according to the character of the subject-matter, unless the will of the people to the contrary is manifest on this point; for, in this respect, all the principles that have been set forth on the obligation of human law in written form can be applied as well to legal custom, since they have—with due proportion—the same bearing upon it.

3. *Custom can establish penal law.* But the question may here be asked, whether consuetudinary law can be binding under a penal sanction, that is, whether it is possible for a custom to establish a penal law. This question can be briefly answered in the affirmative, since what holds true of law in general, holds true of a penal law as well. For what absurdity in reason can be shown in the possibility of a custom binding under a [physical] penalty as well as under [the moral one of] guilt? Indeed, by the very fact that it binds under penalty, it makes the transgressor of the custom liable to penalty; for this liability follows naturally from the guilt. So, for a like reason, determination of the punishment might be established by the same

1. [That by which a thing is what it is.—TR.]

custom; as, for example, that whoever should violate the custom in question could be punished in a certain manner. Thus, the penalty would be just, being fixed (as it were) by the law of custom.

An example in point is at hand in the *Decretals* (Bk. IV, tit. XI, chap. iii), and in the commentaries of Innocent, Abbas [, i.e. Panormitanus], and others on that Chapter. They are there discussing a custom in which one or another non-essential usage in the ritual of the Sacrament of matrimony is observed, and according to which those who have been married otherwise [i.e., without fulfilling the rite] are to be separated for a time as a punishment for their previous departure from the customary rite. These authorities hold that this custom is in both respects a just one, and therefore to be observed.

Likewise, a custom may, not less than the written law, fix the price of some article of merchandise; hence, it may also fix a penalty for a crime. This is the general teaching of writers on penal custom, as may be seen in Rochus (*De Consuetudine*, Sect. 4, nos. 20 *et seq.*), where he cites many others.

A custom can establish a purely penal law. Again, it is my opinion that custom can establish a law of a purely penal character (as it were) by reason of which anyone not observing it may be subject to some punishment, even if no guilt is contracted from his act. On this point, the same reasoning holds for custom as for written law. In that case, however, this sort of custom would seem to be a kind of prescription rather than a law; it would seem, that is, to be rather a kind of tribute which the state or the prince has, through custom, acquired the right to demand under certain conditions.

It could, finally, be established by a custom that whoever did not observe it should be bound in conscience to make reparation, even though no punishment followed, and thus the true character of legal custom would be preserved. Such customs, however, rarely or never occur.

4. The question is also raised frequently, whether consuetudinary law can extend to the effect of invalidating a certain act or contract, or of rendering individuals incompetent for the performance of such acts. This question is usually treated more explicitly in connexion with the matter of matrimony, as Sánchez shows at length ([*De Sancto Matrimonii*

Sacramento,] Bk. VII, disp. iv). The principles, however, there given are nearly the same as those that apply to other forms of contract, as Felinus points out (on *Decretals,* Bk. IV, tit. i, chap. i, nos. 2 and 3).

What is the force of custom in respect of the validity of a contract? Hence, we assert that a custom forbidding certain actions or giving [legal] form thereto, can be introduced with the intention and will that acts done otherwise shall not be valid, and that such a custom, if it be reasonable and be secured by prescription or have the express or tacit approval of the prince, shall have the effect of voiding such a contrary act.

This is the teaching of many Doctors, to whom Felinus and Sánchez refer in the passages above cited, and it is founded upon the *Decretals* (Bk. IV, tit. xi, chap. iii), where (according to the plain context and the truer interpretation) it is assumed that an ecclesiastical custom can introduce a diriment[2] matrimonial impediment, and that those who have contracted a marriage in defiance of the custom are on all accounts to be separated. The same inference is to be drawn from Chapter One of the same Title where [for this effect of a diriment impediment] a custom is specially postulated that would cause scandal, that is to say, the violation of which would cause scandal, and this additional [characteristic] is particularly noted and required by the canonists. But, if the custom be of the sort that introduces a diriment impediment to a marriage, the violation of it cannot but give rise to scandal, and thus scandal is invoked as an indication that such a custom obtains.

An opinion of the canonists is rejected. I disapprove, therefore, of the assertion of certain canonists, that in the foregoing and in similar cases this effect arises more from the necessity of avoiding scandal than from [the legal force of] the custom. For true marriages are not dissolved in order to avoid scandal, nor could the circumstance of scandal void a marriage, unless an impediment were assumed, or a voiding law had been introduced by custom.

5. A similar inference can be drawn from the *Decretals* (Bk. III, tit. iii, chap. vi), together with the Gloss on the word *repugnet* which notes from the text of the law that a person otherwise eligible[3] might through

2. [A diriment matrimonial impediment in the canon law is one which makes an attempted marriage wholly void.—Tr.]

3. [For *aliquam* read *aliquem.*—Reviser.]

custom become ineligible. Thus also the Gloss (on *Authentica*, XLVIII, collection v, tit. 3, chap. i, no. 1, word *auctore* [on *Novels*, XLVII, chap. i, no. 1]) states that by that law the custom can establish what is to be the essential form of the contract, so that its non-observance invalidates the contract. This opinion is followed by other writers, who are mentioned by Felinus (referred to above) and also by Rochus (*De Consuetudine*, Chap. xi, sect. 1, no. 10). Other passages are cited by Antonio Gabrieli ([*Communes Conclusiones,*] Bk. VI, tit. *De Consuetudine,* Concl. 3, especially to no. 4 [no. 8]).

The proof from reason for this assertion is that a custom which is reasonable and prescriptive has all those other effects which human law can have. Therefore, it has this effect also; since no probable reason can be brought forward why custom should not be able to have this effect when it can have the others. For just as the will of the prince verbally expressed can produce this effect, so also can his will tacitly expressed through custom, as is clear from the reason given in the *Digest* (I. iii. 32). In like manner, we can apply here all the laws that speak in a general way of the force of custom and compare it with written law; as does the law referred to above (*Decretals,* Bk. I, tit. IV, chap. xi) in an especially clear manner, as Sánchez rightly proves in the passage cited above. For a fuller discussion of the details of this point, Sánchez's work may be consulted. There remains, then, no difficulty of any weight which demands our attention here.

6. *In what way a custom is to be assimilated to law.* Furthermore, custom is assimilated to law in its effect in respect of the persons whom it can bind by its rule: for just as a law is binding upon those subject to it, so also is custom; and just as a law is not in force outside the territory for which it was enacted, so neither is custom [binding except on those for whom it was introduced]. Whence, if a custom is a universal one of the whole Church, it binds all Christians without distinction; if a custom is that of a single realm or diocese, all dwelling there are bound by it; if it is that of a city, all the citizens, and they alone, are held to its observance: the same is true in due measure of other communities. For it is a general rule that a custom of one community is not binding upon another distinct from it, for the reason that one community has not the power to give law to another, nor does the sovereign give consent thereto.

So true is this, that even a custom of the city or of the diocese of Rome, regarded as Roman, that is, the custom of a particular diocese, is not binding upon other churches, because, as such, the Roman diocese does not act as their superior, except when the Pope commands that the [Roman] custom in question be elsewhere observed. This is also evident from usage, and is noted by Panormitanus (on *Decretals,* Bk. II, tit. IX, chap. v, at the end), and by Torquemada (on *Decretum,* Pt. I, dist. XI, can. iii), and by Rochus (*De Consuetudine,* Sect. 4, no. 18), who cites other examples.

7. *An objection.* An objection can, however, be advanced against our thesis from the words of *Decretals,* Bk. IV, tit. XI, chap. iii, in which a certain bishop is ordered, 'to make inquiry about a custom of his metropolitan church, and of other churches in his neighbourhood, and diligently to imitate the same.' It might be concluded from these words that a custom of one diocese is binding in another, and especially that the custom of the metropolitan church is binding in suffragan sees. The reason given in the law is that it is a serious matter to contemn an ancient custom of the churches of a locality.

Solution. My reply is that this law involves two questions. One is, whether the custom of the metropolitan church must be observed in suffragan churches. On this question it is certain, in the first place, that if a contrary custom is in force in a certain diocese, then that custom is to prevail, as all agree, since it prevails also over the common law, as we shall point out in the following Chapter.

The other is that if a particular diocese follows no custom of its own, then the evident conclusion from the above-cited law is that the custom of the metropolitan see should be observed in that diocese. And this conclusion can be based upon another principle, one accepted by many canonists, namely, that a custom of a city is binding upon subject towns that lie within its territories, if those towns have no customs of their own. This is the opinion of Bartolus (on *Code,* VIII. lii. 2, in *Repetit.* 2, qu. 36, no. 41), of Antonio de Butrio (*De Consuetudine,* Chap. xi)[4] and of Rochus (*ibid.,* Sect. 4, no. 17), who cites the authority of numerous other writers.

4. [For *de Const.* read *de Consuetudine.*—TR.]

8.[5] But this may perhaps be the rule, in the case where a city can bind by its own municipal statutes neighbouring towns which are under its immediate jurisdiction. However, there is no parity between the relation of such a city and town and that of a metropolitan and suffragan church, for a relation of such subordination and immediate jurisdiction does not prevail between the latter.

Just as the special statutes of an archbishop do not bind the suffragan bishops, so neither do the customs of the archiepiscopal see. Whence, just as the statutes enacted by the archbishop for his own diocese are not binding in the sees of his suffragans, so neither does the custom [of the metropolitan see] bind those of the suffragan bishops. It is my opinion, therefore, that the law is to be held as applying to a custom that has been in observance throughout a province, but is not known in a particular diocese of it, for the reason, possibly, that no case has come up to bring to light a practice either in conformity with or contrary to that custom. For it is in such a case, the Pope says, that it is necessary to consult the bishops of the neighbouring dioceses, and especially the metropolitan, and to follow their custom—when, that is, they observe the custom as a general one of the whole province, and not as one that is followed as peculiar to their respective dioceses.

9. *What persons are bound by a custom.* From these observations are to be drawn the answers to the questions treated at length by Bartolus (on *Code,* VIII. lii. 2, *in Repetit.,* last qu.) and Rochus (*De Consuetudine,* Sects. 8 and 9), concerning the persons who fall under the obligation of custom: whether, for instance, it binds a prince or a sovereign senate; or, whether the custom of the city or of the territory binds strangers; or, whether a custom of a state is binding upon its citizens outside its territory. But in these and similar questions, the same rule prevails as holds good in the case of written laws and statutes, on account of the fundamental reason adduced, namely, that the custom with which we are dealing is true law, emanating from the same authority and jurisdiction, differing from law only in its form, which does not change the binding character of custom in any

---

5. [In the Latin text there is an error in the numbering of the sections for the rest of this Chapter.—Tr.]

of these cases. So all the principles which we have laid down with respect to human law on all these points are to be held as applying to custom also. The reader who wishes to inquire into these matters in greater detail may consult the authorities referred to above, and Gregory López ([on *Las Siete Partidas,*] Pt. I, tit. i, law 16, gloss 1 [*glossa* b]), Antonio Gabrieli ([*Communes Conclusiones,*] tr. *De Consuetudine,* Bk. VI, concls. 1 and 2), and others to whom those writers refer. I, also, have dealt with this matter in my work *De Religione* (Tom. I, tract. II, bk. II, chaps. xiii and xiv).[6]

10. *A custom of laymen does not bind clerics.* I shall mention, only briefly, a certain question discussed by every writer on this subject, namely, whether a custom of the laity is binding upon clerics. I shall not rehearse the various opinions of the writers on this point. The opinion commonly held by the canonists is that a custom followed solely among the laity is not binding upon clerics. The reason is that the two form distinct bodies and the clerical is the more eminent community. Again, the clergy are entirely exempt from the authority of laymen.

A mixed custom is one that is binding both upon the clergy and upon the laity. In the case, however, of a mixed custom, one observed both by clerics and laymen, it will be binding upon the clergy, since they have themselves given consent to the custom: they are bound, therefore, not by a lay custom, but by one of their own. This doctrine Rochus sets forth at some length (*De Consuetudine,* Chap. xi, sect. 8, nos. 54 and 65), where he proposes various extensions and limitations of this principle, and introduces many examples of it. Felinus touches upon this matter in two passages (on *Decretals,* Bk. I, tit. II, chap. x, nos. 100 *et seq.,* and Bk. II, tit. xix, chap. xii, no. 3), and Abbas [, i.e. Panormitanus] (on *Decretals, ibid.,* no. 3 [no. 1]) and Alberico de Rosate (tr. *De Statutis,* Pt. II, qu. ix) have also treated of it.

11. *We must observe whose will it is that introduces custom.* It must be noted, however, that since custom chiefly emanates as law not from the people who observe it, but from the prince who gives his consent to it, it is more important to inquire by what power it has been confirmed and stabilized in its legal character, than to inquire into the position of the persons observing it. For the will of the prince or the prelate is the essential cause,

---

6. [Not included in these *Selections.*—Tr.]

that of the people is a motivating cause: the means of effecting and the petition for the consuetudinary law. The answer to the question whether a custom is binding upon clerics, will, therefore, depend very much upon whether it has been confirmed by a prelate of the Church, or by a secular prince. From which authority the custom came into being, can best be determined by a scrutiny of the subject-matter and purpose of the custom, as we have said before. The subject-matter, therefore, of the custom must be examined to determine whether it is spiritual or temporal, and whether it promotes the salvation of souls and the worship of God, or the ends of secular government. The answer to our present question will, I think, be drawn more successfully from a consideration of the authority from which the custom emanates, of its subject-matter, and of its purpose, than from any inquiry as to the persons who make use of the custom; although this latter consideration may be of some assistance also.

12. *First conclusion.* I conclude, then, that if the subject-matter is civil or political, and if it derives its force from the consent of a temporal prince, it is not, strictly speaking, binding upon the clergy; unless, that is, its character is such as not to be opposed to the liberties of the Church, and it relates to the common association of the citizens as such. Under those circumstances, the same opinion is to be adopted on the obligation of the custom as that which we said in an earlier passage would hold of a written civil law. For this assertion is based upon the principles set forth in that earlier passage[7] in which we discussed [the status of the clergy in] civil law: such a custom is, in a word, a civil one, and establishes civil law. The first part of this assertion needs no proof, since a lay prince cannot bind clerics through the exercise of his express will: he cannot, therefore, do so by his tacit will. Again, the clerics themselves cannot give a consent in opposition to their own immunity; and a prelate of the Church is not considered to give such consent. The truth of the second part of this assertion is evident from our earlier discussion of the written law: for the reasoning that is valid on that point is applicable to a custom by which clerics are affected not as clerics, but only as citizens. Such a custom is to be regarded in the same way as a written law would be.

7. [*Vide* Chap. xxxiv of Bk. III, *De Legibus,* not included in these *Selections.*—Tr.]

But if the subject-matter of the custom is of a mixed character, that is, if it pertains to both the civil and the ecclesiastical politics, and if the custom is observed in common by the members of each status or body, then there will prevail two customs (so to speak) and in reality two laws: one civil, having its force from the consent of the lay prince; the other ecclesiastical, having its force from the consent of the prelate of the Church; and each will be binding upon its own subjects, and one can be revoked independently of the other.

When a custom is binding upon clerics. Finally, if the subject-matter of the custom is spiritual, and tends to the welfare of souls, as fasting, &c., it will be really a single custom, and will be binding upon both clerics and laymen, since it depends wholly upon the authority and consent of the prelate of the Church. In this case, the subjects of the custom are considered not as clerics or laymen, but as Christians, without respect to status.

13. It may, again, be asked whether by a similar spiritual custom (so to speak), a usage of the laity only can establish a custom which is also binding upon the clergy. For, according to a rule of the above-cited jurists, the answer must be in the negative; and among the theologians, de la Palu ([on the *Sentences,*] Bk. IV, dist. xv, qu. 4, art. 3) repeats this denial. They base it first upon the ground that clerics follow their own rule of life, as, for example, their own practices with regard to abstinence; and again, upon the ground that clerics have a status similar (as it were) to senators, who are not bound by decrees of the commonalty unless they assent to such decrees; and finally, upon the ground that the monks are not bound by the customs of the secular clergy—notwithstanding that the customs of the latter are holy and religious—and as monks are to the secular clergy, so are the secular clerics to the laymen.

But these reasons are not convincing to me, because the law resulting from a custom of this kind is episcopal law, since it derives its force from the tacit consent of a prelate, and its subject-matter is, of its nature, common both to the clergy and to the laity. Thus, in public fasts, and in the keeping of feasts, the secular clergy do not follow any special legal observances. This fact destroys the force of the first argument given above. The second also lacks force, because no analogy can properly be drawn between such a custom and a decree of the commonalty, for the latter emanates from the people, through their own tribunals, but the law of such custom as we are discussing proceeds from a prelate who is the common superior of both clerics and laymen. The third reason also is not valid, because the secular clergy are not exempt from the jurisdiction of the bishops, as are the religious orders. And with respect to such orders, the question [of their obligation] may be raised, a question which, as it is derived from their exemption, presents the same difficulty in the case of custom, as it does in the case of synodal decrees, which we have already treated.

14. *Second conclusion.* Therefore, I conclude that the obligation arising from a custom of this sort can be extended to the clergy, and that in fact it is so extended, if it is the bishop's will, either tacit or explicit, to establish it as an episcopal law for his diocese. This, without doubt, is within the power of the bishop; and he is to be presumed to have done so when the subject-matter of the custom is, of its nature, common to all, and so equally useful and easy for all concerned that it would be impossible to impose the obligation upon part of the community, and not upon the whole of it, without creating scandal. This is especially true when this obligation is imposed at the request of the entire body of the laity, who, in relation to this custom, are considered, as I have said, not as laymen, but as Christians; and accordingly, they can outnumber the clergy, and, with the bishop's consent, they can bring in a custom that is binding on the clergy, as well as on themselves.

Sometimes, however, a custom may be more properly that of the laity [than of the clergy], either because of the means by which it has been introduced—as, for example, by a special vow made by them, or because of the character of the subject-matter, which is fitted more for them than for the clergy—and in that case the custom will easily be obligatory on them without being such for the clergy, and can also, as such, receive the approval of superiors. And this is to be discerned from the usage itself and from the circumstances.

15. *Of the extension of custom from one case to another, similar one.* Another question which is treated by the aforesaid jurists relates to the effect of custom; namely, whether this obligation of custom is capable of extension from one case to another, on account of the similarity of the

reasons involved. The jurists declare almost generally that an extension of this sort is to be allowed, although later they multiply various explanations and limitations, as may be seen in Rochus Curtius (*De Consuetudine,* Sect. 4, near the beginning), and in Burgos de Paz (Law 1, *Tauri.,* no. 51). Nevertheless, this extension is, in my opinion, of rare occurrence. In the first place, a wider extension is not possible with a legal custom than with a law, since the force of a legal custom with respect to the obligation it establishes is not greater than that of written law—the peculiarities of both kinds of law having been taken into account—as is clear from the previous discussion. I may add, further, that an extension is more difficult of accomplishment in the case of a custom than in that of a written law. This is so because, in the first place, a law is extended for the most part by broadening the effect of its language, according to the meaning and usage which its words have in legal application generally in relation to such and such subject-matter. Whence, since words are lacking to a custom, this mode of extension can have no place, and therefore consuetudinary law cannot be extended in this fashion as written law can be. In the second place, I have, in previous Chapters, observed that this kind of extension is rarely to be admitted, even in the case of written law, unless there is very solid legal ground for so doing. I can only add the further note that in the case of custom it is much more difficult, and for that reason it is of rarest occurrence. For a legal obligation deriving its force from custom alone can be determined only with the greatest difficulty in respect of the locality, of the people concerned, or of the particular subject-matter with which it deals; in what way, then, is it to be easily extended to new localities, persons, subject-matters, except where these are so similar to the old as to be practically identical, or when the extension is made by law; or unless it is reasonably judged that the new is *a fortiori* included in the old, or, as it were, the part is included in the whole? Thus, in the *Code* (VIII. lii (liii). 1), it is stated that 'the governor of a province, having attested by inquiries those practices which have been commonly followed in the city in the same kind of legal controversies, is, having heard the case, to decide . . . &c.' For I consider that that phrase 'in the same' (*in eodem*) signifies 'in identical', and accordingly, I assert that there should be so great a similarity [in the second case to the first,] as to make the two practically identical. Other observations on this point, can be seen in Chapter Two of the preceding Book.[8]

CHAPTER XVII

Can Custom Interpret Law?

1. This interpretation is the second principal effect which the laws grant to custom. It is, however, an effect of that custom which is in accordance with law; for custom which is outside law does not assume the existence of a law to be interpreted; and custom which is opposed to law, rather derogates therefrom. Hence only a custom which is in accordance with law can interpret it.

The reason for this effect is as follows: for the interpretation of a law already in existence, no authority of greater force or clearer expression of intention is requisite, than that which is needed for the introduction of a new law. All the reasons given in the preceding Chapter apply, therefore, with still greater force to this present effect. The laws are clear on this point (*Decretals,* Bk. I, tit. IV, chap. viii; *Digest,* I. iii. 23, 37).

2. *First mode in which custom can interpret law.* In order, however, that this assertion may be amplified and be confirmed with reasons, I observe that a custom can avail for the interpretation of law in two ways; in one way, as a sign or witness thereof, since, so used, a custom in regard to the observance of law testifies that the custom expresses the mind of the lawmaker, and that it has been received as such, and in no other way, since laws are composed of customary usage, according to Isidore as cited in the *Decretum* (Pt. I, dist. 1, chap. i).

In this character, however, a custom cannot furnish a certain and infallible interpretation, since interpretation by custom is no more than human conjecture; but it affords a high probability, and so it is of much assistance in theoretical interpretation; and the more widely spread the custom is and the longer it has endured, the more probable will be the conjecture it furnishes. However, no certain criterion can be fixed for assisting judgment in these matters; decision must be left to the discretion of a prudent mind.

8. [Not included in these *Selections.*—Tr.]

We may add, however, that not only the custom which is concerned with the observance of a law itself after its enactment, but also that which existed prior to its enactment, may be of great assistance in understanding the meaning of that law. Hence, what is stated in the above-cited law (*Digest*, I. iii. 37), namely: 'If there is a question concerning the interpretation of a written law, the first point to be examined is what general rule of law the city formerly applied in cases of this character', can be properly understood as having reference not only to a custom which is subsequent to the law in question, but also to one preceding it. Since, as Isidore holds, and this is cited in *Decretum*, Pt. I, dist. IV, chap. ii, law ought to be framed in harmony with the custom of the country, we can, by referring to the ancient customs of a city, arrive at a probable conjecture as to the sense of the law at the time of its enactment. It is, then, in this sense that the Doctors frequently speak when they say that a law is to be interpreted according to the custom of the locality, even though such interpretation should necessitate some forcing of the strict meaning of the words of the law, because the law must be adapted to the customs of the men [who are bound by it]. This doctrine is stated at length in the Gloss (on *Decretals*, Bk. I, tit. III, chap. xxviii), by Bartolus (on *Digest*, I. i. 9), and also by Panormitanus (on *Decretals*, Bk. III, tit. XXVIII, chap. ix, no. 2).

3. Custom can interpret law in another way—as a cause both of the introduction and settling of such interpretation, and also of the binding force of the law as thus interpreted. The Doctors, cited above, frequently lay down this doctrine, as do others also, to whom Mascardi refers (*De Probationibus*, Vol. II, concl. 1045 in its entirety), and whom he follows. The same is clearly set forth in the *Digest*, I. iii. 38: 'In ambiguities which develop out of existing laws, custom or the attestation of matters which have always been adjudicated in a similar way shall have the force of law.' Hence, just as we have said in an earlier passage that an interpretation made by a law is an authentic one by reason of the efficacy of such law in establishing that interpretation, so the same [in like circumstances] is to be said of custom which has developed to the point at which it obtains the force of law. This is, then, the true reason for that assertion, namely, that since a custom is effective in securing the establishment of law, it can also, for that reason, interpret a law efficaciously, and can do so in the way

in which other laws do. Whatever, then, is necessary that a custom may have legal force, is equally necessary that it may interpret law in this way. What we have said above concerning these matters is, therefore, sufficient.

4. *An observation of the Gloss.* At this point, I shall merely note that the Gloss (on *Digest,* I. iii. 38, word *perpetuo*), concludes from the word *perpetua* in the law, that a period of ten years must elapse, in order that a custom may possess the efficacy of which we have been speaking. The attentive reader will, however, note that the law just cited contains two members. One is 'custom'; the other is 'decisions of judges': and the word *perpetuo* is not attached to the first member—the word 'custom' is used without qualification; but the word *perpetuo* is attached to the second member, in order to make it clear that not simply any decisions will have this force, but only such as have always been concordant. For this reason, no note as to time is set down in the law for the first member; by the general rules [of interpretation] we are to understand the law as referring to custom validated by legal prescription. The word *perpetuo* attached to the second phrase does not signify a number of years, but a perpetual agreement in decisions; that is, that there has been in the decisions handed down on that matter no mutual variation or contradiction; this is the plain meaning of these words in common usage.

What number of such decisions is enough, is not stated in the law, but it can be gathered from what has been said on this point in earlier passages. In principle, the decisions have this efficacy to the extent that they are able to establish custom. So that, if there has been but one, or a smaller number than is sufficient to establish a legitimate custom, then they might establish a probable argument [in favour of the interpretation], but one lacking legal force. Hence, I have often said that a judicial interpretation (so to speak) is reducible to a customary one, that is, to custom. For the decisions handed down by the courts are most of all effectual in that they are received and approved by the common consent of the people. This has been noted by Bartolus and other writers in passages which are frequently cited.

5. *The force of custom in the interpretation of law.* In the light of these considerations, we must understand the opinion of many writers, expounded as follows: custom is of such moment in the interpretation of law, that,

even though it may not be clear from the words or the subject-matter of a law, whether or not the law contains a precept binding under pain of mortal sin, and should therefore, *per se,* be given the more favourable interpretation; nevertheless, if it is clear that a custom [growing out of the observance of the law] has been received as binding under grave obligation, the law is to be held as binding under pain of mortal sin. This is the opinion of Sylvester (word *praeceptum,* no. 2, at end), and that held by Cajetan (on II.–II, qu. 186, art. 9, ad 2, and qu. 147, art. 3, ad 2) in a passage treating in particular of the precept of fasting. Navarrus lays down the same doctrine in [*Enchiridion,*] Chap. xxi, no. 11.

On the same principle, a custom can interpret the word *praecipiendi* (commanding), a term under which a law is enacted, as signifying a serious obligation. Sylvester and Cajetan, in the passages just cited, call attention to this doctrine from the *Constitutions* of Clement (Bk. V, tit. xi, chap. i, § *Item ordo*). The Gloss on that passage makes the same observation.

The reason is that the lawmaker is presumed to employ words according to their common usage. Consequently, I hold conversely that, even though the words and subject-matter of the precept may seem to be such as to make it binding under pain of mortal sin, yet if the custom has interpreted the law otherwise, then it is binding only under pain of venial sin— as Cajetan also has observed. The underlying principle is the same in both these cases. For just as custom is able to introduce law, so it is also able to derogate from law, and this the more so, since the words and the matter of the law can scarcely be [always] so clear as not to leave some ambiguity and room for interpretation. This interpretation, therefore, custom can establish in both ways, namely, in a rigorous or in a gentle sense; but in order to do this efficaciously, it must, as has been said, possess the conditions necessary for the introduction or abrogation of law.

6. *Custom can interpret not only human law, but also divine and natural law.* I add also that it is possible for a custom to interpret not only human law, but divine and natural law as well, as all the Doctors cited above teach. Nevertheless, with these latter kinds of law, the interpretation is effected in a different manner, since custom can interpret human law by restricting or enlarging its scope—as is clear from our remarks in the previous Chapter, and as will be clear from those which will follow in the succeeding

Chapters. Custom interprets divine law, however, only by indicating the intention of the lawgiver; and so, for this interpretation to be certain, the custom must be one that is observed as a tradition of the Universal Church, or one that has had the approval of the Popes.

Custom can also be self-interpreting. Finally, it may be added that a custom can interpret not only written law, but itself also, as is clear from what has been said. The custom can do so because it also manifests the intention of those making use of it, although the custom itself is also to be interpreted by reason, as Rochus notes (*De Consuetudine,* Sect. 4, no. 23) from Baldus (on *Code,* VI. xxviii. 4, at the beginning); and this is evident in the nature of things.

CHAPTER XVIII

Can Custom Abrogate Human Law?

1. *On the abrogation of law through custom.* The reason for doubting that custom can abrogate civil law is based upon the rule laid down by the *Digest* (XLVII. xii. 3, § 5); namely, that a municipal statute which has been enacted subsequent to a civil law, and contrary thereto, does not derogate from it. From this it is concluded that the same must be said of a custom, because the two are judged by identical standards.

Again, an argument of the same tenor might be drawn from the *Code* (VIII. lii (liii). 2), where it is explicitly stated that, although the authority of custom is great, yet it is not such as 'to overcome either reason or law'. It is clear that the jurist must necessarily be speaking here of human law, for natural law is referred to in the first member of the phrase, wherein it is said that custom does not prevail over reason. The same doctrine is also found in the *Decretum* (Pt. I, dist. xi, can. iv), where there are many similar decrees. It is in accord also with that set forth in the *Decretals* (Bk. II, tit. xxvii, chap. viii), which states that, 'although the authority of usage or custom is of no small moment, yet it is never prejudicial to the truth or to law.'

The third and principal reason for doubting the power of custom to abrogate law is that a custom can have no force unless it is reasonable, as is stated in the *Decretals* (Bk. I, tit. iv, chap. xi), and as we have demonstrated above. But a custom, in opposition to law, cannot be reasonable: both because, by the very fact that it is contrary to law, it is against reason; and again because the actions done in pursuance of that custom deviate from right order and cannot work to the favour of those who offend, nor liberate them from the yoke of the law. For these reasons, Hostiensis (on *Decretals,* Bk. I, tit. xxxiv, chap. i [, rubric iv, no. 11])[1] held that a true preceptive law cannot be abrogated by desuetude. But in holding this opinion he stands alone; and he himself departs from it at times.

2. *Human law, whether canonical or civil, can be abrogated by custom.* Notwithstanding the above arguments, the rule is certain that human law, whether canonical or civil, can be abrogated by custom. On this point, all the Doctors are agreed: the theologians, including St. Thomas (I.–II, qu. 97, art. 3); the canonists in their notes on (*De Consuetudine,* Chap. xi)— among them Hostiensis (in *Summa* on that same Chapter); the jurists (on *Digest,* I. iii. 32, and on *Code,* VIII. lii. 1 and 2); and the summists (word *consuetudo*).

With regard to the point [whether canon law can be abrogated by custom the rule] is expressly stated in the *Decretals* (Bk. I, tit. iv, chap. xi). Together with the other general principles there set forth, it is laid down that an ancient custom is to be observed, which rule I cited in a preceding Chapter. The same is expressed in the case of civil law in the *Digest* (I. iii. 32, at the end): 'it is most correctly admitted that not only by the decision of the lawmaker, but by the tacit consent of all, laws may be abrogated through desuetude.' The same principle is embodied in the law of our kingdom (in *Las Siete Partidas,* Pt. I, tit. ii, laws 3 and 5).

The proof of our assertion drawn from reason is the same as that which we developed in proof of an assertion in a preceding Chapter, touching another effect of custom. It is this, that the people do not lack the power to effect the abrogation of law, if the power is explained as it ought to be, and if their will is sufficiently made known by means of the custom itself; hence, nothing is lacking to custom for bringing about this effect.

---

1. [The reference to the Rubric *De Treuga et Pace* should be to the Rubric *De Consuetudine* (*Decretals,* Bk. I, tit. iv).—REVISER.]

3. And first of all, as to the power of the people to effect such abrogation, no difficulty arises with respect to the civil laws of democratic peoples who recognize no superior. This is clear from the principles demonstrated in Chapter xvi; for they apply in our present question also.

Two solutions to the difficulty. A difficulty arises, however, with respect to the civil laws of sovereign princes, and to the canon laws. This difficulty may be met in two ways. First, by saying that these laws are enacted not unconditionally, but with the tacit proviso that the people wish to retain them in force. Such a condition may be understood as present in these laws, either because the prince lacks the power to coerce his people beyond this point by means of his own laws—as some writers hold, at least concerning those legislators who are the source of civil laws; or for the reason that out of his benignity the sovereign has not the will to bind his subjects save under such a limitation—as some believe to be the case even with the canon laws. Consequently, according to this view, we must say that a renewed tacit consent of the prince is not necessary for this sort of abrogation, but that it is provided for in the very framing of the law. But we have already (Book III, chap. xviii, Book IV, chap. xvi)[2] rejected this solution, for the reason that, as a matter of fact, the power to bind their subjects unconditionally is not lacking even to temporal princes; nor is the will to do so, even lacking to the prelates of the Church.

What we demonstrated in the passages just referred to, both from reason and from usage, as to the acceptance of law, is even more certainly true with respect to the abrogation of law already accepted and confirmed by usage: otherwise it would always rest with the will of the people to rid itself without blame of the law of its superior: for such power will rest with the people if the [tacit] condition [of which these writers speak] is included in the law. If this were so, even a subject community could expressly and designedly revoke a law of its prince or prelate, which is absurd.

Hence, we must regard it as certain that this power must be explained as resulting from a union of the people with their prince and lawmaker. The reason is that this power to put aside a law, as it exists in the people

2. [Not included in these *Selections.*—Tr.]

taken alone, is rather a factual than a legal one; on the part of the prince, however, it is also a power to tolerate and give consent to the popular will. Thus, the authority to abolish law is complete in the combination of these two powers: because, in the last resort, its annulment is brought about by the same power that brought it into being—and that this can be done, I have shown in the previous Book.[3]

4. *What power must reside in the people in order that custom may be introduced.* It is, therefore, evident that the principle laid down above has a most important application in respect of this result: namely, that it is not necessary [for these effects] that there exist in the people, viewed separately, the *active* power of making or of repealing law; but that it is sufficient that they have a capacity for receiving law, and that custom be introduced by those to whom the law applies. The reason is that this act of repudiating a law by custom is not one of jurisdiction, or of public authority, but is rather one that proceeds from those under a duty of obedience to the law. Accordingly, these acts [of repudiating law] are (as it were) contrary to the acts of making law, and, therefore, both are concerned about the same thing. And thus, a lay community has the power to establish a custom abrogating an ecclesiastical law. Indeed, even a community of women can have this power as regards a law addressed to them alone, as in the case of the law in *Sext*, Bk. III, tit. xvi, only chapter which—as authorities in this matter point out—enjoins the enclosure of nuns. The reason here is that such a custom does not, on the part of the subjects, abolish the law actively (as it were); it does so only to the extent that it demands from the superior that he abolish the law. That power is, as I have said, in the possession of the superior. It remains for us to take up next a discussion of such questions as touch upon the operations of the will [of the people and of the prince] in this matter.

5. *A twofold will is required for the establishment of the custom [abrogating law].* For the introduction of a custom abrogating law, a twofold will is needed, the one of the people, the other of the prince. The first offers but little difficulty; for a custom is evidence of the general will [of the people]. It is clear from the above discussion that this custom should

3. [Not included in these *Selections.*—Tr.]

be public, and introduced or accepted by a majority of the people. This character of custom is, then, sufficient evidence of voluntary agreement, as is clear from what we have said in another place.[4] Indeed, with respect to the kind of custom we are here discussing, the reasons there given take on an additional force; for the will here indicated to abrogate a law is not a will to bind oneself or to take on a burden, but rather to set one aside. In this kind of custom, no intention to establish a new consuetudinary law is required; there is called for only an intention not to have or retain the law in question, and to resume the earlier status of freedom from legal obligation in this matter. Such an intention is sufficiently manifest by the frequency of the acts, and the agreement and constancy of the people in actions to that end.

6. *A difficulty.* The only difficulty that is likely to be urged here relates to the canon laws made for the whole Church: for it will be necessary that a custom sufficient to derogate from a law of this sort be introduced and accepted by a major part of the Church; such an expectation, however, it is not easy to entertain, and such an agreement of the Church could hardly be manifested.

The reply. My reply is, that if a general law for the whole Church is to be abrogated, nothing less than a custom, universal in the sense we have defined, will suffice; since otherwise it will not carry with it the general agreement of the Church, as such. This mode of abrogation is, therefore, very rare. Yet it is not impossible, since a knowledge of the custom can be effected within the space of forty years, through adequate report and public communication, by means of letters and through notification. Still we must add that, according to the usual practice of the Church and the canonical institutes, it is not to be expected that this abrogation will be accomplished at one and the same time for the entire Church, and by a universal custom; rather, it might be effected by the customs of the different portions thereof, in provinces, dioceses, and other communities which can be governed by their own laws. For if a custom in opposition to a general law prevails among a majority of some one of these communities, then there is a derogation from that law, which is valid for that community,

---

4. [Cf. Chap. xii, § 1, *supra*, p. 628.—Tr.]

even if the general law remain intact for the rest of the Church. Thus the whole difficulty disappears. This doctrine can be applied in due proportion to other common laws, both civil and canonical. This is the teaching of the Gloss (on *Institutes,* I. ii, § 9, word *imitantur*).

7. *For this effect, a privative custom is sufficient.* And therefore, it is not always necessary for this effect [of abrogation] that there be a true custom of fact, that is, a positive custom, one which results from a frequency of actions. A privative custom—which is called desuetude—is sufficient, one, that is, which arises from a repeated omission of an act, and which, of itself, is sufficient against affirmative precepts; for the reason that the very repetition of an omission to act sufficiently indicates a will not to accept such a precept. But it is necessary that the omission be a true [, i.e. formal] one, that is, one in opposition to a legal obligation; it must, also, occur at the time for which the precept commanded the action, since the omission of an action when no action was obligatory is no indication of a will to disregard a law, or refuse to accept it, as is self-evident. This is the doctrine of Panormitanus (on *Decretals,* Bk. III, tit. III, chap. vii [, no. 9]), of Sylvester (word *consuetudine,* Qu. 8) and of Rochus (*De Consuetudine,* Chap. xi, sect. 4, nos. 76 *et seq.*), who deals with this point at great length, as well as of Navarrus (*Consilia,* Bk. II [Bk. I], *De Consuetudine*). We shall discuss this more fully later, in Book VIII,[5] in connexion with the loss of a privilege through non-usage.

8. *For desuetude, the first omissions are necessarily illicit.* From the above, a further conclusion is drawn, namely, that such omissions to act must necessarily be sinful, at least at the beginning; since if the omissions are based on some reasonable excuse—for instance, upon the warrant of some special necessity—they cannot give evidence of a will in opposition to the law. In such a case we shall have not desuetude, but a mere non-usage, which, by universal agreement, is insufficient. The same would be true if the element of ignorance of the law were to intervene, or the element of great fear, and for the same reason. Although, indeed, the fear be not great enough to excuse from fault, it may be sufficient nevertheless to prevent creation of a true custom or a desuetude. An

---

5. [Not included in these *Selections.*—TR.]

act of this kind is not so much an act of the free will as one done under compulsion, and hence it cannot be sufficient indication of a purpose in opposition to law, nor of an absolute will to set the law aside, but only whilst such fear is imminent. And so it would seem to be a sufficiently probable view that in such a case the law is not completely abrogated, but rather that there is, at most, a derogation therefrom: namely, that it is to cease to be of obligation in the presence of so grave an inconvenience and a like imminent danger.

This point is to be especially noted, for a custom of non-observance of a law can often be brought in upon the occasion of such a contingency or necessity, which, of itself, would not be sufficient for excusing from the obligation of the law; but by reason of this custom, assuming the fulfilment of the other requisite conditions, it can be established that the law shall not be binding upon similar occasions, and yet no absolute derogation from the law takes place. Examples of the situation described above are easily supplied in the observance of feasts and of fasts, and similar matters.

9. *A twofold will of the prince is required.* We take up now the question of the will of the prince, a matter to which the doctrine of the preceding Chapter is to be completely applied. In this matter also, the consent of the prince can be understood either as granted through the law itself, or, as personal, and (as it were) given afresh, though tacitly. Either mode is a valid one.

The aforesaid Chap. xi of *Decretals,* Bk. I, tit. IV, has reference to consent of the first sort. The custom must fulfil two conditions to verify consent of that kind, namely, that it be reasonable and prescriptive; these same conditions are set down in the aforesaid laws [3 and 5 of Pt. I, tit. II of *Las Siete Partidas*]. Since no others are postulated, these are sufficient; in the absence of either the law established by the custom would be imperfect and incomplete. Some explanation of these two conditions is necessary to make their nature clear.

Two notes. We have discussed at length the first condition in Chapters Six and Seven of this Book, where we explained what is called an unreasonable custom. At this point, however, two other observations must be specially added: one, that a reason of less force is needed in the custom for producing this effect [, i.e. the abrogation of law], than is required for introducing a law. The reason is that the abolition of a law is a matter of lesser moment than the creation of one. For in the annulment of a law no special utility or rectitude in the subject-matter itself is called for; it is enough that the annulment of the obligation in question be not contrary to the public advantage, since, although some advantage is taken away, there is a corresponding compensation, either in the removal of an occasion of a greater evil, or in conciliating the minds of subjects to a milder government.

10. Whence I add another observation on this point; namely, that it is necessary that in some way or other the custom, or rather the abrogation of law in consequence of custom, should be supported by a reason of some sort. Accordingly, the express repeal of a just law cannot be effected without some upright cause, as has been proved in the preceding book;[6] neither, therefore, can a tacit repeal, such as is made by custom, be effected without a cause of the same character. In like manner, therefore, for the custom to be reasonable, it is insufficient that it be not opposed to natural reason, or to divine law, or that it has not been reprobated by law; but it is necessary that the will to be without such law be justifiable on the part of the subjects for a good reason, such as also justifies the consent of the prince to the abrogation of the law. This is the ground and the necessity of this condition: for unless the custom is in some way reasonable, the prince is not presumed to yield to the desire of his subjects, for he cannot be presumed to have a will to abolish the law without just cause and adequate reason, since he cannot do this without fault, nor should he actually do so. Further remarks on this condition would seem to be unnecessary, though we shall have something more to say on this point when we come to answer the second difficulty that is brought against our assertion.

11. *Second condition.* The second condition, namely, that this custom be prescriptive, has also been explained in former chapters. We shall, therefore, at this point, touch only on the question of the time required for this prescription.

---

6. [Not included in these *Selections.*—TR.]

We assume that it is not necessary for it to be immemorial, as some writers have asserted without a basis in truth, as I have observed in the preceding Chapter. Hence it must be certain that a period of a definite length is called for. Yet we must note a difference between the canon and the civil laws with respect to this matter—one that is taught by all the writers cited above.

A distinction to be noted between canonical and civil laws. For in the case of civil laws, the same time is required for the abrogation of law as for its introduction, namely, ten years. The reason is that the civil law makes no distinction on this point, but requires for both, without distinction, a long time, as is clear from the aforesaid law 32 [*Digest,* I. iii. 32].

In civil law a custom of ten years' standing suffices for the establishment or abrogation of law. But a long time is defined in that law as ten years, as we have noted above. The same definition is more expressly laid down in the *Institutes* (II. vi, § 1 [II. vi, Pref.]). Nor does the law here make any distinction as to the length of the observance necessary by reason of the absence or presence [of the prince]—whatever Sylvester and others may hold—and this, for the reason set forth above. Now it is essential to this prescription that the ignorance of the custom on the part of the prince is supposed; since, if the prince has knowledge of the custom, the prescription is not necessary for this effect of which we are speaking, as I shall immediately prove. But with respect to a prince who is ignorant of the custom, any consideration of his absence or presence is irrelevant; and hence, the law requires the same length of time in both cases without distinction.

The authorities on law generally fix the length of time for this custom at ten rather than twenty years, although this term is not defined in the laws; and the ignorance of the prince may be regarded as a kind of absence—for the reasons we have rehearsed in an earlier passage.[7] Another reason is that in law of this kind the favour of the prince enters as an element, and this is extended when a shorter period for the validation of the custom is fixed. Again, the burden placed upon the people where the revocation of the law is put off for a long time is an element to be taken into account also; and

7. [Cf. Chap. xv, §§ 5 *et seq., supra,* pp. 657 *et seq.*—Tr.]

this burden is lessened by fixing a shorter period. Thus, on either ground, our opinion is in harmony with the law and with the rule of law which says, 'in obscure matters, the course which imposes the least burden is to be followed.'

12. *Concerning laws of the Church, there is a diversity of opinion.* With respect to the laws of the Church on this point, there is a diversity of opinion. For some authorities hold that the same ten-year period is sufficient for these, as in the civil laws. In support of this opinion are quoted Azo (in *Summa*, tit. *De Consuetudine*), Calderinus and others (on *Decretals*, Bk. I, tit. xxxiv, chap. i). These writers are, however, speaking of a law not yet accepted, a point with which I have dealt in Books Three[8] and Four.[9] Though, indeed, there is probably no difference in the prescriptions in either case, since either custom would be counter to the canon law.

That a space of forty years is required for a custom to be prescriptive against canon law. Now the true opinion and the general one is that a period of forty years is required for a custom to be held prescriptive against canon laws.

This is the view of Innocent, on *Decretals*, Bk. I, tit. iv, chap. viii; of Panormitanus (*De Consuetudine*, Chap. xi, no. 11, and on *Decretals*, Bk. I, tit. xxxiv, chap. i, no. 4); of Felinus also (on *Decretals, ibid.*, no. 13); and of Rochus (*De Consuetudine*, Sect. 3, no. 35). It is that set forth by Torquemada (on *Decretum*, Pt. I, dist. i, can. v, qu. 2, and Pt. I, dist. i, can. iv, qu. 4); by Bartolus on *Digest*, I. iii. 32, (in *Repetit.* qu. 2, at the beginning, subquestion 3, no. 14), where in the scholia others are cited; by Jason (on *Digest*, I. iii. 32, col. ii, no. 43); by Antoninus ([*Summa*,] Pt. I, tit. xvi, § 4); by Sylvester (word *consuetudo*, qu. 4); by Angelus de Clavasio ([*Summa*, word *consuetudo*,] no. 8), and by other summists there cited. It is that also defended by Navarrus (*Consilia*, Bk. II, *De Consuetudine*), Corduba ([*Quaestiones*,] Bk. I, qu. xii, ad 4), and Gregory López (on *Las Siete Partidas*, Pt. I, tit. ii, law 5, gloss 4 [*glossa* g]).

---

8. [Only Chapters i–iv and xxxii–xxxiii of Book III are included in these *Selections.*—Tr.]

9. [Not included in these *Selections.*—Tr.]

The proof of this opinion is usually derived from the aforesaid *Decretals*, Bk. I, tit. IV, chap. xi, since it demands [, for abrogation,] a custom validated by a prescription in accordance with law; and in canon law only a custom of forty years' standing is termed such. This is the view of Rochus (*De Consuetudine*, Sect. 3, no. 4), drawn from the Gloss, together with the text of *Sext*, Bk. III, tit. IV, chap. v.

But I do not think that this proof is satisfactory, because the phrase 'validated by a prescription in accordance with law', is a general qualification, and means no more than that the custom must endure for the time and under the conditions prescribed by the law. These words could, then, according as the matter to which they referred varied, indicate equally a prescription of ten or of forty years. Hence, a custom 'validated by prescription in accordance with law', may also be demanded for the introduction of a law outside of, but not opposed to, the common law, in a case where the prince is ignorant of the custom. Because of the unsatisfactory nature of this phrase, the aforesaid writers add that for a legitimate prescription against the Church, a custom of forty years is necessary, according to the *Decretals* (Bk. II, tit. XXVI, chaps. iv and vi), together with other chapters that deal with prescriptions. But a custom opposed to the canons can rightly be said to be against the Church, since it is against the laws of the Church: therefore, a legitimate prescription in such a matter ought to be one of forty years' running.

13. Some writers even add that not only is a period of this length necessary when the custom is contrary to the canon law, but also when it is contrary to the reason of a canon, as is noted by the Gloss (on *Sext*, Bk. I, tit. XVI, chap. v, word *statuimus*) and also by Geminiano on the same Chapter; and he is followed by Peter of Ravenna (Tract. *De Consuetudine*, Sect. I, no. 20). The same view is held by Felinus (on *Decretals*, Bk. II, tit. XXIV, chap. xi, no. 3, and Bk. I, tit. XXXIII, chap. xv, no. 3), where he explains that this assertion is to be understood as referring to a custom contrary to the reason expressed in the law. I add, however, the further note that the reason here referred to must be one so intrinsic and essential to the law that when it ceases to exist the law also must be held as ceasing to exist. This assertion, in the sense of Felinus's qualification of it, is, in that case, a well-grounded one; for a custom opposed to the reason of a law is virtually

opposed to the law itself, and therefore derogates from it. But if the reason of the law is not such as I have noted, but one which can cease to be whilst the law still continues in force, I do not see why a custom opposed to the reason alone of the law should be held to be contrary to the law itself, or why so long a time should be required [for its effect].

Finally, these authors add that because of the character of its subject-matter, a custom may have to be an immemorial one, as when a custom is contrary to the special laws of the prince, and even so a period of forty years will be necessary for the establishment of a custom which is outside the canons, if it should derogate from the law of some particular church.

But even though these observations may be true, they are not properly applicable to the legal custom of which we are speaking, except in so far as a custom of that sort may be bound up with a prescription properly so called on some matter which would require a longer duration.

14. *An abrogation of law is sometimes effected by custom even when the prince is ignorant of the same.* Hence, also, we conclude that a custom fulfilling these two conditions, if it is opposed to an existing law, abrogates that law, even if the custom does not come to the knowledge of the prince. This is the teaching of nearly all the Doctors cited above, and of Covarruvias (on *Decretals,* Bk. IV, *De Matrimoniis,* Pt. II, chap. vi, § 10, nos. 18 and 19 [nos. 35 and 36]), of Dominicus de Sancto Geminiano (on *Decretum,* Pt. I, dist. IV, in § *Leges,* after can. iii, with Gloss), of Archidia-conus (on *Decretum, ibid.*), and others. Felinus in his observations on this point cites these writers. Reference may be made also to all of those whom I have cited in a preceding Chapter.

15. For the same principle applies here. Assuming the existence of a law giving this efficacy to a reasonable and prescriptive custom, there is present by reason thereof a sufficient consent of the prince—by his tacit legal will, so to speak—to the abrogation of the law opposed by the custom. For the operation of such a will, no new knowledge [of the custom], such as is necessary for an expression of his personal will, is required; nor can we add this condition contrary to what the said law lays down. The reason is that for juridical effects no more conditions are to be required than the laws demand; and here the law sets forth these two conditions as sufficient

for this effect; and each condition can be fulfilled without the knowledge of the prince.

The truth of this assertion with respect to the first condition [, i.e. reasonableness,] is self-evident: for a custom is not reasonable merely because it is known to the prince: since any other kind of custom can be equally known or not known by him; and a custom must be postulated of such a reasonable character that it can truly be known as such.

Concerning the second also, the truth of our assertion is clear; for a prescription does not require in the person against whom the prescriptive right is acquired any advertence to the prescription. Furthermore, the nature of human law in a certain way demands this; for it should be adapted to human conduct. Therefore, it is highly expedient that when a people has persevered for a sufficiently long time with a stubborn purpose in a course of conduct opposed to a law, the prince should not urge the law, but should rather cease from enforcing it. Hence, it is justly provided that a prescriptive custom repeals a law [in opposition thereto], irrespective of the knowledge or ignorance of the prince. This matter offers no further difficulty.

16. *What is the force of non-prescriptive custom [with respect to the abrogation of law]?* On the other hand, the question may be raised as to whether a non-prescriptive custom can at times effect the repeal of a law, at least in cases where the prince has knowledge of the custom. For Panormitanus (*De Consuetudine,* Chap. xi, no. 13) is very clearly of the opinion[10] that the fact that the prince has knowledge of the custom is not sufficient to effect a derogation from the law within a shorter time than that required for a prescription. Support for his thesis may be found, first, in the doctrine of the same last chapter of the Title *De Consuetudine* [*Decretals,* Bk. I, tit. IV, chap. xi], which unconditionally demands the fulfilment of the two conditions we have mentioned, in order that a custom may have this effect; therefore, a custom in which one or the other of these conditions is lacking cannot produce this effect, even if the prince have knowledge of the custom. A confirmation of this argument

---

10. [The author refutes these arguments of Panormitanus in later paragraphs. *Vide* pp. 696 *et seq., infra.*—TR.]

is that if the custom is not reasonable, the fact that the prince knows of it in no way enables such custom to repeal the law, according to the most common opinion: therefore, if the custom is non-prescriptive, it will be insufficient, even though it has been brought to the prince's attention. The logical nexus of this argument is evident, because these two conditions are demanded as of equal necessity. A second confirmatory argument offered by Panormitanus is that the most that can be inferred from the fact of the prince's knowledge is that he tolerates the custom, but this, according to the *Decretals* (Bk. III, tit. v, chap. xviii), does not establish consent. It is for this reason that the said author adds that then only should the prince be held to abolish the law when he not only has knowledge of the custom, but follows it himself; for by so doing he gives (as it were) his express consent to it. Finally, I add this further argument: this custom is valid as a kind of prescription; but the time necessary for a prescription is not shortened because of the knowledge of the prescription on the part of the person against whom it is being established. Therefore, . . .

17. *A non-prescriptive custom is sufficient at times for the abrogation of a law.* Nevertheless, I hold that the contrary[11] is true. I assert, then, that a non-prescriptive custom is at times sufficient to derogate from a law, provided the prince has knowledge of the custom, and provided the custom itself is of such a nature, and of such duration as practically to be an indication of his consent to its effect. This seems to be the teaching of St. Thomas (I.–II, qu. 97, art. 3, ad 3) where he demands not a prescription of the custom for this effect, but a sufficient expression of consent by the prince. Soto holds the same opinion (*De Iustitia*, Bk. I, qu. vii, art. 2), as do Bartholomew Medina (on I.–II, qu. 97, art. 3) and Gerson (in the aforesaid treatise *De Vita Spirituali*).

This would also seem to have been the view of Antonio de Butrio (*De Consuetudine*, Chap. xi), for he says that if the Pope has knowledge of a custom in opposition to a law, a period of ten years is sufficient. This statement is approved by Sylvester (word *consuetudo*, Qu. 4), and by Angelus de Clavasio (*Summa*, word *consuetudo*, no. 8). The same is held by the canonists generally with respect to cases where a custom opposes a

---

11. [Contrary to the position just urged by Panormitanus.—Tr.]

canon law which has not yet been accepted, as Felinus records at length [on *Decretals,* Bk. II, tit. xxiv, chap. xi, no. 3 and Bk. I, tit. xxxiii, chap. xv, no. 3].

The same reasoning holds, as I have already pointed out, for a custom [resisting a law of this status, as holds for a custom contrary to a law that has been accepted by those to whom it applies]: and this, both for the reason that such a custom is like the other in that it is in opposition to the Church and her law; and again, because, as I explained above, the observance of a law for a certain period does not increase its legal effect, as such, but is said to confirm it only in fact. Therefore, in respect of their force as law, the principle is the same in both of these cases.

Another proof is that there is no ground for holding that the reason validating the establishment of law should be greater than what is necessary for the abrogation of law. But a non-prescriptive custom of which the prince has knowledge suffices for the introduction of law—as we have demonstrated earlier. Therefore, such a custom is sufficient for the abrogation of law.

The proof of the major premiss and of the logical nexus of this argumentation rests upon the fact that the whole basis of either of these effects lies in the tacit will of the prince; and this will, specific and personal (as it were), can be known not less clearly from a non-prescriptive custom contrary to law, but known to and tolerated by the prince, than from a custom that is outside the law. Therefore, the former custom is no less sufficient for derogation of law than is the latter for the introduction of law. Indeed, there is even more reason for presuming the consent of the prince for the accomplishment of this effect than for the introduction of new law; and this, both for the reason that such abrogation is urgently needed in order to remove from his subjects an occasion of offending against the law which still prevails, and also, because the custom itself brings about such a change in the subjects themselves that through it they have become in a certain fashion unfitted for the observance of the law in question, for the observance of the law ought to be easy and adapted to their general conduct.

Finally, this opinion is confirmed by usage, since many of the laws of the Church are held to have suffered derogation within periods shorter [than forty years], for the reason that the Popes, though not ignorant of the usages, did not manifest their wishes [in favour of the law].

18. *Of the time required for the abrogation of a law through a custom when the prince is ignorant of the same.* On the question of the time required for this effect when the prince has no knowledge of the custom, I think that the opinion that fixes ten years as necessary—although it is defended by Antonio de Butrio and other authorities—is advanced without good reason. For this assertion of Antonio de Butrio cannot have application to the civil laws, because in the case of such laws, even when the prince has no knowledge of the custom, a period longer than ten years is not, as we have said, required for this effect; our assertion, on the other hand, holds true even of civil law, for the reason that when the prince has such knowledge of the custom, the full prescriptive period of ten years fixed by the civil law is not required. And if the words of these writers are to be taken as referring to the canon laws only, they should fix the length of time which should be demanded for this effect [with due proportion] for civil laws. But they cannot, on any good grounds, assign any fixed period as required for such civil laws; hence, neither can the term necessary for this effect in the case of canon laws be fixed, on sound reason, at ten years.

Moreover, there is this general argument [against their position]: the period of duration for this kind of custom has not been determined by any law; therefore, any fixed definition of its necessary duration is unfounded.

A more complete explanation of this point is found in the very fact that since a prescriptive custom is not demanded here, the effect of the custom is dependent not upon the dispositions of a law but upon the prince's consent as judged from the natural [, to be distinguished from the legal] significance of his actions. But with respect to the duration of observance necessary here, judgment finds no guidance in the dispositions of the law or in the nature of things, since the term of observance of such a custom will vary according to circumstances, as I have explained above.

The time here required must be left to the judgment of a prudent mind. Therefore, it is useless to speak of the period as one of ten years. The same assertion holds true of this point, as was made in a like passage on the introduction of a law: the matter must be left to the judgment of a prudent mind. This is the view of Soto, B. Medina, and others.

19. In fact, some canonists have inferred from this conclusion, that when an entire city, or community acts in opposition to some statute made by that community, one act in opposition to the statute will be sufficient to revoke it. The reason is that by this one act the will of the maker of the statute to repeal that statute is sufficiently manifested, since the will that acts against the statute is the same [as that which brought it into being]. This is not the case with law enacted by the will of the prince.

This is the doctrine of Panormitanus (on *Decretals,* Bk. III, tit. IV, chap. XV, no. 9), and of Giovanni d'Andrea (on *Decretals,* Bk. III, tit. V, chap. xxii, and Bk. I, tit. II, chap. viii). The same doctrine is taught by other writers on these laws. But we shall discuss this point, as well as the meaning of the words of these texts, in our discussion on privileges; for under that head the texts are dealt with. Respecting statutes, properly so called, I do not think that sign [of a single act contrary to the statute] is sufficient evidence [of the will of the community to revoke it], unless it is obvious from other circumstances that the community did not perform the action by way of a temporary dispensation from that statute, but rather[12] as an abrogation thereof. It is to be added that a custom [and not merely a single act] is essential also, as I have said, for the abrogation of statutes that require for their validity the confirmation of the prince.

20. *Explanation of* Decretals, *Bk. I, tit. IV, chap. XI.* My reply to the argument[13] based upon the *Decretals* (Bk. I, tit. IV, chap. xi) is that the custom there referred to is one which can, even without the sovereign's knowledge, effect the abrogation of a law; that is, a custom which has that power by reason of its special character and the force and virtue it possesses through the law. But the passage [*Decretals, ibid.*] does not exclude that custom which only serves as a sign [of the general will] and an indication of the will of the sovereign to abrogate a law. For in this sense, not only a custom, but any act of the prince which sufficiently manifests his will, can abrogate law, as is clear from the aforesaid law 32 [*Digest,* I. iii. 32]. It is evident in reason, also; because that power resides in the will of the

---

12. [Read, *sed illud abrogando.*—REVISER.]

13. [Cf. Sect. 16 of this Chapter, *supra,* p. 695.—TR.]

prince, and differences in the manner of its outward expression are purely incidental.

In answer to the first[14] confirmation we deny, at the outset, the equivalence of the examples given: for the condition that a custom be reasonable is necessary from the very nature of the case; but the condition demanding a prescription comes from the law alone, and hence the former condition is the more essential, and holds in every case, since the will of the prince should at all times be and should be presumed to be reasonable, both when it is given expression in a particular case, and when it is manifested in a general way by the disposition of law.

Again, it is maintained that if the will of the prince is sufficiently manifest, even if the custom has no rational basis, so long as it is not contrary to reason, and contains nothing evil, the abrogation would be valid; even though it may have been illicitly made. This doctrine has been set forth in an earlier passage with respect to an express abrogation, but the same is true if we assume that the abrogation is tacit. But such will in the prince is most rarely or never to be admitted when the custom is so much lacking in reason that it would be illicit to yield thereto, and to abrogate the law on account of it, even when it is well known to the prince, since an evil will is not to be presumed in the prince. The contrary, however, would be true if from the very obduracy—even from an unreasonable obduracy—of the people towards the custom, there is given to the prince a moral cause and reason to judge the revocation of the custom would be prudent. For then, even if the prince knows that the people's custom is an unreasonable one, his connivance at the abrogation [of the law] in tacitly tolerating the custom is to be presumed, since under these circumstances the abrogation is just.

Whence to the second confirmatory argument,[15] my reply has already been made in an earlier passage: namely, that in itself the sovereign's toleration is not enough to indicate his consent, but that when other circumstances are present there can then exist a prudent and correct

---

14. [This refers to the confirmation of the argument of Panormitanus, stated in Sect. 16, *supra*, p. 695.—Tr.]

15. [In Sect. 16, *supra*, p. 696.—Tr.]

indication of his consent, and that in the present case, there would be an excellent sign of the will of the prince [to abrogate the law], when, though the prince is conscious of the popular resistance to it, he connives at this resistance: for his doing so whilst the law is in force would be unreasonable and harmful to the people, and hence his permitting the custom to be observed—unless the contrary were made clear—would be presumed to spring from an intention to abrogate the law. The same principle applies as often as the situation is such that abrogation of the law must be deemed the prudent course: in such a situation the knowledge and toleration of the custom by the prince is properly taken as consent.

In reply to the last confirmatory argument,[16] we deny the assumption: for it has already been shown that, in the case mentioned, the custom exerts its effect not as a form of prescription, but as evidence of the consent [of the prince] drawn from his knowledge and tolerance of the custom.

21. *The answer to the first difficulty.* My reply to the first difficulty, found at the opening of the Chapter, which has been taken from Section 5 [*Digest,* XLVII. xii. 3, § 5], is that the words of that law have many interpretations, which we cannot here discuss. Many, however, understand the passage to refer to a situation in which the statute or custom has existed first, and the law is enacted subsequently, and thus it has reference not to our present matter, but to the question to be treated in Chapter XX.

Others construe it to refer to a situation in which a general law exists first, and is followed by a municipal statute. This seems closer to its literal meaning, and it is also a denial of the opinion that the statute remains valid as against the law, which seems to be most probable. For, although Panormitanus, in discussing *De Consuetudine,* Chap. xi, makes the distinction between statutes of the laity and statutes of the clerics to reside in the fact that particular churches cannot enact statutes opposed to the canons, but that cities can enact laws contrary to general law, I do not see the basis for this distinction. Hence, *Digest,* I. i. 9, proves nothing on this point, and the contrary is demonstrated from the aforesaid Section 5 [*Digest,* XLVII. xii. 3, § 5]. This is also clear from what was said *supra* in

16. [In Sect. 16, *supra,* p. 695.—Tr.]

Book III [of this work][17] on the power to make civil laws. I therefore deny that the same reason applies to statute and to custom, as Panormitanus himself admits [*ibid.*] with regard to statutes and customs of clerics.

The reason here would seem to be—even though various reasons are given by the canonists, as by Panormitanus [*ibid.*], and more fully by Rochus (*De Consuetudine,* Sect. 3, no. 7)—that human laws ought to be adapted to the general conduct of the people for whom they are made, and that therefore lawmakers ought, in this matter, to respect a reasonable custom of their subjects. This reason and necessity cease to hold in the case of statutes of custom; for they have been made by inferior powers, which ought to be subordinated to those that are superior; and hence these statutes cannot, by the ordinary law, prevail against the laws of superiors, except by special concession.

22.[18] *Answer to the second difficulty.* In answer to the second difficulty, which is taken from the *Code* (VIII. lii (liii). 2), I note, first, that this law also has been variously explained, as is clear from the Gloss (on *Decretum,* Pt. I, dist. xi, can. iv). The most general and probable reply is that this law must be construed as referring to a custom not having the conditions laid down in the *Decretals* (Bk. I, tit. iv, chap. xi). This is the reading of it given by Jason (in addit. to Gloss, on *Institutes,* I. ii, § 9, word *imitantur*), where the Gloss advances a different explanation. The true meaning of the passage is that a custom is not of so great authority as to prevail in opposition to the will of the prince; and this meaning is indicated by the words of the same law, where it says: '[The authority of custom is not slight, but] it will not prevail by its own force [so as to overcome right reason or positive law]'; that is, by its own force and authority. This assertion is in perfect harmony with the fact that custom may be such as to show that the will of the prince has been changed and this, either by the evidence that it gives of such change, or by virtue of some law [in which the conditions, under which his consent is to be presumed, are laid down].

---

17. [*Supra,* Bk. III, chaps. ii and iii, pp. 429 *et seq.*—Tr.]

18. [This Section and the two following are incorrectly numbered in the Latin text.—Tr.]

23. *The answer to the third difficulty.* In reply to the third difficulty, St. Thomas says (I.–II, qu. 97, art. 3, ad 2), that a custom contrary to a law can be established by means of actions which are morally good, and that the custom will, therefore, be a reasonable one. His reason is that a human law can be disobeyed without fault when necessity arises in some particular cases. Whence, if such occasions are frequent, a custom is established through actions contrary to that law, which proves that the law is not advantageous to the community and, consequently, abrogates the law. This reply is also suggested by Panormitanus (on *Decretals,* Bk. I, tit. xxxiv, chap. i, no. 4); and his opinion follows that of Archidiaconus (on *Decretals, ibid.*).

But this reply does not meet the difficulty. The reason is that those actions are not permitted except by way of *epieikeia* because of a present urgent necessity. But such acts do not establish a custom contrary to law, since they are not contrary thereto, nor do they evince in the people a state of mind in opposition to the law, as has been explained above; nor, again, can an action done in virtue of a custom arising from such acts alone be regarded as licit; it will be such, only upon a similar occasion of need, in which case its justification is provided for by *epieikeia.* But if those occasions occur so frequently as to prove the law to be useless, the law is abrogated, not by reason of the custom, but because it has been proved to be burdensome and of no effect in itself; or else it will cease because the end for which it was enacted ceases to avail generally.[19] So St. Thomas himself says [I.–II, qu. 97, art. 3, ad 2] that: 'Such a custom shows that the law is no longer useful.'

Secondly, St. Thomas replies [*ibid.*] that the law is set aside through custom when the latter has been so firmly established that the law no longer seems possible to observe in accordance with the custom of the country. However, should the matter reach this point, there would be not a real abrogation of law, but rather a cessation of the law through a change in the subject-matter. So great a change, however, is not always necessary

19. [Generally: the teaching of canonists is that if the end or purpose of a law ceases to avail for the people generally, the law ceases; not so if it ceases to avail only in particular cases.—REVISER.]

for the abrogation of a law. For a law is often abrogated if there is a concurrence of the circumstances described above, and this, even if the law might be otherwise justly binding, provided the sovereign's will has not tacitly intervened in one or other of the ways we have mentioned.

St. Thomas, therefore, in the solution he has given, apparently wishes only to indicate the ways in which the cessation of a law can take place through custom; and this, without relation to the consent of the prince, but from the nature of the case, as it were. But such a process is, however, not a true abrogation, but a cessation of law. But in the solution that he gives in the passage (I.–II, qu. 97, art. 3, ad 2) he is rather speaking of abrogation properly so called.

24. *It is possible for a custom begun by actions which are bad, because forbidden to derogate from law.* I shall, then, frame my reply to this objection from the principle laid down in Chapter IV of this Book, namely, that a custom may have its inception through actions which are bad because they are forbidden by law, and yet may establish a custom in derogation of law. This is admitted by Cajetan (on I.–II, qu. 97, art. 3, ad 2), as it is by all other writers. Indeed, it is clear from what we have said that in order to effect this sort of abrogation, the customary actions will inevitably be bad at the outset because they are in opposition to a law which is binding, and this, apart from any excuse or plea of ignorance. The reason why these acts are sufficient for abrogation is that, during the development of the custom, they concur not as a cause, but rather as an indication of the will of the prince or of the law; for they can be an evidence of his will even if they are bad. Again, the final result of such a custom is not evil, namely, that actions of the same sort may be done without fault after the abolition of the law; and it is to this that the prince consents when he abrogates the law. And so this custom, even though it is unreasonable in its mode [of introduction] and initiation, is not essentially such (since these acts can become licit) either in the issue effected or in the results that flow from it. The reasons are that the prince can, on the ground of such custom, prudently and reasonably abrogate the law; that when the custom has matured these acts are licit; and finally that the right to do these actions freely thereafter is a just one—for there arises, as it were, an absence of the law, or rather of the prohibition, which prohibition could be reasonably abolished.

It is added by Cajetan (*ibid.*) and Panormitanus (*ibid.*) that although at the beginning those who act against the law commit a fault, yet their successors can presume that the law has ceased to be observed for some reasonable cause. This certainly seems to be generally probable, especially when the abrogation takes place by means of a long-continued prescription. But I maintain that such a presumption as that is not necessary; for even though all the actions were bad, as being done counter to the law before the completion of the time necessary for prescription, or before there has been a sufficient presumption of a tacit will of the prince, nevertheless, when the prescriptive period has elapsed, or a sufficient manifestation of the prince's will made, the law (*lex*) would be abrogated by force of law (*ius*) in general, or the tacit will of the prince. This tacit will of the prince is just, though the acts of the subjects were bad, as has been stated. It is to be noted that such a custom is not, on the ground that it brings about this effect in this way, to be regarded as equivalent to a prescription—as I have shown in the First Chapter.

25. *An objection.* Some will urge, however, that the law [that was abolished] was reasonable (for this follows from the nature of law, and it is assumed that, in this case in question, the law is a true and valid one), and that hence the opposing custom will be unreasonable, and this not only because it has been introduced by acts that are bad, but because it tended to abolish a reasonable law. This would, then, seem to be a procedure contrary to reason; and since the two are direct contradictories, if one is reasonable, the other must be unreasonable.

The solution. My reply is that the same argument was used previously against the express abrogation of a law, and it was then clear that such could be reasonable and just: hence the solution given there will serve for this objection also. Therefore, I maintain that the law [that is abrogated] is not reasonable in the sense that it is necessary, but only in the sense that it was adapted to bringing about certain effects: but notwithstanding these, the abolition of the law and the custom effecting that abolition may be reasonable under other aspects, which are also good and fitting. It is the usual case of two contrary probabilities: because one may have the advantage of a greater probability, the other is not therefore unreasonable: and this is especially so, because a comparison [between contrary probabilities] usually leaves the matter in doubt.

CHAPTER XIX

Does the Abrogation of a Law through Custom Admit of Any Exception or Extension?

1. For the better understanding of the rule laid down in the preceding Chapter, we must discuss some exceptions to it which are frequently advanced; and towards the end of the Chapter we shall see whether the rule admits of any extension.

First exception. The first exception demanding attention has to do with penal laws by which the penalty is imposed by the fact of transgression. Thus, some writers have held that a law of this kind cannot be abrogated by a prescriptive custom, even when it is a reasonable one, since any action counter to such a law is condemned as soon as it is done and incurs the penalty of the law.

Exception rejected. This opinion is noticed by Giovanni d'Andrea and Panormitanus (on *Decretals,* Bk. I, tit. xxxiv, chap. i). Yet this exception has no legal basis; it is contrary to reason, and therefore the above-cited authorities have rightly rejected it. They do so because even a custom opposed to such a law can be reasonable, as is self-evident; and it may, further, serve as a sufficient indication of a tacit will of the legislator to abrogate that law. For this abrogation may be not less expedient for the common good in the case of a penal law than in that of any other legal rule whatever, when it is not adapted to the general conduct of the people, or when experience has shown that it is not profitable to them. Likewise, the words and reasoning of *Decretals,* Bk. I, tit. iv, chap. xi, apply as equally to this kind of law as to others.

Finally, a confirmation of our argument can be drawn from the example of the law (*Extravagantes Communes,* Bk. V, tit. i, chap. i) which prohibits under censure any remuneration accepted for entrance into religious life; and yet through usage this prohibition has, according to a probable opinion, as we have elsewhere said, been wholly abrogated. This is also the view of Navarrus ([in *Enchiridion,*] Chap. xxvii, no. 106), who gives other examples of this sort.

The reasoning in support of the contrary opinion is of no weight; since, notwithstanding the legal condemnation of the action, and the fact that while the law persists, the penalty is incurred by the transgression, it has actually been possible to nullify the force of the law through usage; either by a prescriptive and reasonable custom, or by the tacit consent of the prince. And when the custom has been thus validated, the act is no longer condemned by the law or liable to penalty.

2. *A doubt and a distinction on the above exception that must be noted.* It is seriously doubted whether a custom can derogate from the penalty of a law, while leaving it still binding in conscience. Some writers, in discussing this point, distinguish between a law that imposes its penalty due to actual transgression, and one that merely provides that punishment must be inflicted; and they assert of this latter sort, that there may be a derogation from that part of the law which deals with the penalty. This opinion is certain and generally accepted. The reason here is one peculiar to this kind of law: the penal section of such a law instructs the judge, and is binding upon him; therefore, just as derogation from other laws is possible, so it is possible from this, in so far as it is a precept addressed to the judge.

Alfonso de Castro (*De Potestate Legis Poenalis,* Bk. II, chap. xii), however, denies that this holds true of a law which directly inflicts a penalty or a censure *ipso facto;* and he cites the authority of Hostiensis (on *Decretals,* Bk. I, tit.[1] xxxiv [, no. 1][2] and Tiraqueau in support of his opinion. The latter, however, is speaking of another matter, as I shall prove shortly. Castro's reason may be that if such a law is not itself abrogated, a fault is always committed in violating it; and that, therefore, the penalty is always incurred. Thus, if excommunication is the penalty [attached to a breach of the law], of necessity it follows the violation of the law, since contumacy against the law precedes its violation.[3] The same is true of the other penal effects that are inflicted by the law itself; and hence there can never be a derogation from the law in respect of these effects alone; nor, therefore, can there ever be a derogation from it in respect of the penalty alone. A confirmatory proof [of Castro's assertion] might be drawn from the consideration that such a custom

---

1. [Read 'tit' for 'cap' in Latin text.—Tr.]

2. [Hostiensis says nothing about this matter in his comment on *De Treuga et Pace* (*Decretals,* I. xxxiv).—Reviser.]

3. [*Contumacia* in canon law is not really expressed by the word 'contumacy'. The Latin word means violation of law that is fully deliberate.—Reviser.]

would be unreasonable, since its tendency would be to allow offences to go unpunished.

3. *A penal law, even when imposing a penalty* ipso facto, *may be abrogated through custom.* Nevertheless, we must assert the contrary opinion, in agreement with Panormitanus, Felinus, and commentators generally (on *Decretals,* Bk. I, tit. xxxiv, chap. i). It is that also of Navarrus (*De Regularibus,* Commentary III, no. 55 [consilium 55], and in *Enchiridion,* Chap. xxvii, no. 106).

The first proof of our assertion is inductive. In earlier times the sons of men of the clerical order were made serfs at birth by the law itself, as a punishment for the incontinence of the father (*Decretum,* Pt. II, causa xv, qu. viii, can. iii); but this penalty was abrogated by desuetude, while the same guilt continues to attach to the offence, as the Gloss on that canon notes. Likewise in *Extravagantes Communes* (Bk. III, tit. iv, only chapter) penalties are imposed for actual transgression, which have disappeared through non-usage, even though the law has continued in force, as may be seen in Navarrus (*Enchiridion,* Chap. xxvii, no. 150), where other examples of this kind of abrogation are to be found. We ourselves daily observe the revocation of the penalties of law without the revocation of the laws themselves—as was recently done by Clement VIII [on the *Constitution* of Pope Sixtus V],[4] concerning that regulating the mode of receiving novices into religious institutes. And since derogation can be effected through the laws, it can be effected through custom, as is clear from principles already laid down.

The reason finally is that derogation from a law is possible without the abrogation of the law. This is in accord with the words of the Gloss (on *Digest,* L. xvi. 102): 'For derogation occurs when a part [of the law] is removed; but abrogation, when the whole is annulled.' There can, then, be derogation from the law through custom, although there is no abrogation, as Navarrus rightly concludes (*Consilia,* Bk. I, *De Consuetudine*). The

---

4. [The *Constitution* of Pope Sixtus V, *Cum de Omnibus,* regulated the reception of novices into Religious Orders (1587). This *Constitution* was modified by Pope Clement VIII, in his *Constitution in Suprema* (1603). Cf. Bullarum RP. PP. collected, Rome, 1747, Tom. IX, p. 370, Tom. XI, p. 409.—REVISER.]

reason is that there is a parity between the force of law and that of custom. Therefore, when, for any reason, the various parts of the law are separable, derogation can be made from one portion, while the other is left unaffected. But the penalty of the law can be separated from the guilt incurred by its violation. Custom can, therefore, derogate from the law respecting the imposition of a penalty, and can leave the guilt incurred by its violation intact. The reason is that the penalty in question is not essentially annexed to the transgression, but proceeds from the will of the prince; and his will may be changed with respect to one part of his law, whilst unchanged with respect to another, as is self-evident, and as is proved by usage. And the prince is bound by the law, as to its directive force, even though he is not bound as to its penalty. The Gloss (on *Decretum,* Pt. I, dist. iv, can. vi, word *consuetudine*) is to this effect also, when it states that even though custom can sometimes release [the sinner] from the temporal punishment due to his sin, it cannot release him from the punishment of hell.[5]

4. *Refutation of the basis of the contrary argument.* I reply, then, to the argument of those who hold the opposite thesis, that so long as the custom has not been validated by prescription, or has not prevailed in opposition to the penalty, then it is true that the latter is incurred by a transgression of the law. Nevertheless, it can happen that even though the penalty is incurred, it is never upheld, and that such non-observance might continue during the running of the time required for prescription, or for the period needed to indicate the will of the prince, who knows of and tolerates the non-observance or non-execution of the penalty; and this is, in a way, sufficient for the abrogation of the penalty—even though no custom opposed to the observance of the law had been established.

In reply to the confirmatory proof [for the contrary assertion] given above,[6] it is to be said that the only effect of such a custom is that the punishment fixed by the law is not at once incurred; but not that the superiors lacked power so to punish offenders and ought not to do so: it does not, therefore, follow that the custom is unreasonable. It is the same case as that

---

5. [Release from temporal penalty by custom must refer to a penalty inflicted by some human authority.—Reviser.]

6. [At the end of Sect. 2 of this Chapter, *supra,* pp. 707–8.—Tr.]

in which the penalty of the law is not one incurred by actual transgression, but is to be imposed by the judge, where, even though there has been a derogation from the existing law to the effect that the judge is not bound to impose the penalty fixed by that law, nevertheless, the new rule does not restrain him from imposing some other punishment, if he deems it expedient. Otherwise, the custom of which we are speaking would be an unreasonable one.

5. *In what sense the aforesaid distinction is true.* Still, the above opinion, or distinction, applies in a certain sense to an unreasonable custom opposed to a law, a matter concerning which many jurists say that even though a custom of that kind cannot abrogate the law, it can, nevertheless, remit its penalty.

This is the opinion expressed in three Glosses (on *Decretals,* Bk. I, tit. IV, chap. vii; on *ibid.,* Tit. XI, chap. ii, word *antiqua,* first reply; and on *ibid.,* Bk. II, tit. xxv, chap. i). It is also that given by Rochus (*De Consuetudine,* Chap. xi, no. 33, to no. 8 of Section 1),[7] where he treats this point at length.

Therefore, I maintain that the distinction between a law which imposes a penalty for actual transgression and one which provides that the penalty may be imposed by a judge, is relevant and useful here.[8] For when a penalty is imposed by the law itself, no abrogation of the penalty nor any derogation therefrom is possible through an unreasonable custom alone; for the consent of the prince to remit the entire punishment cannot be indicated by means of such a custom. Nor, again, can such a custom avail to diminish the penalty of a law, if it is unreasonable in respect of that part of the law—for the same reasoning applies here, as I shall make clear immediately. However, when the penalty is one that is to be imposed by a judge, the custom may afford him an excuse, at least, for the reduction of the penalty, for this is within his authority.

---

7. [This reference will be clear if the reader consults *Tractatus Illustrium* (Venice, 1584), Vol. II, pp. 348 *et seq.,* in which this work of Rochus Curtius is contained.— REVISER.] See the bibliography, under Patristic and Postclassical Works Cited by Suárez, Rochus Curtius, *Enarrationes in capitulo 'cum tanto' de consuetudine* (Lyon, 1550).—ED.

8. [This is the well-known distinction between penalties *latae sententiae* and *ferendae sententiae.*—REVISER.]

6. *Observations.* Nevertheless, it is to be noted, in connexion with this thesis, that an unreasonable custom of a community is one thing, but a private custom of offence by an individual is quite another.

The first observation. For the last-named custom cannot, of itself, have the effect of remitting the penalty, even in the forum of human law, but it rather increases it, because it aggravates the guilt, and is a form of violation which is especially detrimental to the common good. The above-cited authorities [, in setting up their thesis,] are thinking not of a private, but of a public custom.

The second observation. With respect to the latter custom, two other considerations can be urged. The first is that it can be understood as exempting from the penalty, or as diminishing it, in two ways: in one, through the abrogation of the law or by some derogation therefrom, at least as to that part of it which deals with the penalty; in the second, by reason of the circumstances of the customary actions, that is, because of the number of those offending against the law and of the frequency with which the law is violated, there comes into being a proper reason for the reduction or remission of the penalty, even if no derogation is made from the law itself.

The third observation. The second consideration to be urged is, that a custom opposed to a penal law can be unreasonable in two ways. First, by its transgression of the law as a whole; that is, both by the commission of a fault against the provisions of the law itself, and by the remission or non-execution of the penalty provided in the law. Secondly, the custom can be unreasonable in so far as it is a transgression of the law, but not in so far as it fails to carry out the punishment annexed to the law—as might be the case where, even though the malice of the transgression is admitted, the penalty is felt to be too harsh, or too little in accord with the people's ways, or is one that gives occasion to more serious transgressions for some other such reason.

7. *What force an unreasonable custom may have [in the abrogation of a penal law].* I say, then, that a custom which is unreasonable in its disregard of the penal section of a law cannot establish a legal immunity from that penalty by the abrogation of the law.

The proof is that it is impossible for an unreasonable custom to abrogate a law (*Decretals,* Bk. I, tit. IV, chap. xi). No custom can, therefore, in any wise, in so far as it is unreasonable, derogate from a law in respect of any part of that law to which it is contrary; for what is true of such custom in relation to a law as a whole, is true of it with respect to parts of a law. Therefore a custom, unreasonable in its non-execution of a penalty, or in its failure to impose the penalty which is fixed by law, can never derogate from the law in question, even in respect of the law as it imposes a penalty. This assertion is applicable as much to a law which provides that the penalty is to be imposed by a judge (*poena ferenda*), as to one which imposes the penalty for actual transgression, as is clear from the proof given above.

A custom unreasonable as a whole, but which is grounded in reason in respect of the disregard of the penalty of the law, can derogate from the penal portion of the law. I add, however, that even though a custom is unreasonable in so far as it involves a breach of the law, it can, if there is good ground for a disregard of the penalty, derogate from that portion of the law which deals with the penalty—and this, both in respect of the part of a law which imposes its penalty for actual transgression, and of one providing that the penalty be imposed by a judge.

We shall demonstrate our assertion by argument from contraries. Every custom, in so far as it is reasonable, can prevail against that part of the law against which the custom stands in opposition, according to the *Decretals* (*ibid.*). Therefore, a custom which is reasonable in disregarding the penalty of the law will be able to derogate from the portion thereof that fixes the penalty; and this, even though it does not remove completely the obligation of the law, since in the latter regard the custom is, in our assumption, unreasonable.

This inference is logically valid, both because the principle on which the argument rests is, with due proportion, applicable here, and because the useful portion of the law is not impaired by that part of it which is of no value when the two are separable. But in the case of the law we are considering, the penalty is separable from the transgression, as has been explained. Then, finally, the prince may justly give his consent to the remission of the penalty, even though the directive force of the law remains unimpaired; hence, he is to be presumed to do so when there exists a reasonable and prescriptive custom to that effect, or one that has been tolerated for a sufficient length of time.

8. *In what way a custom which is unreasonable, in respect of both parts of the law, may afford some excuse for the non-observance of it.* I observe, finally, that even if the custom is wholly unreasonable as to both portions of the law, it may afford some excuse for the non-observance of it as a modifying circumstance—that is, when the law is not one in which the penalty is incurred by actual transgression, but one which provides that the penalty is to be imposed by a judge. And this, I think, is the sense in which the language of the jurists is to be interpreted. And this becomes clear, first, with respect to individual offenders, from the fact that from a public custom made up of actions in violation of law, especially from such a custom when it is tolerated, there results some ignorance of the law whereby the offence comes to be regarded as less serious; or, if not ignorance of the law, such an insensitiveness to the unlawfulness of the act as to lessen the gravity of the fault and, consequently, the liability to punishment.

Secondly, the example of the violation of the law by great numbers of people presents a very strong temptation (as it were) drawing the transgressor on as by an object of vehement passion; and this fact must usually be accounted as a mitigating circumstance in individual violations of the law. It is this kind of mitigation of the penalty that is discussed by the Gloss (on *Decretals,* Bk. I, tit. IV, chap. vii), as well as by Panormitanus in his comment on the same Chapter (no. 5), and is treated with some fullness by Rochus (*De Consuetudine,* Chap. xi, no. 33).

Again, with respect to the community in general, the multitude of offenders gives rise to the occasion for a failure in executing the penalty, for the reason that it is not easy to punish a whole multitude without scandal, or without causing great disorder and greater harm to the community. Neither is it expedient to punish some, but not others, since this also would give rise to scandal on the ground of favouritism. Even when punishment can, for a particular reason, be visited upon some persons, these are usually few in number, and immunity would then result to the community as a whole.

These two modes of release from the penalty of a law are suggested in the *Decretals* (Bk. I, tit. XI, chap. ii). The latter—in respect of the community as a whole—is set forth by Gregory I (in *Decretum,* Pt. I, dist. IV, can. vi) and is suggested by Augustine, in *Letters,* l [= clxxxv, chap. x, no. 45, Migne ed.], cited in *Decretum*, Pt. I, dist. i, can. xxv, more clearly in *Letters*, lxiv [= xxii, chap. i, no. 3, Migne ed.], cited in *Decretum*, Pt. I, dist. xliv, chap. i. It does not, however, apply in the case of a law which imposes its penalty for actual transgression, for a law of that kind makes no distinction of circumstances, and in all cases rules to the same effect.

9. *A doubt.* Finally, a doubt may be raised in this context as to whether it is possible for a custom to cause a relaxation of the direct obligation of a penal law while leaving the obligation of the penalty intact, thus transforming (so to speak) a mixed law into one wholly penal in character. This point was touched upon by Tiraqueau, in commenting on L. *Si unquam,* word *revertatur,*[9] where, in the twenty-fourth note on the distinction between a *poena lata* and a *poena ferenda* (no. 350), he rehearses the distinction applied by a certain Matthieu in the Preface to the *Constitutions* of Clement [*Universitati*]. For when a law imposes its penalty automatically, Matthieu holds that even though the law itself falls into desuetude, the penalty for its violation is incurred. And in support of his opinion, he [i.e. Tiraqueau,] cites *Decretum* (Pt. I, dist. xi, can. viii, *Sext,* Bk. I, tit. ii, chap. ii)[10] and *Decretals* (Bk. III, tit. xviii) without specific explanation. But I find nothing either in the laws cited or in the whole title that has to do with this question. Matthieu holds, however, that when the law is one which provides that the penalty be imposed by a judge, if the law falls into desuetude, the penalty is also abrogated. In support of this distinction he cites a passage from *Decretum*, Pt. I, dist. iv, can. iii—which also proves nothing. Tiraqueau does not comment upon this opinion, but sends the reader to other writers whose names he gives.

10. *The above reason is rejected.* I can see no truth whatever in this opinion. For the custom to which the thesis [of Matthieu] has reference must be either one that is inchoate and [therefore] insufficient for the abrogation of a law; or it must be one that is perfect and complete. The first kind of custom cannot, of itself, derogate from a law in respect of its primary

---

9. [The reference is to Tiraqueau's commentary on a law (*Si unquam*) issued by the Emperors Constantius and Constans to Orphitus (P. V.), and it is found in the *Code* of Justinian, VIII. lvi. 8, and also in the *Theodosian Code*, VIII. xiii. 3.—Reviser.]

10. [There is, however, nothing in this law on desuetude; it refers to ignorance of penalties.—Reviser.]

obligation, as is evident from the principles that we have established in earlier Chapters, and from *Decretals,* Bk. I, tit. IV, chap. xi. Consequently, such a custom has no bearing on the present point, nor can it have any effect on the abrogation of the direct obligation of a law, nor can it do away with the obligation to pay the penalty of the law, whether that is imposed by the law for actual transgression, or is to be imposed by a judge. It cannot do so, because it has not the force to make actions done in violation of the law guiltless, nor is it of itself sufficient for the abrogation of the penalty of the law.

If, however, Matthieu is here speaking of a matured custom, we must ask another question, namely, whether the distinction he lays down in his assertion with respect to the effect of customs abrogating the direct obligation of the two kinds of penal law, is to be understood as being an actual and necessary, or only a possible one. It is neither: for—to test its necessity—it does not necessarily follow that when the abrogation of the direct obligation of the law has been achieved, a penalty imposed by the law itself is incurred through an action done in observance of a custom opposed to the law. Indeed, the contrary is the more probable consequence; for, with the cessation of the guilt, the penalty then should also lapse—and this seems more frequently to be the actual result. Nor, on the other hand, is it a necessary consequence that when the direct obligation of the law has been abrogated, a penalty to be imposed by a judge should lapse; for the custom can be such that it releases the subject from obedience to the law under the pain of guilt, without, however, releasing him from the obligation to pay a penalty for its violation—as I shall prove immediately. The distinction in question is, therefore, one without foundation.

11. *It is possible that derogation may occur from a law respecting the obligation of guilt, while the penalty remains unimpaired.* The difficulty, therefore, [set down at the beginning of Section 9,] can be raised with respect to both kinds of penal law without distinction, and this, on the ground we have just stated, namely, that when the adequate cause has ceased to exist, its effect ceases to exist: therefore, if the guilt due to the breach of the law is removed through custom, the penalty which follows that guilt is removed also, whether it be a penalty incurred or a penalty to be imposed; for, in

the case of both, guilt is the adequate cause of the penalty. A custom established with any other intention would be unreasonable.

Nevertheless, I hold that it is possible for a custom to derogate from a law with respect to the obligation of incurring guilt, whilst the debt of the penalty remains in some cases, that is, where the penalty does not essentially presuppose the presence of guilt. This, I infer, is the position taken on this point by Navarrus (*Commentaria De Lege Poenali in Cap. Fraternitas, Decretum,* Pt. II, causa xii, qu. ii, chap. xi), as is shown by the tenor of his discourse as a whole and especially by that of the last number (consideration 3), which, even though it is imperfectly stated, gives sufficiently clear evidence for this reading.

The proof for this thesis is that derogation from the law is possible, even though it is not abrogated; and there can, therefore, be derogation from any portion thereof which is separable from the other, while the latter remains in full force. But the imposition of a penalty, or a threat of the same, is independent of the obligation of incurring guilt, as is evident from our earlier discussion of the nature of a penal law. Therefore, a law of a mixed character can be derogated from, in respect of its direct and absolute obligation, in such wise that it remains one of a purely penal nature. Nor is such an effect in itself unjust, since, even though a penalty, taken in its strict meaning, has reference only to guilt; nevertheless, considering it in a broad sense as a burden, or a civil penalty, that is, derived from human sources, it is sufficient that it should be related to a [juridical] cause, and (so to speak) to a juridical culpability. Nor is a custom causing such derogation unreasonable, because there may be good reason for mitigating the obligation.

12. Thus, it is possible that many civil laws—imposing fines, prohibiting freedom of the hunt,[11] or the cutting of timber, or the carrying of certain articles out of the country—although in the beginning they may have been directive in nature, can later, through usage, have become merely penal, and thus have changed their character. The reason is that they were treated as such in practice and it was only in that way [, namely, by non-observance] that prescriptive customs were established against them.

---

11. [Read *venari* for *veneri.*—REVISER.]

I added in my assertion, the qualifying note, 'where the penalty does not essentially presuppose the presence of guilt', in order to exclude from this class of laws those to which censures are attached. For derogation is not possible from the obligation of laws which prohibit under pain of censure incurred by actual transgression, unless there is also a derogation from the censure. This is so because a censure intrinsically presupposes guilt and disobedience, but such presupposition is not implied in every penalty taken in a wide sense. Such laws, however, can be abrogated, either absolutely or merely in respect of the censure, as Navarrus holds in his comments on the *Extravagantes Communes* (Bk. III, tit. IV, only chapter) in the aforesaid *Enchiridion* (Chap. xxvii, no. 150).

For the argument in support of the opposite view is of no weight, since, even though the action stands condemned by reason of the law, and the penalty is immediately incurred by those who offended against the law in the beginning, nevertheless, both the obligation and the punishment, or one of them, can be abrogated by reason of a custom and the tacit consent of the prince.

13. *The second exception.* A second [alleged] exception relates to invalidating[12] laws. For many hold that these cannot be abrogated by custom. This conclusion would seem to be supported by the *Decretals* (Bk. IV, tit. XIV, chap. v), inasmuch as it is there stated that custom cannot abrogate the law of the Church forbidding marriage between blood relations.[13] The same is signified in the *Decretals* (*ibid.,* tit. XI, chap. iii), respecting the custom[14] prohibiting marriages between persons who are spiritually related. No other reason, it would seem, can be assigned for that rule except that the law in question is an invalidating one. This seems to be the opinion of Covarruvias (on *Decretals,* Bk. IV [*De Matrimoniis*], pt. II, chap. vi, § 10,

---

12. [Invalidating laws render an act null and void from the beginning, as in the case of certain contracts; disqualifying laws render the person incapable of certain legal acts, as in the case of marriage.—Reviser.]

13. [Such laws were really disqualifying.—Reviser.]

14. [*Consuetudinem* also appears in the 1619 edition, and we must suppose that Suárez was referring to the impediment of spiritual relationship arising in the first instance from custom, just as marriage between Jew and Gentile was forbidden at first, by custom.—Reviser.]

no. 18),[15] and he cites [in no. 35] Driedo (*De Libertate Christiana,* Bk. X, chap. xi [Bk. I, chap. xi]) in support of it. Sánchez [*De Sancto Matrimonii Sacramento*] refers to many others who favour it also.

These writers, although they are apparently speaking specifically on the subject of matrimony, do, however, infer from that matter a general principle, namely, that a custom cannot qualify a person whom the law has disqualified; but every law invalidating a human action disqualifies persons for that action, or for entering upon the contract referred to, as was affirmed by the Council of Trent (Session XXIV, in the decree *De Matrimonio*), and as we have noted above in Book V.[16] Therefore, if a custom cannot qualify a person who is disqualified, so it will be unable to abrogate a law with this invalidating effect; for by abrogating such a law it would qualify the person. In confirmation of this proof, it may be said that an invalidating law renders a person incapable of performing the act with which the rule of the law is concerned; and a custom cannot cancel such an incapacity of a person. This is the common opinion among jurists. It is also that of Felinus (on *Decretals,* Bk. II, tit. xxvi, chap. xi), of Decio (on *Decretals,* Bk. II, tit. i, chap. xiii, no. 12 [Bk. II, tit. ii, chap. xiii, no. 13]) and of Aimone Cravetta (*De Antiquitatibus Temporum,* Pt. IV, § 3). And a proof for this opinion might be drawn from experience, that is, from the general practice in regard to irregularities, censures, and other like canonical impediments, which cannot be removed by custom.

14. *This exception also must not be admitted.* Nevertheless, neither is this exception, in my opinion, to be admitted, because the *Decretals* (Bk. I, tit. iv, chap. xi), sets forth a principle of general application when it says that a human law can be abrogated by a custom that fulfils the two conditions there stated. But such a law, even though it makes an action null and void, is still a human law. Therefore, if a custom, contrary to this law, fulfils these two conditions, it abrogates the law; if, however, it does not fulfil these conditions, it will effect no exception to that law. To say that there cannot be a reasonable custom counter to an invalidating law, is arbitrary. For such a law can be abrogated for a just reason and is often so

---

15. [Covarruvias, *Opera,* Antwerp, 1627, Tom. I, pt. ii, chap. vii, par. 10, no. 35; reference to Driedo is Bk. I, chap. xi, at end.—REVISER.]

16. [Not included in these *Selections.*—TR.]

abrogated, as is evident in the ancient law prohibiting marriage between persons related within the fifth degree, which has now been abolished.[17] A custom, therefore, contrary to an invalidating law of this kind can be reasonable on the same basis, and consequently can also be either prescriptive, if it endures for a long time, or it can indicate the tacit consent of the prince, if he has knowledge of it. It can, therefore, abrogate a law.

A confirmatory argument can be drawn from the admitted principle that a custom can establish an invalidating law, as we have shown; therefore, it can abrogate such a law. The validity of the argument is clear from the fact that the principle is the same in both cases, as is admitted by Covarruvias (*ibid.*); for the consent of the prince is manifested by the custom for either effect, and in both it is possible for the subject-matter to be just and reasonable, as has been explained.

This opinion is set forth in the Gloss (on *Decretum,* Pt. I, dist. VIII, can. vii, word *consuetudinem*), which states that an ineligible person may be made eligible by custom; that is, by the abrogation of the law through which he had been ineligible (*Decretum,* Pt. I, dist. XII, can. viii). The same view is held by Innocent (on *Decretals,* Bk. IV, tit. XI, chap. i, at end), where he is speaking on the subject of matrimony, and of the diriment impediments [thereto], which are those that are chiefly a matter of doubt. This opinion is followed also by Torquemada (on *Decretum,* Pt. I, dist. XXXII, can. xiii, art. 2, [ad 2, no. 10]), by Hostiensis (in Summa on *Decretals,* Bk. IV, tit. XI [rubric, xi, no. 6]), by Gabriel ([on the *Sentences,*] Bk. IV, dist. xlii, qu. 1, art. 3, doubt 6 [sole qu., concl. 9, doubt 6]) and by Sánchez (*De Sancto Matrimonii Sacramento,* Bk. VII, disp. iv, no. 4 [nos. 6 *et seq.*]).

This also is clearly assumed by the Doctors in their assertion that it is possible for a custom to derogate from a law, which gives not only accidental, but also essential form and solemnity to an action, even in the case where that form and solemnity have been established by positive law. This is also the doctrine of Rochus on this point (*De Consuetudine,* Chap. xi, sect. 2, nos. 34 and 35), where he gives certain other examples on this matter.

---

17. [The Church mitigated her prohibition against marriages between blood relations. At present, the prohibition extends to the third collateral degree.—Reviser.]

15. *The reply to the opposing arguments.* My reply to other arguments set forth for the opposite view is, in the first place, that the authorities who hold that the impediments which make marriage invalid cannot be annulled by custom, are not formally in opposition to us. For their arguments are based not upon the general principle that an invalidating law cannot be abrogated by custom, but upon the special condition of such a custom in the matter of matrimony, in which case their opinion is that this custom is, of itself, essentially evil and unreasonable, or, at least, that it has been condemned by the law. The validity of their view thus qualified should be discussed with relation to the subject matter of matrimony; but we shall have something to say in a general way on this point in connexion with the next alleged exception. It is, however, improbable that those writers who maintain the contrary view have thought that every custom opposed to an invalidating law is unreasonable; and this, both because such custom is not always found condemned by law—as is evident—and, again, because it cannot be held with any probability to be so merely in the nature of the case, as I have shown.

16. *Two ways considered in which a person may become legally qualified, through custom.* We must add that a person legally disqualified may be held to become, through custom, again qualified, in either of two ways. First, through an abrogation of the legal rule by which his disability was brought about; and this, we repeat, can be effected through custom. For if that disqualification be a penalty, it can be removed; just as the penalties imposed directly and *ipso facto* by other penal laws can be abrogated, since the principle involved is the same. If, however, the disability is not a penalty, but is imposed because of something unbefitting, or for some other just cause, then we must determine whether this unbefitting factor or cause continues to exist, or has disappeared. For in the first situation, the custom would be unreasonable, and to that extent ineffective; but in the latter, it would be possible for the custom to derogate from law, and bring it about that such disability should no longer be contracted.

A second view might be held on this point, namely, that a person lacking qualification or capacity can have his disability removed by prescription if he gains by the qualification he lacks, without derogation from a general law. But this mode would seem to be an impossible one. It has, however, no bearing upon the matter we are discussing, since we are concerned not with prescription, but with legal custom properly so called. The argument indeed confirms what we have said earlier about the impossibility of the derogation from a law by the private usage of a single person; for it makes it clear that a prescription cannot be established against the prohibition of such a law.

17. *In what sense the above opinion is to be understood.* And taken in this sense, the principle or axiom of the jurists, to which we referred in our discussion of the last exception,[18] is valid, as is clear from the *Decretals* (Bk. I, tit. IV, chap. iv), which they cite in illustration of it. For simple priests cannot, by means of custom of any sort, acquire the right to administer the Sacrament of Penance,[19] since, notwithstanding any prescription or ancient custom whatever, the divine law denying them that right always remains unaffected, and no human custom can prevail against it. The same is true in respect of the positive law; for no disqualified person—for example, no illegitimate person—can, through his own custom, obtain by prescription a removal of his disability. The reason is that the invalidating ecclesiastical law [in that case] always remains in full force, even though a general custom can effect a derogation from such a law. Thus, the argument for the contrary opinion[20] based upon an induction from the fact that custom cannot remove censures and the like, is of no avail against our thesis. For a custom cannot effect the removal of an excommunication without absolution, solely through some usage; but by derogating from the law which established excommunication as a penalty, can bring it about that this penalty is no longer incurred.[21] The same principle holds in respect of similar impediments.

---

18. [*Cf.* Sect. 13 of this Chapter, *supra,* p. 717.—Tr.]

19. [A simple priest is one who has not received jurisdiction and approbation from his Ordinary to minister the Sacrament of Penance. Attempted administration, outside the danger of death, would have been invalid, because jurisdiction, being a positive grant, cannot be presumed.—Reviser.]

20. [At the end of Sect. 13, *supra,* p. 718.—Tr.]

21. [The absolution or removal of an excommunication is a positive exercise of jurisdiction, and, therefore, no custom could ever take the place of such a positive act.—Reviser.]

18. *The third exception.* The third exception relates to a law which not only enjoins certain actions, but also prohibits and forbids every custom of an opposite nature, and invalidates any such custom, not only past, but future.

The three distinctions to be made. For the discussion of this exception it will be necessary to distinguish three things, as we did in an earlier chapter, namely, the revocation, the prohibition, and the reprobation of a custom.

What effect is produced by the revocation of a custom. For it is certain that, in itself, the express revocation of a custom by a clause attached to a human law, does not prevent the possibility of derogation from such a law, by means of a subsequent custom. The reason is that the law does not prohibit a custom in the future, as we proved above. Therefore, notwithstanding the revocation of the past custom, it is possible for a subsequent one to be just and reasonable as being one that has not been forbidden, and is not in its character essentially bad or lacking all reason: to assume that it must be such would be gratuitous. Therefore it can, by running the proper time, be established by prescription, whether the legislator has no knowledge of it, or whether, having knowledge of the custom, he tolerates it in such wise that his tacit consent is made manifest. Thus, such a custom can have the force of abrogating that kind of law. And so, commonly, exception is not made in the case of a law of this sort, as is evident from the previous discussion, and from what is said by Covarruvias (in *Variarum Resolutionum*, Bk. III, chap. xiii, no. 4). Reference may be made also to the discussion of this point by Burgos de Paz (Law 1, *Tauri.*, nos. 464 and 479).

19. *What effect the prohibition of a custom has.* But in the case of a law forbidding every custom of a contrary nature, even for the future, it might seem that an exception [to our rule] is highly probable [for the following reasons].

The first argument. First, because the custom in question, by the very fact that it is specifically prohibited, would seem to be unreasonable. Hence, it can never be validated by prescription, and so, can never abrogate the law.

The second argument. Secondly, because otherwise those words of the law which forbid a future custom would have no meaning. This is clear from the fact that the actions by which the custom could be established or set on foot, quite apart from the clause in which a future custom is prohibited, have been forbidden by the provisions of the law itself; the repetition of such actions is, therefore, obviously forbidden also. Therefore, for the prohibition of a custom of fact, those words were not necessary. They were, therefore, especially intended as forbidding a custom of law, unless we are to regard them as superfluous. Therefore, they either effectively prohibit this custom, so that its establishment in opposition to the law is impossible, and our thesis is established; or they do not produce this effect, and are meaningless, since, in that case, they add no force to the prohibition of the custom, and there is no other moral effect that they can have.

The third argument. Thirdly, because, in the case of customs of prescription, by the very fact that the law forbids that a certain thing can be claimed by prescription, it is impossible to secure its prescription by any custom whatever (*Digest,* XLI. iii. 24). So, also, by the very fact that the law forbids any custom which is contrary to that law, the effectual result is that no custom can become prescriptive or can prevail.

20. *The fourth argument.* Fourthly, because a custom cannot abrogate a law save by the tacit consent of the prince, as has been said; this consent, however, cannot be presumed where the legislator expressly withholds his consent to a future custom by a prohibition of such custom incorporated in his law. Therefore, . . .

The fifth argument. Fifthly, because if the prince should declare that a law or a privilege can not be abrogated, unless by his express consent, that law or privilege could not be annulled through his tacit consent. But he does that precisely when he forbids the introduction of any custom contrary to his law. Therefore, . . .

The final argument. Finally, because it is possible for a lawmaker to make void future contracts: therefore, he will be able also to make invalid a future custom; and this is his intention when he forbids such a custom, otherwise the prohibition would be, as we have contended, a useless one. Therefore, . . .

This exception[22] is indicated in the Gloss (on *Sext,* Bk. I, tit. II, chap. i); it is also found much more clearly stated in another Gloss (on

22. [*Cf.* Sect. 18, *supra,* p. 722.—TR.]

Extravagantes, Tit. I, chap. ii). It would seem to have been defended also by Antonio de Butrio in his comment (*De Consuetudine* Chap. xi), by St. Antoninus ([*Summa,*] Pt. I, tit. xvi, § 6), by Sylvester (word *consuetudo,* Qu. 6), by Angelus de Clavasio ([*Summa, Consuetudo,*] no. 9), by Baldus and by Bartolus (in Tract. *De Dotibus,* Pt. VI, privil. ii, nos. 18 and 19)[23] and finally, by Soto (*De Iustitia,* Bk. I, qu. vii, art. 2, words *Hoc ergo memoriae*). The same was apparently the view of Covarruvias (*Variarum Resolutionum,* Bk. III, chap. xiii, no. 4), and of many other authorities to whom he refers.

21. *A simple prohibition of a future custom by the law does not make impossible the introduction of such a custom.* Nevertheless, I hold it as the more probable opinion that, if the law does no more than prohibit a future custom, and does not reprobate it, a subsequent custom which has the effect of abrogating the law may be introduced.

This is the doctrine of Navarrus (in Comment. *De Alienatione Rerum Ecclesiasticorum ac De Spoliis,* § 14, no. 8), a doctrine which he drew from the Gloss (on the *Constitutions* of Clement, Bk. I, tit. iii, chap. viii). Vázquez (on I.–II, Disp. 177, last chap.) holds this opinion also, as does Soto but with some qualification. B. Medina (on I.–II, Qu. 97, art. 3) and Gutiérrez (*Practicarum Quaestionum Civilium,* Bk. III, chap. xxxii [quest. xxxi]) agree with this teaching also. Covarruvias [*Variarum Resolutionum, ibid.*] and others do not oppose it, although they do not state it in so definite a way.

The reason for our conclusion must be gathered from the foregoing discussion: namely, that, despite a legal prohibition of that kind, it is possible for the subsequent custom not to be an unreasonable one, as we have demonstrated. And since the condition as to the reasonableness of the custom can be thus fulfilled, so also may that which relates to the sufficiency of its length of observance. And this either by prescription, where the prince has no knowledge of the custom, or by an observance sufficient to indicate the tacit consent of the prince in cases where he has knowledge of and tolerates the custom. This principle is obvious, and has been sufficiently proved above.

23. [*Digest,* Bk. XXIV, chap. iii, in Bartolus, *Prima Super Infortiato,* nos. 18, 19.—REVISER.]

Such a custom can, therefore, bring about the abrogation of that kind of law in two ways. It can do so, first, when the custom is reasonable and prescriptive, by the operation of the principle laid down in the *Decretals* (Bk. I, tit. IV, chap. xi); for no sound reason can be given for not applying it here, the law in question being a human law, however strictly it may prohibit a future custom. Or again it can, at least, avail for this effect, on grounds of natural [as distinguished from legal] reason, when the prince has had knowledge of it and it has run for a sufficient time to be evidence of his tacit will, for his will has the power to effect the revocation of the earlier law, notwithstanding any prohibition embodied in it. For this very prohibition of a future custom issued solely from the consent of the prince; and so, later, when that sovereign or his successor has come to a knowledge of and tolerated the custom [prohibited by the law], and has tacitly consented to it, he changes his former will, and in so doing abrogates the prohibiting law completely. A confirmation of this proof will follow from the refutation of the arguments[24] offered in support of the contrary opinion.

22. *The answer to the first argument.* The first [of the six arguments alleged,] we deny, for the fact that a custom is unreasonable is one thing, but that it is forbidden is quite another: a custom can be prohibited even when it is not unreasonable; and again, a mere prohibition taken by itself does not make a custom unreasonable, as I have demonstrated above.

The answer to the second argument. My reply to the second argument, which is not so easily disposed of, is that the first effect of the legal prohibition is that in the case of doubt—where, that is, the contrary is not clearly evident and established by proof—the custom is presumed to be unreasonable. For since the superior has specifically prohibited the custom, it would seem to be clear that he has done so because he has judged it to be an unreasonable one. This, I have said, is especially true when the matter is doubtful, as can be seen from the arguments offered by Rochus Curtius (*De Consuetudine,* Chap. xi, sect. 7, no. 24). A second possible effect of the prohibition is that the governors and guardians of the laws will be more vigilant, and will not permit the custom in question to be introduced a

---

24. [In Sect. 19, *supra*, p. 722.—Tr.]

second time. A third is that the subjects of the law are probably, because of this specific declaration of the superior's will, bound under an especially strict obligation to abstain from the following of that custom. The fourth and chief effect of such prohibition may be this, namely, that the custom will never, or only very rarely, be able to effect a derogation from the law, save after a long period of time and the establishment of a legal prescription, since in a shorter period, the consent of the prince can hardly be presumed, even if he has knowledge of the custom, or, at all events, many more circumstances must be present and a much longer time than ordinarily is necessary for justifying a presumption of the superior's will as favouring a custom in opposition to such a law; the reason being that he has expressly and specifically declared a contrary will in the prohibiting clause of his law. It is in this sense, I believe, that Soto's opinion on this matter is to be understood.

23. *The answer to the third argument.* The logical nexus of the demonstration in the third argument [Section 19, at the end] for the opposite view is denied.[25] For in the case of a true, private prescription, the will of the prince is never presumed to have changed; nor is there any legal rule that could give justification for the prescription thus prohibited by the law; but the custom at present under discussion has always the support of the law which gives validity to a reasonable and prescriptive custom; as well as that of the principle of natural reason [which gives the same effect to a custom sufficient to manifest] the tacit will of the superior to derogate from the law previously in force.

The answer to the fourth argument. In reply to the fourth argument, I deny the minor premiss. For, even though the prince has expressly prohibited a future custom, he is free to change his will; moreover, he has never withdrawn its force from a prescriptive custom that is reasonable.

The answer to the fifth argument. The major premiss of the fifth argument is true only if the prince holds firmly to his purpose; but he is free to change his mind [, in which case the argument fails]. Again, just as express derogation from laws carrying a prohibiting clause is made by

25. [For the reason, apparently, that there is no parity between a prescription properly so called and a custom of the sort here discussed.—TR.]

terms that are (as it were) retroactive, as by derogation from a law by the special clause: 'Even if the law have such and such a clause'; or, again, by derogation in a general formula, as: 'Under whatsoever form of words the law was enacted'; so, too, in custom, all this retroaction and derogation is implicit, inasmuch as the custom manifests the final will of the prince which can prevail in opposition to every former law. The minor premiss also of this argumentation can be denied, for to forbid the introduction of a future custom, and to rule that a law is not to suffer abrogation except by an express act, are not prohibitions of the same force.

The answer to the sixth argument. With regard to the sixth argument, it can be denied that this prohibition [of a future custom] is equivalent to an invalidation. The reason is that without invalidating the custom, the prohibition can have other effects, as we pointed out in our reply to the second argument.[26] To the objection that at times the word 'invalidate' is used in these clauses—as is to be seen from the above-cited *Extravagantes Communes* (Bk. I, tit. III, chap. ii)—I answer that an invalidation of this kind always depends upon the will of the prince; and that, therefore, since a custom can in the final issue be evidence of a contrary will on the part of the sovereign, a custom can, the invalidating clause notwithstanding, have its effect in that way in this case also—as we have shown in our demonstration that an invalidating law can be abrogated by custom.

24. *How a custom reprobated by a law can prevail against that law.* Coming now to the third principal point[27] of our present inquiry, that is, whether a custom can annul a law that reprobates it, I assert that a contrary custom cannot abrogate a law of this kind unless there has been so great a change in the circumstances that there is certain evidence that this new situation has made the custom one of a different character. An abrogation of this kind is not, therefore, a real exception to the rule that we have laid down.

The first member of our thesis is the common teaching on this point. There is little or no dissent with respect to it, as is evident from the opinion of Panormitanus (on *Decretals,* Bk. II, tit. XIX, chap. ii, nos. 7 and 8), and from that of other commentators on that Chapter. It is found also in the

26. [In Sect. 22, *supra*, p. 725.—Tr.]
27. [Cf. Sect. 18, *supra*, p. 722.—Tr.]

Gloss (on *Sext,* Bk. III, tit. iii, only chapter, word *improbantes* taken with the word *receperit*) and others on that chapter. This doctrine is followed by Navarrus and Covarruvias (*supra,* p. 724), and many other writers to whom they refer. Tiraqueau also defends this thesis in *De Utroque Retractu* (in Preface, Nos. 18 and 19).

The basis of this opinion is that such a custom is always unreasonable, as has been proved above; and that it can never, therefore, possess the conditions for an effective custom laid down in *Decretals,* Bk. I, tit. IV, chap. xi, nor can it be sufficient evidence of the tacit will of the prince.

The second part of our thesis is generally received doctrine, also. Covarruvias gives numerous references to writers who defend this opinion; and Sánchez, many more (*De Sancto Matrimonii Sacramento,* Bk. VII, disp. iv, no. 14).

The reason here is also clear: the law does not always reprobate a custom because it is intrinsically evil; it may do so because of some [annexed] danger, or because such condemnation is judged to be expedient under the circumstances in order to preclude certain effects detrimental to the well-being of the commonwealth or of the Church. In matters of this kind, it frequently happens that a custom which at one time is reasonable, is not so at another; and so, a custom unreasonable in one set of circumstances may not be so in another. Therefore, if the latter kind of reversal occurs in the case of a custom reprobated by law, the custom, notwithstanding the condemnation, ceases to be unreasonable: and this, either because at this later time the custom is, practically, not the custom mentioned by the law, or, because the portion of the law containing the condemnation has completely lapsed in its entire application, and so, too, its effect has lapsed. This law can, therefore, now be abrogated by the custom in question.

The third portion of our thesis is, then, easily proved; for the custom derogating from the law is, under these circumstances, always a reasonable one; and a custom is never incapable of producing this effect, except when it is either unreasonable, or has not been validated by legal prescription, or when it is insufficient as an indication of the will of the prince. There is, therefore, in the abrogation of this kind of law, under these conditions, no exception to the rule that we have laid down.

25. *The fourth exception.* A fourth exception to that rule is maintained by many canonists: namely, that no law [of the Church] regarding matters connected with the Sacraments can be abrogated by a prescriptive custom.

The first proof in support of this thesis is drawn from the *Decretals* (Bk. I, tit. xi, chap. ii), where a custom allowing the promotion of candidates to Sacred Orders outside Quarter tense[28] is condemned. The second is drawn from the *Decretals* (Bk. IV, tit. xi, chap. iii), where similar customs are reprobated; and the third from (*ibid.,* tit. xiv, chap. v), where another such custom is rejected. The fourth is from the *Constitutions* of Clement (Bk. I, tit. vi, chap. iii), wherein is confirmed a custom touching the age of those who are to be raised to Holy Orders, a custom which had been introduced in opposition to the ancient canons, thus indicating that the custom could not have prevailed unless the Pope himself had confirmed it. Whence Hostiensis (in *Summa,* on *Decretals,* Bk. IV, tit. xxi, no. 2 [no. 3], at end) and some others hold that in these matters no custom can prevail unless there has been a law expressly derogating from the previously existing law. Others prefer the rule which requires at least a knowledge of the custom on the part of the Pope and his tacit consent. This is held by Richard Middleton (on the *Sentences,* Bk. IV, dist. xlii, art. 3, qu. 2) and by the Gloss, together with the comments of the Doctors (on *Decretals,* Bk. IV, tit. xxi, chap. iii). It is defended also by many other writers whose names are given by Sánchez.

26. *The above exception is rejected.* Nevertheless, even this exception is not necessary: and this, for the reason that the laws cited give no ground for it. Again the rule of *Decretals,* Bk. I, tit. iv, chap. xi, is of general application; and there would seem to be no sound reason for making an exception in our present case. This is the view of many of the authorities whom I have cited above, and these deny in general the necessity of the prince's knowledge for this effect. De la Palu is especially clear upon this point ([on the *Sentences,*] Bk. IV, dist. xlii, qu. 3, art. 1); and thereon also (*Supplement* to Gabriel on the *Sentences, ibid.,* qu. 2, art. 2 [sole qu., doubt 6]). Sánchez holds this opinion and cites for it the authority of many other

---

28. [That is, the *quatuor tempora,* the beginnings of the ecclesiastical seasons, called Ember Weeks, on the Saturdays of which Sacred Orders could be bestowed.—Reviser.]

writers (*De Sancto Matrimonii Sacramento,* Bk. II [Bk. VII], disp. lxxxii, no. 20). Navarrus enlarges on this point (in *Enchiridion,* Chap. xxii, no. 83 [*De Benedictione Nuptiarum*]), where he censures Rochus for his doubt on this point (*De Consuetudine,* Chap. xi, sect. 4, no. 27). Rochus, however, inclines sufficiently to this opinion, and confirms it, but wishes to dissent modestly from the opinion of the ancient Doctors.

Navarrus develops his proof of this assertion from the same *Decretals,* Bk. I, tit. xi, chap. ii [*Consilia,* Bk. I, *Consilium de Temporibus Ordinationum,* pp. 94 *et seq.*], which Hostiensis cited for his thesis. He does so, on the ground that the ancient custom spoken of in that law is shown to have been valid up to the time of its revocation by the law, by the following words: 'Were it not for the great number [of ordained men] affected, and were it not for an ancient custom of the country, the persons who have been ordained in this manner ought not to be allowed to exercise the ministry, which they have received.' The Gloss here (on word *antiqua,* near the end) understands the word 'ancient' as meaning a reasonable and prescriptive custom, and that [such a custom] had established an excuse from fault, even in that matter. Thus, the first argument for the contrary thesis[29] is answered.

A confirmation of our refutation of Hostiensis's proof is to be found also in the words, 'unless there is a custom of the Church [to the contrary]' (*Decretals,* Bk. IV, tit. xi, chap. i), where the reference is to a matter touching the Sacraments. It is true that the custom there spoken of is one not directly counter to a preceptive law, but one superior to it, or counter to a permissive law. But surely, if it is possible for a custom to introduce a new law and obligation in matters relating to the Sacraments, there is no reason why it cannot abrogate laws relating to such matters.

We have here the principle for the refutation of the second and third arguments, of our opponents. For those laws do not assert that the customs in question could not be valid because they dealt with matters relating to the Sacraments, but because they are either judged to be unreasonable, or are reprobated for causes that were just.

---

29. [In Sect. 25, *supra,* p. 729.—Tr.]

On the other hand, however, the answer to be given to the fourth argument, that drawn from the *Constitutions* of Clement, is that the custom there referred to was confirmed, because the Pope wished to give it his express approbation, and not because it could not have prevailed antecedently against the ancient canons without such approbation.

27. *The rule stated at the beginning of Chap. XVIII suffers no exception.* Whence my final conclusion is that the rule we have given suffers no exception; since, besides those we have considered, no other objections that might be valid against our thesis suggest themselves, nor do the Doctors mention any. In any case, the principles we have set forth would seem to apply with like effect against any other such exception that might be brought up. Hence, Navarrus (*Consilia,* Bk. I: *De Maioritate et Obedientia,* cons. iii) rightly observed that, 'every custom of a reasonable and prescriptive character is valid against any human law whatever'. The addition of the words 'every' and 'whatever' sufficiently signify that in his opinion there is no room for an exception. Finally, whenever a custom, even though it is of long standing and general in character, is stated by the law as not prevailing over a law, a reason is always given for this rejection of the custom: as, that it is unreasonable or a corruption of law, or the like. This is proof that a custom which is reasonable and of a sufficient antiquity lacks nothing for effecting a derogation from a law.

28. *Of the extension of custom. That a custom contrary to law can be extended is denied by Abbas, Jason, Innocent, and Rochus.* It remains now to inquire whether our rule[30] admits of any extension, or enlargement. But on this point the jurists generally, even though they admit extension in the case of a custom outside the law, lay down the rule that a custom contrary to law and abrogating it is not to be extended. This is the view of Abbas [, i.e. Panormitanus,] (on *Decretals,* Bk. I, tit. IV, chap. ii, last no.), as well as that of Innocent on the same law. This opinion is developed at length by Jason also (on *Digest,* I. iii. 32 [, nos. 14, 21]). Rochus gives the question extensive treatment (*De Consuetudine,* Chap. xi, sect. 4, from no. 7 to no. 23), where he sets down nine conditions [under which this rule may hold]. A discussion of these conditions is not necessary here; for, as I have

---

30. [Set forth at the beginning of Chap. XVIII.—Tr.]

said, the principle which applies here is that which applies in the case of written laws or statutes. And therefore, just as one law revoking another is not regarded in itself and generally speaking to be extended, for the reason that it is held to be irksome and, in a certain sense, a burden—as is clear from the principle that the amendment of laws is to be avoided—so also a custom abrogating a law is held to be irksome and, in a certain sense, a departure from normal ways, and is for this reason restricted as to its legal bearing, and is not to be extended. Should the matter of the custom be, however, of such a nature that the custom can be held to be in every way favourable, it may receive that extension which favourable grants allow, provided such extension does not go beyond the bounds of the custom— which, in Baldus's phrase, is to be observed with perfect exactitude (on *Code*, VI. i. 4, no. 20 [no. 17]). Of this sort of extension, as it is treated by the jurists, nothing further need be said here.

29. *What effect has a custom contrary to laws?* There remains, however, the particular question whether a custom contrary to law can not only derogate from law, but introduce new contrary law also. For sometimes a law may be abolished in such a way that it merely ceases to exist; that is, in such a way that it is no longer binding. In this case the acts specified by it are not forbidden, nor, on the other hand, are actions contrary to it prescribed. Again, at times, a law is abolished by (as it were) a contrary disposition; that is, an action that the abolished law forbade is enjoined, or an action that was of obligation under the earlier law is forbidden. I hold that both kinds of derogation can be introduced by legitimate custom.

Solution. The proof of this assertion is that both these effects are possible through the agency of written law: they are, therefore, equally so through custom. Likewise, a custom can be established in opposition to an existing law, for any one of the above-named reasons and purposes, and, at the same time, it may be reasonable and validated by an adequate prescription.

In order, however, to clarify our notions concerning this prescription, there remains the further question whether these two effects may be produced simultaneously, and through one and the same custom, or whether they must be brought about only successively. That they can be brought about successively is very obvious. The reason is that the law can be first abrogated in a purely negative way by a legitimate custom, and this, with the sole purpose of removing the obligation; and afterwards the custom may be continued to be observed with the object of establishing a law. This continuance will be, in effect, a wholly new custom, for from the time when the abrogation of the law occurred, the custom has been a custom not contrary to the law, but outside existing law. As such, then, it will have to run for another period in order to establish a law; that period, however, need not be greater than the usual long time which suffices for the introduction of custom outside law.

30. *A difficulty.* The point of the question is, then, whether both of these results can be accomplished at the same time, and by the same actions. It would seem that this is not possible, for the reason that so long as the existing law stands in opposition, it is impossible for another to be introduced, since the express consent of the prince cannot be in contradiction to his tacit consent. Therefore, it is necessary that the law previously existing be abrogated, in order that another may be introduced. It is, therefore, set down in *Las Siete Partidas* (Pt. I, tit. ii, law 3) that it is not possible for a usage contrary to law to establish a new legal rule, unless the earlier law be first abolished.

Nevertheless, I maintain that a law may be annulled, and its contrary established at the same time, and by the same custom. The proof is that a custom may be reasonable in both respects, and be observed with the intention of bringing in both at the same time; it can therefore, after it has run a sufficient length of time, be validated either by prescription in respect of both its effects, or be evidence of the tacit consent of the prince with respect to both.

A confirmatory proof of this conclusion is that by one action, expressly making a law contrary to a previously existing one, the first can be abolished, and the other expressly established. The same, therefore, is true of a tacit operation of the same kind; for the reason in each case is the same. Nor does the proof to the contrary hold, since for this effect a priority in the order of nature—to use our common terminology—is sufficient. For it is true that a custom contrary to a law cannot establish a new law unless the contrary legal rule is first abolished; it is, however, sufficient if the abolition of the earlier law take place at the same time, and that the abrogation of the prior law occur first—in the order of nature according to our mode of conceiving the matter. For, in that order, the abolition of the earlier law is absolutely the earlier effect, because abolition of the law is a necessary disposition for the establishment of the later one; and this disposition is created not proximately and immediately and (as it were) formally, through the introduction of a new law, but through the abrogation of the old one, and this abrogation can, absolutely speaking, be accomplished without the establishment of a new legal rule. And in this sense, the law [of *Las Siete Partidas*] can be sufficiently intelligible, whatever Gregory López, in his comment thereon, may appear to think.

CHAPTER XX

In What Ways Custom May Be Changed

1. *Of the change of custom.* Although we have given, in the preceding Book,[1] some general attention to the subject of change in written human law, and while the principles there set forth are for the most part applicable to consuetudinary law, we must, nevertheless, take up here the discussion of certain other points which would seem to be peculiar to that kind of law.

Two modes of change. Change in the written law can—as we have seen in an earlier book of this treatise[2]—be effected in two ways: in the one, the change is (as it were) intrinsic, that is, brought about by mere cessation due to conflicting circumstances; in the other, the alteration is induced by the contrary action of some external agency. Custom also can be changed in both these ways. With regard to the first of these, we need add nothing to what we have said in the passage referred to, save that a custom may, of itself, cease to exist on the sole ground of a change in the circumstances affecting the rectitude or the general usefulness of its subject-matter, and this, without a revocation by any external agency. That the subject-matter of a custom can change in this way is self-evident: both from experience, and also from the natural condition of things human. That this change in

1. [Bk. VI, chap. ix, sections 1, 9, *supra*, pp. 477, 486.—Tr.]
2. [Bk. VI, chap. ix, sections 1, 9, *supra*, pp. 477, 486.—Tr.]

the matter of a custom may be such that the custom of itself ceases to be and loses its binding force, is clear from the principle that the custom must always have a good ground in reason, to be established, and must have been introduced to realize some sufficient purpose: the essential nature of law demands this. If, therefore, the matter is so changed that the reason and purpose of the custom disappear, not only in individual cases, but universally, then the obligation of the custom will lapse also.

Indeed, should the change in circumstances be such that the purpose for which the custom was introduced does not so much disappear as work harmful effect, then there may be a positive duty not to observe the custom. This would be the case should the custom begin to be a moral occasion of sin,[3] or be otherwise harmful to the general good of the commonwealth. The same will be true, if, in some particular case, the reason for the custom not only ceases to be, but would even be harmful. This principle we have shown to be true of written law, and it is equally applicable to custom.

Finally, it is clear that this is the only way in which custom can, of itself, cease to exist; since it is not dependent upon any other cause as an active principle to preserve it (as it were) in being. For although the custom may depend upon the will of the prince, the fact that he does not revoke it, is enough for its preservation; and the same is true also of the popular will, in so far as the custom is dependent upon it.

2. *The revocation of a custom.* We shall, therefore, without further discussion of this kind of change, give our exclusive attention to such revocation of custom as is brought about by the prince through a law, or through an express declaration of his will, or that which is effected by the people through an expression of a contrary will. These two kinds of revocation, with which many laws deal, have been set forth in [*Las Siete Partidas,*] Part I, tit. ii, law 6. And by revocation we mean in this connexion not only the complete abrogation, but also the partial derogation of a legal custom, since the two are of a similar nature. It will not be necessary in this discussion of the law of custom to say anything of dispensation, for the reason that it is included either under partial revocation, or, in so far

---

3. [A moral occasion of sin, that is, observance of the custom, would be an incitement to men to do evil. Its influence would be on the passions or will of men.—REVISER.]

as it differs from that, either pertains to the matter of privilege—of which we shall speak in the following Book[4]—or will be the same in principle as dispensation in human law, of which we have spoken at length in a previous Book.[5]

3. *A custom is revoked by a subsequent law in opposition thereto.* My first assertion, then, is that a custom is revoked by a subsequent law in opposition to it, especially when the legislator has knowledge of the custom. This assertion assumes authority in the prince who has power to make laws that may revoke custom. Such is manifest from *Decretals* (Bk. I, tit. ɪᴠ, chap. ix), from *Sext* (Bk. I, tit. ɪɪ, chap. i), and from *Code* (VIII. lii (liii). 2). For what is there stated, namely, that custom has not force sufficient to prevail over law, is especially true in one sense of a law enacted subsequent to a custom. The reason is clear, since the custom has no force save through the consent, at least in a tacit form, of him who has the power to make the law; and therefore, through his will the custom may be revoked, and lose all its force, and even be forbidden, and its contrary prescribed. For if it is possible for the prince, through a subsequent law, to revoke a prior one made by his express will, why is it not possible for him to revoke, by a later rule of law which has his explicit approval, a custom introduced with his tacit consent? On this point, therefore, there is no controversy nor any reason for doubt—if the clause is added: 'Custom to the contrary notwithstanding'—that, then, a custom is undoubtedly revoked, because the legislator could not express his will more unmistakably.

4. *An objection.* An objection may be offered at this point, from the law on *Feuds* [law *De Feudi Cognit.*, Bk. II *Feudorum*, tit. i],[6] which states that, 'The authority of the Roman laws is not of small moment, but it does not extend so far as to override usage and the general customs of the people.'

Objection answered. My reply, in the first place, is that the Gloss understands this to be true of feudal matters alone, but gives no reason for so doing. Cujas, in his notes on this law, understands it to refer to a custom

---

4. [Not included in these *Selections.*—Tʀ.]
5. [Book III, *supra*, p. 388.—Tʀ.]
6. [A collection of Lombard feudal customs was added to the collections of Roman Civil Law, and appears under the title, *Feudorum Libri cum Fragmentis.*—Rᴇᴠɪsᴇʀ.]

confirmed by a decision given in a trial when the custom is impugned. But even this kind of custom may be abolished by law. Others interpret the law in question as referring only to places not under the authority of Rome, where the laws of the Romans have not the force of law, save in so far as they have been accepted by the local sovereigns, and the law says that it is in such localities that custom should have preference over the laws of Rome. But, first of all, this reasoning makes the opinion foolish, for what is strange in the fact that a law of another jurisdiction that has no power to bind, should not prevail in the face of a custom which is binding and peculiar to the place? Again, the reasoning there is far from adequate, as Obertus's note on the law makes clear: 'Decisions on feuds are usually said to be contrary to our own legal rules.' Whence Baldus says that the meaning there is that feudal litigation is to be settled by custom, and not through the written laws, whether of Rome or of the Lombards. Baldus is here referring, it is my opinion, to general laws; for if there were in force special written laws, enacted by competent authority, relating to feudal tenures, these would prevail over custom, in accordance with the rule we have laid down. Hence the meaning is that in feudal questions, the customs peculiar to these must be followed, notwithstanding the provisions of general written laws to the contrary. Or at least these words may be held to apply to prescriptive custom, upon which feudal rights are for the most part founded; and the reason is that the Roman laws are not prejudicial to this sort of custom, inasmuch as they do not abolish rights and ownerships acquired by prescriptive custom.

5. This assertion[7] applies especially to laws which contain the clause 'notwithstanding an existing custom', since no clearer statement of the legislator's will is possible. But when no such clause is added to the law, there is required, first of all, that there be between the law and the custom a contrariety such that the law cannot be obeyed if the custom is observed. For if they can be reconciled in such wise that the law can have its own effect without derogation from the custom—if necessary even by as strict an interpretation as the words of the law will bear, without destroying their proper meaning—the law is to be given an interpretation admitting

7. [*Supra*, p. 735.—TR.]

of such reconciliation. The reason is that the amendment of a law is to be avoided; and much more so that of a custom so far as is possible: and this, both on the ground that a custom becomes (as it were) a second nature, and hence a change in it is not easily made; and again, because the law should be in harmony with the general conduct of the people who observe the laws.

6. *What is required in order that a custom be revoked by a law?* In order, then, that a law revoke a custom by its own force and without the aid of an express revoking clause, it is necessary that the two be in every way repugnant and opposed to each other. Further, the consent of the prince is essential, since through that the revocation is accomplished; and since, for his consent, knowledge of the custom is a prerequisite, he must be presumed to have such knowledge. And it was for this reason that this condition—around which are centred all the difficulties of our present question—was set down by the Pope [as necessary for the revocation of custom by a law], in the *Sext* (Bk. I, tit. ii, chap. i).

7. *First inference: that a general custom is revoked by a general law.* From that text and the condition it lays down, it is inferred, first, that when, for example, a custom is universal—one, that is, which has been observed throughout the entire Church—and a law in opposition to it is enacted for the Universal Church, the custom is wholly annulled by the law, even though the law contain no derogating clause. This is the opinion of Baldus and other commentators (on *Code,* VIII. lii (liii). 2). It is that set forth by Felinus (on *Decretals,* Bk. I, tit. iii, chap. xx, no. 8, words *tertia regula,* and on *Code,* VII. lii. i, no. 4, ampliat. 3). It is to be found in the *Decisions of the Rota* (Decision 2, *De Rescriptis, in novissimis decisionibus,* no. 2), and it is clearly to be drawn from the *Sext* (Bk. I, tit. ii, chap. i, in the passage beginning, *Singularium consuetudines*). For by this phrase [the above-cited chapter of the *Sext*] excludes general [customs and laws], as the Gloss thereon also notes.

The reason is that a subsequent general law revokes a previous one of the same order, even though it makes no mention of the latter, as is stated in the aforementioned chapter [*Sext,* Bk. I, tit. ii, chap. i]. But a universal custom has the same force as a general law, and has the standing of an unwritten rule of the canons, or of the civil law. Therefore, . . .

Likewise, the prince, who is held to have all laws locked within his own breast (as is stated in *Sext,* Bk. I, tit. ii, chap. i and in *Code,* VI. xxiii. 19), is held not to be ignorant of a universal custom; and he is, therefore, assumed to revoke such a custom when he enacts a new law, in the presence of which the custom can no longer persist.

8. *The application of the foregoing rule.* And this rule holds true in due proportion for every diocese with respect to the synodal laws and general customs of that diocese. It is likewise true of the civil laws of the various kingdoms with respect to the general customs that obtain in those kingdoms: the principle is the same. For this reason, Abbas [, i.e. Panormitanus,] says (*De Consuetudine,* Chap. xi, last no.) that if a city makes a statute in opposition to one of its own customs, the latter is then revoked, even though the custom is not mentioned. The reason is that the city is presumed to be aware of its own customs, since they are not introduced without the knowledge of the people. But I think that this assertion is to be taken with the proviso that the city in question shall have absolute authority in legislation; or if it shall have the power of legislation only with the permission of the prince and subject to his confirmation, that the people shall inform him that the law which is to be passed revokes the custom (argument of *Decretals,* Bk. I, tit. IV, chap. ix). The reason is that the prince could not otherwise give his consent to revocation of the custom, since he is not presumed to have knowledge of a private custom. Again, he would permit the enactment of such a statute much less readily and only after very careful consideration, if he were to have notice of the existence of the custom. And finally, by the common law it is provided that a change is not to be made in any custom (*Digest,* I. iii. 23);[8] therefore, in order to enact, with the sovereign's permission, a statute opposed to a custom, the fact of the existence of the custom must be called to his attention.

I note, finally, that the foregoing assertion or conclusion holds true no less in the case of an immemorial custom, than in that of any other custom which has been validated by prescription. For if the law is fully as universal in character as is the custom itself, even though the latter is not

---

8. [*Digest, loc. cit.,* has: *Minime sunt mutanda quae interpretationem certam semper habuerunt.*—REVISER.]

expressly mentioned in the law, it is nevertheless revoked by the said law. The reason is that previously given: the custom in question is presumed not to be unknown, and it possesses no more than the force of a positive common law. In fine, the custom here is held to be revoked not in virtue of a universal derogating clause under which it is to be supposed especially to fall, but by the positive knowledge of it on the part of the prince, who, notwithstanding such knowledge,[9] desires to make a law which cannot be valid unless he revokes the custom in question; therefore, [by enacting the law under these circumstances,] he also revokes the custom.

9. *Second inference.* The second inference from the same condition and rule is that a universal law framed for the whole Church does not revoke the particular customs of dioceses, cities, or provinces, unless there is added to the law the clause *non obstante* (notwithstanding), revoking them in specific or at least in general terms. This statement holds also, in due proportion, for the laws of kingdoms, or of provinces—in so far, that is, as they are universal in those provinces—in their relation to the customs of particular localities of the kingdom or of the province: in these cases also the same principle applies, and there is the same application of jurisdiction.

Thus, therefore, our statement is expressly set forth in the aforesaid *Sext,* Bk. I, tit. II, chap. i. The basis for it in reason there given is that a universal lawgiver is assumed not to know of the particular facts with respect to which the customs of particular localities are ordered. He is, therefore, held not to will the revocation of such customs by a general law, unless he expressly makes reference to them, or, at least, causes a general revocation of all contrary customs by adding the clause *non obstante* (notwithstanding), &c.

The Gloss and the Doctors in their observations (on *Sext,* Bk. I, tit. II, chap. i, and on *Decretals,* Bk. I, tit. IV, chap. xi) agree in holding this opinion, as does Panormitanus in his commentaries on those chapters (no. 24); Rochus (*De Consuetudine,* Sect. 7, no. 30) and Paul de Castro, Jason, and others (on *Digest,* I. iii. 32) take the same view. But Bartolus in commenting on the same law 32 [on *Digest,* I. iii. 32, in lect. no. 5], cites Guido to the contrary, and he himself seems to hold the same opinion

9. [Reading *qui ea* for *qua.*—REVISER.]

with respect to the civil law on the ground of *Digest,* XLVII. xii. 3, § 5, although he admits our opinion with respect to the canon law. Panormitanus also takes the same position (*supra*). Azo defends this opinion in his *Summa.* Hostiensis cites Azo and follows his doctrine (*Summa,* on *Decretals,* Bk. I, tit. iv, no. 10).

But, as a matter of fact, Bartolus disapproves of the doctrine of Guido[10] and, accepting the teaching of the canonists, especially that of Giovanni d'Andrea (on *Sext,* Bk. I, tit. II, chap. i), defends the common opinion. That this is his conclusion and doctrine—in principle—is very clear from *Repetitio,* no. 5. He there makes it clear that, even though this rule is not so expressly stated in the civil as it is in the canon law, nevertheless, the principle of *Sext,* Bk. I. tit. II, chap. i, holds true for all law; and that it does not so much set up a legal rule for one order of law only, but rather declares one that has, according to right reason, application in that of every legislator. And with respect to *Digest,* XLVII. xii. 3, § 5, he replies in a word (in his comment thereon) that we must understand it to refer to custom of which the prince had knowledge, or which he expressly willed to abolish, should it be in existence. This reply amounts to the extending of that text from a statute to custom, if the custom be understood to be one existing antecedent to the law in question. But it has other meanings also, as I have said above. In this meaning, the law (*Las Siete Partidas,* Pt. I, tit. ii, law 6) must also, it would seem, be taken, when it says that it is possible for a subsequent law to abolish a contrary custom, even though Gregory López (*ibid.,* in Gloss 6) understands it to hold absolutely and independently of conditions, citing in support of his opinion the authority of the aforesaid section 5 (*Digest,* XLVII. xii. 3, § 5).

10. *A question raised.* The question arises as to what custom this rule is to be held to apply; to a prescriptive custom only, to one, that is, which has already introduced law, or to one of shorter duration, also? For the above-cited Doctors have nothing on his question, and they set forth their opinion in general terms without explicit reference to these differences in the kind of custom. They would, then, seem to have had in mind legal custom—that is, custom which has introduced a rule of law—and

10. [I.e. Archidiaconus.—Tr.]

furthermore, custom validated by prescription: for they are speaking of a custom of which the prince is presumed to have no knowledge, and custom of that kind cannot establish a legal rule, unless it be validated by prescription. Again, I find the word *praescripta* added to the Gloss (on *Sext,* Bk. I, tit. II, chap. i, word *facti*).

The same conclusion may be drawn from the *Sext* (Bk. I, tit. II, chap. i), where we find the word *derogandi* used; for there can be no derogation in the strict sense of the term except from an earlier law [, in this case, that of a custom validated by prescription]. Conversely, a special custom is held to derogate from a general law for the reason that a special law derogates from a general law; and this, even if the special law was in existence before the general one came into being. This is true, first, as a rule of law; and again, because it is based on the principle that the prince is not presumed to derogate from a special law of which he has no knowledge. Therefore, the custom in question is to be assumed to be such as shall have introduced law. A final argument here is that this rule [of *Sext,* Bk. I, tit. II, chap. i] must have reference to a custom validated by prescription, for no other custom can be designated which, of its nature, should subsist in the face of a later general law.

II. *Certain necessary considerations on the aforesaid chapter of the* Sext. Nevertheless, I must call attention to the fact that in the aforesaid chap. i [*Sext, ibid.*], which rules that particular customs are not revoked by an absolute law framed in general terms,[11] it sets down only one condition with respect to the customs in question, namely, 'provided they are reasonable'; and does not add the condition, 'provided they are validated by prescription.' It is, therefore, not to be added by us. Hence, when the Pope wished validation by prescription to be an essential condition, he never failed to include it, as is clear from the *Decretals* (Bk. I, tit. IV, chap. xi).

Likewise, the reason there given is that the custom [stands in the face of a contrary general law because it] is something in the sphere of fact. I conclude, therefore, that even though it has not developed to the point of

---

11. [The actual words are: *ipsis, dum tamen sint rationabilia, per constitutionem a se noviter editam, nisi expresse caveatur in ipsa, non intelligitur in aliquo derogare.*—REVISER.]

establishing law, the basis of that law exists in it, in respect of the prince's having no knowledge of it, and he is, therefore, presumed not to revoke it.

An objection. One may object that the custom is in that passage termed a custom 'of fact', inasmuch as it is distinguished from a common law, just as a statute is said to be one 'of fact', not because it is not law, both general and particular, but because its enactment has been brought about by special facts. And so this passage is to be taken as referring to prescriptive custom; for, granting that the same reasoning holds true of non-prescriptive as of prescriptive custom, with respect to the ignorance of the prince with regard to the custom, it does not hold true in this respect, that the prince is presumed not to have willed to set up by his law an obligation in opposition to such an inchoate custom of fact. And this, for the reason that, since such custom has not established law, the question of derogation from it—a question which *is* relevant in the case of a custom which has established law—would be without meaning. [The law has, therefore, reference to an established custom 'of fact', in the sense that we defined those words, and not to one that has not yet established law, that is, which is still an inchoate custom of fact.]

The objection is refuted. Granting the difference between the two kinds of custom, I still hold that my inference stands, since in respect of [the principle involved in] the reason laid down by the law—that the prince is not presumed to will the enactment of law inharmonious with the customs of those whom it is to bind—the two are to be regarded in much the same way. And this reasoning holds for any custom which is firmly rooted in observance, even though it has not yet been validated by prescription. This conclusion is further strengthened by the rule of law that a general enactment does not regard what is particular, which the legislator would probably not have wished to affect by his legislation had he been aware of it; and by the fact that the forcing of the people to change a custom which is contrary to a general law, especially a custom which the prince would have taken into very serious account in the framing of his law had he known of it, is attended by difficulties beyond the ordinary. Therefore, it is very improbable that this law intended the revocation of custom of this kind.

12. *In what way the rule of that text receives a broader interpretation.* For the foregoing reasons, I think that the rule stated in the aforesaid chap. i [*Sext*, Bk. I, tit. ii, chap. i] is not to be restricted to a prescriptive custom, but must be understood to extend to any reasonable and just custom which has been confirmed, both by public usage and observance, through a period which would be sufficient for the introduction of a legal rule, if the prince had knowledge of the custom, and if it would appear very probable to a prudent mind that the prince would have given his approval of the custom, provided it had come to his knowledge. Under these conditions, it is most improbable that he would wish to legislate against the custom by a general law, or that he would wish to abolish it—since he has no knowledge of it—without declaring his will in express terms to that effect.

For to this sort of custom, both the words and the principle of the aforesaid chap. i [*Sext, ibid.*] apply exactly. Therefore, the phrase 'to derogate' is rightly used in connexion with this kind of custom also. The reason is, first, that the phrase is commonly used in connexion with other laws of justice which are not truly written laws—for example, when we say that the prince, in conceding a privilege, does not wish to derogate from the [established] rights of a third person; secondly that, such a custom would of its own virtue be sufficient for the establishment of a legal rule, were not this prevented by the sovereign's ignorance of the custom; and finally, that the people already possess a certain right not to be forced to change such a custom, from which the prince is not to be understood as wishing to derogate, unless he gives clear manifestation of such an intention. This, then, is our reply to the argument given against our position.

13. *The answer to the question.*[12] And to the last reason advanced in support of the opinion, I reply that it is true that no fixed period of observance can be set down as marking the custom referred to by that rule; but it can be said, that that period is sufficient which a prudent judgment will regard as such. In principle, the manner of determining a sufficient duration of the custom here in question will be that which we indicated in our discussion of non-prescriptive custom with respect to its establishing law in cases where the prince has knowledge of it. In such cases the sufficient

12. [I.e. the 'final argument' at the end of Sect. 10, *supra*, p. 742.—Tr.]

period of observance is not [always] of the same length, or a fixed one for all customs of that kind; it is, rather, to be determined by a prudent judgment which takes into account the circumstances of the custom. A like duration determined in the same way, is, we hold, sufficient for the custom we are here discussing. All those, certainly, who teach that custom never establishes law, except when the prince has knowledge of it, hold our opinion in principle; for they cannot deny the rule laid down in the aforesaid chap. i [*Sext*, Bk. I, tit II, chap. i.], namely, that a general law does not abrogate a particular custom of which the prince has no knowledge, although, according to their teaching, it has not yet established law.

Finally, it would seem to be accepted usage that in the defence of a particular custom against a general law, the 'long time' necessary for validation by prescription is not to be rigorously considered or urged, but that, rather, the rectitude of the custom and the fact that in the opinion of prudent men it is sufficiently established, are to be urged.

14. *A second difficulty.* A second difficulty with respect to that rule may be raised, namely, whether a particular law enacted without conditions by the Pope, or by some other prince of universal authority, for a certain locality—diocese, &c.—effects a derogation from a particular custom of that locality in opposition to the law in question. The reason for the question is that the law derogates from an antecedent custom, provided the two are (so to speak) properly comparable; as, a general law with a general custom; a particular law with a particular custom. We have already dealt with this question in respect of a general law and a general custom in our discussion of the rule touching that point; and there would seem to be an analogous relation between a particular law and a particular custom. It was for this reason that in setting forth the rule on that point, we stated that a private custom is revoked by a local statute enacted by the community concerned if it has the power to make statutes, even if the custom is not mentioned in the statute. Therefore, the same holds true *a fortiori* of a statute enacted by a superior prince, since his authority is much greater.

15. *A particular custom is not revoked by a particular law made by the Pope, except under certain conditions.* Nevertheless, it would seem that we must assert that the custom is not immediately revoked by a law of this kind, save with the previous consent of the people, or where it is evident

by petition or information, or in some other way, that the law was enacted by the prince with full knowledge of the custom in question. The reason is that the rule of the aforesaid chap. i [*Sext, ibid.*] applies no less in the case of a law of this kind, than in that of a general law; because it is not to be presumed with less reason that the prince is ignorant of the private custom in his making of one law, than in his making of another; nor, supposing that he has no knowledge of the custom, is he to be presumed willing to derogate from it, unless he expresses a will to do so.

Here we have a marked difference between a universal sovereign and a particular and local one, when they exercise legislative authority: in the prince, such ignorance of the local custom is assumed to exist; but in a particular community or governor it is not to be so assumed. Thus the words of the aforesaid chap. i [*Sext, ibid.*] hold generally for every 'constitution newly published by the Pope'. The inference is sound; for, since doubt or obscurity on the point is possible, it is to be held that if the prince had wished that his particular law should prevail, notwithstanding a contrary custom, he would have made known his intention. For this is what is done in most generally accepted usage, and it is in conformity with the law. Hence, when he does not add a clause expressing such an intention, he must be presumed not to have willed to revoke the custom.

This principle must, in practice, be kept in mind with regard to many laws, which are particular with respect to the authority from which they emanate, and also with respect to the community to which that authority is extended, but which are enacted as general for some diocese or congregation, the customs of which, even though they are general for that diocese or congregation, are particular from the standpoint of the prince; they are, therefore, held not to suffer derogation by laws of this kind, unless a derogating clause is incorporated in the law. And so a custom is held not to suffer derogation through a privilege granted by the prince, except when the privilege carries a derogating clause—as will be made clear later in its proper place.

16. *An objection from the Gloss.* An objection may be drawn from the reason set down by the Gloss (on *Sext*, Bk. I, tit. II, chap. i, word *singularium*); namely, that such a law would be useless and superfluous, since it would have no effect in any place. For a general law, even though it

may not abolish a custom in one place, is not useless, for the reason that it would be binding upon the remainder of the whole community. But a law made for a special place or congregation, if it is there obstructed by a particular custom of a contrary nature, will be useless. Likewise, to persist in the observance of that particular custom in contempt of his law would seem to be opposed to the obedience due to the superior prince.

The reply. But the reply can be made, that this law is, of itself, useful and efficacious; but accidentally, by reason, that is, of the prince's lack of knowledge of the custom, it is of no effect. Nor is this [nullification of the law] contrary to the obedience and reverence due to a superior; for it is held to be in accord with his will, as manifested in the common law.

I note, further, that the law in this case is not useless, nor is it wholly lacking in effect; for it obliges the subjects reverently to accept the law, and to have recourse to the superior, calling his attention to their custom, and presenting the reason for it, with the intention of obeying the law, if, notwithstanding his present knowledge of the custom, the superior still wishes that the law should be observed. Meanwhile, however, they are not bound to act against the custom. These reasons are excellently borne out by a parallelism found in the *Decretals* (Bk. I, tit. III, chap. v), and by the observations that are there set down.

17. *What words must be added to a general law, in order that the custom may be held to be abrogated?* Finally, we must make clear what words are to be added to a general law, or a law of the prince, for it to be held as abrogating custom. For in the aforesaid chap. i [*Sext*, Bk. I, tit. II, chap. i] we find the words, 'unless express provision is made in the law'. On this, the only point calling for observation is that, in these cases, the derogation is usually effected through the words, 'notwithstanding a contrary custom', or by others of the same or like import, or a clause of virtually the same meaning. I shall explicitly discuss these clauses in Book VIII,[13] in connexion with the revocation of privileges.

Three opinions as to when an immemorial custom is held to be abrogated. Enough has been said in earlier books of this treatise as to when clauses of this kind do no more than revoke a past custom and when they prohibit,

13. [Not included in these *Selections.*—Tr.]

or even reprobate, a future custom. The only question that remains for us in this matter, is whether an immemorial custom also is to be held abrogated by clauses of this kind expressed in absolute terms; or whether this is true only of customs of whose beginnings we have definite knowledge.

The first opinion. On this point, there are three opinions. The first one affirms absolutely that by means of the clause, 'notwithstanding custom to the contrary', every custom, even an immemorial one, is revoked, even when to that clause the distributive 'whatever', or one similar to it, is not added. This is the doctrine of the Cardinal.[14] The reason that can be given for this opinion is that the negation is sufficiently distributive in itself, since it removes *all* contrary customs.

The second opinion. The second opinion is that, with the addition of the distributive 'whatever', immemorial customs are included in the revocation; but that they are not so included when that word is not used. This opinion is defended by many canonists, and it is to be found in the Glosses cited by Covarruvias. The reason for the exemption of immemorial custom in the first case may be its special character; the ground for holding it revoked in the latter will, then, be that the duplication (as it were) of the distributive is intended to overcome the exemptive character of such custom.

18. *The third opinion.* The third opinion is that, even with the addition of the distributive 'whatever', an immemorial custom is not revoked, unless in the revoking clause the words, 'even if it is immemorial', or their equivalent, are included.

This opinion is held by many jurists. They are referred to by Covarruvias and Tiraqueau, who follow their doctrine; the former does so in *Variarum Resolutionum* (Bk. III, chap. xiii, no. 5); the latter in *De Utroque Retractu* (Tract. II, § 1, gloss 2, no. 25); and it is suggested in Gloss on *Authentica ut de caetero,* chap. i, word *praescriptione* [*Novels,* LV, chap. i, word *praescriptione*]. For, when that law uses the words, 'notwithstanding any prescription, &c.', the Gloss adds, 'Except one of a hundred years', for one of that length is held to be immemorial; indeed, it adds, 'or one of forty years', which is considerable. The import of these words is that

14. [I.e. Gratian.—Reviser.]

whenever a custom is revoked by a law, or a prescription is rejected, the law is to be understood as referring to an ordinary custom, or to a prescription that has run for a 'long time', but not to one that has been observed for the 'very long time', much less to one that is immemorial. Thus also, the civil laws say that discontinuous servitudes cannot be acquired by prescription (*Digest*, VIII. i. 14); nevertheless, this rule does not hold in the case of immemorial prescriptions—and this, without taking into account *Digest*, XLIII. xx. 3, § 4. That law provides us with a basis for proving our assertion almost as strong [as that just cited]. The reasoning here is that, since nothing is known of the beginning of the custom there referred to, so neither is it known whether that right was established by usage alone, or whether it owes its origin to some other cause, such as a privilege, a constitution, or the like. And it is to be noted, for this reason, that a custom of that sort is not abrogated by a law referring in a general way to 'custom'; for the custom of which we treat has a certain superiority of character.

The first conclusion approving this third opinion. It is to be added, that it is for this reason that an immemorial custom has a very special status in law, and carries with it many special privileges; and is, therefore, in accordance with another well-attested interpretation not affected by a general [revocating] clause. Therefore, this opinion can be adopted in practice. Certain conditions, which have to do with the matter of prescription, are commonly set down for the validity of this rule; these, however, we need not rehearse here. They are to be found in the passage of Tiraqueau, cited earlier [*De Utroque Retractu*, Preface, nos. 19 *et seq.*].

19. *The second conclusion: an ancient custom may in due proportion be abrogated by a subsequent one.* Our second main conclusion must be that an ancient custom may be abrogated by a subsequent one, when due proportion is observed; that is, a universal custom by a universal one; and a particular custom by a particular one of the same locality—for customs of different places are not contrary, the one to the other. There may be a derogation, however, from a universal custom by a particular custom of a certain place; and, finally, a custom universal within a certain locality can derogate from a particular one. These conclusions are almost the same as those defended by Hostiensis (in *Summa,* Bk. I, rubric iv, no. 10) and all other writers on this question.

The general proof for this thesis is that in this way customs are compared with one another, just as laws and[15] customs are compared, respect being paid to due proportion between the cases. Thus, in the *Institutes* (I. ii, § 11), we find it stated that, 'The laws which are made by a state are wont often to be altered either by the tacit consent of the people, or by the enactment of a subsequent law.' And just as this is true of rules established by written law, so is it *a fortiori* true of those introduced by unwritten law; for it would seem that a tacit consent is more likely to be changed by a contrary tacit consent, than that an express consent should be changed by a tacit one: yet such can be the case, as we have proved. Therefore, . . .

It is, therefore, most important that the customs be truly contrary to each other; for if they can be brought into harmony, they are, as Hostiensis says, both to be followed. Once we assume their mutual opposition, however, then all parts of our assertion are evident.

Touching the last assertion in our thesis, it is to be noted that there can be no derogating clause attached to a custom, because customs consist of actions, not of words; and that it is for this reason necessary that a universal custom, in order to derogate from a particular one, must be extended to the locality where the latter formerly prevailed. When that takes place, the fact of the derogation is then clear; for contradictory opposition (so to speak) is then perfected, and the people themselves have given their consent. The custom will not have this effect if it remains general only in the other portions of the province or kingdom; for in that case a universal custom cannot be prejudicial to a particular custom to which the people strongly cling, any more than a universal law can derogate from such a custom.

20. *Of the time and the actions required for the revocation of a custom.* It may be asked, what duration is necessary and what number of acts is called for that a subsequent custom may derogate from an earlier one. Our reply must be that neither one nor many contrary actions are sufficient, but that a custom validated by prescription is necessary, or one such as is sufficient for the revocation of a written law. Thus the Gloss 2 (on *Digest*, L. xvii. 171, 166 [54]) is to this effect. This is the doctrine also of Hostiensis

---

15. [Omitting *vel* in the text.—REVISER.]

(on *Decretals,* Bk. I, tit. IV, no. 5, § *qualiter,* words *sed numquid*); of Panormitanus (*De Consuetudine,* Chap. xi, no. 19); of Rochus (*De Consuetudine,* Sect. 4, nos. 69 *et seq.* [nos. 74 *et seq.*]); and of Felinus (on *Decretals,* Bk. I, tit. II, chap. viii, no. 30, at end), where in a scholion the names of many other authorities are given.

The reason here is that no custom can establish new law, unless it is itself validated by prescription, or has the approbation of the prince's consent; and consequently, no custom can abrogate a previous custom, unless it have the same consent of the prince. Therefore, a period of at least ten years is required for abrogation, if the prince has no knowledge of the custom; or a period to be fixed by the judgment of prudent men, if the prince has knowledge of the new custom.

21. It may also be asked, whether a period of forty years is required in ecclesiastical customs in order to effect the revocation of earlier customs. Panormitanus states without reference to a distinction of customs that an observance of ten years is sufficient; and Felinus follows his doctrine. The latter gives as his reason that the later custom is not one contrary to law. This assertion he proves as follows: because either the first custom was contrary to law, and the subsequent one is according to the older law, which had been revoked by the first, and thus a reversion to the more ancient law is facilitated; or, the first custom was outside the law, and so the subsequent custom will be a custom of the same kind: and therefore a period of ten years will always be sufficient for the subsequent custom. Rochus does not approve of this argument (*ibid.*), nor does Barbatia [*Repertorium, De Consuetudine*], and I, also, find it difficult to accept, because it does not take into account at all the character of unwritten law.

The time required in the case of a canonical prescription, and likewise where one custom derogates from another. My opinion, therefore, is, briefly, that if the prior custom was not contrary to the law, but was outside the law, then the subsequent custom will be in absolute opposition to the law, and will therefore demand an observance of the length of time necessary for a canonical prescription. The proof is that the former custom established a legal rule to which the later custom is opposed, nor is it in conformity with any existing law. Likewise, if the prior custom was universal, and the later one was particular, then the truth of my assertion is the more evident, since a universal custom establishes general law. The same thing seems to be true if the earlier custom were a particular custom of that locality, and not in opposition to the general law. For a custom contrary to statutes of the character described above would be in opposition to the law, and would require an observance of the length of time necessary for a canonical prescription. Therefore, the same is true of a custom, for the principle is the same in both cases.

When the period of ten years is sufficient. If, however, the prior custom was opposed to general law, which was not completely abolished by that earlier custom—for the reason that the custom that derogated from it was not a universal, but a particular one—then it is probable that a subsequent prescriptive custom, of ten years' standing, is sufficient. The reason for this is that this prescriptive custom is not of its essence opposed to the law, since the general law, to which a return is made by this custom, always stands. In that case the argument of Felinus stands [on *Decretals,* Bk. I, tit. II, chap. viii, no. 30].

When forty years are required. I could not approve it, however, if the prior custom were universal, and had completely annulled the universal law previously existing; for in that case, I think that a canonical prescription of forty years is necessary against such a custom, because the subsequent custom is then completely contrary to the general law established by the previous custom. For any other law more ancient than either custom is as if it had not existed before the other two, because it has been entirely abolished. Let this suffice for our treatment of custom.

A DEFENCE OF THE CATHOLIC
AND APOSTOLIC FAITH

A DEFENCE OF THE
CATHOLIC AND APOSTOLIC FAITH

IN REFUTATION OF THE ERRORS OF THE ANGLICAN SECT
WITH A REPLY
TO THE APOLOGIE FOR THE OATH OF ALLEGIANCE
and to the admonitory Preface of
His Most Serene Majesty James, King of England

By
FATHER FRANCISCO SUÁREZ
of Granada, Member of the Society of Jesus
Primary Professor of Sacred Theology at the celebrated Academy of Coimbra

Dedicated to Their Most Serene Majesties
the Catholic Kings and Princes of all Christendom

COIMBRA
By privileges of his Catholic Majesty
From the Press of DIOGO GOMEZ DE LOUREYRO
Printer for the Academy
In the Year of Our Lord 1613

Dedication
For Their Most Serene Majesties

THOSE KINGS AND PRINCES WHO ARE THE CHILDREN
AND DEFENDERS OF THE ROMAN CATHOLIC CHURCH

*Francisco Suárez of the Society of Jesus desires temporal
and eternal blessedness*

His Most Serene Majesty James, King of Great Britain, in his recently published work, has called upon the Catholic Kings and Princes, as with a friendly trumpet blast, to share in his own religion, that those whom the King of Kings has bought with His own blood for the defence of the Church of Rome, and whom Christ, the Lord of Lords, has armed with supreme power, might be incited, by the counsel he has imparted, to attack that Church. His Most Serene Majesty, however, has wielded his pen in a vain attempt. For the gates of hell shall not prevail against the Church, nor shall the chill raging of the north wind have power to scatter those who have taken their stand upon the rock of Rome, and have been united by Christ, the corner-stone, in the strongest of bonds, that of true piety. Would that King James, following in the footsteps of his unvanquished royal ancestors, might rather combine with you to exalt the majesty of the Catholic Church, in such fashion as to be not inferior, in the zeal of true piety, to those whose peer he is, in power and sovereignty! Would that he preferred to be numbered among the kings whom divine authority has constituted guardians of that Church, rather than among those whom impious madness has inflamed against the Lord, and against His Christ!

Therefore, since the King of England has published a work testifying to his religion, and since he is waging war upon the Catholic Church, not with the regal majesty adorning him, nor with the clash and might of arms (whereunto the priest of Christ and religious cannot oppose resistance), but rather by the sharp edge of his unaided human talents and pen—I repeat, since this is the case—I have deemed it proper to my office and purpose that I should advance to the line of battle; not with the intention of dimming the lustrous renown of so great a king, an end which I am neither capable nor desirous of achieving, but in order that the mists exhaled from the fetid pools of the Reformers, wherewith he attempts to obscure Catholic truth, may vanish into air and smoke, being dispelled by the rays of true wisdom. That I might accomplish this purpose, I have with all my strength besought that light from God, the Father of light, that knowledge of the uncorrupted truth, which—handed down by Christ the Lord through His Apostles, and expounded by the wakeful toil of the Holy Fathers—should be striven after by one who desires to keep to the true path in his life and his beliefs. May my undertaking be granted the favour of that Divine Spirit in Whose hands lie the hearts of kings. And do you—O Kings and Princes of the Catholic world, who in your sincere affection earnestly desire that His Most Serene Majesty, King James, should be even as you yourselves are—do you receive this work, such as it is, under your patronage, to be defended by your authority. For it is yours, and it is well said that, *We make those things our own, to which we impart our authority.* Therefore, receive the work as your own, that it may be made public, defended by the royal authority of your patronage, adorned by [your] renown and secure from danger; that it may make a brilliant entrance into the world; that it may be deemed not unworthy of kingly eyes. For only under the protection of your name can we oppose this book of ours, wherein we defend God's cause, to that of His Most Serene Majesty. I have, indeed, been inspired by one sole design: the dedication, in dutiful humility, of this product of my labours to you who—as heirs to the sovereignty and piety of your forebears—have devoutly undertaken and unwaveringly administer the guardianship of the Catholic Church. For others, our work may serve as an antidote, but you yourselves, do not lack an antidote (namely, supreme piety, divinely inspired) against the madness of the Reformers; for their poisons, drawn from Stygian streams, are powerless to injure you, who—joined in the bond of divine virtue— are protected as subjects in the unity of the true Catholic faith, under Christ the Lord and His earthly Vicar, the Supreme Pontiff, even as the noblest members of the body are subject to its head. And for so long as your supreme power is firmly founded upon Him, may it grow to a greater imperial glory and aid you toward eternal blessedness.

Coimbra,
On the thirteenth day of June,
In the year 1613.

A Defence of the Catholic and Apostolic Faith

BOOK III

Concerning the Supremacy and Power of the Pope over Temporal Kings

CHAPTER V

Do Christian Kings Possess Supreme Power in Civil, or Temporal Affairs; and [, If So,] by What Right?

1. A given power may be called supreme, when it recognizes no superior. For this word, 'supreme', connotes a denial of the existence of any superior whom the other party—the one said to possess supreme power—is bound to obey.

But it is understood that we are speaking of earthly, or human superiors, inasmuch as we are not instituting a comparison with God. For what human prince, if he were neither an atheist nor a madman, would presume to withdraw himself from divine authority, or even to attempt such a withdrawal? This denial, then, is one which excludes subjection to a human and mortal superior.

However, this denial may be interpreted in a number of different ways. Consequently, in order that the title relating to this question may be understood, and may be distinguished from other questions which could be raised at this point, it is necessary to provide a clear explanation of the manner and meaning of the said denial. For, first, it is possible to deny in an absolute sense all subjection to any human superior, whether in spiritual matters, or in civil ones. Secondly, it is possible to deny subjection in these temporal and civil matters. Moreover, even though the gravest disagreement exists between ourselves and the King of England with respect to the former question (since he desires to be subordinate to no earthly being, even in spiritual matters, a desire which we regard as contrary to the faith and to Christian obedience), nevertheless, we are not treating here of that question; for we have not yet discussed spiritual power, and without knowledge of this power, it is in no wise possible to arrive at an intelligible solution of the said question. Accordingly, we shall postpone its discussion to the closing portion of this Book;[1] and, for the present, we shall apply the term 'supreme temporal power' to that power which is not subject to any other within the same order, or [sphere of] subject-matter.

2. *Two forms of subjection: direct and indirect. The nature of each.* Furthermore, it is customary, in connexion with the question under discussion, to distinguish two forms of subjection, namely, direct and indirect.

That subjection is called direct which is confined within the object and bounds of this [civil] power itself; and that is called indirect which is derived solely from a striving towards an end that is nobler, and pertains to a superior and more excellent authority. For true civil power in its essence, serves directly no other end than the fit condition and temporal felicity of a human commonwealth during this temporal life; and consequently, such power itself is also called temporal. Thus civil power is said to be supreme in its own order, when the ultimate decision in that order and with respect to the end thereof is referred to the said power, within its own sphere, that is to say, within the whole community subject to it; so that all inferior magistrates possessing power in such a community or in a part thereof, are dependent upon such a supreme prince, whereas this supreme sovereign himself is subject to no superior, in regard to the said purpose of civil government. For temporal and civil felicity must of course be related to spiritual and eternal felicity; and therefore, it may happen that the very subject-matter of civil power will require, for the attainment of a spiritual good, such direction and government as would not appear to be demanded otherwise, by reasons of a purely civil nature. Under such circumstances, even though

---

1. [Not included in these *Selections.*—Tr.]

the temporal prince and his power may not be directly subject, in regard to his own acts, to any other power within the same order and serving solely the same [civil] end, nevertheless it may become necessary for this prince to be directed, aided, or corrected in his own field of activity by a higher power that governs men in relation to a more excellent and an eternal end. In that case, the dependence in question is called indirect dependence, since such a superior power is concerned with temporal affairs, not in themselves nor for their own sake, but (as it were) indirectly, and often on account of some other factor.

3. So it is that this denial of subjection in temporal matters, which is thought to be included in the prerogatives of supreme temporal power, is further subdivided into two phases. For one may either deny all subjection, whether direct or indirect, or else deny the direct form only; and thus another twofold question arises. The first [phase of the question] is this: is the power of a Christian king supreme in the former sense; that is to say, does it neither directly nor indirectly recognize any superior in civil and temporal matters? The second [phase] is as follows: is such power supreme, in the latter sense, at least; that is, does it recognize no direct superior in temporal matters? So great is the difference between these two questions that the first relates to the dogmas of the faith, and practically constitutes the crux of the whole controversy between ourselves and the King of England; while the second does not relate to the subject-matter of the faith, nor is there any dissension between us on that point.

Nevertheless, the present discussion is not to be interpreted as referring to the former phase of the question, nor is it to be interpreted as referring to indirect subjection—or rather, exemption from such subjection. For, if the matter is carefully considered, this discussion turns about a question of spiritual power; inasmuch as such indirect subjection can only be subjection to a spiritual power; or (and this is the same thing), inasmuch as any conceivable power to which supreme temporal power is indirectly subject, must be solely spiritual, as we shall see in discussing that [form of power]. Therefore, we shall postpone this question until we come to the said discussion.

Explanation of the sense in which the question is [here] interpreted. The title, then, of the question in hand must be understood to relate exclusively to that supreme power which does not directly recognize any superior within this same [temporal] order. For though, as I have said, there is no dissension between the King and ourselves on this point, nevertheless, in view of the fact that he frequently complains, with regard to Catholics, that we deny the jurisdiction of Christian princes and the obedience due to them, I have come to the conclusion that this question should not be passed by in the present context; my purpose being to show clearly, by the solution of the said question, that the royal power of Christian princes is preserved unimpaired, according to Catholic doctrine, in all those respects in which such power is consistent with natural law.

4. *The first negative opinion.* Therefore, certain Catholics, and especially certain jurists, have held the opinion that within the Church of Christ not only spiritual, but also temporal government is monarchical; that, consequently, in the whole Catholic Church there exists but one supreme temporal prince, who holds, *per se* and directly, supreme civil power over the entire Church; and that this supreme prince is the Pope, by the institution of Christ. Whence these authorities have drawn the further inference that no commonwealth, and no king or emperor, possesses supreme power in temporal matters; since there cannot be two supreme heads within one and the same order, and since therefore, if the Pope holds supreme temporal power, directly and *per se,* it necessarily follows that there is no supreme power in any other temporal prince, inasmuch as there will be no other temporal prince who does not recognize a superior in temporal matters.

Some persons even go so far as to add that all the rights of kingdoms and all powers of dominion were conferred upon Peter, as the vicar of Christ, and that the Roman pontiff accordingly succeeds to these rights, so that supreme civil power resides habitually (to use their own expression) in the Pope alone, although he administers it through other rulers as the result of a tacit or express concession. This is the view expressed by the chief authorities among the early interpreters of Pontifical law: the Gloss, Innocent, Hostiensis, Giovanni d'Andrea, Panormitanus, Felinus, and Decio (on *Decretals,* Bk. II, tit. i, chap. xiii; Bk. IV, tit. xvii, chaps. vii and xiii; Bk. I, tit. xxxiii, chap. vi; Bk. III, tit. xxxiv), and others (on *Decretum,* Pt. I, dist. x, chap. viii and Pt. I, dist. xcvi, chap. vi). Among the interpreters of civil law, the following uphold the same opinion: Bartolus, Oldradus,

Paul de Castro, and others mentioned by Navarrus and Covarruvias (who will be cited below). To these, may be added the names of St. Antoninus ([*Summa Theologica,*] Pt. III, tit. xxii, chap. v, §§ 13 and 17), Alvaro Paez [, *De Planctu Ecclesiae*] and Augustinus [Triumphus] of Ancona [, *Summa de Potestate Ecclesiastica*] as well as many other authorities referred to by those above cited.

5. *The first basis.* They base their opinion, first, upon numerous decrees of the Popes, who apparently uphold this view; decrees to which we shall refer below, in expounding the opinion of the said pontiffs.

A second basis is found in usage, and in the various effects pointing to the existence of the power in question. Examples of this sort are the transference of empire from the Greeks to the Germans, the institution of the mode of electing the emperor, the confirmation of his election, and even, at times, his deposition, all of which are the acts of a superior temporal power. Moreover, if the emperor is not supreme, far less can the other rulers be supreme. Wherefore, kings also have on certain occasions been deposed by the Popes.

A third basis for the same contention is the assumption—so that the Scriptures, too, may be adduced in proof of the said contention—that Christ possessed direct power, not only of a spiritual, but also of a temporal nature. This argument rests, partly, on the fact that He said: 'All power is given to me in heaven and in earth' [*Matthew,* Chap. xxviii, v. 18]; partly, also, on the fact that He was the natural Son of God (*filius Dei naturalis*). Whence the authorities in question infer that He committed both kinds of power alike to His vicar. For in the first place, He Himself made no distinction, but laid upon Peter the general injunction, 'Feed my sheep' [*John,* Chap. xxi, v. 17], and this term 'feeding' embraces civil no less than spiritual government, inasmuch as it is said of David (*2 Kings,* Chap. v [, v. 2]), '[. . .] the Lord said to thee: Thou shalt feed my people Israel [. . .]'; and, in the second place, such [a twofold commission] was expedient for the good government of the Church, as well as for its peace and unity.

Consequently, a fourth argument, founded upon nature, is added, as follows: in one body, there should be only one supreme head, from which, as from a primary source, flow all vital actions, whether they serve the body, or the spirit; and the Church is one mystic body, as has already been explained;[2] therefore, it requires one supreme governor over both orders, and furthermore, both powers must reside in one person, for if they reside in different persons, an infinite number of dissensions and disputes will arise, of a character that can hardly be resolved by human diligence and reason, as actual experience has shown.

6. *The true opinion is laid down.* Nevertheless, we must assert that Christian kings do possess supreme civil power within their own order and that they recognize no other person, within that same temporal or civil order, as a direct superior upon whom they essentially depend in the exercise of their own proper power. Whence it follows that there exists within the Church no one supreme temporal prince over that whole body, that is to say, over all the kingdoms of the Church; but that, on the contrary, there are as many princes as there are kingdoms, or sovereign states.

This is the more widely accepted and approved opinion, among Catholics, and we shall shortly refer to those [authorities who support it].

But the proof of the first part thereof depends upon the proof of the latter part. For if there exists no one temporal head, the inference necessarily drawn is that the many kings are all supreme, in accordance with the proposition which we have already laid down; since it is not our intention at this point to examine specifically the question of whether this or that particular king is supreme, nor to compare the various temporal princes one with another, inasmuch as these are matters quite foreign to our present purpose.

7. *The emperor does not possess supreme temporal power over the Universal Church.* It is for the same reason that we do not deal here with the question of whether or not the emperor[3] is superior in jurisdiction over all Christian provinces and kingdoms, being consequently the supreme monarch of the whole Church. For though this question might be related to the latter part of our assertion, still, it bears scarcely any relation at all to the explanation of the dogmas of the faith. Therefore, we shall briefly assume that—whatever may be the opinion of Bartolus and certain other

2. [In *Defensio Fidei Catholicae*, Bk. I, chap. xvi, § 11, which is not included in these *Selections.*—Tr.]

3. [I.e. The Holy Roman Emperor.—Tr.]

jurists—the emperor does not possess such dominion, or supreme temporal jurisdiction, over the whole Church; for he either never has possessed it, or else, having once done so, has lost the greater portion of it.

Indeed, the proposition that he never did possess this power is very probably correct; inasmuch as he did not receive it in a supernatural or an extraordinary manner from Christ the Lord, nor from the Roman Pontiff, as will become evident, *a fortiori,* from what we say below; neither did he acquire it by any human right, since at no time, whether through election or through a just war, has a single emperor subjected to his sway the whole world, or the whole Church. For even granting that the early Christian emperors were lawful princes over their entire domain, it still does not follow that they were also supreme princes over all Christians, since there may have been many Christian peoples outside of their territories and, as Prosper Aquitanus (*De Vocatione Omnium Gentium,* Bk. II, chap. vi [chap. xvi]) rightly said: 'Christian grace is not content to be bounded by the same limits as Rome; and it has subjected to the sceptre of the Cross of Christ, many peoples whom Rome herself has not conquered with her own arms.' Thus we have also the words of Pope Leo I (*Sermones,* i,[4] *Apostolorum*), regarding Rome: 'That thou mightest govern more widely by divine religion than by earthly domination.' There is, too, the additional argument that this Roman Empire was itself divided into the Eastern and the Western Empires, and that, furthermore, the latter (which alone has remained Christian, the Eastern Empire having been seized by the pagans), though it continues to reside within one person in so far as [imperial] dignity is concerned, has been divided with respect to jurisdiction among many princes and kings. And of these, although some are subject to the emperor, many are regarded as lawfully exempt by right of prescription (to which is adjoined, at the same time, the consent of the peoples concerned), or by a title acquired by just war.

Accordingly, we assume for the present that there are, in addition to the emperor, many temporal kings entirely independent of his jurisdiction, such, for example, as the kings of Spain, of France and of England.

---

4. [Sermon LXXXII, *In Natali Apostolorum Petri et Pauli* in Migne, *P.L.* liv, col. 423.—REVISER.]

8. Therefore, only the assertion concerning the Supreme Pontiff remains to be proved. For if he does not possess true dominion, involving supreme temporal jurisdiction, over all the kingdoms of the Church, it is not possible to conceive of any other person who holds such a primacy, and consequently, there will be a number of kings who are temporally supreme.

The proposition, then, that such temporal jurisdiction over the whole Church is not possessed by the Pope, has been supported, among the theologians, by the following persons, in particular: Major (on the *Sentences,* Bk. IV, dist. xxiv, qu. 3), Cajetan (*Opuscula,* Tom. I, tract. ii, chap. iii [chap. iv] and on II.–II, qu. 43, art. 8), Victoria, in his *Relectiones* [*De Indis,* Sect. II, no. 3; *De Potestate Ecclesiae,* no. 2], Soto (*De Iustitia et Iure,* Bk. IV, chap. ii [Bk. IV, qu. iv. art. 2]) and Bellarmine[5] (*De Potestate Pontificis,* Bk. V, chaps. i *et seq.*), who refers to various other persons as holding the same opinion. And as for the jurists, this proposition is upheld by Covarruvias (on rule *Peccatum,* Pt. II, § 9, no. 7), by Navarrus (at great length on *Decretals,* Bk. II, tit. i, chap. xiii, notab. 3, and when citing several others, no. 41), and by Petrus Bertrandi (tract. *De Origine et Usu Iurisdictionis,* Qu. 3). Furthermore—and this is most important—from the very Popes themselves we obtain in many passages a simple admission of this same truth.

9. *The truth of this assertion is proved by the authority of the Popes.* Accordingly, the truth of the assertion in question should be proved, first of all, on the basis of their laws.

For Pope Nicholas (*Decretum,* Pt. II, causa xxxiii, qu. ii, can. vi) wrote to Archbishop Albinus as follows: 'The holy Church of God has no sword save a spiritual sword.' But the word 'sword', in canon law, customarily denotes temporal power. And therefore, this statement should be interpreted particularly as referring to the direct power and the jurisdiction which the holy Church possesses, of itself and (so to speak) by its intrinsic nature. For, within their own territory, it is possible for the Church, or the Ecclesiastical Prelate, to possess a temporal sword under another, additional title, as the Pope, for example, possesses it within his own proper domain.

---

5. Robert, Cardinal Bellarmine (1542–1621), was a leading Jesuit defender of the pope's possession of an indirect temporal power over princes.

Furthermore, this same Nicholas in a letter to the Emperor Michael (contained in *Decretum,* Pt. I, dist. x, can. viii, and Pt. I, dist. xxxiii [dist. xcvi, can. vi]) declared: 'The emperor has not appropriated papal rights, nor has the Pope usurped the title of emperor, inasmuch as Christ has so separated the functions of the two powers into the respective acts and dignities proper to each,' &c. Pope Gelasius lays down the same doctrine for us, when he writes (*Letters,* x [viii], *To the Emperor Anastasius*) that 'there are two [forces] by which the world is chiefly governed: the sacred authority of the Popes, and kingly power'. Again, Pope Gregory I (Bk. II, indict. xi, letter 61 or chap. c [letter lxv in Migne, *Patrologia Latina,* Vol. lxxvii, col. 662]) addressed these words to the Emperor Mauritius: 'To this end has power over all men been granted to the piety of my lords, namely, in order that the earthly kingdom should serve the kingdom of heaven.' Pope John I, also, in a letter to Justinian (contained in the *Code,* I. i.[6] 8) recognizes the supreme princely authority and royal power of that ruler.

10. Furthermore, Innocent III clearly holds (in *Decretals,* Bk. II, tit. 1, chap. xiii) that the King of the French possesses a supreme temporal jurisdiction which the Pope does not wish to unsettle or diminish; so that he adds: 'For we do not purpose to pass judgment concerning the fief, a matter which it is for the king (*ipsum*) to judge', clearly meaning that this judgment does not pertain to himself [as Pope]—not, at least, in a direct sense—a point which is rightly noted by the Gloss and by Innocent himself. The latter provides a fuller explanation when he adds: 'Save, perhaps, in the case of derogation by common law through a special privilege or through custom.' For in making this exception, Innocent clearly declares that no derogation from kingly rights is effected by divine law. Moreover, this same Pontiff expressly says (*Decretals,* Bk. IV, tit. xvii, chap. xiii) of the French King that this ruler recognizes no superior in temporal affairs; and with respect to the Apostolic See, he observes: 'Within the patrimony of Saint Peter, [the Pope] may order [all things] freely (that is to say, directly and absolutely), for within this territory, he not only exercises the authority of the Supreme Pontiff, but also wields the power of a sovereign prince

---

6. [The Latin text gives this title of the *Code* as *De Sacra Trinitate.* It should read *De Summa Trinitate.*—Tʀ.]

(that is to say, a temporal sovereign)', clearly meaning that, within other realms, he may not order temporal matters thus freely. In like manner, Innocent admits (*Decretals,* Bk. I, tit. xxxiii, chap. vi) that the emperor 'is supreme in temporal matters, within his own domain,'[7] and says of the royal power that 'in carnal matters, it is supreme.'[8] Again (in *Decretals,* Bk. IV, tit. xvii, chap. vii) Alexander III makes the express assertion that it is for the king, not for the Church, to pass judgment regarding temporal possessions; and he refers specifically to the King of England.

It is, then, sufficiently evident that the Roman Pontiffs themselves have never assumed power of the sort in question. This point will be brought out more fully by our later remarks.

11. *The same conclusion finds additional support in reason.* The second and principal proof that the conclusion[9] in question is true consists in the fact that no just title can be assigned by which the Pope properly possesses direct jurisdictional dominion in temporal matters over all the kingdoms of the Church, so that, consequently, he does not possess such jurisdiction, since it cannot be acquired without a just title.

The assumption that no just title can be assigned may be proved as follows: such a title would be based either upon positive divine law, or else upon human law, since it is evident from what has already been said that this title cannot be based directly upon natural law; for we have demonstrated that only a perfect human community incorporated politically in one unified state, is endowed directly by natural law with supreme temporal jurisdiction over itself; whereas the congregation of the Church—though it is the single spiritual, or mystic body of Christ, and possesses in this spiritual sense a unity in faith, in baptism, and in its head—nevertheless is not unified after the manner of a single political congregation; rather

7. [This quotation, as given by Suárez, varies slightly from the text of the *Decretals.*—Tr.]

8. [This quotation, as given by Suárez, varies slightly from the text of the *Decretals.*—Tr.]

9. [I.e. the conclusion that the Pope lacks supreme temporal power, with the corollary that no prince is temporally supreme over the whole Church. (*Vide* the first paragraph of Sect. 8 above.) The first proof of this contention was drawn from the papal decrees themselves. (*Vide* the first sentence of Sect. 9.)—Tr.]

does it contain various kingdoms and commonwealths not possessed of any political unity binding them one with another; therefore, by the force of natural law, there exists within the whole community of the Church no one immediate and supreme jurisdiction of a temporal and universal nature, extending over the Church as a whole; for, on the contrary, there are as many supreme temporal jurisdictions as there are separate political communities which do not form part of one unified political kingdom or commonwealth.

12. *Supreme civil power does not pertain to the Pope by human law.* Whence we draw the equally evident conclusion that the said power does not exist in any ecclesiastical prince, by any human title through which this natural power might have been transferred to such a prince.

For that title would consist in one of several alternatives. It might be a title by election and by the consent of the people; an alternative which (as is self-evident) cannot be applied to the case under discussion, since it has never come to pass that all Christian peoples have of their own volition and by their own consent, subjected themselves to one man as their supreme temporal prince. Or, it might be a title by just war; and this alternative, too, is clearly inapplicable in the case of an ecclesiastical prince. Again, it might be a title by lawful succession; another hypothesis which is untenable in the present instance, if we take our stand strictly upon human law. For it presupposes the existence of a legitimate title and dominion in the predecessor, so that, tracing it back in this fashion, we must necessarily come to some person who acquired such dominion independently of succession, by some other and earlier human title, one which must consist either in the consent of peoples, or else in a war that was just from the beginning, or was made just by the tacit consent of the subject persons, extending throughout the lawfully required period of time; but none of these suppositions is tenable in the case of any Pope, of whatsoever period or past age. Or finally, the title in question might be founded upon some grant made by human agency; and this hypothesis may be answered with very nearly the same reasoning as that applied to the hypothesis of title by succession. For no one can give that which he does not himself possess; and no prince, even of a temporal sort, has ever possessed supreme temporal jurisdiction directly over all Christian provinces and kingdoms (a point on which I have touched, above); therefore, there is no person who can have made such a grant to the Church, nor to the Pope.

13. All these observations are, properly speaking, confirmed by the canon laws which declare that the Pope possesses a legitimate right to, and temporal dominion over the kingdom of Rome—or, as it is called, the patrimony of St. Peter—through a grant made by the Emperor Constantine, as is evident from various passages in the canon law (*Decretum,* Pt. I, dist. xcvi, canons xiii and xiv; *Sext,* Bk. I, tit. vi, chap. xvii and *Decretum,* Pt. II, causa xii, qu. i, can. xv). For these passages clearly point to the conclusion that the Pope possesses direct temporal jurisdiction only over the kingdom and the states pertaining to the patrimony of Peter; a patrimony under which we include all temporal dominion now held by the Pope, whether the whole patrimony was granted by Constantine, or whether it originated with him and was subsequently increased by other kings and princes.

14. *The same point is proved in connexion with divine law.* The title based upon positive divine law is yet to be mentioned, a title which could have originated only through the gift of Christ the Lord, and which could have persisted only through legitimate succession. But no such gift was ever bestowed by Christ the Lord; consequently, there can be no legitimate succession with regard to such temporal jurisdiction; and therefore, jurisdiction of the kind in question does not pertain to the Pope by this title. Moreover, the contention that Christ did not bestow the said jurisdiction upon the Church is proved, first, by the fact that, if He had granted it to any one, He would most surely have granted it to Peter (as I assume, for the present, on the basis of certain statements to be made below, regarding the primacy of the Roman Pontiff); but the inference that Christ did not endow Peter with that jurisdiction is indicated clearly enough by a passage in *Matthew* (Chap. xvi [, v. 19]), wherein, to the words, '[. . .] whatsoever thou shalt bind [. . . ,]' and, 'whatsoever thou shalt loose [. . . ,]' Christ prefixes the promise: '[. . .] I will give to thee the keys of the kingdom of heaven [. . .]'. Therefore, Christ did not promise to Peter the keys of the earthly kingdom; and accordingly, it was spiritual power, not direct temporal dominion or jurisdiction, that He promised. Consequently, the words which Christ straightway adds, '[. . .] whatsoever thou shalt bind

[. . . ,]' and, 'whatsoever thou shalt loose [. . . ,]' should undoubtedly be interpreted in relation to the power which He had promised under the name of the keys. Similarly, the saying, 'Feed my sheep', should be interpreted in relation to that same power, for in these words Christ fulfilled the promise previously made. Nor is there any other passage in which Christ has indicated that He gave temporal dominion, or a kingdom in the literal sense of the word, directly to Peter or to His Church. Nor, indeed, does ecclesiastical tradition indicate that He did so; rather, it supports the opposite view, as we have seen. Consequently, we cannot know through any supernatural channel of the possession of such direct, temporal jurisdiction by the Pope. And therefore, the attribution of this jurisdiction to him is unfounded, inasmuch as he cannot possess it save in some supernatural manner.

15. The most acceptable supposition, then, is as follows: Christ Himself, in His humanity, did not take for Himself an earthly or temporal kingdom with direct, temporal dominion and jurisdiction, such as the emperor or other human princes possess, so that, consequently, He did not bestow that jurisdiction upon His earthly vicar.

We base the antecedent [partly] upon what we have already said in Pt. III of Tom. I, *On the Kingdom of Christ*,[10] and partly upon a brief demonstration of its truth, given here, and drawn from the Scriptural comments on the poverty of Christ the Lord. Take, for example, that passage in *2 Corinthians* (Chap. viii [, v. 9]): '[. . .] you know the grace of our Lord Jesus Christ, that being rich he became poor, for your sakes; that through his poverty you might be rich.' Accordingly, Pope John, when he declares (*Extravagantes Ioannis XXII*, Tit. xiv, chap. iv) that Christ, despite His poverty, did have dominion over some few articles of ordinary use, obviously assumes that He did not take for himself dominion over kingdoms, nor over those other possessions whose ownership constitutes human wealth. Moreover, the same meaning was contained in the words of Christ Himself (*Matthew*, Chap. viii [, v. 20] and *Luke*, Chap. ix [, v. 58]): '[. . .] the son of man hath not where to lay his head.' Again, He

10. [Referring to Suárez's work, *De Verbo Incarnato*, Pt. III, disp. xlviii, § 2, which is not included in these *Selections.*—Tr.]

spoke (*Luke,* Chap. xii [, vv. 13, 14]) with the same meaning of temporal
jurisdiction, when to the one petitioning Him, '[. . .] speak to my brother
that he divide the inheritance with me', He replied: '[. . .] Man, who hath
appointed me judge, or divider, over you?'—as if to say that He had not
assumed these judicial functions nor had He come into the world to exercise temporal jurisdiction; even as Ambrose, Theophylact and Euthymius
have correctly observed.

16. Moreover, our Lord Himself has confirmed this [interpretation],
saying (*John,* Chap. xviii [, v. 36]): '[. . .] My kingdom is not of this
world', meaning that it was not temporal and earthly, as was the kingdom
of Caesar. So this passage is expounded by Cyril (on *John,* Bk. XII, chaps. x
et seq.), by Chrysostom (*Commentary on John,* Homily LXXXII), and most
excellently, by Augustine who says ([*On the Gospel of John,*] Tract. CXV
[, § 2]): 'Hear ye, all ye earthly kingdoms! I do not obstruct your dominion
in this earth; my kingdom is not of this world.'

Wherefore, all the Fathers maintain that Christ took for Himself a spiritual kingdom which was in no way incompatible with true poverty. So it
is that, in the Old Testament (*Zacharias,* Chap. ix [, v. 9]), it is predicted
that there will come a Saviour, Who will be a king, and poor; a prophecy
which the New Testament (*Matthew,* Chap. xxi [, vv. 4 and 5]; and *John,*
Chap. xxii [Chap. xii, vv. 14 and 15]) declares to have been fulfilled in Christ.

In the *Psalms* (ii[, v. 6]), also, it is said of Him: 'But I am appointed king
by him over Sion, his holy mountain,' to which is straightway added the
phrase: 'preaching his commandment,' in order to indicate that this kingdom is spiritual, not earthly. Thus Augustine (*On the Gospel of John,* Tract.
CXV, § 2) asserted that the mountain over which Christ was appointed
king, was not of this world; 'for the believers in Christ, who constitute
His kingdom, are not of this world'.[11] Hilary, too, has declared that this

---

11. [This is a translation of the Latin of our text (*quia credentes in Christum qui sunt
regnum eius, non sunt de hoc mundo*), italicized to indicate that the words are a direct
quotation from Augustine. The passage in Augustine which is evidently referred to,
however, reads as follows in the *Patrologia Latina* of Migne, Vol. XXXV, col. 1939:
*Quod est enim ejus regnum nisi credentes in eum, quibus dicit, De mundo non estis, sicut
et ego non sum de mundo?* (For what does His kingdom consist, if not of those who
believe in Him, to whom He saith: 'Ye are not of this world, even as I am not of the
world?')—Tr.]

DO KINGS HAVE SUPREME POWER IN CIVIL AFFAIRS? 775

kingdom is not the earthly, but the heavenly Jerusalem. Moreover, the angel in like manner foretold [*Luke,* Chap. i, v. 32] concerning Christ: '[. . .] the Lord God shall give unto him the throne of David his father,' straightway adding [vv. 32 and 33]: 'and he shall reign in the house of Jacob forever. And of his kingdom there shall be no end'; for it was to be not a temporal, but a spiritual kingdom, a fact which has been noted by Epiphanius (*Panarium Adversus LXXX Haereses,* XXIX) and also by Jerome (on *Jeremias,* Chap. xxii [, vv. 29, 30] and *Zacharias,* Chap. vi [, vv. 9 *et seq.*]). The reason for this fact is that the temporal kingdom was not necessary to Christ for His honour and majesty, while it was expedient, as an example to us and for our redemption, that He should not take that kingdom for himself.

17. *An objection.* Thus, on the basis of our foregoing remarks, it is easy to prove the truth of our first conclusion,[12] namely, that Christ did not confer upon His vicar, a power which He did not Himself assume.

It will be objected that Christ, although He possessed no temporal kingdom of a perishable and imperfect sort, nevertheless did possess in His humanity, by the grace of [His] union [with the Godhead], a superior dominion, through which He could have used at will all temporal things or kingdoms whatsoever, so that, furthermore, He could have availed Himself of that dominion to bestow temporal kingdoms and a direct temporal jurisdiction upon His vicar.

The solution. We reply that we do not deny that He could have done so, even as He also could have assumed [such kingly power and jurisdiction] for Himself; but we infer that He did not bestow [this gift], since He did not assume for Himself this [temporal kingship and] since He left behind Him on earth only His vicar for that kingdom which He did in actual fact assume for Himself; a kingdom which is spiritual, as we have shown, and which, indeed, attains its perfect consummation in glory, yet has its beginning in this world, in the Church militant. Moreover, inasmuch as Christ Himself held perfect spiritual power without direct temporal jurisdiction, it was likewise possible for Him to impart to His vicar a spiritual jurisdiction that was perfect—that is to say, sufficient—unaccompanied by any

---

12. [*Vide* the first paragraph of Section 15 *supra,* p. 773.—Tr.]

other jurisdiction of a directly temporal nature. And finally, just as it was expedient that Christ Himself should not assume temporal jurisdiction, so also was it fitting that he should refrain from communicating such jurisdiction to His Vicar, lest He should disturb the kings of the earth, or should seem to mingle the spiritual with the secular.

18. Thus we draw our final proof from reasoning, as follows: temporal dominion with direct jurisdiction of a civil nature over the whole Church was not necessary for the spiritual government of the Church, as is self-evident, nor was it even of use for that same purpose; on the contrary, it might rather have proved to be a grave impediment; and therefore, it is improbable that such jurisdiction was granted by Christ.

The truth of the minor premiss is proved, first, by the fact that temporal government differs widely from spiritual government, and involves men in worldly affairs, which are a powerful factor in diverting mankind from spiritual matters, wherefore Paul has declared (2 *Timothy,* Chap. ii [, v. 4]): 'No man, being a soldier to God, entangleth himself with secular businesses [. . .].' Consequently, it is incredible that Christ the Lord should have united these two supreme and universal forms of power in one supreme pontiff of the Church, inasmuch as it is morally impossible that one man should be able to support the burden of universal government in both of these forms.

19. *An objection.* The objection will be made that, according to such reasoning, neither the Pope nor any other bishop can or should be at the same time a temporal prince.

The first reply. We reply, first of all, that it is true that Christ the Lord did not establish such [a twofold principate], nor order its establishment, neither did He bestow a temporal principate upon any of His ministers, or pastors. This point is proved by the foregoing discussion, and confirmed by our remarks concerning the kingly rule of Christ the Lord; [namely,] that He assumed no temporal principate, nor secular power of judgment, whether over the whole world or over some portion thereof, so that, furthermore, that principate and power were not imparted by Him to any of His bishops or vicars. Accordingly, the words which Christ Himself uttered [*Luke,* Chap. xii, v. 14] concerning Himself, '[. . .] who hath appointed me judge [. . .] over you?' are also applicable to every bishop. St. Bernard, too (*De Consideratione ad Eugenium,* Bk. I, chap. vi and Bk. II, chap. vi), proves this same point by means of other testimonies and a lengthy discussion.

We must add, however, that Christ did not forbid that a Pope or bishop should be at the same time a temporal lord. For no prohibition to this effect can be found, a fact on which we have already touched and which will be made still more evident by our later remarks; nor is it to be inferred from the line of reasoning propounded above, inasmuch as it is not in itself an evil that one and the same person should be an ecclesiastical pastor and a temporal prince. On the contrary, even though a temporal charge that is excessive in its demands and of a universal character is not properly compatible with spiritual cares, a temporal principate of a limited nature may nevertheless be not only permissible but even expedient for the conservation of the Church's majesty and authority, for necessary expenses and for similar good ends, as the *Sext* rightly declares (Bk. I, tit. vi, chap. xvii). Therefore, Christ the Lord not forbid this [combination of powers], but left the matter to human management, regulated by right reason and taking into account the requirements of [varying] times.

20. *A second solution.* A different reply may be made, however, to the argument adduced above; [namely, the reply] that the said argument proves merely that the *exercise*[13] of both forms of universal jurisdiction should not have been entrusted to the same person at one and the same time, but that it was nevertheless possible for the twofold jurisdiction to be granted in a primary sense to the Pope, as it has indeed been granted, subject to the law and condition that he shall ordinarily exercise the spiritual jurisdiction directly, and the temporal, through other persons.

The reply is refuted. But this reply may, in its turn, be easily attacked; not only on the ground that such primary jurisdiction cannot, by any title, nor in any convincing manner, be shown to exist (a point which has already been proved),[14] but also on the ground that the said jurisdiction would be either irrelevant or extremely odious.

---

13. [The italics are not in the Latin.—Tr.]
14. [*Supra,* this Chapter, pp. 767 *et seq.*—Tr.]

For, from one standpoint,[15] he who holds this jurisdiction must never make direct use of it in his own person, and thus such jurisdiction will be idle and useless, since it will never be possible for any one to exercise it through the agency of others, until he has first exercised it in his own person, when delegating it, at least, or committing it to another's charge as ordinary [, that is to say, official] jurisdiction. If, on the other hand, it is contended that the jurisdiction in question has indeed been granted to him to be used in this particular manner, I shall furthermore inquire whether the Pope, in committing such jurisdiction, for example, to another, altogether renounces his own share therein, divesting himself completely of all charge over it; or whether his commission of that jurisdiction is such that he nevertheless retains his temporal superiority, together with the power to revoke or at least to limit the charge committed, or even the power to correct or amend at will the acts performed as a part of that charge.

If the primary jurisdiction in question be conceived of in accordance with the former alternative, it is barren and useless. For of what avail is it, that the Pope should possess that power in a primary sense, if he has of necessity been obliged to bestow it upon others, to be exercised by them, and if, having thus bestowed it, he is no longer able to act as a superior within that [temporal] order? On the contrary, it even follows that he no longer possesses the said power, and is merely represented as having possessed it at one time, in order that its derivation in the case of secular princes may be attributed to the Pope, a claim which is regarded as replete with envy and exceedingly odious; and which, for the rest, is both futile and groundless.

21. If, on the other hand, the power in question is to be conceived of, in accordance with the second alternative, as existing in a primary sense in that it may issue as action at any time that is pleasing, or at any time that is opportune, then the hatred and envy involved will be greater still. For [, in the light of such an hypothesis,] temporal princes will no longer be sovereign rulers; the words of poet Sedulius—accepted by the Church and widely celebrated—will be false: 'The Giver of heavenly kingdoms, does not seize

---

15. [Simply *Aut enim*, in the Latin, the correlative of *Aut* apparently being *verô* (on the other hand), in the following sentence.—Tr.]

upon perishable things;'[16] and the Pope will be able to destroy or transfer temporal kingdoms at his own pleasure, and to arrogate to himself at will the function of judging and dispensing in temporal matters, as well as other, similar functions, and he will be able to do so validly, at least. For though such action [on the part of the Pope] might perhaps be undesirable, owing to the resulting disturbance of the [temporal] order, the completed action would nevertheless be valid, since it would be derived from that supreme jurisdiction on which the inferior depends. And such a situation would not only be odious and capable of disturbing (not without cause) the minds of kings, but is, moreover, essentially inconceivable, being opposed to the universal peace of the Church and to her universal and unbroken custom.

Consequently, even those jurists who hold that the Pope does have supreme temporal jurisdiction, do not admit this hypothesis. On the contrary, they absolutely deny, in the case of many acts of temporal jurisdiction, that the Pope is able, outside the bounds of his own temporal domain, to exercise these temporal functions in such a way that his action is even valid. This is the common opinion, for example, of the Doctors, in their commentaries on the *Decretals* (Bk. IV, tit. xvii, chap. xiii).

And finally, if the Pope did thus possess a primary temporal jurisdiction over the whole Church, he would be obliged to exercise solicitude for the proper temporal government of all the kingdoms of the Church, no less than for the spiritual government of all her episcopates, since in due proportion the same reason and the same obligation exist [with respect to both charges]; and consequently, the argument adduced above holds good, that is to say, the argument that this twofold universal care is excessive, practically speaking, for human strength and human capacity, and is entirely contrary to reason and to custom.

22. *The bases of the contrary opinion are destroyed.* Of the basic arguments for the contrary opinion, the first and the second apply only with regard to the indirect power [of the Pope]; and, assuredly, many of the authors cited in defence of that opinion are referring solely to this same superior power, as we shall explain at the end of the present Book.[17]

16. [These are words from the hymn used at Vespers of the Epiphany, beginning *Crudelis Herodes.*—REVISER.]

17. [Not included in these *Selections.*—TR.]

The third basis, on the other hand, is derived from a false principle, since Christ the Lord did not assume temporal dominion for Himself, as has been pointed out.[18]

The fourth basic argument is likewise faulty. For the Church is not a single temporal commonwealth, as it is a spiritual commonwealth, and it therefore requires, not one directly supreme temporal power, but a single spiritual [sovereignty], extending in its application to temporal affairs, as we shall learn below.[19]

CHAPTER XXIII

The Pope May Use Coercive Power against Kings, Even to the Point of Deposing Them from Their Thrones, If There Be a Valid Cause

1. This, as I have said, is the very heart and the chief point of the present controversy.

The chief point of the controversy with the King of England. For King James, who denies the existence of papal jurisdiction over the whole Church and, in particular, over kings, is in truth not greatly troubled with regard to [papal] directive power. He is, on the other hand, anxious and fearful as to the coercive power of the Pope, and especially as to that phase of it which extends to confiscation of his kingdom, since, by persisting in his error, James causes himself to doubt his own security upon his throne, if it should be believed by his subjects that the said power does reside in the Pope.

Accordingly, in order that he may be free to persist in his blindness, he desires to deprive the Church of Christ of every remedy against heretical princes. The same stratagem was devised before him, by Marsilio of Padua[1] and other enemies of the Church.

18. [*Supra,* p. 773, § 15, this Chapter.—Tr.]
19. [Chap. vi of Bk. III, not included in these *Selections.*—Tr.]
1. Marsilius or Marsiglio of Padua (ca. 1275–1342), author of *Defensor Pacis* (1324) and a leading denier of any papal authority in temporal matters.

But the contrary opinion is supported by all the Catholic Doctors whom I have mentioned above, and whom Bellarmine (in the recent treatise already noted, [Tract. *De Potestate Summi Pontificis*]) cites more fully. Nor is this contrary opinion less certainly true than the other statements already made. Indeed, if the latter are carefully weighed, it will not be difficult to refute the error that has been propounded and to defend, moreover, the Catholic truth that is confirmed by custom, by authority and by reason.

2. *Coercive power over wicked kings does indeed reside in the Pope.* For, in the first place, it clearly follows from what has been said above,[2] that there does reside in the Pope coercive power over temporal princes who are incorrigibly wicked, and especially over schismatics and stubborn heretics.

This assertion is proved first by a logical process. He must possess this coercive weapon because directive force is inefficacious without coercive force, as Aristotle points out (*Nicomachean Ethics,* Bk. X, chap. ix [, § 12]); so that if the Pope has directive power over temporal princes, he necessarily has coercive power also, in cases where they have been unwilling to obey the just direction laid down by laws or precepts.

The truth of the inference is proved as follows: those things which are from God, are well ordered and perfectly appointed; and therefore, if God has endowed the Pope with directive power, He will have endowed him with coercive power, inasmuch as any different system would be imperfect and ineffectual. *The Church cannot prescribe acts of a strictly internal nature.* Accordingly, the theologians, by reasoning to the contrary, maintain that the Church has not the power to prescribe acts of a strictly internal nature, since it is not possible to pass judgment regarding such acts, nor, consequently, to impose penalties for them, a process which pertains to coercive power. This is the opinion laid down by St. Thomas (I.–II, qu. 91, art. 4 and qu. 100, art. 9). And therefore, conversely, since the Pope is able, by his command, to direct temporal power efficaciously in its own sphere of action, he is also able to coerce and to punish those princes who disobey his just commands.

---

2. [Bk. III, chap. xxii of *Defensio Fidei Catholicae,* which is not included in these Selections.—Tr.]

3. *This view is supported by the Scriptures.* The foregoing logical argument is doubtless sufficient. However, inasmuch as our opponents demand [further proof, from] the Scriptures, we are also able to draw a clear confirmation of this truth from Scriptural sources.

For Paul,—having first spoken (2 *Corinthians,* Chap. x [, v. 4]) as follows: '[. . .] the weapons of our warfare are not carnal, but mighty to God unto the pulling down of fortifications [. . .]'—subsequently adds [*ibid.,* v. 6]: '[. . .] having in readiness to revenge all disobedience [. . .]' and again, [*ibid.,* v. 8]: 'For if also I should boast somewhat more of our power, which the Lord hath given us unto edification, and not for your destruction, I should not be ashamed.' In these words, indeed, the Apostle clearly maintained that he had received from God the power to avenge and punish all disobedience on the part of any Christian whatsoever, in so far as such vengeance and punishment might be needful for the edification and welfare of the Church. But the power to avenge or punish is a coercive power, as is self-evident. Wherefore, Chrysostom has spoken in this connection (on *Second Corinthians,* Chap. x = Homily XXII) as follows: 'We have received the power to this end, namely, that we may edify. But if any man shall oppose it and struggle against it, being so disposed that he can in nowise be cured by reasoning, then only let us have recourse to yet another power by means of which we shall overthrow and destroy him.' Theophylact also expounds [the words of the Apostle], thus: 'We have in readiness punishment and vengeance. [. . .] To be sure, I have received it (namely, the power in question) principally for the purpose of edification, but if any man proves to be incorrigible, we shall resort to destructive force. [. . .] If I should wish (continues Theophylact) to boast because God hath endowed me more amply, to this end chiefly, that I may have the power to do good, and even if I am forced to inflict punishment as well, I shall not be ashamed; that is to say, I shall not be conducting myself arrogantly nor mendaciously.' Moreover, a similar literal exposition of the passage from 2 *Corinthians* is offered by Theodoret and others, from among the Greek Fathers, and from among the Latin Fathers, by Anselm,[3] Cajetan (on that

---

3. [The Commentary on the Epistles of St. Paul by Herveus Burdigolensis Monachus [Migne, *P.L.,* clxxxi] was attributed to St. Anselm.—REVISER.]

text) and Augustine (*Letters,* 1 = clxxxv, Chap. vi, Migne ed.) where he avails himself of this testimony [on the part of Paul], in order to prove that the Church has power to coerce heretics, by means of punishment, to a recovery of their own sanity.

4. *Coercive power is symbolized in the Scriptures by a rod.* Paul referred symbolically, under the term 'rod', to this same power of punishment, when he said (*1 Corinthians,* Chap. iv [, v. 21]): '[What] will you? shall I come to you with a rod [. . .],' in accordance with the words of Scripture (*Psalms,* ii [, v. 9]): 'Thou shalt rule them with a rod of iron,' and other, similar passages [*The Apocalypse,* Chap. ii, v. 27 and Chap. xix, v. 15], and the Twenty-second Psalm[4] [, v. 4]: '[. . .] Thy rod and thy staff, they have comforted me.' Such is the interpretation offered by Jerome (in his commentary on *Zacharias,* Chap. i); and he expresses the same opinion with regard to the words of Paul already quoted (*To the Galatians,* Chap. vi). A clearer exposition still, is given by Augustine (*Contra Epistolam Parmeniani,* Bk. III, chap. i [, no. 3]), who says: 'Now it is apparent that he is speaking of punishment, to which he refers under the term "rod".' And Ambrose, too, has written (*Letters,* xviii, *To the Sister of Marcellus* [Letter xli, Migne, *P.L.,* xvi, col. IIII: *Frater Sorori*]): 'He whom the rod has barred from participation in the divine sacraments has by clemency been restored, to that participation.' The same writer elsewhere (*De Poenitentia,* Bk. I, chap. xii [chap. xiii]) declares: 'The denunciation of fornication, the indictment against incest, the censuring of swollen passion, and finally, the condemnation of the guilty person—these indicate the meaning of the phrase "to come under the rod".' The view taken by Gregory (*Letters,* Bk. I, epist. iv [epist. xxv]), and that of Tertullian (*On Chastity,* Chap. xiv) are similar, as are the views expressed on the same passage by other commentators whose names I shall omit.

5. Nor do I see what answer can be given in the light of the passages above cited; unless, perchance, it is argued either that Paul is addressing the common people of the Church, who are subject to him, and is not addressing kings, who are his superiors; or else that he is referring to a

---

4. [The Twenty-second of the Douay version of the Bible, but the Twenty-third of the King James version.—Tr.]

power bestowed specifically upon himself and not affording a permissible basis for conclusions as to the ordinary government of the Church.

The arguments of the opponents of this opinion are refuted. Either answer, however, would be futile. For why should Paul's words not apply to Christian kings who are both disobedient and obstinate? Was it, forsooth, because there were no kings within the Church at the time [when he wrote]? But it is possible that at that time there were no Englishmen either, within the Church; and do those words consequently have no application to any Englishman? Perhaps the reason is that kings are superior in temporal power and dignity? But this fact does not prevent them from being subject to the yoke of Christ and to the power of the Church, as we have shown them to be. Therefore, if the power in question is a coercive power over wicked Christians, in accordance with the testimony of Paul, it is also a punitive power over Christian kings. And if the King of England boasts that he is exempt therefrom, let him either confess that he is not a Christian or else let him give proof of a divine privilege and an exemption granted by the word of God; for otherwise, he loses his cause from the standpoint of justice, though he may sustain his position in actual fact. Moreover, even though this power possessed by Paul may have passed away with him in so far as it was related to his person and his apostolic dignity, it does not follow that this same power rested only temporarily in the Church; for it was lodged in Peter in a more perfect manner, by ordinary law, with the purpose of transmitting it, since such power was necessary (as has been demonstrated above)[5] in order to discharge the task of feeding [Christ's sheep] and to govern the Church fittingly.

6. *The power of binding includes coercive power.* Finally, our position is confirmed by the power of binding and loosing, which was granted especially to Peter; for the power to bind includes also coercive and punitive power.

And if our opponents deny this confirmatory argument, they will be obliged to point out the exception, inasmuch as Christ spoke in universal terms, saying [*Matthew*, Chap. xvi, v. 19]: '[. . .] whatsoever thou shalt bind [. . .]'. Moreover, Christ Himself so interpreted that power; for after saying (*Matthew*, Chap. xviii [, v. 17]): '[. . . And] if he will not

---

5. [*Supra*, p. 765; *Defensio Fidei Catholicae*, Bk. III, chap. v, § 5.—TR.]

hear the church, [. . .] let him be to thee as the heathen and publican,'[6] He added [v. 18]: '[. . .] whatsoever you shall bind upon earth, shall be bound also in heaven [. . .]'. It is as if Christ had said: If he will not obey the Church when she binds [him], let him be to thee as the heathen, since the Church shall not lack a power to bind, so efficacious that whatsoever she binds, shall be adjudged bound even in heaven. Accordingly, the Church has always understood from this passage [in *Matthew*] (though Calvin and his followers distort its meaning, as they distort that of other passages) that there resides in her pastors the power to coerce—through the censure of excommunication, at least, which is a spiritual penalty.

Excommunication was practised even in the time of the Apostles. The words of Paul (*1 Corinthians,* Chap. v) afford sufficient evidence that this practice of excommunication was customary within the Church in apostolic times; while the fact that this same practice was preserved in an enduring tradition is attested by all the laws and Councils [of the Church], all the decrees of the Popes, all the writings of the Holy Fathers, and, finally, all [ecclesiastical] histories; so that it would be superfluous to cite [each of] these authorities [individually]. However, it should be noted that Paul shows this form of coercion to be especially necessary against heretics, when he says (*Titus,* Chap. iii [, v. 10]): 'A man that is a heretic, after the first and second admonition,[7] avoid.' The same necessity is indicated by the words of *1 John,* Chap. ii [2 *St. John,* Chap. i, v. 10]): '[. . .] nor say to him, God speed you.'

7. *The Popes have quite frequently availed themselves of the above-mentioned censure, against kings and emperors.* One point only—a point which is of the greatest importance to our contention—I shall not pass over, namely, the fact that the Popes have most certainly made frequent use of the said form of censure when opposing emperors and kings.

For Innocent I excommunicated Arcadius and Eudoxia, because of the crimes committed against St. Chrysostom, as is clear from the last of

---

6. [This quotation, as given by Suárez, varies slightly from the Vulgate.—Tr.]

7. [Our Latin text has *correctionem* (correction, or improvement) which may be a misprint for *correptionem* (reproof), the term used in the Vulgate.—Tr.]

Innocent's epistles (*Letters,* XIV), and also from the statement of Nicephorus Callistus (Bk. XIII, chap. xxxiv). Moreover, Gregory VII (*Registrum,*
Bk. VIII, epist. xxi) records the same event. Gregory II bound the Emperor
Leo and those who followed him in his iconoclasm, by a synodical anathema, a fact recorded by Baronius ([*Annales Ecclesiastici a Christo Nato ad
Annum 1198,*] Anno 726, no. 24), on the authority of Zonaras and others. The same anathema was later confirmed by Gregory III, as Platina
relates. Moreover, Gregory VII excommunicated the Emperor Henry IV,
in the Roman Synod [vii], after repeated admonitions, a fact recorded in
Gregory's *Letters* (Bk. III, epists. v and x). This sentence of excommunication, confirmed by succeeding Popes and by the Councils, was learnedly defended by Cardinal Bellarmine (*Contra Barclaium,* Chap. ix).[8] The
same Gregory VII, in another Roman Council, bound with the chain of
excommunication [incurred] *ipso facto*—as is brought out in another book
of the *Letters* (Bk. VII, after epist. xiv)—the emperors, kings, and other
temporal princes who were usurping the powers of the investiture of bish-
oprics and other ecclesiastical dignities. And this same Pope, according
to Baronius (*Annales,* Anno 1079, no. 40), laid an interdict upon Poland,
because of the most grievous crime committed by her King, in slaying St.
Stanislas. Again, Alexander III excommunicated the Emperor Frederick I,
an incident related by Platina in his account of Alexander III [*De Vitis
Summorum Pontificum Omnium*], where he also records many other evi-
dences of this supreme power on the part of the Pope. Later, Innocent III,
as Platina says (in his biographical account of that Pope), 'branded the
Emperor Otto V with an anathema.' The *Sext* (Bk. II, tit. XIV, chap. ii)
informs us that Gregory IX excommunicated the Emperor Frederick II.
And, finally, John XXII excommunicated Louis of Bavaria, the interloping
Emperor, as Albertus Pighius recounts at length (*De Visibilia Monarchia,*
[in *Hierarchiae Ecclesiasticae Assertio,* Bk. V, chap. xiv]).

Moreover, the power in question was assumed to exist in the Church, by
the Lateran Council held under Innocent III, when that Council ordered

8. Bellarmine's reply *Tractatus de potestate Summi Pontificis in rebus temporalibus,
adversus Gulielmum Barclay* (1610) to *De Potestate Papae in Principes Christianos* (1609)
by the Scottish Catholic jurist William Barclay (1546–1608) who, teaching in France,
denied the legitimacy of the exercise of temporal power by popes over kings.

(Chap. iii) that the secular powers, whatsoever the offices they filled, should be compelled by an ecclesiastical censure—if necessity demanded such a course—to take a public oath as defenders of the faith, &c. This imposition of censures in a form embracing kings and emperors occurs with great frequency and is a rather ancient device, not one newly resorted to, since mention thereof is found in a privilege granted by Gregory I to the Monastery of St. Medardus, as we learn from a postscript to the letters of Gregory.[9] This passage in his letters is also referred to, by another Gregory (the Seventh) who derives from it the same argument (*Registrum*, Bk. VIII, epist. xxi, *Ad Herimannum*).

8. Furthermore, the Emperor Basil confessed that the said power over emperors resided in the Pope, when he said (Eighth Synod, action 6 [in Mansi, *Consilia*, xvi, col. 93]): 'Pope Nicholas, and the Holy Roman Church, have pronounced an anathema against those who resist a decree and sentence of this kind. Moreover, we, being long since aware of this and fearing the promulgation of a decree of anathema, have deemed it necessary to comply with the synodical judgment of the Roman Church.' The same power was recognized by Philip I, King of France, who having been excommunicated by Urban II was later restored [to membership in the Church] by Paschal and sent to Rome, moreover, for absolution, as we read in [the *Annales*] of Baronius (An. 1100 [, no. 19] and 1101 [, no. 7]). King Louis of France likewise acknowledged this power, when he wrote to Alexander III earnestly importuning him to exercise his authority against the King of England because of the death of St. Thomas of Canterbury. Nor did Henry himself, the King of England, dare to resist, for he humbly submitted to the penance imposed upon him by the Pope, as Platina relates. Peter of Blois (*Letters,* cxlv) records a similar instance, in connexion with Queen Eleanor of England, who, in seeking to defend herself and her son (the latter being unjustly held in prison by the King of France), requested the aid of the Pope and the drawing of the spiritual sword against that king. And finally, the existence of such papal power was acknowledged by the King of England, who accused the King of France

9. [The postscript is an appendix to the *Letters* of Pope Gregory I [Migne, *Patrologia Latina*, Vol. lxxvii, col. 1328].—Reviser.]

before Innocent III in order that [the Pope] might reprove the accused[10] and [even] excommunicate him if he would not hearken to the papal admonition.[11] This is the inference which we draw from a passage in the *Decretals* (Bk. II, tit. I, chap. xiii), in which the Pope speaks as follows: 'We do not undertake to judge as to the fief.' And later [*ibid.*]: 'But we do undertake to pass judgment concerning sin, the censuring of which indubitably pertains to us, a censorship which we can and should exercise against any person whatsoever.' And, in accordance [with this same principle of papal power], Innocent III—so Matthew Paris relates ([*Historia Maior,*] Anno 1204 [Anno 1209])—excommunicated King John of England and interdicted his kingdom.

9. Wherefore, they say that Marsilio of Padua himself has not dared deny that the Pope has power to coerce princes and kings, especially those who are heretical, by ecclesiastical censures of excommunication, or even of interdict. Marsilio did, however, deny the Pope's power to proceed further than this, against such rulers. King James, too, in defending his exaction of the oath of allegiance, would seem to resist the power of excommunication less vehemently than he does that of temporal punishment. Thus he bases his defence of the oath chiefly upon the ground that he thereby compels his subjects, not to abjure the papal power of excommunicating kings, but simply to deprive the Pope of kingly dominion and power. For King James holds, as he declares in his Preamble[12] (p. 12): 'On no lawful ground has the Pope acquired the right to depose kings. And this unjust usurpation and secular violence (so James describes it) on the part of the Popes, greatly exceeds the power of excommunication, which is a spiritual censure.' From these words it is sufficiently evident that the King does not oppose the spiritual censure to the same degree as he does temporal coercion.

10. *It is demonstrated that the Pope has power to chastise temporal kings even with temporal punishments.* Accordingly, it remains for us to press

10. [Simply *eum* in the Latin.—TR.]

11. [*Ipsum* in the Latin.—TR.]

12. [I.e. a preamble, as King James himself designated it, to his *Apologie for the Oath of Allegiance.* The full title of the preamble is 'A Premonition to all most Mightie Monarches, Kings, Free Princes and States of Christendom'.—TR.]

still further our argument against him, against Marsilio, and against other persons, by demonstrating that this same papal power may extend to the coercion of kings by means of temporal punishments, and deposition from their thrones, if necessity so demands.

This demonstration can be satisfactorily accomplished on the basis of Scriptural passages already cited,[13] and by practically the same process of reasoning. For Christ the Lord gave to Peter and his successors the power to correct all Christians, even kings, and, consequently, the power to coerce and punish them when they are disobedient and incorrigible. Nor did He limit this to the authority for imposing ecclesiastical censures. Therefore the said power cannot be limited by us nor by any prince within the Church; rather does it pertain to the Pope of Rome to decide and prescribe the fitting punishment for the occasion or necessity that may arise.

We have already given sufficient proof of the first proposition. And the second we can prove by means of Christ's words (which we have quoted many times), if they are correctly interpreted; for His admonition [*John*, Chap. xxi, v. 17], '[. . .] Feed my sheep,' is not limited, and accordingly, since the term 'feed' (*pascendum*) embraces even coercive power, which must necessarily reside in every pastor, the said power is not restricted to the imposition of censures, but rather remains to be shaped through prudence and equitable justice into some [appropriate] form of punishment or coercion. For every shepherd has power to coerce his sheep, not [simply] in some predetermined manner, but in accordance with what may be suitable and expedient for those sheep.

11. Moreover, we draw the same inference from these other words uttered by Christ [*Matthew*, Chap. xvi, v. 19]: '[. . .] whatsoever thou shalt bind [. . .]', inasmuch as this phrase, too, is of a general and indefinite nature.

A way of escape from [Suárez's] conclusion is precluded. And if it be contended that a later passage (*Matthew*, Chap. xviii [, v. 18]) interprets the same phrase and limits its connotations to the binding force of censures, we shall reply that the latter passage does indeed declare that this general power to bind includes the bond of excommunication, but that it does not limit the said power to the sole imposition of this penalty. Our reply

13. [*Supra*, pp. 781–83, §§ 2–3 this Chapter.—TR.]

is based partly on the fact that no such limitation is found in that context; and partly on the fact that forms of censure other than excommunication—such as interdicts, suspensions, and additional penalties of a similar ecclesiastical nature—fall under the power in question, even though the passage cited makes mention only of excommunication. Furthermore, the bond of precept and of law is also included under that same power; and by the very force of these terms, such power, viewed as directive, is not limited to a specific form of direction by personal precept or by fixed law that is binding in this or that particular way, but, on the contrary, embraces all fitting direction, in an unrestricted manner. Therefore, the same conclusion applies to this power in its coercive aspect. And so it is that the existence of such power is deduced from the passage in question by Innocent IV and the Council of Lyons (in *Sext,* Bk. II, tit. xiv, chap. ii).

12. *The same conclusion is drawn from the act of St. Peter.* Moreover, Bede shows (on *Luke,* Bk. III, chap. xl)[14] that [the exercise of] that power is exemplified in the act of Peter, at whose rebuke Ananias and his wife fell dead.[15] Bede asserts that they perished as the result of the words spoken by the Apostle Peter, because it was expedient, even in [the days recorded by] the New Testament, that such punishments should be inflicted occasionally, though with comparative infrequency, for the correction of persons other [than those punished]. Again, there is a statement ascribed to Augustine (*De Mirabilibus Sacrae Scripturae,* Bk. III, last chapter [chap. xvii]) to the effect that this punishment was imposed 'in order to demonstrate the weightiness of Apostolic authority and the gravity of the sin, [. . .] and also to the end that others might be admonished by the example afforded.' Gregory, when treating (*Letters,* Bk. I, epist. xxiv [epist. xxv]) of the office of pastor, and of the benignity, strictness, and zeal for justice demanded by that office, adduces Peter [still] more clearly as an example, saying: 'For so it is, to be sure, that Peter, who was prince over the holy Church by divine authority, refused to be venerated excessively by the just man, Cornelius; yet when he perceived the guilt of Ananias and Saphira, he straightway

---

14. [Bede, On the *Acts of the Apostles,* Chap. v.—Reviser.]

15. See Acts 5:1–10. Ananias and Saphira sought to conceal funds from a sale of land, and, when detected, both fell dead at the accusation of St. Peter.

showed how extensive was the power by which he had been exalted above other men; for by his very utterance, he struck at their life, seeking it out and finding it with the sword of the spirit, and thus confirmed his supreme power in the Church, as the enemy of sin.' Consequently, though this act may have been of an extraordinary nature and performed under the special inspiration and by virtue of the Holy Spirit, nevertheless, as Gregory declares in a subsequent passage: 'The zeal of vengeance revealed the force of power.'

13. *A further confirmation of this conclusion from the words of Paul.* Moreover, Paul points out the existence of this same power, in his *First Epistle to the Corinthians* (Chap. v [, v. 5]), when he has not only excommunicated the fornicator, but has also 'delivered him [. . .] to Satan for the destruction of the flesh, that the spirit may be saved in the day of [our] Lord [Jesus Christ].' For the use of the phrase, 'for the destruction of the flesh', clearly indicates that the culprit was punished with vexation of the flesh, in addition to the spiritual censure, and was forced to do penance in order that his soul might be saved. It is thus that Chrysostom explains the passage cited (in *Orations,* XV [Homily XV], on *First Corinthians,* v. 5, on that text), saying that the fornicator was delivered to an evil spirit for the destruction of the flesh, as was Job (though not for the same cause), in order—says Chrysostom—that '[this demon] might scourge him with a hurtful ulcer or with some other disease.' Theophylact says: 'In order that [the demon] might ravage him with a disease, and cause him to waste away.' And Anselm, too, though he suggests another possible interpretation prefers the one just set forth. For at the end of Chapter xxiv [Chapter iv],[16] when explaining the action of 'the rod', or Apostolic power of coercion, he writes: 'by excommunicating some, by severely rebuking others, and by scourging still others (as becomes a father)'; and in a latter passage (Chapter v), he interprets the phrase, 'destruction of the flesh', as signifying 'a grave bodily affliction brought about by a devil.' He declares, moreover, that Paul possessed a power, 'such that any person whom he had excommunicated would straightway be seized by a devil and tormented

16. [The reference is to the *Commentary of Herveus,* which was attributed to St. Anselm.—REVISER.]

for as long a time and with as much severity as the Apostle might wish.' This particular form of torment demanded a peculiar executive virtue, or power of command, over the evil spirit, of a sort not ordinarily bestowed upon other men [than Paul]; yet it does imply [the possession by Paul's successors of] the authority to coerce not only through excommunication, but also by other means. Again, Pacian suggests (*Paraenesis de [ad] Poenitentiam*) the same interpretation when he infers from the text in question that bodily punishment and affliction are sometimes necessary. Ambrose (*De Poenitentia*, Bk. I, chap. xii [chap. xiii]) takes a similar view, inasmuch as he, like Chrysostom, compares this destruction of the flesh with the trials of Job.

According, then, to this Patristic interpretation of the said text, we find that ecclesiastical correction and punishment consist not in spiritual censure alone, but also, on occasion, in corporeal afflictions, so that the pastors of the Church may resort to temporal punishment for the sake of spiritual welfare.

14. Secondly,[17] we may demonstrate the truth of this conclusion by appealing to the authority and practice of the Church.

Papal usage confirms the truth of this same conclusion. For among those Popes whose excommunication of emperors and kings we have mentioned, we find Gregory II, who caused Rome and the whole of Italy to be withdrawn from the empire of Leo, as Baronius relates (*Annales*, Anno 730, nos. 3 and 4, following Theophanes). And Sigebert (in *Chronicon*, Anno 731) has attributed the same act to Gregory III, saying: 'He convicted the Emperor Leo of error, and took away from him the city of Rome and the Italian (*Hesperiae*) revenues.' Moreover, Gregory VII deprived Henry IV both of his empire and of his kingdom, as is clear from the decree above cited, which runs as follows: 'Blessed Peter, Prince of the Apostles, heed us, we beseech thee'; and further on: 'Therefore, resting on that assurance, and acting for the honour and defence of the Church, as agents of Almighty God, the Father, Son and Holy Ghost, through thy power and authority, I deprive King Henry, son of Henry the Emperor, who with unheard of arrogance has risen against thy Church, of

---

17. [I.e. in addition to the first, or Scriptural basis of demonstration.—Tr.]

his governmental powers over the whole kingdom of Germany and Italy; I free all Christians from the bond of the oath which they have sworn or may swear to him; and I forbid that any of them should serve him as king.' Similarly, Innocent III 'stripped the imperial titles'—as Platina declares—from Otto, whom he also excommunicated. Innocent IV, too, at the Council of Lyons [*Sext,* Bk. II, tit. xiv, chap. ii], deprived Frederick II—who had already been excommunicated by Gregory IX—of his imperial power, not only absolving Frederick's subjects from their oath of allegiance, but also, 'for the rest, strictly prohibiting by apostolic authority that any person should obey or heed him, as Emperor or King.' Moreover, he bound, *ipso facto,* by the censure of excommunication, those persons who should thereafter show favour to Frederick, as Emperor or King, lending him counsel or assistance. Finally, Clement VI deposed Louis of Bavaria—already excommunicated by Clement's predecessors—from the imperial throne which that ruler had unjustly seized; and the election of another and lawful emperor—namely, Charles IV—was brought about by Clement.

15. Furthermore, in addition to these incidents relating to the Empire, Pope Zacharias, in a similar case affecting the Kingdom of France, transferred the royal title from Childeric the King to Pepin, as we read in the letters of Gregory VII (*Registrum,* Bk. VIII, epist. xxi; also in *Decretum,* Pt. II, causa xv, qu. vi, can. iii) and in the *Annales* of Baronius (Anno 751, beginning, and Anno 841, no. 3). In this [latter] context, Baronius tells also of the change transpiring in the kingdom of France in the time of the Emperor Lothaire and his brothers, Charles and Louis. These two, supported by the authority of the bishops, divided the kingdom between them, depriving Lothaire of his share in it, because of his crimes. Boniface VIII, too, issued a declaration depriving Philip the Fair, King of France, of his kingdom, publishing—on that very occasion—the Extravagant beginning '*Unam Sanctam*' (*Extravagantes Communes,* Bk. I, tit. viii, chap. i). This fact is recorded by Aemilius, in his life of that same Philip. In like manner, Gregory VII, when he laid his interdict upon Poland because of the murder of Stanislas, deprived King Bonislas of his realm, as Cromer relates, in his *History of Poland* (Bk. IV). And England herself provides us with a notable example in King John. Because of the monstrous crimes

that this king was committing against religion and against priests and other innocent persons, and also because he refused in a disobedient and stubborn fashion to return to the ways of reason[18]—though Innocent III had frequently admonished him to do so—but rather grew worse from day to day, he was stripped of his kingly dignity by that same Innocent, after lengthy consultation with the Fathers (so Polydorus says); while the peoples subject to him were absolved by the said Pope from their oath of allegiance, and Christian princes, notified of the situation, were admonished that they should pursue him as an enemy of the Church. Daunted by this sentence and stricken with the fear of imminent peril, John at last swore to abide by the will of the Pope, and, having taken the crown from his head, gave it into the hands of Pandulphus, the papal legate, [declaring that] neither he nor his heirs would ever accept it, save from the Pope of Rome. These things are recorded by Polydorus (Bk. XV).

16. Moreover, all the acts above mentioned and others of a similar nature were performed not in a hasty or obscure manner but rather, in some cases, at the largest councils, and sometimes, at general councils, such as that of Lyons. They were performed, too, in the sight of the whole Christian world, which approved them and ordered that they be carried through, so that one cannot possibly conceive of them as acts of usurpation rather than of true authority. Furthermore, the Council of the Lateran (Chap. iii), under Innocent III, assumes the existence of such [papal] power, saying: 'If a temporal lord, after being admonished by the Church, should neglect to purge his domain of heretical vileness, he shall be excommunicated by his metropolitan. And if he should neglect to make amends within the year, this fact shall be reported to the Supreme Pontiff, so that the latter may declare the vassals [of the said lord] to be absolved from that time forth from their obligation of allegiance to him, and may throw open his territory for occupation by Catholics.'

On the basis of all these considerations, one may draw up the following argument: the Universal Church cannot err in those matters which pertain

---

18. [*Resipere* (to savour of) appears to be used here in the place of *resipiscere* (to become reasonable, &c.). Du Cange's *Dictionary* records a fourth conjugation form, *resipire*, with the meaning of *resipiscere*.—Tr.]

to faith and morals; she has given her consent to acts of the sort under discussion and has approved them as being in harmony with divine and natural law; and, similarly, she approves canon laws which impose penalties of the kind in question upon temporal princes, because of the gravest crimes and contumacy on their part, and especially in the case of heresy; therefore, it is as certain that the Pope may coerce and punish temporal princes with such penalties, as it is that the Church cannot err in matters of faith and morals.

17. *The same truth is convincingly demonstrated by reasoning.* Thirdly,[19] the same truth may be proved by reasoning. For this power was required in the supreme head and pastor of the Church, on two grounds: that is to say, both from the standpoint of the emperors or kings and temporal princes of all kinds, and from the standpoint of the peoples subject to them.

The said power is required, on the first ground, in order that the Pope may correct and reform, or may even fittingly punish, a rebellious prince. For both the corrective and punitive functions are proper to the office of a pastor; and it frequently happens that censures alone do not suffice for these purposes, an inadequacy sufficiently brought out by daily experience; therefore, one must conclude that Christ did bestow the power in question upon His Vicar, since He made that Vicar pastor over Christian princes no less than over the rest of Christendom.

Accordingly, in so far as pertains to the first ground, and in cases turning wholly or chiefly upon the reformation of a prince who has sinned, the Popes are wont for the most part to employ censures, since this is the proper curative penalty, of which Christ spoke (*Matthew,* Chap. xviii). And if it so happens that the prince is corrected and reformed as a result of the censure, then it is not the custom of the Church to pursue the strict course of resorting to penalties of a severe and public nature. Nevertheless, the Church can and usually does impose some punishment, both for the reparation of damage, if such damage has perchance been caused by the guilty parties, and also in order that some satisfaction may be given by the latter, to God

---

19. [The first and second bases of proof were respectively, Scriptural passages, and ecclesiastical authority and practice. Cf. the first sentence of Section 14, and the accompanying footnote.—Tr.]

and to the Universal Church. For the obtaining of reparation for damage and of compensation for injuries inflicted is not so much punishment as it is a restitution (so to speak) and discharge of a debt; although coercion to such an end may require superior power. However, the principle of the common good and of legal justice demands that, in addition to this compensation which is due by the rules of commutative justice, some strictly punitive expiation of the offence be exacted, in order that the Church may receive satisfaction and an example may be set before other men, instilling fear into them. Moreover, when the king, disregarding the censure, continues stubbornly and incorrigibly to offend, then graver penalties should be imposed; and almost all the cases mentioned above fall into this category, as St. Thomas has noted (*De Regimine Principum,* Bk. III, chap. x).

18. *A confirmation [of this argument].* This part of our argument may be further confirmed by the fact that the Church does have power, with respect to all others among the faithful—that is, all other baptized Christians—not merely to coerce them through censures in order to correct their faults, but also to avenge offences already committed, by means of other, temporal or corporal punishments, and in the manner suited to an ecclesiastical judge and pastor; wherefore the lawful prelates of the Church, and particularly the Pope, possess this same power with respect to temporal princes, even those of sovereign rank.

The assumption is clearly proved by the unvarying practice of the Church. For the canon laws frequently impose pecuniary penalties, amounting sometimes to a confiscation of property. Again, they at times impose corporal punishments, short of peril to life or limb, such as the punishment of flagellation; at other times, they impose even the penalty of condemnation to the galleys; and, when the death penalty is necessary, the ecclesiastical judges—although, out of regard for the dignity of their position, they do not make a practice of passing such sentence—may nevertheless commit the accused to the charge of a secular judge, instructing the latter to inflict upon the criminal such punishment as is demanded by just laws. All of these facts may be accorded special consideration in connexion with the charge of heresy; for heretics are not only excommunicated by the Church, and subjected to other spiritual punishments, but are also deprived of all their temporal goods, by virtue of the canon laws as well as by the laws of the Emperors. And finally, in the case of a stubborn heretic, or one who has returned to his errors, the imperial laws impose capital punishment, while the canon laws deliver that heretic to the will of the secular judge, that the culprit may receive the punishment suited to the nature of his crime. This point is brought out in the *Decretals* (Bk. V, tit. vii, chap. ix, and similar chapters).

19. *The power to punish by means of temporal penalties is necessary to the Church.* The practice of the Church affords sufficiently convincing proof that these penalties are most just, and the same conclusion finds excellent support in the works of Augustine (*Letters,* xlviii and l [= *Letters,* xciii and clxxxv, Migne ed.] and *Contra epistolam Parmeniani,* Bk. III, chap. ii [, no. 14]). Moreover, the fact that such power must necessarily reside in the Church of Christ as instituted by Him is conclusively proved through reasoning; since if the subjects of the Church could not be coerced with penalties of this [temporal] nature, they might easily scorn the spiritual penalties and do grave injury to themselves and to others. For, as we read in the *Book of Proverbs* (Chap. xxix [, v. 15]): '[. . .] the child that is left to his own will bringeth his mother to shame.' Accordingly, the Christian Church would not have been properly appointed, nor would sufficient provision for it have been made, if it did not possess the power to coerce rebellious members, who are unwilling to submit to its censures. *A way of tacit escape from this conclusion is precluded.* Nor is this issue satisfactorily [evaded] by asserting that the existence of such power in temporal Christian princes is sufficient. For, in the first place, the princes themselves may transgress and be in need of correction, a point which I shall discuss presently. And, in the second place, the punishment of wrongdoing essentially pertains to the civil magistrates exclusively, in so far as those wrongful deeds are opposed to the political ends of the commonwealth, to its peace, and to human justice; but coercion, with respect to those deeds which are opposed to religion and to the salvation of the soul, is essentially a function of spiritual power, so that the authority to make use of temporal penalties for the purposes of such correction must have been allotted in particular to this spiritual power, whether the penalties are to be inflicted directly by the said power, or whether it avails itself of the ministry of its temporal arm that all things may be done decently, in order and efficaciously.

20. *Kings are not more exempt from liability to the said coercive power of the Pope than are other persons.* It remains for us to prove our earlier conclusion, namely, that if the Church possesses the power in question with respect to other Christians, of subordinate rank, it will have received that same power with respect to temporal sovereigns, and it will have done so most especially in the case of Peter and his successors.

The consequent, then, may be proved on the basis of the principle already laid down, that is to say: such sovereigns are as truly the sheep of Peter as are all other [members of the flock]; neither does their temporal dignity nor their temporal power render them immune from the force of the said papal power, nor exempt from liability to the punishment in question, inasmuch as one cannot infer from the words of Christ, nor from any other basic principle, nor by any process of reasoning, that there resides in them such liberty, or rather, such licence to sin. On the contrary, it is far more essential that the Church should possess the said power for the coercion of such princes, than that it should possess the same power for the coercion of their subjects. This is, indeed, the case because in the first place, the princes themselves are the more apt to err, and the more difficult to correct once they have fallen into error, in that they are more free. And, in the second place, the sins of princes—especially those sins which are opposed to the faith and to religion—are more pernicious [than the sins of other Christians]; for princes easily lead their subjects to imitate them, whether by their [bare] example, or by favours and promises, or even by threats and intimidation. Wherefore the Wise Man has rightly said (*Ecclesiasticus,* Chap. x [, vv. 3 and 2]): 'An unwise king shall be the ruin of his people [. . .]', for '[. . .] what manner of man the ruler of a city is, such also are they that dwell therein.'[20] The same doctrine has been upheld by the philosophers who are attracted to it by reason and by practical experience. We have an example in Cicero (*Letters [to his Friends,]* Bk. I [, epist.

---

20. [In the Latin text, the *Nam* (For) which connects these two passages is also italicized, implying that one continuous quotation is given, as follows: *Rex insipiens perdet populum suum. Nam qualis est rector civitatis, tales & habitantes in ea.* In point of fact, parts of two verses are quoted in inverse order, for the Vulgate reads: [. . .] *et qualis rector est civitatis, tales et inhabitantes in ea. Rex insipiens perdet populum suum* [. . .].—TR.]

ix, § 12]), where he follows Plato. Thus it is that this same Cicero has also rightly said in the *Laws* (Bk. III [, chap. xiv, § 32]): 'Vicious princes do not simply harbour vices within themselves, but also infuse those vices into the whole state.' For, in fine, 'Princely transgressions are graver than those of other persons, and therefore, the punishments inflicted upon princes by their pastors should be likewise more grave', as Gregory [the Great] remarked when discussing the pastors themselves (in *Liber Regulae Pastoralis,* Pt. III, chap. v),[21] a remark quoted by Pope Nicholas [the First], opposing Lothaire, King of France,[22] in his letter to that same King (cited in *Decretum,* Pt. II, causa xi, qu. iii, can. iii).

21. Finally, in view of the foregoing, we may readily establish another ground for the existence of such power over kings, namely, that it exists for the defence of the subjects. For it is the function of a pastor not simply to bring back the wandering sheep to the right way and recall them to the fold, but also to ward off the wolves, defending his charges from enemies, lest they be dragged beyond the fold and perish. But a bad king, and especially one who is schismatic and heretical, places his subjects in grave danger of perdition (as is evident from what we have just said), wherefore Claudian has declared [*The Fourth Consulship of Honorius,* Lines 299–300, 302]: 'The whole world adapts itself to the example set by a king. [. . .] Always the inconstant crowd changes with the prince.' Accordingly, it is a function of the papal office to defend the subjects of an heretical or perverse prince, and to free them from that evident peril; and for this reason Christ, Who did and ordered all things well and excellently, conferred upon Peter the power in question, including it under the term 'Feed', and under the power of binding and loosing. Consequently, [the Pope] can, through this power, deprive such a prince of his dominion; he can prevent the latter from injuring the subjects; and he can release those subjects from their oath of allegiance, or declare them to be released, since such an oath is always understood to carry with it the condition that it may be thus dissolved.[23]

---

21. [A footnote to *Decretum,* Pt. II, causa xi, qu. iii, can. iii corrects this reference as follows: Gregory, *Pastoralis,* Pt. III, chap. iv.—Tr.]

22. [Lothaire was King of Lotharingia or Lorraine.—Tr.]

23. [Simply *illa conditio,* in the Latin:—Tr.]

22. This ground for the existence of the said power has seemed, to St. Thomas and other approved theologians, to be so weighty and so moving that it would suffice in itself alone to deprive an infidel king of his dominion and power over the faithful, even if the reason previously expounded—that of vengeance and just punishment—should disappear.

Even if the Pope has not power to punish a heathen king, he does have the power to free Christian subjects from the dominion of that king. For, according to the teachings of Paul [*1 Corinthians*, Chap. v, v. 12], the Church does not judge 'them that are without'; whence these same theologians conclude that the Pope has not power to punish an unbaptized and heathen king, for infidelity or other sins; but, notwithstanding this fact, he does have power, if there are Christian subjects under that king, to deliver them from subjection to their ruler, on the ground that they are in evident peril of moral destruction. Such is the doctrine laid down by St. Thomas (II.–II, qu. 10, art. 10), and implied by Paul (*1 Corinthians*, Chap. vi). For Paul rebukes the believers who go to law before unbelieving judges, assuming that the Church has power to create judges who will decide between the faithful even in temporal questions lest they be compelled to appear before unbelievers, and demanding [*Ibid.*, v. 3], in order to establish this point: 'Know you not that we shall judge angels? how much more things of this world?' These words are cited by Gregory (*Letters,* Bk. VII, epist. xxi),[24] who is led by them to say: 'Is he, then, to whom hath been given the power of opening and closing the gates of heaven, prohibited from judging of earthly matters? This cannot be.'

For the same reason, and in like manner, a Christian wife may—so Paul teaches (*1 Corinthians,* Chap. vii)[25]—be separated from an unbelieving

---

24. [Migne refers the reader to Letter lii, indict. 2 in his *Patrologia Latina,* Vol. lxxvii, col. 875, note.—REVISER.]

25. The Pauline Privilege permits marriage dissolution where both parties to the marriage were nonbaptized throughout the entire duration of their married life. It can be requested when one of the parties either wishes Christian baptism or has been baptized and the other party remains unbaptized: 'To the married I give charge, not I but the Lord, that the wife should not separate from her husband . . . and that the husband should not divorce his wife. . . . But if the unbelieving partner desires to separate, let it be so; in such a case the brother or sister is not bound. For God has called us to peace' (1 Corinthians 7:10–15).

husband if she cannot dwell with him without wronging the Creator. Moreover, on the same principle, children who have been baptized are liberated from the power and the society of unbelieving parents, that they may not be enmeshed anew within the errors of those parents, according to the statement made at the Fourth Council of Toledo (Chap. lix). Accordingly, by a similar, or even more forceful process of reasoning, a Christian king (that is, one subject to the Church by virtue of baptism) may be deprived of his power and dominion over his vassals; and therefore, the ground [of defence for the subjects] is in itself sufficient to endow the Pope with power to punish such Christian princes, lawfully depriving them of their kingdoms and employing for this purpose the sword of other princes, so that sword shall thus be under sword, for the sake of mutual aid in defending and protecting the Church.

23. At this point, I might expound, confirm, and defend still other grounds on which the Pope would be entitled to order temporal matters for just cause; as he has done when transferring the Empire, when establishing the manner of electing the Emperor, when taking charge of that Empire during a vacancy on the imperial throne, and also, on yet other occasions, when laying down the law in temporal cases. But the brevity of a work of this kind forbids a full discussion of all these points; nor are they essential to our purpose and plan. Consequently, I must refer the reader to other authors, who have treated most learnedly of the points in question.

Concerning the Oath of Allegiance Exacted by the King of England

CHAPTER IV

Does the Third Part of the Oath [Exacted by King James] Contain Any Requirement in Excess of Civil Obedience and Contrary to Catholic Doctrine?

1. To the preceding parts of the oath, a third is added, as follows: 'I do further swear that I do from my heart abhor, detest and abjure, as impious and heretical, this [damnable]¹ doctrine and position; that princes which be excommunicated or deprived by the Pope, may be deposed or murdered by their subjects or any other whatsoever.'²

In connexion with these words, three points must be taken into consideration: first, the doctrine itself; secondly, the right by which this [portion of the] oath is exacted of the subjects; and thirdly, the extent of the inconsistency between the words in question and those in which the king promises to show that the said oath exacts nothing beyond [due] civil obedience.

With respect to the first of these points, in view of the fact that the king—anxious for his own security—insists repeatedly upon the well-worn question of whether or not it is permissible for a private individual or for his subjects to kill a tyrannical king, and inasmuch as an understanding

---

1. [This word is omitted in the Latin text of Suárez.—Tr.]

2. [The English translation of this quotation is taken from G. W. Prothero's *Select Statutes and Other Constitutional Documents Illustrative of the Reign of Elizabeth and James I* (3rd ed., Oxford, 1906), p. 259.—Tr.]

of this and other parts of the oath is contingent to a great extent upon a correct solution of that question, I have deemed it necessary to prefix a few words on the subject.

The theologians, then, distinguish two kinds of tyrant.

The two kinds of tyrant. There is one kind of tyrant who has seized the throne, not by a just title but by force and unjustly. These tyrants are not kings and rulers in reality, but simply usurp the position of king and imitate the role of royalty.

There is another sort of tyrant who, although he is the true ruler and holds the throne by a just title, nevertheless rules tyrannically in so far as concerns his use of governmental power. For, to be specific, he either turns all things to his private advantage, neglecting the common advantage, or else unjustly oppresses his subjects by plunder, slaughter, corruption, or the unjust perpetration of other similar deeds, with public effect and on numerous occasions. Such a ruler, for example, was Nero, whom Augustine (*On the City of God,* Bk. V, chap. xix) numbers among those tyrants whose dominion God does at times permit. For Augustine thus reads the passage in *Proverbs* (Chap. viii [, vv. 15–16]): 'By me kings reign and tyrants by me hold sway over the earth.'[3] Moreover, among Christians, that prince is particularly to be included within this class who leads his subjects into heresy, or into any form of apostasy, or into any public schism.

2. *A prince cannot licitly be slain on private authority, even though his government be tyrannical.* The question under discussion, then, has to do chiefly with lawful princes who rule tyrannically, since it is to such princes that the King of England refers, and since he himself is regarded by us as one of this group of lawful sovereigns.

Accordingly, we hold that a [legitimate] prince cannot justly be slain on private authority, on the ground that he rules tyrannically, or because of any crimes whatsoever.

---

3. [St. Augustine gives the citation as *Proverbs,* Chap. viii, v. 15, and quotes the text as follows: *Per me Reges regnant, & tyranni per me tenent terram.* The Vulgate, however, has: *Per me reges regnant, . . . per me principes imperant,* and the English of the Douay version reads: 'By me kings reign, . . . By me princes rule.' Moreover, the quotation would seem to include parts of two verses (15 and 16) rather than the whole of verse 15.—Tr.]

This proposition is commonly accepted and certainly true. It has been laid down by Saint Thomas in the *De Regimine Principum* (Bk. I, chap. vi), where he confirms it by means of excellent moral arguments. The same doctrine is supported by Cajetan (on II.–II, qu. 64, art. 3). And on this same passage of St. Thomas, we have the comments of other modern authors, including Soto (*De Iustitia,* Bk. V, qu. 1, art. 3), Molina (Vol. IV, *De Iustitia,* Tract. III, disp. vi), Azor (Vol. I, bk. viii, chap. xii, qu. 17, and chap. xxvi, qu. 7, and Vol. III, bk. ii, chap. ii, qu. 1, and chap. vii, qu. 30),[4] the Cardinal Toledo (on the *Summa,* Bk. V, chap. vi), and the Summists generally, on the word *Tyrannus.* The jurists—for example Bartolus, Alexander [of Imola], Socinus, the Cardinal[5] and others who are cited and followed by Gigas (throughout the entire treatise *On the Crime of Lesemajesty,* Qu. 65)—agree in upholding the same truth. Lucas of Penna, too (on *Code,* XI. xlvii. 1), supports this assertion, as do Conradus Brunus (*De Seditiosis,* Bk. V, chap. ii, nos. 9 and 10), Thomas Actius (Opusc. *De Ludo Scacchorum sive Latrunculorum,* Qu. 2, no. 50), Restaurus Castaldus (throughout the entire treatise *De Imperatore,* Qu. 82), at length, with excellent effect, and by means of many citations; and Paris de Puteo (tract. *De Sindicatu,* § *An liceat occidere Regem*), who tends toward the conclusion in question, although he expresses himself confusedly, as I shall later point out. Covarruvias (*Epitome of Decretals,* Bk. IV, pt. ii, *De Matrimonio,* chap. iii, § 4, no. 6 [no. 13]) is of a similar opinion. Moreover, this truth is in conformity with the precepts of *1 Peter,* Chap. ii [, v. 13]: 'Be ye subject therefore to every [human] creature for God's sake: whether it be to the king', &c., and later [v. 18]: 'Servants, be subject to your masters [. . .], not only to the good and gentle, but also to the froward.'

3. *The contrary doctrine is condemned as heretical.* The same truth was, indeed, laid down more specifically, and the contrary belief condemned as heretical, at the Council of Constance (Session XV), where (as I have recorded in Book V)[6] there was passed a condemnation of the following

---

4. [Azor, in all these passages, deals with much more than the precise point under discussion.—REVISER.]

5. [Gratian.—TR.]

6. [Not included in these *Selections.*—TR.]

proposition: 'A tyrant may and should be slain licitly and meritoriously by any of his vassals and subjects whomsoever, and even by means of secret snares and subtle blandishments or adulation, notwithstanding any oath sworn to that ruler or any pact made with him, and without awaiting[7] the sentence or mandate of any judge whatsoever.' Furthermore, according to the declaration of the Council, those persons are heretics, and deserving of punishment as such, who persist in defending the said proposition.

For this declaration applies (by the interpretation of all modern authorities) to those rulers who are tyrants simply in their manner of ruling, and not from the standpoint of their title to or usurpation of the throne. This fact is implied by the very language of the decision, since the terms 'vassal' and 'subject' are properly used only in connexion with a true prince and superior; and since, moreover, the phrase, 'notwithstanding any oath sworn' must include even the oaths lawfully taken before true kings, inasmuch as the wording is general. Accordingly, there is no doubt but that the author of the proposition in question is at least referring generally to all tyrants, whether they be tyrants with respect to their titles, or with respect to their manner of ruling. His terminology and elaborations clearly indicate that this is the case. *The error of Wycliffe and of John Huss.* There is, too, the additional argument that the proposition is derived from the doctrines of Wycliffe and John Huss, who held that temporal lords lost their supremacy *ipso facto,* in consequence of any mortal sin whatsoever, and could be rebuked at will by their subjects, on that ground. Such was the interpretation of the said proposition reached by this same Council of Constance (Session VIII). Furthermore, the Council condemns the proposition because of its sweeping universality, and the headlong rashness instantly discernible in all its clauses and amplifications; and it is particularly condemned by that body in so far as it applies to true kings and princes who are ruling in tyrannical fashion.

7. [Suárez here writes *non spectata* (which might be translated 'without reference to'); but the text of the condemnation appearing in the *Enchiridion Symbolorum* (p. 235) and Suárez, too, in subsequent passages on the subject, have *non ex(s)pectata* (without awaiting). *Vide* notes 21 and 23 on p. 818. Moreover, according to the Du Cange *Glossarium,* the two verbs came to be interchangeable in meaning.—Tr.]

The proposition may, indeed, be extended to apply to tyrants, in the strictest sense of the term—those who have unjustly usurped and retained the throne—if [the said proposition] is rashly maintained together with all those additional expressions, namely, the words, 'notwithstanding any oath sworn to that ruler or any pact made with him'. For this is a false belief and one contrary to natural reason, which demands that pacts, and especially pacts which have been solemnized by oath, shall be kept.

4. *The basis of the true doctrine.* Moreover, the principle underlying the assertion in question is as follows: a king ruling in tyrannical fashion might be slain by any private subject whatsoever, either on the ground of just vengeance and punishment, or on that of just defence, whether of the subject himself or of the state.

The first of these grounds is altogether false and heretical, because the power of avenging or punishing offences resides, not in private individuals, but in their superior or in the whole of a perfect community; consequently, a private person who on that ground slays his prince, usurps a jurisdiction and power which he does not rightfully possess; and therefore, he sins against justice. Our major premiss is certain, as a matter of faith, and has been upheld by Augustine, who writes (*On the City of God*, Bk. I, chaps. xvii and xviii):[8] 'It is not permissible for any one to slay, on private authority, a man who is guilty of wrongdoing but whose slaughter is not authorized by any law',[9] and again (Bk. I, chaps. xxi and xxvi): 'He who slays another when unauthorized by public power and not endowed with just dominion over him, is a homicide.'[10] Moreover, the reason underlying this position is, in the first place, the fact that the avenging and punishment of crimes are ordained for the common good of the state, and have therefore been entrusted solely to him who has also been entrusted with public power for the government of the state. Secondly, there is the fact that punishment is the act of a superior and of one possessing jurisdiction, so that, if this act is performed by a private individual, it is one of usurped jurisdiction. Thirdly and finally, if the assertion in question were

---

8. [This quotation is found in Bk. I, chap. xvii, of Augustine's *On the City of God.*—Tr.]

9. [This quotation, as given by Suárez, varies slightly from Augustine's text.—Tr.]

10. [This quotation, as given by Suárez, varies slightly from Augustine's text.—Tr.]

not true,[11] infinite confusion and disorder would result within the state, and the way would be opened to civil discord and to murder.

But if, in accordance with this reasoning, it is homicide to slay a private individual on one's own [unofficial] authority, even if that individual is himself a homicide, a robber, or an assassin, it is a far greater crime to lay hands upon a prince solely on one's own authority, even though he be an unjust and tyrannical prince. In fact, if this were not a crime,[12] there could be no security among kings and princes, since vassals readily devise complaints of unjust treatment on the part of rulers.

5. As to the second ground [for the slaughter of tyrants by private individuals], the ground of defence, it might perhaps be tenable in connexion with certain situations, but it is not tenable in connexion with the question we are discussing, namely: whether or not a king may be slain by a private individual solely because of his tyrannical government.

Thus it is necessary to distinguish between cases of self-defence and those in which one is defending the state. And we must further distinguish, with respect to the former group of cases, between those in which one defends his life or limb (that is to say, his body, which is threatened with grave mutilation), and those in which he is merely defending his external and adventitious goods.

For it would not be permissible to slay a kingly aggressor, solely on the ground of defence of one's external possessions: because, in the first place, the life of the prince—owing to the dignity of his office and the fact that he is, in a unique sense, God's representative and His vicar—must be preferred to such external goods; and furthermore, because the prince possesses a superior form of administrative power over the property of all his subjects, and because although he may possibly exceed the limits set to that power, he may not therefore be resisted to the point where he himself is slain, since it is enough that he should subsequently be bound in justice to make restitution of or compensation for all things forcibly seized, and that a private individual may exact such [restitution or compensation] in so far as he is able to do so without resorting to violence.

---

11. [Simply *alias* (otherwise) in the Latin.—Tr.]
12. [Simply *alias* (otherwise) in the Latin.—Tr.]

Is it permissible, or not, to slay the prince, in defence of one's own life? On the other hand, if one acts in defence of his very life, which the king is attempting to take violently from him, then to be sure, it will ordinarily be permissible for the subject to defend himself, even though the death of the prince result from such defence. For the right to preserve one's own life is the greatest right; nor does the prince, in the situation described, labour under any need that obliges the subject to sacrifice his life for his sovereign's sake, since, on the contrary, the prince himself has voluntarily and by his unjust behaviour placed himself in this perilous position. I say, 'ordinarily', however, for if the state would be thrown into confusion by the death of the king, or would suffer from some other grave injury detrimental to the common welfare, then the charitable love of one's country and a charitable regard for that common welfare, would bind one—even at the peril of his own life—to refrain from slaying the king. But this obligation falls within the order of *charity*, and with that order we are not at present dealing.

6. *What of those cases in which the state is defended?* Again, if the question relates to cases in which the commonwealth itself is to be defended, this [violent method of] defence is impermissible unless we assume that the king is actually attacking the state, with the unjust intention of destroying it and slaughtering the citizens, or that some similar situation exists. Under such circumstances, it will assuredly be permissible to resist the prince, even by slaying him if defence cannot be achieved in any other fashion. One argument in favour of this assertion is as follows: if such action is licit in order to protect one's own life, far more certainly will it be licit for the sake of the common good. A further argument resides in the fact that the state or commonwealth itself is in that case engaged in a just defensive war against an unjust invader, even though he be its own king; so that any citizen whatsoever, acting as a member of that commonwealth, and impelled—whether expressly or tacitly—by it, may therefore defend the said commonwealth, in the course of that conflict, in whatsoever way is possible to him.

However, we are not at present concerned with those cases in which the prince actually wages an offensive war against the state itself, with the intention of destroying it and slaying great numbers of the citizens. Rather are we concerned with those occasions when he rules the state peacefully, but disturbs and injures it in other ways [than by offensive warfare]. And in such cases, defence of the state by violence or by wiles directed against the life of the king is not to be permitted since the state is subjected, on these occasions, to no actual violence, such as might licitly be repelled by violence. Consequently, an attack upon the prince, under these circumstances, would be tantamount to the waging of war upon him, on private authority; and such warfare is in nowise licit, 'because that[13] natural order which is accommodated to the peace of mankind, demands that the authority to engage in a war should reside in the state, or in princes,' as Augustine declares (*Contra Faustum*, Bk. XXII, chap. lxxiv [chap. lxxv]). Another reason supporting the same conclusion is as follows: even as it is not permissible that one should, on his private authority, punish the wrongful deeds of any person by means of that person's death, just so is it impermissible to avert on one's private authority, and by the slaughter of that individual, the wrongful deeds which one fears he may in the future commit; and the principle involved is the same [with respect to both private and princely wrongdoers]; moreover, its validity is manifest in the case of private malefactors; therefore, the said conclusion holds good, and with still greater reason, when applied to offending princes.

7. *It is permissible to slay a tyrant whose title to the throne is tyrannical.* In order, however, that we may elucidate our doctrine more satisfactorily, and may the better apply the foregoing remarks[14] to the clause quoted above[15] from the oath, it will be necessary to make a prior declaration as

---

13. [St. Augustine has *ordo . . . ille,* which defines his meaning perhaps more clearly than does the Suárezian quotation. The latter omits *ille* and varies slightly in other respects from the text of Augustine, which runs: . . . *ordo tamen ille naturalis mortalium paci accommodatus hoc poscit, ut suscipiendi belli auctoritas atque consilium penes Principem sit. . . .* Suárez quotes as follows: *quia ordo naturalis, mortalium paci accommodatus hoc poscit, ut suscipiendi belli authoritatem* [corrected to *auctoritas* in the Paris edition of 1859] *penes rempublicam, seu Principes sit.*—Tr.]

14. [Reading *dicta* with the 1859 Paris edition, not *dictam* with our own Latin text, and that of Mayence, 1619.—Tr.]

15. [*Propositam* in our text. The 1619 and 1859 editions have *praepositam* which is perhaps the clearer term in this context. In any case, the clause here referred to is evidently the entire third part of the oath quoted in the first sentence of this Chapter.—Tr.]

to whether or not the doctrine already laid down holds good with respect to the second group, that is, with respect to rulers whose very title is tyrannical.

For ordinarily a distinction is made between these two classes of tyrants, inasmuch as it is asserted that the tyrant whose title is acquired in tyrannical fashion, may be slain by any private person whatsoever belonging to the state which is subjected to the tyranny, provided that there is no other way in which the said person can free the state from that tyranny.

So St. Thomas has held (on the *Sentences,* Bk. II, dist. xliv, qu. 2, art. 2, main part and conclusion), and his opinion has been adopted by almost all the Doctors above cited. The treatise of Conradus Brunus (*De Seditiosis,* Bk. VI, chap. iii), wherein he records various examples, may also be cited in this connexion, though his examples have been compiled from both just and unjust acts, so that they provide proof with regard not to what is just, but to what is customary. The reason, then, on which the said opinion is founded, is the fact that, under the circumstances described, it is not the king or prince who is slain, but an enemy of the state. Thus it is that St. Thomas (*De Regimine Principum,* Bk. I, chap. vi), similarly defends the deed of Aod, who—though he was merely a private person—slew Eglon, King of Moab, to whom Israel was subject, on the ground that Eglon was not the true King of God's people, but was rather an enemy and a tyrant (*Judges,* Chap. v [Chap. iii]). Abulensis [Tostado] gives the same account (in his commentary on that passage [on *Judges,* Chap. iii], qu. 26), and adds that this tyrant could [licitly] have been slain by any Israelite whatsoever. So, too, did Judith slay Holofernes (*Judith,* Chap. xiii). And Jahel performed a similar deed when she killed Sisara (*Judges,* Chap. iv), a deed for which she is praised (*Judges,* Chap. v). In like manner, St. Thomas approves, in the passage previously cited [on the *Sentences,* Bk. II, dist. xliv, qu. 2, art. 2, main part and conclusion], of the opinion expressed by Cicero when the latter praises [in *Philippics,* I] the slayers of Caesar, usurper of sovereign power, not by a just title, but through violence and tyranny. Accordingly, the Doctors, too, maintain that the crime of lese-majesty is not committed against a tyrant of this sort, since no true majesty resides in him. They furthermore hold that the title of 'prince' does not apply to such tyrants and that consequently the decrees declaring that it is not permissible to slay a prince do not refer to the said tyrants; a fact which is made evident by Gigas in his Treatise *On the Crime of Lese-majesty* (Qu. 65).

8. *A limiting condition.* However, St. Thomas (*on the Sentences,* Bk. II, dist. xliv, qu. 2, art. 2., main part and concl.) adds [, to the proposition that the slaying of these tyrants is permissible,] a limiting condition, as follows: such an act is permissible when no recourse can be had to any superior through whom judgment may be passed upon the usurper. This limitation has force most particularly when the tyranny is practised not by a sovereign prince but by some inferior. For not only [foreign] kings, but also powerful inferior lords are able to usurp through tyranny some form of dominion, or jurisdiction, or magistracy. Accordingly, under such circumstances, although the people may resist an invader while he is in the act of making the attack, nevertheless, when the attack has once been made, and he has obtained possession and the power of dominion, they may not, on their own [private] authority, slay him or begin a new war against him, as long as it is possible for them to have recourse to a superior, inasmuch as they may not draw their swords on their own authority when they have a superior; and still less would this be permissible to every private individual whatsoever. For if it were permissible,[16] general disorder would result, and great confusion would spring up within the state.

The circumstances which must exist in order that a ruler whose title is tyrannical may licitly be slain by a private individual. Furthermore, and for the same reason, even in cases where there is no superior to whom recourse may be had, it is necessary that the tyranny and injustice be public and manifest. For if there is doubt of their reality, it will not be permissible to remove by force the person who is in possession, since in case of doubt his position is the stronger, unless it is at the same time certain that his seizure of possession was tyrannical.

Again, in order that such a tyrant may licitly be slain, this slaying must be necessary to the liberty of the kingdom; for if the tyrant can be removed by any method that is less harsh, it will not be licit to slay him straightway without the sanction of any superior power and an examination of the case.

---

16. [*Alias,* in the Latin.—Tr.]

9. The commonly accepted opinion must also be understood [to include a further limitation, namely]: provided that no treaty, truce, or pact confirmed by oath shall have passed between the tyrant and the people; a point noted by Abulensis [Tostado] (on *Judges,* Chap. iii, qu. 26). For pacts and oaths, even those entered into with enemies, should be observed unless perchance they were manifestly unjust, and exacted by coercion.

Another limitation. Yet another limitation should be added as follows: provided that there is no fear lest the state suffer, in consequence of the slaying of the tyrant, the same ills as those which it endures under his sway, or ills even more grave. Thus Bartolus has declared (in his Treatise *On the Guelphs and Ghibellines,* No. 9)[17] that it is permissible, under the circumstances described, to put to death a tyrant for the sake of the common good, not for one's private advantage. For if any person slays a tyrant in order that he himself may by means of a like tyranny obtain possession of the sovereign power, he cannot but be held guilty of homicide, as well as of fresh tyranny. Again, if it is believed that the son of a tyrant, or another person similarly allied to him, is destined to inflict the same ills upon the state, it will not be permissible [to slay that person], because [in the event of such slaughter] evil is done without hope of effecting thereby a greater good, and because, in such a case, the state is not actually defended, or freed from tyranny, yet these are the sole titles by which that death may be justified.

The last condition. And finally, it is required that the state shall not expressly oppose [the act of tyrannicide]. For, if the state offers an express objection, it does not merely refrain from bestowing authority upon private individuals, but furthermore declares that [such a] defensive act is not desirable for it; and the state must be believed on this point; so that, under these circumstances, it is therefore illicit for a private individual to defend the state by putting the tyrant to death.

10. *The opinion of other authors.* Yet, in spite of the foregoing arguments, there are authors who do not accept the distinction and opinion above set forth, believing rather that it should be unconditionally ruled that private individuals cannot licitly slay a tyrant, whether he be tyrannical solely in

---

17. [In *Consilia, Tractatus, Quaestiones* (1527 Lugduni).—Reviser.]

his exercise of the ruling power, or tyrannical even in the acquisition of his title.

This is the view that Alfonso de Castro takes (*Adversus Omnes Haereses,* Bk. XIV, word *Tyrannus*), inasmuch as he expresses himself uncondition-ally and interprets in this fashion the pronouncements of the Council of Constance. Moreover, all of his doctrines point to that conclusion. Azor has committed himself ([*Moral Institutes,*] Vol. II, bk. XI, chap. v, qu. 10) to the same stand more expressly, rejecting the commonly accepted opin-ion above set forth. His position is founded first, upon the fact that the Council of the Lateran[18] treats of tyranny in absolute and general terms; secondly, upon the assertion (also absolute) of Augustine (*On the City of God,* Bk. I [, chap. xvii]), that it is not permissible to slay any person without public authorization; thirdly, upon the indefinite nature of St. Thomas' statement that the slaying of the tyrant in question is laudable, whereas he does not say that the slaying of the said tyrant by any private individual whomsoever is laudable; and fourthly, upon the fact that no malefactor can rightfully be put to death, nor can he who is in possession be dispossessed forthwith, without first being heard and judged. Nor does evidence of an accomplished crime suffice, unless a pronouncement of sentence precedes [the act of tyrannicide].

11. *Rejection of this opinion.* But these arguments are of little force when opposed to the commonly approved opinion.

For, as I have said, the Council of the Lateran[19] does not lay down the definite and universal negation, that no tyrant may be slain, but simply condemns the universal affirmation that *every* tyrant may be slain, a con-demnation stated not in an absolute form but rather with a number of qualifying terms, so that the declaration of the said Council is reduced to the following loose formula: 'Not every tyrant may be slain before sen-tence has been pronounced against him.' And one cannot draw from this formula any argument in contravention of the common opinion. *A reply to Augustine.* To the words of Augustine I reply that the private individual who slays a tyrant of the kind in question, does not commit this deed

---

18. [Suárez, no doubt, intended to say 'Council of Constance'.—Tr.]
19. [Here also Suárez, no doubt, intended to say 'Council of Constance'.—Tr.]

without public authorization, since he is acting [20]both by the authority of a tacitly consenting state, and[20] by the authority of God, Who has granted to every man, through the natural law, the right to defend himself and his state from the violence inflicted by such a tyrant. To the argument drawn from St. Thomas, we reply that his words are sufficiently clear, for in the body of the article cited [on the *Sentences,* Bk. II, dist. xliv, qu. 2, art. 2] he says: 'When the authority [to do so] exists, any person may repel dominion of this kind'; while in the reply to the fifth objection, St. Thomas makes it clear that he refers to a private individual in using the expression 'any person,' since he so interprets the words of Cicero concerning the slayers of Julius Caesar, and since, moreover, he comes to the following conclusion: 'For he who under such circumstances slays a tyrant, in order to liberate his country, is accorded praise and given a reward.' As to the [fourth and] last argument, we may say that it has force when any one is to be put to death in punishment for his offence, or deprived of those goods which he holds in peace and as possessions at the moment uncontested, whether formally or virtually; but the case with which we are dealing relates to defence, not to punishment; nor is the tyrant in possession peacefully, but rather by actual violence, since the state—though it may perchance refrain from opening battle, owing to its inability to do so—is nevertheless waging incessant and implicit war, as Cajetan rightly notes, in that it offers all the resistance of which it is capable.

12. *A new difficulty is presented.* A new difficulty, however, thus presents itself, namely, the fact that according to the doctrine expounded above there is no difference between the two cases, or two kinds of tyrant. For by that doctrine it is not permissible to slay on private authority even those whose titles are tyrannical, since, on the contrary, public authority is required; yet if the latter form of authority exists, it is also permissible to slay those [true] kings who rule in tyrannical fashion.

Accordingly, I argue further as follows. Even a tyrant whose title is tyrannical should be slain [only] in punishment for his crimes or on

---

20. [This interpretation of the correlatives *vel . . . vel,* attested by Du Cange's *Glossary,* is in the translator's opinion preferable here to the classical interpretation (or . . . or).—Tr.]

the ground of defence. In the former case (as has already been pointed out), he may not be slain simply by any private person acting on private authority, because, in the first place, the imposition of punishment is (as I have remarked above) an act of jurisdiction, to be performed by a superior, and because, secondly, not even the very state that has been wronged by such a tyrant may thus punish him save by the intervention of a public council and after a hearing and an adequate judgment of his case, so that the tacit or presumed consent of the state does not suffice to authorize the commission of this deed by a private individual, but rather, an express declaration made by special—or, at least, by general— commission is required. Wherefore it would be impermissible for a foreigner in a private capacity, or, indeed, for one in a public capacity but not endowed with jurisdiction over the said tyrant, to slay the latter on this [punitive] ground, save by express commission of the injured state. But if the act in question is permitted to a private individual only on the ground of defence, there is, consequently, no distinction between the two kinds of tyrant, since it is also permissible for a private individual to slay on that defensive ground a true king, who tyrannically assails [the rights of] his own kingdom, or state, as we have already pointed out. Moreover, on the same ground, it is not a power tacitly granted by the state to its members that makes such an act of homicide permissible; rather is it rendered permissible by the authority of God, Who through the natural law has bestowed upon every person the right to defend himself, his country and, furthermore, every innocent individual. Therefore, the killing of a tyrant on this ground is permitted not only to the members of a state, but also to foreigners, in either case and with respect to either kind of tyrant, so that no difference exists.

13. *The difficulty is solved.* To the last question I reply that, in the first place, it is true that a tyrant who seizes kingly power without a just title thereto may not justly be slain by any private individual whomsoever, as a measure of vengeance, or punishment. For this negation is conclusively established by the arguments set forth in connexion with the first part of our twofold proposition. Consequently, I grant that with respect to this point no distinction is made between a tyrannical king of the kind in question [and one whose title to power is lawful], in so far as the essential

principle of injustice is concerned; although, in the case of a lawful king, the crime committed is much more grave and constitutes an act of lese-majesty, which does not occur in the case of tyrants of the other group, for such a crime, when committed against them is a simple act of injustice and of usurped jurisdiction. We are thus left to conclude that only the right of self-defence makes it permissible for private individuals to slay [even] this latter sort of tyrant.

There is a great difference, however, between such a tyrant and a wicked [but legitimate] king. For [a true] king, though he may govern in a tyran-nical manner, is not inflicting actual violence upon the state subject to him, so long as he does not begin an unjust war against it; and conse-quently, in so far as he is concerned, no occasion for defence is offered, and no subject may attack him or wage war against him on defensive grounds. A true tyrant, on the other hand, is inflicting continual and actual violence upon the state as long as he unjustly retains the royal power and reigns by force; so that the said state continually wages against him an actual or virtual war, not vengeful in its character (so to speak), but defensive. Moreover, provided the state makes no declaration to the contrary, it is always regarded as willing to be defended by any of its citizens, or, for that matter, even by any foreigner; and therefore, if it cannot be defended in any way save by the slaying of the tyrant, any one of the people can licitly slay him. Thus it is indeed true, strictly speaking, that this act of slaughter is committed, under the circumstances described, not by private but by public authority; or rather, by the authority either of a kingdom willing to be defended by any citizen whomsoever as by its own members or organ, or else by the authority of God, the Author of nature, Who gives to every individual the power of defending the innocent.

Accordingly, even in this respect no true distinction is made between the two kinds of tyrant, since neither of them may be put to death on private authority, public power being, on the contrary, always a necessary factor. The difference between the two cases, however, is as follows: owing to the distinction explained above, the power in question is considered to have been entrusted to every private individual as against a true tyrant, while this is not the case as against a true sovereign [who rules in tyran-nical fashion].

14. *Another difficulty.* But in view of the foregoing, still another difficulty arises, one whose treatment is necessary to our present purposes.

For from the comment just made regarding true tyrants, it follows that the preceding comment regarding [true] kings who govern tyrannically, is applicable only when sentence of deposition has not yet been passed against such a king, and not after the passing of that sentence; this is an inference which will not be pleasing to the King of England, and it is one which merits examination.

For it has a firm basis, first of all, in the Council of Constance, inasmuch as that Council refers only to persons slaying tyrannical princes on private authority 'without awaiting[21] the sentence or mandate of any judge whatsoever' (since it is thus that the Council of Constance condemned the contrary proposition); so that consequently, if any judge possessing lawful jurisdiction with respect to such a [legitimate but tyrannical] king, whosoever that king actually is or may be, has pronounced against the latter a just sentence whereby the said king has *ipso facto* been deposed from his throne—if, I say, this should be the case[22]—the declaration laid down by the Council no longer holds; and therefore, the argument expounded above would cease to be valid, with the result that our comment regarding true kings, in the form previously propounded, would no longer be tenable. For under such circumstances, it is assumed that the sentence which has been awaited[23] is a just and lawful one. Accordingly, the tyrant's assailant acts not upon private authority but by virtue of the said sentence and, consequently, as an instrument of public authority. In short, when a king has been lawfully deposed, he is no longer a legitimate king, or prince; and therefore, the statement [of the Council of Constance], which has reference to legitimate kings, cannot hold true in his case. And furthermore, if

21. [*Vide* footnotes 7, p. 806 and 23 of this page. Suárez has *expectata,* here.—Tr.]

22. [This parenthetical clause translates a single word in the Latin, *tunc.*—Tr.]

23. [*Expectata.* Cf. notes 7, p. 806 and 21 of this page. One is tempted to give the term its late connotation of *spectata,* here, and translate, 'the sentence referred to', or, 'the sentence in question'; but the closely preceding quotation from the declaration of the Council of Constance, in which *expectata* would seem to have the usual classical significance, makes such a translation inadvisable. Probably Suárez's implied meaning is, 'the sentence which has been awaited before the tyrant is put to death.'—Tr.]

after the lawful deposition of such a king he should persist in his obstinacy and forcibly retain the royal power, he will become a tyrant even in regard to his title, since he is not a lawful king, nor is it by just title that he holds kingly power.

The reason for depriving a heretical king of his dominion over the kingdom. This truth is more clearly evident in the case of a heretical king. For in a sense, and by reason of his heresy, such a king is forthwith deprived, *ipso facto,* of his dominion over and proprietary rights in the kingdom, since the latter awaits confiscation, or is to pass *ipso iure* to his lawful Catholic successor; and nevertheless, [this heretical ruler] may not be deprived at once of the kingdom itself, but on the contrary justly continues to possess and administer it, until at least he is condemned through a declaratory judgment of his crime. This point is brought out in the *Sext* (Bk. V, tit. II, chap. xix). On the other hand, once the sentence has been pronounced, he is deprived altogether of the said kingdom, in such a way that he cannot by any just title continue in its possession; and therefore, from that time forth, he may be treated absolutely as a tyrant, and consequently may be put to death by any private individual whatsoever.

15. *A solution of the difficulty.* This difficulty[24] depends upon the assumption that even a king who is supreme in temporal matters may be punished with deposition and sentenced to be deprived of his kingdom; an assumption which the King of England declines to consider, but which is nevertheless true and follows clearly upon the principles laid down in Book III.[25] Moreover, we shall have occasion to repeat it in a subsequent part of our discussion.

To be sure, the question, By whom may such a sentence be imposed? is a grave one. But for the present we shall assume, briefly, that this power to depose a king may reside either in the state itself or in the Pope, although differently in the two cases. *Under what circumstances the state may deprive a [true] king, ruling in tyrannical fashion, of his kingdom.* For it resides in the state solely by way of a defence necessary to the preservation thereof, as

---

24. [See Sect. 14, *supra,* p. 818.—Tr.]
25. [*Supra,* pp. 761 *et seq.; Defensio Fidei Catholicae,* Bk. III, chaps. v and xxiii.—Tr.]

I have already remarked (Bk. III, chap. iii).[26] If, then, a lawful king is ruling in tyrannical fashion, and if the state finds at hand no other means of
self-defence than the expulsion and deposition of this king, the said state,
acting as a whole, and in accordance with the public and general delibera-
tions of its communities and leading men, may depose him. This would
be permissible both by virtue of natural law, which renders it licit to repel
force with force, and also by virtue of the fact that such a situation, [call-
ing for measures] necessary to the very preservation of the state, is always
understood to be excepted from that original agreement by which the state
transferred its power to the king.[27]

      This is the sense that we should give to St. Thomas' declaration (II.–II,
qu. 42, arts. 2 and 3 [art. 2, ad 3]) that it is not seditious to resist a king
who is ruling tyrannically, provided at least that this resistance is offered
through the lawful power of the community itself, and prudently, without
causing greater injury to the people. Moreover, it is thus that St. Thomas
himself has expounded this very point (*De Regimine Principum,* Bk. I,
chap. vi), as have his disciples, Soto (*De Iustitia,* Bk. V, qu. 1, art. 3),
Báñez (on II.–II, qu. 64, art. 3, doubt 1), and Molina (Vol. IV, *De Iustitia,*
Tract. III, disp. vi).

      Others, however, from among the jurists previously cited, take a mixed
view of this matter. For Paris de Puteo, [*De Sindicatu,* § *An liceat occidere
Regem*] and Antonio Massa (tract. *Contra Usum Duelli,* Nos. 78 and 79)
support the statement in question in such a way that they apparently concede even to individual citizens the licence to act thus. Yet, on the other
hand, Restaurus Castaldus ([*De Imperatore,*] aforesaid Qu. 82) supports
the contrary view to such a degree that he would seem to deny such license
even to the community. But [these two extremes of opinion] should be
modified, in accordance with our preceding remarks.

      16. Nevertheless, the power of which we are speaking does indeed reside
in the Pope, as in a superior possessed of jurisdiction for the correction
of kings, even supreme monarchs, these princes being regarded as subject

---

      26. [Not included in these *Selections.*—Tr.]
      27. *Vide* Soto, *De Iustitia,* Bk. V, qu. i, art. 3. Azor, Vol. II, bk. XXI, chap. v, qq. 8
and 9. (This note was in Suárez's original.—Ed.)

to him. This is a point which we have already demonstrated.[28] Accordingly, in the case of crimes relating to spiritual matters, such as the crime of heresy, the Pope has direct power to inflict punishment therefor upon the king, even to the point of deposing the latter from his throne if his obstinacy and a consideration for the common good of the Church should so demand. Again, in the case of faults relating to temporal matters, in so far as these faults constitute sins, they, too, may be corrected by the direct power of the Pope, to the extent, indeed, of their temporal harmfulness to the Christian State; and punishment of these faults may at least be inflicted by his indirect power, in so far as the tyrannical rule of a temporal prince is always pernicious also to the salvation of souls.

17. *A Christian kingdom is dependent upon the Pope when it deposes a tyrannical king.* Moreover, another point should be noted, as follows: even though a state, or human kingdom—regarded solely from the standpoint of its own nature, as it existed once among the Gentiles and exists still among the heathen—possesses the aforesaid power to defend itself against a tyrannical king, and to depose him with a view to such self-defence, in cases of necessity, I repeat, even though this be true, nevertheless, Christian kingdoms, when they so defend themselves, are in a sense dependent upon and subordinate to the Pope.

This assertion is true because, in the first place, the Pope may demand of any [Christian] kingdom that it shall not rise hastily against its king, nor depose him, unless the cause and reason therefor have previously been examined by the Pope himself. The latter possesses this power because of the moral dangers and the loss of souls almost certainly accompanying these popular tumults, and also for the sake of averting sedition and unjust rebellion. Thus history records that in such cases the kingdoms involved have almost always consulted the Pope, or even have petitioned that he should be the one to depose a wrongful king or a tyrant. We are told that this occurred in the case of Childeric, King of France, when Zacharias was Pope (*Decretum,* Pt. II, causa xv, qu. vi, can. iii), and in the case of other persons whom I have mentioned previously.[29] Moreover, the histories of

---

28. [*Supra,* pp. 780 *et seq.; Defensio Fidei Catholicae,* Bk. III, chap. xxiii.—Tr.]
29. [*Supra, Defensio Fidei Catholicae,* pp. 780 *et seq.;* Bk. III, chap. xxiii.—Tr.]

Portugal relate at length that Sancho II, king of that country, was deprived of his royal administrative powers by Innocent IV, when the latter was Pope, although Sancho's kingdom was not taken from him.[30] This incident is recorded also in the *Sext* (Bk. I, tit. VIII, chap. ii).

Secondly, a Christian kingdom is dependent upon the Pope in that the latter not only has power to advise or consent to the deposition by the kingdom of a king destructive to itself, but may even command and compel the said kingdom to take this course, when he shall have concluded that such an act is necessary for the spiritual welfare of the realm and, especially, for the avoidance of heresies and schisms.[31] For under these circumstances the exercise of [his] indirect power with respect to temporal matters for the attainment of a spiritual end is most admissible. Another argument is afforded by the fact that, in a situation of this sort, the Pope *per se* possesses direct power to depose the king; and therefore, he possesses the power by which he may coerce the kingdom, in cases of necessity, to the execution of this purpose, since otherwise his power [of deposition] would be not only inefficacious, but also insufficient. And the final argument is, that such a papal command, under such circumstances, is [in itself] an exceedingly just command.

18. *In what way a king may be punished, after a just declaratory sentence.* Accordingly, granting the truth of this basic assumption, we may assert, with regard to the point last proposed, that, after the rendering of a lawfully authorized condemnatory sentence by which a king is deprived of his realm, or—and this comes to the same thing—after a declaratory sentence for a crime entailing *ipso iure* the punishment in question, the person who has passed the sentence, or the one to whom that person has entrusted the task, does indeed possess the power to deprive the said king of his realm, even by slaying him, if no other means will avail, or if a just sentence includes such an extreme penalty. However, the deposed monarch may not be slain forthwith simply by any private person whatsoever, nor

---

30. Duarte Nunez do Liaõ, *Primeira Parte Dos Chronicas Dos Reis dè Portugal,* alias Capello. (This note was in Suárez's original.—ED.)

31. *Vide* Azor, Vol. III, bk. II, chap. vii, qu. 30. Castro, *De Iusta Haereti. Punit.,* Bk. II, chap. xiv. (This material was in Suárez's original.—ED.)

may he even be driven out by force, until that private individual has been commanded to act thus, or unless a general commission to this effect is contained in the sentence itself or in the law.

The first part of our assertion[32] follows clearly upon the principle above set forth. For he who can justly condemn a given person, is also able to execute—whether by his direct intervention or with such assistance as may be necessary—the punishment he has imposed; otherwise, his power to declare the law, unaccompanied by any effectively coercive power, would be vain. It is for this reason, indeed, as Augustine says (*On the City of God,* Bk. I, chap. xxvi), that an agent of the king acts rightly in slaying a man at the king's command, since under those circumstances he is carrying into effect the power of that monarch, rather than his own. Similarly, then, when a state can justly depose its king, the agents thereof act rightly in coercing that king, or—if it be necessary—in slaying him; for in such a case they are acting not on private, but on public authority. Thus Soto has well said (*De Iustitia,* Bk. V, qu. 1, art. 3), that even though a king who is a tyrant solely in his manner of rule [and not in his title to the throne] may not be slain simply by any one at all, 'nevertheless, when sentence has been passed (these are the words of Soto) any person may be appointed as the agent for its execution.' In like manner, then, if the Pope deposes a king, only those persons whom the Pope himself has charged with the task will have the power to drive out or slay that king. And if the Pope does not enjoin upon [specific] persons the execution of his decree, the said task will fall to the lot of the lawful successor to the royal power; or else, in the event that no such successor has been found, the kingdom itself will be charged with this function. Moreover, the Doctors hold that the same principle is to be observed in connexion with the crime of heresy, when declaration is made by public sentence depriving a heretical king of his kingdom. Castro (*De Iusta Haereticorum Punitione,* Bk. II, chap. vii) and Didacus de Simancas (*Institutiones Catholicae,* Tit. xlvi [, chap. xlv,] no. 75) may be consulted on this point.

32. [The assertion as a whole would seem to include both sentences of the immediately preceding paragraph in the English, and 'the first part' of the assertion is evidently contained in the first, or affirmative sentence. Suárez undertakes to prove the second, or negative statement, in Section 19.—Tr.]

19. The foregoing remarks also afford a ready proof for the second part of our assertion.[33]

A private individual may not on his own personal authority slay a man who has been condemned to death. For even though a given person has been justly condemned to death, he may not be slain at will simply by any private individual whatsoever, unless this individual has been commanded or in some other way impelled to the act of slaughter by one in authority. This condition holds because one person may not kill another, unless the slayer is either a superior possessing in himself the power to do so, or else the agent of such a superior; and he may not be called an agent unless his act is instigated by the authority of his principal. But if all this is true with regard to any malefactor, it will surely hold true with greater reason in the case of a prince.

It will perhaps be argued that these requirements are satisfied by the implicit or tacit instigation of the state, which by virtue of the very fact that it has deposed the king declares its will that he be driven out, coerced, and even—in case he resists—put to death, by the agency of [any or] all persons. Such a contention, however, is false, a fiction devised in defiance of reason. For a judge, in condemning a heretic or malefactor who is a private individual, does not by that very act empower all persons to punish such an individual; and consequently, when the state, or the Pope, condemns a king who is heretical, or tyrannical in some other fashion, such [punitive] licence is not—even in a tacit or implicit sense—granted to every one [indiscriminately]. The consequent is true because there is no just reason to assume the existence of this licence as against a king, more readily than as against other persons. For prudence and just procedure in the actual execution [of a sentence] are always essential; and furthermore, a greater danger of disorder and excess attends the coercion of the person of a prince or king than that which attends the coercion of other individuals. Therefore, if the Pope issues a decree declaring that a given king is heretical and deposing him from his throne, but containing no fuller specifications with regard to the execution of the sentence, all

---

33. [I.e. the negative part, prohibiting completely unauthorized private persons from executing the sentences in question. *Vide* footnote 32, p. 823.—Tʀ.]

other princes are not forthwith empowered to make war upon the deposed monarch, since they are not (so we assume) his temporal superiors, nor does that Pope invest them, by the sole force of his decree, with the power to make such a war.

Consequently (as I was saying) only the lawful Catholic successor of that monarch is invested under these circumstances with the said authority; or, in case he should be disregardful of it, or no such successor should exist, the kingdom as a whole body, provided that it is a Catholic body, will succeed to the right in question. But if this kingdom itself seeks the aid of other princes, they may lend such aid, a fact which is self-evident. Furthermore, if the Pope bestows upon other kings the power to invade the kingdom of the deposed ruler (and the examples which we have adduced in Book III[34] prove that the Pope has quite frequently done this), such an invasion may, under those conditions, be justly undertaken, inasmuch as they lack neither a just cause nor the necessary authority.

20. *The principles expounded above afford convincing proof of the error involved in the oath exacted by King James.* In the light, then, of these true and unquestionable principles, we find clear and convincing proof of the fact that the third part of the oath exacted by King James involves, under various heads, an excessive assumption of power, injustice opposed to righteous custom, and error in contravention of true Catholic doctrine.

To prove the first of these points, i.e. the fact that an excessive assumption of power is involved, I ask: By what authority does the King of England compel his subjects to swear that a certain proposition is heretical, when it has not been so condemned by the Catholic Church? For if the King maintains that the said proposition was condemned by the Council of Constance, we may object, in the first place, that it is impossible for him to make such an assertion consistently, inasmuch as he rejects the authority of the Councils, and particularly that of the modern Councils. By way of a second objection, we may ask where he can find, in the decrees of the Council of Constance, the words, 'princes which be excommunicated or deprived by the Pope'; or these, 'by their subjects or any other whatsoever?' Accordingly, in view of the fact that the addition of these phrases to the

---

34. [*Supra,* pp. 800–801; *Defensio Fidei Catholicae,* Bk. III, chap. xxiii, at end.—Tr.]

proposition in question effects an immense change in it and in its purport, the inference by which [the condemnation of] this [altered] proposition is attributed to the Council, is fallacious and misleading.[35] On the other hand, if King James condemns the said proposition, not on the authority of the Council of Constance, but simply on his own authority, then, beyond any possibility of doubt he exceeds and abuses a power which is not [even rightly] his. Moreover, it is very strange that he should repeatedly disparage the papal power of defining points of faith, while he himself dares to arrogate this same power to himself; for though he does not make this claim in so many words, he professes to do so by his acts. In this arrogation of power, the king is guilty of further inconsistency, inasmuch as he boasts in another passage of this *Apologie for the Oath of Allegiance* that he himself does not, after the fashion of the Popes, fabricate new articles of faith. In fine, since he holds that nothing is of faith save what is contained in the Scriptures, he should show us the Scriptural text condemning the proposition in question as heretical, or the text whereby the contrary proposition is divinely revealed, before we may regard as a heresy the one [condemned by him]. To be sure, Paul said [*Romans,* Chap. xiii, v. i]: 'Let every soul be subject to higher powers'; but nowhere did he add: Let all be subject even to powers that have been excommunicated or deprived [of their authority] by the Pope. Neither may the one injunction be inferred from the other; for they are quite different from each other, not to say mutually opposed (as it were) since a king who has been deposed is no longer a higher power. Wherefore, I further conclude that the profession of the said oath of allegiance, in so far as this [third] part of it is concerned, is tantamount to an acknowledgement of the royal authority and power both to condemn propositions as heretical at the king's own pleasure, and to lay down rules for the faithful, on his own authority, as to what they should believe as proper to the faith and what they should denounce as heretical. On the part of the king, [the exaction of] such an oath is an abuse and

---

35. [The translator has preferred here the ecclesiastical Latin connotation of *illusorius* (implied under *illusio* in Harper's Latin Dictionary), although the classical Latin interpretation would not be inacceptable: 'the inference . . . is a fallacy and a mockery.'—TR.]

usurpation of spiritual power, and on the part of those who take this oath, [its profession] is virtually equivalent to a profession of false faith.

21. *A convincing proof of this same fact, based on the very words of the oath.* Moreover, the very words of the oath are a clear proof of the fact that King James, in exacting the same, exacts more than mere civil obedience; that is to say, more than an oath pledging such obedience.

For something in excess of civil obedience—which is a matter on a far lower plane than the Christian faith—is obviously involved in an oath by which one is pledged to detest a given proposition as heretical. This is particularly the case when the injunction [condemning that proposition] is new to the Church, so that the king [issuing the injunction] does not simply compel Christian subjects to detest a proposition that is in any event already condemned by the Church (an action which is at times permissible to a Catholic king if it is executed in the proper manner), but even compels these subjects to detest a proposition which he himself newly condemns, upon his own authority. Such is the conduct of King James in the present situation.

The foregoing remarks also afford satisfactory proof of [our second point],[36] the fact that the oath in question is unjust on the part of King James, because it exceeds in many ways the proper limits of his power and so becomes a form of coercion by violence, and usurpation of another's jurisdiction.

Again, on the part of the faithful, acquiescence in the said oath is unjust. It is unjust partly for the general reason that they would be swearing either unlawfully or to a lie; since if they believe, solely on the King's authority, that the [rejected] proposition is heretical, their act merits condemnation even on this ground alone. [But such acquiescence is also unjust] for a much more potent reason, namely, because the proposition condemned in this oath is altogether true, and is rendered certain by the true principles of the faith, as we have previously proved;[37] and if, to all outward appearances, the subjects abjure a proposition of this sort, not believing in

---

36. [I.e. the second defect noted in the third part of King James's oath: 'injustice opposed to righteous custom.' *Vide* the first sentence of Section 20 of this Chapter.—Tr.]

37. [*Defensio Fidei Catholicae*, Bk. III, chap. viii, which is not included in these *Selections.*—Tr.]

their hearts that it is heretical, they are guilty of open perjury, a fact that is self-evident. Moreover, the profession of such an oath involves also a special and personal injury affecting the Pope, whose power and right to command obedience they deny, moved by the fear of man.

22. *A twofold error involved in the third part of the oath.* Finally, it is easy to draw from the remarks made above, the inference [embodying our third point][38] as follows: this third part of the oath of allegiance also involves erroneous doctrine.

One error is the contention that the Pope is not endowed with power to depose a heretical or schismatic king who is dragging or perverting his kingdom to the point where it will embrace the same schism or heresy. For this error is upheld by the words of the oath most particularly, and more directly than by any other [words pronounced on that matter], as will be immediately evident to every person reading the oath, and as we have previously proved[39] by manifold arguments.

A second error is not so definitely expressed in the wording, to be sure, but it is implicit in the very substance of the oath, and is virtually included therein, namely, the implication that a temporal king may even exact of his subjects a sworn belief in regard to those matters having to do with the doctrines of the faith and with the renunciation of heresies; and, indeed, the further implication that the decree of the king is to be preferred, even on these points, to the decree of the Pope. And all this is surely equivalent to declaring that a temporal king holds the primacy in spiritual—or ecclesiastical—affairs. For the primacy of Peter includes no greater dignity, nor any that is more necessary to the conservation of the Church and the unity thereof, than the supreme authority to lay down the articles of faith and condemn heresies; an authority which the King of England arrogates to himself, in the words already quoted. Therefore, the profession of the oath in question is an open profession of schism and error; and consequently, true Catholics are bound in conscience to reject the same.

---

38. [I.e. the third defect in this part of the oath: 'error in contravention of true Catholic doctrine.' *Vide* the first sentence of Section 20 of this Chapter, and footnote 36 on p. 827.—Tr.]

39. [*Defensio Fidei Catholicae*, Bk. VI, chaps. i–iii, which are not included in these *Selections.*—Tr.]

A WORK ON THE THREE THEOLOGICAL VIRTUES:
FAITH, HOPE, AND CHARITY

A WORK ON THE THREE THEOLOGICAL VIRTUES FAITH, HOPE AND CHARITY

Divided into Three Treatises, to Correspond with the Number of the Virtues Themselves

by Doctor
FRANCISCO SUÁREZ
of Granada
Member of the Society of Jesus
and Sometime Primary Professor Emeritus of Theology
of the Royal Academy of Coimbra

Dedicated to the Most Illustrious and Most Reverend
LORD D. JOÃO MANOEL
Bishop of Vizeu, &c.

With the Privilege of the Inquisitors, of the Ordinary, and of the King
Printed at Coimbra
By NICOLAUS CARVALHO, Printer to the Academy
In the Year 1621

Dedication

Far more tardily than befits us, most illustrious Bishop, this College of Coimbra, belonging to our Society, and by many titles yours also, offers to you this gift, such as it is. For this College is keenly aware that in you alone there are combined in the highest degree all those qualities by which authors are customarily moved to pay such tribute to their benefactors. They are the glory of your name, and of your truly royal lineage, the distinction of episcopal rank, choice literary culture, and what surpasses and almost eclipses all other titles, an admirable union of all the virtues that adorn a man and a prince. For if it is not unbecoming to pass over other considerations, it would seem to betoken not a human, but (as it were) a divine excellence, that one who excels in every way, should be unassuming in his mode of life, not elated by honours, and, though of an exalted position, not disdainful even of humble friends. For those reasons, indeed, Father Francisco Suárez, while living, had long been aware that he ought by some outstanding product of his talents, to manifest in unique fashion the gratitude due to you before all others. This, I bear witness, was the perpetual and constant wish, this the ardent endeavour, of one whose last wishes it would be wrong, in our judgment, utterly to disregard, especially as he could have found no more favourable advocate for his teachings, no readier champion of his labours.

However, we found at hand no work of this kind by which the debt could be completely discharged, and which could be considered a gift worthy of your acceptance.

But, lo! there now speaks one from above (in my belief, none other than the author), who says: 'You have here the treatise on the theological virtues, by means of which you may carry out the wishes of Suárez, and which you may quite fittingly lay before the illustrious Bishop of Vizeu, so that he who is known to have cultivated these virtues long and well, shall also be the patron of that teaching concerning them, by which the minds of men are disposed to harmony.'

Doubtless, Suárez had foreseen that this posthumous offspring of his talents, when it had come into our possession, and being bereft of its parent, would have need of your protection and your guardianship, so that, should it chance to be exposed to the arrows of the envious, it might be sheltered as by a rampart. For though the author was one whom the plaudits of the world, already universal, had raised above the reach of envy, nevertheless, now that he has attained to that more blessed felicity, far removed from human intercourse, he has been able to look, for this solicitude, to you alone, his strongest and most loving defender.

In truth, however, our College has been moved [also] by this consideration, namely, that the work should by preference be dedicated to you, if not as an [adequate] manifestation of the cherished hope that we may requite our own debt of gratitude, yet as some slight testimony of the sentiments which, each and every one, we entertain for you. Even though you accord but scanty credit to our own labours in connexion with this work, yet the author was one on whose behalf those labours will seem not unfruitful, and to you, most Eminent Lord, before all others, the fruits of that author should be dedicated. *Vale.*

Balthasar Alvarus, Doctor of Theology, of the College
of Coimbra of the Jesuit Society
To the Readers on Behalf of the Author

There are three chief reasons which have urged us not to confine within the enclosure [of our College] these lectures on the theological virtues. First, one might in all justice anticipate that a discussion of theological virtue by so great a theologian would be worthy, indeed, of so eminent an author and so weighty a subject. Secondly, the greater part of this work, which treats of faith, is (as it were) the last offspring of Suárez, generated that he might give a final proof, from his exalted position, of the wealth of his genius and the rich vein of his wisdom. Although, in Spain or in Italy, before he was summoned to this Academy of Coimbra, Suárez dealt more concisely (as he would do in the schools) with the subject-matter of the other two treatises, yet, they cannot fail to evince traces of the author's power and artistry. Thirdly, since—owing to the reasons which we have just mentioned—many copies of those lectures on faith were transcribed incorrectly, and since the number of these copies increased daily, we have decided to make them public, thoroughly freed from copyists' errors, and readily accessible to all students, thanks to the help of the press.

It will, however, appear that in this work one thing is lacking in doctrinal method—though you would hardly find any other writer so successful and scrupulous in the observance of that method—that is to say, the author ought first of all to have discussed the theological virtues in general, and then treated thereafter of the points proper to each. But a reply is ready to hand. For since all habits that accompany grace, chief of which are the theological virtues, go by the name of holiness, there remained hardly anything to be said as applicable to them in common, that would not be applicable also to sanctifying grace. The matter has been treated by Suárez in his work *De Gratia*[1] lately published, in questions such as these: first, are there any such habits *per se* infused and dwelling in the soul? Are the principles of their acts adequate (a point fully treated in Book VI)? Secondly, do the aforesaid habits demand a special co-operation of grace, in order that they may be actualized, or is the general co-operation sufficient (a question accurately treated in Book II)? Then again, thirdly, can these habits become more intense or remiss or be lost altogether (treated in full in Books IX, XI)?

However, if an explanation as to other more common elements in these virtues is desired, it will be published, God willing, in the fourth treatise, that on Passions and Habits, where the treatment by St. Thomas (I.–II, qq. 62 *et seq.*) will be amplified. *Vale*.

---

1. [No part of Suárez's treatise *De Gratia* is included in these *Selections*.—Tr.]

A Work on the Three Theological Virtues: Faith, Hope and Charity

On Faith

რჯ DISPUTATION XVIII რჯ

On the Means Which May Be Used for the Conversion and Coercion of Unbelievers Who Are Not Apostates

[INTRODUCTION]

The means by which unbelievers may be converted, differ in a twofold way. The means by which men may be drawn to virtue and faith, or recalled from vice and unbelief, are partly those which move the will through persuasion, instruction or kindness; and partly those others, which hold man to his duty through punishment or coercion.

Of such means, the former class are, without doubt, more in harmony with faith, because their influence is brought to bear more upon the will, and faith should be voluntary. But the latter class are sometimes necessary, if there is not to be a lack of power; and consequently, we are bound to treat of both groups, beginning with the former. *A twofold coercion: direct, and indirect.* Nevertheless, since the second group depend especially upon authority, which must reside in some individual, in order that he may coerce or punish another, we must first state that this coercion may be twofold, direct and indirect.

As to this issue, in order that coercion may be directly applied, two things are required. One is that it should be derived from the power of jurisdiction; the other is that this means should be used to draw men to the faith. Indirect coercion will be present, when compulsion is exerted not intentionally but in self-defence, or else in order to punish the injustice or crime of another.

Ecclesiastical jurisdiction is twofold in this matter. Therefore, this latter sort of compulsion might be exercised without any power of jurisdiction. With regard to this power, it is well to note at the outset that jurisdiction in the Church is twofold, spiritual and temporal. Hence, unbelievers may be subject to the Church in either of two ways, namely, with respect to the spiritual jurisdiction, as apostates are, or merely with respect to the temporal jurisdiction, as in the case of unbelievers who are not apostates.

SECTION I[1]

Has the Church the Power and Right of Preaching the Gospel to All Unbelievers Everywhere?

1. *Explanation of what constitutes the right and power of preaching.* In the caption introducing this question, two words, power (*potestas*) and right (*ius*), must be noted and distinguished, since they do not mean the same thing. For there are two ways in which one may have the power to perform a given act. First, there is the permissive sense; since one may be allowed to perform an act, although he may have no peculiar right to do so, no proprietary privilege (so to speak) with regard to the practice or act in question, as when I am allowed, for example, to enter the house of another. In the other sense, this power is coupled with right, as in the case of the power to make use of one's own house or of common property. Hence, in the question propounded above,[2] the power referred to must be understood in both senses.

---

1. [It should be borne in mind by the reader that this Disputation and the one following are divided by Suárez into Sections and Sub-sections instead of Chapters and Sections, as elsewhere.—TR.]

2. [I.e. the heading for Section I, 'Has the Church the Power and Right of Preaching the Gospel to All Unbelievers Everywhere?'—TR.]

[The first proposition:] the Church has lawful power to preach the Catholic faith in all regions. Therefore, we must assert, first, that the Church has that power by which it may legitimately preach the Catholic faith everywhere and to all kinds of unbelievers. This is obvious and is clearly a matter of faith, as is proved by the words of Christ in the following passages: (*Matthew,* Chap. xxiv [, v. 14]) 'And this gospel [of the kingdom,] shall be preached in the whole world, for a testimony to all nations'; (Chap. xxviii [, v. 19]), 'Going [therefore], teach ye all nations'; and (*Mark,* Chap. xvi [, v. 15]), 'preach the gospel to every creature.' For He Who gave this command, gave also the power of carrying it out, as the event has proved. Paul said (in the *Epistle to the Colossians,* Chap. i [, v. 6]), speaking of the Gospel: 'It has come unto you, even as it is in all the world bringing forth fruit and growing.' The reason [for the existence of this power] is also clear. For faith is necessary to all for salvation; and therefore, it was likewise necessary that there should be some way of announcing this faith to the whole world, since otherwise there would not be salvation for all according to the ordinary law, in view of the fact that, by the common and ordinary process, faith comes only through hearing and preaching, as Paul bears witness in the *Epistle to the Romans* (Chap. x [, vv. 14 et seq.]). For this reason also Christ Our Lord said (*Luke,* Chap. xxiv [, vv. 46–7]): 'Thus it is written, and thus it behoved Christ to suffer, and to rise again from the dead [, the third day]: And that penance [and remission of sins] should be preached in his name [. . .].' Consequently, this act of preaching the faith is righteous in its very nature and by reason of its object; hence, it is permissible of itself; and therefore, the power of executing that act is everywhere essentially legitimate, and proper to the Church. Finally, the [possession of the power] in question is also in harmony with natural reason. For the reproval of a brother by fraternal correction, and the instruction of the ignorant, especially regarding those things which relate to good conduct are [acts prescribed] by natural law, and the power of performing these acts—nay more, the obligation to do so at an opportune time—is therefore given to all; consequently, when once the fact of revelation and the necessity of faith are assumed, the act of communicating that revelation through speech and teaching, and the permission to do so, follow (as it were) from the natural law, and therefore, the power of preaching is also derived from it.

The inference [from the first proposition]. We may infer incidentally that this simple power (so to speak) normally belongs in some degree to all believers, if they are sufficiently instructed to exercise it, and are not otherwise forbidden. This is obvious, for the reason that [such preaching] is a work of charity, and one of the works of mercy, a fact which will be more fully expounded in connexion with the next proposition.

2. *The second proposition concerns the nature of the Church's power to preach the true faith everywhere.* My second proposition is as follows: the Church has not only the simple and (so to speak) the permissive faculty of preaching the Gospel everywhere, but also the right to preach thus, coupled with a special power. This is evidently the opinion of St. Thomas, as expressed in a passage (II.–II, qu. 10, art. 8), on which Cajetan and other commentators are in agreement; as are other scholastics (on the *Sentences of Peter Lombard,* Bk. II, dist. xli), especially Major (*ibid.,* Dist. xliv, qu. 3), others on the *Sentences* (Bk. IV, dist. iv), including Soto (*ibid.,* Dist. v, the sole question, art. 10), and Victoria (Relectio I: *De Indis,* Sect. II, no. 9 [Relectio V: *De Indis,* Sect. III, no. 9]).

Basis of the second proposition. The basis of that opinion is that Christ our Lord had this power over all men, as His heritage. For that heritage was to be obtained by means of preaching the faith; and since all the nations were not to be instructed by Himself, Christ bestowed the power of giving such instruction, coupled with the corresponding right and authority, to His apostles, and through them to the Church; therefore, the Church has this special right. The entire first proposition of the foregoing argument may easily be drawn from the Old and New Testaments. For in *Psalms,* ii [, v. 6], the Psalmist, speaking in the person of Christ, says: 'But I am appointed king by him over Sion his holy mountain', while the mode of acquiring the kingdom is indicated by the phrase [*ibid.*], 'preaching his commandment'; and then these words are added [*ibid.,* v. 8]: 'Ask of me and I will give thee the Gentiles for thy inheritance, and the uttermost parts of the earth for thy possession,' plainly declaring a plenitude of jurisdiction over the whole world. That this prophecy was fulfilled in and through Christ, Our Lord Himself has testified, saying, *Matthew,* last Chap. [chap. xxviii, v. 18], 'All power is given to me in heaven and in earth'; then follows the command [*ibid.* v. 19],

'Going [therefore], teach ye all nations', whereby He communicates His own right and power to the Apostles. This is Paul's meaning in the words (*2 Corinthians,* Chap. v [, v. 19]), 'hath placed in us the word of reconciliation'; to which he adds [*ibid.,* v. 20], 'For Christ therefore we are ambassadors'; and an ambassador, indeed, represents his prince and shares in his power. Accordingly, Paul also said (*Ephesians,* Chap. iv [, vv. 11–12]), 'And He gave some apostles [. . .] and other some pastors and doctors [. . .] for the edifying of the body of Christ'; and, in his Second *Epistle to Timothy* (Chap. ii [, v. 9]), '[I labour even unto bands, as an evildoer,] but the word of God is not bound'; that is to say, it is not bound, because the Church has this right of spreading the word, and not merely the right, but the necessity and obligation as well, according to the passage (*1 Corinthians,* Chap. ix [, v. 16]), 'For woe is unto me if I preach not the gospel, for a necessity lieth upon me.'[3] Finally, the words of Christ to Peter (*John,* Chap. xxi [, v. 17]), 'Feed my sheep,' support this truth; for the term 'Feed' refers not merely to an indefinite sort of power, but to one coupled with jurisdiction, which is exercised, or rather, is begun, by preaching. Therefore, since this power was given to Peter that it might persist in the Church forever, the Church possesses such right and power.

3. *The reason for this authority, in terms of the end in view, is stated.* Moreover, if we regard the end to be achieved, a reason can be given for the existence of this authority, namely, that the power of teaching the faith was necessary, as I have said, for the salvation of men, and in order that the redemption of Christ might be brought to all men. Therefore, in order that the said power of teaching might be efficacious, it was necessary to communicate it not only with a simple authorization and (as it were) permission, but also with its own proper right and power. The Lord Christ was able to give that power in this way; hence, He did so give it. Furthermore, although the existence of such power cannot be demonstrated by natural reason, it is still entirely in harmony therewith, since, as I have said, the right of teaching the ignorant is (as it were) connatural to every man. Therefore, assuming the necessity for faith, it is entirely consonant with reason that the Author of faith should leave to His ministers and

---

3. [The word order, as given by Suárez, varies somewhat from the Vulgate.—TR.]

especially to His Vicar this special right of instructing men in the doctrines of the faith.

4. *The third proposition: the Church has the right of protecting its preachers, and of punishing those who hinder its preaching.* From this second proposition, a third follows, namely: the Church has the right of defending its preachers, and of subduing those who by force and violence hinder or do not permit this preaching. This is the opinion held by the authors above cited, and especially by Major and by Victoria. It is possible also, in a sense, to confirm this proposition by an example from Paul (*Acts,* Chap. xiii [, vv. 8–11]), who condemned Elymas[4] the sorcerer to a perpetual blindness for resisting the ways of the Lord, as Jerome stated in his letter *To Riparius against Vigilantius* [= *Letters,* cix. 3] and cited in *Decretum,* Pt. II, causa XXIII, qu. viii, can. xiii, where there are many references to the Fathers who confirm this truth; see also *Decretum, ibid.,* can. xi, and other passages therein.

The first reason in proof of this proposition. Reasons in support of this proposition are easily inferred from what we have already said. The first is that if the Church has the right of preaching the Gospel everywhere, then whoever by force or violence prevents the exercise of this right, does an injury to the Church. Therefore, the Church may repel such violence and protect its own right; for this [secondary right] follows naturally from the original right [of preaching], especially since the authority in question is supreme within its own order, as is this right in the Church.

The second reason. Secondly, this same reason is reinforced by another principle of both canon and civil law, namely: when jurisdiction is granted, everything morally necessary for the exercise thereof is granted as well, because otherwise the grant would be minimized and inefficacious (*Digest,* II. i. 2; and likewise *Decretals,* Bk. I, tit. XXIX, chap. v and other similar passages). But the right in question has been given to the Church as a true power and jurisdiction over the whole world, a fact which has been

---

4. St. Paul's condemnation is effective, though it was not designed to be perpetual as Suárez alleges: ' "And now listen—the hand of the Lord is against you, and you will be blind for a while, unable to see the sun." Immediately mist and darkness came over him, and he went about groping for someone to lead him by the hand' (Acts 13:11).

proved by the words of Christ, 'Feed my sheep'; and the exercise of that jurisdiction should begin with the preaching of the Gospel; therefore, it is necessary that the Church should at least have the power of protecting [its preachers].

The third reason. The third reason, which is very cogent, concerns a power that is natural (so to speak) though indirect. For every state has the power to protect innocent persons who suffer grave injury from those stronger than themselves; but whoever hinders the preaching of the Gospel does the gravest injury to many who perchance might have been converted if they had heard it, and who would willingly have heard it, if it had been preached to them; therefore, the Church has the power of protecting those who in that respect are innocent and who suffer a grave injury.

The fourth reason. Finally, there is another analogy showing that the existence of this power is consonant with natural reason. It is as follows: every state has the right of sending ambassadors to treat of peace with another state, and consequently the former has the right of protecting those ambassadors and of avenging an injury if they are ill-treated; therefore, much more has the Church this right with respect to her own ambassadors who are the preachers of the faith, especially since the Church, as was proved above, has the power, given by Christ, to expand and to occupy the whole world.

5. *The power of preaching the faith rests in pastors separately, and is one of common right.* But first we must inquire: In whom is vested this right or power which we have said exists in the Church? This question may be asked either with regard to the immediate power of preaching the Gospel, or secondly, with regard to the right to send forth preachers, or thirdly, with regard to the right of defending those preachers and of removing any obstacle in their way.

As to the first phase of the question, it must be said that this power is vested as one of ordinary right in each of the pastors of the Church respectively; and by delegation it is vested in those only who are legitimately sent forth by those pastors.

The first half of the immediately preceding statement is clearly true, because this power is not only highly necessary to the pastors of the Church, but, more than that, it belongs by virtue of their office to them alone. For the sheep of Christ are to be fed chiefly with the word of faith, and Christ committed His sheep to the charge of these pastors. Moreover, I have said, 'respectively', because the power in question, in so far as it is supreme and universal over the whole world, resides in the Roman Pontiff alone, as Salmerón (on the *Acts of the Apostles,* Vol. XII, tract. xxxviii) well taught.

And by delegation, the power in question resides in those only who are lawfully sent out to preach. In the case of bishops, this power is limited to each one's own diocese, with dependence on the supreme Pontiff. In the case of parish priests, it exists in a proportionate degree, as I assume from other passages.

The second half of the same statement[5] is proved by the custom of the Church. For the practice which has always been observed, from the beginning, is that the ministers of the Gospel should be sent out by the Apostles or by other pastors, according to the passage (2 *Corinthians,* Chap. iii [Chap. viii, v. 22]), 'And we have sent with them our brother,' &c. More explicitly, elsewhere occur these words also (*Romans,* Chap. x [, v. 15]): 'And how shall they preach unless they be sent?' Secondly, this restriction is necessary for the observance of due order, upon which depend the peace and the tranquillity of the Church, and also for the sake of purity of doctrine; for errors would easily be implanted if any person whosoever should assume to himself the power of preaching the faith; and consequently, this office must be exercised by commission from the Church or from its pastors, a rule which is laid down in the *Decretals* (Pt. V, tit. vii, chap. xii). Finally, the right in question pertains to the power of jurisdiction; nor can any one of his own authority usurp the jurisdiction of another, particularly not when this jurisdiction is spiritual and supernatural, and should therefore flow from Christ immediately, or from him to whom Christ directly granted such jurisdiction when he said, 'Feed my sheep', or, 'I send you'.

This must be understood as referring to public preaching, and not to private instruction. However, all this must be understood as referring to public preaching, which is carried on by virtue of special authorization; inasmuch as private instruction and teaching can be conducted by any one of the

---

5. [*Vide* two paragraphs above.—Tr.]

faithful sufficiently learned, when the principle of charity and the occasion should so demand. This is the meaning of the statement in *Ecclesiasticus* (Chap. xvii [, v. 12]), 'And God gave to every one of them commandment concerning his neighbour.' For this sort of instruction is not a usurpation of jurisdiction, since such private teaching is given, not as though by virtue of the pastoral office, but by reason of a duty or counsel of charity. St. Thomas (on *Romans,* Chap. x) adds also that the passage in *Romans* refers to the ordinary [public church] law; for the Holy Spirit, by a private law, may send whomsoever He shall wish, inspiring such a minister with a special impulse to this service. But in that case the Church must be assured by some supernatural act or sign of the validity of this private law, a fact which is brought out in the *Decretals* (Bk. V, tit. vii, chap. xii). Otherwise—that is to say, if any one wishes to exercise this gift contrary to the precept and [right] order of the Church (as Innocent III said in a similar case, *Decretals,* Bk. I, tit. ix, chap. x), such an inspiration must be judged as proceeding from an evil spirit rather than from a good one.

6. *The supreme and universal power of sending forth preachers resides in the supreme Pontiff.* In accordance with the foregoing statements, and in regard to the second phase[6] of the question above propounded it must be asserted that the absolute, supreme and universal right of sending preachers of the Gospel to such unbelievers resides in the supreme Pontiff alone; because he alone is the supreme pastor of the whole flock of Christ, according to the words of Christ, 'Feed my sheep'; and furthermore, because the special duties of extending the bounds of the Church and of disseminating the faith pertain to him, since the other bishops have their jurisdiction limited within definite territorial boundaries. Hence, if there should be any unbelievers of this kind within such territory, any bishop within his own diocese could send to them preachers, or teachers. But as to the territory outside his own diocese, by the ordinary law (as it were) and normally speaking, no bishop below the Pope has this power. However, if necessity presses, or if there should arise a fit occasion for converting any one to the faith, the bishops, as a duty of charity, could send preachers

---

6. [I.e. 'In whom is vested . . . the right to send forth preachers?' See the first paragraph of Sub-section 5 of this Section, *supra,* p. 843.—Tr.]

to neighbouring provinces with the approval and the tacit, or interpretative, consent of the supreme Pontiff, who always in such cases should be consulted as soon as is conveniently possible, that he may, in accordance with his office, provide for the necessity or take advantage of the occasion which has arisen.

7. *The right of protecting preachers from the enemy, even through war and by coercion, resides in the supreme Pontiff; and in what way this is true.* With regard to the third aspect[7] of our question, there is even greater reason to observe that the duty of defending the aforesaid right, even by coercion and war, if such defence should be necessary, belongs solely to the supreme Pontiff. In defence of this statement, we argue, first, that it is his duty to defend the universal rights of the Church. Secondly, such defence involves the waging of war, and therefore normally requires power of a sovereign order; this power does not reside *per se* in temporal princes, for it is derived from a spiritual right which is not granted to them, but is, on the contrary, joined to spiritual power, the latter being indirectly extended to temporal affairs, as was shown elsewhere. Therefore, the power in question resides only in the supreme Pontiff.[8]

It must be added, however, that this power does not so belong to the Pope that it should be exercised by himself or through ecclesiastical persons. For it is no part of the priestly office, nor of the ecclesiastical status, to take up corporeal arms, as was rightly held by Ambrose [*Letters,* xx. 8, *To Marcellina*], who is cited in the *Decretum* (Pt. II, causa XXIII, qu. viii, can. xxi), where, throughout the first six chapters [of the *Causa*], this fact is supported by manifold evidence. Consequently, the Pope has the power of entrusting this defence—that is to say, its execution—to temporal princes, and may even command them to undertake the charge (*Decretum,* Pt. II, causa XXIII, qu. viii, can. viii with other canons in said question viii).

7. [I.e. 'In whom is vested . . . the right of defending . . . preachers and of destroying any impediments in their way?' See the first paragraph of Sub-section 5 of this Section, *supra,* p. 843.—Tr.]

8. *De Legibus,* Bk. III, chap. vi and in other places and *Defensio Fidei,* Bk. III, from chap. xxii. (Suárez's note; the referenced material is not included in these *Selections.*—Ed.)

The supreme Pontiff may entrust this right of defence to kings, and distribute to them the kingdoms of unbelievers. It follows, therefore, as Major and Victoria [*De Indis,* Sect. III, no. 10] rightly observe, that the Pope can distribute among temporal princes and kings the provinces and realms of the unbelievers; not in order that the former may take possession of these regions according to their own will, for that would be tyranny, as I shall explain later, but in order that they may make provision for the sending of preachers of the Gospel to those infidels, and may protect such preachers by their power, even through the declaration of just war, if reason and a rightful cause should require it. For this purpose, then, the Pope may mark off specific boundaries for each prince, which that prince may not later transgress without committing an injustice. This, as we read, was done by Alexander VI in the case of the kings of Portugal and of Castile.

The chief reason of all [for asserting this principle] is the fact that it is expedient that this matter, which most gravely concerns the Church, should be conducted in an orderly manner. For that is most necessary, both for preserving peace among Christian princes, and also in order that each of these princes may procure with the greater care the welfare of the people committed to his charge. Therefore, this prerogative belongs wholly to the Pope as one who gives the first impulse (so to speak); for kings are (as it were) his organs and instruments, and consequently no [temporal prince] can transgress the limits prescribed to him, since he cannot act unless he has received this impulse.

8. *Whether the defence of preachers of the faith is allowed before any injury has been done to them.—The affirmative opinion of some is stated.* A further inquiry may be made regarding this same doctrine, and especially regarding the third proposition: an inquiry that is, as to whether such defence of preaching and of preachers of the Gospel is allowed only after injury has been inflicted by unbelievers, or some obstacle has been placed in the way of the preaching of the faith; or whether that defence is permitted as a precautionary measure (so to speak) and soldiers may be employed in order to prevent injury to the preachers, or in order that their ministry may not be hindered.

The affirmative opinion of certain persons. For some have said that a Christian prince may justly seize the territory of a pagan king on this ground alone, namely, in order that the Gospel may be preached with greater ease and security under a Christian prince.

But since this opinion understood, without limitation, is incredible, as will be made clear from what we shall say later on, some have modified it by declaring that Christian princes may send forth preachers accompanied by a military force, sufficient, not for the waging of war, but in order that the preachers may proceed in security. They add also that a Christian prince may build towers and fortified strongholds in the lands of unbelievers, especially at the national boundaries, in order that entrance and access to such lands may be made easier and more secure for the faithful. Finally, they hold that a prince may collect, from the unbelievers who inhabit the territory in question, whatever expenses he has incurred in such enterprises, since that sum is spent for the benefit of those unbelievers; and that, consequently, he may resort to violence and warfare in order to exact payment, if it is denied, and may proceed even to the occupation of the territory if this should be necessary. That is the opinion of Major ([on the *Sentences,*] Bk. II, dist. xliv, qu. 2 [qu. 3], and it is based solely upon the principle that preferential favour should be shown to the faith.

9. *The negative opinion is approved.* But this teaching is not to be approved, according to the sounder opinion of Victoria, Báñez, and other modern authors, as set forth in the passages cited above.

First, because it has no foundation in the teachings of Christ, but is rather repugnant to his very words (*Matthew,* Chap. x [, v. 16] and *Luke,* Chap. x [, v. 3]), 'Behold I send you as sheep in the midst of wolves', words by which He plainly meant that the preaching of the faith was introduced not by arms, but by gentleness, patience, and the power of the word, and also by living example, according to the assertion of Paul (*2 Corinthians,* Chap. x [, v. 4]), 'For the weapons of our warfare are not carnal, but mighty to God.'

Secondly, the opinion in question is opposed to the custom and practice of the Church, for the Apostles and their successors assuredly did not preach the Gospel in that way, nor were the Popes, even after the conversion of the emperors to the faith, accustomed to send forth preachers to unbelievers in such fashion, a fact which is evident from the case of Gregory, who sent preachers to England, and from similar instances.

Thirdly, the practice under discussion is, in point of fact, not defensive, but aggressive; therefore, it is a virtual coercion to the adoption of the faith, or at least, to a hearing of those who preach the faith; and such coercion, as we shall presently explain, is not permissible.

The first member of this proposition may be explained thus: if preachers are sent with an army, those to whom they are sent may—morally speaking, and not without obvious reason—presume that these preachers have come to seize their territory rather than to provide for their spiritual welfare; hence, even as a general rule, [these unbelievers] may justly defend themselves, action upon a prudent presumption; accordingly, an occasion for a just war is given them, and under these circumstances, the practice in question becomes an aggressive rather than a defensive measure; and on the other hand, if [the unbelievers] are not able to resist, and yield through fear, that, in turn, is coercion, even in the highest degree.

From this explanation is derived a confirmation of the [concluding] statement [of our proposition, namely,] that such means are not fitted for the introduction of the faith. For they lead to its injury and defamation; since the infidels will think, [if we resort to these means,] that our faith gives us the privilege of violating the *ius gentium,* and even the law of nature, by our seizure of the property of others against the will of the owners and by our waging of war without any just ground; and since these same infidels will consequently become more hardened, and more indisposed to receive the faith. Therefore, this mode of introducing the preaching of the faith is not permissible.

10. *In what way Christian princes ought to conduct themselves with unbelievers, in order that the latter may provide opportunity for preaching.* Accordingly, it should be stated that one ought first to try peaceful means, inviting and repeatedly urging infidel princes and states to permit the preaching of the faith in their realms, and to offer or allow security to persons who come into or dwell within their domains for the purpose of performing that task of preaching. This is clearly what Christ Our Lord meant, when He counselled the Apostles whom He was sending forth to preach, that above all things they should proclaim peace (*Matthew,* Chap. x [, v. 12]). But if the unbelieving princes resist, and do not grant entrance, then, in my opinion and on account of the reasons given

above, they may be coerced by the sending of preachers accompanied by an adequate army.

In like manner, if, after the preachers have been received, the infidels should kill them or treat them wrongfully, when the victims are blameless, and for no other reason than that they have preached the Gospel, then an even better reason for just defence and, indeed, for righteous vengeance, has arisen, the latter sometimes being necessary in order that other infidel chiefs may be coerced and may fear to practise like acts of tyranny. For such [defensive action] is in harmony with the natural law and is not opposed to any command of Christ; and if, during the first years of the Church, this mode of coercion was not customarily practised, the reason was, not that this coercion was impermissible, but that the Church in those days had not the temporal means of resisting the enemies of the faith. For in the beginning, Christ our Lord willed to conquer the world by the power of the word and by that of miracles, in order that His own power and the truth of His doctrine might be made more manifest.

SECTION II

Is It Permissible for the Church and Christian Princes to Force These Unbelievers to Give Ear to the Faith?

1. *The affirmative opinion.* With regard to this point, there are two opposing opinions. The first affirms absolutely and unconditionally that such coercion is permissible. This appears to be Major's opinion ([on the *Sentences,*] Bk. II, dist. xliv, qu. 2 [qu. 4]), although he does not state it in set terms.

Argument I in support of the affirmative opinion. Moreover, this view may be suggested by what we have already said (*supra,* p. 840, Sect. I, subsect. 2). For if the infidels could not be forced to listen, then the power to teach would be superfluous, or, at least, in the highest degree useless, since teaching is in vain, if there is no one to hear; but we have said that the Church does possess the power and the right to teach the faith; and therefore it has, accordingly, the power to obtain a hearing through compulsion.

Argument II. Secondly, the force of the foregoing argument is clear from analogy. For Christ said to his Apostles [*John,* Chap. xx, v. 23]: 'Whose sins you shall forgive,' &c., wherefore the Church very properly infers that He commanded the faithful to confess their sins, inasmuch as sins cannot be forgiven unless they are heard and known; hence, by the same reasoning, if He gave to the Church the power of teaching unbelievers, He therefore gave it the power to force unbelievers to hearken, since there can be no teaching without an audience, or since, at least, such teaching would be vain and useless.

Argument III. Hence, the opinion in question is founded, thirdly, upon the principle that when one of two correlatives is granted, the other is granted also; since the one cannot exist without the other, as is usually taught in the matter of privileges in a like connexion. What has been stated elsewhere (*De Legibus,* Bk. VIII, chap. xi)[1] may be consulted. Another principle set forth above has a like bearing on this point, namely, the principle that when jurisdiction has been granted, everything is granted without which that jurisdiction could not well be exercised.

Argument IV. Finally, I contend, in the fourth place, that an argument is derived from what was stated above, namely: it is permissible to employ coercion in order to prevent resistance to the preaching of the faith; but if the pagans are unwilling to listen, in that very unwillingness they resist and impede the preaching of the faith; therefore, . . .

2. *The second and negative opinion.* The second opinion denies unconditionally that the coercion in question is permissible with respect to any unbelievers whomsoever, whether or not they are temporal subjects of the Church or of Christian princes. This opinion was held by Valentia ([*Commentariorum Theologicorum,*] Vol. III, disp. 1, qu. x, point 6, near end), and Salmerón (Vol. XII, tract. xxxviii [, on the *Acts of the Apostles*]) appears to have upheld the same doctrine.

The proofs of the negative opinion are, first, that we do not read that Christ gave this coercive power to the Church; neither does it necessarily accompany the power of preaching, since the latter may have been given with respect to those who wish to hear, and since we often see that a given

1. [Not included in these *Selections.*—Tʀ.]

person has the power, the duty and the right of teaching, but has not the power to compel others to hear him.

Secondly, such coercion does not seem to be in harmony with the example of Christ. For we read (in *Luke*, Chap. ix [, vv. 54–5]), that once, when He went into Samaria, and the Samaritans proved unwilling to receive Him, certain of His disciples said: 'Lord, wilt thou that [we command] fire [to] come down from heaven', &c.; to whom Christ replied: 'You know not of what spirit you are. [The Son of Man came not to destroy souls, but to save',] as if to say that force and threats were not to be used against the Samaritans; and accordingly, He peacefully withdrew. The same principle of conduct may be observed in other passages, also. According to one of those other passages [*Matthew*, Chap. x, v. 14], He said to His Apostles, 'And whosoever shall not receive you, nor hear your words: [. . .] shake off the dust,' &c.

Thirdly, there is an excellent reason, namely, that faith should be voluntary; therefore, the means to faith should also be voluntary; consequently, coercion to the faith in the case of the unbelievers in question is not permissible, as we shall observe in the following Section; and accordingly, coercion to the hearing of the faith is also impermissible. The proof of this deduction is as follows: the essential desirability of the means is the same as that of the end, especially when the means are entirely necessary, and desirable solely on account of the end.

The fourth is the principal argument and is as follows: the coercion which we are discussing is either direct—that is, it employs fear, which it inspires with the intention of forcing these unbelievers to the desired act—or else it is indirect—that is to say, it employs fear which is instilled on some other ground, but one from which it is hoped that the act in question will result, even though this result is not intended directly and for its own sake; this latter method of coercion ordinarily has no place in cases of the sort under discussion, because subject-matter and occasion for such coercion are lacking with respect to unbelievers of the kind in question; the former sort of coercion, indeed, is always illicit; therefore, . . .

The truth of this second proposition is established thus: without jurisdiction, there is no just coercion; the Church has no jurisdiction over unbelievers who are not its [temporal] subjects, while over those infidels who are its subjects it has at most a temporal jurisdiction, which does not extend to spiritual affairs; and to give ear to the preaching of the faith pertains to the spiritual sphere.

3. *The third and true opinion.* A third opinion, which is intermediate between these two, and which distinguishes between infidels subject to Christian princes and those who are not subject, seems to me worthy of approval.

The first proposition. Accordingly, I hold, first, that it is permissible for Christian princes to force their own infidel subjects to hear the faith. Such is the opinion held by Pezant and Báñez (on II.–II, qu. 10, art. 8). Moreover, although the latter author shrinks from the view because he thinks that this practice was never customary on the part of the Church, nevertheless, the example of Rome has great weight with me.

This proposition is proved by means of an example. For the Roman Pontiffs use coercion upon the Jews who are their subjects, compelling those Jews to hear the preaching of the faith once a week, and imposing a penalty upon those who refuse to hear. On this point, one may consult the Bull of Nicholas III which begins '*Vineam*', and that of Gregory XIII beginning '*Sancta Mater Ecclesia.*'

An evasion of the foregoing proof. Some persons, however, reply that this imposition constitutes, not a penalty, but a species of tribute, which may justly be imposed upon such infidels, in their capacity as subjects, but which is remitted by the kindness of the prince in the case of those who hear the preaching; so that the practice in question is not coercion, at least not coercion of a direct kind, but, at most, indirect—or rather a method of inducement through the kindness displayed in the remission of the tribute, a method the use of which is permissible, as we shall explain in the following Section.

This means of evasion is precluded. This evasion of the difficulty, however, although it cannot be clearly refuted, would nevertheless seem to have been devised without any foundation; for that sum of money which is imposed upon those refusing to hear, is levied, not on the extrinsic title of a just tribute, but only on account of an omission, or act of disobedience; and apart from this tax, there are other sufficient tributes which are levied upon such infidels because of their temporal subjection.

4. *The rational proof of the same proposition.* Our proposition, then, may be maintained by an appeal to reason. For there are two ways in which the subjects in question may be compelled to hear the preaching of the word.

First, they are bound by divine command to hear the faith, as Victoria maintained (Pt. I of the aforesaid Relectio, no. 36 [*De Indis,* Sect. II, no. 12]). To be sure, this point does not suffice to justify coercion, at least, direct coercion; for the observance and enforcement of that command do not pertain to temporal jurisdiction, a fact which is self-evident.

Secondly, then, it is possible that there might intervene in this matter some just command issued by the prince himself, for the observance of which he might use coercion upon his subjects. This assumption seems entirely plausible; for the hearing of preaching, is not, in itself and of its own nature, an action that falls within the supernatural sphere, and under the present circumstances subjects could be convinced that it was right and calculated to be for their advantage. Indeed, [such a command on the part of the prince] could even be referred to that welfare of the realm which a temporal prince may and ought to preserve—that is to say, the greater concord and peace of all the subjects: either in order that the unbelievers themselves may be set free from the errors [of whose falsity] they can be convinced because these errors are opposed to natural reason as are those which the Gentiles adopt; or else because such errors are opposed to what they themselves admit and believe, as happens in the case of the Jews; or, finally, because this action [on the part of the prince] may be directed to enabling the subjects to choose the true religion and the true worship of God, since in every human state that is well governed this care must be taken. Therefore, such a mandate, issued by the prince, is just and does not exceed his jurisdiction; and consequently, he may, by imposing a penalty, compel his subjects to obey the mandate in question.

5. *The arguments adduced in connexion with the second opinion do not militate against this proposition.* The arguments adduced in support of the second [and wholly negative] opinion,[2] then, do not militate against this proposition, for they relate only to non-subjects.

2. [*Supra,* p. 851.—Tr.]

Thus, in reply to the first argument, we confess that this act [of coercion] is not to be ascribed to any special power given by Christ, but we maintain that the ordinary power of a temporal prince is sufficient. Therefore, the second argument is fallacious in appealing to the example set by Christ and His Apostles; for they did not assume or make use of a temporal principate. As to the third argument, indeed, regarding coercion to belief, although the introductory statements[3] may be admitted, the final inference[4] is denied: partly on the ground that one may be forced to hear, but not be forced to believe (just as a person may be forced to hear the preaching of the evangelical counsels or that on the grant of indulgences, without on that account being forced either to follow the counsels or to gain the indulgences); and partly on the ground that it is not necessary that the command in question be imposed for the specific reason of belief in a given supernatural faith, but for the general reason of choosing the true religion and of avoiding errors which are repugnant even to reason. The same reply may be made to the fourth argument.

A twofold limitation of the proposition, by Báñez. Báñez, however, adds two limitations to the proposition in question.[5] The first is that this coercion may be allowed solely for the sake of a single hearing of the faith; since otherwise, if it took place frequently, there would be a virtual compulsion to belief. The other limitation is that it be attended by a moderate punishment [in case of disobedience].

The first limitation is rejected. But I disagree as to the first of the two limitations: I do so, partly because the contrary is proved by the Roman custom mentioned above; partly because, practically speaking, the [single exercise of] coercion would be useless, since, for the acceptance of faith, it is not enough that its preaching should be heard once, and especially not, in the case of men who have grown accustomed to their errors; and partly, in fine, because there is no reason, if the coercion has been licit once and has had no effect, to prevent it from being licit again. Neither does

---

3. [I.e. 'faith should be voluntary; therefore, the means to faith should also be voluntary; consequently, coercion to the faith in the case of the unbelievers in question is not permissible. . . . '—TR.]

4. [I.e. 'and accordingly, coercion to the hearing of the faith is also impermissible.'—TR.]

5. [I.e. the first proposition under the third opinion, *supra*, p. 853.—TR.]

there follow from such a procedure any virtual coercion to the faith; for our assertion is not that it is permissible for princes to impose this burden simply at will, but that it is permissible for them to do so with prudence and moderation, and in accordance with the attendant circumstances, as may be seen in the case of the example set by Rome.

The second limitation is approved. The other limitation, however, is decidedly acceptable. For judgement in the case of such coercion should be passed on the same grounds as in the case of a penalty imposed upon one who fails to observe some civil law, the transgression of which, politically speaking, neither causes great disturbance to the state nor is considered to be a very grave matter.

6. *The second proposition.* Secondly, I hold: it is in nowise permissible to coerce unbelievers who are non-subjects, to a hearing of the faith. This proposition is much more nearly a certainty than the first; and is commonly accepted as such, being furthermore proved by the first and second reasons in support of the second opinion, and, especially, by the fourth.

The sources of proof for this proposition. I set forth and urge [the second proposition], in the following manner: all coercion, whether it be direct or indirect, requires in the person exercising it a certain jurisdiction or power over the person coerced, since—in view of the fact that all coercion is executed by the infliction of some ill—it cannot be licit except in virtue of a superior power; but Christian princes have no power or jurisdiction over the unbelievers in question; therefore, . . .

This minor premiss is proved both by the very terms themselves, in that these unbelievers are assumed to be non-subjects; and also by the fact that the Church has no spiritual power over such persons (a point which I shall for the present assume to be true, and which I shall discuss more fully in the next Section); nor has the Church a temporal jurisdiction, since that jurisdiction resides in the princes and kings of the said unbelievers, these rulers being supreme in their own order; and therefore, such coercion cannot under any title be just.

7. Neither do the arguments relating to the first opinion[6] avail against this proposition. For to the first argument, we reply that the power to

6. [*Supra*, p. 850.—Tr.]

preach is not formally a power of jurisdiction, but merely the virtue (so to speak) of enlightening through teaching; so that the efficacy of this power resides, not in any coercive virtue, but in the efficacy of the word and in the showing of the Spirit and power,[7] as Paul said [*1 Corinthians,* Chap. ii]. Nevertheless, it does not follow that this power is fruitless; for it is morally certain that there will be some who will give ear voluntarily, if there is one to preach.

Accordingly, the reply to the second argument, which was derived by analogy and by similitude with the words, 'Whose sins you shall forgive,' is easily evident. For the power to remit sins is one of jurisdiction, and applies to the subject as such; so that, in this respect, there is involved in such power a very different essential principle from that involved in the power to preach. But a certain proportion may be preserved with regard to this point, since, just as the divine precept to confess is joined with the power to give absolution, even so a divine precept to hear and to embrace the faith is imposed together with the power and the right to preach the faith. There is, however, a difference. For the precept enjoining confession falls upon those who are members of the Church, and they can certainly be compelled, through that same Church, to fulfil the said precept; whereas the other precept includes also those persons who are not subject to the Church, and over them the Church can certainly exercise no compulsion.

The answer to the third argument is as follows: the principle there set forth, with regard to correlatives, applies only in the case of those things which are necessary to the use of a power granted in connexion with one of the correlatives; whereas, in the case under discussion, it is not necessary, in order to use the power of preaching, that it should be possible for others to be forced to hear; rather does it suffice that they are licitly able to do so, and that they ought to hear voluntarily. Moreover, the same is true of the other principle adduced.

7. [*Virtus,* translated 'virtue' immediately above, and probably having the same significance here; whereas the 'power' referred to earlier in the same sentence is *potestas,* not *virtus.* The slight inconsistency in translation is due to the fact that the Biblical passage here cited (Douay version) contains the phrase, 'in shewing of the Spirit and power.'—TR.]

Hence, the reply to the fourth argument is evident, since the reasons for maintaining the power to resist those who place unjust impediments in the path of preaching the faith, differ greatly from the reasons for maintaining the power to compel a hearing of the same. For the former power is a means morally necessary, and assumes that an injury which one is allowed to repel, has been committed; whereas neither of these conditions can be found to exist in the latter case, and thus the grounds [for maintaining the existence of this second power] are entirely different.

8. *An objection.* But hereupon a difficulty arises, since it follows from what has been said that if, perchance, in the case of any infidel kingdom both the king and the leaders of the realm are unwilling to admit the preachers of the Gospel, or to permit them to come into the kingdom, the Church cannot use any violent means or coercion in order that the Gospel may be preached there; and this seems unfitting, because such a nation would not be sufficiently provided for; therefore, . . . The truth of the [primary] inference is evident. For in such a case, the entire nation is unwilling to hear the Gospel; and—as has been said—they cannot be compelled to hear it; therefore, . . .

The reply made by certain persons to this objection. As to this argument, some simply concede the inference; since it follows thence, not that men are insufficiently provided for, but only that they are not thus effectually provided for, because under such conditions, men may by their own malice, hinder the means of salvation given them, as it is probable that they will do.

The true solution. What should be done if the king and the leaders of the realm hinder preachers from preaching. Nevertheless, I think that, as a general rule, some coercion is allowable under the circumstances posited. In particular, if any pagan state wishes to hear preachers, and if the pagan king prevents the people from so doing, then the said state may resist him; and in this matter it may be aided by Christian princes, in order that the unwilling king shall permit the preaching of the faith; for in thus [restraining] his subjects he does them an injury, by setting obstacles in the way of their salvation. According to the same reasoning, if the king consents to and desires the preaching, but does not dare to allow it on account of the resistance of the leaders or of the realm at large, the king may bring force to bear upon his subjects; and if he lacks the power, then, in this matter, also, he may be aided by Christian princes, for the reason given above.

Finally, if both the king and kingdom offer simultaneous resistance, I think that they may be forced to permit the preachers of the Gospel to live in their territories; for this tolerance is obligatory under the *ius gentium* and cannot be impeded without just cause. Moreover, that king and that people may be forced to permit these preachers to declare the word of God, without suffering violence or treachery, to those who are willing to hear; since it is probable that there will never be lacking individual persons who will hear voluntarily. For, even if we assume that the king and his kingdom are offering resistance, still, not absolutely all individuals are included under the term 'kingdom', but rather, the Councils or chief men, or else the greater or greatest part of the kingdom; and always, without exception, the Church retains unimpaired its right to preach in that kingdom, and to defend the innocent (so to speak)—to defend, that is, individuals who may wish to hear the word. Accordingly, under such circumstances, there is involved no coercion to the hearing of the faith, but only a coercion to refrain from impeding the preaching of the Gospel, or placing obstacles in the way of those persons who may voluntarily choose to give ear to such preaching.

SECTION III

After a Sufficient Presentation of the Gospel, Is It Allowable to Use Force to Compel Belief on the Part of Those Infidels Who Have Been Sufficiently Instructed?

[1.] *The first opinion.* This question may be discussed both in its relation to those unbelievers who are in every sense non-subjects, and in its relation to those who are temporally subject to the Church. Hence, we have the first opinion, which teaches that it is permissible to use force upon unbelievers, even upon those who are not subjects, in order that they may accept the faith after it has been sufficiently expounded to them. Such is the opinion of Major (on the *Sentences,* Bk. II, dist. ɪᴠ [dist. xʟɪᴠ, qu. 4]); and—so it is said—in the time of Charles V, and with reference to the Jews, a certain Genesius Sepúlveda [, *De Fato et Libero Arbitrio*] strenuously defended the same view.

The first proof. This opinion may find a basis in the words of Christ (*Luke,* Chap. xiv [, v. 23]): 'Compel them to come in', that is, into the Church, as Gregory (Homily XXXIX [Homily XXXVI], *On the Gospel*) and Chrysostom explain (Homily XIV, [*On Matthew*])[1] in their discussion of that point. Therefore, Christ gave the power to compel unbelievers to come into the Church; and that power given by Christ extends to every one. This point is confirmed by the example of Christ, who used force upon Paul to make him submit to the faith. Augustine (*Letters,* xlviii [xciii, no. 5]) makes use of this example in a similar case.

The second proof. I base a second argument upon reason, as follows: these pagans sin grievously in not accepting the faith after it has been sufficiently heard by them; therefore, on account of this sin, they may justly be punished, and through punishment coerced to accept the faith; consequently, men have power to punish the sin in question, for it pertains to the Providence of God so to order human affairs that public crimes shall not remain unpunished; therefore, the power under discussion resides in the Church alone, because that power presupposes the existence of the faith which is found in the true Church and there only.

The third proof. Thirdly, expediency may be adduced as an argument. For through such coercion great good may be anticipated; since, granted perhaps that those who are coerced may be converted less sincerely or even fictitiously, still those who follow,—and who will greatly outnumber the former—will believe the more easily, and many innocent children will be saved through baptism. Therefore, because of this beneficial result, the coercion in question may be allowed. For if any evil follows therefrom, that evil is not wrought, but [merely] permitted, by the Church. This argument may be supported by the authority of Gregory ([*Letters,*] Bk. IV,

---

1. [St. Chrysostom there speaks very indirectly of the Church. His main point is that St. Matthew was speaking of the kingdom of God.—Rᴇᴠɪsᴇʀ.]

letter vi), according to a passage in which, for a similar reason and with regard to a similar case, he uses almost the same words.

2. *The second opinion.* According to the second opinion, the Church and Christian princes may compel acceptance of the faith on the part of those who are temporally subject to them, although this is not the attitude taken with regard to those who are not subjects. Scotus (on the *Sentences,* Bk. IV, dist. iv, qu. 6) upholds this second opinion; while Gabriel and Angelus follow him, but on the condition that the coercion be indirect, not direct, a limitation which will be discussed later.

The opinion in question is founded first of all upon the arguments in favour of the first opinion, which *a fortiori* support this one.

Secondly, the practice of the Church may also be adduced in support of the latter view, for the kings of Spain used the power of which we are speaking. Ferdinand forced the Moors to accept the faith; and before Ferdinand, King Sisebut, he who is called 'most religious', had done likewise in the case of the Jews, and is praised for that deed by the Fourth Council of Toledo (Chap. lvi [Chap. lvii] cited in the *Decretum,* Pt. I, dist. XLV, can. v and the *Decretals,* Bk. III, tit. XLII, chap. iii, last section). The Sixth Council (Chap. iii), and the Seventeenth Council of Toledo (Chap. viii), have also expressed a favourable opinion of the act of Sisebut. The *Decretum* (Pt. II, causa XXIII, qu. vi, can. iv) quotes Gregory, too, as declaring in his *Letters* (Bk. III [Bk. IV], letter xxvi), with regard to the Jews who were subject, that: 'They should be burdened with such a weight of fines that they are compelled through punishment [to accept the faith].' Lastly, there is the rule of Augustine (*Letters,* cciv [clxxiii. 2, in Migne ed.]), 'Wicked men are to be restrained from evil and compelled to do good', cited in *Decretum* (Pt. II, causa XXIII, qu. iv, can. liv). Unbelievers are wicked, and the faith is for them a great good; therefore, they may be forced by their princes to accept this good.

3. *A confirmation as to unbelieving subjects.* Finally, a special argument may be added as to these unbelieving subjects, namely: that the coercion in question is not repugnant to the faith; that with respect to such unbelievers the power to coerce is not lacking, nor is there lacking a suitable reason for such coercion; and that therefore, the coercion is permissible.

The major premiss of this argument may be proved, first of all, from the example of heretics, on whom the Church imposes the faith. Therefore, the sort of coercion under discussion is not repugnant to the faith. Hence, there does not seem to be any solid and true basis for the contention urged by some persons, in this connexion, namely, that faith resulting from coercion is slavish and involuntary, and therefore a sacrilege. For in the example mentioned [that is, in the case of heretics] this contention appears to be proven erroneous. Its erroneous nature may also be proven by reasoning, as follows: when the wish is forced it retains, absolutely speaking, its character as a wish, although relatively it may be involuntary; but it is sufficient for the acceptance of the faith that the act be voluntary, absolutely speaking. To this we may add the consideration that a man is very often induced by punishment and coercion to change his will utterly and absolutely; and therefore, coercion is permissible with respect to many benefits which could not well exist without an absolute wish, as Augustine teaches at some length (in the aforesaid *Letters,* xxiv [*Letters,* cciv, which is clxxiii, no. 2, in Migne ed.]) and as we read in the *Decretum* (Pt. II, causa XXIII, qu. iv, can. xxxviii).

The minor premiss[2] of the chief argument may be proved as follows: the unbelievers in question are assumed to be subjects of Christian princes; and a prince has power to coerce his subjects, especially as to those matters which are necessary for their salvation; moreover, the prince or the immediate prelate may compel a subject to obey not only his own commands, but also the law of a superior sovereign; and therefore, much more certainly may a temporal prince compel his subjects to obey the law of the Supreme Heavenly Prince, and to obey, consequently, the law of faith. Furthermore, a prince may forcibly restrain a pagan subject from blaspheming against the Christian religion, and from inflicting any injury upon it; but those unbelievers have blasphemed in not believing a faith sufficiently set forth to them, for they think and declare that it is false, and therefore may justly be punished and through punishment forced to

2. [I.e. the statement that, 'with respect to such unbelievers the power to coerce is not lacking, nor is there lacking a suitable reason for such coercion'. See the first paragraph of this Sub-section.—TR.]

conversion. This is especially true since these pagans may be convinced that what is set before them is much more prudently credible than the errors in which they themselves live. Therefore, the power in question is not wanting to Christian princes. Finally, and in accordance with the preceding remarks, it is easy to prove the remainder of this minor premiss, namely, that a suitable reason [for such coercion] is not lacking. For it is to be hoped that much good will result from this coercion, either to the parents or to the children or to those who follow, as we have gathered from Gregory [*Letters,* Bk. IV, letter vi]. Neither is there any reason to fear greater evils, for it is worse that unbelievers should persist in their errors than that their conversion should be fictitious. They and not the Church are responsible for that fiction, and consequently, there is no reason to consider this coercion as an evil in itself.

4. *The third and true opinion.* Nevertheless, the third and common opinion of theologians is that unbelievers who are not apostates, whether subjects or not, may not be coerced to embrace the faith, even after it has been sufficiently proposed to them. So St. Thomas teaches (II.–II, qu. 10, arts. 8 and 12); as do also Cajetan [on II.–II, *ibid.*], de la Palu (on the *Sentences,* Bk. IV, dist. iv, qu. 4), Durandus (*ibid.,* qu. 6), Soto (*ibid.,* dist. ix, qu. 1, art. 3 [dist. v, sole question, art. 10]), Richard Middleton (*ibid.,* dist. vi, art. 3, qu. 1), Antoninus ([*Summa Theologica,*] Pt. II, tit. xii, chap. ii), Abulensis [Tostado] (on *Kings,* Bk. I, chap. viii, qq. 34, 182, 183), Sylvester (word *baptismus,* Pt. iv, qu. 6), Alfonso de Castro (*De Iusta Hae-reticorum Punitione,* Bk. II, chap. iv), Victoria, at length (Relect. *De Indis,* Sect. II, no. 15), Salmerón (Vol. XII, tract. xxxvii) and Henríquez (*Summa Theologiae Moralis,* Bk. II, chap. iv, no. 8 [Bk. II, chap. iii, no. 8]). This is absolutely a true and certain opinion, which we shall prove, in separate sections dealing first with non-subjects, then with subjects. Moreover, we shall speak first of direct coercion, and shall then add some remarks as to indirect coercion.

5. *The first proposition: to compel unbelievers who are not subjects to embrace the faith is essentially wrong.* We hold, first, that it is essentially wrong to force unbelievers who are not subjects, to embrace the faith.

The proof of the first proposition. The proof of this proposition is that such coercion cannot occur without lawful power, as is self-evident, since otherwise all wars and all acts of violence could be called just; but the Church does not possess this lawful power with respect to such unbelievers. Therefore, . . .

The first proof [of the minor premiss]. The minor premiss of this argument may be proved as follows: the power in question has not been given by Christ, nor does it reside in the princes of the Church from the very nature of the case—not, at least, with respect to the unbelievers mentioned. The first half of the foregoing statement—namely, the assertion that Christ did not give this special power to the Church—may be proved, first, from what we have said in the preceding section [Sect. ii, subsect. 2], where we demonstrated that Christ did not give such power of forcing these unbelievers to hear the faith, therefore, neither [did He give the power of forcing them] to embrace the faith after hearing it; for the same reasoning is valid in both cases.

The second proof [of the minor premiss]. Secondly, this minor premiss may be proved by a negative argument, since, in the tradition of the Church, there is no trace of such power, either in its practice, or in Scripture; for the words of Christ, 'Compel them to come in' have a meaning very different from this, as I shall show below.

The third proof [of the minor premiss]. Thirdly, the same premiss is established affirmatively by the words of Paul (*1 Corinthians,* Chap. v [, vv. 12–13]), 'For what have I to do to judge them that are without? For them [. . .] God will judge'; words based, surely, upon the fact that these persons are not under our jurisdiction. This was the opinion expressed by Innocent III in the aforesaid *Decretals* (Bk. III, tit. xlii, chap. iii) and enunciated by the Council of Trent (Session XIV, chap. ii), as follows: 'The Church passes judgement upon no man who has not first entered it, through baptism.' Innocent III upholds this same view in another Chapter of the *Decretals* (Bk. IV, tit. xix, chap. viii); and it is the common opinion of Chrysostom, Theophylact, Ambrose, Anselm, St. Thomas, on the text cited (on *1 Corinthians,* Chap. v, v. 13), and of Augustine (*De Verbis Domini,* Sermon VI, chap. vii [in *Sermones supposititii,* Sermon VI, chap. vi, Vol. V, col. 1751 Migne ed.]). Therefore, Paul, *loc. cit.* [*1 Cor.,* v. 13] in order to make it clear that this power was not given to men, added, 'For God will judge them that are without.' The judgment, then, and consequently the punishment and coercion of such unbelievers, have not been committed to men. Wherefore, Christ our Lord instructed the Apostles (*Matthew,* Chap. x [, v. 10]) whom He sent forth to preach, not to carry a staff or a sword; and with respect to this passage, Jerome [on *Matthew,* Chap. x] notes that Christ forbade methods of coercion and taught peace, concluding His instructions with the words: 'Whoever will not receive you, it shall not be remitted to them on the day of judgment', meaning thereby that God has reserved to Himself the punishment of this crime, just as He said elsewhere (*Matthew,* last chap. [*Mark,* Chap. xvi, v. 16]): 'He that believeth not shall be condemned.'

The fourth proof [of the minor premiss]. Fourthly, the same premiss is proved by the canon law, for this coercion is prohibited therein (*Decretals,* Bk. V, tit. vi, chap. ix; *Decretum,* Pt. I, dist. xlv, cans. iii and v). The prohibition, however, arises, not so much from a prohibition of the Church, as from an explanation of the same. Hence, in the *Decretals* (Bk. II, tit. xlii, chap. iii) such coercion is said to be contrary to the Christian religion. Pope Gregory was of the same opinion (*Letters,* Bk. I, letter xci [letter xlvii] and Bk. XI, letter xv [Bk. IX, letter vi]) as were Ambrose (on *Luke,* Chap. x), and Chrysostom (on *Matthew,* Chap. xxxiv).

The fifth proof [of the minor premiss]. From the foregoing, the strongest argument is derived, namely, that if the power in question had been specially granted by Christ it would not be vested immediately in temporal princes, because Christ granted no power immediately to them. Therefore, this power would reside in the bishops, and especially in the supreme Pontiff. But the pastors of the Church themselves do not acknowledge the possession of this power, nor have they ever used it; and Christ our Lord said to Peter simply this: 'Feed my sheep.' Therefore, it is certain that Christ has not given this power to the Church.

6. *The sixth proof of the same premiss.* Finally, an argument may be derived from the end in view; for such a coercive method of drawing men to the faith would not befit the Church; on the contrary, it would be much more expedient that the first acceptance and profession of the faith should be absolutely and entirely spontaneous.

This spontaneity is desirable, first, in order that the power of the divine word and of the grace of God may be manifested in this work of conversion, which is especially the work of God, as Christ said (*John,* Chap. vi [, v. 29]). Accordingly, Paul wrote (*2 Corinthians,* Chap. x [, v. 4]): 'For the weapons of our warfare are not carnal', &c., and again (*1 Corinthians,* Chap. i [, v. 26]): '[there are not many wise according to the flesh,] not many mighty [, not many noble].'

The same spontaneous element is desirable, secondly, because the coercive method in question would involve many disadvantages, since it would, as a general rule, be followed by feigned conversions and innumerable acts of sacrilege. The unbelievers also would be much scandalized and would blaspheme the Christian religion if, by any human power, they were forced to embrace that religion, which is entirely supernatural. Therefore, the special supernatural power of which we are speaking has not been given to the Church.

Again, as to the fact, no proof is needed that this power, in so far as concerns pagans who are not subjects, does not reside in the Church from the very nature of the case; for this truth is expressed in the terms themselves, since from the very fact that we assume that these pagans are not subjects—at least, not temporal subjects—we consequently imply that the Church has no temporal power over them; therefore, it has no other power with respect to them from the nature of the case; for there exists no other power derived from the law of nature over human beings as members of a human state. Moreover, even the power in question comes not immediately from God or from the law of nature, but mediately through man's devising and from the *ius gentium.* Therefore, to no state or prince is this power given with respect to aliens, but only with respect to the members of that particular state; and these unbelievers, in addition to the fact that they are not members of the Church, are supposedly not even members of a secular state under the rule of a Christian prince. Therefore, the power in question does not extend to them.

7. *The second proposition.* Secondly, the following proposition must be laid down: the Church may not exercise compulsion even upon those pagans who are temporally subject to it, in order that they shall embrace the faith. This proposition is easily proved from the preceding one, since the reference is to direct compulsion, which requires power and jurisdiction. For from what has been said, it is evident that the Church

has not such power over the infidels in question, by any special grant from Christ; inasmuch as the proofs adduced above are universal, and the canon laws, when they forbid any coercion [of subjects] and declare it to be contrary to the Christian religion, refer to pagan subjects in particular. Yet the Church is not forbidden to wield temporal power over these pagan subjects, for the latter can be members of a civil state, although the supreme temporal power of that state resides in a Christian prince. Nevertheless, that power does not extend to the act of punishing such subjects because of their sin in not embracing the faith after it has been sufficiently proposed to them; for the power in question, being proximately derived from men, is accordingly directed only to a natural end, and especially to preserving the peace of the state, and natural justice, and the virtue appropriate to such an end; whereas the aforementioned sin of unbelief is a matter entirely apart from that purpose and end, so that the punishment of it does not fall within the scope of this [temporal] power. Therefore, the power of coercion to effect an acceptance of the faith cannot rightfully be claimed by virtue of such [temporal] power; for that coercion cannot be justly exerted unless it be in the form of a just punishment for an offence opposed [to the acceptance of faith]. Hence we see, even in the case of the Church, that to whatever extent it may justly compel unbelieving apostates to return to the faith, to precisely that same extent it may justly punish them on account of apostasy from the faith professed by them in baptism; and therefore, wherever the power for the punishment of unbelief is wanting, there is lacking also the power to compel an acceptance of the faith. This fact is further confirmed by all the arguments from inexpediency which have been adduced in this, and in the preceding Sub-section.

8. *The third proposition: indirect coercion to compel acceptance of the faith is not intrinsically evil.* From this proof it may easily be understood that the preceding proposition refers to direct coercion exerted directly to this end, namely, the prevention of unbelief and the acceptance of the faith. Accordingly, we must make an additional statement as to indirect coercion, to the effect that such coercion is not in itself and intrinsically evil, if applied under the proper conditions. This is the opinion of Saint Antoninus, Angelus in passages already cited, and Valentia (Vol. III, disp. i,

[qu. x,] point 6, [ad 4]); and the same view is to be derived from Gregory (*Letters,* Bk. VII, letter xxx [Bk. II, letter xxxii] and Bk. IV, letter vi [letter xxvi]), for in the first mentioned place he advises that a portion of the just tribute be remitted to pagan subjects, so that through kindness they may be drawn to the faith; and in the latter place, he says that if some of the pagans become too contumacious, they are to be loaded with burdens in order to recall them to their senses, a course of action which is indirect coercion. He states a like view elsewhere (*Letters,* Bk. III, letter xxvi, cited in *Decretum,* Pt. II, causa XXIII, qu. vi, can. iv).

The reason for the proposition stated above. The reason [supporting the proposition that such indirect coercion is not intrinsically evil] is as follows: coercion is indirect when any right [asserted] or punishment inflicted under one particular title or on account of a given offence is secondarily directed by the one exercising [the right, or inflicting the penalty,] to the end of inducing another to exercise some act of the will; and in the case under consideration, the power to punish or to exercise compulsion on account of a just end is not lacking, while the secondary end, consisting in the conversion of another to the faith, is not evil, but, on the contrary, is in itself virtuous. Therefore, the act of indirect coercion [to this secondary end] is not in itself evil, but can be justified. The truth of the major premiss and of the consequent is clear. The minor is also proved by the fact that the Christian princes in the case under discussion may justly punish the pagan subjects on account of offences other [than unbelief], or they may impose tributes upon such subjects. Therefore, if the princes should judge that this [imposition of penalties or of tribute] would be useful for the conversion of the subjects, they may bear in mind this additional intention and may impose the burden in the manner best adapted to such a [secondary] end.

9. *Under what circumstances indirect coercion should be used.* However, as I have said, this indirect coercion should be applied under the proper conditions; for there are two conditions, above all others, which must be observed.

One is that in imposing any burden or in inflicting any evil, the bounds of justice are not to be transgressed, since if they should be transgressed, the coercion would, for that reason, be inequitable. Take, for example, the statement of Gregory, [*Letters,* Bk. IV, letter xxvi] to the effect that

greater taxes could be imposed on such pagans for the purpose in question, provided, however, that these taxes be just; for within the limits of
just taxation one tax may be heavier than another even to the maximum
amount, which, for the rest, is termed 'rigorous'; up to that limit, then, a
tax may be increased, but no further. The same is true as to punishment,
which may be increased or diminished at the will of the prince; and thus
a rigorous punishment, which is nevertheless just, may be imposed. In
the same way, Catholic princes have, when there is just cause, the power
to prohibit unbelievers from dwelling in their kingdoms: as when [such
fellow-countrymen] would be dangerous to the faithful; or after unbelievers have been conquered in a just war, so that they may be expelled on that
ground and punished (as it were) by exile; or surely, if they are strangers
and aliens, and may [on that account] be forbidden to acquire a domicile in the kingdom. In such cases, then, a Christian prince may prohibit
unbelievers from dwelling in his realm unless they are converted, as was
stated in the Sixth Council of Toledo (Chap. iii); and that act on his part
is, indeed, a form of indirect coercion. It is necessary, however, that this
act of expulsion be just.

10. *Prudence must be observed in the use of indirect coercion to convert
unbelievers to the faith.* The other condition [to the proper exercise of indirect coercion] is that the end of conversion shall be sought prudently. For
the kind of coercion in question, even though indirect, carries with it the
danger of a counterfeit conversion, and therefore thorough precautions
must be taken lest unbelievers be admitted to the faith and to the Sacraments without sufficient examination, and without a moral certitude that
their conversion is real. On this point it must be especially noted, that
to take such precautions is the duty of the pastors of the Church, rather
than of temporal princes; for the princes may work piously in this way,
by striving for the just conversion of unbelievers, but it is not for them to
admit to baptism those who are thus converted and ask for baptism. This
function pertains rather to the pastors of the Church, and therefore it is
for the latter to test and examine such conversions, and to avert in all cases
the moral peril of a pretence.

11. *Indirect coercion to the faith properly takes place only with respect to
pagan subjects.* From all of the above it may be gathered that this indirect

coercion, strictly speaking, takes place only in regard to subjects, because lawful power to inflict ills upon non-subjects is lacking, unless they are first reduced to subjection by reason of an offence committed in a kingdom not their own, or by the title of a just war.

However, I have used the term 'strictly speaking', because even though non-subjects may not positively (as it were) be afflicted with punishments and loaded with burdens, nevertheless, they may be deprived of gratuitous benefits, advantages, or favours; and such means also may be well adapted to drawing them to the faith or to a favourable inclination toward it, and may be considered as a kind of indirect coercion. Without doubt, coercion exercised only in this way is permissible, because no jurisdiction or superior power is required in order to deprive any one of such benefits. Moreover, since it is entirely permissible to entice these unbelievers to the faith by kindness and good deeds, when there is hope of success, as is evident from the statements made by Gregory (*Letters,* Bk. XIII, letter xii [in Migne, *P.L.,* p. 1268, col. 2]); therefore, conversely, when kindness is of no avail, these same pagans may rightfully be deprived of such benefits, in order that 'vexation may give them understanding' [*Isaias,* Chap. xxviii, v. 19]; for this vexation is legitimate, as I have already explained.

12. *In answer to the first argument in support of the first opinion [Subsect. 1], the passage in* Luke, *xiv [, v. 23] is explained literally.* The first argument in support of the first opinion[3] was derived from the words of Christ, 'Compel them to come in', words which Augustine (in *Letters,* xlviii and l [xciii. 2 and clxxxv]) interprets as referring to real compulsion by means of a penalty. However, he applies the passage in question to heretics and apostates; for he explains that the first group who have been invited, are the Jews; the second, who have simply been called, are the Gentiles; while the third, who are under compulsion, are the heretics. Concerning the latter, we shall answer, first, that it is indeed permissible to use force upon them. But the literal interpretation would seem, in my opinion, to be that adopted by Chrysostom and others, who say that this passage refers to the

---

3. [I.e., the opinion that: 'it is permissible to use force upon unbelievers, even upon those who are not subjects, in order that they may accept the faith after it has been sufficiently expounded to them.' *Vide* the first paragraph of Sub-section 1, p. 859.—Tr.]

end of the world, at which time, in order to complete the number of the elect, there will be used a kind of compulsion upon the number lacking—compulsion, not by means of punishments or real violence, but by the might of signs and miracles and by the efficacy of preaching and of inner grace. Such was the power manifested in the conversion of Paul, which is cited as an example by the authorities above-mentioned.

The answer to the second argument for the same opinion. The second argument in support of the first opinion is based upon the power of punishing wrongdoing, to which we reply that God has not given men the power of punishing all the evil deeds of mankind; since He has reserved some of these deeds for His own tribunal, because otherwise the human race could not be governed with peace and justice. And among these sins which God has reserved for His own judgement, is the sin of unbelief, in those who have not professed the faith through baptism. This inference we may well derive from the words of Christ and of Paul, quoted above; for without such a divine reservation, even greater evils would necessarily result.

The reply to the third argument. Therefore, as to the third argument, based upon expediency and upon the fact that the successors of such unbelievers might, [by the coercion in question,] be more easily and more surely converted, it should be replied, first of all, that evil should not be done in order to bring about good. Furthermore, experience has taught that such success is not obtained by that kind of coercion, but rather, that the contrary is true. Hence, Gregory did not adduce the argument of expediency, save in the case of indirect coercion, to be exercised only in a lawful manner and with due circumspection.

13. *The arguments in favour of the second opinion, and set forth in Sub-sections 2 and 3, are answered.* As to the arguments in favour of the second opinion,[4] the examples set by the Spanish kings which are cited, chiefly regard indirect coercion applied in virtue of a just title, such as was the practice of Catholic kings. For if formerly Sisebut somewhat exceeded due

---

4. [I.e. the opinion that, 'the Church and Christian princes may compel acceptance of the faith on the part of those who are temporally subject to them, although this is not the attitude taken with regard to those who are not subjects.' *Vide* the first sentence of Sub-section 2 of this Section, p. 861.—Tr.]

limits, his intention only and not his action is to be praised; and similarly if, perchance, a proper moderation is not observed in indirect coercion, although that fault may be excused on the ground of good faith, yet the result proves that the act was not fitting.

As for the second argument in support of the second opinion, the argument regarding the law of a superior, the reply is that this holds good with respect to subjects and in connexion with delegation by a sovereign prince; but, as I have explained, God has not committed such power to men.

Finally, it is not enough that the faith should be capable of being made clearly credible; for authority (*potestas*) is requisite to coercion, and authority is lacking in the case under discussion.

SECTION IV

May Unbelievers Be Forced to Abandon Those of Their Errors and False Rites Which Are Contrary Not Only to Faith but Also to Reason?

1. *Two kinds of unbelief are distinguished.* In the subject-matter of faith we have distinguished, in former Chapters, between two main categories— one concerning the entirely supernatural mysteries; another concerning a group of either divine or moral truths which can also be known through a natural process [, that is, by reason]. Therefore, a twofold kind of unbelief may, in like manner, be distinguished; the unbelief which is opposed to supernatural truths only, and with which we have hitherto been chiefly concerned; and the unbelief which is opposed also to natural reason, and concerning which something remains to be said.

Whether unbelievers may be forced to abandon errors which are contrary to natural understanding. Now in regard to the latter point, we may also assume, from what has already been said, that unbelievers may not be coerced to accept this [set of truths] as revealed, and as something to be believed by faith; but we ask whether or not, in this matter, they may at least be compelled to think correctly in accordance with reason or with some kind of human faith, and consequently to abandon external rites contrary thereto, such as idolatry and the like. In the consideration of this question, the usual distinction must be made, with respect to those unbelievers who are civil subjects of the Church, or of Christian princes.

2. *The first opinion affirms [that compulsion may be used] even against non-subjects.* Concerning non-subjects, Major (on the *Sentences,* Bk. II, dist. xliv, qu. 4) and Sepúlveda (*De Fato et Libero Arbitrio*), then, have logically maintained that pagan idolaters may be forced by the Church to worship the one God and to relinquish the rites of idolatry, and that if these pagans refuse [to do so], they may justly be punished and deprived of their liberty and their kingdoms.

The basis of this view. Possibly, the basis of this view is the fact that a Christian state has the right to defend the divine honour, and to suppress and avenge blasphemies against God; but idolatry is a serious offence to the Almighty and connotes blasphemies against Him, as St. Thomas (II.–II, qu. 94, art. 3, ad 1) teaches; therefore, . . . The major premiss of the argument is also derived from St. Thomas (*ibid.,* Qu. 10, arts. 8 and 11), where he asserts specifically that unbelievers may be forcibly prevented from uttering blasphemies against God's name. The same opinion can also be supported by reasoning, as follows: one man may licitly defend the life or the honour of another; and therefore, still more rightfully may a man defend the honour of God.

The first confirmation of the view in question. The first confirmation of such a view is this: if the heathen sacrifice grown men or children to their gods, they may be forcibly compelled to abandon this practice, at least on the ground of defence of the innocent; therefore, Christian princes may take the same measures towards any heathen people, on behalf of the honour of God.

The second confirmation. The second confirmation is that the Romans have been praised for the reason that they made subjects of the barbarian nations, in order to recall those nations to a better way of living; as is evident from Augustine (*On the City of God,* Bk. V, chaps. xii and xvii), and from St. Thomas (*De Regimine Principum,* Bk. III, chaps. iv *et seq.*).[1]

---

1. *De Regimine Principum* after Book 2, chapter 4 (so including book 3) is in fact by Tolomeo of Lucca (ca. 1227–ca. 1327), a papalist writer.

The third confirmation. The final confirmation is that certain peoples are so barbarous, so unfitted to acquire naturally the knowledge of God, that they seem fashioned by nature for a state of slavery, as Aristotle (*Politics*, Bk. I, chap. i [, §§ 4–6] and chap. iii [Bk. I, chap. ii, § 15]) has remarked; therefore, even on this ground, they might be forced to true knowledge and to an upright way of life.

3. *The second and true opinion denies the truth of the statement defined above.* Nevertheless, the true and certain opinion is that those unbelievers who are not subjects, cannot normally be forced even to change their errors and their rites. This is the view of the commentators on the above cited articles in St. Thomas, namely, on [II.–II, qu. 10,] arts. 8 and 11, and by Cajetan (on II.–II, qu. 66, art. 8), Victoria in the aforesaid Relectio, no. 40 [*De Indis,* Sect. II, no. 16], Soto (on the *Sentences,* Bk. IV, dist. v, sole question, art. 10), Covarruvias (on *Sext,* in rule *peccatum,* De Reg. Jur., Pt. II, § 10, no. 3), Valentia (Vol. III, disp. i, qu. 10, point 7), and Aragón (on II.–II, qu. 10, art. 8).

The proof of the true opinion, through an example. This true opinion may be proved, first, by appeal to divine example; for when God wished to destroy or punish the people living in the Promised Land, He willed, not that they should be conquered by the Israelites solely on account of idolatry, but that they should thus be conquered on account of the wrong they had committed in denying to the children of Israel a peaceful transit through their lands, and because of other similar wrongs; a fact which one deduces from the Book of *Numbers* (Chap. XX). Augustine, too, has noted this point (on *Numbers,* Qu. xliv [in *Questions on Heptateuch,* Bk. IV, qu. xliv]; on *Josue,* Qu. x [in *Questions on Heptateuch,* Bk. VI, qu. x]); and it is also brought out in the *Decretum* (Pt. II, causa XXIII, qu. ii, cans. ii and iii). From this example the general rule is inferred that it is not permissible for a prince to make war on the peoples in question, save in order to avert or vindicate some injury inflicted upon himself or upon his subjects. Therefore, the sole purpose of overthrowing idolatry is not a sufficient ground for a just exercise of coercion. Hence, Pope Nicholas, in reply to the questions of the Bulgarians, said: 'As to those who sacrifice to idols, we can say nothing more than that such persons must be reclaimed by reason rather than by force.'

The proof of the true opinion, through reason. The reason supporting the true opinion is the same as that which has been suggested in previous passages, namely, that the Church has no jurisdiction over the unbelievers in question, and that coercion or punishment without jurisdiction is unjust; for both these points have been proved. Therefore, just as one private individual may not punish or coerce another private individual, and just as one Christian king may not be accorded such treatment by another Christian [king], nor an infidel ruler by another infidel [ruler], so neither may an infidel state, supreme in its own order, be punished by the Church on account of its crimes, even if those crimes are contrary to natural reason; and consequently, it may not be compelled to give up idolatry or similar rites.

4. *The reply to the grounds on which the first opinion is based.* Neither is it pertinent that such sins (as was noted in the basic argument [for the first opinion])[2] are sins against God. For as I have already said, God has not made men judges to avenge all wrongs done to Him by any man; on the contrary, He has willed that due order be observed in this respect, [namely,] that subjects should obey their princes, while, on the other hand, He has reserved sovereign princes for His own tribunal in those matters which relate to the natural order, because greater evils would result from the opposite course.

Moreover, in reply to the observations made concerning blasphemy, it should be said in the first place that idolatry is not formal blasphemy, but only virtually and inclusively such. It should also be said that a Christian prince may compel the unbelievers to cease from blaspheming, when their blasphemy is in contempt of the Church and to the injury of the Christian religion, because from such an act on their part there arises a just ground for war; even as these same infidels may be forcibly prevented from harming Christians, and from dragging the latter into error or compelling them to desert the faith; whereas the case is far otherwise when the sins of infidels, although contrary to religion, are against God alone.

2. [I.e. the opinion that even in the case of non-subjects, 'pagan idolaters may be forced by the Church to worship the one God and to relinquish the rites of idolatry', &c. *Vide* Sub-section 2 of this Section, p. 873.—Tr.]

The reply to the first confirmation [of the first opinion]. The reply, then, to the first confirmation [of the first opinion][3] is evident. It was in view of this reply, moreover, that I inserted [the limiting term,] 'normally', in my statement [of the second opinion].[4] For, in order to defend the innocent, it is allowable to use violence against the infidels in question, that they may be prevented from sacrificing infants to their gods; inasmuch as such a war is permissible in the order of charity and is, indeed, a positive duty if it can be conveniently waged. It should be added that this course of action is licit, not only in order to free children, but also for the purpose of freeing adults, even though the latter may consent and wish to be sacrificed to idols; because in this respect, they are worse than madmen, and because, moreover, they are not the lords of their own lives, so that, accordingly, any man can be restrained by another from committing suicide. But what has been stated [concerning sacrifice] must be limited to cases where such killing is unjust. For if infidels had a custom of sacrificing to idols only those criminals who were justly condemned to death, such infidels could not be coerced solely on that ground, since in this practice they would sin, not against justice, but against religion only, and the excuse of defending the innocent would therefore cease to avail.

5. *The answer to the second and third confirmations [of the first opinion].* The reply to the second confirmation [of the first opinion][5] is this: the practice of the Romans is praised, not as being virtuous in an absolute sense, but as a lesser evil possessing some semblance of virtue because of its material object. As for the saying of Aristotle quoted in the last [and third] confirmation,[6] it would indeed be duly applicable, if there existed any people so barbarous that they were neither united in a civil society, nor capable of exercising government. For in that case, it would be not on the ground of religion, but on that of the defence of humanity (so to speak) that they might be forcibly subjected to the government of some state. But, in my opinion, no people so barbarous have yet been found.

---

3. [*Vide* Sub-section 2 of this Section, p. 873.—TR.]
4. [*Vide* the first sentence of Sub-section 3 of this Section, p. 874.—TR.]
5. [*Vide* Sub-section 2 of this Section, p. 873.—TR.]
6. [*Vide* Sub-section 2 of this Section, p. 873.—TR.]

6. *Infidels who are subjects of a Christian prince can be forced by the latter to profess the cult of the true God.* As to infidels of the kind in question, who are nevertheless subjects of Christian princes, it should be said that, in the first place, they may be forced by such princes to profess the worship of the true God, and consequently to cease from professing errors contrary to natural reason and to the faith. So St. Thomas teaches, as do the other theologians, in the passages cited.

The first proof of this assertion, from Deuteronomy, *Chap. xiii.* Moreover, the truth of this assertion can be proved, first, from a passage of *Deuteronomy* (Chap. xiii), wherein God orders that unbelievers of this kind—namely, unbelievers who are in any way subjects [of a faithful state]—shall be put to death on account of such wrong-doing. On this passage, and others like it, one may consult Cyprian's *Exhortation to Martyrdom* (Chap. v), and other references given there by Pamelius.[7]

The second proof of the same assertion based upon the practice of the Church. Secondly, the assertion in question can be proved from the practice of the Church, since from the beginning, the Christian emperors followed this course in so far as the circumstances of the times rendered it advisable. For Constantine forthwith ordered that the temples of the idols should be closed and that idolatry should be abolished, as we may gather from Eusebius (*On the Life of Constantine,* Bk. II, chaps. xliii and xliv and Bk. IV, chap. xxiii), Rufinus (*Ecclesiastical History,* Bk. II, chap. xix), and Nicephorus (in Bk. VIII, chap. xxxiii and also in Bk X, chap. xxxix), where he cites a similar order issued by Jovinian.[8] Later, indeed, Theodosius entirely destroyed the temples, according to Rufinus (Bk. II, Chaps. xxii and xxiii]), and Nicephorus (Bk. XII, chap. xxv). Subsequently, the same Theodosius framed many laws in which he condemned the worshippers of idols and which are to be found in the *Theodosian Code* (tit. *On the Pagans* [*Code,* XVI. x]). Moreover, he was imitated by Justinian in his *Code,* same title [*Code,* I. xi]. Augustine (*Letters,* xlviii, l and xxiv [Migne ed. *Letters,*

---

7. [Jacobus Pamelius (Jac. de Joigny de Pamele, 1536–87), Flemish priest, edited the works of Cyprian.—Tr.]

8. [Suárez probably refers to Jovian or Jovianus Flavius Claudius who became Emperor of Rome in 363 A.D.—Tr.]

xciii, clxxxv and cci]) approved of these laws, while Ambrose, too (*Letters,* xxx [xl]), and many Councils also, approved of the practice in question: for the Fifth Council of Carthage (Chap. xv [Chap. xvi]) declared that the Emperor must be petitioned to destroy the remnants of idolatry; the same view was upheld by the African Council under Boniface (Chap. xxv); the Third Council of Toledo (Chap. xvi) ordered that idolatry be uprooted from the lands of the faithful, a decree which was also issued by the Twelfth Council of Toledo (Chap. xi), and the Sixteenth (Chap. ii); and finally the Council of Elvira (Chap. xli) ordered that Christians having pagan servants should not allow the latter to keep idols in their homes.

7. *The assertion set forth [in Sub-section 6] is confirmed by reasoning.* The reason [for the opinion under discussion[9]] is that these Christian princes do not lack jurisdiction with respect to the unbelievers in question, since the latter are assumed to be subjects, and since the action of which we are speaking does not exceed the limits of that jurisdiction.

A second reason [for the same opinion] is as follows: it is the duty of a civil state, by virtue of reason and the natural law, to provide for the true worship of God within its borders; accordingly, in that same state there exists a directive power for the government of men with respect to this sort of worship; consequently, that state possesses also a coercive power for the punishment of offences contrary to such worship and for the coercion of men, lest they become involved in errors of the kind (for a directive power would be ineffective, and of insufficient use to the state, without an accompanying coercive power); and this coercive power, in so far as it is natural, resides in Christian princes; therefore, Christian princes may thereby exert force upon their own subjects, in the manner above-mentioned, even if the latter are unbelievers. The entire argument is clear. Its foundation, moreover, which is expressed in the first antecedent, is laid down by St. Thomas (*De Regimine Principum,* Bk. I, chap. xiv, and Bk. II, last chapter). This assertion is, furthermore, a self-evident truth. For the

---

9. [I.e. the belief that infidels who are subjects of Christian princes, 'may be forced by such princes to profess the worship of the true God, and consequently to cease from professing errors contrary to natural reason and to the faith.' *Vide* the first sentence of Sub-section 6 of this Section, p. 877.—Tr.]

power in question is of God, as Paul testifies in *Romans* (Chap. xiii [, v. 1]), adding, immediately thereafter, the words, 'And those [powers] that are, are ordained of God.' Hence, this power has pre-eminently been given for the honour and worship of the one God, of Whom human princes are the ministers, as Paul says, in the chapter cited. The confirmation of our argument is that the purpose of such power is to maintain the state in peace and justice, which cannot be done unless the state is also induced to live virtuously; but men cannot live according to moral and natural virtue, without true religion and the worship of the one God; therefore, natural power and the jurisdiction of a human state are extended to include this purpose.

8. *The first corollary of the immediately preceding statements.* From this reasoning I infer, first, that even a pagan—that is, a non-Christian—king, if he has a knowledge of the true God, may use force upon his own subjects to cause them to believe that truth, either by their own reasoning if they are intelligent, or by putting human faith in more learned men, if they are ignorant; and consequently, he may compel those same subjects to cease from the worship of idols and from similar superstitions contrary to natural reason. The proof of this inference is that there resides in such a king all power which, according to natural reason, is suitable for a human state.

The second corollary of the same statements. Secondly, it follows from that series of statements that the princes in question not only have the aforesaid power, but are moreover bound to use it in the manner indicated. The proof of this second corollary is as follows: by virtue of their office they are under an obligation to govern their subjects well, in accordance with the purpose for which they possess power; and good government demands this use [of such power], as has been proved; hence, this obligation is more weighty in the case of Christian princes, because they have a greater knowledge of truth, and because in Christian kingdoms this coercion is especially necessary in view of the welfare of the Christian subjects also; consequently, princes of the kind in question are bound to frame laws prohibiting offences in this matter [of worship], for they cannot inflict punishment for such offences, if they observe a due order, unless they first prohibit the offences in their laws.

The third corollary of those statements. Thirdly, it follows that such power is to be exercised by public, not private authority; and hence a private citizen who is a Christian may not force another and infidel citizen to refrain from the worship of idols; neither may that Christian citizen, acting on his own private authority, destroy those idols, [a prohibition] which is indicated by the civil law (*Code,* I. xi. 3 and 6). In this sense, also, one should understand Canon 60 of the Council of Elvira, according to which a Christian who breaks an idol and does so on his own private authority, is not reputed a martyr, even though he be slain for that action, because he thrust himself forward indiscreetly and on his own initiative, as Mendoza explains at length, in dealing with the said Council ([*Vetustissimum et Nobilissimum Concilium Illiberitanum cum Discursibus* . . . ,] Bk. III, chap. xlv).

9. *Are the rites of unbelievers to be tolerated in Christian kingdoms?* Finally, there remains for discussion an obvious question connected with the foregoing, a question of which St. Thomas (II.–II, qu. 10, art. 11) treats, namely: are the rites of unbelievers to be tolerated in the kingdoms of the faithful? From what has been said, it would seem that such rites ought not to be tolerated; for they are superstitious and injurious to God, Whose true worship the princes of those kingdoms are bound to advance.

However, St. Thomas makes a valid distinction between two kinds of rites: those which are contrary to natural reason, and opposed to God as known by the light of nature, for example, idolatry, and so forth; and those others which are indeed superstitions, by comparison with the Christian faith and its precepts, but which are not intrinsically evil or contrary to natural reason, for example, rites of the Jews, and perhaps even many of the rites of the Saracens and of similar infidels who worship only the one true God.

As to the first group, then, the inference stated at the beginning of this sub-section[10] is valid; for the Church ought not to tolerate these among her infidel subjects, a point proved by all the passages which we have cited and by the fact that, in such toleration or permission, there is no advantage either to the unbelievers themselves or to the Christian state. This assertion must be understood, however, only in a general sense; for it often happens

---

10. [Sub-sect. 9; i.e. the inference that, 'such rites ought not to be tolerated', &c.—Tr.]

that a Christian king is not able to destroy these rites entirely, without great loss to his kingdom or to the other Christian subjects, in which event he may, without sin, connive at and allow [the continued observance of the rites]. This concession has its foundation in the words of Christ (*Matthew*, Chap. xiii [, v. 29]) as set forth in the parable in which the servants asked the head of the household whether the cockle should be rooted up, whereat the latter replied: 'No, lest perhaps rooting up the cockle, you root up the wheat also together with it'. So it is that the Church often tolerates grave sins even in the faithful, lest schisms still more grave result. Such is the doctrine upheld by Augustine refuting Parmenianus *Contra Epistolam Parmeniani*, Bk. III, chap. ii [, no. 13]), and set forth in *Decretum* (Pt. II, causa XXIII, qu. iv, can. xix). The reason for this view is clear, namely: prudence teaches that of many evils the least should be chosen, while the rule of charity demands that correction should not be exercised save for a fruitful result; and therefore, much less should coercion be exercised when greater harm would ensue.

10. *Unbelievers are not to be compelled, even when they are subjects, to abandon rites which are merely in opposition to the faith.* As to the other rites of unbelievers, those which are opposed only to the faith but not to natural reason, it is a certainty that unbelievers, even though subjects, should not be compelled to abandon them; on the contrary, such rites should be tolerated by the Church. So St. Gregory teaches (*Letters*, Bk. I, letter xxxiv [Bk. XIII, letter xii]), especially with respect to the Jews, when he forbids that the latter be deprived of their synagogues, and urges (Bk. XI, letter xv) that they be permitted to engage in their ceremonies therein. He likewise teaches that the Jews should be permitted to celebrate their solemn rites.

The proof of this assertion. The reason for such a view is that these rites are not intrinsically evil according to the natural law, and that therefore, the temporal power of the prince does not *per se* include the authority to prohibit them; since no reason for the prohibition can be given, save that the rites in question are contrary to the faith, and this is not a sufficient reason in the case of those who are not spiritually subject to the power of the Church.

The confirmation. The confirmation of this argument is the fact that such a prohibition would be (so to speak) a coercion to the acceptance of the faith; and this coercion, as we have said, is not permissible. The foregoing argument applies in general to the Saracens and to the other unbelievers who know and worship the one true God, in so far as pertains to those rites which are not contrary to natural reason.

Why the Jews are to be permitted to celebrate their own rites in Christian states. However, the Church has always considered that this tolerance is especially advisable in dealing with the Jews, because the errors of the latter furnish a testimony to the faith in many particulars. In the first place, the Jews admit that the Messiah was promised, and they accept the Scriptures from which we clearly prove that the promise has been fulfilled. Secondly, we see fulfilled in them what the Prophets and Christ foretold regarding their desertion of Him and their hardness of heart. Finally, Augustine has said (*On the City of God,* Bk. XVIII, chap. xlvi) that the Jews should be preserved and allowed to live in their own sects, in order that they in turn may preserve a testimony to the Scriptures such as the Church received, even from her enemies; and, in this connexion, Augustine quotes the words of Paul (*Romans,* Chap. xi [, v. 11]), 'But by their offence, salvation is come to the Gentiles'; and also a passage from the *Psalms* (lviii [, v. 12]), 'Slay them not, lest at any time my people forget, scatter them by Thy power, &c.' Augustine cites similar examples in his first sermon, on *Psalm* xl, near the end.

11. However, it should be added that the Church has allowed these rites within certain bounds and limitations.

Within what limits these rites should be allowed to the Jews. The first and general limitation is that such rites are not to be celebrated to the scandal of the faithful; a fact which one may gather from the *Decretals* (Bk. V, tit. VI, chaps. iii, iv, vii and xv) and from the *Code* (I. ix, throughout many laws there given). Among the Laws of Spain, too, there are many of the same sort ([*Las Siete Partidas,*] Pt. VII, tit. XXIV, laws I et seq. and Pt. I, tit. IV, law 63).

Secondly, and specifically, although the Jews are permitted to retain and to keep in repair their old synagogues, they are nevertheless forbidden to erect new synagogues. On this point, see the *Code* (I. ix. 18), and the *Decretals* (Bk. V, tit. VI, chaps. iii and vii).

Thirdly, although it is forbidden that their synagogues should be taken away from them, nevertheless, if these are once so taken, and consecrated as churches, they are not to be restored, and the loss must be made good in some other way; as Gregory indicates in *Letters* (Bk. VII, letter lviii [Bk. IX, letter lv]).

Fourthly, the Jews are not allowed to do anything which has not been ordained in their law, a limitation which is laid down by Gregory in the same Letter lviii [lv].

Fifthly, they are not allowed to have their synagogues in the neighbourhood of Christian churches, according to the same Gregory (Bk. XII, letter xviii [Bk. I, letter x]).

Sixthly, on the day of the Passover, Jews are forbidden to go out in public; nay more, they are ordered to keep their doors and windows closed, as we read in the *Decretals* (Bk. V, tit. VI, chaps. iv and xv). According to this same authority, they are also commanded to wear an outward sign by which they may be externally distinguished from the faithful. And in general, they are to be severely punished if they do anything or make any public manifestation, in opposition to the honour of the Christian religion; a fact which is also brought out in the *Decretals* (Bk. V, tit. VI, chap. xv) and in the *Decretum* (Pt. II, causa XXIII, qu. viii, cans. viii *et seq.*), and in the civil laws cited above.

Finally, for the reason already expounded, the ancient rabbinical books which were written sincerely and without any hatred of the Christian religion are tolerated; but the Books of the Hebrews, who later corrupted the Scriptures, are banned, as Cajetan has noted (on II.–II, qu. 10, art. 11).

SECTION V

May the Unbelievers in Question Be Deprived of All Superior Power Which They Hold over Christians, That Is to Say, over the Faithful?

1. *The fourfold power of unbelievers over Christians.* This power may be manifold, but it can be reduced to four heads. First, there is the power of jurisdiction, whether it be supreme as in kings, or inferior as in their ministers. The second sort is the power of true dominion, to which absolute

slavery corresponds. The third is the power which may be called domestic, to which service corresponds. The fourth is the *patria potestas*.

The question stated above may be applied to all these forms of power, but we shall speak chiefly of princes; and that point being made clear, the other headings will be disposed of easily. Moreover, all these forms may be treated as relating to non-subjects [as well as subjects]; and in either case a twofold procedure is distinguishable by which the holders may be deprived of this power—that is, they may be deprived directly, merely by reason of the unbelief of the superiors, or because of the faith of the subjects; or only indirectly, on account of other intrinsic purposes.

2. *The opinion of certain persons, who affirm the right even of direct deprivation.* In the first place, then, as to those non-Christian princes some or many of whose subjects are converted to the faith, there is the opinion of certain persons who hold that these unbelievers may be absolutely and directly deprived by the Church of their power over their Christian subjects. Hostiensis (*Summa*, Bk. III, *De Voto*, p. 263, at end) has been cited as supporting this opinion; but he does not really hold such a view, although in other matters he differs from what we have said above, expressing himself in a somewhat inconsistent manner. Alvaro Paez (*De Planctu Ecclesiae*, Bk. I, chap. xviii [chap. lix]), however, inclines more definitely to the view in question. The ground on which that opinion is based is the contention that it is not fitting, but on the contrary, seems wholly disgraceful, that the faithful should be governed by unbelievers. This statement is made in the *Decretals* (Bk. V, tit. vi, chap. i) and is derived from Paul's writings (*1 Corinthians*, Chap. vi). Moreover, there are cited in favour of this view other Scriptural testimonies which I shall not discuss here, since I speak of them in another passage presently to be cited. However, the opinion in question is wholly false.

3. *The first proposition: unbelieving princes may not be deprived of their jurisdiction over their Christian subjects, simply and directly [on the ground of unbelief].* The following proposition must, then, be laid down at the outset: unbelieving princes may not simply and directly on the ground [of unbelief], be deprived by the Church of the power and jurisdiction which they hold over Christian subjects. This is the common opinion, and it is drawn from a passage in the works of St. Thomas above cited

([II.–II,] qu. 10, art. 10), in connexion with which Cajetan and all the more recent commentators uphold such a view; as do the other Scholastics, especially Durandus (on the *Sentences,* Bk. II, dist. xliv, qu. 3), the canonists, in general, on the *Decretals* (Bk. III, tit. xxxiv, chap. viii), St. Antoninus (Pt. II, title x, chap. xv, § 1, at end [tit. xii, chap. iii, § 1, at end]), Sylvester (word *infidelitas,* Qu. 4), Waldensis (*Doctrinale Antiquitatum Fidei,* Bk. II, chaps. lxxxi *et seq.*), Driedo (*De Libertate Christiana,* Bk. III, chap. ix, at end), Victoria (Relect. *De Indis, passim*), Soto (*De Iustitia,* Bk. IV, qu. ii, art. 2) and Salmerón (Vol. XIII, tracts. xxxvii and xxxviii [Vol. XII, tract. xxxviii]). Other authorities, who will be referred to below, support the same opinion.

4. *The basis of the first proposition stated as a dilemma.* The basis of this truth rests on the fact that either the princes in question may be deprived *de facto* of such jurisdiction and power, on the ground that they do not possess this jurisdiction and power by divine right, or else they are unworthy on account of their unbelief to hold the power which they may actually have, and consequently may justly be deprived of it; but neither of these arguments is valid; therefore, . . .

An exposition of the first part of the dilemma. The first part of the minor premiss, which I have elsewhere proved at length (*Defensio Fidei,* Bk. III, chap. iv, no. 1),[1] is most certainly true. Briefly, the argument is as follows: Christ our Lord has not deprived the aforementioned princes of the power in question; nor does baptism—whether *ipso iure* or *de facto*—exempt the Christian from the power of his king, even though the latter be an unbeliever.

The proof of this argument is sufficiently evident, both in the fact that neither from Scripture nor from tradition can such deprivation or exemption be derived; and, more especially, in the fact that both Scripture and tradition clearly uphold the contrary practice. This is true of Scripture, because Paul said (*Romans,* Chap. xiii [, v. 1]): 'Let every soul be subject to higher powers'; an admonition which, under the expression 'every soul', manifestly includes the faithful, and under 'higher powers', includes the emperor and the princes of those days, who were unbelievers; wherefore

---

1. [Not included in these *Selections.*—Tr.]

in the *Epistle to Titus* (Chap. iii [, v. 1]), Paul also said, 'Admonish them to obey princes',[2] and Peter wrote (*1 Peter,* Chap. ii [, v. 13]), 'Be ye subject,' &c. Again, as to tradition, [viewed in relation to our argument,] it is well-known from the ancient custom of the Church, which I have elsewhere pointed out, in the work cited [*Defensio Fidei*], in accordance with the comments of many of the Fathers. To these citations I now add only the name of Polycarp as quoted by Eusebius (*Ecclesiastical History,* Bk. IV, chap. xiv, or xv [chap. xv]). The former, speaking of non-Christian princes, says, 'We are taught to render to the magistrates and the powers constituted by God, in proportion to their dignity of rank, such honour as is in no way detrimental to our salvation or to our religion.' St. Thomas (II.–II, qu. 10, art. 10) also defends this view very cogently by argument, when he reasons as follows: the political power in question springs from natural law and the *ius gentium,* whereas faith springs from divine and supernatural law; and the one law does not destroy or alter the other; neither is the natural law founded on the divine positive law; rather is it in a way subject thereto, constituting (as it were) the presupposition of the latter; and therefore, positive power is not founded on faith in such a way that one may lose that power on account of unbelief nor, on the other hand, is positive subjection, i.e. [subjection in the political sense] to one who is an unbeliever, repugnant to faith or to the baptismal character, so that, consequently this subjection is not automatically dissolved [by faith and baptism].

5. *An exposition of the latter part of the dilemma.* The other part[3] of the proposition which we have stated as a dilemma follows clearly from what has been said above. For the unbelieving princes of whom we speak, may not rightfully be deprived of their possessions without some just ground; and included within those possessions is the jurisdiction which they are assumed to have over Christian subjects; therefore, they may not be deprived of such jurisdiction, simply and directly [on the ground of unbelief].

2. [The Vulgate reads: 'Admonish them to be subject to princes and powers, to obey at a word', &c.—Tr.]

3. [I.e. the assumption that the princes in question, 'are unworthy on account of their unbelief to hold the power which they may actually have, and consequently may justly be deprived of it.' *Vide* the first sentence of Sub-section 4 of this Section, p. 885.—Tr.]

The truth of the antecedent in both its parts is self-evident. The proof of the consequent is as follows: there is no just ground on which such an act of deprivation may be committed; for the pretext would be specifically that very unbelief, since strictly speaking, no other ground exists or can be conceived; and in truth, unbelief is not, *per se,* a just ground: For if we consider it purely as an absence of faith, we must admit that, as I have said, such a lack does not destroy the basis of political power; and if, on the other hand, unbelief is considered as a sin worthy of such punishment, even so, it is not within the power of the Church to punish these unbelievers, since the Church has no jurisdiction over them, as I have also proved. Therefore, just as they may not be punished by the loss of other temporal goods, in view of the fact that their ownership of those goods is not based upon faith, similarly, they may not be deprived of the power in question.

A demonstration by analogy. Proof of this fact may be derived by analogy. For if there were two sovereign princes who were unbelievers, and one of them worshipped the true God as known by the light of nature, while the other prince was an idolater some of whose subjects worshipped the true God, the latter prince could not, on the ground of his idolatry, be deprived by the former of his jurisdiction over such subjects, since the prince who worshipped the true God would have no jurisdiction over the other, and since the idolatrous prince would not lose his jurisdiction over the subjects in question owing to the mere fact of his idolatry. There is, then, an indication from natural law that this order must be preserved, because that preservation is expedient to the welfare and peace of the world and to a just equity; but the power given to the Church does not interfere with natural rights, since it has [rather] been given for edification and is to be used in the way best adapted to the preservation of the faith; therefore, the Church has not been given the aforementioned power of deprivation, a power which would serve for destruction instead [of serving for edification], inasmuch as it would result in harm to the faith and in scandal to those who are not of the faith.

6. *The second proposition: the Church may indirectly deprive non-Christian princes of their power over those of their subjects who are believers.* Nevertheless, we must state, in the second place, that the Church may

indirectly[4] deprive these non-Christian princes of their power over those subjects who are believers, if the welfare or defence of the latter makes this necessary. St. Thomas so teaches (II.–II, qu. 10, art. 10), as do others cited above; and I also have touched upon this subject in the *Defensio Fidei* (Bk. III, chap. xxiii, no. 21).[5]

The reason supporting this proposition. The reason in support of this second proposition is as follows: the baptized faithful, by the fact of their faith and their baptism, are subjects of the Church in spiritual matters, so that the Church has the power to rule them to the extent that is necessary or highly expedient for the welfare of their souls; and therefore, if it should become necessary to this end, to free such persons from the power of non-Christian lords, the Church may do so, and consequently may deprive those non-Christian princes of their power over the persons in question. For he who gives the form, gives also those things that are consequent upon the form; and whoever gives power and jurisdiction in order to attain any end, gives consequently, all the means necessary to reach that end.

A confirmation. This argument is confirmed by the example of a marriage contracted between unbelievers, one of whom is later converted to the faith. For if either party wishes to remain in wedlock without injury to God, the other may not sever the bond; but if, on the other hand, the unbelieving spouse is the occasion to the Christian partner of evil living, then the latter both may and ought to be separated from that unbeliever, as Paul declares (*1 Corinthians,* Chap. vii [, v. 15]). Thus the unbelieving partner, indirectly (as it were) and for the good of the faith, is deprived of the power and dominion which he has over his spouse. Therefore, the same holds true to a far greater degree in the case which we are discussing; for the marriage bond is of its nature more nearly indissoluble than the bond of political subjection.

7. It should be noted, however, that there are two ways in which such Christians may be freed from the power of unbelievers.

The first mode of freeing the faithful from the power of non-Christian princes, viz. through change of domicile. The first primarily affects the

---

4. [I.e. incidentally, in the process of attaining some other end.—Tr.]
5. [*Supra,* p. 799.—Tr.]

subjects themselves, who may change their domicile and pass over to the realms of Christian princes; for then it follows of necessity that they are no longer subject to their former prince. This method is easy and entirely just; and therefore, it may be employed by any Christian subject, acting on his own authority, for he is not bound to remain always in the same territory. Consequently, if any prince attempts to prevent his Christian subjects from thus transferring their domicile, he may be forcibly resisted by Christian princes, and justly subdued in war in defence of these subjects, because they are being deprived of their right which they wish to exercise.

8. *The second mode of depriving an unbelieving prince either of his sovereignty, or of his power over the faithful.* These unbelieving princes may be deprived of their power over their Christian subjects in another way, which affects [primarily] the princes themselves; that is, though the subjects in question remain in that territory, the prince may be deprived [either of his sovereignty],[6] or at least of his power over such subjects. But this result could hardly be effected without a change of ruler, so that the second method is more difficult [to follow than the first]; and therefore, although the power [to employ that method] is not lacking [to the faithful], nevertheless, great caution is necessary in its employment. In the first place, [if this second method is to be used,] the faithful should constitute a great multitude; or, if they be few, it must be practically impossible for them to change their domicile to a place where they may practise their faith without scandal. Furthermore, the successful issue of the enterprise must be morally certain, lest it come to pass that in wishing to eradicate the cockle, these Christian subjects should pull up the wheat.

Durandus requires that some injuries be committed on the part of the prince [before the second mode may be employed]. Durandus [on the *Sentences,* Bk. II, dist. xliv, qu. 3] holds, moreover, that it is necessary, [in order to justify the method in question,] that the non-Christian prince shall first have been the cause of injuries and obstacles to the faith—such as attempting to entice his subjects to unbelief, or impelling them to observe his own rites,

6. [The bracketed English phrase has been supplied from the Latin phrase, *vel regno,* which occurs in the marginal note, but not in the body of the text.—Tr.]

or prohibiting them from practising the Catholic rites and from obeying their own spiritual pastors, or similar injuries—since both necessity and the ground of justice would then exist.

Yet the moral peril of injury is sufficient. St. Thomas ([II.–II, qu. 10,] art. 10), however, thinks that, although these factors may, in a general sense, be necessary for the exercise of the power in question, yet the Church has the power, even before the infliction of this kind of injury, to remove such non-Christian sovereigns solely on the ground of moral peril to the faithful. This opinion I too have approved, in the aforesaid *Defensio Fidei* (Bk. III, chap. xxx, no. 6),[7] because, in moral questions peril must be guarded against before any specific injury occurs, a principle which certainly is very true when the peril is imminent and concerns the moral order. Therefore, as regards the matter specifically under discussion [—that is, the second mode of depriving an infidel prince of power—] all the circumstances in any particular case must be taken into consideration, and [in view of them], such peril to the faithful must be judged to exist [before resort to that second method is justifiable].

9. *In whom this indirect power resides.* Furthermore, I note that this indirect power, which we hold, exists in the Church for the removal of the above-mentioned princes, is a public power and not a private one, a fact which is self-evident. Therefore, it may be considered as residing either in the Pope, or in some sovereign Catholic king. The Pope has, by reason of his supreme spiritual jurisdiction, the power to secure and watch over the salvation of souls; whereas this power exists in a temporal prince only as a means of defending his neighbours, and especially the faithful, for such a prince has no spiritual jurisdiction.

Consequently, a temporal king may not use this power on his own authority until a non-Christian prince has inflicted violence upon his own Christian subjects, since measures of defence are not lawful before an act of aggression occurs. But both the Pope, and a king as moved by the Pope and as his instrument (so to speak) may well take preventive measures solely on the ground of peril, since the power of jurisdiction extends to the prevention of evils lest they occur.

7. [Not included in these *Selections.*—Tr.]

These remarks will suffice as to sovereign princes. In due proportion, the same conclusions might easily be applied to other and intermediate rulers, as well as in the case of all unbelievers not subject to the Church who exercise jurisdiction over the faithful.

10. *The third proposition: infidel masters, not subjects of the Church, cannot be deprived of their dominion over their Christian slaves, directly [on the ground of unbelief].* In view of the foregoing, it is easy to deal with the second division [of power],[8] that which relates to Christian slaves and their infidel masters. For, following a similar line of reasoning, we must state that these masters, who are not in any other respect subjects of the Church, may not be deprived of their Christian slaves, directly [on the ground of unbelief], whereas they may indirectly[9] be deprived of those slaves.

The first half of this proposition is certainly true and commonly accepted. With regard to it, and in addition to the authors already cited, Sylvester (word *furtum,* Qu. 6), may be consulted; and by him, at that place, Rosella ([word *furtum,*] No. 25) is quoted, although in another passage (*ibid.,* No. 24) Rosella seems to hold a different opinion. In the latter case, however, he was probably speaking of Christian slaves captured in an unjust war; otherwise he would be speaking incorrectly and contradicting himself. Angelus de Clavasio ([*Summa,* word *dominus,*] No. 56) may also be consulted on this point. The statement in question is upheld, too, by Navarrus (*Summa,* chap. xvii, nos. 103 and 104), Covarruvias (on *Sext,* rule *Peccatum, De Reg. Jur.,* Pt. II, § 11, no. 6), and Molina (*De Iustitia,* Bk. I, disp. xxxix).

The argument supporting this statement is similar to that given above. For Christians who before baptism were subject to unbelievers are not released from temporal servitude to the latter by the simple force of divine law, that is, of baptism; and, therefore, infidel masters, who are not in any other respect subjects of the Church, may not, directly [on the ground of unbelief,] be deprived by the Church of their dominion. The truth of the

---

8. [*Secundum membrum,* referring to true dominion, the second of the four divisions mentioned in the first paragraph of this Section. The various series of numbers used by Suárez in the course of the section are somewhat confusing.—Tr.]

9. [I.e. incidentally.—Tr.]

antecedent, Paul clearly assumes, when he says in the *Epistle to the Ephesians* (Chap. vi [, v. 5]): 'Servants be obedient to them that are your lords according to the flesh [. . .] as to Christ.' This injunction is repeated in the *Epistle to the Colossians* (Chap. iii [, v. 22]), in that to *Titus* (Chap. ii [, v. 9]), and in the *First Epistle of Peter* (Chap. ii [, v. 18]). Wherefore Augustine (on *Psalms,* cxxiv [, no. 7]), also, rightly says: 'Christ did not make free men out of slaves, but made good slaves out of bad ones.' He upholds this same doctrine at some length in his thirty-first sermon, on *Psalm* cxviii, and under His name in *Questions on the Old and New Testaments* (Qu. xxxv). From what has been said above, the truth of the consequent is also evident, namely, that these non-Christians, since they are not subjects of the Church, may not justly be deprived of their slaves.

11. *Nevertheless, these infidel masters may suffer such deprivation, indirectly.* The second half of our third proposition,[10] indeed, that half which relates to the power [to deprive infidel masters] on indirect grounds of their dominion over Christian slaves—is applicable when non-Christian masters are hostile to their Christian slaves, especially if that hostility involves matters of faith. In that case, these very slaves have the right to defend themselves, or to recover their original freedom if they can do so through flight; and certainly, in view of the arguments already set forth, the princes of the Church have the right, in this connexion, to exercise coercion upon unbelievers.

The same holds true as to servants. From the above statements, we derive sufficient enlightenment as to what should be said on the third point,[11] which relates to servants and the power of the head of the household over them; for the solution [in this case] should preserve a similar proportion.

May the children of unbelievers be baptized against the will of their parents? With respect to the fourth point, however [—that which relates to the *patria potestas*—] there arises a serious question, of which St. Thomas ([II.–II. qu. 10,] art. 12) treats, namely: may these unbelievers who are non-subjects be forcibly deprived of their infant children in order that the latter may be baptized? But this question pertains to the subject of baptism, with

10. [*Vide* the first paragraph of Sub-section 10 of this Section, p. 891.—Tr.]
11. [I.e. domestic power. *Vide* the first paragraph of Sub-section 1, pp. 883–84.—Tr.]

which I have dealt in Vol. III, disp. xxv, § 3 [*De Sacramentis*].[12] Enough has been said, then, as to unbelievers who are not subjects.

12. *The fourth proposition.* We must consider, secondly,[13] [whether] unbelievers who are [themselves] subjects of Christian princes [may be deprived of power over Christians]. Under this head those four topics discussed above may be examined and treated.

Infidel judges under a Christian king may be deprived of their power either directly or indirectly. As to the first point, indeed—that which relates to jurisdiction—the question has no application with respect to a sovereign prince; for we are assuming that these unbelievers are subjects of some Christian sovereign. Therefore, we have only to inquire as to the inferior judges or governors; and on this point it should be stated briefly that the Church can deprive such unbelievers, either directly or indirectly, of all jurisdiction of this kind over Christians, or—what amounts to the same thing—it may determine that in a Christian kingdom the faithful shall not be governed temporally by infidel judges or other infidel officials.

The first proof: from reason. The direct power to do so clearly exists, because it is a Christian prince who has jurisdiction over the subjects in question, and he may require in his judges and officials such qualifications as he deems necessary for honour, or for distributive justice, or for the peace and safety of his state. On this ground, then, it is easily possible to exclude certain persons from the offices mentioned. The existence of the indirect power, on the other hand, is a self-evident fact; for the act in question is highly expedient to the welfare of the faith, an argument which proves the existence, not only of the power, but even of the obligation.

13. *The second proof: from Paul.* This teaching agrees with the words of Paul (*1 Corinthians,* Chap. vi [, v. 6]), 'But brother goeth to law with brother and that before unbelievers', clearly reproving such behaviour as indecorous; at least, in cases in which it can be avoided. To the same effect is his saying elsewhere (*2 Corinthians,* Chap. vi [, v. 14]), 'Bear not the yoke

---

12. [Not included in these *Selections.*—TR.]

13. [I.e. 'secondly', as opposed to 'In the first place', the opening phrase of Subsection 2 (p. 884), where Suárez introduces the discussion relating to non-Christian princes whose subjects are converted to the faith.—TR.]

with unbelievers'. For although there may be other interpretations of this passage, this also is a probable one; or, in any case, the phrase may well be adapted to such an interpretation by a parity of reasoning.

The third proof: from law. Furthermore the existence of this power may be clearly proved from the application of human laws. For in the *Code* (I. ix. 18), Justinian forbids the Jews to hold public offices affecting Christians. Innocent III makes a similar ruling in the *Decretals* (Bk. V, tit. vi, chap. xvi), when he imposes a penalty upon Jews who accept or hold such offices. Moreover, the application of this rule is extended to the pagans,[14] that is, to Saracens, as may be learned from the last chapter of the same title [, i.e. *Decretals,* Bk. V, tit. vi, chap. xviii], in which Portugal is expressly enjoined to obey this law, with an additional statement to the effect that she may not sell tribute or royal grants to the Jews except when the latter are joined [in partnership] with some Christian, who will take care lest injury be done to believers. A similar law is laid down by the Third Council of Toledo (Chap. xiv [cited in] *Decretum,* Pt. I, dist. xxiv, can. i [Pt. I, dist. liv, can. xiv]); and in the Fourth Council of Toledo (Chap. lxiv [cited in] *Decretum,* Pt. II, causa xvii, qu. iv, can. xxxi), it has been enacted that those who entrust such offices to Jews should be excommunicated. The reason given is that, relying on this authority, the Jews take occasion to do injury to the faithful. Finally, the same rule is laid down in the First Council of Macon (Chap. xiii).

14. *The fifth proposition: Christians may not be slaves of those unbelievers who are subjects of the Church or of Christian princes.* Secondly, as to slavery, it should be stated that the faithful may not be slaves of the unbelievers in question, [i.e. of those unbelievers who are subject to a Christian prince or state,] and consequently the Church has been able[15] to deprive her infidel subjects of such power over Christians. So the Emperor Justinian also ordered, in the *Code* (I. x, only law); and in the *Decretals* (Bk. V, tit. vi, chap. v) there is a similar rule with respect to Jews. Gregory, too (*Letters,* Bk. II, letter xxxvi or Chap. lxxvi [Bk. III, letter xxxviii]) and the

---

14. [*Paganos,* where one would expect *infideles.* Cf. note to first paragraph of Subsection 15, *infra,* p. 896.—Tr.]

15. [*Potuisse.* Possibly Suárez intended *posse.*—Tr.]

Decretum (Pt. I, dist. LIV, cans. xiii and xiv, with other Chapters of the same dist. LIV), have rulings to this effect.

A special reason for such provisions may be inferred from the danger that would result to the faithful themselves if they should be allowed to dwell under the dominion of unbelievers. Another reason is that occasions of blasphemy, contempt of faith, and injury to the faithful might arise from such a relation.

These reasons pertain rather to the question of indirect power, although I may add that they have to do also with the direct power of Christian princes. For, in the first place, a Christian king may issue a general decree to apply throughout his realm, to the effect that Christians are not to be made the slaves even of other Christians, a rule which many kingdoms even now observe; because, though the civil power is not directly derived from the faith, nevertheless, when it is joined thereto, it is directed, and (so to speak) elevated thereby, so that it may do much for the welfare of the faith; therefore, the same law may far more readily be decreed with regard to unbelieving masters. Secondly, a king may impose upon his subjects such tribute and burdens as he deems necessary for good government; therefore, in like manner, he may impose upon infidel subjects the burden of an incapacity to be masters of Christians.

By what right the Christian slaves of unbelievers are freed from servitude. So it has been ordained that if an unbeliever, the slave of another unbeliever, is converted to the faith, by that very conversion he shall be emancipated. In the same way, if a Christian is bought by an infidel as a slave for purposes of servitude, he shall become free, by the very nature of the transaction, and the buyer shall lose his purchase money. But if the said Christian be bought for purposes of trading, he shall be sold to a believer within three months; otherwise, he becomes free. The same provision is laid down in the *Code* (I. ix, last law [only law] and I. iii, last law, last section [*Code,* I. iii. 54 (56), §§ 8 *et seq.*]).

However, the canonists note, with respect to one of the chapters cited above (*Decretals,* Bk. V, tit. VI, chap. ii), that these rulings do not prevent a Christian from working as a farm-servant, whether as a newcomer to the lands or estates of an unbeliever, or as one born thereon, for the following reasons: the permission to do so may be inferred from the passage in question; moreover, such labour is not servitude, and consequently is not included under the aforesaid prohibition; and finally, in the case of farm-servants there does not exist the same peril [to the faith], or likelihood of scandal, since the believer and the unbeliever do not live together or engage in frequent and familiar intercourse by reason of such occupation.

15. *The sixth proposition: the Church has the power to command that Christians shall not act as servants of unbelievers who are subject to her; and the Church does in fact so order.* Thirdly, on the question of servants it must be stated that the Church has this same power to prohibit Christians from acting even as free servants of unbelievers. This assertion may be proved without difficulty by applying to the present case the reasons given above,[16] an application which is easily made and which I therefore omit. Usage also confirms the same assertion. For this principle is laid down in a Chapter of the *Code* (I. iii. 55, § 5 [54, §§ 8 *et seq.*]), already cited; and its application is extended to the pagans,[17] in the *Decretals* (Bk. V, tit. vi, chap. viii [chap. xiii]), in a passage where the Saracens are expressly mentioned.

What should be said regarding the power of parents over their children. Finally, with respect to the *patria potestas,* it is certain that the son of an unbeliever, as soon as he is baptized, must in view of that very fact be freed from the power of his unbelieving parent, for the sake of the safety of the faith, and because by reason of baptism he is now under the law of the Church. This rule has been laid down in the Councils of Toledo, cited above, and is proved by the *Decretals* (Bk. III, tit. xlii, chap. iii). Whether the infant children of these unbelieving subjects may be baptized when the parents are unwilling, and whether the former may be taken from the parents with that end in view, are, however, disputed questions, which I have discussed [in *De Sacramentis*], Vol. III, pt. iii, disp. xxv, §§ 4, 5 and 6, to which the reader may refer.[18]

---

16. [*Vide* 894; the fifth proposition in the preceding Sub-section.—Tr.]

17. [*Paganos* again occurs where *infideles* would seem to be the more appropriate term. Cf. note 14, p. 894.—Tr.]

18. [Not included in these *Selections.*—Tr.]

SECTION VI

Whether Every Other Form of Communication between Christians and Unbelievers Is or May Be Prohibited

1. *The three kinds of communication between Christians and unbelievers.* Three kinds of communication between Christians and unbelievers must be distinguished: the first may be called formal, that is, communication in the works of unbelief; the second is communication in the works of our religion, and in a way this approximates to formal communication; the third is purely secular and human, and with respect to faith and unbelief, it is merely material [, i.e. incidental].

2. *The first kind of communication, in works of unbelief, is forbidden by the natural law.* The first kind is certainly forbidden by the divine and the natural law. This prohibition, by its very nature, is directed primarily to Christians; yet it may be applied to the unbeliever himself, either because unbelief is itself forbidden thereby, or—again—because the act of drawing a Christian into the intercourse or co-operation in question, is *per se* an evil act. However, this negative command regarding Christians is issued primarily to us, to whom these words were addressed (*1* [2] *Corinthians,* Chap. vi [, vv. 14, 16, 15]): 'For what fellowship hath light with darkness [. . .] or what agreement hath the temple of God with idols [. . .] or what part hath the faithful with the unbeliever?' Paul repeated this admonition in the same Epistle (*1 Corinthians,* Chap. x [, v. 20]): 'I would not that you should be made partakers with devils.' And a similar sense may be given to the passage (*2 Corinthians,* Chap. vi [, v. 14]): 'Bear not the yoke with unbelievers.' The same prohibition, both in its general form and with reference to many specific points, is found in the Sacred Canons (69, 70)[1] of the Apostles, in the Canons (61, 62) of the Trullan Synod, held after the Sixth [General] Council, in the Collection (71 to 75) of Martin, Bishop of Braga, compiled after the Second Council of Braga, and in the Council of Laodicea (Canons 37 *et seq.*), and also in the *Decretum* (Pt. II, causa xxvi, qu. v, can. iii).

1. [Canons 70, 71 in the edition of Funk.—REVISER.]

A proof by reasoning. Now the reason [for this prohibition] is that such intercourse is both irreligiously superstitious and opposed to the profession of the faith. Therefore, all that we said above about the necessity of professing the faith has due application at this place, as have our remarks in Vol. I: *De Religione* (Tract. III, bk. II)[2] on the sin of superstition.

The appearance and moral suspicion of communication are to be avoided. We need only add that not merely actual communication [with unbelievers] must be avoided, but also the appearance and moral suspicion of the same, such as the frequenting of the synagogues and temples of unbelievers, especially at the hours when their rites are celebrated. For this practice may give rise to scandal and provide occasion for the suspicion that those temples and rites are acceptable or approved.

All co-operation in the works of unbelievers is still more to be avoided. Azor (*Moral Institutes,* Vol. I, bk. VIII, chap. xxii, qu. 3 and bk. IX, chap xi, qu. 3) may be consulted on this point, as may also my own work, the *Defensio Fidei* (Bk. VI, chap. ix),[3] in which I have added that all co-operation is much more to be avoided [than is communication]. However, it is difficult to determine whether or not any co-operation takes place in particular cases: as when [Christians] sell to Jews or to pagans any animal or other object necessary for the sacrifices of the latter. But with respect to this point, one must observe the rule that if a thing cannot possibly be put to a good use, the sale of the same is co-operation; whereas if the object in question can be put to a licit use and in itself is neither good nor bad, then, normally, its sale is not co-operation. This is the rule laid down by Cajetan (on II.–II, qu. 10, art. 4), a rule which conforms with the opinion expressed by St. Thomas (II.–II, qu. 169, art. 2, ad 4); moreover, the same view is held by Sylvester, Angelus de Clavasio, and others (on word *infidelitas*); while I, too, have touched upon this subject in the aforesaid Chap. ix [*Defensio Fidei,* Bk. VI, chap. ix],[4] and have discussed it at length in the treatise on *The Sacraments in General,*[5] and

2. [Not included in these *Selections.*—Tr.]
3. [Not included in these *Selections.*—Tr.]
4. [Not included in these *Selections.*—Tr.]
5. [Not included in these *Selections.*—Tr.]

on *Oaths*,[6] and in other passages; for this question is indeed of a very general application.

3. *The second kind of communication is prohibited by the natural law.* The second kind of communication of unbelievers with believers, that which takes place in connexion with sacred matters and with the works of our own religion, is at times forbidden by divine and natural law as being intrinsically evil.

An instance of such a forbidden act is the admission of an unbeliever to partake of the Sacraments, this act of admission being absolutely and directly prohibited to believers; but unbelievers, too, are forbidden to obtrude themselves into the rites in question, and accordingly, they may be punished as injurious to the Christian religion, if they do so forcibly.

Under this part of our discussion, we may include the prohibition of marriage with unbelievers, although an infidel who has been converted to the faith may remain in wedlock already contracted with another infidel, provided that no offence[7] to the Creator results therefrom. Nevertheless, a baptized Christian is forbidden to contract marriage with an unbeliever, as I assume from the treatment of the subject of matrimony. It is true indeed that this prohibition is ecclesiastical rather than divine; and yet it seems to have been enacted not only on account of peril [to the faith], but also because of reverence for marriage, which, among the faithful, has been elevated to the character of a Sacrament.

Accordingly, other acts of communication of this sort are forbidden by human law; for example, it is prohibited that unbelievers should be present at the sacrifice of the Mass, or should behold the Sacrament of the Eucharist, prohibitions recorded by St. Thomas (*Summa*, Pt. III, qu. 80, art. 4, ad 4) commenting on Dionysius (*Ecclesiastica Hierarchia*, Chap. vii). This view is supported by Clement (*Constitutions*, Bk. VIII, chaps. viii and xii), whereon Turrianus comments at length; by the Fourth Council of Carthage (Chap. lxxxiv); and in the *Decretum* (Pt. III, dist. IV [dist. I, can.

---

6. [Not included in these *Selections.*—Tr.]

7. ['Offence'. The Latin words *contumelia, injuria,* are used indifferently to express any grievous sin which the unbaptized partner induces, or might induce, the Christian partner to commit.—Reviser.]

lxvii]). According to the latter passage, unbelievers are allowed to be present at that portion of the Mass which is called the Mass of the Catechumens, and far more readily are they allowed to be present at discourses on sacred matters delivered for their benefit; just as it is also permissible to pray privately for them or even to instruct them in the mysteries of religion.

Is it permissible to debate with unbelievers, on sacred matters? In this connexion, there arose also a question of which St. Thomas treats ([II.–II,] qu. 10, art. 7), namely: is it permissible to debate with unbelievers, on sacred matters? The discussion of this point, I shall reserve for Disputation XX [, i.e. *De Remediis Ecclesiae contra Haereses et Haereticos,*] Sect. i),[8] in which we are to ask the same question with regard to heretics, because that aspect of the question involves the same principle. For the present, I shall state briefly that such debating is not in itself evil, since it is often essential to the conversion of those unbelievers; but it should be conducted under proper circumstances, of which we shall speak in the Disputation above-mentioned.

4. *The third kind of communication, that which takes place in secular affairs, is not inherently evil, nor is it forbidden by divine law; but incidentally, in certain cases, it may be forbidden.* The third kind of communication is secular, or human, and it is with this kind in particular that we are now dealing. In this connexion, three points should be briefly discussed.

The first is that the sort of communication in question is not in itself evil or forbidden by divine law. This is certain; for Paul (*1 Corinthians,* Chap. vii [, vv. 12–14]) permits complete domestic and human communication between a Christian spouse and an unbelieving partner, and in the same *Epistle to the Corinthians* [Chap. x, v. 27] he allows the faithful to eat with unbelievers, upon invitation from the latter, a fact which both Chrysostom thereon (in Homily XXV [on *First Corinthians,* Chaps. vii and x] and Homily XXV, on *Hebrews*) and St. Thomas ([II.–II, qu. 10,] art. 9) note. Furthermore, a general prohibition with regard to such matters would not be expedient, because the conversion of unbelievers would thereby be rendered practically impossible. This would be the result, in the first place, in so far as preachers are concerned; for how could they approach

8. [Not included in these *Selections.*—Tr.]

those unbelievers for the purpose of instructing them, without first having had human intercourse with them? Therefore, this kind of communication is not only not prohibited, but even encouraged, as we learn from the *Decretals* (Bk. V, tit. vi, chap. x) and from the *Decretum* (Pt. II, causa xi, qu. i, can. xl), following Gregory (*Letters,* Bk. III, letter xxvi). Secondly, in so far as the unbelievers themselves are concerned, how could a father be converted to the faith, if he were to be immediately cut off from communication with his children or with his entire family, or even with his friends? This kind of communication, then, is not evil in itself; neither do we find that it is forbidden by divine law. The fact is simply that any believer is bound by virtue of the natural and the divine law to avoid that kind of human communication or converse with unbelievers which threatens peril to himself or is scandalous to others. This distinction as to different sorts of human intercourse is clear from general principles, but in a particular case it is based upon circumstances and the exercise of prudence.

5. *Nevertheless, the third kind of communication may be forbidden by ecclesiastical law.* Hence, secondly,[9] it must be stated that the Church can prohibit this sort of communication between Christians and unbelievers. This is evident, because there is no lack of jurisdiction for the making of such a law; and the subject-matter is also capable of being placed under such a prohibition, since the latter may be conducive to the peace and security of the faithful. Therefore, that prohibition must, as a general rule, be held to fall directly upon Christians alone, because, as St. Thomas noted (II.–II, qu. 10, art. 9), they are the true subjects of the Church. We must add, however, that the law in question may also [in special cases] be directly applied to non-believing subjects, either in punishment for some offence—as is the case with many laws which we shall presently cite—or in order to promote sound external government of the state, or even for the sake of the security of the faithful. Consequently, there are times when a Christian prince can, for the sake of religion, place a ban, directed even to foreign and non-subject unbelievers, upon this intercourse within his own kingdom.

---

9. [I.e. this is the second of the three points to be discussed in connexion with secular, or human, communication. *Vide* the first paragraph of the immediately preceding Sub-section, p. 900.—Tr.]

6. Thirdly,[10] the statement must be made that the Church has, in actual fact, laid down many prohibitions with respect to the sort of communication under discussion.

Moreover, familiarity with the Jews is in actual fact forbidden. In the first place, indeed, familiarity with Jews is placed under a general prohibition. On this point, the *Decretals* (Bk. V, tit. vi, chap. viii) may be consulted. In fact, it would seem that absolutely all converse and communication with them was forbidden by the Fourth Council of Toledo (Chap. lxi [Chap. lxii]). However, that prohibition has reference, not to all the faithful, universally, but to those who have been newly converted to the faith from among the ranks of the Jews themselves. To these new Christians, converse with those of their own people who persevere in Judaism is forbidden, because of the peril attending such converse. Therefore, this prohibition should be understood to refer to frequent, or continued converse, which may result in peril. Thomas Sánchez (*Opus Morale in Praecepta Decalogi,* Bk. II, chap. xxxi), following St. Thomas, Sylvester, and others, limits this general prohibition in such a way as to exclude its application in the case of those believers who are firm in the faith and with respect to whom there can be no fear of moral peril. However, if the prohibition contained in a law is general, it does not cease to bind in an individual case, even if the purpose of the law does, in a purely negative sense, cease to be realized in the individual case, as I assume from the treatise on laws. I therefore think that there is a limitation to the prohibition in the case of those persons whose care it is to convert such infidels as we speak of, because the purpose of the law then does not simply cease to be realized in a negative sense, but in addition, it ceases by contrariety.[11]

---

10. [This is the third of the three points to be taken up in connexion with secular, or human, communication. *Vide,* Sub-section 4, p. 900.—Tr.]

11. [I.e. harm to the individual. The above is what is taught by all theologians on law, viz. if law ceases to secure its purpose negatively in a given case, it still binds; if, however, it ceases *contrarie,* as is said, it ceases to bind, i.e. if a law does some real extrinsic harm to a person, it would *not* bind him. This is clearly seen in the laws of fasting and abstinence. If such a law would make a person unwell, it is said to cease *contrarie.* However, the law against reading certain books may cease *negatively,* but never *contrarie.*—Reviser.]

7. *Secondly, living in the same house with Jews is specifically forbidden.*
Secondly,[12] living in the same house with Jews is specifically forbidden
(*Decretum*, Pt. II, causa XXVIII, qu. i, can. xiii; *Decretals*, Bk. V, tit. VI,
chap. v). The reason for this prohibition is the avoidance of harm.

An objection. But the objection may be made that a Christian can own
a slave who is an unbeliever, and that consequently, he can live with that
unbeliever. The antecedent is supported in the *Decretals* (*ibid.*, chap. xiii).

The solution. Our reply is as follows: either this fact constitutes an
exception to the prohibition set forth above; or else it cannot properly be
said that the master dwells with the slave, but rather the converse, so that
the prohibition in question does not apply to such a master; or, at least,
a certain equality of fellowship and familiar intercourse is required for
'dwelling together', in the true sense of the phrase, so that the Christian
master, in accordance with other laws above-mentioned, must avoid also
this equal association with an unbelieving slave.

Furthermore, it is forbidden to eat at the same table with Jews. Thirdly, a
Christian is forbidden to invite an unbeliever to his banquet table, or to
accept such an invitation from the latter; for this also is dangerous association. This prohibition was especially directed against Jews in the Third
Council of Orleans (Chap. xxiii [Chap. xiii]), and in the Council of Agde
(Chap. xl cited in *Decretum*, Pt. II, causa XXVIII, qu. i, can. xiv), the special
reason being given that Jews discriminate among different sorts of food,
a practice which is not permissible to Christians. However, as a special
concession, this eating in common is permitted to preachers who are sent
forth to convert unbelievers.

The eating of unleavened bread is also forbidden. Fourthly, in these same
laws, and in the Apostolic canons cited above, Christians are specifically
forbidden to eat the unleavened bread of the Jews; an act which is evil in
itself, if it is understood to involve the consumption of such food as a Jewish rite; but this rule is also interpreted as a prohibition, in order to avoid
suspicion and peril [to the faith], against any partaking of the azyme with

12. [This introduces the second of the prohibitions mentioned at the beginning of
the preceding Sub-section. Six more, making eight in all, are discussed in the immediately succeeding pages.—TR.]

the Jews themselves or receiving it from them. When there is no danger of scandal, however, and especially if necessity requires, the eating of this food as ordinary bread is not forbidden, as the eating of idolothytes is forbidden in the *Decretum* (Pt. II, causa XXXII, qu. iv, can. viii).

8. *It is forbidden, moreover, to call in Jews in case of illness.* Fifthly, in case of illness, Christians are forbidden to call in Jews; at least they are forbidden to do so for the purpose of [medical] treatment (Sixth Synod, Chap. XI, cited in *Decretum,* Pt. II, causa XXVIII, qu. I, can. xiii). This rule may have been made not merely because of special peril to the soul, but also to avoid bodily contact. Hence, a further rule has been laid down against receiving medicine from Jews, a prohibition which is chiefly understood to mean medicine is not to be received at their hands and administered by them, lest familiarity and peril result. But these and like prohibitions should be interpreted as applying only when the case is not one of necessity, since necessity knows no law.

It is likewise forbidden to frequent the baths in the company of Jews, if this be done in accordance with a previous agreement. Sixthly, Christians are further ordered not to bathe with Jews at the same time at the same public baths, a prohibition which is laid down in the above-mentioned Chapter xiii [*Decretum, ibid.*]. This rule should be understood as applying only in a general sense, namely, as referring to the act of walking to the baths with them, that is to say, [the act of bathing together] as the result of an intention to do so. For this deliberate practice involves true social intercourse and familiarity, against which, on account of the danger involved therein, all the prohibitions under discussion are especially directed. If a Christian, then, should come accidentally to a public bath where a Jew is bathing at the time, the rule has no application, and it is not necessary that the Christian should on that account forgo what is convenient to him, or postpone it.

Furthermore, it is forbidden that Christian women should nurse Jewish children. Seventhly, it may be especially noted that Christian women are forbidden to act as nurses for Jewish children, a fact which is brought out in the *Decretals* (Bk. V, tit. VI, chap. viii). However, this qualifying phrase is added: 'in their homes'—that is, in the homes of the Jews—so that apparently, the rule in question is made solely to guard against the practice of dwelling together. Consequently, the inference may be drawn that a Christian woman is not forbidden to nurse a Jewish child in her own home; since the words of the law do not include such a case and should not be so extended. However, although this is true in so far as the strict letter of the law is concerned, nevertheless, the situation in question should be avoided because of the familiarity and peculiar affection which, as a general rule, result therefrom.

9. *It is also forbidden to make heirs or legatees of Jews.* Eighthly, it is forbidden that Christians, in their wills, should name Jews as their heirs and legatees. This is the doctrine of the canonists (*Decretals,* Bk. V, tit. vi, chap. v), and especially of Felinus (on *Decretals, ibid.,* no. 3), the Gloss thereon, and Sylvester (on the word *iudaeus,* Qu. 1 [, no. 2]). The *Code* (I. ix. 1) may be cited on the same rule; but in the *Code* the prohibition refers only to the Jews as a whole, that is, as a community, and prohibitions expressed in such terms are not usually extended to apply to individuals, as the Gloss thereon indicates. In this case, however, the extended application is allowed in the interests of the faith and of religion. Yet another chapter in the *Decretals* (Bk. V, tit. vii, chap. v) and one in the *Decretum* (Pt. II, causa xxiv, qu. ii, can. vi) may be mentioned in this connexion, in which the said prohibition is imposed upon bishops, in particular, while in the *Decretals* (Bk. V, tit. vii, chap. vi) it is extended to clerics.

The Doctors, however, apply that rule to all Catholics, either by the same process of reasoning, or at least *a fortiori;* and such should be the practice observed by all Catholics, especially since there exists a general warning lest they render aid and favour of this sort to Jews. This was the ruling of the Fourth Council of Toledo (Chap. lvii).

One must note, with respect to these and like questions, that the prohibitions involved are grave, both because of their subject-matter and because of the purpose they serve; and that by their nature, and generally speaking, they are binding under pain of mortal sin, although occasionally, when the particular instance happens to be of slight importance, the transgression may become venial.

Moreover, since a prohibition of the sort under discussion is part of the common law [of the Church], dispensations therefrom cannot usually be given by bishops; but when in any given case the necessity is urgent and delay would be dangerous, then, according to the common teaching on law, the granting of such dispensations is within the power of a bishop.

10. *Are these prohibitions extended to apply to all unbelievers?* Finally, it may be asked whether the laws in question are to be interpreted as applying universally to all unbelievers, or whether they have reference only to the Jews.

The cause of the doubt is that the laws cited speak expressly of the Jews, so that some persons hold that, the said laws being penal in nature, there should be no extension of their application. A special reason which is customarily given is that, according to the *Decretals* (Bk. V, tit. vi, chap. xiii), the Jews are not only subjects but also slaves. Hostiensis (*Summa,* Bk. V, *De Iudaeis,* p. 349) holds that the passage in question refers only to one's own purchased slaves, a view which certain of the Summists adopt. However, such a limitation is certainly not contained in the text, where, on the contrary, it is stated that the Jews have indeed inherently merited this slavery, but that in point of fact they are tributaries with the civil status of subordinate subjects, as Panormitanus (on *Decretals,* Bk. V, tit. vi, chap. xiii) notes with reference to this point, and as St. Thomas (II.–II, qu. 10, art. 12, ad 3 and Pt. III, qu. 68, art. 10, ad 2) and Soto (on the *Sentences,* Bk. IV, dist. v, sole question, art. 10, ad 2) have also explained. Therefore, the true reason for this discrimination against the Jews is thought to be the fact that intercourse with the Jews involves more peril on account of their greater pertinacity and their hatred of the Christian religion.

Nevertheless, it is my opinion that the prohibitions which we are discussing, apply also to the Saracens[13]—that is, the Mohammedans—both because such an extension of their force is repeatedly indicated in the civil and canon law (*Code,* I. iii. 57, § 5 [I. iii. 54 (56), §§ 8 (3) *et seq.*] and *Decretals,* Bk. V, tit. vi, chaps. viii, xvi, xv, xix, v); and also because there is an analogy in the reasoning applicable to both cases, inasmuch as these [Mohammedan] unbelievers are also enemies of the Christians, and attempt with all their strength to pervert the faithful.

As for other unbelieving pagans, however, they do not seem to have been included in the aforementioned laws, a fact which has been noted by

---

13. [The *Code* refers to 'pagans'.—Tr.]

Sánchez ([*Opus Morale in Praecepta Decalogi,* Bk. II,] chap. xxxi, no. 25), of whose opinion I approve in so far as relates to this matter. Many statements concerning these prohibitions may also be found in the writings of the jurists on the laws in question, in the comments of the Summists (on the word *iudaeus*), and in the statements of St. Antoninus (Pt. II, tit. XII, chap. iii), as well as in those of Azor and Sánchez, already cited; and these authorities quote many others.

The foregoing may suffice on the subject of unbelief.

On Charity

To the Gentle Reader

The primary cause, gentle reader, of the unusually brief form in which the following treatises on Hope and Charity are published, was the fact that even the members of the very school over which Suárez presided at Rome, during the time when he lectured on these subjects, became wearied of extremely diffuse and excessively elaborate dissertations, wherefore he readily bowed to the precepts and wishes of that school, such was the simple sincerity of this noble Doctor.

Furthermore, this treatment is brief, because he disregarded not a few matters that are usually dealt with, especially on the subject of Charity, for these matters are either entirely or in great measure applicable to grace, a subject which Suárez, in his work thereon, had very cogent reasons for thinking to be distinct from Charity (*De Gratia,* Bk. VI, chap. xii).[1] Such matters concern the supernatural entity of Charity, the production, increase, and loss of habits, the power of sanctifying and meriting. These are explained at length in that same work, and partially, in his treatise on the resuscitation of merit (section 3).[2] Grace itself, which of its nature precedes Charity, demanded that all of those matters should have a prior claim to treatment, and if the reader should here find them to be missing, they will be fully supplied in the passages indicated above.

However, the fact that these treatises, if compared with others which the author has already published, are briefer, is no indication that they

---

1. [Not included in these *Selections.*—Tr.]
2. [*Opusculum; Relectio de Meritis mortificatis,* &c., Disp. I, sect. iii, which is not included in these *Selections.*—Tr.]

are in any respect unsuited to the character of his genius and judgment. On the contrary, we venture to assert that when the author employs this concise method of composition, he appears, not merely to be equal to, but in a certain sense, to surpass himself. For the discursive reasonings of his profound genius and keen discernment, as well as the cogency of the arguments set forth by him, which attain a felicitous amplitude in other works of his, are here compressed into small compass, and more readily understood, without any loss of efficacy and force. Consequently, these treatises contain the pith and marrow of the subjects at hand, as you yourself, gentle reader, will (I hope) admit, when you have made the test of experiment. Nor will it be difficult, if you observe the similarity of this work[3] with others, its order and method, to divine the author of both the one and the others, recognizing (as it were) the lion by its claws.

In addition, in order that all this matter may be readily intelligible even to those who are not very well versed in the works of Suárez, we indicate in the margins of these disputations on Hope and Charity identical or similar points which Suárez discusses elsewhere more at length.[4] For the author will thus come to his own assistance, where there might seem to be need, without help sought from any other source.

DISPUTATION XIII

On War

[INTRODUCTION]

War in a general sense is manifold. An external contest at arms which is incompatible with external peace is properly called war, when carried on between two sovereign princes or between two states. When, however, it is a contest

---

3. [*Hujus operis,* referring evidently to both disputations (those on Hope and Charity).—Tr.]

4. [Of the volume *De Triplici Virtute Theologica,* only Disp. XVIII of the treatise *On Faith,* and Disp. XIII of the treatise *On Charity* are included in these *Selections.*—Tr.]

between a prince and his own state, or between citizens and their state, it is termed sedition. When it is between private individuals it is called a quarrel or a duel. The difference between these various kinds of contest appears to be material rather than formal, and we shall discuss them all, as did St. Thomas (II.–II, qq. 40, 41, 42) and others who will be mentioned below.

SECTION I

Is War Intrinsically Evil?

1. The first heresy [in connexion with this subject] consists in the assertion that it is intrinsically evil and contrary to charity to wage war.[5] Such is the heretical belief attributed by Augustine to the Manichaeans (*Against Faustus,* Bk. XXII, chap. lxxiv), whom Wycliffe followed, according to the testimony of Waldensis (*De Sacramentalibus* [which is Vol. III of *Doctrinale Antiquitatum Fidei*] last title, next to last chapter). The second error is the assertion that war is specifically forbidden to Christians, and especially, war against Christians.[6] So Eck maintains (*Enchiridion Locorum Communium,* Chap. xxii);[7] and other persons of our own time, who are heretics, advance the same contention. They distinguish, however, two kinds of war, the defensive and the aggressive, which we shall discuss in Sub-section 6 of this Section. The conclusions that follow will elucidate the matter.

2. *The first conclusion, which is negative, and a matter of faith.* Our first conclusion is that war, absolutely speaking, is not intrinsically evil, nor is it forbidden to Christians. This conclusion is a matter of faith and is laid down in the Scriptures, for in the Old Testament, wars waged by most holy men are praised (*Genesis,* Chap. xiv [, vv. 19–20]): 'Blessed be Abram [. . . .] And blessed be God by whose protection the enemies are in thy hands.' We find similar passages concerning Moses, Josue, Samson, Gedeon, David, the Machabees, and others, whom God often ordered to

5. On this and the following error see Bellarmine, *De Laicis,* Bk. III, chaps. xiv and xvi. Molina, *De Iustitia,* Disp. xc. (This note was in Suárez's original.—ED.)

6. In opposition to these heretics, others are also cited by Cenedo, *Collect.,* LIX, pt. i. (This note was in Suárez's original.—ED.)

7. [Eck speaks of the lawfulness of Christians waging war against Turks and heretics.—REVISER.]

wage war upon the enemies of the Hebrews. Moreover, the apostle Paul (*Hebrews,* Chap. xi [, v. 33]) said that by faith the saints conquered kingdoms. The same principle is confirmed by further testimony, that of the Fathers quoted by Gratian (*Decretum,* Pt. II, causa XXIII, qq. 1 and 2), and also that of Ambrose (*On Duties,* various chapters).

The first objection: based on 1 Paralipomenon, *xxviii.* However, one may object, in the first place, that the Lord said to David [1 *Paralipomenon,* Chap. xxviii, v. 3]: 'Thou shalt not build my temple because thou art a man who has shed blood.[8]

The second objection: based on Matthew, *Chap. xix* [John, *Chap. xviii*] *and on* Isaias, *Chaps. ii and xi.* Secondly, it will be objected that Christ said to Peter (*John,* Chap. xviii [, v. 11]): 'Put up thy sword into the scabbard,' &c.; and that Isaias also said (*Isaias,* Chap. ii [, v. 4]): 'They shall turn their swords into ploughshares [. . .] neither shall they be exercised any more to war'; and, in another Chapter (Chap. xi [, v. 9]): 'They shall not hurt nor shall they kill in all [my] holy mountain.' The Prophet is speaking, indeed, of the time of the coming of the Messiah, at which time, especially, it will be made clear, what is permissible and what is not permissible.

The third objection: based on the Council of Nicaea, and a letter of Pope Leo. Thirdly, at the Council of Nicaea (Chap. xi [, can. xii]), a penalty was imposed upon Christians who, after having received the faith, enrolled themselves for military service. Furthermore, Pope Leo (*Letters,* xcii [Letter clxvii, inquis. xii]) wrote that war was forbidden to Christians, after a solemn penance.

The fourth objection: based on reasoning. Fourthly, war morally brings with it innumerable sins; and a given course of action is considered in itself evil and forbidden, if it is practically always accompanied by unseemly circumstances and harm to one's neighbours. [Furthermore,] one may add that war is opposed to peace, to the love of one's enemies, and to the forgiveness of injuries.

3. *The answer to the first objection.* We reply to the first objection that [the Scriptural passage in question] is based upon the unjust slaying of Uriah; and, also, upon the particularly great reverence owed to the Temple.

---

8. [Suárez's quotation of *Paralipomenon,* Chap. xxviii, v. 3, reads: *Non aedificabis mihi templum, quia vir sanguinum es.* The same passage in the Vulgate reads: *Non aedificabis domum nomini meo, eo quod sis vir bellator, et sanguinem fuderis.*—Tr.]

The answer to the second objection. [As for the second objection, we may answer, first, that] Christ our Lord is speaking of one who on his own initiative wishes to use the sword, and in particular, of one who so desires, against the will of his prince. Moreover, the words of Isaias, especially in Chap. xi, are usually understood as referring to the state of glory. Secondly, it is said that future peace was symbolized in the coming of the Messiah, as is explained by Jerome on this point [on *Isaias,* Chap. xi], Eusebius (*Demonstrations,* Bk. I, chap. i), and other Fathers [of the Church]; or, at least, that Isaias is referring to the spiritual warfare of the Apostles and of the preachers of the Gospel, who have conquered the world not by a material but by a spiritual sword. This is the interpretation found in Justin Martyr, in his *Second Apology* for the Christians, and in other writers.

The answer to the third objection. The Council of Nicaea, indeed, dealt especially with those Christians who, for a second time, were assuming the uniform of pagan soldiers which they had once cast off. And Pope Leo, as the Gloss (on *Decretum,* Pt. II, causa xxxIII, qu. iii (*De Paenitentia*), dist. v, cans. iv and iii) explains, was speaking of those Christians who, after a public penance had been imposed upon them, were returning to war, before the penance had been completed. Furthermore, it may have been expedient for the early Church to forbid those who had recently been converted to the faith, to engage in military service immediately, in company with unbelievers, and under pagan officers.

The answer to the fourth objection. To the argument drawn from reason, Augustine replies (*On the City of God,* Bk. XIX, last chapter [Chap. vii]) that he deems it advisable to avoid war in so far as is possible, and to undertake it only in cases of extreme necessity, when no alternative remains; but he also holds that war is not entirely evil, since the fact that evils follow upon war is incidental, and since greater evils would result if war were never allowed.

The answer to the confirmation. Wherefore, in reply to the confirmation of the argument in question one may deny that war is opposed to an honourable peace; rather, it is opposed to an unjust peace, for it is more truly a means of attaining peace that is real and secure. Similarly, war is not opposed to the love of one's enemies; for whoever wages war honourably hates, not individuals, but the actions which he justly punishes. And the same reasoning is true of the forgiveness of injuries, especially since this forgiveness is not enjoined under every circumstance, for punishment may sometimes be exacted, by legitimate means, without injustice.

4. *The second conclusion, which is twofold.* Secondly, I hold that defensive war not only is permitted, but sometimes is even commanded. The first part of this proposition follows from the first conclusion, which even the Doctors cited above accept; and it holds true not only for public officials, but also for private individuals, since all laws allow the repelling of force with force (*Decretals,* Bk. V, tit. xxxix, chap. iii). The reason supporting it is that the right of self-defence is natural and necessary. Whence the second part of our second proposition is easily proved. For self-defence may sometimes be prescribed, at least in accordance with the order of charity; a fact which I have elsewhere pointed out, in Disputation IX [: *De Ordine circa Personas Servando in Praecepto Charitatis,* &c., Chaps. xxv, xl, § 3].[9] The same is true of the defence of the state, especially if such defence is an official duty. See the statement of Ambrose (*On Duties,* Bk. I, chap. vii). If any one objects that in the *Epistle to the Romans* (Chap. xii [, v. 19]) these words are found: 'Revenge not yourselves, my dearly beloved', and that this saying is in harmony with the passage (*Matthew,* Chap. v [, v. 39]): 'If one strike thee on the right cheek, turn to him also the other', we shall reply with respect to the first passage, that the reference is to vengeance, so that another version reads [*Romans,* Chap. xii, v. 19]: 'Not avenging yourselves', and that the Greek word, ἐκδικοῦντες, has both significations; but the meaning is clear from what follows: 'For it is written: Revenge is mine', &c. The meaning of the second passage cited is the same, if it is interpreted as a precept; although it may also be understood, in accordance with Augustine's explanation (Vol. IV in the book *On Lying,* Chap. xv and elsewhere), as referring to the preparation of the soul, at least when such a process is necessary; for otherwise [the passage in question is] merely a counsel [of perfection, and not a commandment].[10]

5. My third conclusion is, that even when war is aggressive, it is not an evil in itself, but may be right and necessary. *Proof from authority.* This is

---

9. [Not included in these *Selections.*—Tr.]

10. [St. Augustine here means that one must be prepared to be struck on the other cheek, if this is a necessary part of persecution for the faith; when it is not necessary, the words of St. Matthew, cited above, express a counsel, not a precept.—Reviser.]

clear from the passages of Scripture cited above, which make no distinction [between aggressive and defensive wars]. The same fact is evidenced
by the custom of the Church, one that has quite frequently been approved
by the Fathers and the Popes, according to an extensive collection of all
such instances, made by Roffensis[11] (*Contra Lutherum* [*Assertionis Lutheranae Confutationem,*] Art. 4 [Art. 34]). In this connexion, we may refer also
to Torquemada (on *Decretum,* Pt. II, causa XXIII, qu. i, nos. 1 and 2), as
well as to many other passages, in *Decretum, ibid.,* qu. viii, cans. vii *et seq.*

A proof from reasoning. The reason supporting our third conclusion is that
such a war[12] is often necessary to a state, in order to ward off acts of injustice
and to hold enemies in check. Nor would it be possible, without these wars,
for states to be maintained in peace. Hence, this kind of warfare is allowed
by natural law; and even by the law of the Gospel, which derogates in no
way from natural law, and contains no new divine commands save those
regarding faith and the Sacraments. The statement of Luther that it is not
lawful to resist the punishment of God is indeed ridiculous; for God does
not will the evils [against which war is waged,] but merely permits them; and
therefore He does not forbid that they should be justly repelled.

6. *What is a defensive war; and what, an aggressive war?* It remains for
us to explain what constitutes an aggressive war, and what, on the other
hand, constitutes a defensive war; for sometimes that which is merely an
act of defence may present the appearance of an aggressive act. Thus, for
example, if enemies seize the houses or the property of others, but have
themselves suffered invasion[13] from the latter, that is no aggression but
defence. To this extent, civil laws (*Code,* VIII. iv. 1 and *Digest,* XLIII.
xvi. 1 and 3) are justified in conscience also, when they provide that if
any one tries to dispossess me of my property, it is lawful for me to repel
force with force. For such an act is not aggression, but defence, and may
be lawfully undertaken even on one's own authority. The laws in question are extended[14] to apply to him who, while absent, has been ejected

11. [John Fisher, Cardinal, and Bishop of Rochester, lately canonized.—Tr.]
12. [I.e. an aggressive war.—Tr.]
13. [*Invaderit* should be replaced by *invaserint.* Cf. the edition of Paris, 1858.—Tr.]
14. [Read *extenduntur* in the Latin text, as in the 1858 edition above cited.—Reviser.]

from a tenure which they call a natural one, and who, upon his return, is prevented from recovering that tenure. For [the same laws decree] that any one who has been despoiled may, even on his own authority, have recourse to arms, because such an act is not really aggression, but a defence of one's legal possession. This rule is laid down in *Decretals*, Bk. II, tit. xiii, chap. xii.

A note. Consequently, we have to consider whether the injustice is, practically speaking, simply about to take place; or whether it has already done so, and redress is sought through war. In this second case, the war is aggressive. In the former case, war has the character of self-defence, provided that it is waged with a moderation of defence which is blameless.[15] Now the injury is considered as beginning, when the unjust act itself, even physically regarded, is beginning; as when a man has not been entirely deprived of his rightful possession; or even when he has been so deprived, but immediately—that is, without noteworthy delay—attempts to defend himself and to reinstate himself in possession. The reason for this is as follows: When any one is, to all intents and purposes, in the very act of resisting, and attempts—in so far as is possible—to protect his right, he is not considered as having, in an absolute sense, suffered wrong, nor as having been deprived of his possession. This is the common opinion of the Doctors as stated by Sylvester (word *bellum*, Pt. II), and also by Bartolus and the jurists on the aforesaid *Digest*, XLIII. xvi. 3, § 9 [§§ 1 *et seq.*].

7. *The fourth conclusion.* Our fourth proposition is this: in order that a war may be justly waged, a number of conditions must be observed, which may be grouped under three heads. First, the war must be waged by a legitimate power; secondly, the cause itself and the reason must be just; thirdly, the method of its conduct must be proper, and due proportion must be observed at its beginning, during its prosecution and after victory. All of this will be made clear in the following sections. The underlying principle of this general conclusion, indeed, is that, while a war is not in itself evil, nevertheless, on account of the many misfortunes which

---

15. [That is, when the act of self-defence is not excessive, and out of all proportion to the attack.—REVISER.]

it brings in its train, it is one of those undertakings that are often carried on in evil fashion; and that therefore, it requires many [justifying] circumstances to make it righteous.[16]

SECTION II

Who Has the Legitimate Power of Declaring War?

1. Our question relates to aggressive war; for the power of defending oneself against an unjust aggressor is conceded to all.

The first conclusion. I hold first: that a sovereign prince who has no superior in temporal affairs, or a state which has retained for itself a like jurisdiction, has by natural law legitimate power to declare war. This is the opinion held by St. Thomas (II.–II, qu. 40, art. 1); and he is supported by all. Reference may be made to Covarruvias (on *Sext,* rule *peccatum,* Pt. 11, § 9), who cites many laws, as well as certain theological divines.

The first proof. A reason in support of this conclusion is, first, that this sort of war is at times permitted by the natural law, as we have demonstrated;[1] hence, the power of declaring such a war must rest with some one; and therefore it must rest, most of all, with the possessor of sovereign power, for it is particularly his function to protect the state, and to command the inferior princes [within the realm].

The second proof. A second reason is that the power of declaring war is (so to speak) a power of jurisdiction, the exercise of which pertains to punitive justice, which is especially necessary to a state for the purpose of constraining wrongdoers; wherefore, just as the sovereign prince may punish his own subjects when they offend others, so may he avenge himself on another prince or state which by reason of some offence becomes subject to him; and this vengeance cannot be sought at the hands of another judge, because the prince of whom we are speaking has no superior in temporal affairs; therefore, if that offender is not prepared to give satisfaction, he may be compelled by war to do so.

---

16. On this conclusion, see Bellarmine, *De Laicis,* Bk. III, Chap. xv; and Molina, *De Iustitia,* Disps. X *et seq.* (This note was in Suárez's original.—Ed.)

1. [*Vide* second paragraph of Sub-section 5 of Section I, *supra,* p. 915.—Tr.]

In this first conclusion, I used the words, 'or a state', in order that I might include every kind of polity; for the same reasoning holds true of all polities. Only it must be noted of a monarchical régime that, after a state has transferred its power to some one person, it cannot declare war without that person's consent, because it is no longer supreme; unless the prince should chance to be so negligent in avenging or defending the state as to cause public and very grave harm to that state, for, in such a case, the commonwealth as a whole could take vengeance and deprive the sovereign of the authority in question. For the state is always regarded as retaining this power within itself, if the prince fails in his duty.

2. *The second conclusion.* I hold, secondly, that an inferior prince, or an imperfect state, or whosoever in temporal affairs is under a superior, cannot justly declare war without the authorization of that superior. A reason for the conclusion is, first, that a prince of this kind can claim his right from his superior, and therefore has not the right to declare war; since, in this respect, he has the character of a private person. For it is because of the reason stated that private persons cannot declare war. A second reason in support of this same conclusion is that such a declaration of war is opposed to the rights of the sovereign prince, to whom that power has been specially entrusted; for without such power he could not govern peacefully and suitably.

Victoria [*De Iure Belli,* no. 9], indeed, sets certain limitations to what has been here stated,[2] and Cajetan and others seem to hold the same opinion.

The first limitation of this conclusion, from Victoria. The first limitation to this second conclusion is as follows: provided no contrary practice shall have been observed by very ancient custom. This provision may have force when a war has been declared against those who are not subjects of the king who governs the declarer of war. But if on the other hand the war should be declared against another portion of the same realm, the custom in question would certainly appear to be contrary to the natural law; for when there exist a tribunal and an authority superior to both parties, it is contrary to the law of nature to strive for one's own right by force, and

---

2. [*Haec verò limitat Victoria suprà.*—Tr.]

acting (as it were) on one's own authority. Moreover, in the case of private persons, such an attempt is without doubt contrary to natural law; and yet, in the case which we have supposed, these two members of the same state, although they may be of more importance [than single individuals], are nevertheless in the position of private persons.

The second limitation. To the same conclusion, Victoria [*ibid.*] sets a second limitation, namely: provided that the sovereign prince is not negligent in avenging a wrong. For, if he is negligent, an inferior prince may avenge himself.

Such a course of action is not entirely commendable. Nevertheless this course of action is not [entirely] commendable, especially when the conflict occurs between two portions of one and the same state. For, although a private person, when he cannot obtain his rights at the hands of a public tribunal, may secretly and without scandal protect himself, nevertheless he may not do so by force and through war; and still less may he avenge himself [after an injury has actually been inflicted], if he is not able to obtain such vengeance through the judge. For a punishment inflicted by one's own private authority is intrinsically evil, and tumults and wars might easily be provoked within a state, on this pretext. But the right of punishment possessed by a portion of the state, or that possessed by a mere private person, are equally imperfect, and in the former case, there is greater likelihood of the harm in question; therefore, licence [to exact private vengeance] must not be granted to a portion of a state or to a private person, save only within the limits of just defence.

3. *Note 1.* But it must be added, first, that [provided the need for declaring war arises,] it is sometimes sufficient to interpret the wish of the sovereign in the cases above-mentioned, if the matter is pressing, and recourse [to the sovereign] is not immediately possible; particularly if the war is to be undertaken against foreigners, and above all if these foreigners are on other grounds overt enemies of the sovereign.

Note 2. Secondly, I must also note that if at any time enemies of this kind are seized within the boundaries of some imperfect state, not only is a just defensive war against them then permissible, but so also are aggression, vengeance, and punishment; for by reason of the wrong committed in the territory of that state they have made themselves its subjects.

Note 3. Finally, it should be added that more things are allowable to a given state or commonwealth with regard to its own defence than to a given private individual; because the good defended in the former case is common to many, and is of a higher grade, and also because the power of a state is by its very nature public and common; therefore, it is not strange that more things are permissible to a state than to an individual.

4. *A little question with respect to the first and second conclusions. The mark of supreme jurisdiction.* But it may be asked, what is a perfect state; or, who is a sovereign prince? The reply is, first, that all kings are in this respect sovereign. Innocent III so states (*Decretals,* Bk. IV, tit. xvii, chap. xiii). Many counts also claim this sovereign power. Hence, certain of the canonists are mistaken in saying that only absolute power is sovereign in this fashion. Consequently, the issue depends on the mode of jurisdiction exercised by each particular prince, or state; and it is the mark of supreme jurisdiction when, under such a prince or such a state, there exists a tribunal before which all cases of litigation in that realm are decided, and from which there is no appeal to any superior tribunal.

But when there is room for an appeal, that is the mark of an imperfect state, since an appeal is the act of an inferior towards a superior. Hence it must be noted, first, that not all the states which are subject to one and the same king are necessarily of the imperfect sort. For it may happen that such a bond of union has been effected incidentally, a fact indicated by a diversity in laws, taxes, and so forth. And this distinction between a perfect and an imperfect state, although it is of no great importance in relation to the power of which we now treat, since the latter is already vested in the king, has, nevertheless, an important relation to the power which such a state may possess in opposition to its own king, if he lapses into tyranny. For if the state be a perfect one, it has power against its own king, even when the latter rules also over other kingdoms. But the case is otherwise if the state be an imperfect one, and a portion of one kingdom; for then nothing can be done without the consent of the whole. All of the foregoing statements, since they are founded upon natural law, are applicable to both Christians and unbelievers.

5. *Christian kings are subject to the Pope.* In the case of Christian kings, however, a second point must be noted, namely, that the supreme Pontiff, although he has no direct power in temporal affairs outside of his own

domain, nevertheless does possess such power indirectly, as is indicated in certain passages of the *Decretals* (Bk. I, tit. vi, chap. xxxiv; Bk. II, tit. i, chap. xiii). Therefore, under this title, he has a right to require that a cause of war be referred to him, and the power to give a judgment thereon, which the parties in question are bound to obey, unless his decision be manifestly unjust. For such [authority on the part of the Pope] is certainly necessary for the spiritual welfare of the Church and for the avoidance of almost infinite evils. Accordingly, Soto said (on *Romans,* Chap. xii [, v. 18]), that war between Christian princes is rarely just, since they have at hand another ready means of settling their mutual disputes.

But sometimes the Pope does not interpose his authority, lest perchance greater evils result. In that event, to be sure, sovereign princes are not bound to secure any authorization from the Pope, and may urge their own right as long as they are not forbidden to do so. Nevertheless, they should take care lest they themselves be a cause of the fact that the Pope dares not intervene; for in that case they will not be free from blame.

6. *The third conclusion; and the reason in support of it.* Thirdly, I hold that a war which, according to the preceding conclusion, is declared without legitimate authority, is contrary not only to charity, but also to justice, even if a legitimate cause for it exists. The reason supporting this conclusion is that such an act is performed without legitimate jurisdiction, and is consequently an illegitimate act. Therefore, it follows that a war of this kind gives rise to an obligation of making restitution for all ensuing damages.

The first corollary. Therefore, it is indeed true that if any one merely recovers his own property in such a war, he will not be bound to restore that property; but he will be held liable for all injuries and losses inflicted upon others. The reason for such a distinction is that in the latter case he has done an injustice, since there was no just cause for all that damage; whereas, in recovering his own property, he has not, strictly speaking, committed an injustice,—save possibly in the means used, from which, in a strict sense, there arises no obligation to make restitution.

The second corollary; from Sylvester. Whence follows the conclusion noted by Sylvester (word *bellum,* Pt. I, qu. 10 [qu. 11, no. 4]), that he who makes war without the authorization in question, even if he has, in other respects, a just ground for so doing, nevertheless incurs the penalties imposed upon those who wage an unjust war; so that if, for example, he be an incendiary, he will incur the excommunication promulgated against incendiaries.

7. *The solution of a doubt which arises.* But it may be asked whether a Christian king or prince subject only to the Pope sins against justice or merely against his duty of obedience, if he wages a just war, of the kind in question, in defiance of the papal prohibition. For it is upon this point that the judgment regarding the obligation of making restitution depends.

My reply is that so long as the Pope does not so issue his prohibition as to remand the case for his own hearing, constituting himself as its judge, the prince does not sin against justice in prosecuting his own rights, irrespective of whether or not the Pope has done wrong in not [thus] forbidding the war. The reason is that in such a case, the prince [, notwithstanding the want of papal approval,] nevertheless retains his own jurisdiction and power. If the Pope, however, by his own authority and power justly issues a prohibition against the war in question as being opposed to the spiritual welfare of the Church and thereby, as he may, deprives the prince of all right to make war; then, the prince [who persists in waging the war] will sin against justice, and will be under a binding obligation to make restitution. The reason for this assertion is that under such circumstances he no longer has any title whereby he may justly, through war, cause harm to another prince; and therefore, when he causes such harm, he does so in opposition even to commutative justice, and consequently justice demands that reparation for those injuries shall be made. Neither is the situation affected by the fact that, when the Pope deprives the aforesaid prince of the right to make war, he acts only by means of his indirect power, provided that he is acting on the genuine ground of the common good, as we assume to be the case.

SECTION III

Is It Permissible Even for Clerics to Declare War and to Engage Therein?

1. *The question is expounded.* Since it may be that sovereign power in temporal affairs resides in ecclesiastical princes, it is necessary to discuss the question of whether the aforesaid right is common to all of them; and at

the same time we shall consider the inquiry of St. Thomas (II.–II, qu. 40, art. 2) as to whether it is permissible for clerics and bishops to engage in battle, a question which concerns offensive, not defensive war. For just as the latter sort of war is allowed by the law of nature, even so it is not forbidden by positive law, whether one is defending his life, or his property, or the life and property of another—especially if that other be his father,[1] or if the matter relate to the common good. The above-mentioned question, however, relates only to positive law, both divine and human. For the acts of waging and declaring war are not in themselves forbidden to any one by the natural law, unless perhaps to those persons who are unable to render military service, as, normally, women are said to be. But even in the case of women, there is no absolute prohibition, and without doubt they may declare war, if they are sovereign princes. Hence we shall speak only of positive law, which alone is applicable to ecclesiastical persons.

2. *The first conclusion: unquestioned, and commonly held.* I hold, in the first place, that episcopal Prelates of the Church, if there are any such who are sovereign in temporal affairs, may licitly, and even without fear of irregularity, declare war, assuming the presence of the other required conditions. This conclusion is unquestioned and commonly held.

The reason supporting this conclusion. The reason [supporting it] is that such a right is inherent in the complete and perfect sovereign power which resides in princes of this character. Moreover, the fact that such a course of action is not forbidden to them is evident from many decrees (*Decretum,* Pt. II, causa XXIII, qu. viii). Again, these princes themselves do not directly incite men to homicide or mutilation, but rather to an act of fortitude.

A confirmation: concerning which see the work De Censuris,[2] *Disp. XLVII, sect. 1, from no. 5.* The conclusion is confirmed by the fact that the princes in question are, for a like reason, allowed to set up judges who may rightfully give judgment in criminal cases. Furthermore, Sylvester adds (word *bellum,* Pt. III, no. 2) that this right may pertain to bishops by virtue of

---

1. [*Patris,* an erratum for *patriae* (native land)?—Tr.]
2. [This work of Suárez is not included in these *Selections.*—Tr.]

their spiritual power, though indirectly, for the reason that it is essential to spiritual welfare. This statement may easily be credited in the case of the supreme Pontiff; but in the case of other [ecclesiastical] princes, not sovereign in temporal affairs, it can exist only on the ground of self-defence; for with respect to offensive war, the latter are not supreme in spiritual matters, and may easily have recourse to their supreme head.

3. *The second conclusion: twofold in form.* I hold, secondly, that although by divine law clerics are not necessarily forbidden to engage in war, nevertheless, by ecclesiastical law, they are forbidden to do so.

The first member of the conclusion is proved by the fact that there exists no divine precept to this effect, whether in Scripture or in tradition; neither is the prohibition absolutely inherent in the priestly office; nor is [clerical participation in warfare] intrinsically repugnant to right reason. This argument is confirmed by the analogous consideration that a cleric is not forbidden by the divine law to be judge in a case involving bloodshed.

The second member is supported by the Decretum. The second part of the same conclusion is incontrovertible; and it is derived from *Decretum,* Pt. I, dist. L, can. v, wherein Pope Nicholas forbids [clerics to engage in war], under penalty of suspension. Many canons relating to this matter are contained in *Decretum,* Pt. II, causa XXIII, qu. iv. Arguments from reason and congruity in support of this prohibition are obvious. In connexion with this, St. Thomas may be consulted (II.–II, qu. 40, art. 2).

4. *A consequent of this conclusion.* It follows from the first part of this conclusion that the supreme Pontiff can grant a dispensation from the precept in question because it is a human one. Gratian held the contrary opinion (*Decretum,* Pt. II, causa XXIII, qu. viii, at the beginning), but without any grounds therefor.

The inference in question is also clearly to be drawn from many chapters of the [canon] law; and the granting of dispensation is usually held to be justified by a case of grave necessity, if the common good of the Church is at stake, for in such cases clerics may even be obliged by natural law to engage in war of the kind under discussion. It is, indeed, true that this kind of war is then more allied to defence than to aggression; for in an aggressive war there is not normally so great a necessity. See Cajetan (on II.–II, qu. 40, art. 2) and Covarruvias (*On the Constitutions of Clement*, c. *si furiosus*, Pt. II, § 3, no. 2).

5. *The third conclusion.* Thirdly, I hold that the precept in question is binding under pain of mortal sin, on those who have been ordained to holy orders. First, because the matter is most serious, and because it is forbidden under the gravest penalties and censures [that clerics should engage in war]. That this precept is indeed binding upon all those who are ordained to holy orders, even upon subdeacons, is the common opinion of St. Thomas (II.–II, qu. 40, art. 2), Cajetan (*ibid.*), Sylvester (word *bellum*, Pt. III, qu. 2 [qu. 3]), Antoninus ([*Summa Theologica,*] Pt. III, tit. xxviii, chap. ii, § 6), Covarruvias (*loc. cit.*), and others also (on *Decretals*, Bk. V, tit. xii, chap. xxiv). The reason for this opinion is readily apparent, namely: that such persons are already at the threshold of the sacred ministry and are bound to its [duties].

As to others, however, constituted in minor orders, since they participate but imperfectly in the clerical state, it is probable either that they are in no way bound, especially if they have already entirely renounced that state; or else, at most, that they are bound under pain of venial sin. This is the opinion of Soto (*De Iustitia*, Bk. V, qu. i, art. 4) and Covarruvias (*On the Constitutions of Clement*, c. *si furiosus*, Pt. II, § 3, no. 2), except with reference to those who chance to hold an ecclesiastical benefice; for in the latter event, such individuals are already *ex officio* ministers of the Church, and under an obligation—as so many persons believe—to aspire to higher orders, or, at least, not to create any impediment to those orders while they will to remain in their office. Therefore, these individuals are bound under a grave penalty.[3]

Note. However, it must be noted that this sin on the part of clerics is not precisely a sin against justice, but rather one against religion or obedience; and hence, if the other conditions of a just war are fulfilled, such clerics are in no wise bound to make any restitution, [in case they have committed the sin in question]. Sylvester (on word *bellum*, Pt. III,

---

3. Sánchez, *De Sancto Matrimonii Sacramento*, Bk. VII, Disp. XLV, discusses at some length this obligation to aspire to higher orders. (This note was in Suárez's original.—Ed.)

qu. 4), indeed, holds a contrary opinion, saying: 'Just as a prince could not authorize a cleric to wage war, so he could not authorize him to engage in plunder.'[4]

Refutation of Sylvester's view. But this argument is not conclusive. For [the prince], although he may not have been able to grant [to clerics] the authority to engage in war legitimately, can nevertheless give [them] the power to engage therein without violating justice; provided the Pope does not, in the manner explained at the end of the preceding section, deprive him of the right to do so; and this authorization on the part of the prince is enough to free [the said clerics] from the obligation of making restitution; just as the same principle is clear in the case of a cleric who, as a minister of justice, puts some one to death, since he does not thereby sin against justice, and is not bound to make restitution.

6. *Whether clerics engaged in war incur an irregularity.* But what of irregularity?[5] This question is answered as follows: if a war is unjust, and if, in the course of the same, any person is slain or mutilated, then all the soldiers incur irregularity, whether they be priests or not, and whether they kill directly or through the help of others. This is the opinion of Sylvester, as stated in a passage (on word *bellum,* Pt. III, qu. 3), wherein he cites certain laws which, to be sure, are not sufficiently convincing to me. Nevertheless, since the matter is doubtful, his position is the safer one; for this reason, that all those fighting in such a manner are held to be co-operating in the homicide, because practically all are guilty of unjust co-operation, proximate or remote.

If, on the other hand, the war be a just one, we must make a further distinction. For if the cleric sins by becoming a combatant, and kills another person by his own hand, he contracts an irregularity; for clearly, he is a voluntary homicide; but if he himself does not kill, although others do so, then he incurs no irregularity, a fact which may be gathered

4. [Although this passage is printed in the Latin text as a quotation, it is in fact a paraphrase of Sylvester. Suárez has: *quia Princeps sicut non potuit dare clerico authoritatem bellandi, ita nec praedandi,* while Sylvester reads thus: *quia sicut bellandi ita rapiendi non potuit ei suus dominus auctoritatem dare.*—TR.]

5. *Vide De Censuris,* Disp. XLVII, sect. vi, by the author. (This note was in Suárez's original; the referenced material is not included in these *Selections.*—ED.)

from the *Decretals* (Bk. V, tit. xii, chap. xxiv; *ibid.,* tit. xxv, chap. iii; *ibid.,* chap. iv). The basis of the foregoing distinction is the fact that the war is in itself just, and the harm done follows incidentally, so that, under the circumstances, this harm is not to be morally imputed to any one and therefore may be imputed only to that person who was the physical cause of the same. If a cleric, however, while legitimately a combatant, kills or mutilates some one by his own hand, but does so in absolutely necessary defence of his life, he does not contract an irregularity.

Apart from this case, indeed, Cajetan holds (on II.–II, qu. 40, art. 2) that irregularity is always incurred [by clerics in the situation described]. Navarrus ([*Consilia seu Responsa,*] Chap. xxvii, no. 213), is of the same opinion. The reason for their view is that self-defence is the only exception mentioned in the law (*Constitutions of Clement,* Bk. V, tit. iv, only chapter). Moreover, their view is confirmed by the fact that in *Decretals,* Bk. V, tit. xii, chap. xxiv, and in connexion with a certain just war in defence of [the subjects'] own town, the reply of the Pope was to the effect that it was advisable for clerics engaging in that war to refrain from the ministry of the altar. So it is that St. Thomas (II.–II, qu. 64, art. 7, ad 3) simply cites this text, [in his discussion of the question]. It is true that the reason for the Pope's reply might possibly have been that those clerics had exceeded the limits of self-defence. And therefore, there are some who hold, not without reason, that he who fights legitimately does not incur irregularity, even if he be a cleric and commit homicide. Others limit this exemption from irregularity to cases [of homicide] in defence of the common good, a motive which is not merely equal to, but higher than defence of one's own life, and which might, upon occasion, make it obligatory [for clerics] to engage in war. In such a situation, then, it seems to me practically certain that there is no irregularity, an opinion which is confirmed by that of Sylvester (on word *bellum,* Pt. III, qu. 2). For, in the first place, it is not reasonable that evil consequences should result from an action to which one is absolutely bound in charity. Furthermore, Cajetan, for this same reason, has said (on II.–II, qu. 33, art. 7) that he who brings an accusation in a criminal case, if he is bound to do so, does not incur irregularity. If, however, the war be legitimate, but not a matter of obligation, then the question is very doubtful; because in that case there is not the pressure of unavoidable necessity.

Consequently, under such circumstances, it is safer [for clerics who propose to engage in the contest] to obtain a dispensation. We must note, however, that if, at any time, a cleric is permitted, by a papal dispensation, to engage personally in warfare, he contracts no irregularity in the course of that warfare; for a dispensation with respect to the principal act is held to cover any consequence that accompanies that act.

7. *A twofold objection.* On the other hand, one may argue thus: the foregoing discussion would imply that it is not fitting for clerics to take any part in war, or to exhort soldiers to do battle; and that clerics who do so, incur irregularity. Moreover, the same would seem to hold true of clerics who advise other persons to go to war.[6] One may reply that the latter part of the objection presents no difficulty, because such advice is not in itself evil, nor is it forbidden. On the contrary, it is the custom of the Church [to give counsel of this sort], as is evident from a passage in the *Decretum* (Pt. II, causa xxiii, qu. ii [, can. iii]); for [in so doing, the Church] exhorts men not to homicide, but to an act of fortitude and justice, even as one rightfully admonishes a judge to make a just decision. However, Sylvester (earlier, on word *bellum,* Pt. III, qu. 2) holds otherwise, asserting that [such a course of action on the part of clerics] is permissible only in a defensive war, and that even in a war of this kind irregularity is incurred, if a cleric urges on the soldiers during the actual progress of the combat. With this view, Hostiensis agrees (on *Decretals,* Bk. V, tit. xxxvii, chap. v).

As to the first part of the objection, it should be observed that the exhortations mentioned are not evil in themselves; nor are they forbidden by law; for custom indicates that the contrary is true. It is more fitting, however, that [clerics] should not deliver these exhortations without the permission of the bishop or superior, a fact which is brought out in the *Decretum* (Pt. II, causa xxiii, qu. viii, cans. xxvii and xxvi). Similarly, I believe it more correct to hold that no irregularity is incurred in such cases, unless the cleric intentionally and directly incites to homicide. But if he merely exhorts the combatants to act bravely, irregularity is not incurred;

---

6. The answer to the said objections treated in *De Censuris,* Disp. XLVII, sect. vi, no. 8. (This note was in Suárez's original; the referenced material is not included in these *Selections.*—ED.)

for the law does not expressly state that it is incurred, nor does the cleric morally co-operate in homicide, and, in short, the same reasoning holds good [with regard to exhortation] as that which we applied to the matter of advising. This is the view of Navarrus ([*Consilia seu Responsa* or *Enchiridion,*] Chap. xxvii, no. 216) and Covarruvias, as already cited [on the *Constitutions of Clement,* c. *si furiosus,* Pt. II, § 3, no. 2].

On such dispensations vide De Censuris, *Disp. IV, sect. ii.*[7] Finally, it may be asked, Who has the power to grant dispensations in the case of such an irregularity? On this question see Sylvester, as cited above, and Cajetan (word *irregularitas*). I reply briefly that only the supreme Pontiff can grant a dispensation, unless the matter is occult, in which case, the power is expressly granted by the Council of Trent to the bishops (Session XXIV, chap. [canon] vi, *De Reformatione*). Such a situation, however, rarely occurs in connexion with questions of war, and it is with these matters that we are dealing.

SECTION IV

What Is a Just Cause of War, on the Basis of Natural Reason?

This question and the following are treated at length by Molina, De Iustitia, *Treatise II, disps. cii, civ, cv, cvi.* There was an old error current among the Gentiles, who thought that the rights of nations were based on military strength, and that it was permissible to make war solely to acquire prestige and wealth; a belief which, even from the standpoint of natural reason, is most absurd.

1. *The first conclusion.* Therefore I hold, first: that there can be no just war without an underlying cause of a legitimate and necessary nature. The truth of this conclusion is indubitable and clearly evident. Now, that just and sufficient reason for war is the infliction of a grave injustice which cannot be avenged or repaired in any other way. This, the consensus of opinion of all the theologians, is also to be deduced from the *Decretum* (Pt. II,

---

7. [Not included in these *Selections.*—Tr.]

tit. XXIII, chap. ii) and from a mass of evidence collected by Covarruvias on the *Constitutions of Clement,* c. *si furiosus,* Pt. II, § 3, no. 2].

The first reason. The first reason in support of such a conclusion is the fact that war is permissible [only] that a state may guard itself from molestation; for in other respects, war is opposed to the welfare of the human race on account of the slaughter, material losses, and other misfortunes which it involves; and therefore, if the cause in question should cease to exist, the justice of war would also cease to exist.

The second reason. Secondly, in war, men are despoiled of their property, their liberty, and their lives; and to do such things without just cause is absolutely iniquitous, for if this were permissible, men could kill one another without cause.

The third reason. Thirdly, the sort of war which we are chiefly discussing is aggressive war, and it is frequently waged against non-subjects. Consequently, it is necessary that the latter shall have committed some wrong on account of which they render themselves subjects. Otherwise, on what ground could they be deserving of punishment or subject to an alien jurisdiction?

Furthermore, if the grounds or purposes which the Gentiles had in view (for example, ambition, avarice, and even vainglory or a display of ferocity) were legitimate and sufficient, any state whatsoever could aspire to these ends; and hence, a war would be just on both sides, essentially and apart from any element of ignorance. This supposition is entirely absurd; for two mutually conflicting rights cannot both be just.

2. But in order that this matter may be explained more clearly, there are several points which should be noted.

Note 1. First, it is not every cause that is sufficient to justify war, but only those causes which are serious and commensurate with the losses that the war would occasion. For it would be contrary to reason to inflict very grave harm because of a slight injustice. In like manner, a judge can punish, not all offences whatsoever, but only those which are opposed to the common peace and to the welfare of the realm. In this connexion, however, we must remember that not infrequently a wrong which appears to be slight is in fact serious, if all the circumstances are weighed, or if other and similar wrongs are permitted [as a consequence], since thereby great harm may gradually ensue. Thus, for example, to seize even the smallest town, or to make raids, &c., may sometimes constitute a grave injustice, especially when the prince who has done the wrong treats with scorn the protest that is made.

3. *Note 2.* Secondly, it must be noted that there are various kinds of injuries which are causes of a just war. These may be grouped under three heads. One of the heads would be the seizure by a prince of another's property, and his refusal to restore it. Another head would be his denial, without reasonable cause, of the common rights of nations, such as the right of transit over highways, trading in common, &c. The third would be any grave injury to one's reputation or honour. It should be added that it is a sufficient cause for war if an injury of this kind be inflicted either upon a prince himself or upon his subjects; for the prince is guardian of his state and also of his subjects. Furthermore, the cause is sufficient if the wrong be inflicted upon any one who has placed himself under the protection of a prince, or even if it be inflicted upon allies or friends, as may be seen in the case of Abraham (*Genesis,* Chap. xiv), and in that of David (*1 Kings,* Chap. xxviii). 'For a friend is a second self', says Aristotle (*Nicomachean Ethics,* Bk. IX, chaps. iv and ix). But it must be understood that such a circumstance justifies war only on condition that the friend himself would be justified in waging the war, and consents thereto, either expressly or by implication. The reason for this limitation is that a wrong done to another does not give me the right to avenge him, unless he would be justified in avenging himself and actually proposes to do so. Assuming, however, that these conditions exist, my aid to him is an act of co-operation in a good and just deed; but if [the injured party] does not entertain such a wish, no one else may intervene, since he who committed the wrong has made himself subject not to every one indiscriminately, but only to the person who has been wronged. Wherefore, the assertion made by some writers, that sovereign kings have the power of avenging injuries done in any part of the world, is entirely false, and throws into confusion all the orderly distinctions of jurisdiction; for such power was not [expressly] granted by God and its existence is not to be inferred by any process of reasoning.

4. *Note 3.* Thirdly, we must note that, in regard to an injury inflicted, two arguments may be alleged, [to justify a declaration of war]. The first

is [that such a declaration is justifiable], in order that reparation for the losses suffered should be made to the injured party. For this cause, indeed, it is not to be questioned that war may legitimately be declared; for if this declaration is to be permitted because of an injury [already done], then it is in the highest degree permissible when the object is that each one may secure himself against loss. Many examples illustrating this point are to be found in the Scriptures (*Genesis,* Chap. xiv, and similar passages). The other argument is [that war should be declared] in order that the offender may be duly punished; a contention which presents its own difficulty.

5. *The second and commonly accepted conclusion.* Secondly, then, I hold that a war may also be justified on the ground that he who has inflicted an injury should be justly punished, if he refuses to give just satisfaction for that injury, without resort to war. This conclusion is commonly accepted. In connexion with it, and with the preceding conclusion, we must assume that the opposing party is not ready to make restitution, or to give satisfaction; for if he were so disposed, the warlike aggression would become unjust, as we shall demonstrate in the following sections.

Its exposition and proof. First: from Scripture. The conclusion is proved, first, by certain Scriptural passages (*Numbers,* Chap. xxv; *2 Kings,* Chaps. x and xi), according to which, unconditional punishment for offences was carried into execution, by the command of God.

The second proof, by reasoning. The reason in support of this same conclusion is that, just as within a state some lawful power to punish crimes is necessary to the preservation of domestic peace; so in the world as a whole, there must exist, in order that the various states may dwell in concord, some power for the punishment of injuries inflicted by one state upon another; and this power is not to be found in any superior, for we assume that these states have no commonly acknowledged superior; therefore, the power in question must reside in the sovereign prince of the injured state, to whom, by reason of that injury, the opposing prince is made subject; and consequently, war of the kind in question has been instituted in place of a tribunal administering just punishment.

6. *The first objection, drawn from* Romans, *xii. Its solution.* But, on the other hand, one may object, first: that to fight in this manner seems opposed to the admonitions in the *Epistle to the Romans* (Chap. xii

[, v. 17]): 'To no man rendering evil for evil', and [*ibid.,* v. 19]: 'Not avenging yourselves.' The reply to the objection is that the passages quoted refer
to acts performed by private authority and with the intention of doing
evil for its own sake, to another. But if the acts in question be done under
legitimate and public authority, with the intention of holding an enemy
to his duty and of reducing to its due order that which was disorderly,
then they are not only not prohibited but even necessary. Hence, in that
same Epistle (*Romans,* Chap. xiii [, v. 4]), we find this additional passage:
'For he beareth not the sword in vain. For he is God's minister: to work
vengeance upon evildoers.'[1]

The second objection. Secondly, it is objected that [if our second general
conclusion be true,] then, as a consequence, the same party in one and
the same case is both plaintiff and judge, a situation which is contrary to
the natural law. The truth of the conclusion is evident, since the prince
who has been wronged, assumes the role of judge by his act of aggression.

The first confirmation of this objection. The objection is confirmed, in
the first place, by the fact that the right to avenge themselves is denied to
private individuals, for this reason, namely, that they would practically
exceed the bounds of justice; and yet the same danger exists in the case of
a prince who avenges himself.

The second confirmation of the second objection. A second confirmation
of the same objection is that, by a like reasoning, any private person who
might be unable to secure such punishment through a judge could take
the law into his own hands, executing it on his own authority; since this
privilege is granted to princes, on the sole ground that there is no other
way of securing a just vengeance.

7. *The solution.* Our reply is, that it cannot be denied that in this matter
[of public vengeance], one and the same person assumes, in a sense, the
role of plaintiff and that of judge; even as we perceive that God, to Whom
there is some analogy in the public authority, assumes this double role.
But the cause [of such an assumption on the part of public authority] is

---

1. [Suárez's quotation for the latter part of this passage reading: *ad vindictam malè
factorum,* varies somewhat from the version found in the Vulgate which reads: *vindex
in iram ei qui malum agit.*—Tr.]

simply that this act of punitive justice has been indispensable to mankind, and that no more fitting method for its performance could, in the order of nature and humanly speaking, be found. This is especially true, since we must presuppose, prior to the war, the contumacy of the offending party in not wishing to give satisfaction; for then (contumacy being established) if he finds himself in subjection to the offended party, he may impute his own misfortune to himself.

The reply to the first confirmation. Neither is this case analogous to that of a private individual. For in the first place, such an individual is guided by his own [unaided] judgment, and therefore he will easily exceed the limits of vengeance; whereas public authority is guided by public counsel, to which heed must be paid, and consequently authority of this sort may more easily avoid the disadvantages arising from personal inclination. In the second place, this power of punishment has for its essential purpose not private but public good, and hence it has been committed not to the private individual, but to the public body. Therefore, if the latter is unable or unwilling to punish [an injury], the private individual shall patiently endure his loss. From the foregoing remarks, then, our reply to the first confirmation of the objection is evident.

The reply of certain authorities to the second confirmation is examined. As to the second confirmation, it has been said by some persons that in the situation referred to, a private individual is allowed to avenge himself secretly; and in the *Code* there is a title, *Quando liceat sine judice* [. . .] *se vindicare* [. . .] (when it is permitted to avenge oneself without recourse to a judge = *Code,* III. xxvii). But this must be understood as referring to restitution for losses suffered; for in so far as it refers to the punishment of an offence, it is an inadmissible error. An act of punitive justice, indeed, is an exercise of that jurisdiction which private individuals do not possess, and cannot obtain through an offence committed by another. For if they could possess it, there would be no need to employ the public power of jurisdiction; or at least, since this power of jurisdiction is derived from men themselves, each one would have had the power to refrain from transferring it to the state official, retaining it, on the contrary, for himself; a conclusion which would be opposed to the natural law, and to the good governance of the human race.

A clear reply. Therefore, we deny the consequent involved in the second confirmation. For laws regard those things which are true in an absolute sense, and private individuals, absolutely speaking, may obtain a ready revenge for offences because there is a public authority, while the fact that sometimes they are not able to do so, is an accidental occurrence which, for that reason, must necessarily be endured, as we have said. But the relationship between two sovereign powers is based on an absolute necessity. It is in the light of this necessity that certain civil glosses cited by Covarruvias (on *Sext*, rule *Peccatum*, Bk. I, pt. ii, § 9), should be interpreted. On this point, Victoria (*De Potestate Civili*, no. 6 [*De Iure Belli*, no. 56]) and Soto (*De Iustitia*, Bk. IV, qu. iv, art. 1) may also be consulted.

8. *The truth of a third conclusion is manifest.* Thirdly, I hold that whoever begins a war without just cause, sins not only against charity, but also against justice; and hence he is bound to make reparation for all the harm that results. The truth of this conclusion is manifest.

A doubt which arises. The only question which arises in connexion with this point is whether or not there may sometimes exist a cause for war which absolves one from the charge of injustice, but not from the charge of sinning against charity. The reply must be that such a situation rarely occurs; and yet it is by no means inconceivable. For just as it happens among private individuals that one person may take what is due to him from another, an act which is not opposed to justice, but which is opposed to charity at times (namely, when the debtor incurs very serious losses in consequence, while the property in question is not in great degree necessary to the creditor); even so, a similar situation might arise between princes or states. In this connexion, however, it should be noted that in a war of the kind described, it is possible to consider, first, the loss to the state against which the war is waged; secondly, the loss to the state which commences the war; thirdly and finally, the possible loss to the entire Church.

A discussion of the cases in which harm to the Church would result from war. With respect to this third contingency, we may easily find support for our assertion. For although a Christian king may declare war on some particular just ground, it will nevertheless be possible for him to sin against the charity due to the Church, in pursuing his rights. For example, he may foresee the consequent growth in power of the enemies of the faith, and so forth; so that, in that case, it may be a sin to wage war, and yet there arises no obligation to make restitution, since the particular just ground that he has extinguishes such an obligation.

Discussion of the cases in which harm to the enemy would result. When the harm is of the kind first mentioned, [a harm, that is, to the state against which war is waged,] then there is no great obligation to make restitution, since the malicious intent of the state inflicting the original injury was the cause of the loss in question. Nevertheless, if in a particular case the latter state should be unable to give satisfaction or make restitution without suffering great injury, and if such satisfaction should not be necessary to the prince of the other state, then the latter, by insisting that satisfaction be given, would clearly be acting against charity.

A discussion of the cases in which harm would result to the party that commences hostilities. Finally, turning to the second case mentioned, if one prince begins a war upon another, even with just cause, while exposing his own realm to disproportionate loss and peril, then he will be sinning not only against charity, but also against the justice due to his own state. The reason for this assertion is as follows: a prince is bound in justice to have greater regard for the common good of his state than for his own good; otherwise, he will become a tyrant. So a judge who condemns to hanging a criminal deserving of execution but very necessary to the state, would act in a manner opposed to his official obligations, and, consequently, to justice. Similarly, a physician would sin against the justice required by his profession if he should give medicine which would heal a present disease but would cause more serious diseases to ensue.

9. *A modification of the last statement.* However, with respect to this last point, we must take into consideration the fact that a single king who rules over several kingdoms, can often make war for the sake of one of these to the detriment of another. For though the various kingdoms may be distinct from one another, nevertheless, inasmuch as they are subject to one head, they can and should be of mutual aid, since the defence of one contributes to the benefit of another and in this way, the principle of equality is preserved. For in its own emergency, one kingdom might require the aid of another. In addition to all these considerations, the mere fact that

their [common] prince is rendered more powerful, is in itself extremely advantageous to each of the kingdoms involved. In short, greater peace, and other advantages, may perhaps accrue to a state so supported; and many other [similar] points can easily be perceived upon reflection. There are, then, numerous considerations which may oblige a prince to abandon his right to make war lest his realm suffer loss.

10. *The conclusion of Cajetan.* Furthermore, we should call attention to the conclusion, drawn from these primary considerations by Cajetan (on II.–II, qu. 96, art. 4 [qu. 40, art. 1]), namely, that for a war to be just, the sovereign ought to be so sure of the degree of his power, that he is morally certain of victory. The first reason for this conclusion is the fact that otherwise the prince would incur the evident peril of inflicting upon his state losses greater than the advantages involved. In the same way, says Cajetan, a judge would do wrong in attempting the arrest of a criminal without a force that, to his certain knowledge, could not be overpowered. Secondly, whoever begins a war assumes an active role; and the one who assumes such a role must always be the stronger, in order to vanquish the one who plays a passive part.

How much truth is there in this conclusion? But this condition [of certitude] does not appear to me to be absolutely essential. First, because, from a human standpoint, it is almost impossible of realization. Secondly, because it is often to the common interest of the state not to await such a degree of certitude, but rather to test its ability to conquer the enemy, even when that ability is somewhat doubtful. Thirdly, because if the conclusion were true, a weaker sovereign could never declare war upon a stronger, since he is unable to attain the certitude which Cajetan demands.

Therefore, the following rules should be laid down. A prince [who declares war] is, indeed, bound to attain the maximum certitude possible regarding victory. Furthermore, he ought to balance the expectation of victory against the risk of loss, and ascertain whether, all things being carefully considered, expectation is preponderant. If so great a degree of certitude is impossible of attainment, he ought at least to have either a more probable expectation of victory, or one equally balanced as to the chances of victory or defeat, and that, in proportion to the need of the state and the communal welfare. But if the expectation of victory is less apt to be realized than the chance of defeat, and if the war is offensive in character, then in almost every case that war should be avoided. If [, on the other hand,] the war is defensive, it should be attempted; for in that case it is a matter of necessity, whereas the offensive war is a matter of choice. All of these conclusions are sufficiently clear in the light of the principles of conscience and justice.

SECTION V

Can Christian Princes Have Any Just Ground for War beyond That Which Natural Reason Dictates?

1. *The first opinion: affirmative.* The first opinion [which we shall discuss in this connexion] is affirmative, and is defended by Hostiensis, Panormitanus, and other canonists (on *Decretals,* Bk. III, tit. xxxiv, chap. viii), as well as by Alvaro Paez (*De Planctu Ecclesiae,* Bk. I, chap. xxxvii [chap. xiii and Bk. II, chap. xlvi]), Gabriel (on the *Sentences,* Bk. IV, dist. xv, qu. 4) and other authorities to whom Covarruvias refers (on *Sext,* rule *Peccatum,* Pt. II, § 10).

But these authors do not all express themselves in the same manner, for they mention varying grounds for the opinion in question.

The first ground which may be advanced is rejected by the author, in the treatise De Fide *(Disp. xviii).*[1] The first ground is that of simple unbelief [on the part of the enemy], that is, a refusal to accept the true religion. But this is a false ground, a point with which we deal in the treatise *De Fide.*[2]

The second ground is also rejected. The second ground is that God may be avenged for injuries which are done to Him by sins against nature, and by idolatry. Alfonso de Castro (*De Iusta Haereticorum Punitione,* Bk. II, chap. xiv) supports this latter contention. But this opinion is also false, and it is so first of all, even if we speak of 'vengeance', in the strict sense. For God did not give to all men the power to avenge the injuries they do to Him, since He can easily avenge Himself, if He

---

1. [*Supra*, p. 856.—Tr.]
2. See note 1.

so wills. Moreover, it would not have been well for the human race had men received this power from God, for the greatest disorder would have resulted therefrom. The same argument holds true with respect to the plea of defending [the majesty of God]; since the sins against Him would thus be multiplied rather than prevented. On this same ground, moreover, Christian princes could declare war even upon one another, for many of these princes also are offenders against God. Likewise, since such a ground of aggression could never be sufficiently established, those who were so attacked could justly defend themselves, and the war would thus become just for both sides.

2. *An objection based upon* Leviticus, *xviii.* The objection may be made that the people of Israel were permitted to make war against idolaters on this very ground, as is clear from the Old Testament (*Leviticus,* Chap. xviii [, vv. 24–8]).

Its solution by Augustine, Epiphanius and Cassian. I reply that various grounds are assigned for [the justification of] the war in question. Augustine (*Sermones,* CXV, *De Tempore* [also CV = *Sermones De Scripturis,* xxxiv, in Vol. V, Appendix, col. 1811, Migne ed.]), Epiphanius ([*Panarium Adversus LXXX Haereses,* Lib. II, tom. ii,] haeres lxvi, [no. lxxxiii]) and Cassian (*Collationes,* V, chap. xxiv) hold that the [disputed] land belonged by hereditary right to the children of Israel as descendants of Sem, to whom Noe had given it as an inheritance, and that it had been forcibly seized by Cham, the brother of Sem. I neither accept nor reject this ground, because the arguments adduced on both sides are insufficient.

The solution of other authorities is approved. Others say that the title in question was a gift of God, and this is indeed a valid title. Augustine adds, however (*Questions on Josue,* Qu. 20 [= *Questions on Heptateuch,* Bk. VI, qu. 20]), that although this title was just, nevertheless, since it could not be proved, other reasons, more firmly and clearly established, have always been sought, namely: that the enemy forbade [the Israelites] passage over common highways; or again, that the former were the aggressors, and began the war. It may also be said that these enemies were not only idolaters, but homicides, since it was their custom to sacrifice innocent little children; hence, on the ground of the defence of the innocent, it was permissible to subdue them in war.

3. *A further explanation of the second ground mentioned above.* It must be noticed, however, that the second ground mentioned[3] has been virtually accepted by a number of authorities, with respect to cases in which it happens that a state worshipping the one God inclines toward idolatry through the wickedness of its prince; these authorities claim that it is allowable to make war upon that prince.[4] Their contention would be valid if the prince forcibly compelled his subjects to practice idolatry; but under any other circumstances, [such a ground] would not be a sufficient cause for war, unless the whole state should demand assistance against its sovereign. For where compulsion does not intervene, defence has no place.

This position is supported, first, by the fact that, if the reasoning in question were valid, it would always be permissible to declare such a war on the ground of protecting innocent little children. Secondly, on the basis of that same reasoning, Christian princes would always be permitted to wage war among themselves, upon their own authority. Finally, by whatever arguments this ground for war may be justified, [the title urged] is not confined to Christians alone, but is possessed in common with all unbelievers who worship only the one God; and accordingly, these unbelievers could rightfully defend those who wished to worship the same God, and who were forced by others into idolatry.

4. *The third ground is absolutely rejected.* A third ground for war is advanced, namely, the supreme temporal dominion [of Christians]. That is to say, the authorities mentioned above maintain either that unbelievers are not true owners of their possessions; or else that the Christian Emperor, or—at least—the supreme Pontiff, has direct temporal dominion over the whole world.

But all such claims are vain inventions, a point which we discuss elsewhere, on the subject of dominion and laws.[5] In the second place, even if we grant that such a title does indeed exist, still it would be

---

3. [That is, the avenging of God for sins which are against nature, or idolatrous.—Tr.]

4. Concerning this second ground, see *De Fide,* Disp. XVIII, sect. iv. (This note was in Suárez's original; *supra,* p. 871.—Ed.)

5. See *De Legibus,* Bk. III, chap. vii [chap. vi], *Defensio Fidei,* Bk. III, chaps. i, iv, v. (This note was in Suárez's original.—Ed.) [Of these chapters, only chap. v of Bk. III of the *Defensio Fidei* is included in these *Selections. Vide supra,* p. 761.—Tr.]

impossible either to demonstrate its existence to the satisfaction of infidels, or to force them to believe in the existence of such dominion; and therefore, they could not be forced to obey. Finally, on that same ground, the Pope or the Emperor could make war [even] upon all Christian princes. Wherefore, it must be observed that although the Pope has indirectly supreme power in temporal affairs, nevertheless, the existence of such temporal power is always based, essentially, upon the assumption of direct power in spiritual matters; and therefore, this indirect power does not essentially extend to unbelievers, over whom no direct spiritual dominion exists even in the Pope himself. But I use the term, 'essentially' (*per se loquendo*), because 'incidentally' (*per accidens*) the case may be otherwise, as I shall presently show.

5. *A fourth ground is examined.* A fourth ground urged is that unbelievers are barbarians and incapable of governing themselves properly; and that the order of nature demands that men of this condition should be governed by those who are more prudent, as Aristotle (*Politics,* Bk. I, chap. i) has taught, saying (*ibid.,* chap. v [Bk. I, chap. iii, § 8]) that a war is by nature just, when it is waged against men born to be under obedience but unwilling to accept that condition; a ground [for war] which is approved by Major (on the *Sentences,* Bk. II, dist. xliv, qu. 3), and at great length by Sepúlveda (Bk. VII, chap. ii [*De Regno et Regis Officio,* Bk. III, near end]).

In the first place, however, such a contention cannot have a general application; for it is evident that there are many unbelievers more gifted by nature than are the faithful, and better adapted to political life. Secondly, in order that the ground in question may be valid, it is not enough to judge that a given people are of inferior natural talents; for they must also be so wretched as to live in general more like wild beasts than like men, as those persons are said to live who have no human polity, and who go about entirely naked, eat human flesh, &c. If there are any such, they may be brought into subjection by war, not with the purpose of destroying them, but rather that they may be organized in human fashion, and justly governed. However, this ground for war should rarely or never be approved, except in circumstances in which the slaughter of innocent people, and similar wrongs take place; and therefore, the ground in question is more properly included under defensive than under offensive wars.

Finally, Aristotle, in the passage cited above, declares that a war of this sort is permissible only when those men who are subdued in order that they may be governed, are as different from the rest of mankind as is the body from the soul; a proposition from which one must conclude, however, that the said ground for war, if it really exists, is valid not only for Christians, but also for every sovereign who wishes to defend the law of nature, which, when understood in an absolute sense, gives rise to that ground.

6. *The true solution of this question, by means of three conclusions.* Therefore, the assertion must be made that there is no ground for war so exclusively reserved to Christian princes that it has not some basis in, or at least some due relation to, natural law, being therefore also applicable to princes who are unbelievers.

The first conclusion. By way of explaining this assertion, I conclude, first, that a Christian prince may not declare war save either by reason of some injury inflicted or for the defence of the innocent. We have already given sufficient proof of this fact, by rejecting all the invalid grounds for war, [advanced above]. The arguments we have adduced are a proof of this same fact; for the law of grace has not destroyed, but on the contrary completes the natural law.

7. *The second conclusion.* Secondly, I must say that the defence of the innocent is permissible in a special sense to Christian princes, and that the same proposition holds true, proportionately, with respect to avenging injuries. For if a state subject to an unbelieving prince wishes to accept the law of Christ and the unbelieving sovereign prevents that acceptance, then Christian princes have the right to defend that innocent people; but if the same kingdom wishes to submit to the law of unbelievers—for example, to the Mohammedan—and its prince is opposed to this submission, then an unbelieving Turkish prince would not have a similar right of war against that other sovereign. The reason for this distinction is that to prevent the acceptance of the law of Christ does indeed involve grievous injustice and harm, whereas there is no injury at all in prohibiting the acceptance of another law. Likewise, if [a given people] are willing to listen [to the Gospel], they may be convinced through reason that this is the more credible faith and that it ought to be believed; and therefore, it is just to assist them, under these circumstances.

Similar examples may be adduced, relating to the first[6] part of our conclusion, as when injuries are inflicted upon preachers of the Gospel; or certainly when unbelieving princes act to the harm of the faithful, for this is an injury to the Church which she has a special right to repel and avenge. This right is in part supernatural, that is, in so far as the power from God to preach the Gospel is concerned, and in this sense, it surely is not possessed by unbelievers; all of which we have sufficiently proved in treating of faith (*De Fide,* Disp. XVIII, sect. 1).[7]

8. *The third conclusion.* I hold, thirdly, that all of the foregoing considerations are so founded on the natural reason that they may, to a certain extent and in due proportion, be applied to unbelievers. The explanation of this conclusion is that if any state wishes to worship the one God and observe the law of nature, or to listen to preachers who teach these things, and if the sovereign of that state forcibly prevents it from doing so, there would spring up in consequence a just ground for war to be waged by some other prince, even if the latter should be an unbeliever, and guided solely by natural reason; because that war would be a just defence of innocent persons.

In like manner, if any nation should worship the one God and observe the laws of nature, while another nation practised idolatry and lived contrary to natural reason, then the former state would have the right to send missionaries to instruct [the citizens of the latter state], and to free them from their errors. And if this action were forcibly prevented, then war could justly follow; first, for the reason that such a right is entirely in harmony with nature; secondly, because the defence of the innocent would be involved in that procedure, since, speaking generally, there would not fail to be some who wished to be taught the natural truths necessary for an upright and virtuous life, and who would be wickedly impeded in the attainment of this wish, and finally, because of other reasons which we

---

6. [*Sic (primam);* but the reference is apparently to the second conclusion, which relates to 'avenging injuries'. *Vide* the first sentence of Sub-section 7 of Section V, *supra,* p. 942.—TR.]

7. [*Supra,* p. 838.—TR.]

have set forth in our discussion of faith (*De Fide,* Disp. XVIII)[8] and which, in due proportion, are applicable to the point under discussion.

SECTION VI

What Certitude as to the Just Cause of War Is Required in Order That War May Be Just?

Three kinds of persons must here be distinguished, to wit: the sovereign king and prince, the leading men and generals, and the common soldiers. It is to be assumed that practical certitude is required of all these persons, a certitude which may be expressed in the statement: 'It is lawful for me to make war.' The whole doubt is concerned with theoretical certitude, which is to be expressed as follows: 'This cause of war is just in itself', or, 'This thing which I seek through war is rightfully mine'.

1. *The first conclusion: which is twofold.* I hold, first, that the sovereign ruler is bound to make a diligent examination of the cause and its justice, and that after making this examination, he ought to act in accordance with the knowledge thus obtained.

The proof of the first part. The basis of the first part of this conclusion is that war is a matter of the gravest character; and reason demands that in any matter whatsoever, deliberation and diligence should be applied, commensurate with its importance. Furthermore, a judge, in order to pass judgment in a private matter, ought to make diligent investigation; hence, the necessity for such diligence exists in due proportion in a public cause of war. Finally, if the ruler were not bound to make this investigation, the rashness of princes would easily result in universal disturbance. With regard to the first part of this assertion, then, there is no difficulty.

2. *The second part of this conclusion is explained.* The explanation of the second part of the conclusion is as follows. Let us suppose that the ground for a war is the fact that a certain king claims a certain city as belonging to him, or as falling newly to him by hereditary right. Now if, when the matter has been carefully examined, the truth of that claim is clearly

---

8. [*Supra,* p. 837.—Tr.]

established, what I have asserted is obviously true. But when the case of each side contains [an element of] probability, then the king ought to act as a just judge.

What should the king do when the claims of one side are more plausible than those of the other side? Therefore, if he finds that the opinion favouring his own side is the more probably true, he may, even justly, prosecute his own right; because, so I believe, the more probable opinion should always be preferred in passing judgment. For that is an act of distributive justice, in which the more worthy party is to receive the preference; and he is the more worthy party who enjoys the more probable right, as we shall explain below at greater length. For the same reason, however, if the more probable opinion favours the opposing side, the prince in question may on no account proceed to war.

3. *What should the king do, when the doubt is equal on both sides and the opposing side is in possession?* If, finally, after diligent investigation, the probabilities on both sides are found to be equal, or if, at least, equal uncertainty exists—whatever the ground of the uncertainty—then, if the opposing party is in possession, he ought to have the preference, because even in a judicial process, that party is favoured, inasmuch as he has the greater right. On this account, the party who is not in possession cannot proceed to war against the possessor; while the latter, on the other hand, is secure [in his conscience] and may justly defend himself.

Adrian (on the *Sentences,* Bk. IV, concerning restitution, and in *Quaestiones Quodlibeticae,* Qu. ii, art. 2), however, maintains an opinion contrary to this last statement. 'For that person' (he says) 'is in doubt as to whether he is retaining the property of another. Therefore, he is not secure [in his conscience].'[1] Soto (*De Iustitia,* Bk. IV, qu. v, last arg.) also says that the one who is in doubt is bound to divide with the other party, or to give satisfaction to that other in proportion to the doubt. This would be true if in the beginning he had taken possession, while doubting [the justice of his action]; for that sort of possession confers no kind of right. But if,

---

1. [If certainty of true ownership cannot be attained, the possessor, being in doubt, must relieve his conscience by giving the thing (possessed) to the poor (*loc. cit. 1ᵐ punctum, secundo dico*).—REVISER.]

on the other hand, he held possession at the beginning in good faith, if a doubt has arisen since that time, and if he has made diligent inquiries into the truth but has not been able to ascertain it, then he may, [with a] secure [conscience], continue in possession of the whole of the property in question; for the doubt remains purely theoretical, and such possession confers absolutely the right to the whole of the thing possessed, a fact which we have established universally and more fully, in our discussion of conscience ([*De Bonitate et Malitia Humanorum Actuum,*] Treatise III, disp. xii, §§ 5 and 6).[2] The same fact is stated specifically by Covarruvias (on *Sext,* rule *possessor,* Pt. II, § 7) and by Victoria (aforesaid Relectio [*De Iure Belli,* no. 29]). Soto (Relectio: *De Secreto,* Memb. iii. qu. 2)[3] does likewise. Nevertheless, Victoria observes that a possessor of the kind in question is bound, when the doubt arises, to inquire diligently into the truth; and that, if he refuses to do so, he can be forced into this inquiry by the other party, even through war, for the principles of justice and right judgment do indeed demand that such an investigation be made.

4. *What should the king do when neither side is in possession?* Another aspect of the question regards the situation in which no one is in possession and the doubts and probabilities balance each other. The more common opinion seems to be that either party has the right to seize first the thing in dispute. In accordance with this opinion, the war would become just simultaneously, on both sides; but this point is of no importance, when ignorance intervenes. The reason, indeed, which is offered in support of this opinion is that in a similar case a judge could award the property by his own decision to either one of the parties to the litigation, as he might choose.

However, I am unable to persuade myself that a judge may act thus in the case supposed. For certainly, under those circumstances, the judge is merely a distributor of property over which he personally has no right; consequently, if the rights of the parties in question are at all times entirely equal, there is no reason which would allow him to allot the whole

---

2. [Not included in these *Selections.*—Tr.]

3. [Soto, *De ratione tegendi et detegendi secretum,* relectio theologica (Salamanca, 1574).—Reviser.]

property to either party; and therefore, the judge is bound to divide the property. Or, if this cannot be advantageously done, it will be necessary to satisfy both sides, in some fashion. Hence, in a question involving war, the princes shall be bound to this same attitude. Accordingly, they must either divide between them the thing in dispute, or cast lots for it, or settle the matter in some other way. But if one party should attempt to seize the whole possession to the exclusion of the other party, by that very act he would be doing the other a wrong which the latter might justly repel, thus seizing, on this just ground of war, the entire disputed possession.

5. *It is more probably true that in case of doubt as to the justice of a war, a prince is bound to submit the matter to the judgment of a good man.* But the question may be asked whether, in cases of this kind, sovereign princes are bound to submit the matter to the decision of good men. This question, moreover, arises from the standpoint of natural law only, so that, in our discussion, we shall not include the authority of the Pope, of which we have already spoken.[4]

Indeed, I am of the opinion that the affirmative answer to this question is, in all probability, correct. For the said princes are bound to avoid war in so far as is possible, and by upright means. Therefore, if no danger of injustice is to be feared, the above-mentioned [arbitration] is plainly the best means of decision, and consequently resort should be had to it.

This opinion is confirmed as follows: it is impossible that the Author of nature should have left human affairs, governed as they are by conjecture more frequently than by any sure reason, in such a critical condition that all controversies between sovereigns and states should be settled only by war; for such a condition would be contrary to prudence and to the general welfare of the human race; and therefore it would be contrary to justice. Furthermore, if this condition prevailed, those persons would as a rule possess the greater rights who were the more powerful; and thus such rights would have to be measured by arms, which is manifestly a barbarous and absurd supposition.

6. *Note 1. Concerning the decision that is given.* In this connexion, however, we must observe, first, that a sovereign prince is not bound by the

4. [Cf. Sub-section 5 of Section II, *supra*, p. 920.—Tʀ.]

decision of those whom he himself has not constituted as judges. There-fore, it would be necessary for the arbitrators to be chosen with the consent of both sides. Resort to this method, indeed, is a most rare occurrence, inasmuch as [these princes] seldom favour it; for very frequently one or other of the princes holds the foreign judges in suspicion.

Note 2. Secondly, it should be noted that a sovereign prince, if he is acting in good faith, may ascertain his own rights through prudent and learned men [of his own choice]; then he may follow their judgment (if by it his rights are made clear to him); and under these circumstances he will not be bound to abide by the judgment of other [and foreign arbitra-tors]. The reason in support of this statement is that the rights in question must be judicially ascertained in the same manner as a just decision of a court; and in the latter sort of decision, [only] two objectives are involved. One is an examination of the cause and acquaintance with the rights of both sides; for which process, not jurisdiction, but knowledge and discre-tion, are necessary. For since this decision is not sought through war, but, on the contrary, a substitute for war [i.e. a judicial inquiry] is employed, there is no occasion to call in any arbitrator. The other objective is the enforcement of the right after it has been made clear. For this, jurisdiction is indeed required; but such jurisdiction is inherent in a sovereign prince when in other respects he is sufficiently certain of his right. In that case, then, there is no reason binding him to await the judgment of another, although he ought to accept just settlements if they are presented to him.

7. *The second conclusion, in two parts: relating to generals.* Secondly, I hold that generals and other chief men of the kingdom, whenever they are summoned for consultation to give their opinion on beginning a war, are bound to inquire diligently into the truth of the matter; but if they are not called, they are under no greater obligation to do so than others who are common soldiers. The first part of this conclusion is clearly true; because these generals, having been summoned, are bound in justice to give a just opinion, for if they did not do so, any injustice that there might be in the war will be laid to their charge. The proof of the second part of the conclu-sion is the fact that, when they are not summoned [to give advice], their part in the affair becomes simply that of private soldiers, since they are merely set in action by others, but do not control action; while it is only

incidental (*per accidens*) that they are wealthy or of noble birth. Neverthe-less, Victoria (*De Iure Belli,* no. 24) adds that such generals are bound in charity to inquire into the justice of the war, in order to give warning when it shall be necessary. But if this obligation is derived from charity alone, it will exist only in case of necessity; and therefore, generally speaking, apart from these cases where there is such need, they will not be so bound.

8. *The third conclusion: relating to common soldiers.* I hold thirdly, that: common soldiers, as subjects of princes, are in no wise bound to make diligent investigation, but rather may go to war when summoned to do so, provided it is not clear to them that the war is unjust. This conclusion may be proved by the following arguments: first, when the injustice of the war is not evident to these soldiers, the united opinion of the prince and of the realm is sufficient to move them to this action; secondly, subjects when in doubt (i.e. doubt of a theoretical character) are bound to obey their superiors (*Decretum,* Pt. II, causa xxiii, qu. i, can. iv, which is cited from Augustine, *Against Faustus,* Bk. XXII, chap. lxxv). This last statement is based upon the best of reasons, namely, the fact that in cases of doubt the safer[5] course should be chosen; therefore, since the prince possesses rightful authority, the safer course is to obey him.

The assertion is confirmed by the fact that the official subordinate of a judge may execute a sentence without any previous examination, provided that sentence is not manifestly unjust. Such is the common opinion of Cajetan (*Summma,* word *bellum*), Soto (*De Iustitia,* Bk. IV, qu. vii, art. 2), Victoria (*De Iure Belli,* no. 25), and Sylvester (word *bellum,* Pt. I, qu. 9 [qu. 5]).[6]

9. *A limitation of the third conclusion; by Sylvester.* Nevertheless, Sylves-ter would seem to limit this conclusion. For he says that, if the common soldiers have doubts, they are bound to make inquiries in order to dispel those doubts; but, if they cannot do so, it will be permissible for them to fight. *Adrian likewise limits this conclusion, in a different way; or rather*

---

5. [I.e. morally safer.—Tr.]

6. See Suárez in a similar passage in regard to an executor, vol. *De Censuris,* Disp. III, sect. xv, from no. 9. (This note was in Suárez's original; the referenced material is not included in these *Selections.*—Ed.)

he [absolutely] denies it. Adrian (*Quaestiones Quodlibeticae,* II) indeed, absolutely denies that it is permissible to go to war with such doubts; both because it is never permissible to act with a doubtful conscience; and because soldiers who did act thus would be choosing the [morally] more dangerous course, since they would be exposing themselves to the peril of unjust slaughter and plundering; whereas, if they abstained from going, they would sin only by disobedience, and justice imposes a more rigorous obligation than that of obedience.

Adrian is answered. The reply to this objection, however, is that the doubt in such a case is not practical but speculative, and therefore this does not render the conscience doubtful. Furthermore, it would not be safer to disobey; for as a natural result of such disobedience, it would become impossible for princes to defend their rights, and this would be a serious and general misfortune.

Sylvester is answered. With regard to Sylvester's limitation, we should observe: first, that the doubt may be a purely negative one, namely, that the soldiers are entirely ignorant of the basis of the justice or injustice underlying the war; in which case they are in no wise bound to make inquiry, being sufficiently supported by the fact that they have relied upon the authority of their sovereign; secondly, that the doubt may be positive, having its source in conflicting arguments adduced in favour of one side and the other. Indeed, if the arguments showing the war to be unjust were such that the soldiers themselves were unable to give a satisfactory answer, then they would be bound to inquire into the truth in some way. Even this obligation, however, is to be imposed, not readily, but only in case those arguments render the justice of the war extremely doubtful, for in that case, it would seem that the soldiers have inclined towards a moral judgment that the war was unjust; otherwise, however, if they have probable reason for thinking that the war is just, they may legitimately conform their conduct to these reasons.

10. *The more common opinion with respect to mercenary soldiers, who are not subjects.* A greater difficulty arises in connexion with soldiers who are not subjects and who are called mercenaries. The opinion commonly held seems to be that these soldiers are bound to inquire into the justice of a war, before they enlist. This is the opinion of Sylvester (on word *bellum,*

Pt. I, qu. 10), who even states definitely that such soldiers, when doubt-ful, cannot legitimately engage in the war. Cajetan (*Summa,* word *bellum*) holds almost the same view; although he makes this limitation: 'Unless they receive their pay in time of peace also, and are bound to go forth to war whenever called.' For in that case, [according to Cajetan], mercenaries may conduct themselves as if they were subjects, since they are really such, by reason of the pay which they receive. *The basis of the opinion above set forth.* The basis of the foregoing opinion is the fact that in such a situation it is safer for one who is not a subject to abstain from fighting; because if he so abstains he does not expose himself to any peril; whereas, if he does fight, he exposes himself to all the dangers enumerated by Adrian; and in doubtful matters the safer part should be chosen.

The first confirmation from the rule of law and from Ambrose. This asser-tion is confirmed, first, by the *Sext* (Bk. V, tit. xii, *De Regulis Iuris,* rule 19) and the *Digest* (L. xvii. 38 [36]), which states that he is not exempt from blame who thrusts himself, with peril to another, into affairs that do not concern him; wherefore Ambrose (*On Duties,* Bk. III, chap. ix and cited in *Decretum,* Pt. II, causa xiv, qu. v, can. x) makes the general statement that no one ought to assist one party to the prejudice of another.

The second confirmation. It is confirmed secondly by the fact that, in a similar kind of doubt, and for the reason set forth above, the laws hold that a spouse who is in doubt [as to the title to the act] may render the conjugal debt, but may not ask for it. By the same reasoning, it may also be said that princes who are kinsmen or friends may not assist one another until they have duly examined the cause.

11. However, such an opinion comes into conflict with the following difficulties.

The first argument against this opinion. First, it would be necessary for each individual mercenary soldier to inquire into the cause of the war. But such an investigation is contrary to all custom, and humanly speaking, is impossible; for, as I have said above, the reason for the war cannot be explained to all, nor are all capable of appreciating that explanation.

The second argument. Secondly, [if the opinion in question were valid,] even soldiers who were subjects could not take part in a doubtful war without examining the cause, save when they were under strict orders of such sort that they would be disobedient in not going; for in that case their obedience would alone excuse them. But as long as they were not under orders, it would be [morally] safer not to fight. However, this consequent is contrary to all custom, and that[7] obligation [to investigate the cause of war] would be harmful to the state.

The third argument. Thirdly, if permanent mercenaries could, previously to a war, bind themselves to fight even in doubtful cases by giving their consciences into the keeping of the prince's conscience, why could not those mercenaries do the same who enlist at the outbreak of a war? For, from a moral standpoint, the same principle is involved in the performance of an action and in binding oneself to perform it.

The confirmation of the third argument. The confirmation of this argument lies in the fact that just as one is not allowed to proceed to an unjust war, neither is he allowed to undertake the obligation of serving in such a war, nor even in any war indiscriminately, whether just or unjust; and the reason for these restrictions is that to fight in an unjust war is to act unjustly. Therefore, conversely, if one is permitted to bind himself to service in a doubtful war, the obligation involved in such a case is not wicked; and therefore, it would be permissible so to bind oneself for pay, here and now, although no previous obligation exists. Nor does it seem to be of much importance that a given [mercenary] was already regarded as a subject before the war, by reason of his pay. For one might say the same thing in the case of a contract made on the eve of the outbreak of the war, since, at such a time also, soldiers bind themselves to obedience in all matters in which obedience is legitimate; so that it makes no difference from the standpoint of justice, whether this contract was made before the war, or whether it is made now, [at the moment when the conflict begins].

The fourth argument. Fourthly, in a similar doubtful situation, any person is permitted to sell arms to these princes and to the soldiers; nevertheless, if they do so, the same danger is present, namely, that the act may contribute to the injury of innocent persons, if by any chance, the war is in fact unjust. The antecedent is commonly accepted as true. The proof of the consequent is, that both kinds of co-operation are very pertinent

7. [Reading *illa* for *alia*.—REVISER.]

to actual wars; and although soldiers seem, in a sense, to co-operate more immediately, nevertheless the persons who furnish arms are ordinarily able to do more harm.

The fifth argument. Fifthly, any individual is permitted to enter the service of a merchant, on a wage contract, with the intention of co-operating with the latter in those of his contracts whose injustice is not manifest to the employee; neither is that employee under an obligation to examine the nature of the contracts; and accordingly one should adopt a similar view with respect to the case under discussion.

The sixth argument. Lastly, there is one argument that is commonly applicable to all the cases mentioned above, namely, in all of them, the first and essential element is that one who is not a subject, submits himself to another for the sake of payment, and in so doing, inflicts no injury upon any person; neither, generally speaking, does he expose himself to the danger of any wrongdoing. And for the rest, he is [simply] exercising his right, when he sells his own property or his own labour, a right of which he certainly is not bound to deprive himself to his own detriment. With regard to these [mercenary] soldiers, there is, in addition, a special argument; for each of them has the authority of the prince and that of the whole state to support him, a fact which involves a great probability [that their conduct is just].

Hence, all the circumstances being weighed, it would by no means seem that mercenaries who serve in that contingency,[8] are choosing the course that is [morally] less safe.

12. *The author's decision: in two parts.* These arguments are clearly convincing; nor do I find any difference in actual fact between subjects and non-subjects. So it is that Victoria (*supra,* in his Relectio [*De Iure Belli*], no. 24 [no. 25]), too, speaks simply of 'soldiers', without distinction.

With respect to a negative doubt. However, since the question is one of moral conduct, and in order that we may proceed with less risk of error, I lay down this conclusion: if the doubt [as to the justice of a war] is purely negative,[9] it is probable that the soldiers in question may [rightfully] take

8. [I.e. when there is great probability that the war is just.—REVISER.]

9. 'Negative and positive doubt': with positive doubt, there is equally balanced evidence for and against; negative doubt arises from the absence of evidence on either side.

part in that war without having made any examination of the question, all responsibility being thrown upon the prince to whom they are subject. We assume, to be sure, that this prince enjoys a good reputation among all men. This is clearly the opinion supported by Victoria and agreed to by other Thomists.

With respect to a positive doubt. If, however, the doubt is positive, and if both sides advance plausible arguments, then, in my opinion, [those who are about to enlist] should make an inquiry into the truth of the matter. If they are unable to ascertain the truth, they will be bound to follow the course of action which is more probably just, and to aid him who is more probably in the right. For when the case involves doubt with respect to a fact, such as loss affecting one's neighbour, or with respect to the defence of the innocent, that course which appears to be more probably just should be followed, in accordance with the rules on conscience above set forth (Sub-sect. 6). To this end, indeed, it will be sufficient if the soldiers consult prudent and conscientious men upon the question of whether or not they are in an absolute sense able to take part in such a war. And if the soldiers in question form a single political body, and have their own chiefs, the inferiors will certainly satisfy all requirements, if each person examines the question of the justice of the war, through his own chief or prince, and follows the judgment of that authority. Finally, if the arguments on both sides contain an equal [element of] probability, the soldiers may under such circumstances conduct themselves as if the doubt were purely negative; for the balance is then equal, and the authority of the prince turns the scale. Sylvester, too (on the word *bellum*, Pt. I), has clearly suggested this conclusion.

The foregoing may suffice for the question under discussion.

SECTION VII

What Is the Proper Mode of Conducting War?

1. *Notes for the solution of this question.* Three periods must be distinguished [with respect to every war]: its inception; its prosecution, before victory is gained; and the period after victory. The three classes of persons already

mentioned must also be distinguished, namely: the sovereign prince; the intermediate group of leaders; and the soldiers of the rank and file.

A fourfold relationship is outlined. All of these persons may be considered in certain specific relationships. First, with respect to the enemy, that is to say: how may these classes justly conduct themselves toward the enemy? Secondly, with respect to their mutual relations: how should the king conduct himself toward his soldiers? Thirdly, [and again in connexion with their mutual relations,] how should the soldiers conduct themselves toward their kings? Fourthly, how should they conduct themselves toward other persons, for example, those persons in whose houses the soldiers are quartered during the march?

At present, we are dealing in the main with the first question; but we shall also treat briefly of the others.

2. *On the fourth relationship.* With respect to the fourth relationship, then, we may repeat briefly the admonition of John the Baptist (*Luke,* Chap. iii [, v. 14]): 'Do violence to no man; [. . .] and be content with your pay.' Hence, none of these soldiers may take anything from his hosts, beyond that which has been determined by the king; otherwise, he sins against justice and is bound to make restitution. The same is true if he does any other damage to houses, fields, &c. To be sure, the leaders [of intermediate rank] and the princes are bound, by virtue of their office, to prevent such acts in so far as they are able. If they fail to do so, the whole duty of making restitution falls upon them, in default of the soldiers.

On the third relationship. Concerning the third head, just as the kings are under an obligation to give pay to the soldiers, so the latter are bound to discharge all the duties pertaining to their office. Hence, justice requires of them brave conduct, even to such a degree that they shall not take to flight, nor desert their stations or fortifications; a matter concerning which there are many laws (in *Digest,* XLIX. xvi). Cajetan, also, should be consulted in his brief treatise on the subject (*Opusculum,* Bk. IV, last question but one [Bk. III, treatise ix: *De Vinculo Obedientiae*]); for he holds that commanders of forts are under an obligation not to surrender through any fear of death or starvation, since they have made a contract with the prince not to do so, and since they receive their payment because of this contract, whence there arises an obligation binding them in justice.

Finally, with regard to the mutual relationship of the private soldiers, we may remark that, apart from the ordinary rules of justice, they are especially bound after victory to make a just distribution in sharing the booty. What that just distribution may be, however, it is not possible for us to determine; for in every kingdom the rules laid down by the monarchs or generals should be observed, or, at least, those rules which may have been established by usage and custom.

Only the first head, then, still remains for discussion.

3. *On the first relationship. The first conclusion, in two parts.* I hold, first that before a war is begun the [attacking] prince is bound to call to the attention of the opposing state the existence of a just cause of war, and to seek adequate reparation therefor; and if the other state offers such adequate reparation, he is bound to accept it, and desist from war; for if he does not do so, the war will be unjust. If, on the other hand, the opposing prince refuses to give satisfaction, the first prince may begin to make war.

It is commonly accepted. The latter part of the conclusion is clearly true. This conclusion is commonly accepted in its entirety, and the latter part is clearly true because, assuming the obstinacy of the opposing prince or state, and the other conditions specified, there is no [other] point that calls for consideration.

The first part is proved by citing authorities and by reasoning. The first part is derived from Augustine (in *Decretum*, Pt. II, causa XXIII, qu. i, can. iii [which is cited from Augustine, *Letters*, clxxxix, no. 4, *To Boniface*]; *Decretum, ibid.,* qu. ii, can. ii [cited from Augustine, *On Josue* in *Questions on the Heptateuch*, Bk. VI, qu. 10, Migne ed.]). Moreover, this view is accepted by all Doctors: Major (on the *Sentences*, Bk. IV, qu. 20); Driedo (*De Libertate Christiana*, Bk. II, chap. vi); Cajetan (on the word *bellum*) and Sylvester (*ibid.,* qu. iv, concl. 2 [qu. i, concl. 2]). And it would seem that the same principle may correctly be inferred from a passage in *Deuteronomy* (Chap. xx [, v. 1]): 'If thou go out to war [against thy enemies and see horsemen and chariots, and the numbers of the enemy's army greater than thine, thou shalt not fear them: because thy God is with thee]'. The reason supporting this part of our conclusion is that any other manner of making war would be unjust, and therefore the cause of war itself would become unjust. For where a full and sufficient satisfaction is voluntarily offered, there is no ground for violence; especially not, since reason demands that punitive justice be exercised with the least possible harm to all, provided, however, that the principle of equality be observed. Moreover, one sovereign has no coercive power over another sovereign, unless the latter acts unjustly, as is the case when he is unwilling to give satisfaction.

4. *Cajetan's limitation of this conclusion.* But Cajetan limits this conclusion by stipulating the following condition: namely, that the satisfaction in question shall be offered before the actual encounter in war. For after the war has commenced, he who brings it to a victorious conclusion is not bound to accept such satisfaction; since, in that conflict, he is as a judge who, once the action has been undertaken, finds the cause within his jurisdiction, having acquired the right to proceed to the end, so that the vanquished party has only himself to blame, in that he did not offer satisfaction at the proper time.

This limitation is examined. But, I ask, what does Cajetan mean by 'actual encounter in warfare?' If he refers to the last actual battle in which the whole war is to find its conclusion, there is no doubt that, if the affair has already been entered into and victory is beginning to favour the side of the just belligerent, the latter is not bound, under such circumstances, to accept any reparation short of complete victory; for such victory now seems to be in all probability close at hand, and, indeed, to treat of peace at that juncture is, to all intents and purposes, impossible.

If, on the other hand, by actual encounter in warfare, Cajetan means a war in which several conflicts have occurred, I do not see how it may be asserted with any solid assurance that, under these circumstances, [the just belligerent] has the cause under his jurisdiction any more than he had before the commencement of the war. For previously, he had the same right to begin the war that he now has to proceed with it; and the sole difference is that the injury has grown greater, and that consequently an increased right to a greater satisfaction has arisen. Moreover, the arguments set forth above apply equally to both of the situations in question. For the continuance as well as the beginning of the war ought to be dictated by necessity. And, in addition to all these considerations, there is the fact that, [in the wake of both situations,] similar wrongs against the general welfare follow, wrongs which should be avoided while preserving intact one's individual rights. These are preserved when satisfaction is offered, because nothing further than this satisfaction can be claimed even when victory is achieved, a point which we shall discuss below.[1] In short, the right to make war is prejudicial to others,[2] and the punishment inflicted through war is of the severest kind; therefore, that punishment ought to be inflicted as sparingly as is possible.

5. *The [author's] solution, which is absolutely contrary to Cajetan's limitation. It is more fully explained.* Therefore, the opinion contrary to Cajetan's appears to be in every respect nearer the truth, with the sole proviso that complete satisfaction shall include the following conditions: all property unjustly withheld shall be restored; secondly, reimbursement must be made for all expenses due to injuries inflicted by the enemy, so that, once the war has been begun, a claim may justly be made for all its costs, to date; thirdly, something may be demanded as a penalty for the injury inflicted, for in war, regard must be had not only for commutative justice, but also for punitive justice; and finally, a demand may justly be made for whatever shall seem necessary to preserve and also to guard peace, in the future, since the chief end of war is to establish such a future peace. It should also be added that the state of war has its rightful source in justice and that, consequently, if war is made contrary to justice, there arises from that fact an obligation to make reparation for this injury.

6. *The second conclusion.* I hold, secondly, that after war has been begun, and during the whole period thereof up to the attainment of victory, it is just to visit upon the enemy all losses which may seem necessary either for obtaining satisfaction or for securing victory, provided that these losses do not involve an intrinsic injury to innocent persons, which would be in itself an evil. Of this injury, we shall treat below, in the sixth conclusion. The reason in support of this conclusion is as follows: if the end is permissible, the necessary means to that end are also permissible; and hence it follows that in the whole course, or duration, of the war hardly anything

---

1. [*Infra,* p. 959, Sub-section 7.—TR.]

2. [*Jus belli odiosum.* The expression has a legal connotation, namely, that one man's right may restrict the action of another, and is, therefore, prejudicial to the latter.—REVISER.]

done against the enemy involves injustice, except the slaying of the innocent. For all other damages are usually held to be necessary for attaining
the end to which the war is directed.

7. *The third conclusion: commonly applicable, and undoubtedly true.*
In the third place, I hold that after the winning of victory, a prince is
allowed to inflict upon the conquered state such losses as are sufficient for
a just punishment and satisfaction, and reimbursement for all losses suffered. This conclusion is commonly accepted and undoubtedly true, both
because the exaction of such penalties is the object of war, and also because
in a righteous judgment at law this same course of conduct is permissible. But it should be observed that in computing the sum required for
this satisfaction, one should include all the losses by the state in question
throughout the war, i.e. the deaths of men, conflagrations, &c.

*The first observation: An additional comment is not improperly attached to
this observation, by Sylvester and by Victoria.* In the first place, however, the
additional comment made by Sylvester (word *bellum,* Pt. I, qu. 9 [qu. 10])
and by Victoria (above-cited Relectio, no. 20 [*De Iure Belli,* no. 51]) is not
unacceptable, namely, that movable goods captured by soldiers during the
war are not to be reckoned by the prince as part of the restitution. For this
rule has become a part of the *ius gentium,* through common custom. The
reason underlying it is that, since the soldiers' lives are exposed to dangers
so numerous and so grave, they should be allowed something; and the
same is true of their prince.

The second observation. Secondly, it is necessary to observe with regard
both to this, and the previous conclusions,[3] that soldiers are not allowed
to seize anything on their own authority, whether after or even before the
victory is won; because they have in themselves no power, but possess it
solely through their prince, as his agents, so that they may not justly take
anything without his express or implied authorization.

*The third observation, involving a twofold corollary based upon this con-
clusion.* Thirdly: it follows from this conclusion that, if all the penalties
just enumerated seem insufficient in view of the gravity of the wrong,

3. [I.e. the first conclusion, Sub-section 3 of this Section; and the second conclusion,
Sub-section 6 of the same.—Tr.]

then, after the war has been entirely ended, certain guilty individuals among the enemy may also, with justice, be put to death; and, although the slaying of a great multitude would be thus permissible only when there was most urgent cause, nevertheless, even such slaughter may sometimes be allowed, in order to terrify the rest, as is indicated in the following passage from *Deuteronomy* (Chap. xx [, vv. 13–14]): 'When the Lord thy God shall deliver the city into thy hands, thou shalt slay all that are therein of the male sex, with the edge of the sword, excepting women and children,' &c. And from this passage it follows that with much more reason the guilty who have been vanquished may be reduced to captivity and all their property seized.

The fourth observation: whereby various laws regarding this conclusion are made clear. Fourthly, it is to be noted that one should interpret in accord with this conclusion the civil laws which assert that, through the *ius gentium,* it has been established that all the property of the enemy, both movable and immovable, passes to the victors. This fact is brought out in the *Digest* (XLIX. xv. 24, 28), the *Code* (VIII. liii. 36), and the *Decretum* (Pt. I, dist. 1, cans. ix and x). The same point is made by Ambrose (on *Abraham,* Bk. I, chap. iii), and by St. Thomas (*De Regimine Principum,* Bk. III), while Covarruvias (on *Sext,* rule *peccatum,* Pt. II, § 13 [§ 11, nos. 6–7]) discusses the subject at length. Moreover, similar laws are found in *Deuteronomy* (Chaps. xi and xx), as Abulensis notes thereon [on *Deuteronomy,* Qu. 3]. But all of these passages must be interpreted in conformity with the rule previously laid down, namely, that a just equality must be preserved, and regard must be had for the future peace; a matter of which we shall treat below. For it is necessary to preserve in war the same quality as in a just judgment; and in such a judgment, the offender cannot be visited with every sort of punishment nor deprived of all his property without any restriction, but may be punished only in proportion to his fault.

8. *The first doubt: concerning goods which did not belong to the enemy.* A doubt, however, arises; for it sometimes happens that among the goods of the enemy there are found many of which they themselves are not the owners. May these goods, then, be seized, if they are necessary for reparation? *First, a decision is given as to immovables.* The reply is, that if the property is immovable, [the victors] certainly cannot retain it; for those

from whom it was taken were not the owners; therefore, the victors themselves do not acquire any ownership therein; and consequently, they must restore such goods to the true owners. This is the rule laid down in certain laws of the *Digest* (XLIX. xv. 20, § 1, XLI. i. 44).

A decision is given, secondly, as to movables, from the standpoint of the law of nature. However, the civil laws apparently lay down the contrary rule in regard to movable property, as Covarruvias contends at length (on *Sext, rule peccatum,* Pt. II, § 11, nos. 6–7). But, putting aside the positive law, if such property has been acquired through theft, so that the title thereto does not vest in those in whose custody that property is found, but rather in its former owners, the reason stated above proves incontestably that the said property must be restored to those former owners. Nevertheless, the victorious soldiers may demand a just reward for their labours, and may exact it from the true owners of the property in question; or the victorious prince may make the demand, if it so happens that he has already recompensed his soldiers. The foregoing is, indeed, a provision of the natural law.

9. *Next, a decision is given from the standpoint of positive law.* But positive laws in favour of those making war against the enemies of the state could have granted to the soldiers themselves the ownership of such property, when it has been found by those soldiers to be already in the peaceful possession of the enemy. Accordingly, the effect of these laws could have been to deprive the former owners of their title to the property, for the benefit of the state, to which such a practice may often be advantageous, particularly with respect to movables, the true ownership of which it is difficult to ascertain, while it is nevertheless desirable that the rights of ownership should in some other way be rendered unimpeachable. This is the case especially when the property in question comes into the hands of subjects, a practice which, according to Covarruvias, was allowed by the laws of Spain. For, as a general rule, it would be rather difficult to believe that this practice prevailed, since the laws of one country cannot bind [the citizens of] other countries, nor deprive aliens of their rights of ownership. Thus the civil laws seem, in this respect, to have sprung from the unjust manner in which wars were at that time carried on. *The unjust mode of war employed by the ancient Romans.* For the Romans believed that the wars

which they waged against the enemies of the state were just on both sides; and in fact, they preferred to fight as if upon the tacit and mutual understanding that the conqueror should become absolute master. Hence, they were accustomed to consider that all property of the enemy, whatsoever its origin, passed absolutely to the captors; and that the latter would thus possess this property, whatever might be its source. This standpoint is clearly brought out in the *Digest* (XLIX. xv. 5, § 2). Accordingly, they thought it unnecessary to restore these goods to the former owners, since the enemies of the latter,[4] as soon as they had taken the property, had acquired the title to it. Furthermore, arguing conversely, the laws deny this right [of postliminium] to pirates and robbers. On this point see the *Digest* (XLIX. xv. 19). Assuming that all this is true, the question of whether or not such a practice would imperil the conscience is a matter which will be better explained below, in Sub-section 22 [of this Section].

10. *The second doubt: who on the enemy's side are liable to punishment?* But another doubt remains, namely: whether it is equally allowable to inflict damages of this kind upon all those who are numbered among the enemy. In answering this question we must note that some of these persons are said to be guilty, and others innocent. It is implicit in natural law that the innocent include children, women, and all unable to bear arms; by the *ius gentium,* ambassadors, and among Christians, by positive [canon] law (*Decretals,* Bk. I, tit. xxxiv, chap. ii), religious persons, priests, &c. And Cajetan (on *Decretum,* Pt. II, causa xxiii, qu. iv [causa xxiv, qu. iii, can. xxv, word *bellum*]) holds, indeed, that this provision of law has been abolished by custom, which should be observed. All other persons are considered guilty; for human judgment looks upon those able to take up arms as having actually done so. Now, the hostile state is composed of both classes of persons, and therefore, all these persons are held to be enemies (*Digest,* XLIX. xv. 24). In this respect, strangers and foreigners, since they form no part of the state and therefore are not reckoned among the enemy unless they are allies in the war, differ from the persons above mentioned.

---

4. [Who had subsequently become the enemies of the Romans.—Tr.]

11. *The fourth conclusion.* Assuming that the foregoing is true, I hold, fourthly,[5] that if the damages inflicted upon the guilty are sufficient for restitution and satisfaction, those damages cannot justly be extended to affect the innocent. This fact is self-evident as a result of what has already been said, for one may not demand greater satisfaction than that which is just. The only question that might arise is whether or not victorious soldiers are always bound to observe this order in their procedure, taking vengeance upon the guilty and their property rather than upon the innocent. The reply is briefly that, other things being equal, and within the limits of the same class of property, they are so bound. For the principle of equity clearly imposes this rule, a fact which will become more evident from what follows.

12. *The fifth conclusion and the reason underlying it.* Fifthly, I hold that if such a course of action is essential to complete satisfaction, it is permissible to deprive the innocent of their goods, even of their liberty. The reason is that the innocent form a portion of one whole and unjust state; and on account of the crime of the whole, this part may be punished even though it does not of itself share in the fault.

The confirmation. This argument is confirmed as follows: first, it is on this very ground that the children of the Saracens are made slaves by the Christians; secondly, a son is sometimes punished for a crime committed by his father, as we have said in the treatise on faith, in dealing with heresy (Disp. XXII, sect. v, and Disp. XXIV, sect. iii, no. 3).[6] In this connexion, the canon law (*Sext,* Bk. V, *De Regulis Iuris,* rule 23) states that, 'No one is punished save for guilt or for a just cause';[7] from which one infers the falsity of the opinion expressed by Sylvester (word *bellum,* Pt. I, qu. 10 [qu. 11]) that, after victory is attained, the property of the innocent must be restored to them; unless he is speaking of cases in which property has evidently been seized in excess of the amount required for satisfaction, for

---

5. [The Latin reads: *hoc posito. 11. Dico quarto;* i.e. the new section actually begins after the phrase 'Assuming that the foregoing is true.'—Tr.]

6. [Disputations XXII and XXIV are not included in these *Selections.*—Tr.]

7. [This quotation, as given by Suárez, varies slightly from the text of the canon law.—Tr.]

in that case, if anything is to be restored, reason demands that a beginning be made with what was taken from the innocent; but if the property seized does not exceed the required amount, then, just as it was permissible to take such property, so also it is permissible to retain it, as Victoria has noted [Relectio, *De Iure Belli,* no. 40].

13. In this connexion, however, some [special circumstances] existing among Christians must be noted. First: by the *ius gentium* the custom has been introduced among Christians that prisoners of war are not to be made slaves by *mancipium,* although they may justly be detained until they are sufficiently punished or redeemed by a just ransom; a point which is confirmed by a royal decree ([*Las Siete Partidas,*] Pt. II, tit. XXIX, law I). But since this privilege was introduced for the benefit of the faithful, it is not always extended to apostates. Therefore, if war be waged against those baptized persons who have entirely forsaken the faith, as is the case with those who pass over to paganism, such persons may be made slaves by *mancipium.* This is the custom. For they themselves wholly deny Christ, and consequently, they may not reasonably profit by the privilege of Christians. However, it has been customary for heretics to enjoy this privilege, since in a sense, at least, they confess Christ. For [this privilege], inasmuch as it has been introduced by custom, is to be interpreted equally in the light of custom. Covarruvias (on *Sext,* rule *peccatum,* § 9, no. 4 [Pt. II, § 10, no. 3]), indeed, quoting Innocent and others, seems not to have spoken truly with respect to wars waged against apostate subjects, in which the latter, [according to him,] may not be enslaved by *mancipium,* 'since', says Covarruvias, 'it is not properly war, but (as it were) an exercise of ordinary jurisdiction'.

In the war against Granada, however, we see that the contrary procedure was adopted, with the approval of all the most learned and conscientious men. Ayala, too, takes this stand ([*De Iure et Officiis Bellicis et Disciplina Militari,*] Bk. I, chap. ii, no. 15): The argument in favour of such a view is that the apostates in question are subjects and that, therefore, they may justly be punished. Moreover, if [the practice in question] is permissible with respect to foreigners over whom there is less jurisdiction, why is it not permissible with respect to subjects? Finally, it is false to assert that the action described above is not war; for when subjects are rebels the ordinary mode of procedure is to subdue them anew through war.

14. Secondly, we must note that among Christians the immunity of ecclesiastical persons and property has also been introduced, both because of reverence, and because these persons or goods seem to form a kind of spiritual realm distinct from the temporal state and exempt from temporal jurisdiction.

Furthermore, Sylvester (word *bellum,* at end) adds that all property, to whomever it may belong, if it is placed within a church, enjoys this same privilege; for consecrated places cannot be attacked. But this last statement is true only in a general sense. Therefore, if men seek retreat in such places solely to protect their own lives, they should enjoy ecclesiastical immunity; but if an enemy use a church as a citadel or as a defensive camp, that church may be attacked and burned, even if some disadvantages follow therefrom; for such disadvantages would be of an incidental nature. However, with respect to other temporal goods, there is no fixed rule; although, in such cases, the customary practice should be observed.

15. Sixthly, I hold that innocent persons as such may in nowise be slain, even if the punishment inflicted upon their state would, otherwise, be deemed inadequate; but incidentally they may be slain, when such an act is necessary in order to secure victory.

The reason supporting this conclusion is that the slaying of innocent persons is intrinsically evil. However, one may object that this is true with respect to killing upon private authority and without just cause, but that the case in question involves both public authority and a just cause. Nevertheless, such a plea must be rejected when the slaughter is not necessary for victory (a condition which we have already assumed to exist), and when the innocent can be distinguished from the guilty.

The conclusion is confirmed by the difference existing between life and other possessions. For the latter fall under human dominion; and the state as a whole has a higher right to them than single individuals; hence, individuals may be deprived of such property because of the guilt of the whole realm. But life does not fall under human dominion, and therefore, no one may be deprived of his life save by reason of his own guilt. For this reason, undoubtedly, a son is never killed on account of the sin of his father; which is in accordance with the passage in *Deuteronomy* (Chap. xxiv [, v. 16]), and *Exodus* (Chap. xxiii [, v. 7]), 'Do not put to death the innocent.' [Another] confirmatory argument is that, if the innocent were able to defend themselves, they would act justly in so doing; hence, an attack upon them is unjust. There is a final confirmation of the same conclusion in the act of Ambrose, who visited Theodosius with a major excommunication because of a like slaying of the innocent; a fact which is recorded in the *Decretum* (Pt. II, causa XI, qu. iii, can. lxix).

Who are the innocent, with respect to the conclusions under discussion? But one may ask, who actually are the innocent, with respect to this issue? My reply is that they include not only the persons enumerated above, but also those who are able to bear arms, if it is evident that, in other respects, they have not shared in the crime nor in the unjust war; for the natural law demands that, generally speaking,[8] no one who is actually known to be free from guilt, shall be slain. But what shall we say, if certain persons are not known to have participated either [in the crime or in the unjust war], and if there exists only the presumption that they were able to bear arms? On this point, I shall speak shortly.

16. *An argument from Scripture against this conclusion.* However, there is an argument [opposed to the sixth conclusion] which runs as follows: In two passages of the Old Testament (*Josue,* Chap. vi [, v. 17] and *1 Kings,* Chap. xv [, v. 3]) the people of God were ordered to kill all of the enemy, not excepting the children. Again, according to the account in the Book of *Judges* (Chap. xx), as many as possible of the tribe of Benjamin were slain indiscriminately by the Israelites, even after victory.[9] In *Deuteronomy* (Chap. xx [, vv. 16–17]) we read that after a city had been captured authority was given to kill all the enemy, including the women and children.

The reply to the first two passages. As to the first two passages cited, the reply must be that only God could have given such an order, and

---

8. [*Per se;* i.e. apart from specific cases in which such slaughter is needful, for incidental reasons.—Tr.]

9. [*Citra victoriam* is a rather obscure expression, but the context appears to favour the translation given above.—Tr.]

accordingly, that this command was a special judgment of God designed to terrify the nations in question and caused by their iniquity, as may be gathered from *Deuteronomy* (Chap. ix).

To the third passage. In the event described in the third passage [, that concerning the slaughter of the Benjamites,] the children of Israel acted wrongfully. On this point, see Abulensis [Tostado] ([on *Judges,*] Chap. xv, qu. xxxvii).

St. Thomas's reply to the fourth passage. St. Thomas (I.–II, qu. 105, art. 3, ad 4), explains the fourth passage as meaning that permission was given to kill all who refused to accept peace; therefore he would seem to conclude that this permission applied only to the slaughter of the guilty. *The sense in which this passage is more commonly taken.* Nevertheless, the commentators generally appear to think that it applied to the slaughter of all adult males who might have been capable of bearing arms; for the presumption of guilt existed with respect to all of them and therefore their destruction was lawful, if there was no proof of their innocence. Abulensis adds another reason [for the authority to slay, mentioned in this fourth passage], namely, that [otherwise] the enemies in question might renew the warfare against the Chosen People. *Refutation of the reason given by Abulensis in favour of the permission mentioned in* Deuteronomy, *xx.* But this reason, simply in itself, is not sufficient; and consequently, Abulensis (above cited, Qu. xxxvii) himself later refutes it on the ground that no one may be punished for a prospective sin, provided that he is not otherwise deserving of death; this refutation being especially applicable because the presumption in question does not of itself seem to warrant the slaughter of human beings, since in a criminal trial particularly there should be sufficient proof, and since, furthermore, he who is not proved guilty is presumed to be innocent. Finally, it is practically certain that, among a whole multitude, some may be found who neither consented to the war nor gave any assistance in it, but who, on the contrary, urged the acceptance of peace; and therefore, all may not be indiscriminately slain.

A reply especially adapted to the first part of the above-cited permission. These arguments prove beyond a doubt that, after victory has been attained, those only who are clearly guilty may be slain. As for the law above referred to [see *Josue,* Chap. vi, v. 17; *1 Kings,* Chap. xv, v. 3 and

Judges, Chap. xx], we may say that this was a positive law laid down by a special act of God's will.

What of the second part? With regard to the second part of that same law,[10] indeed, we may even observe that it was given in time of actual combat and upon an occasion of the kind when, according to the customary phrase, a rebellious city is justly handed over 'to blood and to the sword'. For sometimes this is permissible, either on account of the enormity of the offence, or for the correction [by example] of other cities; since, to be sure, upon such occasions it is scarcely possible to distinguish the innocent from the guilty, except through age and sex. Hence, the slaughter of all those whose innocence is not clearly evident for reasons of age or sex is, in general, permitted, as long as the actual combat continues; but the case will be otherwise after the cessation of combat, and the attainment of victory.

17. *The reason supporting the latter part of the [sixth] conclusion.* The latter part of the [sixth] conclusion is also commonly accepted, and is clearly true in the case of certain means essential to victory, which, however, necessarily involve the death of innocent persons, as in the burning of cities and the destruction of fortresses. For, absolutely speaking, whoever has the right to attain the end sought by a war, has the right to use these means to that end. Moreover, in such a case, the death of the innocent is not sought for its own sake, but is an incidental consequence; hence, it is considered not as voluntarily inflicted but simply as allowed by one who is making use of his right in a time of necessity.

A confirmation of this argument, from the inconvenience that would otherwise follow, and from an example. A confirmation of this argument lies in the fact that it would be impossible, through any other means, to end the war. In like manner, a pregnant woman may use medicine necessary to preserve her own life, even if she knows that such an act will result in the death of her unborn child. From these arguments it is to be inferred that, save in time of necessity, the means in question are not legitimate.

18. *Arguments against the second part of the sixth conclusion.* On the other hand, one may argue, first: that in the case described, one really

---

10. [*De posteriori vero parte illiusmet legis.* This appears to be interpolated in the Latin text.—REVISER.]

co-operates, in a positive sense, in bringing about the death of an innocent person; hence, one cannot be excused from sin.

In the second place: it may be alleged that to kill an innocent person is as intrinsically evil as to kill oneself; and to kill oneself in this manner, even incidentally,[11] is evil; as, for example, when soldiers demolish a citadel and a wall, although they know with certainty that they will be crushed at the moment [when the fortifications fall]. An indication of this fact is that Samson, who committed such an act [of self-destruction], is exonerated by the Fathers, Augustine (*On the City of God,* Bk. I, chaps. xxi and xxvi), Bernard (*De Praecepto et Dispensatione* [Chap. iii]), St. Thomas (II.–II, qu. 64, from no. 5 [art. 5], ad 4) only because he acted at the prompting of the Holy Spirit.

In the third place: evil may not be done that good may ensue.

Fourthly: [in the parable of our Lord] (*Matthew,* Chap. xiii [, v. 29]) it is forbidden to pull up the tares lest the wheat should be pulled up with them.

Fifthly: the innocent persons in question would be justified in defending themselves if they were able to do so; hence the aggression against them is unjust.[12]

Sixthly: the [last] argument mentioned in favour of the sixth conclusion may be reversed to prove the contrary contention; for a mother is not allowed to use a particular medicine, if she knows with certainty that it will cause the death of her unborn child, and especially not after the infusion into that child of a rational soul. This seems to be the opinion more commonly held by Antoninus ([*Summa Theologica,*] Pt. III, tit. vi [tit. vii], chap. ii), Sylvester (word *medicus,* Qu. 4), Navarrus ([*Summa,*] Chap. xxv, no. 62). The reason supporting it is that, if help cannot be given to one person without injuring another, it is better to help neither person. On this point, see the *Decretum* (Pt. II, causa xiv, can. i [Pt. II, causa xiv, qu. v, can. x]).

19. The reply to the first of the foregoing arguments is as follows: if the matter be viewed from a physical standpoint, the victor does not really

---

11. [*Per accidens,* i.e. incidentally to the attainment of a justifiable end.—Tr.]

12. [According to the principle that war (or combat) cannot be justly waged on both sides.—Tr.]

kill, for he is not the cause of the death in an essential, but merely in an incidental sense; and even in the moral order, he is not guilty of homicide, because he is exercising his own right, nor is he bound to avoid to [his own] great detriment, the resulting harm to his neighbour.

As for the second argument, I deny that [the act in question] is intrinsically evil, basing my denial on that same ground, namely, that the person described does not in fact kill himself, but merely permits his own death. The question of whether or not this may be allowed under such circumstances must be considered in the light of the order of charity; that is to say, one must consider whether the good at stake in the case is to such an extent the common good,[13] that there is an obligation to expose oneself in its defence to a peril so great. There are some who think that Samson's action may be excused from this point of view; but such a reason would not seem to serve as a sufficient excuse for that action, because, if the matter is looked at from a purely human standpoint, the punishment of one's enemies would not seem to be a good so great as to justify Samson in killing himself therefor, even though his death would be only incidental [to the attainment of his end].

With respect to the third argument, it is true that morally evil deeds may not be performed that good may ensue, but it is permissible to inflict the evils of punishment [for that purpose]; though, [in point of fact,] in the present case, the evils in question are not so much brought about [with deliberation], as they are allowed to follow [incidentally].

As to the fourth argument: in the first place, I deny that the case [set forth in *Matthew*, Chap. xiii, on the tares and wheat] involved a legitimate necessity [of pulling up the tares]. Moreover, there was no power to do so. Again, the pulling up of the tares was inexpedient to the end sought by the head of the household.

To the fifth argument, some persons reply that, under such circumstances, the war may incidentally be just for both sides. Excluding cases of ignorance, however, this seems impossible. Accordingly, my reply is that

---

13. [The Latin reads: *an ibi intercedat tam commune bonum.* If for *tam,* we substituted *tantum,* the translation would be: 'Whether the common good at stake is so great that, &c.'—REVISER.]

the innocent persons in question may indeed protect themselves in so far as mere self-defence is concerned: by preventing the burning of the city, for example, or the destruction of the citadel, &c. For such actions involve solely the protection of their own lives, and may lawfully be performed. I maintain, however, that they may not adopt an aggressive defence (so to speak) combating those who are justly engaged in the war; for, in point of fact, such combatants are doing them no injury. But these innocent persons may fight against those who are responsible for the war, since the latter are truly doing them an injury.

As for the last argument, the judgment set forth above must be understood to relate to a situation in which the medicine is not indeed absolutely necessary to save the mother's life, but is perhaps necessary simply as an aid to her better health; for in such a case the life of the child should be given the preference. This would seem to be the teaching of Ambrose (on *Duties,* Bk. III, chap. ix). That same judgment must also be held to refer to medicine administered with the deliberate intention of killing the foetus. But otherwise, if a case of necessity coupled with a right intention be present, then without doubt it is permissible [to take the medicine]. This is clearly true, even apart from the arguments adduced above; because, if the mother were allowed to die, then, in most cases, both she and the child would perish; therefore, it is preferable, if possible, to save the mother's life while permitting the child to die, rather than to allow the death of both. The matter would, indeed, be somewhat doubtful, if it involved a comparison of the mother's physical existence with the spiritual life of the child; for possibly the latter could be baptized [if he were not deprived of physical life]. With respect to this question, however, the order of charity mentioned above must be observed.

20. Seventhly, I hold that, in addition to all the losses which have previously been enumerated and which may be claimed as necessary to satisfaction, a prince who has obtained a just victory may do everything with the property of the enemy that is essential to the preservation of an undisturbed peace in the future, provided that he spare the lives of the enemy. Therefore, if it is necessary, he may on this ground seize cities, provinces, &c.

That is the doctrine supported by all, and the rational basis thereof is derived from the very purpose of an honourable war; since war is permissible especially for this reason, namely, as a way (so to speak) to an upright peace.

This reasoning is confirmed by the fact that within the state itself, wrongdoing is punished in accordance with what is necessary for the public peace with the result that, frequently, some person is ordered into exile, or visited with a similar punishment, &c. From this example, one infers that, if a [precautionary] measure of this sort is taken under circumstances such that it may at the same time come into the category of a penalty, this step should be taken on both of these grounds;[14] nor is it permissible to multiply without cause the harm inflicted upon the enemy.

21. Finally, I hold that a war will not be unjust, if all the precautions which we have enumerated are observed in it, and if at the same time the other general conditions of justice are fulfilled; and yet, such a war may contain some evil element opposed to charity or to some other virtue. The first part of this conclusion is sufficiently proved by what has already been said (Sect. IV, sub-sect. 8). Some examples confirming the second part have been mentioned above, examples relating to cases in which a war is undertaken in opposition to charity, but not in opposition to justice. Another illustration would be a situation in which the conditions above set forth are fulfilled, yet the war springs from hatred.

22. However, some doubts which need elucidation are attached to this conclusion. The first doubt is as follows: if both sides voluntarily engage in war, without just cause, should that war be considered as opposed to charity, or as opposed to justice; and does it give rise to a consequent obligation to make restitution? Covarruvias (on *Sext,* rule *peccatum,* Pt. II, § 21 [§ 12]) indicates that a war of this kind is contrary to justice; for he says that goods captured therein must be restored, since an unjust war creates no right.

But, while there is no doubt that in the sight of God such a war is, in its essence, opposed to justice, because of the homicides—actual or potential—which are involved in it, nevertheless, there would seem to be no injustice involved, in so far as regards the combatants themselves.

---

14. [I.e. the grounds of precaution in the interests of future peace, and punishment for past wrongdoing.—Tr.]

For injustice is in no wise done to a person who knowingly consents [to an action]; and [, in the situation under discussion,] the two sides are voluntarily fighting with each other, since, as I assume, the war is waged by mutual agreement, and after proclamation.

In the second place, for the very reason that the parties in question make this agreement, they surrender (as it were) their own rights, and join in a pact to the effect that the victorious party shall acquire the property of the vanquished; and once this compact—unjust though it is in the sight of God—has been made, the victors become the true owners of such property, since they possess it by the will of the former owners. Therefore, [the victors are not bound to make restitution for property thus acquired].

In the third place, for these same reasons, there exists no obligation to make reparation, not, at all events, for the losses inflicted; and therefore, the conquerors may also reimburse themselves from the property of the enemy, at least to the extent of the expenses which those conquerors have incurred in the war.

Finally, because of the mutual and voluntary agreement, there arises in the case of a private duel which is voluntary on both sides, no obligation to make restitution, nor any act of injustice. Therefore, . . .

These arguments, then, would seem to prove that there results no obligation of making restitution for losses inflicted—not, at least, in a war of the kind in question; but as to other questions of property, the case is doubtful. Nevertheless, it is extremely probable that the same rule holds with regard to this matter, also; just as a game which is in other respects wrong, but in which there is no injustice committed among the players, may result in the transference of property from one to another without any consequent obligation to make restitution. The same may be said of adultery, if a price is given in exchange for it; however, we do not deny that the opposite opinion may perhaps be correct; and much less do we deny that it is [morally] safe.

23. A second doubt, according to St. Thomas (II.–II, qu. 40, art. 3), is whether stratagems are permissible in war. To this we must briefly reply, in agreement with him, that they are permissible in so far as relates to the prudent concealment of one's plans; but not with respect to the telling

of lies. Regarding this point, what we have said elsewhere (Disp. XIV, sect. iv)[15] on the concealment of one's religious faith should be consulted.

From the foregoing, another doubt is resolved *a fortiori,* the doubt as to whether it is permissible in war to break faith plighted with the enemy.[16] For we must say that, generally speaking, such an act is not permissible, since it involves patent injustice; and consequently, if the enemy suffers loss for this reason, full reparation should be made. However, all this is true only provided that the promise shall have been made from the beginning of the war, by a just and mutual agreement (as it were) in such a way as to be binding; and it is also necessary that this promise shall have remained and persisted in full vigour and force, since, if one side has perchance broken faith, the other side will be entirely freed from its own obligation. For the equity of law demands that this condition be understood to exist. The same holds true if any change in circumstances has occurred, such that the promises in question cannot be kept without grave loss. In that event, the opposing side must be warned that it is not possible to keep the promise made to it; and, after [either side] has issued this declaration, it is freed from the pledge. However, such a declaration is seldom to be permitted.

24. *The third doubt: drawn from the same St. Thomas. The author treats of this point more fully in* De Diebus Festis [*in* De Virtute et Statu Religionis,] *Bk. II, chap. xxviii, no. 7.*[17] A third doubt, also derived from St. Thomas (II.–II, qu. 40, art. 4), turns upon the question: is fighting permissible on feast days? The reply is that such fighting is permissible, in cases of urgent necessity. Cajetan adds that, if mass is heard, there is no mortal sin involved in fighting on feast days, even when there is no necessity for so doing; although such an act may be a venial sin, because it is characterized by a certain lack of proportion, especially if the fighting could be postponed without detriment. Sylvester (word *bellum,* Pt. I) extends this permission to the season of Lent, relying on the canon law (*Decretum,* Pt. II, causa xxiii, qu. viii, can. xv; *Decretals,* Bk. I, tit. xxxiv, chap. i), but

---

15. [Not included in these *Selections.*—Tr.]
16. *Vide* Bk. VI of the *Defensio Fidei,* chap. ix. (This note was in Suárez's original; the referenced material is not included in these *Selections.*—Ed.)
17. [Not included in these *Selections.*—Tr.]

custom does not sanction that view, a fact which is noted in the Gloss on the passages above cited.

25. *The fourth doubt is resolved by means of examples.* A fourth doubt concerns the question of whether or not a Christian prince sins in calling to his aid infidel sovereigns, or, conversely, in giving them aid in a war which is otherwise just. We must answer that such an action is not in itself a sin, since it is not opposed to any virtue, and since examples [of this sort of conduct] are supplied by the Scriptures in the case of David (*1 Kings,* Chap. xxviii) and the Machabees (*1 Machabees,* Chaps. viii and xi).

This point is also proved by reasoning. Furthermore, it is permissible in war to employ the aid of wild animals; therefore, why not the aid of unbelievers? Conversely, it is permissible to sell arms to unbelievers for use in just wars; hence it is permissible to aid them. Sometimes, however, such a course of action may militate against charity, because it involves public scandal, or some peril to believers, or even lack of trust in divine aid. In this connexion, an example may be found in the Old Testament (*2 Paralipomenon,* Chap. xvi), where King Asa is gravely rebuked and is punished for having sought the human aid of another and infidel prince, through his want of trust in divine aid. Abulensis [Tostado] should also be consulted, in this connexion (on *1 Kings,* Chap. xxviii, qu. 17).

SECTION VIII

Is Sedition Intrinsically Evil?

1. *What is sedition?* Sedition is the term used to designate general warfare carried on within a single state, and waged either between two parts thereof or between the prince and the state. *The first conclusion.* I hold, first, that sedition involving two factions of the state is always an evil on the part of the aggressor, but just on the defensive side. The truth of the latter statement is self-evident. The truth of the former is proved by the fact that no legitimate authority to declare war is discernible in such a situation, for this authority, as we have seen (Section II [*supra,* p. 917]), resides in the sovereign prince.

The objection to the contrary is answered. The objection will be made that, sometimes, a prince will be able to delegate this authority, if urgent public necessity demands that he do so. In such a case, however, the prince himself, and not a part of the state, is held to be the aggressor; so that no sedition will exist in the sense in which we are using the term. But what if one part of the state actually suffers injury from another part, and is unable to secure its right through the prince? My reply is that this injured part may do nothing beyond that which a private individual may do, as can easily be gathered from what we have said above.[1]

2. *The second conclusion, on which see* Defensio Fidei, *Bk. VI, chap. iv.*[2] I hold, secondly, that a war of the state against the prince, even if it be aggressive, is not intrinsically evil; but that the conditions necessary for a war that is in other respects just must nevertheless be present in order that this sort of war may be righteous. This conclusion holds true only when the prince is a tyrant, a situation which may occur in one of two ways, as Cajetan notes (on II.–II, qu. 64, art. 1, ad 3 [art. 3]). In the first place, the prince may be a tyrant in regard to his [assertion of tyrannical] dominion, and power; secondly, he may be so merely in regard to his acts of government.

When the first kind of tyranny occurs, the whole state, or any portion thereof, has the right [to revolt] against the prince. Hence, it follows that any person whatsoever may avenge himself and the state against [such] tyranny. The reason supporting these statements is that the tyrant in question is an aggressor, and is waging war unjustly against the state and its separate parts, so that, in consequence, all those parts have the right of defence. Such is the opinion expressed by Cajetan (*loc. cit.*); and this conclusion may also be derived from a passage in St. Thomas's works (on the *Sentences,* Bk. II, dist. xliv, qu. 2, art. 2).

John Huss upheld the same doctrine with respect to the second kind of tyrant, and, indeed, with respect to every unjust superior. But this teaching was condemned at the Council of Constance (Sessions VIII and XV). Consequently, it is most certain that no private person, nor any imperfect power, may justly begin an aggressive war against this kind of tyrant, and that such a war would be sedition in the true sense of the term.

---

1. [Cf. Section II, sub-section 2, of this Disputation, *supra,* p. 918, especially the third paragraph.—Tr.]

2. [*Supra,* p. 803.—Tr.]

The proof of these assertions is as follows: the prince in question is, we assume, the true sovereign; and inferiors have not the right of declaring war, but only that of defending themselves, a right which does not apply in connexion with this sort of tyrant; for the latter does not always do wrong to individuals, and in any attack which [these individuals] might make, they would be obliged to confine themselves to necessary self-defence. The state as a whole, however, may rise in revolt against such a tyrant; and this uprising would not be a case of sedition in the strict sense, since the word is commonly employed with a connotation of evil. The reason for this distinction is that under the circumstances described the state, as a whole, is superior to the king, for the state, when it granted him his power, is held to have granted it upon these conditions: that he should govern in accord with the public weal, and not tyrannically; and that, if he did not govern thus, he might be deposed from that position of power.

[In order that such rebellion may justly occur,] however, the situation must be one in which it is observed that the king does really and manifestly behave in a tyrannical manner; and the other conditions laid down for a just war must concurrently be present. On this point, see St. Thomas (*De Regimine Principum*, Bk. I, chap. vi).

3. *The third conclusion.* I hold, thirdly, that a war of the state against a king who is tyrannical in neither of these two ways, is sedition in the truest sense and intrinsically evil. This is certainly true, as is evident from the fact that, in such a case, both a just cause and a [rightful] authority are lacking. From this, conversely, it is also evident that the war of a prince against a state subject to himself, may be just, from the standpoint of rightful authority, if all the other required conditions be present, but that, in the absence of those conditions, that same war is entirely unjust.

LAST SECTION [SECTION IX]

Is a Private War, That Is to Say, a Duel, Intrinsically Evil?

1. A private contest of this sort, which in Greek is called μονομαχία (single combat), may be entered into, in one of two ways: either suddenly (as

it were) and by chance, and viewed in this light, the treatment of such contests is part of the subject-matter of homicide; or else, by the agreement and consent of both parties. In the latter case, if certain public conditions are satisfied, the contest is called a duel (*duellum*); but if the affair is conducted privately, it is termed a *diffidatio*[1] or single combat, that is, in our common tongue,[2] a *desafío*.

The first conclusion. I hold, first: that if a just cause be lacking, a duel is always wicked. This is clearly true, since such a contest is a kind of war, and since it is even possible that in the course of that contest the death of a human being may occur.

Again, a duel may be fought in order to display prowess and courage; or in order to win a reputation, as is wont to be the case, from time to time, among soldiers during a war. Duels fought for such reasons are also evil, because the participants rashly expose themselves both to the peril of death and to the peril of killing another.

This view is confirmed by the fact that a sham battle[3] is a mortal sin, if it involves evident danger of death; for those who die therein are denied the right of ecclesiastical burial, in accordance with the canon law (*Decretals,* Bk. V, tit. xiii, chap. i); therefore, . . .

For a like reason, the same opinion should be held with respect to duels fought for the sake of revealing some truth or clearing oneself of some charge. This is the doctrine laid down by Cajetan (on II.–II, qu. 95, art. 8 [, ad 3]), and supported by *Decretals* (Bk. V, tit. xxxv, chap. i), by the *Decretum* (Pt. II, causa ii, qu. v, can. xxii), by Torquemada thereon, and by Henry of Ghent (*Quodlibeta,* IX [V], qu. 32). The reason supporting this view is that such contests are not really a means of revealing truth and innocence, seeing that sometimes an innocent man is slain in a duel. Neither, [in situations of this sort,] is there sufficient reason to justify killing another; and therefore, there is not sufficient reason for making an attack. Furthermore, such conduct is contrary to the charity due to

---

1. [An impromptu armed combat following a challenge.—Tr.]

2. [*Vulgo;* in this case, Spanish.—Tr.]

3. [*Bellicum exercitium* (a warlike exercise). Or Suárez may have had in mind a tournament, to which his canon law reference applies.—Tr.]

oneself; for if the person who issues the challenge is innocent, he exposes himself to the peril of death; and, on the other hand, if he is guilty, his sin is far greater in that he attempts to clear himself in a superstitious manner. Finally, in these contests, God Himself is tempted, since His aid is hoped for, through unfitting means.[4]

2. *The second conclusion and the proof thereof.* I hold, secondly: that every private duel, that is, [every contest of this sort] that is not characterized by all the conditions of a just war, is intrinsically evil. This is the common opinion of the Summists (on word *duellum*).

The first point. Regarding the challenger to a duel, indeed, the truth of such an assertion is admitted without any limitation or distinction, and may be proved as follows: the killing of any man on mere private authority is intrinsically wicked, except in the necessary defence of one's own person and property; and the challenger to a private duel sets out to kill upon his private authority; therefore, . . .

A second point. Secondly, the same proof applies in regard to one who accepts a challenge; for in his very acceptance he wills to undertake the slaying of that other person who issues the challenge.

Confirmation from both forms of law.[5] This argument is confirmed by the fact that such duels are, in general, condemned by the law, as laid down in the *Code* (XI. xliv. 1); while the Council of Trent (Session XXV, *De Reformatione* [, chap. xix]) has also imposed the penalty of excommunication, and many other penalties, upon those who fight, counsel, participate as spectators, &c., in connexion with these duels. In a certain Bull of Pius IV [*Contra Pugnantes in Duello,* &c., Nov. 13, 1564],[6] such excommunication is reserved [for absolution] to the Pope, save with respect to the persons of the emperors or kings [who are not included in the penalty]. And although these laws may seem to refer only to public duels, Gregory XIII [Bull *Ad Tollendum,* Dec. 5, 1582][7] nevertheless extends such duels to include single

---

4. See the author [Suárez,] *De Irreligiositate,* no. 8 [in *De Virtute et Statu Religionis,* Tract. III, Bk. I, chap. iii]. (This note was in Suárez's original; the referenced material is not included in these *Selections.*—ED.)

5. [I.e. civil and ecclesiastical.—TR.]

6. [Bullarium Romanum VII, p. 85 (Turin, 1862).—REVISER.]

7. [Bullarium Romanum VIII, p. 400 (Turin, 1862).—REVISER.]

combats between individuals; but he does not reserve [to himself the absolution of] the excommunication.

3. *A limiting clause which some writers impose upon this conclusion.* It is to be noted, indeed, that some writers have limited this conclusion with reference to the person who accepts the challenge, if he does so in order to defend his honour and for the reason that, otherwise (that is, if he did not accept the challenge received), he would incur disgrace.

The basis of their limitation. An argument in favour of this stand is based upon analogy: for a nobleman attacked by another is not bound to flee, but may lawfully stand his ground and kill his aggressor in self-defence; and this merely to protect the honour befitting his rank; therefore, in like manner, . . .

This is the point of view suggested by Navarrus in one passage of his work (*Summa* [*Enchiridion sive Manuale Confessariorum,*] Chap. xv, at end); although in another Chapter (Chap. xi, no. 39), he expresses a different opinion.

This limiting clause is rejected: first, by citing authorities. However, the contrary is in every respect true, as is evident from the laws above cited, and especially from the Bull of Pius IV, in which the following words are to be noted: 'To allow [duelling], for whatsoever cause, even for one not disapproved by the [civil] laws, or on whatsoever pretext', &c.[8]

Furthermore, it is rejected by reasoning. The reason, *a posteriori,* for such a stand is derived from nature;[9] for, in the judgment of every prudent person, each of the combatants in the situation described, chooses, contrary to right reason, to smite his adversary. Furthermore, I maintain that the alleged disgrace is not truly such, although the ignorant crowd may judge it to be disgrace. The reason, *a priori* for this same opinion, is clear, to wit: [acceptance of a challenge] is not an act of defence but one of aggression, since there is occasion for defensive acts only when force is repelled by force and since no force has entered into the case in

---

8. [The words are not in the Const. of Pope Pius IV (1560), but very similar words are found in the Const. of Pope Julius II (*Regis pacifici,* Feb. 24, 1509).—Reviser.]

9. [*Naturalis.*—Tr.]

question.[10] Therein lies the difference between this case and the analogous one that was adduced. For in the latter instance, the nobleman suffers actual violence, and is forced into an action which would not otherwise be permissible to him; whereas, in the former instance, [as we have said,] there is no use of force. Moreover, in that [supposedly analogous] situation, a man is provoked to an act of simple defence; but in this matter [of the duel], one is provoked to an act of aggression, and such a challenge may be refused, for a righteous reason. Such is the stand taken by Cajetan (on II.–II, qu. 95, art. 8, ad 3) and in his *Summa* (word *duellum*), and Armilla thereon ([on word *duellum*,] no. 1). See also Soto (*De Iustitia*, Bk. V, qu. i, art. 8, clause *quod si hinc*), and Abulensis [Tostado] (on *1 Kings,* Chap. xvii, last qu.).

4. Secondly, there is an exception to the conclusion in question,[11] in the case of an innocent person who is unjustly accused and condemned—or who, at least, is going to be sentenced to death—if that person is challenged by his accuser to a duel, and wishes to substitute the peril of such a contest, for the certain death to which he must shortly submit as the result of a judicial decision. For, under these circumstances, his agreement to undertake the duel would seem to be an act of just [self-]defence. This is the opinion held by de Lyra (on *1 Kings,* Chap. xvii), Navarrus ([*Summa* or *Enchiridion*], Chap. xi, no. 39 and Chap. xv, no. 9), and Cajetan (on II.–II, qu. 95, art. 8 and [*Summa,*] on word *duellum*).

The latter, however, adds a provisional clause to the effect that this duel shall be undertaken, not upon one's own authority, but upon that of the prince.

The proof of the second limiting clause is as follows: the accuser in question attacks an innocent man with the sword of justice; therefore, self-defence is permissible to that innocent person; and consequently, it is also permissible for him to avail himself of the means of defence, which in the case supposed is none other than the duel.

---

10. [I.e. the case in which a given person has been challenged to a duel.—Tr.]

11. [I.e. the second conclusion: 'Every private duel that is not in every way characterized by the conditions of a just war is intrinsically evil.' *Supra,* sub-section 2 of this Section.—Tr.]

This argument is confirmed by the fact that, occasionally, as we have said above,[12] what is material aggression is formal defence; so that this fact, too, must be considered, in connexion with the situation described.

5. But this [second] exception is not established to my satisfaction. Moreover, it is rejected by Sylvester (word *duellum*), Abulensis [Tostado] (*supra*), and Antoninus ([*Summa Theologica,*] Pt. III, tit. IV, § [chap.] iii), with other authorities there cited. Soto (*De Iustitia,* Bk. V, qu. I, art. 8, near end) appears to hold the same view.

If, indeed, we put aside [the cases sanctioned by] the authority of the prince, we may argue that, in reality, the act in question is not one of defence but one of aggression. For defence is possible only where force is applied by an actual aggressor; and the accuser, in this instance, does not resort to force, since he does not compel the other to fight, but merely invites him to do so, being an aggressor, strictly speaking, only in his false accusation; whereas calumny is repelled not by violence, but by the manifestation of truth. Moreover, if the latter course of action cannot be followed, it is in no wise permissible to resort to irregular means which are not truly means. On the contrary, death must be patiently endured just as if an innocent person were found guilty because of false witnesses.[13]

This argument is confirmed [, first,] by the fact that, if the acceptance of a duel under these circumstances had a defensive character, then, surely, the challenge also would have the same character, provided no other means [of exonerating oneself] were available. For this act [of challenging, on the part of the accused], also, would amount to the repelling, by violence, of the violence inflicted with the sword of justice. And therefore, such a challenge [on the part of the accused] to a duel [of this sort] would be permissible; a proposition which, however, the very authorities cited above deny. [Secondly,] a further consequent [of the assertion which we are rejecting] would be that the accused, should he be able to do so, might legitimately kill his accuser in secret, if he hoped thereby to escape death. This consequent would clearly follow, since in a just defence it is allowable to anticipate a future situation.

12. [Cf. Section I, sub-section 6, of this Disputation.—Tr.]
13. Salon also agrees with this, on II.–II, qu. 64, art. 3, controvers. 3. (This note was in Suárez's original.—Ed.)

Another [and third] consequent of the assertion in question would be that one could licitly accept the challenge in question in order to prevent any other person from depriving him through a judicial decision of his reputation or his entire fortune. For not only in defence of one's life, but also in defence of one's external possessions, it is permissible to kill another. This consequent is rejected by Cajetan, who argues as follows: armed defence is permissible only when one person makes an armed attack upon another; in a criminal action, however, while the aggressor does not attack with his own weapons, still he does attack with the sword of the judge; but this is not true of a civil action, wherein the sole weapon employed is an unjust judgment. However, this point is of no significance; for in the first place, as far as the moral question is concerned, such a distinction is wholly of a material nature, and consequently has no application to upright conduct.

Therefore, other authorities make an assertion which, even if it is less probably true, is nevertheless more logical; since they admit that the same reasoning holds for both sides.[14] This assertion is that, when an innocent person is to be condemned, even if it be [merely] to serious loss of reputation or of fortune, he may accept or issue a challenge to a duel. Furthermore, Cajetan even makes a false assumption; for if some unarmed person should attempt to steal my property, and if I were unable to ward off the injury without arms, it would be entirely permissible for me to use weapons for that act of self-defence; and therefore, in like manner, it would be allowable for me to avert by armed defence the above-mentioned loss of reputation or property, while accepting my calumniator's challenge to a duel. There are some, however, who deny that the cases are similar, on this ground, namely, that no one is allowed to expose himself to the peril of death for the sake of external possessions. The denial which they rest upon such a basis is erroneous. For, indeed, as was pointed out in Sub-section 3 [of this Section] the nobleman [in the case supposed] is not bound to flee, although, by awaiting the aggressor in order to protect the honour befitting his rank, he exposes himself to the danger of death.

---

14. Among these authorities are Molina, *Treatise III, De Iustitia Commutativa,* Disp. XVII, no. 7; and Sánchez, with others whom he cites, *Decalogue,* Bk. II, chap. xxxix, no. 8. (This note was in Suárez's original.—ED.)

6. *The second and principal rejection of the limiting clause.* Finally, the defendant who is thus falsely accused may not slay his accuser; and therefore, he may not attempt to do so by means of a duel. The truth of the consequent is evident; for it is not permissible to attempt that which it is not permissible to do. The truth of the antecedent also becomes clear, both from what has been said above, and from the following example: if Peter, for instance, knew that Paul had given money to another person in order that the latter might slay Peter, it would not be permissible for Peter, acting on his own authority, to slay Paul, even if he believed that there was no other way in which he could escape death at the hands of that third person; and this would be true for no other reason than that Paul would not, in his own person, be inflicting violence; therefore, and in like manner, one who has been falsely accused before a judge may not for that reason slay his accuser.

A confirmation. In fine, the foregoing is confirmed by the fact that much unjust slaughter would undoubtedly result, to the great detriment of the state, from the acceptance of the contrary opinion. For any one might easily persuade himself that he was being unjustly accused in court and that there remained no other means of protecting his life, honour, or property, than that he should slay his accuser. It would also follow that, if one person should, out of invincible ignorance, accuse another—in good faith, to be sure, but nevertheless falsely—the accused could slay that innocent accuser, in order to protect his own life or reputation. For even such an accuser attacks another person with the sword of the judge, no less than if he were making the accusation out of malice; since, in point of fact, he also is about to take from that other, through a false accusation, his life or his good fame. Consequently, although the opinion opposed to that which we are defending may seem convincing from a theoretical point of view, still, it is by no means admitted in practice.

7. *A further rejection of the limiting clause, as qualified by Cajetan's proviso.* Cajetan's statement, indeed, that it is permissible to accept the challenge in question, at least, with the permission of the prince, does not seem to be sufficiently sound. For a prince may not justly give such authorization, since according to the allegations and the proofs, he is certain either that the accused person is innocent or that he is guilty, or that neither the one

nor the other fact [is manifest]. If the first alternative be true, then the sovereign is bound to acquit the accused and cannot righteously involve him in the peril of a duel. In the third case, exactly the same assertion applies. For the laws and the principle of justice demand that when the accuser does not prove his charge, the defendant shall be discharged; and in case of doubt, the defendant is to be favoured. If, however, the second alternative shall prevail, the judge is bound to condemn the accused, according to the ordinary law.

Evasion is precluded. Moreover, if it be argued that a sovereign prince, out of the plenitude of his power, may set free even a convicted person, especially if privately he knows that person to be innocent, we say in rebuttal, not even then may he permit the duel; for if the prince has the power to acquit, right reason demands that he shall wholly acquit this person and not expose him to the peril of a duel. There is the additional consideration that, with respect to the accuser, an injustice would be committed. For, even though the prince may be able to acquit an innocent person who has been found guilty, still he may in no wise punish a guilty person who has not been convicted of guilt; and the accuser, in his turn, even though he may be in fact a calumniator, nevertheless has not been convicted of this offence in court; and if, eventually, he is punished, it will at least be through a just punishment, and not through a duel. It may be urged that the contest in question is not a punishment nor a wrong, because, so we assume, the duel is voluntarily sought or accepted. I reply, indeed, that it is true that on this account no wrong is done to the private person involved; but a wrong is nevertheless done to the state and to good government, whenever, in violation of due process of law, any person is exposed to the peril of death without sufficient public cause.

The final argument is refuted, and the second conclusion defended as generally applicable. Finally, if it should be contended that in any given situation, the sovereign may allow such a duel in order to avoid greater evils, just as in actual fact prostitutes are tolerated; even so, he can in no way confer the right and the power to engage justly in this practice of duelling, although he may not have been sinful in permitting it [, in a particular instance]. For the innocent or accused person in the case has no right, acting for himself and on his own authority, either to slay or to

attack the other; and consequently, the prince cannot grant such power
to innocent persons of this sort. The truth of the consequent is evident,
since the sovereign may not grant that any one shall, without sin, kill
another person, unless the latter has previously been legally convicted and
condemned, circumstances which do not exist in the situation supposed.
Therefore, the conclusion propounded above[15] is applicable in general
without qualification.

8. *The third conclusion: commonly held and consisting of two parts.* Thirdly,
I hold that a private armed contest—that is, one fought by two or by a few
individuals—is not intrinsically wicked, if engaged in by public authority;
on the contrary, if in other respects the contest in question comprehends
the conditions of a just war, it may be justified, for in that event it has the
nature of war—at least, war of a limited sort—rather than that of a duel.
This is the commonly accepted conclusion.

The first part is proved. The prior part of the conclusion is proved, in
the first place, as follows: slaying on public authority and for a just cause
is not intrinsically evil; hence, it will not be evil to resort to the means
necessary in order to effect that slaying (in which means there is included
the [private armed] contest in question.)

Confirmation I. This argument is confirmed by the fact that a war in
which many persons are engaged, and which is characterized by the conditions laid down above, may be just; and therefore, the same assertion holds
true of a contest carried on among a few persons; for a mere difference in
the number of persons involved does not affect the righteousness or the
justice of a cause.

Confirmation II. Secondly, the argument in question is confirmed as
follows: any one condemned to capital punishment may legitimately, on
the authorization of the prince, be put to death by any private person
whatsoever, if it shall prove necessary for such an authorization to be
given; and under these circumstances, the private agent will not be guilty
of any sin in such killing, since he acts as a minister of justice; therefore,
in the case described, the same procedure will be permissible.

---

15. [I.e. the second conclusion. See Sub-sections 2 and 4 of this Section.—Tr.]

9. *The proof of the latter part.* Now the latter part of [this third] conclusion may be established, in the first place, from the [special] use of the word duel (*duellum*). Ordinarily, indeed, the term refers to a combat which is entirely private, i.e. undertaken solely upon private authority and on account of a private matter. Such a duel, to be sure, is intrinsically wicked. But the combat of which we are speaking, although it may in appearance be private, because it involves only a few persons, is nevertheless held to be public in point of fact, for the reason that it is undertaken under public authority and for a public cause; and therefore, it is not characterized by the intrinsic wickedness of the duel, but has, on the contrary, the true character of war. Accordingly, in order that such a contest may licitly be undertaken, it must be clothed with the conditions characterizing a just war; and this may come about in either one of two ways.

The first way in which this kind of a duel may be justifiable. First, the whole business of a war may be reduced to an armed contest among a few combatants. No doubt exists on the question of whether or not such [a cause] is righteous, provided that, in addition to the fact that the war is just, precaution is taken by the prince not to make victory more doubtful than it would have been in case of actual warfare. Cajetan [on II.–II, qu. 95, art. 8, comment. x], indeed, maintains that the prince is not allowed to reduce a war to an engagement among a few combatants, unless he is sure that he would be defeated in the general war. But the rule already laid down[16] is more widely applicable and contains more truth. For when the hope of victory is not diminished and does not become less sure because the war has been reduced to a duel, no harm or wrong is done to any one, and for the rest, a great deal of slaughter is avoided. Accordingly, [the arrangement in question] will be righteous and just. However, since this sort of advantageous transformation of the war is a rare occurrence, prudence must be used in allowing it. For if the prince does perchance allow such [a procedure] rashly and without sufficient cause, he will not sin, to be sure, against the justice owed to the enemy state, provided that, in other respects, he is waging a just war; but he will be sinning against the due rights of his own

---

16. [I.e. the rule that the prince may resort to such a procedure, if the chance of victory is not rendered more doubtful thereby.—Tr.]

state, for which, by virtue of his office, he is bound to make careful provision and take careful thought; and he will also be sinning against those subjects whom he exposes to the peril of a duel without reasonable cause.

The second way in which this kind of duel may be justified. In a second way, the contest in question may be righteous. Not because the entire war is (so to speak) virtually contained therein, but because it is a portion of a war, justly undertaken and begun, which it is perhaps expedient to carry forward in this fashion to the attainment of victory, inasmuch as the act of reducing the war to a duel deprives the enemy of certain of their bravest soldiers or else disheartens that enemy, while, on the other hand, one's own men may be heartened; or there may be other, similar reasons, which will possibly arise. Thus Navarrus taught ([*Summa,*] Chap. xv, at end). However, the true reason [for the legitimacy of the contest] is that a lawful cause and power underly it, in this case. Moreover, if the war as a whole is legitimate, the same is true of a part thereof; and this armed contest is (as it were) a certain portion of the whole, and a portion, so we assume, which is necessary or useful to attaining the end of the war in its entirety; therefore, . . .

The foregoing argument proves that it is as permissible to propose such a contest as it is to accede to the proposal; for if that contest is allowable in itself, it will also be allowable to obtain the authorization to engage in it, from the possessor of authority. Cajetan (word *duellum*), however, seems to hold an opinion opposed to this one regarding the second manner [in which the contests in question may be justified]. But Navarrus explains the statement of Cajetan as referring to those occasions when the war is confined to a few combatants, without justice and without cause.

10. Now it is maintained in opposition to the above conclusion, first, that whoever offers a challenge to such a duel, provided he is waging a righteous war, consequently invites and incites another to an action which the latter cannot without sin accept; hence the challenger himself sins by the act of provocation.

Secondly, he exposes innocent people to the peril of death, an act which in its very essence would seem to be evil.

Thirdly, he binds himself not to defend his own people, if they are vanquished by their adversaries or are in most evident danger; yet, to bind oneself thus seems to be opposed to natural law, which places us under the obligation of protecting the innocent.

In reply to the first objection, we must say that the prince in question provokes not to evil [as such], but to a lesser [alternative] evil; for he is directly concerned with seeking his own rights; and he may, on the ground that the other side is sinning, and for the purpose of preventing war on a large scale, seek to substitute for that war a lesser evil, such as this engagement involving peril to only a few persons.

To the second objection, one may reply that sometimes it is permissible to endanger the lives of innocent persons, for the sake of the common welfare. For in the general engagement, also, innocent persons—in much greater number—are exposed to the peril of death. In individual cases, however, care must be taken that these single combats be entered into only with serious reason and that, as far as possible, the peril be diminished.

To the third objection it may be replied that, just as the duty of defending the innocent is a precept that binds, not without intermission, but only when it can advantageously be carried out; so, conversely, to bind oneself in a given situation to refrain from defending the innocent, is not intrinsically wicked, and may be allowed when such an obligation is entered upon, under circumstances that to the prudent mind may render the defence of the innocent impossible for the reason that it would clearly involve grave and general disadvantage; these being, indeed, the circumstances assumed in the course of our argument.

We might deal at this point with the penalties inflicted for duelling, as well as with the punishment of those who encourage the practice; matters which are, however, more suitably discussed in connexion with censures.[17] Here, then, we may conclude the entire treatise on charity, written for the glory of God and of His Virgin Mother.

PRAISE BE TO GOD

---

17. *Vide* Suárez, Vol. *De Censuris*,[18] Disp. XXIII, sect. vii, no. 11; Disp. XXXI, sect. iv, no. 48. (This note was in Suárez's original; the referenced material is not included in these *Selections.*—ED.)

18. [This work is not included in these *Selections.*—TR.]

BIBLIOGRAPHY

Works of Francisco Suárez

De legibus ac deo legislatore. Coimbra, 1612.

Defensio fidei catholicae et apostolicae adversus anglicanae sectae errores, cum responsione ad apologiam pro iuramento fidelitatis, et praefationem monitoriam serenissimi Iacobi Angliae regis. Coimbra, 1613.

De triplice virtute theologica, fide, spe et charitate. Edited by Balthasar Alvarez. Coimbra, 1621.

Opera omnia. Edited by D. M. André and C. Berton. 26 vols. Paris: Louis Vivès, 1856–78. *De legibus* is volumes 5–6, *De fide, spe et charitate* is volume 12, and *Defensio fidei catholicae* is volume 24.

Defensio fidei Book III I: Principatus politicus o la soberania popular. Corpus Hispanorum De Pace, vol. 2. Edited by E. Elorduy and L. Pereña. Madrid: Consejo Superior de Investigaciones Científicas, 1965.

Lectiones de fide, anno 1583 in Collegio Romano habitas. Edited by K. Deuringer. Granada: Facultad de Teologica, 1967.

De fide. Secunda pars, Roma, 1583. Edited by K. Deuringer. Archivo Teologico Granadino, 32 (1969), pp. 79–232, and 33 (1970), pp. 191–305.

De legibus ac deo legislatore. Corpus Hispanorum De Pace. 8 vols. Edited by L. Pereña, V. Abril, C. Baciero, E. Elorduy, A. Garcia, and C. Villanueva. Madrid: Consejo Superior de Investigaciones Científicas, 1971–81.

Defensio fidei Book VI De iuramento fidelitatis. Corpus Hispanorum De Pace, vol. 19. Edited by L. Pereña, V. Abril, C. Baciero, A. Garcia, and C. Villanueva. Madrid: Consejo Superior de Investigaciones Científicas, 1978.

Collections

Patristic Writings

Migne, J. P., ed. *Patrologia Graeca.* 161 vols. Paris, 1857–66.

Migne, J. P., ed. *Patrologia Latina.* 221 vols. Paris, 1844–55 and 1862–65.

Civil Law

Krueger, P., T. Mommsen, and R. Schoell, eds. *Corpus iuris civilis.* 3 vols. Berlin: Weidmann, 1954.

Canon Law

Richter, A. L., and E. Friedberg, eds. *Corpus iuris canonici.* 2 vols. Leipzig: Tauchnitz, 1879.

General Councils

Tanner, N., and G. Alberigo, eds. *Decrees of the Ecumenical Councils.* 2 vols. Washington: Georgetown University Press, 1990.

Patristic and Postclassical Works Cited by Suárez

Abbas. *See* Panormitanus.

Abulensis. *See* Tostado, Alonso.

Actius, Thomas. *See* Azzio, Tommaso.

Adrian (of Utrecht, 1459–1523; Pope Adrian VI, Dutch theologian at Louvain, cardinal, and pope). *Commentarius in lib. 4 sententiarum Petri Lombardi.* Paris, 1512.

———. *Quaestiones quodlibeticae.* Louvain, 1518.

Aemilius Veronensis, Paulus (Paolo Emilio da Verona, ca. 1455–1529; Italian historian). *De rebus gestis Francorum usque ad annum 1488.* Paris, 1539.

Ailly, Peter d' (1350–1420; French theologian, philosopher, and cardinal). *Quaestiones super 1, 3 et 4 sententiarum.* Paris, 1515.

Alberico de Rosate (ca. 1290–ca. 1360). *De statutis.* Lyon, 1552.

Albert of Bologna (Alberto Bolognetti, 1538–85; Italian cardinal and jurist). *De lege, iure et aequitate disputationes.* Rome, 1570.

Albertus Magnus (Albert the Great, ca. 1193–1280; 'the Universal Doctor,' bishop and doctor of the Church, German schoolman and philosopher).

In Aristotelis ethica. In vol. 7 of *Opera omnia,* ed. by E. Borgnet. 38 vols. Paris, 1890.

Alexander of Hales (d. 1245; Franciscan theologian and philosopher). *Summa universae theologiae.* Nuremberg, 1481–82.

Alexander of Imola (Alessandro Tartagni, 1424–77; also called Imolensis, Italian jurist at Padua, Ferrara, and Bologna). *Consiliorum seu responsorum lib. 7.* Venice, 1595.

Alliaco, Petrus de. *See* Ailly, Peter d'.

Almain, Jacobus (ca. 1480–1515; French theologian). *In 3 lib. sententiarum.* Lyon, 1527.

———. *Libellus de auctoritate ecclesiae.* Paris, 1512.

———. *Moralia.* Paris, 1526.

Altisiodorensis, Gulielmus (William of Auxerre, d. 1231; French theologian). *Summa aurea in 4. lib. sententiarum.* Paris, 1500.

Ambrose, St. (ca. 340–97; bishop of Milan and doctor of the Church). Works found in vols. 14–17 of J. P. Migne, ed. *Patrologia Latina,* 221 vols. Paris, 1844–55 and 1862–65.

———. *Commentaria in epistolam ad Romanos.*

———. *Commentaria in 2 epistolas ad Corinthios.*

———. *De Abraham.*

———. *De officiis ministrorum.*

———. *De paradiso.*

———. *De poenitentia.*

———. *Epistolae.*

———. *Expositio evangelii secundum Lucam.*

———. *Hexaemeron.*

Ancharano, Petrus de (ca. 1330–1416; Italian canonist). *Consilia sive iuris responsa.* Venice, 1585.

———. *In V decretales libros facundissima commentarii.* Bologna, 1581.

Andrea, Giovanni d' (Joannes Andreas, ca. 1275–1348; Italian canonist). *Commentaria in decretales et sextum.* Venice, 1581.

Angelus de Clavasio (Angelo Carletti di Chivasso, 1411–95). *Summa angelica de casibus conscientiae.* Strasbourg, 1495.

Angelus de Ubaldis or Angelo Baldi (Baldeschi, 1327–1407). *In I atque II digesti veteris partem commentariae.* Venice, 1580.

Angest, Jerome (Hieronymus de Hangest, d. 1538; French theologian). *Moralia magna.* Lyon, 1541.

Anselm, St. (ca. 1033–1109; Italian ecclesiastic, doctor of the Church, archbishop of Canterbury). Works found in vol. 158 of J. P. Migne, ed. *Patrologia Latina,* 221 vols. Paris, 1844–55 and 1862–65.

———. *Cur deus homo.*

———. *De conceptu virginali et originali peccato.*

———. *De voluntate dei.*

———. *Proslogium.*

Antoninus, St. (Antoninus of Florence, Antonio Pierozzi, Antonio de Forciglioni, 1389–1459; Florentine theologian, archbishop of Florence). *Summa theologiae moralis.* Venice, 1477.

Aquinas. *See* Thomas Aquinas, St.

Aquitanus, Prosper (ca. 390–ca. 455; Prosper of Aquitaine). *De vocatione omnium gentium.* In vol. 51 of J. P. Migne, ed. *Patrologia Latina,* 221 vols. Paris, 1844–55 and 1862–65.

Aragón, Petrus de (d. 1584; Spanish theologian). *Commentaria in secundam secundae divi Thomae.* Lyon, 1596.

Archidiaconus (Guido de Baysio, ca. 1250–1313). *Apparatus super sexto.* Milan, 1490.

———. *Rosarium seu in decretorum volumen commentaria.* Strasbourg, 1472.

Augustine, St. (Aurelius Augustinus, 354–430; saint, doctor of the Church, bishop of Hippo). Works found in vols. 32–45 of J. P. Migne, ed. *Patrologia Latina,* 221 vols. Paris, 1844–55 and 1862–65. Works attributed to Augustine include *De mirabilibus sacrae scripturae* by Augustinus Hibernicus (fl. seventh century); *Quaestiones veteris et novi testamenti* by pseudo-Ambrose (fl. fourth century).

———. *Confessiones.*

———. *Contra duas epistolas Pelagianorum.*

———. *Contra epistolam Parmeniani.*

———. *Contra Faustum Manichaeum.*

———. *Contra mendacium ad Consentium.*

———. *Contra Secundinum Manichaeum.*

———. *De baptismo.*

———. *De catechizandis rudibus.*

———. *De civitate dei.*

———. *De diversis quaestionibus ad Simplicianum.*

———. *De diversis quaestionibus octaginta tribus.*

———. *De doctrina Christiana.*

———. *De fide et operibus.*

———. *De Genesi ad litteram.*

———. *De gratia Christi et de peccato originali.*

———. *De gratia et libero arbitrio.*

———. *De libero arbitrio.*

———. *De mendacio.*

———. *De mirabilibus sacrae scripturae* (attributed to Augustine).

———. *De moribus ecclesiae catholicae et de moribus Manichaeorum.*

———. *De natura boni, contra Manichaeos.*

———. *De natura et gratia.*

———. *De octo Dulcitii quaestionibus.*

———. *De peccatorum meritis et remissione et de baptismo parvulorum.*

———. *De sermone domini in monte.*

———. *De trinitate.*

———. *De vera religione.*

———. *Enarrationes in psalmos.*

———. *Enchiridion.*

———. *Epistolae.*

———. *In Joannis evangelium tractatus.*

———. *Quaestiones in Heptateuchum.*

———. *Quaestiones veteris et novi testamenti* (attributed to Augustine).

———. *Retractationes.*

———. *Sermones.*

Augustinus Triumphus (Agostino Trionfo, Augustinus of Ancona, 1243–1328). *Summa de potestate ecclesiastica.* Cologne, 1475.

Ayala, Balthazar (ca. 1548–84; Spanish jurist and statesman). *De iure et officiis bellicis et disciplina militari.* Douai, 1582.

Azo, Portius (d. ca. 1230). *Ad singulas leges XII librorum codicis Iustinianaei commentarius.* Paris, 1577.

Azor, Juan (1533–1603; Spanish Jesuit and theologian, taught at Piacenza, Alcalá, and Rome). *Institutionum moralium,* vol. 3. Lyon, 1622.

Azpilcueta, Martin de. *See* Navarrus.

Azzio, Tommaso (fl. 1603; Italian jurist). *De ludo scacchorum in legali methodo tractatus.* Pesaro, 1583.

Baius, Michael (Michel de Bay, 1513–89; Louvain theologian). *Opera.* Cologne, 1696.

Balbus, Joannes Franciscus (fl. 1510; Italian jurist). *De praescriptionibus.* Lyon, 1567.

Baldus de Ubaldis (Baldeschi, ca. 1327–1400; Perugian jurist and glossator; taught law at Perugia, Padua, and Pavia; brother of Angelus and Petrus de Ubaldis). *Opera omnia: in ius universum civile commentarii, consilia, tractatus et reportorium Bartoli.* Basel, 1562.

Báñez, Domingo (1528–1604; Spanish Dominican). *Scholastica commentaria in primam partem et secundam secundae sancti Thomae.* Lyon, 1588.

Barbatia, Andreas de (Barbazza, 1399–1479). *Repertorium principalium emergentium quaestionum super prima parte principali decretalium.* Venice, 1508.

Barbosa, Augustinus (1589–1649; Portuguese jurist). *Opera.* 19 vols. Lyon, 1657–65.

Barclay, William (1546–1608; Scottish jurist, professor at Pont-à-Mousson and then at Angers). *De potestate papae.* Pont-à-Mousson, 1609.

Baronius, Caesar (1538–1607; cardinal, oratorian, and church historian). *Annales ecclesiastici a Christo nato ad annum 1198.* Rome, 1588–1607.

Bartolus of Sassoferrato (ca. 1313–57; Italian jurist and professor at Pisa and Perugia). *Super digesto veteri, infortiato, digesto novo, codice, consilia, tractatus, quaestiones.* Lyon, 1527.

Basil the Great (ca. 329–79; saint, doctor of the Church, bishop of Caesarea). Works found in vols. 29–32 of J. P. Migne, ed. *Patrologia Graeca,* 161 vols. Paris, 1857–66.

———. *Commentarium in Isaiam.*

———. *De spiritu sancto.*

———. *Homiliae.*

———. *Regulae brevius tractatae.*

———. *Regulae fusius tractatae.*

Bassolis, Joannes de (d. 1347). *Commentaria in quatuor libros sententiarum.* Paris, 1516–17.

Baysio, Guido de. *See* Archidiaconus.

Beauvais, Vincent de. *See* Vincent of Beauvais.

Bede (the Venerable, ca. 673–735). *In quatuor evangelia.* In vol. 92 of J. P. Migne, ed. *Patrologia Latina,* 221 vols. Paris, 1844–55 and 1862–65.

Bellarmine, St. Robert (1542–1621; cardinal and Jesuit, archbishop of Capua). Works found in *Opera omnia,* ed. J. Fèvre. 12 vols. Paris: Vivès, 1870–74.

———. *De gratiae reparatione et statu iustificationis per Christum.*

———. *De laicis.*

———. *De potestate summi pontificis in rebus temporalibus adversus Gulielmum Barclaium.*

———. *De romano pontifice.*

———. *De verbo dei scripto et non scripto.*

Bernard, St. (1090–1153; abbot of Clairvaux). Works found in vol. 182 of J. P. Migne, ed. *Patrologia Latina,* 221 vols. Paris, 1844–55 and 1862–65.

———. *De consideratione ad Eugenium.*

———. *De praecepto et dispensatione.*

Bertrandus, Petrus (1280–1349; cardinal, bishop of Autun). *De origine et usu iurisdictionum sive de duabus potestatibus temporali scilicet ac spirituali.* Venice, 1584.

Biel, Gabriel (ca. 1420–95; Nominalist theologian). *Collectorium in IV lib. sententiarum.* Lyon, 1514.

Biesius, Nicolas (1516–72). *De republica libri quatuor.* Antwerp, 1556.

Boethius, Anicius Manlius Severinus (480–525). *De consolatione philosophiae.* Basel, 1570.

Bolognetti, Alberto. *See* Albert of Bologna.

Bonaventure, St. (1221–74; Giovanni di Fidanza, doctor of the Church, cardinal). *In libros quatuor sententiarum* in *Opera omnia.* 9 vols. Florence: Quaracchi, 1882–1902.

Brisson, Barnabé (1531–91; French jurist, counsellor of state to Henry III). *De verborum quae ad ius pertinent significatione.* Lyon, 1559.

Brunus, Conradus (Konrad Braun, ca. 1495–1563). *De seditionibus libri sex.* Mainz, 1550.

Butrio, Antonio de (1338–1408). *Super lib. I decretalium.* Venice, 1578.

Cajetan, Cardinal (Thomas de Vio, 1469–1534; cardinal and Dominican theologian). *Commentaria in sancti Thomae Aquinatis.* Venice, 1588.

———. *De romani pontificis institutione et auctoritate.* In Cajetan. *Opuscula omnia.* Lyon, 1587.

———. *De vinculo obedientiae.* In Cajetan. *Opuscula omnia.* Lyon, 1587.

———. *In epistolam secundum ad Corinthios commentarius.* In Cajetan. *Opera omnia quotquot in sacrae scripturae expositionem reperiuntur.* Lyon, 1639.

Calderinus, Joannes (1300–1368). *Divini ac humani iuris repertorium.* Basel, 1474.

Canisius, Peter (Pieter Kannees, 1521–97). *Commentariorum de verbi dei corruptelis tomi duo.* Ingolstadt, 1583.

Cano, Melchior (ca. 1509–60). *De sacramentis in genere et de poenitentia.* Milan, 1580.

Cassian, Joannes (ca. 360–ca. 435). *Collationes patrum.* In vol. 49 of J. P. Migne, ed. *Patrologia Latina,* 221 vols. Paris, 1844–55 and 1862–65.

Castaldus, Restaurus (Ristoro Castaldi, d. 1564). *Tractatus de imperatore.* Lyon, 1549.

Castrensis, Paulus. *See* Castro, Paul de.

Castro, Alfonso de (Alphonsus a Castro, ca. 1495–1558). Works found in *Opera omnia.* Paris, 1571.

———. *Adversus omnes haereses.*

———. *De iusta haereticorum punitione.*

———. *De potestate legis poenalis.*

Castro, Paul de (d. ca. 1441). *Super codice, digesto veteri, infortiato, digesto novo.* Lyon, 1527.

Cenedo, Peter Jerome (d. 1603). *Collectanea iuris canonici.* Zaragoza, 1592.

Chrysostom, St. John (ca. 347–407; Greek doctor of the Church, bishop of Constantinople). Works found in vols. 47–64 of J. P. Migne, ed. *Patrologia Graeca,* 161 vols. Paris, 1857–66.

———. *Homiliae in epistolam ad Hebraeos.*

———. *Homiliae in epistolam ad Romanos.*

———. *Homiliae in epistolam primam ad Corinthios.*

———. *Homiliae in epistolam secundam ad Corinthios.*

———. *Homiliae in Ioannem.*

———. *Homiliae in Lucam.*

———. *Homiliae in Matthaeum.*

Clavasio, Angelus de. *See* Angelus de Clavasio.

Clement I (d. 100; pope, saint). *Constitutiones apostolicae* (falsely attributed). In Migne, *Patrologia Graeca,* vol. 1.

Clement of Alexandria (Titus Flavius Clemens, ca. 150–ca. 215). *Stromata.* In vols. 8–9 of J. P. Migne, ed. *Patrologia Graeca,* 161 vols. Paris, 1857–66.

Clichtovus, Jodocus (Josse Clichthove, ca. 1472–1543). *Ioannis Damasceni orthodoxae fidei Iodoci Clictovei enarratio.* Basel, 1548.

Code of Justinian (*Codex Justinianus*). *See* Krueger, Mommsen, and Schoell, *Corpus iuris civilis, under* Collections: Civil Law.

Connan, François (1508–51). *Commentariorum iuris civilis.* Paris, 1553.

Conrad. *See* Koellin, Conrad.

Constitutions of Clement (*Clementines, Constitutiones Clementis papae V, Libri Clementinarum*). *See* Richter and Friedberg, *Corpus iuris canonici, under* Collections: Canon Law.

Cordoba, Antonio de (1485–1578). *Opera.* Venice, 1569.

Corneus, Petrus Philippus (Pier Filippo Corneo, 1420–1493). *Consilia.* Trino, 1513.

Covarruvias y Leyva, Diego de (1512–77; jurist and theologian and pupil of Francisco de Vitoria). *Opera omnia.* Frankfurt, 1583.

Cravetta, Aimone (1504–69). *De antiquitate temporis.* Lyon, 1562.

Cromer, Martin (1512–89; Polish historian, bishop of Ermland). *De origine et rebus gestis Polonorum libri XXX.* Basel, 1555.

Cujas, Jacques (Jacobus Cujacius, 1522–90). *De feudis libri V.* Lyon, 1566.

Cynus (Cino) of Pistoia (1270–1337). *Lectura super codice.* Pavia, 1485.

Cyprian, St. (Thascius Caecilius Cyprianus, ca. 200–258; bishop of Carthage and martyr). Works found in vol. 4 of J. P. Migne, ed. *Patrologia Latina*, 221 vols. Paris, 1844–55 and 1862–65.

———. *De exhortatione martyrii.*

———. *De singularitate clericorum* (pseudo-Cyprian).

Cyril, St. (ca. 376–444; bishop of Alexandria and doctor of the Church). Works found in vols. 68–77 of J. P. Migne, ed. *Patrologia Graeca*, 161 vols. Paris, 1857–66.

———. *Commentarius in Ioannem.*

———. *Commentarius in Isaiam prophetam.*

———. *Contra Julianum.*

d'Ailly, Peter. *See* Ailly, Peter d'.

Damascenus, Joannes. *See* Joannes Damascenus.

d'Andrea, Giovanni. *See* Andrea, Giovanni d'.

Decio, Filippo (Philippus Decius, 1454–1535). *Super decretalibus.* Lyon, 1536.

———. *Super digesto.* Lyon, 1538.

Decretals of Pope Gregory IX (Decretales Gregorii papae IX). See Richter and Friedberg, *Corpus iuris canonici, under* Collections: Canon Law.

Decretum Gratiani. See Richter and Friedberg, *Corpus iuris canonici, under* Collections: Canon Law.

Digest of Justinian (Justiniani digesta). See Krueger, Mommsen, and Schoell, *Corpus iuris civilis, under* Collections: Civil Law.

Dionysius the Areopagite. *See* Pseudo-Dionysius.

Dominicus de Sancto Geminiano (1375–1424). *Commentaria in decretum.* Venice, 1504.

———. *Summa.* Venice, 1584.

———. *Super decretalium prima et secunda partes.* Venice, 1491–93.

Driedo, Joannes (ca. 1480–1535; Louvain theologian). *De libertate Christiana.* Louvain, 1540.

Duns Scotus, John (ca. 1266–1308; Franciscan theologian). *In quatuor libros sententiarum.* Venice, 1477.

Durandus a Sancto Porciano (Durandus of St. Pourçain, ca. 1275–ca. 1334). *Commentarii in 4 libros sententiarum.* Venice, 1571.

———. *De origine iurisdictionum et de legibus.* Paris, 1506.

Eck, Johann (Johannes Eckius, 1486–1543). *Enchiridion locorum communium adversus Lutheranos.* Antwerp, 1536.

Emilio, Paolo. *See* Aemilius Veronensis, Paulus.

Epiphanius (ca. 310–403; monk, bishop of Salamis). *Panarium sive arcula adversus 80 haereses.* In vols. 41–43 of J. P. Migne, ed. *Patrologia Graeca*, 161 vols. Paris, 1857–66.

Eusebius (ca. 263–340; bishop of Caesarea). Works found in vols. 19–24 of J. P. Migne, ed. *Patrologia Graeca,* 161 vols. Paris, 1857–66.

———. *Demonstrationis evangelicae libri X.*

———. *Historia ecclesiastica.*

———. *Vita Constantini.*

Evodius (d. 424; bishop of Uzalis). *De fide.* In vol. 42 of J. P. Migne, ed. *Patrologia Latina,* 221 vols. Paris, 1844–55 and 1862–65.

Extravagantes Communes. See Richter and Friedberg, *Corpus iuris canonici, under* Collections: Canon Law.

Extravagantes Ioannis XXIII. See Richter and Friedberg, *Corpus iuris canonici, under* Collections: Canon Law.

Felinus (Felino Sandeo, 1444–1503; bishop of Lucca, Italian canonist). *In libros decretalium commentaria.* Milan, 1504.

Ficino, Marsilio (1433–99; humanist and neo-Platonist philosopher). *Opera.* Florence, 1491.

Fisher, John. *See* Roffensis, Joannes.

Fontanus, Jacobus (fl. 1530). *Sextus decretalium liber Aegidii Perrini opera suae genuinae integritati restitutus. Jacobus Fontani cura illustratus.* Lyon, 1554.

Franchis, Philippus de (d. 1471). *Super sexto libro decretalium.* Venice, 1499.

Fulgosius, Raphael (1367–1427). *In primam pandectarum partem commentarium.* Lyon, 1554.

Fumo, Bartolomeo (d. 1555). *Summa casuum conscientia aurea armilla.* Antwerp, 1576.

Gabriel. *See* Biel, Gabriel.

Gabrieli, Antonio (d. 1555). *Communes conclusiones lib. VII.* Venice, 1584.

Gandavensis, Henricus. *See* Henry of Ghent.

Garcia, Fortunius (1494–1534). *De ultimo fine utriusque iuris canonici et civilis.* Bologna, 1517.

———. *Repetitionum seu commentariorum in varia iurisconsultorum responsa.* Lyon, 1553.

Gelasius I (d. 496; pope). *Epistolae.* In vol. 59 of J. P. Migne, ed. *Patrologia Latina,* 221 vols. Paris, 1844–55 and 1862–65.

Geminianus. *See* Dominicus de Sancto Geminiano.

Genesius. *See* Sepúlveda, Joannes Genesius.

Gerson, Joannes (Jean Charlier de, 1363–1429; theologian and chancellor of University of Paris). Works found in *Oeuvres complètes,* ed. P. Glorieux. 10 vols. Paris, 1960–73.

———. *Alphabetum divini amoris.*

———. *De potestate ecclesiastica et de origine iuris et legum tractatus.*

———. *De vita spirituali animae.*

Gigas, Hieronymus (Girolamo Giganti, d. 1560). *De crimine laesae majestatis.* Venice, 1557.

Gómez, Antonio (1501–97). *Opus super legibus Tauri.* Salamanca, 1575.

Gregory I, the Great (ca. 540–604, pope). Works found in vols. 75–79 of J. P. Migne, ed. *Patrologia Latina,* 221 vols. Paris, 1844–55 and 1862–65.

———. *Epistolae.*

———. *In evangelia.*

———. *Moralia in Job.*

———. *Regulae pastoralis.*

Gregory VII (Hildebrand of Soana, ca. 1015–85; pope). *Registrum.* In vol. 148 of J. P. Migne, ed. *Patrologia Latina,* 221 vols. Paris, 1844–55 and 1862–65.

Gregory of Nazianzus (ca. 329–ca. 389; bishop of Constantinople). *De paschate.* In vols. 35–38 of J. P. Migne, ed. *Patrologia Graeca,* 161 vols. Paris, 1857–66.

Gregory of Rimini (Ariminiensis, ca. 1300–1358). *In lib. II sententiarum.* Venice, 1503.

Gregory of Valencia (ca. 1540–1603; Spanish Jesuit and professor at Ingolstadt). *Commentariorum theologicorum tomi quatuor.* Lyon, 1619.

Gutiérrez, Joannes (d. 1618). *Practicarum quaestionum civilium libri V.* Frankfurt, 1607.

Hales, Alexander. *See* Alexander of Hales.

Henríquez, Enrique (1536–1608; Portuguese Jesuit and theologian, taught at Córdoba and Salamanca, teacher of Suárez). *Summa theologiae moralis.* Venice, 1597.

Henry of Ghent (Henricus Gandavensis, ca. 1217–93). *Quodlibeta.* Paris, 1518.

Hostiensis, Henricus (Henry of Segusio, ca. 1200–1271). *Summa aurea.* Strasbourg, 1512.

Hugh of St. Victor (ca. 1096–1141). *De sacramentis Christianae fidei.* In vol. 176 of J. P. Migne, ed. *Patrologia Latina,* 221 vols. Paris, 1844–55 and 1862–65.

Innocent I (d. 417; pope). *Epistolae.* In vol. 20 of J. P. Migne, ed. *Patrologia Latina,* 221 vols. Paris, 1844–55 and 1862–65.

Innocent IV (Sinibaldo Fieschi, ca. 1195–1254; pope). *Apparatus seu commentaria in 5 libros decretalium.* Strasbourg, 1478.

Institutes of Justinian (Justiniani Institutiones). See Krueger, Mommsen, and Schoell, *Corpus iuris civilis, under* Collections: Civil Law.

Irenaeus, St. (ca. 140–ca. 202; bishop of Lyon). *Adversus haereses.* In vol. 7 of J. P. Migne, ed. *Patrologia Graeca,* 161 vols. Paris, 1857–66.

Isidore of Seville, St. (ca. 560–636; bishop of Seville). *Etymologiarum sive originum libri XX.* Venice, 1483.

James I (1566–1625; king of England and Scotland). *Apologie for the Oath of Allegiance, together with a Premonition of his Majesties, to all most Mightie Monarches, Kings, free Princes and States of Christendome.* London, 1608.

Jason Mainus (Giasone del Maino, 1435–1519). *Additiones ad Christopheri Porci in 3 priores institutionum libros.* Venice, 1580.

——. *Prima super digesto veteri.* Lyon, 1542.

——. *Primum super codice.* Lyon, 1542.

Jerome, St. (Eusebius Sophronius Hieronymus, ca. 347–420). Works found in vols. 22–30 of J. P. Migne, ed. *Patrologia Latina,* 221 vols. Paris, 1844–55 and 1862–65.

——. *Adversus Jovinianum.*

——. *Apologeticum adversus Rufinum.*

——. *Epistolae.*

——. *In epistolam ad Titum.*

——. *In Isaiam prophetam.*

——. *In Jeremiam prophetam.*

——. *In Matthaeum.*

——. *In Zachariam prophetam.*

Joannes Damascenus (John Damascene, ca. 676–754). *Expositio fidei orthodoxae.* In vol. 94 of J. P. Migne, ed. *Patrologia Graeca,* 161 vols. Paris, 1857–66.

Juárez, Rodericus. *See* Suárez, Rodrigo.

Justin Martyr (ca. 100–ca. 165). *Apologia secunda pro Christianis.* In vol. 6 of J. P. Migne, ed. *Patrologia Graeca,* 161 vols. Paris, 1857–66.

Koellin, *or* Kollin, Conrad (1476–1536; German theologian, cited as Conrad). *Expositio commentaria in primam secundae angelici doctoris, sancti Thomae Aquinatis per Conradum Koellin.* Cologne, 1512.

Kromer, Martin. *See* Cromer, Martin.

Lactantius, Lucius Caecilius Firmianus (ca. 240–ca. 320). *Epitome divinarum institutionum libri VII.* In vol. 7 of J. P. Migne, ed. *Patrologia Latina,* 221 vols. Paris, 1844–55 and 1862–65.

Lapo da Castiglioncho (ca. 1316–81). *Allegationes iuris.* Venice, 1498.

Ledesma, Peter (1544–1616). *Theologia moralis.* Cologne, 1630.

Leo I, the Great (ca. 391–461; saint, pope). Works found in vol. 54 of J. P. Migne, ed. *Patrologia Latina,* 221 vols. Paris, 1844–55 and 1862–65.

——. *Epistolae.*

——. *Sermones.*

Lombard, Peter (ca. 1096–1164; Master of the Sentences, bishop of Paris). *Magistri Petri Lombardi sententiae in quatuor libris distinctae.* 2 vols. Grotta-ferrata: Collegii Sancti Bonaventurae ad Claras Aquas, 1971–81.

López, Gregorio (sixteenth century, Spanish jurist). *Las siete partidas del sabio rey don Alonso nono nuevamente glosadas por el licenciado Gregorio López.* . . . Salamanca, 1555.

Lucas de Penna (ca. 1325–ca. 1390; Portuguese jurist). *Super tres libros codicis, X, XI, XII.* Paris, 1509.

Major, Joannes (John Mair, ca. 1467–1550). *In quatuor magistri sententiarum.* Paris, 1509.

Marsilius of Padua (ca. 1275–1342). *Defensor pacis.* Basel, 1522.

Mascardi, Josephus de Sarzana (d. 1588). *De probationibus.* Lyon, 1589.

Massa, Antonio (Massanus or Massetanus, d. 1435). *Contra usum duelli.* Rome, 1554.

Mathieu, Pierre (Petrus Matthaeus, 1563–1621). *Liber septimus decretalium.* Paris, 1705.

Matienzo, Joannes (sixteenth century). *Commentaria Ioannis Matienzo in librum quintum recollectionis legum Hispaniae.* Madrid, 1580.

Matthew Paris (Matthaeus Parisiensis, ca. 1200–1259). *Chronica,* ed. H. R. Louard. London: Longman, 1872–83.

Mazzolini. *See* Sylvester Prierias.

Medina, Bartolome de (1527–81). *Expositio in primam secundae angelici doctoris divi Thomae Aquinatis.* Venice, 1580.

Medina, Joannes (1490–1546). *De poenitentia, restitutione et contractibus.* Ingol-stadt, 1581.

Mendoza, Fernando de (b. 1566). *Vetustissimum et nobilissimum concilium Illi-beritanum cum discursibus.* . . . Lyon, 1665.

Menochio, Jacopo (Jacobus Menochius, 1532–1607). *De arbitrariis iudicium quaestionibus et causis.* Frankfurt, 1576.

Middleton, Richard. *See* Richard of Middleton.

Molina, Luis de (1535–1600; Spanish Jesuit). *De iustitia et iure.* Mainz, 1602.

Molina [Morales], Luis de (fl. sixteenth century; Spanish jurist). *De Hispano-rum primogeniorum origine et natura.* Lyon, 1588.

Mozolini. *See* Sylvester Prierias.

Navarrus (Martin de Azpilcueta, 1491–1586; Doctor Navarrus, Spanish canonist and moral theologian). *Opera omnia.* Venice, 1618–21.

Nazianzen, Gregory of. *See* Gregory of Nazianzus.

Netter, Thomas. *See* Waldensis.

Nicephorus, Callistus. *See* Xanthopulus, Nicephorus Callistus.

Nicholas of Lyra (ca. 1270–1340). *Commentaria in vetero testamento.* Basel, 1507.

Novels of Justinian (*Justiniani novellae*). *See* Richter and Friedberg, *Corpus iuris canonici, under* Collections: Canon Law.

Novocastro, Andreas a (André of Neufchâteau, d. ca. 1400). *Commentarius in IV lib. sententiarum.* Paris, 1514.

Nuñez do Liao, Duarte (d. 1608; Portuguese historian). *Primeira parte das chronicas dos reis de Portugal.* Lisbon, 1600.

Ockham, William of (or Occam; ca. 1288–ca. 1348). *Super quatuor sententiarum libris.* Lyon, 1495.

Origen (ca. 185–ca. 255). *Opera omnia.* In vols. 11–17 of J. P. Migne, ed. *Patrologia Graeca,* 161 vols. Paris, 1857–66.

Pacian (310–91; bishop of Barcelona). *Paraenesis ad poenitentiam.* Paris, 1533.

Palude, Petrus de (Peter Paludanus, ca. 1275–1342). *Commentaria in 4 libros sententiarum.* Paris, 1518.

Panormitanus, *or* Abbas *or* Siculus (Nicolò de' Tudeschi, 1386–1445; Italian canonist, archbishop of Palermo). *Commentaria in primum–quintum decretalium libros.* Venice, 1569.

———. *Consilia.* Lyon, 1537.

———. *Lectura in sextum.* Venice, 1564.

Paz, Cristóbal de (fl. late sixteenth century; Spanish jurist). *Scholia ad leges regias styli.* Madrid, 1608.

Paz, Marcus Salon de (fl. 1560; Spanish jurist). *Ad leges Taurinas insignes commentarii.* Poissy, 1568.

Pelayo, Alvaro (Alvarus Pelagius, ca. 1280–1352; Spanish Franciscan, bishop of Sylves). *De planctu ecclesiae.* Ulm, 1474.

Peter of Blois (ca. 1135–ca. 1211). *Epistolae.* Brussels, 1480.

Peter of Ravenna (Petrus Ravennas, ca. 1448–1508). *Enarrationes in tit. de consuetudine.* Lyon, 1550.

Petrus de Ubaldis (Petrus de Baldeschi, ca. 1330–ca. 1406; Perugian civilist, brother of Angelus and Baldus de Ubaldis). *Super canonica episcopali et parochiali.* Perugia, 1474.

Pezant (Pesantius), Alexander (fl. early seventeenth century). *Brevia commentaria et disputationes in universam theologiam divi Thomae Aquinatis.* Venice, 1606.

Pighius, Albertus (Albert Pigghe, 1490–1542). *De visibilia monarchia* in *Hierarchiae ecclesiasticae assertio.* Cologne, 1572.

Pinellus, Benedictus. *Selectae iuris interpretationes, conciliationes et variae resolutiones.* Lyon, 1670.

Platina, Bartolomeo (born Bartolomeo Sacchi, 1421–81; Italian historian). *De vitis summorum pontificum omnium.* Cologne, 1562.

Polydorus Vergillius (Polydore Vergil, 1470–1555). *Anglicae historiae libri XVI.* Basel, 1534.

Prosper Aquitanus. *See* Aquitanus, Prosper.

Pseudo-Dionysius (late fifth to early sixth century). *De caelesti hierarchia.* In vols. 3–4 of J. P. Migne, ed. *Patrologia Graeca,* 161 vols. Paris, 1857–66.

Puteo, Paris de (Paride del Pozzo, 1410–93). *De sindicatu.* Venice, 1505.

Rebuffi, Pierre (Petrus Rebuffus, 1487–1557; French jurist). *Commentaria in constitutiones seu ordinationes regias.* Lyon, 1599.

Ribera, Franciscus (1537–91). *Commentarii in 12 prophetas minores.* Cologne, 1599.

Richard of Middleton (Richardus de Mediavilla, d. ca. 1300). *Super quatuor libros sententiarum.* Venice, 1478.

Rochus Curtius (fl. 1470). *Enarrationes in capitulo 'cum tanto' de consuetudine.* Lyon, 1550.

Roffensis, Joannes (St. John Fisher, 1469–1535; bishop of Rochester executed by Henry VIII). *Assertionis Lutheranae confutatio.* Cologne, 1523.

Rosate, Alberico de. *See* Alberico de Rosate.

Rufinus Aquileiensis (Rufinus of Aquileia, ca. 345–ca. 411). Works found in vol. 21 of J. P. Migne, ed. *Patrologia Latina,* 221 vols. Paris, 1844–55 and 1862–65.

———. *Historiae ecclesiasticae.*

———. *Historia monachorum.*

Salazar, Peter de (fl. 1612). *De usu et consuetudine tractatus.* Frankfurt, 1600.

Saliceto, Bartolomeo da (d. 1411). *In Justiniani codicem.* Lyon, 1532.

Salmerón, Alfonso (1515–85). *Commentarii in evangelicam historiam et in acta apostolorum et epistolam.* Cologne, 1602–4.

Sánchez, Tomás (1550–1610). *De sancto matrimonii sacramento disputationum libri X.* Madrid, 1605.

———. *Opus morale in praecepta decalogi.* Antwerp, 1614.

Sandeo, Felino. *See* Felinus.

Scotus, Joannes Duns. *See* Duns Scotus, John.

Senis, Fredericus de (Frederico Petrucci, d. ca. 1343). *Disputationes, quaestiones et consilia.* Siena, 1489.

Sepúlveda, Joannes Genesius (Juan Ginés de Sepúlveda, 1490–1573). *De fato et libero arbitrio.* Rome, 1526.

———. *De regno et regis officio.* Lerida, 1571.

Sext (*Liber sextus decretalium Bonifacii papae VIII*). *See* Richter and Friedberg, *Corpus iuris canonici, under* Collections: Canon Law.

Sigebert of Gembloux (Sigebertus, ca. 1030–1112). *Chronica.* In vol. 160 of J. P. Migne, ed. *Patrologia Latina,* 221 vols. Paris, 1844–55 and 1862–65.

Sigonius, Carolus (Carlo Sigonio, ca. 1524–84; Italian historian and antiquary). *De regno Italiae.* Venice, 1574.

Silvester. *See* Sylvester Prierias.

Simancas, Diego (1518–83). *Institutiones Catholicae.* Valladolid, 1552.

Socinus, Bartholomaeus (Bartolomeo Sozzini, 1436–1507). *Consilia.* Venice, 1579.

Soto, Domingo de (1494–1560; Spanish Dominican and student of Francisco de Vitoria). *De iustitia et iure libri X.* Salamanca, 1553–54.

———. *De ratione tegendi et detegendi secretum.* Salamanca, 1541.

———. *In epistolam divi Pauli ad Romanos commentarius.* Antwerp, 1550.

———. *In quatuor sententiarum libros commentarii.* Salamanca, 1557–60.

Suárez (Juárez or Xuárez), Rodrigo (fl. 1494). *In commentaria ad prooemium fori.* Valladolid, 1696.

Sylvester Prierias (Silvestro Mazzolini de Prierio, ca. 1456–1523; Italian Dominican). *Summa Sylvestrina, quae summa summarum merito nuncupatur.* Rome, 1516.

Tertullian (Quintus Septimius Florens Tertullianus, ca. 160–ca. 230). Works found in vols. 1–2 of J. P. Migne, ed. *Patrologia Latina,* 221 vols. Paris, 1844–55 and 1862–65.

———. *Adversus Judaeos.*

———. *De corona militis.*

———. *De exhortatione castitatis.*

Theodoret (ca. 393–ca. 457). Works found in vols. 81–83 of J. P. Migne, ed. *Patrologia Graeca,* 161 vols. Paris, 1857–66.

———. *Graecarum affectionum curatio.*

———. *In epistolam secundam ad Corinthios commentarius.*

Theodosian Code (*Codex Theodosianus*). In *Codex Theodosianus cum Perpetuis Commentarius Iacobi Gothofredi.* Leipzig, 1736–41.

Theophylact (Theophylactus, ca. 1050–1109). Works found in vol. 124 of J. P. Migne, ed. *Patrologia Graeca,* 161 vols. Paris, 1857–66.

———. *Commentarius in epistolam ad Romanos.*

———. *Commentarius in epistolam primam ad Corinthios.*

———. *Commentarius in epistolam secundam ad Corinthios.*

———. *Enarratio in evangelium sancti Lucae.*

Thomas Aquinas, St. (ca. 1225–74). Works found in Thomas Aquinas, *Opera omnia* (Leonine edition), 50 vols. Rome: Ex Typographia Polyglotta S.C. de Propaganda Fide, 1882–.

———. *De regimine principum.*

———. *De veritate.*

———. *In decem libros ethicorum Aristotelis ad Nicomachum.*

———. *In epistolam ad Romanos.*

———. *In quatuor libros sententiarum.*

———. *Quaestiones quodlibetales.*

———. *Summa theologiae.*

Tiraqueau, André (Andreas Tiraquellus, 1488–1558; French jurist). *Commentarii de nobilitate et iure primogenitorum.* Paris, 1549.

———. *Commentarius in legem si unquam, de revocandis donationibus.* Paris, 1535.

———. *De utroque retractu.* Paris, 1549.

Toledo, Francisco (or Toletus, 1532–96; Jesuit and cardinal). *Summa casuum conscientiae, sive de instructione sacerdotum.* Lyon, 1599.

Torquemada, Juan de (Joannes de Turrecremata, 1388–1468; Dominican, cardinal, and canonist). *In Gratiani decretorum primam et secundam.* Lyon, 1519.

———. *Summa de ecclesia.* Rome, 1489.

Torres, Francisco. *See* Turrianus, Franciscus.

Tostado, Alonso (Alonso Fernández de Madrigal, Tostatus Abulensis, 1410–55; bishop of Avila). *Opera omnia.* 13 vols. Cologne, 1613.

Trovamala, Baptista (d. 1484). *Summa rosella de casibus conscientiae.* Venice, 1495.

Tudeschi, Nicolò de'. *See* Panormitanus.

Turrianus, Franciscus (Francisco Torres, 1504–84; Spanish Jesuit). *Apostolicarum constitutionum.* Antwerp, 1578.

Valdés, Diego de (fl. latter half of sixteenth century; Spanish historian and canonist). *Ad volumen repetitionum doctissimi Roderici Suárez additiones.* Poissy, 1590.

———. *In commentaria ad prooemium fori Roderici Xuárez additiones.* Medina, 1596.

Valla, Lorenzo (1406–57). *Elegantiarum Latinae linguae libri VI.* Rome and Venice, 1471.

Vázquez, Gabriel (1549–1604; Spanish Jesuit). *Commentariorum ac disputationum in partes sancti Thomae tomi VIII.* Alcalá, 1598–1615.

Vega, Andreas de (d. ca. 1560; Spanish Franciscan). *Tridentini decreti de iustificatione expositio et defensio.* Venice, 1548.

Vergillius, Polydorus. *See* Polydorus Vergilius.

Viguerius, Joannes (Jean Viguier, fl. 1550). *Institutiones theologicae.* Paris, 1550.

Vincent of Beauvais (Vincentius Bellovacensis, ca. 1190–1264; French Dominican). *Speculum morale.* Strasbourg, 1476.

Vitoria, Francisco de (ca. 1483–1546; Spanish Dominican). *Relectiones XII theologicae libri II.* Lyon, 1557.

Vives, Luis (Joannes Ludovicus Vives, 1493–1540). *Commentarii ad divi Aurelii Augustini De civitate dei.* Hamburg, 1661.

Waldensis (Thomas Netter, ca. 1375–1430; English Carmelite). *De sacramentalibus* in *Doctrinales antiquitatum fidei ecclesiae Catholicae.* Paris, 1532.

William of Auvergne (William of Paris, ca. 1180–1249; bishop of Paris). *De fide et legibus* in *Opera.* Nuremberg, 1496.

William of Occam. *See* Ockham, William of.

Xanthopulus, Nicephorus Callistus (Nikephoros Kallistos Xanthopoulos, fl. 1320). *Ecclesiasticae historiae libri 18.* In vol. 145 of J. P. Migne, ed. *Patrologia Graeca,* 161 vols. Paris, 1857–66.

Zonaras, Joannes (fl. twelfth century; Byzantine theologian and historian). *Epitome historiae.* In vol. 135 of J. P. Migne, ed. *Patrologia Graeca,* 161 vols. Paris, 1857–66.

SUGGESTIONS FOR
FURTHER READING

Brett, Annabel. *Liberty, Right and Nature: Individual Rights in Later Scholastic Thought.* Cambridge: Cambridge University Press, 1997.

Costello, Frank. *The Political Philosophy of Luis de Molina, S.J. (1535–1600).* Rome: Bibliotheca Instituti Historici S.I., 1974.

Haakonssen, Knud. 'Natural Law in the Seventeenth Century.' In Knud Haakonssen, *Natural Law and Moral Philosophy: From Grotius to the Scottish Enlightenment,* pp. 15–62. Cambridge: Cambridge University Press, 1996.

Hamilton, Bernice. *Political Thought in Sixteenth-Century Spain: A Study of the Political Ideas of Vitoria, Soto, Suárez, and Molina.* Oxford: Oxford University Press, 1963.

Höpfl, Hanno. *Jesuit Political Thought: The Society of Jesus and the State, c. 1540–1630.* Cambridge: Cambridge University Press, 2004.

Lloyd, Howell. 'Constitutionalism.' In H. Burns and Mark Goldie, eds., *The Cambridge History of Political Thought 1450–1700,* pp. 254–97. Cambridge: Cambridge University Press, 1991.

Pink, Thomas. 'Action, Will, and Law in Late Scholasticism.' In Jill Kraye and Risto Saarinen, eds., *Moral Philosophy on the Threshold of Modernity,* pp. 31–50. Dordrecht: Springer, 2005.

———. 'Natural Law and the Theory of Moral Obligation.' In Sara Heinämaa, ed., *Psychology and Philosophy: Inquiries into the Soul from Late Scholasticism to Contemporary Thought,* pp. 97–114. Dordrecht: Springer, 2009.

———. 'Suárez, Hobbes, and the Scholastic Tradition in Action Theory.' In Thomas Pink and M. W. F. Stone, eds., *The Will and Human Action,* pp. 127–53. London: Routledge, 2004.

Rommen, H. *Die Staatslehre des Franz Suárez.* München-Gladbach: Volksvereins-Verlag, 1926.

Salmon, J. H. M. 'Catholic Resistance Theory, Ultramontanism, and the Royalist Response, 1580–1620.' In J. H. Burns and Mark Goldie, eds., *The Cambridge History of Political Thought 1450–1700*, pp. 219–53. Cambridge: Cambridge University Press, 1991.

Scorraille, Raoul de. *François Suárez de la Compagnie de Jésus*. 2 vols. Paris: Lethielleux, 1912.

Tierney, Brian. 'Rights, Community, and Sovereignty.' In Brian Tierney, *The Idea of Natural Rights*, pp. 288–316. Atlanta, Ga.: Scholars Press, 1997.

Tutino, Stefania. *Empire of Souls: Robert Bellarmine and the Christian Commonwealth*. Oxford: Oxford University Press, 2010.

INDEX

Abbas. *See* Panormitanus

abolition versus suspension of law, 499

Abraham (biblical patriarch), 29, 67, 90, 119, 146, 327, 332, 343, 349, 419, 931, 960

abrogation: of custom by law, 568–72, 722, 747–50; of custom by subsequent custom, 749–50; derogation of law without, 708–9; exception or extension and, 706–34; of human law by custom, 683–705; ignorance of prince regarding, 694–704; of invalidating laws by custom, 717–21; non-prescriptive custom and, 695–98; of penal law imposing penalty by fact of transgression, 706–17

absolute necessity, 37

absolute versus regulated power of God, 164

Abulensis. *See* Tostado, Alonso

Actius, Thomas [Tommaso Azzio], 805

Acts (biblical book): 4:12, 150; 5:1–10, 790n15; 6:14, 535; 7:53, 190; 13:8–11, 842; 15:1, 507, 535

acts and actions: for abrogation of custom, 750–52; external versus internal, 49; good and evil as inherent quality of, 217–20; good versus bad, 553–67; human, 12n2,

21n14; ignorance or error, custom not established by acts done in, 629–30; moral acts, law as measure of, 21–23, 88; necessary for making of law, 55–64; repetition of acts, custom introduced by, 609–14, 663–65; voluntary nature of acts establishing custom, 628–38. *See also* intellect; moral actions; will

Adam (biblical patriarch), 21, 63, 90, 145, 431, 434

Adrian VI (pope), 137, 945, 949–50, 951

Ad Tollendum (papal bull), 979

Aemilius Veronensis [Paolo Emilio da Verona], 793

aequitas. See equity

affirmative law, 54

affirmative precepts, 260–61, 295–96

Agde, Council of (506), 903

aggression, acceptance of duel as act of, 982

aggressive war, 914–16, 917, 930

Ailly, Peter d' [Petrus de Alliaco], 210, 328, 578

Alberico de Rosate, 674

Albert of Bologna, 201, 307, 313, 397

Albertus Magnus, 378

Alexander III (pope), 565, 770, 786, 787

Alexander VI (pope), 847

This book is set in Adobe Garamond, a modern adaptation by Robert Slimbach of the typeface originally cut around 1540 by the French typographer and printer Claude Garamond. The Garamond face, with its small lowercase height and restrained contrast between thick and thin strokes, is a classic 'old-style' face and has long been one of the most influential and widely used typefaces.

Printed on paper that is acid-free and meets the requirements of the American National Standard for Permanence of Paper for Printed Library Materials, z39.48–1992. ⊗

Book design by Louise OFarrell, Gainesville, Florida
Typography by Apex CoVantage, Madison, Wisconsin
Printed and bound by Sheridan Books, Inc.,
Chelsea, Michigan